THIRD EDITION

Business Communication

PROCESS AND PRODUCT

MARY ELLEN GUFFEY

Los Angeles Pierce College

South-Western College Publishing
an International Thomson Publishing company I(T)P®

Cincinnati • Albany • Boston • Detroit • Johannesburg • London • Madrid • Melbourne • Mexico City
New York • Pacific Grove • San Francisco • Scottsdale • Singapore • Tokyo • Toronto

Team Leader: Dave Shaut
Acquisitions Editor: Pamela M. Person
Developmental Editor: Mary Draper
Marketing Manager: Sarah Woelfel
Production Editor: Kelly Keeler
Manufacturing Coordinator: Dana Began Schwartz
Internal Design: Liz Harasymczuk Design
Cover Design: Liz Harasymczuk Design
Cover Photographer or Illustrator: © Charlie Hill/Superstock
Photo Manager: Cary Benbow
Production House: WordCrafters Editorial Services, Inc.
Compositor: GGS Information Services, Inc.
Printer: R.R. Donnelley & Sons

Printed in the United States of America
2 3 4 5 6 7 8 9 10

International Thomson Publishing Europe
Berkshire House
168-173 High Holborn
London, WC1V7AA, United Kingdom

Nelson ITP, Australia
102 Dodds Street
South Melbourne Albert Complex
Victoria 3205 Australia

Nelson Canada
1120 Birchmount Road
Scarborough, Ontario
Canada M1K 5G4

International Thomson Publishing Southern Africa
Building 18, Constantia Square
138 Sixteenth Road, P.O. Box 2459
Halfway House, 1685 South Africa

International Thomson Editores
Seneca, 53
Colonia Polanco
11560 México D.F. México

International Thomson Publishing Asia
60 Alberta Street #15-01
Singapore 189969

International Thomson Publishing Japan
Hirakawa-cho Kyowa Building, 3F
2-2-1 Hirakawa-cho, Chiyoda-ku
Tokyo 102, Japan

Library of Congress Cataloging-in-Publication Data

Guffey, Mary Ellen.
Business communication : process & product / Mary Ellen Guffey. — 3rd ed.
p. cm.
Includes bibliographical references and index.
ISBN 0-324-00766-3
1. Business writing. 2. English language—Business English. 3. Business communication. I. Title.
HF5718.3.G838 2000
651.7—dc21 99-29250
CIP

This book is printed on acid-free paper.

About the Author

A dedicated professional, Mary Ellen Guffey has taught business communication and business English topics for over thirty years. She received a bachelor's degree, *summa cum laude,* in business education from Bowling Green State University; a master's degree in business education from the University of Illinois, where she held a fellowship; and a doctorate in business and economic education from the University of California, Los Angeles (UCLA). She has taught at the University of Illinois, Santa Monica College, and Los Angeles Pierce College.

She is the author of *Business Communication: Process and Product,* 2e, a leading textbook in the field. She has also written *Business English,* 6e, which serves more students than any other book in its field; *Essentials of College English,* and *Essentials of Business Communication,* 4e, the leading text/workbook in its market. Dr. Guffey serves on the review boards of *The Delta Pi Epsilon Journal* and *The Business Communication Quarterly* of the Association of Business Communication.

A teacher's teacher and leader in the field, Dr. Guffey acts as a partner and mentor to hundreds of business communication instructors across the country. Her workshops, seminars, newsletters, articles, teaching materials, and Web sites help novice and veteran business communication instructors achieve effective results in their courses. She privately maintains comprehensive Web sites for students and instructors. Her print and on-line newsletters are used by thousands of instructors in this country and abroad.

Brief Contents

Detailed Contents

UNIT 2 The Writing Process 99

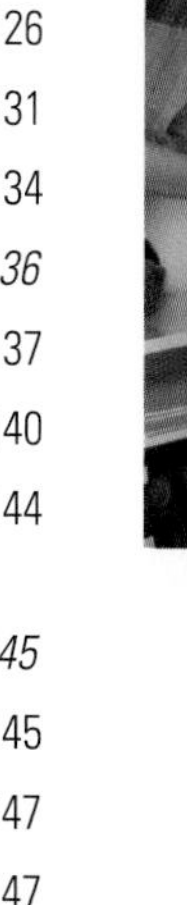

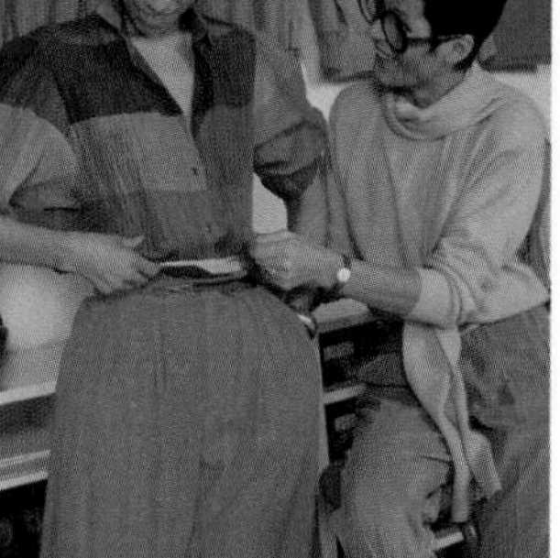

¡Y
Quie

EPSI PE

UNIT 5 Presentations 459

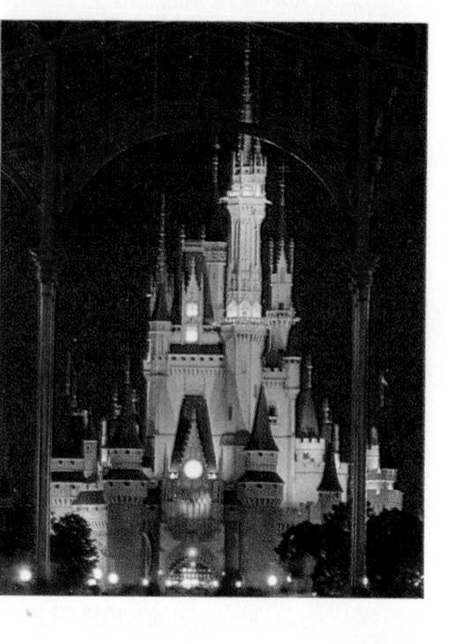

The Business Communication Foundation

A time-tested, interactive learning/testing system that delivers comprehensive student and instructor resources.

Process

Analyze-Anticipate-Adapt

Research-Organize-Compose

Revise-Proofread-Evaluate

Mary Ellen Guffey's unique 3-x-3 process approach provides students a practical strategy for solving communication problems and creating successful communication products. New coverage of multicultural communication and teamwork, plus unique three-part case studies of prominent companies expand student understanding of real-world situations.

Product

Memos. Letters. E-Mail. Résumés. Reports. Presentations.

Through direct application of the strategic 3-x-3 process to all forms of business communication, students attain the tools they need to create well-crafted documents and presentations. New e-mail, Web browsing, critical thinking, and teamwork assignments reflect the increasing role of technology in business communication.

Partnership

Mary Ellen Guffey, your students, and you.

Mary Ellen Guffey actively responds to your needs and suggestions while offering a vast array of print and on-line teaching resources. Dedicated Web sites for instructors and students offer continuously updated teaching and learning resources for success inside and outside the classroom.

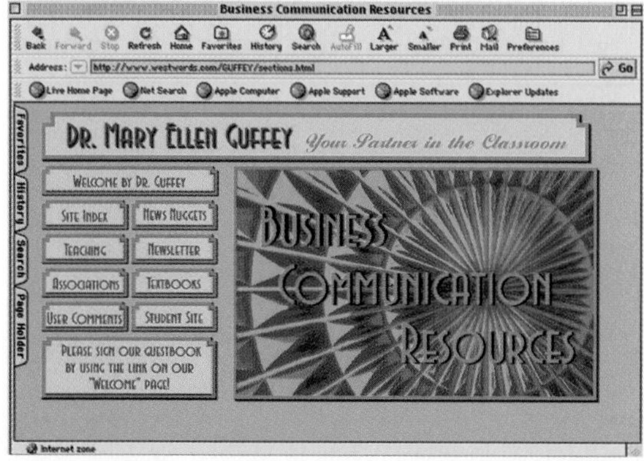

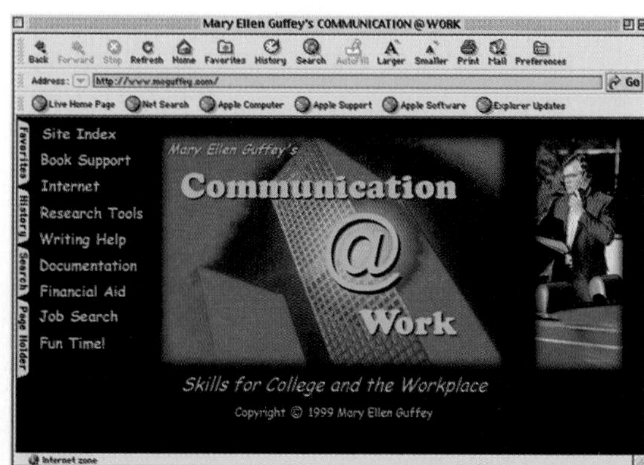

Voice Mail: 1-800-876-2350, 2, Ext. 7495
E-mail: meguffey@west.net
Fax: 805-964-8614

Web Site for Instructors: http://www.westwords.com/instructor.html
Web Site for Students: http://www.meguffey.com

South-Western College Publishing
Academic Resource Center: 1-800-423-0563
E-mail: examcopy@swpco.com

Dear Friends and Colleagues:

I am pleased to present to you the third edition of ***Business Communication: Process and Product***. As you may know, thanks to the support of instructors and the enthusiastic acceptance of students across the country, the first two editions of this text experienced tremendous success. ***Business Communication: Process and Product*** is the market leader in the business communication market.

Although it may have been risky to make changes to an already popular text, I feel the improvements made in this third edition provide an even greater emphasis on student interaction in real business situations. As change is constant, I also wanted to update many technology and multicultural discussions, as well as find ways to facilitate the learning experience in the classroom.

While retaining my focus on the process and product of business communication, I have enhanced the application of concepts to real-world situations. Included are new chapters on multicultural communication and teamwork; new letter and memo-writing assignments; new activities for team, Web, critical thinking, and e-mail issues; and new "Tech Talk" boxes to support the increasing importance of the Web as a communication vehicle.

Although I've added new material, I've condensed other areas to hold the book to the same overall length as the second edition - 16 chapters. Most important, ***Business Communication: Process and Product*** is supplemented with the best publisher ancillaries, the latest complimentary teaching materials, and the most useful student and instructor Web sites in the field.

In the Visual Sampler that follows, key features of ***Business Communication: Process and Product*** are illustrated to introduce you to the process of successful business communication and the conversion of that process into effective products.

I sincerely hope you enjoy this new edition and all of your business communication experiences.

Cordially,

Mary Ellen Guffey

Mary Ellen Guffey

MARY ELLEN GUFFEY

YOUR PARTNER IN THE CLASSROOM AND ON-LINE

Research Resources

Links to over 120 on-line national and world newspapers are provided, as well as links to comprehensive search tools, reference tools, magazines and journals, and Usenet news groups.

Book Support

Interactive chapter reviews; PowerPoint summaries; vocabulary, spelling, and sentence structure skill builders, Web-oriented critical thinking exercises, and other textbook-specific support.

Financial Aid

An updated list provides links to multiple sources of information about locating & applying for financial aid.

Job Search

Students will find an updated collection of preferred Web sites that link to job search information, résumé-writing services, résumé job banks, classified ads, and internship resources.

Fun Time

Lighten up with jokes, puzzles, games, and fun diversions.

Student Web Site

An Unparalleled Resource for Students: http://www.meguffey.com

- **Two NEW On-line Chapters.** Technology and Employment Interviewing chapters supplement the textbook for additional coverage of these key topics.
- **Interactive Chapter Reviews.** Students can assess their knowledge of each chapter by answering practice test questions. Every response generates feedback and explanation to enhance student comprehension and learning.
- **Interactive Skill Builders,** written by the author, review and reinforce basic skills in spelling, vocabulary, and sentence competency.
- **Internet Resources.** Find links to the best search engines and recently published information on the Internet. Included are sites that help teach a basic understanding of the Internet, how to search, and how to assess the quality of Web pages and data. These sites are constantly monitored and updated for the most current information.
- **PowerPoint™ slides** provide a colorful, animated, and quick summary of principal chapter concepts. Slides are immediately viewable—no downloading!

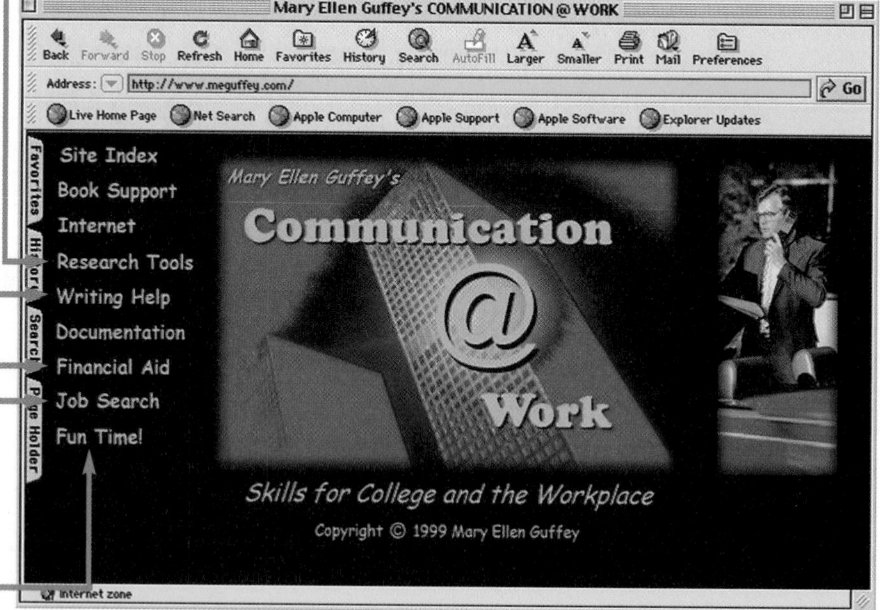

Student Testimonials:

- *"Guffey's Web site is very helpful. The practice exams really made a difference in improving my studying."* – Chet Barney, Utah State University
- *"I like the use of real people to accentuate the examples.* ***Business Communication: Process and Product*** *is bright and colorful, and the Web site is helpful in tandem with the book."* – Julia Boyd, Motlow State Community College

Instructor Web Site

An Invaluable Resource for Instructors:

http://www.westwords.com/instructor.html

- **Unrivaled Author Support.** Guffey is the only author to develop and maintain all of the materials at her Web sites privately. All inquiries come directly to her and are answered immediately, providing a direct line to a knowledgeable, accessible, and concerned author.
- **Additional useful resources include** links to professional organizations, information about all four Guffey textbooks, and user comments.

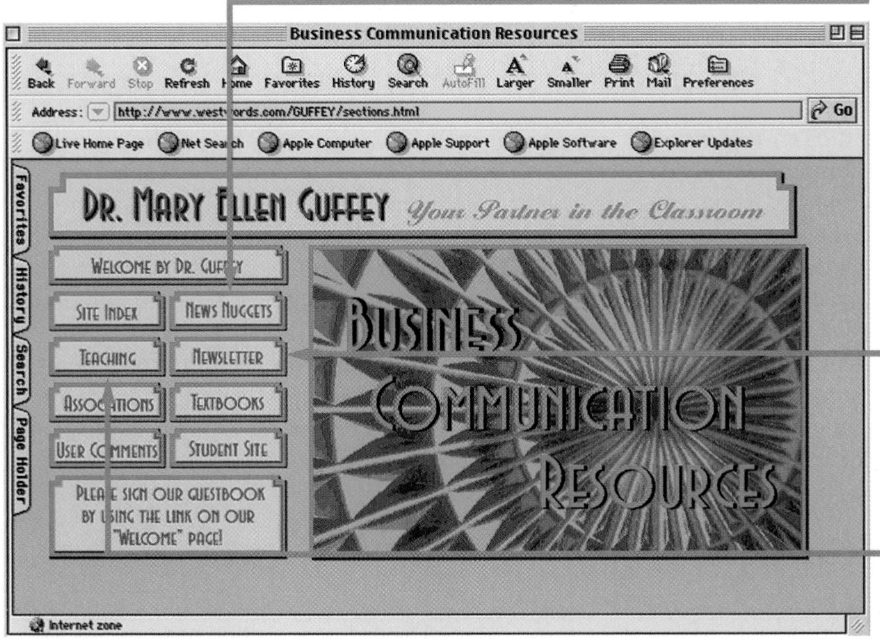

News Nuggets

summarize what is happening in the news and relate it to the business communication classroom. Instructors will find endless enrichment items from a wide range of newspapers, magazines, journals, and Internet sources.

Newsletter

provides archived copies of selected articles from Guffey's print newsletter *Business Communication News*. Instructors can also sign up for the *On-Line Guffey Report*, a monthly on-line newsletter that contains fast-paced summaries of relevant current events, lecture ideas, teaching tips, and new business communication writing problems and case studies.

Teaching Materials

Guffey provides change-of-pace quizzes, PowerPoint™ Web instructional modules, down-loadable teaching units, and an order form for additional complimentary materials that come directly from the author. These items are available at a password-protected portion of the Guffey Instructor Web site. See your ITP sales representative or the Instructor's Manual for the password.

Instructor Testimonials:

- *"Your textbook and your Web page both make my job MUCH easier. They also make me a better teacher."* – Dr. David Williams, Director, Business Communication Center, University of Oklahoma, Norman
- *"I am very impressed with the number of materials and sites available. The teaching resources are wonderful - very useful and informative."* – Margaret S. Walters, University of Houston, Clear Lake

UNMATCHED AUTHOR SUPPORT

Mary Ellen Guffey: Your Business Communications Partner

Mary Ellen Guffey's commitment to providing an exceptional business communication experience for professors and students alike is best exemplified through the support she offers beyond the text. Through her unique instructor and student Web sites, timely newsletters, and customized teaching materials, Guffey is a valuable resource both in and out of the classroom. With Guffey you know that you have access to a personal teaching consultant who actively responds to your needs and suggestions.

3-X-3 WRITING PROCESS

A Foundation for Success

The 3-x-3 writing process is a practical approach to written and oral communication that provides a sensible strategy for solving business communication problems and creating successful communication products. Mary Ellen Guffey is the first author to develop such a process. With strong graphics as visual guides, this multistage process of analyzing-anticipating-adapting, researching-organizing-composing, and revising-proofreading-evaluating is consistently applied to all forms of business communication. Learn about each of these nine steps in Chapters 4, 5, and 6, and then apply the 3-x-3 process to create communication products in the chapters that follow. Through consistent utilization and unique visualization techniques, Mary Ellen Guffey provides the foundation for an invaluable business communication problem-solving strategy.

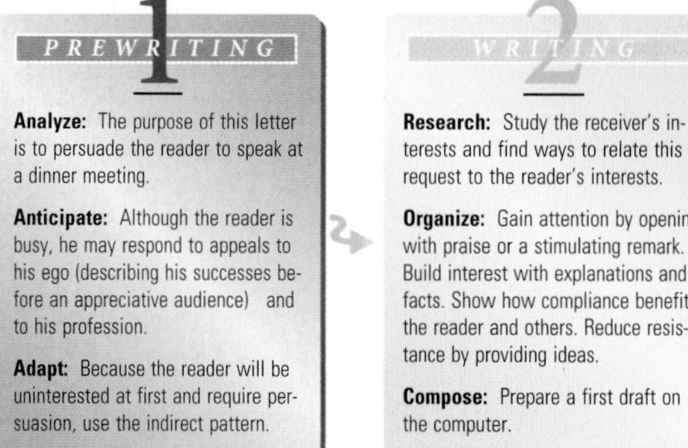

1
PREWRITING
Analyze: The purpose of this letter is to persuade the reader to speak at a dinner meeting.
Anticipate: Although the reader is busy, he may respond to appeals to his ego (describing his successes before an appreciative audience) and to his profession.
Adapt: Because the reader will be uninterested at first and require persuasion, use the indirect pattern.
2
WRITING
Research: Study the receiver's interests and find ways to relate this request to the reader's interests.
Organize: Gain attention by opening with praise or a stimulating remark. Build interest with explanations and facts. Show how compliance benefits the reader and others. Reduce resistance by providing ideas.
Compose: Prepare a first draft on the computer.
3
POSTWRITING
Revise: Revise to show direct and indirect benefits more clearly.
Proofread: Use quotes around "R" to reflect their usage. In the fourth paragraph use a semicolon in the compound sentence. Start all lines at the left for a block-style letter.
Evaluate: Will this letter convince the reader to accept the invitation?

COMMUNICATION TECHNOLOGY

Communication on the Cutting-Edge

Communicating successfully in the business world today includes communicating effectively by computer. ***Business Communication: Process and Product*** helps the business communicator understand and prepare for electronic communication challenges. New **"Tech Talk"** boxes provide important information on the technology tools and issues common in today's workplace.

TECH TALK

UNDERSTANDING NATURAL LANGUAGE, KEYWORD, AND BOOLEAN SEARCHING

Natural language searches involve posing a search question as you would normally state it. For example, "Is there a correlation between employee morale and productivity?" Using AltaVista for this search question produced nearly 5 million documents. Although the total is overwhelming, the most relevant "hits" were listed first. And the first ten items were all relevant. An increasing number of Web search engines and databases support natural language searching. It's particularly handy for vague or broad questions.

Keyword searches involve using the principal words in which you are interested. From the above question, you might choose to search on the phrase "employee morale" or "employee productivity." Omit useless words such as articles, conjunctions, and prepositions. Some search tools allow you to enclose keyword sequences (such as *employee morale*) in quotation marks to ensure that the specified words appear together and not separately.

Boolean searches involve joining keywords with "operators" (connectors) that include or exclude specific topics. For example, "employee AND morale." Using Boolean operators enables you to narrow your search and thus improve its precision. The following Boolean operators are most common:

AND — Identifies only documents containing all of the specified words. **employee AND productivity AND morale**

OR — Identifies documents containing at least one of the specified words: **employee OR productivity OR morale**

NOT — Excludes documents containing the specified word: **employee productivity NOT morale**

NEAR — Finds documents containing target words or phrases within a specified distance, for instance, within 10 words: **employee NEAR productivity**

Career Application

Using a search engine that supports natural language, keyword, and Boolean searching (such as AltaVista), try an experiment. Explore the same topic using (1) a natural language question, (2) key words, and (3) Boolean operators. Which method produced the most relevant hits?

Communicating by computer also involves using technology effectively. Internet assignments, plus specific examples on using the Internet effectively and efficiently, preparing multimedia presentations, and using electronic applications and formats are included throughout the text. Most important, as a user of *Business Communication: Process and Product*, you will have access to text-specific Web sites (one developed specifically for instructors, one for students) as resources!

REAL-WORLD CASE STUDIES

Real-World Applications

Applying a concept to a real-life situation is the best way to learn and retain important information. Through unique three-part case studies, companies such as Amazon.com, Pepsi-Cola, and Nike are put in the spotlight and business communication problem-solving skills are applied to their real-world situations. At the beginning of each chapter, "Communication in Process" introduces the featured company and its business communication scenario. Part two, "Communication in Progress", outlines the company response and poses critical thinking questions. At the end of each chapter, "Process to Product" provides the opportunity to play the role of employee and take the next step in resolving the communication issue.

TEAMWORK

Communicating In Teams

Team-based work environments present new challenges to today's business communicators. New Chapter 2, "Communicating in Teams: Listening, Nonverbal, Collaboration, and Meeting Skills" explores the dynamics of team communication. Its many tips, techniques, and strategies prepare students to collaborate effectively on campus and work projects.

CROSS-CULTURAL, WORKFORCE DIVERSITY

Communicating in a Complex World

Today's increasingly global economy and diverse work environment have added a unique dimension to business communication. Mary Ellen Guffey addresses these issues in a new chapter, **Chapter 3, "Communicating Across Cultures,"** that applies practical skills for communicating in the global environment. This chapter helps business communicators recognize the growing need for multicultural sensitivity, and it provides helpful coping strategies that encourage awareness, tolerance, and accommodation.

CHAPTER • 3 •

Communicating Across Cultures

LEARNING OBJECTIVES

1 Discuss three significant trends related to the increasing importance of multicultural communication.

2 Define *culture.* Describe five significant characteristics of culture, and compare and contrast five key dimensions of culture.

3 Explain the relationship between ethnocentrism, tolerance, and stereotypes in achieving multicultural sensitivity. Identify the six stages of multicultural transformation.

CRITICAL THINKING FOCUS

Exercising the Mind

More than ever before, employees must put their **critical thinking skills** to work in order to analyze situations, make decisions, and solve problems. Through the incorporation of chapter-opening case studies and end-of-chapter problem-solving activities, Mary Ellen Guffey equips the business communicator with these higher-level skills and prepares them for career success.

END-OF-CHAPTER MATERIALS

Applying the Concepts

Chapter concepts are strengthened and applied through comprehensive end-of-chapter materials directly related to the learning objectives. Every chapter offers a wide assortment of short, long, easy, and difficult exercises, activities, and problems. Selected problems are identified as **Team, Web, Critical Thinking** and **E-mail**, to provide a variety of stimulating assignment choices. Nearly 90 percent of the letter- and memo-writing problems are new, and many are related to current events.

CHAPTER REVIEW

1. What is the difference between *cognitive* and *affective* conflict? (Obj. 1)
2. What is *groupthink*? (Obj. 1)
3. Why can diverse teams be more effective than homogeneous teams? (Obj. 2)
4. Why are team decisions based on consensus better than decisions reached by majority rule? (Obj. 2)
5. In times of team crisis, is it better to have shared leadership or one leader? (Obj. 2)
6. What is the best way to set team deadlines when time is short to complete a project? (Obj. 3)
7. In completing a team-written report, should all team members work together to write the report? Why or why not? (Obj. 3)
8. Workers spend what percentage of their communication time listening? What percentage do executives spend? (Obj. 4)
9. Define *lag time.* (Obj. 4)
10. Describe the four elements in the listening process. (Obj. 4).
11. Define *nonverbal communication.* (Obj. 5)
12. When verbal and nonverbal messages disagree, which message does the receiver consider more truthful? Give an example. (Obj. 5)
13. How does good eye contact help a speaker/sender? How does it benefit a listener/receiver? (Obj. 5)
14. What is the ideal size for a problem-solving meeting, and who should be invited? (Obj. 6)
15. Why is teleconferencing becoming increasingly popular among businesspeople? (Obj. 6)

CRITICAL THINKING

1. How would you compare the advantages and disadvantages of teams in today's workplace? (Objs. 1, 2, and 3)
2. How are listening skills important to employees, supervisors, and executives? Who should have the best listening skills? (Obj. 4)
3. What arguments could you give for or against the idea that body language is a science with principles that can be interpreted accurately by specialists? (Obj. 5)
4. How would you comment on this statement? "If you can't orchestrate a meeting, then you are of little use to an organization." (Obj. 6)
5. **Ethical issue:** You're disturbed that Randy, one member of your team, is selling Amway products to other members of the team. He shows catalogs and takes orders at lunch, and he distributes products after work and during lunch. He also leaves an order form on the table during team meetings. What should you do? What if Randy were selling Girl Scout cookies?

ACTIVITIES

2.1 Team Formation and Discussion (Objs. 1, 2, and 3)

Team

In groups of four or five, conduct a team discussion using one of the topics below. Appoint a team leader and a recorder. Discuss a topic for 10 minutes (or as long as your instructor directs). Then as a group, draft an outline of the major points discussed and the decision your team reached. Your instructor may ask you to report your decisions to the class or prepare a group memo describing your team's discussion and decision.

a. Should an employee be allowed to sell products such as Amway items or Girl Scout cookies at work? (See Critical Thinking Question 5 for more details.)
b. Should an employee be allowed to send personal e-mail messages during breaks or lunch hours? How about using company computers after hours to prepare a college report? What if your supervisor gives her permission but asks you to keep quiet about it?
c. Should companies have the right to monitor e-mail messages sent by employees? If so, is it necessary for an organization to inform the employees of its policy?

2.2 Web Detectives (Objs. 1 and 2)

Web Team

Assume your employer has asked you to investigate competitors' Web sites and report what you find. Team up with another class member. Select any two competing companies (say, Coke and PepsiCo or Nike and Reebok). Examine their Web sites and compare what you find. What services do they offer? How easy is it to navigate each site? How attractive is the format? Is one site clearly better than the other? Why? As a team, report your findings in a memo to your instructor.

C.L.U.E.

Back to the Basics

Competent Language Usage Essentials. Review and reinforce grammar and language principles with the help of C.L.U.E. This business writer's handbook contains 50 of the most used and abused language elements, along with frequently misspelled and misused words. Try-out exercises help students learn C.L.U.E. principles, while additional end-of-chapter review exercises continue to reinforce the basics.

APPENDIX A

C.L.U.E. Competent Language Usage Essentials:

A Business Communicator's Guide

In the business world, people are often judged by the way they speak and write. Using the language competently can mean the difference between individual success and failure. Often a speaker sounds accomplished; but when that same individual puts ideas in print, errors in language usage destroy his or her credibility. One student observed, "When I talk, I get by on my personality; but when I write, the flaws in my communication show through. That's why I'm in this class."

What C.L.U.E. Is

This appendix provides a condensed guide to competency in language usage essentials (C.L.U.E.). Fifty guidelines review sentence structure, grammar, usage, punctuation, capitalization, and number style. These guidelines focus on the most frequently used—and abused—language elements. Presented from a business communicator's perspective, the guidelines also include realistic tips for application. And frequent checkpoint exercises enable you to try out your skills immediately. In addition to the 50 language guides in this appendix, you'll find a list of 160 frequently misspelled words plus a quick review of selected confusing words.

The concentrated materials in this guide will help novice business communicators focus on the major areas of language use. The guide is not meant to teach or review *all* the principles of English grammar and punctuation. It focuses on a limited number of language guidelines and troublesome words. Your objective should be mastery of these language principles and words, which represent a majority of the problems typically encountered by business writers.

How to Use C.L.U.E.

Your instructor may give you a language diagnostic test to help you assess your competency. After taking this test, read and work your way through the 50 guidelines. Concentrate on areas where you are weak. Memorize the spelling list and definitions for the confusing words located at the end of this appendix.

Two kinds of exercises are available for your practice. (1) *Checkpoints,* located in this appendix, focus on a small group of language guidelines. Use them to test your comprehension as you complete each section. (2) *Review exercises,* located in

APPLIED CAREER SKILLS COVERAGE

Communication at Work

Career Coach boxes offer practical advice and information on translating communication skills to future careers. Topics such as "He Said, She Said: Gender Talk and Gender Tension" and "Five Strategies for Reaching Group Decisions" take a closer look at communication issues and challenges in the workplace.

CAREER COACH

HE SAID, SHE SAID: GENDER TALK AND GENDER TENSION

Has the infiltration of gender rhetoric done great damage to the workplace? Are men and women throwing rotten tomatoes at each other as a result of misunderstandings caused by stereotypes of "masculine" and "feminine" attitudes? Deborah Tannen's book *You Just Don't Understand: Women and Men in Conversation,* as well as John Grey's *Men Are From Mars, Women Are From Venus,* caused an avalanche of discussion (and some hostility) by comparing the communication styles of men and women. Here are some of their observations (greatly simplified):[42]

	Women	Men
Object of talk	Establish rapport, make connections, negotiate inclusive relationships	Preserve independence, maintain status, exhibit skill and knowledge
Listening behavior	Attentive, steady eye contact; remain stationary; nod head	Less attentive; sporadic eye contact; move around
Pauses	Frequent pauses, giving chance for others to take turns	Infrequent pauses; interrupt each other to take turns
Small talk	Personal disclosure	Impersonal topics
Focus	Details first, pulled together at end	Big picture
Gestures	Small, confined	Expansive
Method	Questions, apologies; "we" statements; hesitant, indirect, soft speech	Assertions; "I" statements; clear, loud, take-charge speech

Gender theorists suggest that one reason women can't climb above the glass ceiling is that their communication style is less authoritative than that of men.

Career Application

In small group or class discussion, consider these questions. Do men and women have different communication styles? Which style is more appropriate for today's team-based management? Do we need a kind of communicative affirmative action to give more recognition to women's ways of talking? Should training be given to men and women encouraging the interchang ing on the situation?

Spotlight on Communicators features professionals and business leaders and their comments on the communication strategies that helped them to achieve their goals.

Each chapter highlights tips from prominent communicators. Their advice is directly related to chapter concepts, providing real-world applications of communication at work.

Spotlight on **Communicators**

Katie Couric, co-host of the "Today" show and former Pentagon reporter, does her homework before she conducts interviews. Disarmingly cheerful and humorous, she can also be hard-hitting and uncompromising in her blunt questioning of newsmakers. Yet she always strives to be positive, courteous, and fair—important characteristics of every

MODEL DOCUMENTS

An abundance of perfectly formatted **model documents** reinforce student understanding of communication concepts. Colorful pointers on the letters, memos, and reports lead to concise annotations that explain communication strategies and applications of theory.

Complete coverage of **employment communication** products including up-to-date model résumés and letters of application, plus job-search skills from interview through follow-up, provides useful tools and guidance for the job seeker.

FIGURE 4.4 Customer Response Letter

February 23, 2000

Mrs. Elaine Hough
9403 Farwest Drive SW
Tacoma, WA 98498

Dear Mrs. Hough:

Your letter was a strong endorsement of our belief that we made the right choice when we devoted our company to traditional, classic styles — and that it's still the right choice.

Opens response to inquiry by agreeing with customer

Explains evolving merchandise line from company's and reader's view

It's true we've made changes. In the past few years, with the markets soft and tastes changing, we reexamined our merchandise, with a view to continuing to serve valued customers while introducing ourselves to new ones. We decided that our styles needed freshening and that we would offer clothes that didn't chase after trends but did have a feel for what was current.

Our commitment to the classics hasn't weakened, as I hope you'd agree, having seen recent catalogs. But we've defined "classic" more inclusively than in the past. We're using new fabrics, new colors, a more relaxed fit. There's more imagination in our product mix now, but the sweaters, rugbys, blouses, button-downs, and other basics for which you've relied on us are still here. You may not find each one in every catalog, and you may notice the new products more than those you've seen before. The classics are still here, and the selection will be growing.

Uses conversational language to convey warmth and sincerity

Emphasizes areas of agreement.

I've arranged to send you just the four catalogs a year you wanted. I hope you'll keep an eye on them. I think that, more and more, you'll be able to come to us for the styles you want.

Concludes by giving customer what she wants and promoting future business

Sincerely,

Brian Finnegan
Customer Relations

LANDS' END, INC.
1 LANDS' END LANE DODGEVILLE, WI 53595
(608)935-9341

ETHICAL CONSIDERATIONS

Communicating Ethically

To stress the importance of ethical considerations in all communication settings, the first chapter immediately introduces ethical challenges and tools for doing the right thing. These tools are then integrated throughout the book. This approach puts ethical conduct in context, rather than isolating these issues from the reality of day-to-day business interactions.

Additionally, **Ethical Insights** boxes in selected chapters address ethical issues or dilemmas in communication and provide strategies for communicating information within a complex business environment. Every chapter includes an **Ethical Issues** question for class discussion.

ETHICAL INSIGHTS

ARE INFLATED RÉSUMÉS WORTH THE RISK?

A résumé is expected to showcase a candidate's strengths and minimize weaknesses. For this reason, recruiters expect a certain degree of self-promotion. But some résumé writers step over the line that separates honest self-marketing from deceptive half-truths and flat-out lies. Distorting facts on a résumé is unethical; lying is illegal. And either practice can destroy a career.

Although recruiters can't check everything, most will verify previous employment and education before hiring candidates. Over half will require official transcripts. And after hiring, the checking process may continue. At one of the nation's top accounting firms, the human resources director described the posthiring routine: "If we find a discrepancy in GPA or prior experience due to an honest mistake, we meet with the new hire to hear an explanation. But if it wasn't a mistake, we terminate the person immediately. Unfortunately, we've had to do that too often."[22]

No job seeker wants to be in the unhappy position of explaining résumé errors or defending misrepresentation. Avoiding the following common problems can keep you off the hot seat:

- **Inflated education, grades, or honors.** Some job candidates claim degrees from colleges or universities when in fact they merely attended classes. Others increase their grade-point averages or claim fictitious honors. Any such dishonest reporting is grounds for dismissal when discovered.

- **Enhanced job titles.** Wishing to elevate their status, some applicants misrepresent their titles. For example, one technician called himself a "programmer" when he had actually programmed only one project for his boss. A mail clerk who assumed added responsibilities conferred upon herself the title of "supervisor." Even when the description seems accurate, it's unethical to list any title not officially granted.

- **Puffed-up accomplishments.** Some job seekers inflate their employment experience or achievements. One clerk, eager to make her photocopying duties sound more important, said that she assisted the *vice president in communicating and distributing employee directives.* An Ivy

RESOURCES THAT ENHANCE INSTRUCTION AND LEARNING

Integrated Learning/Testing System.
Learning objectives summarize key chapter concepts and anchor a comprehensive learning/testing system. The chapter learning objectives are marked by special icons, reviewed point by point in the chapter summary and review, and noted in the assignment material. Most important, this well-organized system enables instructors to select appropriate problem-solving activities and test items to reflect their course objectives.

NEW! **Instructor's CD-ROM.**
Utilizing key course resources is now easier than ever! The Instructor's CD combines popular text supplement material in one easy-to-use format. You'll have complete access to letter- and memo-writing solutions from the Instructor's Manual, the entire transparency acetate packet (chapter outlines, bonus lecture material, before-and-after documents, and solutions to select chapter activities), PowerPoint™ presentation slides for all chapters, and Test Banks with feedback for every question, right at your fingertips.

Instructor's Manual. (0-324-01372-8)
This comprehensive resource includes model course schedules, chapter synopses, teaching ideas, lecture enrichment material, classroom management techniques, answers for chapter review questions, suggested discussion guides for critical thinking questions, solution guides for case study questions and applications, and solutions for most end-of-chapter exercises and activities. New to this edition are solutions for all letter- and memo-writing assignments in the book. Written by the author, these solutions are properly formatted and can be used as transparency masters.

Student Study Guide. (0-324-01375-2)
To promote student success in the course as well as in future careers, this hands-on study guide provides students with a variety of exercises and sample test questions that review chapter concepts and key terms. The study guide also helps students enrich their vocabularies, master frequently misspelled words, and develop language competency with bonus C.L.U.E exercises. Nearly all exercises are self-checked so students receive immediate feedback. The Study Guide is especially helpful for short-term, evening, or distance-learning classes. Its question-oriented format ensures better performance on chapter tests.

PowerPoint™ Presentation Slides. (0-324-01373-6)
This lecture resource, with 600 text-specific slides, offers one of the largest and most comprehensive presentation programs in the market. It provides summaries, explanations, and illustrations of key chapter concepts, plus lecture enrichment material not included in the text.

Transparency Acetates and Masters. (0-324-01378-7)
Written by the author, 167 acetates and masters summarize, supplement, and highlight course concepts. These one-, two-, and four-color acetates and masters provide outlines, text figures, enrichment material, and solutions to key problems. Moreover, the Instructor's Manual includes 128 additional pages of letter and memo solutions presented as transparency masters. This makes a total of 295 masters and acetates - the biggest and best package on the market.

Print Test Bank. (0-324-01377-9)
Organized by the integrated learning/testing system, each chapter of the test bank contains between 60 and 150 test questions. A special feature of this new edition is the inclusion of feedback for the response to each question. Every chapter opens with a correlation table that identifies questions by chapter learning objective and by content: factual, conceptual, or application. Page references to the text ensure quick reference.

Thomson Learning Testing Tools™. (0-324-01380-9)
All items from the printed test bank are available on disk through Thomson Learning Testing Tools, an automated testing program that allows instructors to create exams by selecting provided questions, modifying existing questions, and adding questions. It is available in Windows and MS-DOS versions and is provided free of charge to instructors at educational institutions that adopt ***Business Communication: Process and Product*,** 3e by Mary Ellen Guffey (0-324-01380-9). Instructors can also have tests created and printed by calling International Thomson Publishing Academic Resource Center at 1-800-423-0563 (8:30 a.m. - 6:00 p.m. EST).

Videos.
Business communication issues are brought to life by a series of videos that highlight and reinforce key chapter concepts, especially the themes of the third edition.

Distance Learning Resources.
Numerous distance learning instructors have made ***Business Communication: Process and Product*,** 3e their textbook choice because of its comprehensive learning/testing system, its technologically savvy approach, and its numerous on-line resources. Distance learning students have direct access to PowerPoint slides, interactive chapter review questions, interactive skill builders, electronic citation formats, and many other student-oriented electronic resources.

Premier Student Web Site (http://www.meguffey.com).
The first to offer Internet student resources, Guffey's Student Web site continues to lead the field with over 3,000 student-oriented Web pages. Students will find updated links to the best Web search engines; financial aid information; Internet history, use, and evaluation information; and preferred career information including job search, résumé, classified ads, and internship sites. Students can circle the globe by clicking links to national and world newspapers. PowerPoint™ slides that are immediately viewable encourage students to preview and review chapter concepts. Review exercises with immediate feedback enable students to assess their comprehension of chapter concepts and prepare for class tests. For students who need to build basic language proficiency, Guffey provides a set of on-line Skill Builders that focus on spelling, vocabulary, and sentence competency.

Leading Instructor Web Site (http://www.westwords.com/instructor.html).
Now password-protected, the Guffey Instructor site provides access to newsletter articles, change-of-pace quizzes, textbook information, links to professional organizations, and digests of relevant current event items that can enrich business communication lectures. Best of all are the downloadable teaching units on such topics as listening, peer evaluation, analytical reports, and HTML instruction. Instructors may obtain a password to this valuable resource from the Instructor's Manual or their ITP sales representative.

Newsletters and Complimentary Teaching Materials.
All adopters receive a complimentary subscription to our twice-yearly newsletter, *Business Communication News*. It highlights current issues and news of interest in the business communication course as well as offers complimentary teaching materials that may be ordered directly from the author. In addition, instructors may receive *The On-Line Guffey Report*, a monthly electronic newsletter sent directly to e-mail boxes of instructors who sign up. It provides relevant news nuggets, classroom teaching tips, lecture ideas, and bonus case studies. Mary Ellen Guffey remains the number one business communication author when it comes to accessibility, complimentary teaching materials, and on-line resources.

ENHANCE YOUR COURSE WITH THESE OUTSTANDING RESOURCES

HOW 8: Handbook for Office Workers. (0-538-86319-6)
By Lyn Clark and James Clark
This handbook is the most comprehensive reference manual available for writing, formatting, and transmitting business documents. It is designed to assist office professionals and business writers in preparing successful written business communications. Completely updated, it reflects the most current use of technology in the office, including e-mail and the Internet.

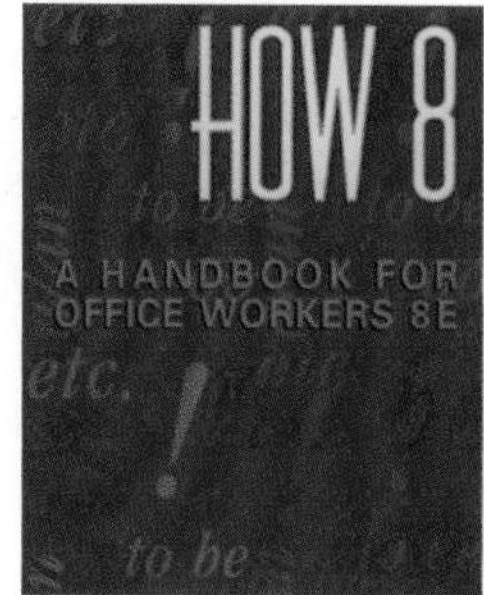

The Professional Writer's Electronic Resource (PoWER) CD-ROM. (0-538-87895-9)
By Mary Ellen Guffey, Lyn Clark, and James Clark
This on-line reference and interactive study guide reviews and reinforces grammar, spelling, punctuation, mechanics, and usage in all forms of communication. The software includes pretests, posttests, examples, lessons, and exercises.

Business Communications, the Real World, and Your Career. (0-324-01426-0)
By James Sequin
This brief text teaches students how to use the business communication skills they learn in college to obtain the career they want and advance professionally. It is a perfect supplement to any business communication course or for instructors teaching in any discipline who want to show their students how to apply skills from their coursework in their professional lives. Special attention is given to life-long learning and career development, including networking and communications skill building.

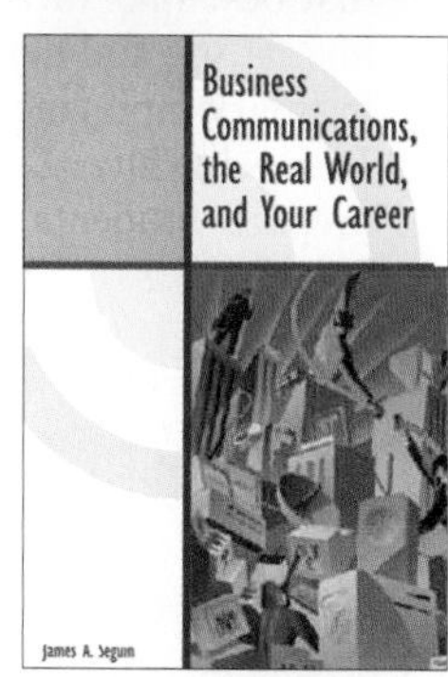

Start Now. Succeed Later: Making College Count for Career Search Success.
By Pat O'Brien, (0-324-01540-2)
This highly approachable, graphics-intensive book helps students to understand what they need to do throughout their college experience to build the skills necessary to ultimately achieve success in the job interview process. Highlighted are key skills that students should begin building now, through academics, extra-curricular activities, and relevant work experience, to maximize their career opportunities. Combining clear and immediate directions on developing these skills with examples and interviews with recruiting executives, this text gives students the tools they need to turn their college experiences into future job success.

Wired Résumés. **http://www.wired-resumes.com**
By Tim Krause
Wired Résumés is the first and only Web site that allows instructors to walk students through the process of creating a professional quality on-line resume – and ***Wired Résumés Guide*** assures success for all.

<Wired Resumes>

Wired Résumés Guide. **http://www.wired-resumes.com** (0-324-01538-0)
By Tim Krause
Tim Krause, co-director of Business Writing at Purdue University, contributor to *Business Communication Quarterly,* and electronic communication specialist with Cargill Industries, gives you and your students all the help you need to successfully navigate the Wired Resumes Web site regardless of skill or experience level.

Career Strategies. (0-324-01403-1)
By Thomas Clark
This workbook is designed to take the reader through the process of assesssing skills and talents, developing a networking data bank, preparing job search marketing tools, and answering interview questions effectively.

Résumés, Cover Letters and Interviewing: Setting the Stage for Success.
By Clifford Eischen and Lynn Eischen (0-324-01404-X)
This practical how-to manual takes students step by step through the process of crafting a polished résumé. It is the only résumé manual on the market specifically geared toward those students who will be entering the job market with a two-year degree. Numerous examples allow students to develop a résumé that best suits their professional goals. Information on electronic résumé formatting and delivery prepares students to use today's business technologies in their employment search. In addition to résumé building and preparation, ***Résumés, Cover Letters and Interviewing: Setting the Stage for Success*** also prepares students for the interview process.

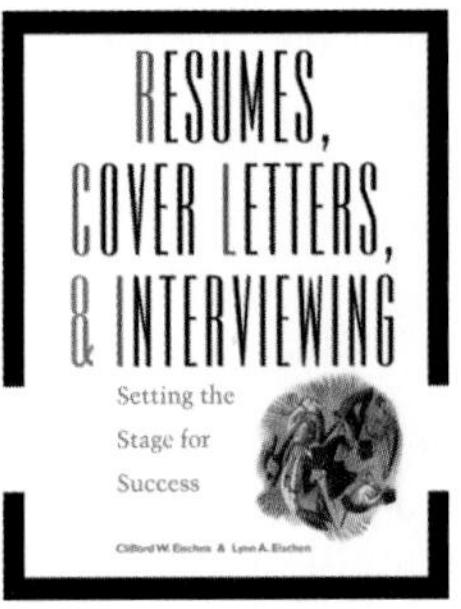

Appreciation for Support

Probably no other book has had as great a level of professional support in its development as *Business Communication: Process and Product.* I am exceedingly grateful to the reviewers and other experts, shown in the accompanying list, who contributed their pedagogic and academic expertise in shaping this book.

In addition to these friends and colleagues, sincere thanks go to Wadsworth Publishing Company for propelling the first edition to its number one position. In helping us maintain that top position with the second and third editions, I extend sincere thanks to many professionals at South-Western College Publishing, including Pamela Person, Dave Shaut, Kelly Keeler, Sarah Woelfel, Mary Draper, Craig Ramsdell, Dana Schwartz, and Cary Benbow.

My heartfelt appreciation also goes to Marilyn Lammers, California State University, Northridge, for developing an excellent integrated testing system; to Thomas Marshall, Robert Morris College, for working with me to construct an exceptional Instructor's Manual; and to Lorraine Korkosz for providing much-needed office support.

Finally, I express my deep gratitude to my husband, Dr. George R. Guffey, emeritus professor of English, University of California, Los Angeles, for supplying extraordinary computer expertise and Internet skills, as well as love, strength, and wisdom.

Mary Ellen Guffey

To receive newsletters and materials or to comment and make suggestions, you may reach Dr. Guffey in the following ways:

Mail: Dr. Mary Ellen Guffey, P.O. Box 6011, Malibu, CA, 90264

Voice Mail: 1-800-876-2350, 2, Ext. 7495

E-mail: meguffey@westwords.com

Student Web site: www.meguffey.com

Instructor Web site: www.westwords.com/instructor.html

Acknowledgments

Leslie Adams, Houston Baptist University
Kehinde A. Adesina, Contra Costa College
Asberine Parnell Alford, Suffolk Community College, Selden, New York
Virginia Allen, Joliet Junior College
Cynthia Anderson, Youngstown State University
Vanessa D. Arnold, University of Mississippi
Lois J. Bachman, Community College of Philadelphia
Rebecca Barksdale, University of Central Florida
Sandra Berill, Arkansas State University
Randi Blank, Indiana University
Martha E. Bradshaw, Southeastern Louisiana University
Bernadine Branchaw, Western Michigan University
Maryanne Brandenburg, Indiana University of Pennsylvania
Paula E. Brown, Northern Illinois University
Phyllis C. Bunn, Delta State University
Mary Ann Burris, Pueblo Community College
Roosevelt D. Butler, College of New Jersey
Jane Campanizzi-Mook, Franklin University
Nancy J. Cann
James F. Carey, Onondaga Community College
Leila Chambers, Cuesta College
Patricia H. Chapman, University of South Carolina
Judie C. Cochran, Grand Canyon University
Randy E. Cone, University of New Orleans
James Conley, Eastern Michigan University
Billie Miller Cooper, Cosumnes River College, Sacramento
Jane G. Corbly, Sinclair Community College
Martha Cross, Delta State University
Linda Cunningham, Salt Lake Community College
Bertha Dee-Babcock, University of San Francisco
Dorothy Drayton, Texas Southern University
Anna Easton, Indiana University
Lorena B. Edwards, Belmont University, Nashville
Donald E. English, Texas A&M University
Margaret Erthal, Southern Illinois University at Edwardsville
Terry M. Frame, University of South Carolina
Kerry J. Gambrill, Florida Community College
Judith L. Graham, Holyoke Community College
Carolyn G. Gray, The University of Texas at Austin
Diane Gruber, Arizona State University West
David Hamilton, Bemidji State University
Paul Hegele, Elgin Community College
Rovena L. Hillsman, California State University, Sacramento
Shirely Houston, University of Nebraska
Warren B. Humphrey, University of Central Florida
Robert G. Insley, University of North Texas
Edna Jellesed, Lane Community College
Carolyn Spillers Jewell, Pembroke State University
Pamela R. Johnson, California State University, Chico
Eric Johnstone, Montana State University
Diana K. Kanoy, Central Florida Community College
Margaret S. Kilcoyne, Northwestern State University
G. Scott King, Sinclair Community College
Suzanne P. Krissler, Orange County Community College
Linda L. Labin, Husson College
Richard Lacy, California State University–Fresno
Suzanne Lambert, Broward Community College South
Marilyn L. Lammers, California State University, Northridge
Lorita S. Langdon, Columbus State Community College
Joyce N. Larsen, Front Range Community College
Barbara Lea, West Valley College
Claire E. Legowski, North Dakota State University
Mary E. Leslie, Grossmont College
Mary Jean Lush, Delta State University
Sonia Maasik, University of California, Los Angeles
Bruce MacBeth, Clarion University of Pennsylvania
Georgia E. Mackh, Cabrillo College
Andrew Madson, Milwaukee Area Technical College

Maureen L. Margolies, University of Cincinnati, Raymond Walters College
Thomas A. Marshall II, Robert Morris College
John F. Mastriani, El Paso Community College
Diana McKowen, Indiana University
Mary C. Miller, Ashland University
Nancy B. Moody, Sinclair Community College
Wayne A. Moore, Indiana University of Pennsyvania
Paul William Murphey, Southwest Wisconsin Technical College
Alexa B. North, State University of West Georgia
Lin Nassar, Oakland Community College
Beverly H. Nelson, University of New Orleans
John P. Nightingale, Eastern Michigan University
Alexa B. North, Georgia State University
Rosemary Olds, Des Moines Area Community College
James S. O'Rourke IV, University of Notre Dame
Calvin R. Parks, Nothern Illinois University
Pamela A. Patey, Riverside Community College
William Peirce, Prince George's Community College and University of Maryland University College
Joan Policano, Onondaga Community College
Paula J. Pomerenke, Illinois State University
Karen Sterkel Powell, Colorado State University
Gloria Power, Delgado Community College
Richard P. Profozich, Prince George's Community College, Largo, Maryland
Carolyn Mae Rainey, Southeast Missouri State University
Richard G. Raspen, Wilkes University
Virginia L. Reynolds, Cleveland State University
Ruth D. Richardson, University of North Alabama
Joseph H. Roach, Middlesex County College
Terry D. Roach, Arkansas State University, Jonesboro
Betty Jane Robbins, University of Oklahoma
Linda Sarlo, Rock Valley College
Christine A. Saxild, Mt. Senario College
Joseph Schaffner, State University of New York at Alfred
Annette Schley, North Seattle Community College
Betty L. Schroeder, Northern Illinois University
Carolyn M. Seefer, Diablo Valley Community College
Marilyn Simonson, Lakewood Community College
Sue C. Smith, Palm Beach Community College
Kathleen M. Sole, University of Phoenix
Charles L. Snowden, Sinclair Community College
Gayle A. Sobolik, California State University, Fresno
Jeanette Spencer, Arkansas State University
Judy Steiner-Williams, Indiana University
Ted D. Stoddard, Brigham Young University
Roni Szeliga, Gateway Technical College, Wisconsin
Leslie S. Talley, University of Central Florida
Barbara P. Thompson, Columbus State Community College
Sally J. Tiffany, Milwaukee Area Technical College
Mary L. Tucker, Colorado State University
Richard F. Tyler, Anne Arundel Community College
Doris A. Van Horn Christopher, California State University, Los Angeles
David Victor, Eastern Michigan University
Lois Ann Wagner, Southwest Wisconsin Technical College
John L. Waltman, Eastern Michigan University
Marion Webb, Cleveland State University
Carol M. Williams, Pima County Community College District
Jane D. Williams, J. Sargeant Reynolds Community College
Rosemary B. Wilson, Washtenaw Community College
Beverly C. Wise, State University of New York at Morrisville
William E. Worth, Georgia State University
Myron D. Yeager, Chapman University

UNIT • 1 •

Communication Foundations

CHAPTER 1

Communicating at Work

CHAPTER 2

Communicating in Teams: Listening, Nonverbal Communication, Collaboration, and Meeting Skills

CHAPTER 3

Communicating Across Cultures

CHAPTER • 1 •

Communicating at Work

LEARNING OBJECTIVES

1. Identify changes in the workplace and the importance of communication skills.

2. Describe the process of communication.

3. Discuss barriers to interpersonal communication and the means of overcoming those barriers.

4. Analyze the functions and procedures of communication in organizations.

5. Assess the flow of communication in organizations including barriers and methods for overcoming those barriers.

6. List the goals of ethical business communication and describe important tools for doing the right thing.

COMMUNICATION IN PROCESS

CASE STUDY

Pillsbury's Restructuring "Discombobulates" Employees

A new age dawned at Pillsbury in the 1990s. The food giant underwent staggering changes that shook it to its very flour-milling roots. Like many companies at that time, it experienced mergers and acquisitions, a shake-up of senior management, and downsizing in some divisions. With over 18,000 employees worldwide, Pillsbury maintains its headquarters in the Pillsbury Center, Minneapolis, shown on page 2. It controls many well-known trademarks including Green Giant, Häagen-Dazs, Old El Paso, and Progresso. It also claims America's most famous spokescritter, the Pillsbury Doughboy, and, until recently, owned Burger King.

"The company got a new CEO in the fall of 1991," explained Lou de Ocejo, senior vice president of human resources and corporate affairs. "We went through a fairly extensive structural change in how we run the business—we focused on competencies in food technology, brands marketing, and that type of thing, [moving] away from the old focus, which was on divisions within the company and functional silos." Instead of working in "silos" such as research, production, personnel, or shipping, people became part of cross-functional teams. "When we made that change," said de Ocejo, "it was very traumatic. Philosophically, it was a good idea, but the lines of authority got blurred, and new things became important. People became discombobulated—who's my boss? Where do I go?"

Worse yet, as a company Pillsbury wasn't growing. Business was flat. Moreover, it was fundamentally a U.S. business. Suddenly, this company that had seen all roads begin and end in Minneapolis had to regroup and look beyond its regional home. "Roads were beginning and ending in Argentina and Bombay," said de Ocejo.[1] Expanding its global market, managing broad restructuring, and pumping up sagging employee morale became urgent concerns in the new age of Pillsbury.

In any organization, when employees fear that their jobs will change or even disappear, morale plummets. Rumors fly, and productivity sinks. Excessive caution and mistrust prevail. That's why, in times of upheaval, communication—and lots of it—becomes paramount.

www.pillsbury.com

Ensuring That You Succeed in the New Workplace

Employees at many organizations are experiencing the kind of change and upheaval felt at Pillsbury. In fact, the entire work world you are about to enter is changing dramatically. The kind of work you'll do, the tools you'll use, the form of management, the environment where you'll work, the people with whom you'll interact—all are undergoing a profound transformation. Many of the changes in this dynamic workplace revolve around processing and communicating information. As a result, the most successful players in this new world of work will be those with highly developed communication skills.

1

The abilities to read, listen, speak, and write effectively, of course, are not inborn. Thriving in the dynamic and demanding work world depends on many factors, some of which you cannot control. But one factor that you do control is how well you communicate. The goals of this book and this course are to teach you basic business communication skills, such as how to write a memo or letter and how to make a presentation. You will also learn additional powerful communication skills, as summarized in Figure 1.1. Because they will equip you with the skills most needed in today's dynamic workplace, *this book and this course may well be the most important in your entire college curriculum.*

Succeeding in today's world of work demands that you read, listen, speak, and write effectively.

FIGURE 1.1 Succeeding in Today's Dynamic and Demanding Workplace

This Business Communication Book and This Course Will Help You

- Apply a universal process that helps you solve communication problems now and throughout your entire career
- Learn specific writing techniques and organizational strategies to compose clear, concise, and purposeful business messages
- Master effective speaking skills for getting your ideas across to small and large groups
- Learn to be a valuable team player
- Work productively with the Internet and other rapidly evolving communication technologies
- Recognize the importance of nonverbal communication cues
- Value diversity and function with sensitivity in multicultural work environments
- Develop tools for meeting ethically challenging situations
- Feel confident that you will always have excellent document models to follow now and on the job
- Land the job of your dreams by providing invaluable job-search, résumé-writing, and interviewing tips

The book provides you with not only the process but also the products of effective communication. You'll be able to use it throughout your training for its many models of successful business and professional documents. When you are ready to enter the job market, you'll find it to be an invaluable source of excellent résumés and cover letters. On the job you'll refer to it for examples of business letters, e-mail messages, reports, and other documents. That's why many students decide that this is one book they will keep.

This book and your instructor provide you with the principles, processes, products, and practice that you need to succeed.

To become an effective communicator, though, you need more than a good book. You also need practice—with meaningful feedback. You need someone such as your instructor to tell you how to modify your responses so that you can improve. We've designed this book and its supplements to provide you and your instructor with principles, processes, products, and practice—everything necessary to make you a successful business communicator in today's dynamic workplace.

Yes, the workplace is undergoing profound changes. As a businessperson and especially as a business communicator, you will undoubtedly be affected by many transformations. Some of the most significant changes include global competition, flattened management hierarchies, and team-based projects. Other changes reflect our constantly evolving information technology, new work environments, a diverse workforce, and the emergence of a knowledge-based economy. The following brief look at this new world of work reveals how directly your success in it will be tied to possessing excellent communication skills.

Heightened Global Competition

Small, medium, and large companies increasingly find themselves competing in global rather than local markets. Improved systems of telecommunication, advanced forms of transportation, and saturated local markets—all of these developments have encouraged companies to move beyond familiar territories to emerging markets around the world. PepsiCo fights Coca-Cola for new customers in India. Toys R Us opens shop in Japan. FedEx learns the ropes in South America. And Burger King challenges McDonald's for fast-food supremacy in Europe.[2]

Communication is more complicated with people who have different religions, customs, and lifestyles.

Doing business in far-flung countries means dealing with people who are very different from you. They have different religions, engage in different customs, live different lifestyles, and rely on different approaches in business. Now add the complications of multiple time zones, vast distances between offices, and different languages. No wonder global communicators can blunder.[3] Take, for example, FedEx's offer of a money-back guarantee in South America. The concept was so unfamiliar to the culture that people automatically thought something must be wrong with the service.[4] FedEx quickly withdrew the offer.

Successful communication in these new markets requires developing new skills such as cultural knowledge and sensitivity, flexibility, patience, and tolerance. Because these are skills and traits that most of us need to polish, you will receive special communication training to help you deal with intercultural business transactions.

Flattened Management Hierarchies

In response to intense global competition and other pressures, businesses have for years been cutting costs and flattening their management hierarchies. This flattening means that fewer layers of managers separate decision makers from line workers. In traditional companies, information flows through many levels of managers. In flat organizations, however, where the lines of communication are shorter, decision makers can react more quickly to market changes. Toymaker Mattel transformed itself from an "out-of-control money loser" into a record-breaking money maker by taking the advice of employees and cutting six layers from its organizational hierarchy.[5]

Flatter organizations demand that every employee be a skilled communicator.

But today's flatter organizations also bring greater communication challenges. In the past, authoritarian and hierarchical management structures did not require that every employee be a skilled communicator. Managers simply passed along messages to the next level. Today, however, front-line employees as well as managers participate in decision making. Their input and commitment are necessary for their organizations to be successful in global markets. Moreover, everyone has become a writer and a communicator.[6] Secretaries no longer "clean up" their bosses' writing. Nearly all employees have computers and write their own messages. Even though writing on the job is an important skill, myths and misconceptions about it persist, as discussed in the accompanying Career Coach box.

Expanded Team-Based Management

Along with flatter chains of command, companies are also turning to the concept of team-based operations. Nearly 80 percent of employers in all industries have adopted some form of quality circles or self-directed teams. At the Frito-Lay plant in Lubbock, Texas, workers formerly loaded bags of potato chips into cartons. Now organized into work teams, they are responsible for everything from potato processing to equipment maintenance. They even interview new hires and make quality control decisions.[7] At Cigna Corporation, a huge national insurance company, three organizational layers were flattened, and teams were formed to reduce backups in processing customer claims. Formation of these teams forced technology specialists to communicate constantly with business specialists. Suddenly, computer programmers had to do more than code and debug; they had to listen, interpret, and explain. All members of the team had to analyze problems and negotiate solutions.[8]

CAREER COACH

FIVE COMMON MYTHS ABOUT WRITING ON THE JOB

A myth is an unfounded belief or misconception. You may have seen movies or heard friends talk about some occupations, leading you to accept without scrutiny certain myths about writing on the job. These myths may affect the way you prepare for your career. Here are five common myths about writing and the facts that refute them.

Myth: Because I'm in a technical field, I'll work with numbers, not words.

Fact: In truth, 90 percent of all business transactions involve written communication.[9] Conducting business in any field—even in technical and specialized areas such as information technology, accounting, engineering, marketing, hotel management, and so forth—involves some writing. "You can have the greatest technical skills in the world, but without solid communication skills, who will know and can understand?" said Kevin Jetton, executive vice president of the Association of Information Technology Professionals.[10] Moreover, with promotions, writing tasks will increase.

Myth: Secretaries will clean up my writing problems.

Fact: In today's world of tightened budgets, only a few upper-level executives still have secretaries or assistants who type their messages. Most managers and executives now write their own e-mail messages, memos, and letters on their computers because it's faster and more efficient. For those who do have administrative help, it's wise to remember that even the most highly skilled secretary cannot remedy fundamental problems in organization, emphasis, and tone.

Myth: Technical writers do most of the real writing on the job.

Fact: Some companies employ technical writers to prepare manuals, documentation, and public documents such as annual reports. Rarely, however, do these specialists write everyday messages (internal reports, letters, memos) for employees. Instead, sales representatives, programmers, accountants, engineers, technicians, and other professionals must rely on their own skills to communicate their ideas.

Myth: Computers can fix any of my writing mistakes.

Fact: Today's style, grammar, and spell checkers are wonderful aids to business writers. They can highlight selected trouble areas and occasionally suggest revisions. What they can't do, though, is write the document and ensure its total accuracy. Spell checkers, for example, may not distinguish between confusing words such as *their/there/they're* or *principal/principle.* Other checkers can't locate or correct most grammar, punctuation, style, tone, and organizational errors. Only trained writers can do that.

Myth: I can use form letters for most messages.

Fact: Books and computer programs can provide dozens of ready-made letters or pattern paragraphs for which businesspeople merely fill in the blanks. When these letters are appropriate and well written, they can be useful time-savers. Often, however, such letters are poorly written and ill suited for specific situations. Most messages demand that writers create their own original thoughts.

Career Application

Interview a specialist in your career area. What kinds of messages does she or he write? How often? After promotions, do these specialists have different writing tasks?

When companies form cross-functional teams, individuals must work together and share information. What's tough is that these individuals often don't share the same background, knowledge, or training. Some companies must hire communication coaches to help existing teams get along. They work on developing interpersonal, negotiation, and collaboration techniques. But companies would prefer to hire new workers who already possess these skills. That's why so many ads say "must possess good communication skills."

Innovative Communication Technologies

E-mail, voice mail, fax, videoconferencing, and the Web are revolutionizing the way we exchange information.

Because technology is completely revolutionizing the way we communicate, recruiters are also looking for people with good computer skills. We now exchange information by e-mail, voice mail, and fax. Through teleconferencing and videoconferencing, we can conduct meetings with associates around the world. And no self-respecting businessperson today would make a presentation without using sophisticated presentation software. Moreover, we now make tremendous use of the Internet and the Web for collecting information, serving customers, and promoting products and services. Like many companies, cataloger L. L. Bean first launched its Web site, shown in Figure 1.2, as a simple information site. Now it offers on-line shopping and richer, lengthier content including guides to eight national parks.

Just as companies are scrambling to use the Web most effectively, individual businesspeople are eagerly embracing the new technologies and revamping the way they communicate. E-mail has already become the most often used means of communication, according to the American Management Association.[11] To use these new resources most effectively, you, as a skilled business communicator, must develop a tool kit of new communication skills. For example, you will want to know how to design documents for screen appeal, how to select the best medium for a message, and how to use on-line search tools efficiently.

FIGURE 1.2 **L. L. Bean Web Site Serves Customers**

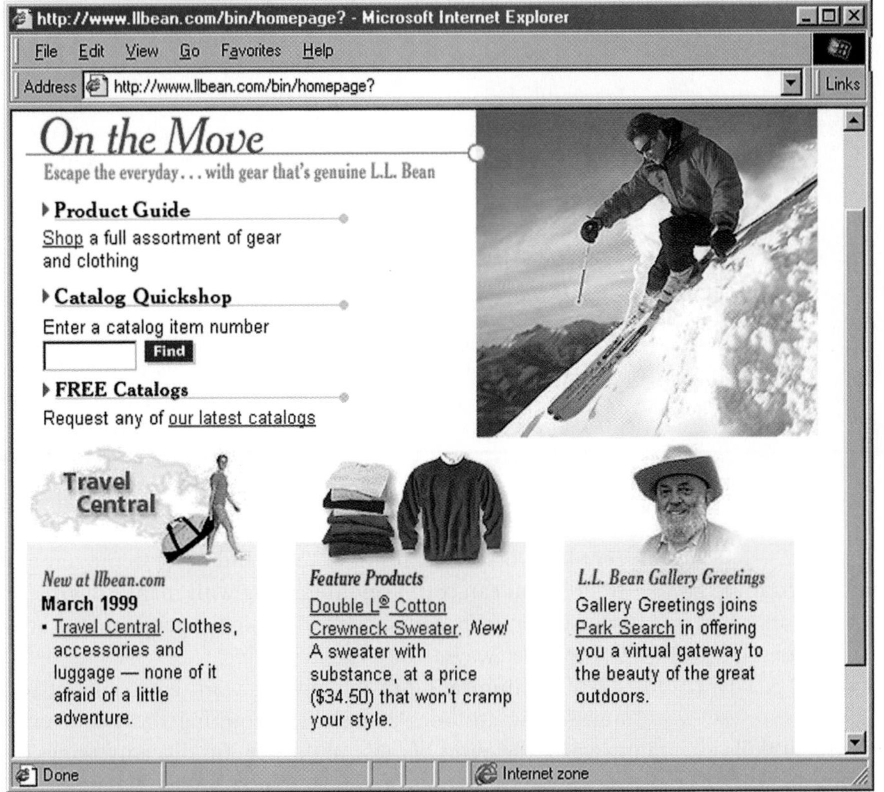

L. L. Bean offers customer service, catalog sales, and information about the national parks.

New Work Environments

Global competition, restructuring, and mobile technologies are encouraging flexible working arrangements such as telecommuting and hotelling.

As a result of global competition and restructuring, it's no surprise that we are also seeing dramatic changes in work environments. Thanks to mobile technologies, millions of Americans now *telecommute.* They have flexible working arrangements so that they can work at home at least part of the time. Many workers live thousands of miles from the office, and others carry their work with them as they travel.[12] Some Big Six accounting firms are even instituting the practices of *hotelling* and *hot-desking.*[13] *Hotelling* describes the practice of an open office with unassigned desks. Employees do not have personal work spaces; they reserve a desk for the days or hours they will be in the office. *Hot-desking* refers to a desk that's still warm from its previous occupant (similar to *hot-bunking* for sailors on crowded ships). Hotelling makes sense for companies with staffs that spend most of their time outside the office, such as accountants who work at clients' businesses. Why should a company rent offices for empty desks gathering dust in expensive office buildings?

Although hotelling and hot-desking will probably never become commonplace, many office workers are admittedly working in tighter quarters and under greater stress. Some are in open offices divided into small work cubicles, resulting in the need for new rules of office etiquette and civility. For example, instead of wandering into a cubicle, visitors should knock on the frame (they have no doors) to ask permission to enter.[14] Tight quarters, intense cost-cutting measures, demands for increased productivity, and the fast-paced world of information technology—all are creating stress for today's workers. Combined with new responsibilities of team problem solving, business communicators can expect to need interpersonal skills that deal with heightened levels of emotion. Especially important are listening to and empathizing with fellow employees. Equally significant is respecting others' periodic need for uninterrupted, focused work time.[15] And employees at home may face added communication challenges since staying connected with the office often requires exchanging more messages than if they were face to face with their colleagues.

One unspoken benefit of teams is their role in making diversity more successful. Teams encourage members to get to know each other as they work together to solve problems.

Increasingly Diverse Workforce

Changes in today's work environments include more than new technology, team management, and different work routines. You can also expect to see hoards of new faces. No longer, say the experts, will the workplace be predominantly male or Anglo oriented. By the year 2005, women and minority men will make up 62 percent of the workforce.[16] Moreover, workers from the ages of 55 to 64 will increase from 9 percent of the workforce in 1994 to 12 percent by 2005.[17] As a result of these and other demographic trends, you can count on interacting with many coworkers who differ from you in race, ethnicity, gender, age, and many other ways.

Communicating in this diverse work environment requires new attitudes and skills. Acquiring these new employment skills is certainly worth the effort because of the benefits diversity brings to consumers, work teams, and business organizations. A diverse staff is better able to read trends and respond to the increasingly diverse customer base in local and world markets. In the workplace, diversity also makes good business sense. Teams made up of different people with different experiences are more likely to create the different products that consumers demand. Customers also want to deal with companies that respect their values. They are more likely to say, "If you're a company whose ads don't include me, or whose workforce doesn't include me, I won't buy from you."[18] Learning to cooperate and communicate successfully with diverse coworkers should be a major priority for all businesspeople.

Communicating with workers who differ in race, ethnicity, gender, and age requires new attitudes and skills.

Thriving in the Age of Knowledge

We're now witnessing the emergence of an advanced economy based on information and knowledge. Physical labor, raw materials, and capital are no longer the key ingredients in the creation of wealth. Now, the vital raw material in our economy, say futurists Alvin Toffler and Oren Harari, is knowledge.[19] Tomorrow's wealth depends on the development and exchange of knowledge. And individuals entering the workforce offer their knowledge, not their muscles. Knowledge workers, says management guru Peter Drucker, get paid for their education and their ability to learn.[20] Knowledge workers engage in mind work. They deal with symbols: words, figures, and data.

Knowledge workers deal with symbols, such as words, figures, and data.

Spotlight on **Communicators**

"We are entering an age where intangible assets like expertise, intelligence, speed, agility, imagination, maneuverability, networks, passion, responsiveness and innovation—all facets of 'knowledge'—become more important than the tangibles of traditional balance-sheet perspectives," contends Oren Harari, management expert and futurist. The emerging knowledge economy, he asserts, is "brain-based."

What does all this mean for you? As a future knowledge worker, you can expect to be generating, processing, and exchanging information. Currently three out of four jobs involve some form of mind work, and that number will increase sharply in the future. Management and employees alike will be making decisions in such areas as product development, quality control, and customer satisfaction.

You will be asked to think critically. This means having opinions that are backed by reason and evidence. When your boss or team leader says, "What do you think we ought to do?" you want to be able to supply good ideas. The accompanying Career Coach box provides a five-point critical thinking plan to help you solve problems and make decisions. But having a plan is not enough. You also need chances to try the plan out and get feedback from colleagues and your boss (your instructor, for the time being). At the end of each chapter, you'll find activities and problems that will help you develop and apply your critical thinking skills.

In the new world of work, you can look forward to being in constant training to acquire new skills that will help you keep up with improved technologies and procedures. You can also expect to be taking greater control of your career. Gone are the nine-to-five jobs, lifetime security, predictable promotions, and even the conventional workplace, as you have learned earlier. Don't presume that companies will provide you with a clearly defined career path or planned developmental experiences. And don't wait for someone to "empower" you. You have to empower yourself.[21] To thrive in the new work world, you must be flexible and continually willing to learn new skills that supplement the strong foundation of basic skills you acquire in college.

Constantly changing technologies and work procedures mean continual training for employees.

Probably the most important foundation skill for knowledge workers in the new environment is the ability to communicate. This means being able to listen and to express your ideas effectively in writing and in speech. As you advance in your career, communication skills become even more important. The number one requirement for promotion to management is the ability to communicate. Corporate president Ben Ordover explained how he makes executive choices: "Many people climbing the corporate ladder are very good. When faced with a hard choice between candidates, I use writing ability as the deciding factor. Sometimes a candidate's writing is the only skill that separates him or her from the competition."[22]

CAREER COACH

SHARPENING YOUR SKILLS FOR CRITICAL THINKING, PROBLEM SOLVING, AND DECISION MAKING

Gone are the days when management expected workers to check their brains at the door and do only as told. As a knowledge worker, you'll be expected to use your brains in thinking critically. You'll be solving problems and making decisions. Much of this book is devoted to solving problems and communicating those decisions to management, fellow workers, clients, the government, and the public.

Faced with a problem or an issue, most of us do a lot of worrying before separating the issues or making a decision. All that worrying can become directed thinking by channeling it into the following procedure.

1. **Identify and Clarify the Problem.** Your first task is to recognize that a problem exists. Some problems are big and unmistakable, such as failure of an air-freight delivery service to get packages to customers on time. Other problems may be continuing annoyances, such as regularly running out of toner for an office copy machine. The first step in reaching a solution is pinpointing the problem area.
2. **Gather Information.** Learn more about the problem situation. Look for possible causes and solutions. This step may mean checking files, calling suppliers, or brainstorming with fellow workers. For example, the air-freight delivery service would investigate the tracking systems of the commercial airlines carrying its packages to determine what went wrong.
3. **Evaluate the Evidence.** Where did the information come from? Does it represent various points of view? What biases could be expected from each source? How accurate is the information gathered? Is it fact or opinion? For example, it is a fact that packages are missing; it is an opinion that they are merely lost and will turn up eventually.
4. **Consider Alternatives and Implications.** Draw conclusions from the gathered evidence and pose solutions. Then weigh the advantages and disadvantages of each alternative. What are the costs, benefits, and consequences? What are the obstacles, and how can they be handled? Most important, what solution best serves your goals and those of your organization? Here's where your creativity is especially important.
5. **Choose and Implement the Best Alternative.** Select an alternative and put it into action. Then, follow through on your decision by monitoring the results of implementing your plan. The freight company decided to give its unhappy customers free delivery service to make up for the lost packages and downtime. Be sure to continue monitoring and adjusting the solution to ensure its effectiveness over time.

Career Application

Managers at Pillsbury could hardly believe it when they heard from customers that their Pillsbury Chocolate Chip Cookies (a refrigerated dough product sold in 18-ounce packages) had walnuts in it. This product isn't supposed to contain walnuts. Something obviously went wrong in production. Fortunately, only a small number of packages were involved. However, consumption of this product could be dangerous to walnut-sensitive people. In teams of three or four, discuss the five steps above in analyzing and reacting to this problem. Should Pillsbury admit its mistake? If so, how could it communicate the news to the public? What alternatives does it have in rectifying its mistake? Be prepared to present a summary of your team's itemized responses to your class.[23]

Examining the Process of Communication

Since communication is a central factor in the emerging knowledge economy and a major consideration for anyone entering today's workforce, we need to look more closely at the total process of communication. Just what is communication? For our purposes communication is the *transmission of information and meaning from one individual or group to another.* The crucial element in this definition is meaning. Communication has as its central objective the transmission of meaning. The process of communication is successful only when the receiver understands an idea as the sender intended it. Both parties must agree not only on the information transmitted but also on the meaning of that information. This entire book is devoted to one objective: teaching you the skills of communication so that you can transmit meaning along with information. How does an idea travel from one person to another? Despite what you may have seen in futuristic science fiction movies, we can't just glance at another person and transfer meaning directly from mind to mind. We engage in a sensitive process of communication that generally involves five steps, discussed here and depicted in Figure 1.3.

Sender Has Idea

The communication process has five steps: idea formation, message encoding, message transmission, message decoding, and feedback.

The process of communication begins when the person with whom the message originates—the *sender*—has an idea. The form of the idea will be influenced by complex factors surrounding the sender: mood, frame of reference, background, culture, and physical makeup, as well as the context of the situation and many other factors. The way you greet people on campus, for example, depends a lot on how you feel, whom you are addressing (a classmate, a professor, a campus worker), and what your culture has trained you to say ("Hi," "Howdy," "How ya doing?" or "Good morning").

The form of the idea, whether a simple greeting or a complex idea, is shaped by assumptions based on the sender's experiences. A manager sending a message to employees assumes they will be receptive, while direct mail advertisers assume that receivers will give only a quick glance to their message. Ability to accurately predict how a message will affect its receiver and skill in adapting that message to its receiver are key factors in successful communication.

FIGURE 1.3 **The Communication Process**

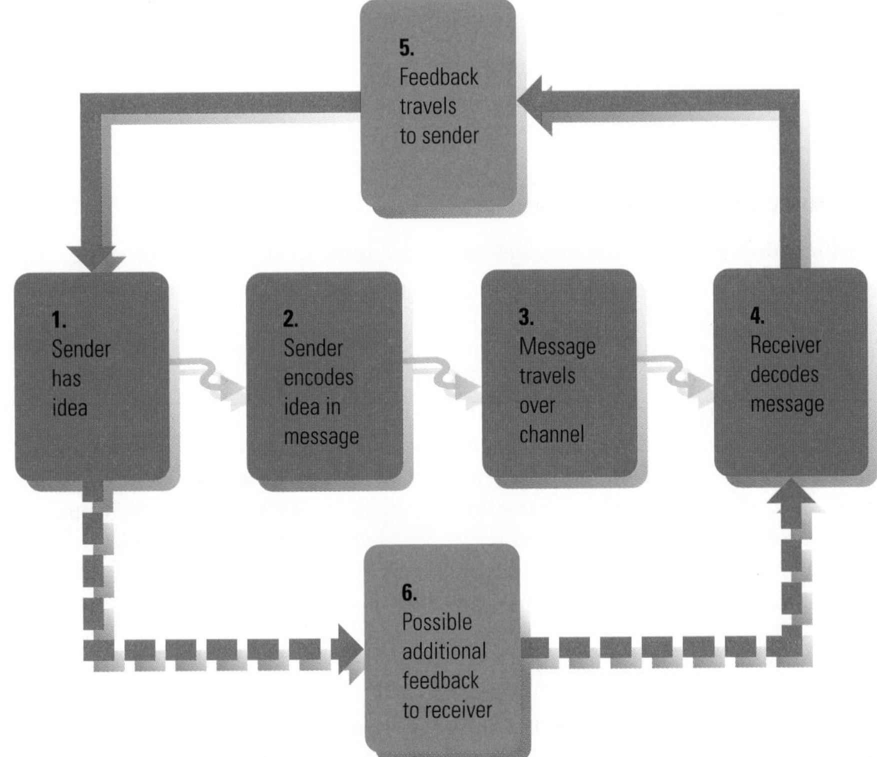

Sender Encodes Idea in Message

The next step in the communication process involves *encoding.* This means converting the idea into words or gestures that will convey meaning. A major problem in communicating any message verbally is that words have different meanings for different people. When misunderstandings result from missed meanings, it's called *bypassing.* Recognizing how easy it is to be misunderstood, skilled communicators choose familiar words with concrete meanings on which both senders and receivers agree. In selecting proper symbols, senders must be alert to the receiver's communication skills, attitudes, background, experiences, and culture: How will the selected words affect the receiver? For example, a Dr. Pepper cola promotion failed miserably in Great Britain because American managers had not done their homework. They had to change their "I'm a Pepper" slogan after learning that *pepper* is British slang for *prostitute.*[24] Because the sender initiates a communication transaction, he or she has primary responsibility for its success or failure. Choosing appropriate words or symbols is the first step.

Message Travels Over Channel

Channels are the media—computer, telephone, letter, fax, and so on—that transmit messages.

The medium over which the message is physically transmitted is the *channel.* Messages may be delivered by computer, telephone, letter, memorandum, report, announcement, picture, spoken word, fax, pager, or through some other channel. Because communication channels deliver both verbal and nonverbal messages, senders must choose the channel and shape the message carefully. A company may use its annual report, for example, as a channel to deliver many messages to stockholders. The verbal message lies in the report's financial and organizational news. Nonverbal messages, though, are conveyed by the report's appearance (showy versus bland), layout (ample white space versus tightly packed columns of print), and tone (conversational versus formal).

Anything that interrupts the transmission of a message in the communication process is called *noise.* Channel noise ranges from static that disrupts a telephone conversation to typographical errors in a letter or e-mail message. Such errors damage the credibility of the sender. Channel noise might even include the annoyance a receiver feels when the sender chooses an improper medium for sending a message, such as announcing a loan rejection via postcard or firing an employee by e-mail.

Spotlight on **Communicators**

As the founder of ASK, a $400 million computer software company in Silicon Valley, Sandra Kurtzig recognized the power of encoding and decoding messages accurately. The best ideas in the world, she warns, are useless if they can't be communicated clearly and concisely to others.

Receiver Decodes Message

The individual for whom the message is intended is the *receiver.* Translating the message from its symbol form into meaning involves *decoding.* Only when the receiver understands the meaning intended by the sender—that is, successfully decodes the message—does communication take place. Such success, however, is difficult to achieve because no two people share the same life experiences and because many barriers can disrupt the process.

Decoding can be disrupted internally by the receiver's lack of attention to or bias against the sender. It can be disrupted externally by loud sounds or illegible words. Decoding can also be sidetracked by semantic obstacles, such as misunderstood words or emotional reactions to certain terms. A memo that refers to all the women in an office as "girls," for example, may disturb its receivers so much that they fail to comprehend the total message.

Feedback Travels to Sender

The verbal and nonverbal responses of the receiver create *feedback,* a vital part of the communication process. Feedback helps the sender know that the message was received and understood. If, as a receiver, you hear the message "How are you," your feedback might consist of words ("I'm fine") or body language (a smile or a wave of the hand). Although the receiver may respond with additional feedback to the sender (thus creating a new act of communication), we'll concentrate here on the initial message flowing to the receiver and the resulting feedback.

Asking questions encourages feedback that clarifies communication.

Senders can encourage feedback by asking questions such as, *Am I making myself clear?* and *Is there anything you don't understand?* Senders can further improve feedback by timing the delivery appropriately and by providing only as much information as the receiver can handle. Receivers can improve the process by paraphrasing the sender's message with comments such as, *Let me try to explain that in my own words.* The best feedback is descriptive rather than evaluative. For example, here's a descriptive response: *I understand you want to launch a used golfball business.* Here's an evaluative response: *Your business ideas are always weird.* An evaluative response is judgmental and doesn't tell the sender if the receiver actually understood the message.

Overcoming Interpersonal Communication Barriers

3

The communication process is successful only when the receiver understands the message as intended by the sender. It sounds quite simple. Yet, it's not. How many times have you thought that you delivered a clear message, only to learn later that your intentions were totally misunderstood? Most messages that we send reach their destination, but many are only partially understood.

Obstacles That Create Misunderstanding

Barriers to successful communication include bypassing, differing frames of reference, lack of language or listening skills, emotional interference, and physical distractions.

You can improve your chances of communicating successfully by learning to recognize barriers that are known to disrupt the process. The most significant barriers for individuals are bypassing, frames of reference, lack of language skill, and distractions.

Bypassing. One of the biggest barriers to clear communication involves words. Each of us attaches a little bundle of meanings to every word, and these meanings are not always similar. *Bypassing* happens when people miss each other with their meanings.[25] Let's say your boss asks you to "help" with a large customer mailing. When you arrive to do your share, you learn that you are expected to do the whole mailing yourself. You and your boss attached different meanings to the word *help.* Bypassing can lead to major miscommunication because people assume that meanings are contained in words. Actually, meanings are in people. For communication to be successful, the receiver and sender must attach the same symbolic meanings to their words.

Miscommunication often results when the sender's frame of reference differs markedly from the receiver's.

Frame of Reference. Another barrier to clear communication is your *frame of reference.* Everything you see and feel in the world is translated through your individual frame of reference. Your unique frame is formed by a combination of your experiences, education, culture, expectations, personality, and many other elements. As a result, you bring your own biases and expectations to any communication situation. Because your frame of reference is totally different from everyone else's, you will never see things exactly as others do. American owners attempting to modernize a Mexican assembly plant, for example, perceived failure when they saw a report indicating a slow pace of change. The Mexican managers, on the other hand, saw the report and congratulated themselves on their splendid progress. Wise business communicators strive to prevent communication failure by being alert to both their own frames of reference and those of others.

Successful communication requires good oral and written language skills.

Lack of Language Skill. No matter how extraordinary the idea, it won't be understood or fully appreciated unless the communicators involved have good language skills. Each individual needs an adequate vocabulary, a command of basic punctuation and grammar, and skill in written and oral expression. Moreover, poor listening skills can prevent us from hearing oral messages clearly and thus responding properly.

Distractions. Other barriers include emotional interference and physical distractions. Shaping an intelligent message is difficult when you're feeling joy, fear, resentment, hostility, sadness, or some other strong emotion. To reduce the influence of emotions on communication, both senders and receivers should focus on the content of the message and try to remain objective. Physical distractions such as faulty acoustics, noisy surroundings, or a poor telephone connection can disrupt oral communication. Similarly, sloppy appearance, poor printing, careless formatting, and typographical or spelling errors can disrupt written messages.

Overcoming the Obstacles

To overcome obstacles, communicators must anticipate problems in encoding, transmitting, and decoding.

Careful communicators can conquer barriers in a number of ways. Half the battle in communicating successfully is recognizing that the entire process is sensitive and susceptible to breakdown. Like a defensive driver anticipating problems on the road, a good communicator anticipates problems in encoding, transmitting, and decoding a message. Effective communicators also focus on the receiver's environment and frame of reference. They ask themselves questions such as, *How is that individual likely to react to my message?* or *Does the receiver know as much about the subject as I do?*

Misunderstandings are less likely if you arrange your ideas logically and use words precisely. Mark Twain was right when he said, "The difference between an almost-right word and the right word is like the difference between lightning and the lightning bug." But communicating is more than expressing yourself well. A large part of successful communication is listening. Management advisor Peter Drucker observed that "too many executives think they are wonderful with people because they talk well. They don't realize that being wonderful with people means listening well."[26]

Overcoming interpersonal barriers often involves questioning your preconceptions. Successful communicators continually examine their personal assumptions, biases, and prejudices. The more you pay attention to subtleties and know "where you're coming from" when you encode and decode messages, the better you'll communicate. An American software company, for example, failed unnecessarily in Japan because it simply translated its glossy brochure from English into Japanese. The Americans didn't realize that in Japan such brochures are associated with low-priced consumer products. The software producer wrongly assumed that since glossy was upscale here, it would be perceived similarly in Japan.

Good communicators ask questions to stimulate feedback.

Finally, effective communicators create an environment for useful feedback. In oral communication this means asking questions such as, *Do you understand?* and *What questions do you have?* as well as encouraging listeners to repeat instructions or paraphrase ideas. To a listener, it means providing feedback that describes rather than evaluates. And in written communication it means asking questions and providing access: *Do you have my telephone number in case you have questions?* or *Please jot your answers down on my letter and return it in the enclosed envelope.*

Communicating in Organizations

4

Until now, you've probably been thinking about the communication you do personally. But business communicators must also be concerned with the bigger picture, and that involves sharing information in organizations. Creating and exchanging knowledge are critical to fostering innovation, the key challenge in today's knowledge economy. On the job you'll be exchanging information by communicating internally and externally.

Internal and External Functions

Internal communication often consists of e-mail, memos, and voice messages; external communication generally consists of letters.

Internal communication includes sharing ideas and messages with superiors, coworkers, and subordinates. When those messages must be written, you'll probably choose e-mail or a printed memorandum, such as the American Airlines memo shown in Figure 1.4. When you are communicating externally with customers, suppliers, government, and the public, you will generally send letters on company stationery, such as American's letter also shown in Figure 1.4.

Some of the functions of internal communication are to issue and clarify procedures and policies, inform management of progress, persuade employees or management to make changes or improvements, coordinate activities, and evaluate and reward employees. External functions are to answer inquiries about products or services, persuade customers to buy products or services, clarify supplier specifications, issue credit, collect bills, respond to government agencies, and promote a positive image of the organization.

In all of these tasks employees and managers use a number of communication skills: reading, listening, speaking, and writing. As college students, you probably realize that you need to improve these skills to the proficiency level required for success in today's knowledge society. This book and this course will provide you with practical advice on how to do just that.

Organizational communication has three basic functions: to inform, to persuade, and/or to promote goodwill.

Now, look back over the preceding discussion of internal and external functions of communication in organizations. Although there appear to be a large number of diverse business communication functions, they can be summarized in three simple categories, as Figure 1.5 shows: (1) to inform, (2) to persuade, and/or (3) to promote goodwill.

New Emphasis on Interactive Communication

The flattening of organizations coupled with the development of sophisticated information technology has greatly changed the way we communicate internally and externally. We're seeing a major shift away from one-sided and rather slow forms of communication, such as memos and letters. More companies are seeking customer and employee input to learn ways to improve business. To convey information to various audiences, organizations prefer more interactive, fast-results communication, such as e-mail, voice mail, intranets (company versions of the Internet), Web sites, video transmission, and videoconferencing. You'll be learning more about these forms of communication in subsequent chapters. Despite the range of interactive technologies, communicators are still working with two basic forms of communication: oral and written. Each has advantages and disadvantages.

Oral Communication. Nearly everyone agrees that the best way to exchange information is orally in face-to-face conversations or meetings. Oral communication

FIGURE 1.4 Internal and External Forms of Communication

AmericanAirlines®

EXECUTIVE OFFICE

March 4, 2000

Ms. Christie Bonner
1792 Southern Avenue
Mesa, AZ 85202

Dear Ms. Bonner:

Congratulations for taking steps to overcome your fear of flying! Your eloquent words are testimony to the effectiveness of our AAir Born program; and more important, they underline how liberating the experience can be. I know the door is now open for you to enjoy many satisfying travel experiences.

Probably the most pleasant part of my responsibilities at American is receiving compliments from our customers about the service provided by our employees. I have passed along your kind words about those individuals who made such a difference to you in realizing your dream of flight. We appreciate the opportunity to recognize their fine performance.

On behalf of all of us associated with the AAir Born program, thank you very much, Ms. Bonner. We look forward to welcoming you aboard again soon.

Sincerely,

Janice Moore

Janice Moore
Staff Supervisor

Letters on company stationery communicate with outsiders. Notice how this one builds a solid relationship between American Airlines and a satisfied customer.

Eudora Pro - [Bob Markum, NEWS RELEASE ABOUT NASHVILLE C]

File Edit Mailbox Message Transfer Special Tools Window Help

Standard MIME QP RR Send

To: Bob Markum <bmarkum@aa.com>
From: Tim Smith <tsmith@aa.com>
Subject: NEWS RELEASE ABOUT NASHVILLE CREW BASE
Cc:
Bcc:
Attached: News_Release.txt

As an attachment, Bob, I'm sending a draft of the news release announcing the Nashville crew base. Please look it over and make any changes you like. We've tried to keep it short and to the point. Captain Bill Baker has agreed to do the media conference late Tuesday morning since your schedule is so tight.

Because *Flagship News* is close to its deadline and would like to run a brief story on the announcement, I'll need your response by August 12. Thanks for your help.

Tim

E-mail messages and printed memorandums typically deliver messages within organizations. They use a standardized format and are direct and concise.

FIGURE 1.5 Functions of Business Communication

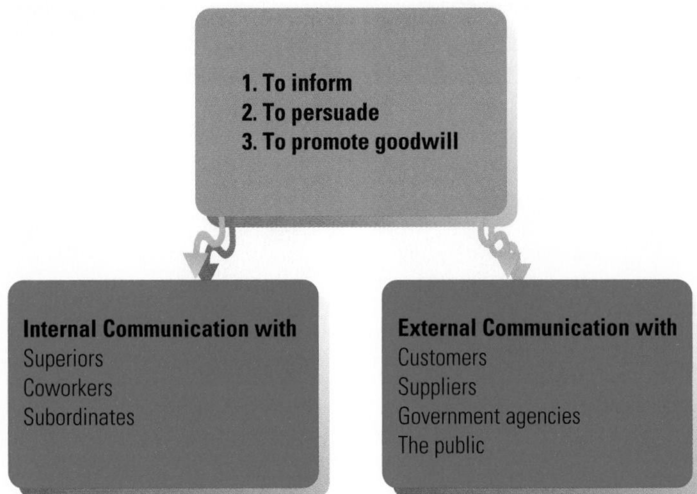

has many advantages. For one thing, it minimizes misunderstandings because communicators can immediately ask questions to clarify uncertainties. For another, it enables communicators to see each other's facial expressions and hear voice inflections, further improving the process. Oral communication is also an efficient way to develop consensus when many people must be consulted. Finally, most of us enjoy face-to-face interpersonal communication because it's easy, feels warm and natural, and promotes friendships.

Oral communication minimizes miscommunication but provides no written record.

The main disadvantages of oral communication are that it produces no written record, sometimes wastes time, and may be inconvenient. When individuals meet face to face or speak on the telephone, someone's work has to be interrupted. And how many of us are able to limit a conversation to just business? Nevertheless, oral communication has many advantages. The forms and advantages of both oral and written communication are summarized in Figure 1.6.

Written Communication. Written communication is impersonal in the sense that two communicators cannot see or hear each other and cannot provide immediate feedback. Most forms of business communication—including e-mail, announcements, memos, faxes, letters, newsletters, reports, proposals, and manuals—fall into this category.

Organizations rely on written communication for many reasons. It provides a permanent record, a necessity in these times of increasing litigation and extensive government regulation. Writing out an idea instead of delivering it orally enables communicators to develop an organized, well-considered message. Written documents are also convenient. They can be composed and read when the schedules of both communicators permit, and they can be reviewed if necessary.

Written communication provides a permanent record but lacks immediate feedback.

Written messages have drawbacks, of course. They require careful preparation and sensitivity to audience and anticipated effects. Words spoken in conversation may soon be forgotten, but words committed to hard or soft copy become a public record—and sometimes an embarrassing one. A former IBM chairman, for example, must have had second thoughts about his e-mail memo blasting managers for complacency and product defects. When leaked to the press, the memo shook up the financial world and damaged IBM's image and morale.

FIGURE 1.6 Forms of Organizational Communication

Oral Communication	Written Communication
Form	**Form**
Phone call	Announcement
Conversation	Memo, E-mail, fax
Interview	Letter
Meeting	Report, proposal
Conference	Newsletter
Advantages	**Advantages**
Immediate feedback	Permanent record
Nonverbal clues	Convenience
Warm feeling	Economy
Forceful impact	Careful message
Multiple input	Easy distribution

Written messages demand good writing skills, which can be developed through training.

Another drawback to written messages is that they are more difficult to prepare. They demand good writing skills, and such skills are not inborn. But writing proficiency can be learned. Because as much as 90 percent of all business transactions may involve written messages and because writing skills are so important to your business success, you will be receiving special instruction in becoming a good writer and a good communicator.

Avoiding Information Overload and Productivity Meltdown

The large volume of messages and communication channel choices overhwelms many workers.

Although technology provides a myriad of communication channel choices, the sheer volume of messages is overwhelming many employees. A study of 1,035 employees at America's most successful companies revealed that workers were sending or receiving an incredible 190 messages a day, as shown in Figure 1.7.[27] A similar poll by Gallup disclosed that workers averaged 178 voice mail, e-mail, and fax messages each day.[28] Workers often feel that they're getting no work done because interruptions average once every ten minutes. "Messaging is at the core of virtually all business processes, and managing it now controls people's daily priorities and focus," said Meredith Fischer. She is vice president of corporate marketing at Pitney Bowes, which specializes in communication products and services.[29]

Information overload and resulting productivity meltdown are becoming serious problems for workers and their employers. One mid-level manager at a global company solves his overload problem by deleting all the messages in his e-mail inbox when it gets too full. "If it's important," he reasons, "people will get back to me."[30] That technique, however, flirts with disaster. While some software programs can now automatically sort messages into limited categories, one expert says that "human brainpower"—not new technology—is the key to managing e-mail overload.[31] Suggestions for controlling the e-mail monster are shown in the accompanying Tech Talk box.

TECH TALK

TIPS FOR CONTROLLING THE E-MAIL MONSTER

- Send only business messages that you would have sent in a memo format.
- Check your e-mail in-box only at specific times each day, say at 9 a.m. and again at 4 p.m.
- Print important memos to read during free time away from your desk.
- Avoid using the copy function and sending unnecessary replies.
- Pick up your incoming messages on-line, but answer them off-line. Take time to think about your responses. Compose them on your word processor and upload them to your mail program, thus saving valuable network connection time.
- Devise a logical storage system, and religiously move incoming mail into electronic folders.
- Subscribe only to listservs (automated mailing lists) in which you are really interested. (Some high-volume Internet listservs disgorge 30 or more messages a day.)[32]

FIGURE 1.7 **Volume and Source of Daily Messages for Average Worker**

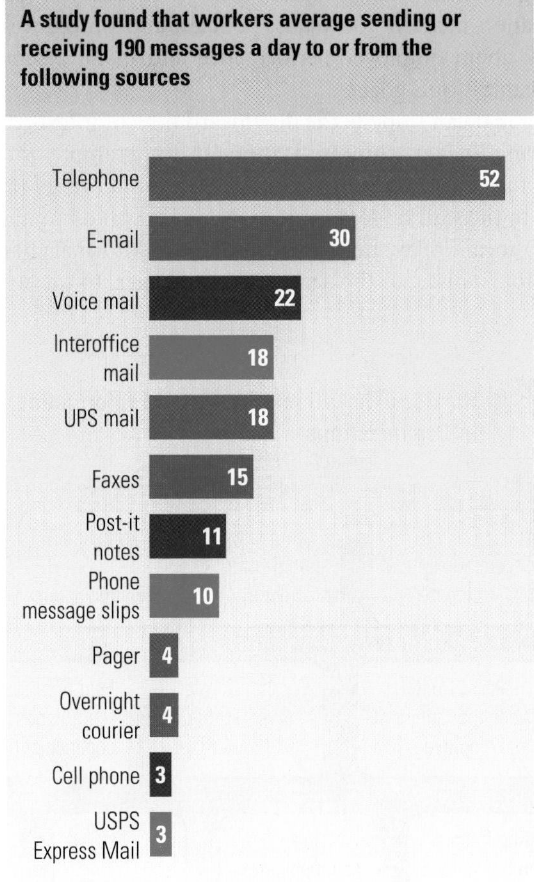

Source: Pitney Bowes Inc.

Although communication tools like e-mail and voicemail were expected to make workers more productive, the truth is that many employees feel stressed and unable to function. Solutions? Some workers are beginning to telecommute. Working from home means fewer interruptions. Others are blocking out work time when they turn off pagers and cell phones and log off the Internet.

Improving the Flow of Information in Organizations

5

Information within organizations flows through formal and informal communication channels. A free exchange of information helps organizations respond rapidly to changing markets, increase efficiency and productivity, build employee morale, serve the public, and take full advantage of the ideas of today's knowledge workers. However, barriers can obstruct the flow of communication, as summarized in Figure 1.8.

Formal Channels

Formal communication channels follow an organization's chain of command.

Formal channels of communication generally follow an organization's hierarchy of command, as shown in Figure 1.9. Information about policies and procedures originates with executives and flows down through managers to supervisors and finally to lower-level employees. Many organizations have formulated official communication policies that encourage regular open communication, suggest means for achieving it, and spell out responsibilities. Official information among workers typically flows through formal channels in three directions: downward, upward, and horizontally.

Job plans, policies, instructions, feedback, and procedures flow downward from managers to employees.

Downward Flow. Information flowing downward generally moves from decision makers, including the CEO and managers, through the chain of command to workers. This information includes job plans, policies, and procedures. Managers also provide feedback about employee performance and instill a sense of mission in achieving the organization's goals.

One obstacle that can impede the downward flow of information is distortion resulting from long lines of communication. If, for example, the CEO in Figure 1.9 wanted to change an accounting procedure, she or he would probably not send a memo directly to the staff or cost accountants who would implement the change. Instead, the CEO would relay the idea through proper formal channels—from the office president for finance, to the accounting manager, to the senior accountant,

FIGURE 1.8 Barriers That Block the Flow of Information in Organizations

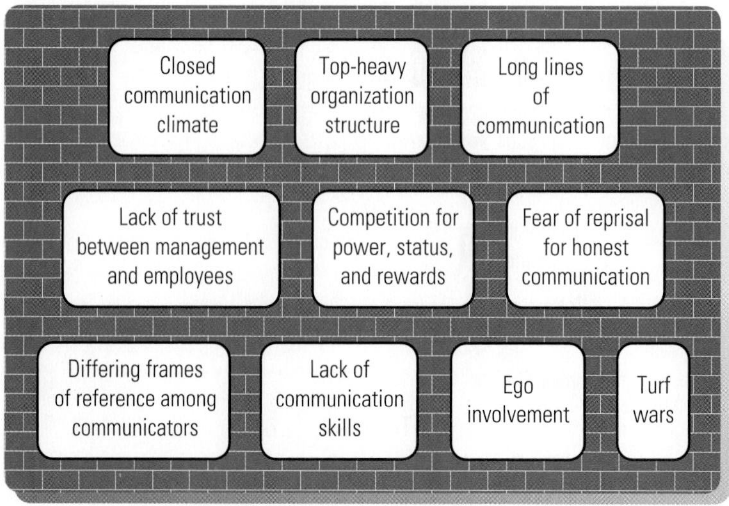

FIGURE 1.9 Formal Communication Channels

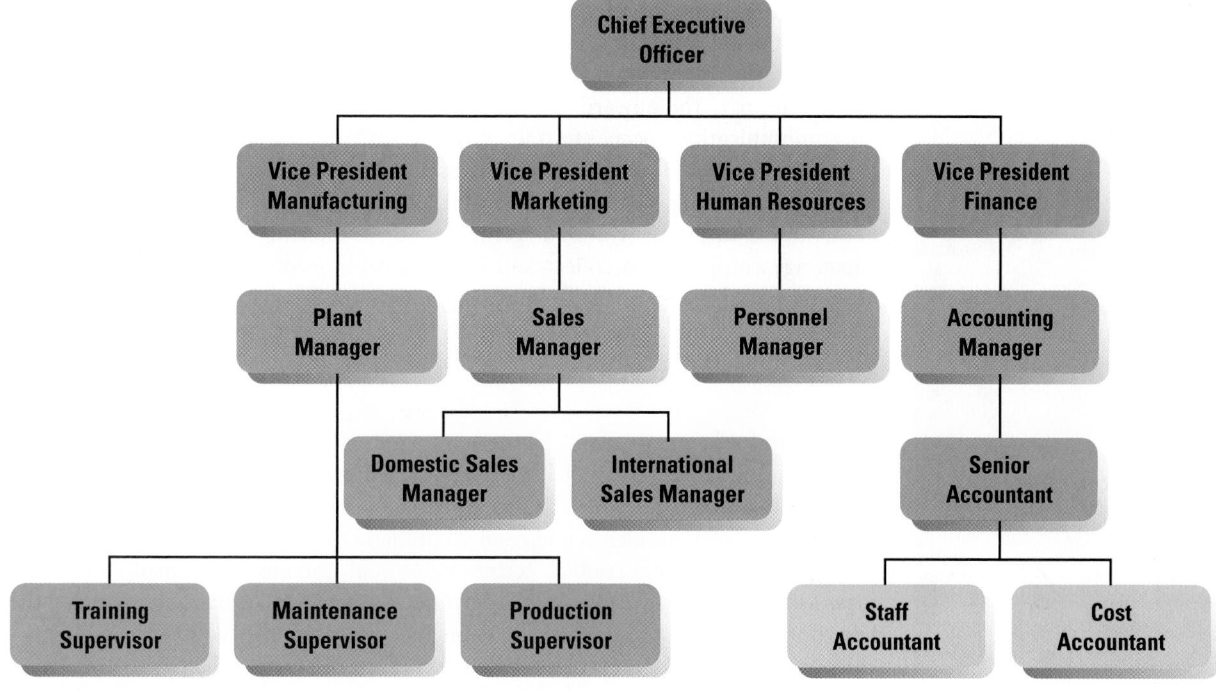

and so on—until the message reached the affected employees. Obviously, the longer the lines of communication, the greater the chance that a message will be distorted.

To improve communication and to compete more effectively, many of today's companies have "reengineered" themselves into smaller operating units and work teams. Rather than being bogged down with long communication chains, management speaks directly to team leaders, thus speeding up the entire process.[33] Management is also improving the downward flow of information through newsletters, announcements, meetings, videos, and company intranets. Instead of hoarding information at the top, today's managers recognize how essential it is to let workers know how well the company is doing and what new projects are planned.

Feedback from employees forms the upward flow of communication in most organizations.

Upward Flow. Information flowing upward provides feedback from nonmanagement employees to management. Subordinate employees describe progress in completing tasks, report roadblocks encountered, and suggest methods for improving efficiency. Channels for upward communication include phone messages, e-mail, memos, reports, departmental meetings, and suggestion systems. Ideally, the heaviest flow of information should be upward with information being fed steadily to decision makers.

A number of obstacles, however, can interrupt the upward flow of communication. Employees who distrust their employers are less likely to communicate openly. Employees cease trusting managers if they feel they are being tricked, manipulated, criticized, or treated unfairly. Unfortunately, in the current workplace, some employees no longer have a strong trusting attitude toward employers. Downsizing, cost-cutting measures, the tremendous influx of temporary workers, discrimination and harassment suits, outrageous compensation packages for chief executives, and many other factors have eroded the feelings of trust and pride that

Spotlight on **Communicators**

General Electric CEO John F. Welch, one of the most highly regarded executives in the country, contends that people won't do their best unless they believe they'll be treated fairly and without favoritism. To create that kind of trust, he advises laying out your values and then "walking the talk." Maintaining trust means doing what you say you will do, consistently, over time.

employees once felt toward their employers and their jobs. Other obstacles include fear of reprisal for honest communication, lack of adequate communication skills, and differing frames of reference. Imperfect communication results when individuals are not using words or symbols with similar meanings, when they cannot express their ideas clearly, or when they come from different backgrounds.

To improve the upward flow of communication, some companies are (1) hiring communication coaches to train employees, (2) asking employees to report customer complaints, (3) encouraging regular meetings with staff, (4) providing a trusting, nonthreatening environment in which employees can comfortably share their observations and ideas with management, and (5) offering incentive programs that encourage employees to collect and share valuable feedback. Companies are also building trust by setting up hotlines for anonymous feedback to management and by installing ombudsman programs. An *ombudsman* is a mediator who hears employee complaints, investigates, and seeks to resolve problems fairly.

Horizontal Flow. Lateral channels transmit information horizontally among workers at the same level, such as between the training supervisor and maintenance supervisor in Figure 1.9. These channels enable individuals to coordinate tasks, share information, solve problems, and resolve conflicts. Horizontal communication takes place through personal contact, telephone, e-mail, memos, voice mail, and meetings. Most traditional organizations have few established regular channels for the horizontal exchange of information. Reengineered companies with flattened hierarchies and team-based management, however, have discovered that when employees combine their knowledge with that of other employees, they can do their jobs better. Much of the information in these organizations is traveling horizontally between team members.[34]

Obstacles to the horizontal flow of communication, as well as to upward and downward flow, include poor communication skills, prejudice, ego involvement, and turf wars. Some employees avoid sharing information if doing so might endanger their status or chances for promotion within the organization. Competition within units and an uneven reward system may also prevent workers from freely sharing information.

To improve horizontal communication, companies are training and rewarding employees.

To improve horizontal communication, companies are (1) training employees in teamwork and communication techniques, (2) establishing reward systems based on team achievement rather than individual achievement, and (3) encouraging full participation in team functions. However, employees must also realize that they are personally responsible for making themselves heard, for really understanding what other people say, and for getting the information they need. Developing those business communication skills is exactly what this book and this course will do for you.

Informal Channels

Informal organizational communication transmits unofficial news through the grapevine.

Not all information within an organization travels through formal channels. Often, it travels in informal channels called the *grapevine.* These channels are usually based on social relationships in which individuals talk about work when they are having lunch, meeting at the water cooler, working out, golfing, or carpooling to work. Alert managers find the grapevine an excellent source of information about employee morale and problems. They have also used the grapevine as a "break it to them gently" device, planting "rumors," for example, of future layoffs or other changes.

Researchers studying communication flow within organizations know that the grapevine can be a major source of information. One study found that as much as two thirds of an employee's information comes from informal channels.[35] Is this bad? Yes and no. The grapevine can be a fairly accurate and speedy source of organization information. However, grapevine information is often incomplete because it travels in headlines: "Robinson Canned" or "Jerk on the Fourth Floor Promoted."[36] When employees obtain most of their company news from the grapevine, it's a pretty sure bet that management is not releasing sufficient information through formal channels.

A recent interesting theory holds that sensitivity to the office grapevine is age related. Marilyn Moats Kennedy, career specialist and author, reported that focus groups of workers under 30 revealed that they are uninterested in the grapevine. They don't want to hear any speculations or rumors because, "What can you do about that stuff, anyway?" They value plain talk and facts, yet some of them consider it fashionable "to disbelieve all company intelligence, whether it comes by memo or whisper."[37] They describe company newsletters as "The Fairy Tale Times." Older workers, too, have become skeptical of company announcements. This skepticism has grown since the downsizing and reorganization traumas of the early 1990s when some companies deceived workers about layoffs and closing plants.

The truth is that most employees want to know what's going on. In fact, one study found that regardless of how much information organization members reported receiving, they wanted more.[38] Many companies today have moved away from a rigid authoritarian management structure in which only managers were privy to vital information, such as product success and profit figures. Employees who know the latest buzz feel like important members of the team.[39] Through formal lines of communication, smart companies are keeping employees informed. Thus, the grapevine is reduced to carrying gossip about who's dating whom and what restaurant is cool for lunch.

Employees prefer to receive vital company information through formal channels.

CASE STUDY

PROCESS IN PROGRESS

Pillsbury Revisited

In the early 1990s few formal channels of communication were in place at Pillsbury. When new management arrived and the company was restructured, all that changed. "We started a business-focused employee newspaper," said Lou de Ocejo, human resources vice president. "We started having CEO luncheons every month, and communication meetings with all functions at least once a quarter. We tried to do a lot of things to tell people what this new age at Pillsbury was all about." Most difficult, though, was getting employees to talk back. Manage-ment wanted to know what was going right and what was going wrong. It wanted product ideas and suggestions for improving procedures. But employees in most organizations are cautious, despite pep talks from managers about how their doors are always open.

Then Pillsbury installed a unique feedback tool, a hotline called "InTouch." This toll-free, third-party voice mail service allows employees to leave anonymous messages about any subject at any time. At first employees were cynical, but over time they began to respond. More than 2,300 messages have now been recorded. Employees reported such problems as faulty work systems and ineffective supervisors. But they also provided many new product ideas and cost-saving suggestions, such as recommendations for pizza toppings and ways to recycle surplus paper. "Getting this feedback wasn't fun the first time out, and sometimes it still isn't," reported Lou de Ocejo, "but the system does just what we need it to do."

Critical Thinking

- Why are informal channels of communication dangerous in times of organizational upheaval?
- What obstacles may interrupt the downward, upward, and horizontal flow of information in organizations undergoing restructuring, such as Pillsbury?
- How could Pillsbury's InTouch voice mail system break down common barriers to communication?

Facing Increasing Ethical Challenges

6

The work world is indeed changing. One of the most remarkable changes involves ethics in the workplace. At one time the expression "business ethics" drew a big laugh. Many considered it an *oxymoron,* a combination of contradictory words. How could a business, which is obviously governed by profits, also be ethical? Yet, corporations made a remarkable turnabout in the 1990s. Following the "greed is good" era of the 1980s, businesspeople became increasingly concerned with ethics. An estimated 95 percent of Fortune 500 corporations as well as many smaller companies have now adopted ethics statements or codes of conduct.[40]

Ethical awareness grows as companies recognize that ethical practices make good business sense.

What caused this explosion of ethical awareness? According to one poll, many companies were primarily interested in incorporating ethics into their organizations because they wished to be more socially responsible.[41] Actually, however, many businesses simply recognized that ethical practices make good business sense. Ethical companies endure less litigation, less resentment, and less government regulation.[42] As a result, companies are adding ethics officers, hotlines, workshops, training programs, and codes of conduct. If you go to work for a large company, chances are good that you'll be asked to comply with its code of conduct.

The business world suffers from a poor public image resulting from unethical behavior by some organizations.

Despite this trend, however, the business world continues to be plagued by unethical behavior and a poor public image. Texaco suffered irreparable damage to its good name as a result of tapes revealing an atmosphere of discrimination among a group of its senior executives. And executives at the huge food products company Archer Daniels Midland paid millions of dollars in government fines resulting from price fixing. But it's not just executives who are tempted. One recent study revealed that 56 percent of the employees surveyed felt some pressure to act unethically or illegally. Another 48 percent admitted they had engaged in one or more unethical and/or illegal actions during the past year. The most common violations were as follows:[43]

Employees revealed common ethical violations.

- Cutting corners on quality
- Covering up incidents
- Abusing or lying about sick days
- Deceiving customers
- Lying to a supervisor or underling
- Taking credit for a colleague's ideas

With downsized staffs and fewer resources, employees feel pressure to increase productivity—by whatever means. Knowingly or not, managers under pressure to make profit quotas may send the message to workers that it's OK to lie, cheat, or steal to achieve company goals.[44] Couple these pressures with a breakdown in the traditional attitudes of trust and loyalty toward employers, and it's easy to see why ethical lapses are causing concern in the workplace.

Ethical behavior means doing the *right* thing given the circumstances.

Just what is ethical behavior? Ethics author Mary E. Guy defined ethics as "that behavior which is the *right* thing to do, given the circumstances."[45] Ethical behavior involves four principles: honesty, integrity, fairness, and concern for others. "These four principles are like the four legs of a stool," explained ethics authority Michael Josephson. "If even one leg is missing, the stool wobbles, and if two are missing, the stool falls. It's not enough to pride oneself on your honesty and integrity if you're not fair or caring." Consider a manager who would never dream of behaving dishonestly on the job or off. Yet this same manager forces a key employee to choose between losing her job and staying home with a sick child. The manager's lack of caring and failure to consider the circumstances create a shaky ethical position that would be difficult to justify.

Five Common Ethical Traps

In making ethical decisions, business communicators commonly face five traps that can make arriving at the right decision more difficult.[46]

The False Necessity Trap. People act from the belief that they're doing what they must do. They convince themselves that they have no other choice, when in fact it's generally a matter of convenience or comfort. Consider the Beech-Nut Corporation's actions when it discovered that its supplier was providing artificial apple juice. Beech-Nut canceled its contracts but continued to advertise and sell the adulterated "apple" juice as a 100 percent natural product in its baby food line. Apparently falling into the false necessity trap, Beech-Nut felt it had no choice but to continue the deception.

Carol R. Marshall helped aerospace giant Lockheed Martin develop a popular ethics training program featuring Dilbert. Many companies recognize that ethical business practices translate into better employee morale, improved customer satisfaction, and increased profits. Marshall's Dilbert game presents typical business dilemmas forcing employees to make ethical decisions in common office situations.

The Doctrine-of-Relative-Filth Trap. Unethical actions sometimes look good when compared with the worse behavior of others. What's a little fudging on an expense account compared with the pleasure cruise the boss took and charged as a business trip? Or how about using your PC at work to send a little personal e-mail (just a few quick notes) and perhaps do some much-needed research on an SUV you are considering buying? After all, the fellows in Engineering told you that they spend hours on their PCs checking sports scores, playing games, and conducting recreational Web surfing. They even have bookmarked "Don's Boss Page" so that they can look busy while cruising the Internet.[47] Your minor infraction is insignificant compared with what's happening regularly in Engineering.

The Rationalization Trap. In falling into the rationalization trap, people try to explain away unethical actions by justifying them with excuses. Consider employees who "steal" time from their employers by taking long lunch and coffee breaks, claiming sick leave when not ill, and completing their own tasks on company time. It's easy to rationalize such actions: "I deserve an extra-long lunch break because I can't get all my shopping done on such a short lunch hour" or "I'll just write my class report at the office because the computer printer is much better than mine, and they aren't paying me what I'm worth anyway."

The Self-Deception Trap. Applicants for jobs often fall into the self-deception trap. They are all too willing to inflate grade-point averages or exaggerate past accomplishments to impress prospective employers. One applicant, for example, claimed experience as a broker's assistant at a prestigious securities firm. A background check revealed that he had interviewed for the securities job but was never offered it.[48] Another applicant claimed that in his summer job he was "responsible for cross-corporate transferral of multidimensional client receivables." In other words, he moved boxes from sales to shipping. Self-deception can lead to unethical and possibly illegal behavior.

The Ends-Justify-the-Means Trap. Taking unethical actions to accomplish a desirable goal is a common trap. Consider a manager in a Medicare claims division of a large health insurance company who coerced clerical staff into working overtime without pay. The goal was the reduction of a backlog of unprocessed claims. Despite the worthy goal, the means of reaching it was unethical.

Spotlight on **Communicators**

Teresa McBride, National Minority Small Business Person of the Year, founded her Albuquerque-based computer consulting company on a firm basis of ethics, honesty, and trust. The youthful entrepreneur vows to deliver according to a customer's requirements or she will refer the customer to someone who can, even a competitor. Emphasis on ethics helps explain the phenomenal success of her multimillion-dollar business and its past recognition as one of the country's fastest-growing Hispanic-owned businesses.

Goals of Ethical Business Communication

Business communicators can minimize the danger of falling into ethical traps by setting specific ethical goals. Although the following goals hardly comprise a formal code of conduct, they will help business writers maintain a high ethical standard.

Telling the Truth. Ethical business communicators do not intentionally make statements that are untrue or deceptive. We become aware of dishonesty in business when violators break laws, notably in advertising, packaging, and marketing. The Federal Trade Commission, for example, ordered Kraft Foods to cancel a deceptive advertisement claiming that each Kraft Singles processed cheese slice contained as much calcium as five ounces of milk, an untrue statement.[49] In a similar case, the FTC charged Stouffer Foods with misrepresentation for its claim that Lean Cuisine entrées always contain less than 1 gram of sodium. In a fine-print footnote, careful consumers learn that 1 gram is equivalent to 1,000 milligrams, which is the commonly used unit of measurement for sodium.[50] The FTC also has cracked down on the makers of exercise equipment, such as Abflex, because three minutes a day on the "ab" machine doesn't come close to producing a "washboard stomach," as the manufacturer claimed.[51]

Half-truths, exaggerations, and deceptions constitute unethical communication. But conflicting loyalties in the workplace sometimes blur the line between right and wrong. Let's say you helped the marketing director, who is both your boss and your friend, conduct consumer research about a new company product. When you see the final report, you are astonished at how the findings have been distorted to show a highly favorable product approval rating. You are torn between loyalty to your boss (and friend) and loyalty to the company. Tools for helping you solve such ethical dilemmas will be discussed shortly.

Labeling Opinions. Sensitive communicators know the difference between facts and opinions. Facts are verifiable and often are quantifiable; opinions are beliefs held with confidence but without substantiation. It's a fact, for example, that women are starting new businesses twice as fast as men.[52] It's an opinion, though, that increasing numbers of women are abandoning the corporate employment arena to start these businesses. Such a statement can't be verified. Stating opinions as if they were facts is unethical.

***Facts* are verifiable; *opinions* are beliefs held with conviction.**

Being Objective. Ethical business communicators recognize their own biases and strive to keep them from distorting a message. Suppose you are asked to investigate laptop computers and write a report recommending a brand for your office. As you visit stores and watch computer demonstrations, you discover that an old high school friend is selling Brand X. Because you always liked this individual and have faith in his judgment, you may be inclined to tilt your recommendation in his direction. However, it's unethical to misrepresent the facts in your report or to put a spin on your arguments based on friendship. To be ethical, you could note in your report that you have known the person for ten years and that you respect his opinion. In this way, you have disclosed your relationship as well as the reasons for your decision. Honest reporting means presenting the whole picture and relating all facts fairly.

Communicating Clearly. Ethical business communicators feel an obligation to write clearly so that receivers understand easily and quickly. Some states have even passed "Plain English" laws that require businesses to write policies, warranties, and contracts in language comprehensible to average readers. Plain English means short sentences, simple words, and clear organization. Communicators who intentionally obscure the meaning with long sentences and difficult words are being unethical. A thin line, however, separates unethical communication from ethical communication. Some might argue that writers and speakers who deliver wordy, imprecise messages requiring additional correspondence or inquiry to clarify the meaning are acting unethically. However, the problem may be one of experience and skill rather than ethics. Such messages waste the time and resources of both senders and receivers. However, they are not unethical unless the intent is to deceive.

"Plain English" laws require simple, understandable language in policies, contracts, warranties, and other documents.

Giving Credit. As you probably know, using the written ideas of others without credit is called *plagiarism.* Ethical communicators give credit for ideas by (1) referring to originators' names within the text, (2) using quotation marks, and (3) documenting sources with endnotes, footnotes, or internal references. (You'll learn how to do this in Chapter 12 and Appendix C.) One student writer explained his reasons for plagiarizing material in his report by rationalizing, "But the encyclopedia said it so much better than I could!" This may be so, yet such an argument is no justification for appropriating the words of others. Quotation marks and footnotes could have saved the student. In school or on the job, stealing ideas or words from others is unethical.

Plagiarists use the ideas of others without giving credit.

Tools for Doing the Right Thing

In composing messages or engaging in other activities on the job, business communicators can't help being torn by conflicting loyalties. Do we tell the truth and risk our jobs? Do we show loyalty to friends even if it means bending the rules? Should we be tactful or totally honest? Is it our duty to make a profit or to be socially responsible? Acting ethically means doing the right thing given the circumstances. Each set of circumstances requires analyzing issues, evaluating choices, and acting responsibly.

Acting ethically means doing the right thing given the situation.

Resolving ethical issues is never easy, but the task can be made less difficult if you know how to identify key issues. The following questions may be helpful.

- **Is the action you are considering legal?** No matter who asks you to do it or how important you feel the result will be, avoid anything that is prohibited by law. Giving a kickback to a buyer for a large order is illegal, even if you suspect that others in your field do it and you know that without the kickback you will lose the sale.
- **How would you see the problem if you were on the opposite side?** Looking at all sides of an issue helps you gain perspective. Consider the issue of mandatory drug testing among employees. From management's viewpoint such testing could stop drug abuse, improve job performance, and lower health insurance premiums. From the employees' viewpoint mandatory testing reflects a lack of trust of employees and constitutes an invasion of privacy. By weighing both sides of the issue, you can arrive at a more equitable solution.

Business communicators can help resolve ethical issues through self-examination.

- **What are alternate solutions?** Consider all dimensions of other options. Would the alternative be more ethical? Under the circumstances, is the alternative feasible? Can an alternate solution be implemented with a minimum of disruption and with a high degree of probable success? In the situation involving your boss's distortion of consumer product research, you could go to the head of the company and tell what you know. A more tactful alternative, however, would be to approach your boss and ask if you misunderstood the report's findings or if an error might have been made.

Discussing an ethical problem with a coworker or colleague might lead to helpful alternatives.

- **Can you discuss the problem with someone whose advice you trust?** Suppose you feel ethically bound to report accurate information to a client even though your boss has ordered you not to do so. Talking about your dilemma with a coworker or with a colleague in your field might give you helpful insights and lead to possible alternatives.
- **How would you feel if your family, friends, employer, or coworkers learned of your action?** If the thought of revealing your action publicly produces cold sweats, your choice is probably not a wise one. Losing the faith of your friends or the confidence of your customers is not worth whatever short-term gains might be realized.

Perhaps the best advice in ethical matters is contained in the Golden Rule: Do unto others as you would have others do unto you. The ultimate solution to all ethics problems is treating others fairly and doing what is right to achieve what is good. In succeeding chapters you will find additional discussions of ethical questions as they relate to relevant topics.

Strengthening Your Communication Skills

You can improve your communication skills by making use of the model documents, practice exercises, procedures, tips, strategies, summaries, and checklists in this book.

You've just taken a brief look at the changing workplace, the process of communication, the flow of communication in organizations, and ethical challenges facing business communicators today. Each topic provided you not only with the latest information about an issue but also with tips and suggestions that will help you function successfully in the changing workplace. After all, it's not enough to know the problems; you also need to know some of the solutions. Our goal is to help you recognize the problems and also to equip you with techniques for overcoming the obstacles that others have faced. This book is crammed with model documents, practice exercises, procedures, tips, strategies, suggestions, summaries, and checklists—all meant to ensure that you develop the superior communication skills that are so vital to your success as a businessperson today.

Remember, communication skills are not inherent; they must be learned. Remember also to take advantage of the unique opportunity you now have. You have an expert who is willing to work with you to help improve your writing, speaking, and other communication skills. Many organizations pay thousands of dollars to communication coaches and trainers to teach employees the very skills that you are learning in this course. Your coach is your instructor. Get your money's worth! Pick his or her brains. With this book as your guide and your instructor as your coach, you will find that this course, as we mentioned earlier, could very well be the most important in your entire college curriculum.

Summary of Learning Objectives

1 Identify changes in the workplace and the importance of communication skills. The workplace has undergone profound changes, such as the emergence of heightened global competition, flattened management hierarchies, expanded team-based management, innovative communication technologies, new work environments, and an increasingly diverse workforce. In this dynamic workplace you can expect to be a knowledge worker; that is, you will deal with words, figures, and data.

PROCESS TO PRODUCT

Applying Your Skills at Pillsbury

CASE STUDY

As part of a group of college interns, you work for Lou de Ocejo in the office of Human Resources and Corporate Affairs at Pillsbury in the early 1990s. He is considering purchasing the InTouch voice mail system. However, it costs $3 per employee per year. He's not sure it's worth the cost, and he wonders if employees will really use it. He's also afraid that it might degenerate into a gripe box. Because he values your input, he wants the intern team to discuss the following questions.

- What are the major advantages and disadvantages of Pillsbury's anonymous voice mail system?
- Do the advantages outweigh the disadvantages? Why?
- In what ways could Pillsbury's management encourage employees to use the InTouch system? What channels of communication should it use?

Your Job

In teams of three to five, discuss your responses to your boss's questions. Summarize your conclusions and (1) appoint one team representative to report to the class or (2) write individual memos describing your conclusions. (See Chapter 8 and Appendix B for tips on writing memos.)

The most important foundation skill for knowledge workers is the ability to communicate. You can improve your skills by studying the principles, processes, and products of communication as provided in this book and in this course.

2 **Describe the process of communication.** The sender encodes (select) words or symbols to express an idea. The message is sent verbally over a channel (such as a letter, e-mail message, or telephone call) or is expressed nonverbally, perhaps with gestures or body language. "Noise"—such as loud sounds, misspelled words, or other distractions—may interfere with the transmission. The receiver decodes (interprets) the message and attempts to make sense of it. The receiver responds with feedback, informing the sender of the effectiveness of the message. The objective of communication is the transmission of meaning so that a receiver understands a message as intended by the sender.

3 **Discuss barriers to interpersonal communication and the means of overcoming those barriers.** Bypassing causes miscommunication because people have different meanings for the words they use. One's *frame of reference* creates a filter through which all ideas are screened, sometimes causing distortion and lack of objectivity. *Weak language skills* as well as *poor listening skills* impair communication efforts. *Emotional interference*—joy, fear anger, and so forth—hampers the sending and receiving of messages. *Physical distractions*—noisy surroundings, faulty acoustics, and so forth—can disrupt oral communication. You can reduce or overcome many interpersonal communication barriers if you (a) realize that the communication process is imperfect, (b) adapt your message to the receiver, (c) improve your language and listening skills, (d) question your preconceptions, and (e) plan for feedback.

4 **Analyze the functions and procedures of communication in organizations.** Internal functions of communication include issuing and clarifying procedures and policies, informing management of progress, persuading others to make changes or improvements, and interacting with employees. External functions of communication include answering inquiries about products or services, persuading customers to buy products or services, clarifying supplier specifications, and so forth. Oral, face-to-face communication is most effective, but written communication is often more expedient. The volume of messages today is overwhelming many employees, who must institute techniques to control information overload and productivity meltdown.

5 **Assess the flow of communication in organizations including barriers and methods for overcoming those barriers.** Formal channels of communication follow an organization's hierarchy of command. Information flows downward from management to workers. Long lines of communication tend to distort information. Many organizations are improving the downward flow of communication through newsletters, announcements, meetings, videos, and company intranets. Information flows upward from employees to management, thus providing vital feedback for decision makers. Obstacles include mistrust, fear of reprisal for honest communication, lack of adequate communication skills, and differing frames of reference. To improve upward flow, companies are improving relations with staff, offering incentive programs that encourage employees to share valuable feedback, and investing in communication training programs. Horizontal communication is between workers at the same level. Obstacles include poor communication skills, prejudice, ego involvement, competition, and turf wars. Techniques for overcoming the obstacles include (a) training employees in communication and teamwork techniques, (b) establishing reward systems, and (c) encouraging full participation in team functions. Informal channels of communication, such as the grapevine, deliver unofficial news—both personal and organizational—among friends and coworkers.

6 **List the goals of ethical business communication and describe important tools for doing the right thing.** Ethical business communicators strive to (a) tell the truth, (b) label opinions so that they are not confused with facts, (c) be objective and avoid distorting a message, (d) write clearly and avoid obscure language, and (e) give credit when using the ideas of others. When you face a difficult decision, the following questions serve as valuable tools in guiding you to do the right thing: (a) Is the action you are considering legal? (b) How would you see the problem if you were on the opposite side? (c) What are alternate solutions? (d) Can you discuss the problem with someone whose advice you trust? (e) How would you feel if your family, friends, employer, or coworkers learned of your action?

CHAPTER REVIEW

1. How are business communicators affected by the emergence of global competition, flattened management hierarchies, and expanded team-based management? (Obj. 1)
2. How are business communicators affected by the emergence of innovative communication technologies, new work environments, and an increasingly diverse workforce? (Obj. 1)
3. What are knowledge workers? Why are they hired? (Obj. 1)
4. Define *communication* and explain its most critical factor. (Obj. 2)
5. Describe the five steps in the process of communication. (Obj. 2)
6. List four barriers to interpersonal communication. Be prepared to discuss each. (Obj. 3)
7. Name five specific ways in which you can personally reduce barriers in your communication. (Obj. 3)
8. What are the three main functions of organizational communication? (Obj. 4)
9. What are the advantages of oral, face-to-face communication? (Obj. 4)
10. What are the advantages of written communication? (Obj. 4)
11. Within organizations how do formal and informal channels of communication differ? (Obj. 5)
12. Describe three directions in which communication flows within organizations and what barriers can obstruct each. (Obj. 5)
13. How can barriers to the free flow of information in organizations be reduced? (Obj. 5)
14. Discuss five thinking traps that block ethical behavior. (Obj. 6)
15. When faced with a difficult ethical decision, what questions should you ask yourself? (Obj. 6)

CRITICAL THINKING

1. Why should business and professional students strive to improve their communication skills, and why is it difficult or impossible to do it on their own? (Obj. 1)
2. Recall a time when you experienced a problem as a result of poor communication. What were the causes of and possible remedies for the problem? (Objs. 2 and 3)
3. How would you respond to this complaint? Some companies say that the more information they provide to employees, the more employees want. (Objs. 4 and 5)
4. How would you describe the communication climate in an organization to which you belonged or for which you worked? (Objs. 4 and 5)
5. How are the rules of ethical behavior that govern businesses different from those that govern your personal behavior? (Obj. 6)
6. **Ethical Issue:** Suppose your superior asked you to alter year-end financial data, and you knew that if you didn't you might lose your job. What would you do if it were a small amount? A large amount?

ACTIVITIES

1.1 Communication Assessment: How Do You Stack Up? (Objs. 2 and 3)

You know more about yourself than anyone else. That makes you the best person to assess your present communication skills. Take an honest look at your current skills and rank them using the following chart. How well you communicate will be an important factor in your future career—particularly if you are promoted into management, as many college graduates are. For each skill, circle the number from 1 (indicating low ability) to 5 (indicating high ability) that best reflects your perception of yourself.

Writing Skills	**Low**				**High**
1. Possess basic spelling, grammar, and punctuation skills	1	2	3	4	5
2. Am familiar with proper memo, letter, and report formats for business documents	1	2	3	4	5
3. Can analyze a writing problem and quickly outline a plan for solving the problem	1	2	3	4	5
4. Am able to organize data coherently and logically	1	2	3	4	5
5. Can evaluate a document to determine its probable success	1	2	3	4	5

Reading Skills	**Low**				**High**
1. Am familiar with specialized vocabulary in my field as well as general vocabulary	1	2	3	4	5
2. Can concentrate despite distractions	1	2	3	4	5
3. Am willing to look up definitions whenever necessary	1	2	3	4	5
4. Am able to move from recreational to serious reading	1	2	3	4	5
5. Can read and comprehend college-level material	1	2	3	4	5
Speaking Skills					
1. Feel at ease in speaking with friends	1	2	3	4	5
2. Feel at ease in speaking before a group of people	1	2	3	4	5
3. Can adapt my presentation to the audience	1	2	3	4	5
4. Am confident in pronouncing and using words correctly	1	2	3	4	5
5. Sense that I have credibility when I make a presentation	1	2	3	4	5
Listening Skills					
1. Spend at least half the time listening during conversations	1	2	3	4	5
2. Am able to concentrate on a speaker's words despite distractions	1	2	3	4	5
3. Can summarize a speaker's ideas and anticipate what's coming during pauses	1	2	3	4	5
4. Provide feedback, such as nodding, paraphrasing, and asking questions	1	2	3	4	5
5. Listen with the expectation of gaining new ideas and information	1	2	3	4	5

Now analyze your scores. Where are you strongest? Weakest? How do you think outsiders would rate you on these skills and traits? Are you satisfied with your present skills? The first step to improvement is recognition of a need. Put check marks next to the five traits you feel you should begin working on immediately.

1.2 E-Mail or Printed Memo: Getting to Know You (Objs. 1 and 2)

Send an e-mail or write a memo of introduction to your instructor. See Appendix B for memo formats and Chapter 8 for tips on preparing an e-mail message. In your message include the following:

- **a.** Your reasons for taking this class
- **b.** Your career goals (both temporary and long-term)
- **c.** A brief description of your employment, if any, and your favorite activities
- **d.** An assessment and discussion of your current communication skills, including your strengths and weaknesses
- **e.** A brief discussion of your familiarity with e-mail, the Internet, and other communication technologies

1.3 Small-Group Presentation: Getting to Know You (Objs. 1 and 2)

Your instructor may divide your class into small groups or teams. At your instructor's direction, either (a) interview another group member and introduce that person to the group or (b) introduce yourself to the group. Think of this as an informal interview for a team assignment or for a job. You'll want to make notes from which to speak. Your introduction should include information such as the following:

- **a.** Where did you grow up?
- **b.** What work and extracurricular activities have you engaged in?
- **c.** What are your interests and talents? What are you good at doing?
- **d.** What have you achieved?
- **e.** How familiar are you with various computer technologies?
- **f.** What are your professional and personal goals? Where do you expect to be five years from now?

1.4 Want Ads: Analyzing Job Requirements (Obj. 1)

At the direction of your instructor, conduct a survey of print or electronic job advertisements in your field. Consult the Sunday edition of a large newspaper or visit the Guffey student Web site **<meguffey.com>**. At the Web site click on "Internship, Job-Search, and Résumé-Creation Information." Then select one of the links to job listings. Find five or more job listings in which you might be interested. If possible, print the results of your search. If you cannot print, make notes on what you found and how you found it. Study the skills requested. How often do the ads mention communication, teamwork, and computer skills? What tasks do the ads mention? Your instructor may ask you to submit your findings and/or report to the class.

1.5 Information Flow: What's the Latest Buzz? (Obj. 5)

Consider an organization to which you belong or a business where you've worked. How did members learn what was going on in the organization? What kind of information flowed through formal channels? What were those channels? What kind of information was delivered through informal channels? Was the grapevine as accurate as official channels? What barriers obstructed the flow of information? How could the flow be improved?

1.6 Communication Process: Analyzing the Process (Obj. 2)

Review the communication process and its barriers as described in the text. Now imagine that you are the boss in an organization where you've worked and you wish to announce a new policy aimed at improving customer service. Examine the entire communication process from sender to feedback. How will the message be encoded? What assumptions must you make about your audience? How should you announce the new policy? How can you encourage feedback? What noise may interfere with transmission? What barriers should you expect? How can you overcome them? Your instructor may ask you to write a memo describing your responses to these questions.

1.7 Document Analysis: Barriers to Communication (Objs. 3, 4, and 5)

The following memo was actually written in a large business organization. Comment on its effectiveness, tone, and potential barriers to communication.

TO: All Department Personnel

SUBJECT: FRIDAY P.M. CLEAN-UP

Every Friday afternoon starting at 3 p.m. there is suppose to be a departmental clean-up. This practice will commence this Friday and continue until otherwise specified.

All CC162 employees will partake in this endeavor. This means not only cleaning his own area, but contributing to the cleaning of the complete department.

Thank you for your cooperation.

1.8 Communicating in Organizations: Reducing Information Overload (Obj. 4)

Eric S. has been working at HotStuff Software for six months. He loved e-mail when he first joined HotStuff, but now it's overwhelming him. Every day he receives between 200 and 300 messages, some important and some junk. To keep caught up, Eric checks his e-mail every hour— sometimes more often if he's expecting a response. He joined five listservs (automated mailing lists) because they sounded interesting and helpful. But when a topic really excites the subscribers, Eric's e-mail box is jammed with 50 or 60 postings at once. Reading all his messages prevents him from getting his real work done. If he ignores his e-mail, though, he may miss something important. What really frustrates him is what to do with messages that he must retain until he gathers the necessary information to respond. What suggestions can you make to lessen Eric's e-mail overload?

1.9 Communication Process: Avoiding Misunderstanding (Obj. 2)

Communication is not successful unless the receiver understands the message as the sender meant it. Analyze the following examples of communication failures. What went wrong?

- **a.** A supervisor issued the following announcement: "Effective immediately the charge for copying services in Repro will be raised ½ to 2 cents each." Receivers scratched their heads.
- **b.** The pilot of a military airplane about to land decided that the runway was too short. He shouted to his engineer,"Takeoff power!" The engineer turned off the engines; the plane crashed.
- **c.** The following statements actually appeared in letters of application for an advertised job opening. One applicant wrote, "Enclosed is my résumé in response to Sunday's New York Times." Another wrote, "Enclosed is my résumé in response to my

search for an editorial/creative position." Still another wrote, "My experience in the production of newsletters, magazines, directories, and on-line data bases puts me head and shoulders above the crowd of applicants you have no doubtedly been inundated with."

d. The following sign in English appeared in an Austrian hotel that catered to skiers: "Not to perambulate the corridors in the hours of repose in the boots of ascension."

1.10 Ethics: Where Do You Stand? (Obj. 6)

How do your ethics compare with those of businesspeople across the country? Complete the following survey and then compare your responses with the results obtained from readers of *Business Month* magazine.[53] Be prepared to discuss your responses in class.

a. Corporate ethics should be as important a priority as profits.

☐ Strongly agree ☐ Agree ☐ Undecided
☐ Disagree ☐ Strongly disagree

b. In an overzealous attempt to help their companies, officials at two generic drug makers lied to the FDA. Is this kind of dishonesty ever acceptable?

☐ Yes, because ______________________________
____
____

☐ No, because ______________________________
____
____

c. It's OK to bend the rules if the survival of your job is at stake.

☐ Always ☐ Often ☐ Occasionally
☐ Never

d. How would you rate the following infractions, where 1 represents the most offensive and 5 the least offensive infraction?

___ cheating on an expense report

___ playing dirty tricks on a competitor

___ paying bribes in a country where it's the accepted custom

___ lying to protect a friend

e. Although he voted to deny shareholders a lucrative $200-a-share takeover offer, Time Inc.'s CEO entered into a different merger deal guaranteeing himself a ten-year contract for at least $14.6 million. Was this ethical?

☐ Yes ☐ No ☐ Don't know

1.11 A Code of Ethics for Ruby's Natural by Nature.

Team | Web

You and another recent graduate were recently hired by Ruby's Natural by Nature, a small premium ice cream company in Brooklyn, New York. It makes terrific ice cream that is certified to be organic and contains no pesticides, hormones, or antibodies. Your boss, Ruby Fowler, not only wants to produce wholesome ice cream products, but she also wants to ensure that her company and employees act ethically. She thinks that Ruby's Natural by Nature needs some kind of code of ethics, credo, or mission statement. She asks you and your partner to search the Web for anything you can find that might help her write a code, credo, or mission statement for the company. She is most interested, of course, in companies that are in the food industry. You immediately think of Ben & Jerry's, which probably has a code of ethics or mission statement since social responsibility is high on its list of priorities. A quick way to find the Web site address of Ben & Jerry's is to search the business database of Hoovers **<hoovers.com>**, which lists thousands of companies. For a selected list of corporate codes of ethics, try "Business Ethics Resources on WWW" **<www.ethics.ubc.ca/resources>**. If necessary, use one or two search engines to look for other codes—from food companies, if possible. Print three or four codes, credos, or mission statements. Individually or as a team, write a memo or an e-mail message to CEO Ruby Fowler summarizing the topics covered in the codes. Be sure to include the Web addresses of the codes you cite. See Appendix C for memo formats and Chapter 8 for tips on preparing memos and e-mail messages.

Note About Using the Web

Some of the Web addresses (URLs) shown in this text will change. With each new printing, we will try to update our Web addresses. However, if a Web site is unavailable, please use a search engine to locate its new address or to find a relevant substitute. Remember, on the job you will rarely be given specific URLs. You'll be using search engines to track down information on your own.

If you are new to the Web, try using a tutorial, such as that provided at **<www.learnthenet>**. This tutorial provides basic information such as what to expect when you click on hypertext links. But you'll also find more advanced information, such as a guide to digging for data and evaluating what you find on the Web. Not everything you will find is reliable. Anyone can publish anything on the Web, so you must learn to be skeptical. For example, tourists drove six hours to Mankato, Minnesota, in search of caves, sunny beaches, and hot springs described on a Web site. Turns out that the Web site was a spoof created by people who were fed up with Minnesota's cold winters. The lesson to be learned here is that the Web may be the home of whoppers as well as reliable data. In Chapter 11 you will learn more about evaluating Web information sources. At the Guffey Student Web site **<meguffey.com>**, you can find links to terrific sites that teach you how to use the Internet as well as links to many helpful research tools. Check it out!

C.L.U.E. REVIEW 1

Each chapter includes an exercise based on Appendix A, "Competent Language Usage Essentials (C.L.U.E.)." This appendix is a business communicator's condensed guide to language usage, covering 50 of the most used, and abused, language elements. It also includes a list of 160 frequently misspelled words and a quick review of selected confusing words. The following exercise is packed with errors based on concepts and spelling words from the appendix. If you are rusty on these language essentials, spend some time studying the guidelines and examples in Appendix A. Then, test your skills with the chapter C.L.U.E. exercises. You will find the corrections for these exercises at the end of the appendix. Remember, these exercises contain only usage and spelling words from Appendix A. On a separate sheet, edit the following sentences to correct faults in grammar, punctuation, spelling, and word use.

1. After he checked many statements our Accountant found the error in colume 2 of the balance sheet.
2. Because Mr. Lockwoods business owned considerable property. We were serprised by it's lack of liquid assets.
3. The mortgage company checked all property titles separatly, however it found no discrepancies.
4. When Ms. Diaz finished the audit she wrote 3 letters. To appraise the owners of her findings.
5. Just between you and I whom do you think could have ordered all this stationary.
6. Assets and liabilities is what the 4 buyers want to see, consequently we are preparing this years statements.
7. Next spring my brother and myself plan to enroll in the following courses marketing english and history.
8. Dan felt that he had done good on the exam but he wants to do even better when it's given again next Fall.
9. Our records show that your end of the month balance was ninety-six dollars and 30 cents.
10. When the principle in the account grows to large we must make annual withdrawals.

CHAPTER • 2 •

Communicating in Teams:
Listening, Nonverbal Communication, Collaboration, and Meeting Skills

LEARNING OBJECTIVES

1. Discuss the importance of communicating in a team-oriented workplace, the four phases of team development, and the role of conflict.

2. Identify the characteristics of successful teams.

3. List techniques for organizing team-based written and oral presentations.

4. Explain how to become an effective team listener.

5. Analyze how information is transmitted through nonverbal messages and discuss how to improve nonverbal communication skills.

6. Discuss how to plan and participate in face-to-face and electronic meetings.

COMMUNICATION IN PROCESS

CASE STUDY

Harley-Davidson Cruises Toward Team-Based Management

For nearly a century Harley-Davidson motorcycles cruised the open road, the ultimate symbol of freewheeling joy and machismo. But though the Harley-Davidson Motor Company is wallowing in "hog heaven" profits now, the company was near death's door in the early 1980s. Poor quality was a major problem. Bikers took perverse joy in pointing to any oil puddle on the road and speculating that a Harley had recently been parked there. Plagued with reliability and other problems, the company lost significant market share to Honda, Suzuki, Kawasaki, and Yamaha.

Under new ownership, however, Harley-Davidson narrowly averted bankruptcy to emerge as a classic American Cinderella story. Its remarkable turnaround resulted from a number of factors, including a fanatical brand of customer loyalty. Many customers actually have the company logo tattooed on their bodies! More relevant to its comeback, though, were extensive changes in organization and management. With new owners the Harley-Davidson Motor Company created a flatter, more interdependent organizational structure. It moved away from the traditional model of independent leaders issuing orders to dependent followers. New managers emphasized empowered work teams called "circles," leading to greater employee involvement in decision making.

Although new leadership and a flatter organization boosted Harley-Davidson to its current position as the leading global supplier of premium quality, heavyweight motorcycles, it's not out of the woods yet. Upstart companies with new factories want to cash in on the world's robust appetite for cruising and touring machines. And Harley hankers after the younger market, where it is pitching its more affordable "Sportster" model. Some advertisements even attempt to soften its image with less testosterone and leather and more "poetry" of the open road. Meeting local and global competition, developing new markets without abandoning its core market, and maintaining quality are continuing challenges for Harley-Davidson. Its move away from a strong hierarchical organization to management by collaborating teams has enabled it to respond to these challenges, but not always smoothly.

www.harley-davidson.com

Communicating in a Team-Oriented Workplace

1

Many organizations develop teams to compete globally, meet higher standards, and increase profits.

Like employees at the Harley-Davidson Motor Company, you will probably eventually find yourself working in some kind of team-oriented environment. You may already be part of one or more teams. That's good, because experience on a team has become one of the top requests among recruiters looking over job candidates. To function effectively on a team, however, you'll need a number of skills. In this chapter you'll learn to polish your listening and nonverbal communication skills. You'll also study how to collaborate in team writing projects and how to participate in productive meetings.

As organizations in the past decade were downsized, restructured, and reengineered, one reality became increasingly clear. Companies were expected to compete globally, meet higher standards, and increase profits—but often with fewer people and fewer resources.[1] Striving to meet these seemingly impossible goals, organizations began developing teams. In most models of future organizations, teams, not individuals, function as the primary performance unit.[2]

Teams generally accomplish more than individuals can.

Why this emphasis on teams? Teams improve communication by sharing information within an organization. Because of their versatility, they do work that ordinary groups or single individuals could not accomplish. They make better use of resources. Teams increase productivity by delivering better quality goods and services and by developing improved processes. Employees working in successful teams report improved job satisfaction, increased pride in their jobs, and higher self-esteem.[3] Best of all for organizations, effective teams solve problems more creatively and more efficiently.[4] Take, for example, the production of one of the world's lightest, smallest, and highest-quality cellular phones. When they developed it, Motorola teams blew away the Japanese competition by designing a superior phone. And the new phone had only a few hundred parts compared with thousands of parts in rival phones.[5] Teams, not individuals, worked together to create the cellular phone breakthrough.

As you prepare for your business and professional career, you need to know more about how teams work. Primary concerns are the four phases of team development, the role of conflict, and the characteristics of successful teams.

Spotlight on **Communicators**

"Teamwork is the starting point for treating people right," says Dave Thomas, founder of Wendy's Old Fashioned Hamburgers. "Most people think that teamwork is only important when competing against other teams. But competition is only part of the picture. In most things we do in life, people have to work with rather than against each other to get something done. Win-win situations and partnerships are the most important results of teamwork. The best teams in the world are the ones that help people become better and achieve more than they ever thought they could on their own."

The Four Phases of Team Development

Teams may be formed to complete a single task or to function as permanent ongoing groups. Regardless, successful teams normally go through four predictable phases, as identified by psychologist B. A. Tuckman. These phases include **forming, storming, norming,** and **performing.**[6] Some teams get lucky and move quickly from forming to performing. But most teams struggle through disruptive, although ultimately constructive, team-building stages.

Forming. During the first stage of team development, individuals get to know each other. They often are overly polite and feel a bit awkward. As they search for similarities and attempt to bond, they begin to develop trust in each other. Members will discuss fundamental topics such as why the team is necessary, who "owns" the team, whether membership is mandatory, how large the team should be, and what talents team members can contribute. The team leader functions primarily as a traffic director. Teams should resist the efforts of some members to sprint through the first stages and vault to the performing stage. Moving slowly through the stages is necessary in building a cohesive, productive unit.

Storming. During the second phase, members define their roles and responsibilities, decide how to reach their goals, and iron out the rules governing how they interact. Unfortunately, this stage often produces conflict, resulting in **storming.** A good team leader, however, should step in to set limits, control the chaos, and offer suggestions. The leader will be most successful if she or he acts like a coach rather than a cop. Teams composed of dissimilar personality types may take longer to progress through the storming phase. Tempers may flare, sleep may be lost, leaders may be deposed. But most often the storm passes, and a cohesive team emerges.

In the norming stage, tensions subside, roles clarify, and information flows between team members.

Norming. Once the sun returns to the sky, teams enter the *norming* stage. Tension subsides, roles clarify, and information begins to flow between members. The group periodically checks its agenda to remind itself of its progress toward its goals. People are careful not to shake the hard-won camaraderie and formation of a single-minded team purpose. Formal leadership is unnecessary since everyone takes on leadership functions. Important data is shared with the entire group, and mutual interdependence becomes typical. The team begins to move smoothly in one direction. Members make sure that procedures are in place to resolve future conflicts.

Teams that work together successfully—whether on the Whitbread Round the World yacht race or in offices around the world—go through developmental stages before they function harmoniously.

Performing. In Tuckman's team growth model, some teams never reach the final stage of *performing.* Problems that may cause them to fail are shown in Figure 2.1. For those that survive the first three phases, however, the final stage is gratifying. Team members have established a pace and a shared language. They develop loyalty and a willingness to resolve all problems. A "can-do" mentality pervades as they progress toward their goal. Fights are clean, and team members continue working together without grudges. Best of all, information flows freely, deadlines are met, and production exceeds expectations.

The Role of Conflict and Groupthink

Cognitive conflict centers on issues and is considered healthy and functional.

As teams develop, they should expect conflict to arise—not only in the storming phase but also at other times. How a team manages that conflict determines whether a team survives; it also affects the quality of its performance and its decisions. Teams may experience two kinds of conflict. *Cognitive conflict* centers on issues[7] and is considered healthy and functional. Cognitive conflict arouses discussion and stimulates creative thinking. It makes team members get involved as they examine, compare, and reconcile their differences. Cognitive conflict also promotes acceptance of a team decision. Team members "buy into" the decision and are more willing to implement it when they have been able to speak their minds.

Affective conflict centers on feelings and personalities and is considered disruptive.

Affective conflict aims not at issues but at feelings and personalities. It is disruptive and dysfunctional. Affective conflict tends to be emotional and focuses on people, not on substantive matters. Such conflict may erupt into name-calling and criticism, which destroys team unity. Research shows that the best decisions are made by teams that experience healthy differences of opinion but are able to keep their conflict aimed at issues. As one member of a successful team remarked, "We scream a lot, then laugh, and then resolve the issues."[8]

Without conflict and free discussions, teams may fall victim to *groupthink.* This is a term coined by theorist Irving Janis to describe faulty decision-making processes by team members who are overly eager to agree with one another. Several conditions can lead to groupthink: team members with similar backgrounds, a lack of methodical procedures, a demand for a quick decision, and a strong leader who favors a specific decision. Symptoms of groupthink include pressures placed on a member

FIGURE 2.1 **Why Teams Don't Work: Typical Problems, Symptoms, and Solutions**

Problem	Symptom	Solution
Confused goals	People don't know what they're supposed to do	Clarify team purpose and expected outcomes
Mismatched needs	People with private agendas are working at cross-purposes	Get hidden agendas on table by asking what people personally want from teaming
Unresolved roles	Team members are uncertain what their jobs are	Inform team members what is expected of them
Senseless procedures	Team is at the mercy of an employee handbook from hell	Throw away the book and develop procedures that make sense
Bad leadership	Leader is tentative, inconsistent, or foolish	Leader must learn to serve the team and keep its vision alive or give up role
Antiteam culture	Organization is not committed to the idea of teams	Team for the right reasons or don't team at all; never force people onto a team
Poor feedback	Performance is not being measured; team members are groping in the dark	Create system of free flow of useful information to and from all team members

Based on Harvey Robbins and Michael Finley, *Why Teams Don't Work: What Went Wrong and How to Make It Right* (Princeton, NJ: Peterson's/Pacesetter Books, 1995), pp. 14–15.

Groupthink means that team members agree without examining alternatives or considering contingency plans.

who argues against the group's shared beliefs, self-censorship of thoughts that deviate from the group consensus, collective efforts to rationalize, and an unquestioned belief in the group's inherent morality. Teams suffering from groupthink fail to examine alternatives, are biased in collecting and evaluating information, and ignore the risks of the preferred choice. They may also forget to work out a contingency plan in case the preferred choice fails.[9]

Effective teams avoid groupthink by striving for team diversity—in age, gender, backgrounds, experience, and training. They encourage open discussion, search for relevant information, evaluate many alternatives, consider how a decision will be implemented, and plan for contingencies in case the decision doesn't work out.

Characteristics of Successful Teams

2

The use of teams has been called the "solution" to many ills in the current workplace.[10] Someone even observed that as an acronym TEAM means "Together, Everyone Achieves More."[11] Yet, many teams do not work well together. In fact, some teams can actually increase frustration, lower productivity, and create employee dissatisfaction. Experts who have studied team workings and decisions have discovered that effective teams share some or all of the following characteristics.

Small Size, Diverse Makeup. For most functions the best teams range from 2 to 25 members, although 4 or 5 is optimum for many projects. Larger groups have trouble interacting constructively, much less agreeing on actions.[12] For the most creative decisions, teams generally have male and female members who differ in age, social background, training, and experience. Members should bring complementary skills to a team. Paul Fireman, founder of sports shoe manufacturer Reebok, wisely remarked, "If you put five centers on the basketball court, you're going to lose the game. You need, we all need, people of different strengths and talents—and that means, among other things, people of different backgrounds."[13] Diverse teams can produce innovative solutions with broader applications than homogeneous teams can.

Small, diverse teams often produce more creative solutions with broader applications than homogeneous teams.

Spotlight on **Communicators**

"Teamwork is absolutely essential," says community and industry leader Roy Richards Jr., who is CEO of Southwire Company, North America's largest producer of aluminum and copper rod, wire, and cable. "Two heads are better than one and 200 are better than 10. The greatest bulk of ideas is at the bottom of the organization and not at the top, and therefore the empowerment of all our employees and the networking of all their ides is necessary for us to move forward and upward and to always improve."

Agreement on Purpose. An effective team begins with a purpose. Xerox scientists who invented personal computing developed their team purpose after the chairman of Xerox called for an "architecture of information." A team at Sealed Air Corporation developed its purpose when management instructed it to cut waste and reduce downtime.[14] Working from a general purpose to specific goals typically requires a huge investment of time and effort. Meaningful discussions, however, motivate team members to "buy into" the project.

Agreement on Procedures. The best teams develop procedures to guide them. They set up intermediate goals with deadlines. They assign roles and tasks, requiring all members to contribute equivalent amounts of real work. They decide how they will reach decisions using one of the strategies shown in the accompanying Career Coach box. Procedures are continually evaluated to ensure movement toward attainment of the team's goals.

Ability to Confront Conflict. Poorly functioning teams avoid conflict, preferring sulking, gossip, or backstabbing. A better plan is to acknowledge conflict and address the root of the problem openly. Although it may feel emotionally risky, direct confrontation saves time and enhances team commitment in the long run. To be constructive, however, confrontation must be task oriented, not person oriented. An open airing of differences, in which all team members have a chance to speak their minds, should center on strengths and weaknesses of the different positions and ideas—not on personalities. After hearing all sides, team members must negotiate a fair settlement, no matter how long it takes. The best decisions are based on consensus: all members agree.

Use of Good Communication Techniques. The best teams exchange information and contribute ideas freely in an informal environment. Team members speak clearly and concisely, avoiding generalities. They encourage feedback. Listeners become actively involved, read body language, and ask clarifying questions before responding. Tactful, constructive disagreement is encouraged. Although a team's task is taken seriously, successful teams are able to inject humor into their interactions.

Good teams exchange information freely and collaborate rather than compete.

Ability to Collaborate Rather than Compete. Effective team members are genuinely interested in achieving team goals instead of receiving individual recognition. They contribute ideas and feedback unselfishly. They monitor team progress, including what's going right, what's going wrong, and what to do about it. They celebrate individual and team accomplishments.

CAREER COACH

FIVE STRATEGIES FOR REACHING GROUP DECISIONS

The manner in which teams reach decisions greatly affects the morale and commitment of a team, as well as the implementation of any team decision. In our culture the majority usually rules. But is this method most effective?

- **Majority:** Group members vote; a majority wins. Advantage: Results in a quick decision.
- **Consensus:** Discussion continues until all team members air their opinions and, ultimately, agree. Advantages: Produces creative, high-quality discussion and elicits commitment by all members to implement the decision.
- **Minority:** Usually takes the form of a subcommittee delegated to investigate and make a recommendation for action. Advantages: Useful when everyone cannot get together to make a decision or when time is short.
- **Averaging:** Members haggle, bargain, cajole, and negotiate a middle position. Involves compromise. Advantages: Individual errors and extreme opinions tend to cancel each other out.
- **Authority Rule With Discussion:** Boss or individual in command listens to team members' ideas, but final decision is his or hers. Advantages: Encourages lively discussion and results in participatory decision making.

Career Application

In teams of three or four, discuss the advantages and disadvantages of each of the above methods. What methods are most effective for routine decisions? For serious, complex, and important decisions? Why do you think that majority usually rules in our culture?

Shared Leadership. Effective teams often have no formal leader. Instead, leadership rotates to those with the appropriate expertise as the team evolves and moves from one phase to another. Many teams operate under a democratic approach. This approach can achieve buy-in to team decisions, boost morale, and create fewer hurt feelings and less resentment. But in times of crisis, a strong team member may need to step up as leader.

Checklist for Developing Team Effectiveness

Establish small teams. Teams with fewer members are thought to function more efficiently and more effectively than larger teams.

Encourage diversity. Innovative teams typically include members who differ in age, gender, and background. Team members should possess technical expertise, problem-solving skills, and interpersonal skills.

Determine purpose, procedures, and roles. Members must understand the task at hand and what is expected of them. Teams function best when operating procedures are ironed out early on and each member has a specific role.

Acknowledge and manage conflict. Conflict is productive when it motivates a team to search for new ideas, increase participation, delay premature decisions, or discuss disagreements. Keep conflict centered on issues rather than on people.

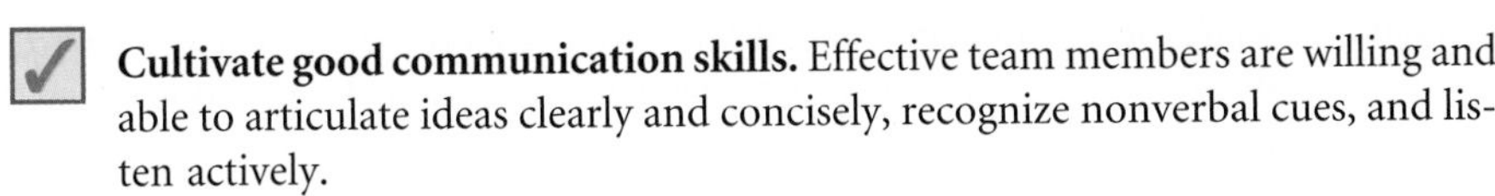

Cultivate good communication skills. Effective team members are willing and able to articulate ideas clearly and concisely, recognize nonverbal cues, and listen actively.

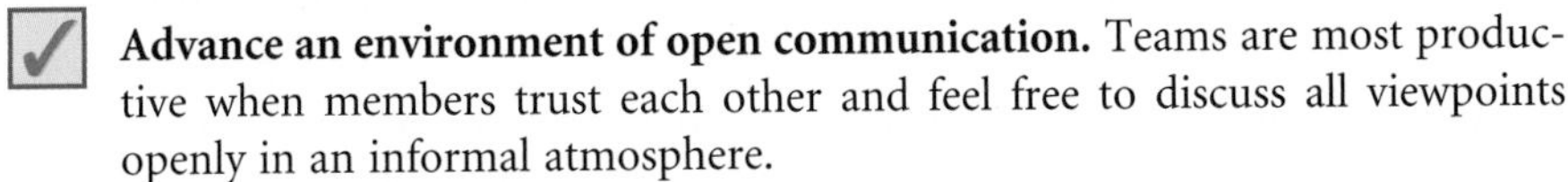

Advance an environment of open communication. Teams are most productive when members trust each other and feel free to discuss all viewpoints openly in an informal atmosphere.

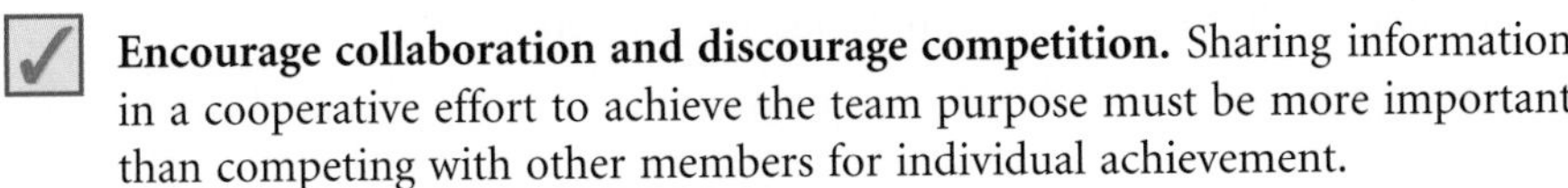

Encourage collaboration and discourage competition. Sharing information in a cooperative effort to achieve the team purpose must be more important than competing with other members for individual achievement.

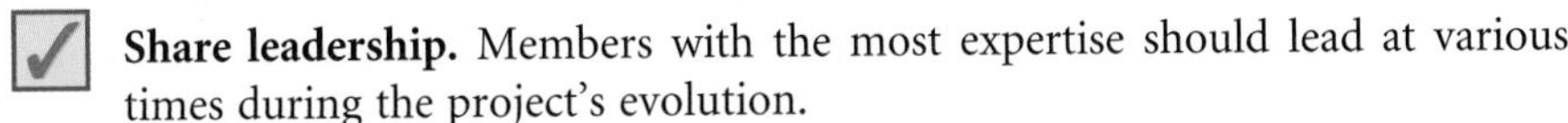

Share leadership. Members with the most expertise should lead at various times during the project's evolution.

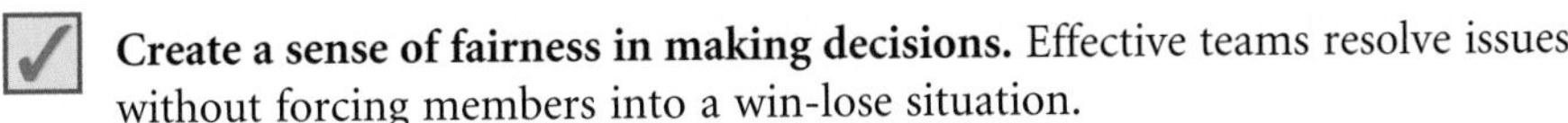

Create a sense of fairness in making decisions. Effective teams resolve issues without forcing members into a win-lose situation.

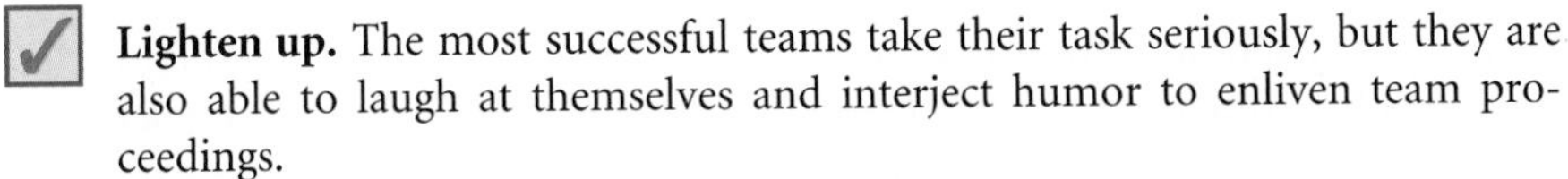

Lighten up. The most successful teams take their task seriously, but they are also able to laugh at themselves and interject humor to enliven team proceedings.

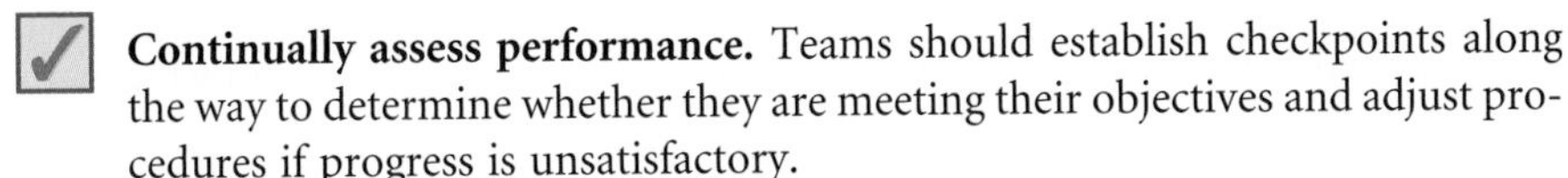

Continually assess performance. Teams should establish checkpoints along the way to determine whether they are meeting their objectives and adjust procedures if progress is unsatisfactory.

Organizing Team-Based Written and Oral Presentations

3

Companies form teams for many reasons. The goal of some teams is an oral presentation to pitch a new product or to win a high-stakes contract. Before Bill Gates and his Microsoft team roll out their latest PC operating system, you can bet that team members spend months preparing the presentation so that everything flows smoothly. The goal of other teams is to investigate a problem and submit recommendations to decision makers in a report. At Kodak, for example, the "Zebra Team" advised management regarding the development and marketing of all black-and-white film products. The end product of any team is often a written report or an oral presentation.

Guidelines for Team Writing and Oral Presentations

Team projects proceed more smoothly when members agree on ground rules.

Whether your team's project produces written reports or oral presentations, you generally have considerable control over how the project is organized and completed. If you've been part of any team efforts before, you also know that such projects can be very frustrating—particularly when some team members don't carry their weight or when members cannot resolve conflict. On the other hand, team projects can be harmonious and productive when members establish ground rules and follow guidelines related to preparing, planning, collecting information for, organizing, rehearsing, and evaluating team projects.

Preparing to Work Together. Before you begin talking about a specific project, it's best to discuss some of the following issues in regard to how your group will function.

- Name a meeting leader to plan and conduct meetings, a recorder to keep a record of group decisions, and an evaluator to determine whether the group is on target and meeting its goals.

Teams must decide whether they will be governed by consensus, by majority rule, or by some other method.

- Decide whether your team will be governed by consensus (everyone must agree), by majority rule, or by some other method.
- Compare schedules of team members in order to set up the best meeting times. Plan to meet often. Make team meetings a top priority. Avoid other responsibilities that might cause disruption during these meetings.
- Discuss the value of conflict. By bringing conflict into the open and encouraging confrontation, your team can prevent personal resentment and group dysfunction. Confrontation can actually create better final products by promoting new ideas and avoiding groupthink. Conflict is most beneficial when team members are allowed to air their views fully.
- Discuss how you will deal with team members who are not pulling their share of the load.

Planning the Document or Presentation. Once you've established ground rules, you're ready to discuss the final document or presentation. Be sure to keep a record of the following decisions your team makes.

- Establish the specific purpose for the document or presentation. Identify the main issues involved.
- Decide on the final format. For a report determine what parts it will include, such as an executive summary, figures, and an appendix. For a presentation, decide on its parts, length, and graphics.
- Discuss the audience(s) for the product and what questions it would want answered in your report or oral presentation. If your report is persuasive, consider what appeals might achieve its purpose.

In planning a team document or presentation, develop a work plan, assign jobs, and set deadlines.

- Develop a work plan (see Chapter 11). Assign jobs. Set deadlines. If time is short, work backward from the due date. For oral presentations build in time for content and creative development as well as for a series of rehearsals.
- For oral presentations give each team member a written assignment that details his or her responsibilities for researching content, producing visuals, developing handout materials, building transitions between segments, and showing up for rehearsals.
- For written reports decide how the final document will be composed: individuals working separately on assigned portions, one person writing the first draft, the entire group writing the complete document together, or some other method.

Unless facts are accurate, reports and presentations will fail.

Collecting Information. The following suggestions help teams generate and gather accurate information. Unless facts are accurate, the most beautiful report or the best high-powered presentation will fail.

- Brainstorm for ideas; consider cluster diagramming (see Figure 5.2 in Chapter 5).
- Assign topics. Decide who will be responsible for gathering what information.
- Establish deadlines for collecting information.
- Discuss ways to ensure the accuracy of the information collected.

Organizing, Writing, and Revising. As the project progresses, your team may wish to modify some of its earlier decisions.

- Review the proposed organization of your final document or presentation and adjust it if necessary.
- Compose the first draft of a written report or presentation. If separate team members are writing segments, they should use the same word processing and/or presentation graphics program to facilitate combining files.
- Meet to discuss and revise the draft(s) or rehearse the presentation.
- If individuals are working on separate parts of a written report, appoint one person (probably the best writer) to coordinate all the parts, striving for consistent style and format. Work for a uniform look and feel to the final product.
- For oral presentations be sure each member builds a bridge to the next presenter's topic and launches it smoothly. Strive for logical connections between segments.

For team reports assign one person to coordinate all the parts and make the style consistent.

One person should be responsible for finding and correcting errors.

Editing, Rehearsing, and Evaluating. Before the presentation is made or the final document is submitted, complete the following steps.

- For a written report give one person responsibility for finding and correcting grammatical and mechanical errors.
- For a written report meet as a group to evaluate the final document. Does it fulfill its purpose and meet the needs of the audience? Successful group documents emerge from thoughtful preparation, clear definition of contributors' roles, commitment to a group-approved plan, and willingness to take responsibility for the final product.
- For oral presentations assign one person the task of merging the various files, running a spell checker, and examining the entire presentation for consistency of design, format, and vocabulary.
- Schedule at least five rehearsals, say the experts.[15] Consider videotaping one of the rehearsals so that each presenter can critique his or her own performance.
- Schedule a dress rehearsal with an audience at least two days before the actual presentation. Practice fielding questions.

CASE STUDY

PROCESS IN PROGRESS

Harley-Davidson Revisited

Blitzing country curves or cruising highway straight stretches, Harley bikers own the road. And the Harley-Davidson Motor Company wants to keep it that way. Staying ahead of ever-growing local and global competition is a major concern. After surviving serious quality problems and competition from Japanese motorcycles, the company now commands 56 percent of the U.S. heavyweight or "hog" market. Much of its current success, say managers, results from its switch to team-based management.

But the switch has been difficult. Clyde Fessler, vice president for business development, admitted as much when he said, "We would probably all agree that the shift from hierarchy to circles has not been easy—practicing consensus decision-making never is. However, defining the roles and responsibilities of each functional circle and each circle member has brought clarity, which in turn stimulates dialogue, trust, and eventually, non-threatening confrontation."

Collaborative, interdependent teams work more slowly than a single, decisive leader in a hierarchy. "But," said Fessler, "they can be more innovative and resourceful and, ultimately, more effective in today's complex business climate."[16]

Critical Thinking

- What stages of development could Harley-Davidson teams have expected to pass through as they were formed?
- Why are decisions by consensus harder to achieve than those from a majority vote or from an authoritative leader?
- Since team-based management is slower and more painful than management from a strong leader and line managers, why would a company like Harley-Davidson adopt this strategy?

More information about writing business reports and making individual presentations appears in subsequent chapters of this book.

Becoming an Effective Team Listener

4

A vital part of every successful team is high-quality communication. And three quarters of high-quality communication involves listening.[17] In addition to helping you interact with teams, listening skills are important in getting along with colleagues, managers, family, and friends. Although our discussion centers on business and employment needs, many of the listening tips you learn will be equally effective in your personal life.

Most of us listen at only 25 percent efficiency.

Most workers spend 30 to 45 percent of their communication time listening,[18] while executives spend 60 to 70 percent of their communication time listening.[19] Although executives and workers devote the bulk of their communication time to listening, research suggests that they're not very good at it. In fact, most of us are poor listeners. Some estimates indicate that only half of the oral messages heard in a day are completely understood. Experts say that we listen at only 25 percent efficiency. In other words, we ignore, forget, distort, or misunderstand 75 percent of everything we hear.

We are inefficient listeners because of lack of training, competing sounds, slowness of speech, and daydreaming.

Such listening inefficiency may result from several factors. Lack of training is one significant reason. Few schools give as much emphasis to listening as they do to the development of reading, speaking, and writing skills. In addition, our listening skills may be less than perfect because of the large number of competing sounds and stimuli in our lives that interfere with concentration. Finally, we are inefficient listeners because of the slowness of speech. While most speakers talk at about 150 words per minute, listeners can process oral communication at over 400 words per minute. This lag time causes daydreaming, which in turn reduces listening efficiency.

Examining the process of listening, as well as its barriers, may shed some light on ways to improve your listening efficiency and retention.

The Listening Process and Its Barriers

The four stages of listening are perception, interpretation, evaluation, and action.

Listening takes place in four stages—perception, interpretation, evaluation, and action—as illustrated in Figure 2.2. Barriers, however, can obstruct the listening process. These barriers may be mental or physical.

Perception. The listening process begins when you hear sounds and concentrate on them. Stop reading for a moment and become conscious of the sounds around you. Do you notice the hum of an electrical appliance, background sounds from a TV program, muffled traffic noise, or the murmur of distant voices? Until you "tuned in" to them, these sounds went unnoticed. The conscious act of listening begins when you focus on the sounds around you and select those you choose to hear. You tune in when you (1) sense that the message is important, (2) are interested in the topic, or (3) are in the mood to listen. Perception is reduced by impaired hearing, noisy surroundings, inattention, and pseudolistening. *Pseudolistening* occurs when listeners "fake" it. They look as if they are listening, but their minds are wandering far off.

Interpretation. Once you have focused your attention on a sound or message, you begin to interpret, or decode, it. As described in Chapter 1, interpretation of a message is colored by your cultural, educational, and social frames of reference. The meanings you attach to the speaker's words are filtered through your expectations and total life experiences. Thus, your interpretation of the speaker's meaning may

FIGURE 2.2 **The Listening Process and Its Barriers**

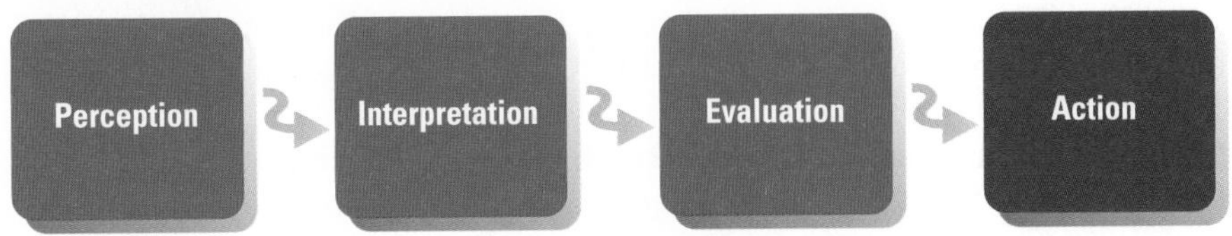

LISTENING BARRIERS

Mental Barriers	Physical and Other Barriers
Inattention Prejudgment Frame of reference Closed-mindedness Pseudolistening	Hearing impairment Noisy surroundings Speaker's appearance Speaker's mannerisms Lag time

be quite different from what the speaker intended because your frame of reference is different.

Evaluation involves separating fact from opinion and judging messages objectively.

Evaluation. After interpreting the meaning of a message, you analyze its merit and draw conclusions. To do this, you attempt to separate fact from opinion. Good listeners try to be objective, and they avoid prejudging the message. In a study of college students, one researcher determined that closed-mindedness and opinionated attitudes functioned as major barriers to listening. Certain students were not good listeners because their prejudices prevented them from opening up to a speaker's ideas.[21] The appearance and mannerisms of the speaker can also affect a listener's evaluation of a message. A juror, for example, might jump to the conclusion that an accused man is guilty because of his fierce expression or his substandard English. Thus, to evaluate a message accurately and objectively, you should (1) consider all the information, (2) be aware of your own biases, and (3) avoid jumping to hasty conclusions.

Action. Responding to a message may involve storing the message in memory for future use, reacting with a physical response (a frown, a smile, a laugh), or supplying feedback to the speaker. Listener feedback is essential because it helps clarify the message so that it can be decoded accurately. Feedback also helps the speaker to find out whether the message is getting through clearly. In one-to-one conversation, of course, no clear distinction exists between the roles of listener and speaker—you give or receive feedback as your role alternates.

Tips for Better Team Listening

Listening in teams is more difficult than listening in college classes where experienced professors present well-organized lectures and repeat important points. Team listening is more challenging because information is often exchanged casually. It may be disorganized, unclear, and cluttered with extraneous facts. Moreover, team members are usually friends. Because they are familiar with one another, they may not be as polite and respectful as they are with strangers. Friends tend to interrupt, jump to conclusions, and take each other for granted. Team members cannot do this, de-

Spotlight on **Communicators**

Celebrated talk show host Oprah Winfrey owes much of her success to her artful application of the simple process and listening and responding. "Communicating with people is how I always developed any kind of value about myself," says the most successful female entertainer in the world. On her show she is able to block out external distractions, become actively involved, listen empathically without interrupting, paraphrase her guests' ideas, and ask clarifying questions to draw out deep meanings and issues that underlie their everyday lives.

spite their familiarity with each other. They must remember that their job is to listen carefully and to understand what is being said so that they can do their work well. The following suggestions can help you improve your listening effectiveness—both as a team member and as a business communicator in general.

Control External and Internal Distractions. Move to an area where you can hear without conflicting noises or conversations. Block out surrounding physical distractions. Internally, try to focus totally on the speaker. If other projects are on your mind, put them on the back burner temporarily. When you are emotionally upset, whether angry or extremely happy, it's a good idea to postpone any serious listening.

Become Actively Involved. Show that you are listening closely by leaning forward and maintaining eye contact with the speaker. Don't fidget or try to complete another task at the same time you are listening. Listen to more than the spoken words. How are they said? What implied meaning, reasoning, and feelings do you hear behind the spoken words? Does the speaker's body language (eye contact, posture, movements) support or contradict the main message?

Identify Important Facts. Team members may intersperse critical information with casual conversation. Unrelated topics pop up—ball scores, a customer's weird request, a computer glitch, the boss's extravagant new sports utility van. Your task is to select what's important and register it mentally. What step is next in your project? Who does what? What is your role?

Don't Interrupt. While someone else has the floor, don't interrupt with a quick reply or opinion. And don't show nonverbal disagreement such as negative head shaking, rolling eyes, sarcastic snorting, or audible sighs. Good team members let speakers have their say. Interruptions are not only impolite, but they also prevent you from hearing the speaker's complete thought. Listeners who interrupt with their opinions sidetrack discussions and cause hard feelings.

Ask Clarifying Questions. Good team members wait for the proper moment and then ask questions that do not attack the speaker. Instead of saying, "But I don't understand how you can say that," a good listener seeks clarification with questions such as, "Please help me understand by explaining more about . . . ." Because questions can put you in the driver's seat, think about them in advance. Use open questions (those without set answers) to draw out feelings, motivations, ideas, and suggestions. Use closed fact-finding questions to identify key factors in a discussion.[22] And, by the way, don't ask a question unless you are ready to be quiet and listen to the answer.

Paraphrasing means rephrasing the speaker's ideas in your own words.

Paraphrase to Increase Understanding. To make sure you understand a speaker, rephrase and summarize a message in your own words. Be objective and nonjudgmental. Remember that your goal is to understand what the speaker has said—not to show how mindless the speaker's words sound when parroted. Remember, too, that the rest of the team will also benefit from a clear summary of what was said.

Take Advantage of Lag Time. While you are waiting for a speaker's next idea, use the time to review what the speaker is saying. Separate the central idea, key points, and details. Sometimes you may have to supply the organization. You can also use lag time to silently rephrase and summarize the speaker's message in your own words. Most important, keep your mind focused on the speaker and his or her ideas—not on all the other work waiting for you.

Take Notes to Ensure Retention. Don't trust your memory. A wise person once said that he'd rather have a short pencil than a long memory. If you have a hallway conversation with a team member and don't have a pencil handy, make a mental note of the important items. Then write them down as soon as possible. Even with seemingly easily remembered facts or instructions, jot them down to ease your mind and also to be sure you understand them correctly. Two weeks later you'll be glad that you did. Be sure you have a good place to store notes of various projects, such as file folders, notebooks, or computer files.

Working as part of a team, these four La Sierra University students won top honors in a competition sponsored by Students in Free Enterprise. One of their collaborative projects, "Rent a Brain," offered consulting services to local businesses. Team efforts require listening with an open mind, observing nonverbal cues, and interpreting the feelings of the speaker.

Checklist for Improving Listening

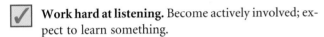

- ✓ **Stop talking.** Accept the role of listener by concentrating on the speaker's words, not on what your response will be.
- ✓ **Work hard at listening.** Become actively involved; expect to learn something.
- ✓ **Block out competing thoughts.** Concentrate on the message. Don't allow yourself to daydream during lag time.
- ✓ **Control the listening environment.** Move to a quiet area where you won't be interrupted by telephone calls or visitors. Check to be certain that listeners can hear speakers.
- ✓ **Maintain an open mind.** Know your biases and try to correct for them. Be tolerant of less-abled and different-looking speakers. Provide verbal and nonverbal feedback. Encourage the speaker with comments such as "Yes," "I see," "OK," and "Uh huh," and ask polite questions. Look alert by leaning forward.
- ✓ **Paraphrase the speaker's ideas.** Silently repeat the message in your own words, sort out the main points, and identify supporting details. In conversation sum up the main points to confirm what was said. Take selective notes. If you are hearing instructions or important data, record the major points; then, verify your notes with the speaker.
- ✓ **Listen between the lines.** Observe nonverbal cues and interpret the feelings of the speaker: What is really being said?
- ✓ **Capitalize on lag time.** Use spare moments to organize, review, anticipate, challenge, and weigh the evidence.

Jot down notes to make sure you understand and remember.

Communicating Through Nonverbal Messages

5

Understanding the messages of team members, as well as those of anyone else with whom you are communicating, often involves more than merely listening to the spoken words. Nonverbal clues, in fact, can speak louder than words. Eye contact, facial expression, body movements, space, time, distance, appearance—all of these nonverbal clues influence the way the message is interpreted, or decoded, by the re-

FIGURE 2.3 Elements in Message Meaning

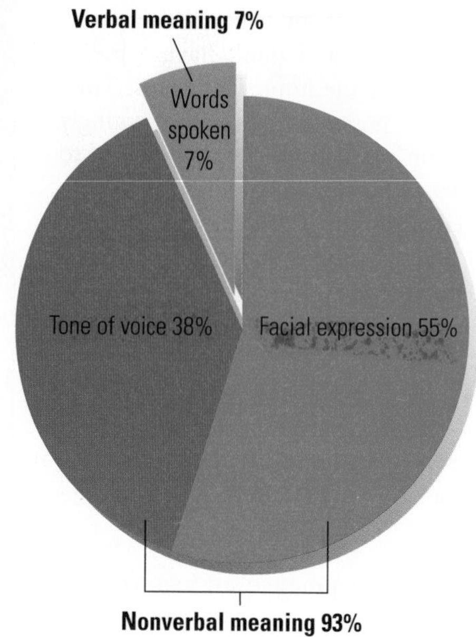

ceiver. In studies of interpersonal communication, researchers have found that only 7 percent of the "attitudinal" meaning of a message comes from the words spoken. An astounding 93 percent of the meaning, as shown in Figure 2.3, results from nonverbal cues.[23]

Nonverbal cues can contain up to 93 percent of the meaning of a message.

Nonverbal communication includes all unwritten and unspoken messages, both intentional and unintentional. These silent signals exert a strong influence on the receiver. Yet, interpreting them is by no means a science. Does a downward glance indicate modesty, embarrassment, or fatigue? Does a constant stare reflect coldness, insensitivity, or dullness? Messages are especially difficult to decipher when the verbal and nonverbal codes contradict each other. How would you interpret the following?

- Allison assures the team that she has enough time to complete her assigned research, but she misses two deadlines.
- Stewart protests that he's not really angry but slams the door when he leaves.
- Kyoko claims she's not nervous about a team presentation, but her brow is furrowed and she perspires profusely.

When verbal and nonverbal messages clash, receivers tend to believe the nonverbal messages.

The nonverbal messages in these situations speak louder than the words uttered. As numerous studies indicate, when verbal and nonverbal messages conflict, receivers put more faith in the nonverbal cues. In one experiment speakers delivered a positive message but averted their eyes as they spoke. Listeners perceived the overall message to be negative. Moreover, listeners thought that gaze aversion suggested nonaffection, superficiality, lack of trust, and nonreceptivity.[24] Successful communicators recognize the power of nonverbal messages. While it's unwise to attach arbitrary meanings to specific gestures or actions, some of the cues broadcast by body language are helpful in interpreting the general feelings and attitudes of the sender. For example, body language can suggest defensiveness, cooperation, nervousness, frustration, weakness, and power, as Figure 2.4 points out.

Listeners are understandably confused when a speaker's nonverbal cues contradict the verbal message. Let's look more closely at the powerful effect eye contact, facial expressions, posture, and gestures have on communication.

FIGURE 2.4 Body Language Cues

Defensiveness

Crossing arms, glancing sideways, touching or rubbing nose, rubbing eyes, buttoning coat, drawing away

Nervousness

Clearing throat, making "whew" sound, whistling, smoking, pinching flesh, fidgeting, covering mouth, jiggling money or keys, tugging ears, wringing hands

Cooperation

Leaning forward, opening hands, sitting on edge of chair, making hand-to-face gestures, unbuttoning coat

Power, Confidence

Making expansive movements, sitting upright, steepling hands, placing hands behind back or in coat pockets with thumbs out, acting affable, turning one's back, sitting in relaxed, almost sprawling position

Weakness, Insecurity

Making small movements, hunching over, pinching flesh, chewing pen, twiddling thumbs, biting fingernails, leaning forward with feet together on floor

Frustration

Taking short breaths, making "tsk" sound, wringing hands, clenching fists, pointing index finger, running fingers through hair, rubbing back of neck

Eye contact, facial expressions, and posture and gestures can all convey meaning.

Eye Contact. The eyes have been called the "windows to the soul." Even if communicators can't look directly into the soul, they consider the eyes to be the most accurate predictor of a speaker's true feelings and attitudes. Most of us cannot look another person straight in the eyes and lie. As a result, we tend to believe people who look directly at us. We have less confidence in and actually distrust those who cannot maintain eye contact. Sustained eye contact suggests trust and admiration; brief eye contact signifies fear or stress. Prolonged eye contact, however, can be intrusive and intimidating. One successful CEO says that he can tell from people's eyes whether they are focused, receptive, or distant. He also notes the frequency of eye blinks when judging a person's honesty.[25]

Good eye contact enables the message sender to determine if a receiver is paying attention, showing respect, responding favorably, or feeling distress. From the receiver's perspective, good eye contact reveals the speaker's sincerity, confidence, and truthfulness. Since eye contact is a learned skill, however, you must be respectful of people who do not maintain it. You must also remember that nonverbal cues, including eye contact, have different meanings in various cultures. You'll learn more about the cultural influence of nonverbal cues in Chapter 3.

Facial Expression. The expression on a communicator's face can be almost as revealing of emotion as the eyes. Researchers estimate that the human face can display over 250,000 different expressions.[26] Although a few people can control these expressions and maintain a "poker face" when they want to hide their feelings, most of us display our emotions openly. Raising or lowering the eyebrows, squinting the eyes, swallowing nervously, clenching the jaw, smiling broadly—these voluntary and involuntary facial expressions supplement or entirely replace verbal messages.

Nonverbal messages often have different meanings in different cultures.

Posture and Gestures. An individual's general posture can convey anything from high status and self-confidence to shyness and submissiveness. Leaning toward a speaker suggests attraction and interest; pulling away or shrinking back denotes fear, distrust, anxiety, or disgust. Similarly, gestures can communicate entire thoughts via simple movements. But remember that these nonverbal cues may have vastly different meanings in different cultures. A team member who signals success by forming the thumb and forefinger into a circle would be in deep trouble in Germany or parts of South America. The harmless OK sign is actually an obscene reference in those areas.[27]

Tuning in on nonverbal messages requires an awareness of their existence and an appreciation of their importance. To take stock of how effective you are in nonverbal communication, ask a classmate to critique your use of eye contact, facial expressions, and body movements. Another way to analyze your nonverbal style is to videotape yourself making a presentation and study your performance. This way you can make sure your nonverbal cues send the same message as your words.

How Time, Space, and Territory Send Silent Messages

People convey meaning in how they structure and organize time and how they order the space around themselves.

In addition to nonverbal messages transmitted by your body, three external elements convey information in the communication process: time, space, and distance.

Time. How we structure and use time tells observers about our personality and attitudes. For example, when Maritza Perez, a banking executive, gives a visitor a prolonged interview, she signals her respect for, interest in, and approval of the visitor or the topic to be discussed. By sharing her valuable time, she sends a clear nonverbal message. Likewise, when David Ing twice arrives late for a team meeting, it could mean that the team assignment is unimportant to David, that the meeting has low priority, that David is a self-centered person, or that he has little self-discipline. These are assumptions that typical Americans might make. In other cultures and regions, though, punctuality is viewed differently.

The way an office is arranged can send nonverbal messages about the openness of its occupant.

Space. How we arrange things in the space around us tells something about ourselves and our objectives. Whether the space is a dorm room, an office, or a department, people reveal themselves in the design and grouping of furniture within that space. Generally, the more formal the arrangement, the more formal and closed the communication environment. An executive who seats visitors in a row of chairs across from his desk sends a message of aloofness and desire for separation. A team leader who arranges chairs informally in a circle rather than in straight rows or a rectangular pattern conveys her desire for a more open, egalitarian exchange of ideas. A manager who creates an open office space with few partitions separating workers' desks seeks to encourage an unrestricted flow of communication and work among areas.

Territory. Each of us has certain areas that we feel are our own territory, whether it's a specific spot or just the space around us. Your father may have a favorite chair in which he is most comfortable, a cook might not tolerate intruders in his or her kitchen, and veteran employees may feel that certain work areas and tools belong to them. We all maintain zones of privacy in which we feel comfortable. Figure 2.5 categorizes the four zones of social interaction among Americans, as formulated by anthropologist Edward T. Hall. Notice that we are a bit standoffish; only intimate friends and family may stand closer than about 1½ feet. If someone violates that territory, we feel uncomfortable and defensive and may step back to reestablish our space. An episode in the popular *Seinfeld* program aptly described a close-talker as a "space invader."[28]

How Appearance Sends Silent Messages

Your appearance and the appearance of your documents convey nonverbal meanings.

The physical appearance of a business document, as well as the personal appearance of an individual, transmits immediate and important nonverbal messages.

Appearance of Business Documents. The way a letter, memo, or report looks can have either a positive or a negative effect on the receiver. Envelopes through their postage, stationery, and printing can suggest routine, important, or junk mail. Letters and reports can look neat, professional, well organized, and attractive—or just the opposite. Sloppy, hurriedly written documents convey negative nonverbal messages regarding both the content and the sender. In succeeding chapters you'll learn how to create documents that send positive nonverbal messages through their appearance, format, organization, readability, and correctness.

Appearance of People. The way you look—your clothing, grooming, and posture—telegraphs an instant nonverbal message about you. Based on what they see, viewers make quick judgments about your status, credibility, personality, and potential. Businesspeople who look the part are more likely to be successful in working with teams, other colleagues, and customers. Because appearance is such a powerful force in business, some aspiring professionals are turning for help to image consultants (who charge up to $500 an hour!).

What specific advice do image consultants give? Try to invest in conservative, professional-looking clothing and accessories; quality is much more important than quantity. Avoid flashy garments, clunky jewelry, garish makeup, and overpowering colognes, because, as one image consultant remarked, "they speak volumes without your ever saying a word."[29] Pay attention to good grooming, including a neat hairstyle, body cleanliness, polished shoes, and clean nails. Project confidence in your posture both standing and sitting.

FIGURE 2.5 Four Space Zones for Social Interaction

Zone	Distance	Uses
Intimate	0 to 1½ feet	Reserved for members of the family and other loved ones.
Personal	1½ to 4 feet	For talking with friends privately. The outer limit enables you to keep someone at arm's length.
Social	4 to 12 feet	For acquaintances, fellow workers, and strangers. Close enough for eye contact yet far enough for comfort.
Public	12 feet and over	For use in the classroom and for speeches before groups. Nonverbal cues become important as aids to communication.

The cues we send nonverbally are probably more important than those we send verbally.

Nonverbal communication can outweigh words in the way it influences how team members and other colleagues perceive us. You can harness the power of silent messages by reviewing the tips in the following checklist, paying special attention to the last two.

Checklist of Techniques for Improving Nonverbal Communication Skills

 **Establish and maintain eye contact.** Remember, in America appropriate eye contact signals interest, attentiveness, strength, and credibility.

 **Use posture to show interest.** Encourage communication interaction by leaning forward, sitting or standing erect, and looking alert.

 **Reduce or eliminate physical barriers.** Move out from behind a desk or lectern; shorten lines of communication; arrange meeting chairs in a circle.

 **Improve your decoding skills.** Watch facial expressions and body language to understand the complete verbal and nonverbal message being communicated.

 **Probe for more information.** When you perceive nonverbal cues that contradict verbal meanings, politely seek additional clues (*I'm not sure I understand, Please tell me more about . . .*, or *Do you mean that . . .*).

 **Avoid assigning nonverbal meanings out of context.** Make nonverbal assessments only when you understand a situation or a culture.

 **Associate with people from diverse cultures.** Learn about other cultures to widen your knowledge and tolerance of intercultural nonverbal messages.

 **Appreciate the power of appearance.** Keep in mind that the appearance of your business documents, your business space, and yourself send immediate positive or negative messages to receivers.

 **Observe yourself on videotape.** Ensure that your verbal and nonverbal messages are in sync by taping and evaluating yourself making a presentation.

 **Enlist friends and family.** Ask them to monitor your conscious and unconscious body movements and gestures to help you become a more effective communicator.

Planning and Participating in Productive Meetings

6

As businesses become more team oriented and management becomes more participatory, people are attending more meetings than ever. One survey of managers found that they were devoting as many as two days a week to various gatherings.[30] Yet, meetings are almost universally disliked. Typical comments include "We have too many of them," "They don't accomplish anything," and "What a waste of time!" In spite of employee reluctance and despite terrific advances in communication and team technology, face-to-face meetings are not going to disappear. In discussing the future of meetings, Akio Morita, chairman of the Sony Corporation, said that he expects "face-to-face meetings will still be the number one form of communication in the twenty-first century."[31] So, get used to them. Meetings are here to stay. Our task, then, as business communicators, is to learn how to make them efficient, satisfying, and productive.

Because you can expect to attend many meetings, learn to make them efficient, satisfying, and productive.

Meetings, by the way, consist of three or more individuals who gather to pool information, solicit feedback, clarify policy, seek consensus, and solve problems. But meetings have another important purpose for you. They represent opportunities. Because they are a prime tool for developing staff, they are career-critical. "If you can't orchestrate a meeting, you're of little use to the corporation," says Morris Schechtman, head of a leadership training firm.[32] At meetings judgments are formed and careers are made. Therefore, instead of treating them as thieves of your valuable time, try to see them as golden opportunities to demonstrate your leadership, communication, and problem-solving skills. So that you can make the most of these opportunities, here are techniques for planning and conducting successful meetings.

Deciding Whether a Meeting Is Necessary

Call meetings only when necessary, and invite only key people.

No meeting should be called unless the topic is important, can't wait, and requires an exchange of ideas. If the flow of information is strictly one way and no immediate feedback will result, then don't schedule a meeting. For example, if people are merely being advised or informed, send an e-mail, memo, or letter. Leave a telephone or voice mail message, but don't call a costly meeting. Remember, the real expense of a meeting is the lost productivity of all the people attending. To decide whether the purpose of the meeting is valid, it's a good idea to consult the key people who will be attending. Ask them what outcomes are desired and how to achieve those goals. This consultation also sets a collaborative tone and encourages full participation.

Selecting Participants

The number of meeting participants is determined by the purpose of the meeting, as shown in Figure 2.6. If the meeting purpose is motivational, such as an awards ceremony for sales reps of Mary Kay Cosmetics, then the number of participants is unlimited. But to make decisions, according to studies at 3-M Corporation, the best number is five or fewer participants.[33] Ideally, those attending should be people who will make the decision and people with information necessary to make the decision. Also attending should be people who will be responsible for implementing the decision and representatives of groups who will benefit from the decision.

FIGURE 2.6 Meeting Purpose and Number of Participants

Purpose	Ideal Size
Intensive problem solving	5 or fewer
Problem identification	10 or fewer
Information reviews and presentations	30 or fewer
Motivation	Unlimited

Distributing Advance Information

Pass out a meeting agenda showing topics to be discussed and other information.

At least two days in advance of a meeting, distribute an agenda of topics to be discussed. Also include any reports or materials that participants should read in advance. For continuing groups, you might also include a copy of the minutes of the previous meeting. To keep meetings productive, limit the number of agenda items. Remember, the narrower the focus, the greater the chances for success. A good agenda, as illustrated in Figure 2.7, covers the following information:

- Date and place of meeting
- Start time and end time

FIGURE 2.7 Typical Meeting Agenda

AGENDA

Quantum Travel International

Staff Meeting September 4, 1999

10 to 11 a.m.

Conference Room

		Person	Proposed Time
I.	Call to order; roll call		
II.	Approval of agenda		
III.	Approval of minutes from previous meeting		
IV.	Committee reports		
	A. Web site update	Kevin	5 minutes
	B. Tour packages	Lisa	10 minutes
V.	Old business		
	A. Equipment maintenance	John	5 minutes
	B. Client escrow accounts	Alicia	5 minutes
	C. Internal newsletter	Adrienne	5 minutes
VI.	New business		
	A. New accounts	Sarah	5 minutes
	B. Pricing policy for trips	Marcus	15 minutes
VII.	Announcements		
VIII.	Chair's summary, adjournment		

- Brief description of each topic, in order of priority, including the names of individuals who are responsible for performing some action
- Proposed allotment of time for each topic
- Any premeeting preparation expected of participants

Getting the Meeting Started

Start meetings on time and open with a brief introduction.

To avoid wasting time and irritating attendees, always start meetings on time—even if some participants are missing. Waiting for latecomers causes resentment and sets a bad precedent. For the same reasons, don't give a quick recap to anyone who arrives late. At the appointed time, open the meeting with a 3- to 5-minute introduction that includes the following:

- Goal and length of the meeting
- Background of topics or problems
- Possible solutions and constraints
- Tentative agenda
- Ground rules to be followed

A typical set of ground rules might include arriving on time, communicating openly, being supportive, listening carefully, participating fully, confronting conflict frankly, following the agenda, and adhering to Robert's Rules of Order. At this point, ask if participants agree with you thus far. The next step is to assign one attendee to take minutes and one to act as a recorder. The recorder stands at a flipchart or whiteboard and lists the main ideas being discussed and agreements reached.

Moving the Meeting Along

Keep the meeting moving by avoiding issues that sidetrack the group.

After the preliminaries, the leader should say as little as possible. Like a talk show host, an effective leader makes "sure that each panel member gets some air time while no one member steals the show."[34] Remember that the purpose of a meeting is to exchange views, not to hear one person, even the leader, do all the talking. If the group has one member who monopolizes, the leader might say, "Thanks, Kurt, for that perspective, but please hold your next point while we hear how Ann would respond to that." This technique also encourages quieter participants to speak up.

To avoid allowing digressions to sidetrack the group, try generating a "Parking Lot" list. This is a list of important but divergent issues that should be discussed at a later time. Another way to handle digressions is to say, "Folks, we are getting off track here. Forgive me for pressing on, but I need to bring us back to the central issue of . . . ."[35] It's important to adhere to the agenda and the time schedule. Equally important, when the group seems to have reached a consensus, is to summarize the group's position and check to see whether everyone agrees.

Dealing With Conflict

Before reaching decisions, most groups go through a "storming" or conflict stage. Conflict is natural and even desirable, but it can cause awkwardness and uneasiness. In meetings, conflict typically develops when people feel unheard or misunderstood. If two people are in conflict, the best approach is to encourage each to make a complete case while group members give their full attention. Let each one question the other. Then, the leader should summarize what was said, and the group should offer comments. The group may modify a recommendation or suggest alternatives before reaching consensus on a direction to follow.

Ending With a Plan

End the meeting with a summary of accomplishments.

End the meeting at the agreed time. The leader should summarize what has been decided, who is going to do what, and by what time. It may be necessary to ask people to volunteer to take responsibility for completing action items agreed to in the meeting. No one should leave the meeting without full understanding of what was accomplished. One effective technique that encourages full participation is "once around the table." Everyone is asked to summarize briefly his or her interpretation of what was decided and what happens next. Of course, this closure technique works best with smaller groups. The leader should conclude by asking the group to set a time for the next meeting. He or she should also assure the group that a report will follow and thank participants for attending.

Following Up Actively

Follow up by reminding participants of their assigned tasks.

If minutes were taken, they should be distributed within a couple of days after the meeting. It is up to the leader to see that what was decided at the meeting is accomplished. The leader may need to call people to remind them of their assignments and also to volunteer to help them if necessary.

Meetings are a necessary evil for today's team-oriented workplace. The following checklist can help you use them effectively and perhaps accelerate your career.

Checklist for Planning and Participating in Productive Meetings

Before the Meeting

Consider alternatives. Unless a topic is important and pressing, avoid calling a meeting. Perhaps an e-mail message, telephone call, or announcement would serve the purpose as well.

Invite the right people. To make decisions, invite those people who have information and authority to make the decision and implement it.

Distribute an agenda. Prepare and distribute an agenda that includes the date and place of the meeting, the starting and ending time, a brief description of each topic, the names of people responsible for any action, and a proposed time allotment for each topic.

During the Meeting

Start on time and introduce the agenda. Discuss the goal and length of the meeting, provide background of topics for discussion, suggest possible solutions and constraints, propose a tentative agenda, and clarify the ground rules for the meeting.

Appoint a secretary and a recorder. Ask one attendee to make a record of the proceedings, and ask another person to record discussion topics on a flipchart or whiteboard.

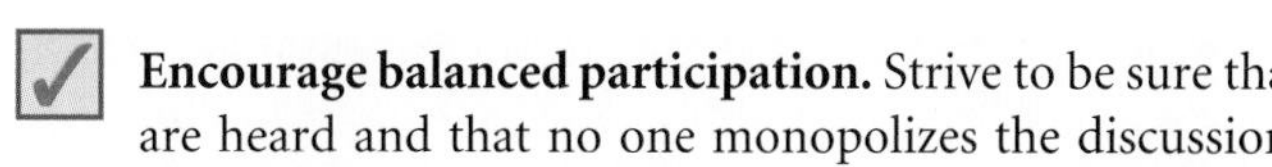

Encourage balanced participation. Strive to be sure that all participants' views are heard and that no one monopolizes the discussion. Avoid digressions by steering the group back to the topics on the agenda.

Confront conflict frankly. If people disagree, encourage each to explain his or her position completely. Then, restate each position and ask for group comments. The group may modify a recommendation or suggest alternatives before agreeing on a plan of action.

Summarize along the way. When the group seems to reach a consensus, summarize and see whether everyone agrees.

Ending the Meeting and Following Up

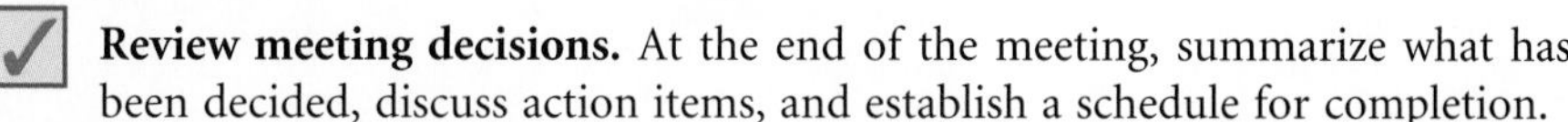

Review meeting decisions. At the end of the meeting, summarize what has been decided, discuss action items, and establish a schedule for completion.

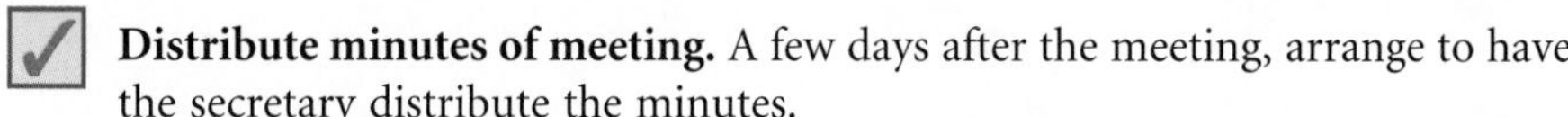

Distribute minutes of meeting. A few days after the meeting, arrange to have the secretary distribute the minutes.

Remind people of action items. Follow up by calling people to see if they are completing the actions recommended at the meeting.

Using Groupware to Facilitate Meetings and Decision Making

***Groupware* is a collection of computer tools to facilitate meetings and decision making.**

Groupware is a dazzling and growing collection of computer tools to facilitate meetings and decision making. This term refers to a number of related technologies that help groups exchange information, collaborate in writing projects, and reach consensus. For example, groupware is helpful in the planning and management of focus groups, executive retreats, strategic planning sessions, product development meetings, team-building seminars, and other meetings and training programs. Groupware is also effective when members of organizations must work together to solve problems, write mission statements, and develop proposals. Three common groupware options include teleconferencing/videoconferencing, e-mail meetings, and electronic meetings.[36]

Videoconferencing and Teleconferencing. Although *videoconferencing* generally refers to technologies primarily associated with viewing and *teleconferencing* refers to technologies primarily associated with speaking, often the terms are used interchangeably. Both technologies enable individuals to conduct meetings without getting together face to face.

Videoconferencing and teleconferencing enable individuals to meet without coming together face to face.

Images in videoconferencing may be viewed on a large screen in a conference room, on television screens in multiple rooms, or on desktop computers with small cameras installed. Group members may be able to see documents and objects as well as notes recorded on electronic live boards. Some technologies enable participants to interact at the same time even when they are in different places. Such meetings are increasingly popular because they reduce travel expenses, travel time, and fatigue. Take Syntec Corporation, for example. This large multinational pharmaceutical company figures that it saves $1,700 in travel expenses each time an employee attends a video meeting instead of actually making a business trip. The real savings,

Videoconferencing technologies allow Microsoft chair Bill Gates, located in Redmond, Washington, to appear with NBC dignitaries (including anchors Jane Pauley and Brian Williams) in New York as they launch MSNBC, the cable and Internet news service.

though, are in travel time and exhaustion. "We are a research-oriented company operating in every continent except Africa with a very high percentage of professionals," says the CEO. "The time of our people is worth a lot more than saving $1,700 a day in travel costs. Our primary goal is to avoid travel."[37]

E-mail meetings allow individuals to respond at different times.

E-mail Meetings. Participants can exchange words and data, but not pictures, in e-mail meetings. These meetings are usually unmediated; that is, they function without the services of a facilitator to direct the exchange of information. E-mail meetings enable participants to respond at different times, thus erasing time constraints for global team members. Like teleconferencing, e-mail meetings can increase participation by avoiding the dominance of overly vocal or very powerful team members. E-mail meetings also reduce writing inhibitions and decrease transmission time when circulating documents. However, e-mail meetings may suffer from excessive informality, lack of confidentiality, and lack of assurance that participants will read the messages.

Electronic meeting software facilitates brainstorming, decision making, and transmission of ideas throughout an organization.

Electronic Meetings. Electronic meeting software (also known as EMS or *meetingware*) uses networked computers to automate traditional meeting functions. A typical session uses a large screen at the front of the room. This screen functions as an electronic flipchart displaying participant ideas and responses. Meetingware allows facilitators to poll meeting participants, capture large amounts of verbatim feedback, analyze voting results, and create detailed reports including meeting minutes.

Meetingware is especially helpful when large groups must reach decisions quickly. Why? All members can participate simultaneously instead of listening politely as each member explains his or her ideas. The software saves time in sending ideas and decisions up and down an organization's communication hierarchy. At Hewlett-Packard meetingware accelerated product development by 30 percent. Structured electronic meetings were 20 to 30 percent shorter than face-to-face meetings. In addition to speeding the pace of meetings, meetingware engaged partici-

PROCESS TO PRODUCT

CASE STUDY

Applying Your Skills at Harley-Davidson

In turning around its fortunes, Harley-Davidson was able to expand its market share, eliminate its debt, and, most important, regain the respect of its customers. Keys to its success were establishing team-based management techniques and gaining employee involvement. As employees were moved to work groups, team members would set their own schedules and be cross-trained. One critical need was training employees in the techniques of how to run meetings and how consensus decision making works. According to training manager Darlene Rindo, "the basic idea is that while not everyone in the group will agree with a decision, they have to be able to go out and support it on the factory floor. That means never moving on to another agenda item without reaching closure."[38]

Your Job

As an assistant to the training manager at Harley-Davidson, you have been asked to prepare a summary of suggestions for developing effective meetings. Discuss how to prepare for meetings, how to conduct meetings, and how to follow up after meetings. Your suggestions will eventually become part of a training video called "Meetings Harley Style." Suggest ways to illustrate your points in a video. Present your ideas in an oral report (with chalkboard, flip chart, transparency, or electronic graphics) or submit your ideas in a memo with descriptive side headings.

pants in ways that traditional meeting tools do not. Meetingware also elicits higher-quality input from attendees and helps keep group decisions on track. However, this software is so complex that a facilitator is required to instruct participants and organize sessions.

Strengthening Your Teamwork Skills Now

At one time or another in your current or future job and certainly in your college career, you will be working on a team. It may be a temporary team created to complete one specific task, such as developing a new product or completing a project. It could be a permanent team with a continuing function, such as overseeing a complete line of products. In your personal life you could be a committee member or part of the governing body for your church, a social group, or a housing group. Most certainly, however, in your professional life you will be part of a team effort. You may be thinking, "Yeah, down the road a bit I might need some of these skills, but why worry about them now?"

The truth is that you need to start developing teamwork skills now. You can't just turn them on when you want them. They need to be studied, modeled, nurtured, and practiced. You've just taken a look at the inner workings of teams, including the four phases of team development, the role of conflict, the characteristics of successful teams, listening skills, nonverbal communication skills, and participating in productive meetings. In this book, in this course, and throughout your college career, you will have opportunities to work with teams. Begin to analyze their dynamics. Who has the power and why? Who are the most successful team

Teamwork skills need to be studied, modeled, nurtured, and practiced.

members and why? What would make a team function more effectively? How can you improve your teamwork skills?

Remember, job recruiters consider team skills among the most important requirements for many of today's jobs. You can become the number one candidate for your dream job by developing team skills and acquiring experience now.

Summary of Learning Objectives

1 **Discuss the importance of communicating in a team-oriented workplace, the four phases of team development, and the role of conflict.** Because they can be more productive and effective than individuals, many organizations are forming teams. Teams typically go through four stages of development. In the *forming* stage, they get to know each other and discuss general topics. In the second stage, *storming,* they define their roles, goals, and governing procedures. Tempers may flare as conflict erupts. Once team members work through this stage, they enter the *norming* stage in which tension subsides, roles clarify, and information begins to flow. Finally, in the *performing* stage, teams develop loyalty and progress toward their goals. Conflict that centers on issues can generate new ideas and help the group progress toward consensus. Open discussion of conflict prevents *groupthink,* a condition that leads to faulty decisions.

2 **Identify the characteristics of successful teams.** The most effective teams are usually small and diverse; that is, they are made up of people representing different ages, genders, and backgrounds. Successful teams agree on their purpose and procedures. They are able to channel conflict into constructive discussion and reach consensus. They encourage open communication, listen actively, provide feedback, and have fun. Members are able to collaborate rather than compete, and leadership is often a shared responsibility depending on the situation and expertise required.

3 **List techniques for organizing team-based written and oral presentations.** In preparing to work together, teams should limit their size, name a meeting leader, and decide whether they wish to make decisions by consensus, majority rule, or some other method. They should work out their schedules, discuss the value of conflict, and decide how to deal with team members who do not do their share. They should decide on the purpose, form, and procedures for preparing the final document or presentation. They must brainstorm for ideas, assign topics, establish deadlines, and discuss how to ensure information accuracy. In composing the first draft of a report or presentation, they should use the same software and meet to discuss drafts and rehearsals. For written reports one person should probably compose the final draft, and the group should evaluate it. For group presentations they need to work for consistency of design, format, and vocabulary. At least five rehearsals, one of which should be videotaped, will enhance the final presentation.

4 **Explain how to become an effective team listener.** Team members (as well as others) can become better listeners by controlling external and internal distractions, becoming actively involved, and identifying important facts. Good listeners do not interrupt speakers who have the floor. They ask clarifying questions at appropriate times, and they paraphrase to ensure that they understand what the speaker has said. While waiting for the speaker's next idea, good listeners analyze the speaker's central idea, key points, and details. To enhance memory and retention, effective listeners take notes or record important points as reminders for future reference or action.

5 **Analyze how information is transmitted through nonverbal messages and discuss how to improve nonverbal communication skills.** Nonverbal messages are sent by our eyes, face, and body. For example, sustained eye contact indicates trust or admiration; brief eye contact may signify fear or stress. Expressions on a communicator's face can supplement or entirely replace verbal messages. Posture can indicate status, confidence, shyness, or submissiveness. Gestures also send nonverbal messages, many of which are culture dependent. Moreover, how a communicator uses time, space, and territory sends messages that require no words. The amount of space we need for social interaction can be another means of sending messages nonverbally. Communicators may improve their nonverbal communication skills by maintaining eye contact, looking alert, eliminating physical barriers that separate them from their listeners, and improving their comprehension of nonverbal signals. They should evaluate nonverbal messages only in context, seek feedback, associate with diverse people, recognize the power of appearance, see themselves on videotape, and ask friends and family to monitor their body language.

6 **Discuss how to plan and participate in face-to-face and electronic meetings.** Call a meeting only when urgent two-way communication is necessary. Limit participants to those directly involved. Distribute an agenda in advance, start the meeting on time, and keep the discussion on track. Confront conflict openly by letting each person present his or her views fully before having the group decide which direction to take. End the meeting on time and summarize what was accomplished. Follow up by distributing minutes of the meeting and verifying that action items are being accomplished. *Groupware* is a collection of computer tools that facilitate meetings and decision making. Among groupware options are teleconferencing and e-mail meetings, both of which allow individuals to discuss topics although team members may be geographically dispersed. Another option is electronic meeting software (*meetingware*), which automates traditional meeting functions, such as brainstorming, capturing feedback, analyzing voting results, and creating reports including meeting minutes.

CHAPTER REVIEW

1. What is the difference between *cognitive* and *affective* conflict? (Obj. 1)
2. What is *groupthink*? (Obj. 1)
3. Why can diverse teams be more effective than homogeneous teams? (Obj. 2)
4. Why are team decisions based on consensus better than decisions reached by majority rule? (Obj. 2)
5. In times of team crisis, is it better to have shared leadership or one leader? (Obj. 2)
6. What is the best way to set team deadlines when time is short to complete a project? (Obj. 3)
7. In completing a team-written report, should all team members work together to write the report? Why or why not? (Obj. 3)
8. Workers spend what percentage of their communication time listening? What percentage do executives spend? (Obj. 4)
9. Define *lag time.* (Obj. 4)
10. Describe the four elements in the listening process. (Obj. 4).
11. Define *nonverbal communication.* (Obj. 5)
12. When verbal and nonverbal messages disagree, which message does the receiver consider more truthful? Give an example. (Obj. 5)
13. How does good eye contact help a speaker/sender? How does it benefit a listener/receiver? (Obj. 5)
14. What is the ideal size for a problem-solving meeting, and who should be invited? (Obj. 6)
15. Why is teleconferencing becoming increasingly popular among businesspeople? (Obj. 6)

CRITICAL THINKING

1. How would you compare the advantages and disadvantages of teams in today's workplace? (Objs. 1, 2, and 3)
2. How are listening skills important to employees, supervisors, and executives? Who should have the best listening skills? (Obj. 4)
3. What arguments could you give for or against the idea that body language is a science with principles that can be interpreted accurately by specialists? (Obj. 5)
4. How would you comment on this statement? "If you can't orchestrate a meeting, then you are of little use to an organization." (Obj. 6)
5. **Ethical issue:** You're disturbed that Randy, one member of your team, is selling Amway products to other members of the team. He shows catalogs and takes orders at lunch, and he distributes products after work and during lunch. He also leaves an order form on the table during team meetings. What should you do? What if Randy were selling Girl Scout cookies?

ACTIVITIES

2.1 Team Formation and Discussion (Objs. 1, 2, and 3)

Team

In groups of four or five, conduct a team discussion using one of the topics below. Appoint a team leader and a recorder. Discuss a topic for 10 minutes (or as long as your instructor directs). Then as a group, draft an outline of the major points discussed and the decision your team reached. Your instructor may ask you to report your decisions to the class or prepare a group memo describing your team's discussion and decision.

a. Should an employee be allowed to sell products such as Amway items or Girl Scout cookies at work? (See Critical Thinking Question 5 for more details.)

b. Should an employee be allowed to send personal e-mail messages during breaks or lunch hours? How about using company computers after hours to prepare a college report? What if your supervisor gives her permission but asks you to keep quiet about it?

c. Should companies have the right to monitor e-mail messages sent by employees? If so, is it necessary for an organization to inform the employees of its policy?

2.2 Web Detectives (Objs. 1 and 2)

Web **Team**

Assume your employer has asked you to investigate competitors' Web sites and report what you find. Team up with another class member. Select any two competing companies (say, Coke and PepsiCo or Nike and Reebok). Examine their Web sites and compare what you find. What services do they offer? How easy is it to navigate each site? How attractive is the format? Is one site clearly better than the other? Why? As a team, report your findings in a memo to your instructor.

2.3 Bad Listening Habits (Obj. 4)

Concentrate for three days on your listening habits in class and on the job. What bad habits do you detect? Be prepared to discuss five bad habits and specific ways you could improve your listening skills. Your instructor may ask you to report your analysis in a memo.

2.4 Listening and Retention (Obj. 4)

Listen to a 30-minute segment of TV news using your normal listening habits. When you finish, make a list of the major items you remember, recording names, places, and figures. A day later watch the same 30-minute segment but put to use the good-listening tips in this chapter, including taking selective notes. When the segment is completed, make a list of the major items you remember. Which experience provided more information? What made a major difference for you?

2.5 Silent Messages (Obj. 5)

Analyze the kind of silent messages you send your instructor, your classmates, and your employer. How do you send these messages? What do they mean? Be prepared to discuss them in small groups or in a memo to your instructor.

2.6 Body Language (Obj. 5)

What attitudes do the following body movements suggest to you? Do these movements always mean the same thing? What part does context play in your interpretations?

- **a.** Whistling, wringing hands
- **b.** Bowed posture, twiddling thumbs
- **c.** Steepled hands, sprawling sitting position
- **d.** Rubbing hand through hair
- **e.** Open hands, unbuttoned coat
- **f.** Wringing hands, tugging ears

2.7 Document Appearance (Obj. 5)

Select a business letter and envelope that you have received at home or work. Analyze their appearance and the nonverbal messages they send. Consider the amount of postage, method of delivery, correctness of address, kind of stationery, typeface(s), format, and neatness. What assumptions did you make when you saw the envelope? How about the letter itself?

2.8 Gender Differences (Obj. 5)

Many researchers in the field of nonverbal communication report that women are better at accurately interpreting nonverbal signals than are men. Conduct a class survey. On a scale of 1 (low) to 5 (high), how would you rank men in general on their ability to interpret the meaning of eye, voice, face, and body signals? Then rank women in general. Tabulate the class votes. Why do you think gender differences exist in the decoding of nonverbal signals?

2.9 Planning a Meeting (Obj. 6)

Assume that the next meeting of your associated students organization will discuss preparations for a career day in the spring. The group will hear reports from committees working on speakers, business recruiters, publicity, reservations of campus space, setup of booths, and any other matters you can think of. As president of your ASO, prepare an agenda for the meeting. Compose your introductory remarks to open the meeting. Your instructor may ask you to submit these two documents or use them in staging an actual meeting in class.

2.10 Analyzing a Meeting (Obj. 6)

Attend a structured meeting of a college, social, business, or other organization. Compare the manner in which the meeting is conducted with the suggestions presented in this chapter. Why did the meeting succeed or fail? Prepare a memo for your instructor or be ready to discuss your findings in class.

2.11 Searching the Web for Videoconferencing Data (Obj. 6)

Web

Your boss wants to find a way to reduce travel costs of staff members. He asks you to investigate videoconferencing technology. The first place you turn for research is the Web, and you discover that a surprising number of organizations offer videoconferencing services at their Web sites. Search for two organizations that provide information about videoconferencing technology, its applications, and costs. What services do they provide? How much does it cost to make a point-to-point conference call or to set up an entire in-house system? Gather preliminary data and condense it into a one-page memo (your boss doesn't like to read long memos).

C.L.U.E. REVIEW 2

On a separate sheet edit the following sentences to correct faults in grammar, punctuation, spelling, and word use.

1. If swimming is especialy good for you're figure how do you explain whales.
2. Although you may be on the right track you can get run over if you just set there.
3. Ellen and myself examined all simular accounts on a case by case basis.
4. Although both reports was wrote by Jeff and I, they carried the bosses signature.
5. The Vice President said, "Meetings are places where minutes may be kept but hours are lost."
6. At least fourteen patience were admitted after the accident, however, only four required treatment.
7. If the company is sold about one hundred and fifty employees will be out-of-work.
8. The meeting is scheduled for 4:00 p.m. consaquently Melissa and myself may be a little late.
9. Did you know that seventy percent of americans have visited disneyland or disney world.
10. I have allready checked the Web but I visited only one Government cite.

CHAPTER • 3 •

Communicating Across Cultures

LEARNING OBJECTIVES

1 Discuss three significant trends related to the increasing importance of multicultural communication.

2 Define *culture.* Describe five significant characteristics of culture, and compare and contrast five key dimensions of culture.

3 Explain the relationship between ethnocentrism, tolerance, and stereotypes in achieving multicultural sensitivity. Identify the six stages of multicultural transformation.

4 Illustrate how to improve nonverbal and oral communication in multicultural environments.

5 Illustrate how to improve written messages in multicultural environments.

6 Discuss multicultural ethics, including ethics abroad, bribery, prevailing customs, and methods for coping.

7 Explain the challenge of capitalizing on workforce diversity, including its dividends and its divisiveness. List tips for improving harmony and communication among diverse workplace audiences.

CASE STUDY

COMMUNICATION IN PROCESS

Corning and Vitro: A Marriage Made in Hell

When the marriage was first announced, it seemed like a blessed union. U.S. glassware leader Corning joined with the giant Mexican glass manufacturer Vitro in a cross-border alliance. Both companies were customer oriented. Both were aggressive global marketers, and both still had founding families in control.

But the honeymoon was short-lived. Perhaps the split-up could have been foreseen. Corning's modern offices in upstate New York feature streamlined glass structures. In sharp contrast, Vitro's headquarters in historic Monterrey are a replica of a sixteenth-century convent, with artwork, arched ceilings, gardens, and fountains.

Beyond conflicting styles of architecture, deeper disparities separated the two companies. Corning managers complained that important deadlines were often missed because only top managers could make decisions at Vitro. Mexicans faulted the Americans for being too direct and pushy. Vitro managers, practicing politeness, appeared to the Americans to be unwilling to recognize problems and weaknesses. The Mexicans generally thought that Corning moved too fast; the Americans grumbled that Vitro was too slow. And the need to react to a fast-changing market only added to the difficulties.

Clashes in management style also caused problems. Vitro and other Mexican businesses are hierarchical. This means that decisions are often left either to a member of the controlling family or to top executives. Middle managers may not even be asked their opinions. After the split, Vitro president Eduardo Martens remarked, "Business in Mexico is done on a consensus basis. [It's] very genteel and sometimes slow by U.S. standards."[1] Summing up, one analyst pronounced it "a marriage made in hell."

www.corning.com

www.vto.com

The Increasing Importance of Multicultural Communication

1

The "global village" predicted many years ago is increasingly becoming a reality. National and even local businesses find that their markets frequently extend across borders. Especially in North America, this movement toward global markets has swelled to a torrent. To better compete, many organizations form multinational alliances, such as that between Corning, the U.S. global glassmaker and fiber optics manufacturer, and Groupo Vitro, Mexico's largest industrial group. Some alliances end in divorce, as in the Corning-Vitro marriage. Those that flourish, however, have generally confronted and overcome many obstacles.

Learning more about how culture affects behavior helps you reduce friction and misunderstandings.

Some of the most significant obstacles involve misunderstandings and contrary views resulting from multicultural differences. In your current or future work, you may find that your employers, fellow workers, or clients are from other countries. You may travel abroad for your employer or on your own. Learning more about the powerful effect that culture has on behavior will help you reduce friction and misunderstanding in your dealings with people from other cultures. Before examining strategies for helping you surmount intercultural obstacles, let's take a closer look at three significant trends: (1) globalization of markets, (2) technological advancements, and (3) a multicultural workforce.

Globalization of Markets

Doing business beyond our borders is now commonplace. Procter & Gamble is selling disposable diapers in Asia; Rubbermaid would like to see its plastic products in all European kitchens; and Unilever promotes its detergents around the world. Not only are market borders blurring, but acquisitions, mergers, and alliances are obscuring the nationality of many companies. Firestone is owned by Japan's Bridgestone; Sylvania is controlled by German lighting giant OSARM; and even the Pillsbury doughboy dances to the tune of foreign conglomerate Diageo. Half of Xerox's employees work on foreign soil, and half of Sony's employees are not Japanese.

As markets expand, national boundaries and national allegiance mean less and less. When the German manufacturer Daimler-Benz, makers of Mercedes luxury cars, merged with U.S. carmaker Chrysler, one executive commented: "There are no German and American companies. There are only successful and unsuccessful companies."[2]

National boundaries mean less as businesses expand through mergers, alliances, and acquisitions.

To be successful in this interdependent global village, American companies are increasingly finding it necessary to adapt to other cultures. In China and Korea, Procter & Gamble learned to promote unisex white diapers. Although Americans preferred pink for girls and blue for boys, Korean and Chinese housewives balked at pink diapers. In a society where intense sexism favors boys, shoppers preferred white diapers that did not signal their child's sex.[3] In Europe, Rubbermaid met resistance when it offered products in neutral blues and almond, favorite American colors. Southern Europeans prefer red, while customers in Holland want white.[4] To sell its laundry products in Europe, Unilever learned that Germans demand a product that's gentle on lakes and rivers. Spaniards wanted cheaper products that get shirts white and soft. And Greeks preferred small packages that were cheap and easy to carry home.[5] To sell ketchup in Japan, H. J. Heinz had to overcome a cultural resistance to sweet flavors. Thus, it offered Japanese homemakers cooking lessons instructing them how to use the sugary red sauce on omelets, sausages, and pasta.[6]

American companies in global markets must adapt to other cultures.

What's caused this rush toward globalization of markets and blurring of national identities? One significant factor is the passage of favorable trade agreements. The General Agreement on Tariffs and Trade (GATT) promotes open trade globally, while the North American Free Trade Agreement (NAFTA) expands free trade between Canada, the United States, and Mexico. NAFTA created the largest and richest free-trade region on earth.[7] The opening of Eastern Europe and the shift away from communism in Russia have also fueled the progress toward expanding world markets.

Another important factor in the new global market is the explosive growth of the middle class. Parts of the world formerly considered underdeveloped now boast robust middle classes. And these consumers crave everything from cola to cellular phones. But probably the most important factor in the rise of the global market is the development of new transportation and information technologies.

Favorable trade agreements and the growth of the middle class fuel the expansion of global markets.

Technological Advancements

Amazing new transportation and information technologies are major contributors to the development of our global interconnectivity. Supersonic planes now carry goods and passengers to other continents overnight. As a result, produce shoppers in Japan can choose from the finest apples, artichokes, avocados, and pears only hours after they were picked in California. Americans enjoy bouquets of tulips, gerbera daisies, and exotic lilies soon after harvesting in Holland and Colombia. In fact, 70 percent of the cut flowers in the United States now come from Colombia in South

Advancements in transportation and information technologies contribute to global interconnectivity.

America. Continent-hopping planes are so fast and reliable that most of the world is rapidly becoming an open market.

Equally significant in creating the global village are incredible advancements in communication technologies. The Internet now permits instantaneous oral and written communication across time zones and continents. Managers in Miami or Milwaukee can use high-speed data systems to swap marketing plans instantly with their counterparts in Milan or Munich. Software firms in Silicon Valley depend on programmers in India to solve intricate computer problems and return the solutions overnight via digital transmission. Fashion designers at Liz Claiborne can snap a digital photo of a garment and immediately transmit the image to manufacturers in Hong Kong and Djakarta, Indonesia.[8] They can even include a video clip to show a tricky alteration.

Companies use the Web to sell products, provide support, offer service, investigate the competition, and link to suppliers.

Moreover, the Web is emerging as a vital business tool. Companies depend on the Web to sell products, provide technical support, offer customer service, investigate the competition, and link directly to suppliers. Many multinational companies are now establishing country-specific Web sites, as discussed in the accompanying Tech Talk box and illustrated by the Sony Music Germany site shown in Figure 3.1.

Internal web networks called *intranets* streamline business processes and improve access to critical company information. Through intranets employees have access to information that formerly had to be printed, such as a company phone book, training manuals, job postings, employee newsletters, sales figures, price lists, and even confidential reports, which can be password-protected. The Internet and the Web are changing the way we do business and the way we communicate. These advancements in communication and transportation have made markets more accessible and the world of business more efficient and more globally interdependent.

Unlike Sony Music Germany, few multinational companies are addressing the needs of their international audiences. Instead, they offer a North American experience with interactions only in English. But 80 percent of European corporate sites are multilingual, with English as the preferred second language.

FIGURE 3.1 Web Screen of Sony Music Germany

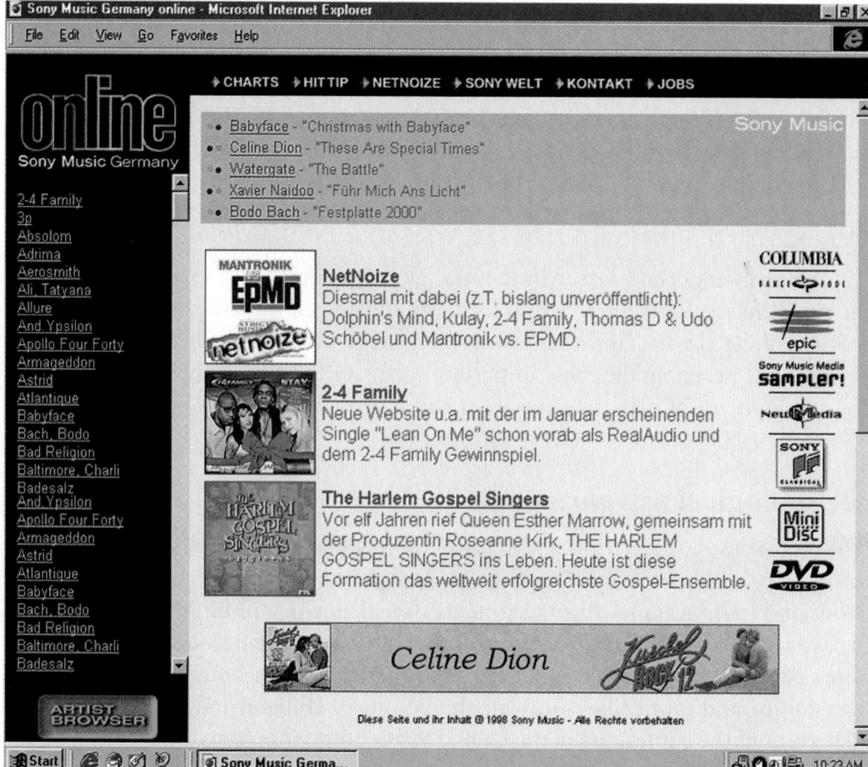

TECH TALK

BEING MULTICULTURALLY CORRECT ON THE WEB

Early Web sites were almost always in English and meant for Americans. But as on-line access grows around the world, multinational companies are taking a second look at their sites. Sony Music Entertainment, Inc., for example, now boasts 13 country-specific Web sites. French fans can see which Sony artists are "en tournée" in Nice; and German fans, as shown in Figure 3.1, can see which Sony records topped the local album charts "diese woche." United Parcel Service, Inc., allows customers in 13 European countries to track packages in their native languages. And Reebok considers its multilingual Web presence a necessity in expanding its global sales and marketing. What should companies do when they decide to go global on the Web?

- **Learn the local lingo.** Other countries have developed their own Web jargon and iconography. *Home page* is "pagina inicial" (initial page) in Spanish and "page d'accueil" (welcome page) in French. Experts warn against simply translating English words page by page.
- **Check icons.** American Web surfers easily recognize the mailbox, but in Europe a more universal icon would be an envelope. Test images with locals.
- **Relax restrictions on consistency.** Allow flexibility to meet local tastes. For example, McDonald's main site greets visitors with the golden arches and a Ronald McDonald-red background. The Japanese site, though, complements the McDonald's red and gold with pinks and browns, which are more pleasing in their culture.
- **Keep the message simple.** Whether in English or the local language, use simple, easily translated words. Avoid slang, jargon, acronyms, or ambiguous expressions.
- **Develop the site together.** The best foreign Web sites for multinational companies are developed when domestic and foreign webmasters work together. Start early and build rapport, recommends Judy Newby, McDonald's webmaster in Oakbrook, Illinois.[9]

Career Application

Compare the foreign and domestic sites of several multinational companies such as Sony Music Entertainment, IBM, United Parcel Service, Reebok, and McDonald's. Are design, content, and navigation similar? Is any English used?

Multicultural Workforce

Immigration makes cross-cultural communication skills increasingly necessary.

As world commerce mingles more and more, another trend gives cross-cultural communication increasing importance. People are on the move. Lured by the prospects of peace, prosperity, education, or a fresh start, persons from many cultures are moving to countries promising to fulfill their dreams. For generations the two most popular destinations have been the United States and Canada.

Because of increases in legal (and illegal) immigration, foreign-born persons are an ever-growing portion of the total U.S. population. In March of 1997 the Census Bureau reported that the total U.S. population was about 270 million people. Of this number about 27 million are foreign-born. This means that 10 percent of the total population comes from other countries.[10] Barring a change in government policy, we can expect to see a million new immigrants arrive in the United States every year. Estimates suggest that by 2006 immigrants will account for half of all new U.S. workers.[11]

This influx of immigrants is reshaping American and Canadian society. Earlier immigrants were thought to be part of a "melting pot" of ethnic groups. Today, they are more like a "tossed salad" or "spicy stew," with each group contributing its own unique flavor. Instead of the exception, cultural diversity is increasingly the norm. As we seek to accommodate multiethnic neighborhoods, multinational companies, and a multicultural workforce, we can expect some changes to happen smoothly. Other changes will involve conflict and resentment, especially for people losing their positions of power and privilege. Learning how to manage multicultural conflict is an important part of the education of any business communicator.

Understanding Culture

2

Every country or region within a country has a unique common heritage, joint experience, or shared learning. This shared background produces the culture of a region, country, or society. For our purposes, *culture* may be defined as the complex system of values, traits, morals, and customs shared by a society. Culture teaches people how to behave, and it conditions their reactions.

The Computer as Cultural Metaphor

People are like computers who are controlled by operating systems—our culture.

In some respects we are like computers that are controlled by operating systems—our culture. Anthropologists Edward T. Hall and Mildred Reed Hall suggested that culture is "a system for creating, sending, storing, and processing information." Sounds rather like the standard definition for a computer, doesn't it? This useful metaphor helps us better understand how culture operates. Think of your body as the hardware of a computer. Computers may have more than one operating system, such as DOS, Mac, Unix, or Windows. They also have software that controls specific applications, such as word processing, spreadsheets, and presentations. When you are functioning under one operating system, say as a European North American, you behave like others in that group. But at times you may be controlled by another operating system, say, when you are in a situation where you are functioning as a female. Society programs men and women to act differently. Gender, race, age, religion, and many other factors affect our behavior. These factors are like operating systems that program us to behave in certain patterns.

Just as computers with differing operating systems have difficulty communicating, so do people from differing cultures.

Just as a Unix operating system has trouble communicating with a DOS machine, so do people from one culture have difficulty getting through to those from another culture. Because individuals have more than one operating system, they do not always behave as expected. And just as operating systems can control many software applications, people are further differentiated by the software application that may be operating at any given time. For example, work cultures differ remarkably from one organization to another. When people conditioned to work in casual surroundings are placed in work cultures that are more formal and regimented, they may experience culture shock.

The important thing to remember is that culture is a powerful operating force that conditions the way we think and behave. And yet, we are not truly computers. As thinking individuals, we are extraordinarily flexible and are capable of phenomenal change. The purpose of this chapter is to broaden your view of culture and open your mind to flexible attitudes so that you can avoid frustration when cultural adjustment is necessary.

Characteristics of Culture

Understanding basic characteristics of culture helps us make adjustments and accommodations.

Culture is shaped by attitudes learned in childhood and later internalized in adulthood. As we enter this current period of globalization and multiculturalism, we should expect to make adjustments and adopt new attitudes. Adjustment and accommodation will be easier if we understand some basic characteristics of culture.

Culture Is Learned. Rules, values, and attitudes of a culture are not inherent. They are learned and passed down from generation to generation. For example, in many Middle Eastern and some Asian cultures, same-sex people may walk hand-in-hand in the street, but opposite-sex people may not do so. In Arab cultures conversations are often held in close proximity, sometimes nose to nose. But in Western cultures if a person stands too close, one may react as if violated: "He was all over me like a rash." Cultural rules of behavior learned from your family and society are conditioned from early childhood.

IMAGINE
Growing up, I got good at taking direction.
"Say your line here." "Hit your mark there." And "Drink your milk."
That's good advice for kids and adults. The calcium in milk helps bones
grow till you're about 35 and helps keep them strong long after.
So I still drink milk. Only now, I'm the one giving direction.
MILK
Where's *your* mustache?"

The "Got Milk" advertising punch line amused English speakers, but in Spanish it means "Are you lactating?" To counter the illogical and culturally unappealing message, a new Spanish-language milk campaign featured a family-centered message titled "Generations." Advertisers are increasingly aware of the need to shape campaigns that are logical and appealing across cultures.

Cultures Are Inherently Logical. The rules in any culture originated to reinforce that culture's values and beliefs. They act as normative forces. For example, in Japan the original Barbie doll was a failure for many reasons, one of which was her toothy smile.[12] Japan is a country where women cover their mouths with their hands when they laugh so as not to expose their teeth. Exposing one's teeth is not only immodest but also aggressive. Although current cultural behavior may sometimes seem silly and illogical, nearly all serious rules and values originate in deep-seated beliefs. Rules about exposing teeth or how close to stand are linked to values about sexuality, aggression, modesty, and respect. Acknowledging the inherent logic of a culture is extremely important when learning to accept behavior that differs from one's own cultural behavior.

Culture Is the Basis of Self-Identity and Community. Culture is the basis for how we tell the world who we are and what we believe. People build their identities through cultural overlays to their primary culture. North Americans, for example, make choices in education, career, place of employment, and life partner. Each of these choices brings with it a set of rules, manners, ceremonies, beliefs, language, and values. They add to one's total cultural outlook, and they represent major expressions of a person's self-identity.

Culture determines our sense of who we are and our sense of community.

Culture Combines the Visible and Invisible. To outsiders, the way we act—those things that we do in daily life and work—are the most visible parts of our culture. In Japan, for instance, harmony with the environment is important. Thus, when attending a flower show, a woman would wear a dress with pastel rather than primary colors to avoid detracting from the beauty of the flowers. And in India people avoid stepping on ants or insects because they believe in reincarnation and are careful about all forms of life.[13] These practices are outward symbols of deeper values that are invisible but that pervade everything we think and do.

Attitudes, behaviors, and beliefs in a culture change as a result of migration, disasters, and wars.

Culture Is Dynamic. Over time, cultures will change. Changes are caused by advancements in technology and communication, as discussed earlier. Change is also caused by events such as migration, natural disasters, and wars. The American Civil War, for instance, produced far-reaching cultural changes for both the North and the South. Another major event in this country has been the exodus of people living on farms. When families moved to cities, major changes occurred in the way family members interacted. Attitudes, behaviors, and beliefs change in open societies more quickly than in closed societies.

Dimensions of Culture

The more you know about culture in general and your own culture in particular, the better able you will be to adapt to a multicultural perspective. A typical North American has habits and beliefs similar to those of other members of Western, technologically advanced societies. In our limited space in this book, it's impossible to cover fully the infinite facets of culture. But we can outline some key dimensions of culture and look at them from different views.

Remember, though, that these are generalizations, intended to help us take a broad view. Individuals in a group may share many important characteristics of its culture. Yet, they are still individuals and, unlike computers, they may act independently of the group. Remember, too, that people may function under different operating systems and act differently from the norm because of a specific situation.

So that you will better understand your culture and how it contrasts with other cultures, we will describe five key dimensions of culture: context, individualism, formality, communication style, and time orientation.

Low-context cultures (North America, Western Europe) depend less on the environment of a situation to convey meaning than do high-context cultures (such as those in Japan, China, and Arab countries).

Context. Context is probably the most important cultural dimension and also the most difficult to define. It's a concept developed by cultural anthropologist Edward T. Hall. In his model, context refers to the stimuli, environment, or ambience surrounding an event. Communicators in low-context cultures (such as those in North America, Scandinavia, and Germany) depend little on the context of a situation to convey their meaning. They assume that listeners know very little and must be told practically everything. In high-context cultures (such as those in Japan, China, and Arab countries), the listener is already "contexted" and does not need to be given much background information.[14] To identify low- and high-context countries, Hall arranged them on a continuum, as shown in Figure 3.2.

People in low-context cultures tend to be logical, analyical, and action oriented.

Low-context cultures tend to be logical, analytical, and action oriented. Business communicators stress clearly articulated messages that they consider to be objective, professional, and efficient. High-context cultures are more likely to be intuitive and contemplative. Communicators in high-context cultures pay attention to more than the words spoken. They emphasize interpersonal relationships, nonverbal expression, physical setting, and social setting. They are more aware of the communicator's history, status, and position. Communication cues are transmitted by posture, voice inflection, gestures, and facial expression. Establishing relationships is an important part of communicating and interacting.

In terms of thinking patterns, low-context communicators tend to use *linear logic.* They proceed from Point A to Point B to Point C and finally arrive at a conclusion. High-context communicators, however, may use *spiral logic,* circling around a topic indirectly and looking at it from many tangential or divergent viewpoints. A conclusion may be implied but not argued directly. For a concise summary of important differences between low- and high-context cultures, see Figure 3.2.

Members of many low-context cultures value independence and freedom from control.

Individualism. An attitude of independence and freedom from control characterizes individualism. Members of low-context cultures, particularly Americans, tend to value individualism. They believe that initiative and self-assertion result in personal achievement. They believe in individual action and personal responsibility, and they desire a large degree of freedom in their personal lives.

Members of high-context cultures are more collectivist. They emphasize membership in organizations, groups, and teams; they encourage acceptance of group values, duties, and decisions. They typically resist independence because it fosters

FIGURE 3.2 Comparing Low- to High-Context Cultures

Low Context	High Context
Tends to prefer direct verbal interaction	Tends to prefer indirect verbal interaction
Tends to understand meaning at one level only	Tends to understand meanings embedded at many sociocultural levels
Is generally less proficient in reading nonverbal cues	Is generally more proficient in reading nonverbal cues
Values individualism	Values group membership
Relies more on logic	Relies more on context and feeling
Employs linear logic	Employs spiral logic
Says *no* directly	Talks around point; avoids saying *no*
Communicates in highly structured (contexted) messages, provides details, stresses literal meanings, gives authority to written information	Communicates in simple, ambiguous, noncontexted messages; understands visual messages readily

Low-Context Cultures ← German, German-Swiss, North American, Scandinavian, French, English, Spanish, Italian, Greek, Mexican, Chinese, Arab, Japanese → **High-Context Cultures**

competition and confrontation instead of consensus. In group-oriented cultures like many Asian societies, for example, self-assertion and individual decision making are discouraged. "The nail that sticks up gets pounded down" is a common Japanese saying.[15] Business decisions are often made by all who have competence in the matter under discussion. Similarly, in China managers also focus on the group rather than on the individual, preferring a "consultative" management style over an autocratic style.[16]

Many cultures, of course, are quite complex and cannot be characterized as totally individualistic or group oriented. For example, European Americans are generally quite individualistic, while African Americans are less so, and Latin Americans are closer to the group-centered dimension.[17]

Tradition, ceremony, and social rules are more important in some cultures.

Formality. Members of some cultures place less emphasis on tradition, ceremony, and social rules than do members of other cultures. Americans, for example, dress casually and are soon on a first-name basis with others. Their lack of formality is often characterized by directness. In business dealings Americans come to the point immediately; indirectness, they feel, wastes time, a valuable commodity in American culture.

This informality and directness may be confusing abroad. In Mexico, for instance, a typical business meeting begins with handshakes, coffee, and an expansive conversation about the weather, sports, and other light topics. An invitation to "get down to business" might offend a Mexican executive.[18] In Japan signing documents and exchanging business cards are important rituals. In Europe first names are never used without invitation. In Arab, South American, and Asian cultures, a feeling of friendship and kinship must be established before business can be transacted.

In Western cultures people are more relaxed about social status and appearance of power.[19] Deference is not generally paid to individuals merely because of their wealth, position, seniority, or age. In many Asian cultures, however, these characteristics are important and must be respected. Marriott Hotel managers, for example, have learned never to place a lower-level Japanese employee on a floor above a higher-level executive from the same company.

Words are used differently by people in low- and high-context cultures.

Communication Style. People in low- and high-context cultures tend to communicate differently with words. To Americans and Germans, words are very important, especially in contracts and negotiations. People in high-context cultures, on the other hand, place more emphasis on the surrounding context than on the words describing a negotiation. A Greek sees a contract as a formal statement announcing the intention to build a business for the future. The Japanese treat contracts as statements of intention, and they assume changes will be made as a project develops. Mexicans treat contracts as artistic exercises of what might be accomplished in an ideal world. They do not expect contracts to apply consistently in the real world. An Arab may be insulted by merely mentioning a contract; a man's word is more binding.[20]

Americans tend to take words literally, while Latins enjoy plays on words; and Arabs and South Americans sometimes speak with extravagant or poetic figures of speech that may be misinterpreted if taken literally. Nigerians prefer a quiet, clear form of expression; and Germans tend to be direct but understated.[21]

Americans value a direct, straightforward communication style.

In communication style Americans value straightforwardness, are suspicious of evasiveness, and distrust people who might have a "hidden agenda" or who "play their cards too close to the chest."[22] Americans also tend to be uncomfortable with silence and impatient with delays. Some Asian businesspeople have learned that the longer they drag out negotiations, the more concessions impatient Americans are likely to make.

Western cultures have developed languages that use letters describing the *sounds* of words. But Asian languages are based on pictographical characters representing the *meanings* of words. Asian language characters are much more complex than the Western alphabet; therefore, Asians are said to have a higher competence in the discrimination of visual patterns.

North Americans tend to correlate time with productivity, efficiency, and money.

Time Orientation. North Americans consider time a precious commodity to be conserved. They correlate time with productivity, efficiency, and money. Keeping people waiting for business appointments wastes time and is also rude.

In other cultures time may be perceived as an unlimited and never-ending resource to be enjoyed. An American businessperson, for example, was kept waiting two hours past a scheduled appointment time in South America. She wasn't offended, though, because she was familiar with Hispanics' more relaxed concept of time.

Asians tend to need time for deliberation and contemplation.

Although Asians are punctual, their need for deliberation and contemplation sometimes clashes with our desire for speedy decisions. They do not like to be rushed. A Japanese businessperson considering the purchase of American appliances, for example, asked for five minutes to consider the seller's proposal. The potential buyer crossed his arms, sat back, and closed his eyes in concentration. A scant 18 seconds later, the American resumed his sales pitch to the obvious bewilderment of the Japanese buyer.[23]

Achieving Multicultural Sensitivity

Being aware of your own culture and how it contrasts with others is an important first step in achieving multicultural sensitivity. Another step involves recognizing barriers to multicultural accommodation and striving to overcome them. Some of these barriers occur quite naturally and require conscious effort to surmount. You might be thinking, why bother? Probably the most important reasons for becoming multiculturally competent are that your personal life will be more satisfying and your work life will be more productive, gratifying, and effective.

Avoiding Ethnocentrism

The belief in the superiority of one's own race is known as *ethnocentrism,* a natural attitude inherent in all cultures. If you were raised in North America, many of the dimensions of culture described previously probably seem "right" to you. For example, it's only logical to think that time is money and you should not waste it. Everyone knows that, right? That's why an American businessperson in an Arab or Asian country might feel irritated at time spent over coffee or other social rituals before any "real" business is transacted. In these cultures, however, time is viewed differently. And personal relationships must be established and nurtured before credible negotiations may proceed.

Ethnocentrism causes us to judge others by our own values. We expect others to react as we would, and they expect us to behave as they would. Misunderstandings naturally result. A North American who wants to set a deadline for completion of negotiations is considered pushy by an Arab. That same Arab, who prefers a handshake to a written contract, is seen as naïve and possibly untrustworthy by a North American. These ethnocentric reactions can be reduced through knowledge of other cultures and development of increased multicultural sensitivity.

Consider the dilemma of the international consulting firm of Burns & McCallister, described in the accompanying Ethical Insights box. In refusing to send women to negotiate in certain countries, the company enraged some women's rights groups. But was Burns & McCallister actually respecting the cultures of those countries?

Spotlight on **Communicators**

Isadore Sharp, chairman and founder of the Four Seasons luxury hotel chain, plans to extend operations worldwide. Especially aware of intercultural sensitivity, Four Seasons is looking for overseas managers with strong listening skills, alertness to body language, and open minds. In working abroad, Four Seasons managers must be able to suspend judgment because right and wrong may not be the same as they would be at home.

Bridging the Gap

Developing cultural competence often involves changing attitudes. Remember that culture is learned. Through exposure to other cultures and through training, such as you are receiving in this course, you can learn new attitudes and behaviors that help bridge gaps between cultures.

Because culture is learned, you can learn new attitudes and behaviors through training.

Tolerance. One desirable attitude in achieving multicultural sensitivity is that of *tolerance.* Closed-minded people cannot look beyond their own ethnocentrism. But as global markets expand and as our own society becomes increasingly multiethnic, tolerance becomes especially significant. Some job descriptions now include statements such as "Must be able to interact with ethnically diverse personnel."

To improve tolerance, you'll want to practice *empathy.* This means trying to see the world through another's eyes. It means being less judgmental and more eager to seek common ground. For example, one of the most ambitious cross-cultural business projects ever attempted joined Siemens AG, the giant German technology firm, with Toshiba Corporation of Japan and IBM. Scientists from each country worked at the IBM facility on the Hudson River in New York State to develop a revolutionary computer memory chip. All sides devoted extra effort to overcome communication and other problems. The Siemens employees had been briefed on America's "ham-

ETHICAL INSIGHTS

FIRM LANDS IN HOT WATER FOR CAVING IN TO CULTURAL PREJUDICES

The international management consulting firm of Burns & McCallister found itself in cultural hot water. The problem? It refused to send female executives abroad to negotiate contracts in certain countries. Although the company has earned kudos for its fair treatment of women in this country, it declines to send female partners to negotiate contracts in certain countries.

Silent Women. In some cultures women may work in clerical positions, but they are not allowed to speak in a meeting of men. Contacts with clients must be through male partners or account executives. Japan, for example, has a two-track hiring system with women represented in only 3 percent of all professional positions. Other women in the workforce are uniformed office ladies who do the filing and serve tea.

Company Justification. In defense of its ban on sending women to negotiate in certain cultures, the head of Burns & McCallister said: "Look, we're about as progressive a firm as you'll find. But the reality of international business is that if we try to use women, we don't get the job. It's not a policy on all foreign accounts. We've just identified certain cultures in which women will not be able to successfully land or work on accounts. This restriction does not interfere with their career track."

Women's Rights. The National Organization for Women (NOW) argues that Burns & McCallister should apply its American standards throughout the world. Since women are not restricted here, they should not be restricted abroad. Our culture treats women fairly and other cultures should recognize and respect that treatment. Unless Burns & McCallister stands up for its principles, change can never be expected.

Career Application Organize a debate or class discussion focused on these questions. On what grounds do you support or oppose the position of Burns & McCallister to prohibit women from negotiating contracts in certain cultures? Should American businesses impose their cultural values abroad? Should Burns & McCallister sacrifice potential business to advance a high moral position? If the career advancement of women within the firm is not affected by the policy, should women care? Do you agree with NOW that change cannot occur unless Burns & McCallister takes a stand?

***Empathy,* which means trying to see the world through another's eyes, helps you be more tolerant and less judgmental.**

burger style of management." When American managers must criticize subordinates, they generally start with small talk, such as "How's the family?" That, according to the Germans, is the bun on the top of the hamburger. Then they slip in the meat, which is the criticism. They end with encouraging words, which is the bun on the bottom. "With Germans," said a Siemens cross-cultural trainer, "all you get is the meat. And with the Japanese, it's all the soft stuff—you have to *smell* the meat."[24] Along the continuum of high-context, low-context cultures, you can see that the Germans are more direct, the Americans are less direct, and the Japanese are very subtle.

Recognizing these cultural differences enabled the scientists to work together with greater tolerance. They also sought common ground when trying to solve disagreements, such as one involving work space. The Toshiba researchers were accustomed to working in big crowded areas like classrooms where constant supervision and interaction took place. But IBMers worked in small isolated offices. The solution was to knock out some walls for cooperative work areas while also retaining smaller offices for those who wanted them. Instead of passing judgment and telling the Japanese that solitary workspaces are the best way for serious thinkers to concentrate, the Americans acknowledged the difference in work cultures and sought common ground. Accepting cultural differences and adapting to them with tolerance and empathy often results in a harmonious compromise.

Saving Face. In business transactions North Americans often assume that economic factors are the primary motivators of people. It's wise to remember, though, that strong cultural influences are also at work. *Saving face,* for example, is important in many parts of the world. Face refers to the image a person holds in his or her social network. Positive comments raise a person's social standing, but negative comments lower it. People in low-context cultures are less concerned with face. Germans and North Americans, for instance, value honesty and directness; they generally come right to the point and "tell it like it is." Mexicans, Asians, and members of other high-context cultures, on the other hand, are more concerned with preserving social harmony and saving face. They are indirect and go to great lengths to avoid giving offense by saying *no.* The Japanese, in fact, have 16 different ways to avoid an outright *no.* The empathic listener recognizes the language of refusal and pushes no further.

Patience. Being tolerant also involves patience. If a foreigner is struggling to express an idea in English, Americans must avoid the temptation to finish the sentence and provide the word that they presume is wanted. When we put words into their mouths, our foreign friends often smile and agree out of politeness, but our words may in fact not express their thoughts. Remaining silent is another means of exhibiting tolerance. Instead of filling every lapse in conversation, North Americans, for example, should recognize that in Asian cultures people deliberately use periods of silence for reflection and contemplation.

CASE STUDY

PROCESS IN PROGRESS

Corning and Vitro Revisited

The marriage and subsequent divorce of glassmakers Corning of New York State and Vitro of historic Monterrey, Mexico, illustrates the difficulty of joining two cultures. Corporate consultant Richard N. Sinkin believes that cultural differences are the number one reason for failure in Mexican–U.S. business ventures. For example, take the matter of contracts. In the United States contracts are law, but in Mexico Sinkin says they "are kind of ideal things that you strive to achieve."

Many companies involved in joint ventures resort to borrowing from both cultures to fashion a new corporate culture. For example, Bank One of Columbus, Ohio, worked with Bancomer, one of Mexico's largest banks, to set up a consumer credit card operation. But different approaches to working procedures disrupted the operation. Mexican bankers were accustomed to long working hours, typically from 9 a.m. until 9 p.m. They took leisurely meals, sometimes lasting two hours. They also requested evening meetings, to which they were often late. The American bankers ate their lunches at their desks and wanted to be home in the evening. In forging a new culture, both groups agreed to changes, including full lunches in the company dining rooms. Evening meetings were held, but latecomers had to drop a few pesos for every tardy minute into a piggy bank set in the middle of the meeting table.

Critical Thinking

- What typical North American cultural values may clash with Mexican values in business alliances?
- How could Corning and Vitro have worked to improve their cooperative effort?
- Should the more powerful partner have imposed its culture and management style on the weaker? Why or why not?

Moving Beyond Stereotypes

Our perceptions of other cultures sometimes cause us to form stereotypes about groups of people. A *stereotype* is an oversimplified behavioral pattern applied uncritically to groups. For example, the Swiss are hard-working, efficient, and neat; Germans are formal, reserved, and blunt; Americans are loud, friendly, and impatient. As an American, are you loud, friendly, and impatient? Probably not, and you resent being lumped into this category. When you meet and work with people from other cultures, remember that they, too, resent

A *stereotype* is an oversimplified behavioral pattern applied uncritically to groups.

being stereotyped. In achieving multicultural sensitivity, we must look beneath surface stereotypes and labels to discover individual personal qualities.

Six Stages of Multicultural Transformation

***Ethnorelativism* suggests that absolute standards of rightness and goodness cannot be applied to cultural behavior.**

Achieving multicultural sensitivity and acceptance is not easy for people raised in closed communities where they had few opportunities to interact with other cultures. Moving from a state of ethnocentrism to one of ethnorelativism requires motivation and effort. *Ethnorelativism* refers to an attitude that absolute standards of rightness and goodness cannot be applied to cultural behavior. Cultural differences are neither good nor bad; they are merely different.[25] Those making this transformation will probably pass through six stages,[26] as shown in Figure 3.3.

In moving from ethnocentrism to ethnorelativisim, one may pass through stages of denial, defense, minimization, acceptance, adaptation, and integration.

1. **Denial.** We deny that cultural differences exist among people. We avoid learning other languages, we avoid topics that cause cultural discomfort, and we distort novel ideas.
2. **Defense.** We attempt to protect our own worldview to counter the perceived threat of cultural difference. For example, we may use words such as *backward* and *primitive* to describe cultures that differ from our own. We insist that only our language be spoken in the workplace.
3. **Minimization.** We attempt to protect the core of our own worldview by concealing differences in the shadow of cultural similarities. For example, one might say, "They may talk, dress, and eat differently, but underneath they're just like us." Surface similarities are recognized while deep differences are trivialized.
4. **Acceptance.** We begin to accept the existence of behavioral differences and underlying cultural differences. We begin to adopt a "live and let live" philosophy.
5. **Adaptation.** We become empathic toward cultural differences and become bicultural or multicultural. We may live and work in communities where multiple languages may be spoken and various cultural practices exist side by side.
6. **Integration.** We apply ethnorelativism to our own identity and can experience difference as an essential and joyful aspect of all life. We look upon cultural differences as a means of enriching our lives.

FIGURE 3.3 Six Stages in Multicultural Transformation

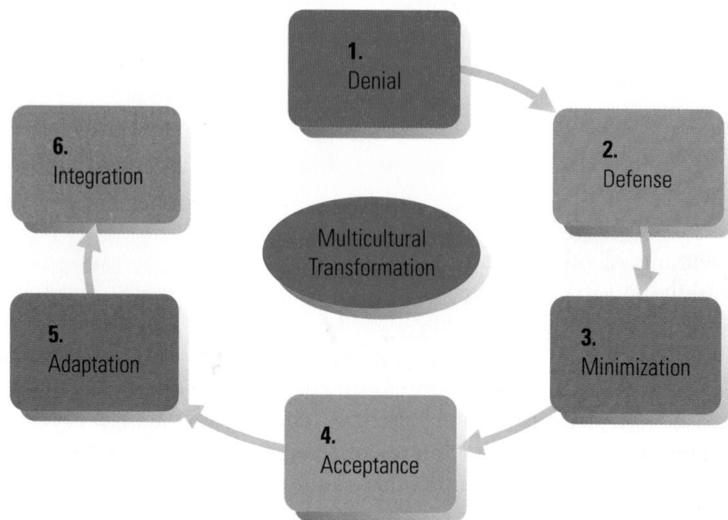

Improving Communication With Multicultural Audiences

Thus far we've discussed the increasing importance of multicultural sensitivity as a result of globalization of markets, increasing migration, and technological advancements. We've described characteristics and dimensions of cultures, and we've talked about avoiding ethnocentrism. You've studied the six stages in multicultural transformation. Our goal was to motivate you to unlock the opportunities offered by multiculturalism. Remember, the key to future business success may very well lie in finding ways to work harmoniously with people from different cultures.

4

Business success may depend on working harmoniously with people from different cultures.

Adapting Messages to Multicultural Audiences

As business communicators, we need to pay special attention to specific areas of communication to enhance the effectiveness of multicultural messages. To minimize the chance of misunderstanding, we'll look more closely at nonverbal communication, oral messages, and written messages.

Nonverbal Communication. Verbal skills in another culture can generally be mastered if one studies hard enough. But nonverbal skills are much more difficult to learn. Nonverbal behavior includes the areas described in Chapter 2, such as eye contact, facial expression, posture, gestures, and the use of time, space, and territory. The messages sent by body language and the way we arrange time and space have always been open to interpretation. Does a raised eyebrow mean that your boss doubts your statement or just that she is seriously considering it? Does that closed door to an office mean that your coworker is angry or just that he is working on a project that requires concentration? Deciphering nonverbal communication is difficult for people who are culturally similar, and it is even more troublesome when cultures differ.

Understanding nonverbal communication is difficult when people are from different cultures.

In Western cultures, for example, people perceive silence as a negative trait. It suggests rejection, unhappiness, depression, regret, embarrassment, or ignorance. However, the Japanese admire silence and consider it a key to success. A Japanese proverb says, "Those who know do not speak; those who speak do not know." Over 60 percent of Japanese businesswomen said that they would prefer to marry silent men.[27] Silence is equated with wisdom.

Although nonverbal behavior is ambiguous within cultures and even more problematic between cultures, it nevertheless conveys meaning. If you've ever had to talk with someone who does not share your language, you probably learned quickly to use gestures to convey basic messages. Since gestures can create very different reactions in different cultures, one must be careful in using and interpreting them. In some societies it is extremely bad form to point one's finger, as in giving directions. Other hand gestures can also cause trouble. The "thumbs up" symbol may be used to indicate approval in North America, but in Iran and Ghana it is a vulgar gesture.[28]

Gestures can create different reactions in multicultural environments.

As businesspeople increasingly interact with their counterparts from other cultures, they will become more aware of these differences. Some behaviors are easy to warn against, such as touching people from the Middle East with the left hand (because it is considered unclean and is used for personal hygiene). We're also warned not to touch anyone's head (even children) in Thailand, as the head is considered sacred. Numerous lists of cultural do's and don'ts have been compiled. However, learning all the nuances of nonverbal behavior in other cultures is impossible, and such lists are merely the tip of the cultural iceberg.

Associating with people from different cultures broadens multicultural competence.

Although we can't ever hope to understand fully the nuances of meaning transmitted by nonverbal behavior in various cultures, we can grow more tolerant, more flexible, and eventually, more competent. An important part of achieving nonverbal competence is becoming more aware of our own nonverbal behaviors and their meanings. Much of our nonverbal behavior is learned in early childhood from our families and from society, and it is largely unconscious. Once we become more aware of the meaning of our own gestures, posture, eye gaze, and so on, we will become more alert and more sensitive to variations in other cultures. Striving to associate with people from different cultures can further broaden our multicultural competence.

In achieving competence, one multicultural expert, M. R. Hammer, suggests that three processes or attitudes are effective. *Descriptiveness* refers to the use of concrete and specific feedback. As you learned in Chapter 1 in regard to the process of communication, descriptive feedback is more effective than judgmental feedback. For example, using objective terms to describe the modest attire of Muslim women is more effective than describing it as unfeminine or motivated by oppressive and unequal treatment of females. A second attitude is *nonjudmentalism,* which goes a long way in preventing defensive reactions from communicators. Most important in achieving effective communication is *supportiveness.* This attitude requires us to support others positively with head nods, eye contact, facial expression, and physical proximity.[29]

Keep your gestures to a minimum or follow the lead of native businesspeople.

From a practical standpoint, when interacting with businesspeople in other cultures, it's always wise to follow their lead. If they avoid intense eye contact, don't stare. If no one is putting his or her elbows on a table, don't be the first to do so. Until you are knowledgeable about the meaning of gestures, it's probably a good idea to keep yours to a minimum. Learning the words for *please, yes* and *thank you,* some of which are shown in Figure 3.4, is even better than relying on gestures.[30] Achieving multicultural competence in regard to nonverbal behavior may never be totally attained, but sensitivity, nonjudgmentalism, and tolerance go a long way toward improving interactions.

When English is a second language, don't assume that speakers understand everything you say.

Oral Messages. Although it's best to speak a foreign language fluently, many of us lack that skill. Fortunately, global business transactions are often conducted in English, though the level of proficiency may be limited among those for whom it is a second language. Americans abroad make a big mistake in thinking that people who speak English always understand what is being said. Comprehension can be fairly superficial. The following suggestions are helpful for situations in which one or both communicators may be using English as a second language.

- **Learn foreign phrases.** In conversations, even when English is used, foreign nationals appreciate it when you learn greetings and a few phrases in their language. See Figure 3.4 for a list of basic expressions in some of the world's major languages. Practice the phrases phonetically so that you will be understood.

Use simple English and avoid puns, sports references, slang, and jargon when communicating with people for whom English is a second language.

- **Use simple English.** Speak in short sentences (under 15 words), and try to stick to the 3,000 to 4,000 most common English words. For example, use *old* rather than *obsolete* and *rich* rather than *luxurious* or *sumptuous.* Eliminate puns, sports and military references, slang, and jargon (special business terms). Be especially alert to idiomatic expressions that can't be translated, such as *burn the midnight oil* and *under the weather.*
- **Speak slowly and enunciate clearly.** Avoid fast speech, but don't raise your voice. Overpunctuate with pauses and full stops. Always write numbers for all to see.
- **Observe eye messages.** Be alert to a glazed expression or wandering eyes—these tell you the listener is lost.

FIGURE 3.4 **Basic Expressions in Other Languages**

Country	Good Morning	Please	Thank You	Yes	No	Goodbye
Arabic	saBAH al-khayr	minFUDlak	shookRAAN	NAA-am	LAA	MAA-a salAAMuh
French	Bonjour [bohnzhoor]	S'il vous plaît [see voo pleh]	Merci (beaucoup) [mare-see (bo-coo)]	Oui [weeh]	Non [nonh]	Au revoir [oh vwar]
German	Guten morgen [Goo-ten more-gen]	Bitte [Bitt-eh]	Danke [Dahnk-eh]	Ja [Yah]	Nein [Nine]	Auf Wiedersehen [auwf vee-dur-zain]
Italian	Buon giorno	Per favore/per piacere	Grazie (tante)	Si	No	Arrivederia (Arrivederci, informal)
Japanese	Ohayoo [Ohio (go-ZAI-mahss) or simply Ohio]	oh-NEH-ga-ee she-mahss (when requesting)	Arigato [Ah-ree-GAH-tow (go-ZAI-mahss)]	High, so-dess	Ee-yeh	Sayonara
Norwegian	God morgen	Vaer sa snill [var so snill]	Takk [tahk]	Ja [yah]	Nei [nay]	Adjo [adieu]
Russian	Do'braye oo-tra	Pa-JAH-loos-tah	Spa-SEE-bah	Dah	N'yet	DasviDANya
Spanish	Buenos días [BWEH-nos DEE-ahs]	Con permiso [Con pair-ME-soh], Por favor [Pohr fah-VOHR]	Gracias [GRAH-seeahs]	Sí [SEEH]	No [NOH]	Adiós

- **Encourage accurate feedback.** Ask probing questions, and encourage the listener to paraphrase what you say. Don't assume that a *yes,* a nod, or a smile indicates comprehension.
- **Check frequently for comprehension.** Avoid waiting until you finish a long explanation to request feedback. Instead, make one point at a time, pausing to check for comprehension. Don't proceed to B until A has been grasped.
- **Accept blame.** If a misunderstanding results, graciously accept the blame for not making your meaning clear.
- **Listen without interrupting.** Curb your desire to finish sentences or to fill out ideas for the speaker. Keep in mind that North Americans abroad are often accused of listening too little and talking too much.
- **Remember to smile!** Roger Axtell, international behavior expert, calls the smile the single most understood and most useful form of communication in either personal or business transactions.[31]
- **Follow up in writing.** After conversations or oral negotiations, confirm the results and agreements with follow-up letters. For proposals and contracts, engage a translator to prepare copies in the local language.

To improve communication when English is a second language, speak slowly, enunciate clearly, observe eye messages, encourage feedback, check for comprehension, accept blame, don't interrupt, remember to smile, and follow up important conversations in writing.

Written Messages. In sending letters and other documents to businesspeople in other cultures, try to adapt your writing style and tone appropriately. For example, in cultures where formality and tradition are important, be scrupulously polite. Don't even think of sharing the latest joke. Humor translates very poorly and can cause misunderstanding and negative reactions. Familiarize yourself with accepted channels of communication. Are letters, e-mail, and faxes common? Would a direct or indirect organizational pattern be more effective? The following suggestions, cou-

5

pled with the earlier guidelines, can help you prepare successful written messages for multicultural audiences.

To improve written messages, adopt local formats, use short sentences and short paragraphs, avoid ambiguous expressions, strive for clarity, use correct grammar, cite numbers carefully, and accommodate readers in organization, tone, and style.

- **Adopt local formats.** Learn how documents are formatted and addressed in the intended reader's country. Use local formats and styles.
- **Use short sentences and short paragraphs.** Sentences with fewer than 15 words and paragraphs with fewer than 7 lines are most readable.
- **Avoid ambiguous expressions.** Include relative pronouns (*that, which, who*) for clarity in introducing clauses. Stay away from contractions (especially ones like *Here's the problem*). Avoid idioms (*once in a blue moon*), slang (*my presentation really bombed*), acronyms (*ASAP* for *as soon as possible*), abbreviations (*DBA* for *doing business as*) jargon (*input, bottom line*), and sports references (*play ball, slam dunk, ballpark figure*). Use action-specific verbs (*purchase a printer* rather than *get a printer*).
- **Strive for clarity.** Avoid words that have many meanings (the word *light* has 18 different meanings!). If necessary, clarify words that may be confusing. Replace two-word verbs with clear single words (*return* instead of *bring back; delay* instead of *put off; maintain* instead of *keep up*).
- **Use correct grammar.** Be careful of misplaced modifiers, dangling participles, and sentence fragments. Use conventional punctuation.
- **Cite numbers carefully.** For international trade it's a good idea to learn and use the metric system. In citing numbers use figures (*15*) instead of spelling them out (*fifteen*). Always convert dollar figures into local currency. Avoid using figures to express the month of the year. See Figure 3.5 for additional guidelines on data formats.
- **Accommodate reader in organization, tone, and style.** Organize your message to appeal to the reader. If flowery tone, formal salutations, indirectness, references to family and the seasons, or unconditional apologies are expected, strive to accommodate.

Making the effort to communicate with sensitivity across cultures pays big dividends. "Much of the world wants to like us," says businessman and international consultant Kevin Chambers. "When we take the time to learn about others, many will bend over backward to do business with us."[32] The following checklist summarizes suggestions for improving communication with multicultural audiences.

Checklist for Improving Multicultural Sensitivity and Communication

Study your own culture. Learn about your customs, biases, and views and how they differ from those in other societies. This knowledge can help you better understand, appreciate, and accept the values and behavior of other cultures.

Learn about other cultures. Education can help you alter cultural misconceptions, reduce fears, and minimize misunderstandings. Knowledge of other cultures opens your eyes and teaches you to expect differences. Such knowledge also enriches your life.

FIGURE 3.5 **Typical Data Formats**

	United States	United Kingdom	France	Germany	Portugal
Dates	May 15, 2000 5/15/00	15th May 2000 15/5/00	15 mai 2000 15.05.00	15. Mai 2000 15.5.00	00.05.15
Time	10:32 p.m.	10:32 PM	22.32 22 h 32	22:32 Uhr 22.32	22H32m
Currency	$123.45 US$123.45	£123.45 GB£123.45	123F45 123,45F 123.45 euros	DM 123,45 123,45 DM 123.45 euros	123$45 ESC 123.45 123.45 euros
Large numbers	1,234,567.89	1,234,567.89	1.234.567,89 1 234 567	1.234.567,89	1.234.567,89
Phone numbers	(205) 555-1234	(081) 987 1234 0255 876543	(15) 61-87-34-02 (15) 61.87.34.02	(089) 2 61 39 12	056-244 33 056 45 45 45

✓ **Curb ethnocentrism.** Avoid judging others by your personal views. Get over the view that the other cultures are incorrect, defective, or primitive. Try to develop an open mindset.

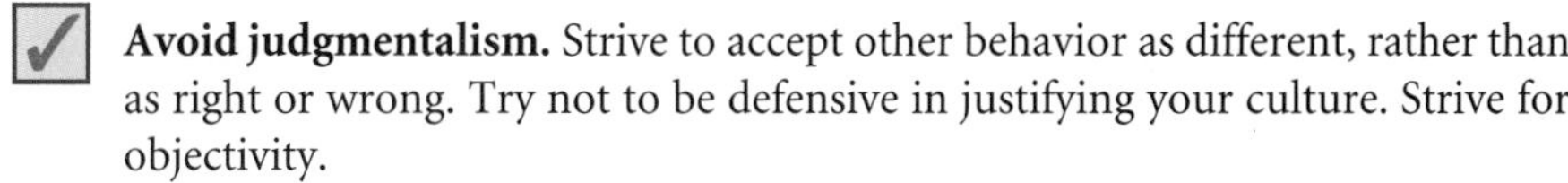

✓ **Avoid judgmentalism.** Strive to accept other behavior as different, rather than as right or wrong. Try not to be defensive in justifying your culture. Strive for objectivity.

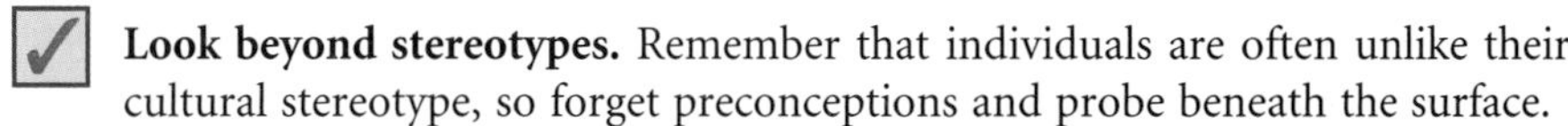

✓ **Look beyond stereotypes.** Remember that individuals are often unlike their cultural stereotype, so forget preconceptions and probe beneath the surface.

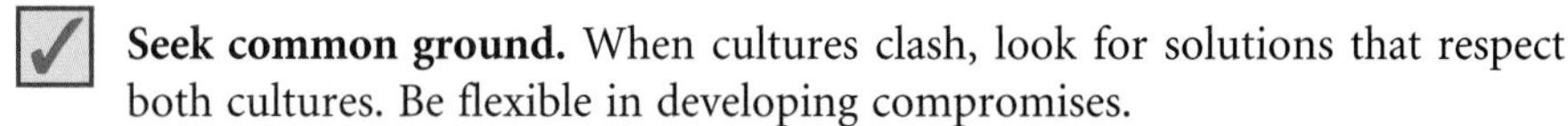

✓ **Seek common ground.** When cultures clash, look for solutions that respect both cultures. Be flexible in developing compromises.

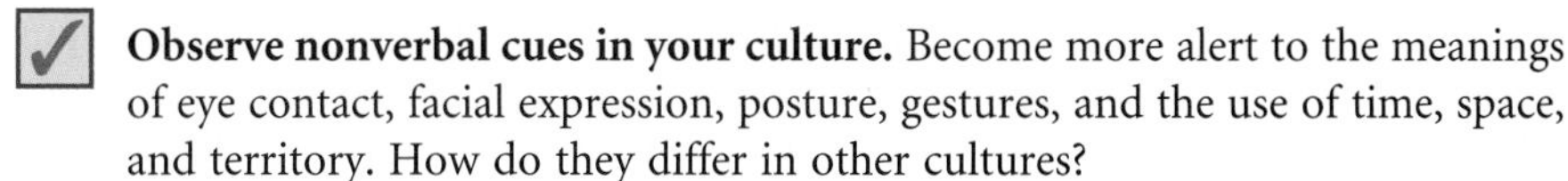

✓ **Observe nonverbal cues in your culture.** Become more alert to the meanings of eye contact, facial expression, posture, gestures, and the use of time, space, and territory. How do they differ in other cultures?

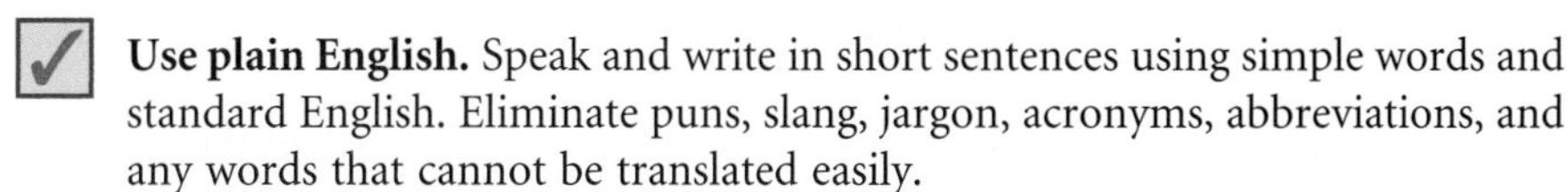

✓ **Use plain English.** Speak and write in short sentences using simple words and standard English. Eliminate puns, slang, jargon, acronyms, abbreviations, and any words that cannot be translated easily.

✓ **Encourage accurate feedback.** In conversations ask probing questions and listen attentively without interrupting. Don't assume that a *yes* or a smile indicates assent or comprehension.

✓ **Adapt to local preferences.** Shape your writing to reflect the reader's document styles, if appropriate. Express currency in local figures. Write out months of the year for clarity.

Coping With Multicultural Ethics

A perplexing problem faces conscientious organizations and individuals who do business around the world. Whose values, culture, and, ultimately, laws do you follow? Do you heed the customs of your country or those of the country where you are engaged in business? Some observers claim that when American businesspeople venture abroad, they're wandering into an "ethical no-man's land, where each encounter holds forth a fresh demand for a 'gratuity,' or baksheesh.[33]

Business Practices Abroad

When Americans conduct business abroad, their ethics are put to the test.

As companies do more and more business around the globe, their assumptions about ethics are put to the test. Businesspeople may face simple questions regarding the appropriate amount of money to spend on a business gift or the legitimacy of payments to agents and distributors to "expedite" business. Or they may encounter out-and-out bribery, child-labor abuse, environment mistreatment, and unscrupulous business practices.

In South America many U.S. companies are "locked out" of the market because of a closed bidding system that favors the region's large, nationalized companies. In other countries U.S. businesses are out of the running because they refuse to pay the bribes required to get the business. The founder of Control Data Corporation said, "No question about it. We were constantly in the position of saying how much we were willing to pay" to complete even routine business services.[34]

The least corrupt countries are New Zealand, Denmark, Finland, Sweden, and Canada.

All countries, of course, are not corrupt. *The New York Times* compiled a ranking of corruption in 41 countries. Based on a number of polls and surveys of businesspeople and journalists, the index presents a "Global Gauge of Greased Palms," as shown in Figure 3.6. The least corrupt countries are New Zealand, Denmark, Finland, Sweden, and Canada. The most corrupt were Indonesia, China, Pakistan, Venezuela, and Brazil. The United States ranked between Germany and France, in the upper third.

Laws Forbidding Bribery

The United States leads the global fight against corruption.

The United States is not highest on the index of least corruptible countries. Yet, it has taken the global lead in fighting corruption. Over two decades ago the U.S. government passed the Foreign Corrupt Practices Act of 1977. It prohibits payments to foreign officials for the purpose of obtaining or retaining business. But the law applied only to U.S. companies. Thus, they were at a decided disadvantage when competing against less scrupulous companies from other nations. U.S. companies complained that they lost billions of dollars in contracts every year because they refused to bribe their way to success.

Most other industrialized countries looked the other way when their corporations used bribes. They considered the "greasing of palms" just a cost of doing business in certain cultures. In fact, German corporations were even allowed to deduct bribes as a business expense when they calculated taxes. But in this country, bribery is a criminal offense; and corporate officials found guilty are fined and sent to jail.

After years of U.S. negotiating, however, the tide is turning. Many of the world's industrialized countries formally agreed in 1997 to a new global treaty. It bans the practice of bribery of foreign government officials. The treaty covers 29 countries belonging to the Organization for Economic Cooperation and Development (OECD).[35]

FIGURE 3.6 Global Gauge of Greased Palms

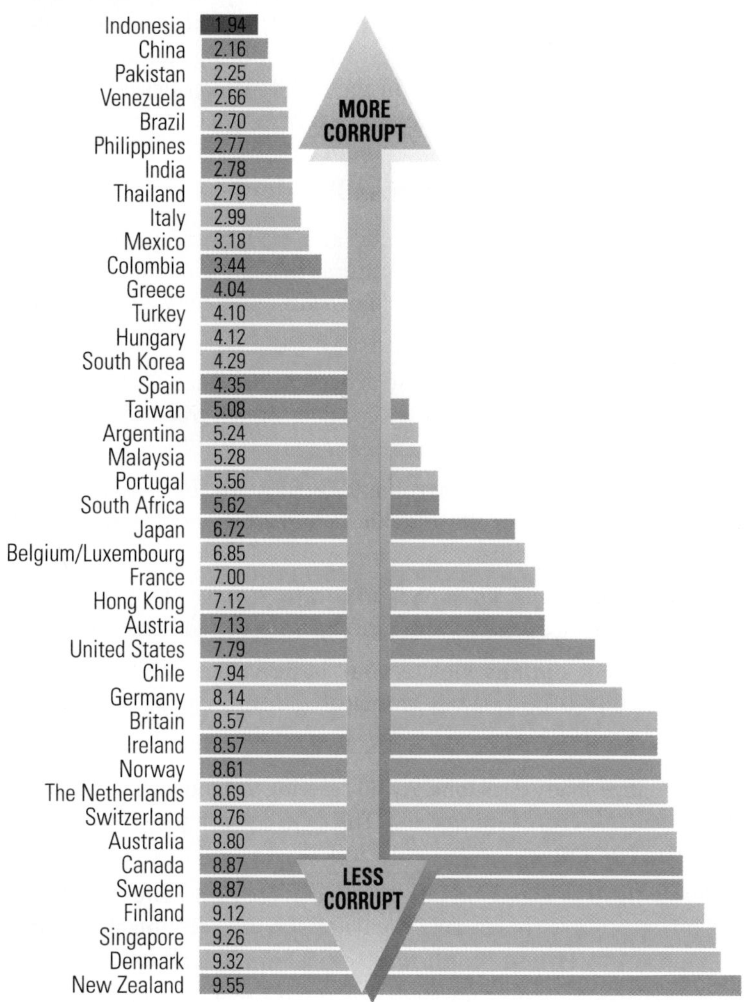

Reprinted with permission of *The New York Times.*

The international corruption index is a compilation of polls and surveys put together by Transparency International, a Berlin-based watchdog organization whose purpose is curbing the increasingly rampant corruption stunting the development of poor countries.

Whose Ethics Should Prevail?

Although world leaders agree that bribery of officials is wrong, they do not agree on other ethical behavior.

Although world leaders seem to agree that bribery of officials is wrong, many other shady areas persist. Drawing the lines of ethical behavior here at home is hard enough. When faced with a cultural filter, the picture becomes even murkier. Most people agree that mistreating children is wrong. But in some countries, child labor is not only condoned, it is considered necessary for a family to subsist. While most countries want to respect the environment, they might also sanction the use of DDT because crops would be consumed by insects without it.

In some cultures "grease" payments to customs officials may be part of their earning—not blackmail. In parts of Africa, a "family" celebration at the conclusion of a business deal includes a party for which you are asked to pay. This payment is a sign of friendship and lasting business relationship, not a personal payoff. In some Third World countries, requests for assistance in developing technologies or reducing hunger may become part of a business package.[36]

The exchanging of gifts is another tricky subject. In many non-Western cultures, the gift exchange tradition has become a business ritual. Gifts are not only a sign of gratitude and hospitality, but they also generate a future obligation and trust. Americans,

Gifts may be a sign of gratitude and hospitality, but they also suggest future obligation.

of course, become uneasy when gift-giving seems to move beyond normal courtesy and friendliness. If it even remotely suggests influence-peddling, they back off.

Whose ethics should prevail across borders? Unfortunately, no clear-cut answers can be found. Americans are sometimes criticized for being ethical "fanatics," wishing to impose their "moralistic" views on the world. Also criticized are ethical "relativists" who contend that no absolute values exist.[37]

Making Ethical Decisions Across Borders

Instead of trying to distinguish "good ethics" and "bad ethics," perhaps the best plan is to look for practical solutions to the cultural challenges of global business interaction. Following are suggestions that acknowledge different values but also respect the need for moral initiative.[38]

- **Broaden your view.** Become more sensitive to the values and customs of other cultures. Look especially at what they consider moral, traditional, practical, and effective.
- **Avoid reflex judgments.** Don't automatically judge the business customs of others as immoral, corrupt, or unworkable. Assume they are legitimate and workable until proved otherwise.

Finding practical solutions to ethical problems is most important.

- **Find alternatives.** Instead of caving in to government payoffs, perhaps offer nonmonetary public service benefits, technical expertise, or additional customer service.
- **Refuse business if options violate your basic values.** If an action seriously breaches your own code of ethics or that of your firm, give up the transaction.
- **Work in the fresh air.** Conduct all relations and negotiations as openly as possible.
- **Don't rationalize shady decisions.** Avoid agreeing to actions that cause you to say, "This isn't *really* illegal or immoral," "This is in the company's best interest," or "No one will find out."

Businesspeople abroad can choose many alternatives that acknowledge different values but also respect the need for moral initiative.

- **Resist legalistic strategies.** Don't use tactics that are legally safe but ethically questionable. For example, don't call "agents" (who are accountable to employers) "distributors" (who are not). When faced with a multicultural ethical dilemma, you can apply the same five-question test you learned in Chapter 1. Even in another culture, these questions can guide you to the best decision.

1. Is the action you are considering legal?
2. How would you see the problem if you were on the opposite side?
3. What are alternate solutions?
4. Can you discuss the problem with someone whose advice you trust?
5. How would you feel if your family, friends, employer, or coworker learned of your action?

Capitalizing on Workforce Diversity

7

At the same time that North American businesspeople are interacting with people from around the world, the domestic workforce is becoming more diverse. This diversity has many dimensions—race, ethnicity, age, religion, gender, national origin, physical ability, and countless other qualities. No longer, say the experts, will the workplace be predominantly Anglo oriented or male. By 2005 groups now considered minorities (African Americans, Hispanics, Asians, Native Americans) will make up 27 percent of the workforce. Women are projected to be 47 percent of the work-

Presentations in an intercultural setting, especially to an audience that uses English infrequently, require sensitivity. Wise speakers use simple language, speak slowly, watch for eye messages, and encourage frequent feedback.

force by 2006.[39] Moreover, about 40 percent of the workforce will be over 45 years of age, a dramatic jump from 31 percent today. And because of technological advances, more physically challenged people are joining the workforce.

Dividends of Diversity

A diverse workforce benefits consumers, work teams, and business organizations.

As society and the workforce become more diverse, successful interaction and communication among the various identity groups brings distinct challenges and dividends in three areas.

Consumers. A diverse staff is better able to read trends and respond to the increasingly diverse customer base in local and world markets. Diverse consumers now want specialized goods and services tailored to their needs. Teams made up of different people with different experiences are better able to create the different products that these markets require. Consumers also want to deal with companies that respect their values.

Work Teams. As you learned in Chapter 2, employees today work in teams. Team members with different backgrounds may come up with more creative and effective problem-solving techniques than homogeneous teams. At Procter & Gamble a senior marketing executive hit the nail on the head when he said, "I don't know how you can effectively market to the melting pot that this country represents without a workforce and vendors who have a gut-level understanding of the needs and wants of all of these market segments. . . . When we started getting a more diverse workforce, we started getting richer [marketing] plans, because they came up with things that white males were simply not going to come up with on their own."[40]

Business Organizations. Companies that set aside time and resources to cultivate and capitalize on diversity will suffer fewer discrimination lawsuits, fewer union clashes, and less government regulatory action. Most important, though, is the growing realization among organizations that diversity is a critical bottom-line business strategy to improve employee relationships and to increase productivity. Developing a diverse staff that can work together cooperatively is one of the biggest challenges facing business organizations today.

Divisiveness of Diversity

Diversity can cause divisiveness, discontent, and clashes.

Diversity can be a positive force within organizations. But all too often it can also cause divisiveness, discontent, and clashes. Many of the identity groups, the so-called workforce "disenfranchised," have legitimate gripes.

The *glass ceiling* is an invisible barrier of attitudes, prejudices, and "old boy networks" that block women from reaching important positions.

Women complain of the *glass ceiling*, that invisible barrier of attitudes, prejudices, and "old boy networks" blocking them from reaching important corporate positions. Some women feel that they are the victims of sexual harassment, unequal wages, sexism, and even their style of communication. See the accompanying Career Coach box to learn more about gender talk and gender tension. On the other hand, men, too, have gender issues. One manager described gender discrimination in his office: "My boss was a woman and was very verbal about the opportunities for women to advance in my company. I have often felt she gave much more attention to the women in the office than the men."[41]

Older employees feel that the deck is stacked in favor of younger employees. Minorities complain that they are discriminated against in hiring, retention, wages, and promotions. Physically challenged individuals feel that their limitations should not hold them back, and they fear that their potential is often prejudged. Individuals with different religions feel uncomfortable working alongside each other. A Jew, for example, may be stressed if he has to train a Palestinian from Saudi Arabia. Similarly, a manager confessed, "I am half Jewish on my father's side. Very often someone will make a comment about Jews and I am always faced with the decision of speaking up or not."[42]

Tips for Improving Communication Among Diverse Workplace Audiences

A diverse workforce may reduce productivity unless trained to value differences.

Integrating all this diversity into one seamless workforce is a formidable task and a vital one. Harnessed effectively, diversity can enhance productivity and propel a company to success well into the twenty-first century. Mismanaged, it can become a tremendous drain on a company's time and resources. How companies deal with diversity will make all the difference in how they compete in an increasingly global environment. And that means that organizations must do more than just pay lip service to these issues. Harmony and acceptance do not happen automatically when people who are dissimilar work together. The following suggestions can help you and your organization find ways to improve communication and interaction.

- **Seek training.** Especially if an organization is experiencing problems in managing diversity, awareness-raising sessions may be helpful. Spend time reading and learning about workforce diversity and how it can benefit organizations. Look upon diversity as an opportunity, not a threat. Cross-cultural communication, team building, and conflict resolution are skills that can be learned in diversity training programs.
- **Understand the value of differences.** Diversity makes an organization innovative and creative. Sameness fosters an absence of critical thinking called "groupthink," which you learned about in Chapter 2. Case studies, for example, of the Kennedy Administration's decision to invade Cuba and of the *Challenger* shuttle disaster suggest that groupthink prevented alternatives from being considered.[43] Diversity in problem-solving groups encourages independent and creative thinking.
- **Don't expect conformity.** Gone are the days when businesses could say, "This is our culture. Conform or leave."[44] Paul Fireman, CEO of Reebok, stresses seeking people who have new and different stories to tell. "And then you have to make real room for them, you have to learn to listen, to listen closely, to their stories.

CAREER COACH

HE SAID, SHE SAID: GENDER TALK AND GENDER TENSION

Has the infiltration of gender rhetoric done great damage to the workplace? Are men and women throwing rotten tomatoes at each other as a result of misunderstandings caused by stereotypes of "masculine" and "feminine" attitudes? Deborah Tannen's book *You Just Don't Understand: Women and Men in Conversation,* as well as John Grey's *Men Are From Mars, Women Are From Venus,* caused an avalanche of discussion (and some hostility) by comparing the communication styles of men and women. Here are some of their observations (greatly simplified):[45]

	Women	Men
Object of talk	Establish rapport, make connections, negotiate inclusive relationships	Preserve independence, maintain status, exhibit skill and knowledge
Listening behavior	Attentive, steady eye contact; remain stationary; nod head	Less attentive; sporadic eye contact; move around
Pauses	Frequent pauses, giving chance for others to take turns	Infrequent pauses; interrupt each other to take turns
Small talk	Personal disclosure	Impersonal topics
Focus	Details first, pulled together at end	Big picture
Gestures	Small, confined	Expansive
Method	Questions, apologies; "we" statements; hesitant, indirect, soft speech	Assertions; "I" statements; clear, loud, take-charge speech

Gender theorists suggest that one reason women can't climb above the glass ceiling is that their communication style is less authoritative than that of men.

Career Application

In small group or class discussion, consider these questions. Do men and women have different communication styles? Which style is more appropriate for today's team-based management? Do we need a kind of communicative affirmative action to give more recognition to women's ways of talking? Should training be given to men and women encouraging the interchangeable use of these styles depending on the situation?

It accomplishes next to nothing to employ those who are different from us if the condition of their employment is that they become the same as us. For it is their differences that enrich us, expand us, provide us the competitive edge."[46]

Challenge others' biases and stereotypes politely but firmly.

- **Create zero tolerance for bias and stereotypes.** Cultural patterns exist in every identity group, but applying these patterns to individuals results in stereotyping. Assuming that African Americans are good athletes, that women are poor at math, that French Canadians excel at hockey, or that European American men are insensitive fails to admit the immense differences in people in each group. Check your own use of stereotypes and labels. Don't tell sexist or ethnic jokes at meetings. Avoid slang, abbreviations, and jargon that imply stereotypes. Challenge others' biases politely but firmly.
- **Learn about your cultural self.** Begin to think of yourself as a product of your culture, and understand that your culture is just one among many. Try to stand outside and look at yourself. Do you see any reflex reactions and automatic thought patterns that are a result of your upbringing? These may be invisible to

CASE STUDY

PROCESS TO PRODUCT

Applying Your Skills in Mexico

Let's assume you are a manager for a North American company with an assembly line plant in Monterrey, Mexico. Workers have a long tradition of taking *el puente* or "the bridge," which extends a formal holiday into a mini-vacation. If, for example, a holiday falls on a Tuesday, workers take Monday off also, thus "bridging" the gap to the holiday. Mexican managers see no problem with workers who take *el puente.* American managers, however, want to fire them or dock their pay because of the decreased productivity near holidays.

Your Job

As a member of a team of North American and Mexican managers, discuss and evaluate possible options. Can a new culture be forged here? Select the best option. Your team may be asked to explain its decision to the class or to write an individual summary of the pros and cons for each option. Be prepared to support your choice of the best option.

you until challenged by difference. Remember, your culture was designed to help you succeed and survive in a certain environment. Be sure to keep what works and yet be ready to adapt as environments change.

- **Make fewer assumptions.** Be careful of seemingly insignificant, innocent workplace assumptions. For example, don't assume that everyone wants to observe the holidays with a Christmas party and a decorated tree. Celebrating only Christian holidays in December and January excludes those who honor Hanukkah, Kwanza, and the Chinese New Year. Moreover, in workplace discussions don't assume that everyone is married or wants to be or is even heterosexual, for that matter. For invitations, avoid phrases such as *managers and their wives.* Spouses or partners is more inclusive. Valuing diversity means making fewer assumptions that everyone is like you or wants to be like you.

In times of conflict, look for areas of agreement and build on similarities.

- **Build on similarities.** Look for areas where you and others not like you can agree or at least share opinions. Be prepared to consider issues from many perspectives, all of which may be valid. Accept that there is room for different points of view to coexist peacefully. Although you can always find differences, it's much harder to find similarities. Look for common ground in shared experiences, mutual goals, and similar values. Concentrate on your objective even when you may disagree on how to reach it.[47]

Summary of Learning Objectives

1 Discuss three significant trends related to the increasing importance of multicultural communication. Three trends are working together to crystallize the growing need for developing multicultural sensitivities and improved communication techniques. First, the globalization of markets means that you can expect to be doing business with people from around the world. Second, technological advancements in transportation and information are making the world smaller and more intertwined. Third, more and more immigrants from other cultures are settling in North America, thus changing the complexion of the workforce. Successful interaction requires awareness, tolerance, and accommodation.

2 **Define *culture.* Describe five significant characteristics of culture, and compare and contrast five key dimensions of culture.** *Culture* is the complex system of values, traits, morals, and customs shared by a society. Like a computer, each of us is shaped by the operating system of our culture. Some of the significant characteristics of culture include the following: (1) culture is learned, (2) cultures are inherently logical, (3) culture is the basis of self-identity and community, (4) culture combines the visible and invisible, and (5) culture is dynamic. Members of low-context cultures (such as those in North America, Scandinavia, and Germany) depend on words to express meaning, while people in high-context cultures (such as those in Japan, China, and Arab countries) rely more on context (social setting, a person's history, status, and position) to communicate meaning. Other key dimensions of culture include individualism, degree of formality, communication style, and time orientation.

3 **Explain the relationship between ethnocentrism, tolerance, and stereotypes in achieving multicultural sensitivity. Identify the six stages of multicultural transformation.** *Ethnocentrism* refers to a feeling that the culture you belong to is superior to all others and holds all truths. To function effectively in a global economy, we must develop knowledge of and tolerance for other cultures. We also need to move beyond stereotypes, which are oversimplified behavioral patterns applied uncritically to groups. To achieve multicultural sensitivity, we should discover and value individual personal qualities. The first stage of multicultural transformation is *denial,* in which we refuse to admit that cultural differences exist among people. The second stage, *defense,* involves protecting our own worldview to counter the perceived threat of cultural difference. In the third stage, *minimization,* we conceal differences in the shadow of cultural similarities; differences are trivialized. The fourth stage includes *acceptance,* wherein we begin to accept the existence of behavioral differences. In the fifth stage, *adaptation,* we become empathic toward cultural differences; and in the sixth stage, *integration,* we look upon cultural differences as a means of enriching our lives.

4 **Illustrate how to improve nonverbal and oral communication in multicultural environments.** We can minimize nonverbal miscommunication by recognizing that meanings conveyed by eye contact, posture, and gestures are largely culture dependent. Nonverbal messages are also sent by the use of time, space, and territory. Becoming aware of your own nonverbal behavior and what it conveys is the first step in broadening your multicultural competence. In improving oral messages, you can learn foreign phrases, use simple English, speak slowly and enunciate clearly, observe eye messages, encourage accurate feedback, check for comprehension, accept blame, listen without interrupting, smile, and follow up important conversations in writing.

5 **Illustrate how to improve written messages in multicultural environments.** To improve written messages, adopt local formats, use short sentences and short paragraphs, avoid ambiguous expressions, strive for clarity, use correct grammar, and cite numbers carefully. Also try to accommodate the reader in organization, tone, and style.

6 Discuss multicultural ethics, including ethics abroad, bribery, prevailing customs, and methods for coping. In doing business abroad, businesspeople should expect to find differing views about ethical practices. Although deciding whose ethics should prevail is tricky, the following techniques are helpful. Broaden your understanding of values and customs in other cultures, and avoid reflex judgments regarding the morality or corruptness of actions. Look for alternative solutions, refuse business if the options violate your basic values, and conduct all relations as openly as possible. Don't rationalize shady decisions, resist legalistic strategies, and apply a five-question ethics test when faced with a perplexing ethical dilemma.

7 Explain the challenge of capitalizing on workforce diversity, including its dividends and its divisiveness. List tips for improving harmony and communication among diverse workplace audiences. Having a diverse workforce can benefit consumers, work teams, and business organizations. However, diversity can also cause divisiveness among various identity groups. To promote harmony and communication, many organizations develop diversity training programs. As an individual, you must understand and accept the value of differences. Don't expect conformity, and create zero tolerance for bias and stereotypes. Learn about your cultural self, make fewer assumptions, and seek common ground when disagreements arise.

CHAPTER REVIEW

1. Why is it increasingly important for businesspeople to develop multicultural communication skills? (Obj. 1)
2. How is culture like a computer? (Obj. 2)
3. What is culture and how is culture learned? (Obj. 2)
4. Describe five major dimensions of culture. (Obj. 2)
5. Briefly, contrast high- and low-context cultures. (Obj. 2)
6. What is *ethnocentrism*? (Obj. 3)
7. What is a *stereotype*? Give original examples. (Obj. 3)
8. Describe the six stages of multicultural transformation. (Obj. 3)
9. Name three processes that are effective in achieving competence in dealing with nonverbal messages in other cultures. (Obj. 4)
10. Describe five specific ways in which you can improve oral communication with a foreigner. (Obj. 4)
11. Describe five specific ways in which you can improve written communication with a foreigner. (Obj. 5)
12. What is the Foreign Corrupt Practices Act? (Obj. 6)
13. List seven techniques for making ethical decisions across borders. (Obj. 6)
14. Name three groups who benefit from workforce diversity and explain why. (Obj. 7)
15. Explain five strategies for improving communication among diverse workplace audiences. (Obj. 7)

CRITICAL THINKING

1. Since English is becoming the world's language and since the United States is a dominant military and trading force, why should Americans bother to learn about other cultures? (Objs. 1, 2, and 7)
2. If the rules, values, and attitudes of a culture are learned, can they be unlearned? Explain. (Obj. 2)
3. An international business consultant quipped that Asians spend money on entertainment while Americans spend money on attorneys. What are the implications of this statement for business communicators? (Objs. 2, 3, and 6)
4. Some economists argue that the statement that "diversity is an economic asset" is an unproved and perhaps unprovable assertion. Should social responsibility or market forces determine whether an organization strives to create a diverse workforce? Why? (Obj. 7)

5. **Ethical Issue:** In many countries government officials are not well paid, and "tips" (called "bribes" in the United States) are a way of compensating them. If such payments are not considered wrong in those countries, should you pay them as a means of accomplishing your business? (Objs. 2 and 6)

ACTIVITIES

3.1 From Waterloo, Wisconsin, Trek Bicycles Goes Global (Objs. 1, 3, and 7)

The small town of Waterloo, Wisconsin (population 2,888), is about the last place you would expect to find the world's largest specialty bicycle maker. But Trek Bicycles started its global business in a red barn smack in the middle of Wisconsin farm country. Nearly 40 percent of the sales of the high-tech, Y-frame bicycles come from international markets. And future sales abroad look promising. Europeans buy 15 million bikes a year, while Americans and Canadians together purchase only 10 million. In Asia bicycles are a major means of transportation. To accommodate domestic and international consumers, Trek maintains a busy Web site at **<www.trekbikes.com>**.

Like many companies, Trek encountered problems in conducting multicultural transactions. For example, in Mexico, cargo was often pilfered while awaiting customs clearance. Distributors in Germany were offended by catalogs featuring pictures of Betty Boop, a cartoon character that decorated Allied bombers during World War II. In Singapore a buyer balked at a green bike helmet, explaining that when a man wears green on his head it means his wife is unfaithful. In Germany, Trek had to redesign its packaging to reduce waste and meet environmental requirements. Actually, the changes required in Germany helped to bolster the company's overall image of environmental sensitivity. Based on principles you studied in this chapter, name several broad lessons that other entrepreneurs can learn from Trek's international experiences.[48]

3.2 Interpreting Multicultural Proverbs (Objs. 2 and 3)

Proverbs, which tell truths with metaphors and simplicity, often reveal fundamental values held by a culture. Discuss the following proverbs and explain how they relate to some of the cultural values you studied in this chapter. What additional proverbs can you cite and what do they mean?

Japanese proverbs

The pheasant would have lived but for its cry.
The nail that sticks up gets pounded down.
To say nothing is a flower.

North American proverbs

The squeaking wheel gets the oil.
A stitch in time saves nine.
A bird in the hand is worth two in the bush.
A man's home is his castle.

German proverbs

No one is either rich or poor who has not helped himself to be so.
He who is afraid of doing too much always does too little.

3.3 Negotiating Traps (Objs. 2, 3, 4 and 5)

Discuss the causes and implications of the following common mistakes made by North Americans in their negotiations with foreigners.

a. Assuming that a final agreement is set in stone
b. Lacking patience and insisting that matters progress more quickly than the pace preferred by the locals
c. Thinking that an interpreter is always completely accurate
d. Believing that individuals who speak English understand every nuance of your meaning
e. Ignoring or misunderstanding the significance of rank

3.4 Global Economy (Obj. 1)

Fred Smith, CEO of Federal Express, said, "It is an inescapable fact that the U.S. economy is becoming much more like the European and Asian economies, entirely tied to global trade." Read your local newspapers for a week and peruse national news magazines (*Time, Newsweek, Business Week, U.S. News,* and so forth) for articles that support this assertion. Your instructor may ask you to (a) report on many articles or (b) select one article to summarize. Report your findings orally or in a memo to your instructor. This topic could be expanded into a long report for Chapters 13 or 14.

3.5 Learning About Other Cultures: Multicultural Panel (Objs. 1–7)

Team

Locate two or three students from other countries (possibly members of your class or international students on campus) who could report on differences between their cultures and North American culture. In addition to context, individualism, formality, communication style, and time, consider such topics as the importance of family and gender roles. Study attitudes toward education, clothing, leisure time, and work. You may want to try some questions such as these:

a. What U.S. behavior or practices shocked you when you first arrived?

b. What are some things visitors should or shouldn't do in your country?

c. What is your educational system like?

d. What do you consider a proper greeting for a friend? For a teacher? For your boss?

e. What could we say or do to increase your comfort in social or business settings?

Conduct a panel discussion. At the chalkboard or on an overhead transparency, you might wish to develop a chart contrasting American values with those of the interviewees. See Activity 14.6 in Chapter 14 for a research report focussed on this topic.

3.6 Designing a Cell Phone Manual for Low- and High-Context Cultures (Obj. 2)

Critical Thinking

Sometime in the early twenty-first century, many are predicting that China will emerge as the world's largest consumer of electronics products.[49] Well aware of this prediction, Siemens AG, a German cellular telephone manufacturer, is preparing to sell its popular German model to the Chinese. To develop the cell phone user manual, it conducted focus groups with Chinese and German consumers. The traditional German manual was translated into Chinese, and both German and Chinese focus groups were given nine tasks to perform using the same manual.

The focus groups produced contrasting results. When Chinese users first approach a manual, they want to see basic operations illustrated in color on single pages with pictures. They reported having "no patience" to learn functions they might not use. They also noted that they learned to use the phone by asking friends, but if they had a problem they would never admit it to a friend. The Germans, on the other hand, wanted a manual that would present a clear but detailed overview of all the phone functions, not just basic operations. They thought that it would be useful in the long run to know all the different functions. The Germans read the words in the manual carefully, sometimes complaining when sentences were illogical or contradictory.

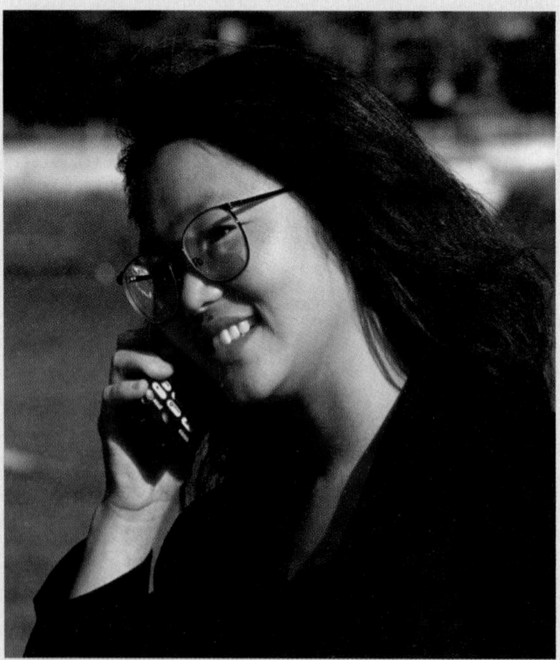

The Chinese preferred the "help" key to the printed manual. One said, "It gives you a very foolish feeling to use the phone at the same time you use the manual. It is ridiculous." The Chinese requested a videotape to show operations, and they also recommended that the size of the characters in the manual correlate with the importance of the information.

Based on your knowledge of high- and low-context cultures, how do the reactions of these focus groups reflect cultural expectations? If you were the researcher in this study, would you suggest to Siemens that a totally different user manual be developed for the Chinese market? What design recommendations would you make regarding the Chinese manual?

3.7 Analyzing a Problem International Letter (Obj. 5)

Study the following letter[51] to be sent by an American firm to a potential supplier in another country. Identify specific weaknesses that may cause trouble for multicultural readers.

Dear Madeleine:

Because of the on-again/off-again haggling with one of our subcontractors, we have been putting off writing to you. We were royally turned off by their shoddy merchandise, the excuses they made up, and the way they put down some of our customers. Since we have our good name to keep up, we have decided to take the bull by the horns and see if you would be interested in bidding on the contract for spare parts.

By playing ball with us, your products are sure to score big. So please give it your best shot and fire off your price list ASAP. We'll need it by 3/8 if you are to be in the running.

Yours,

3.8 Talking Turkey: Avoiding Ambiguous Expressions (Obj. 5)

When a German firm received a message from an American firm saying that it was "time to talk turkey," it was puzzled but decided to reply in Turkish, as requested. Assume you are a businessperson engaged in exporting and importing.

As such, you are in constant communication with suppliers and customers around the world. In messages sent abroad, what kinds of ambiguous expressions should you avoid? In teams or individually, list three to five original examples of idioms, slang, acronyms, sports references, abbreviations, jargon, and two-word verbs.

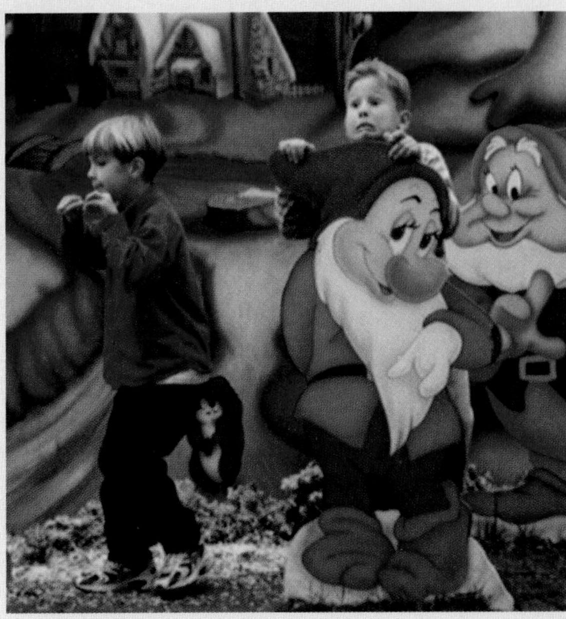

3.9 Making Grease Payments Abroad (Obj. 6)

Critical Thinking

The Foreign Corrupt Practices Act prohibits giving anything of value to a foreign official in an effort to win or retain business. However, the FCPA does allow payments that may be necessary to expedite or secure "routine governmental action." For instance, a company could make "grease" payments to obtain permits and licenses or to process visa or work orders. Also allowed are payments to provide telephone service, power and water supply, and loading and unloading of cargo. In light of what you have learned in this chapter, how should you act in the following situations? Are the actions legal or illegal?[52]

a. Your company is moving toward final agreement on a contract in Pakistan to sell farm equipment. As the contract is prepared, officials ask that a large amount of funds be included to enable the government to update its agriculture research. The extra amount is to be paid in cash to the three officials you have worked with. Should your company pay?

b. You have been negotiating with a government official in Niger regarding an airplane maintenance contract. The official asks to use your Diner's Club card to charge $2,028 in airplane tickets as a honeymoon present. Should you do it to win the contract?

c. You are trying to collect an overdue payment of $163,000 on a shipment of milk powder to the Dominican Republic. A senior government official asks for $20,000 as a collection service fee. Should you pay?

d. Your company is in the business of arranging hunting trips to East Africa. You are encouraged to give guns and travel to officials in a wildlife agency that has authority to issue licenses to hunt big game. The officials have agreed to keep the gifts quiet. Should you make the gifts?

e. Your firm has just moved you to Malaysia, and your furniture is sitting on the dock. Cargo handlers won't unload it until you or your company pays off each local dock worker. Should you pay?

f. In Mexico your firm has been working hard to earn lucrative contracts with the national oil company, Pemex. One government official has hinted elaborately that his son would like to do marketing studies for your company. Should you hire the son?

g. Your company is trying to open its new office in Chile. But local officials will not allow the power or telephone connections until you make cash payments to two local officials. Should you pay?

h. Keeping Disney's consumer products division supplied with a multitude of items, ranging from figurines of the Seven Dwarfs to the latest movie tie-in promotion items, involves many manufacturers around the world. As a representative of a vendor supplying Magic Kingdom souvenirs, you are approached by a Chinese "distributor." He promises to make all the grease payments necessary to facilitate low-cost production of your souvenirs in his country. You would make no payments directly to locals. Should you pay?

3.10 Diversity Role-Playing: Hey, We're All Clones! (Obj. 7)

Reebok International, the athletic footwear and apparel company, swelled from a $12-million-a-year company to a $3-billion footwear powerhouse in less than a decade. "When we were growing very, very fast, all we did was bring another friend into work the next day," recalls Sharon Cohen, Reebok vice president. "Everybody hired nine of their friends. Well, it happened that nine white people hired nine of their friends, so guess what? They were white, all about the same age. And then we looked up and said, 'Wait a minute. We don't like the way it looks here.'"[53] Assume you are a manger for a successful, fast-growing company like Reebok. One day you look around and notice that everyone looks alike. Pair off with a classmate to role-play a discussion in which you strive to convince another manager that your organization would be better if it were more diverse. The other manager (your classmate), however, is satisfied with the status quo. Suggest advantages for diversifying the staff. The opposing manager argues for homogeneity.

3.11 Locating Diversity Training Consultants (Obj. 7)

Web

Management thought it was doing the right thing in diversifying its staff. But now signs of friction are appearing. Staff meetings are longer, and conflicts have arisen in solving problems. Some of the new people say they aren't taken seriously and that they are expected to blend in and become just like everybody else. A discrimination suit was filed in one department. CEO William Somers asks you, a human resources officer, to present suggestions for overcoming this staff problem. Make a list of several suggestions, based on what you have learned in this chapter. In addition, go to the Web and locate three individuals, teams, or firms who you think might be possibilities for developing a diversity training program for your company. Prepare a memo or an e-mail to Mr. Somers outlining your suggestions and listing your recommendations for possible diversity training consultants. Describe the areas of expertise of each potential consultant.

3.12 Searching International Newspapers for Business News (Objs. 1–6)

Web

Using the Guffey Student Web Site **<meguffey.com>**, click on "Recommended Research Tools" and "U.S. and World Newspapers." You'll find English editions of international newspapers from such countries as Ethiopia, Japan, Thailand, China, the Philippines, Sri Lanka, Egypt, South Africa, Israel, Hong Kong, Turkey, South Korea, Zambia, Russia, Turkey, and many others. Assume that your company seeks to expand its markets overseas. Your boss asks you to check three newspapers (your choice) every week to keep track of business-related events. She's interested in a variety of subjects and is always intrigued by whatever you uncover. Select three to five articles to summarize in a memo to your boss, Susan Plutsky. Include a short description of each newspaper.

C.L.U.E. REVIEW 3

On a separate sheet edit the following sentences to correct faults in grammar, punctuation, spelling, and word use.

1. To avoid embarassing any employee the personell manager and myself has decided to talk personal to each individual.
2. 3 assistants were sent on a search and destroy mission in a conscience effort to remove at least fifteen thousand old documents from the files.
3. Electronic mail, now used by ¾ of Americas largest companys transmits messages quick and cheap.
4. An article entitled whats new with managers appeared in reader's digest which is read by 60,000,000 americans.
5. Your account is now sixty days overdue consequently we have only 1 alternative left.
6. The marketing managers itinirary listed the following three destinations seattle portland and eugene.
7. Each of the beautifully-printed books available at pickwick book company have been reduced to thirty dollars.
8. We reccommend therefor that a committee study our mail procedures for a 3 week period, and submit a report of itís findings.
9. Their going to visit there relatives in columbus ohio over the memorial day holiday.
10. The hotel can acommodate three hundred convention guests but it has parking facilities for only one hundred cars.

UNIT • 2 •

The Writing Process

CHAPTER • 4 •

Preparing to Write Business Messages

LEARNING OBJECTIVES

1. Describe three basic elements that distinguish business writing and summarize the three phases of the 3-×-3 writing process.

2. Explain how the writing process may be altered and how it is affected by team projects and technology.

3. Clarify what is involved in analyzing a writing task and selecting a communication channel.

4. Describe anticipating and profiling the audience for a message.

5. Specify six writing techniques that help communicators adapt messages to the task and audience.

6. Explain why four areas of communication hold legal responsibilities for writers.

COMMUNICATION IN PROCESS

Kinko's Trades Quirky Campus Image for Buttoned-Down Corporate Look

If you still think of Kinko's as quirky self-serve copy shops, "you're stuck in the Seventies, man," says *Fortune* magazine.[1] Actually, Kinko's is growing globally, employs over 23,000 "co-workers" in over 860 U.S. stores, and offers a multitude of business services.

Its founder Paul ("Kinko") Orfalea got his start hawking school supplies from an oversized knapsack to students in dormitories at the University of California, Santa Barbara. He is fond of telling stories about his lackluster college career. After attending his first philosophy class, he said, "God, I don't understand any of that. . . . I'm never going to make it in this world." And he did have a problem. Orfalea (pronounced "Or-fa-la") suffered from such severe dyslexia that as a child he was barely able to read or write. "Some people say they have dyslexia," he confided, rolling his eyes. "I got the real thing!"[2] Although not particularly gifted as a student, he was definitely talented as a businessperson.

While finishing his degree, Orfalea (whose nickname comes from his kinky red hair) noticed a copy machine in the university library. Seeing its potential, he leased one and set up business in a tiny vacated hamburger stand near campus. His cheap prices drew in the students, and before long he expanded his copy store concept to other campuses. Kinko's now combines printer, publisher, computer, and post office services with high-volume duplicating, color copying, faxing, and most recently, videoconferencing.

Without benefit of fancy market research, Orfalea developed a keen sense of customer needs. "Early on, we learned our customers were a little uptight and very confused," he said. "They didn't know what they wanted, and they wanted it yesterday." He painted stores blue to soothe stressed customers, and despite a "hippie-like management structure," he had employees dress "more like Republicans."[3] He also was quick to recognize a trend toward home businesses. Kinko's became "your branch office," supplying increasing numbers of self-employed people with quality services. They had quick access to sophisticated equipment they couldn't afford to purchase themselves. As Orfalea became more small-business oriented, he moved his stores away from campus locations to suburban and business centers.

Now Orfalea has his eye on another branch of consumers: corporate types that occupy Fortune 500 offices. He sees corporate outsourcing as the future growth market for Kinko's. His goal is to convince big companies that Kinko's can give better reprographic service than their own in-house departments. It also means developing a mobile sales staff and changing the image of Kinko's. No longer does Kinko's merely copy student papers or support small business operations. It wants to do big jobs for big companies. And that requires a change in image. Revamping its image and adapting to a new audience demands special communication talents and procedures.

www.kinkos.com

Approaching the Writing Process Systematically

1

As Kinko's moves into a new marketing arena, its representatives must finely tune their communication skills to project a new image and capture new clients. Preparing and writing any business message—whether a letter, an e-mail memo, or a Kinko's sales presentation—is easier when the writer or presenter has a systematic plan to follow.

The Basics of Business Writing

Business writing is purposeful, economical, and reader oriented.

Business writing differs from other writing you may have done. High school or college compositions and term papers may have required you to describe your feelings, display your knowledge, and meet a minimum word count. Business writing, however, has different goals. In preparing business messages and oral presentations, you'll find that your writing needs to be:

- **Purposeful.** You will be writing to solve problems and convey information. You will have a definite purpose to fulfill in each message.
- **Economical.** You will try to present ideas clearly but concisely. Length is not rewarded.
- **Reader oriented.** You will concentrate on looking at a problem from the reader's perspective instead of seeing it from your own.

Business writers seek to *express* rather than to *impress*.

These distinctions actually ease the writer's task. In writing most business documents, you won't be searching your imagination for creative topic ideas. You won't be stretching your ideas to make them appear longer. One writing consultant complained that "most college graduates entering industry have at least a subliminal perception that in technical and business writing, quantity enhances quality."[4] Wrong! Get over the notion that longer is better. Conciseness is what counts in business. Furthermore, you won't be trying to dazzle readers with your extensive knowledge, powerful vocabulary, or graceful phrasing. The goal in business writing is to *express rather than impress.* You will be striving to get your ideas across naturally, simply, and clearly.

In many ways business writing is easier than academic writing, yet it still requires hard work, especially from beginners. But following a process, studying models, and practicing the craft can make nearly anyone a successful business writer and speaker. This book provides all three components: process, products (models), and practice. First, you'll focus on the process of writing business messages.

The 3-×-3 Writing Process for Business Messages and Oral Presentations

The phases of the 3-×-3 writing process are prewriting, writing, and revising.

This book divides the writing process into three distinct phases: prewriting, writing, and revising. As shown in Figure 4.1, each phase is further divided into three major activities. The 3-×-3 process provides you with a systematic plan for developing all your business communications from simple memos and informational reports to corporate proposals and oral presentations.

The time spent on each phase varies with the deadline, purpose, and audience for the message. Let's consider how the 3-×-3 writing process might work in a typical business situation. Suppose you must write a letter to a department store buyer about an order that you, as a manufacturer of jeans, cannot fill. The first phase (prewriting) prepares you to write and involves analyzing, anticipating, and adapting. In analyzing the situation, you decide to focus your letter on retaining the order. That can best be done by persuading the buyer to accept a different jeans model. You anticipate that the buyer will be disappointed that the original model is unavailable. What's more, she will probably be reluctant to switch to a different model. Thus, you must find ways to adapt your message to reduce her reluctance and convince her to switch.

The second phase (writing) involves researching, organizing, and then composing the message. To collect facts for this letter, you would probably investigate the buyer's past purchases. You would check to see what jeans you have in stock that

FIGURE 4.1 **The 3-×-3 Writing Process**

she might accept as a substitute. You might do some brainstorming or consult your colleagues for their suggestions about how to retain this order. Then, you would organize your information into a loose outline and decide on a strategy or plan for revealing your information most effectively. Equipped with a plan, you're ready to compose the first draft of the letter.

Collecting data, organizing it, and composing a first draft make up the second phase of the writing process.

The third phase of the process (revising) involves revising, proofreading, and evaluating your letter. After writing the first draft, you'll revise the message for clarity, conciseness, tone, and readability. You'll proofread carefully to ensure correct spelling, grammar, punctuation, and format. Finally, you'll evaluate the message to see whether it accomplishes your goal.

Although our diagram of the writing process shows the three phases equally, the time you spend on each varies. One expert gives these rough estimates for scheduling a project: 25 percent worrying and planning (Phase 1), 25 percent writing (Phase 2), 45 percent revising, and 5 percent proofreading (Phase 3). These are rough guides, yet you can see that good writers spend most of their time revising. Much depends, of course, on your project, its importance, and your familiarity with it. What's critical to remember, though, is that revising is a major component of the writing process.

In the writing process, revising requires the most time.

This process may seem a bit complicated for the daily messages and oral presentations that many businesspeople prepare. Does this same process apply to memos and short letters? And how do collaborators and modern computer technologies affect the process?

Adapting and Altering the Process. Although good writers proceed through each phase of the writing process, some steps may be compressed for short, routine messages. Brief, everyday documents enlist the 3-×-3 process, but many of the steps are performed quickly, without prolonged deliberation. For example, prewriting may take the form of a few moments of reflection. The writing phase may consist of looking in the files quickly, jotting a few notes in the margin of the original document, and composing at your computer. Revising might consist of reading a printout, double-checking the spelling and grammar, and making a few changes. Longer, more involved documents—such as persuasive memos, sales letters, management reports, proposals, and résumés—require more attention to all parts of the process.

2

One other point about the 3-×-3 writing process needs clarification. It may appear that you perform one step and progress to the next, always following the same order. Most business writing, however, is not that rigid. Although writers perform the tasks described, the steps may be rearranged, abbreviated, or repeated. Some writers revise every sentence and paragraph as they go. Many find that new ideas occur after they've begun to write, causing them to back up, alter the organization,

Steps in the writing process may be rearranged, shortened, or repeated.

Spotlight on **Communicators**

Warren Buffet, the second richest man in the U.S. and one of the most successful investors of all time, values plain English. When writing annual reports, he pretends that he's talking to his sisters. "I have no trouble picturing them. Though highly intelligent, they are not experts in accounting or finance. They will understand plain English but jargon may puzzle them. . . . To succeed, I don't need to be Shakespeare; I must, though, have a sincere desire to inform. No sisters to write to? Borrow mine: Just begin with 'Dear Doris and Bertie,'" he advises.

and rethink their plan. You should expect to follow the 3-×-3 process closely as you begin developing your business communication skills. With experience, though, you'll become like other good writers and presenters who alter, compress, and rearrange the steps as needed.

Working With Teams. At one time or another you can expect to collaborate on a project. Estimates are that 40 to 50 percent of the workforce could be in some kind of team environment by the turn of the century.[5] A study of business professionals showed that nine out of ten sometimes write as part of a team.[6] Collaborative composition is especially necessary for (1) big tasks, (2) items with short deadlines, and (3) team projects that require the expertise or consensus of many people. Businesspeople sometimes collaborate on short documents, such as memos, letters, information briefs, procedures, and policies. But more often, teams work together on big documents and presentations. For example, let's say that a product development team at Mattel comes up with a new line of educational computer toys for infants. The team will probably have to prepare a proposal that persuades management to manufacture and market the new toys. This proposal would be developed and written by many members of a team.

Team-written documents and presentations produce better products.

Team-written documents and presentations are standard in most organizations because collaboration has many advantages. Most important, collaboration produces a better product. Many heads are better than one. In addition, team members and organizations benefit from team processes. Working together helps socialize members. They learn more about the organization's values and procedures. They are able to break down functional barriers, and they improve both formal and informal chains of communication. Additionally, they "buy into" a project when they are part of its development. Members of effective teams are eager to implement their recommendations.

In preparing big projects, teams may not actually function together for each phase of the writing process. Typically, team members gather at the beginning to brainstorm. They iron out answers to questions about purpose, audience, content, organization, and design of their document or presentation. They develop procedures for team functioning, as you learned in Chapter 2. Then, they often assign segments of the project to individual members. Thus, teams work together closely in Phase 1 (prewriting) of the writing process. However, members generally work separately in Phase 2 (writing), when they conduct research, organize their findings, and compose a first draft. During Phase 3 (revising) teams may work together to synthesize their drafts and offer suggestions for revision. They might assign one person the task of preparing the final document and another the job of proofreading. The revision and evaluation phase might be repeated several times before the final product is ready for presentation.

Computer technology helps you generate ideas, conduct research, and organize facts.

Working With Technology. The composition process—whether you are writing a business document, preparing an oral presentation, or creating a Web page—is further affected by today's amazing computer tools. Software exists to help you generate ideas, conduct research electronically, and organize facts into outlines. In fact, many phases of the writing process—such as keyboarding, revision, and collaboration—are simplified and supported by word processing programs, discussed more fully in the accompanying Tech Talk box.

Wonderful as these powerful technological tools are, however, they do not automatically produce effective letters, persuasive oral presentations, or cool Web sites. They can neither organize data into concise and logical presentations nor shape ideas

TECH TALK

SEVEN WAYS COMPUTER SOFTWARE CAN HELP YOU CREATE BETTER WRITTEN MESSAGES, ORAL PRESENTATIONS, AND WEB PAGES

Although computers and software programs cannot actually do the writing for you, they provide powerful tools that make the composition process easier and the results more professional. Here are seven ways your computer can help you improve your written documents, oral presentations, and even Web pages.

1. **Fighting writer's block.** Because word processors enable ideas to flow almost effortlessly from your brain to a screen, you can expect fewer delays resulting from writer's block. You can compose rapidly, and you can experiment with structure and phrasing, later retaining and polishing your most promising thoughts. Many authors "sprint write," recording unedited ideas quickly, to start the composition process and also to brainstorm for ideas on a project. Then, they tag important ideas and use computer outlining programs to organize those ideas into logical sequences.

2. **Collecting information electronically.** As a knowledge worker in an information economy, you will need to find information quickly. Much of the world's information is now accessible by computer. You can locate the titles of books, as well as many full-text articles from magazines, newspapers, and government publications. Massive amounts of information are available from the Internet, CD-ROMS, and on-line services. Through specialized information-retrieval services (such as ABI-INFORM or Dow Jones News/Retrieval Service), you can have at your fingertips up-to-the-minute legal, scientific, scholarly, and business information. The most amazing source of electronic information is the Web, with its links to sites around the world, some incredibly helpful and others worthless. You'll learn more about these exciting electronic resources in Unit 4.

3. **Outlining and organizing ideas.** Most high-end word processors include some form of "outliner," a feature that enables you to divide a topic into a hierarchical order with main points and subpoints. Your computer keeps track of the levels of ideas automatically so that you can easily add, cut, or rearrange points in the outline. This feature is particularly handy when you're preparing a report or organizing a presentation. Some programs even enable you to transfer your outline directly to slide frames to be used as visual aids in a talk.

4. **Improving correctness and precision.** Nearly all word processing programs today provide features that catch and correct spelling and typographical errors. Poor spellers and weak typists universally bless their spell checkers for repeatedly saving them from humiliation. Most high-end word processing programs today also provide grammar checkers that are markedly improved over earlier versions. They now detect many errors in capitalization, word use (such as *it's, its*), double negatives, verb use, subject-verb agreement, sentence structure, number agreement, number style, and other writing faults. However, most grammar programs don't actually correct the errors they detect. You must know how to do that. Still, grammar checkers can be very helpful. In addition to spelling and grammar programs, thesaurus programs help you choose precise words that say exactly what you intend.

5. **Adding graphics for emphasis.** Your letters, memos, and reports may be improved by the addition of graphs and artwork to clarify and illustrate data. You can import charts, diagrams, and illustrations created in database, spreadsheet, graphics, or draw-and-paint programs. Moreover, ready-made pictures, called clip art, can be used to symbolize or illustrate ideas.

6. **Designing and producing professional-looking documents, presentations, and Web pages.** Most high-end word processing programs today include a large selection of scalable fonts (for different character sizes and styles), italics, boldface, symbols, and styling techniques to aid you in producing consistent formatting and professional-looking results. Moreover, today's presentation software enables you to incorporate showy slide effects, color, sound, pictures, and even movies into your talks for management or customers. Web document builders also help you design and construct Web pages.

(continued)

7. **Using collaborative software for team writing.** Assume you are part of a group preparing a lengthy proposal to secure a government contract. You expect to write one segment of the proposal yourself and help revise parts written by others. Special word processing programs with commenting and strikeout features allow you to revise easily and to identify each team member's editing. These collaborative programs, called groupware, as you learned in Chapter 2, also include decision-support tools to help groups generate, organize, and analyze ideas more efficiently than in traditional meetings.

Career Application

Individually or in teams, identify specific software programs that perform the tasks described here. Prepare a table naming each program, its major functions, and its advantages and disadvantages for business writers in your field.

into persuasive arguments. Only a well-trained author can do that. Nevertheless, today's technology enhances every aspect of writing. Therefore, skill in using software is essential for anyone whose job requires composition.

Analyzing the Task

3

Whether you're writing with a team, composing by yourself, or preparing an oral presentation, the product of your efforts can be improved by following the steps described in the 3-×-3 writing process. Not only are you more likely to get your message across, but you'll feel less anxious and your writing will progress more quickly. The remainder of this chapter concentrates on the prewriting phase of composition: analyzing, anticipating, and adapting.

In analyzing the composition task, you'll first need to identify the purpose of the message and select the best channel or form in which to deliver it.

Identifying Your Purpose. As you begin to compose a message, ask yourself two important questions: (1) Why am I sending this message? and (2) What do I hope to achieve? Your responses will determine how you organize and present your information.

Most business communication has both primary purposes (to inform or persuade) and secondary purposes (to promote goodwill).

Your message may have primary and secondary purposes. For college work your primary purpose may be merely to complete the assignment; secondary purposes might be to make yourself look good and to get a good grade. The primary purposes for sending business messages are typically to inform and to persuade. A secondary purpose is to promote goodwill: you and your organization want to look good in the eyes of your audience.

Most business messages do nothing more than *inform.* They explain procedures, announce meetings, answer questions, and transmit findings. Some business messages, however, are meant to *persuade.* These messages sell products, convince managers, motivate employees, and win over customers. Informative messages are developed differently than persuasive messages.

Selecting the Best Channel. After identifying the purpose of your message, you need to select the most appropriate communication channel. As you learned in Chapter 1, some information is most efficiently and effectively delivered orally. Other messages should be written, and still others are best delivered electronically. Whether to set up a meeting, send a message by e-mail, or write a report depends on some of the following factors:

- Importance of the message
- Amount and speed of feedback required
- Necessity of a permanent record
- Cost of the channel
- Degree of formality desired

Choosing an appropriate channel depends on the importance of the message, the feedback required, the need for a permanent record, the cost, and the degree of formality needed.

The foregoing factors could help you decide which of the channels shown in Figure 4.2 is most appropriate for delivering a message. Kinko's account managers, for example, would probably choose face-to-face conversations or group meetings as the most effective communication channel in delivering their changed-image message.

Anticipating the Audience

Some messages miss the mark. Consider a letter that responds to a six-year-old boy who requested a toy rocket launcher from a breakfast cereal company. "Due to the overwhelming response this promotion has generated, we have unfortu-

FIGURE 4.2 Choosing Communication Channels

Channel	Best Use
Face-to-face conversation	When you want to be persuasive, deliver bad news, or share a personal message.
Telephone call	When you need to deliver or gather information quickly, when nonverbal cues are unimportant, and when you cannot meet in person.
Voice mail message	When you wish to leave important or routine information that the receiver can respond to when convenient.
Fax	When your message must cross time zones or international boundaries, when a written record is significant, or when speed is important.
E-mail	When you need feedback but not immediately. Insecurity makes it problematic for personal, emotional, or private messages. Effective for communicating with a large, dispersed audience.
Face-to-face group meeting	When group decisions and consensus are important. Inefficient for merely distributing information.
Video or teleconference	When group consensus and interaction are important but members are geographically dispersed.
Memo	When you want a written record to clearly explain policies, discuss procedures, or collect information within an organization.
Letter	When you need a written record of correspondence with customers, the government, suppliers, or others outside an organization.
Report or proposal	When you are delivering considerable data internally or externally.

Before writing a letter or preparing a presentation, think carefully about your audience. Visualizing the receiver and anticipating a reaction to your message helps you determine the words to use, the amount of detail to include, the best method of organization, and many other important factors.

nately depleted our stock temporarily. We are, therefore, holding your request pending stock replenishment." The breakfast cereal company's representative had no sense of audience; as a result, the language was totally inappropriate.

A good writer anticipates the audience for a message: What is the reader like? How will that reader react to the message? Although you can't always know exactly who the reader is, you can imagine some characteristics of the reader. The breakfast cereal company writer could have pictured a typical young boy and imagined the vocabulary and expectations he might have. Even writers of direct mail sales letters have a general idea of the audience they wish to target. Picturing a typical reader is important in guiding what you write. One copywriter at Lands' End, the catalog company, pictures his sister-in-law whenever he writes product descriptions for the catalog. By profiling your audience and shaping a message to respond to that profile, you are more likely to achieve your communication goals.

By profiling your audience before you write, you can identify the appropriate tone, language, and channel.

Profiling the Audience. Visualizing your audience is a pivotal step in the writing process. The questions in Figure 4.3 will help you profile your audience. How much time you devote to answering these questions depends greatly on your message and its context. An analytical report that you compose for management or an oral presentation before a big group would, of course, demand considerable audience anticipation. On the other hand, a memo to a coworker or a letter to a familiar supplier might require only a few moments of planning. No matter how short your message, though, spend some time thinking about the audience so that you can tailor your words to your readers or listeners. "The most often unasked question in business and professional communication," claims a writing expert, "is as simple as it is important: HAVE I THOUGHT ENOUGH ABOUT MY AUDIENCE?"[7]

FIGURE 4.3 Asking the Right Questions to Profile Your Audience

PRIMARY AUDIENCE

Who is my primary reader or listener?

What is my personal and professional relationship with that person?

What position does the individual hold in the organization?

How much does that person know about the subject?

What do I know about that person's education, beliefs, culture, and attitudes?

Should I expect a neutral, positive, or negative response to my message?

SECONDARY AUDIENCE

Who might see this message after the primary audience?

How do these people differ from the primary audience?

Responding to the Profile. Anticipating your audience helps you make decisions about shaping the message. You'll discover what kind of language is appropriate, whether you're free to use specialized technical terms, whether you should explain everything, and so on. You'll decide whether your tone should be formal or informal, and you'll select the most desirable channel. Imagining whether the receiver is likely to be neutral, positive, or negative will help you determine how to organize your message.

Another result of profiling your audience will be knowing whether a secondary audience is possible. If so, you'll provide more background information and be more specific in identifying items than would be necessary for the primary audience only. Analyzing the task and anticipating the audience assists you in adapting your message so that it will accomplish what you intend.

Adapting to the Task and Audience

5

After analyzing your purpose and anticipating your audience, you must convey your purpose to that audience. Adaptation is the process of creating a message that suits your audience.

One important aspect of adaptation is *tone.* Conveyed largely by the words in a message, tone reflects how a receiver feels upon reading or hearing a message. For example, think how you would react to these statements:

You must return the form by 5 p.m.

Would you please return the form by 5 p.m.

Ways to adapt to the audience include choosing the right words and tone, spotlighting reader benefits, cultivating a "you" attitude, and using sensitive, courteous language.

The wording of the first message establishes an aggressive or negative tone—no one likes being told what to do. The second message is reworded in a friendlier, more positive manner. Poorly chosen words may sound demeaning, condescending, discourteous, pretentious, or demanding. Notice in the Lands' End letter in Figure 4.4 that the writer achieves a courteous and warm tone. The letter responds to a customer's concern about the changing merchandise mix available in Lands' End catalogs. The customer also wanted to receive fewer catalogs. The writer explains the company's expanded merchandise line and reassures the customer that Lands' End has not abandoned its emphasis on classic styles.

Skilled communicators create a positive tone in their messages by using a number of adaptive techniques, some of which are unconscious. These include spotlighting receiver benefits, cultivating a *you* attitude, and avoiding gender, racial, age, and disability bias. Additional adaptive techniques include being courteous, using familiar words, and choosing precise words.

Empathic communicators envision the receiver and focus on benefits to that person.

Spotlighting Receiver Benefits. Focusing on the audience sounds like a modern idea, but actually one of America's early statesmen and authors recognized this fundamental writing principle over 200 years ago. In describing effective writing, Ben Franklin observed, "To be good, it ought to have a tendency to benefit the reader."[8] These wise words have become a fundamental guideline for today's business communicators. Expanding on Franklin's counsel, a contemporary communication consultant gives this solid advice to his business clients: "Always stress the benefit to the readers of whatever it is you're trying to get them to do. If you can show them how you're going to save *them* frustration or help them meet their goals, you have the makings of a powerful message."[9]

Adapting your message to the receiver's needs means putting yourself in that person's shoes. It's called *empathy.* Empathic senders think about how a receiver will

FIGURE 4.4 Customer Response Letter

February 23, 2000

Mrs. Elaine Hough
9403 Farwest Drive SW
Tacoma, WA 98498

Dear Mrs. Hough:

Your letter was a strong endorsement of our belief that we made the right choice when we devoted our company to traditional, classic styles — and that it's still the right choice.

It's true we've made changes. In the past few years, with the markets soft and tastes changing, we reexamined our merchandise, with a view to continuing to serve valued customers while introducing ourselves to new ones. We decided that our styles needed freshening and that we would offer clothes that didn't chase after trends but did have a feel for what was current.

Our commitment to the classics hasn't weakened, as I hope you'd agree, having seen recent catalogs. But we've defined "classic" more inclusively than in the past. We're using new fabrics, new colors, a more relaxed fit. There's more imagination in our product mix now, but the sweaters, rugbys, blouses, button-downs, and other basics for which you've relied on us are still here. You may not find each one in every catalog, and you may notice the new products more than those you've seen before. The classics are still here, and the selection will be growing.

I've arranged to send you just the four catalogs a year you wanted. I hope you'll keep an eye on them. I think that, more and more, you'll be able to come to us for the styles you want.

Sincerely,

Brian Finnegan
Customer Relations

LANDS' END, INC.
1 LANDS' END LANE DODGEVILLE, WI 53595
(608)935-9341

Opens response to inquiry by agreeing with customer

Explains evolving merchandise line from company's and reader's view

Uses conversational language to convey warmth and sincerity

Emphasizes areas of agreement.

Concludes by giving customer what she wants and promoting future business

The most successful messages are receiver-focused.

decode a message. They try to give something to the receiver, solve the receiver's problems, save the receiver money, or just understand the feelings and position of that person. Which of the following messages are more appealing to the receiver?

Sender-Focused	**Receiver-Focused**
To enable us to update our stockholder records, we ask that the enclosed card be returned.	So that you may promptly receive dividend checks and information related to your shares, please return the enclosed card.
Our warranty becomes effective only when we receive an owner's registration.	Your warranty begins working for you as soon as you return your owner's registration.

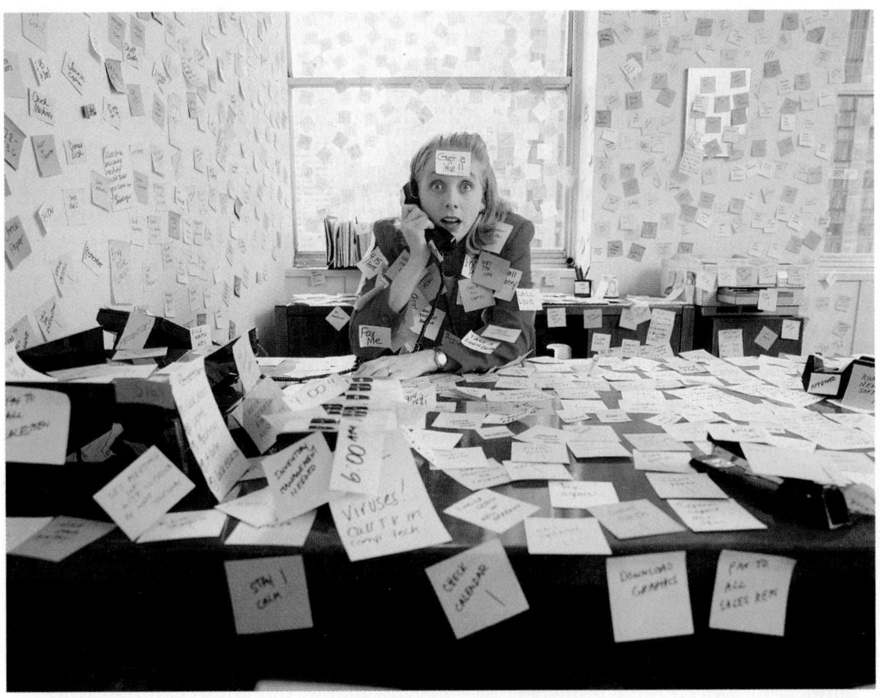

Many receivers of business messages today are frazzled and suffering from information overload. Capturing the attention of such receivers requires a message that is "you" oriented and emphasizes reader benefits. How can your message help solve the receiver's problems?

Sender-Focused	Receiver-Focused
We offer an audiocassette language course that we have complete faith in.	The sooner you order the audiocassette language program, the sooner the rewards will be yours.
The Human Resources Department requires that the enclosed questionnaire be completed immediately so that we can allocate our training resource funds.	You can be one of the first employees to sign up for the new career development program. Fill out the attached questionnaire and return it immediately.

Cultivating the "You" View. Notice how many of the previous receiver-focused messages included the word *you.* In concentrating on receiver benefits, skilled communicators naturally develop the "you" view. They emphasize second-person pronouns (*you, your*) instead of first-person pronouns (*I/we, us, our*). Whether your goal is to inform, persuade, or promote goodwill, the catchiest words you can use are *you* and *your.* Compare the following examples.

"I/We" View	"You" View
I have scheduled your vacation to begin May 1.	You may begin your vacation May 1.
We have shipped your order by UPS, and we are sure it will arrive in time for the sales promotion January 15.	Your order will be delivered by UPS in time for your sales promotion January 15.
I'm asking all of our employees to respond to the attached survey regarding working conditions.	Because your ideas count, please complete the attached survey regarding working conditions.

To see if you're really concentrating on the reader, try using the "empathy index." In one of your messages, count all the second-person references. Then, count

Spotlight on **Communicators**

In dealing with customers, John H. Johnson always concentrated on what they wanted rather than what he wanted. His focus on the "you" view helped him build *Ebony* and *Jet* magazines, along with *Fashion Fair* cosmetics, into million-dollar businesses. He was a master at profiling potential customers and cultivating the "you" view. "I want to know where they came from, what are their interests, [and] what can I talk to them about." He strove to establish rapport with people by having mutual interests.

CASE STUDY

PROCESS IN PROGRESS

Kinko's Revisited

Kinko's famously eccentric founder Paul Orfalea built a hugely successful copy services chain by following a simple marketing strategy. Build a store, keep it open 24 hours a day, and customers will come. Just walk into a Kinko's any time of the day or night. Chances are you'll find college students using computers, businesspeople copying proposals, and job seekers printing résumés. More recently, though, Kinko's began to cultivate a new kind of market—Fortune 500 corporations who are more accustomed to having the office brought to them.

These potential customers required a totally new strategy. Instead of waiting for customers to pop in the door, Kinko's now has to solicit business actively, preferably from multibillion-dollar companies. Many of these companies have their own in-house business services departments, which Kinko's hopes to shut down. Convincing big companies that duplicating work can be done better at Kinko's is no easy task. Kinko's 550 salespeople, called account managers, do a lot of "cold-calling" to generate business. Although they often get the cold shoulder, occasionally they hit pay dirt. For example, in Seattle, after knocking on 50 doors, one account manager knocked on the door of a consulting company. Inside, employees were frantically preparing training packets for a Monday morning course, and they were behind schedule on Friday afternoon. Kinko's came to the rescue and gained a new client.

A major challenge for the growing platoon of account managers is learning about Kinko's new corporate audience and communicating successfully Kinko's new image. The goal of Kinko's management is to increase corporate sales to 30 percent of the company's total revenue.

Critical Thinking

- In planning a presentation or proposal for a potential customer, why is analyzing the task and anticipating the audience such an important part of preparation?
- If a Kinko's account manager is working on a presentation or a proposal for a potential customer, such as Bank of America, what kinds of questions should he or she ask to profile the audience?
- How important is it to consider receiver benefits before communicating a message, particularly the kinds of sales messages that Kinko's account managers must send?

all the first-person references. Your empathy index is low if the *I*'s and *we*'s outnumber the *you*'s and *your*'s.

But the use of *you* is more than merely a numbers game. Second-person pronouns can be overused and misused. Readers appreciate genuine interest; on the other hand, they resent obvious attempts at manipulation. Some sales messages, for example, are guilty of overkill when they include *you* dozens of times in a direct mail promotion. Furthermore, the word can sometimes create the wrong impression. Consider this statement: *You cannot return merchandise until you receive written approval. You* appears twice, but the reader feels singled out for criticism. In the following version the message is less personal and more positive: *Customers may return merchandise with written approval.* In short, avoid using *you* for general statements that suggest blame and could cause ill will.

In recognizing the value of the *you* attitude, however, writers do not have to sterilize their writing and totally avoid any first-person pronouns or words that show their feelings. Skilled communicators are able to convey sincerity, warmth, and enthusiasm by the words they choose. Don't be afraid to use phrases such as *I'm happy* or *We're delighted,* if you truly are. When speaking face to face, communicators show sincerity and warmth with nonverbal cues such as a smile and pleasant voice tone. In letters, memos, and e-mail messages, however, only expressive words and phrases can show these feelings. These phrases suggest hidden messages that say to readers and customers "You are important, I hear you, and I'm honestly trying to please you."

Using Bias-Free Language. In adapting a message to its audience, be sure your language is sensitive and bias-free. Few writers set out to be offensive. Sometimes, though, we all say things that we never thought might be hurtful. The real problem is that we don't think about the words that stereotype groups of people, such as *the boys in the mail room* or *the girls in the front office.* Be cautious about expressions that might be biased in terms of gender, race, ethnicity, age, and disability.[10]

Avoiding Gender Bias. You can defuse gender time bombs by replacing words that exclude or stereotype women (sometimes called *sexist language*) with neutral, inclusive expressions. The following examples show how sexist terms and phrases can be replaced with neutral ones.

Gender Biased	**Improved**
female doctor, woman attorney, cleaning woman	doctor, attorney, cleaner
waiter/waitress, authoress, stewardess	server, author, cabin attendant
mankind, man-hour, man-made	humanity, working hours, artificial
office girls	office workers
the doctor . . . he	doctors . . . they
the teacher . . . she	teachers . . . they
executives and their wives	executives and their spouses
foreman, flag-man, workman	lead workers, flagger, worker
businessman, salesman	businessperson, sales representative
Each worker had his picture taken.	Each worker had a picture taken. Each worker had his or her picture taken. All workers had their pictures taken.

Generally, you can avoid gender-biased language by leaving out the words *man* or *woman,* by using plural nouns and pronouns, or by changing to a gender-free word (*person* or *representative*).

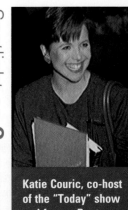

Spotlight on Communicators

Katie Couric, co-host of the "Today" show and former Pentagon reporter, does her homework before she conducts interviews. Disarmingly cheerful and humorous, she can also be hard-hitting and uncompromising in her blunt questioning of newsmakers. Yet she always strives to be positive, courteous, and fair—important characteristics of every good communicator.

Avoiding Racial or Ethnic Bias. You need to indicate racial or ethnic identification only if the context demands it.

Racially or Ethnically Biased	**Improved**
An Indian accountant was hired.	An accountant was hired.
James Lee, an African American, applied.	James Lee applied.

Avoiding Age Bias. Again, specify age only if it is relevant, and avoid expressions that are demeaning or subjective.

Age Biased	**Improved**
The law applied to old people.	The law applied to people over 65.
Sally Kay, 55, was transferred.	Sally Kay was transferred.
a spry old gentleman	a man
a little old lady	a woman

Avoiding Disability Bias. Unless relevant, do not refer to an individual's disability. When necessary, use terms that do not stigmatize disabled individuals.

Sensitive communicators avoid gender, racial or ethnic, and disability biases.

Disability Biased	**Improved**
afflicted with, suffering from, crippled by	has
defect, disease	condition
confined to a wheelchair	uses a wheelchair

The preceding examples give you a quick look at a few problem expressions. The real key to bias-free communication, though, lies in your awareness and commitment. Always be on the lookout to be sure that your messages do not exclude, stereotype, or offend people.

CAREER COACH

EIGHT EASY WAYS TO MAKE READERS AND LISTENERS ANGRY

Communicators in all career areas run the risk of angering receivers by using certain expressions that have hidden meanings. Here are techniques and expressions to avoid because they are guaranteed to offend your audience.

1. **Call them stupid (even if done unintentionally):**

   If you had read the instruction booklet . . .

   You are probably ignorant of the fact that . . .

2. **Suggest that they are lying (even if you don't say so directly):**

   You claim that you returned the item.

   According to you, the item stopped working.

3. **Issue commands and orders:**

   You must comply with our regulations.

   We expect you to complete all portions of the form.

4. **Confuse a person's name or gender:**

   Dear Ms. Lee: We understand, Mr. Lee, that . . .

   Dear Phoung: As a lady of fine tastes, you . . .

5. **Indicate that they are complainers:**

   You complain that . . .

   We have received your complaint describing . . .

6. **Blame them:**

   Obviously you overlooked . . .

   You forgot to . . .

   You neglected to . . .

   You failed to . . .

7. **Write in a language that requires interpretation:**

   When your financial status ameliorates, your application will be given expeditious scrutiny.

   Because of current electronic compositional instrumentation, you need no longer fear exposure of your grammatical foibles.

8. **Issue ultimatums:**

   This will be the last memo sent on this subject. Anyone arriving late faces immediate disciplinary action!

   Either comply with the regulations or face the consequences!

Career Application

Collect actual memos, letters, or other documents that illustrate unintentionally offensive language. Bring the documents to class for discussion and revision.

Positive language creates goodwill and gives more options to readers.

Expressing Yourself Positively. Certain negative words create ill will because they appear to blame or accuse readers. For example, opening a letter to a customer with *You claim that* suggests that you don't believe the customer. Other loaded words that can get you in trouble are *complaint, criticism, defective, failed, mistake,* and *neglected.* Often the writer is unconscious of the effect of these words. Take a look at the accompanying Career Coach box to see eight easy ways to make your readers and listeners angry. To avoid these angry reactions, restrict negative words and try to find positive ways to express ideas. You provide more options to the reader when you tell what can be done instead of what can't be done.

Negative	Positive
You failed to include your credit card number, so we can't mail your order.	We'll mail your order as soon as we receive your credit card number.
Your letter of May 2 claims that you returned a defective headset.	Your May 2 letter describes a headset you returned.
You cannot park in Lot H until April 1.	You may park in Lot H starting April 1.
You won't be sorry that . . .	You will be happy that . . .
The problem cannot be solved without the aid of top management	With the aid of top management, the problem can be solved.

Negative expressions can often be rephrased to sound positive.

Being Courteous. Maintaining a courteous tone involves not just guarding against rudeness but also avoiding words that sound demanding or preachy. Expressions like *you should, you must,* and *you have to* cause people to instinctively react with "Oh, yeah?" One remedy is to turn these demands into rhetorical questions that begin with *Will you please* . . . . Giving reasons for a request also softens the tone.

Less Courteous	More Courteous
You must complete this report before Friday.	Will you please complete the report by Friday.
You should organize a car pool in this department.	Organizing a car pool will reduce your transportation costs and help preserve the environment.

Even when you feel justified in displaying anger, remember that losing your temper or being sarcastic will seldom accomplish your goals as a business communicator to inform, to persuade, and to create goodwill. When you are irritated, frustrated, or infuriated, keep cool and try to defuse the situation. Concentrate on the real problem. What must be done to solve it?

Even when you are justifiably angry, courteous language is the best way to achieve your objectives.

You May Be Thinking This	Better to Say This
This is the second time I've written. Can't you get anything right?	Please credit my account for $843. My latest statement shows that the error noted in my letter of June 2 has not been corrected.
Am I the only one who can read the operating manual?	Let's review the operating manual together so that you can get your documents to print correctly next time.
Hey, don't blame me! I'm not the promoter who took off with the funds.	Please accept our sincere apologies and two complimentary tickets to our our next event. Let me try to explain why we had to substitute performers.

Simplifying Your Language. In adapting your message to your audience, whenever possible use short, familiar words that you think they will recognize. Don't, however, avoid a big word that conveys your idea efficiently and is appropriate for the audience. Your goal is to shun pompous and pretentious language. Instead, use "GO" words. If you mean *begin,* don't say *commence* or *initiate.* If you mean *give,* don't write *render.*[11] By substituting everyday, familiar words for unfamiliar ones, as shown here, you help your audience comprehend your ideas quickly.

The simpler the language, the better.

Spotlight on **Communicators**

The hardest part of her job is making complicated financial information easy to read and understand, admits successful *Newsweek* columnist and financial advisor Jane Bryant Quinn. Diligent revision helps her clarify her thinking and her language. Whether writing about borrowing, investing, or insuring, she constantly adapts to her audience and looks for familiar language. "I'm always asking myself, 'Will the reader understand this word, this phrase?'"

Unfamiliar	Familiar
commensurate	equal
conceptualization	idea
interrogate	question
materialize	appear
remunerate	pay
terminate	end

At the same time, be selective in your use of jargon. *Jargon* describes technical or specialized terms within a field. These terms enable insiders to communicate complex ideas briefly, but to outsiders they mean nothing. Human resources professionals, for example, know precisely what's meant by *cafeteria plan* (a benefits option program), but most of us would be thinking about lunch. Geologists refer to *plate tectonics*, and physicians discuss *metastatic carcinomas*. But these terms mean little to most of us. Use specialized language only when the audience will understand it. And don't forget to consider secondary audiences: Will those potential readers understand any technical terms used?

Using Precise, Vigorous Words. Strong verbs and concrete nouns give readers more information and keep them interested. Don't overlook the thesaurus (or the thesaurus program on your computer) for expanding your word choices and vocabulary. Whenever possible, use specific words as shown here.

Imprecise, Dull	More Precise
a gain in profits	a jump in profits a 23 percent hike in profits
it takes memory	it hogs memory it requires 32 megabytes of RAM
to think about	to identify, diagnose, analyze to probe, examine, inspect

Using familiar but precise words helps receivers understand.

By reviewing the tips in the following checklist, you can master the steps of writing preparation. As you review these tips, remember the three basics of prewriting: analyzing, anticipating, and adapting.

Checklist for Adapting a Message to Its Audience

 **Identify the message purpose.** Ask yourself why you are communicating and what you hope to achieve. Look for primary and secondary purposes.

 **Select the most appropriate form.** Determine whether you need a permanent record or whether the message is too sensitive to put in writing.

 **Profile the audience.** Identify your relationship with the reader and your knowledge about that individual or group. Assess how much the receiver knows about the subject.

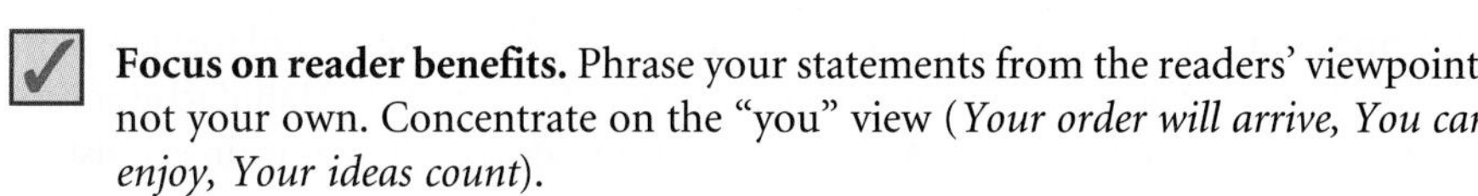

- **Focus on reader benefits.** Phrase your statements from the readers' viewpoint, not your own. Concentrate on the "you" view (*Your order will arrive, You can enjoy, Your ideas count*).

- **Avoid gender and racial bias.** Use bias-free words (*businessperson* instead of *businessman*; *working hours* instead of *man-hours*). Omit ethnic identification unless the context demands it.

- **Avoid age and disability bias.** Include age only if relevant. Avoid potentially demeaning expressions (*spry old gentleman*), and use terms that do not stigmatize disabled people (*he is disabled* instead of *he is a cripple* or *he has a handicap*).

- **Express ideas positively rather than negatively.** Instead of *Your order can't be shipped before June 1,* say *Your order can be shipped June 1.*

- **Use short, familiar words.** Use technical terms and big words only if they are appropriate for the audience (*end* not *terminate, required* not *mandatory*).

- **Search for precise, vigorous words.** Use a thesaurus if necessary to find strong verbs and concrete nouns (*announces* instead of *says, brokerage* instead of *business*).

Adapting to Legal Responsibilities

6

One of your primary responsibilities in writing for an organization or for yourself is to avoid language that may land you in court. In our current business environment, lawsuits abound, many of which center on the use and abuse of language. You can protect yourself and avoid litigation by knowing what's legal and by adapting your language accordingly. Be especially careful when communicating in the following four areas: investments, safety, marketing, and human resources. Because these information areas generate the most lawsuits, we will examine them more closely.[12]

Investment Information

Careful communicators should familiarize themselves with information in four information areas: investments, safety, marketing, and human resources.

Writers describing the sale of stocks or financial services must follow specific laws written to protect investors. Any messages—including letters, newsletters, and pamphlets—must be free from misleading information, exaggerations, or half-truths. One company in Massachusetts inadvertently violated the law by declaring that it was "recession-proof." After going bankrupt, the company was sued by angry stockholders claiming that they had been deceived. Another company, Lotus Development Corporation, caused a flurry of lawsuits by withholding information that revealed problems in a new version of its 1-2-3 program. Stockholders sued, charging that managers had deliberately concealed the bad news, thus keeping stock prices artificially high. Experienced financial writers know that careless language and even poor timing may provoke litigation.

Safety Information

Writers describing potentially dangerous products worry not only about protecting people from physical harm but also about being sued. During the past three decades,

Warnings on dangerous products must be written especially clearly.

litigation arising from product liability has been the most active area of tort law (tort law involves wrongful civil acts other than breach of contract).[13] Manufacturers are obligated to warn consumers of any risks in their products. These warnings must do more than suggest danger; they must also clearly tell people how to use the product safely. In writing warnings, concentrate on major points. Omit anything that is not critical. In the work area describe a potential problem and tell how to solve it. For example, *Lead dust is harmful and gets on your clothes. Change your clothes before leaving work.*

Clearly written safety messages use easy-to-understand words, such as *doctor* instead of *physician, clean* instead of *sanitary,* and *burn* instead of *incinerate.* Technical terms are defined. For example *Asbestos is a carcinogen (something that causes cancer).*[14] Effective safety messages also include highlighting techniques, such as using headings and bullets. In coming chapters you'll learn more about these techniques for improving readability.

Marketing Information

Sales and marketing messages must not make claims that can't be verified.

Sales and marketing messages are illegal if they falsely advertise prices, performance capability, quality, or other product characteristics. Marketing messages must not deceive the buyer in any way. A Southern California entrepreneur, for example, promoted a Band-Aid-like device, Le Patch, as "a dramatic breakthrough in weight control technology." When worn around the waist, Le Patch was supposed to reduce appetite. The claims, however, could not be proved; and the promoter was charged with misrepresenting the product. Sellers of services must also be cautious about the language they use to describe what they will do. Letters, reports, and proposals that describe services to be performed are interpreted as contracts in court. Therefore, language must not promise more than intended. Here are some dangerous words (and recommended alternatives) that have created misunderstandings leading to lawsuits.[15]

Dangerous Word	Court Interpretation	Recommended Alternative
inspect	to examine critically, to investigate and test officially, to scrutinize	to review, to study, to tour the facility
determine	to come to a decision, to decide, to resolve	to evaluate, to assess, to analyze
assure	to render safe, to make secure, to give confidence, to cause to feel certain	to facilitate, to provide further confidence, to enhance the reliability of

Human Resources Information

The safest employment recommendations contain positive, job-related information.

The vast number of lawsuits relating to employment makes this a treacherous area for business communicators. In evaluating employees in the workplace, avoid making unsubstantiated negative comments. It's also unwise to assess traits (*she is unreliable*) because they require subjective judgment. Concentrate instead on specific incidents (*in the last month she missed four work days and was late three times*). Defamation lawsuits have become so common that some companies no longer provide letters of recommendation for former employees. To be safe, give recommendations only when the former employee authorizes the recommendation. For more information about letters of recommendation, see pages 191–193.

PROCESS TO PRODUCT

Applying Your Skills at Kinko's

The new marketing strategy at Kinko's is to attract corporate clients with such services as high-speed duplicating for big jobs, color and graphics printing using the best equipment available, proposal and brochure packets, and videoconferencing services. Kinko's has even installed its own network called "Kinkonet." This service enables clients to use digital technologies and modems to compose reports or other materials and have them printed wherever they are needed, say, for instance, in Amsterdam.

Your Job

You have been hired as a communication trainer to assist Greg Soulages, vice president of sales for Kinko's. He realizes that his newly hired product managers do not always think in terms of adapting a message to its audience. He asks you to give the new hires some pointers on specific techniques for improving their presentations and proposals. Before the training session, though, Soulages asks you to submit a list of points you will emphasize in your talk. Individually or in small groups, review suggestions in this chapter for adapting a message to its audience. Prepare a list of at least six points to submit to Vice President Soulages. For each point, try to supply an example from a case in which Kinko's is trying to convince Bank of America to have its next set of color brochures printed by Kinko's instead of having them prepared in-house.

Statements in employee handbooks also require careful wording, because a court might rule that such statements are "implied contracts." Consider the following handbook remark: "We at Hotstuff, Inc., show our appreciation for hard work and team spirit by rewarding everyone who performs well." This seemingly harmless statement could make it difficult to fire an employee because of the implied employment promise.[16] Companies are warned to avoid promissory phrases in writing job advertisements, application forms, and offer letters. Phrases that suggest permanent employment and guaranteed job security can be interpreted as contracts.[17]

In adapting messages to meet today's litigious business environment, be sensitive to the rights of others and to your own rights. The key elements in this adaptation process are awareness of laws, sensitivity to interpretations, and careful use of language.

Summary of Learning Objectives

1 **Describe three basic elements that distinguish business writing and summarize the three phases of the 3-×-3 writing process.** Business writing differs from academic writing in that it strives to solve business problems, it is economical, and it is reader oriented. Phase 1 of the writing process (prewriting) involves analyzing the message, anticipating the audience, and considering ways to adapt the message to the audience. Phase 2 (writing) involves researching the topic, organizing the material, and composing the message. Phase 3 (revising) includes proofreading and evaluating the message.

2 **Explain how the writing process may be altered and how it is affected by team projects and technology.** The writing process may be compressed for short messages; steps in the process may be rearranged. Team writing, which is necessary for large projects or when wide expertise is necessary, alters the writing process. Teams often work together in brainstorming and working out their procedures and assignments. Then individual members write their portions of the report or presentation during Phase 2. During Phase 3 (revising) teams may work together to combine their drafts. Technology assists writers with word processing, revision, and collaboration tools.

3 **Clarify what is involved in analyzing a writing task and selecting a communication channel.** Communicators must decide why they are delivering a message and what they hope to achieve. Although many messages only inform, some must also persuade. After identifying the purpose of a message, communicators must choose the most appropriate channel. That choice depends on the importance of the message, the amount and speed of feedback required, the need for a permanent record, the cost of the channel, and the degree of formality desired.

4 **Describe anticipating and profiling the audience for a message.** A good communicator tries to envision the audience for a message. What does the receiver know about the topic? How well does the receiver know the sender? What is known about the receiver's education, beliefs, culture, and attitudes? Will the response to the message be positive, neutral, or negative? Is the secondary audience different from the primary audience?

5 **Specify six writing techniques that help communicators adapt messages to the task and audience.** Skilled communicators strive to (a) spotlight reader benefits, (b) look at a message from the receiver's perspective (the "you" view), (c) use sensitive language that avoids gender, racial, ethnic, and disability biases, (d) state ideas positively, (e) show courtesy, and (f) use short, familiar, and precise words.

6 **Explain why four areas of communication hold legal responsibilities for writers.** Actions and language in four information areas generate the most lawsuits: investments, safety, marketing, and human resources. In writing about investments, communicators must avoid misleading information, exaggerations, and half-truths. Safety information, including warnings, must tell people clearly how to use a product safely and motivate them to do so. In addition to being honest, marketing information must not promise more than intended. And communicators in the area of human resources must use careful wording (particularly in employment recommendations and employee handbooks) to avoid potential lawsuits.

CHAPTER REVIEW

1. Name three ways in which business writing differs from other writing. (Obj. 1)
2. Describe the components in each stage of the 3-×-3 writing process. (Obj. 1)
3. List five factors to consider when selecting a communication channel. (Obj. 3)
4. Why should you "profile" your audience before composing a message? (Obj. 4)
5. What is *empathy,* and how does it apply to business writing? (Obj. 5)
6. Discuss the effects of first- and second-person pronouns. (Obj. 5)
7. What is gender-biased language? Give examples. (Obj. 5)
8. Name replacements for the following gender-biased terms: *waitress, stewardess, foreman.* (Obj. 5)
9. When should a writer include racial or ethnic identification, such as *Ellen Lee, an Asian, . . .?* (Obj. 5)
10. Revise the following expression: *He is crippled by muscular dystrophy.* (Obj. 5)
11. Revise the following expression to show more courtesy: *You must submit your budget before noon.* (Obj. 5)
12. What is *jargon,* and when is it appropriate for business writing? (Obj. 5)
13. What's wrong with using words such as *commence, mandate,* and *interrogate*? (Obj. 5)
14. What four information areas generate the most lawsuits? (Obj. 6)
15. How can business communicators protect themselves against litigation? (Obj. 6)

CRITICAL THINKING

1. Business communicators are encouraged to profile or "visualize" the audience for their message. How is this possible if you don't really know the people who will receive a sales letter or who will hear your business presentation? (Obj. 4)
2. How can the 3-×-3 writing process help the writer of a business report as well as the writer of an oral presentation? (Obj. 1)
3. If adapting your tone to the receiving audience and developing reader benefits are so important, why do we see so much writing that does not reflect these suggestions? (Objs. 3 to 5)
4. Discuss the following statement: "The English language is a landmine—it is filled with terms that are easily misinterpreted as derogatory and others that are blatantly insulting. . . . Being fair and objective is not enough; employers must also appear to be so."[18] (Obj. 5)
5. **Ethical Issue:** Suppose your superior asked you to change year-end financial data, and you knew that if you didn't, you might lose your job. What would you do if it were a small amount? A large amount?

ACTIVITIES

4.1 Document for Analysis (Obj. 5)

Discuss the following memo, which is based on an actual document sent to employees. How could you apply what you learned in this chapter to improving this memo?

TO: All Employees Using HP 5000 Computers

It has recently come to my attention that a computer security problem exists within our organization. I understand that the problem is twofold in nature:

a. You have been sharing computer passwords.

b. You are using automatic log-on procedures.

Henceforth, you are prohibited from sharing passwords for security reasons that should be axiomatic. We also must forbid you to use automatic log-on files because they empower anyone to have access to our entire computer system and all company data.

Enclosed please find a form that you must sign and return to the aforementioned individual, indicating your acknowledgement of and acquiescence to the procedures described here. Any computer user whose signed form is not returned will have his personal password invalidated.

4.2 Selecting Communication Channels (Obj. 3)

Using Figure 4.2 (page 107), suggest the best communication channels for the following messages. Assume that all channels shown are available. Be prepared to explain your choices.

a. As department manager, you wish to inform four department members of a training session scheduled for three weeks from now.

b. As assistant to the vice president, you are to investigate the possibility of developing internship programs with several nearby colleges and universities.

c. You wish to send price quotes for a number of your products in response to a request from a potential customer in Taiwan.

d. You must respond to a notice from the Internal Revenue Service insisting that you did not pay the correct amount for last quarter's employer's taxes.

e. As a manager, you must inform an employee that continued tardiness is jeopardizing her job.

f. Members of your task force must meet to discuss ways to improve communication among 5,000 employees at 32 branches of your large company. Task force members are from Los Angeles, Orlando, San Antonio, White Plains, and Columbus (Ohio).

g. You need to know whether Paula in Printing can produce a special pamphlet for you within two days.

4.3 Analyzing Audiences (Obj. 4)

Using the questions in Figure 4.3 (page 108), write a brief analysis of the audience for each of the following communication tasks.

a. Your letter of application for a job advertised in your local newspaper. Your qualifications match the job description.

b. An e-mail memo to your boss persuading her to allow you to attend a computer class that will require you to leave work early two days a week for ten weeks.

c. An unsolicited sales letter promoting life insurance to a targeted group of executives.

d. A letter from the municipal water department explaining that the tap water may taste and smell bad; however, it poses no threats to health.

e. A letter from a credit card organization refusing credit to an applicant.

4.4 Reader Benefits and the "You" View (Obj. 5)

Revise the following sentences to emphasize the reader's perspective and the "you" view.

a. To prevent us from possibly losing large sums of money, our bank now requires verification of any large check presented for immediate payment.

b. We take pride in announcing a new schedule of low-cost flights to Hawaii.

c. So that we may bring our customer records up to date and eliminate the expense of duplicate mailings, we are asking you to complete the enclosed card.

d. For just $300 per person, we have arranged a three-day trip to Las Vegas that includes deluxe accommodations, the "City Lights" show, and selected meals.

e. I give my permission for you to attend the two-day workshop.

f. We're requesting all employees to complete the enclosed questionnaire so that we may develop a master schedule for summer vacations.

g. I think my background and my education match the description of the manager trainee position you advertised.

h. We are offering an in-house training program for employees who want to improve their writing skills.

i. We are pleased to announce an arrangement with Compaq that allows us to offer discounted computers in the student bookstore.

j. We have approved your application for credit.

k. We are pleased to announce that we have selected you to join our trainee program.

l. Our safety policy forbids us from renting power equipment to anyone who cannot demonstrate proficiency in its use.

m. We will reimburse you for all travel expenses.

n. To enable us to continue our policy of selling name brands at discount prices, we cannot give cash refunds on returned merchandise.

o. We offer a free catalog of computer and office supplies that saves money and shopping time for readers.

4.5 Language Bias (Obj. 5)

Revise the following sentences to eliminate gender, racial, age, and disability stereotypes.

a. Any applicant for the position of fireman must submit a medical report signed by his physician.

b. We hired Todd Shimoyama, a Japanese American, for the position of communications coordinator.

c. Because she is confined to a wheelchair, we look for restaurants without stairs.

d. Every employee is entitled to see his personnel file.

e. Some restaurants have a special menu for old people.

f. How many man-hours will the project require?

g. James is afflicted with arthritis, but his crippling rarely interferes with his work.

h. Debbie Sanchez, 24, was hired; and Tony Morris, 57, was promoted.

i. All conference participants and their wives are invited to the banquet.

j. Our company encourages the employment of handicapped people.

k. Representing the community are a businessman, a lady attorney, and a female doctor.

l. A salesman would have to use all his skills to sell those condos.

m. Their child suffers from cerebral palsy.

n. Armando is an excellent Hispanic computer technician.

o. Every attorney has 10 minutes for his summation.

4.6 Positive Expression (Obj. 5)

Revise the following statements to make them more positive.

a. If you fail to pass the examination, you will not qualify.

b. In the message you left at our Web site, you claim that you returned a defective headset.

c. Although you apparently failed to read the operator's manual, we are sending you a replacement blade for your food processor. Next time read page 18 carefully so that you will know how to attach this blade.

d. We can't process your application because you neglected to insert your social security number.

e. Construction cannot begin until the building plans are approved.

f. Because of a mistake in its address, your letter did not arrive until January 3.

g. In response to your e-mail complaint, we are investigating our agent's poor behavior.

h. It is impossible to move forward without community support.

i. Customers are ineligible for the 10 percent discount unless they show their membership cards.

j. You won't be disappointed with the many electronic services we now offer.

4.7 Courteous Expression (Obj. 5)

Revise the following messages to show greater courtesy.

a. You must sign and return this form immediately.

b. This is the last time I'm writing to try to get you to record my January 6 payment of $500 to my account. Anyone who can read can see from the attached documents that I've tried to explain this to you before.

c. As manager of your department, you will have to get your employees to use the correct forms.

d. To the Staff: Can't anyone around here read instructions? Page 12 of the operating manual for our copy machine very clearly describes how to remove jammed paper. But I'm the only one who ever does it, and I've had it! No more copies will be made until you learn how to remove jammed paper.

e. If you had listened to our agent more carefully, you would know that your policy does not cover accidents outside the United States.

4.8 Familiar Words (Obj. 5)

Revise the following sentences to avoid unfamiliar words.

a. Pursuant to your invitation, we will interrogate our manager.

b. To expedite ratification of this agreement, we urge you to vote in the affirmative.

c. In a dialogue with the manager, I learned that you plan to terminate our agreement.

d. Did the steering problem materialize subsequent to our recall effort?

e. Once we ascertain how much it costs, we can initiate the project.

4.9 Precise Words (Obj. 5)

From the choices in parentheses, select the most precise, vigorous words.

a. If you find yourself (*having, engaged in, juggling*) many tasks, find ways to remind yourself of them.

b. He is (*connected to, associated with, employed by*) the Dana Corporation.

c. We plan to (*acknowledge, publicize, applaud*) the work of exemplary employees.

d. The splendid report has (*a lot of, many, a warehouse of*) facts.

e. All the managers thought the new software was (*good, nice, helpful*).

For the following sentences provide more precise alternatives for the italicized words.

f. If necessary, we will (a) *drop* overtime hours in order to (b) *fix* the budget.

g. The CEO (a) *said* that only (b) *the right kind of* applicants should apply.

h. After (a) *reading* the report, I decided it was (b) *bad.*

i. Jenny said the movie was (a) *different,* but her remarks weren't very (b) *clear* to us.

j. I'm (a) *going* to Little Rock tomorrow, and I plan to (b) *find out* the real problem.

k. Most (a) *people* don't have much (b) *feeling toward* brand names unless the brands are heavily promoted.

l. The (a) *news* made us feel particularly (b) *positive.*

4.10 Legal Language (Obj. 6)

To avoid possible litigation, revise the italicized words in the following sentences taken from proposals.

a. We will *inspect* the building plans before construction begins.

b. Our goal is to *assure* completion of the project on schedule.

c. We will *determine* the amount of stress for each supporting column.

C.L.U.E. REVIEW 4

On a separate sheet edit the following sentences to correct faults in grammar, punctuation, spelling, and word use.

1. If I was you I would schedule the conference for one of these cities Atlanta Memphis or Nashville.

2. The committees next meeting is scheduled for May fifth at three p.m., and should last about two hours.

3. Were not asking you to altar the figures, we are asking you to check there accuracy.

4. Will you please fax me a list of our independant contractors names and addresses?

5. The vacation calender fills up quick for the Summer months, therefore you should make your plans early.

6. After the inspector issues the waver we will be able to procede with the architects plan.

7. If we can't give out neccessary information what is the point in us answering the telephone.

8. Every new employee will receive their orientation packet, and be told about their parking priviledges.

9. About eighty-five percent of all new entrants into the workforce in the 1990s is expected to be: women, minorities and immigrants.

10. Our Vice President in the Human Resources Development Department asked the Manager and I to come to her office at three-thirty p.m.

CHAPTER • 5 •

Organizing and Writing Business Messages

LEARNING OBJECTIVES

1. Contrast formal and informal methods for researching data and generating ideas.
2. Specify how to organize data into lists and alphanumeric or decimal outlines.
3. Compare direct and indirect patterns for organizing ideas.
4. Discuss composing the first draft of a message, focusing on techniques for creating effective sentences.
5. Define a paragraph and describe three classic paragraph plans and techniques for composing meaningful paragraphs.

CASE STUDY

COMMUNICATION IN PROCESS

Liz Claiborne Finds That Achieving Human Rights in Apparel Industry Is Like Bottling Fog

Over the past two decades Liz Claiborne, Inc., quietly became the largest women's apparel company in the world. One of only two companies started by a woman to crack the Fortune 500, it is the leading "power brand" in the women's apparel field. But CEO Paul Charron knows all too well that the fashion industry is fickle and that his core consumers—the women of America—are discriminating, intelligent, and "have no loyalties to brands."[1]

To maintain its dominance in department stores, Liz Claiborne designers turn out a new line of products every five weeks. Moreover, Liz Claiborne is moving into menswear, which now makes up 25 percent of its total revenues. However, as the apparel industry moves toward the new millennium, it continues to undergo massive changes in all areas. Competition is greater, production costs are higher, and profits are tougher to earn. These trends force the apparel industry to continue along the path of efficiency, consolidation, and cost-cutting.

Apparel makers quickly learned that the best way to cut costs involved shifting production to other countries. Apparel imports from Mexico recently soared by 40 percent, while imports from other countries jumped 16 percent. But along with cheaper costs came sweatshop conditions and human rights violations by contractors.

Although committed to making profits and providing value to its customers, Liz Claiborne also cares about ethics, integrity, and human rights. CEO Charron says, "We have been very active on the President's Commission [of the Apparel Industry Partnership] and very aggressive about making sure that all of our contractors take a very positive approach to human rights. Studies may show that the consumer doesn't care about any phase in the product development cycle—just what corresponds to her needs. But for us, it is a very big deal to have integrity about how our manufacturing partners treat our workers."

To implement its commitment to human rights, Liz Claiborne instituted a code of conduct forbidding, among other things, forced labor, harassment, abuse, discrimination, and the use of child labor. Although this code is spelled out in brochures and at the Liz Claiborne Web site, communicating its meaning to contractors—and achieving compliance—is a continuing challenge. One authority said that enforcing worker rights in the 100 or more nations engaged in international apparel trade was like "trying to bottle fog."[2]

www.lizclaiborne.com

Researching Data and Generating Ideas

1

Before writing, conduct formal or informal research to collect or generate necessary data.

Business communicators at Liz Claiborne, Inc., face daily challenges that require data collection, idea generation, and concept organization. These activities are part of the second phase of the writing process, which includes researching, organizing, and composing.

No smart businessperson would begin writing a message before collecting all the needed information. We call this collection process *research,* a rather formal-sounding term. For simple documents, though, the procedure can be quite informal. Research is necessary before beginning to write because the information you collect helps shape the message. Discovering significant data after a message is half completed often means starting over and reorganizing. To avoid frustration and inaccurate messages, collect information that answers a primary question:

- *What does the receiver need to know about this topic?*

When the message involves action, search for answers to secondary questions:

- *What is the receiver to do?*
- *How is the receiver to do it?*
- *When must the receiver do it?*
- *What will happen if the receiver doesn't do it?*

Whenever your communication problem requires more information than you have in your head or at your fingertips, you must conduct research. This research may be formal or informal.

Formal Research Methods

Formal research may involve searching libraries and electronic databases or investigating primary sources (interviews, surveys, and experimentation).

Long reports and complex business problems generally require some use of formal research methods. Let's say you are a market specialist for Coca-Cola, and your boss asks you to evaluate the impact on Coke sales of private-label or generic soft drinks (the bargain-basement-brand knockoffs sold at Kmart and other outlets). Or, let's assume you must write a term paper for a college class. Both tasks require more data than you have in your head or at your fingertips. To conduct formal research, you could:

- **Search manually.** You'll find helpful background and supplementary information through manual searching of resources in public and college libraries. These traditional sources include periodical indexes for lists of newspaper, magazine, and journal articles, along with the card catalog for books. Other manual sources are book indexes, encyclopedias, reference books, handbooks, dictionaries, directories, and almanacs.
- **Access electronically.** Like other facets of life, the research process has been changed considerably by the computer. Much of the printed material just described is now available from the Internet, databases, or compact discs that can be accessed by computer. College and public libraries subscribe to retrieval services that permit you to access thousands of bibliographic or full-text databases. You'll learn more about using the Internet and other electronic information resources in Unit 4.
- **Investigate primary sources.** To develop firsthand, primary information for a project, go directly to the source. For the Coca-Cola report, for example, you could find out what consumers really think by conducting interviews or surveys, by putting together questionnaires, or by organizing focus groups. Formal research includes scientific sampling methods that enable investigators to make accurate judgments and valid predictions.

Good sources of primary information are interviews, surveys, questionnaires, and focus groups.

- **Experiment scientifically.** Another source of primary data is experimentation. Instead of merely asking for the target audience's opinion, scientific researchers present choices with controlled variables. Assume, for example, that Coca-Cola wants to determine at what price and under what circumstances consumers would switch from Coca-Cola to a generic brand. The results of such experimentation would provide valuable data for managerial decision making.

Because formal research techniques are particularly necessary for reports, you'll study resources and techniques more extensively in Unit 4.

Informal Research and Idea Generation

Most routine tasks—such as composing e-mail messages, memos, letters, informational reports, and oral presentations—require data that you can collect informally.

Spotlight on Communicators

Generating ideas takes top priority for Gerry Laybourne, who, after serving as president of cable network's Nickelodeon/Nick at Nite and president of Disney/ABC Cable network, started her own media company. Three techniques work for her: being unafraid of making mistakes or looking silly, refusing to censor ideas, and brainstorming with her staff. Because she feels that many heads are better than one, she encourages brainstorming and follows it up with team-centered management.

For some projects, though, you rely more on your own ideas instead of—or in addition to—researching existing facts. Here are some techniques for collecting informal data and for generating ideas:

- **Look in the files.** Before asking others for help, see what you can find yourself. For many routine messages you can often find previous documents to help you with content and format.
- **Talk with your boss.** Get information from the individual making the assignment. What does that person know about the topic? What slant should be taken? What other sources would he or she suggest?
- **Interview the target audience.** Consider talking with individuals at whom the message is aimed. They can provide clarifying information that tells you what they want to know and how you should shape your remarks.
- **Conduct an informal survey.** Gather unscientific but helpful information via questionnaires or telephone surveys. In preparing a memo report predicting the success of a proposed fitness center, for example, circulate a questionnaire asking for employee reactions.
- **Brainstorm for ideas.** Alone or with others, discuss ideas for the writing task at hand, and record at least a dozen ideas without judging them. Small groups are especially fruitful in brainstorming because people spin ideas off one another.
- **Develop a cluster diagram.** Prepare a cluster diagram (discussed in the next section) to help you generate and organize ideas. Clustering allows your mind to open up and free associate.

Collecting Information and Generating Ideas on the Job

Let's follow Susanne Tully to see how she collected data and generated ideas for two projects at Liz Claiborne, the women's clothing manufacturer. One of Susanne's tasks is simple, and one is complex.

Writing an Informational E-Mail Memo. Susanne's first task is to write an informational memo, shown in Figure 5.1. It describes a photo contest sponsored by Liz Claiborne. For this memo Susanne began by brainstorming with her staff, other employees, and her boss to decide on a photo contest theme. After naming a theme, "Together We Win," inspired by the Special Olympics, she consulted the files to see who had won prizes in last year's contest. She also double-checked with management to ensure that the prize money of $500, $250, and $100 remained the same. Then she made the following quick scratch list outlining the points she wanted to cover in her memo.

Photo Contest E-Mail Memo

1. Announce theme; give examples
2. Encourage all employees to participate
3. Review prizes; name last year's winner
4. Limit: one entry each
5. Details in November; call Rosemary for more info

Many business messages, like Susanne's finished memo, require only simple data-collection and idea-generation techniques.

FIGURE 5.1 Informational E-Mail Memo at Liz Claiborne

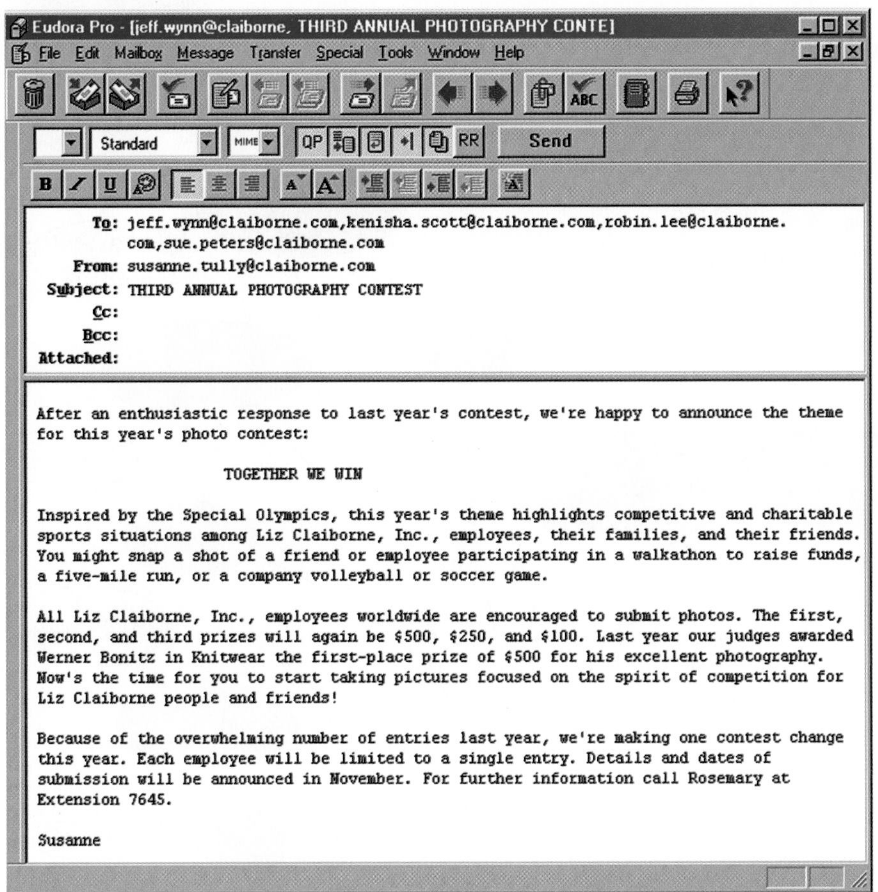

Preparing a Recruitment Brochure. Susanne's second project, though, demanded both formal and informal research, along with considerable creativity. She needed to produce a recruitment brochure that explained career opportunities for college students at Liz Claiborne. She had definite objectives for the brochure: it should be colorful, exciting, concise, lightweight (because she had to carry stacks of them to college campuses!), and easily updated. Moreover, she wanted the brochure to promote Liz Claiborne, describing its progressive benefits, community involvement, career potential, and corporate values program (called "Priorities").

Some of her thoughts about this big project are shown in the cluster diagram in Figure 5.2. Cluster diagramming sparks our creativity; it encourages ideas to spill forth because the process is unrestricted. From the jumble of ideas in the initial cluster diagram, main categories—usually three to five—are extracted. At this point some people are ready to make an outline; others need further visualization, such as a set of subclusters, shown in Figure 5.3. Notice that four major categories (Purpose, Content, Development, and Form) were extracted from the initial diagram. These categories then became the hub of related ideas. This set of subclusters forms the basis for an outline, to be discussed shortly.

To collect data for this project, Susanne employed both formal and informal research methods. She studied recruiting brochures from other companies. She talked with college students to ask what information they sought in a brochure. She conducted more formal research among the numerous division presidents and execu-

FIGURE 5.2 Using Cluster Diagram to Generate Ideas for Liz Claiborne College Recruiting Brochure

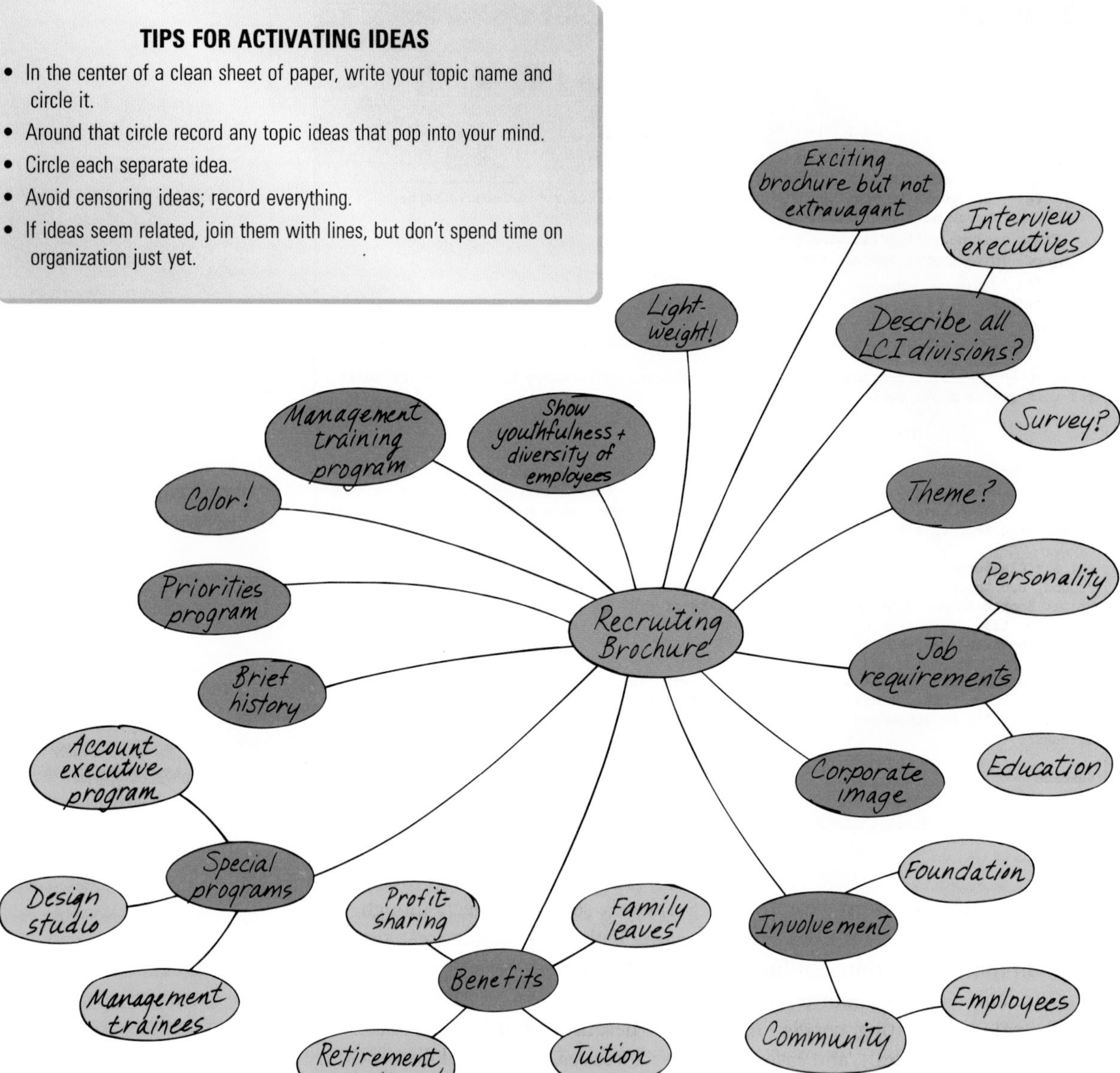

tives within her company to learn what really went on in all the departments, such as Information Systems, Operations Management, Production, and Design. She also had to learn the specific educational and personality requirements for careers in those areas. Working with an outside consultant, she prepared a questionnaire, which was used in personal interviews with company executives. The interviews included some open-ended questions, such as "How did you start with the company?" It also contained more specific questions about the number of employees in their departments, intended career paths, degree requirements, personality traits desired, and so forth. Organizing the mass of data collected was the next task.

FIGURE 5.3 **Organizing Ideas from Cluster Diagram into Subclusters**

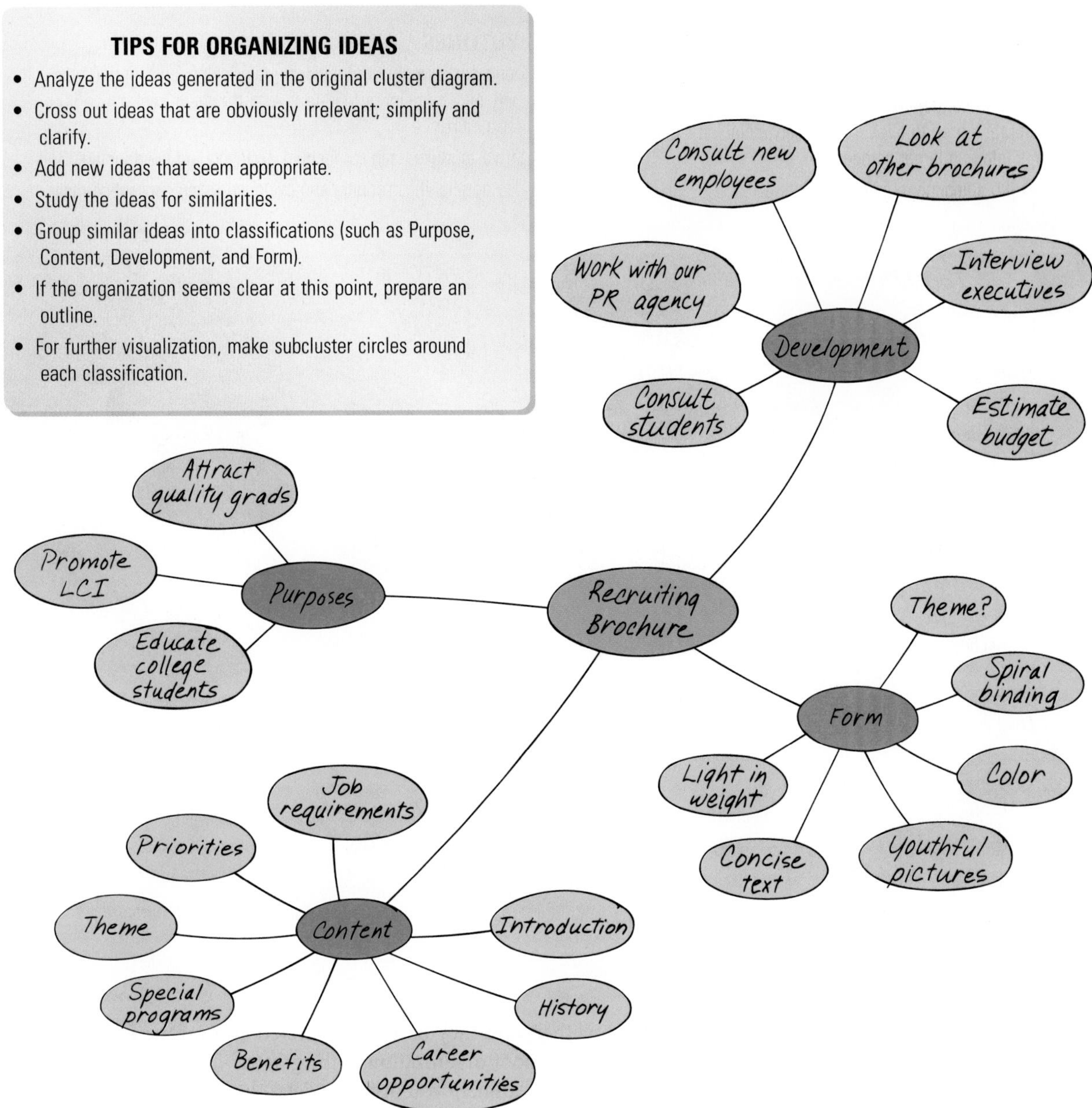
TIPS FOR ORGANIZING IDEAS
• Analyze the ideas generated in the original cluster diagram.
• Cross out ideas that are obviously irrelevant; simplify and clarify.
• Add new ideas that seem appropriate.
• Study the ideas for similarities.
• Group similar ideas into classifications (such as Purpose, Content, Development, and Form).
• If the organization seems clear at this point, prepare an outline.
• For further visualization, make subcluster circles around each classification.
Recruiting Brochure
Development
Consult new employees
Look at other brochures
Work with our PR agency
Interview executives
Consult students
Estimate budget
Purposes
Attract quality grads
Promote LCI
Educate college students
Form
Theme?
Spiral binding
Color
Light in weight
Concise text
Youthful pictures
Content
Job requirements
Priorities
Theme
Introduction
Special programs
History
Benefits
Career opportunities

Organizing Data

The process of organization may begin before you collect data, as it did for Susanne, or occur simultaneously with data collection. For complex projects, organization may be ongoing. Regardless of when organization occurs, its primary goals are grouping and patterning. Well-organized messages group similar items together; ideas follow a sequence that helps the reader understand relationships and accept the writer's views. Unorganized messages proceed free-form, jumping from one thought to another. Such messages fail to emphasize important points. Puzzled readers can't see

2

FIGURE 5.4 **Two Outlining Formats**

TIPS FOR MAKING OUTLINES

- Define the main topic (purpose of message) in the title.
- Divide the main topic into major components or classifications (preferably three to five). If necessary, combine small components into one larger category.
- Break the components into subpoints.
- Don't put a single item under a major component; if you have only one subpoint, integrate it with the main item above it or reorganize.
- Strive to make each component exclusive (no overlapping).
- Use details, illustrations, and evidence to support subpoints.

Format for Alphanumeric Outline	***Format for Decimal Outline***
Title: Major Idea, Purpose	Title: Major Idea, Purpose
I. First major component	1.0. First major component
A. First subpoint	1.1. First subpoint
1. Detail, illustration, evidence	1.1.1. Detail, illustration, evidence
2. Detail, illustration, evidence	1.1.2. Detail, illustration, evidence
B. Second subpoint	1.2. Second subpoint
1.	1.2.1
2.	1.2.2
II. Second major component	2.0. Second major component
A. First subpoint	2.1. First subpoint
1.	2.1.1
2.	2.1.2
B. Second subpoint	2.2. Second subpoint
1.	2.2.1
2.	2.2.2
III. Third major component	3.0. Third major component
A.	3.1
1.	3.1.1
2.	3.1.2
B.	3.2
1.	3.2.1
2.	3.2.2
(This method is simple and familiar.)	*(This method relates every item to the overall outline.)*

Writers of well-organized messages group similar ideas together so that readers can see relationships and follow arguments.

how the pieces fit together, and they become frustrated and irritated. Many communication experts regard poor organization as the greatest failing of business writers. Two simple techniques can help you organize data: the scratch list and the outline.

Listing and Outlining

Alphanumeric outlines show major and minor ideas; decimal outlines show how ideas relate to one another.

In developing simple messages, some writers make a quick scratch list of the topics they wish to cover, as Susanne did for her memo in Figure 5.1. Writers often jot this scratch list in the margin of the letter or memo to which they are responding—and the majority of business messages are written in response to other documents. These writers then compose a message at their computers directly from the scratch list.

Most writers, though, need to organize their ideas—especially if the project is complex—into a hierarchy, such as an outline. The beauty of preparing an outline is that it gives you a chance to organize your thinking before you get bogged down in word choice and sentence structure.[3] Figure 5.4 shows two outline formats: al-

In organizing this Liz Claiborne recruitment brochure, Susanne Tully and her staff achieved coherence and readability by converting each topic from the outline into a consistent, reader-centered heading. Notice the emphasis on "you," an important lesson for every business communicator to learn.

phanumeric and decimal. The familiar alphanumeric format uses Roman numerals, letters, and numbers to show major and minor ideas. The decimal format, which takes a little getting used to, has the advantage of showing how every item at every level relates to the whole. Both outlining formats force you to focus on the topic, identify major ideas, and support those ideas with details, illustrations, or evidence. Many computer outlining programs now on the market make the mechanics of the process a real breeze.

The hardest part of outlining is grouping ideas into components or categories—ideally three to five in number. By the way, these major categories will become the major headings in your report. If you have more than five components, look for ways to combine smaller segments into broader topics. The following example shows how a portion of the Liz Claiborne brochure subcluster (Figure 5.3) can be organized into an alphanumeric outline.

I. Introduction
    A. Brief history of Liz Claiborne
        1. Founding, Fortune 500 status
        2. Product lines
    B. Corporate environment
        1. System of values: "Priorities"
        2. Team spirit; corporate image
II. Career opportunities
    A. Operations management
        1. Traffic
        2. International trade and corporate customs
        3. Distribution

FIGURE 5.5 Typical Major Components in Business Outlines

Letter or Memo
I. Opening
II. Body
III. Close

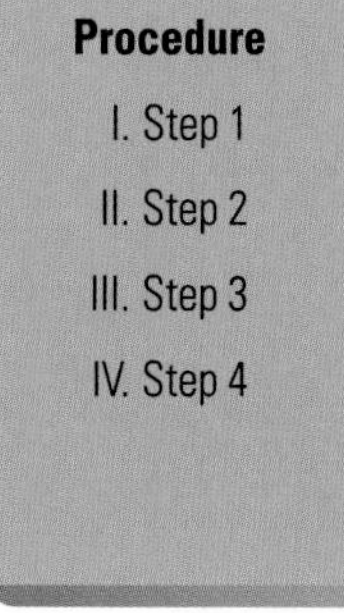

Procedure
I. Step 1
II. Step 2
III. Step 3
IV. Step 4

Informational Report
I. Introduction
II. Facts
III. Summary

Analytical Report
I. Introduction/ problems
II. Facts/finding
III. Conclusions
IV. Recommendations (if requested)

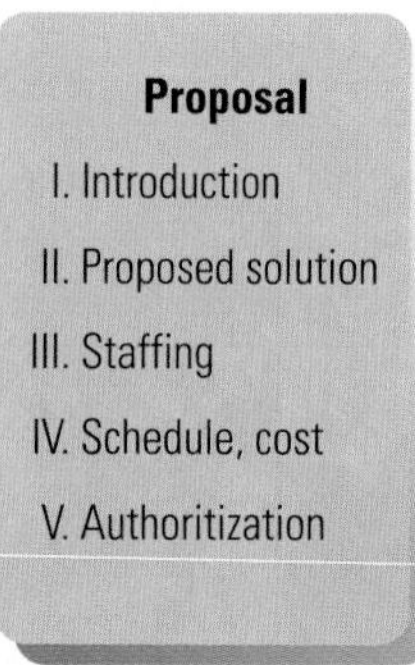

Proposal
I. Introduction
II. Proposed solution
III. Staffing
IV. Schedule, cost
V. Authorization

B. Accounting and finance
    1. General accounting
    2. Internal audit
    3. Treasury and risk management
C. Special opportunities
    1. Management training program
    2. Account executive sales training program
    3. Design studio

Every major category in an outline should have at least two subcategories.

Notice that each major category is divided into at least two subcategories, which in turn are fleshed out with examples, details, statistics, case histories, and other data. In moving from major point to subpoint, you are progressing from large abstract concepts to small concrete ideas. And each subpoint could be further subdivided with more specific illustrations if you desired. You can determine the appropriate amount of detail by considering what your audience (primary and secondary) already knows about the topic and how much persuading you must do.

How you group ideas into components depends on your topic and your channel of communication. The finished Liz Claiborne recruitment brochure, shown on page 133, required careful editing so that each component fit into the page layout. Business documents, on the other hand, do not have rigid page constraints. They usually contain typical components arranged in traditional patterns, as shown in Figure 5.5.

Business messages typically follow either the (1) direct pattern, with the main idea first, or (2) the indirect pattern, with the main idea following explanation and evidence.

Thus far, you've seen how to collect information, generate ideas, and prepare an outline. How you order the information in your outline, though, depends on what pattern or strategy you choose.

Organizing Ideas Into Patterns

3

Two organizational patterns provide plans of action for typical business messages: the direct pattern and the indirect pattern. The primary difference between the two patterns is where the main idea is placed. In the direct pattern the main idea comes first, followed by details, explanation, or evidence. In the indirect pattern the main idea follows the details, explanation, and evidence. The pattern you select is determined by how you expect the audience to react to the message, as shown in Figure 5.6.

FIGURE 5.6 **Audience Response Determines Pattern of Organization**

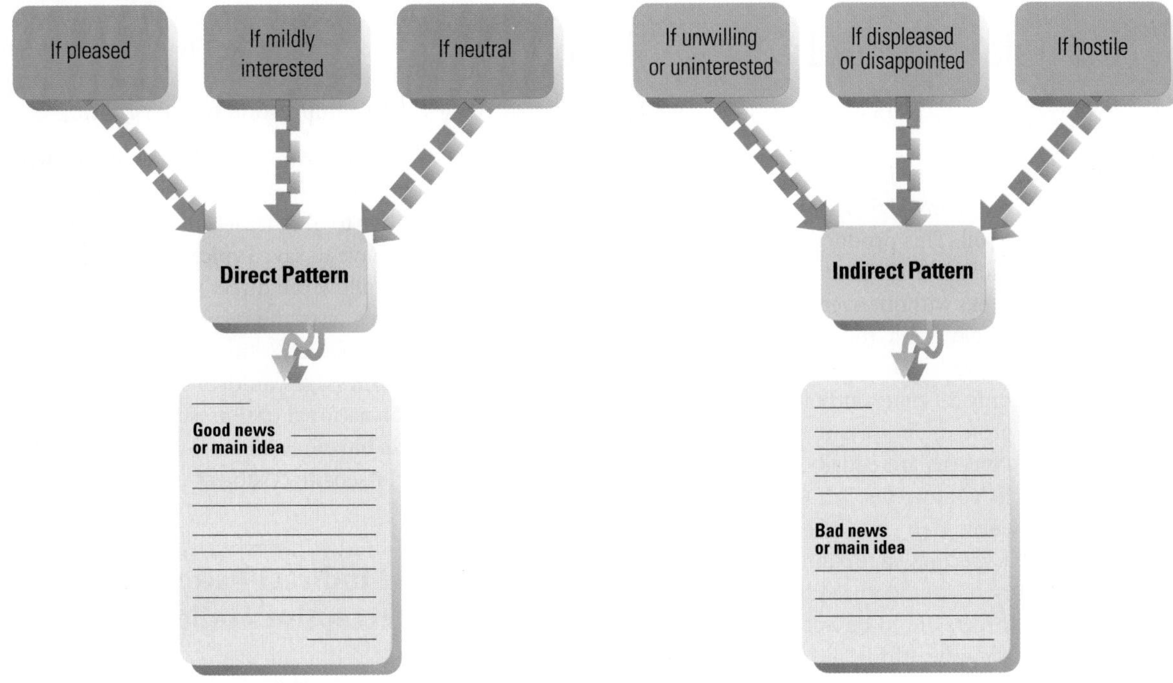

The Direct Pattern for Receptive Audiences

In preparing to write any message, you need to anticipate the audience's reaction to your ideas and frame your message accordingly. When you expect the reader to be pleased, mildly interested, or, at worst, neutral—use the direct pattern. That is, put your main point—the purpose of your message—in the first or second sentence. Compare the direct and indirect patterns in the following memo openings. Notice how long it takes to get to the main idea in the indirect opening.

Indirect Opening

Our company has been concerned with attracting better-qualified prospective job candidates. For this reason, the Management Council has been gathering information about an internship program for college students. After considerable investigation, we have voted to begin a pilot program starting next fall.

Direct Opening

The Management Council has voted to begin a college internship pilot program next fall.

Explanations and details should follow the direct opening. What's important is getting to the main idea quickly. This direct method, also called *frontloading,* has at least three advantages:

Frontloading saves the reader time, establishes the proper frame of mind, and prevents frustration.

- **Saves the reader's time.** Many of today's businesspeople can devote only a few moments to each message. Messages that take too long to get to the point may lose their readers along the way.
- **Sets a proper frame of mind.** Learning the purpose up front helps the reader put the subsequent details and explanations in perspective. Without a clear opening, the reader may be thinking, "Why am I being told this?"

CASE STUDY

PROCESS IN PROGRESS

Liz Claiborne, Inc., Revisited

Stiff competition and consumer demand for ever-lower prices have forced many U.S. apparel manufacturers to shift production off U.S. soil. This production may even be done in sweatshops, such as those in Honduras. The worst sweatshops demand 80-hour work weeks without overtime pay. Bosses routinely shout at workers and may send them home for talking on the job. Women may be fired if they get pregnant or join trade unions. And they earn only 29 cents an hour.

Although profit is important to managers at Liz Claiborne, human rights concerns are equally compelling. To prevent labor abuses among its contractors, Liz Claiborne formulated and distributed a formal written code of conduct in 1994. Among other requirements, it specifies that contractors may not use forced labor (such as prison or indentured labor) or hire anyone under 15 years of age. Workers are to be treated with respect, and working conditions must be healthful and safe. However, Liz Claiborne works with about 250 suppliers in over 28 countries around the world. Enforcing its standards worldwide requires an ongoing effort. When complaints from human rights activists and others arrive, Liz Claiborne must investigate and respond to each inquiry.

Critical Thinking

- When a business communicator responds to an inquiry, such as a letter asking about human rights violations among contractors, is "research" necessary?
- What is the difference between formal and informal research?
- What are some of the best methods for generating ideas about solving a problem?

- **Prevents frustration.** Readers forced to struggle through excessive verbiage before reaching the main idea become frustrated. They resent the writer. Poorly organized messages create a negative impression of the writer.

This frontloading technique works best with audiences that are likely to be receptive to or at least not disagree with what you have to say. Typical business messages that follow the direct pattern include routine requests and responses, orders and acknowledgments, nonsensitive memos, e-mail messages, informational reports, and informational oral presentations. All these tasks have one element in common: none has a sensitive subject that will upset the reader.

The Indirect Pattern for Unreceptive Audiences

When you expect the audience to be uninterested, unwilling, displeased, or perhaps even hostile, the indirect pattern is more appropriate. In this pattern you don't reveal the main idea until after you have offered explanation and evidence. This approach works well with three kinds of messages: (1) bad news, (2) ideas that require persuasion, and (3) sensitive news, especially when being transmitted to superiors. The indirect pattern has these benefits:

The indirect pattern respects the feelings of the audience, facilitates a fair hearing, and minimizes a negative reaction.

- **Respects the feelings of the audience.** Bad news is always painful, but the trauma can be lessened when the receiver is prepared for it.
- **Ensures a fair hearing.** Messages that may upset the reader are more likely to be read when the main idea is delayed. Beginning immediately with a piece of bad news or a persuasive request, for example, may cause the receiver to stop reading or listening.
- **Minimizes the negative reaction.** A reader's overall reaction to a negative message is generally improved if the news is delivered gently.

Typical business messages that could be developed indirectly include letters and memos that refuse requests, deny claims, and disapprove credit. Persuasive requests, sales letters, sensitive messages, and some reports and oral presentations also benefit from the indirect strategy. You'll learn more about how to use the indirect pattern in Chapters 9 and 10.

In summary, business messages may be organized directly, with the main idea first, or indirectly, with the main idea delayed. Although these two patterns cover many communication problems, they should be considered neither universal nor inviolate. Every business transaction is distinct. Some messages are mixed: part good news, part bad; part goodwill, part persuasion. In upcoming chapters you'll practice applying the direct and indirect patterns in typical situations. Then, you'll have the skills and confidence to evaluate communication problems and vary these patterns depending on the goals you wish to achieve.

Composing the First Draft

4

Once you've researched your topic, organized the data, and selected a pattern of organization, you're ready to begin composing. Communicators who haven't completed the preparatory work often suffer from "writer's block" and sit staring at a piece of paper or at the computer screen. It's difficult to get started without organized ideas and a plan. Composition is also easier if you have a quiet environment in which to concentrate. Businesspeople with messages to compose set aside a given time and allow no calls, visitors, or other interruptions. This is a good technique for students as well.

When composing the first draft, write quickly and save revision for later.

As you begin composing, keep in mind that you are writing the first draft, not the final copy. Experts suggest that you write quickly (*sprint writing*). Get your thoughts down now and refine them in later versions.[4] As you take up each idea, imagine that you are talking to the reader. Don't let yourself get bogged down. If you can't think of the right word, insert a substitute or type "find perfect word later."[5] Sprint writing works especially well for those composing on a computer because it's simple to make changes at any point of the composition process. If you are handwriting the first draft, double-space so that you have room for changes.

Creating Effective Sentences

Sentences must have subjects and verbs and must make sense.

As you create your first draft, you'll be working at the sentence level of composition. Although you've used sentences all your life, you may be unaware of how they can be shaped and arranged to express your ideas most effectively. First, let's review some basic sentence elements.

Complete sentences have subjects and verbs and make sense.

SUBJECT VERB — SUBJECT VERB

This report is clear and concise. Our employees write many reports.

Clauses have subjects and verbs, but phrases do not.

Clauses and phrases, the key building blocks of sentences, are related groups of words. Clauses have subjects and verbs; phrases do not.

PHRASE — PHRASE

The CEO of that organization sent a letter to our staff.

PHRASE — PHRASE

By reading carefully, we learned about the merger.

CLAUSE — CLAUSE

Because she writes well, Tracy answers most customer letters.

CLAUSE — CLAUSE

If we accumulate too many letters, we assign other writers.

Independent clauses may stand alone; dependent clauses may not.

Clauses may be divided into two groups: independent and dependent. Independent clauses are grammatically complete. Dependent clauses depend for their meaning on independent clauses. In the two preceding examples the clauses beginning with *If* and *Because* are dependent. Dependent clauses are often introduced by words such as *if, when, because,* and *as.*

INDEPENDENT CLAUSE
Tracy uses simple language.

DEPENDENT CLAUSE — INDEPENDENT CLAUSE
When she writes to customers, Tracy uses simple language.

By learning to distinguish phrases, independent clauses, and dependent clauses, you'll be able to punctuate sentences correctly and avoid three basic sentence faults: the fragment, the run-on sentence, and the comma splice. In Appendix A, we examine these writing problems in greater detail. For now, however, let's look at some ways to make your sentences more readable.

Effective sentences are short and stress important ideas.

Using Short Sentences. Because your goal is to communicate clearly, you're better off limiting your sentences to about 20 or fewer words. The American Press Institute reports that reader comprehension drops off markedly as sentences become longer.[6] Thus, in crafting your sentences, think about the relationship between sentence length and comprehension:

Sentences of 20 or fewer words have the most impact.

Sentence Length	Comprehension Rate
8 words	100%
15 words	90%
19 words	80%
28 words	50%

Instead of stringing together clauses with *and, but,* and *however,* break some of those complex sentences into separate segments. Business readers want to grasp ideas immediately. They can do that best when thoughts are separated into short sentences. On the other hand, too many monotonous short sentences will sound "grammar schoolish" and may bore or even annoy the reader. Strive for a balance between longer sentences and shorter ones. Your computer probably can point out long sentences and give you an average sentence length.

Emphasizing Important Ideas. You can stress prominent ideas in three ways. The first is to place an important idea at the beginning of a sentence. Notice how the following sentence obscures the date of the meeting by burying it: *All production and administrative personnel will meet May 23, at which time we will announce a new plan of salary incentives.* To emphasize the date, start the sentence with it: *On May 23 all personnel will meet . . .* A secondary position of importance is the end of a sentence: *All personnel will meet to discuss salary incentives on May 23.* Remember this guideline when composing paragraphs as well; put the main idea at the start and then follow up with supporting material.

A second way to emphasize an important idea is to be sure that it acts as the subject in a sentence. Notice the difference between the sentences *Michelle wrote the environmental report* and *The environmental report was written by Michelle.* Michelle receives the emphasis in the first version; the report receives it in the second.

A third way to emphasize an idea is to place it in a short sentence. Important ideas can get lost when enveloped by numerous competing words. How quickly can

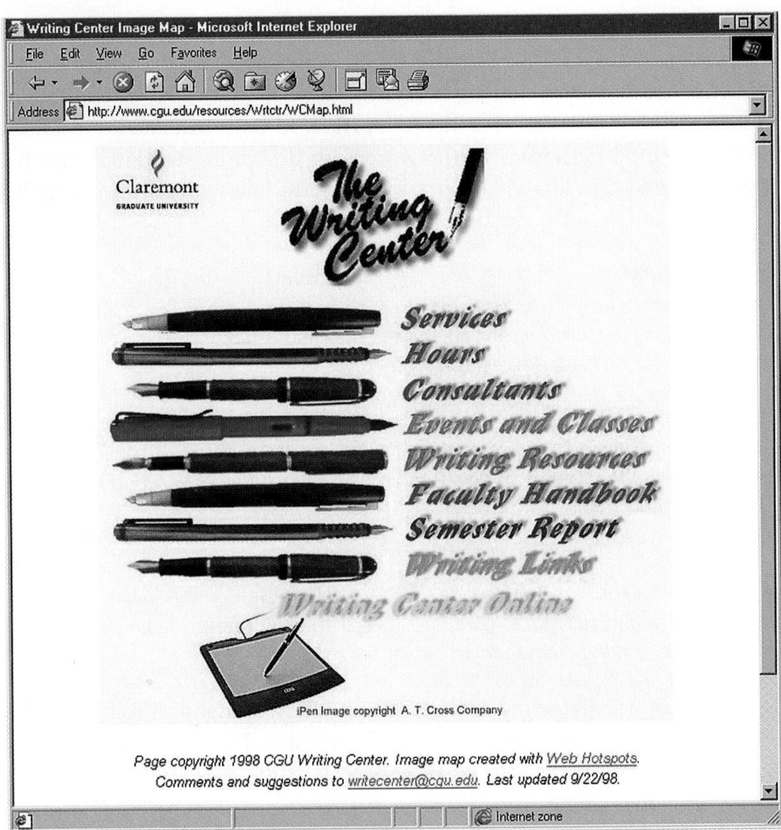

Many educational institutions provide on-line writing laboratories (OWLs) that offer "handouts" with grammar and writing tips as well as links to writing resources. Some even work with students on-line to solve writing problems. Links to favorite writing labs are available at the Guffey Student Web site **<www.meguffey.com>**.

you grasp the important idea in this sentence? *This announcement is to inform all employees and guests that the hotel's restaurant will be closed Thanksgiving Day, although we do plan to resume restaurant services Friday at 7 a.m.* To give impact to the main idea, present it in a short sentence: *The hotel's restaurant will be closed Thanksgiving Day.* Then, provide explanations and details.

Active-voice sentences are direct and easy to understand.

Using the Active Voice. In the active voice the subject performs the action: *Brandon selected new computers.* In the passive voice the subject receives the action: *New computers were selected by Brandon.* Passive-voice sentences deemphasize the performer of the action. The performer is in a phrase (*by Brandon*) or is totally absent (*New computers were selected*). If you suspect that a verb is passive but you're not sure, try the "by whom?" test: *New computers were selected [by whom?].* If you can fill in the performer of the action, the sentence is probably passive. What difference does it make if the verb is active or passive? Active-voice sentences are more direct because they reveal the performer immediately. They're easier to understand and shorter. Most business writing should be in the active voice.

Passive-voice sentences are useful for tact and to direct attention to actions instead of people.

Using the Passive Voice Selectively. Although we prefer active verbs in business writing, passive verbs are useful in certain instances. For example, when the performer is unknown or insignificant, use passive voice: *Drug tests are given to all applicants.* Who performs the drug tests is unimportant. You can also use the passive voice to tactfully deflect attention away from the people involved: *Three totals were calculated incorrectly.* Notice that this sentence stresses the problem while concealing the person who committed the error.

Avoiding Dangling and Misplaced Modifiers. For clarity, modifiers must be close to the words they describe or limit. A modifier dangles when the word or phrase it describes is missing from its sentence. A modifier is misplaced when the word or phrase it describes is not close enough to be clear. In both instances, the solution is to position the modifier closer to the word(s) it describes or limits. Introductory verbal phrases are particularly dangerous; be sure to follow them immediately with the words they can logically describe or modify.

Dangling Modifier	**Improved**
To win the lottery, a ticket must be purchased. (*The introductory verbal phrase must be followed by a logical subject.*)	To win the lottery, you must purchase a ticket.
Driving through Malibu Canyon, the ocean suddenly came into view. (*Is the ocean driving through Malibu Canyon?*)	As we drove through Malibu Canyon, the ocean suddenly came into view.
Speaking before the large audience, my knees began to knock. (*Are your knees making a speech?*)	Speaking before the large audience, I felt my knees begin to knock.

Try this trick for detecting and remedying these dangling modifiers. Ask the question *who?* or *what?* after any introductory phrase. The words immediately following should tell the reader *who* or *what* is performing the action. Try the "who?" test on the previous danglers.

Misplaced Modifier	**Improved**
Seeing his error too late, the envelope was immediately resealed by Mark. (*Did the envelope see the error?*)	Seeing his error too late, Mark immediately resealed the envelope.
A wart appeared on my left hand that I want removed. (*Is the left hand to be removed?*)	A wart that I want removed appeared on my left hand.
The busy personnel director interviewed only candidates who had excellent computer skills in the morning. (*Were the candidates skilled only in the morning?*)	In the morning the busy personnel director interviewed only candidates who had excellent computer skills.

5 Drafting Meaningful Paragraphs

From composing sentences, we progress to paragraphs. A paragraph is one or more sentences designated as a separate thought group. To avoid muddled paragraphs, writers must recognize basic paragraph elements, conventional sentence patterns, and ways to organize sentences into one of three classic paragraph patterns. They must also be able to polish their paragraphs by linking sentences and using transitional expressions.

Discussing One Topic. Well-constructed paragraphs discuss only one topic. They reveal the primary idea in a main sentence that usually, but not always, appears first.

Other ideas, connected logically with transitional expressions (verbal road signs), support or illustrate that idea.

Effective paragraphs focus on one topic, link ideas to build coherence, and use transitional devices to enhance coherence.

Organizing Sentences into Paragraphs. Paragraphs are generally composed of three kinds of sentences:[7]

- **Main sentence:** expresses the primary idea of the paragraph.
- **Supporting sentence:** illustrates, explains, or strengthens the primary idea.
- **Limiting sentence:** opposes the primary idea by suggesting a negative or contrasting thought; may precede or follow the main sentence.

These sentences may be arranged in three classic paragraph plans: direct, pivoting, and indirect.

Using the Direct Paragraph Plan. Paragraphs arranged in the direct plan begin with the main sentence, followed by supporting sentences. Most business messages use this paragraph plan because it clarifies the subject immediately. This plan is useful whenever you must define (a new product or procedure), classify (parts of a whole), illustrate (an idea), or describe (a process). Simply start with the main sentence; then strengthen and amplify that idea with supporting ideas, as shown here:

The direct paragraph pattern is appropriate when defining, classifying, illustrating, or describing.

Main Sentence	A social audit is a report on the social performance of a company.
Supporting Sentences	Such a report may be conducted by the company itself or by outsiders who evaluate the company's efforts to produce safe products, engage in socially responsible activities, and protect the environment. Many companies publish the results of their social audits in their annual reports. Ben & Jerry's Homemade, for example, devotes a major portion of its annual report to its social audit. The report discusses Ben & Jerry's efforts to support environmental restoration. Moreover, it describes workplace safety, employment equality, and peace programs.

You can alter the direct plan by adding a limiting sentence if necessary. Be sure, though, that you follow with sentences that return to the main idea and support it, as shown here:

Main Sentence	Flexible work scheduling could immediately increase productivity and enhance employee satisfaction in our entire organization.
Limiting Sentence	Such scheduling, however, is impossible for all employees.
Supporting Sentences	Managers would be required to maintain their regular hours. For many other employees, though, flexible scheduling permits extra time to manage family responsibilities. Feeling less stress, employees are able to focus their attention better at work; hence they become more relaxed and more productive.

Using the Pivoting Paragraph Plan. Paragraphs arranged in the pivoting plan start with a limiting sentence that offers a contrasting or negative idea before delivering the main sentence. Notice in the following example how two limiting sentences

The pivoting paragraph pattern is appropriate when comparing and contrasting.

about drawbacks to foreign service careers open the paragraph; only then do the main and supporting sentences describing rewards in foreign service appear. The pivoting plan is especially useful for comparing and contrasting ideas. In using the pivoting plan, be sure you emphasize the turn in direction with an obvious *but* or *however.*

Limiting Sentences	Foreign service careers are certainly not for everyone. Many are in remote countries where harsh climates, health hazards, security risks, and other discomforts exist.
Main Sentence	However, careers in the foreign service offer special rewards for the special people who qualify.
Supporting Sentences	Foreign service employees enjoy the pride and satisfaction of representing the United States abroad. They relish frequent travel, enriching cultural and social experiences in living abroad, and action-oriented work.

The indirect paragraph pattern is appropriate when delivering bad news or when persuasion is necessary.

Using the Indirect Paragraph Plan. Paragraphs arranged in the indirect plan start with the supporting sentences and conclude with the main sentence. This useful plan enables you to build a rationale, a foundation of reasons, before hitting the audience with a big idea—possibly one that is bad news. It enables you to explain your reasons and then in the final sentence draw a conclusion from them. In the following example the vice president of a large accounting firm begins by describing the trend toward casual dress and concludes with a recommendation that his firm change its dress code. This indirect plan works well for describing causes followed by an effect.

Supporting Sentences	According to a recent poll, more than half of all white-collar workers are now dressing casually at work. Many high-tech engineers and professional specialists have given up suits and ties, favoring khakis and sweaters instead. In our own business our consultants say they stand out like "sore thumbs" because they are attired in traditional buttoned-down styles, while the businesspeople they visit are usually wearing comfortable, casual clothing.
Main Sentence	Therefore, I recommend that we establish an optional "business casual" policy allowing consultants to dress casually, if they wish, as they perform their duties both in and out of the office.

You'll learn more techniques for implementing direct and indirect writing strategies when you prepare letters, memos, e-mail messages, reports, and oral presentations in subsequent chapters.

Coherent paragraphs link ideas by sustaining the main idea, using pronouns, dovetailing sentences, and using transitional expressions.

Linking Ideas to Build Coherence. Paragraphs are coherent when ideas are linked, that is, when one idea leads logically to the next. Well-written paragraphs take the reader through a number of steps. When the author skips from Step 1 to Step 3 and forgets Step 2, the reader is lost. You can use several techniques to keep the reader in step with your ideas.

Sustaining the Key Idea. This involves simply repeating a key expression or using a similar one. For example:

FIGURE 5.7 Transitional Expressions to Build Coherence

To Add or Strengthen	To Show Time or Order	To Clarify	To Show Cause and Effect	To Contradict	To Contrast
additionally	after	for example	accordingly	actually	as opposed to
again	before	for instance	as a result	but	at the same time
also	earlier	I mean	consequently	however	by contrast
besides	finally	in other words	for this reason	in fact	conversely
likewise	first	that is	so	instead	on the contrary
moreover	meanwhile	this means	therefore	rather	on the other hand
further	next	thus	thus	still	
furthermore	now	to put it another way	under the circumstances	though	
	previously			yet	

Our philosophy holds that every customer is really a guest. All new employees to our theme parks are trained to treat *guests* as *VIPs*. These *VIPs* are never told what they can or cannot do.

Notice how the repetition of *guest* and *VIP* connects ideas.

Using Pronouns. Familiar pronouns, such as *we, they, he, she,* and *it,* help build continuity, as do demonstrative pronouns, such as *this, that, these,* and *those.* These words confirm that something under discussion is still being discussed. For example:

Using pronouns strategically helps build coherence and continuity.

All new park employees receive a two-week orientation. They learn that every staffer has a vital role in preparing for the show. This training includes how to maintain enthusiasm.

Be careful with *this, that, these,* and *those,* however. These words usually need a noun with them to make their meaning absolutely clear. In the last example notice how confusing *this* becomes if the word *training* is omitted.

Dovetailing Sentences. Sentences are "dovetailed" when an idea at the end of one connects with an idea at the beginning of the next. For example:

Dovetailing sentences means connecting ending and beginning ideas.

New hosts and hostesses learn about the theme park and its *facilities.* These *facilities* include telephones, food services, bathrooms, and attractions, as well as the location of *offices.* Knowledge of administrative *offices* and internal workings of the company, such as who's who in administration, ensures that staffers will be able to *serve guests* fully. *Serving guests,* of course, is our number one priority.

Dovetailing of sentences is especially helpful with dense, difficult topics. This technique, however, should not be overused.

Using Transitional Expressions to Build Coherence. Transitional expressions are another excellent device for achieving paragraph coherence. These words, some of which are shown in Figure 5.7, act as verbal road signs to readers and listeners. Transitional expressions enable the receiver to anticipate what's coming, to reduce

Transitional expressions help readers anticipate what's coming, reduce uncertainty, and speed comprehension.

uncertainty, and to speed up comprehension. They signal that a train of thought is moving forward, being developed, possibly detouring, or ending. Transitions are especially helpful in persuasive writing.

As Figure 5.7 shows, transitions can add or strengthen a thought, show time or order, clarify ideas, show cause and effect, contradict thoughts, and contrast ideas. Thus, you must be careful to select the best transition for your purpose. Look back at the examples of direct, pivoted, and indirect paragraphs to see how transitional expressions and other devices build paragraph coherence. Remember that coherence in communication rarely happens spontaneously; it requires effort and skill.

Paragraphs with fewer than eight lines are inviting and readable.

Composing Short Paragraphs. Although no rule regulates the length of paragraphs, business writers recognize the value of short paragraphs. Paragraphs with fewer than eight lines look inviting and readable, whereas long, solid chunks of print appear formidable. If a topic can't be covered in fewer than eight printed lines (not sentences), consider breaking it up into smaller segments.

The following checklist summarizes the key points of writing a first draft.

Checklist for Composing Sentences and Paragraphs

For Effective Sentences

 **Use short sentences.** Keep in mind that sentences with fewer than 20 words are easier to read. Use longer sentences occasionally, but rely primarily on short sentences.

 **Emphasize important ideas.** Place main ideas at the beginning of short sentences for emphasis.

 **Apply active and passive verbs carefully.** Use active verbs (*She sent the e-mail* instead of *The e-mail was sent by her*) most frequently; they immediately identify the doer. Use passive verbs to be tactful, to emphasize an action, or to conceal the performer.

 **Eliminate misplaced modifiers.** Be sure that introductory verbal phrases are followed by the words that can logically be modified. To check the placement of modifiers, ask *who?* or *what?* after such phrases.

For Meaningful Paragraphs

 **Develop one idea.** Use main, supporting, and limiting sentences to develop a single idea within each paragraph.

 **Use the direct plan.** Start most paragraphs with the main sentence followed by supporting sentences. This direct plan is useful in defining, classifying, illustrating, and describing.

 **Use the pivoting plan.** To compare and contrast ideas, start with a limiting sentence; then, present the main sentence followed by supporting sentences.

 **Use the indirect plan.** To explain reasons or causes first, start with supporting sentences. Build to the conclusion with the main sentence at the end of the paragraph.

CASE STUDY

PROCESS TO PRODUCT

Applying Your Skills at Liz Claiborne, Inc.

Liz Claiborne, Inc., strives to do business ethically. As its Web site declares, "That includes promoting fair and just treatment for all those who produce our products." Officials feel they are making real progress in preventing labor abuses and human rights violations. However, the issue is complicated by cultural and economic differences, as well as by distance. The real problem boils down to convincing suppliers that Liz Claiborne is serious about enforcing its code of conduct. Although all contractors receive the code, not all share this information with workers. To see the code, access the site map and click on "Workers' Rights" at **<www.lizclaiborne.com>**.

Your Job

Your boss at Liz Claiborne has a brilliant idea. Why not develop a Spanish-language video explaining the company's policies and give it directly to workers who manufacture the clothing? But your boss is going out of the country for two weeks and dumps the project in your lap. Before leaving, she asks you and your staff to generate ideas for the project. She fully expects to develop the content of the video when she returns, but in the meantime she wants you to get started. In small groups brainstorm for ideas about where you can collect information for this project. Based on what you learned in this chapter, list possible sources of information from informal research. Your instructor may further ask you to brainstorm about potential problems in developing this video. If directed, make a cluster diagram showing the results of your brainstorming.

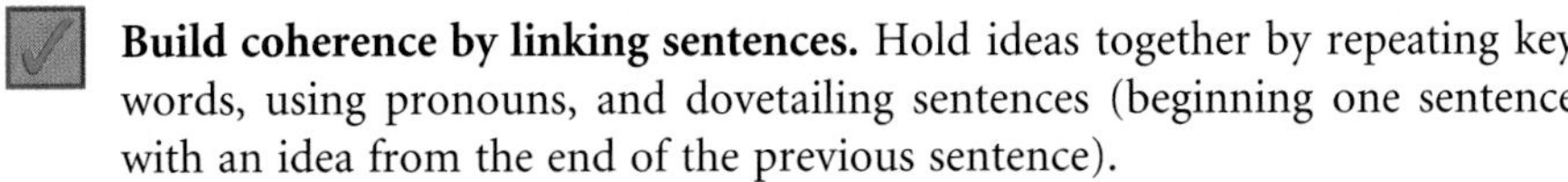

- ✓ **Build coherence by linking sentences.** Hold ideas together by repeating key words, using pronouns, and dovetailing sentences (beginning one sentence with an idea from the end of the previous sentence).
- ✓ **Provide road signs with transitional expressions.** Use verbal signals to help the audience know where the idea is going. Words like *moreover, accordingly, as a result,* and *thus* function as idea pointers.
- ✓ **Limit paragraph length.** Remember that paragraphs with fewer than eight printed lines look inviting. Consider breaking up longer paragraphs if necessary.

Summary of Learning Objectives

1 **Contrast formal and informal methods for researching data and generating ideas.** Formal research for long reports and complex problems may involve searching library data manually or electronically, as well as conducting interviews, surveys, focus groups, and experiments. Informal research for routine tasks may include looking in company files, talking with your boss, interviewing the target audience, conducting informal surveys, brainstorming for ideas, and cluster diagramming.

2 **Specify how to organize data into lists and alphanumeric or decimal outlines.** One method for organizing data in simple messages is to list the main topics to be discussed. Organizing more complex messages usually requires an outline. To prepare an outline, divide the main topic into three to five major components. Break the components into subpoints consisting of details, illustrations, and evidence. For an alphanumeric outline arrange items using Roman numerals (I, II), capital letters (A, B), and numbers (1, 2). For a decimal outline show the ordering of ideas with decimals (1., 1.1, 1.1.1).

3 **Compare direct and indirect patterns for organizing ideas.** The direct pattern places the main idea first. This pattern is useful when audiences will be pleased, mildly interested, or neutral. It saves the reader's time, sets the proper frame of mind, and prevents reader frustration. The indirect pattern places the main idea after explanations. This pattern is useful for audiences that will be unwilling, displeased, or hostile. It respects the feelings of the audience, encourages a fair hearing, and minimizes negative reactions.

4 **Discuss composing the first draft of a message, focusing on techniques for creating effective sentences.** Compose the first draft of a message in a quiet environment where you won't be interrupted. Compose quickly, preferably at a computer. Plan to revise. As you compose, remember that sentences are most effective when they are short (under 20 words). A main idea may be emphasized by making it the sentence subject, placing it first, and removing competing ideas. Effective sentences use active verbs, although passive verbs may be necessary for tact or deemphasis. Effective sentences avoid dangling and misplaced modifiers.

5 **Define a paragraph and describe three classic paragraph plans and techniques for composing meaningful paragraphs.** A paragraph consists of one or more sentences designated as a separate thought group. Typical paragraphs follow one of three plans. Direct paragraphs (main sentence followed by supporting sentences) are useful to define, classify, illustrate, and describe. Pivoting paragraphs (limiting sentence followed by main sentence and supporting sentences) are useful to compare and contrast. Indirect paragraphs (supporting sentences followed by main sentence) build a rationale and foundation of ideas before presenting the main idea. Paragraphs may be improved through the use of coherence techniques and transitional expressions.

CHAPTER REVIEW

1. How does a writer "brainstorm"? (Obj. 1)
2. What is a cluster diagram, and when might it be useful? (Obj. 1)
3. Describe an alphanumeric outline. (Obj. 2)
4. What is the relationship between the major categories in an outline and those in a report written from the outline? (Obj. 2)
5. Distinguish between the direct and indirect patterns of organization for typical business messages. (Obj. 3)
6. Why should most messages be "frontloaded"? (Obj. 3)
7. List some business messages that should be frontloaded and some that should not be frontloaded. (Obj. 3)
8. Why should writers plan for revision? How can they do it? (Obj. 4)
9. Distinguish an independent clause from a dependent clause. Give examples. (Obj. 4)
10. Name three ways to emphasize important ideas in sentences. (Obj. 4)
11. Distinguish between active-voice sentences and passive-voice sentences. Give examples. (Obj. 4)
12. Give an original example of a dangling or misplaced modifier. Why are introductory verbal phrases dangerous? (Obj. 4)
13. Describe three kinds of sentences used to develop ideas in paragraphs. (Obj. 5)
14. Describe three paragraph plans. Identify the uses for each. (Obj. 5)
15. What is coherence, and how is it achieved? (Obj. 5)

CRITICAL THINKING

1. Why is cluster diagramming considered an intuitive process while outlining is considered an analytical process? (Obj. 1)
2. Why is audience analysis so important in choosing the direct or indirect pattern of organization for a business message? (Obj. 3)
3. In what ways do you imagine that writing on the job differs from the writing you do in your academic studies? Consider process as well as product. (Obj. 1)
4. Why are short sentences and short paragraphs appropriate for business communication? (Obj. 4)
5. **Ethical Issue:** Discuss the ethics of the indirect pattern of organization. Is it manipulative to delay presentation of the main idea in a message?

ACTIVITIES

5.1 Document for Analysis (Objs. 3, 4 and 5)

First, read the following memo to see if you can understand what the writer requests from all Southeast Division employees. Then, discuss why this memo is so hard to read. How long are the sentences? How many passive-voice constructions can you locate? How effective is the paragraphing? Can you spot four dangling or misplaced modifiers? In the next activity you'll improve the organization of this message.

TO: All Southeast Division Employees

[1]Personal computers and all the software to support these computers are appearing on many desks of Southeast Division employees. [2]After giving the matter considerable attention, it has been determined by the Systems Development Department (SDD) that more control should be exerted in coordinating the purchase of hardware and software to improve compatibility throughout the division so that a library of resources may be developed. [3]Therefore, a plan has been developed by SDD that should be followed in making all future equipment selections and purchases. [4]To make the best possible choice, SDD should be contacted as you begin your search because questions about personal computers, word processing programs, hardware, and software can be answered by our knowledgeable staff, who can also provide you with invaluable assistance in making the best choice for your needs at the best possible cost.

[5]After your computer and its software arrive, all your future software purchases should be channeled through SDD. [6]To actually make your initial purchase, a written proposal and a purchase request form must be presented to SDD for approval. [7]A need for the purchase must be established; benefits that you expect to derive resulting from its purchase must be analyzed and presented, and an itemized statement of all costs must be submitted. [8]By following these new procedures, coordinated purchasing benefits will be realized by all employees. [9]I may be reached at X466 if you have any questions.

5.2 Organizing Data (Obj. 2)

Use either a cluster diagram or an outline to organize the garbled message in Activity 5.1. Beyond the opening and closing of the message, what are the three main points the writer is trying to make? Should this message use the direct pattern or the indirect pattern? Your instructor may ask you to discuss how this entire message could be revised or to actually rewrite it.

5.3 Collaborative Brainstorming (Obj. 1)

In teams of four or five, analyze a problem on your campus such as the following: unavailable classes, unrealistic degree requirements, lack of student intern programs, poor parking facilities, inadequate registration process, lack of diversity among students on campus, and so forth. Use brainstorming techniques to generate ideas that clarify the problem and explore its solutions. Each team member should prepare a cluster diagram to record the ideas generated. Either individually or as a team, organize the ideas into an outline with three to five main points and numerous subpoints. Assume that your ideas will become part of a letter to be sent to an appropriate campus official or to your campus newspaper discussing the problem and your solution.

5.4 Individual Brainstorming (Objs. 1 and 2)

Critical Thinking

Analyze a problem that exists where you work or go to school, such as long lines at the copy or fax machines, overuse of express mail services, understaffing during peak customer service hours, poor scheduling of employees, inferior or inflexible benefit package, outdated office or other equipment, or one of the campus problems discussed in Activity 5.3. Select a problem about which you have some knowledge. Assume your boss or department chair wants you to submit a short report analyzing the problem. Prepare a cluster diagram to develop ideas. Then, organize the ideas into an outline with three to five main points and numerous subpoints.

5.5 Outlining (Obj. 2)

The following topics will be part of a report that a consultant is submitting to a group of investors who requested information about starting a new radio station in Scottsdale, Arizona. Arrange the topics into a coherent alphanumeric outline. Clue: the items are already in the right order.

Problem: determining program format for new radio station KFSD-FM

Background: current radio formats available to listeners in Scottsdale

Background: demographics of target area (population, age, sex, income)

Survey results: music preferences

Survey finds that top two favorites are easy listening and soft rock

Next two favorites are country and rock

Other kinds of music mentioned in survey: classical, jazz

Survey results: newscast preferences

News emphasis: respondents prefer primarily national news but with some local items

Respondents say yes to news but only short, hourly newscasts

Analysis of findings: discussion of all findings in greater detail

Recommendations: hybrid format combining easy listening and soft rock

Recommendations: news in 3- to 5-minute newscasts hourly; cover national news but include local flavor

We recommend starting new station immediately.

5.6 Collaborative Letter (Objs. 3–5)

Team

Divide into teams of three to five people who have similar majors. Work together to compose an inquiry letter requesting career information from someone in your field. Include questions about technical and general courses to take, possible starting salaries, good companies to apply to, technical skills required, necessary interpersonal skills, computer tools currently used, and tips for getting started in the field. Although this is a small project, your team can work more harmoniously if you apply some of the suggestions from Chapter 2. For example, appoint a meeting leader, recorder, and evaluator.

Your instructor may vary this project by asking teams to compose group letters to campus administrators discussing problems on campus; to newspaper editors reacting to news items or editorial positions; or to local, state, or federal elected officials discussing policies that you support or oppose.

5.7 Sentence Elements (Obj. 4)

In the following sentences underscore and identify dependent clauses (DC), independent clauses (IC), and phrases (P). Circle subjects and verbs in clauses.

- **a.** We watched a television commercial, and the food looked delicious.
- **b.** Although it looks delicious, the food in commercials often is inedible.
- **c.** Food stylists use amazing techniques to create vivid colors and textures.
- **d.** When viewers see ice cream, they probably are looking at a mixture of lard, powdered sugar, and food coloring.

e. For each plate of food filmed, stylists have typically prepared 20 plates.

5.8 Sentence Length (Obj. 4)

Break the following sentences into shorter sentences. Use appropriate transitional expressions.

a. If firms have a substantial investment in original research or development of new products, they should consider protecting those products with patents, although all patents eventually expire and what were once trade secrets can become common knowledge in the industry.

b. As soon as consumers recognize a name associated with a product or service, that name is entitled to legal protection as a trademark; in fact, consumers may even create a trademark where none existed or create a second trademark by using a nickname as a source indicator, such as the name "Coke," which was legally protected even before it had ever been used by the company.

c. Although no magic formula exists for picking a good trademark name, firms should avoid picking the first name that pops into someone's head; moreover, they should be aware that unique and arbitrary marks are best, while descriptive terms such as "car" or "TV repair" are useless, and surnames and geographic names are weak because they lack distinction and exclusivity.

5.9 Active and Passive Voice (Obj. 4)

In the following sentences convert passive-voice verbs to active-voice verbs. Add subjects if necessary. Be prepared to discuss which sentence version is more effective.

a. A decision to focus on customer service was made by the board.

b. First, the product line was examined to determine if it met customers' needs.

c. In the past, products had been built to the company's internal expectations of market needs.

d. When it was realized that changes were in order, a new product line was designed.

e. After just-in-time inventory procedures were introduced, our inventories were cut in half.

f. Our company was recently named "Vendor of the Year" by Texas Instruments.

Now convert active-voice verbs to passive-voice verbs, and be prepared to discuss which sentence version is more effective.

g. We cannot authorize repair of your VCR since you have allowed the warranty period to expire.

h. I cannot give you a cash refund for merchandise that you purchased over 60 days ago.

i. Kaiser Hospital does not accept patients who are not members.

j. You must submit all reports by Friday at 5 p.m.

k. Joan added the two columns instead of subtracting them, thus producing the incorrect total.

5.10 Dangling and Misplaced Modifiers (Obj. 4)

Remedy any dangling or misplaced modifiers in the following sentences. Add subjects as needed, but retain the introductory phrases. Mark "C" if correct.

a. To stay in touch with customers, telephone contacts were encouraged among all sales reps.

b. By making sales reps a part of product design, a great deal of money was saved.

c. Acting as president, the contract was immediately signed by Rachel.

d. To receive a bachelor's degree, complete 120 units of study. (*Tricky!*)

e. Noxious fumes made the office workers sick coming from the storage tanks of a nearby paint manufacturer.

f. Using available evidence, it becomes apparent that the court has been deceived by the witness.

g. Having found the misplaced report, the search was ended.

h. The presidential candidate announced his intentions to run as a national candidate in his hometown of Blue Bell, Pennsylvania.

i. Although T-Mart is a self-service department store, every effort is made to give customers personalized, patient service. (*Tricky!*)

j. Ignoring the warning prompt on the screen, the computer was turned off resulting in the loss of data.

5.11 Transitional Expressions (Obj. 5)

Add transitional expressions to the following sentences to improve the flow of ideas (coherence).

a. Computer style checkers rank somewhere between artificial intelligence and artificial ignorance. They are like clever children: smart but not wise. Business writers should be fully aware of the limitations and the usefulness of style checkers.

b. Our computerized file includes all customer data. It provides space for name, address, and other vital information. It has an area for comments, a feature that comes in handy and helps us keep our records up-to-date.

c. No one likes to turn out poor products. We began highlighting recurring problems. Employees make a special effort to be more careful in doing their work right the first time. It doesn't have to be returned to them for corrections.

d. In-depth employment interviews may be structured or unstructured. Structured interviews have little flexibility. All candidates are asked the same questions in the same order. Unstructured interviews allow a free-flowing conversation. Topics are prepared for discussion by the interviewer.

e. Fringe benefits consist of life, health, and dental insurance. Some fringe benefits might include paid vacations and sick pay. Other fringe benefits include holidays, funeral leave, and emergency leave. Paid lunch, rest periods, tuition reimbursement, and child care are also sometimes provided.

f. Service was less than perfect for many months. We lacked certain intangibles. We didn't have the customer-specific data that we needed. We made the mistake of removing all localized, person-to-person coverage. We are returning to decentralized customer contacts.

5.12 Paragraph Organization (Obj. 5)

The following poorly written paragraphs follow the indirect plan. Locate the main sentence in each paragraph. Then revise each paragraph so that it is organized directly. Improve coherence by using the techniques described in this chapter.

a. Many of our customers limp through their business despite problems with their disk drives, printers, and peripherals. We cannot service their disk drives, printers, and peripherals. These customers are unable to go without this equipment long enough for the repair. We've learned that there are two times when we can get to that equipment. We can do our repairs in the middle of the night or on Sunday. All of our staff of technicians now works every Sunday. Please authorize additional budget for my department to hire technicians for night and weekend service hours.

b. Air express is one of the ways SturdyBilt power mowers and chain saws may be delivered. Air express promises two-day delivery but at a considerable cost. The cheapest method is for retailers to pick up shipments themselves at our nearest distribution center. We have distribution centers in St. Louis, Phoenix, and Los Angeles. Another option involves having our trucks deliver the shipment from our distribution center to the retailer's door for an additional fee. These are the options SturdyBilt provides for the retailers purchasing our products.

C.L.U.E. REVIEW 5

Edit the following sentences to correct faults in grammar, punctuation, spelling, and word use.

1. Although, we formally used a neighborhood printer for all our print jobs we are now saving almost five hundred dollars a month by using desktop publishing.
2. Powerful softwear however cannot garantee a good final product.
3. To develop a better sense of design we collected desireable samples from: books, magazines, brochures, and newsletters.
4. We noticed that, poorly-designed projects often was filled with cluttered layouts, incompatible typefaces, and to many typefaces.
5. Our layout design are usually formal but ocasionally we use an informal layout design which is shown in figure six.
6. We usually prefer a black and white design; because color printing is much more costly.
7. Expensive color printing jobs are sent to foreign countries, for example china Italy and Japan.
8. Jeffreys article which he entitled "The Shaping of a corporate image" was excepted for publication in "the journal of communication."
9. Every employee will persenally receive a copy of his Performance Evaluation which the President said will be the principle basis for promotion.
10. We will print three hundred and fifty copies of the newsletter, to be sent to whomever is currently listed in our database.

CHAPTER • 6 •

Revising Business Messages

LEARNING OBJECTIVES

1. Identify revision techniques that make a document clear, conversational, and concise.

2. Describe revision tactics that make a document vigorous and direct.

3. Discuss revision strategies that improve readability.

4. List problem areas that good proofreaders examine carefully.

5. Compare the proofreading of routine and complex documents.

6. Evaluate a message to judge its success.

CASE STUDY

COMMUNICATION IN PROCESS

Spanish-Speaking Chihuahua Sparks Overhaul of Taco Bell Menu

Taco Bell's low-priced Mexican fast-food menu wasn't drawing much consumer traffic until a little Spanish-speaking Chihuahua entered the picture. Suddenly people began lining up for tacos and burritos. The hip little spokespooch with the downtrodden attitude became a hero to underdogs from coast to coast, especially among Taco Bell's core 18- to 35-year-old customers. So popular was the little dog that its image decorated the best-selling adult novelty T-shirt on record. Some restaurant experts have credited Taco-Bell's high-profile ad campaign featuring the Chihuahua with increasing customer awareness of Mexican food as an alternative to burgers and chicken. One food industry executive said, "Burgers are your dad's food, and Mexican is the choice of the new generation."[1]

The big bump in awareness and sales couldn't have come at a better time. Spun off from PepsiCo, Taco Bell is now part of Tricon Global Restaurants Inc., based in Louisville, Kentucky. In addition to Taco Bell, Tricon also acquired KFC and Pizza Hut. Tricon owns nearly 30,000 company and franchise restaurants, making it the largest restaurant company in the world in terms of number of locations. But it still lags behind McDonald's in the all-important category of sales. Tricon aims to become the world's dominant quick-service restaurant company, and a thriving Taco Bell is pivotal to reaching this goal.

Happily for Taco Bell, consumers are increasingly choosing Mexican foods. Surveys show that 90 percent of Americans have tried Mexican foods, and a whopping 85 percent eat it often or at least occasionally. As one expert said, "Mexican food has successfully crossed 'white-bread lines,'" a fact confirmed in the early 1990s when salsa sales began to surpass those of ketchup.[2] Taco Bell's problem is extending the consumer buzz over its celebrity Chihuahua into a long-term market surge.

Although Taco Bell aims to increase its market share of the fast-food market, it also is keenly aware of two important facts: (1) it sells a quasi-Mexican food, and (2) its customers are mainstream Americans. This means that its products cannot veer too far from what appeals to the masses. Yet, it wants to move away from low-priced meals toward larger-portion sandwiches and other higher-priced innovative items. That's why management is looking for exciting menu ideas that capitalize on trends in Mexican foods. A newly hired culinary product manager is charged with the task of coming up with menu suggestions and communicating them to management.

www.tacobell.com

Revising Messages

1

The final phase of the 3-×-3 writing process focuses on revising, proofreading, and evaluating. Revising means improving the content and sentence structure of your message. Proofreading involves correcting its grammar, spelling, punctuation, format, and mechanics. Evaluating is the process of analyzing whether your message achieved its purpose. One would not expect people in the restaurant business to require these kinds of skills. Yet, the new culinary product manager at Taco Bell—and many other similar businesspeople—realize that their ideas are worth little unless they can be communicated effectively to fellow workers and to management. In the communication process the techniques of revision can often mean the difference between the acceptance or rejection of ideas.

While the composition process differs for individuals and situations, this final phase should occupy a significant share of the total time you spend on a message. As you learned earlier, some experts recommend devoting about half the total composition time to revising and proofreading.[3]

Rarely is the first or even second version of a message satisfactory. One authority says, "Only the amateur expects writing perfection on the first try."[4] The revision stage is your chance to make sure your message says what you mean. Many professional writers compose the first draft quickly without worrying about language, precision, or correctness. Then they revise and polish extensively. Other writers, however, prefer to revise as they go—particularly for shorter business documents.

Important messages—such as those you send to management or to customers or turn in to instructors for grades—deserve careful revision and proofreading. When you finish a first draft, plan for a cooling-off period. Put the document aside and return to it after a break, preferably after 24 hours or longer.[5]

Whether you revise immediately or after a break, you'll want to examine your message critically. You should be especially concerned with ways to improve its clarity, conciseness, vigor, and readability.

Spotlight on **Communicators**

General Colin Powell believes that effective leaders apply the KISS principle in keeping things simple. They articulate vivid, overarching goals and values. Their visions and priorities are lean and compelling, not cluttered and buzzword-laden. One of General Powell's favorite quotations illustrates his conviction: "Great leaders are almost always great simplifiers, who can cut through argument, debate and doubt, to offer a solution everybody can understand."

Keeping It Clear

One of the first revision tasks is assessing the clarity of your message. A clear message is one that is immediately understood. To achieve clarity, resist the urge to show off or be fancy. Remember that your goal is not to impress an instructor. Instead, the goal of business writing is to *express,* not *impress.* This involves two simple rules: (1) keep it simple and (2) keep it conversational.

Why do some communicators fail to craft simple, direct messages? For several reasons:

- Untrained executives and professionals worry that plain messages don't sound important.
- Subordinates fear that plain talk won't impress the boss.
- Unskilled writers create foggy messages because they've not learned how to communicate clearly.
- Unethical writers intentionally obscure a message to hide the truth.

Whatever the cause, you can eliminate the fog by applying the familiar KISS formula: Keep It Short and Simple! One way to achieve clear writing is to use active-voice sentences that avoid foggy, indirect, and pompous language.

To achieve clarity, remember to KISS Keep It Short and Simple!

Foggy	**Clear**
Employees have not been made sufficiently aware of the potentially adverse consequences involved regarding these chemicals.	Warn your employees about these chemicals.
To be sure of obtaining optimal results, it is essential that you give your employees the implements that are necessary for completion of the job.	To get the best results, give employees the tools they need to do the job.

Spotlight on **Communicators**

Even though he works in the complex field of data and information processing, executive Mike Simmons insists on simplicity. "I'm a nut on plain vanilla. . . . It took me years to learn how not to use acronyms to talk about our business." As chief information officer of Bank of Boston, he realizes that plenty of smart people don't know anything about data processing. To avoid irritating those people, he stresses simplicity, directness, and jargon-free communication.

Keeping It Conversational

Clarity is further enhanced by language that sounds like conversation. This doesn't mean that your letters and memos should be chatty or familiar. Rather, you should strive to sound professional, yet not artificial or formal. This means avoiding legal terminology, technical words, and third-person constructions (*the undersigned, the writer*). Business messages should sound warm, friendly, and conversational—not stuffy and formal.[6] To sound friendly, include occasional contractions (*can't, doesn't*) and first-person pronouns (*I/we*). This warmth is appropriate in all but the most formal business reports. You can determine if your writing is conversational by trying the kitchen test. If it wouldn't sound natural in your kitchen, it probably needs revision. Note how the following formal sentences were revised to pass the kitchen test.

Formal	**Conversational**
As per your verbal instruction, steps will be undertaken immediately to investigate your billing problem.	At your suggestion I'm investigating your billing immediately.
Our organization would like to inform you that your account is being credited in the aforementioned sum.	We're crediting your account for $78.

Keeping It Concise

Another revision task is making certain that a message makes its point in the fewest possible words. One of the shortest and most effective business letters ever written contained only 19 words. Composed by business tycoon Cornelius Vanderbilt, the following masterpiece in brevity was sent to a pair of business associates who tried to swindle him while he vacationed in Europe:

> Gentlemen:
>
> You have undertaken to cheat me. I won't sue you, for the law is too slow. I'll ruin you.
>
> Yours truly,
>
> Cornelius Vanderbilt

Main points are easier to understand in concise messages.

Messages without flabby phrases and redundancies are easier to comprehend and more emphatic because main points stand out, as Vanderbilt's letter proves. Efficient messages also save the reader valuable time.

Many busy executives today won't read wordy reports. Chairman Martin Kallen, of Monsanto Europe, "flipped" because too much paper was clogging the company. He complained that reports were too long, too frequent, and too unread. He then decreed that all writing be more concise, and he refused to read any report that was not summarized in two or fewer pages.[7] Similarly, Procter & Gamble, the giant household products manufacturer, for years required all memos to be limited to one page. The president returned long messages, urging writers to "boil it down to something I can grasp." And Microsoft Chairman Bill Gates is said to stop reading e-mail messages after three screens.

Short messages require more effort than long, flabby ones.

But concise writing is not easy. As one expert copyeditor observed, "Trim sentences, like trim bodies, usually require far more effort than flabby ones."[8] To turn out slim sentences and lean messages, you do not have to be brusque, rude, or simple-minded. Instead, you must take time in the revision stage to "trim the fat." And before you can do that, you must learn to recognize it. Locating and excising wordiness involves (1) removing opening fillers, (2) eliminating redundancies, (3) reducing compound prepositions, and (4) purging empty words.

Removing Opening Fillers. Openers like *there is* and *it is* fill in sentences but generally add no meaning. These fillers reveal writers spinning their wheels until deciding where the sentence is going. Train yourself to question these constructions. About 75 percent of sentence-opening fillers can be eliminated, almost always resulting in more emphatic and more efficient sentences.

Wordy There are three things I want you to do.

Concise I want you to do three things.

Wordy It is important to start meetings on time.

Concise Starting meetings on time is important.

Eliminating Redundancies. Expressions that repeat meaning or include unnecessary words are redundant. To say *unexpected surprise* is like saying "surprise surprise" because *unexpected* carries the same meaning as *surprise.* Excessive adjectives, adverbs, and phrases often create redundancies and wordiness. The following list represents a tiny segment of the large number of redundancies appearing in business writing today. What word in each expression creates the redundancy?

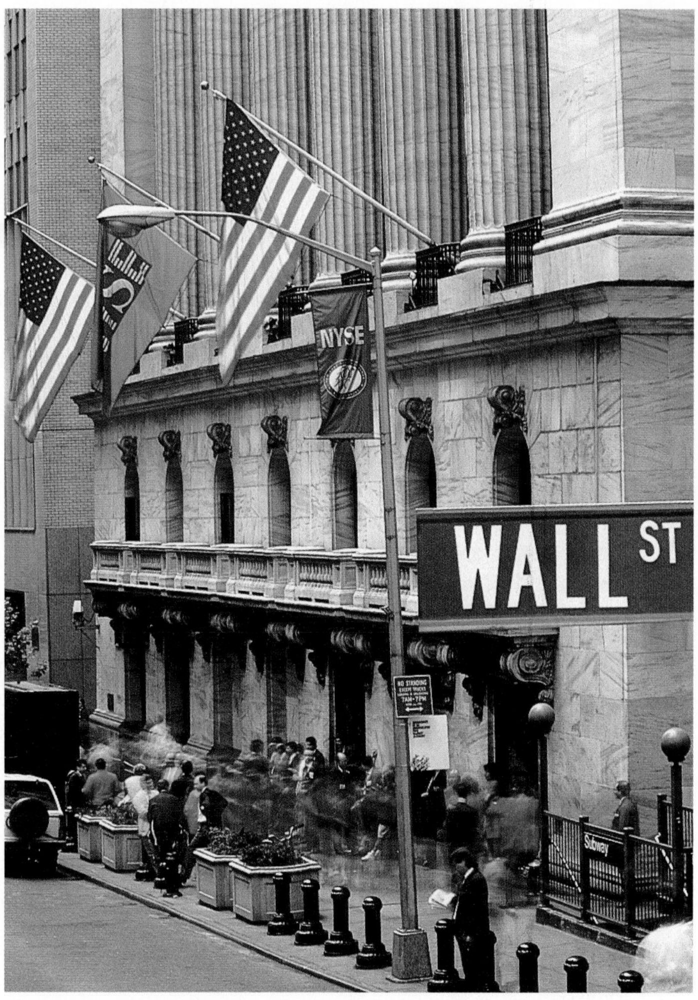

Stock brokerage firms on Wall Street have a new rule book to follow. The Securities Exchange Commission has decreed that contracts, policies, and investment literature must now be written in Plain English. The S.E.C. even published The Plain English Handbook teaching businesses how to avoid redundancies, long sentences, wordy phrases, passive voice, and abstract words. The handbook also emphasizes graphic highlighting techniques to improve readability.

Redundancies to Avoid

advance warning	exactly identical	perfectly clear
alter or change	few in number	personal opinion
assemble together	free and clear	potential opportunity
basic fundamentals	grateful thanks	positively certain
collect together	great majority	proposed plan
consensus of opinion	integral part	refer back
contributing factor	last and final	serious interest
dollar amount	midway between	true facts
each and every	new changes	visible to the eye
end result	past history	unexpected surprise

Redundancies convey a meaning more than once.

Spotlight on **Communicators**

Sam Walton, one of America's most successful merchants, said, "If you had to boil down the Wal-Mart system to one single idea, it would probably be communication, because it is one of the real keys to our success." His brand of communication meant sharing management strategies with sales associates in direct, vigorous, and simple talk, as in his sales plan: "Buy it low, stack it high, sell it cheap."

Reducing Compound Prepositions. Single words can often replace wordy prepositional phrases. In the following examples notice how the shorter forms say the same thing but more efficiently.

Wordy Compound Preposition	Shorter Form
as to whether	whether
at a later date	later
at this point in time	now
at such time, at which time	when
by means of, in accordance with	by
despite the fact that	although
due to the fact that, inasmuch as	because
in view of the fact that	because
for the amount of	for
in advance of, prior to	before
subsequent to	after
the manner in which	how
until such time as	until

Many familiar phrases contain empty words.

Purging Empty Words. Familiar phrases roll off the tongue easily, but many contain expendable parts. Be alert to these empty words and phrases: *case, degree, the fact that, factor, instance, nature,* and *quality.* Notice how much better the following sentences sound when we remove all the empty words:

~~In the case of~~ *USA Today* ~~the newspaper~~ improved its readability.

Because of ~~the degree of~~ active participation by our sales reps, profits soared.

We are aware ~~of the fact~~ that many managers need assistance.

Except for ~~the instance of~~ Mazda, Japanese imports sagged.

She chose a career in a field that was analytical ~~in nature~~. (Or, *She chose a career in an analytical field.*)

Student writing in that class is excellent ~~in quality~~.

Good writers avoid saying what is obvious.

Also avoid saying the obvious. In the following examples notice how many unnecessary words we can omit through revision:

~~When it arrived~~, I cashed your check immediately. (*Announcing the check's arrival is unnecessary. That fact is assumed in its cashing.*)

~~We need printer cartridges; therefore~~, please send me two dozen laser cartridges. (*The first clause is obvious.*)

~~This is to inform you that~~ the meeting will start at 2 p.m. (*Avoid unnecessary lead-in.*)

Finally, look carefully at clauses beginning with *that, which,* and *who.* They can often be shortened without loss of clarity. Search for phrases, such as *it appears that.* Such phrases can be reduced to a single adjective or adverb, such as *apparently.*

successful
Changing the name of a company ~~that is successful~~ is always risky.
∧

All employees ~~who are among those~~ completing the course will be reimbursed.

final
Our proposal, ~~which was~~ slightly altered ~~in its final form~~, won approval.
^

weekly
We plan to schedule meetings ~~on a weekly basis~~.
^

Revising for Vigor and Directness

2

Much business writing has been criticized as lifeless, cautious, and "really, really boring."[9] This boredom results not so much from content as from wordiness and dull, trite expressions. You've already studied ways to improve clarity and conciseness. You can also reduce wordiness and improve vigor by (1) kicking the noun habit and (2) dumping trite business phrases.

Kicking the Noun Habit

Much business writing is plagued by wordiness and triteness.

Some writers become addicted to nouns, needlessly transforming verbs into nouns (*we make a recommendation of* instead of *we recommend*). This bad habit increases sentence length, drains verb strength, slows the reader, and muddies the thought. Notice how efficient, clean, and forceful the verbs below sound compared with their noun phrase counterparts.

Overusing noun phrases lengthens sentences, saps verbs, and muddies the message.

Wordy Noun Phrase	**Verb**
conduct a discussion of	discuss
create a reduction in	reduce
engage in the preparation of	prepare
give consideration to	consider
make an assumption of	assume
make a discovery of	discover
perform an analysis of	analyze
reach a conclusion about	conclude
take action on	act

Dumping Trite Business Phrases

To sound "businesslike," many writers repeat the same stale expressions that other writers have used over the years. Your writing will sound fresher and more vigorous if you eliminate these phrases or find more original ways to convey the idea.

Avoid trite expressions that are overused in business writing.

Trite Phrase	**Improved Version**
as per your request	as you request
pursuant to your request	at your request
enclosed please find	enclosed is
every effort will be made	we'll try
in accordance with your wishes	as you wish
in receipt of	have received
please do not hesitate to	please
thank you in advance	thank you
under separate cover	separately
with reference to	about

Revising for Readability

3

To help receivers anticipate and comprehend ideas quickly, two special writing techniques are helpful: (1) parallelism, which involves balanced writing, and (2) highlighting, which makes important points more visible. And to ensure that your document is readable, consider applying the Fog Index, a readability measure described later.

Developing Parallelism

Parallelism means matching nouns with nouns, verbs with verbs, phrases with phrases, and so on.

As you revise, be certain that you express similar ideas in balanced or parallel construction. For example, the phrase *clearly, concisely, and correctly* is parallel because all the words end in *-ly*. To express the list as *clearly, concisely, and with correctness* is jarring because the last item is not what the receiver expects. Instead of an adverb, the series ends with a noun. To achieve parallelism, match nouns with nouns, verbs with verbs, phrases with phrases, and clauses with clauses. Avoid mixing active-voice verbs with passive-voice verbs.

Not Parallel	Improved
The policy affected all vendors, suppliers, and those involved with consulting.	The policy affected all vendors, suppliers, and consultants. (*Series matches nouns.*)
Good managers analyze a problem, collect data, and alternatives are evaluated.	Good managers analyze a problem, collect data, and evaluate alternatives. (*Series matches verb forms.*)

Be alert to a list or series of items; the use of *and* or *or* should signal you to check for balanced construction. When elements cannot be balanced fluently, consider revising to subordinate or separate the items.

Not Parallel	Improved
Foreign service employees must be able to communicate rapidly, concisely, and be flexible in handling diverse responsibilities.	Foreign service employees must be able to communicate rapidly and concisely; they must also be flexible in handling diverse responsibilities.

Applying Graphic Highlighting

Graphic devices such as lists, bullets, headings, and white space spotlight important ideas.

One of the best ways to improve comprehension is through graphic highlighting techniques. Spotlight important items by setting them off with

Lists offset from the text and introduced with bullets have a strong visual impact.

- Letters, such as (a), (b), and (c), within the text
- Numerals, such as 1, 2, and 3, listed vertically
- Bullets—black squares, raised periods, or other figures
- Headings
- Capital letters, underscores, boldface, and italics

Ideas formerly buried within sentences or paragraphs stand out when targeted with one of these techniques. Readers not only understand your message more rapidly and easily but also consider you efficient and well organized. In the following sentence notice how highlighting with letters makes the three items more visible and emphatic.

Without Highlighting
Nordstrom attracts upscale customers by featuring quality fashions, personalized service, and a generous return policy.

Highlighted With Letters
Nordstrom attracts upscale customers by featuring (a) quality fashions, (b) personalized service, and (c) a generous return policy.

If you have the space and wish to create even greater visual impact, you can list items vertically. Capitalize the word at the beginning of each line. Don't add end punctuation unless the statements are complete sentences. And be sure to use parallel construction whenever you itemize ideas. In the following examples, each item in the bulleted list follows an adjective/noun sequence. In the bulleted list, each item begins with a verb. Notice, too, that we use bullets when items have no particular order or importance. Numbers, however, are better to show a definite sequence.

Highlighted With Bullets
Nordstrom attracts upscale customers by featuring the following:

- Quality fashions
- Personalized service
- Generous return policy

Numbers for Sequence
Nordstrom advises recruiters to follow these steps in hiring applicants:

1. Examine application
2. Interview applicant
3. Check references

CASE STUDY

PROCESS IN PROGRESS

Taco Bell Revisited

The newly hired culinary product manager at Taco Bell has her job cut out for her. Management expects her to anticipate trends in Mexican foods and improve restaurant menus. Part of the challenge is recognizing trends that consumers haven't even picked up yet and then working these trends into restaurant products. In her words, "We want to kick it up a notch, but we still have to deliver to mainstream America." She needs to read the market and then create new menu ideas to follow the launch of the Gordita ("little fat one"), a flat bread taco that proved to be the chain's most successful product launch ever. The new chef is eager to incorporate some of the rich, complex flavors of authentic Mexican cuisine. But she must do it in ways that are acceptable to mainstream America. Although she has excellent culinary references, the new chef has not been trained in communication. She has plenty of ideas to put into a memo or a presentation. Her job now depends on how well she can communicate these ideas to management.

Critical Thinking

- Based on what you learned in this chapter, what specific advice can you give about keeping a message clear? Should a business message be conversational? How is a conversational tone achieved?
- Why is conciseness important, and what techniques can be used to achieve it?
- Would you advise the culinary chef to be direct with her ideas? What advice can you give for improving the directness and readability of a business message?

Headings are another choice for highlighting information. They force the writer to organize carefully so that similar data are grouped together. And they help the reader separate major ideas from details. Moreover, headings enable a busy reader to skim familiar or less important information. They also provide a quick preview or review. Although headings appear more often in reports, they are equally helpful in complex letters and memos. Here, they informally summarize items within a message:

Headings help writers to organize information and enable readers to absorb important ideas.

Highlighted With Headings
Nordstrom focuses on the following areas in the employment process:

- **Attracting applicants.** We advertise for qualified applicants, and we also encourage current employees to recommend good people.
- **Interviewing applicants.** Our specialized interviews include simulated customer encounters as well as scrutiny by supervisors.
- **Checking references.** We investigate every applicant thoroughly, including conversations with former employers and all listed references.

Spotlight on **Communicators**

Well-known Washington Post columnist William Raspberry, surprised at the news that he had won the Pulitzer Prize, frequently promotes the value of language skills: "Misused words, haphazard sentences, failed subject-verb agreement can distract people from our ideas and get them concentrating on our inadequacies. Good English, carefully spoken and written, can open more doors than a college degree. Bad English can slam doors we don't even know about."

Readability formulas like the Fog Index are based on word and sentence lengths.

To highlight individual words, use CAPITAL letters, <u>underlining</u>, **bold** type, or *italics*. Be careful with these techniques, though, because they SHOUT at the reader. Consider how the reader will react.

The following chapters supply additional ideas for grouping and spotlighting data. Although highlighting techniques can improve comprehension, they can also clutter a message if overdone. Many of these techniques also require more space, so use them judiciously.

Measuring Readability

Experts have developed methods for measuring how easy, or difficult, a message is to read. Probably the best known is Robert Gunning's Fog Index, which measures long words and sentence length to determine readability. The accompanying Career Coach box shows you how to apply eight steps in figuring the Fog Index for a piece of writing, such as the sample business letter shown.

Our calculation indicates that this sample letter has a reading grade level of 10. The foggier a message, the higher its reading level. Magazines and newspapers that strive for wide readership keep their readability between levels 8 and 12. (*USA Today* is 10.6, *The New York Times* is 12.6,[10] and *People* magazine ranges between 8.4 and 11.2.) By occasionally calculating the Fog Index of your writing, you can ensure that you stay within the 8 to12 range. Remember that long words—those over two syllables—and long sentences make your writing foggy.

Readability formulas, however, don't always tell the full story. Although they provide a rough estimate, those based solely on word and sentence counts fail to measure meaningfulness. Even short words (such as *skew, onus,* and *wane*) can cause trouble if readers don't recognize them. More important than length are a word's familiarity and meaningfulness to the reader. In Chapter 3 you learned to adapt your writing to the audience by selecting familiar words. Other techniques that can improve readability include well-organized paragraphs, transitions to connect ideas, headings, and lists.

The task of revision, summarized in the following checklist, is hard work. It demands objectivity and a willingness to cut, cut, cut. Though painful, the process is also gratifying. It's a great feeling when you realize your finished message is clear, concise, and readable.

Checklist for Revising Messages

 **Keep the message simple.** Express ideas directly. Don't show off or use fancy language.

 **Be conversational.** Include occasional contractions (*hasn't, don't*) and first-person pronouns (*I/we*). Use natural-sounding language.

 **Avoid opening fillers.** Omit sentence fillers such as *there is* and *it is* to produce more direct expression.

 **Shun redundancies.** Eliminate words that repeat meanings, such as *mutual cooperation.* Watch for repetitious adjectives, adverbs, and phrases.

 **Tighten your writing.** Check phrases that include *case, degree, the fact that, factor,* and other words and phrases that unnecessarily increase wordiness. Avoid saying the obvious.

CAREER COACH

APPLYING THE FOG INDEX TO DETERMINE READABILITY

One way to calculate the "readability" of a document is by applying the Gunning Fog Index. Here's how you can figure it manually for the business letter shown here. (This same calculation can be performed by many computer software programs.)

- **Step 1: Select the passage.** Choose a continuous passage of between 100 and 130 words.
- **Step 2: Count the total words.** Count numbers, dates, and abbreviations as separate words. Our business letter sample has 110 words.
- **Step 3: Count the sentences.** Count all independent clauses separately. For example, *He applied, and he was hired* counts as two sentences. Our sample has seven sentences, marked with superscript numbers.
- **Step 4: Find the average sentence length.** Divide the total number of words by the number of sentences (110 divided by 7 equals 16 words).
- **Step 5: Count the number of long words.** A word is long if it has three or more syllables. Exclude (a) capitalized words, (b) compound words formed from short words (*nevertheless*), and (c) verbs made into three syllables by the addition of *-ed* or *-es* (*located, finances*). In our sample the long words are underlined.
- **Step 6: Find the percentage of long words.** Divide the number of long words by the number of total words (10 divided by 110 equals .09 or 9 percent).
- **Step 7: Add the results.** Add the average sentence length (16) and the percentage of long words (9). The result is 25.
- **Step 8: Multiply.** Multiply by 0.4 (25 × 0.4 equals 10). The reading level of this letter is 10.

Dear Mrs. Lawrence:

[1]Yes, I can meet with you Thursday, April 3, at 10 a.m. to discuss possible ways to finance the purchase of a new home in San Diego. [2]Before we meet, though, you might like to <u>consider</u> two <u>possible</u> plans.

[3]The first plan finances your purchase with a swing loan, which has a fixed <u>interest</u> rate for a short period of time. [4]A second plan requires you to <u>refinance</u> your present <u>residence</u>. [5]We have located five programs from three <u>different institutions</u> that would do this. [6]Enclosed is a <u>summary</u> of these five plans. [7]I look forward to seeing you Thursday to find a way for you to own a home in San Diego.

Sincerely,

The reading level of this short letter is 10. This level indicates that the reader needs ten years of schooling to understand the letter. Your goal should be to keep your writing between the levels of 8 and 12. Two factors that most influence reading level are sentence length and word length.

Career Application

Compare the reading levels of several publications. Calculate the Fog Index for short passages from two of your college textbooks, your local newspapers, a business document (letter, memo, report), and an insurance policy. Discuss in class the appropriateness of the reading levels for each document.

Don't convert verbs to nouns. Keep your writing vigorous by avoiding the noun habit (*analyze* not *make an analysis of*).

Avoid trite phrases. Keep your writing fresh, direct, and contemporary by skipping such expressions as *enclosed please find* and *pursuant to your request.*

Strive for parallelism. Help receivers anticipate and comprehend your message by using balanced writing (*planning, drafting, and constructing* not *planning, drafting, and construction*).

Highlight important ideas. Use graphic techniques such as letters, numerals, bullets, headings, capital letters, underlining, boldface, and italics to spotlight ideas and organization.

In some ways business communicators can learn to improve the readability of their messages by emulating magazine articles. Magazine writers enhance comprehension by writing concisely, using short sentences, controlling paragraph length, including headings, and developing parallelism (expressing similar ideas in similar grammatical constructions).

 **Test readability.** Check your writing occasionally to identify its reading level. Remember that short, familiar words and short sentences help readers comprehend.

Proofreading for the Finishing Touch

4

Once you have the message in its final form, it's time to proofread it. Don't proofread earlier because you may waste time checking items that eventually are changed or omitted.

Proofreading before a document is completed is generally a waste of time.

What to Watch for in Proofreading

Careful proofreaders check for problems in these areas:

- **Spelling.** Now's the time to consult the dictionary. Is *recommend* spelled with one or two *c*'s? Do you mean *affect* or *effect*? Use your computer spell checker, but don't rely on it totally. See the accompanying Tech Talk box to learn more about the benefits and hazards of computer spell checkers.
- **Grammar.** Locate sentence subjects; do their verbs agree with them? Do pronouns agree with their antecedents? Review the C.L.U.E. principles in Appendix A if necessary. Use your computer's grammar checker, but be suspicious. See the Tech Talk box on page 165.
- **Punctuation.** Make sure that introductory clauses are followed by commas. In compound sentences put commas before coordinating conjunctions (*and, or, but, nor*). Double-check your use of semicolons and colons.
- **Names and numbers.** Compare all names and numbers with their sources because inaccuracies are not immediately visible. Especially verify the spelling of the names of individuals receiving the message. Most of us immediately dislike someone who misspells our name.

TECH TALK

SPELL CHECKERS ARE WONDERFUL, BUT . . .

Nearly all high-end word processing programs now include sophisticated spell checkers. Also called dictionaries, these programs compare your typed words with those in the computer's memory. Microsoft uses a wavy red line to underline misspelled words caught "on the fly."

Although some writers dismiss spell checkers as an annoyance,[11] most of us are only too happy to have our typos and misspelled words detected. The real problem is that spell checkers (and grammar checkers, which are discussed in a subsequent box) don't find all the problems. In the following poem, for example, only two problems were detected (*your* and *it's*):

I have a spell checker
That came with my PC.
It plainly marks four my review
Mistakes I cannot sea.

I've run this poem threw it,
I'm sure your pleased too no.
Its letter perfect in it's weigh
My checker tolled me sew.[12]

The lesson to be learned here is that you can't rely totally on any spell checker. Misused words may not be highlighted because the spell checker doesn't know what meaning you have in mind. That's why you're wise to print out every message and proofread it word by word.

Career Application

Use the latest version of Word as you write an assignment for this class. Note any words that it underlined with wavy red lines. Then, have a friend or classmate proofread it to see what the computer missed.

- **Format.** Be sure that your document looks balanced on the page. Compare its parts and format with those of standard documents shown in Appendix B. If you indent paragraphs, be certain that all are indented.

How to Proofread Routine Documents

5

Routine documents need a light proofreading.

Most routine documents require a light proofreading. You may be working with a handwritten or a printed copy or on your computer screen. If you wish to print a copy, make it a rough draft (don't print it on letterhead stationery). In time, you may be able to produce a "first-time-final" message, but beginning writers seldom do.

For handwritten or printed messages, read the entire document. Watch for all of the items just described. Use standard proofreading marks, shown in Figure 6.1, to indicate changes.

For computer messages you can read the document on the screen, preferably in WYSIWYG mode (what you see is what you get). Use the down arrow to reveal one line at a time, thus focusing your attention at the bottom of the screen. A safer proofreading method, however, is reading from a printed copy. You're more likely to find errors and to observe the tone. "Things really look different on paper," observed veteran writer Louise Lague at *People* magazine. "Don't just pull a letter out of the printer and stick it in an envelope. Read every sentence again. You'll catch bad line endings, strange page breaks, and weird spacing. You can also get a totally different feeling about what you've said when you see it in print. Sometimes you can say something with a smile on your face; but if you put the same thing in print, it won't work."[13]

FIGURE 6.1 **Proofreader's Marks**

Most proofreaders use these standard marks to indicate revisions.

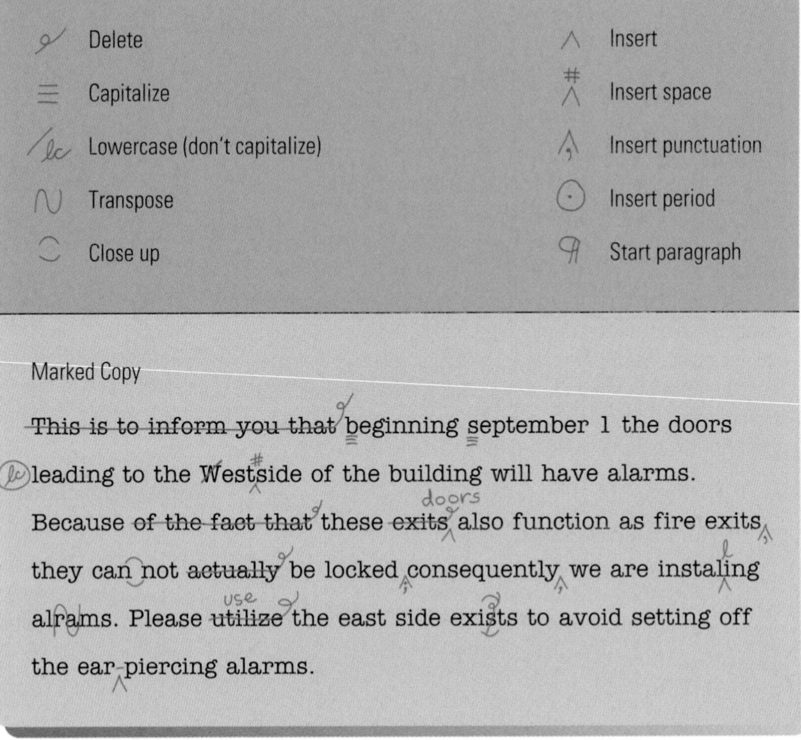

Delete
Capitalize
Lowercase (don't capitalize)
Transpose
Close up
Insert
Insert space
Insert punctuation
Insert period
Start paragraph
Marked Copy
This is to inform you that beginning september 1 the doors
leading to the Westside of the building will have alarms.
Because of the fact that these exits also function as fire exits
they can not actually be locked consequently we are instaling
alrams. Please utilize the east side exists to avoid setting off
the ear piercing alarms.
doors
use

How to Proofread Complex Documents

Long, complex, or important documents demand more careful proofreading using the following techniques:

For both routine and complex documents, it's best to proofread from a printed copy, not on a computer screen.

- Print a copy, preferably double-spaced, and set it aside for at least a day. You'll be more alert after a breather.
- Allow adequate time to proofread carefully. A common excuse for sloppy proofreading is lack of time.
- Be prepared to find errors. One student confessed, "I can find other people's errors, but I can't seem to locate my own." Psychologically, we don't expect to find errors, and we don't want to find them. You can overcome this obstacle by anticipating errors and congratulating, not criticizing, yourself each time you find one.

Complex documents should be proofread at least twice.

- Read the message at least twice—once for word meanings and once for grammar/mechanics. For very long documents (book chapters and long articles or reports), read a third time to verify consistency in formatting.
- Reduce your reading speed. Concentrate on individual words rather than ideas.
- For documents that must be perfect, have someone read the message aloud. Spell names and difficult words, note capitalization, and read punctuation.
- Use standard proofreading marks, shown in Figure 6.1, to indicate changes.

Your computer word processing program may include a style or grammar checker. These programs generally analyze aspects of your writing style, including

TECH TALK

GRAMMAR CHECKERS: THEY'VE COME A LONG WAY, BABY

When first introduced, grammar and style checkers were not too helpful. They were limited in scope, awkward to use, and identified many questionable "errors." But today's built-in grammar checkers detect an amazing number of legitimate writing lapses. Microsoft's Word 97 marks faults in word use (such as *there, their*), capitalization, punctuation, subject-verb agreement, sentence structure, singular and plural endings, repeated words, wordy expression, gender-specific expressions, and many other problems.

How does a grammar checker work? Let's say you typed the sentence, "The office and its equipment is for sale." You would see a wavy green line appear under *is.* When you point your cursor at "Tools" in the tool bar and click on "Spelling and Grammar," a box opens up. It identifies the subject-verb agreement error and suggests the verb *are* as a correction. When you click on "Change," the error is corrected. Pretty nifty, eh?

The capabilities of these grammar checkers are truly astounding, given the complexity of the English language. However, before you decide that all your writing problems are solved, think again. Even Word's sophisticated program misses plenty of errors, and it also mismarks some correct expressions. For example, in one document the checker suggested that *company's goals* be changed to *companies goals,* which is clearly wrong. It also thought that the word *italics* should be capitalized.

Despite their limitations, grammar checkers definitely enhance the proofreading process. They find many errors—especially for inexperienced writers. But keep in mind that they are far from perfect. Be prepared to question their suggestions. If in doubt, consult your instructor, a good reference manual, your college writing lab, or one of the on-line writing labs.

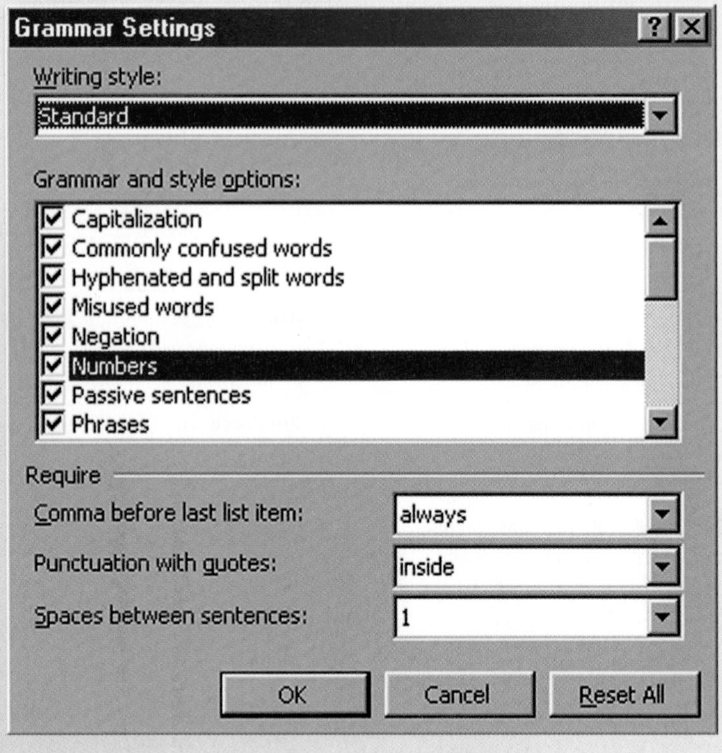

The Word grammar feature allows you to select the writing style you prefer (casual, standard, formal, or technical) and customize many options, as shown here. A click inside a box inserts or removes a check mark indicating your choice.

Career Application

Use a word processing program with a built-in grammar checker in preparing letters and memos for this class. Analyze the suggestions made by the checker. Revise your documents using your judgment about what changes improve message effectiveness.

readability level and use of passive voice, trite expressions, split infinitives, and wordy expressions. Some of them, such as Word 97, use sophisticated technology (and a lot of computer memory) to identify significant errors. In addition to finding spelling and typographical errors, Word 97 will find subject-verb lack of agreement, word misuse, spacing irregularities, punctuation problems, and many other faults. But it won't find everything, as you see in the accompanying Tech Talk box.

Evaluating the Product

6

A good way to evaluate messages is through feedback.

As part of applying finishing touches, take a moment to evaluate your writing. How successful will this message be? Does it say what you want it to? Will it achieve your purpose? How will you know if it succeeds?

As you learned in Chapter 1, the best way to judge the success of your communication is through feedback. Thus, you should encourage the receiver to respond to your message. This feedback will tell you how to modify future efforts to improve your communication technique.

Your instructor will also be evaluating some of your writing. Although any criticism is painful, try not to be defensive. Look on these comments as valuable advice tailored to your specific writing weaknesses—and strengths. Many businesses today spend thousands of dollars bringing in communication consultants to improve employee writing skills. You're getting the same training in this course. Take advantage of this chance—one of the few you may have—to improve your skills. The best way to improve your skills, of course, is through instruction, practice, and evaluation.

Your instructor and this book provide you with the three keys to success: instruction, practice materials, and evaluation.

In this class you have all three elements: instruction in the writing process (summarized in Figure 6.2), practice materials, and someone willing to guide and evaluate your efforts. Those three elements are the reasons that this book and this course may be the most valuable in your entire curriculum. Because it's almost impossible to improve your communication skills alone, grab this chance!

FIGURE 6.2 The Complete 3-×-3 Writing Process

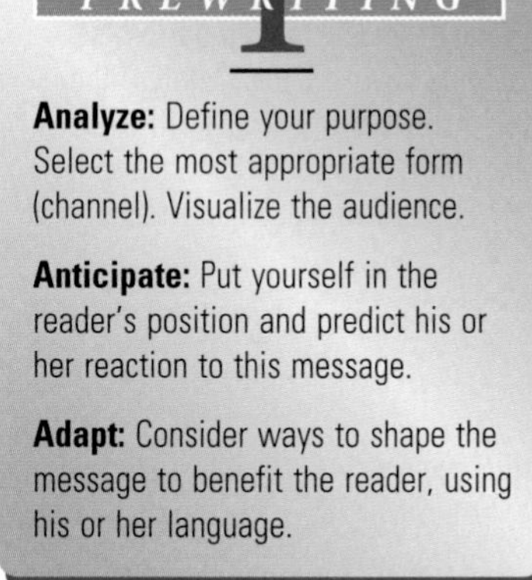

1
PREWRITING
Analyze: Define your purpose. Select the most appropriate form (channel). Visualize the audience.
Anticipate: Put yourself in the reader's position and predict his or her reaction to this message.
Adapt: Consider ways to shape the message to benefit the reader, using his or her language.

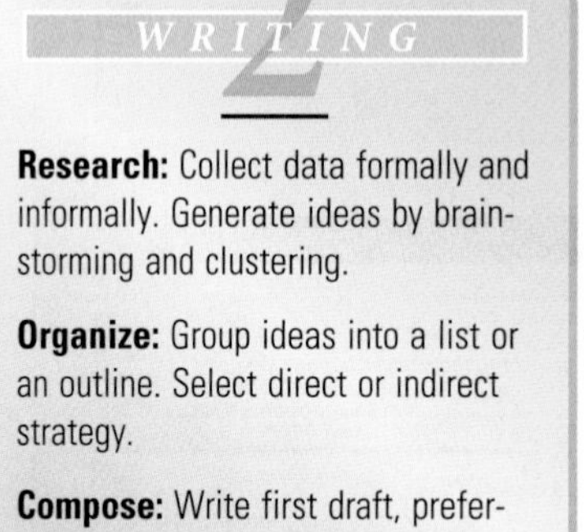

3

REVISING

Revise: Revise for clarity, tone, conciseness, and vigor. Revise to improve readability.

Proofread: Proofread to verify spelling, grammar, punctuation, and format. Check for overall appearance.

Evaluate: Ask yourself if the final product will achieve its purpose.

Summary of Learning Objectives

1 **Identify revision techniques that make a document clear, conversational, and concise.** Clear documents use active-voice sentences and simple words and avoid negative expressions. Clarity is further enhanced by language that sounds like conversation, including occasional contractions and first-person pronouns (*I/we*). Conciseness can be achieved by excluding opening fillers (*There are*), redundancies (*basic essentials*), and compound prepositions (*by means of*).

PROCESS TO PRODUCT

Applying Your Skills at Taco Bell

CASE STUDY

Upgrading the menu at Taco Bell is an exciting challenge for the new culinary product manager. In response to management's request, she comes up with terrific ideas for capitalizing on eating trends and converting them to mainstream tastes. She has been asked to submit a memo summarizing her longer report, which will be presented at a management meeting next week.

Although the new culinary product manager has exceptional talent in the field of cuisine, she realizes that her writing skills are not as well developed as her cooking skills. She comes to the corporate communications department and shows your boss the first draft of her memo. Your boss is a nice guy; and, as a favor, he revises the first two paragraphs, as shown in Figure 6.3.

Your Job

Your boss, the head of corporate communications, has many important tasks to oversee. Thus, he hands the product manager's memo to you, his assistant, and tells you to finish cleaning it up. He adds, "Her ideas are right on target, but the main points are totally lost in wordy sentences and solid paragraphs. Revise this and concentrate on conciseness, parallelism, and readability. Don't you think some bulleted lists would help this memo a lot?" Revise the remaining four paragraphs of the memo using the techniques you learned in this chapter. Type a copy of the complete memo to submit to your boss.

2 **Describe revision tactics that make a document vigorous and direct.** Writers can achieve vigor in messages by revising wordy phrases that needlessly convert verbs into nouns. For example, instead of *we conducted a discussion of,* write *we discussed.* To make writing more direct, good writers replace trite business phrases, such as *please do not hesitate to,* and similar expressions, such as *please.*

3 **Discuss revision strategies that improve readability.** One revision technique that improves readability is the use of balanced constructions (*parallelism*). For example, *collecting, analyzing, and illustrating data* is balanced and easy to read. *Collecting, analysis of, and illustration of data* is more difficult to read because it is unbalanced. Parallelism involves matching nouns with nouns, verbs with verbs, phrases with phrases, and clauses with clauses. Another technique that improves readability is graphic highlighting. It incorporates devices such as lettered items, numerals, bullets, headings, capital letters, underlining, italics, and bold print to highlight and order ideas. A readability scale, such as the Fog Index, is helpful in measuring how easy or difficult a document is to read.

4 **List problem areas that good proofreaders examine carefully.** Proofreaders must be especially alert to these problem areas: spelling, grammar, punctuation, names, numbers, and document format.

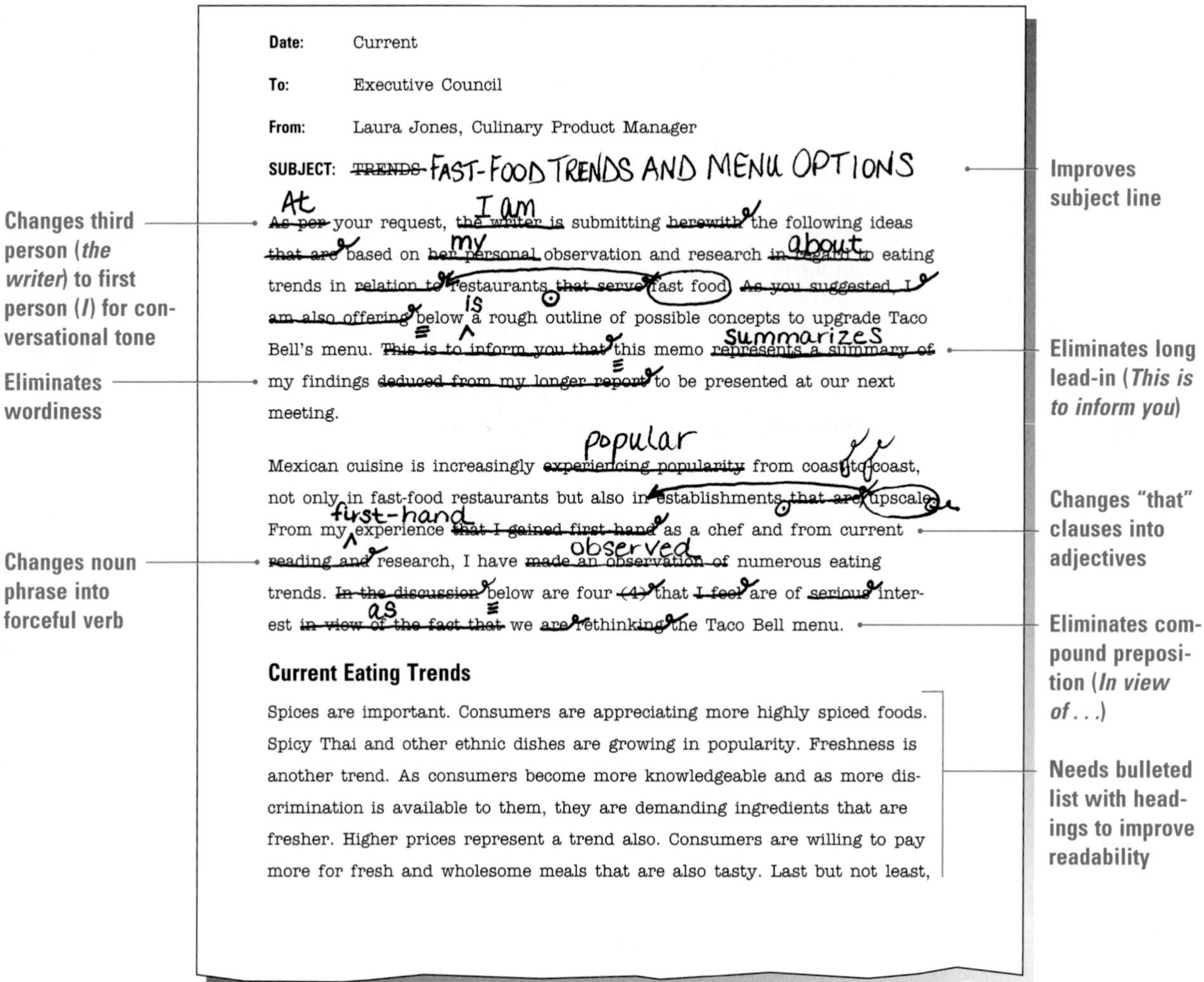
FIGURE 6.3 Partially Revised First Draft

Date: Current

To: Executive Council

From: Laura Jones, Culinary Product Manager

SUBJECT: ~~TRENDS~~ FAST-FOOD TRENDS AND MENU OPTIONS

~~As per~~ At your request, ~~the writer is~~ I am submitting ~~herewith~~ the following ideas ~~that are~~ based on ~~her personal~~ my observation and research ~~in regard to~~ about eating trends in ~~relation to~~ restaurants ~~that serve~~ fast food. ~~As you suggested, I am also offering~~ below is a rough outline of possible concepts to upgrade Taco Bell's menu. ~~This is to inform you that~~ this memo ~~represents a summary of~~ summarizes my findings ~~deduced from my longer report~~ to be presented at our next meeting.

Mexican cuisine is increasingly ~~experiencing popularity~~ popular from coast to coast, not only in fast-food restaurants but also in ~~establishments that are~~ upscale establishments. From my first-hand experience ~~that I gained first-hand~~ as a chef and from current ~~reading and~~ research, I have ~~made an observation of~~ observed numerous eating trends. ~~In the discussion~~ below are four ~~(4)~~ that ~~I feel~~ are of ~~serious~~ interest ~~in view of the fact that~~ as we ~~are~~ rethinking the Taco Bell menu.

Current Eating Trends

Spices are important. Consumers are appreciating more highly spiced foods. Spicy Thai and other ethnic dishes are growing in popularity. Freshness is another trend. As consumers become more knowledgeable and as more discrimination is available to them, they are demanding ingredients that are fresher. Higher prices represent a trend also. Consumers are willing to pay more for fresh and wholesome meals that are also tasty. Last but not least,

Improves subject line
Changes third person (*the writer*) to first person (*I*) for conversational tone
Eliminates long lead-in (*This is to inform you*)
Eliminates wordiness
Changes "that" clauses into adjectives
Changes noun phrase into forceful verb
Eliminates compound preposition (*In view of . . .*)
Needs bulleted list with headings to improve readability

5 **Compare the proofreading of routine and complex documents.** Routine documents may be proofread immediately after completion. They may be read line by line on the computer screen or, better yet, from a printed draft copy. More complex documents, however, should be proofread after a breather. To do a good job, you must read from a printed copy, allow adequate time, reduce your reading speed, and read the document at least three times—for word meanings, for grammar/mechanics, and for formatting.

6 **Evaluate a message to judge its success.** Encourage feedback from the receiver so that you can determine whether your communication achieved its goal. Try to welcome any advice from your instructor on how to improve your writing skills. Both techniques contribute to helping you evaluate the success of a message.

a final trend includes big appetites. Other fast-food restaurants are cashing in on sandwiches that are satisfying, such as the Whopper, the Big Mac, and the Big Jack. In this respect, teenagers are our prime targets.

Given the increasing degree of acceptance of Mexican cuisine and the rich array of flavors and textures in Mexican cuisine, we find that we have many possibilities for the expansion of our menu. Despite the fact that my full report contains a number of additional trends and menu ideas, I will concentrate below on four significant concepts.

Needs to reduce wordy phrases

New Menu Concepts

First, I am of the opinion that we should add **More Grilled Items.** Offer spicy chicken marinated in lime juice or chipotle-rubbed ahi tuna served with cranberry mango salsa. A second idea involves **Larger-Portion Sandwiches.** Consider a "Machaca Taco," an oversized taco featuring shredded beef. Another possibility is "Mad Mex," a wild burrito served with a smoky rojo sauce. Third, concentrate on Higher Quality, More Expensive Dishes. Consider churrascos, made with prime beef tenderloin basted with a South American pesto sauce. Lastly, we should consider a Self-Serve Salsa Bar. In relation to this, we could offer exotic fresh salsas with bold flavors and textures.

Needs bulleted list with headings to highlight main points

Revise for conciseness

I would be more than happy to have a discussion of these ideas with you in greater detail and to have a demonstration of them in the kitchen. Thanks for this opportunity to work with you in the expansion of our menu in a move to ensure that Taco Bell remains tops in Mexican cuisine.

Must convert noun phrases to verbs

Needs to eliminate empty words

CHAPTER REVIEW

1. Approximately how much of the total composition time should be spent revising, proofreading, and evaluating? (Obj. 1)
2. What is the KISS method? In what three ways can it apply to business writing? (Obj. 1)
3. What is a redundancy? Give an example. Why should writers avoid redundancies? (Obj. 1)
4. Why should communicators avoid openings such as *there is*? (Obj. 1)
5. What shorter forms could be substituted for the expressions *by means of, despite the fact that,* and *at this point in time*? (Obj. 1)
6. Why should a writer avoid the opening *This memo is to inform you that our next committee meeting is Friday*? (Obj. 1)
7. Why should a writer avoid an expression such as *We hope you will give consideration to our proposal*? (Obj. 2)
8. What's wrong with businesslike expressions such as *enclosed please find* and *as per your request*? (Obj. 2)
9. Discuss five ways to highlight important ideas. (Obj. 3)
10. What two characteristics increase the Fog Index of written matter? (Obj. 3)
11. What is parallelism, and how can you achieve it? (Obj. 3)

12. Name five specific items to check in proofreading. Be ready to discuss methods you find useful in spotting these errors. (Obj. 4)

13. In proofreading, what major psychological problem do you face in finding errors? How can you overcome this barrier? (Obj. 4)

14. List four or more techniques for proofreading complex documents. (Obj. 5)

15. How can you overcome defensiveness when your writing is criticized constructively? (Obj. 6)

CRITICAL THINKING

1. Why is it difficult to recommend a specific process that all writers can follow in composition? (Obj. 1)

2. Would you agree or disagree with the following statement by writing expert William Zinsser? "Plain talk will not be easily achieved in corporate America. Too much vanity is on the line." (Objs. 1 and 2)

3. To be conversational, should business writing be exactly as we talk? Support your opinion. (Obj. 1)

4. Why should the proofreading process for routine documents differ from that for complex documents? (Objs. 4 and 5)

5. **Ethical Issue:** What advice would you give in this ethical dilemma? Lisa is serving as interim editor of the company newsletter. She receives an article written by the company president describing, in abstract and pompous language, the company's goals for the coming year. Lisa thinks the article will need considerable revising to make it readable. Attached to the president's article are complimentary comments by two of the company vice presidents. What action should Lisa take?

ACTIVITIES

6.1 Document for Analysis (Objs. 1 and 3)

Revise the following memo to improve its clarity, conciseness, vigor, and readability. How many wordy constructions can you spot?

TO: All Management

This memo is addressed to all members of management to advise you that once a year we like to remind management of our policy in relation to the matter of business attire. In this policy there is a recommendation that all employees should wear clothing that promotes a businesslike atmosphere and meets requirements of safety.

Employees who work in offices and who, as part of their jobs, meet the public and other outsiders should dress in a professional manner, including coat, tie, suit, dress, and so forth. In areas of industrial applications, supervisors may prohibit loose clothing (shirttails, ties, cuffs) that could become entangled in machinery that moves.

Where it is necessary, footwear should provide protection against heavy objects or sharp edges at the level of the floor. In the manufacturing and warehousing areas, prohibited footwear includes the following: shoes that are open toe, sandals, shoes made of canvas or nylon, tennis shoes, spiked heels, and heels higher than $1\frac{1}{2}$ inches.

Each and every manager has the responsibility for the determination of suitable business attire, and employees should be informed of what is required.

6.2 Document for Analysis (Objs. 4 and 5)

Use proofreading marks to indicate needed corrections in the following letter. Check spelling, typos, grammar, punctuation, names and numbers, and format.

Dear Ms. Willis,

We appreciate you interest in employe leasing through U.S. Staff Network. Our programs and our service has proved to be powerful management tools for business owners, like you.

Our seventeen year history, Ms. Williams, provide the local service and national strength neccesary to offer the best employee leasing programs available, we save business owners time, and money, employee hassles and employer liability.

Your employees' will receive health care benifits, retirement plan choices and a national credit union. As a small business owner you can eliminate personel administration. Which involves alot of goverment paperwork today.

Whether you have one or 1,000 employees and offer no benefits to a full-benefits package employee leasing will get you back to the basics of running your business more profitably. I will call you to arrange a time to meet, and talk about your specific needs.

Cordially,

6.3 Computing Fog Index (Obj. 3)

As an in-class project or for homework, do the following: (1) Compute the Fog Index for the following letter. (2) Then revise the letter using proofreading marks. Reduce its length and improve its readability by eliminating redundancies, wordiness, and trite expressions. Use simple, clear words. Shorten sentences. (3) Prepare a clean copy of the revised letter. (4) Finally, calculate the Fog Index for your revision.

Dear Mr. Sato:

Pursuant to your request, the undersigned is transmitting to you herewith the attached materials and documents with regard to the improvement of security in your business. To ensure the improvement of your after-hours security, you should initially make a decision with regard to exactly what you contemplate must have protection. You are, in all probability, apprehensive not only about your electronic equipment and paraphernalia but also about your company records, information, and data.

Inasmuch as we feel you will want to obtain protection for both your equipment and data, we will make suggestions for taking a number of judicious steps to inhibit crime. First and foremost, we recommend that you install defensive lighting. A consultant for lighting, currently on our staff, can design both outside and inside lighting, which brings me to my second point. Exhibit security signs, due to the fact that nonprofessional thieves are often as not deterred by posted signs on windows and doors. As my last and final recommendation, you should install space alarms, which are sensors that look down over the areas that are to receive protection, and activate bells or additional lights, thus scaring off intruders.

After reading the enclosed materials, please call me to further discuss the protection of your business.

Sincerely,

6.4 Interview (Objs. 1–6)

To learn more about on-the-job writing, interview someone—preferably in your field of study. Ask questions such as these: *What kind of writing do you do? What kind of planning do you do before writing? Where do you get information? Do you brainstorm? Make lists? Do you compose with pen and paper, a computer, or a dictating machine? How long does it take you to compose a routine one- or two-page memo or letter? Do you revise? How often? Do you have a preferred method for proofreading? When you have questions about grammar and mechanics, what or whom do you consult? Does anyone read your drafts and make suggestions? Can you describe your entire composition process? Do you ever work with others to produce a document? How does this process work? What makes writing easier or harder for you? Have your writing methods and skills changed since you left school?* Your instructor may ask you to present your findings orally or in a written report.

6.5 Clarity (Obj. 1)

Revise the following sentences to make them direct, simple, and conversational.

a. As per your written instruction, we will undertake the task of studying your investment program.

b. A request that we are making to managers is that they not spend all their time in their departments and instead visit other departments one hour a month.

c. We in management are of the opinion that employees have not been made sufficiently aware of the problem of computer security.

d. Our organization is honored to have the pleasure of extending a welcome to you as a new customer.

e. Please be advised that it is our intention to make every effort to deliver your order by the date of your request, December 1.

f. Enclosed herewith please find the proposal which we have the honor to submit to your esteemed organization in regard to the acquisition and purchase of laptop computers.

g. It has been established that the incontestable key to the future success of QuadCam is a deep and firm commitment to quality.

h. It is our suggestion that you do not attempt to move forward until you seek and obtain approval of the plan from the team leader prior to beginning this project.

i. It has been determined by the staff that our process of check verification for customers must be simplified.

j. Past experience has indicated that employees who have had the opportunity to attend training sessions benefit most greatly when those sessions are not overly long.

k. If doubt is entertained regarding an optimal solution to the problem of acquiring new equipment, may I suggest that we refer the problem to a newly appointed team.

l. It is the personal opinion of this writer that when deadlines have the characteristics of negotiation, they are no longer effective.

6.6 Conciseness (Obj. 1)

Suggest shorter forms for the following expressions.

a. at this point in time

b. in reference to

c. in regard to

d. without further delay

e. on an annual basis

f. in the event that

g. a report for which you have no use

h. a project manager who took great care

i. arranged according to numbers

j. a program that is intended to save time

6.7 Conciseness (Obj. 1)

Revise and shorten the following sentences.

a. There are three people who volunteered for the new team.

b. As per your suggestion, we will not attempt to make alterations or changes in the proposal at this point in time.

c. Because of the fact that his visit was an unexpected surprise, we were totally unprepared to make a presentation of profit and loss figures.

d. It is perfectly clear that meetings held on a weekly basis are most effective.

e. Despite our supposition that the bill appeared erroneous, we sent a check in the amount of $250.

f. We have received your letter, and we are sending the brochures you request.

g. A great majority of companies are unaware of the fact that college interns cannot displace regular employees.

h. There are numerous benefits that can result from a good program that focuses on customer service.

i. Because of the degree of active employee participation, we are of the opinion that our team management program will be successful.

j. At this point in time in the program, I wish to extend my grateful thanks to all the support staff who helped make this occasion possible.

k. There is a short questionnaire enclosed that is designed to help us take action on the proposed environment plan.

l. In accordance with your wishes, we are sending you under separate cover two contract forms.

m. Although our sales figures for July are high in number, past experience has indicated that this is not an unusual condition for the middle of summer.

n. This is to inform you that service should be our first and foremost goal.

o. It is certain that our team will give consideration to the fact that funds are limited.

p. For each and every single customer who complains, there are 10 to 15 other ones out there who are not bothering to speak up about their dissatisfaction or unhappiness.

q. Our consultants can assist you in answering questions that you may have about our fitness equipment.

r. It is our expectation that we will see increases in sales when our sales associates learn the new system.

s. Those who function as suppliers may not have a full understanding of the problem.

t. Except in the instance of FatBurger, most fast-food chains are aware of the fact that many consumers want choices on the menu that are healthful.

u. Two weeks in advance of its planned date of release, the announcement regarding our relocation was leaked to the press.

v. This is just to let you know that applications will be accepted at a later date for employees who are at the entry level.

w. Did the CEO give you any indication as to whether she was coming?

x. There are many words that are useless that can be eliminated through revision that is carefully done.

6.8 Vigor (Obj. 2)

Revise the following sentences to reduce noun conversions, trite expressions, and other wordiness.

a. We must make the assumption that you wish to be transferred.

b. Please give consideration to our latest proposal, despite the fact that it comes into conflict with the original plan.

c. The committee reached the conclusion that a great majority of students had a preference for mail-in registration.

d. Please conduct an investigation of employee turnover in that department for the period of June through August.

e. After we engage in the preparation of a report, our recommendations will be presented in their final form before the Executive Committee.

f. There are three members of our staff who are making every effort to locate your lost order.

g. Whether or not we make a continuation of the sales campaign is dependent upon its success in the city of Houston.

h. If you need further assistance, please do not hesitate to call me at 889-1901.

i. Please forward any bills in connection with the construction, in accordance with our agreement, to the address of my attorney.

j. Members of the team have taken into consideration every one of the factors that has the capacity to affect the purchase.

6.9 Parallelism (Obj. 3)

Revise the following sentences to improve parallelism. If elements cannot be balanced fluently, use appropriate subordination.

a. Your goal should be to write business messages that are concise, clear, and written with courteousness.

b. Ensuring equal opportunities, the removal of barriers, and elimination of age discrimination are our objectives.

c. Ms. Thomas tries to read all e-mail messages daily, but responses may not be made until the following day.

d. Last year Mr. Alvarro wrote letters and was giving presentations to promote investment in his business.

e. Because of its air-conditioning and since it is light and attractive, I prefer this office.

f. For this position we assess oral and written communication skills, how well individuals solve problems, whether they can work with teams, and we're also interested in interpersonal skills, such as cultural awareness and sensitivity.

6.10 Highlighting (Obj. 3)

Revise the following statements using the suggested highlighting techniques. Improve parallel construction and reduce wordiness if necessary.

a. Revise using letters, such as (a) and (b), within the sentence.

The benefits for employees that our organization offers include annual vacations of two weeks, insurance for group life, provision for insurance coverage of medical expenses for the family, and a private retirement fund.

b. Revise using a vertical list with bullets.

The American Automobile Association makes a provision of the following tips for safe driving. You should start your drive well rested. You should wear sunglasses in bright sunshine. To provide exercise breaks, plan to stop every two hours. Be sure not to drink alcohol or take cold and allergy medications before you drive.

c. Revise using a vertical list with numbers.

Our attorney made a recommendation that we take several steps to avoid litigation in regard to sexual harassment. The first step we should take involves establishing an unequivocal written statement prohibiting sexual harassment within our organization. The second thing we should do is make sure training sessions are held for supervisors regarding a proper work environment. Finally, some kind of procedure for employees to lodge complaints is necessary. This procedure should include investigation of complaints.

6.11 Proofreading (Objs. 4 and 5)

Use proofreading marks to mark spelling, grammar, punctuation, capitalization, and other errors in the following sentences.

a. To be elligible for this job, you must: (1) Be a U.S. citizen, (2) Be able to pass a through back ground investigation, and (3) Be available for world wide assignment.

b. Some businesses view "quality" as a focus of the organization rather then as a atribute of goods or services.

c. Its easy to get caught up in internal problems, and to overlook customers needs.

d. Incidently we expect both the ceo and the president to give there speechs before noon.

e. This is to inform you that wordiness destroys clarity therefore learn to cut the fat from your writing.

f. A clothing outlet opened at lakeland plaza in june, however business isslow.

C.L.U.E. REVIEW 6

Edit the following sentences to correct faults in grammar, punctuation, spelling, and word use.

1. Business documents must be written clear to insure that readers comprehend the message quick.
2. We expect Mayor Wilson to visit the govenor in an attempt to increase the cities share of State funding.
3. The caller could have been him but we don't know for sure. Since he didn't leave his name.
4. The survey was sited in an article entitled "Whats new in softwear, however I can't locate it now.
5. All three of our companys auditors—Jim Lucus, Doreen Delgado, and Brad Kirby—critisized there accounting procedures.
6. Anyone of the auditors are authorized to procede with an independant action, however, only a member of the management counsel can alter policy.
7. Because our printer has been broke everyday this week; were looking at new models.
8. Have you all ready ordered the following? a dictionary a reference manual and a style book.
9. In the morning Mrs Williams ordinarilly opens the office, in the evening Mr Williams usualy closes it.
10. When you travel in england and ireland I advice you to charge purchases to your visa credit card.

UNIT •3•

Business Correspondence

CHAPTER • 7 •

Routine Letters and Goodwill Messages

LEARNING OBJECTIVES

1. List three characteristics of good letters and describe the direct pattern for organizing letters.
2. Write letters requesting information and action.
3. Write letters placing orders.
4. Write letters making claims.
5. Write letters complying with requests.
6. Write letters of recommendation.
7. Write letters granting claims and making adjustments.
8. Write goodwill messages.
9. Modify international letters to accommodate other cultures.

Ben & Jerry's Uses Routine Letters to Sweeten Relations With Customers

America's love affair with numbingly rich ice cream may have finally plateaued. Health worries and changing tastes have apparently cut the breakneck growth of superpremium ice creams. Yet, Ben & Jerry's Homemade, premier purveyor of the superpremiums, remains one of the country's most visible ice cream companies.

In growing from a 12-flavor miniparlor in Burlington, Vermont, into a Fortune 500 company called a "national treasure," Ben & Jerry's has been showered with publicity. The flood of press notices flows not so much from its rapid ascent or its funky flavor hits like "Chunky Monkey," "Cherry Garcia," and its latest concoction, "Dilbert's World Totally Nuts"(butter almond ice cream with roasted hazelnuts, praline pecans, and white fudge-coated almonds). Of great media interest is the New Age business philsophy of founders Ben Cohen and Jerry Greenfield. Unlike most entrepreneurs, their aim is to build a successful business but, at the same time, be a force for social change.

Despite a falloff in its rate of growth, Ben & Jerry's continues to strive to operate in a way that improves local and global quality of life. It contributes 7½ percent of its pretax profits to charitable causes, ranging from cash grants for Vermont community groups to support for national progressive grassroots causes. Equally important is its mission to create career opportunities, financial rewards, and a fun-filled work environment for employees.

Such a visible company with a popular national product and a strong social stance naturally generates a lot of correspondence. Customer letters typically fall into three categories: (1) "fan" mail, (2) information requests, and (3) claims. Fan mail contains praise and testimonials: "Tried the new Cherry Garcia Frozen Yogurt and . . . I want to go to Vermont and shake your sticky hands." Information requests may involve questions about ingredients or food processing, and some letters comment on Ben & Jerry's social positions. Claim letters generally contain a complaint and require immediate response. Responding to customer letters in all three categories is a critical element in maintaining customer goodwill and market position for Ben & Jerry's.[1]

www.benjerry.com

Strategies for Routine Letters

1

Letters, such as those sent by Ben & Jerry's to its customers, are a primary channel of communication for delivering messages *outside* an organization. In this book we'll divide letters into three groups: (1) routine letters communicating straightforward requests, replies, and goodwill messages; (2) persuasive messages including sales pitches; and (3) negative messages delivering refusals and bad news.

Routine letters to outsiders encourage product feedback, project a favorable company image, and promote future business.

This chapter concentrates on routine, straightforward letters through which we conduct everyday business and convey goodwill to outsiders. Such letters go to suppliers, government agencies, other businesses, and, most importantly, customers. The letters to customers receive a high priority because these messages encourage product feedback, project a favorable image of the company, and promote future business.

Publisher Malcolm Forbes understood the power of business letters when he said, "A good business letter can get you a job interview, get you off the hook, or get you money. It's totally asinine to blow your chances of getting *whatever* you want—with a business letter that turns people off instead of turning them on."[2] This chapter teaches you what turns readers on. You'll study the characteristics of good letters, techniques for organizing direct requests and responses, and ways to apply the 3-×-3 writing process. You'll learn how to write six specific kinds of direct letters, along with special goodwill messages. Finally, you'll study how to modify letters to accommodate other cultures.

Characteristics of Good Letters

Although routine letters deliver straightforward facts, they don't have to sound and look dull or mechanical. At least three characteristics distinguish good business letters: clear content, a tone of goodwill, and correct form.

Clear letters feature short sentences and paragraphs, transitional expressions, familiar words, and active-voice verbs.

Clear Content. A clearly written letter separates ideas into paragraphs, uses short sentences and paragraphs, and guides the reader through the ideas with transitional expressions. Moreover, a clear letter uses familiar words and active-voice verbs. In other words, it incorporates the writing techniques you studied in Chapters 4, 5, and 6.

But many business letters are not written well. As many as one third of business letters do nothing more than seek clarification of earlier correspondence. Clear letters avoid this problem by answering all the reader's questions or concerns so that no further correspondence is necessary. Clear letters also speak the language of the receiver. One expert says, "The only sure-fire way to avoid miscommunication is to determine your audience's characteristics" and write in his or her language.[3] This doesn't mean "dumbing down" your remarks. It means taking into consideration what your reader knows about the subject and using appropriate words.

Letters achieve a tone of goodwill by emphasizing a "you" view and reader benefits.

A Tone of Goodwill. Good letters, however, have to do more than deliver clear messages; they also must build goodwill. Goodwill is a positive feeling the reader has toward an individual or an organization. By analyzing your audience and adapting your message to the reader, your letters can establish an overall tone of goodwill.

To achieve goodwill, look for ways to present the message from the reader's perspective. In other words, emphasize the "you" view and point out benefits to the reader. In addition, be sensitive to words that might suggest gender, racial, age, or disability bias. Finally, frame your ideas positively because they will sound more pleasing and will give more information than negative constructions. For example, which sounds better and gives more information? *We cannot send your order until April 1* or *We can send your order April 1.*

Appropriate letter formats send silent but positive messages.

Correct Form. A business letter conveys silent messages beyond that of its printed words. The letter's appearance and format reflect the writer's carefulness and experience. A short letter bunched at the top of a sheet of paper, for example, looks as if it was prepared in a hurry or by an amateur.

For your letters to make a good impression, you need to select an appropriate format. The block style shown in Figure 7.1 is a popular format. Other letter formats are illustrated later in this chapter and shown in Appendix C. In the block style the parts of your letter—dateline, inside address, body, and so on—are set flush left on the page. Also, the letter is formatted so that it is centered on the page and framed by white space. Most letters will have margins of 1 to 1½ inches.

Finally, be sure to use ragged-right margins; that is, don't allow your computer to justify the right margin and make all lines end evenly. Unjustified margins improve readability, say experts, by providing visual stops and by making it easier to tell where the next line begins. Although book publishers use justified right margins, as you see on this page, your letters should be ragged right. Study Figure 7.1 for more tips on making your letters look professional.

FIGURE 7.1 **Business Letter Formatting**

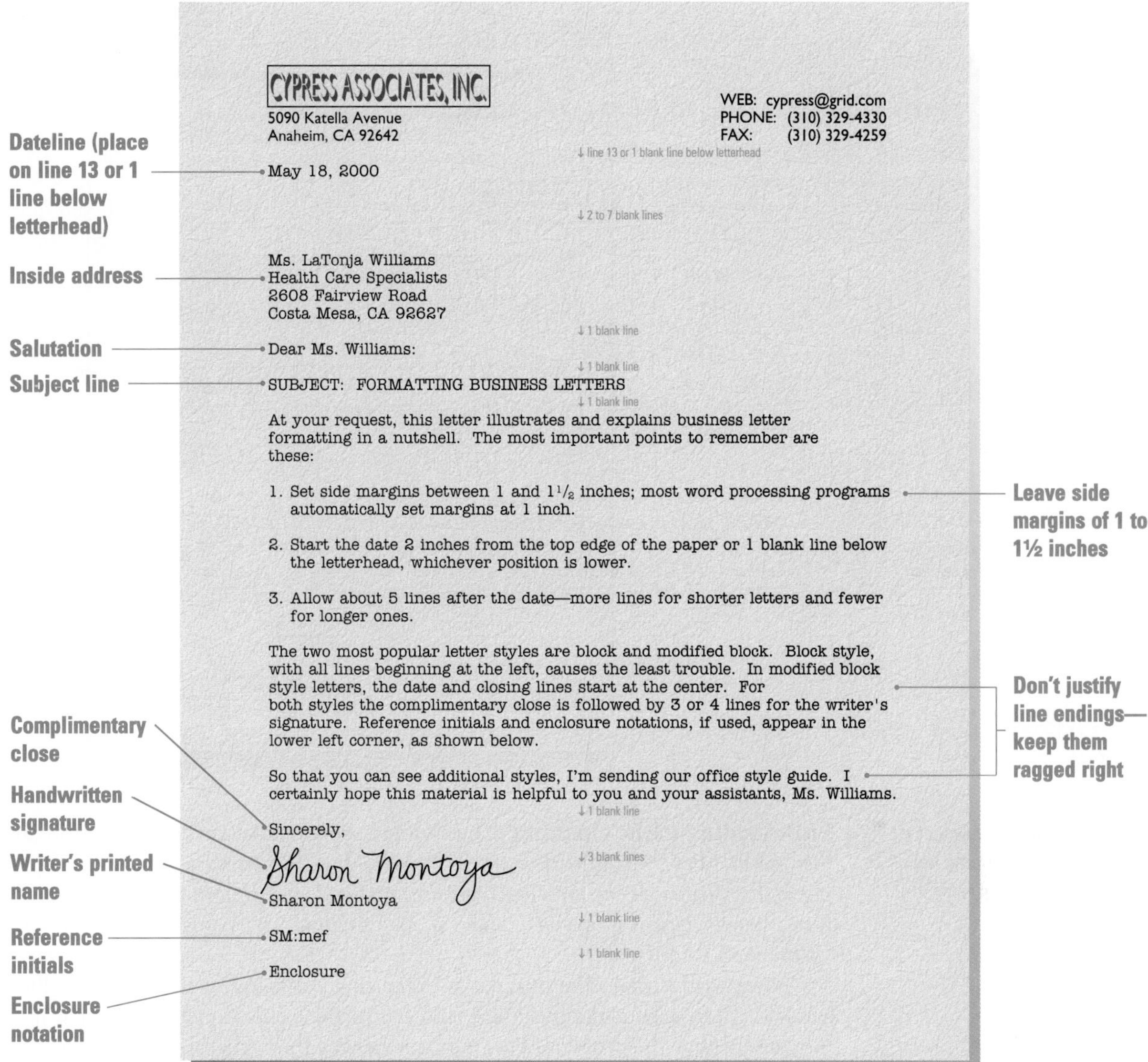

CYPRESS ASSOCIATES, INC.
5090 Katella Avenue
Anaheim, CA 92642

WEB: cypress@grid.com
PHONE: (310) 329-4330
FAX: (310) 329-4259

May 18, 2000

Ms. LaTonja Williams
Health Care Specialists
2608 Fairview Road
Costa Mesa, CA 92627

Dear Ms. Williams:

SUBJECT: FORMATTING BUSINESS LETTERS

At your request, this letter illustrates and explains business letter formatting in a nutshell. The most important points to remember are these:

1. Set side margins between 1 and 1 1/2 inches; most word processing programs automatically set margins at 1 inch.

2. Start the date 2 inches from the top edge of the paper or 1 blank line below the letterhead, whichever position is lower.

3. Allow about 5 lines after the date—more lines for shorter letters and fewer for longer ones.

The two most popular letter styles are block and modified block. Block style, with all lines beginning at the left, causes the least trouble. In modified block style letters, the date and closing lines start at the center. For both styles the complimentary close is followed by 3 or 4 lines for the writer's signature. Reference initials and enclosure notations, if used, appear in the lower left corner, as shown below.

So that you can see additional styles, I'm sending our office style guide. I certainly hope this material is helpful to you and your assistants, Ms. Williams.

Sincerely,

Sharon Montoya

Sharon Montoya

SM:mef

Enclosure

Using the Direct Pattern for Routine Letters

The everyday transactions of a business consist mainly of routine requests and responses. Because you expect the reader's response to be positive or neutral, you won't need special techniques to be convincing, to soften bad news, or to be tactful. Thus, in composing routine letters, you can organize your message, as shown in Figure 7.2, into three parts:

Most business messages are routine requests or routine responses.

- **Opening:** a statement that announces the purpose immediately
- **Body:** details that explain the purpose
- **Closing:** a request for action or a courteous conclusion

FIGURE 7.2 **Three-Part Direct Pattern for Routine Requests and Responses**

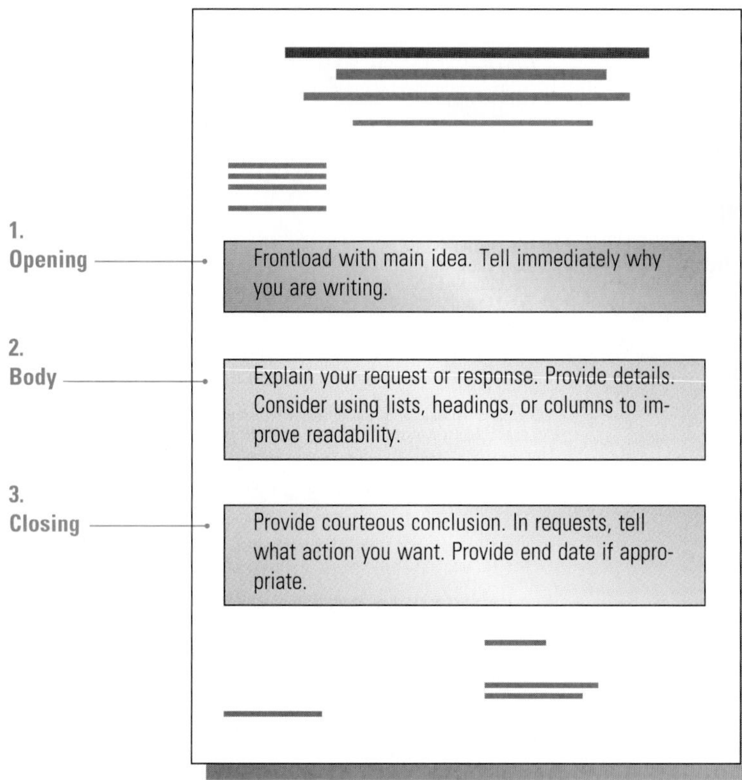

1. Opening
Frontload with main idea. Tell immediately why you are writing.
2. Body
Explain your request or response. Provide details. Consider using lists, headings, or columns to improve readability.
3. Closing
Provide courteous conclusion. In requests, tell what action you want. Provide end date if appropriate.

Everyday business messages "frontload" by presenting the main idea or purpose immediately.

Frontloading in the Opening. You should begin everyday messages in a straightforward manner by frontloading the main idea. State immediately why you are writing so that the reader can anticipate and comprehend what follows. Remember, every time a reader begins a message, he or she is thinking, "Why was this sent to me?" "What am I to do?"

Some writers make the mistake of organizing a message as if they were telling a story.[4] They start at the beginning and follow the same sequence in which they thought through the problem. This means reviewing the background, discussing the reasons for action, and then requesting an action. Most business letters, though, are better written "backwards." Start with the action desired or the main idea. Don't get bogged down in introductory material, history, justifications, or old-fashioned "business" language.[5] Instead, reveal your purpose immediately. Compare the following indirect and direct openers to see the differences:

Indirect Opening	Direct Opening
Our company is experiencing difficulty in retaining employees. We also need help in screening job applicants. Our current testing program is unsatisfactory. I understand that you offer employee testing materials, and I have a number of questions to ask.	Please answer the following questions about your personnel testing materials.

Most simple requests should open immediately with a statement of purpose (*Please answer these questions about. . . .*). Occasionally, however, complex requests may require a sentence or two of explanation or background before the purpose is revealed. What you want to avoid, though, is delaying the purpose of the letter beyond the first paragraph.

Explaining in the Body. After a direct opening that tells the reader why you are writing, present details that explain your request or response. This is where your planning pays off, allowing you to structure the information for maximum clarity and readability. Here you should consider using some graphic devices to highlight the details: a numbered or bulleted list, headings, columns, or boldface or italic type.

The body explains the purpose for writing, perhaps using graphic devices to highlight important ideas.

If you have considerable information, you'll want to develop each idea in a separate paragraph with effective transitions to connect them. The important thing to remember is to keep similar ideas together. The biggest problem in business writing is poor organization, and the body of a letter is where that failure becomes apparent.

Being Specific and Courteous in the Closing. In the last paragraph of direct letters, readers look for action information: schedules, deadlines, activities to be completed. Thus, at this point, you should specify what you want the reader to do. If appropriate, include an end date—a date for completion of the action. If possible, give reasons for establishing the deadline. Research shows that people want to know why they should do something—even if the reasons seem obvious. Moreover, people want to be treated courteously (*Please answer these questions before April 1, when we must make a final decision*), not bossed around (*Send this information immediately*).

The closing courteously specifies what the receiver is to do.

Applying the 3-×-3 Writing Process to Routine Letters

Although routine letters may be short and straightforward, they benefit from attention to the composition process. "If you force yourself to think through what you want to say and to whom you want to say it," observed a communication consultant in *Business Week*, "the writing task becomes infinitely easier."[6] Here's a quick review of the 3-×-3 writing process to help you think through its application to routine letters.

Before writing routine letters, make yourself analyze your purpose and anticipate the response.

Analysis, Anticipation, and Adaptation. Before writing, spend a few moments analyzing your task and audience. Your key goals here are (1) determining your purpose, (2) anticipating the reaction of your audience, and (3) visualizing the audience. Too often, letter writers start a message without enough preparation. Alice Blachly, a veteran letter writer at Ben & Jerry's, realizes the problem. She says, "If I'm having trouble with a letter and it's not coming out right, it's almost always because I haven't thought through exactly what I want to say."[7]

Research, Organization, and Composition. Collect information and make a list of the points you wish to cover. For short messages such as an answer to a customer's inquiry, jot your notes down on the document you are answering. For longer documents that require formal research, use a cluster diagram or the outlining techniques discussed in Chapter 5. When business letters carry information that won't upset the receiver, you can organize them in the direct manner described earlier. And be sure to plan for revision. A writer can seldom turn out an excellent message on the first attempt. For easier revision, keyboard your message on your computer.

Revision, Proofreading, and Evaluation. When you finish the first draft, revise for clarity. The receiver should not have to read the message twice to grasp its meaning. Proofread for correctness. Check for punctuation irregularities, typos, misspelled words, or other mechanical problems. *Always* take time to examine the words highlighted by your spell checker. Finally, evaluate your product. Before any letter leaves her desk at Ben & Jerry's, writer Alice Blachly always rereads it and puts herself in the shoes of the reader: "How would I feel if I were receiving it?"

Direct Request Letters

2

A direct letter may open with a question or a polite request.

Many of your routine business letters will fall into one of three categories: (1) asking for information or action, (2) placing orders for products, or (3) making a claim requiring an adjustment when something has gone wrong. In this section you'll learn how to write good letters for each of these circumstances. Before you write any letter, though, consider its costs in terms of your time and workload. Whenever possible, don't write! Instead of asking for information, could you find it yourself? Would a telephone call, an e-mail message, or a brief visit to a coworker solve the problem quickly? If not, use the direct pattern to present your request efficiently.

Requesting Information and Action

The majority of your business letters will request information or action. Suppose you have questions about a payroll accounting service your company is considering or you need to ask a customer to supply missing data from an order. For these routine messages put the main idea first. If your request involves several questions, you could open with a polite request, such as *Will you please answer the following questions about your payroll service.* Note that although this request sounds like a question, it's actually a disguised command. Since you expect an action rather than a reply, punctuate this polite command with a period instead of a question mark.

Questions in a direct letter should be parallel (balanced grammatically).

Clarifying Requests. In the letter body explain your purpose and provide details. If you have questions, express them in parallel form so that you balance them grammatically. To elicit the most information, pose open-ended questions (*What computer lock-down device can you recommend?*) instead of yes-or-no questions (*Do you carry computer lock-down devices?*). If you are asking someone to do something, be sure your tone is polite. When possible, focus on benefits to the reader (*To ensure that you receive the exact sweater you want, send us your color choice*). In the closing tell the reader courteously what is to be done. If a date is important, set an end date to take action and explain why. Some careless writers end request letters simply with *Thank you,* forcing the reader to review the contents to determine what is expected and when. You can save the reader time by spelling out the action to be taken. Avoid other overused endings such as *Thank you for your cooperation* (trite) and *If you have any questions, do not hesitate to call me* (suggests that you didn't make yourself clear).

Direct request letters maintain a courteous tone, spell out what needs to be done, and focus on reader benefits.

Showing Appreciation. It's always appropriate to show appreciation, but try to do so in a fresh and efficient manner. For example, you could hook your thanks to the end date (*Thanks for returning the questionnaire before May 5, when we will begin tabulation*). You might connect your appreciation to a statement developing reader benefits (*We are grateful for the information you will provide because it will help us serve you better*). Or you could describe briefly how the information will help you (*I appreciate this information that will enable me to . . .*). When possible, make it easy for the reader to comply with your request (*Here's my e-mail address so that you can reach me quickly*).

Let's now analyze the first draft of a direct request letter written by office manager Melanie Marshall. She wants information about computer security devices, but the first version of her letter is confusing and inefficient. Melanie makes a common mistake: starting the message with a description of the problem instead of starting with the main idea. The most effective messages tell a story from the reader's perspective, not the writer's.*

Poorly Written First Draft

Our insurance rates will be increased soon if we don't install security devices on our computer equipment. We have considered some local suppliers, but none had exactly what we wanted.

Starts with background information and explanation instead of request.

We need a device that can be used to secure separate computer components at a workstation including a computer, keyboard, and monitor. We currently own 18 computers, keyboards, and monitors, along with six printers.

Fails to organize information into logical order.

We wonder if professionals are needed to install your security devices. We're also interested in whether the devices can be easily removed when we need to move equipment around. We are, of course, very interested in prices and quantity discounts, if you offer them.

Confuses reader by jumping around among many topics. Fails to ask specific questions.

Thank you for your attention to this matter.

Ends with cliché. Does not reveal what to do and when to do it.

Melanie's second version, shown in Figure 7.3, begins more directly. The opening sentence introduces the purpose immediately so that the reader quickly knows why the letter was sent. Melanie then provides background information. Most important, she organizes all her requests into specific questions, which are sure to bring a better result than her previous diffuse request. Study the 3-×-3 writing process outlined in Figure 7.3 to see the plan Melanie followed in improving her letter.

Placing Orders

3

Letters placing orders specify items or services, quantities, dates, prices, and payment method.

You may occasionally need to write a letter that orders supplies, merchandise, or services. Generally, such purchases are made by telephone, catalog order form, fax, or Web page. Sometimes, however, you may not have a telephone number, order form, or Web address—only a street address. To order items by letter, supply the same information that an order blank would require. In the opening let the reader know immediately that this is a purchase authorization and not merely an information inquiry. Instead of *I saw a number of interesting items in your catalog,* begin directly with order language such as *Please send me by UPS the following items from your fall merchandise catalog.*

If you're ordering many items, list them vertically in the body of your letter. Include as much specific data as possible: quantity, order number, complete description, unit price, and total price. Show the total amount, and figure the tax and shipping costs if possible. The more information you provide, the less likely that a mistake will be made.

In the closing tell how you plan to pay for the merchandise. Enclose a check, provide a credit card number, or ask to be billed. Many business organizations have credit agreements with their regular suppliers that enable them to send goods without prior payment. In addition to payment information, tell when the merchandise

*Some unformatted letters and memos such as that shown here will appear in this textbook. They illustrate content rather than form. Documents that illustrate form are shown in figures, such as Figure 7.3.

FIGURE 7.3 Direct Request Letter

The Three Phases of the Writing Process

1 PREWRITING

Analyze: The purpose of this letter is to gain specific data about devices to lock down computer equipment.

Anticipate: The audience is expected to be a busy but receptive customer service representative.

Adapt: Because the reader will probably react positively to this inquiry, the direct pattern is best.

2 WRITING

Research: Determine how much equipment must be locked down and what questions must be answered. Learn name of receiver.

Organize: Open with general inquiry about security devices. In the body give details; arrange any questions logically. Close by courteously providing a specific deadline.

Compose: Draft the first copy on a computer.

3 REVISING

Revise: Improve the clarity by grouping similar ideas together. Improve readability by listing and numbering questions. Eliminate wordiness.

Proofread: Look for typos and spelling errors. Check punctuation and placement. Indent the second line of all listed items for a clean look.

Evaluate: Is this message attractive and easily comprehended?

---

inner Circle graphics

5489 North Clark Street, Chicago, IL 60640

(708) 488-3310 phone (708) 488-3319 fax

February 3, 2000

Ms. Sue Ivorson, Customer Service
Micro Supplies and Software
P.O. Box 800
Fort Atkinson, WI 53538

Dear Ms. Ivorson: — **Addresses receiver by name**

Please provide information and recommendations regarding security equipment to prevent the theft of office computers, keyboards, monitors, and printers. — **Introduces purpose immediately**

Our office now has 18 computer workstations and 6 printers that we must secure to desks or counters. Answers to the following questions will help us select the best devices for our purpose. — **Explains need for information**

1. What device would you recommend that can secure a workstation consisting of a computer, monitor, and keyboard?
2. What expertise and equipment are required to install and remove the security device?
3. How much is each device? Do you offer quantity discounts, and if so, how much?

Groups open-ended questions into list for quick comprehension and best feedback

Your response before February 15 will help us meet an April 1 deadline from our insurance company for locking down this equipment. — **Courteously provides end date and reason**

Sincerely,

Melanie Marshall

Melanie Marshall
Office Manager

should be sent and express appreciation. The following letter from the human resources department of a business illustrates the pattern of an order letter.

Please send by express mail the following items from your summer catalog.

Opens directly with authorization for purchase, method of delivery, and catalog source.

250	No. OG-18	Payroll greeting cards	$102.50
250	No. OG-22	Payroll card envelopes	21.95
100	No. OM-01	Performance greeting cards	80.00
	Subtotal		$204.45
	Tax at 7%		14.31
	Shipping		24.00
	Total		$242.76

Uses columns to make quantity, catalog number, description, and price stand out.

Calculates totals to prevent possible mistakes.

My company would appreciate receiving these cards immediately since we are starting an employee recognition program February 12. Enclosed is our check for $242.76. If additional charges are necessary, please bill my company.

Expresses appreciation and tells when items are expected. Identifies method of payment.

Making Straightforward Claims

4

Claim letters open with a clear problem statement, support the claim with specifics, and close with a statement of goodwill.

In business many things can go wrong—promised shipments are late, warranted goods fail, or service is disappointing. When you as a customer must write to identify or correct a wrong, the letter is called a *claim.* Straightforward claims are those to which you expect the receiver to agree readily. But even these claims often require a letter. While your first action may be a telephone call or a visit to submit your claim, you may not be satisfied with the result. Written claims are often taken more seriously, and they also establish a record of what happened. Straightforward claims use a direct approach. Claims that require persuasion are presented in Chapter 9.

Most businesses today honestly want to please their customers. To compete globally and to pump up local markets, American industry is particularly sold on the idea of improving the quality of its service. Since winning a new customer is three times as expensive as retaining a current one, businesses especially want to hear what customers have to say—even when it's a complaint. One industry expert observed, "You're most likely to hear from customers when they have a complaint, and that's a good thing. They're not only giving you a chance to help them, but they're initiating a dialogue, which is exactly what you want to have with your best customers."[8]

Opening Directly. When you, as a customer, have a legitimate claim, you can expect a positive response from a company. Smart businesses today want to hear from their customers. That's why you should open a claim letter with a clear statement of the problem or with the action you want the receiver to take. You might expect a replacement, a refund, a new order, credit to your account, correction of a billing error, free repairs, free inspection, or cancellation of an order. When the remedy is obvious, state it immediately (*Please send us 24 Royal hot-air popcorn poppers to replace the 24 hot-oil poppers sent in error with our order shipped January 4*). When the remedy is less obvious, you might ask for a change in policy or procedure or simply for an explanation (*Because three of our employees with confirmed reservations were refused rooms September 16 in your hotel, would you please clarify your policy regarding reservations and late arrivals*).

Providing details without getting angry improves the effectiveness of a claim letter.

Explaining. In the body of a claim letter, explain the problem and justify your request. Provide the necessary details so that the difficulty can be corrected without further correspondence. Avoid becoming angry or trying to fix blame. Bear in mind that the person reading your letter is seldom responsible for the problem. Instead, state the facts logically, objectively, and unemotionally; let the reader decide on the causes. Include copies of all pertinent documents such as invoices, sales slips, catalog descriptions, and repair records. (By the way, be sure to send copies and NOT your originals, which could be lost.) When service is involved, cite names of individuals spoken to and dates of calls. Assume that a company honestly wants to satisfy its customers—because most do. When an alternative remedy exists, spell it out (*If you are unable to send 24 Royal hot-air popcorn poppers immediately, please credit our account now and notify us when they become available*).

Written claims submitted promptly are taken more seriously than delayed ones.

Closing. Conclude a claim letter with a courteous statement that promotes goodwill and expresses a desire for continued relations. If appropriate, include an end date (*We realize that mistakes in ordering and shipping sometimes occur. Because we've enjoyed your prompt service in the past, we hope that you will be able to send us the hot-air poppers by January 15*). Finally, in making claims, act promptly. Delaying claims makes them appear less important. Delayed claims are also more difficult to verify. By taking the time to put your claim in writing, you indicate your seriousness. A written claim starts a record of the problem, should later action be necessary. Be sure to keep a copy of your letter.

Figure 7.4 shows a first draft of a hostile claim that vents the writer's anger but accomplishes little else. Its tone is belligerent, and it assumes that the company intentionally mischarged the customer. Furthermore, it fails to tell the reader how to remedy the problem. The revision tempers the tone, describes the problem objectively, and provides facts and figures. Most important, it specifies exactly what the customer wants done.

To sum up, use the direct pattern with the main idea first when you expect little resistance to letters making requests. The following checklist reviews the direct strategy for information and action requests, orders, and adjustments.

Checklist for Writing Direct Requests

Information or Action Request Letters

- ✓ **Open by stating the main idea.** To elicit information, ask a question or issue a polite command (*Will you please answer the following questions. . . .*).

- ✓ **Explain and justify the request.** In seeking information, use open-ended questions structured in parallel, balanced form.

- ✓ **Request action in the closing.** Express appreciation, and set an end date if appropriate. Avoid clichés (*Thank you for your cooperation*).

Order Letters

- ✓ **Open by authorizing the purchase.** Use order language (*Please send me . . .*), designate the delivery method, and state your information source (such as a catalog, advertisement, or magazine article).

- **List items in the body.** Include quantity, order number, description, unit price, extension, tax, shipping, and total costs.

FIGURE 7.4 Direct Claim Letter

First Draft

Dear Good Vibes:

You call yourselves Good Vibes, but all I'm getting from your service is bad vibes! I'm furious that you have your salespeople slip in unwanted service warranties to boost your sales.

When I bought my Panatronic VCR from Good Vibes, Inc., in August, I specifically told the salesperson that I did NOT want a three-year service warranty. But there it is on my VISA statement this month! You people have obviously billed me for a service I did not authorize. I refuse to pay this charge.

How can you hope to stay in business with such fraudulent practices? I was expecting to return this month and look at CD players, but you can be sure I'll find an honest dealer this time.

Sincerely,

Sounds angry; jumps to conclusions

Forgets that mistakes happen

Fails to suggest solution

Revision

1201 Lantana Court
Lake Worth, FL 33461
September 3, 2000

Personal business letter style

Mr. Sam Lee, Customer Service
Good Vibes, Inc.
2003 53rd Street
West Palm Beach, FL 33407

Dear Mr. Lee:

Please credit my VISA account, No. 0000-0046-2198-9421, to correct an erroneous charge of $299.

States simply and clearly what to do

Explains objectively what went wrong

On August 8 I purchased a Panatronic VCR from Good Vibes, Inc. Although the salesperson discussed a three-year extended warranty with me, I decided against purchasing that service for $299. However, when my credit card statement arrived this month, I noticed an extra $299 charge from Good Vibes, Inc. I suspect that this charge represents the warranty I declined.

Doesn't blame or accuse

Documents facts

Enclosed is a copy of my sales invoice along with my VISA statement on which I circled the charge. Please authorize a credit immediately and send a copy of the transaction to me at the above address.

Suggests continued business once problem is resolved

I'm enjoying all the features of my Panatronic VCR and would like to be shopping at Good Vibes for a CD player shortly.

Uses friendly tone

Sincerely,

Keith Cortez

Keith Cortez

Enclosure

 **Close with the payment data.** Tell how you are paying and when you expect delivery. Express appreciation.

Claim Letters

 **Begin with the purpose.** Present a clear statement of the problem or the action requested—such as a refund, replacement, credit, explanation, or correction of error.

 **Explain objectively.** In the body tell the specifics of the claim. Provide copies of necessary documents.

 **End by requesting action.** Include an end date if important. Add a pleasant, forward-looking statement. Keep a copy of the letter.

Direct Reply Letters

When you can respond favorably to requests, use the direct pattern.

Occasionally, you will receive requests for information or action. In these cases your first task is deciding whether to comply. If the decision is favorable, your letter should let the reader know immediately by using the direct pattern and frontloading the good news.

This section focuses on routine reply letters in three situations: (1) complying with requests for information or action, (2) writing letters of recommendation, and (3) granting claims and making adjustments.

Complying With Requests

Often, your messages will respond favorably to requests for information or action. A customer wants information about a product. A supplier asks to arrange a meeting. Another business inquires about one of your procedures or about a former employee. In complying with such requests, you'll want to apply the same direct pattern you used in making requests.

Letters responding to requests may open with a subject line to identify the topic immediately.

The opening of a direct reply letter might contain a subject line, which helps the reader recognize the topic immediately. Usually appearing one blank line below the salutation, the subject line refers in abbreviated form to previous correspondence and/or summarizes a message (*Subject: Your Letter of August 5 About Award Programs*). It often omits articles (*a, an, the*), is not a complete sentence, and does not end with a period. Knowledgeable business communicators use a subject line to refer to earlier correspondence so that in the first sentence, the most emphatic spot in a letter, they are free to emphasize the main idea.

Opening Directly. In the first sentence of a direct reply letter, deliver the information the reader wants. Avoid wordy, drawn-out openings such as *I have before me your letter of August 5, in which you request information about. . . .* More forceful and more efficient is an opener that answers the inquiry (*Here is the information you wanted about . . .*). When agreeing to a request, announce the good news promptly (*Yes, I will be happy to speak to your class on the topic of . . .*).

In the body of your reply, supply explanations and additional information. Because a letter written on company stationery is considered a legally binding contract, be sure to check facts and figures carefully. If a policy or procedure needs authorization, seek approval from a supervisor or executive before writing the letter.

Arranging Information Logically. When answering a group of questions or providing considerable data, arrange the information logically and make it readable by using lists, tables, headings, boldface, italics, or other graphic devices. When customers or prospective customers inquire about products or services, your response should do more than merely supply answers. You'll also want to promote your organization and products. Often, companies have particular products and services they want to spotlight. Thus, when a customer writes about one product, provide helpful information that satisfies the inquiry, but consider introducing another product as well. Be sure to present the promotional material with attention to the "you" view and to reader benefits (*You can use our standardized tests to free you from time-consuming employment screening*). You'll learn more about special techniques for developing sales and persuasive messages in Chapter 9.

Responding to customer inquiries provides a good opportunity to promote your business.

In concluding, make sure you are cordial and personal. Refer to the information provided or to its use. If further action is required, describe the procedure and help the reader with specifics (*The Small Business Administration publishes a number of helpful booklets. Its Web address is. . . .*).

Illustrating Reply Letters. In replying to a customer's request for information, the writer in Figure 7.5 begins with a subject line that immediately identifies the topic and refers to previous correspondence. She uses the first sentence to present the most important information. Then she itemizes her list of responses to the customer's questions. If she had written these responses in paragraph form, they would have been less emphatic and more difficult to read. She goes on to describe and promote the product, being careful to show how it would benefit the customer. And she concludes by referring specifically to pages in an enclosed pamphlet and providing a number for the customer's response.

A direct reply letter, shown in Figure 7.6, responds to a request from a young Ben & Jerry's customer. The opening announces the letter's purpose immediately and also establishes rapport with the reader by describing similarities between the reader's Ben & Jerry's club and its parent organization. The body of the letter includes a bulleted list and an explanation of the items being sent. Notice how the writer invites future business by enclosing "ballots," on which consumers suggest to local grocers favorite ice cream flavors to be stocked. The cordial, personalized closing concludes a direct reply letter that is sure to build goodwill and promote future business while delivering the information sought.

Treating Mixed Messages. The direct pattern is also appropriate for messages that are mostly good news but may have some negative elements. For example, a return policy has time limits; an air fare may contain holiday restrictions; a speaker can come but not at the time requested; an appliance can be repaired but not replaced. When the message is mixed, emphasize the good news by presenting it first (*Yes, I would be delighted to address your marketing class on the topic of . . .*). Then, explain why a problem exists (*My schedule for the week of October 10 takes me to Washington and Philadelphia, where I am . . .*). Present the bad news in the middle (*Although I cannot meet with your class at that time, perhaps we can schedule a date during the week of . . .*). End the message cordially by returning to the good news (*Thanks for the invitation. I'm looking forward to arranging a date in October when I can talk with your students about careers in marketing*).

In mixed-news messages the good news should precede the bad.

Your goal is to present the negative news clearly without letting it become the focus of the message. Thus, you want to spend more time talking about the good news. And by placing the bad news in the middle of the letter, you deemphasize it. You'll learn other techniques for presenting bad news in Chapter 10.

FIGURE 7.5 **Customer Reply Letter**

PREWRITING 1

Analyze: The purpose of this letter is to provide helpful information and to promote company products.

Anticipate: The reader is the intelligent owner of a small business who needs help with personnel administration.

Adapt: Because the reader requested this data, she will be receptive. Use the direct pattern.

WRITING 2

Research: Gather facts to answer the business owner's questions. Consult brochures and pamphlets.

Organize: Prepare a scratch outline. Plan for a fast, direct opening. Use bulleted answers to the business owner's three questions.

Compose: Write the first draft on a computer. Strive for short sentences and paragraphs.

REVISING 3

Revise: Eliminate jargon and wordiness. Look for ways to explain how the product fits the reader's needs. Revise for "you" view.

Proofread: Double-check the form of numbers (*July 12, page 6, 8 to 5 PST*).

Evaluate: Does this letter answer the customer's questions and encourage an order?

SONOMA SOFTWARE, INC.
520 Sonoma Parkway
Petaluma, CA 94539
www.sonoma.com

July 15, 2000

Mr. Jeffrey M. White
White-Rather Enterprises
1349 Century Boulevard
Wichita Falls, TX 76308

Dear Mr. White:

SUBJECT: YOUR JULY 12 INQUIRY ABOUT PERSONNEL SOFTWARE

Identifies previous correspondence and subject

Puts most important information first

Yes, we do offer personnel record-keeping software specially designed for small businesses like yours. Here are answers to your three questions about this software:

Lists answers to sender's questions in order asked / *Emphasizes "you" view*

1. Our Personnel Manager software provides standard employee forms so that you are always in compliance with current government regulations.

2. You receive an interviewer's guide for structured employee interviews, as well as a scripted format for checking references by telephone.

3. Yes, you can update your employees' records easily without the need for additional software, hardware, or training.

Links sales promotion to reader benefits

This software was specially designed to provide you with expert forms for interviewing, verifying references, recording attendance, evaluating performance, and tracking the status of your employees. We even provide you with step-by-step instructions and suggested procedures. You can treat your employees as if you had a professional human resources specialist on your staff.

Helps reader find information by citing pages / *Makes it easy to respond*

On page 6 of the enclosed pamphlet you can read about our Personnel Manager software. To receive a preview copy or to ask questions about its use, just call 1-800-354-5500. Our specialists are eager to help you weekdays from 8 to 5 PST. If you prefer, visit our Web site to receive more information or to place an order.

Sincerely,

Amy Villanueva

Amy Villanueva
Senior Marketing Representative

Enclosure

FIGURE 7.6 Direct Reply from Ben & Jerry's

January 18, 2000

Ms. Jennifer Ball
1401 Churchville Lane
Bel Air, MD 21014

Dear Jennifer:

We're delighted to hear of your Ben & Jerry's Club at Franklin Middle School and to send the items you request!

Your club sounds as though it resembles its parent in many ways. We, too, can't seem to control our growth; and we, too, get a little out of control on Friday afternoons. Moreover, the simplicity of your club rules mirrors the philosophy of our co-founder, who says, "If it's not fun, why do it?"

Enclosed are the following items:

- A list of all flavors available in pints. If you can't find these flavors at your grocer's, I'm sending you some "ballots" for your club's use in encouraging your grocer to stock your favorites.
- The latest issue of Ben & Jerry's "Chunk Mail." We're also putting you on our mailing list so that your club will receive our Chunk Mail newsletter regularly.

We hope, Jennifer, that you'll soon tour our plant here in Vermont. Then, you can be on an equal footing with your prez and sport one of our tour buttons. This seems only appropriate for the consensus-building, decision-making model you are pioneering in your Ben & Jerry's Club!

Sincerely,

Alice

Alice Blachly
Consumer Affairs

Enc: Flavor list, ballots, Chunk Mail

P.O. BOX 240, WATERBURY, VERMONT 05676 (802) 244-6957 FAX (802) 244-5944
100% Post-Consumer Recycled Paper

Personalizes reply and builds goodwill with reference to writer's letter

Opens directly with response to customer's request

Itemizes and explains enclosures requested by customer

Ties in cordial closing with more references to customer's letter

Writing Letters of Recommendation

Letters of recommendation may be written to nominate people for awards and for membership in organizations. More frequently, though, they are written to evaluate present or former employees. The central concern in these messages is honesty. Thus, we should avoid exaggerating or distorting a candidate's qualifications to cover up weaknesses or to destroy the person's chances. Ethically and legally, we have a duty to the candidate as well as to other employers to describe that person truthfully and objectively. We don't, however, have to endorse everyone who asks. Since recommendations are generally voluntary, we can—and should—resist writing letters for individuals we can't truthfully support. Ask these people to find other recommenders who know them better.

ETHICAL INSIGHTS

USING CAUTION IN WRITING LETTERS OF RECOMMENDATION

Fearing lawsuits, many companies prohibit their managers from recommending ex-employees. Instead, they provide only the essentials, such as date of employment and position held. Is it ethical for employers to refuse such requests? In truth, employers have little reason to fear providing honest references. *U.S. News & World Report* revealed that only 12 employment-related defamation suits involving job references were filed between 1985 and 1990, and these figures have changed very little in recent years.[9]

An even more worrisome ethical problem involves companies that fail to provide references revealing problems with employees. A growing trend in lawsuits are judgments against employers who conceal knowledge of demonstrated violent or dangerous behavior of former employees. Take, for example, a past employer who does not reveal information about a child molester who applies for work with a school. One executive admitted that he felt ethically bound to reveal serious deficiencies in former employees, even if his company prohibited the writing of recommendations. "When it comes to . . . anything that can cause really serious problems, I'll find a way to send up a red flag." Like many employers, this executive believes that the consequences of withholding critical data "can just be too great—for the new employer, for its customers and other employees—and for us."[10]

Regardless of the problems involved, most ethical and conscientious businesspeople recognize that references serve a valuable purpose in conveying personnel data. Yet, they are cautious in writing them. Here are six guidelines that a careful writer can follow in writing recommendations:

- **Respond only to written requests.** Moreover, don't volunteer information, particularly if it's negative.
- **State that your remarks are confidential.** While such a statement does not prevent legal review, it does suggest the intentions of the writer.
- **Provide only job-related information.** Avoid commenting on behavior or activities away from the job.
- **Avoid vague or ambiguous statements.** Keep in mind that imprecise, poorly explained remarks (*she left the job suddenly*) may be made innocently but could be interpreted quite differently.
- **Supply specific evidence for any negatives.** Support any damaging information with verifiable facts.
- **Stick to the truth.** Avoid making any doubtful statements. Truth is always a valid defense against libel or slander.

Career Application

You are the manager of productions at a mid-sized graphics company. A well-regarded former employee asks for your recommendation, which you want to write. However, your boss has recently prohibited the writing of any letters of recommendation. You feel strongly that you should write this recommendation. What should you do?

Letters of recommendation present honest, objective evaluations of individuals and help match candidates to jobs.

Some businesspeople today refuse to write recommendations for former employees because they fear lawsuits. See the accompanying Ethical Insights box for tips on using caution in these letters. Other businesspeople argue that recommendations are useless because they're always positive. Despite the general avoidance of negatives, well-written recommendations do help match candidates with jobs. Hiring companies learn more about a candidate's skills and potential. As a result, they are able to place a candidate properly. Therefore, you should learn to write such letters because you will surely be expected to do so in your future career.

Opening. Begin with the name of the candidate and the position sought, if it is known. State that your remarks are confidential, and suggest that you are writing at the request of the applicant. Describe your relationship with the candidate, as shown here:

Ms. Cindy Rosales, whom your organization is considering for the position of media trainer, requested that I submit confidential information on her behalf. Ms. Rosales worked under my supervision for the past two years in our Video Training Center.

The opening establishes the reason for writing and the relationship of the writer.

Letters that recommend individuals for awards may open with more supportive statements, such as *I'm very pleased to nominate Robert Walsh for the Employee-of-the-Month award. For the past sixteen months, Mr. Walsh served as staff accountant in my division. During that time he distinguished himself by. . . . .*

Body. Describe the applicant's job performance and potential. Employers are particularly interested in such traits as communication skills, organizational skills, people skills, ability to work with a team, ability to work independently, honesty, dependability, ambition, loyalty, and initiative. In describing these traits, be sure to back them up with evidence. One of the biggest weaknesses in letters of recommendation is that writers tend to make global, nonspecific statements[11] (*He was careful and accurate* versus *He completed eight financial statements monthly with about 99 percent accuracy*). Employers prefer definite, task-related descriptions:

The body of a letter of recommendation should describe the candidate's job performance and potential in specific terms.

As a training development specialist, Ms. Rosales demonstrated superior organizational and interpersonal skills. She started as a Specialist I, writing scripts for interactive video modules. After six months she was promoted to team leader. In that role she supervised five employees who wrote, produced, evaluated, revised, and installed 14 computer/videodisc training courses over a period of eighteen months.

A good recommendation describes general qualities ("organizational and interpersonal skills") backed up by specific evidence that illustrates those qualities.

Be especially careful to support any negative comments with verification (not *He was slower than other customer service reps* but *He answered 25 calls an hour, while most service reps average 40 calls an hour*). In reporting deficiencies, be sure to describe behavior (*her last two reports were late and had to be rewritten by her supervisor*) rather than evaluate it (*she is unreliable and her reports are careless*).

Conclusion. In the final paragraph, offer an overall evaluation. Tell how you would rank this person in relation to others in similar positions. Many managers add a statement indicating whether they would rehire the applicant. If you are strongly supportive, summarize the candidate's best qualities. In the closing you might also offer to answer questions by telephone. Such a statement, though, could suggest that the candidate has weak skills and that you will make damaging statements orally but not in print. Here's how our sample letter might close:

Ms. Rosales is one of the most productive employees I have supervised. I would rank her in the top 10 percent of all the media specialists with whom I have worked. Were she to return to Bridgeport, we would be pleased to rehire her. If you need additional information, call me at (517) 440-3019.

The closing of a recommendation presents an overall ranking and may provide an offer to supply more information by telephone.

General letters of recommendation, written when the candidate has no specific position in mind, often begin with the salutation TO PROSPECTIVE EMPLOYERS. More specific recommendations, to support applications to known positions, address an individual. When the addressee's name is unknown, consider using the simplified letter format, shown in Figure 7.7, which avoids a salutation.

The letter shown in Figure 7.7 illustrates a complete employment letter of recommendation and shows a summary of writing tips. After naming the applicant and the position sought, the letter describes the applicant's present duties. Instead of merely naming positive qualities (*he is personable, possesses superior people skills, works*

FIGURE 7.7 **Employment Recommendation Letter**

Tips for Writing Letters of Recommendation

- Identify the purpose and confidentiality of the message.
- Establish your relationship with the applicant.
- Describe the length of employment and job duties, if relevant.
- Provide specific examples of the applicant's professional and personal skills.
- Compare the applicant with others in his or her field.
- Offer an overall rating of the applicant.
- Summarize the significant attributes of the applicant.
- Draw a conclusion regarding the recommendation.

Good Samaritan Hospital
2404 Euclid Avenue
Cleveland, OH 44114-2900
216-939-8700

• NAHF
NATIONAL ASSOCIATION
OF HEALTH FACILITIES

February 21, 2000

Vice President, Human Resources
Healthcare Enterprises
3529 Springfield Street
Cincinnati, OH 45890

Illustrates simplified letter style — RECOMMENDATION OF LANCE W. OLIVER

Identifies applicant and position — **Mentions confidentiality of message** — **Tells relationship to writer**

At the request of Lance W. Oliver, I submit this confidential information in support of his application for the position of assistant director in your Human Resources Department. Mr. Oliver served under my supervision as assistant director of Guest Relations at Good Samaritan Hospital for the past three years.

Supports general qualities with specific details

Mr. Oliver was in charge of many customer service programs for our 770-bed hospital. A large part of his job involved monitoring and improving patient satisfaction. Because of his personable nature and superior people skills, he got along well with fellow employees, patients, and physicians. His personnel record includes a number of "Gotcha" citations, given to employees caught in the act of performing exemplary service.

Describes and interprets accomplishments

Mr. Oliver works well with a team, as evidenced by his participation on the steering committee to develop our "Service First Every Day" program. His most significant contributions to our hospital, though, came as a result of his own creativity and initiative. He developed and implemented a patient hot line to hear complaints and resolve problems immediately. This enormously successful telephone service helped us improve our patient satisfaction rating from 7.2 last year to 8.4 this year. That's the highest rating in our history, and Mr. Oliver deserves a great deal of the credit.

Summarizes main points and offers evaluation

We're sorry to lose Mr. Oliver, but we recognize his desire to advance his career. I am confident that his resourcefulness, intelligence, and enthusiasm will make him successful in your organization. I recommend him without reservation.

Mary E. O'Rourke

MARY E. O'ROURKE, DIRECTOR, GUEST RELATIONS

MEO:rtd

well with a team, is creative, and *shows initiative*), these attributes are demonstrated with specific examples and details.

Granting Claims and Making Adjustments

7

Businesses generally respond favorably to claims because of legal constraints and the desire to maintain customer goodwill.

Even the best-run and best-loved businesses occasionally receive claims or complaints from consumers. Most businesses grant claims and make adjustments promptly—they replace merchandise, refund money, extend discounts, send coupons, and repair goods. Businesses make favorable adjustments to legitimate claims for two reasons. First, consumers are protected by contractual and tort law for recovery of damages.[12] Thus, for example, if you find an insect in a package of frozen peas, the food processor of that package is bound by contractual law to replace it. And if you suffer injury, the processor may be liable for damages. Second, and more obviously, most organizations genuinely want to satisfy their customers and retain their business.

Customer goodwill and retention have an important effect on profits. One study showed that losing a customer reduces profits by $118. Keeping that customer satisfied, however, costs only $20.[13] When customers are unhappy, they don't return. A staggering 91 percent of disgruntled customers swear they will never do business again with a company that does not resolve their complaint.[14] What's worse, today's unhappy customers are wired; they have the Web to broadcast their protests to the world. In fact, entire Web sites, such as "Down With Snapple" and "Walmart Sucks.com," are devoted to blasting errant companies.[15] Small wonder that businesses are increasingly concerned with improving customer service and listening to what customers are saying.

Wise organizations value complaints not only as a chance to retain customers but also as a significant source of feedback. Comments from complainers often provide more useful information than expensive customer surveys and focus groups.

Favorable responses to customer claims follow the direct pattern; unfavorable responses follow the indirect pattern.

In responding to customer claims, you must first decide whether to grant the claim. Unless the claim is obviously fraudulent or represents an excessive sum, you'll probably grant it. When you say yes, your adjustment letter will be good news to the reader, so you'll want to use the direct pattern. When your response is no, the indirect pattern might be more appropriate. Chapter 10 discusses the indirect pattern for conveying negative news.

Adjustment letters seek to right wrongs, regain customer confidence, and promote further business.

You'll have three goals in adjustment letters:

- Rectifying the wrong, if one exists
- Regaining the confidence of the customer
- Promoting further business

Opening sentences tell the good news quickly.

Opening With the Good News. The opening of a positive adjustment letter should approve the customer's claim immediately. Notice how quickly the following openers announce the good news:

> You're right! We agree that the warranty on your American Standard Model UC600 dishwasher should be extended for six months.
>
> The enclosed $250 refund check demonstrates our desire to satisfy our customers and earn their confidence.
>
> You will be receiving shortly a new Techtronic cordless telephone to replace the one that shattered when dropped recently.
>
> Please take your Sanyo cassette tape deck to A-1 Appliance Service, 220 Orange Street, Pasadena, where it will be repaired at no cost to you.

Occasionally, customers merely want to lodge a complaint and know that something is being done about it. Here's the opening from a bank responding to such a complaint:

> We agree with you completely. Some of our customers have recently spent too much time "on hold" while waiting to speak to a customer service representative. These delays are unacceptable, and we are taking strong measures to eliminate them.

In making an adjustment, avoid sounding resentful or grudging. Once you decide to grant a claim, do so willingly. Remember that a primary goal in adjustments is retaining customer loyalty. Statements that sound reluctant (*Although we generally refuse to extend warranties, we're willing to make an exception in this case*) may cause greater dissatisfaction than no response at all.

Explain what caused the problem and the measures taken to avoid future recurrence.

Explaining the Reasons. In the body of an adjustment letter, your goal is to win back the confidence of the customer. You can do this by explaining what caused the problem (if you know) or by describing the measures you are taking to avoid recurrences of the problem, such as in the following:

> In preparing our products, we take special care to see that they are wholesome and free of foreign matter. Approved spraying procedures in the field control insects when necessary during the growing season. Our processing plants use screens, air curtains, ultraviolet lights, and other devices to exclude insects. Moreover, we inspect and clean every product to ensure that insects are not present.

Notice that this explanation does not admit error. Many companies sidestep the issue of responsibility because they feel that such an admission damages their credibility or might even encourage legal action. Others admit errors indirectly (*Oversights may sometimes occur*) or even directly (*Once in a while a product that is less than perfect goes out*). The major focus of attention, however, should be on explaining how you are working to prevent the recurrence of the problem, as illustrated in the following:

> Waiting "on hold" is as unacceptable to us as it is to you. This delay was brought about when we installed a new automated system. Unfortunately, it took longer than we expected to implement the system and to train our people in their new roles. We are now taking strong measures to eliminate the problem. We have made a significant investment in new technology that will free our customer representatives from routine calls so that they can help you with those banking needs that require personal attention. We are also rerouting calls and modifying the way they are handled.

Explain what went wrong without admitting liability or making excuses.

When an explanation poses no threat of admitting liability, provide details. But don't make your explanation sound like an excuse. Customers resent it when organizations don't take responsibility or try to put the blame elsewhere. When Intel Corp. was swamped with a flood of unfavorable responses regarding a flawed Pentium chip, President Andy Grove posted a letter to the Internet. His letter said, "I'd like to comment a bit on the conversations that have been taking place here. First of all, I'm truly sorry for the anxiety created among you by our floating-point issue." He went on to explain how Intel had tested the chip and appointed a group of mathematicians and scientists to study the problem. Eventually, Intel decided to replace all flawed chips. His letter concluded, "Please don't be concerned that the passing of time will deprive you of the opportunity to get your problem resolved. We will stand behind these chips for the life of your computer."[16] The tone of a response is extremely important, and Grove sounded sincere in his explanation.

Apologize if it seems natural and appropriate.

Should You Apologize? Another sticky issue is whether to apologize. Notice that Andy Grove of Intel apologized in his Internet letter. Studies of adjustment letters received by consumers show that a majority do contain apologies, either in the opening or in the closing.[17] Many business writing experts, however, advise against apologies, contending that they are counterproductive and merely remind the customer of unpleasantness related to the claim. However, if it seems natural to you to apologize, do so. People like to hear apologies. It raises their self-esteem and shows the humility of the writer.[18] Don't, however, fall back on the familiar phrase, "I'm sorry for any inconvenience we may have caused." It sounds mechanical and totally insincere. Instead try something like this: *We understand the frustration our delay has caused you. We're sorry you didn't receive better service,* or *You're right to be disappointed.* If you feel that an apology is appropriate, do it early and briefly, as Andy Grove did in his Internet response. Remember that the primary focus of your letter is on (1) how you are complying with the request, (2) how the problem occurred, and (3) how you are working to prevent its recurrence.

Focus on complying with request, explaining reasons, and preventing recurrence.

The language of adjustment letters must be particularly sensitive, since customers are already upset. Here are some don'ts:

- Don't use negative words (*trouble, regret, misunderstanding, fault, error, inconvenience, you claim*).
- Don't blame customers—even when they may be at fault.
- Don't blame individuals or departments within your organization; it's unprofessional.
- Don't make unrealistic promises; you can't guarantee that the situation will never recur.

To regain the confidence of your reader, consider including resale information. Describe a product's features and any special applications that might appeal to the reader. Promote a new product if it seems appropriate.

Close with appreciation, thanks for past business, and expression of desire to be of service.

Closing an Adjustment Letter. To close an adjustment letter, assume that the problem has been resolved and that future business will continue. You might express appreciation that the reader wrote, extend thanks for past business, refer to your desire to be of service, or mention a new product. Here are some effective adjustment letter closings for various purposes:

> You were most helpful in informing us of this situation and permitting us to correct it. We appreciate your thoughtfulness in writing to us.
>
> Thanks for writing. Your satisfaction is important to us. We hope that this refund check convinces you that service to our customers is our number one priority. Our goal is to earn your confidence and continue to justify that confidence with quality products and excellent service.
>
> Your cordless telephone will come in handy when you're playing and working outside this summer. For additional summer enjoyment take a look at the portable CD player on page 37 of the enclosed catalog. We value your business and look forward to your future orders.

FIGURE 7.8 **Adjustment Letter**

Rose World
One Rose Lane
Ashland, Oregon 95402
1-800-543-2000

June 3, 2000

Mr. James Bronski
1390 Moorpark Avenue
San Jose, CA 95127

Dear Mr. Bronski:

You may choose six rose bushes as replacements, or you may have a full cash refund for the roses you purchased last year.

The quality of our plants and the careful handling they receive assure you of healthy, viable roses for your garden. Even so, plants sometimes fail without apparent cause. That's why every plant carries a guarantee to grow and to establish itself in your garden.

Along with this letter is a copy of our current catalog for you to select six new roses or reorder the favorites you chose last year. Two of your previous selections—Red Velvet and Rose Princess—were last season's best-selling roses. For fragrance and old-rose charm, you might like to try the new David Austin English Roses. These enormously popular hybrids resulted from crossing full-petaled old garden roses with modern repeat-flowering shrub roses.

To help you enjoy your roses to the fullest, you'll also receive a copy of our authoritative *Home Gardener's Guide to Roses*. This comprehensive booklet provides easy-to-follow planting tips as well as sound advice about sun, soil, and drainage requirements for roses.

To receive your free replacement order, just fill out the order form inside the catalog and attach the enclosed certificate. Or return the certificate, and you will receive a full refund of the purchase price.

The quality of Rose World plants reflects the expertise of over a century of hybridizing, growing, harvesting, and shipping top-quality garden stock. Your complete satisfaction is our primary goal. If you're not happy, Mr.Bronski, we're not happy. To ensure your satisfaction and your respect, we maintain our 100 percent guarantee policy.

Sincerely,

Michael Vanderer

Michael Vanderer
General Manager

mv: meg

Enclosures

Approves customer's claim immediately

Tactfully skirts the issue of what caused plant failure

Avoids blaming customer

Offers resale information to assure customer of wise choice

Includes some sales promotion without overkill

Projects personal, conversational tone by using contractions and reader's name

Tells reader clearly what to do next

Shows pride in the company's products and concern for its customers

Strives to regain customer's confidence in both products and service

The adjustment letter in Figure 7.8 offers to replace dead rose bushes. It's very possible that grower error caused the plants to die, yet the letter doesn't blame the customer. Notice, too, how resale information and sales promotion material are introduced without seeming pushy. Most important, the tone of the letter suggests that the company is in the customer's corner and wants to do what is right.

Although the direct pattern works for many requests and replies, it obviously won't work for every situation. With more practice and experience, you'll be able to alter the pattern and apply the writing process to other communication problems. The following checklist summarizes the process of writing direct replies.

Checklist for Writing Direct Replies

Complying With Requests

 **Use a subject line.** Identify previous correspondence and the topic of this letter.

 **Open directly.** In the first sentence deliver the information the reader wants (*Yes, I can meet with your class* or *Here is the information you requested*). If the message is mixed, present the best news first.

 **In the body provide explanations and additional information.** Arrange this information logically, perhaps using a list, headings, or columns. For prospective customers build your company image and promote your products.

 **End with a cordial, personalized statement.** If further action is required, tell the reader how to proceed and give helpful details.

Writing Letters of Recommendation

 **Open with identifying information.** Name the candidate, identify the position, and explain your relationship. State that you are writing at the request of the candidate and that the letter is confidential.

 **In the body add supporting statements.** Describe the applicant's present duties, job performance, skills, and potential. Back up general qualities with specific evidence. Verify any negative statements.

 **Close with an overall ranking of the candidate.** (*Of all the people I have known in this position, Jim ranks . . .*). Offer to supply more information by telephone.

Granting Claims and Adjustments

 **Open with approval.** Comply with the customer's claim immediately. Avoid sounding grudging or reluctant.

 **In the body win back the customer's confidence.** Explain the cause of the problem or describe your ongoing efforts to avoid such difficulties. Focus on

CASE STUDY

PROCESS IN PROGRESS

Ben & Jerry's Revisited

Customer letters arriving at Ben & Jerry's get special attention from Alice Blachly, one of the consumer affairs coordinators. To fan letters, Blachly responds with handwritten cards or printed letters that promote good feelings and cement a long-lasting bond between Ben & Jerry's and its satisfied consumers. To letters with questions, Blachly locates the information and responds. For example, a consumer worried that cottonseed oil, formerly contained in the nut-butter portion of Rainforest Crunch ice cream, might be contaminated by pesticides. Blachly checked with company quality assurance experts and also investigated articles about cottonseed oil before responding. Other consumers might wonder about Ben & Jerry's position on the treatment of cows by Vermont dairy farmers.

However, letters with consumer complaints, such as "My pint didn't have quite enough cookie dough," get top priority. "We have trained our consumers to expect the best," says Blachly, "so they are disappointed when something goes wrong. And we are disappointed, too. We refund the purchase price, and we explain what caused the problem, if we know."

Critical Thinking

- When customers write to Ben & Jerry's for information and the response must contain both positive and negative news, what strategy should the respondent follow?
- If a customer writes to complain about something for which Ben & Jerry's is not responsible (such as ice in frozen yogurt), should the response letter contain an apology? Why or why not?
- Why is letter-writing an important function for a company like Ben & Jerry's?

your efforts to satisfy customers. If you apologize, do so early and briefly. Avoid negative words, accusations, and unrealistic promises. Consider including resale and sales promotion information.

Close positively. Express appreciation to the customer for writing, extend thanks for past business, anticipate continued patronage, refer to your desire to be of service, and/or mention a new product if it seems appropriate.

Writing Winning Goodwill Messages

Goodwill messages, which include thanks, recognition, and sympathy, seem to intimidate many communicators. Finding the right words to express feelings is sometimes more difficult than writing ordinary business documents. Writers tend to procrastinate when it comes to goodwill messages, or else they send a ready-made card or pick up the telephone. Remember, though, that the personal sentiments of the sender are always more expressive and more meaningful to readers than are printed cards or oral messages. Taking the time to write gives more importance to our well-wishing. Notes also provide a record that can be reread, savored, and treasured.

In expressing thanks, recognition, or sympathy, you should always do so promptly. These messages are easier to write when the situation is fresh in your mind. They also mean more to the recipient. And don't forget that a prompt thank-you note carries the hidden message that you care and that you consider the event to be important. The best goodwill messages—whether thanks, congratulations, praise, or sympathy—concentrate on the five Ss. These goodwill messages are

- **Selfless.** Be sure to focus the message solely on the receiver, not the sender. Don't talk about yourself; avoid such comments as *I remember when I. . . .*
- **Specific.** Personalize the message by mentioning specific incidents or characteristics of the receiver. Telling a colleague *Great speech* is much less effective than *Great story about McDonald's marketing in Moscow.* Take care to verify names and other facts.
- **Sincere.** Let your words show genuine feelings. Rehearse in your mind how you would express the message to the receiver orally. Then transform that conversational language to your written message. Avoid pretentious, formal, or flowery language (*It gives me great pleasure to extend felicitations on the occasion of your firm's 20th anniversary*).
- **Spontaneous.** Keep the message fresh and enthusiastic. Avoid canned phrases (*Congratulations on your promotion, Good luck in the future*). Strive for directness and naturalness, not creative brilliance.
- **Short.** Although goodwill messages can be as long as needed, try to accomplish your purpose in only a few sentences. What's most important is remembering an individual. Such caring does not require documentation or wordiness. Individuals and business organizations often use special note cards or stationery for brief messages.

Thanks

When someone has done you a favor or when an action merits praise, you need to extend thanks or show appreciation. Letters of appreciation may be written to customers for their orders, to hosts and hostesses for their hospitality, to individuals for kindnesses performed, and especially to customers who complain. After all, complainers are actually providing you with "free consulting reports from the field."

8

Spotlight on **Communicators**

Brent Frei, co-founder and CEO of Onyx Software Corporation, works to keep the lines of communication open between employees, management, and customers. His company makes enterprise relationship management software that enhances organizational communication. When a company is small, he says, the boss knows everyone. But when a company grows, managers must promote communication through an open-door policy, frequent talks with employees, and goodwill messages.

Complainers who feel that they were listened to often become the greatest promoters of an organization.[19]

Because the receiver will be pleased to hear from you, you can open directly with the purpose of your message. The letter in Figure 7.9 thanks a speaker who addressed a group of marketing professionals. Although such thank-you notes can be quite short, this one is a little longer because the writer wants to lend importance to the receiver's efforts. Notice that every sentence relates to the receiver and offers enthusiastic praise. And, by using the receiver's name along with contractions and positive words, the writer makes the letter sound warm and conversational.

Written notes that show appreciation and express thanks are significant to their receivers. In expressing thanks, you generally write a short note on special notepaper or heavy card stock. The following messages provide models for expressing thanks for a gift, for a favor, and for hospitality.

To Express Thanks for a Gift
Thanks, Laura, to you and the other members of the department for honoring me with the elegant Waterford crystal vase at the party celebrating my twentieth anniversary with the company.

The height and shape of the vase are perfect to hold roses and other bouquets from my garden. Each time I fill it, I'll remember your thoughtfulness in choosing this lovely gift for me.

To Send Thanks for a Favor
I sincerely appreciate your filling in for me last week when I was too ill to attend the planning committee meeting for the spring exhibition.

Without your participation much of my preparatory work would have been lost. It's comforting to know that competent and generous individuals like you are part of our team, Mark. Moreover, it's my very good fortune to be able to count you as a friend. I'm grateful to you.

To Extend Thanks for Hospitality
Jeffrey and I want you to know how much we enjoyed the dinner party for our department that you hosted Saturday evening. Your charming home and warm hospitality, along with the lovely dinner and sinfully delicious chocolate dessert, combined to create a truly memorable evening.

Most of all, though, we appreciate your kindness in cultivating togetherness in our department. Thanks, Jennifer, for being such a special person.

Spotlight on **Communicators**

A mere thank-you followed by general comments is rather hollow, says Andrew S. Grove, CEO of Intel, the nation's principal computer chip maker. He suggests making the thanks match the deed. Ask yourself what was special, unusual, extraordinary, or over and above the call of duty—and then describe it. Being specific, warm, and sincere are as important as the difference between a personal note and a computerized form letter.

Response

Should you respond when you receive a congratulatory note or a written pat on the back? By all means! These messages are attempts to connect personally; they are efforts to reach out, to form professional and/or personal bonds. Failing to respond to notes of congratulations and most other goodwill messages is like failing to say "You're welcome" when someone says "Thank you." Responding to such messages is simply the right thing to do. Do avoid, though, minimizing your achievements with comments that suggest you don't really deserve the praise or that the sender is exaggerating your good qualities.

Take the time to respond to any goodwill message you may receive.

To Answer a Congratulatory Note
Thanks for your kind words regarding my award, and thanks, too, for sending me the newspaper clipping. I truly appreciate your thoughtfulness and best wishes.

To Respond to a Pat on the Back
Your note about my work made me feel good. I'm grateful for your thoughtfulness.

FIGURE 7.9 Thank You Letter for a Favor

1 PREWRITING

Analyze: The purpose is to express appreciation to a business executive for presenting a talk before professionals.

Anticipate: The reader will be more interested in personalized comments than in general statements showing gratitude.

Adapt: Because the reader will be pleased, use the direct pattern.

2 WRITING

Research: Consult notes taken during the talk.

Organize: Open directly by giving the reason for writing. Express enthusiastic and sincere thanks. In the body provide specifics. Refer to facts and highlights in the talk. Supply sufficient detail to support your sincere compliments. Conclude with appreciation. Be warm and friendly.

Compose: Write the first draft.

3 REVISING

Revise: Revise for tone and warmth. Use the reader's name. Include concrete detail but do it concisely. Avoid sounding gushy or phony.

Proofread: Check the spelling of the receiver's name; verify facts. Check the spelling of *gratitude, patience, advice, persistence,* and *grateful.*

Evaluate: Does this letter convey sincere thanks?

Dallas–Fort Worth Chapter
American Marketing Association
P.O. Box 3598
Dallas, TX 74209

March 20, 2000

Mr. Bryant Huffman
Marketing Manager, Western Division
Toys "R" Us, Inc.
Dallas, TX 75232

Dear Bryant:

You have our sincere gratitude for providing the Dallas–Fort Worth chapter of the AMA with one of the best presentations our group has ever heard.

Tells purpose and delivers praise

Personalizes the message by using specifics rather than generalities

Your description of the battle Toys "R" Us waged to begin marketing products in Japan was a genuine eye-opener for many of us. Nine years of preparation establishing connections and securing permissions seems an eternity, but obviously such persistence and patience pays off. We now understand better the need to learn local customs and nurture relationships when dealing in Japan.

In addition to your good advice, we particularly enjoyed your sense of humor and jokes—as you must have recognized from the uproarious laughter. What a great routine you do on faulty translations!

Spotlights the reader's talents

Concludes with compliments and thanks

We're grateful, Bryant, for the entertaining and instructive evening you provided our marketing professionals. Thanks!

Cordially,

Joyce Barnes

Joyce Barnes
Program Chair, AMA

JRB:grw

Sympathy

Most of us can bear misfortune and grief more easily when we know that others care. Notes expressing sympathy, though, are probably more difficult to write than any other kind of message. Commercial "In sympathy" cards make the task easier—but they are far less meaningful. Grieving friends want to know what you think—not what Hallmark's card writers think. To help you get started, you can always glance through cards expressing sympathy. They will supply ideas about the kinds of thoughts you might wish to convey in your own words. In writing a sympathy note, (1) refer to the death or misfortune sensitively, using words that show you understand what a crushing blow it is; (2) in the case of a death, praise the deceased in a personal way; (3) offer assistance without going into excessive detail; and (4) end on a reassuring, forward-looking note. Sympathy messages may be typed, although handwriting seems more personal. In either case, use notepaper or personal stationery.

Sympathy notes should refer to the misfortune sensitively and offer assistance.

To Express Condolences

We are deeply saddened, Gayle, to learn of the death of your husband. Bill's kind nature and friendly spirit endeared him to all who knew him. He will be missed.

Mentions the loss tactfully and recognizes good qualities of the deceased.

Although words seem empty in expressing our grief, we want you to know that your friends at QuadCom extend their profound sympathy to you. If we may help you or lighten your load in any way, you have but to call.

Assures receiver of your concern. Offers assistance.

We know that the treasured memories of your many happy years together, along with the support of your family and many friends, will provide strength and comfort in the months ahead.

Concludes on positive, reassuring note.

Checklist for Writing Goodwill Messages

General Guidelines: The Five Ss

Be selfless. Discuss the receiver, not the sender.

Be specific. Instead of generic statements (*You did a good job*), include special details (*Your marketing strategy to target key customers proved to be outstanding*).

Be sincere. Show your honest feelings with conversational, unpretentious language (*We're all very proud of your award*).

Be spontaneous. Strive to make the message natural, fresh, and direct. Avoid canned phrases (*If I may be of service, please do not hesitate . . .*).

Keep the message short. Remember that, although they may be as long as needed, most goodwill messages are fairly short.

Giving Thanks

Cover three points in gift thank-yous. (1) Identify the gift, (2) tell why you appreciate it, and (3) explain how you will use it.

Be sincere in sending thanks for a favor. Tell what the favor means to you. Avoid superlatives and gushiness. Maintain credibility with sincere, simple statements.

 **Offer praise in expressing thanks for hospitality.** Compliment, as appropriate, the (1) fine food, (2) charming surroundings, (3) warm hospitality, (4) excellent host and hostess, and (5) good company.

Answering Congratulatory Messages

 **Respond to congratulations.** Send a brief note expressing your appreciation. Tell how good the message made you feel.

 **Accept praise gracefully.** Don't make belittling comments (*I'm not really all that good!*) to reduce awkwardness or embarrassment.

Extending Sympathy

 **Refer to the loss or tragedy directly but sensitively.** In the first sentence mention the loss and your personal reaction.

 **For deaths, praise the deceased.** Describe positive personal characteristics (*Howard was a forceful but caring leader*).

 **Offer assistance.** Suggest your availability, especially if you can do something specific.

 **End on a reassuring, positive note.** Perhaps refer to the strength the receiver finds in friends, family, colleagues, or religion.

Writing International Letters

International letters should conform to the organizational, format, and cultural conventions of the receiver's country.

The letter-writing suggestions you've just studied work well for correspondence in this country. You may wish, however, to modify the organization, format, and tone of letters going abroad.

American businesspeople appreciate efficiency, straightforwardness, and conciseness in letters. Moreover, American business letters tend to be informal and conversational. Foreign correspondents, however, may look upon such directness and informality as inappropriate, insensitive, and abrasive. Letters in Japan, for example, may begin with deference, humility, and references to nature:

> *The season for cherry blossoms is here with us and everybody is beginning to feel refreshed. We sincerely congratulate you on becoming more prosperous in your business.*[20]

Letters in Germany commonly start with a long, formal lead-in, such as *Referring to your kind inquiry from the 31st of the month, we take the liberty to remind you with this letter. . . .*[21] Italian business letters may refer to the receiver's family and children. And French correspondents would consider it rude to begin a letter with a request before it is explained. French letters typically include an ending with this phrase (or a variation of it): *I wish to assure you [insert reader's most formal title] of my most respectful wishes [followed by the writer's title and signature]*.[22] Foreign letters are also more likely to include passive-voice constructions (*your letter has been received*), exaggerated courtesy (*great pleasure, esteemed favor*), and obvious flattery (*your eminent firm*).[23]

Foreign letters may use different formatting techniques. Whereas American business letters are typewritten and single-spaced, in other countries they may be

PROCESS TO PRODUCT

CASE STUDY

Applying Your Skills at Ben & Jerry's

Alice Blachly, customer affairs coordinator at Ben & Jerry's, is overloaded with work. She asks you, her assistant, to help out and hands you a stack of letters. The top one is from a customer who complains that she didn't get quite enough cookie and chocolate chunks in her last pint. She also wants to know whether Ben & Jerry's has ever considered a sugar-free ice cream, and she concludes by saying that she agrees with Ben & Jerry's stand on peace. Blachly tells you to explain that, although we work hard and long at it, the chunking equipment for nuts, chocolate, and cookies is as not always as consistent as B & J would like and that you will report the problem of cookie and chocolate chunks to production. She tells you to refund the estimated purchase price for one pint of ice cream. As she walks away, she says that B & J experimented with a sugar-free ice cream, but it was so far below its taste standards that it never got beyond lab tests.

Your Job

Respond to all three of the comments in the letter of Diane Gruber, 1968 West Griswold Road, Phoenix, AZ 85051. Although her complaint was gentle, it is, nevertheless, a complaint that warrants an adjustment. In your response strive to maintain her goodwill and favorable opinion of Ben & Jerry's.

handwritten and single- or double-spaced. Address arrangements vary as well, as shown in the following:

Always learn about local preferences before sending letters abroad.

German	**Japanese**
Herr [title, Mr., on first line]	Ms. Atsuko Takagi [title, name]
Deiter Woerner [name]	5-12 Koyo-cho 4 chome [street, house number]
Fritz-Kalle-Strasse 4 [street, house number]	Higashinada-ku [city]
6200 Wiesbaden [postal district, city]	Tokyo 194 [prefecture, postal district]
Germany [country]	Japan [country]

Dates and numbers can be particularly confusing, as shown here:

American	**Some European Countries**
June 3, 2000	3rd of June 2000
6/3/00	3.6.00
$5,320.00 U.S.	$5,320,00 U.S.

To be safe, spell out the names of months instead of using figures. Verify sums of money and identify the currency unit.

Check sums of money and dates carefully.

Because the placement and arrangement of letter addresses and closing lines vary greatly, you should always research local preferences before writing. For important letters going abroad, it's also wise to have someone familiar with local customs read and revise the message. An American graduate student learned this lesson when she wrote a letter, in French, to a Paris museum asking for permission to do research. She received no response. Before writing a second time, she took the letter to her French tutor. "No, no, mademoiselle! It will never do! It must be more respectful. You must be very careful of individuals' titles. Let me show you!" The second letter won the desired permission.

Summary of Learning Objectives

1 **List three characteristics of good letters, and describe the direct pattern for organizing letters.** Good letters are characterized by clear content, a tone of goodwill, and correct form. Letters carrying positive or neutral messages should be organized directly. That means introducing the main idea (the purpose for writing) immediately in the opening. The body of the letter explains and gives details. Letters that make requests close by telling what action is desired and establishing a deadline (end date) for that action.

2 **Write letters requesting information and action.** The opening immediately states the purpose of the letter, perhaps asking a question. The body explains and justifies the request. The closing tells the reader courteously what to do and shows appreciation.

3 **Write letters placing orders.** The opening introduces the order and authorizes a purchase (*Please send me the following items . . .*). The body lists the desired items including quantity, order number, description, unit price, and total price. The closing describes the method of payment, tells when the merchandise should be sent, and expresses appreciation.

4 **Write letters making claims.** The opening describes the problem clearly or tells what action is to be taken. The body explains and justifies the request without anger or emotion. The closing, which might include an end date, describes the desired action.

5 **Write letters complying with requests.** A subject line identifies previous correspondence, while the opening immediately delivers the good news. The body explains and provides additional information. The closing is cordial and personalized.

6 **Write letters of recommendation.** The opening identifies the candidate, the position, your relationship, and the confidentiality of the letter. The body describes the candidate's job duties, performance, skills, and potential. The closing provides an overall ranking of the candidate and offers to give additional information by telephone.

7 **Write letters granting claims and making adjustments.** The opening immediately grants the claim without sounding grudging. To regain the confidence of the customer, the body may explain what went wrong and how the problem will be rectified. However, it may avoid accepting responsibility for any problems. The closing expresses appreciation, extends thanks for past business, refers to a desire to be of service, and/or mentions a new product. An apology is optional.

8 **Write goodwill messages.** Goodwill messages deliver thanks, praise, or sympathy. They should be selfless, specific, sincere, spontaneous, and short. Gift thank-yous should identify the gift, tell why you appreciate it, and explain how you will use it. Thank-yous for favors should tell, without gushing, what they mean to you. Expressions of sympathy should mention the loss tactfully; recognize

good qualities in the deceased (in the case of a death); offer assistance; and conclude on a positive, reassuring note.

9 **Modify international letters to accommodate other cultures.** Letters going to individuals in some areas, such as Japan and Europe, should probably use a less direct organizational pattern and be more formal in tone. They should also be adapted to appropriate regional letter formats.

CHAPTER REVIEW

1. What is goodwill? Briefly describe five ways to develop goodwill in a letter. (Obj. 1)
2. Why is it best to write most business letters "backwards"? (Obj. 1)
3. What kind of questions elicit the most information? Give an example. (Obj. 2)
4. Why is the direct letter strategy appropriate for most business messages? (Obj. 2)
5. For order letters what information goes in the opening? In the body? In the closing? (Obj. 3)
6. What is a claim? (Obj. 4)
7. Why are most companies today particularly interested in listening to customers? (Obj. 4)
8. In complying with requests, why is it especially important that all facts are correct on letters written on company stationery? (Obj. 5)
9. When answering many questions for a customer, how can the information be grouped to improve readability? (Obj. 5)
10. What information should the opening of a letter of recommendation contain? (Obj. 6)
11. What is an appropriate salutation for a letter of recommendation when the candidate has no specific position in mind? (Obj. 6)
12. What are a writer's three goals for adjustment letters? (Obj. 7)
13. Name four things to avoid in adjustment letters. (Obj. 7)
14. Name five characteristics of goodwill messages. (Obj. 8)
15. Name three elements of business letters going abroad that might be modified to accommodate readers from other cultures. (Obj. 9)

CRITICAL THINKING

1. What's wrong with using the indirect pattern for writing routine requests and replies? If in the end the reader understands the message, why make a big fuss over the organization? (Obj. 1)
2. Is it insensitive to include resale or sales promotion information in an adjustment letter? (Obj. 7)
3. Why is it important to regain the confidence of a customer in an adjustment letter? How can it be done? (Obj. 7)
4. How are American business letters different from those written in other countries? Why do you suppose this is so? (Obj. 9)
5. **Ethical Issue:** Let's say you've drafted a letter to a customer in which you apologize for the way the customer's account was fouled up by the accounting department. You show the letter to your boss, and she instructs you to remove the apology. It admits responsibility, she says, and the company cannot allow itself to be held liable. You're not an attorney, but you can't see the harm in a simple apology. What should you do? Refer to the section "Tools for Doing the Right Thing" in Chapter 1 to review the five questions you might ask yourself in trying to do the right thing.

ACTIVITIES

7.1 Direct Openings (Objs. 1–8)

Revise the following openings so that they are more direct. Add information if necessary.

a. Please allow me to introduce myself. I am Todd Thompson, and I am the assistant manager of Body Trends, a fitness equipment center in Miami Shores. My manager has asked me to make inquiry about the upright and semi-recumbent cycling machines that we saw advertised in the June issue of *Your Health* magazine. I have a number of questions.

b. Because I've lost your order blank, I have to write this letter. I hope that it's all right to place an order this way. I am interested in ordering a number of things from your summer catalog, which I still have although the order blank is missing.

c. Pursuant to your letter of January 15, I am writing in regard to your inquiry about whether or not we offer our European-style patio umbrella in colors. This unique umbrella receives a number of inquiries. Its 10-foot canopy protects you when the sun is directly overhead, but it also swivels and tilts to virtually any angle for continuous sun protection all day long. It comes in two colors: off white and forest green.

d. Your letter of March 21, which was originally sent to *Mountain Bike Action,* has been referred to my desk for response. In your letter you inquire about the mountain bike featured on the cover of the magazine in April. That particular bike is a Series 70 Paramount and is manufactured by Schwinn.

e. I am pleased to receive your inquiry regarding the possibility of my acting as a speaker at the final semester meeting of your business management club on April 30. The topic of on-line résumés interests me and is one on which I think I could impart helpful information to your members. Therefore, I am responding in the affirmative to your kind invitation.

f. Thank you for your recent order of November 2. We are sure you will enjoy the low-profile brushed-cotton ball caps that you ordered from our spring catalog. Your order is currently being processed and should leave our production facility in Denver early next week. We use UPS for all deliveries in southern California. Because you ordered caps with your logo embroidered in a two-tone combination, your order cannot be shipped until November 12. You should not expect it before November 15.

g. We have just received your letter of March 12 regarding the unfortunate troubles you are having with your Magnum videocassette recorder. In your letter you ask if you may send the flawed VCR to us for inspection. Although we normally handle all service requests through our local dealers, in your circumstance we are willing to take a look at your unit here at our Richmond plant. Therefore, please send it to us so that we may determine what's wrong.

7.2 Subject Lines (Objs. 1–8)

Write efficient subject lines for each of the messages in Activity 7.1. Add dates and other information if necessary.

7.3 Letter Formatting (Obj. 1)

On a sheet of paper draw two rectangles about 4 by 6 inches. Within these rectangles show where the major parts of letters go: letterhead, dateline, inside address, salutation, body, complimentary close, signature, and author's name. Use lines to show how much space each part would occupy. Illustrate two different letter styles, such as block and personal business style. Be prepared to discuss your drawings. Consult Appendix C for format guidelines.

7.4 Document for Analysis: Information Request (Obj. 2)

Analyze the following letter. List its weaknesses. If your instructor directs, revise the letter.

Dear Sir:

I am a new member of the Corporate Travel Department of my company, QuadCom, and I have been assigned the task of writing to you to inquire about our next sales meeting. We would like to find a resort with conference facilities, which is why I am writing to the Scottsdale Hilton.

We are interested in banquet facilities where we can all be together, but we will also need at least four smaller meeting rooms. Each of these rooms should accommodate about 75. We hope to arrange our conference August 4 through August 9, and we expect about 250 sales associates. Most of our associates will be flying in so I'm interested in what airport is closest and transportation to and from the airport.

Does the Scottsdale Hilton have public address systems in the meeting rooms? How about audio-visual equipment and computer facilities for presentations? Thank you for any information you can provide.

Sincerely,

7.5 Document for Analysis: Claim Request (Obj. 4)

Analyze the following letter. List its weaknesses. If your instructor directs, revise the letter.

Dear Service Manager Kent Fowler:

This is to inform you that you can't have it both ways. Either you provide customers with cars with full gas tanks or you don't. And if you don't, you shouldn't charge them when they return with empty tanks!

In view of the fact that I picked up a car in Raleigh August 22 with an empty tank, I had to fill it immediately. Then I drove it until August 25. When I returned to Charlotte, I naturally let the tank go nearly empty, since that is the way I received the car in Raleigh.

But your attendant in Charlotte charged me to fill the tank—$26.50 (premium gasoline at premium prices)! Although I explained to him that I had received it with an empty tank, he kept telling me that company policy required that he charge for a fill-up. My total bill came to $266.50, which, you must agree, is a lot of money for a rental period of only three days. I have the signed rental agreement and a receipt showing that I paid the full amount and that it included $26.50 for a gas fill-up when I returned the car.

Inasmuch as my company is a new customer and inasmuch as we had hoped to use your agency for our future car rentals because of your competitive rates, I trust that you will give this matter your prompt attention.

Disappointedly yours,

7.6 Document for Analysis: Favorable Adjustment (Obj. 7)

Analyze the following letter. List its weaknesses. If your instructor directs, revise the letter.

Dear Mr. Yoder:

I have before me your letter in which you complain about a missing shipment. May I suggest that it is very difficult for us to deliver merchandise when we have been given an erroneous address.

Our investigators made an investigation of your problem shipment and arrived at the determination that it was sent immediately after we received the order. According to the shipper's records, it was delivered to the warehouse address given on your stationery: 3590 University Avenue, St. Paul, Minnesota 55114. Unfortunately, no one at that address would accept delivery, so the shipment was returned to us. I see from your current stationery that your company has a new address: 2293 Second Avenue, St. Paul, Minnesota 55120. With the proper address, we probably could have delivered this shipment.

When an order cannot be delivered, we usually try to verify the shipping address by telephoning the customer. Apparently, we could not find you.

Although we feel that it is entirely appropriate and right to charge you shipping and restocking fees, as is our standard practice on returned goods, in this instance we will waive those fees. We hope this second shipment finally catches up with you.

Sincerely,

7.7 Information Request: Touring Europe on a Shoestring (Obj. 2)

Web

You just saw a great TV program about cheap travel in Europe, and you think you'd like to try it next summer. The program described how some people want to get away from it all; others want to see a little of the world. Some want to learn a different language; some want to soak up a bit of culture. The "get-away" group, the program advised, should book a package trip to a Contiki resort where they relax and soak up the sun. But "culture vultures" and FITS (free independent travelers) should select the countries they want to visit and plan their own trips. You decide to visit France, Spain, and Portugal (or any other countries you select).

Begin planning your trip by gathering information from the country's tourist office. Many details need to be worked out. What about visas? How about inoculations (ouch!)? Since your budget will be limited, you need to stay in youth hostels whenever possible. Where are they? Are they private? Some hostels accept only people who belong to their organization. You really need to get your hands on a list of hostels for every country before departure. You are also interested in any special transport passes for students, such as a Eurail Pass. And while you are at it, find out if they have any special guides for student travelers. All this information can be secured from a tourist office. Using the Internet, you found an address for information: France Tourist Office, 444 Madison Avenue, New York, NY 10020-2452 **<http://www.fgtousa.org>**. If you prefer another country, find its tourist office address. Write a letter requesting information. Because this is a personal business letter, include your return address above the date. See Appendix C, page A-40.

7.8 Information Request: Finding the Perfect $6 Million Gift (Obj. 2)

Critical Thinking

"It's a bit like watching the fattest kid in high school waddle up to the starting line and dash off a four-minute mile, leaving all the big jocks gasping for breath." That's how *Fortune* magazine described the amazing comeback of Warner-Lambert Co. This multinational company—best known in recent times for its Listerine, bubble gum, Sudafed, and Schick razors—had been the leader in pharmaceuticals back in the 1950s. However, it grew pudgy and complacent without new drugs to capture current markets—until the early 1990s. At that time Warner's scientists, quietly working behind the scenes, unveiled two blockbuster drugs that reduced cholesterol and fought diabetes. These new drugs, together with new management, transformed a bloated giant into a front-running pharmaceutical company. Almost overnight it became one of the 100 most valuable companies in the world.

CEO Melvin R. Goodes decided that he wanted to reward the hard work of all 42,000 Warner-Lambert employees with some kind of recognition. He dreamed of a gift that would unite all the firm's employees in 140 locations under "one cultural umbrella." A committee met in an effort to select the perfect gift that would be appropriate for all employees, male and female. But no decision could be reached. "We have a regular recognition program, and we do lots of sales incentives," said Vice President Sandra Levine. But she and CEO Goodes wanted an extraordinary gift to celebrate the company's extraordinary turnaround.

They knew the thank-you gift and the recognition program would have to be appropriate for employees in 45 countries around the globe. Yet they had no idea what to give nor how to proceed with such a gigantic recognition program. "Our workforce is scattered all over the globe working on such different products as fish food, chewing gum, and diabetes medicine," said Levine. Yet, she and Goodes wanted all the gifts to be presented on the same day, a day that would make history at Warner-Lambert.

Because this task is way beyond the reach of her staff, Levine decides to engage the O. C. Tanner Recognition Company to help develop a giant thank-you program. She asks you, her assistant, to draft a letter to this company requesting information about their services. She wonders if O. C. Tanner is prepared to handle communications in 13 languages: English, Italian, Portuguese, German, French, Spanish, Dutch, Arabic, Thai, Japanese, Chinese (two character systems), and Indonesian. "I want to connect with everyone and I think you can only really do that in their language," says Levine. She and CEO Goodes hope to include, along with the gift, a video with a prepared message congratulating the employees on their achievements. And they want the gift to be something that can be inscribed with the company's logo and these words: "We're making the world feel better." The budget for the program is $6 million.

Your task is to organize an information request that not only explains what your company wants but also asks specific questions about what O. C. Tanner can do. Draft a letter for the signature of Vice President Sandra Levine. The letter goes to Jonathon E. Hodges, O. C. Tanner Recognition Company, P.O. Box 3440, Salt Lake City, CO 84001.[24]

7.9 Information Request: Backpacking Cuisine (Obj. 2)

Assume that you are Benjamin Spring, manager of a health spa and also an ardent backpacker. You are organizing a group of hikers for a wilderness trip to Canada. One item that must be provided is freeze-dried food for the three-week trip. You are unhappy with the taste and quality of backpacking food products currently available. You expect to have a group of hikers who are older, affluent, and natural-food enthusiasts. Some are concerned about products containing preservatives, sugar, and additives. Others are on diets restricting cholesterol, fat, and salt.

You heard that Outfitters, Inc., offers a new line of freeze-dried products. You want to know what they offer and whether they have sufficient variety to serve all the needs of your group. You need to know where their products can be purchased and what the cost range is. You'd also like to try a few of their items before placing a large order. You are interested in how they produce the food products and what kinds of ingredients they use. If you have any items left over, you wonder how long they can be kept and still be usable. Write an inquiry letter to Tia Osborne, Outfitters, Inc., 1169 Willamette Street, Eugene, OR 97401.

7.10 Information Request: Saving an Old Printer (Obj. 2)

You were delighted when your friend Kevin, in the graphics arts department, announced that his department was getting rid of its old DeskJet Plus printer. He said it was in great working condition. Your department could really use another printer, and the operations manager approved the transfer. The only problem is that graphics arts used Windows 95, and your department is still using Windows 3.1. Kevin said he didn't have a Windows 3.1 driver, which your computer requires. Naturally, you went straight to the Hewlett-Packard Web site to check its downloadable drivers, but you could not find one listed for the DeskJet Plus.

You decide to write to Hewlett-Packard to see whether you overlooked a driver available at the H-P Web site. If one is not available there, you wonder whether H-P could send you a driver on a 3½-inch disk. If that's impossible, you wonder whether a driver for a later version of the DeskJet might work with your printer and Windows 3.1. Write to Rick Richardson, Customer Service, Hewlett-

Packard, 3000 Hanover Street, Palo Alto, CA 94305. Provide your e-mail address, as well as your land address.

7.11 Information Request: River Rafting on the Web (Obj. 2)

Web

As the program chair for the campus Ski Club, you have been asked by the president to investigate river rafting. The Ski Club is an active organization, and its members want to schedule a summer activity. A majority favored rafting. Use a browser to search the Web for relevant information. Select five of the most promising Web sites offering rafting. If possible, print a copy of your findings. Then, summarize your findings in a letter to Brian Krauss, Ski Club president. The next meeting of the Ski Club is May 8, but you think it would be a good idea if you could discuss your findings with Brian before the meeting. Write to Brian Krauss, SIU Ski Club, 303 Founders Hall, Carbondale, IL 62901.

7.12 Information Request: Computer Code of Conduct (Obj. 2)

Web

As an assistant in the campus computer laboratory, you have been asked by your boss to help write a code of conduct for use of the laboratory facilities. This code will spell out what behavior and activities are allowed in your lab. The first thing you are to do is conduct a search of the Internet to see what other college or university computing labs have written as conduct codes. Using at least two search engines, explore the Web employing variations of the key words "computer code of conduct." Print two or three codes that seem appropriate. Write a letter (or e-mail message, if your instructor agrees) to the director of an educational computer laboratory asking for further information about its code and its effectiveness. Include at least five significant questions. Attach your printouts to your letter.

7.13 Information Request: On-Line Microbrewery (Obj. 2)

Play the part of brewmaster Carol Fischer, owner of Crystal Ale Microbrewery, 7345 East State Street, Portland, OR 97208. Your Crystal Ale beers have won local taste awards. However, sales are dismal, perhaps because your beer is pricier than mass-produced beers and because you have a meager advertising and sales budget.

Then you hear about MicroBeer On-Line, a service that sells microbrewed beer via the World Wide Web. When you visit the Web site, you find descriptions of beer from many microbreweries, along with ratings for each beer. An order page enables customers to order beer directly from the Web site.

You wonder if you might sell your beer via MicroBeer On-Line, but you're not exactly sure how the service works. For example, who writes the product descriptions, and who rates the beer? Furthermore, because you offer some seasonal varieties of Crystal Ale, you are concerned about being able to change the selection of beer offered on the service. Of course, you also need to know the specifics of working with MicroBeer On-Line. For example, how much does it cost to sell on-line? In addition, since Crystal Ale badly needs customers, you would like to know how many customers Crystal Ale might gain through MicroBeer On-Line. You have many questions! You could e-mail Mr. Fahlk, but you prefer a paper copy as a permanent record of the correspondence. Write a letter to Peter Fahlk, Webmaster, MicroBeer On-Line, 300 East Parkway Avenue, San Diego, CA 92138. Provide an end date and a logical reason for it.

7.14 Order Letter: Camera Jumble (Obj. 3)

Analyze the following ineffective request for merchandise. Revise the letter and place your return address above the date. Send the letter to Cameratone, Inc., 140 Northern Boulevard, Flushing, NY 11354-1400. Add any necessary information.

Dear Sir:

I saw a number of items in your summer/fall catalog that would fit my Lentax ME camera. I am particularly interested in your Super Zoom 55-200mm lens. Its number is SF39971, and it costs $139.95. To go with this lens I will need a polarizing filter. Its number is SF29032 and costs $22.95 and should fit a 52mm lens. Also include a 05CC magenta filter for a 52mm lens. That number is SF29036 and it costs $9.95. Please send also a Hikemaster camera case for $24.95. Its number is SF29355.

I am interested in having these items charged to my credit card. I'd sure like to get them quickly because my vacation starts soon.

Sincerely,

7.15 Order Letter: Office Supplies to Go (Obj. 3)

You are Hector Rivera, manager, Lasertronics, Inc., 2004 Henrietta Road, Rochester, NY 14623. You want to order some items from an office supply catalog, but your catalog is one year old and you have lost the order form. Because you're in a hurry, you decide to place a fax order. Rather than write for a new catalog, you decide to take a chance and order items from the old catalog, realizing that prices may be somewhat different. You want three Panasonic electric pencil sharpeners, Item 22-A, at $19.95 each. You want one steel desktop organizer, 60 inches long, Item No. 23-K. Its price is $117.50. Order two Roll-a-Flex files for 2- by 4-inch cards at $14.50 each. This is Item 23-G. The next item is No. 29-H, file folders, box of 100, letter size, at $5.29. You need ten boxes. You would like to be invoiced for this purchase, and you prefer UPS delivery. Even though the prices may be somewhat higher, you decide to list the prices shown in your catalog so that you have an idea of what the total order will cost. Write a letter to Monarch Discount Office Furniture, 2890 Monarch Road, Lethbridge, Alberta T1K 1L6. Between the date and the inside address, type TRANSMITTED BY FAX.

7.16 Claim Letter: Deep Desk Disappointment (Obj. 4)

Assume that you are Monica Keil, president, Keil Consulting Services, 423 E. Willamette Avenue, Colorado Springs, CO 80903. Since your consulting firm was doing very well, you decided to splurge and purchase a fine executive desk for your own office. You ordered an expensive desk described as "North American white oak embellished with hand-inlaid walnut cross-banding." Although you would not ordinarily purchase large, expensive items by mail, you were impressed by the description of this desk and by the money-back guarantee promised in the catalog.

When the desk arrived, you knew that you had made a mistake. The wood finish was rough, the grain looked splotchy, and many of the drawers would not pull out easily. The advertisement had promised "full suspension, silent ball-bearing drawer slides." You are disappointed with the desk and decide to send it back, taking advantage of the money-back guarantee. You want your money refunded. You're not sure whether the freight charges can be refunded, but it's worth a try. Supply any details needed. Write a letter to Rodney Harding, Marketing Manager, Idaho Wood Products, P.O. Box 488, Sandpoint, ID 83864.

7.17 Claim Letter: Earth First Runs Dry (Obj. 4)

Assume that you are Megan Phillips, public relations assistant for a grassroots environmental organization, Earth First, 5314 River Road, Evergreen, CO 80439. You are responsible for printing 250 flyers for an upcoming Earth First rally, but the ink cartridges for your two Stellar printers aren't working properly. Although the cartridges are clearly full, no ink is dispensed. When you tried to return the faulty cartridges to your local office supply store, The Office Center, the store refused to take them because you had purchased the cartridges more than 30 days ago.

On the advice of the store manager, you purchase two new cartridges that enable you to print your flyers on time. However, you are frustrated about spending Earth First's meager funds on faulty equipment. The store manager said that many customers recently had returned Stellar ink cartridges. You hope Stellar isn't losing its commitment to quality. After all, you are particularly fond of Stellar ink

cartridges, since they are the only cartridges on the market that use environmentally safe soy-based ink. Decide what will resolve your complaint: a cash refund of $126.50, replacement cartridges, or some other action. Send a claim letter, the cartridges, and a copy of your receipt to Stellar Printers, 908 East State Street, New York, NY 10001.

7.18 Claim Letter: Undersized French Doors (Obj. 4)

As Julie Chen, owner of Smart Interiors, you recently completed a kitchen remodel that required double-glazed, made-to-order oak French doors. You ordered them, by telephone, on July 2 from Custom Wood, Inc. When they arrived on July 25, your carpenter gave you the bad news: the doors were cut too small. Instead of measuring a total of 11 feet 8 inches, the doors measured 11 feet 4 inches. In your carpenter's words, "No way can I stretch those doors to fit these openings!" You waited three weeks for these doors, and your clients wanted them installed immediately. Your carpenter said, "I can rebuild this opening for you, but I'm going to have to charge you for my time." His extra charge came to $455.50.

You feel that the people at Custom Wood should reimburse you for this amount since it was their error. In fact, you actually saved them a bundle of money by not returning the doors. You decide to write to Custom Wood and enclose a copy of your carpenter's bill. You wonder whether you should also include a copy of Custom Wood's invoice, even though it does not show the exact door measurements. You are a good customer of Custom Wood, having used their quality doors and windows on many other jobs. You're confident that it will grant this claim. Write a claim letter to Jay Brandt, Marketing Manager, Custom Wood, Inc., 401 Main Street, Waterford, MI 48327.

7.19 Claim Letter: The Real Thing (Obj. 4)

Select a product or service that has disappointed you. Write a claim letter requesting a refund, replacement, explanation, or whatever seems reasonable. Generally, such letters are addressed to customer service departments. For claims about food products, be sure to include bar-code identification from the package, if possible. Your instructor may ask you to actually mail this letter. Remember that smart companies want to know what their customers think, especially if a product could be improved. Give your ideas for improvement. When you receive a response, share it with your class.

7.20 Request Response: McDonald's Goes Green (Obj. 5)

Team

Diane LaSala, director of Customer Service for McDonald's Corporation, has received a letter from Sandi Escalante, an environmentalist. Ms. Escalante wants to know what McDonald's is doing to reduce the huge amounts of waste products that its restaurants generate. She argues that these wastes not only deplete world resources but also clog our already overburdened landfills. Diane LaSala thinks that this is a good opportunity for her student interns to sharpen their reasoning and writing skills on the job. She asks you and the other interns to draft a response to the inquiry telling how McDonald's is cleaning up its act. Here are some of the facts that Diane supplies your group.

Actually, McDonald's has been quite active in its environmental efforts. Working with the Environmental Defense Fund, McDonald's has initiated a series of 42 resolutions that are cutting by more than 80 percent the huge waste stream from its 12,000 restaurants. McDonald's efforts meant making changes in packaging, increasing their recycling campaign, trying more composting, and retraining employees.

McDonald's was one of the food industry leaders in abandoning the polystyrene "clamshell" box for hamburgers and sandwiches. Formerly using an average of 20 pounds of polystyrene a day per restaurant, McDonald's now uses only 10 percent of that figure. McDonald's suppliers have been asked to use corrugated boxes that contain at least 35 percent recycled content. Moreover, suppliers will be asked to make regular reports to McDonald's that measure their progress in reaching new waste-reduction goals. Other environmental efforts include testing a starch-based material in consumer cutlery to replace plastic forks, knives, and spoons. Many restaurants have also begun trial composting of eggshells, coffee grounds, and food scraps. McDonald's is also starting a nationwide program for recycling corrugated boxes. In addition, the company is testing reusable salad lids and shipping pallets, pump-style bulk dispensers for condiments, and refillable coffee mugs.

McDonald's has retrained its restaurant crews to give waste reduction equal weight with other priorities, such as quickness, cleanliness, and quality service. The company is trying to reduce the waste both behind the counter (which accounts for 80 percent of the total waste) and over the counter. Prepare a letter that can be used for similar inquiries. To promote goodwill, you might wish to throw in a few coupons for free sandwiches. Send this letter to Sandi Escalante, 3233 Garden Drive, Springfield, MO 65807.[25]

7.21 Request Response: Scannable Résumés (Obj. 5)

Team | **Critical Thinking** | **Web**

Your team has been asked to devise a form letter to send to job applicants who inquire about the résumé-scanning techniques used by ABI Footwear, 14238 Fruitvale Avenue, Saratoga, CA 95070. The following poorly written letter was pulled from the file. Your team is to produce an informative letter that can be sent to anyone who inquires. Discuss how this letter could be improved. Decide what information is necessary to send to potential job applicants. Search for additional information that might be helpful.

Dear Mr. Madzar:

Your letter of April 11 has been referred to me for a response. We are pleased to learn that you are considering employment here at ABI Footwear, and we look forward to receiving your résumé, should you decide to send same to us.

You ask if we scan incoming résumés. Yes, we certainly do. Actually, we use SmartTrack, an automated résumé-tracking system. SmartTrack is wonderful! You know, we sometimes receive as many as 300 résumés a day, and SmartTrack helps us sort, screen, filter, and separate the résumés. It also processes them, helps us organize them, and keeps a record of all of these résumés. Some of the résumés, however, cannot be scanned, so we have to return those—if we have time.

The reasons that résumés won't scan may surprise you. Some applicants send photocopies or faxed copies, and these can cause misreading, so don't do it. The best plan is to send an original copy. Some people use colored paper. Big mistake! White paper (8½ × 11-inch) printed on one side is the best bet. Another big problem is unusual type fonts, such as script or fancy gothic or antique fonts. They don't seem to realize that scanners do best with plain, readable fonts such as Helvetica or Universe in a 10- to 14-point size.

Other problems occur when applicants use graphics, shading, italics, underlining, horizontal and vertical lines, parentheses, and brackets. Scanners like plain "vanilla" résumés! Oh yes, staples can cause misreading. And folding of a résumé can also cause the scanners to foul up. To be safe, don't staple or fold, and be sure to use wide margins and a quality printer (no dot matrixes!!).

When a hiring manager within ABI Footwear decides to look for an appropriate candidate, he is told to submit key words to describe the candidate he has in mind for his opening. We tell him (or sometimes her) to zero in on nouns and phrases that best describe what they want. Thus, my advice to you is to try to include those words that highlight your technical and professional areas of expertise.

If you do decide to submit your résumé to ABI Footwear, be sure you don't make any of the mistakes described herein that would cause the scanner to misread it.

Sincerely,

7.22 Request Response: Tell Me About Your Major (Obj. 5)

A friend in a distant city is considering moving to your area for more education and training in your field. This individual wants to know about your program of study. Write a letter describing a program in your field (or any field you wish to describe). What courses must be taken? Toward what degree, certificate, or employment position does this program lead? Why did you choose it? Would you recommend this program to your friend? How long does it take? Add any information you feel would be helpful.

7.23 Request Response: Backpacking Cuisine (Obj. 5)

As Tia Osborne, owner of Outfitters, Inc., producer of freeze-dried backpacking foods, answer the inquiry of Benjamin Spring (described in Activity 7.9). You are eager to have Mr. Spring sample your new all-natural line of products containing no preservatives, sugar, or additives. You want him to know that you started this company two years ago after you found yourself making custom meals for discerning backpackers who rejected typical camping fare. Some of your menu items are excellent for individuals on restricted diets. Some dinners are cholesterol-, fat-, and salt-free, but he'll have to look at your list to see for himself.

You will send him your complete list of dinner items and the suggested retail prices. You will also send him a sample "Saturday Night on the Trail," a four-course meal that comes with fruit candies and elegant appetizers. All your food products are made from choice ingredients in sanitary kitchens that you personally supervise. They are flash frozen in a new vacuum process that you patented. Although your dried foods are meant to last for years, you don't recommend that they be kept beyond 18 months because they may deteriorate. This could happen if a package were punctured or if the products became overheated. Your products are currently available at Malibu Sports Center, 19605 Pacific Coast Highway, Malibu, CA 90265. Large orders may be placed directly with you. You offer a 5 percent discount on direct orders. Write a response to Benjamin Spring, 322 East Chapman, Fullerton, CA 92634.

7.24 Request Response: MicroBeer On-Line (Obj. 5)

As Peter Fahlk, webmaster for MicroBeer On-Line, respond to a letter from a potential customer, microbrewer Carol Fischer (see Activity 7.13). In addition to answering Ms. Fischer's questions, you hope to gain her company, Crystal Ale Microbrewery, as a new customer by highlighting the benefits of MicroBeer On-Line. Of course, you want to clarify for Ms. Fischer that MicroBeer On-Line doesn't brew beer; it simply advertises and collects orders on its Web site. Orders are then forwarded to microbrewers, who fill the orders, ship the product to the consumer, and fork over 4 percent of on-line sales receipts to MicroBeer. (The fee of 4 percent of sales is well under the amount allocated for advertising in most company budgets).

Although you can't predict how many customers each brewer will gain through MicroBeer On-Line, you do know that the service reaches thousands of consumers a day, 365 days a year, 24 hours a day. Small brewers appreciate MicroBeer On-Line because it brings in orders while brewers concentrate on brewing their specialty beers. Furthermore, by cutting out middlemen and reducing distribution costs, MicroBeer On-Line enables brewers to maintain reasonable beer prices. Consumers particularly appreciate MicroBeer's product write-ups and beer ratings by Ted Groebles, a well-known brewmaster. However, since Groebles is able to review only a reasonable number of beers at a time, MicroBeer limits its service to 50 breweries and about 250 beers. Brewers may sell up to five beers on the service, and the beers may change seasonally.

It is very inexpensive for MicroBeer to run its Web site; the cost of setting up the Web site was less than the cost of four half-page ads in a major newspaper. Gaining new customers, however, hasn't been easy, so MicroBeer now offers short-term contracts to brewers new to the service. Brewers may call you personally at (517) 756-1456 for more information

Write to Carol Fischer, Crystal Ale Microbrewery, 7345 East State Street, Portland, OR 97208. Answer the questions in her inquiry (Activity 7.13). Along with your reply, send her your brochure "MicroBeer On-Line."

7.25 Letter of Recommendation: Recommending Yourself (Obj. 6)

You are about to leave your present job. When you ask your boss for a letter of recommendation, to your surprise he tells you to write it yourself and then have him sign it. [Actually, this is not an unusual practice today. Many businesspeople find that employees are very perceptive and accurate when they evaluate themselves.] Use specifics from a current or previous job. Describe your duties and skills. Be sure to support general characteristics with specific examples.

7.26 Order Response: Office Supplies to Go (Obj. 7)

Respond to the order placed by Hector Rivera, Manager, Lasertronics, Inc., 2004 Henrietta Road, Rochester, NY 14623 (described in Activity 7.15). Yes, all of the prices listed in your old catalog have increased. That's the bad news. The good news is that you have in stock nearly everything he ordered. The only item not immediately available is the desktop organizer, Item No. 23-K. That has to be shipped from the manufacturer in Pittsburgh, Pennsylvania. You've been having trouble with that supplier lately, perhaps because of heavy demand. However, you think that the organizer will be shipped no later than three weeks from the current date. You're pleased to have Lasertronics' order. They might be interested in your new line of office supply products at discount prices. Send him a new catalog and call his attention to the low, low price on continuous-form computer paper. It's just $39.95 for a box containing 2,700 sheets of 9½- by 11-inch, 20-pound printout paper. All the items he ordered, except the organizer, are on their way by UPS and should arrive in three days.

7.27 Claim Response: Undersized French Doors (Obj. 7)

Critical Thinking

As Jay Brandt, manager of Custom Wood, Inc., you have a problem. Your firm manufactures quality precut and custom-built doors and frames. You have received a letter dated August 3 from Julie Chen (described in Activity 7.18). Ms. Chen is an interior designer, and she complains that the oak French doors she recently ordered for a client were made to the wrong dimensions.

Although they were the wrong size, she kept the doors and had them installed because her clients were without outside doors. However, her carpenter charged an extra $455.50 to install them. She claims that you should reimburse her for this amount, since your company was responsible for the error. You check her July 2 order and find that the order was filled correctly. In a telephone order, Ms. Chen requested doors that measured 11 feet 4 inches and that's what you sent. Now she says that the doors should have been 11 feet 8 inches. Your policy forbids refunds or returns on custom orders. Yet, you remember that around July 2 you had two new people working the phones taking orders. It's possible that they did not hear or record the measurements correctly. You don't know whether to grant this claim or refuse it. But you do know that you must look into the training of telephone order takers and be sure that they verify all custom order measurements. It might also be a good idea to have your craftsmen call a second time to confirm custom measurements.

Ms. Chen is a successful interior designer and has provided Custom Wood with a number of orders. You value her business but aren't sure how to respond. In your letter remind her that Custom Wood has earned a reputation as the manufacturer of the finest wood doors and frames on the market. Your doors feature prime woods, and the craftsmanship is meticulous. The designs of your doors have won awards, and the engineering is ingenious. You have a new line of greenhouse windows that are available in three sizes. Include a brochure describing these windows. Decide how to treat this claim and then write to Julie Chen, Smart Interiors, 3282 Richmond Road, Highland Hills Village, OH 44122.

7.28 Claim Response: Deep Desk Disappointment (Obj. 7)

As Rodney Harding, sales manager, Idaho Wood Products, it is your job to reply to customer claims, and today you must respond to Monica Keil, president, Keil Consulting Services, 423 E. Willamette Avenue, Colorado Springs, CO 80903 (described in Activity 7.16). You are disappointed that she is returning the executive desk (Invoice No. 3499), but your policy is to comply with customer wishes. If she doesn't want to keep the desk, you will certainly return the purchase price plus shipping charges. On occasion, desks are damaged in shipping, and this may explain the marred finish and the sticking drawers.

You want Ms. Keil to give Idaho Wood Products another chance. After all, your office furniture and other wood products are made from the finest hand-selected woods by master artisans. Since she is apparently furnishing her office, send her another catalog and invite her to look at the traditional conference desk on page 10-E. This is available with a matching credenza, file cabinets, and accessories. She might be interested in your furniture-leasing plan, which can produce substantial savings. You promise that you will personally examine any furniture she may order in the future. Write her a letter granting her claim.

7.29 Claim Response: Earth First Runs Dry (Obj. 7)

As Antonio Garcia, customer service manager for Stellar Printers, 908 East State Street, New York, NY 10001, reply to a claim letter from Megan Phillips, public relations assistant, Earth First, 5314 River Road, Evergreen, CO 80439 (see Activity 7.17). Explain to Ms. Phillips that Stellar Printers will refund to Earth First $126.50 for the two faulty cartridges it purchased. The cartridges were apparently among the 10 percent of cartridges shipped to retailers in December and January that were made with a new type of protective tape. The tape worked well in manufacturing, and it was much cheaper for Stellar to use. Unfortunately, when printer owners removed the protective tape as instructed, residue from the tape clogged the cartridges' ink holes, causing the cartridges to malfunction even though they were still full of ink.

You would like Earth First to know that Stellar is committed to improving the quality of its soy-based ink cartridges, but not at the expense of customer satisfaction. Clearly the protective tape wasn't a successful product improvement, and customer feedback from companies such as Earth First has helped Stellar to improve product quality. In February, Stellar stopped using the defective tape. Instead, it returned to its original protective tape to seal cartridges. This tape never failed. Cartridges with the new tape were removed from store shelves. Write a letter granting the claim.

7.30 Thanks for a Favor: Got the Job! (Obj. 8)

After completing your degree, you have taken a job in your field. One of your instructors was especially helpful to you when you were a student. This instructor also wrote an effective letter of recommendation that was instrumental in helping you obtain your job. Write a letter thanking your instructor.

7.31 Thanks for a Favor: The Century's Biggest Change in Job Finding (Obj. 8)

Team

Your business communication class was fortunate to have author Joyce Lain Kennedy speak to you. She has written many books including *Electronic Job Search Revolution, Hook Up, Get Hired!, and Electronic Résumé Revolution.* Ms. Kennedy talked about writing a scannable résumé, using keywords to help employers hire you, keeping yourself visible in databases on the Internet, and how to find on-line classified ads. The class especially liked hearing the many examples of real people who had found jobs on the Internet. Ms. Kennedy shared many suggestions from human resources people, and she described how large and small employers are using computers to read résumés and track employees. You know that she did not come to plug her books, but when she left, most class members wanted to head straight for a bookstore to get some of them. Her talk was a big hit. Individually or in small groups, draft a thank-you letter to Joyce Lain Kennedy, P.O. Box 3502, Carlsbad, CA 92009.

7.32 Thanks for the Hospitality: Holiday Entertaining (Obj. 8)

Write a thank-you letter to your boss (supervisor, manager, vice president, president, or chief executive officer) or to the head of an organization to which you belong. Assume that you and other members of your staff or organization were entertained at an elegant dinner during the winter holiday season. Include specific details that will make your letter personal and sincere.

7.33 Responding to Good Wishes: Saying Thank You (Obj. 8)

Write a short note thanking a friend who sent you good wishes when you recently completed your degree.

7.34 Extending Sympathy: To a Spouse (Obj. 8)

Imagine that a coworker was killed in an automobile accident. Write a letter of sympathy to his or her spouse.

C.L.U.E. REVIEW 7

Edit the following sentences to correct faults in grammar, punctuation, spelling, and word use.

1. The extrordinary increase in sales is related to us placing the staff on a commission basis and the increase also effected our stock value.
2. She acts as if she was the only person who ever received a complement about their business writting.
3. Karen is interested in working for the U.S. foreign service. Since she is hopping to travel.
4. Major Hawkins whom I think will be elected has all ready served three consecative terms as a member of the gulfport city counsel.
5. After Mr. Freeman and him returned from lunch the customer's were handled more quick.
6. Our new employees cafeteria, which opened six months ago has a salad bar that everyone definitly likes.
7. On Tuesday Ms Adams can see you at two p.m., on Wednesday she has a full skedule.
8. His determination courage and sincerity could not be denied however his methods were often questioned.
9. After you have checked the matter farther report to the CEO and I.
10. Mr. Garcia and her advised me not to dessert my employer at this time. Although they were quite sympathetic to my personel problems.

CHAPTER • 8 •

Routine Memos and E-Mail Messages

LEARNING OBJECTIVES

1. Discuss the characteristics of and writing process for successful routine memos and e-mail messages.
2. Analyze the organization of memos and e-mail messages.
3. Explain how to use e-mail effectively, including practices, netiquette, and formatting.
4. Write information and procedure memos and e-mail messages.
5. Write request and reply memos and e-mail messages.
6. Write confirmation memos and e-mail messages.

CASE STUDY

COMMUNICATION IN PROCESS

Getting Facts on Record at Shore Memorial Hospital

"In my business, I must have things on record," says Cathy Trimble, Wellness Center coordinator at Shore Memorial Hospital. "This is a large bureaucracy, and I work with many people in many departments. People sometimes forget telephone conversations or remember selectively. When my boss says, 'Hey, the head of that department claims she knows nothing about the health fair you are coordinating,' I want to have a record of what really happened. It's a great feeling to be able to respond, 'But here's a copy of the memo I sent to her three weeks ago describing the fair.'"

Shore Memorial Hospital, with over 1,500 employees, serves residents and tourists visiting the Ocean City and Atlantic City, New Jersey, area. As Wellness coordinator, Trimble organizes preventive health programs such as community health fairs and workshops on stress management, blood pressure control, and weight management. The hospital also offers services in corporate settings, where it conducts health risk assessments for employees of large companies.

Whether she's organizing a kids' health fair at a local mall or developing an executive health assessment program at Harrah's Hotel Casino in Atlantic City, Trimble is immersed in hundreds of scheduling and organizing details. In the Harrah's program, for example, she is responsible for setting up vision, hearing, blood, urine, blood pressure, body fat, and flexibility screenings. She also schedules all the hospital professionals needed to conduct these screenings and the follow-up consultations.

An important form of communication that aids Trimble in scheduling and organizing the many details of her job is the memo, whether it is printed or an electronic message. "I must have a record of decisions and procedures. It's not enough to call someone on the phone and make arrangements; sending a confirmation memo verifies the details and keeps the record straight." Because she cares about the effectiveness of her memos, Trimble pays attention to her writing. She's learned to avoid the "mystery story" approach, which forces readers to plow through six or seven paragraphs before they understand why the memo was written.[1]

www@shorememorial.org

Writing Routine Memos and E-Mail Messages

1

E-mail messages and interoffice memorandums are favorites for internal communication.

In most organizations today, employees spend more time writing e-mail messages and memos than they spend writing anything else.[2] Memos were always a favorite means of internal communication, but e-mail is rapidly becoming the communication medium of choice. According to the United States Postal Service, nearly 40 percent of all business and personal correspondence now bypasses the USPS by traveling over the Internet.[3] Small wonder. It costs only about $1 to send 19 e-mail messages,[4] and they arrive almost instantaneously.

Developing skill in writing memos and e-mail brings you two important benefits. First, well-written documents are likely to achieve their goals. Second, such documents enhance your image within the organization. Individuals identified as competent, professional writers are noticed and rewarded; most often, they are the ones promoted into management positions.

This chapter concentrates on routine memos and e-mail messages. These straightforward messages, such as those frequently written by Cathy Trimble at Shore

Technology allows increasing numbers of employees to work at home and telecommute to the office. As a result, more and more messages—especially memos—need to be written to keep the lines of communication open between remote employees and the office.

Memorial Hospital, open with the main idea first because their topics are not sensitive and require little persuasion. You'll study the characteristics, writing process, organization, and forms for preparing procedure, information, request, reply, and confirmation memos.

Characteristics of Successful Memos and E-Mail Messages

Because memos and e-mail messages are standard forms of communication within most organizations, they will probably become your most common business communication medium. These indispensable messages inform employees, request data, supply responses, confirm decisions, and give directions. Good memos and e-mail messages generally share certain characteristics.

Routine memos inform employees, request data, give responses, confirm decisions, and provide directions.

To, From, Date, Subject Headings. Memos and e-mail messages contain guide-word headings as shown in Figure 8.1. These headings help readers immediately identify the date, origin, destination, and purpose of a message.

Single Topic. Good memos and e-mail messages generally discuss only one topic. Notice that Cathy Trimble's memo in Figure 8.1 talks only about the executive program at Harrah's. Limiting the topic helps the receiver act on the subject and file it appropriately. A memo writer who, for example, describes a computer printer problem and also requests permission to attend a conference runs a 50 percent failure risk. The reader may respond to the printer problem but forget about the conference request.

Conversational Tone. The tone of memos and e-mail messages is expected to be conversational because the communicators are usually familiar with one another. This means using occasional contractions (*I'm, you'll*), ordinary words, and first-person pronouns (*I/we*). Yet, the tone should also be professional. E-mail is so fast and so easy to use that some writers have been seduced into an "astonishing lack of professionalism."[5] Although warm and friendly, e-mail messages should not be emotional. They should never include remarks that would not be said to the face of an

FIGURE 8.1 Interoffice Memo

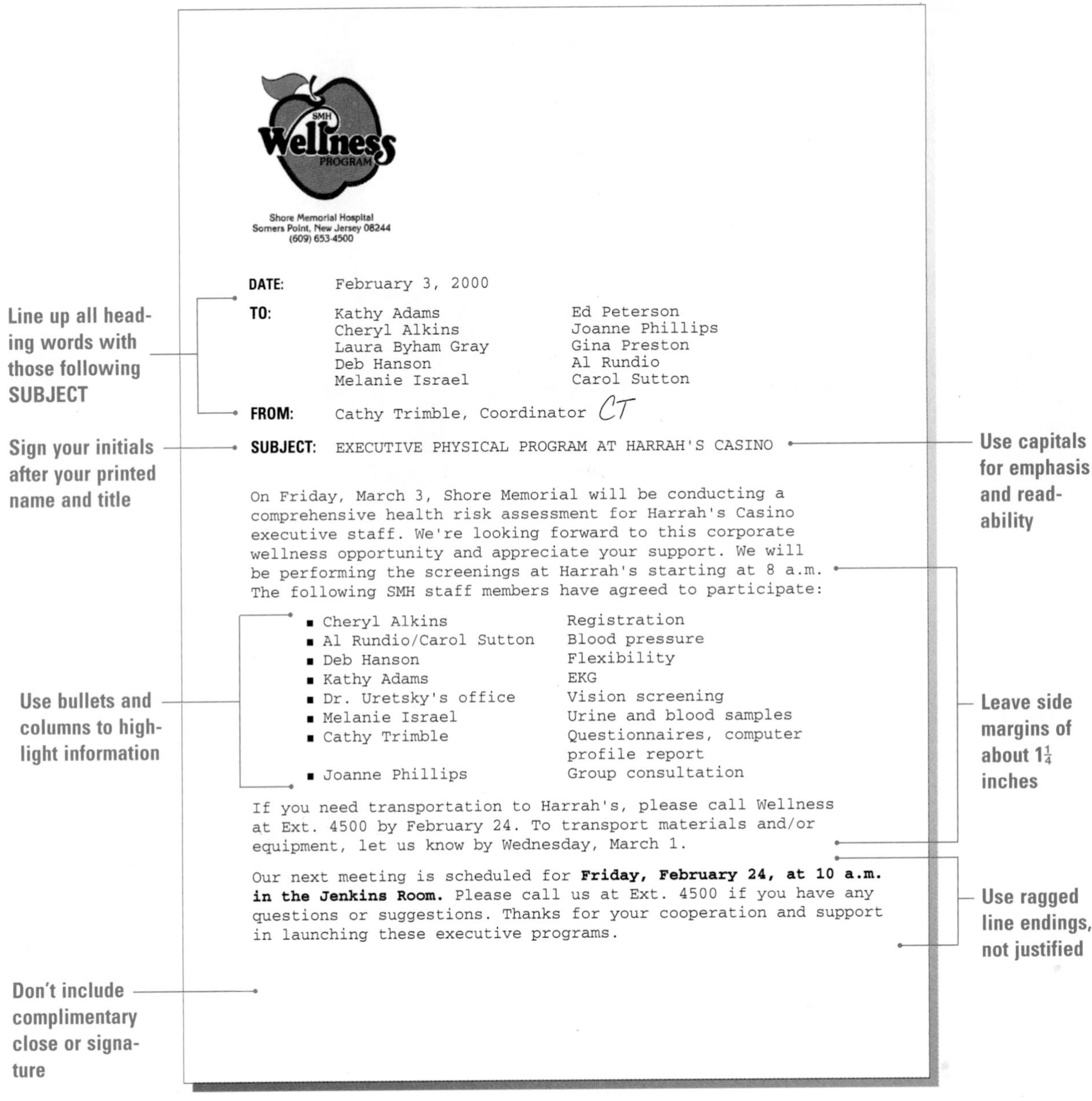

Shore Memorial Hospital
Somers Point, New Jersey 08244
(609) 653-4500

DATE: February 3, 2000

TO: Kathy Adams, Cheryl Alkins, Laura Byham Gray, Deb Hanson, Melanie Israel, Ed Peterson, Joanne Phillips, Gina Preston, Al Rundio, Carol Sutton

FROM: Cathy Trimble, Coordinator *CT*

SUBJECT: EXECUTIVE PHYSICAL PROGRAM AT HARRAH'S CASINO

On Friday, March 3, Shore Memorial will be conducting a comprehensive health risk assessment for Harrah's Casino executive staff. We're looking forward to this corporate wellness opportunity and appreciate your support. We will be performing the screenings at Harrah's starting at 8 a.m. The following SMH staff members have agreed to participate:

- Cheryl Alkins — Registration
- Al Rundio/Carol Sutton — Blood pressure
- Deb Hanson — Flexibility
- Kathy Adams — EKG
- Dr. Uretsky's office — Vision screening
- Melanie Israel — Urine and blood samples
- Cathy Trimble — Questionnaires, computer profile report
- Joanne Phillips — Group consultation

If you need transportation to Harrah's, please call Wellness at Ext. 4500 by February 24. To transport materials and/or equipment, let us know by Wednesday, March 1.

Our next meeting is scheduled for **Friday, February 24, at 10 a.m. in the Jenkins Room.** Please call us at Ext. 4500 if you have any questions or suggestions. Thanks for your cooperation and support in launching these executive programs.

SMH
Wellness
PROGRAM
Line up all heading words with those following SUBJECT
Sign your initials after your printed name and title
Use bullets and columns to highlight information
Don't include complimentary close or signature
Use capitals for emphasis and readability
Leave side margins of about $1\frac{1}{4}$ inches
Use ragged line endings, not justified

Effective memos contain guide-word headings, focus on a single topic, are concise and conversational, and use graphic highlighting.

individual. Naturally, they should also follow the standard writing techniques that you've been learning for other business messages.

Conciseness. As functional forms of communication, routine memos and e-mail messages contain only what's necessary to convey meaning and be courteous. Often, they require less background explanation and less attention to goodwill efforts than do letters to outsiders. Be particularly alert to eliminating wordiness. Avoid opening fillers (*there is, it is*), long lead-ins (*I am writing this memo to inform you that*), and wordy phrases (*because of the fact that*).

Graphic Highlighting. To make important ideas stand out and to improve readability, memo and e-mail writers make liberal use of graphic highlighting techniques. The content of many printed memos is enhanced by numbered or bulleted items, headings, tables, and other techniques you studied in Chapter 6. E-mail messages may not transmit italics, bolding, or double sets of columns. However, you can improve readability with good paragraphing, bullet or asterisk points, and side headings, especially for longer messages. Readers hate to scroll through screen after screen of solid writing. Although corporate America has fallen in love with e-mail, users are less and less tolerant of writers who fail to follow writing conventions. They won't tolerate unattractive, unintelligible, and "impenetrable data dumps."[6]

Graphic highlighting includes numbered and bulleted lists and headings.

Writing Process

"One of the most amazing features of the information revolution," says one technology vice president, is that the "momentum has turned back to the written word."[7] Businesspeople are writing more messages than ever before, and many of them are memos and e-mail. Like letters, good memos require careful preparation. Although they often seem routine, memos and e-mail messages may travel farther than you expect. Consider the market researcher in Illinois, new to her job and eager to please her boss, who was asked to report on the progress of her project. Off the top of her head, she dashed off a quick summary of her work in an e-mail memo to her boss. Later that week a vice president asked her boss how the project was progressing. Her boss forwarded the market researcher's hurried memo. The resulting poor impression was difficult for the new employee to overcome.

Businesspeople are writing more messages than ever before.

Careful writing takes time—especially at first. By following a systematic plan and practicing your skill, however, you can speed up your efforts and greatly improve the product. Bear in mind, moreover, that the effort you make to improve your communication skills can pay big dividends. Frequently, your speaking and writing abilities determine how much influence you'll have in your organization. As with other writing tasks, memo writing follows the familiar three-phase writing process.

A systematic plan helps you write faster and more effectively.

Analysis, Anticipation, and Adaptation. In Phase 1 (prewriting) you'll need to spend some time analyzing your task. It's amazing how many of us are ready to put our pens or computers into gear before engaging our minds. Ask yourself three important questions:

Analyzing the purpose of a message helps determine whether a permanent record is required.

- **Do I really need to write this memo or e-mail?** A phone call or a quick visit to a nearby coworker might solve the problem—and save the time and expense of a written message. On the other hand, some written messages are needed to provide a permanent record. Another decision is whether to write a hard-copy memo or send an electronic one. Many offices are moving toward a *paperless workplace,* as discussed in the accompanying Tech Talk box.
- **Why am I writing?** Know why you are writing and what you hope to achieve. This will help you recognize what the important points are and where to place them.
- **How will the reader react?** Visualize the reader and the effect your message will have. Consider ways to shape the message to benefit the reader.

Research, Organization, and Composition. In Phase 2 (writing) you'll first want to check the files, gather documentation, and prepare your message. Make an outline of the points you wish to cover. For short messages you can jot down notes on the document you are answering. Be sure to prepare for revision, because excellence is rarely achieved on the first effort.

TECH TALK

NOT EXACTLY A PAPERLESS OFFICE, BUT CLOSE

Promises, promises. We've been hearing for years that the paperless office was just around the corner, but it never seems to happen. Perhaps we should settle for a "paper-reduced" workplace, which is increasingly possible through advances in networking and software. A paperless work environment requires two components.

- A device such as a scanner to convert paper documents into electronic ones so that they can be handled by a computer.
- A software program, like a document manager, to file and retrieve documents when needed.

The real problem is convincing people to give up paper. Some organizations have been partially successful. For example, Nordstrom is saving a million dollars every year in paper costs by making internal reports electronically accessible. Aetna Life & Casualty Co. saves millions of dollars by creating manuals and other texts only on computers. Moreover, companies are increasingly using *intranets,* which are internal Web sites, to publish and store company files and data. They're also saving paper by using e-mail for all internal messages.

Career Application

Discuss the statement that "paper is like cholesterol in the blood stream. Good paper is what you need to communicate with others . . . . and bad paper is the internal stuff that clogs up the arteries" (John Loewenberg, Information Services, Aetna Life & Casualty). What constitutes "good" paper and what is "bad"?

Revision, Proofreading, and Evaluation. Careful and caring writers revise their messages, proofread the final copy, and make an effort to evaluate the success of their communication.

- **Revise for clarity.** Viewed from the receiver's perspective, are the ideas clear? Do they need more explanation? If the memo is passed on to others, will they need further explanation? Consider having a colleague critique your message if it is an important one.
- **Proofread for correctness.** Are the sentences complete and punctuated properly? Did you overlook any typos or misspelled words? Remember to use your spell checker and grammar checker to proofread your message before sending it.
- **Plan for feedback.** How will you know if this message is successful? You can improve feedback by asking questions (such as *Do you agree with these suggestions?*) and by making it easy for the receiver to respond.

Organization of Memos and E-Mail Messages

2

Whether hard-copy or electronic, routine memos generally contain four parts: (1) a subject line that summarizes the message, (2) an opening that reveals the main idea immediately, (3) a body that explains and justifies the main idea, and (4) an action closing. Remember that routine messages deliver good news or standard information.

Subject Line. In letters a subject line is optional; in memos it is mandatory. The subject line should summarize the central idea. It provides quick identification for the reader and for filing. As you learned in Chapter 7, the subject line is usually written in an abbreviated style, often without articles (*a, an, the*). It need not be a complete sentence, and it does not end with a period. E-mail subject lines are particularly important, since meaningless ones may cause readers to delete the message without ever opening it. Good subject lines, such as the following, are specific, eye-catching, and talking (contain a verb form):

Direct memos contain a SUBJECT line, an opener stating the main idea, a body with explanation and justification, and an action closing.

SUBJECT: Three Promotional Items to Showcase at Our Next Trade Show (rather than *Trade Show*)

SUBJECT: Beefing Up Our Messaging Capabilities (rather than *New Software*)

SUBJECT: Staff Meeting to Discuss Summer Vacation Schedules (rather than *Meeting*)

Opening. Most memos and e-mails cover nonsensitive information that can be handled in a straightforward manner. "The memos that grab me tell right away what the writer has in mind," says corporate executive Doris Margonine.[8] Begin by frontloading; that is, reveal the main idea immediately. Even though the purpose of the memo or e-mail is summarized in the subject line, that purpose should be restated—and amplified—in the first sentence. Some readers skip the subject line and plunge right into the first sentence. Notice how the following indirect memo openers can be improved by frontloading.

Most direct memos convey nonsensitive information and thus frontload the main idea in the opening.

Indirect Opening	**Direct Opening**
For the past six months the Human Resources Development Department has been considering changes in our employees' benefit plan.	Please review the following proposal regarding employees' benefits, and let me know by May 20 if you approve these changes.
As you may know, employees in Document Production have been complaining about eye fatigue as a result of the overhead fluorescent lighting in their center.	If you agree, I'll order six high-intensity task desk lamps at $189 each for use in the Document Production Center.

Body. The body provides more information about the reason for writing. It explains and discusses the subject logically. Design your data for easy comprehension by using numbered lists, headings, tables, and other graphic highlighting techniques. Compare the following versions of the same message. Observe how the graphic devices of columns, headings, and white space make the main points easy to comprehend.

Hard-to-Read Paragraph Version
Effective immediately are the following air travel guidelines. Between now and December 31, only account executives may take company-approved trips. These individuals will be allowed to take a maximum of two trips, and they are to travel economy or budget class only.

Improved Version With Graphic Highlighting
Effective immediately are the following air travel guidelines:

- Who may travel: Account executives only
- How many trips: A maximum of two trips
- By when: Between now and December 31
- Air class: Economy or budget class only

Memos should close with (1) action information including dates and deadlines, (2) a summary, or (3) a closing thought.

Closing. Generally end with (1) action information, dates, or deadlines; (2) a summary of the message; or (3) a closing thought. Here again the value of thinking through the message before actually writing it becomes apparent. This is where readers look for deadlines and action language. An effective memo or e-mail closing might be, *Please submit your report by June 15 so that we can have your data before our July planning session.*

In more complex messages a summary of main points may be an appropriate closing. If no action request is made and a closing summary is unnecessary, you might end with a simple concluding thought (*I'm glad to answer your questions* or *This sounds like a useful project*). Although you needn't close messages to coworkers with goodwill statements such as those found in letters to customers or clients, some closing thought is often necessary to prevent a feeling of abruptness. Closings can show gratitude or encourage feedback with remarks such as *I sincerely appreciate your cooperation* or *What are your ideas on this proposal?* Other closings look forward to what's next, such as *How would you like to proceed?* As with routine letters, avoid trite expressions. Overused endings such as *Please let me know if I may be of further assistance* sound mechanical and insincere.

Putting It All Together. Now let's put it all together. The following memo is the first draft of a message Steven Timms, Mail Services supervisor, wrote to his supervisor. Although it contains solid information, the message is so wordy and poorly organized that the reader will have trouble grasping its significance.

Poorly Written First Draft

MEMO TO: Andrea Kanarek

Repeats information the reader already knows. Fails to open with information the reader wants.

This memo is in response to your recent inquiry about mail costs. Your message of April 30 said that you wanted a brief explanation of what is being done in Mail Services to cut back on overall costs. I can tell you that I've been doing many things to cut costs.

Fails to help reader see the three main points. Overuses "I." Uses wordy expressions, such as "making a proposal" instead of *proposing*.

For one thing, I'm trying very hard to locate duplicate names and addresses inadvertently included in our mailing lists. This problem is particularly difficult when we merge multiple mailing lists. Another thing I'm doing relates to envelope size. Departments that use envelopes larger than $6\frac{1}{8}$ by $11\frac{1}{2}$ are costing us a lot of money, which they do not realize. Therefore, I am making a proposal to all departments to limit envelope size.

Fails to provide any form of concusion.

Finally, I'm looking into the possibility of presorting some of our first- and third-class mail. Mailings that are presorted are charged less.

Steven's revised message appears in Figure 8.2. To improve readability, he used bullets and boldfaced headings that emphasize the three actions he's taking to cut costs in his department. Notice, too, that he developed a more conversational tone and replaced "I" with "we" to reflect team effort. Compare the revision with Steven's first draft. Which memo will make a better impression on his boss?

Using E-Mail Effectively

3

Corporate America is rapidly embracing communication by e-mail (sometimes called *messaging* as in "Why don't you message me?"). In fact, the growth of e-mail has far outpaced that of telephones when they first appeared. The Electronic Messaging Association predicted that more than 94 million users would send over

FIGURE 8.2 **Information Memo**

The Three Phases of the Writing Process

Analyze: The purpose of this memo is to describe briefly how costs are being cut in the Mail Services Department.

Anticipate: The audience is the writer's boss, who is familiar with the topic and who appreciates brevity.

Adapt: Because the reader requested this message, the direct pattern is most appropriate.

Research: Gather data showing how Mail Services is reducing costs.

Organize: In the opening, summarize the purpose and announce that three actions are being taken to reduce costs. In the body, list and explain the three measures being taken. In the closing, review the actions and look forward to the next step.

Compose: Prepare the first draft.

Revise: Highlight the three main actions. Make the bulleted ideas parallel. Reduce the emphasis on "I."

Proofread: Use figures in "$6\frac{1}{8}$ by $11\frac{1}{2}$" envelope size. Use hyphens in "first- and third-class discounts."

Evaluate: Does this memo supply concise information the boss wants in an easy-to-read form?

DATE: May 2, 2000

TO: Andrea Kanarek
Operations Manager

FROM: Steven W. Timms SWT
Mail Services Supervisor

SUBJECT: YOUR APRIL 30 MEMO ABOUT REDUCING MAIL COSTS

Subject line identifies previous memo and summarizes purpose

Opening states purpose concisely

As you requested, here is a brief summary of three measures Mail Services is taking to reduce overall mailing costs.

Body organizes main points for readability

- Eliminating Duplicate Addresses. For mass mailings we're redoubling our efforts to locate duplicate entries, particularly when we merge multiple mailing lists.
- Limiting Envelope Size. We're asking all departments to use envelopes no larger than $6^1/8$ by $11^1/2$ inches. Larger envelopes cost more.
- Using Presorting Discounts. To take advantage of first- and third-class discounts, we're considering presorting large mailings by zip code and by carrier route.

These are cost-reduction steps we've taken thus far. If you'd like more detailed information, I'd be happy to talk with you about our efforts or to prepare a more formal report.

Closing summarizes and looks forward to next action

SEARCH
E-MAIL
STORE LOCATOR
REMINDER SERVICE
Hallmark
Seasons & Reasons
Ornaments & Collectibles
Our Company
Shoebox
Hallmark Business Expressions
Hallmark Connections
Hallmark Hall of Fame
Electronic Greetings
Shop Online
Multicultural Products
Seasons and Reasons
Check out What's New for Easter at local Hallmark Stores. Post your holiday stories on our bulletin board. Visit the Card Lover's Corner to see our newest card lines.
Shop Online
Send friends and family animated electronic greetings. We have more than 1,000 free greetings. Order your spring flowers and gifts from Hallmark today.
Write to the Easter Bunny!
Send a Hallmark animated greeting!
Keepsake Ornaments and Collectibles
Keepsake Ornaments for Spring are arriving in stores now. Talk collecting in the Ornament Bulletin Board. See the latest Kiddie Car Classics and other great collectibles.
Shoebox
The Grays introduce a weekly cartoon strip, as your other favorites -- Toon in Here, Crabby Road Joke of the Day, and Funny, But No continue to offer Shoebox humor online. Check out some Shoebox holiday cards and don't miss your chance to create a personalized Maxine poster.
Multicultural Products
Meet the Feldmans. Win a seder plate. Share Simone's Scene. Visit Mahogany Hot Spot and win free cards for a year.
Hallmark Business Expressions
Request a catalog or find out how we can create a custom card just for your business.
Hallmark Hall of Fame
Check our recent productions and see which productions can now be purchased on video.
Hallmark Connections
Design your cards at home with Microsoft® Graphics Studio Greetings 99. Our bright and colorful Computer Papers help you shake the winter blues. Free Software templates make it even easier to use our papers. Visit one of our retail stores for even more options from Custom Printing.
Our Company
Learn the history of Hallmark Cards. Find out how to get a job here. Check out the latest news and headlines including updates to our Hallmark International section.
Hallmark Gold Crown Stores
Find the nearest Hallmark Gold Crown store with our locator service. Check your Gold Crown Card point total online.
Hallmark's Reminder Service
Our free Reminder Service ensures you'll never forget important dates.
KIDS
Visit our friends at Crayola for some colorful fun!
Ask Carla the Card Queen
Our online relationship expert answers your questions.
Crayola
OVER

Hallmark Cards projects a warm and fuzzy feeling at its Web site **<http://www.hallmark.com>**, but its internal policy on e-mail is all business. Employees are to use e-mail only as a business tool. The policy also cautions employees that e-mail messages should never be considered confidential. Like Hallmark, many companies strive to establish e-mail policies that offer protection without being overly restrictive.

5.5 trillion e-mail messages in 1999.[9] But some users have legitimate complaints about e-mail "brain dumping" and information overload. Although the benefits of e-mail far outweigh its disadvantages, organizations can take measures to make e-mail more efficient and less burdensome for users, as discussed earlier (see Tech Talk box in Chapter 1).

Early users were encouraged to "ignore stylistic and grammatical considerations." They thought that "words on the fly," as e-mail messages were considered, required little editing or proofing. Correspondents used emoticoms (such as sideways happy faces) to express their emotions. And some e-mail today is still quick and dirty. But as this communication channel matures, messages are becoming more proper and more professional. Today, the average e-mail message may remain in the company's computer system for up to five years. And in some instances the only impression a person has of the e-mail writer is from a transmitted message. That's why it's important to take the time to organize your thoughts, compose carefully, and be concerned with correct grammar and punctuation.

Smart e-mail business communicators are also learning its dangers. They know that their messages can travel (intentionally or unintentionally) long distances. A quickly drafted note may end up in the boss's mailbox or be forwarded to an adversary's box. Making matters worse, computers—like elephants and spurned lovers—never forget.[10] Even erased messages can remain on disk drives. This was learned by Colonel North during the Iran-Contra hearings and more recently by Monica Lewinsky in relation to "deleted files" extracted from her home computer.[11] In another highly publicized case, comments made by police over an internal e-mail system were recovered and became evidence in the Rodney King beating case. "It's as if people put their brains on hold when they write e-mail," said one expert. They think that e-mail "is a substitute for a phone call, and that's the danger."[12]

Smart E-Mail Practices

E-mail is most effective in delivering simple messages. Complex data should probably be sent in hardcopy documents. Despite its dangers and limitations, e-mail is increasingly the way to send business messages. The following pointers will help you use it safely and effectively, while the suggestions in the Career Coach box will help you with e-mail courtesy.

- **Get the address right.** E-mail addresses are often complex, usually illogical, and always unforgiving. Omit one character or misread the letter *l* for the number *1*, and your message bounces. Solution: Use your electronic address book for people you write frequently. And double-check every address that you key in manually. Also be sure that you don't reply to a group of receivers when you intend to answer only one.
- **Avoid misleading subject lines.** With an abundance of spam (junk mail) clogging most inboxes, make sure your subject line is relevant and helpful. Generic tags like *Hello* and *Great Deal* may cause your message to be deleted before it is opened.
- **Be concise.** Don't burden readers with unnecessary information. Remember that monitors are small and typefaces are often difficult to read. Organize your ideas tightly. Messages over three screens would have to be very compelling to keep a reader's interest.
- **Don't send anything you wouldn't want published.** Because e-mail seems like a telephone call or a person-to-person conversation, writers sometimes send sensitive, confidential, inflammatory, or potentially embarrassing messages. Beware! E-mail creates a permanent record that often does not go away even when deleted. And every message is a corporate communication that can be used against you or your employer. Don't write anything that you wouldn't want your boss, your family, or a judge to read.
- **Don't use e-mail to avoid contact.** E-mail is inappropriate for breaking bad news or for resolving arguments. For example, it's improper to fire a person by e-mail. It's also not a good channel for dealing with conflict with supervisors, subordinates, or others. If there's any possibility of hurt feelings, pick up the telephone or pay the person a visit.
- **Never respond when you're angry.** Always allow some time to cool off before shooting off a response to an upsetting message. You often come up with different and better alternatives after thinking about what was said. If possible, iron out differences in person.
- **Care about correctness.** Initially, senders and receivers of e-mail were casual about spelling, grammar, and punctuation. Today, though, e-mail is becoming a mainstream channel of communication. And people are still judged by their writing, whether electronic or paper-based. Sloppy e-mail messages (with missing apostrophes, haphazard spelling, and stream-of-consciousness writing) make readers work too hard. They resent not only the information but also the writer.
- **Resist humor and tongue-in-cheek comments.** Without the nonverbal cues conveyed by your face and your voice, humor can easily be misunderstood.
- **Limit any tendency to send blanket copies.** Send copies only to people who really need to see a message. And remember that it's unnecessary to document every business decision and action with an electronic paper trail.
- **Use design to improve readability of longer messages.** When a message requires several screens, help the reader with headings, bulleted listings, side headings, and perhaps an introductory summary that describes what will follow. Although these techniques lengthen a message, they shorten reading time.
- **Consider cultural differences.** When using this borderless tool, be especially clear and precise in your language. Remember that figurative clichés (*pull up stakes, playing second fiddle,*) sports references (*hit a home run, play by the rules*) and slang (*cool, stoked*) cause confusion abroad.

Spotlight on **Communicators**

Noël Irwin Hentschel is a busy lady. She's CEO of American Tours International, the largest inbound tour operator in the U.S., and the mother of seven children.

Looking for ways to save time, she reads e-mail messages only once. Then she decides to store, print and file a hard copy, or delete. She also makes computer templates of all documents created regularly. When concentrating on critical projects, she recommends closing your door or hanging out a "Please Don't Disturb" sign.

CAREER COACH

E-MAIL NETIQUETTE: COURTESY IN CYBERSPACE

You may eventually be among those who receive and send hundreds of e-mail messages every week. Don't let its heavy use numb your respect for those who read your messages. Here are a few simple rules of e-mail etiquette:

- **Use correct formatting.** Avoid writing in all caps, which is like SHOUTING! And don't write in all lowercase letters, which makes sentences hard to decipher.
- **Respond immediately if requested.** It's courteous to respond right away if you are asked to do so. If you must gather information before replying fully, explain in a brief reply.
- **Use design to help readers.** Include headings, listings, subheadings, and side titles to assist readers in locating information at a glance.
- **Identify messages that are information only and require no response.** Receivers really appreciate knowing which messages require action and which are FYI (For Your Information).
- **Don't read messages waiting to be picked up at a printer.** It's impolite to read other people's e-mail at a printer.
- **Don't send personal messages on company computers.** Unless your company specifically allows it, never use your employer's computers for personal messages or entertainment.
- **Avoid forwarding without permission.** Don't send an individual's message on to another person without the writer's approval.
- **Announce attachments.** If you're sending a lengthy attachment, tell your receiver. You might also ask what format is preferred.
- **Don't automatically return the sender's message.** When replying, cut and paste those parts that include strategic wording. But avoid irritating your recipients by returning their original messages, as well as all the preceding "thread" on a topic.

- **Double-check before hitting the *Send* button.** Have you included everything? Avoid the necessity of sending a second message, which makes you look pretty careless. Use spell-check and reread for fluency before sending.
- **Protect against e-mail break-ins.** Don't give your password to anyone else (except perhaps a trusted assistant who sorts your messages). Change your password frequently. Beware of anyone claiming by phone or e-mail to be a technician or administrator working on the system.

Formatting E-Mail Messages

Because e-mail is a developing communication channel, its formatting and usage conventions are still fluid. Users and authorities do not always agree on what's appropriate for salutations and closings, for instance. The following suggestions, however, can guide you in formatting most e-mail messages, but always check with your organization to observe its practices.

Guide Words. Following the guide word *To*, some writers insert just the recipient's electronic address, such as *mlammers@accountpro.com.* Other writers prefer to include the receiver's full name plus the electronic address, as shown in Figure 8.3. By including full names in the *To* and *From* slots, both receivers and senders are better able to identify the message. By the way, the order of *To, From, Date, Subject,* and other guide words, varies depending on your e-mail program and whether you are sending or receiving the message.

FIGURE 8.3 E-Mail Request

Tips for E-Mail Formatting

- After *To,* type the receiver's electronic address. If you include the receiver's name, enclose the address in angle brackets.
- After *From,* type your name and electronic address, if your program does not insert it automatically.
- After *Subject,* provide a clear description of your message.
- Insert the addresses of anyone receiving carbon or blind copies.
- Include a salutation (such as *Dear Marilyn, Hi Marilyn, Greetings*) or weave the receiver's name into the first line (see Figure 8.5). Some writers omit a salutation.
- Set your line length for no more than 80 characters. If you expect your message to be forwarded, set it for 60 characters.
- Use word-wrap rather than pressing *Enter* at line ends.
- Double-space (press *Enter*) between paragraphs.
- Do not type in all caps or in all lowercase letters.
- Include a complimentary close, your name, and your address if you wish.

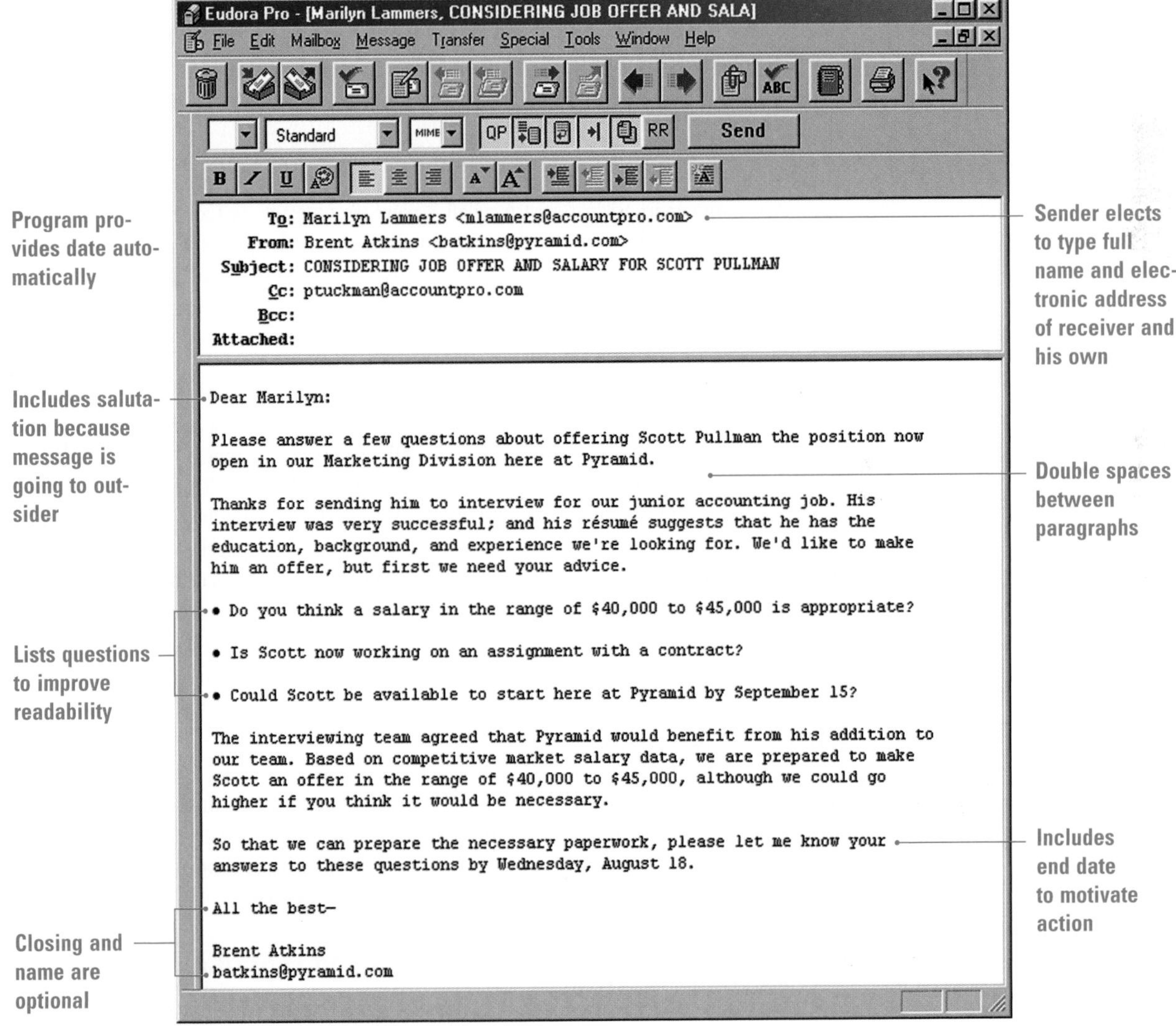

The position of *To, From, Date,* and *Subject* vary depending on your e-mail program.

Most e-mail programs automatically add the current date after *Date.* On the *Cc* line (which stands for *carbon* or *courtesy copy*) you can type the address of anyone who is to receive a copy of the message. Remember, though, to send copies only to those people directly involved with the message. Most e-mail programs also include a line for *Bcc* (*blind carbon copy*). This sends a copy without the addressee's knowledge. Sending blind copies, however, is dangerous because you just might make an address error, and the addressee could learn of the intended *bcc.* On the subject line, identify the subject of the memo. Be sure to include enough information to be clear and compelling.

Salutations for e-mail messages are optional, and practice is as yet unsettled.

Salutation. What to do about a salutation is sticky. Many writers omit a salutation because they consider the message a memo. In the past, hard-copy memos were sent only to company insiders, and salutations were omitted. However, many e-mail messages now go to outsiders, and omitting a salutation seems curt and unfriendly. Thus, if you think it is appropriate, include a salutation such as *Dear Jake; Hi, Jake; Greetings;* or just *Jake:.* Including a salutation is also a visual cue to where the message begins. Many messages are transmitted or forwarded with such long headers that finding the beginning of the message can be difficult. A salutation helps, as shown in Figure 8.3. Other writers do not use a salutation; instead, they use the name of the recipient in the first sentence.

Body. The body of an e-mail message should be typed with upper- and lowercase characters—never in all uppercase or all lowercase characters. Cover just one topic, and try to keep the total message under three screens in length. To assist you, many e-mail programs have basic text-editing features, such as cut, copy, paste, and word-wrap. However, avoid boldface and italics because they create a string of control characters that may cause chaos on the recipient's computer.

Closing lines may include the writer's name, title, and organization.

Closing Lines. Conclude an external message, if you like, with a closing such as *Cheers* or *All the best* followed by your name and e-mail address (because some systems do not transmit your address automatically). If the recipient is unlikely to know you, it's not a bad idea to include your title and organization. Some veteran e-mail users include a *signature file* with identifying information embellished with keyboard art. Use restraint, however, because signature files take up precious space. Writers of e-mail messages sent within organizations may omit closings and even skip their names at the ends of messages because receivers recognize them from identification in the opening lines.

Kinds of Memos

4

Business communicators write many different kinds of memos and e-mail messages to conduct the operations of organizations. This chapter focuses on routine messages that can be grouped in three categories: (1) procedure and information memos, (2) request and reply memos, and (3) confirmation memos.

Procedure and information memos typically flow downward and convey clear information about daily operations.

Procedure and Information Memos and E-Mail Messages

Most internal messages describe procedures and distribute information. These messages typically flow downward from management to employees and relate to the daily operation of an organization. When the topics are nonsensitive, follow the overall memo plan: clear subject line, direct opening, concise explanation, and action closing. They have one primary function: conveying your idea so clearly that no further explanation (return message, telephone call, or personal visit) is necessary.

PROCESS IN PROGRESS

Shore Memorial Hospital Revisited

At Shore Memorial Hospital, Wellness Center director Cathy Trimble writes many memos and e-mail messages to direct employees and to monitor projects. Her pet peeve involves "mystery" memos that she sometimes receives. They conceal their purpose until well into the message. To avoid falling into this trap herself, she concentrates major points in the first paragraph. She also aims for a "high scan factor." This means using bullets, numbered lists, and columns to make main points stand out. "People shouldn't have to read through four or five paragraphs to figure out, for example, what they need to bring to where they're going. Bulleted and numbered items are great for fast reading and also for quick reference, when you want to look back over a document and refresh your memory."

Even though most of her messages are internal, Trimble takes the time to compose carefully. She has good advice for beginning writers. "Before you do any writing on the job, try to get sample documents from the files. You can then see how formal an organization's writing style is, and you can learn about formats. Look for a good communicator whose messages you admire, and study that person's style. You should also try to persuade a fellow worker to read your messages critically before you send them."

Critical Thinking

- How is the writing process or organizational strategy for memos different from that for letters?
- Can writers of e-mail messages be more casual than those who write letters or hard-copy memos?
- What are the pros and cons of adopting the writing style of a colleague who is a good communicator?

In writing information and procedure memos, be careful of tone. Today's managers and team leaders seek employee participation and cooperation, but they can't achieve that rapport if they sound like dictators or autocrats. Avoid making accusations and fixing blame. Rather, explain changes, give reasons, and suggest benefits to the reader. Assume that employees want to contribute to the success of the organization and to their own achievement. Remember, too, that saying something negatively (*Don't park in Lot A*) is generally less helpful than saying it positively (*Park in Lot B until Lot A is repaired*).

The following procedure memo about large printing bills is disappointing both in content and tone.

Ineffective Memo

MEMO TO: Staff Members

Lately, very large expenditures for printing jobs have been submitted, particularly bills being paid to PrintMasters. These bills are suspiciously large and can no longer be honored without careful scrutiny.

Fails to reveal the purpose of the memo (new procedures). Uses accusatory language.

Henceforth, all employees may not send out printing jobs without prior written notice. Using PrintMasters as our sole source must stop. Therefore, authorization is now required for all printing. Two copies of any printing order must be submitted to Kelly before any job is commenced. Please see Kelly if you have any questions.

Concentrates on what should *not* be done instead of what should be done. Word choice (*must stop, is now required*) conveys authoritarian tone.

Thank you for your cooperation.

Sounds insincere.

The following improved version of this memo delivers essentially the same message. It reflects, however, a more cooperative tone and illustrates clear thinking and expression.

Improved Memo

MEMO TO: Staff

Opening reveals purpose and offers brief explanation.

To improve budget planning and to control costs, please follow the new procedures listed below in submitting future requests for outside printing jobs.

Body uses conversational language in justifying reasons for change in procedures.

In our business, of course, printing is a necessary expenditure. However, our bills seem very high lately, particularly those from PrintMasters. The following procedures should help protect us from being overcharged:

Listing of steps in chronological order tells readers exactly how to implement the new procedure. Beginning each numbered item with a verb improves readability and comprehension.

1. Determine your exact printing specifications for a particular job.
2. Secure two estimates for the job.
3. Submit the written estimates to Kelly.
4. Place the order after receiving approval.

Following these new procedures will result in more competitive pricing and perhaps may even provide you with new creative printing options.

The preceding procedure memo applies a direct strategy in telling how to complete a task. Information memos also use that straightforward approach in supplying details about organization activities, services, and actions. The following memo describes four child-care options. Notice how the information was designed for maximum visual impact and readability. Imagine how it would have looked if it had been presented in one or two big paragraphs.

Effective Memo

MEMO TO: Staff

Straightforward opening immediately sets forth the purpose from the reader's viewpoint.

Members of your employee council have met with representatives from management in considering the following four options to provide child care.

Since these items reflect no particular order, they are bulleted to present a slightly cleaner appearance than a numbered list.

- *On-site day-care centers.* This option accommodates employees' children on the premises. Weekly rates would be competitive with local day-care facilities. This option is most costly but is worth pursuing, particularly if local facilities are deficient.
- *Off-site centers in conjunction with other local employers.* We are looking into the possibility of developing central facilities to be shared with nearby firms.
- *Neighborhood child-care centers.* We would contract with local centers to buy open slots for employees' children, perhaps at a discount.
- *Sick-child services.* This plan would provide employees with alternatives to missing work when children are ill. We are investigating sick-child programs at local hospitals and services that send workers to employees' homes to look after sick children.

Ends with forward-looking statement. No action is required.

As soon as we gather more information about these options, we will pass that data along to you.

Request and Reply Memos and E-Mail Messages

5

Request and reply memos follow the direct pattern in seeking or providing information.

In requesting routine information or action within an organization, the direct approach works best. Generally, this means asking for information or making the request without first providing elaborate explanations and justifications. Remember that readers are usually thinking, "Why me? Why am I receiving this?" Readers can understand the explanation better once they know what you are requesting.

If you are seeking answers to questions, you have two options for opening the memo: (1) ask the most important question first, followed by an explanation and then the other questions, or (2) use a polite command, such as *Please answer the following questions regarding . . . .*

In the body of the memo, you can explain and justify your request or reply. When many questions must be asked, list them, being careful to phrase them similarly. Be courteous and friendly. In the closing include an end date (with a reason, if possible) to promote a quick response. For simple requests some writers encourage their readers to jot responses directly on the request memo. In answering e-mail messages, writers may request a quick reply.

The request shown below seeks information from managers about the use of temporary office workers. It begins with a polite command followed by numbered questions. Notice that the writer develops reader's benefits by describing how the data collected will be used to help the reader. Notice, too, the effort to promote the feeling that the writer is part of a team working with employees to achieve their common goals.

Effective Memo

MEMO TO: Department Managers

Please answer the questions listed below about the use of temporary help in your department. — **Opens with polite command.**

With your ideas we plan to develop a policy that will help us improve the process of budgeting, selecting, and hiring temporaries. — **Explains the purpose concisely.**

1. What is the average number of temporary office workers you employ each month?
2. What is the average length of a temporary worker's assignment in your department? — **Lists parallel questions for easy reading and comprehension.**
3. What specific job skills are you generally seeking in your temporaries?
4. What temporary agencies are you now using?

By replying before January 20, you will have direct input into the new policy, which we will be developing at the end of the month. This improved policy will help you fill your temporary employment needs more quickly and more efficiently. — **Includes end date, along with reason and reader benefit.**

Writers sometimes fall into bad habits in answering memos. Here are some trite and long-winded openers that are best avoided:

In response to your message of the 15th . . . (*States the obvious.*)

Thank you for your memo of the 15th in which you . . . (*Suggests the writer can think of nothing more original.*)

Overused and long-winded openers bore readers and waste their time.

I have before me your memo of the 15th in which you . . . (*Unnecessarily identifies the location of the previous message.*)

Pursuant to your request of the 15th . . . (*Sounds old-fashioned.*)

This is to inform you that . . . (*Delays getting to the point.*)

Please refer to your memo of . . . (*Asks reader to search for original document. Always supply a copy if necessary or summarize its points.*)

Direct opening statements can also be cheerful and empathic.

Instead of falling into the trap of using one of the preceding shopworn openings, start directly by responding to the writer's request. If you agree to the request, show your cheerful compliance immediately. Consider these good-news openers:

Yes, we will be glad to . . . (*Sends message of approval by opening with "Yes."*)

Here are answers to the questions you asked about . . . (*Sounds straightforward, businesslike, and professional.*)

You're right in seeking advice about . . . (*Opens with two words that every reader enjoys seeing and hearing.*)

We are happy to assist you in . . . (*Shows writer's helpful nature and goodwill.*)

The information you requested is shown on the attached . . . (*Gets right to the point.*)

After a direct and empathic opener, provide the information requested in a logical and coherent order. If you're answering a number of questions, arrange your answers in the order of the questions. In the favorable reply shown in Figure 8.4, information describing dates, speakers, and topics is listed in columns with headings. Although it requires more space than the paragraph format, this arrangement vastly improves readability and comprehension.

In providing additional data, use familiar words, short sentences, short paragraphs, and active-voice verbs. When alternatives exist, make them clear. Consider using graphic highlighting techniques, as shown in Figure 8.4, for both the speakers' schedules and the two program choices offered further along in the letter. Imagine how much more effort would be required to read and understand the letter without the speaker list or the numbered choices.

If further action is required, be specific in spelling it out. What may be crystal clear to you (because you have been thinking about the problem) is not always immediately apparent to a reader with limited time and interest. Figure 8.4 not only illustrates a readable, well-organized reply memo, it also reviews formatting tips.

Confirmation Memos and E-Mail Messages

6

Confirmation memos—also called *to-file reports* or *incident reports*—record oral decisions, directives, and discussions. They create a concise, permanent record that could be important in the future. Because individuals may forget, alter, or retract oral commitments, it's wise to establish a written record of significant happenings. Such records are unnecessary, of course, for minor events. The confirmation e-mail message shown in Figure 8.5 reviews the significant points of a sales agreement discussed in a telephone conversation. When you write to confirm an oral agreement, remember these tips:

- Include names and titles of involved individuals.

FIGURE 8.4 Reply Memo

Tips for Formatting Hard-Copy Memos

- Set one tab to line up all entries evenly after SUBJECT.
- Leave two blank lines between SUBJECT line and first line of memo text.
- Single-space all but the shortest memos. Double-space between paragraphs.
- For memos printed on plain paper, leave a top margin of 2 inches for full-page memos and 1 inch for half-page memos.
- Use $1\frac{1}{4}$-inch side margins.
- If a memo requires two pages, use a second-page heading that includes the addressee's name, page number, and date.
- Handwrite your initials after your typed name.

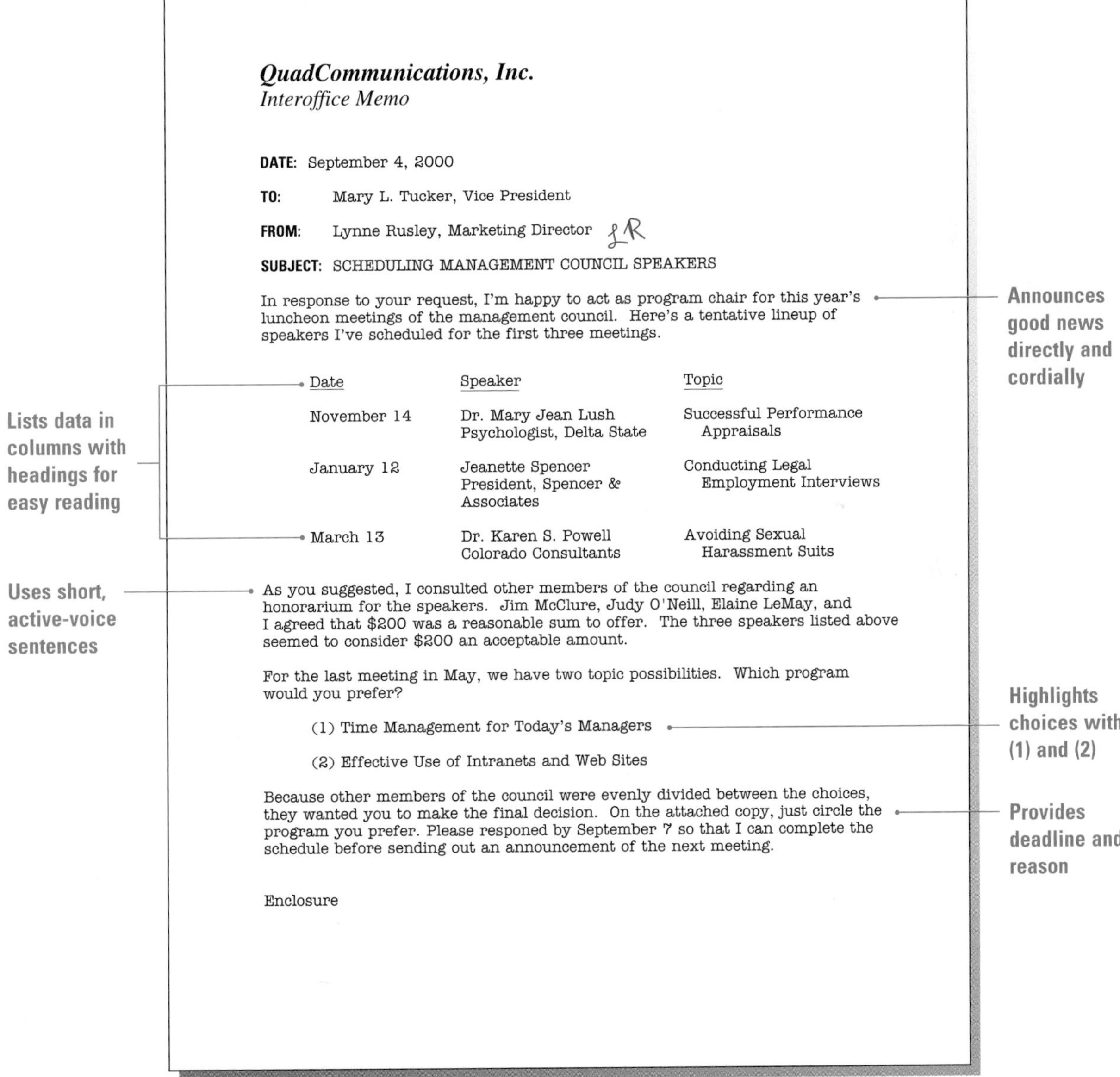

QuadCommunications, Inc.
Interoffice Memo

DATE: September 4, 2000

TO: Mary L. Tucker, Vice President

FROM: Lynne Rusley, Marketing Director LR

SUBJECT: SCHEDULING MANAGEMENT COUNCIL SPEAKERS

In response to your request, I'm happy to act as program chair for this year's luncheon meetings of the management council. Here's a tentative lineup of speakers I've scheduled for the first three meetings.

Date	Speaker	Topic
November 14	Dr. Mary Jean Lush Psychologist, Delta State	Successful Performance Appraisals
January 12	Jeanette Spencer President, Spencer & Associates	Conducting Legal Employment Interviews
March 13	Dr. Karen S. Powell Colorado Consultants	Avoiding Sexual Harassment Suits

As you suggested, I consulted other members of the council regarding an honorarium for the speakers. Jim McClure, Judy O'Neill, Elaine LeMay, and I agreed that $200 was a reasonable sum to offer. The three speakers listed above seemed to consider $200 an acceptable amount.

For the last meeting in May, we have two topic possibilities. Which program would you prefer?

(1) Time Management for Today's Managers

(2) Effective Use of Intranets and Web Sites

Because other members of the council were evenly divided between the choices, they wanted you to make the final decision. On the attached copy, just circle the program you prefer. Please responed by September 7 so that I can complete the schedule before sending out an announcement of the next meeting.

Enclosure

Announces good news directly and cordially
Lists data in columns with headings for easy reading
Uses short, active-voice sentences
Highlights choices with (1) and (2)
Provides deadline and reason

FIGURE 8.5 **Confirmation E-Mail**

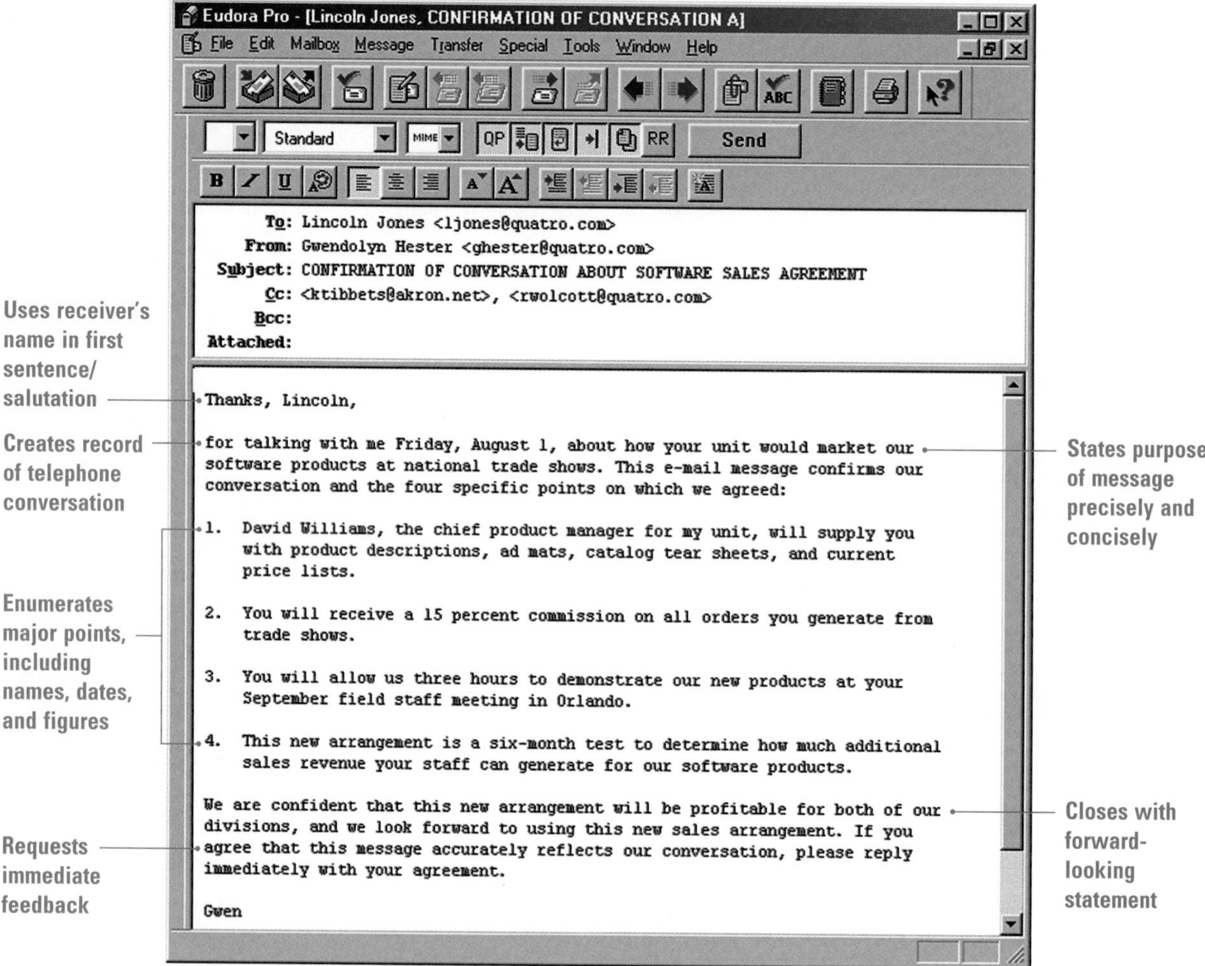
Eudora Pro - [Lincoln Jones, CONFIRMATION OF CONVERSATION A]

To: Lincoln Jones <ljones@quatro.com>
From: Gwendolyn Hester <ghester@quatro.com>
Subject: CONFIRMATION OF CONVERSATION ABOUT SOFTWARE SALES AGREEMENT
Cc: <ktibbets@akron.net>, <rwolcott@quatro.com>
Bcc:
Attached:

Thanks, Lincoln,

for talking with me Friday, August 1, about how your unit would market our software products at national trade shows. This e-mail message confirms our conversation and the four specific points on which we agreed:

1. David Williams, the chief product manager for my unit, will supply you with product descriptions, ad mats, catalog tear sheets, and current price lists.

2. You will receive a 15 percent commission on all orders you generate from trade shows.

3. You will allow us three hours to demonstrate our new products at your September field staff meeting in Orlando.

4. This new arrangement is a six-month test to determine how much additional sales revenue your staff can generate for our software products.

We are confident that this new arrangement will be profitable for both of our divisions, and we look forward to using this new sales arrangement. If you agree that this message accurately reflects our conversation, please reply immediately with your agreement.

Gwen

Uses receiver's name in first sentence/ salutation
Creates record of telephone conversation
Enumerates major points, including names, dates, and figures
Requests immediate feedback
States purpose of message precisely and concisely
Closes with forward-looking statement

Confirmation memos provide a permanent record of oral discussions, decisions, and directives.

- Itemize major issues or points concisely.
- Request feedback regarding unclear or inaccurate points.

Another type of confirmation memo simply verifies receipt of materials or a change of schedule. It is brief and often kept on file to explain your role in a project. For example, suppose you are coordinating an interdepartmental budget report. Carla Ramos from Human Resources calls to let you know that her portion of the report will be a week late. To confirm, you would send Carla the following one-sentence memo: *This message verifies our telephone conversation of November 5 in which you said that your portion of the budget report will be submitted November 14 instead of November 7.* Be sure to print a copy if you are using e-mail. Notice that the tone is objective, not accusatory. However, if you are later asked about why your project is running late (and you probably will be), you'll have a record of the explanation. In fact, you should probably send a copy to your superior so that he or she can intervene if necessary.

Some critics complain that too many "cover-your-tail" memos are written, thus creating excessive and unnecessary paperwork.[13] However, legitimate memos that confirm and clarify events have saved many thoughtful workers from being misunderstood or blamed unfairly.

Sometimes taken lightly, office memos and e-mail messages, like other business documents, should be written carefully. Once they leave the author's hands, they are essentially published. They can't be retrieved, corrected, or revised. Review the following checklist for tips in writing memos that accomplish what you intend.

Confirmation memos can save employees from being misunderstood or blamed unfairly.

Checklist for Writing Routine Memos and E-Mail Messages

Subject Line

 **Summarize the central idea.** Make the subject line read like a newspaper headline—brief but clear.

 **Use an abbreviated style.** Omit articles (*a, an, the*), and do not try to make the subject line a complete sentence. Omit an ending period.

Opening

 **State the purpose for writing.** Include the same information that's in the subject line, but expand it.

 **Ask questions immediately.** If you are requesting information, begin with the most important question or use a polite command (*Please answer the following questions about . . .*).

 **Supply information directly.** If responding to a request, give the reader the requested information immediately in the opening. Explain later.

Body

 **Explain details.** Arrange information logically. For complex topics use separate paragraphs developed coherently.

 **Enhance readability.** Use short sentences, short paragraphs, and parallel construction for similar ideas.

 **Supply graphic highlighting.** Provide bulleted and/or numbered lists, tables, or other graphic devices to improve readability and comprehension.

 **Be cautious.** Remember that memos and e-mail messages often travel far beyond their intended audiences.

Closing

 **Request action.** If appropriate, state specifically what you want the reader to do. Include a deadline, with reasons, if possible.

 **Summarize the memo or provide a closing thought.** For long memos provide a summary of the important points. If neither an action request nor a summary is necessary, end with a closing thought.

 **Avoid cliché endings.** Use fresh remarks rather than overused expressions such as *If you have additional questions, please do not hesitate to call* or *Thank you for your cooperation.*

Spotlight on **Communicators**

While CEO of Warnaco, a $789 million maker of intimate apparel and men's shirts, Linda J. Wachner kept abreast of activity in the seven divisions of her company through memos. Every Friday night division heads faxed her a one-page memo outlining any problems that might have cropped up in shipping or delivery. These informative memos gave her a preview of what to expect on Monday morning so that she was ready to attack problems head-on.

CASE STUDY

PROCESS TO PRODUCT

Applying Your Skills at Shore Memorial Hospital

One of Cathy Trimble's jobs is making sure that Shore Memorial's webmaster receives updated information on various Wellness Center events. She asks you, her assistant, to transform the following jumble of information into a proper memo.

One new event for the Calendar of Events at the hospital Web site is a stop-smoking program sponsored by Smokeless. A free orientation is given on the first night. This national program is hospital-based and will be offered by Maria Spear. She is a certified Smokeless instructor. $120. Starts September 22 and meets eight times. 7 to 9 p.m. Scheduled for the SMH Rainbow Room.

Another new program is a workshop offered by Joanne Phillips, R.N., and Kim Cipkins in the SMH Jenkins Room. One is a cardiac educator/nurse and the other is a registered dietitian. High blood cholesterol and dietary interventions will be discussed. Fee: $5. 7 to 10 p.m. This workshop is called "Eat to Your Heart's Content." Dietary fats, interpreting food labels, and the modification of recipes will be discussed. Just one night, October 2.

The final new program doesn't have a name yet. Trimble wants you to think of one. It's aimed at divorced people—the legal, social, and financial aspects of being a single parent. This first session focuses on finances. Five sessions are planned. Colleen Kelly, RIA, will conduct the workshop, which costs $5 per night. 7 to 9 p.m. September 20. Meet in Conference Center.

Your Job

For Cathy Trimble's signature, in teams or individually, prepare a memo to webmaster Kevin von Gillern. Describe the three new programs for the fall Calendar of Events. Decide whether to sequence the information in paragraph form or some other format. To prevent errors, Trimble wants the webmaster to send her a printout of the listings before they are posted. Set an end date and give a reason. If any information is missing, supply it.

Summary of Learning Objectives

1 **Discuss the characteristics of and writing process for successful memos and e-mail messages.** Successful memos and e-mails begin with TO, FROM, SUBJECT, and DATE, and they generally cover just one topic. They are written conversationally and concisely. Their content often can be highlighted with numbered or bulleted lists, headings, and tables. Before writing, determine if you really must write. If you must, analyze your purpose and audience. Collect information, prepare an outline, and compose the first draft on a word processor. Revise for clarity and correctness. Encourage feedback from the reader.

2 **Analyze the organization of memos and e-mail messages.** The subject line summarizes the central idea, while the opening repeats that idea and amplifies it. The body explains and provides more information. The closing includes (a) action information, dates, and deadlines; (b) a summary of the memo; and/or (c) a closing thought.

3 **Explain how to use e-mail effectively, including practices, netiquette, and formatting.** Careful e-mail users do not transmit sensitive, confidential, inflammatory, or potentially embarrassing messages. Each message is concise and correctly addressed. It contains a descriptive subject line. Longer messages use headings, bulleted lists, and summaries to improve readability. Writers are careful about spelling, grammar, and usage. Courteous writers respond if requested, identify messages that are information only, avoid forwarding without permission, and avoid using company facilities for private messages. E-mail messages should be single-spaced with double-spacing between paragraphs. Salutations and closings are optional.

4 **Write information and procedure memos and e-mail messages.** Messages delivering information or outlining procedures follow the direct memo plan with the main idea stated immediately. Ideas must be explained so clearly that no further explanation is necessary. The tone of the memo should encourage cooperation.

5 **Write request and reply memos and e-mail messages.** Messages requesting action or information open with a specific request, followed by details. Memos that reply to requests open with information the reader most wants to learn. The body contains details, and the closing may summarize the important points or look forward to a subsequent event or action.

6 **Write confirmation memos and e-mail messages.** Sometimes called "to-file reports" or "incident reports," confirmation messages create a permanent record of oral decisions, directives, and discussions. They should include names and titles of involved individuals, major issues discussed, and a request for approval by the receiver.

CHAPTER REVIEW

1. Name five characteristics of successful memos and e-mail messages. (Obj. 1)
2. What is graphic highlighting, and why is it particularly useful in memos and e-mail messages? (Obj. 1)
3. Briefly describe the writing process for memos and e-mail messages. (Obj. 1)
4. What three questions should you ask yourself before writing a memo or e-mail message? (Obj. 1)
5. Name three ways to close a memo or e-mail message. (Obj. 2)
6. What are some of the dangers for users of e-mail? (Obj. 3)
7. Suggest at least ten pointers that you could give to a first-time e-mail user. (Obj. 3)
8. Name at least five rules of e-mail etiquette that show respect for others. (Obj. 3)
9. What are three possibilities in handling the salutation for an e-mail message? (Obj. 3)
10. What tone should managers avoid in writing procedure or information memos and e-mail messages? (Obj. 4)
11. Why should writers of information memos and e-mail messages strive to express ideas positively instead of negatively? (Obj. 4)
12. Should a request memo or e-mail message open immediately with the request or with an explanation? Why? (Obj. 5)
13. What's wrong with a message opener such as *This is to inform you that . . .*? (Obj. 5)
14. What is a confirmation memo or e-mail message? What other names could it be given? (Obj. 6)
15. What three elements should most confirmation memos and e-mail messages include? (Obj. 6)

CRITICAL THINKING

1. How can the writer of a business memo or an e-mail message develop a conversational tone and still be professional? Why do e-mail writers sometimes forget to be professional? (Objs. 1–3)
2. What factors would help you decide whether to write a memo, send an e-mail, make a telephone call, leave a voice-mail message, or deliver a message in person? (Objs. 1 and 2)
3. Why are lawyers and technology experts warning companies to store, organize, and manage computer data, including e-mail, with sharper diligence? (Obj. 3)
4. Discuss the ramifications of the following statement: Once a memo or any other document leaves your hands, you have essentially published it. (Objs. 2–6)
5. **Ethical Issue:** Should managers have the right to monitor the e-mail messages of employees? Why or why not? What if employees are warned that e-mail could be monitored? If a company sets up an e-mail policy, should only in-house transmissions be monitored? Only outside transmissions?

ACTIVITIES

8.1 Openers for Memos and E-Mail Messages (Objs. 1–3)

Revise the following memo openers so that they are more direct.

a. At the meeting of the management council last Thursday, you mentioned a very interesting study that you conducted last year. It reported data regarding employee turnover, and you said that it revealed some intriguing findings. Please send me a copy of your study.

b. I appreciate your asking me for my ideas on processing data electronically. In the nearly 15 years since EDI (electronic data interchange) was first introduced, large companies have always wanted their smaller suppliers to use it. But now with Internet-based systems, it's much more usable and less expensive. I've worked out six suggestions for how your company can switch to Internet-based EDI. They are discussed below.

c. I have before me your memo of the 16th in which you request permission to attend the Web Site Design Seminar sponsored by Presentation Planners. As I understand it, this is a two-day seminar scheduled for February 25 and 26. Your reasons for attending were well stated and convincing. You have my permission to attend.

d. As you are aware, the document specialists in our department have been unhappy about their chairs and their inability to adjust the back height. The chairs are uncomfortable and cause back fatigue. As a result, I looked into the possibility of purchasing new adjustable chairs that I think will be just right for these employees. New chairs have been ordered for all these employees. The new chairs should be arriving in about three weeks.

8.2 Subject Lines (Objs. 1–3)

Write effective subject lines for the messages represented by the openings in Activity 8.1.

8.3 Graphic Highlighting Techniques (Objs. 1 and 3)

Revise the following hard-to-read paragraphs. Include an introductory statement or a title before presenting the data in bulleted or numbered lists.

a. A recent survey of car buyers uncovered some very interesting information about what electronic options they really wanted in new cars. Some technology visionaries have been saying that car buyers wanted a lot of fancy electronic gadgets, but the survey showed that only 5.1 percent, for example, wanted a trip computer. Most car buyers mentioned cruise control (79.1 percent). A total of 61.1 percent said that they wanted antilock brakes. A smaller percentage (50.5 percent) wanted keyless entry. Farther down the list we found that buyers wanted CD players (34.1 percent).

b. Our employee leasing program has proven to be an efficient management tool for business owners because we take care of everything. Our program will handle your payroll preparation. Moreover, benefits for employees are covered. We also know what a chore calculating worker's compensation premiums can be, so we do that for you. And we make all the necessary state and federal reports that are required today.

c. We are concerned about your safety in using our automated teller machines (ATMs) at night, so we think you should consider the following tips. Users of ATMs are encouraged to look around—especially at night—before using the service. If you notice anything suspicious, the use of another ATM is recommended. Or you could come back later. Another suggestion that we give our customers involves counting your cash. Be sure that the cash you receive is put away quickly. Don't count it as soon as you get it. It's better to check it in the safety of your car or at home. Also, why not take a friend with you if you must use an ATM at night? We also suggest that you park in a well-lighted area as close to the actual location of the ATM as possible.

8.4 Document for Analysis: Procedure Memo (Obj. 4)

Analyze the following memo. List its weaknesses. If your instructor directs, revise the memo.

Poorly Written Memo

DATE: Current

TO: Staff Members

FROM: Randy Eastman, Manager

SUBJECT: TIME MANAGEMENT SUGGESTIONS

Recently I had the pleasure of attending an excellent time management seminar in which we managers were told about some interesting strategies for managing the glut of information from which we all suffer. Since many of you have been complaining about all the time you spend on e-mail and voice mail, I thought I would send you some of the best pointers we were given. These might help you increase your productivity and decrease your frustration.

When it comes to e-mail, we were urged to practice e-mail "triage." This means glancing through all incoming mail quickly and separating the messages you need to answer immediately, as well as determining which messages can wait and which ones can be deleted. Generally, you can do this by checking subject lines and the names of senders. To cut down on the amount of time you spend on your e-mail, you should check e-mail messages only once or twice each day and at specific times so that you develop a routine. This simple practice can save you a lot of wasted time. Another technique involves time management but also courtesy. Be sure to respond briefly to all important e-mails, even if you can say only that you are looking into a matter.

When it comes to voice mail, check it at least three times a day. This prevents "message bump"—having the same person call you several times with the same request. Another idea for saving time with voice mail is to try skipping to the beep when you want to leave a message. Hit the star or pound key on your phone.

By the way, we need a volunteer to attend a conference on preventing violence in the workplace. Thank you for your cooperation.

8.5 Document for Analysis: Request Memo (Obj. 5)

Analyze the following memo. List its weaknesses. If your instructor directs, revise it.

Poorly Written Memo

DATE: Current

TO: All Employees

FROM: Elizabeth Mendoza, Human Resources

SUBJECT: NEW HOLIDAY PLAN

In the past we've offered all employees 11 holidays (starting with New Year's Day in January and proceeding through Christmas Day the following December). Other companies offer similar holiday schedules.

In addition, we've given all employees one floating holiday. As you know, we've determined that day by a companywide vote. As a result, all employees had the same day off. Now, however, management is considering a new plan that we feel would be better. This new plan involves a floating holiday that each individual employee may decide for herself or himself. We've given it considerable thought and decided that such a plan could definitely work. We would allow each employee to choose a day that he or she wants. Of course, we would have to issue certain restrictions. Selections would have to be subject to our staffing needs within individual departments. For example, if everyone wanted the same day, we could not allow everyone to take it. In that case, we would allow the employee with the most seniority to have the day off.

Before we institute the new plan, though, we wanted to see what employees thought about this. Is it better to continue our current companywide uniform floating holiday? Or should we try an individual floating holiday? Please let us know what you think as soon as possible.

8.6 Document for Analysis: Confirmation E-Mail (Obj. 6)

Analyze the following e-mail message. List its weaknesses. If your instructor directs, revise it.

Poorly Written E-Mail Message

To: WilliamMorrison@commercial.com

From: TracyAnnPhillips@aol.com

Subject: COMMERCIALS

It was good to talk to you on the telephone yesterday after exchanging letters with you and after reading so much about Bermuda. I was very interested in learning about the commercials you want me to write. As I understand it, Mr. Morrison, you want a total of 240 one-minute radio commercials. These commercials are intended to rejuvenate the slumping tourist industry in Bermuda. You said that these commercials would be broadcast from March 30 through June 30. You said these commercials would be played on three radio stations. These stations are in five major cities on the East Coast. The commercials would be aimed at morning and evening drive time, for drivers who are listening to their radios, and the campaign would be called "Radio Bermuda."

I am sure I can do as you suggested in reminding listeners that Bermuda is less than two hours away. You expect me to bring to these commercials the color and character of the island. You want me to highlight the attractions and the civility of Bermuda, at least as much as can be done in one-minute radio commercials. In my notes I wrote that you also mentioned that I should include references to tree frogs and royal palm trees. Another item you suggested that I include in some of the commercials was special Bermuda food, such as delicacies like shark on toast, conch fritters, and mussel stew.

I wanted to be sure to write these points down so that we both agreed on what we said in our telephone conversation. I am eager to begin working on these commercials immediately, but I would feel better if you looked over these points to see if I have it right. I look forward to working with you.

8.7 Information Memo: What I Do on the Job (Obj. 4)

Some employees have remarked to the boss that they are working more than other employees. Your boss has decided to study the matter by collecting memos from everyone. He asks you to write a memo describing your current duties and the skills required for your position. If some jobs are found to be overly demanding, your boss may redistribute job tasks or hire additional employees. Based on your own work or personal experience, write a well-organized memo describing your duties, the time you spend on each task, and the skills needed for what you do. Provide enough details to make a clear record of your job. Use actual names and describe actual tasks. Report to the head of the organization. The organization could be a campus club or committee on which you serve. Don't make your memo a list of complaints. Just describe what you do in an objective tone. And by the way, your boss appreciates brevity. Keep your memo under one page.

8.8 Information Memo: Party Time (Obj. 4)

As Wendy Nguyen, you have been asked to draft a memo to the office staff about the upcoming December holiday party. Decide what kind of party you would like. Include information about where the party will be held, when it is, what the cost will be, a description of the food to be served, whether guests are allowed, and with whom to make reservations.

8.9 Information Memo: Trading Obscenities (Obj. 4)

The National Association of Securities Dealers sent a notice to its 5,515 members warning against "the use of profane or obscene language" by brokers. Such language, the NASD cautions, could lead to censures, fines, or suspension from the association. Apparently, at many brokerage firms traders can't go through a single sentence without interjecting a string of obscenities. Profanity seems to be part of the job. But now more women are becoming stockbrokers, and the crude language could lead to sexual harassment suits. Smith Barney, Inc., for example, was hit with a highly publicized suit over a fraternity-like "boom-boom room" where female brokers felt threatened by the vulgar language being used. To be fair, it should be noted that not all the complaints come from women. In fact, in many cases Wall Street women are said to be able to hold their own in the swearing department. Nevertheless, the new directive from NASD aims to require its members to police communication between brokers and their clients. It also wants to cut out the use of obscenities between traders.

Although NASD is clear about the problem, it's not so clear about the solution. It offers no guidelines or suggestions for implementing its directive. When asked if some four-letter words were subject to steeper fines than others, NASD's general counsel Alden Adkins said, "It's hard to specify." The current directive from NASD stems from a Federal Trade Commission regulation banning abusive and deceptive telemarketing techniques, including the use of profane or obscene language by people selling things over the telephone.[14] NASD is just getting around to enforcing the "obscene language" portion of the FTC ruling.

As Mark Mandel, manager of a prestigious East Coast brokerage house, write a memo to the numerous brokers on your staff informing them of the NASD directive. Avoid blaming the entire staff for vulgar language. Actually, only a few of your brokers use obscenities regularly. However, you do have to emphasize the seriousness of the directive. Strive to gain their cooperation.

8.10 Information Memo: Retirement Questions (Obj. 4)

Team

The following memo was assigned by a writing consultant as an exercise to train your team in writing skills. In small groups discuss its weaknesses and then compose, either individually or as a team, an improved version.

Poorly Written Memo

DATE: Current

TO: All Employees

FROM: Mark Grist, Employee Benefits Division

SUBJECT: RETIREMENT

We are aware that many employees do not have sufficient information that relates to the prospect of their retirement. Many employees who are approaching retirement age have come to this office with specific questions about their retirement. It would be much easier for us to answer all these questions at once, and that is what we will try to do.

We would like to answer your questions at a series of retirement planning sessions in the company conference room. The first meeting is September 6. We will start at 4 p.m., which means that the company is giving you one hour of released time to attend this important session. We will meet from 4 to 6 p.m. when we will stop for dinner. We will begin again at 7 p.m. and finish at 8 p.m.

We have arranged for three speakers. They are: our company benefits supervisor, a financial planner, and a psychologist who treats retirees who have mental problems. The three sessions are planned for: September 6, October 4, and November 1.

8.11 Information Memo: It's a Dog-Eat-Pasta World (Obj. 4)

As Karen Munson, marketing director for Premier Pet Products, you have just completed the planning stages of a campaign, organized by your advertising agency, the Wootton Group of Virginia Beach, Virginia. The management council of Premier gave the go-ahead to Wootton for a unique effort to push pasta as an ideal food for pets. You have worked out the following details of the promotion. The most visible element of the campaign is a "Teach Your Dog to Say Pasta" contest. Dog owners will be encouraged to send in videotapes of their dogs barking "pasta." Sounds weird, but several dog owners swear that their dogs can do it.

To promote the contest, Wootton is running 60-second radio spots about the contest in several target markets around the country. Contestants call 1-800-PASTA-DOG. The goal is to convince dog owners that pasta is good for dogs and that dogs like pasta. Tied in with the promotion are product names such as Woof-A-Roni dog treats. Other promotional events will be held in grocery store "barking lots" in as many as 30 cities this summer. Hot dogs will be sold, of course, and dogs will participate in Frisbee games and costume contests. The promotions will end in August. The owner of the talking-dog contest winner will receive a two-week trip to Italy, where dogs are said to be crazy about pasta.[15]

Your task is to write to Vice President Matt Brooks. Tell him of the campaign that you and the advertising agency have developed. Vice President Brooks was part of the management decision to push pasta for dogs, but he knows nothing about the promotional campaign. Prepare a well-organized memo listing the elements of the promotion.

8.12 Information Memo or E-Mail*: Wilderness Retreat (Obj. 4)

E-Mail

Assume you are Mark Peters, president of a small printing operation employing 25 workers. On Friday, June 7, your print shop employees will join you at an expense-paid, one-day retreat that you hope will improve teamwork among the workers. The retreat will be led by Wilderness Retreats, which offers companies outdoor team training designed to build employee trust, teamwork, and loyalty. Employees will meet at work at 8 a.m., and a Wilderness Retreats van will pick them up and take them to a nearby national forest. Employees will spend the day on team-building activities, including a map-reading exercise that will require employee teams to find their way through a wooded area to a "home base." The retreat will provide a catered picnic lunch and time for socializing. The group will return to work by 4 p.m. Since the print shop will be closed during the retreat, you consider the retreat a work day and expect all employees to attend. Employees should dress casually. They'll be outside most of the day. Write a memo to employees announcing the retreat.

*All e-mail activities may be used as memos if e-mail is unavailable.

8.13 Information Memo or E-Mail:* Sweet Rewards (Obj. 4)

E-Mail

The summer Candy Show is a "must-attend" trade show for all manufacturers of sweets, including cereals and even fruit drinks. This year's event, held in Chicago, produced a number of trends including novelty items, tie-ins with books and movies, and high-tech products. "Nobody sells just candy anymore," observed one visitor. "You need a gimmick, such as a connection with a cartoon character, a book or movie, a sports team, or something high-tech." Among the novelty items were Crispy Candies (chocolate-covered rice) by M&M/Mars. A novelty item by Amural featured Chocolate Chip Cookie Doh, a candy that looks like raw cookie dough. Concord brought out edible candy stampers, an interesting concept. Some novelties combined candy with toys. For example, Cap Toy introduced White Ranger, a spin-top candy, and Candy Popper, a battery-operated spin toy.

After novelty products, the most popular new items incorporated tie-in products. For example, a Willy Wonka candy line featured an animated character and a Web site said to have a "substantial" advertising budget. Another tie-in product was a Dilbert Desktop Dispenser for M&Ms, as well as numerous candies connected with current films. Sports licenses were also hot, such as a Team NFL gum bank. Some of the most interesting new products involved high-tech items, such as the Web site for Willy Wonka candy. Amural Confections featured a refillable "gum-puter," available in three different flavors.

As Peter Kim **<pkim@candy.com>**, assistant marketing director at a large Midwestern candy manufacturer, you have been sent to this year's Candy Show to observe what's hot. You are exhausted after visiting nearly all the exhibits in two days. But you must respond to your boss's request that you use your laptop computer to send her an e-mail message summarizing what you saw. She asked you to pick out three trends that could affect your company's product development. Describe each trend briefly and give examples. You'll provide a full report when you return to the office. Address an e-mail message to Tanya Smith **<tsmith@candy.com>**.[16]

8.14 Procedure Memo: Ticket-Free Parking (Obj. 4)

Assume that you are Tran Crozier, director of the Human Resources Division of IBM at Franklin Lakes, New York. Both day- and swing-shift employees need to be reminded of the parking guidelines. Day-shift employees must park in Lots A and B in their assigned spaces. If they have not registered their cars and received their white stickers, the cars will be ticketed.

Day-shift employees are forbidden to park at the curb. Swing-shift employees may park at the curb before 3:30 p.m. Moreover, after 3:30 p.m., swing-shift employees may park in any empty space—except those marked Tandem, Handicapped, Van Pool, Car Pool, or Management. Day-shift employees may loan their spaces to other employees if they know they will not be using the space.

One serious problem is lack of registration (as evidenced by white stickers). Registration is done by Employee Relations. Any car without a sticker will be ticketed. To encourage registration, Employee Relations will be in the cafeteria May 12 and 13 from 11:30 a.m. to 1:30 p.m. and from 3 p.m. to 5 p.m. to take applications and issue white parking stickers.

Write a memo to employees that reviews the parking guidelines and encourages them to get their cars registered. Use itemization techniques and strive for a tone that fosters a sense of cooperation rather than resentment.

8.15 Procedure Memo: Hot Calls in August (Obj. 4)

Play the part of Sally Chernoff, division sales manager of DataCom Electronics. The company's long-distance telephone bills have been skyrocketing. Sales reps use the telephone to make "hot" calls to close deals or to persuade hard-sells. However, Paul Wilson, vice president, Sales, is not sure that the cost of these calls is worth the return. He suggested sharply reducing or even eliminating *all* long-distance calls made by sales reps, but you want to collect information first. You propose a plan.

For the month of August, all sales reps are to place their long-distance calls through the company operator (rather than dialing direct). They are to keep a log of all calls, including the date, time, city, and reason for the call. In September you'd like them to give you that telephone log. Then you can analyze the data and perhaps solve this telephone budget crisis. Privately, you hope that the cumbersome procedure will, by itself, decrease the number of calls.

Write a memo to all sales reps describing this procedure. Attach a telephone log. Include reader benefits and itemization techniques.

8.16 Request Memo or E-Mail: Smokers vs. Nonsmokers (Obj. 5)

E-Mail

As Lindsay English, director of human resources, write a memo to all department managers of General Wheat, a large foods company. The city of Milwaukee has mandated

*All e-mail activities may be used as memos if e-mail is unavailable.

that employees "shall adopt, implement, and maintain a written smoking policy which shall contain a prohibition against smoking in restrooms and infirmaries." Employers must also "maintain a nonsmoking area of not less than two thirds of the seating capacity in cafeterias, lunchrooms, and employee lounges, and make efforts to work out disputes between smokers and nonsmokers." Make this announcement to your department managers. Tell the managers that you want them to set up departmental committees to mediate any smoking conflicts before the complaints surface. Explain why this is a good policy.

8.17 Reply Memo or E-Mail: Enforcing Smoking Ban (Obj. 5)

E-Mail

You are Bruni Comenic, manager of accounting services for General Wheat, responding to Ms. English's memo in the preceding activity. You could have called Ms. English, but you prefer to have a permanent record of this message. You are having difficulty enforcing the smoking ban in restrooms. Only one men's room serves your floor, and 9 of your 27 male employees are smokers. You have already received complaints, and you see no way to enforce the ban in the restrooms. You have also noticed that smokers are taking longer breaks than other employees. Smokers complain that they need more time because they must walk to an outside area. Smokers are especially unhappy when the weather is cold, rainy, or snowy. Moreover, smokers huddle near the building entrances, thus creating a negative impression for customers and visitors. Your committee members can find no solutions; in fact, they have become polarized in their meetings to date. You need help from a higher authority. Appeal to Ms. English for solutions. Perhaps she should visit your department.

8.18 Reply Memo or E-Mail: What's New at the P.O. (Obj. 5)

E-Mail Web

As Leticia Lopez, assume that you work for MagicMedia, Inc., a large software manufacturer. The office manager, Patricia Wildey, asks you to seek two kinds of information from the U.S. Postal Service. First, she wants to learn exactly how envelopes should be addressed according to USPS guidelines. Second, she wants to know how to get a passport, since she will be traveling to Europe on business in the spring. The easiest way to obtain both sets of information is by visiting the USPS Web site **<http://www.usps.gov/postofc>**. If that is impossible, go to a local office. Write a one-page memo summarizing your findings.

8.19 Reply Memo: Chocolates on the Web (Obj. 5)

E-Mail Web

Again act as Peter Kim, assistant marketing director at a large Midwestern candy manufacturer. Your boss asks you to check out a competitor's World Wide Web site **<http://www.godiva.com>**. Godiva chocolates, according to your boss, has a much-acclaimed Web site. You are to access the site, examine what it offers, and report your findings. Godiva is an upscale chocolatier offering its delights in the best department stores, as well as through its own stores and catalog. Your boss wonders if a Web site might be a good investment for your company. In an e-mail message, report to your boss (your instructor, in this instance) how Godiva uses the site and what it features.

8.20 Reply Memo: Rescheduling Interviews (Obj. 5)

Your boss, Fred Knox, had scheduled three appointments to interview applicants for an accounting position. All of these appointments were for Friday, October 7. However, he now must travel to Philadelphia on that weekend. He asks you to reschedule all the appointments for one week later. He also wants a brief summary of the background of each candidate.

You call each person and arrange these times. Paul Scheffel, who has been an accountant for 15 years with Bechtel Corporation, agreed to come at 10:30 a.m. Mark Cunningham, who is a CPA and a consultant to many companies, will come at 11:30. Geraldine Simpson, who has a B.A. degree and 8 years of experience in payroll accounting, will come at 9:30 a.m. You're wondering if Mr. Knox forgot to include Don Stastry, operations personnel officer, in these interviews. Mr. Stastry usually is part of the selection process. Write a memo to Mr. Knox including all the vital information he needs.

8.21 Request Memo or E-Mail: Dress-Down Day for Us? (Obj. 5)

According to a poll funded by Levi Strauss & Co, more than half of all white-collar workers now can dress casually at work. The dress-down trend reflects larger changes in work patterns. Top-down management is less prevalent, and more people work at home or have flexible hours. Even John Molloy, the guru of the 1980s "dress for success" movement, now works with "befuddled executives" teaching them what to wear in a casual world.

Play the role of Thomas Marshall, CEO of Marshall & Associates, a sedate accountancy firm. You have had some inquiries from your accountants and other employees about the possibility of dressing casually—not all the time, but occasionally. You decide to ask a few key people what they think about establishing a casual-dress day. It sounds like a good idea, especially if it makes people feel more at ease in the office. But you worry that it might look unprofessional and encourage sloppy work and horsing around. Moreover, you are concerned about what people might wear, such as shorts, tank tops, T-shirts with slogans, baseball caps, and dirty athletic clothes. Would a dress-down policy make the office atmosphere less professional? Perhaps a written dress code will be necessary if a casual-dress policy is allowed.

To solicit feedback, you write the same memo to two partners and your office manager. Ask for their opinions, but do so with specific questions. Be sure to include an end date so that you can decide on a course of action before the next management council meeting. Address the same memo or e-mail to Mary E. Leslie **<mel@marsh.com>**, Sam W. Miller **<sam@marsh.com>**, and Jonathon Galston **<jon@marsh.com>**.[17]

8.22 Reply E-Mail: Dress-Down Discussion and Decision (Obj. 5)

Team | Critical Thinking | E-mail

Casual dress in professional offices seems to be increasingly common. Get together in groups to discuss a suitable response to the request made in Activity 8.21. Should the accountancy firm allow employees one dress-down day a week? Why or why not? If you decide to recommend a dress-down day, consider whether a dress code is appropriate. Give reasons. Then decide whether a dress-down day would affect the professional environment of the office. You can tell from the CEO's words that he favors a limited dress-down program. But your team should make up its own mind. Once you reach consensus, respond to the boss either in individual memos or a team-written memo. Be sure to answer the questions and issues raised in Activity 8.21. Your reply memo should go to CEO Thomas Marshall **<tmarshall@marsh.com>**.

8.23 Reply Memo: Someone's Going to Get Dumped On (Obj. 5)

Team | Web

The IS (Information Systems) network manager at Lionel Trains in Chesterfield, Michigan, worried that his company would have to upgrade its Internet connection because operations were noticeably slower than in the past. Upon checking, however, he discovered that extensive recreational Web surfing among employees was the real reason for the slowdown. Since the company needed a good policy on using e-mail and the Internet, he assigned your team the task of investigating existing policies. Your team leader, Thad Tucker, who has quite a sense of humor, said, "Adopting an Internet policy is a lot like hosting a convention of pigeons. Both will result in a lot of squawking, ruffled feathers, and someone getting dumped on." Right! No one is going to like having e-mail and Internet use restricted. It is, indeed, a dirty job, but someone has to do it.

Your team's task is to check Web sites, individually, to locate examples or models of company e-mail and Internet policies. For best results use several search engines and try variations of the search term "Company E-Mail Policy." Print out any helpful material. Then meet as a group and select six to eight major topics that you think should be covered in a company policy. Your investigation will act as a starting point in the long process of developing a policy that provides safeguards but is not overly restrictive. You are not expected to write the policy at this time. But you could attach copies of anything interesting. Your boss would especially like to know where he could see or purchase model company policies. Send a reply memo or an e-mail message to Rick Rodriquez, your team leader.[18]

8.24 Confirmation Memo or E-mail: Looking Over the Employee's Shoulder (Obj. 6)

E-Mail

At lunch one day you had a stimulating discussion with Barbara Wilson, your company attorney, about e-mail privacy. You brought up the topic because you will be attending a conference shortly on Internet uses and abuses, and you will be serving on a panel discussing e-mail privacy. As you recall, Ms. Wilson emphasized the fact that the employer owns the workplace. She said, "It owns the desks, machines, stationery, computers, and everything else. Employees have no legal right to use the employer's property for personal business."

Equally important, however, is the recognition of a right to privacy, even in the workplace. "If an employee can demonstrate that the employer violated his or her reasonable *expectation* of privacy," said Ms. Wilson, "then he or she can hold the employer liable for that violation." You also remember a rather startling comment. Ms. Wilson said that an employer may listen to or read only as much of a communication as is necessary for the employer to determine whether it is personal or business. You wonder if you remembered this conversation accurately. Since one of the topics your panel will discuss is whether employers may monitor e-mail, you decide to write to Ms. Wilson to confirm what she said.[19]

8.25 Confirmation Memo: Dream Vacation (Obj. 6)

Play the role of Jack Mendoza. You had a vacation planned for September 2 through 16. But yesterday your wife suggested delaying the vacation for several weeks so that you could travel through New England when the fall colors are most beautiful. She said it would be the vacation of her dreams, and you agree. Perhaps you could change your vacation dates. Alas, you remember that you're scheduled to attend the Hampshire marketing exhibit September 29–30. But maybe Melanie Grasso would fill in for you and make the presentation of the company's newest product, JuiceMate. You see your boss, Mas Watanabe, in the hall and decide to ask if you can change your vacation to September 28 through October 12. To your surprise, he agrees to the new dates. He also assures you that he will ask Melanie to make the presentation and encourage her to give a special demonstration to the Dana Corporation, which you believe should be targeted.

Back in your office, you begin to worry. What if Mas forgets about your conversation? You can't afford to take that chance. Write a confirmation memo that summarizes the necessary facts and also conveys your gratitude.

C.L.U.E. REVIEW 8

Edit the following sentences to correct all language faults, including grammar, punctuation, spelling, and word use.

1. Mr. Krikorian always tries however to wear a tie and shirt that has complimentary colors.
2. The federal trade commission are holding hearings to illicit information about IBMs request to expand marketing in twenty-one city's.
3. Consumer buying and spending for the past 5 years, is being studied by a Federal team of analysts.
4. Because we recommend that students bring there own supplies; the total expense for the trip should be a miner amount.
5. Wasnt it Mr Cohen not Ms Lyons who asked for a tuition waver.
6. As soon as we can verify the figures either my sales manager or myself will call you, nevertheless, you must continue to disperse payroll funds.
7. Our human resources department which was formerally in room 35 has moved it's offices to room 5.
8. We have arranged interviews on the following dates, Wednesday at 330 pm Thursday at 1030 am and Friday at 415 pm.
9. The Post Dispatch our local newspaper featured as its principle article a story entitled, Smarter E-Mail is here.
10. Every one on the payroll, which includes all dispatchers and supervisers were cautioned to maintain careful records everyday.

CHAPTER • 9 •

Persuasive and Sales Messages

LEARNING OBJECTIVES

1. Apply the 3-×-3 writing process to persuasive messages.
2. Explain the components of a persuasive message.
3. Request favors and action effectively.
4. Write convincing persuasive messages within organizations.
5. Request adjustments and make claims successfully.
6. Compose successful sales messages.
7. Describe the basic elements included in effective news releases.

COMMUNICATION IN PROCESS

CASE STUDY

Amazon.com Learns How to Persuade Its Web Customers

Amazon.com is undoubtedly the hottest success story in the short history of the Web. Billing itself as "Earth's Biggest Bookstore," Amazon enjoyed sales that grew an astounding 838 percent in one year. Founder Jeff Bezos chose Amazon's name for its image of colossal size as well as for its alphabetical advantage.

On opening day the Earth's Biggest Bookstore touted over one million copies for sale, yet its shelves held a scant 2,000 volumes. Filling orders meant acquiring books quickly from two large distributors. This method saved Bezos the cost of maintaining a huge inventory. Now, however, Amazon's inventory has swollen to nearly 1½ million books, and its books fill two huge warehouses in Seattle. Controlling its own inventory means that Amazon can extract buying discounts from publishers, and it can also save time by shipping books directly to customers.

Although Amazon's books are flying off the shelves and Bezos has built a blockbuster brand identity almost overnight, Amazon has not yet seen any profits. But that has not stopped it from expanding into CDs and videos. These items, along with books, are perfect for cybershopping. They are information-rich commodities, and they are easy to order on-line and can be shipped straight from a distributor to a customer.

Service and convenience to customers are the keys to Amazon's amazing success. Bezos recognized early on the potential of the Web, but he also knew its major drawback. Booting up a computer and hacking through a maze of computer screens requires much more effort than picking up a telephone to order. He had to learn what his customers wanted, and he had to find ways to persuade them that his Web site was the easiest, fastest, safest, and most economical way to buy books—and CDs and videos and gifts.[1]

www.amazon.com

Strategies for Making Persuasive Requests

Successful persuasion results from a reasonable request and a well-presented argument.

The ability to persuade is one of life's important skills. Persuading means using argument or discussion to change an individual's beliefs or actions. Persuasion, of course, is a very important part of any business that sells goods or services. And selling on-line, such as Jeff Bezos must do with Amazon.com, is even more challenging than other forms of persuasion because of the technology barrier that must be overcome. However, many of the techniques that Bezos uses at Amazon.com are similar to those you will use in persuasion at home, at school, and on the job.

Doubtless you've had to be persuasive to convert others to your views or to motivate them to do what you want. The outcome of such efforts depends largely on the reasonableness of your request, your credibility, and the ability to make your request attractive to the receiver. In this chapter you will learn many techniques and strategies to help you be successful in any persuasive effort.

When you think that your listener or reader is inclined to agree with your request, you can start directly with the main idea. But when the receiver is likely to resist, don't reveal the purpose too quickly. Ideas that require persuasion benefit from a slow approach that includes ample preparation.

Let's say you want to replace your outdated office PC with a new, powerful computer that is fast as lightning and enables you to link to the Web more easily. In a memo to your boss, Laura, who is likely to resist this request because of budget constraints, you wisely decide not to open with a direct request. Instead, you gain her attention and move to logical reasons supporting your request. This indirect pattern is effective when you must persuade people to grant you favors, accept your recommendations, make adjustments in your favor, or grant your claims.

Effective sales messages reflect thorough product knowledge, writer credibility, and specific reader benefits.

The same is true for sales messages. Instead of making a sales pitch immediately, smart communicators prepare a foundation by developing credibility and hooking their requests to benefits for the receiver. In persuasive messages other than sales, you must know precisely what you want the receiver to think or do. You must also anticipate what appeals to make or "buttons to push" to motivate action. Achieving these goals in both written and oral messages requires special attention to the initial steps in the process.

Applying the 3-×-3 Writing Process to Persuasive Messages

1

Persuasion means changing people's views, and that's a difficult task. Pulling it off demands planning and perception. The 3-×-3 writing process provides you with a helpful structure for laying a foundation for persuasion. Of particular importance here are (1) analyzing the purpose, (2) adapting to the audience, (3) collecting information, and (4) organizing the message.

Persuasive messages require careful analysis of the purpose for writing.

Analyzing the Purpose. The purpose of a persuasive message is to convert the receiver to your ideas or to motivate action. A message without a clear purpose is doomed. Not only must you know what your purpose is and what response you want, but you must know these things when you start writing a letter or planning a presentation. Too often, ineffective communicators reach the end of a message before discovering exactly what they want the receiver to do. Then they must start over, giving the request a different "spin" or emphasis. Because your purpose establishes the strategy of the message, determine it first.

Let's return to your memo requesting a new computer. What exactly do you want your boss to do? Which of these actions do you expect Laura to take? (1) Meet with you so that you can show her how much computer time is lost with slow software and poor Internet connections? (2) Purchase a Brand X computer for you now? (3) Include your computer request in the department's five-year equipment forecast? By identifying your purpose up front, you can shape the message to point toward it. This planning effort saves considerable rewriting time and produces the most successful persuasive messages.

Effective persuasive messages focus on audience needs or goals.

Adapting to the Audience. While you're considering the purpose of a persuasive message, you also need to concentrate on the receiver. How can you adapt your request to that individual so that your message is heard? Zorba the Greek wisely observed, "You can knock forever on a deaf man's door." A persuasive message is equally futile unless it meets the needs of its audience. In a broad sense, you'll be seeking to show how your request helps the receiver achieve some of life's major goals or fulfills key needs: money, power, comfort, confidence, importance, friends, peace of mind, and recognition, to name a few.

On a more practical level, you want to show how your request solves a problem, achieves a personal or work objective, or just makes life easier for your audience. In your request for a new computer, for example, you could appeal to your boss's expressed concern for increasing productivity. If you were asking for a four-day work schedule, you could cite the need for improved efficiency and better employee morale.

CAREER COACH

SEVEN RULES EVERY PERSUADER SHOULD KNOW

Successful businesspeople create persuasive memos, letters, reports, and presentations that get the results they want. Yet, their approaches are all different. Some persuaders are gentle, leading readers by the hand to the targeted recommendation. Others are brisk and authoritative. Some are objective, examining both sides of an issue like a judge deciding a difficult case. Some move slowly and carefully toward a proposal, while others erupt like a volcano in their eagerness to announce a recommendation.

Because of the immense number of variables involved, no single all-purpose strategy works for every persuasive situation. You wouldn't, for example, use the same techniques in asking for a raise from a stern supervisor as you would use in persuading a close friend to see a movie of your choice. Different situations and different goals require different techniques. The following seven rules suggest various strategies—depending on your individual need.

- **Consider whether your views will create problems for your audience.** A student engineer submitted a report recommending a simple change at a waste-treatment facility. His recommendation would save $200,000 a year, but the report met with a cool reception. Why? His supervisors would have to explain to management why they had allowed a waste of $200,000 a year! If your views make trouble for the audience, think of ways to include the receivers in your recommendation if possible. Whatever your strategy, be tactful and empathic.
- **Don't offer new ideas, directives, or recommendations for change until your audience is prepared for them.** Receivers are threatened by anything that upsets their values or interests. The greater the change you suggest, the more slowly you should proceed. For example, if your boss is enthusiastic about a new marketing scheme (that would cost $50,000 to develop), naturally you will go slowly in shooting it down. If, on the other hand, your boss has little personal investment in the scheme, you could be more direct in your attack.
- **Select a strategy that supports your credibility.** If you have great credibility with your audience, you can proceed directly. If not, you might want to establish that credibility first. *Given* credibility results from position or reputation, such as that of the boss of an organization or a highly regarded scientist. *Acquired* credibility is earned. To acquire credibility, successful persuaders often identify themselves, early in the message, with the goals and interests of the audience (*As a small business owner myself . . .*). Another way to acquire credibility is to mention evidence or ideas that support the audience's existing views (*We agree that small business owners need more government assistance*). Finally, you can acquire credibility by citing authorities who rate highly with your audience (*Richard Love, recently named Small Businessperson of the Year, supports this proposal*).
- **If your audience disagrees with your ideas or is uncertain about them, present both sides of the argument.** You might think that you would be most successful by revealing only one side of an issue—your side, of course. But persuasion doesn't work that way. You'll be more successful—particularly if the audience is unfriendly or uncertain—by disclosing *all* sides of an argument. This approach suggests that you are objective. It also helps the receiver remember your view by showing the pros and cons in relation to one another. Thus, if you want to convince the owners of a realty firm that an expensive new lockbox system is a wise investment, be truthful about any shortcomings, weaknesses, and limitations.
- **Win respect by making your opinion or recommendation clear.** Although you should be truthful in presenting both sides of an argument, don't be shy in supporting your conclusions or final proposals. You will, naturally, have definite views and should persuade your audience to accept them. The two-sided strategy is a means to an end, but it does not mean compromising your argument. One executive criticized reports from his managers because they presented much data and concluded, in effect, with "Here is what I found out and maybe we should do this or maybe we should do that." Be decisive and make specific recommendations.
- **Place your strongest points strategically.** Some experts argue that if your audience is deeply concerned with your subject, you can afford to begin with your weakest points. Because of its commitment, the audience will stay with you until you reach the strongest points at the end

(continued)

For an unmotivated audience, begin with your strongest points to get them interested. Other experts feel that a supportive audience should receive the main ideas or recommendations immediately, to avoid wasting time. Whichever position you choose, don't bury your recommendation, strongest facts, or main idea in the middle of your argument.

- **Don't count on changing attitudes by offering information alone.** "If customers knew the truth about our costs, they would not object to our prices," some companies reason. Well, don't bet on it. Companies have pumped huge sums into advertising and public relations campaigns that provided facts alone. Such efforts often fail because learning something new (that is, increasing the knowledge of the audience) is rarely an effective way to change attitudes. Researchers have found that presentations of facts alone may strengthen opinions—but primarily for people who already agree with the persuader. The added information reassures them and provides ammunition for defending themselves in discussions with others.

Career Application

Consider a career-oriented problem in a current or past job: customer service must be improved, workers need better training, inventory procedures are inefficient, equipment is outdated, worker scheduling is arbitrary, and so forth. Devise a plan to solve the problem. How could the preceding rules help you persuade a decision maker to adopt your plan? In a memo to your instructor or in class discussion, outline the problem and your plan for solving it. Describe your persuasive strategy.

To adapt your request to the receiver, consider these questions that receivers will very likely be asking themselves:[2]

Why should I?	Who cares?
What's in it for me?	Says who?
So what?	What's in it for you?

Adapting to your audience means being ready to answer these questions. It means learning about audience members and analyzing why they might resist your proposal. It means searching for ways to connect your purpose with their needs. If completed before you begin writing, such analysis goes a long way toward overcoming resistance and achieving your goal. The accompanying Career Coach box presents additional strategies that can make you a successful persuader.

The key components of a persuasive request are gaining attention, showing the worth of the proposal, overcoming resistance, and motivating action.

Researching and Organizing Data. Once you've analyzed the audience and considered how to adapt your message to its needs, you're ready to collect data and organize it. You might brainstorm and prepare cluster diagrams to provide a rough outline of ideas. For your computer request, if your strategy was to show that a new computer would increase your productivity, you would gather data to show how much time and effort could be saved with the new machine. To overcome resistance to cost, you would need information about prices. To ensure getting exactly what you want, you would study many computer configurations.

The next step is organizing your data. Suppose you have already decided that your request will meet with resistance. Thus, you decide not to open directly with your request. Instead, you use the four-part indirect pattern, listed below and shown graphically in Figure 9.1:

- Gain attention
- Build interest
- Reduce resistance
- Motivate action

FIGURE 9.1 **Four-Part Indirect Pattern for Persuasion**

Gaining Attention	Building Interest	Reducing Resistance	Motivating Action
Free offer	Rational appeals	Testimonials	Gift
Promise	Emotional appeals	Satisfied users	Incentive
Question	Dual appeals	Guarantee	Limited offer
Quotation	Product description	Warranty	Deadline
Proverb	Reader benefits	Free trial	Guarantee
Product feature	Cold facts mixed with warm feelings	Sample	Repetition of selling feature
Testimonial		Performance tests	
Startling statement		Polls, awards	
Action setting			

The indirect pattern discussed and illustrated here suggests a specific plan for making persuasive requests.

Blending the Components of a Persuasive Message

Although the indirect pattern appears to contain separate steps, successful persuasive messages actually blend these steps into a seamless whole. However, the sequence of the components may change depending on the situation and the emphasis. Regardless of where they are placed, the key elements in persuasive requests are (1) gaining the audience's attention, (2) convincing them that your proposal is worthy, (3) overcoming resistance, and (4) motivating action.

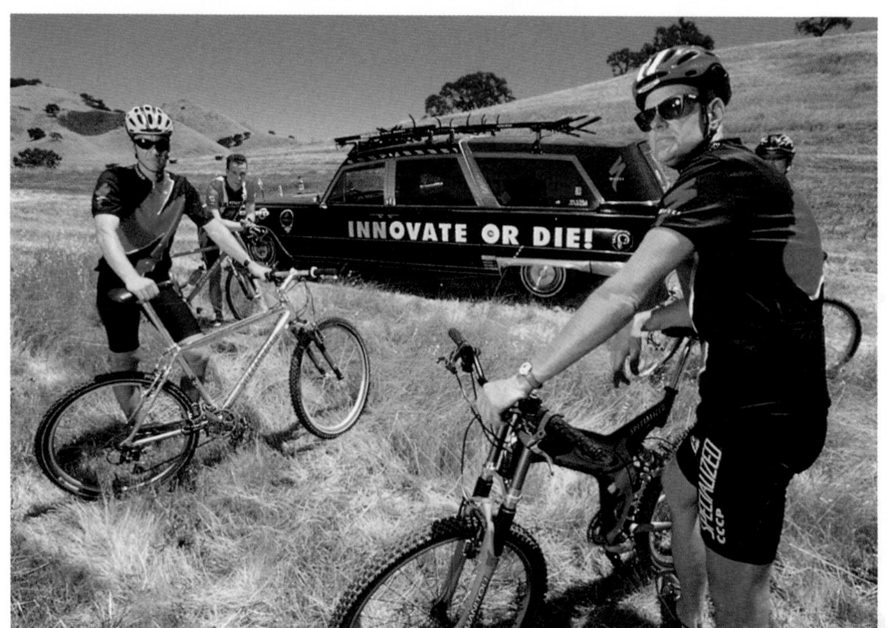

"Innovate or Die," the attention-grabbing motto of Specialized Bicycle Components, reminds founder Mike Sinyard and his management team that innovation is critical. Even with superior products, he realized that his company couldn't remain a leader without constantly developing new ideas and improvements. Emblazoning his motto on a hearse gains attention, the first step in creating a persuasive message.

Successful openers to persuasive requests are brief, targeted, and interesting.

Gaining Attention. To grab attention, the opening statement in a persuasive request should be brief, relevant, and engaging. When only mild persuasion is necessary, the opener can be low-key and factual. If, however, your request is substantial and you anticipate strong resistance, provide a thoughtful, provocative opening. The following examples suggest possibilities.

- **Problem description.** In a recommendation to hire temporary employees: *Last month legal division staff members were forced to work 120 overtime hours, costing us $6,000 and causing considerable employee unhappiness.* With this opener you've presented a capsule of the problem your proposal will help solve.
- **Unexpected statement.** In a memo to encourage employees to attend an optional sensitivity seminar: *Men and women draw the line at decidedly different places in identifying what behavior constitutes sexual harassment.* Note how this opener gets readers thinking immediately.
- **Reader benefit.** In a proposal offering writing workshops to an organization: *For every letter or memo your employees can avoid writing, your organization saves $78.50.* Companies are always looking for ways to cut costs, and this opener promises significant savings.
- **Compliment.** In a letter inviting a business executive to speak: *Because our members admire your success and value your managerial expertise, they want you to be our speaker.* In offering praise or compliments, however, be careful to avoid obvious flattery.
- **Related fact.** In a memo encouraging employees to start car pooling: *A car pool is defined as two or more persons who travel to work in one car at least once a week.* An interesting, relevant, and perhaps unknown fact sets the scene for the interest-building section that follows.
- **Stimulating question.** In a plea for funds to support environmental causes: *What do Jay Leno, the Sequoia redwood tree, and the spotted owl have in common?* Readers will be curious to find the answer to this intriguing question.

The body of a persuasive request may require several paragraphs to build interest and reduce resistance.

Building Interest. After capturing attention, a persuasive request must retain that attention and convince the audience that the request is reasonable. To justify your request, be prepared to invest in a few paragraphs of explanation. Persuasive requests are likely to be longer than direct requests because the audience must be convinced rather than simply instructed. You can build interest and conviction through the use of the following:

- Facts, statistics
- Expert opinion
- Direct benefits
- Examples
- Specific details
- Indirect benefits

Showing how your request can benefit the audience directly or indirectly is a key factor in persuasion. If you were asking alumni to contribute money to a college foundation, for example, you might promote *direct benefits* such as listing the donor's name in the college magazine or sending a sweatshirt with the college logo. Another direct benefit is a tax write-off for the contribution. An *indirect benefit* comes from feeling good about helping the college and knowing that students will benefit from the gift. Nearly all charities rely in large part on indirect benefits—the selflessness of givers—to promote their causes.

Reducing Resistance. One of the biggest mistakes in persuasive requests is the failure to anticipate and offset audience resistance. How will the receiver object to your request? In brainstorming for clues, try *What if?* scenarios. Let's say you are trying to convince management that the employees' cafeteria should switch from paper and plastic plates and cups to ceramic. What if they say the change is too expensive? What if they argue that they are careful recyclers of paper and plastic? What if they contend that ceramic dishes would increase cafeteria labor and energy costs tremendously? What if they protest that ceramic is less hygienic? For each of these *What if?* scenarios, you need a counterargument.

Unless you anticipate resistance, you give the receiver an easy opportunity to dismiss your request. Countering this resistance is important, but you must do it with finesse (*Although ceramic dishes cost more at first, they actually save money over time*). You can minimize objections by presenting your counterarguments in sentences that emphasize benefits: *Ceramic dishes may require a little more effort in cleaning, but they bring warmth and graciousness to meals. Most important, they help save the environment by requiring fewer resources and eliminating waste.* However, don't spend too much time on counterarguments, thus making them overly important. Finally, avoid bringing up objections that may never have occurred to the receiver in the first place.

Another factor that reduces resistance is credibility. Receivers are less resistant if your request is reasonable and if you are believable. When the receiver does not know you, you may have to establish your expertise, refer to your credentials, or demonstrate your competence. Even when you are known, you may have to establish your knowledge in a given area. In making your request for a new computer, you might have to establish your credibility by showing your boss articles you have read about the latest computers and how much more efficient you could be with better Internet connections. Some charities establish their credibility by displaying on their stationery the names of famous people who serve on their boards. The credibility of speakers making presentations is usually outlined by someone who introduces them.

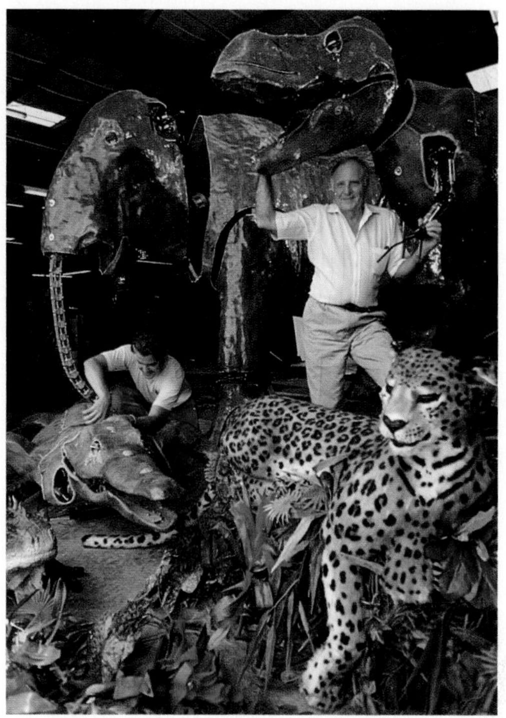

Gerald King gambled on purchasing a debt-ridden manufacturer of mechanical rides for theme parks. But he had to overcome the resistance of four partners in redirecting the company's core business from making rides to fabricating lifelike animatronic figures. He was persuasive in motivating action because he saw an opportunity to sell his lifelike figures in theme parks, water parks, other recreation facilities, and even shopping malls.

Persuasive requests reduce resistance by addressing *What if?* questions and establishing credibility.

Motivating Action. After gaining attention, building interest, and reducing resistance, you'll want to inspire the receiver to act. This is where your planning pays dividends. Knowing exactly what action you favor before you start to write enables you to point your arguments toward this important final paragraph. Here you will make your recommendation as specifically and confidently as possible—without seeming pushy. A proposal from one manager to another might conclude with, *So that we can begin using the employment assessment tests by May 1, please send a return e-mail immediately.* In making a request, don't sound apologetic (*I'm sorry to have to ask you this, but . . .*), and don't supply excuses (*If you can spare the time, . . .*). Compare the following closings for a persuasive memo recommending training seminars in communication skills.

Persuasive requests motivate action by specifying exactly what should be done.

Too General
We are certain we can develop a series of training sessions that will improve the communication skills of your employees.

Too Timid
If you agree that our training proposal has merit, perhaps we could begin the series in June.

FIGURE 9.2 **Components of a Persuasive Message**

Gaining Attention	Building Interest	Reducing Resistance	Motivating Action
Summary of problem	Facts, figures	Anticipate objections	Describe specific request
Unexpected statement	Expert opinion	Offer counterarguments	Sound confident
Reader benefit	Examples	Play *What if?* scenarios	Make action easy to take
Compliment	Specific details	Establish credibility	Offer incentive
Related fact	Direct benefits	Demonstrate competence	Don't provide excuses
Stimulating question	Indirect benefits	Show value of proposal	Repeat main benefit

Too Pushy
Because we're convinced that you will want to begin improving the skills of your employees immediately, we've scheduled your series to begin in June.

Effective
You will see decided improvement in the communication skills of your employees. Please call me at 439-2201 by May 1 to give your approval so that training sessions may start in June, as we discussed.

Note how the last opening suggests a specific and easy-to-follow action. Figure 9.2 summarizes techniques for overcoming resistance and crafting successful persuasive messages.

Being Persuasive but Ethical

Ethical business communicators maintain credibility and respect by being honest, fair, and objective.

Business communicators may be tempted to make their persuasion even more forceful by fudging on the facts, exaggerating a point, omitting something crucial, or providing deceptive emphasis. Consider the case of a manager who sought to persuade employees to accept a change in insurance benefits. His memo emphasized a small perk (easier handling of claims) but deemphasized a major reduction in total coverage. Some readers missed the main point—as the manager intended. Others recognized the deception, however, and before long the manager's credibility was lost. A persuader is effective only when he or she is believable. If receivers suspect that they are being manipulated or misled, or if they find any part of the argument untruthful, the total argument fails. Persuaders can also fall into traps of logic without even being aware of it. Take a look at the accompanying Ethical Insights box to learn about common logical fallacies that you will want to avoid.

Persuasion becomes unethical when facts are distorted, overlooked, or manipulated with an intent to deceive. Of course, persuaders naturally want to put forth their strongest case. But that argument must be based on truth, objectivity, and fairness.

In prompting ethical and truthful persuasion, two factors act as powerful motivators. The first is the desire to preserve your reputation and credibility. Once lost, a good name is difficult to regain. An equally important force prompting ethical behavior, though, is your opinion of yourself. One stockbroker admits that she's in the

ETHICAL INSIGHTS

WHAT'S FAIR IN PERSUASION? AVOIDING COMMON LOGICAL FALLACIES

While being persuasive, we must be careful to remain ethical. In our eagerness to win others over to our views, we may inadvertently overstep the bounds of fair play. Philosophers through the years have pinpointed a number of logical fallacies. Here are three you'll want to avoid in your persuasive messages. For an on-line discussion of many logical fallacies, try **<www.assiniboinec.mb.ca/user/downes/fallacy/falla.htm>** or use a Web search engine to find "Stephen's Guide to the Logical Fallacies."

- **Circular reasoning.** When the support given for a contention merely restates the contention, the reasoning is circular. For example, *Investing in the stock market is dangerous for short-term investors because it is unsafe.* The evidence (*because it is unsafe*) offers no proof. It merely circles back to the original contention. Revision: *Investing in the stock market is dangerous for short-term investors because stock prices fluctuate widely.*
- **Begging the question.** A statement such as *That dishonest CEO should be replaced* begs the question. Merely asserting that the CEO is dishonest is not enough. Be sure to supply solid evidence for such assertions. Revision: *That CEO is dishonest because he awards contracts only to his friends. A good manager would require open bidding.*
- **Post hoc (after, thus, because).** Although two events may have happened in immediate sequence, the first did not necessarily cause the second. For example, *The company switched to team-based management, and its stock price rose immediately afterward.* Switching to teams probably had no effect on the rise in stock price. Revision: *At about the same time the company switched to team-based management, its stock price began to rise, although the two events are probably unrelated.*

Career Application

In teams or in class discussion, cite examples of how these fallacies could be used in persuasive messages or sales letters. Provide a logical, ethical revision for each.

business to make money, but she still has to be able to look herself in the mirror each morning. "We've gone through the '80s, when it was tough for morality. Now we're in the process of doing a complete turnaround; people are saying that honesty is what's really important. If you're unethical, you may make all the money in the world. But you won't retain family, friends, or lasting business relationships."[3]

Writing Successful Persuasive Requests

3

Convincing someone to change a belief or to perform an action when that individual is reluctant requires planning and skill—and sometimes a little luck. When the request is in writing, rather than face to face, the task is even more difficult. The indirect pattern, though, can help you shape effective persuasive appeals that (1) request favors and action, (2) persuade within organizations, and (3) request adjustments and make claims.

Requesting Favors and Actions

Persuading someone to do something that largely benefits you is not easy. Fortunately, many individuals and companies are willing to grant requests for time,

CASE STUDY

PROCESS IN PROGRESS

Amazon.com Revisited

Jeff Bezos, founder and CEO of Amazon.com, knew that persuading customers to buy on-line was going to be difficult. They had to have computers, they had to be willing to use a new technology, and they had to overcome fears about security and loss of privacy. But he also knew that people are time-starved, thrifty, and eager for convenience. As Amazon grew, Bezos learned that its customers have higher-than-average incomes and education, and they tend to be male—but this is changing, says Bezos. They also tend to be busy, which makes the convenience factor important. And their access to the Web is often at work. Shopping on-line is not done at home, where their lives are already overloaded with responsibilities.

In anticipating the fears of his audience, Bezos developed a secure method for giving credit information. Through focus groups, he devised techniques to allow customers to fill their on-line shopping carts with a minimum of hassle. He overcame people's reluctance to use technology by capitalizing on its possibilities, such as offering an inventory of 2 million books. Repeat customers are immediately greeted by name, and they receive recommendations based on their previous purchases. He also anticipated the needs of his customers by providing huge amounts of "content," such as reviews of books and experts' music lists. This information facilitates quick, easy, and appropriate purchase decisions.

Critical Thinking

- How does knowledge of Amazon's customers help shape its persuasive efforts?
- Why is it difficult to change attitudes (such as the fear of giving your credit card number to an on-line company) by offering information only?
- How is the four-part plan for persuasion effective for sales messages such as Amazon might send to its customers?

money, information, special privileges, and cooperation. They grant these favors for a variety of reasons. They may just happen to be interested in your project, or they may see goodwill potential for themselves. Often, though, they comply because they see that others will benefit from the request. Professionals sometimes feel obligated to contribute their time or expertise to "pay their dues."

Shaping direct and indirect appeals is an important part of the persuasive process.

You may find that you have few direct benefits to offer in your persuasion. Instead, you'll be focusing on indirect benefits, as the writer does in Figure 9.3. In asking a manager to speak before a marketing meeting, the writer has little to offer as a direct benefit other than a $300 honorarium. But indirectly, the writer offers enticements such as an enthusiastic audience and a chance to help other companies solve overseas marketing problems. This persuasive request appeals primarily to the reader's desire to serve his profession—although a receptive audience and an opportunity to talk about one's successes have a certain ego appeal as well. Together, these appeals—professional, egoistic, monetary—make a persuasive argument rich and effective.

As another example, consider the persuasive message on page 260, which asks a company to participate in a survey requesting salary data. This is usually a touchy subject. Few organizations are willing to reveal how much they pay their employees. Yet, this request may succeed because of the explanation provided and the benefit offered (free salary survey data).

Persuasive Favor Request

1 PREWRITING

Analyze: The purpose of this letter is to persuade the reader to speak at a dinner meeting.

Anticipate: Although the reader is busy, he may respond to appeals to his ego (describing his successes before an appreciative audience) and to his professionalism.

Adapt: Because the reader will be uninterested at first and require persuasion, use the indirect pattern.

2 WRITING

Research: Study the receiver's interests and find ways to relate this request to his interests.

Organize: Gain attention by opening with praise or a stimulating remark. Build interest with explanations and facts. Show how compliance benefits the reader and others. Reduce resistance by providing ideas for the dinner talk.

Compose: Prepare first draft on a computer.

3 REVISING

Revise: Revise to show direct and indirect benefits more clearly.

Proofread: Use quotes around "R" to reflect the company usage. In the fourth paragraph, use a semicolon in the compound sentence. Start all lines at the left for block-style letter.

Evaluate: Will this letter convince the reader to accept the invitation?

Dallas–Fort Worth Chapter
American Marketing Association
P.O. Box 3598
Dallas, TX 74209

January 28, 2000

Mr. Bryant Hoffman
Marketing Manager, Western Division
Toys "R" Us, Inc.
Dallas, TX 75232

Dear Mr. Hoffman:

One company is legendary for marketing American products successfully in Japan. *(Piques reader's curiosity; Gains attention)*

That company, of course, is Toys "R" Us. The triumph of your thriving toy store in Amimachi, Japan, has given other American marketers hope. But this success story has also raised numerous questions. Specifically, how did Toys "R" Us circumvent local trade restrictions? How did you solve the complex distribution system? And how did you negotiate with all the levels of Japanese bureaucracy? *(Builds interest)*

The members of the Dallas–Fort Worth chapter of the American Marketing Association asked me to invite you to speak at our March 19 dinner meeting on the topic of "How Toys 'R' Us Unlocked the Door to Japanese Trade." By describing your winning effort, Mr. Hoffman, you can help launch other American companies who face the same quagmire of Japanese restrictions and red tape that your organization overcame. Although we can offer you only a small honorarium of $300, we can assure you of a big audience of enthusiastic marketing professionals eager to hear your war story. *(Notes indirect benefit; Notes direct benefit)*

Our relaxed group doesn't expect a formal address; they are most interested in what steps Toys "R" Us took to open its Japanese toy outlet. To make your talk easy to organize, I've enclosed a list of questions our members submitted. Most talks are about 45 minutes long. *(Offsets reluctance by making the talk informal and easy to organize; Reduces resistance)*

Can we count on you to join us for dinner at 7 p.m. March 19 at the Cattleman's Inn in Grand Prairie? Just call me at (214) 860-4320 by February 15 to make arrangements. *(Motivates action; Makes acceptance as simple as a telephone call)*

Sincerely,

Joyce Barnes

Joyce Barnes
Program Chair, AMA

JCB:grw
Enclosure

Dear Ms. Masi:

Gains attention with two short questions that suggest problems the reader knows.

Has your company ever lost a valued employee to another organization that offered 20 percent more in salary for the same position? Have you ever added a unique job title but had no idea what compensation the position demanded?

Discusses a benefit that leads directly to the frank request for help. Notice that the request is coupled with a reader's benefit.

To remain competitive in hiring and to retain qualified workers, companies rely on survey data showing current salaries. My organization collects such data, and we need your help. Would you be willing to complete the enclosed questionnaire so that we can supply companies like yours with accurate salary data?

Anticipates and counters resistance to confidentiality and time/effort objections.

Your information, of course, will be treated confidentially. The questionnaire takes but a few moments to complete, and it can provide substantial dividends for professional organizations that need comparative salary data.

Offers free salary data as a direct benefit. Describes the benefit in detail to strengthen its appeal.

To show our gratitude for your participation, we'll send you comprehensive salary surveys for your industry and your metropolitan area. Not only will you find basic salaries, you'll also learn about bonus and incentive plans, special pay differentials, expense reimbursements, perquisites such as a company car and credit card, and special payments such as beeper pay.

Appeals to professionalism. Motivates action with a deadline and a final benefit that relates to the opening questions.

Comparative salary data are impossible to provide without the support of professionals like you. Please complete the questionnaire and return it in the prepaid envelope before November 1, our fall deadline. You'll no longer be in the dark about how much your employees earn compared with others in your industry.

Notice that the last paragraph gives details about how to comply with the request. It also takes advantage of an "emphasis spot" (the end of a letter) to provide a final benefit reminder echoing the opening questions.

An offer to work as an intern, at no cost to a company, would seem to require little persuasion. Actually, though, companies hesitate to participate in internship programs because student interns require supervision, desk space, and equipment. They also pose an insurance liability threat.

In Figure 9.4 college student Melanie Harris seeks to persuade Software Enterprises to accept her as an intern. In the analysis process before writing, Melanie thought long and hard about what benefits she could offer the reader and how she could present them strategically. She decided that the offer of a trained college student's free labor was her strongest benefit. Thus, she opens with it, as well as mentioning the same benefit in the letter body and in the closing. After opening with the main audience benefit, she introduces the actual request ("Could you use the part-time services of a college senior . . . ?").

In the interest section, Melanie tells why she is making the request and describes its value in terms of direct and indirect benefits. Notice how she transforms obstacles (lack of equipment or desk space) into helpful suggestions about how her services would free up other staff members to perform more important tasks. She delays mentioning a negative (being able to work only 15 hours a week and only in the afternoon) until she builds interest and reduces resistance. And she closes confidently and motivates action with reference to both direct and indirect benefits.

4

Persuading Within Organizations

Instructions or directives moving downward from superiors to subordinates usually require little persuasion. Employees expect to be directed in how to perform their jobs. These messages (such as information about procedures, equipment, or cus-

FIGURE 9.4 Persuasive Action Request

4320 Mountlake Terrace Drive
Lynnwood, WA 98250
January 12, 2000

Ms. Nancy Ashley, Director
Human Resources Department
Software Enterprises, Inc.
268 Redmond Avenue
Bellevue, WA 98420

Dear Ms. Ashley:

How often do college-trained specialists offer to work for nothing? — **Uses strongest benefit for stimulating opener**

Introduces request after presenting main benefit — Very infrequently, I imagine. But that's the offer I'm making to Software Enterprises. During the next 14 weeks, could you use the part-time services of a college senior with communication and computer skills?

Builds interest with direct benefits — To gain work experience and to earn three units of credit, I would like to become an intern at Software Enterprises. My skills in Word and Excel, as well as training in letter and report writing, could be put to use in your Customer Service, Human Resources, Legal, Documentation, or other departments.

By granting this internship, your company not only secures the skills of an enthusiastic and well-trained college student, but it also performs a valuable service to Edmonds College. Your cooperation provides an opportunity for students to acquire the kind of job training that college classrooms simply cannot give. — **Notes direct benefit** / **Notes indirect benefit**

If equipment and desk space at Software Enterprises are limited, you may want me to fill in for employees who can then be freed up for other projects, training, or release time. In regard to supervision you'll find that I require little direction once I start a project. Moreover, you don't need to worry about insurance, as our college provides liability coverage for all students at internship sites. — **Anticipates three obstacles and answers each**

Introduces a negative in a positive way — Although I'm taking classes in the mornings, I'm available to work afternoons for 15 hours a week. Please examine the attached résumé to confirm my preparation and qualifications. — **Refers to enclosure only after presenting main points**

Couples action request with reference to direct and indirect benefits — Do you have any questions about my proposal to become an intern? To talk with me about it, please call 893-2155. I could begin working for you as early as February 1. You gain a free employee, and you also provide an appreciative local college student with much-needed job training.

Sincerely,

Melanie E. Harris

Melanie E. Harris

Enclosure

tomer service) follow the direct pattern, with the purpose immediately stated. However, employees are sometimes asked to perform in a capacity outside their work roles or to accept changes that are not in their best interests (such as pay cuts, job transfers, or reduced benefits). In these instances, a persuasive memo using the indirect pattern may be most effective.

Internal persuasive memos present honest arguments detailing specific reader benefits.

The goal is not to manipulate employees or to seduce them with trickery. Rather, the goal is to present a strong but honest argument, emphasizing points that are important to the receiver. In business, honesty is not just the best policy—it's the *only policy*. Especially within your own organization, people see right through puffery and misrepresentation. For this reason, the indirect pattern is effective only when supported by accurate, honest evidence.

Evidence is also critical when subordinates submit recommendations to their bosses. "The key to making a request of a superior," advises communication consultant Patricia Buhler, "is to know your needs and have documentation [facts, figures, evidence]." Another important factor is moderation. "Going in and asking for the world [right] off the cuff is most likely going to elicit a negative response," she adds.[4]

The following draft of a request for a second copy machine fails to present convincing evidence of the need. Although the request is reasonable, the argument lacks credibility because of its high-pressure tactics and lack of proof.

Ineffective Memo

TO: Patricia Karathanos, Vice President
FROM: Mike Montgomery, Marketing
SUBJECT: COPIERS

Begins poorly by reminding reader of negative past feelings.

Although you've opposed the purchase of additional copiers in the past, I think I've found a great deal on a copier that's just too good to pass up but we must act before May 1!

Sounds high-pressured and poorly conceived.

Copy City has reconditioned copiers that are practically being given away. If we move fast, they will provide many free incentives—like a free copier stand, free starter supplies, free delivery, and free installation.

Presents persuasive arguments illogically. Fails to tell exactly how much money could be saved.

We must find a way to reduce copier costs in my department. Our current copier can't keep up with our demand. Thus, we're sending secretaries or sales reps to Copy Quick for an average of 10,000 copies a month. These copies cost 5 cents a page and waste a lot of time. We're making at least eight trips a week, adding up to a considerable expense in travel time and copy costs.

Doesn't suggest specific action for reader to take.

Please give this matter your immediate attention and get back to me as soon as possible. We don't want to miss this great deal!

The preceding memo will probably fail to achieve its purpose. Although the revised version in Figure 9.5 is longer, it's far more effective. Remember that a persuasive message will typically take more space than a direct message because proving a case requires evidence. Notice that the subject line in Figure 9.5 tells the purpose of the memo without disclosing the actual request. By delaying the request until he's had a chance to describe the problem and discuss a solution, the writer prevents the reader's premature rejection.

The strength of this revision, though, is in the clear presentation of comparison figures showing how much money can be saved by purchasing a remanufactured copier. Although the organization pattern is not obvious, the revised memo begins with an attention-getter (frank description of problem), builds interest (with easy-to-read facts and figures), provides benefits, and reduces resistance. Notice that the conclusion tells what action is to be taken, makes it easy to respond, and repeats the main benefit to motivate action.

5 Complaint Letters: Requesting Adjustments and Making Claims

Persuasive adjustment letters make claims about damaged products, mistaken billing, inaccurate shipments, warranty problems, return policies, insurance snafus, faulty merchandise, and so on. Generally, the direct pattern is best for requesting straightforward adjustments (see Chapter 7). When you feel your request is justified and will be granted, the direct strategy is most efficient. But if a past request has been

FIGURE 9.5 **Persuasive Memo**

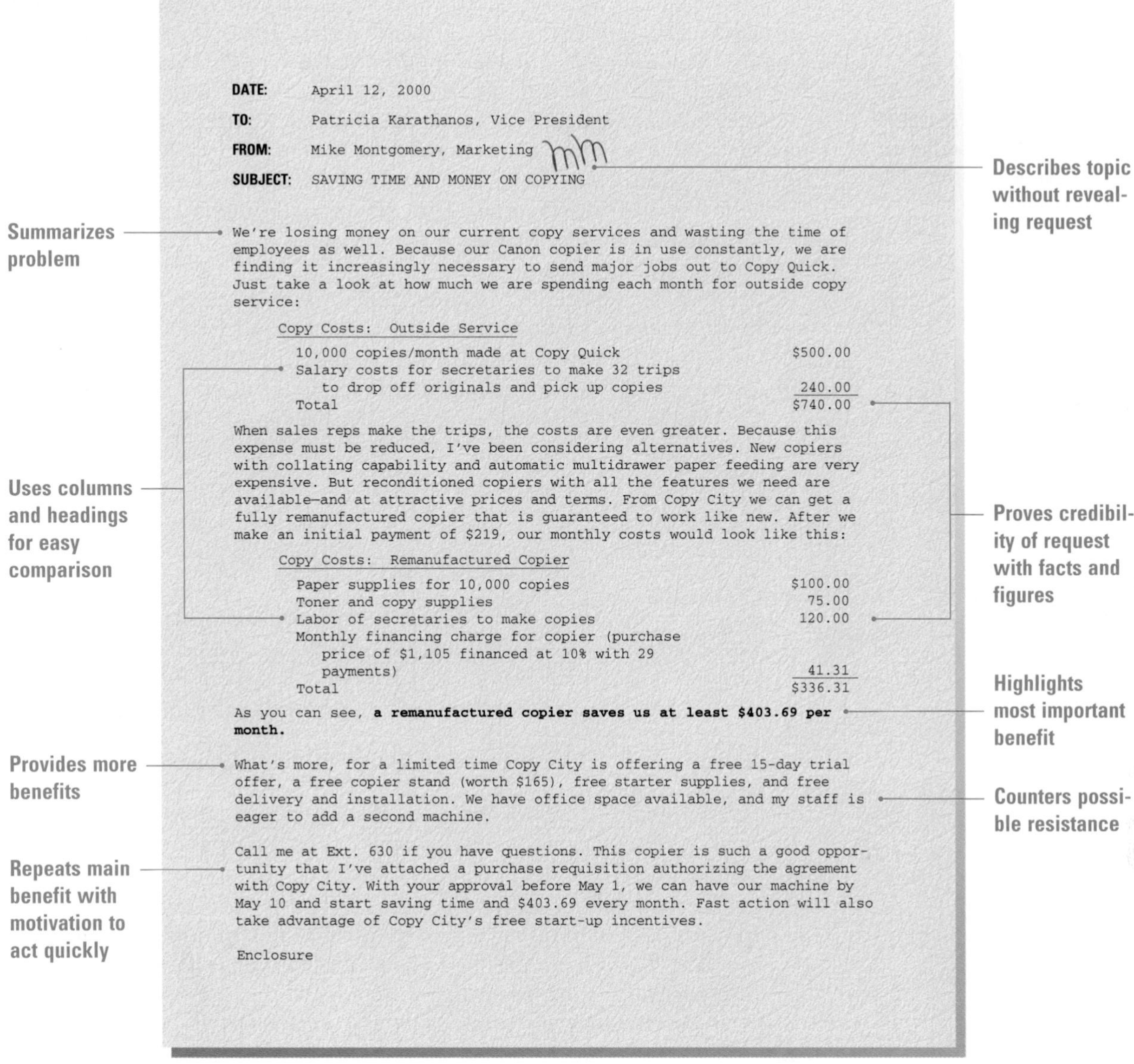
DATE: April 12, 2000

TO: Patricia Karathanos, Vice President

FROM: Mike Montgomery, Marketing *MM*

SUBJECT: SAVING TIME AND MONEY ON COPYING

We're losing money on our current copy services and wasting the time of employees as well. Because our Canon copier is in use constantly, we are finding it increasingly necessary to send major jobs out to Copy Quick. Just take a look at how much we are spending each month for outside copy service:

Copy Costs: Outside Service	
10,000 copies/month made at Copy Quick	$500.00
Salary costs for secretaries to make 32 trips to drop off originals and pick up copies	240.00
Total	$740.00

When sales reps make the trips, the costs are even greater. Because this expense must be reduced, I've been considering alternatives. New copiers with collating capability and automatic multidrawer paper feeding are very expensive. But reconditioned copiers with all the features we need are available—and at attractive prices and terms. From Copy City we can get a fully remanufactured copier that is guaranteed to work like new. After we make an initial payment of $219, our monthly costs would look like this:

Copy Costs: Remanufactured Copier	
Paper supplies for 10,000 copies	$100.00
Toner and copy supplies	75.00
Labor of secretaries to make copies	120.00
Monthly financing charge for copier (purchase price of $1,105 financed at 10% with 29 payments)	41.31
Total	$336.31

As you can see, **a remanufactured copier saves us at least $403.69 per month.**

What's more, for a limited time Copy City is offering a free 15-day trial offer, a free copier stand (worth $165), free starter supplies, and free delivery and installation. We have office space available, and my staff is eager to add a second machine.

Call me at Ext. 630 if you have questions. This copier is such a good opportunity that I've attached a purchase requisition authorizing the agreement with Copy City. With your approval before May 1, we can have our machine by May 10 and start saving time and $403.69 every month. Fast action will also take advantage of Copy City's free start-up incentives.

Enclosure

Describes topic without revealing request
Summarizes problem
Uses columns and headings for easy comparison
Proves credibility of request with facts and figures
Highlights most important benefit
Provides more benefits
Counters possible resistance
Repeats main benefit with motivation to act quickly

refused or ignored or if you anticipate reluctance, then the indirect pattern is appropriate.

Effective complaint/adjustment letters make reasonable claims backed by solid evidence.

In a sense, an adjustment letter is a complaint letter. Someone is complaining about something that went wrong. Some complaint letters just vent anger; the writers are mad, and they want to tell someone about it. But if the goal is to change something (and why bother to write except to motivate change?), then persuasion is necessary. Effective adjustment letters make a reasonable claim, present a logical case with clear facts, and adopt a moderate tone. Anger and emotion are not effective persuaders.

You'll want to open an adjustment letter with some sincere praise, an objective statement of the problem, a point of agreement, or a quick review of what you have done to resolve the problem. Then you can explain precisely what happened or why your claim is legitimate. Don't provide a blow-by-blow chronology of details; just hit the highlights. Be sure to enclose copies of relevant invoices, shipping orders, warranties, and payments. And close with a clear statement of what you want done: refund, replacement, credit to your account, or other action. Be sure to think through the possibilities and make your request reasonable.

Adjustment requests should adopt a moderate tone, appeal to the receiver's sense of responsibility, and specify needed actions.

The tone of the letter is important. You should never suggest that the receiver intentionally deceived you or intentionally created the problem. Rather, appeal to the receiver's sense of responsibility and pride in its good name. Calmly express your disappointment in view of your high expectations of the product and of the company. Communicating your feelings, without rancor, is often your strongest appeal.

Janet Walker's letter, shown in Figure 9.6, follows the persuasive pattern as she seeks to return three answering machines. Notice that she uses simplified letter style (skipping the salutation and complimentary close) because she doesn't have a person's name to use in addressing the letter. Note also her positive opening; her calm, well-documented claims; and her request for specific action.

The following checklist reviews pointers for helping you make persuasive requests of all kinds.

Checklist for Making Persuasive Requests

Gain attention. In requesting favors, begin with a compliment, statement of agreement, unexpected fact, stimulating question, reader benefit, summary of the problem, or candid plea for help. For claims and complaints, also consider opening with a review of action you have taken to resolve the problem.

Build interest. Prove the accuracy and merit of your request with solid evidence, including facts, figures, expert opinion, examples, and details. Suggest direct and indirect benefits for the receiver. Avoid sounding high-pressured, angry, or emotional.

Reduce resistance. Identify what factors will be obstacles to the receiver; offer counterarguments. Demonstrate your credibility by being knowledgeable. In requesting favors or making recommendations, show how the receiver or others will benefit. In making claims, appeal to the receiver's sense of fairness and desire for goodwill. Express your disappointment.

Motivate action. Confidently ask for specific action. For favors include an end date (if appropriate) and try to repeat a key benefit.

Planning and Composing Sales Messages

Traditional direct mail marketing involves the sale of goods and services through letters, catalogs, brochures, and other messages delivered by land mail. Electronic marketing, on the other hand, involves sales messages delivered by e-mail, Web sites, and, less frequently, by fax. To some marketers, e-mail sounds like "the promised land," guaranteeing instant delivery and at only pennies per message. However, unsolicited e-mail, called "spam," has generated an incredible backlash from recipients, who want their e-mail addresses to remain private and unviolated. One of the leading direct mail marketers correctly sensed the pulse of the times when he remarked,

FIGURE 9.6 Request for Adjustment (Complaint Letter)

Tips for Requesting Adjustments and Making Complaints

- Begin with a compliment, point of agreement, statement of the problem, or brief review of action you have taken to resolve the problem.
- Provide identifying data.
- Prove that your claim is valid; explain why the receiver is responsible.
- Enclose document copies supporting your claim.
- Appeal to the receiver's fairness, ethical and legal responsibilities, and desire for customer satisfaction.
- Describe your feelings and your disappointment.
- Avoid sounding angry, emotional, or irrational.
- Close by telling exactly what you want done.

CHAMPION AUTOMOTIVES
309 Porterville Plaza, Lansing, Michigan 48914 (517) 690-3500

November 21, 2000

Customer Service
Raytronic Electronics
594 Stanton Street
Mobile, AL 36617

SUBJECT: CODE-A-PHONE MODEL 100S — *Uses simplified letter style when name of receiver is unknown*

Begins with compliment — Your Code-A-Phone Model 100S answering unit came well recommended. We liked our neighbor's unit so well that we purchased three for different departments in our business.

Describes problem calmly — After the three units were unpacked and installed, we discovered a problem. Apparently our office fluorescent lighting interferes with the electronics in these units. When the lights are on, heavy static interrupts every telephone call. When the lights are off, the static disappears.

We can't replace the fluorescent lights, so we tried to return the Code-A-Phones to the place of purchase (Office Mart, 2560 Haslett Avenue, Lansing, MI 48901). A salesperson inspected the units and said they could not be returned since they were not defective and they had been used.

Suggests responsibility — Because the descriptive literature and instructions for the Code-A-Phones say nothing about avoiding use in rooms with fluorescent lighting, we expected no trouble. *Stresses disappointment* — We were quite disappointed that this well-engineered unit—with its time/date stamp, room monitor, and auto-dial features—failed to perform as we hoped it would.

Tells what action to take — If you have a model with similar features that would work in our offices, give me a call. Otherwise, please authorize the return of these units and refund the purchase price of $519.45 (see enclosed invoice). *Appeals to company's desire to preserve good reputation* — We're confident that a manufacturer with your reputation for excellent products and service will want to resolve this matter quickly.

Janet Walker

JANET WALKER, PRESIDENT

JPW:ett
Enclosure

Spotlight on **Communicators**

To launch Pitney Bowes' new computerized mail system, Marketing Vice President Kathleen Synnott had to persuade both coworkers and customers that the new system made sense. Internally, her persuasion centered on economics, emphasizing the need for the company to reinvent its product. With customers, her sales message concentrated on benefits, showing how the new mail-meter system could allow mail of mixed sizes to be weighed, stamped, and prepared for the post office in minutes. She advises anyone selling a product to know it thoroughly.

"Nothing is more powerful than goodwill—except ill will."[5] Unsolicited e-mail seems to create enormous ill will today. Although marketing by e-mail may one day eclipse traditional direct mail, for today's markets, traditional sales messages are still key. Sellers feel that "even with all the new media we have available today, a letter remains one of the most powerful ways to make sales, generate leads, boost retail traffic, and solicit donations."[6]

Professionals who specialize in traditional direct mail services have made a science of analyzing a market, developing an effective mailing list, studying the product, preparing a sophisticated campaign aimed at a target audience, and motivating the reader to act. You've probably received many direct mail packages, often called "junk" mail. These packages typically contain a sales letter, a brochure, a price list, illustrations of the product, testimonials, and other persuasive appeals.

We're most concerned here with the sales letter: its strategy, organization, and evidence. Because sales letters are generally written by specialists, you may never write one on the job. Why, then, learn how to write a sales letter? In many ways, every letter we create is a form of sales letter. We sell our ideas, our organizations, and ourselves. Learning the techniques of sales writing will help you be more successful in any communication that requires persuasion and promotion. Furthermore, you'll recognize sales strategies, thus enabling you to become a more perceptive consumer of ideas, products, and services.

Applying the 3-×-3 Writing Process to Sales Messages

Marketing professionals analyze every aspect of a sales message because consumers reject most direct mail offers. Like the experts, you'll want to pay close attention to the preparatory steps of analysis and adaptation before writing the actual message.

Successful sales messages require research on the product or service offered and analysis of the purpose for writing.

Analyzing the Product and Purpose. Before writing a sales letter, you should study the product carefully. What can you learn about its design, construction, raw materials, and manufacturing process? About its ease of use, efficiency, durability, and applications? Be sure to consider warranties, service, price, and special appeals. At the same time, evaluate the competition so that you can compare your product's strengths against the competitor's weaknesses.

Now you're ready to identify your central selling points. At Amazon.com the central selling point is size. Its slogan "Earth's Biggest Bookstore" translates into the widest selection of books anywhere. Another seller focused on service and used a testimonial: "When we went looking for copiers, service was our number one concern . . . and Pitney Bowes was our number one choice." Analyzing your product and the competition helps you determine what to emphasize in your sales letter.

Another important decision in the preparatory stage involves the specific purpose of your letter. Do you want the reader to call for a free video and brochure? Fill out an order form? See a demonstration? Send a credit card authorization? Before you write the first word of your message, know what features of the product you will emphasize and what response you want.

Adapting to the Audience. Blanket mailings sent "cold" to occupants generally produce low responses—typically only 2 percent. That means that 98 percent of us usually toss direct mail sales letters directly into the garbage. But the response rate can be increased dramatically by targeting the audience through selected mailing lists. These lists can be purchased or compiled. Let's say you're selling fitness equipment. A good mailing list might come from subscribers to fitness or exercise magazines. By directing your message to a selected group, you can make certain assumptions about the receivers. You would expect similar interests, needs, and demographics (age, income, and other characteristics). With this knowledge you can adapt the sales letter to a specific audience.

Crafting a Winning Sales Message

Your primary goal in writing a sales message is to get someone to devote a few moments of attention to it.[7] You may be promoting a product, a service, an idea, or yourself. In each case the most effective messages will (1) gain attention, (2) build interest, (3) reduce resistance, and (4) motivate action. This is the same recipe we studied earlier, but the ingredients are different.

Gaining Attention. One of the most critical elements of a sales letter is its opening paragraph. This opener should be short (one to five lines), honest, relevant, and stimulating. Marketing pros have found that eye-catching typographical arrangements or provocative messages, such as the following, can hook a reader's attention:

- **Offer:** *A free trip to Hawaii is just the beginning!*
- **Promise:** *Now you can raise your sales income by 50 percent or even more with the proven techniques found in . . .*
- **Question:** *Do you yearn for an honest, fulfilling relationship?*
- **Quotation or proverb:** *Necessity is the mother of invention.*
- **Product feature:** *Volvo's snazzy new convertible ensures your safety with a roll bar that pops out when the car tips 40 degrees to the side.*
- **Testimonial:** "The Journal *surprises, amuses, investigates, and most of all educates.*" (*The New Republic* commenting on *The Wall Street Journal.*)
- **Startling statement:** *Let the poor and hungry feed themselves! For just $100 they can.*
- **Personalized action setting:** *It's 4:30 p.m. and you've got to make a decision. You need everybody's opinion, no matter where they are. Before you pick up your phone to call them one at a time, pick up this card: AT&T Teleconference Services.*

Other openings calculated to capture attention might include a solution to a problem, an anecdote, a personalized statement using the receiver's name, or a relevant current event.

Spotlight on Communicators

In writing winning sales messages, beware of impossible promises, warns Herb Kelleher, cofounder and CEO of Southwest Airlines. He believes his company has the quickest baggage delivery in the industry—only eight minutes from jetway to pickup. But when his marketing staff proposed making such a promise in the Southwest promotions, Kelleher balked. On rare occasions Southwest wouldn't be able to deliver, he reasoned, and broken promises are not easily forgotten.

Building Interest. In this phase of your sales message, you should describe clearly the product or service. In simple language emphasize the central selling points that you identified during your prewriting analysis. Those selling points can be developed using rational or emotional appeals.

Openers for sales messages should be brief, honest, relevant, and provocative.

Rational appeals are associated with reason and intellect. They translate selling points into references to making or saving money, increasing efficiency, or making the best use of resources. In general, rational appeals are appropriate when a product is expensive, long-lasting, or important to health, security, and financial success. Emotional appeals relate to status, ego, and sensual feelings. Appealing to the emotions is sometimes effective when a product is inexpensive, short-lived, or nonessential. Many clever sales messages, however, combine emotional and rational strategies for a dual appeal. Consider these examples:

Rational Appeal
You can buy the things you need and want, pay household bills, pay off higher-cost loans and credit cards—as soon as you're approved and your Credit-Line account is opened.

Spotlight on **Communicators**

From San Francisco, Charles Schwab runs the nation's biggest discount stock brokerage firm and the most successful online trading firm. To sell his financial services, he makes both rational and emotional appeals. Rationally, he promises customers investment services at discount prices, sometimes undercutting industry giants by as much as 60 percent. Emotionally, he promises personalized, ethical service. His sincere soft-sell approach educates and assures investors, thus reducing resistance and fear.

Emotional Appeal

Leave the urban bustle behind and escape to sun-soaked Bermuda! To recharge your batteries with an injection of sun and surf, all you need is your bathing suit, a little suntan lotion, and your Credit-Line card.

Dual Appeal

New Credit-Line cardholders are immediately eligible for a $100 travel certificate and additional discounts at fun-filled resorts. Save up to 40 percent while lying on a beach in picturesque, sun-soaked Bermuda, the year-round resort island.

A physical description of your product is not enough, however. Zig Ziglar, thought by some to be America's greatest salesperson, points out that no matter how well you know your product, no one is persuaded by cold, hard facts alone. In the end, he contends, "People buy because of the product benefits."[8] Your job is to translate those cold facts into warm feelings and reader benefits. Let's say a sales letter promotes a hand cream made with aloe and cocoa butter extracts, along with Vitamin A. Those facts become, "Nature's hand helpers—including soothing aloe and cocoa extracts, along with firming Vitamin A—form invisible gloves that protect your sensitive skin against the hardships of work, harsh detergents, and constant environmental assaults."

Reducing Resistance. Marketing pros use a number of techniques to overcome resistance and build desire. When price is an obstacle, consider these suggestions:

- Delay mentioning price until after you've created a desire for the product.
- Show the price in small units, such as the price per issue of a magazine.
- Demonstrate how the reader saves money by, for instance, subscribing for two or three years.
- Compare your prices with those of a competitor.

In addition, you need to anticipate other objections and questions the receiver may have. When possible, translate these objections into selling points (*If you've never ordered software by mail, let us send you our demonstration disks at no charge*). Other techniques to overcome resistance and prove the credibility of the product include the following:

Techniques for reducing resistance include testimonials, guarantees, warranties, samples, and performance polls.

- **Testimonials:** *"I learned so much in your language courses that I began to dream in French."—Holly Franker, Beaumont, Texas*
- **Names of satisfied users** (with permission, of course): *Enclosed is a partial list of private pilots who enthusiastically subscribe to our service.*
- **Money-back guarantee or warranty:** *We offer the longest warranties in the business—all parts and service on-site for two years!*
- **Free trial or sample:** *We're so confident that you'll like our new accounting program that we want you to try it absolutely free.*
- **Performance tests, polls, or awards:** *Last year our microwave oven won customer satisfaction polls in the U.S., U.K., Germany, and France.*

Motivating Action. All the effort put into a sales message is wasted if the reader fails to act. To make it easy for readers to act, you can provide a reply card, a stamped and preaddressed envelope, a toll-free telephone number, an easy Web site, or a

FIGURE 9.7 Components of a Sales Letter

Gain Attention	Build Interest	Reduce Resistance	Motivate Action
Open with brief, relevant, and engaging statement that does not reveal the request immediately.	Retain attention and convince the reader that the request is reasonable. Generally, present strongest benefit before making request.	Anticipate reader objections and offer counterarguments. Picture benefits from the reader's view.	Encourage reader to act by coupling strongest benefit with easy, clear method of responding. May offer incentive.

Techniques for motivating action include offering a gift or incentive, limiting an offer, and guaranteeing satisfaction.

promise of a follow-up call. Because readers often need an extra push, consider including additional motivators, such as the following:

- **Offer a gift:** *You'll receive a free calculator with your first order.*
- **Promise an incentive:** *With every new, paid subscription, we'll plant a tree in one of America's Heritage Forests.*
- **Limit the offer:** *Only the first 100 customers receive free checks.*
- **Set a deadline:** *You must act before June 1 to get these low prices.*
- **Guarantee satisfaction:** *We'll return your full payment if you're not entirely satisfied—no questions asked.*

The final paragraph of the sales letter carries the punch line. This is where you tell readers what you want done and give them reasons for doing it. Most sales letters also include postscripts because they make irresistible reading. Even readers who might skim over or bypass paragraphs are drawn to a P.S. Therefore, use a postscript to reveal your strongest motivator, to add a special inducement for a quick response, or to reemphasize a central selling point.

Figure 9.7 summarizes useful techniques for developing the four components of successful sales letters.

Because direct mail is an expensive way to advertise, messages should present complete information in a personalized tone for specific audiences.

Putting It All Together. Direct mail advertising accounts for about 15 percent of all money spent on advertising in the United States. Sales letters are a preferred marketing medium because they can be personalized, directed to target audiences, and filled with a more complete message than other advertising media. But direct mail is expensive. That's why the total sales message is crafted so painstakingly.

Let's examine a sales letter, shown in Figure 9.8, addressed to a target group of small-business owners. To sell the new magazine *Small Business Monthly,* the letter incorporates all four components of an effective persuasive message. Notice that the personalized action-setting opener places the reader in a familiar situation (getting into an elevator) and draws an analogy between failing to reach the top floor and failing to achieve a business goal. The writer develops a rational central selling point (a magazine that provides valuable information for a growing small business) and repeats this selling point in all the components of the letter. Notice, too, how a testimonial from a small-business executive lends support to the sales message, and how the closing pushes for action. Since the price of the magazine is not a selling feature, it's mentioned only on the reply card. This sales letter saves its strongest motivator—a free booklet—for the high-impact P.S. line.

Whether you actually write sales letters on the job or merely receive them, you'll better understand their organization and appeals by reviewing this chapter and the tips in the checklist on page 271.

FIGURE 9.8 **Sales Letter**

The Three Phases of the Writing Process

Analyze: The purpose of this letter is to persuade the reader to return the reply card and subscribe to Small Business Monthly.
Anticipate: The targeted audience consists of small-business owners. The central selling point is providing practical business data that will help their businesses grow.
Adapt: Because readers will be reluctant, use the indirect pattern.

Research: Gather facts to promote your product, including testimonials.
Organize: Gain attention by opening with a personalized action picture. Build interest with an analogy and a description of magazine features. Use a testimonial to reduce resistance. Motivate action with a free booklet and an easy-reply card.
Compose: Prepare first draft for pilot study.

Revise: Use short paragraphs and short sentences. Replace words like malfunction with words like *glitch.*
Proofread: Indent long quotations on the left and right sides. Italicize or underscore titles of publications. Hyphenate *hard-headed* and *first-of-its-kind.*
Evaluate: Monitor the response rate to this letter to assess its effectiveness.

small business monthly
28 North Ferry Road • Waterford, CT 06386

April 15, 2000

Mr. James Wehrley
1608 Montlieu Avenue
High Point, NC 27262

Dear Mr. Wehrley:

[Puts reader into action setting] You walk into the elevator and push the button for the top floor. The elevator glides upwards. You step back and relax. **[Gains attention]**

But the elevator never reaches the top. A glitch in its electronics prevents it from processing the information it needs to take you to your destination.

[Suggests analogy] Do you see a similarity between your growing company and this elevator? You're aiming for the top, but a lack of information halts your progress. Now you can put your company into gear and propel it toward success with a new publication—*Small Business Monthly.*

[Emphasizes central selling point] This first-of-its-kind magazine brings you marketing tips, hard-headed business pointers, opportunities, and inspiration. This is the kind of current information you need today to be where you want to be tomorrow. One executive wrote: **[Builds interest]**

[Uses testimonial for credibility]

> As president of a small manufacturing company, I read several top business publications, but I get my "bread and butter" from *Small Business Monthly.* I'm not interested in a lot of "pie in the sky" and theory. I find practical problems and how to solve them in *SBM.*
>
> —Mitchell M. Perry, Bowling Green, Ohio

Mr. Perry's words are the best recommendation I can offer you to try *SBM.* In less time than you might spend on an average business lunch, you learn the latest in management, operations, finance, taxes, business law, compensation, and advertising. **[Reduces resistance]**

[Repeats central sales pitch in last sentence] To evaluate *Small Business Monthly* without cost or obligation, let me send you a free issue. Just initial and return the enclosed card to start receiving a wealth of practical information that could keep your company traveling upward to its goal. **[Motivates action]**

Cordially,

Cheryl Owings

Cheryl Owings
Vice President, Circulation

[Spotlights free offer in P.S. to prompt immediate reply] P.S. Act before May 15 and I'll send you our valuable booklet *Managing for Success,* revealing more than 100 secrets for helping small businesses grow.

Checklist for Writing Sales Letters

 **Gain attention.** Offer something valuable, promise the reader a result, pose a stimulating question, describe a product feature, present a testimonial, make a startling statement, or show the reader in an action setting. Other attention-getters are a solution to a problem, an anecdote, a statement using the receiver's name, and a relevant current event.

 **Build interest.** Describe the product in terms of what it does for the reader: save or make money, reduce effort, improve health, produce pleasure, boost status. Connect cold facts with warm feelings and needs.

 **Reduce resistance.** Counter reluctance with testimonials, money-back guarantees, attractive warranties, trial offers, or free samples. Build credibility with results of performance tests, polls, or awards. If price is not a selling feature, describe it in small units (*only 99 cents an issue*), show it as savings, or tell how it compares favorably with the competition.

 **Motivate action.** Close with a repetition of the central selling point and clear instructions for an easy action to be taken. Prompt the reader to act immediately with a gift, incentive, limited offer, deadline, and/or guarantee of satisfaction. Put the strongest motivator in a postscript.

Youthful entrepreneur Brad Daniel relies on news releases, such as that in Figure 9.9, to spread word of his growing gift store and franchise enterprises. Brad was 19 and in college when he opened his first store near the University of Florida in Gainesville. Six years and 23 stores later, he has acquired considerable sales and public relations savvy. Often his news releases are tailored to a specific audience. This one is aimed at a local newspaper where a new store is to open. Readers are particularly interested in how one of his gift stores may benefit them.

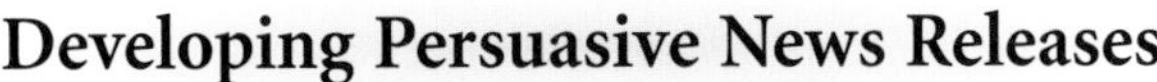

Developing Persuasive News Releases

News (press) releases announce information about your company to the media: new products, new managers, new facilities, participation in community projects, awards given or received, joint ventures, donations, or seminars and demonstrations. Naturally, you hope that this news will be published and provide good publicity for your company. But this kind of largely self-serving information is not always appealing to magazine and newspaper editors or to TV producers. To get them to read beyond the first sentence, try these suggestions:

7

Effective news releases feature an attention-getting opener, place key information up front, appeal to the target audience, and maintain visual interest.

- Open with an attention-getting lead or a summary of the important facts.
- Include answers to the five Ws and one H (who, what, when, where, why, and how) in the article—but not all in the first sentence!
- Appeal to the audience of the target media. Emphasize reader benefits written in the style of the focus publication or newscast.
- Present the most important information early, followed by supporting information. Don't put your best ideas last because they may be chopped off or ignored.
- Make the release visually appealing. Limit the text to one or two double-spaced pages with attractive formatting.
- Look and sound credible—no typos, no imaginative spelling or punctuation, no factual errors.

FIGURE 9.9 **News Release**

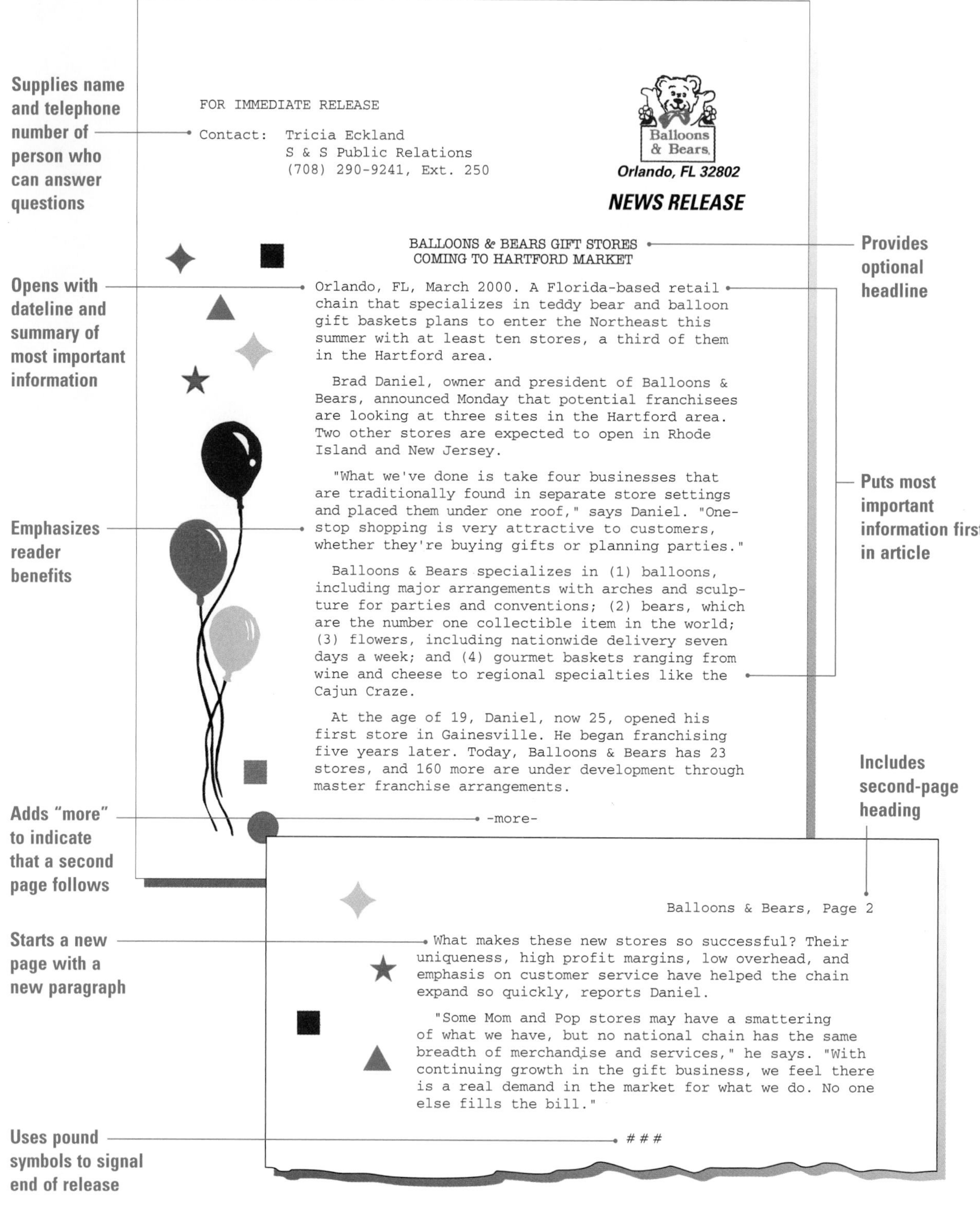

Supplies name and telephone number of person who can answer questions
FOR IMMEDIATE RELEASE
Contact: Tricia Eckland
S & S Public Relations
(708) 290-9241, Ext. 250
Balloons & Bears
Orlando, FL 32802
NEWS RELEASE
BALLOONS & BEARS GIFT STORES
COMING TO HARTFORD MARKET
Provides optional headline
Opens with dateline and summary of most important information
Orlando, FL, March 2000. A Florida-based retail chain that specializes in teddy bear and balloon gift baskets plans to enter the Northeast this summer with at least ten stores, a third of them in the Hartford area.
Brad Daniel, owner and president of Balloons & Bears, announced Monday that potential franchisees are looking at three sites in the Hartford area. Two other stores are expected to open in Rhode Island and New Jersey.
"What we've done is take four businesses that are traditionally found in separate store settings and placed them under one roof," says Daniel. "One-stop shopping is very attractive to customers, whether they're buying gifts or planning parties."
Emphasizes reader benefits
Puts most important information first in article
Balloons & Bears specializes in (1) balloons, including major arrangements with arches and sculpture for parties and conventions; (2) bears, which are the number one collectible item in the world; (3) flowers, including nationwide delivery seven days a week; and (4) gourmet baskets ranging from wine and cheese to regional specialties like the Cajun Craze.
At the age of 19, Daniel, now 25, opened his first store in Gainesville. He began franchising five years later. Today, Balloons & Bears has 23 stores, and 160 more are under development through master franchise arrangements.
Includes second-page heading
Adds "more" to indicate that a second page follows
-more-
Balloons & Bears, Page 2
Starts a new page with a new paragraph
What makes these new stores so successful? Their uniqueness, high profit margins, low overhead, and emphasis on customer service have helped the chain expand so quickly, reports Daniel.
"Some Mom and Pop stores may have a smattering of what we have, but no national chain has the same breadth of merchandise and services," he says. "With continuing growth in the gift business, we feel there is a real demand in the market for what we do. No one else fills the bill."
Uses pound symbols to signal end of release
# # #

PROCESS TO PRODUCT

Applying Your Skills at Amazon.com

CASE STUDY

As the holiday season approaches, Jeff Bezos wants to add a seasonal component to Amazon, just as typical retail bookstores do. Although he avoids antagonizing customers with frequent sales messages, he thinks he can offer a welcome service with an on-line sales message describing the many gift possibilities at Amazon. Bezos has excellent ideas about what should go into an on-line sales letter, but he wants the corporate communication people to actually organize and write it.

Amazon's new gift store offers hundreds of favorite toys, gifts for kids, personal electronics, gadgets, and computer and video games. (You might name a few of your favorites.) Bezos' favorite new feature is Gift-Click, which enables customers to select a gift while Amazon takes care of everything. Customers just type in the recipient's e-mail address. Amazon finds the physical address, selects, wraps, and sends the gift.

The new video store has more than 60,000 VHS titles. Amazon provides comprehensive video information, expert reviews, movie quotes, and trivia. In the new releases section, customers can browse hundreds of genres. And, of course, Amazon offers over 3 million book and CD titles—at savings up to 40 percent. Amazon offers a money-back guarantee on everything it sells. As Bezos says, "We gift wrap and ship gifts wherever you want—right up to the last minute." Amazon even offers gift certificates that can be sent on Christmas Day! Talk about a procrastinator's dream come true!

Your Job

In teams or individually, write the on-line sales letter from Jeff Bezos to all Amazon customers. Since Bezos wants this to look like a letter, should it contain a salutation and complimentary closing? What central selling point should be emphasized? What could serve as a motivator in a P.S.? Your instructor may wish to show you a letter similar to the one Amazon actually sent.

The most important ingredient of a press release, of course, is news. Articles that merely plug products end up in the circular file. The news release in Figure 9.9 emphasizes the most newsworthy aspects of an announcement of a new gift store specializing in balloons and bears.

Summary of Learning Objectives

1 **Apply the 3-×-3 writing process to persuasive messages.** The first step in the writing process for a persuasive message is analysis of the audience and purpose. Writers must know exactly what they want the receiver to do or think. The second step involves thinking of ways to adapt the message to the audience. Particularly important is expressing the request so that it may benefit the reader. Next, the writer must collect data and organize it into an appropriate strategy. An indirect strategy is probably best if the audience will resist the request.

2 **Explain the components of a persuasive message.** The most effective persuasive messages gain attention by opening with a problem, unexpected statement, reader benefit, compliment, related fact, stimulating question, or

similar device. They build interest with facts, expert opinions, examples, details, and additional reader benefits. They reduce resistance by anticipating objections and presenting counterarguments. They conclude by motivating a specific action and making it easy for the reader to respond. Skilled communicators avoid distortion, exaggeration, and deception when making persuasive arguments.

3 **Request favors and action effectively.** When writing to ask for a favor, the indirect pattern is appropriate. This means delaying the request until after logical reasons have been presented. Such memos should emphasize, if possible, benefits to the reader. Appeals to professionalism are often a useful technique. Writers can counter any anticipated resistance with explanations and motivate action in the closing.

4 **Write convincing persuasive messages within organizations.** In writing internal messages that require persuasion, the indirect pattern is appropriate. These messages might begin with a frank discussion of a problem. They build interest by emphasizing points that are important to the readers. They support the request with accurate, honest evidence.

5 **Request adjustments and make claims successfully.** When writing about damaged products, mistaken billing, or other claims, the indirect pattern is appropriate. These messages might begin with a sincere compliment or an objective statement of the problem. They explain concisely why a claim is legitimate. Copies of relevant documents should be enclosed. The message should conclude with a clear statement of the action to be taken.

6 **Compose successful sales messages.** Before writing a sales message, it's necessary to analyze the product and purpose carefully. The letter begins with an attention-getting statement that is short, honest, relevant, and stimulating. It builds interest by describing the product or service clearly in simple language, incorporating appropriate appeals. Testimonials, a money-back guarantee, a free trial, or some other device can reduce resistance. A gift, incentive, deadline, or other device can motivate action.

7 **Describe the basic elements included in effective news releases.** Effective news releases usually open with an attention-getting lead or summary of the important facts. They attempt to answer the questions who, what, when, where, why, and how. They are written carefully to appeal to the audience of the target media. The best news releases present the most important information early, make the release visually appealing, and look and sound credible.

CHAPTER REVIEW

1. List the four steps in the indirect pattern for persuasive messages. (Objs. 1 and 2)
2. List six or more techniques for opening a persuasive request for a favor. (Obj. 3)
3. List techniques for building interest in a persuasive request for a favor. (Obj. 3)
4. Describe ways to reduce resistance in persuasive requests. (Obj. 2)
5. How should a persuasive request end? (Objs. 2 and 3)
6. When does persuasion become unethical? (Obj. 2)
7. What are the differences between direct and indirect reader benefits? Give an original example of each (other than those described). (Obj. 3)
8. When would persuasion be necessary in messages moving downward in organizations? (Obj. 4)
9. Why are persuasive messages usually longer than direct messages? (Objs. 1–7)
10. When is it necessary to use the indirect pattern in requesting adjustments or making claims? (Obj. 5)
11. What percentage of response can be expected from an untargeted direct mail campaign? (Obj. 6)
12. Name eight or more ways to attract attention in opening a sales message. (Obj. 6)
13. How do rational appeals differ from emotional appeals? Give an original example of each. (Obj. 6)
14. Name five or more ways to motivate action in closing a sales message. (Obj. 6)
15. List five or more topics that an organization might feature in a press release. (Obj. 7)

CRITICAL THINKING

1. How are requests for action and sales letters similar and how are they different? (Objs. 3 and 6)
2. What are some of the underlying motivations that prompt individuals to agree to requests that do not directly benefit themselves or their organizations? (Objs. 2–7)
3. In view of the burden that "junk" mail places on society (depleted landfills, declining timber supplies, overburdened postal system), how can "junk" mail be justified? (Obj. 6)
4. Why is it important to know your needs and have documentation when you make requests of superiors? (Obj. 5)
5. **Ethical Issue:** Identify and discuss direct mail sales messages that you consider unethical.

ACTIVITIES

9.1 Document for Analysis: Weak Persuasive Invitation (Obj. 3)

Analyze the following document. List its weaknesses. If your instructor directs, revise it.

Ineffective Letter

Dear Dr. Thomas:

Because you're a local Atlanta author, we thought it might not be too much trouble for you to speak at our GSU Management Society banquet May 5.

Some of us business students here at Georgia State University admired your book *Beyond Race and Gender,* which appeared last spring and became such a hit across the nation. One of our professors said you were now the nation's diversity management guru. What exactly did you mean when you said that America is no longer a melting pot of ethnic groups—it's now an "American mulligan stew"?

Because we have no funds for honoraria, we have to rely on local speakers. The Reverend James R. Jones and Vice Mayor Rebecca A. Timmons were speakers in the past. Our banquets usually begin at 6:30 with a social hour, followed by dinner at 7:30 and the speaker from 8:30 until 9:00 or 9:15. We can arrange transportation for you and your wife if you need it.

We realize that you must be very busy, but we hope you'll agree. Please let our advisor, Professor Alexa North, have the favor of an early response.

9.2 Document for Analysis: Weak Persuasive Memo (Obj. 4)

Analyze the following document. List its weaknesses. If your instructor directs, revise it.

Poorly Written Memo

TO: Jay S. Jacobs, VP, Human Resources

Sue Simmons and I, along with other Intercontinental employees, have been eager to return to college, but we can't afford the costs of tuition and books.

Many of us were forced to go to work before we could complete our college degrees. We know that the continuing education divisions of some universities provide good courses that we could take at night. Sue and I—

and we think many other employees as well—would like to enroll for these courses. Would Intercontinental be interested in helping us with a tuition-reimbursement program?

We've heard about other local companies (Bank of America, First Federal, GE, and others) that offer reimbursement for fees and books when employees complete approved courses with a C or higher. Sue and I have collected information, including a newspaper clipping that we're enclosing. Surveys show that tuition-reimbursement programs help improve employee morale and loyalty. They also result in higher productivity because employees develop improved skills.

We'd like a chance to talk over this worthwhile employee program with you at your convenience.

9.3 Document for Analysis: Weak Adjustment Request (Obj. 5)

Analyze the following document. List its weaknesses. If your instructor directs, revise it.

Poorly Written Letter

Gentlemen:

Three months ago we purchased four of your CopyMaster Model S-5 photocopiers, and we've had nothing but trouble ever since.

Our salesperson, Kevin Woo, assured us that the S-5 could easily handle our volume of 3,000 copies a day. This seemed strange since the sales brochure said that the S-5 was meant for 500 copies a day. But we believed Mr. Woo. Big mistake! Our four S-5 copiers are down constantly; we can't go on like this. Because they're still under warranty, they eventually get repaired. But we're losing considerable business in downtime.

Your Mr. Woo has been less than helpful, so I telephoned the district manager, Keith Sumner. I suggested that we trade in our S-5 copiers (which we got for $2,500 each) on two S-55 models (at $13,500 each). However, Mr. Sumner said he would have to charge 50 percent depreciation on our S-5 copiers. What a ripoff! I think that 20 percent depreciation is more reasonable since we've had the machines only three months. Mr. Sumner said he would get back to me, and I haven't heard from him since.

I'm writing to your headquarters because I have no faith in either Mr. Woo or Mr. Sumner, and I need action on these machines. If you understood anything about business, you would see what a sweet deal I'm offering you. I'm willing to stick with your company and purchase your most expensive model—but I can't take such a loss on the S-5 copiers. The S-5 copiers are relatively new; you should be able to sell them with no trouble. And think of all the money you'll save by not having your repair technicians making constant trips to service our S-5 copiers! Please let me hear from you immediately.

9.4 Sales Letter Analysis (Obj. 6)

Select a one- or two-page sales letter received by you or a friend. Study the letter and then answer these questions:

a. What techniques capture the reader's attention?

b. Is the opening effective? Explain.

c. What are the central selling points?

d. Does the letter use rational, emotional, or a combination of appeals? Explain.

e. What reader benefits are suggested?

f. How does the letter build interest in the product or service?

g. How is price handled?

h. How does the letter anticipate reader resistance and offer counterarguments?

i. What action is the reader to take? How is the action made easy?

j. What motivators spur the reader to act quickly?

9.5 Persuasive Favor/Action Request: Celebrity Auction (Obj. 3)

Team **Critical Thinking**

Your professional or school organization (such as the Associated Students Organization) must find ways to raise money. The president of your group appoints a team and asks it to brainstorm for ways to meet your group's pledge to aid the United Way's battle against adult illiteracy in your community. After considering and discarding a number of silly ideas, your team comes up with the brilliant idea of a celebrity auction. At a spring function, items or services from local and other celebrities would be auctioned. Your organization approves your idea and asks your team to begin by writing a letter persuading an important person in your professional organization (or your college president) to donate one hour of tutoring in a subject he or she chooses. If you have higher aspirations, write to a movie star or athlete of your choice (perhaps one who is part of your organization or who attended your school). Persuade the star to donate an item (perhaps a prop from a recent movie) that could be auctioned at your spring function. The campaign against adult illiteracy has targeted an estimated 10,000 people in your community who cannot read or write. As a team, decide what to request and then write an appropriate persuasive letter to secure that item.

9.6 Persuasive Favor/Action Request: Inviting a Winner (Obj. 3)

As program chair of Women in Business, a national group of businesswomen, you must persuade Joann R. Schulz to be the speaker at your annual conference April 14 in New Orleans. Ms. Schulz was recently named Small Business Person of the Year by the president. She is the first woman to receive the award in the 27-year history of the Small Business Administration. After her 44-year-old husband died of a heart attack, Ms. Schulz threw herself into their fledgling company and eventually transformed it from a small research company into an international manufacturer of devices for treatment of eye problems. Under her leadership, her St. Petersburg, Florida, company grew from 3 to 75 employees in six years and now sells more than $5 million worth of artificial lenses in 22 countries.

In overcoming adversity, Ms. Schulz has remarked, "We have an old saying in my family that if you break eggs, you make an omelette." You're certain that she would be an excellent speaker. SBA Administrator Patricia Saiki said about Schulz, "Her firm's dramatic growth is evidence of her determination and can-do spirit that exemplify the best of American entrepreneurship." Central to Ms. Schulz's business and personal success is her outlook, says Paul Getting of the St. Petersburg Area Chamber of Commerce: "She radiates positive thoughts and vibrations." Although you can offer Ms. Schulz only $1,000, you have heard that she is eager to encourage female entrepreneurs. You feel she might be receptive to your invitation. Write to Ms. Joann R. Schulz, President, NBR Industries, 3450 West 16 Street, St. Petersburg, FL 33201.

9.7 Persuasive Favor/Action Request: Dining Gratuity Guidelines (Obj. 3)

As a server in the Tejas Grill, you have occasionally been "stiffed" by customers who left no tip. You know your service is excellent, but some customers just don't get it. They seem to think that tips are optional, a sign of appreciation. For servers, however, tips are 80 percent of their income. In a recent *New York Times* article, you learned that some restaurants—like the new 16-32 Coach House in New York—automatically add a 15 percent tip to the bill. In Santa Monica the Lula restaurant prints "gratuity guidelines" on checks, showing customers what a 15 or 20 percent tip would be. You also know that American Express recently developed a gratuity calculation feature on its terminals. This means that diners don't even have to do the math! Your fellow servers have asked you, who they know is studying business communication, to write a serious letter to Doug Young, general manager of Tejas (3210 Congress Avenue, Austin, TX 78704), persuading him to adopt mandatory tipping guidelines. Talk with fellow servers (your classmates) to develop logical persuasive arguments. Follow the four-part plan developed in this chapter.

9.8 Persuasive Action Request: Getting Your Congressional Representative to Listen and Act (Obj. 3)

Web

Assume you are upset about an issue, and you want your representative or senator to know your position. Choose a national issue about which you feel strongly: student loans, social security depletion, human rights in other countries, federal safety regulations for employees, environmental protection, affirmative action, gun control, taxation of married couples, the federal deficit, or some other area regulated by Congress. Obtain your representative's address by visiting The Zipper **<http://www.voxpop.com>**. This Web site provides the land mail addresses of the congresspeople for your zip code. It also gives an e-mail address, if available. However, although e-mail messages are fast, they don't carry as much influence as personal letters. Therefore, it's better to write a persuasive letter to your congressional representative outlining your feelings.

For best results, consider these tips. (1) Use the proper form of address (*The Honorable John Smith, Dear Senator Smith* or *The Honorable Joan Doe, Dear Representative Doe*). (2) Identify yourself as a member of his or her state or district. (3) Immediately state your position (*I urge you to support/oppose . . . because*). (4) Present facts and illustrations and how they affect you personally. If legislation were enacted, how would you or your organization be better off or worse off? Avoid generalities. (5) Offer to provide further information. (6) Keep the letter polite, constructive, and brief.

9.9 Persuasive Action Request: Solving the Problem of Chaotic Service Lines at McDonald's (Obj. 3)

Team **Critical Thinking**

As Parker Williams, the franchise owner of a popular local McDonald's restaurant, you are unhappy about one thing. At rush times customers complain about the chaotic multiple waiting lines to approach the service counter. You once saw two customers nearly get into a fistfight over cutting into a line. Customers often are so intent on looking for ways to improve their positions in line that they fail to examine the menu and are clueless when their turn arrives. At moderately busy times, no lines form at all and shy customers are served last.

You get together with a small group of other franchise owners to discuss the problem. Your goal is to work out a solution to the problem and then write a letter to other owners to convince them of your decision. A district meeting of McDonald's owners is scheduled in one month, and you would like to see action taken. All restaurant owners in a district must agree on a plan, if a change is made.

In teams, discuss the pros and cons of multiple lines versus a single-line (serpentine) system. It seems like a simple thing, but for many businesses it is a major decision. In fact, some academics devote their careers to studying the psychology of lines. Within your group, discuss the advantages of each system (or any other system). What do banks do? How about the competition, such as Wendy's, Burger King, and other fast-food restaurants? Is this totally an issue of speed? Some McDonald's executives contend that the multiline system accommodates higher volumes of customers more quickly. But the problem of perception is equally important. What happens when you open the door to a restaurant and see a long, long single line? Do you stick around to learn how fast the line is moving?

Within your group decide on a course of action based on your own experience in fast-food restaurants and other service organizations. Perhaps a trial program at a group of restaurants would be possible. Write a letter to other franchise owners in your region persuading them to agree with your position at the next district meeting. Although a similar letter will go to many franchise owners, address the first one to Matthew and Cynthia Ames, co-owners of a McDonald's at 13711 Beamer, Houston, TX 77089. Your letter should gain attention, build interest, reduce resistance, and motivate action.[9]

9.10 Persuasive Internal Request: Hosting America's Little People (Obj. 4)

As Christine Harris, group sales manager of The Riverfront Hotel, it's your job to promote the hotel to convention planners. You have a potential customer in America's Little People, an organization for people of small stature. It wants to host its July 9–15 convention in your hotel. Although you are happy to book the convention's 900 attendees, you must first convince the hotel's general manager, James Stockbridge. To host the convention, the hotel must alter its facilities by making check-in desks, toilets, elevator buttons, and other facilities accessible to people as short as three feet. The staff, furthermore, must be trained to serve without patronizing or alienating members of America's Little People.

The benefits of hosting the convention would be many. Like most meetings for individuals with disabilities, this convention would yield higher-than-average returns. Apparently, conventioneers with disabilities typically spend more money on dining and hotel services, and their conventions last longer than most. The America's Little People convention would last six days—twice as long as most at The Riverfront. Moreover, the organization has promised to schedule most evening meals at the hotel. Typical conventions book only one or two hotel meals. Room fees (600 rooms at $89 per night for five nights) would equal $534,000; and meals would likely bring in another $100,000. Since the organization would pay regular fees for meeting rooms and equipment, the total convention revenues could reach nearly $700,000. And if the convention went well, the organization would likely book future conventions at The Riverfront. You've read about other hotels who serve convention clientele with special needs.

Hotels equipped to serve individuals with disabilities can attract long-term convention business not available to other hotels. One competing hotel won the convention for the American Association for the Blind, and it has had return business for three years. The Riverfront could use such a niche; its convention business has been lagging. Several years ago it lost two main convention accounts, Smith's Brothers Candies and the National Women's Society.

Your task is to convince Mr. Stockbridge to host the America's Little People convention. Get a commitment from Mr. Stockbridge to meet on September 1 with Carol Martin, president of America's Little People. Ms. Martin can define the organization's convention needs and discuss training for The Riverfront staff. You'll also seek permission to secure a cost estimate for the hotel alterations from The Design Group. The contractor has experience building to ADA specifications, and the $3,000 estimate fee can be applied to the alteration bill.

If you schedule the cost estimate before September 15, you will have plenty of time to reply to America's Little People. Its deadline is November 15. Once Mr. Stockbridge has talked with the organization president and costs have been established, you feel certain he will agree to the alterations. As Christine Harris, group sales manager, write a memo to James Stockbridge, general manager, persuading him to do as you wish.

9.11 Persuasive Internal Request: Convincing the Boss (Obj. 4)

In your own work or organization experience, identify a situation in which persuasion is necessary. Should a procedure be altered to improve performance? Would a new or different piece of equipment help you perform your work more efficiently? Do you want to work other hours or perform other tasks? Do you deserve a promotion? Could customers be better served by changing something? Do you have a suggestion to improve profitability?

Once you have identified a situation, write a persuasive memo to your boss or organizational head. Use actual names and facts. Employ the concepts and techniques in this chapter to convince your boss that your idea should prevail. Include direct and indirect appeals, anticipate and counter objections, and emphasize reader benefits. End with a specific action to be taken.

9.12 Persuasive Internal Request: Overusing Overnight Shipments (Obj. 4)

As office manager of Cupertino Software, write a memo persuading technicians, engineers, programmers, and other employees to reduce the number of overnight or second-day mail shipments. Your Federal Express and other shipping bills have been sky high, and you feel that staff members are overusing these services.

Encourage employees to send messages by fax. Sending a fax costs only about 35 cents a page to most long-distance areas and nothing to local areas. There's a whopping difference between 35 cents and $15 for FedEx service! Whenever possible, staff members should obtain the FedEx account number of the recipient and use it for charging the shipment. If staff members plan ahead and allow enough time, they can use UPS ground service, which takes three to five days.

Ask the staff to consider whether the recipient is *really* going to use the message as soon as it arrives. Does it justify an overnight shipment? You'd like to reduce overnight delivery services voluntarily by 50 percent over the next two months. Unless a sizeable reduction occurs, the CEO is threatening severe restrictions in the future. Address the memo to all employees.

9.13 Persuasive Internal Request: Supporting Project H.E.L.P. (Obj. 4)

E-Mail

As employee relations manager of The Prudential Insurance Company, one of your tasks is to promote Project H.E.L.P. (Higher Education Learning Program), an on-the-job learning opportunity. Project H.E.L.P. is a combined effort of major corporations and the Newark Unified School District. You must recruit 12 employees who will volunteer as instructors for 50 or more students. The students will spend four hours a week at the Prudential Newark facility earning an average of five units of credit a semester.

This semester the students will be serving in the Claims, Word Processing, Corporate Media Services, Marketing, Communications, Library, and Administrative Support departments. Your task is to convince employees in these departments to volunteer. They will be expected to supervise and instruct the students. In return, employees will receive two hours of release time per week to work with the students. The program has been very successful thus far. School officials, students, and employees alike express satisfaction with the experience and the outcomes. Write a persuasive memo or e-mail message with convincing appeals that will bring you 12 volunteers to work with Project H.E.L.P.

9.14 Persuasive Internal Request: Scheduling Meetings More Strategically (Obj. 4)

The following memo (with names changed) was actually sent. Can you improve it? Expect the staff to be somewhat resistant because they've never before had meeting restrictions.

Poorly Written Memo

DATE: March 13, 1994

TO: All Managers and Employees

FROM: Lynn Wasson, CEO

SUBJECT: SCHEDULING MEETINGS

Please be reminded that travel in the greater Los Angeles area is time consuming. In the future we're asking that you set up meetings that

1. Are of critical importance
2. Consider travel time for the participants
3. Consider phone conferences (or video or e-mail) in lieu of face-to-face meetings
4. Meetings should be at the location where most of the participants work and at the most opportune travel times
5. Traveling together is another way to save time and resources.

We all have our traffic stories. A recent one is that a certain manager was asked to attend a one hour meeting in Burbank. This required one hour travel in advance of the meeting, one hour for the meeting, and two and a half hours of travel through Los Angeles afterward. This meeting was scheduled for 4 p.m. Total time consumed by the manager for the one hour meeting was four and a half hours.

Thank you for your consideration.

9.15 Persuasive Internal Request: Rapid Reviews Land Top Recruits (Obj. 5)

As Cassandra Carpenter, associate director of Human Resources at Techtronics computer consulting, you must improve company recruitment and retention rates soon. Employee turnover at the company is higher than 20 percent, and filling vacancies can take up to a year. Recruiting trends in the high-tech industry are clear. Record low unemployment rates, a burgeoning computer industry, and too few computer systems graduates have made the hiring game extremely competitive. To stay ahead, most firms have pumped up recruiting tactics, using hiring bonuses, unusually high salaries, extra vacation, and early reviews and raises to win the best employees. "I asked for a six-month review from ComputerTech," said one especially promising candidate, "and they agreed to it. They'll even offer a raise after three months if my performance is up to it."

You're certain that your boss will never agree to giving new employees salary raises after only three months on the job. However, offering reviews and pay raises at six months would enable you to snare the best hires without paying top dollar up front. Company pay scales simply don't allow for outlandish starting salaries, and reviews typically are given after 12 months. By offering early reviews for the best candidates, you could honor the internal pay scales while offering applicants the opportunity for early raises.

At a recent recruiting seminar, you learned that many companies are resorting to early reviews because they must. Nearly 30 percent of all high-tech companies offer them. Raises based on those reviews range from 2 percent to 8 percent, and a few star employees manage to gain even more. Companies using the tactic report great results. One company apparently reduced its usual 10 percent turnover to 1 percent for those who received raises. Those expecting early reviews performed well right away because they wanted the early pay raise. When they got it, they stayed on.

You are determined to make early reviews part of your hiring arsenal, and you plan to pitch the plan to your boss, Director of Public Relations Jonathon Richards, in a persuasive memo. You have checked with his assistant, and he is available for a meeting on Wednesday, November 15 at 10:30. You would like to meet with him then to discuss the issue, but your memo should precede the visit. Write a convincing memo that wins the appointment.

9.16 Claim Request: Excessive Attorney Fees (Obj. 5)

You are the business manager for McConnell's, a producer of gourmet ice cream. McConnell's has 12 ice cream parlors in the San Francisco area and a reputation for excellent ice cream. Your firm was approached by an independent ice cream vendor who wanted to use McConnell's name and recipes for ice cream to be distributed through grocery stores and drugstores. As business manager you worked with a law firm, Lancomb, Pereigni, and Associates, to draw up contracts regarding the use of McConnell's name and quality standards for the product. When you received the bill from Louis Lancomb, you couldn't believe it. The bill itemized 38 hours of attorney preparation, at $300 per hour, and 55 hours of paralegal assistance, at $75 per hour. The bill also showed $415 for telephone calls, which might be accurate because Mr. Lancomb had to converse with McConnell's owners, who were living in Ireland at the time. However, you doubt that an experienced attorney would require 38 hours to draw up the contracts in question.

Perhaps some error was made in calculating the total hours. Moreover, you have checked with other businesses and found that excellent legal advice can be obtained for $150 per hour. McConnell's would like to continue using the services of Lancomb, Pereigni, and Associates for future legal business. Such future business is unlikely if an adjustment is not made on this bill. Write a persuasive request to Louis Lancomb, Attorney at Law, Lancomb, Pereigni, and Associates, 2690 Mission Street, San Francisco, CA 94103.

9.17 Claim Request: Kodak Ruins His Round-the-World Trip (Obj. 5)

Pictures of himself in front of the Great Pyramids of Giza, shots of the famous Blue Mosque in Istanbul, and photographs of himself dancing with children around a fire in a Thailand village—all lost because of a faulty shutter mechanism on his camera. Brian P. Coyle, a 27-year-old resident of Orlando, Florida, made a once-in-a-lifetime trip around the world last fall. To record the sights and adventures, he invested in a Kodak Advantix camera. This is the camera featured by Eastman Kodak Company in television ads showing an American tourist snapping a shot of his gorgeous Italian date in Venice. When she is gone, he discovers that he misloaded the film, and he shouts, "I should have had a Kodak Advantix camera!"

In fact, Coyle selected the Advantix because of this easy-load feature, which worked well. But when he returned, he discovered that 12 of the 15 rolls of film he shot were ruined. He learned later that the camera shutter had malfunctioned. Needless to say, Coyle is very unhappy. After all, half of the fun of a trip lies in the memories summoned forth by photographs that can be enjoyed years after one returns. The emotional value of his pictures is far greater than the film on which they are recorded. He decides that he won't settle for 12 rolls of new film and perhaps replacement of the camera. He wants Kodak to send him around the world to repeat his trip. He figures that it is the only way he can recapture and record his lost adventure. He figures it would cost him about $20,000 to repeat his 27-day trip.

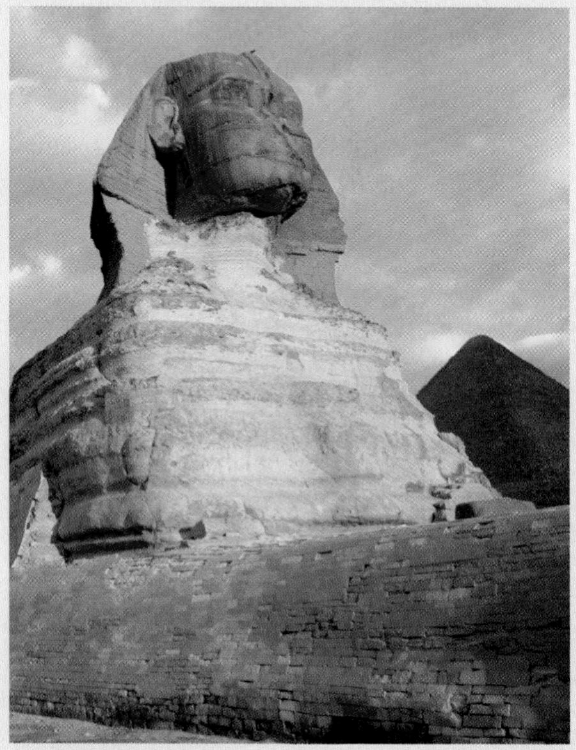

Coyle asks you, who he knows is studying business communication, to help him write a convincing letter to Kodak. You respond that it's highly unlikely that Kodak will grant this claim, and Coyle says, "Hey, what have I got to lose? Kodak ruined my trip, and I think a lot of travelers would be interested in hearing about my troubles with Kodak's Advantix camera." You and he decide to write the letter and send it along with the defective camera, purchase papers, and 12 rolls of ruined film. (Should you send it by Certified Mail with a return receipt requested?) Write a persuasive claim to Mr. Charles Smith, Customer Relations, Eastman Kodak Company, 258 West Main Street, Rochester, NY 14605.[10]

9.18 Sales Letter: Fitness at Crown Pizza (Obj. 6)

Assume you are Mike Forrest, sales representative, Fitness Associates, 135 East Stokely Boulevard, Milwaukee, WI 53217. Fitness Associates sells fitness equipment and services to businesses. You need to write a letter that generates new sales, and Crown Pizza looks especially promising. Through a friend, you've learned that Crown Pizza is striving to reduce health care bills by downsizing its employee insurance plan. However, you hope to convince the company that it would benefit from an on-site fitness center.

Health research shows that 34 million Americans are overweight, and estimated costs for the nation in deaths related to obesity exceed $39 million. Employers and employees could save $1,200 a year for each person's medical costs if overweight employees shed their excess weight. The workout programs of Fitness Associates can help employees to do just that. With regular exercise at an on-site fitness center, employees lose weight and improve overall health. As employee health improves, absenteeism is reduced and overall productivity increases. And employees love working out before or after work. They make the routine part of their workday, and they often have work buddies who share their fitness regimen.

Though many companies resist spending money to save money, fitness centers need not be large or expensive to be effective. Studies show that moderately sized centers coupled with motivational and training programs yield the greatest success. For just $30,000, Fitness Associates will provide exercise equipment including stationary bikes, weight machines, and treadmills. Their fitness experts will design a fitness room, set up the fitness equipment, and design appropriate programs. Best of all, the one-time cost is usually offset by cost savings within one year of center installation. For additional fees FA can also provide fitness consultants for employee fitness assessments. FA specialists will also train employees on proper use of equipment and clean and manage the facility—for an extra charge, of course.

Write a sales letter to Ms. Kathleen Stewart, Human Resources Vice President, Crown Pizza Company, 145 South Superior Street, Milwaukee, WI 53211. Ask for an appointment to meet with her. Send her a brochure detailing the products and services that Fitness Associates provides. As an incentive, offer a free fitness assessment for all employees if Crown Pizza installs a fitness facility by December 1.

9.19 Sales Letter: Promoting Your Product or Service (Obj. 6)

Identify a situation in your current job or a previous one in which a sales letter is (was) needed. Using suggestions from this chapter, write an appropriate sales letter that promotes a product or service. Use actual names, information, and examples. If you have no work experience, imagine a business you'd like to start: word processing, student typing, pet grooming, car detailing, tutoring, specialty knitting, balloon decorating, delivery service, child care, gardening, lawn care, or something else. Write a letter selling your product or service to be distributed to your prospective customers. Be sure to tell them how to respond.

9.20 Sales Letter: Wooing L. L. Bean With Wild West Buffalo Footwear

Your boss Harrison Trask is an excellent shoe manufacturer and salesman, but he's not so good at writing business letters. He hired you as his assistant, and he knows that you just finished your degree. He asks you to write a persuasive letter to L. L. Bean to get an order for his newest men's shoes. The trick is that Trask isn't really selling just the shoes. He's selling the lure of the Wild West, the buffalo that roam the range, and the mythical cowboy and Indian drama that men dream about as boys.

Trask himself didn't stop dreaming of the West when he began selling Buster Browns and other shoes in San Francisco. In fact, he lived a bit of the dream each summer when he traveled to Yellowstone National Park to fish the Madison River. There the water ran clear, the wilderness loomed large, and buffalo grazed so close that you could hear them breathe. It wasn't long before Trask put love and vocation together and set out to create shoes that would capture a bit of the Western mystique—shoes made of buffalo hide.

The hides were readily available, Trask learned. More than 11,000 hides are thrown out each year after the buffalo have been slaughtered for their low-cholesterol meat. Trask developed relationships with suppliers, who directed up to 80 percent of their hides to his company. He also secured a manufacturer in Arkansas. Then he partnered with John Brewer, his best friend and also a sales manager at L.A. Gear. Together they developed two styles of men's shoes. The first was the Gallatin, a casual lace-up that men could wear for leisure or dress. It sells for $145. The second, a boot-cut version called the Madison, sells for $165. Both are made of soft and durable buffalo hide.

By selling their shoes to small, specialty retailers across the country, the two men have made H. S. Trask & Co. quite successful. The company has been profitable since 1995, and current year profits are expected to exceed $10 million. Specialty stores such as Paragon Sporting Goods in New York City and Schnee's Boots and Shoes in Bozeman, Montana, have sold small orders of the shoes. A sporting goods catalog called Orvis ordered the shoes at a Trask trade show booth. These successes in hand, Trask would like to sell to a larger market.

Send sample Gallatin and Madison shoes along with your letter. Your letter should request an order of 200 pairs of each style. Such a large order qualifies for a 5 percent quantity discount. The brochure you will enclose describes the shoe features in detail. For your boss's signature, write a sales letter to Mr. Howard Smith, L. L. Bean, Inc., Freeport, ME 04033.[11]

9.21 News Release: Vintage Nikes Wanted in Japan (Obj. 7)

Team

Ever hear of the Nike "Dunk," a brightly colored basketball shoe sold in the 1980s? Although it bombed in the U.S., a pair of Dunks might now sell for $2,000 in Japan, where vintage (translation: old) athletic footwear is all the rage. Why would anyone pay exorbitant prices for smelly, old athletic shoes? Here's how Robert Smith, of Farley Enterprises, explains the craze. Japanese young people are forced to wear look-alike outfits six days a week. But out of school, they desperately want to break out of the school uniform mold to look different. And they're not interested in standard Nike, Reebok, and Adidas items that anyone can pick up at an outlet. Instead, they clamor for unique, hard-to-find older sneakers, such as the Nike Dunk in bright purple or neon yellow.

St. Louis-based Farley Enterprises has been scouring the U.S. seeking vintage articles for the Japanese market. Although the company continues to offer old Levi's jeans (small sizes preferred) and aged Hawaiian shirts, its main interest right now is in older but well-known Nikes. As Smith says, "Nike has spent a lot more money on advertising, and everyone knows who Michael Jordan is." For anyone willing to part with an old pair of Nike Dunks, Farley would offer as much as $500 (maybe more for a really clean pair). But Farley is also interested in other vintage athletic shoes. In fact, the company has gone so far as to search through running magazines for the names of athletes who might have kept their old shoes around. One Toronto-based wholesaler of used clothing made $2.3 million in 1996 exporting vintage items to Japan.

As an intern for Farley Enterprises, you have been asked to work with two other interns in writing an effective news release for local newspapers and radio and TV stations around the country. Discuss what should be included in the news release and the best way to develop the information. Be sure to describe Farley's search efforts. Encourage people to call 1-800-VINTAGE if they have distinctive, old athletic shoes or old Levis. As a contact person, you can be reached at 1-314-867-4673. Individually or as a team, write a persuasive news release.[12]

9.22 News Release: It's New! (Obj. 7)

In a company where you now work or for an organization you belong to, identify a product or service that could be publicized. Consider writing a press release announcing a new course at your college, a new president, new equipment, or a campaign to raise funds. Write an announcement for your local newspaper.

C.L.U.E. REVIEW 9

Edit the following sentences to correct faults in grammar, punctuation, spelling, and word use.

1. 2 loans made to Consumer products corporation must be repaid within 90 days. Or the owners will be in default.
2. One loan was for property apprised at forty thousand dollars, the other was for property estimated to be worth ten thousand dollars.
3. Our Senior Marketing Director and the sales manager are quite knowledgable about communications hardware, therefore they are traveling to the Computer show in northern California.
4. We congradulate you on winning the award, and hope that you will continue to experience simular success, in the future.
5. Mr. Salazar left three million dollars to be divided among 4 heirs; one of whom is a successful manufacture.
6. If the CEO and him had behaved more professional the chances of a practicle settlement would be considerably greater.
7. Just inside the entrance, is the desk of the receptionist and a complete directory of all departments'.
8. Every new employee must recieve their permit to park in lot 5-A or there car will be sited.
9. When we open our office in Montreal we will need at least 3 people whom are fluent in french and english.
10. Most companys can boost profits almost one hundred percent by retaining just 5% more of there permenant customers.

CHAPTER •10•

Negative Messages

LEARNING OBJECTIVES

1. Describe the goals of business communicators in delivering bad news.

2. Identify the causes of legal problems in business writing.

3. Explain the components of a bad-news message.

4. Compare the direct and indirect patterns for breaking bad news. List situations in which the direct pattern is better.

5. Identify routine requests and describe a strategy for refusing such requests.

6. Describe a strategy for sending bad news to customers while retaining their goodwill.

7. Explain the best strategy for managing negative organization news.

8. Compare strategies for revealing bad news in different cultures.

CASE STUDY

COMMUNICATION IN PROCESS

Pepsi Sometimes Says No

"It's amazing how a soft drink can become so much a part of people's lives that they feel passionate about it," reveals Cathy Dial, manager of Consumer Relations at Pepsi-Cola. Cathy deals with many passionate consumers every day at Pepsi-Cola headquarters in Somers, New York. Her office employs 23 representatives who respond to at least 1,000 telephone calls and 100 letters every day. The majority of these contacts are inquiries about promotions or products, and she can respond with positive information. But sometimes she has to deliver disappointing news or must refuse a request.

"The refillable bottle is a really passionate issue for some consumers," says Dial. Although the entire beverage industry moved away from returnable glass bottles, some consumers insist that Pepsi offer them. Dial receives letters saying, "Pepsi just doesn't taste the same in cans or plastic bottles; I want my bottle back!"

Other inquiries are from consumers who think they have won a prize in a promotion. In one contest a few years ago, the word *Van* appeared under a Pepsi bottle cap. Many consumers saw the word and called or wrote to claim their automobile. "Actually," explains Dial, "*Van* meant that consumers were entitled to a 10 percent discount at Van's Shoes. In a situation like this, our job is to carefully explain the rules of the promotion to consumers and thank them for participating."

Sometimes people complain about sponsorship of TV shows that have celebrities or messages that they don't like or agree with. Dial's office also receives passionate letters from individuals asking Pepsi-Cola to contribute money to their charity, to provide soft drinks for a function, or to sponsor events. Pepsi-Cola's employees give generously of their own time, and the company also is a frequent contributor to the United Way, American Cancer Society, many scholarship funds, and other causes. But it cannot support every request it receives. At times, Cathy Dial at Pepsi-Cola must deliver disappointing news.[1]

www.pepsico.com

Strategies for Breaking Bad News

The sting of bad news can be reduced by giving reasons and communicating sensitively.

Breaking bad news is a fact of business life for Cathy Dial at Pepsi-Cola and for nearly every business communicator. Because bad news disappoints, irritates, and sometimes even angers the receiver, such messages must be written carefully. The bad feelings associated with disappointing news can be reduced if (1) the reader knows the reasons for the rejection and (2) the bad news is revealed with sensitivity. You've probably heard people say, "It wasn't so much the bad news that I resented. It was the way I was told!"

This chapter concentrates on how to use the indirect pattern in delivering negative messages. You'll apply that pattern to messages that refuse routine requests, deliver bad news to customers, and deal with negative organization news. The indirect strategy is especially appealing to relationship-oriented writers. They care about how a message will affect its receiver. The direct strategy, which you learned in earlier chapters, frontloads the main idea, even when it's bad news. The direct strategy may be more appealing to efficiency-oriented writers who don't want to waste time with efforts to soften the effects of bad news.[2] The major focus of this chapter will be on developing the indirect strategy, since it is frequently used for bad-news messages. But you'll also learn to identify instances in which the direct pattern may be preferable in announcing bad news.

Spectacularly beautiful Denver International Airport introduced an automated baggage system that worked well on paper. But during the first heavy holiday period, the new system damaged some 500 bags, causing considerable customer anguish. Messages that deliver bad news to customers and to others are generally best developed using the indirect strategy.

Goals in Communicating Bad News

1

As a business communicator who must deliver bad news, you have many goals, the most important of which are these:

In communicating bad news, key goals include getting the receiver to accept it, maintaining goodwill, and avoiding legal liability.

- **Acceptance.** Make sure the reader understands and *accepts* the bad news. The indirect pattern helps in achieving this objective.
- **Positive image.** Promote and maintain a good image of yourself and your organization. Realizing this goal assumes that you will act ethically.
- **Message clarity.** Make the message so clear that additional correspondence is unnecessary.
- **Protection.** Avoid creating legal liability or responsibility for you or your organization.

These are ambitious goals, and we're not always successful in achieving them all. The patterns you're about to learn, however, provide the beginning communicator with strategies and tactics that many writers have found successful in conveying disappointing news sensitively and safely. With experience, you'll be able to vary these patterns and adapt them to your organization's specific writing tasks.

Using the Indirect Pattern to Prepare the Reader

The indirect pattern softens the impact of bad news by giving reasons and explanations first.

Revealing bad news indirectly shows sensitivity to your reader. Whereas good news can be revealed quickly, bad news is generally better when broken gradually. By preparing the reader, you soften the impact. A blunt announcement of disappointing news might cause the receiver to stop reading and toss the message aside. The indirect strategy enables you to keep the reader's attention until you have been able to explain the reasons for the bad news. The most important part of a bad-news letter is the explanation, which you'll learn about shortly. The indirect plan consists of four parts, as shown in Figure 10.1:

- **Buffer.** Offer a neutral but meaningful statement that does not mention the bad news.

FIGURE 10.1 **Four-Part Indirect Pattern for Bad News**

Buffer: Open with a neutral but meaningful statement that does not mention the bad news.
Reasons: Explain causes of the bad news before disclosing it.
Bad News: Reveal bad news without emphasizing it. Provide alternative or compromise, if possible.
Closing: End with a personalized, forward-looking, pleasant statement. Avoid referring to the bad news.

- **Reasons.** Give an explanation of the causes for the bad news before disclosing it.
- **Bad news.** Provide a clear but understated announcement of the bad news that may include an alternative or compromise.
- **Close.** Include a personalized, forward-looking, pleasant statement.

Avoiding Three Causes of Legal Problems

2

Before we examine the components of a bad-news message, let's look more closely at how you can avoid exposing yourself and your employer to legal liability in writing negative messages. Although we can't always anticipate the consequences of our words, we should be alert to three causes of legal difficulties: (1) abusive language, (2) careless language, and (3) the "good-guy syndrome."

Abusive language becomes legally actionable when it is false, harmful to the person's good name, and "published."

Abusive Language. Calling people names (such as *deadbeat, crook,* or *quack*) can get you into trouble. *Defamation* is the legal term for any false statement that harms an individual's reputation. When the abusive language is written, it's called *libel*; when spoken, it's *slander.*

To be actionable (likely to result in a lawsuit), abusive language must be (1) false, (2) damaging to one's good name, and (3) "published"—that is, spoken within the presence of others or written. Thus, if you were alone with Jane Doe and accused her of accepting bribes and selling company secrets to competitors, she couldn't sue because the defamation wasn't published. Her reputation was not damaged. But if anyone heard the words or if they were written, you might be legally liable.

In a new wrinkle, you may now be prosecuted if you transmit a harassing or libelous message by e-mail on a computer bulletin board. Such electronic transmission is considered to be "published." Moreover, a company may incur liability for messages sent through its computer system by employees. That's why many companies do not allow employees to post Internet messages using the company's return address. Employees must add a "not speaking for the company" disclaimer to private messages transmitted over networks.[3]

Obviously, competent communicators avoid making unproven charges and letting their emotions prompt abusive language—in print or electronically.

Careless language includes statements that could be damaging or misinterpreted.

Careless Language. As the marketplace becomes increasingly litigious, we must be certain that our words communicate only what we intend. Take the case of a factory worker injured on the job. His attorney subpoenaed company documents and discovered a seemingly harmless letter sent to a group regarding a plant tour. These words appeared in the letter: "Although we are honored at your interest in our company, we cannot give your group a tour of the plant operations as it would be too noisy and dangerous." The court found in favor of the worker, inferring from the letter that working conditions were indeed hazardous.[4] The letter writer did not intend to convey the impression of dangerous working conditions, but the court accepted that interpretation.

This case points up two important cautions. First, be careful in making statements that are potentially damaging or that could be misinterpreted. Be wary of explanations that convey more information than you intend. Second, be careful about what documents you save. Attorneys may demand, in pursuing a lawsuit, all company files pertaining to a case. Even documents marked "Confidential" or "Personal" may be used.

Remember, too, that e-mail messages are especially risky. You may think that a mere tap of the delete key makes a file disappear. No way! Messages continue to exist on backup storage devices in the files of the sender and the recipient. "Everyone needs to understand that anything typed onto the system remains out there forever," says attorney Ronald J. James. "There is no such thing as a delete key."[5]

Spotlight on **Communicators**

On the way to developing the world's largest prestige cosmetics firm, Estee Lauder learned valuable lessons for dealing with anger and remaining in control. "When you're angry," she suggests, "never put it in writing. It's like carving your anger in stone." She preferred face-to-face confrontations or, better yet, cooling off before reacting.

The Good-Guy Syndrome. Most of us hate to have to reveal bad news—that is, to be the bad guy. To make ourselves look better, to make the receiver feel better, and to maintain good relations, we are tempted to make statements that are legally dangerous. Consider the case of a law firm interviewing job candidates. One of the firm's partners was asked to inform a candidate that she was not selected. The partner's letter said, "Although you were by far the most qualified candidate we interviewed, unfortunately, we have decided we do not have a position for a person of your talents at this time." To show that he personally had no reservations about this candidate and to bolster the candidate, the partner offered his own opinion. But he differed from the majority of the recruiting committee. When the rejected interviewee learned later that the law firm had hired two male attorneys, she sued, charging sexual discrimination. The court found in favor of the rejected candidate, agreeing that a reasonable inference could be made from the partner's letter that she was the "most qualified candidate."[6]

Avoid statements that make you feel good but may be misleading or inaccurate.

Two important lessons emerge. First, business communicators act as agents of their organizations. Their words, decisions, and opinions are assumed to represent those of the organization. Thus, if you want to communicate your personal feelings or opinions, use your home computer or write on plain paper (rather than company letterhead) and sign your name without title or affiliation. Second, volunteering extra information can lead to trouble. Thus, avoid supplying data that could be misused, and avoid making promises that can't be fulfilled. Don't admit or imply responsibility for conditions that caused damage or injury. Even apologies (*We're sorry that a faulty bottle cap caused damage to your carpet*) may suggest liability.

Use organizational stationery for official business only, and beware of making promises that can't be fulfilled.

In Chapter 4 we discussed four information areas that generate the most lawsuits: investments, safety, marketing, and human resources. In this chapter we'll make specific suggestions for avoiding legal liability in writing responses to claim letters, credit letters, and personnel documents. You may find that in the most critical areas (such as collection letters or hiring/firing messages) your organization provides language guidelines and form letters approved by legal counsel. As the business environment becomes more perilous, we must be not only sensitive to receivers but also keenly aware of risks to ourselves and to the organizations we represent.

Developing Bad-News Messages

Legal issues aside, let's move on to the central focus of this chapter—how to deliver a bad-news message. You may use a direct method with the main idea announced immediately, as you learned in earlier chapters. Many writers, however, prefer to use an indirect strategy, which delays the bad news until after explanations have been given. In your own writing, you can use whichever strategy seems most appropriate

FIGURE 10.2 **Delivering Bad News Sensitively**

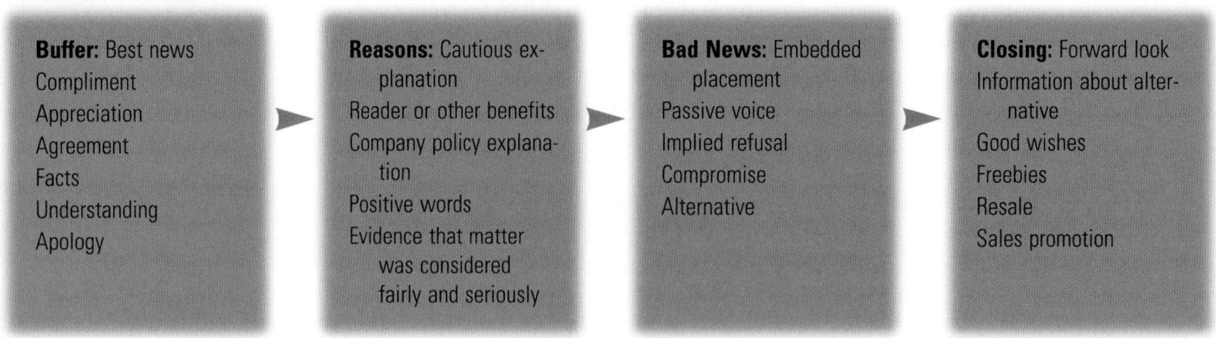

Buffer: Best news
Compliment
Appreciation
Agreement
Facts
Understanding
Apology
Reasons: Cautious explanation
Reader or other benefits
Company policy explanation
Positive words
Evidence that matter was considered fairly and seriously
Bad News: Embedded placement
Passive voice
Implied refusal
Compromise
Alternative
Closing: Forward look
Information about alternative
Good wishes
Freebies
Resale
Sales promotion

To reduce negative feelings, use a buffer opening for sensitive bad-news messages.

to the situation and to your organization. In this chapter you'll now learn how to develop and apply the indirect strategy. Its four components, as shown in Figure 10.2, include buffer, reasons, bad news, and closing.

Buffering the Opening. A buffer is a device to reduce shock or pain. To buffer the pain of bad news, begin with a neutral but meaningful statement that makes the reader continue reading. The buffer should be relevant and concise and provide a natural transition to the explanation that follows. The individual situation, of course, will help determine what you should put in the buffer. Avoid trite buffers such as *Thank you for your letter.* Here are some possibilities for opening bad-news messages.

Best News. Start with the part of the message that represents the best news. For example, in a memo that announces a new service along with a cutback in mail room hours, you might write, *To ensure that your correspondence goes out with the last pickup, we're starting a new messenger pickup service at 2:30 p.m. daily beginning June 1.*

Openers can buffer the bad news with compliments, appreciation, agreement, relevant facts, and understanding.

Compliment. Praise the receiver's accomplishments, organization, or efforts. But do so with honesty and sincerity. For instance, in a letter declining an invitation to speak, you could write, *The Thalians have my sincere admiration for their fund-raising projects on behalf of hungry children. I am honored that you asked me to speak Friday, November 5.*

Appreciation. Convey thanks to the reader for doing business, for sending something, for conveying confidence in your organization, for expressing feelings, or simply for providing feedback. Suppose you had to draft a letter that refuses employment. You could say, *I appreciated learning about the hospitality management program at Cornell and about your qualifications in our interview last Friday.* Avoid thanking the reader, however, for something you are about to refuse.

Agreement. Make a relevant statement with which both reader and receiver can agree. A letter that rejects a loan application might read, *We both realize how much the export business has been affected by the relative strength of the dollar in the past two years.*

Facts. Provide objective information that introduces the bad news. For example, in a memo announcing cutbacks in the hours of the employees' cafeteria, you might say, *During the past five years the number of employees eating breakfast in our cafeteria has dropped from 32 percent to 12 percent.*

Understanding. Show that you care about the reader. Notice how in this letter to customers announcing a product defect, the writer expresses concern: *We know that you expect superior performance from all the products you purchase from OfficeCity. That's why we're writing personally about the Exell printer cartridges you recently ordered.*

Apology. As you learned in Chapter 7, an apology may be appropriate. A study of actual letters responding to customer complaints revealed that 67 percent carried an apology of some sort.[7] If you do apologize, do it early, briefly, and sincerely. For example, a manufacturer of super premium ice cream might respond to a customer's complaint with, *We're genuinely sorry that you were disappointed in the price of the ice cream you recently purchased at one of our scoop shops. Your opinion is important to us, and we appreciate your giving us the opportunity to look into the problem you describe.*

Good buffers avoid revealing the bad news immediately. Moreover, they do not convey a false impression that good news follows. Additionally, they provide a natural transition to the next bad-news letter component—the reasons.

Bad-news messages should explain reasons before stating the negative news.

Presenting the Reasons. The most important part of a bad-news letter is the section that explains why a negative decision is necessary. Without sound reasons for denying a request or refusing a claim, a letter will fail, no matter how cleverly it is organized or written. As part of your planning before writing, you analyzed the problem and decided to refuse a request for specific reasons. Before disclosing the bad news, try to explain those reasons. Providing an explanation reduces feelings of ill will and improves the chances that the reader will accept the bad news.

Being Cautious in Explaining. If the reasons are not confidential and if they will not create legal liability, you can be specific: *Growers supplied us with a limited number of patio roses, and our demand this year was twice that of last year.* In refusing a speaking engagement, tell why the date is impossible: *On January 17 we have a board of directors meeting that I must attend.* Don't, however, make unrealistic or dangerous statements in an effort to be the "good guy."

Citing Reader or Other Benefits if Plausible. Readers are more open to bad news if in some way, even indirectly, it may help them. In refusing a customer's request for free hemming of skirts and slacks, Lands' End wrote: "We tested our ability to hem skirts a few months ago. This process proved to be very time-consuming. We have decided not to offer this service because the additional cost would have increased the selling price of our skirts substantially, and we did not want to impose that cost on all our customers."[8] Readers also accept bad news better if they recognize that someone or something else benefits, such as other workers or the environment: *Although we would like to consider your application, we prefer to fill managerial positions from within.* Avoid trying to show reader benefits, though, if they appear insincere: *To improve our service to you, we're increasing our brokerage fees.*

Readers accept bad news more readily if they see that someone benefits.

Explaining Company Policy. Readers resent blanket policy statements prohibiting something: *Company policy prevents us from making cash refunds* or *Contract bids may be accepted from local companies only* or *Company policy requires us to promote from within.* Instead of hiding behind company policy, gently explain why the policy makes sense: *We prefer to promote from within because it rewards the loyalty of our employees. In addition, we've found that people familiar with our organization make the quickest contribution to our team effort.* By offering explanations, you demonstrate that you care about readers and are treating them as important individuals.

Choosing Positive Words. Because the words you use can affect a reader's response, choose carefully. Remember that the objective of the indirect pattern is holding the reader's attention until you've had a chance to explain the reasons justifying the bad news. To keep the reader in a receptive mood, avoid expressions that might cause the reader to tune out. Be sensitive to negative words such as *claim, error, failure, fault, impossible, mistaken, misunderstand, never, regret, unwilling, unfortunately,* and *violate.*

Showing That the Matter Was Treated Seriously and Fairly. In explaining reasons, demonstrate to the reader that you take the matter seriously, have investigated carefully, and are making an unbiased decision. Consumers are more accepting of disappointing news when they feel that their requests have been heard and that they have been treated fairly. Avoid passing the buck or blaming others within your organization. Such unprofessional behavior makes the reader lose faith in you and your company.

Techniques for cushioning bad news include positioning it strategically, using the passive voice, implying the refusal, and suggesting alternatives or compromises.

Cushioning the Bad News.

Although you can't prevent the disappointment that bad news brings, you can reduce the pain somewhat by breaking the news sensitively. Be especially considerate when the reader will suffer personally from the bad news. A number of thoughtful techniques can cushion the blow.

Positioning the Bad News Strategically. Instead of spotlighting it, sandwich the bad news between other sentences, perhaps among your reasons. Don't let the refusal begin or end a paragraph—the reader's eye will linger on these high-visibility spots. Another technique that reduces shock is putting a painful idea in a subordinate clause: *Although another candidate was hired, we appreciate your interest in our organization and wish you every success in your job search.* Subordinate clauses often begin with words like *although, as, because, if,* and *since.*

Using the Passive Voice. Passive-voice verbs enable you to depersonalize an action. Whereas the active voice focuses attention on a person (*We don't give cash refunds*), the passive voice highlights the action (*Cash refunds are not given because . . .*). Use the passive voice for the bad news. In some instances you can combine passive-voice verbs and a subordinate clause: *Although franchise scoop shop owners cannot be required to lower their ice cream prices, we are happy to pass along your comments for their consideration.*

Accentuating the Positive. As you learned earlier, messages are far more effective when you describe what you can do instead of what you can't do. Rather than *We will no longer allow credit card purchases,* try a more positive appeal: *We are now selling gasoline at discount cash prices.*

Implying the Refusal. It's sometimes possible to avoid a direct statement of refusal. Often, your reasons and explanations leave no doubt that a request has been denied. Explicit refusals may be unnecessary and at times cruel. In this refusal to contribute to a charity, for example, the writer never actually says no: *Because we will soon be moving into new offices in Glendale, all our funds are earmarked for moving and furnishings. We hope that next year we'll be able to support your worthwhile charity.* The danger of an implied refusal, of course, is that it is so subtle that the reader misses it. Be certain that you make the bad news clear, thus preventing the need for further correspondence.

Suggesting a Compromise or an Alternative. A refusal is not so depressing—for the sender or the receiver—if a suitable compromise, substitute, or alternative is available. In denying permission to a class to visit a historical private residence, for instance, this writer softens the bad news by proposing an alternative: *Although private tours of the grounds are not given, we do open the house and its gardens for one charitable event in the fall.*

You can further reduce the impact of the bad news by refusing to dwell on it. Present it briefly (or imply it), and move on to your closing.

Closings to bad-news messages might include a forward look, an alternative, good wishes, freebies, and resale or sales promotion information.

Closing Pleasantly. After explaining the bad news sensitively, close the message with a pleasant statement that promotes goodwill. The closing should be personalized and may include a forward look, an alternative, good wishes, freebies, resale information, or an off-the-subject remark.

Forward Look. Anticipate future relations or business. A letter that refuses a contract proposal might read: *Thanks for your bid. We look forward to working with your talented staff when future projects demand your special expertise.*

Alternative. If an alternative exists, end your letter with follow-through advice. For example, in a letter rejecting a customer's demand for replacement of landscaping plants, you might say: *I will be happy to give you a free inspection and consultation. Please call 746-8112 to arrange a date for my visit.*

Good Wishes. A letter rejecting a job candidate might read: *We appreciate your interest in our company, and we extend to you our best wishes in your search to find the perfect match between your skills and job requirements.*

Freebies. When customers complain—primarily about food products or small consumer items—companies often send coupons, samples, or gifts to restore confidence and to promote future business. In response to a customer's complaint about a frozen dinner, you could write, *Your loyalty and your concern about our frozen entrées is genuinely appreciated. Because we want you to continue enjoying our healthful and convenient dinners, we're enclosing a coupon that you can take to your local market to select your next Green Valley entrée.*

Resale or Sales Promotion. When the bad news is not devastating or personal, references to resale information or promotion may be appropriate: *The computer workstations you ordered are unusually popular because of their stain-, heat-, and scratch-resistant finishes. To help you locate hard-to-find accessories for these workstations, we invite you to visit our Web site where our on-line catalog provides a huge selection of surge suppressors, multiple outlet strips, security devices, and PC tool kits.*

Avoid endings that sound canned, insincere, inappropriate, or self-serving. Don't invite further correspondence (*If you have any questions, do not hesitate . . .*), and don't refer to the bad news. To review these suggestions for delivering bad news sensitively, take another look at Figure 10.2.

When to Use the Direct Pattern

Many bad-news letters are best organized indirectly, beginning with a buffer and reasons. The direct pattern, with the bad news first, may be more effective, though, in situations such as the following:

- **When the receiver may overlook the bad news.** With the crush of mail today, many readers skim messages, looking only at the opening. If they don't find substantive material, they may discard the message. Rate increases, changes in ser-

The direct pattern is appropriate when the receiver might overlook the bad news, when directness is preferred, when firmness is necessary, or when the bad news is not damaging.

vice, new policy requirements—these critical messages may require boldness to ensure attention.

- **When organization policy suggests directness.** Some companies expect all internal messages and announcements—even bad news—to be straightforward and presented without frills.
- **When the receiver prefers directness.** Busy managers may prefer directness. Such shorter messages enable the reader to get in the proper frame of mind immediately. If you suspect that the reader prefers that the facts be presented straightaway, use the direct pattern.
- **When firmness is necessary.** Messages that must demonstrate determination and strength should not use delaying techniques. For example, the last in a series of collection letters that seek payment of overdue accounts may require a direct opener.
- **When the bad news is not damaging.** If the bad news is insignificant (such as a small increase in cost) and doesn't personally affect the receiver, then the direct strategy certainly makes sense.

Rate increases represent bad news to customers. However, small increases, such as that announced in the FedEx letter shown in Figure 10.3, can be announced directly. Notice that FedEx includes many letter components discussed earlier. The letter presents the rate increase but immediately points out that other service rates remain the same or are decreasing. In fact, the entire balance of the letter promotes reader benefits, including committed delivery, 24-hour access to shipment information, money-back guarantees, an enhanced Web site, and Sunday delivery. The letter emphasizes the "you" view throughout and closes with a forward-looking thought. Clever organizations like FedEx can turn bad news into an opportunity to sell their services.

FedEx placed its rate increase right up front. Generally, however, American writers prefer to use an indirect strategy, especially for more serious bad news. On the other hand, some researchers report that *where* the writer places the bad news is not nearly so important as the *tone* of the message.[9] Many of the techniques you've just learned will help you achieve a sensitive, personal tone in messages delivering negative news.

Applying the 3-×-3 Writing Process

The 3-×-3 writing process is especially important in crafting bad-news messages because of the potential consequences of poorly written messages.

Thinking through the entire process is especially important in bad-news letters. Not only do you want the receiver to understand and accept the message, but you want to be careful that your words say only what you intend. Thus, you'll want to apply the familiar 3-×-3 writing process to bad-news letters.

Analysis, Anticipation, and Adaptation. In Phase 1 (prewriting) you need to analyze the bad news so that you can anticipate its effect on the receiver. If the disappointment will be mild, announce it directly. If the bad news is serious or personal, consider techniques to reduce the pain. Adapt your words to protect the receiver's ego. Instead of *You neglected to change the oil, causing severe damage to the engine,* switch to the passive voice: *The oil wasn't changed, causing severe damage to the engine.* Choose words that show you respect the reader as a responsible, valuable person.

Research, Organization, and Composition. In Phase 2 (writing) you can gather information and brainstorm for ideas. Jot down all the reasons you have that ex-

FIGURE 10.3 FedEx Uses Direct Strategy for Rate Increase

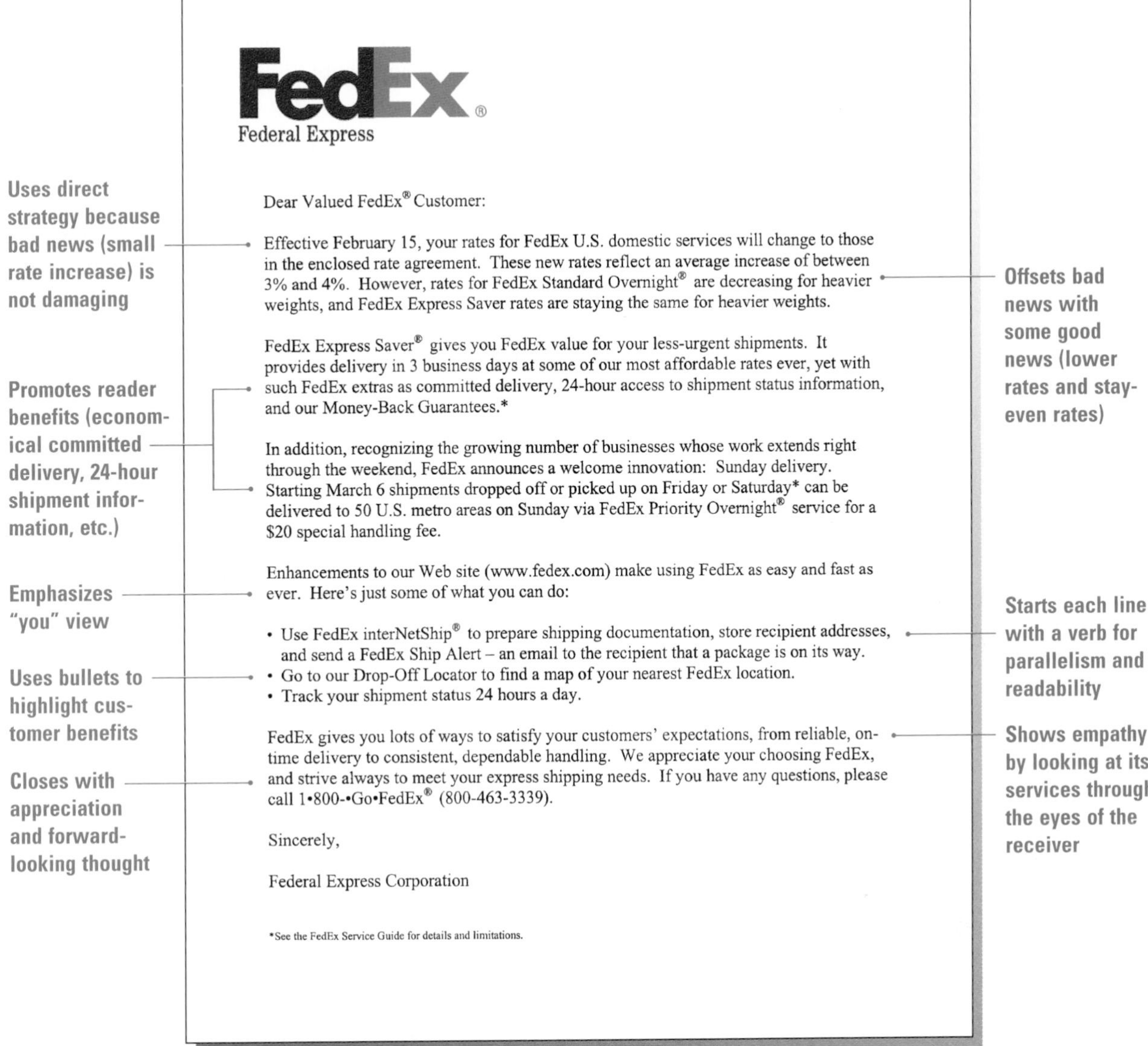

FedEx
Federal Express
Uses direct strategy because bad news (small rate increase) is not damaging
Promotes reader benefits (economical committed delivery, 24-hour shipment information, etc.)
Emphasizes "you" view
Uses bullets to highlight customer benefits
Closes with appreciation and forward-looking thought
Offsets bad news with some good news (lower rates and stay-even rates)
Starts each line with a verb for parallelism and readability
Shows empathy by looking at its services through the eyes of the receiver

Dear Valued FedEx® Customer:

Effective February 15, your rates for FedEx U.S. domestic services will change to those in the enclosed rate agreement. These new rates reflect an average increase of between 3% and 4%. However, rates for FedEx Standard Overnight® are decreasing for heavier weights, and FedEx Express Saver rates are staying the same for heavier weights.

FedEx Express Saver® gives you FedEx value for your less-urgent shipments. It provides delivery in 3 business days at some of our most affordable rates ever, yet with such FedEx extras as committed delivery, 24-hour access to shipment status information, and our Money-Back Guarantees.*

In addition, recognizing the growing number of businesses whose work extends right through the weekend, FedEx announces a welcome innovation: Sunday delivery. Starting March 6 shipments dropped off or picked up on Friday or Saturday* can be delivered to 50 U.S. metro areas on Sunday via FedEx Priority Overnight® service for a $20 special handling fee.

Enhancements to our Web site (www.fedex.com) make using FedEx as easy and fast as ever. Here's just some of what you can do:

- Use FedEx interNetShip® to prepare shipping documentation, store recipient addresses, and send a FedEx Ship Alert – an email to the recipient that a package is on its way.
- Go to our Drop-Off Locator to find a map of your nearest FedEx location.
- Track your shipment status 24 hours a day.

FedEx gives you lots of ways to satisfy your customers' expectations, from reliable, on-time delivery to consistent, dependable handling. We appreciate your choosing FedEx, and strive always to meet your express shipping needs. If you have any questions, please call 1•800-•Go•FedEx® (800-463-3339).

Sincerely,

Federal Express Corporation

*See the FedEx Service Guide for details and limitations.

plain the bad news. If four or five reasons prompted your negative decision, concentrate on the strongest and safest ones. Avoid presenting any weak reasons; readers may seize on them to reject the entire message. After selecting your best reasons, outline the four parts of the bad-news pattern: buffer, reasons, bad news, closing. Flesh out each section as you compose your first draft.

Revision, Proofreading, and Evaluation. In Phase 3 (revising) you're ready to switch positions and put yourself into the receiver's shoes. Have you looked at the problem from the receiver's perspective? Is your message too blunt? Too subtle? Does the message make the refusal, denial, or bad-news announcement clear? Prepare the final version, and proofread for format, punctuation, and correctness.

Refusing Routine Requests

Every business communicator will occasionally have to say no to a request. Depending on how you think the receiver will react to your refusal, you can use the direct or the indirect pattern. If you have any doubt, use the indirect pattern.

Rejecting Requests for Favors, Money, Information, and Action

Most of us prefer to be let down gently when we're being refused something we want. That's why the reasons-before-refusal pattern works well when you must turn down requests for favors, money, information, action, and so forth.

Let's say you must refuse a request from Mark Stevenson, one of your managers, who wants permission to attend a conference. You can't let him go because the timing is bad; he must be present at budget planning meetings scheduled for the same two weeks. Normally, you'd try to discuss this with Mark in person. But he's been traveling among branch offices recently, and you haven't been able to catch him in. Your first inclination might be to send a quickie memo, as shown below, and "tell it like it is."

Ineffective Memo

MEMO TO: Mark Stevenson

Announces the bad news too quickly and painfully. → We can't allow you to attend the conference in September, Mark. Perhaps you didn't know that budget planning meetings are scheduled for that month.

Gives reasons, but includes a potentially dangerous statement about the "shaky" system. Overemphasizes the refusal and apology. → Your expertise is needed here to help keep our telecommunications network on schedule. Without you, the entire system—which is shaky at best—might fall apart. I'm sorry to have to refuse your request to attend the conference. I know this is small thanks for the fine work you have done for us. Please accept my humble apologies.

Makes a promise that might be difficult to keep. → In the spring I'm sure your work schedule will be lighter, and we can release you to attend a conference at that time.

In revising, you realize that this message is going to hurt and that it has possible danger areas. Moreover, you see that this memo misses a chance to give Mark positive feedback.

Compliments can help buffer the impact of request refusals.

An improved version of the memo, shown in Figure 10.4, starts with a buffer that delivers honest praise (*pleased with your leadership and your genuine professional commitment*). By the way, don't be stingy with compliments; they cost you nothing. As a philosopher once observed, *We don't live by bread alone. We need buttering up once in a while.* The buffer also includes the date of the meeting, used strategically to connect the reasons that follow. You will recall from Chapter 5 that repetition of a key idea is an effective transitional device to provide smooth flow between components of a message.

The middle paragraph provides reasons for the refusal. Notice that they focus on positive elements: Mark is the specialist; the company relies on his expertise; and everyone will benefit if he passes up the conference. In this section it becomes obvious that the request will be refused. The writer is not forced to say *No, you may not attend.* Although the refusal is implied, the reader gets the message.

The closing suggests a qualified alternative (*if our work loads permit, we'll try to send you then*). It also ends positively with gratitude for Mark's contributions to the

FIGURE 10.4 **Refusing a Request**

The Three Phases of the Writing Process

Analyze: The purpose of this memo is to refuse a respected employee's request without damaging good relations.

Anticipate: The audience is a valued manager who wants to attend a conference.

Adapt: Because the reader will probably be hurt and disappointed at this message, the indirect pattern is best.

Research: Gather necessary data, including reasons explaining the refusal.

Organize: In the buffer, praise the manager's contributions. Mention the conference date to provide a transition. In the reasons section, explain why the request cannot be granted. Imply the refusal. Close by suggesting a feasible alternative. Show appreciation.

Compose: Prepare the first draft.

Revise: Respect the reader's feelings by softening the tone. Show that the refusal is in the reader's best interests. Don't apologize; you've done nothing wrong.

Proofread: Verify spelling of troublesome words. Use commas after beginning clauses and around "Mark" (direct address)

Evaluate: Will this message make the reader understand and accept the refusal?

DATE: July 2, 2000

TO: Mark Stevenson
Manager, Telecommunications

FROM: Ann Wells-Freed AWF
VP, Management Information Systems

SUBJECT: REQUEST TO ATTEND SEPTEMBER CONFERENCE

The Management Council and I are extremely pleased with the leadership you have provided in setting up live video transmission to our regional offices. Because of your genuine professional commitment, Mark, I can understand your desire to attend the conference of the Telecommunication Specialists of America September 23 to 28 in Atlanta.

The last two weeks in September have been set aside for budget planning. As you and I know, we've only scratched the surface of our teleconferencing projects for the next five years. Since you are the specialist and we rely heavily on your expertise, we need you here for those planning sessions.

If you're able to attend a similar conference in the spring and if our work loads permit, we'll try to send you then. You're a valuable player, Mark, and I'm grateful you're on our MIS team.

Buffer: Includes sincere praise

Transition: Uses date to move smoothly from buffer to reasons

Reasons: Tells why refusal is necessary

Bad news: Implies refusal

Closing: Contains realistic alternative, praise, and appreciation

organization and with another compliment (*you're a valuable player*). Notice that the improved version focuses on explanations and praise rather than on refusals and apologies.

The success of this message depends on attention to the entire writing process, not just on using a buffer or scattering a few compliments throughout. Review the components of the 3-×-3 writing process and how they relate to request refusals by studying the boxes at the top of Figure 10.4.

Routine request refusals focus on explanations and praise, maintain a positive tone, and offer alternatives.

Just as managers must refuse proposals from employees, they must also reject requests for contributions of money, time, equipment, or other support. Requests for contributions to charity are common. Most big companies receive hundreds of requests annually—from consumers as well as from employees. Although the causes may be worthy, resources are usually limited. If you were required to write frequent refusals, you might prepare a form letter, changing a few variables as needed. See the accompanying Tech Talk box to learn how you can personalize form letters by using word processing equipment.

As you read the following letter, think about how it could be adapted, using word processing equipment, to serve other charity requests.

Dear Ms. Brown:

Opens with acknowledgment of inquiry and praise for the writer. Doesn't say yes or no.

We appreciate your letter describing the good work your Tri-Valley chapter of the National Reye's Syndrome Foundation is doing in preventing and treating this serious affliction. Your organization is to be commended for its significant achievements resulting from the efforts of dedicated members.

Repeats the key idea of *good work.* Explains that a decline in sales requires a cutback in gifts. Reveals refusal gently without actually stating it.

Supporting the good work of your organization and others, although unrelated to our business, is a luxury we have enjoyed in past years. Because of sales declines and organizational downsizing, we're forced to take a much harder look at funding requests that we receive this year. We feel that we must focus our charitable contributions on areas that relate directly to our business.

Closes graciously by looking forward to next year.

We're hopeful that the worst days are behind us and that we'll be able to renew our support for worthwhile projects like yours next year.

Declining Invitations

When we must decline an invitation to speak or attend a program, we generally try to provide a response that says more than *I can't* or *I don't want to.* Unless the reasons are confidential or business secrets, try to explain them. Because responses to invitations are often taken personally, make a special effort to soften the refusal. In the following letter, an accountant must say no to the invitation from a friend's son to speak before the young man's college business club. The refusal is embedded in a long paragraph and deemphasized in a subordinate clause (*Although I must decline your invitation*). The reader naturally concentrates on the main clause that follows. In this case that main clause contains an alternative that draws attention away from the refusal.

Notice that the tone of a refusal is warm, upbeat, and positive. This refusal starts with conviviality and compliments.

Effective Memo

Dear William:

Opens cordially with buffer statement praising reader's accomplishments.

News of your leadership position in Epsilon Phi Delta, the campus business honorary club, fills me with delight and pride. Your father must be proud also of your educational and extracurricular achievements.

Explains the writer's ignorance on the topic of ethics. Lessens the impact of the refusal by placing it in a subordinate clause (*Although your invitation must be declined*) using the passive voice. Concentrates attention on the alternative.

You honor me by asking me to speak to your group in the spring about codes of ethics in the accounting field. Because our firm has not yet adopted such a code, we have been investigating the codes developed by other accounting firms. I am decidedly not an expert in this area, but I have met others who are. Although your invitation must be declined, I would like to recommend Dr. Carolyn S. Marshall, who is a member of the ethics subcommittee of the Institute of Internal Auditors. Dr. Marshall is a professor who often addresses

TECH TALK

USING TECHNOLOGY TO PERSONALIZE FORM LETTERS

If you had to send the same information to 200 or more customers, would you write a personal letter to each? Probably not! Responding to identical requests can be tedious, expensive, and time-consuming. That's why many businesses turn to form letters for messages like these: announcing upcoming sales, responding to requests for product information, and updating customers' accounts.

But your letters don't have to sound or look as if a computer wrote them. Word processing equipment can help you personalize those messages so that receivers feel they are being treated as individuals. Here's how the process works.

First, create a form letter (main document), inserting codes or "data fields" at each point where information will vary. Next, prepare a list of "variable" information, such as the customer's name and address, item ordered, balance due, or due date. These two documents (files) are then merged to create a personalized letter for each individual. It's usually wise to minimize the variable information within the body of your message to keep the merging operation as simple as possible.

Form Letter (Main Document)

Current Date
[Title] [FirstName] [LastName]
[Address 1]
[City], [State] [PostalCode]

Dear [Title] [LastName]:

Thanks for your recent order from our fall catalog.

One item that you requested, [Item], has proved to be very popular this season. Occasionally, we are able to appeal to our manufacturers to make more of a popular item. In this instance, though, our pleas went unanswered.

More than anything, we hate to disappoint customers like you, [Title] [LastName]. We pledge to do better with your future orders.

Sincerely,

Cindy Scott

List of Variable Information in Data Source

[Title] Mr.
[FirstName] Drew
[LastName] Jamison
[Street] 17924 Dreyfuss Avenue
[City] Evansville
[State] IN
[PostalCode] 47401
[Item] No. 8765 Ivory Pullover.

Completed Form Letter

Current Date

Mr. Drew Jamison
17924 Dreyfuss Avenue
Evansville, IN 47401

Dear Mr. Jamison:

Thanks for your recent order from our fall catalog.

One item that you requested, No. 8765 Ivory Pullover, has proved to be very popular this season. Occasionally, we are able to appeal to our manufacturers to make more of a popular item. In this instance, though, our pleas went unanswered.

More than anything, we hate to disappoint customers like you, Mr. Jamison. We pledge to do better with your future orders.

Sincerely,

Cindy Scott

Career Application

Bring in a business letter that could be adapted as a form letter. Using it as a guide, prepare a rough draft of the same message indicating the exact locations of all necessary variables. Then ask someone from your class or your campus computer center to demonstrate how this letter would be set up and merged using word processing software.

groups on the subject of ethics in accounting. I spoke with her about your club, and she indicated that she would be happy to consider your invitation.

Ends positively with compliments and assistance for arranging the substitute speaker.

It's good to learn that you are guiding your organization toward such constructive and timely program topics. Please call Dr. Marshall at (415) 389-2210 if you would like to arrange for her to address your club.

Although the direct refusal in this letter is softened by a subordinate clause, perhaps the refusal could have been avoided altogether. Notice how the following statement implies the refusal: *I'm certainly not an expert in this area, but I have met others who are. May I recommend Dr. Marshall. . . .* If no alternative is available, focus on something positive about the situation: *Although I'm not an expert, I commend your organization for selecting this topic.*

The following checklist reviews the steps in composing a letter refusing a routine request.

Checklist for Refusing Routine Requests

Open indirectly with a buffer. Pay a compliment to the reader, show appreciation for something done, or mention some mutual understanding. Avoid raising false hopes or thanking the reader for something you will refuse.

Provide reasons. In the body explain why the request must be denied—without revealing the refusal. Avoid negativity (*unfortunately, unwilling,* and *impossible*) and potentially damaging statements. Show how your decision benefits the reader or others, if possible.

Soften the bad news. Reduce the impact of bad news by using (1) a subordinate clause, (2) the passive voice, (3) a long sentence, or (4) a long paragraph. Consider implying the refusal, but be certain it is clear. Suggest an alternative, if a suitable one exists.

Close pleasantly. Supply more information about an alternative, look forward to future relations, or offer good wishes and compliments. Maintain a bright, personal tone. Avoid referring to the refusal.

Sending Bad News to Customers

Messages with bad news for customers follow the same pattern as other negative messages. Customer letters, though, differ in one major way: they usually include resale or sales promotion emphasis. Customer bad-news messages typically handle problems with orders, denial of claims, or credit refusals.

Handling Problems With Orders

In handling problems with orders, the indirect pattern is appropriate unless the message has some good-news elements.

Not all orders can be filled as received. Suppliers may be able to send only part of an order or none at all. Substitutions may be necessary, or the delivery date may be delayed. Suppliers may suspect that all or part of the order is a mistake; the customer may actually want something else. In writing to customers about problem orders, it's generally wise to use the direct pattern if the message has some good-news elements. But when the message is disappointing, the indirect pattern is more appropriate.

Problems with customer orders can sometimes be resolved by telephone. Large companies, though, more often rely on written messages. If the message contains any good news, begin with that. For messages that are primarily disappointing, use the indirect method, beginning with a buffer and an explanation.

Let's say you represent Live and Learn Toys, a large West Coast toy manufacturer, and you're scrambling for business in a slow year. A big customer, Child Land, calls in August and asks you to hold a block of your best-selling toy, the Space Station. Like most vendors, you require a deposit on large orders. September rolls around, and you still haven't received any money from Child Land. You must now write a tactful letter asking for the deposit—or else you will release the toy to other buyers. The problem, of course, is delivering the bad news without losing the customer's order and goodwill. Another challenge is making sure the reader understands the bad news. The following letter sandwiches the bad news (*without a deposit, we must release this block to other retailers*) between resale information and sales promotion information.

Effective Letter

Dear Mr. Ronzelli:

You were smart to reserve a block of 500 Space Stations, which we have been holding for you since August. As the holidays approach, the demand for all our learning toys, including Space Station, is rapidly increasing.

Opening compliments the receiver while establishing the facts.

Toy stores from Florida to California are asking us to ship these Space Stations. One reason the Space Station is moving out of our warehouses so quickly is its assortment of gizmos that children love, including a land rover vehicle, a shuttle craft, a hovercraft, astronauts, and even a robotic arm. As soon as we receive your deposit of $4,000, we'll have this popular item on its way to your stores. Without a deposit by September 20, though, we must release this block to other retailers. Use the enclosed envelope to send us your check immediately. You can begin showing this fascinating Live and Learn toy in your stores by November 1.

Reasons justify the coming bad news. Instead of focusing on the writer's needs (*we have a full warehouse* and *we need your deposit*), the reasons concentrate on motivating the reader. After the reasons, the bad news is clearly spelled out.

Please visit our Web site, which replaces our paper catalog, for pictures, descriptions, and prices of other popular Live and Learn toys. We were voted one of the best on-line toy stores—with higher ratings than even FAO Schwarz, Etoys, and all the biggies. We look forward to your check as well as to continuing to serve all your toy needs.

Closing promotes the company's Web site and looks ahead to future business.

Millionaire publisher Malcolm Forbes recognized that being agreeable while disagreeing is truly an art. He advised being positive and "nice." Contrary to the cliché, genuinely nice people most often finish first or very near it. He suggested using the acid test, particularly for a bad-news message. After you finish, read it out loud. You'll know if it sounds natural, positive, and respectful.

Denying Claims

Customers occasionally want something they're not entitled to or that you can't grant. They may misunderstand warranties or make unreasonable demands. Because these customers are often unhappy with a product or service, they are emotionally involved. Letters that say no to emotionally involved receivers will probably be your most challenging communication task. As publisher Malcolm Forbes observed, "To be agreeable while disagreeing—that's an art."[10]

Fortunately, the reasons-before-refusal plan helps you be empathic and artful in breaking bad news. Obviously, in denial letters you'll need to adopt the proper tone. Don't blame customers, even if they are at fault. Avoid *you* statements that sound preachy (*You would have known that cash refunds are impossible if you had read your contract*). Use neutral, objective language to explain why the claim must be refused. Consider offering resale information to rebuild the customer's confidence in your products or organization. In Figure 10.5 the writer denies a customer's claim for the difference between the price the customer paid for speakers and the price he saw advertised locally (which would have resulted in a cash refund of $151). While the catalog service does match any advertised lower price, the price-matching policy applies *only* to exact models. This claim must be rejected because the advertisement the customer submitted showed a different, older speaker model.

The letter to Matthew Tyson opens with a buffer that agrees with a statement in the customer's letter. It repeats the key idea of product confidence as a transition to the second paragraph. Next comes an explanation of the price-matching policy. The writer does not assume that the customer is trying to pull a fast one. Nor does he suggest that the customer is a dummy who didn't read or understand the price-matching policy. The safest path is a neutral explanation of the policy along with precise distinctions between the customer's speakers and the older ones. The writer also gets a chance to resell the customer's speakers and demonstrate what a quality product they are. By the end of the third paragraph, it's evident to the reader that his claim is unjustified.

Refusing Credit

Goals when refusing credit include maintaining customer goodwill and avoiding actionable language.

As much as companies want business, they can extend credit only when payment is likely to follow. Credit applications, from individuals or from businesses, are generally approved or disapproved on the basis of the applicant's credit history. This record is supplied by a credit-reporting agency, such as Experian (formerly TRW). After reviewing the applicant's record, a credit manager applies the organization's guidelines and approves or disapproves the application.

If you must deny credit to prospective customers, you have four goals in conveying the refusal:

- Avoiding language that causes hard feelings
- Retaining customers on a cash basis
- Preparing for possible future credit without raising false expectations
- Avoiding disclosures that could cause a lawsuit

Because credit applicants are likely to continue to do business with an organization even if they are denied credit, you'll want to do everything possible to encourage that patronage. Thus, keep the refusal respectful, sensitive, and upbeat. To avoid possible litigation, some organizations give no explanation of the reasons for the refusal. Instead, they provide the name of the credit-reporting agency and suggest that inquiries be directed to it. Here's a credit refusal letter that uses a buffer

FIGURE 10.5 **Denying a Claim**

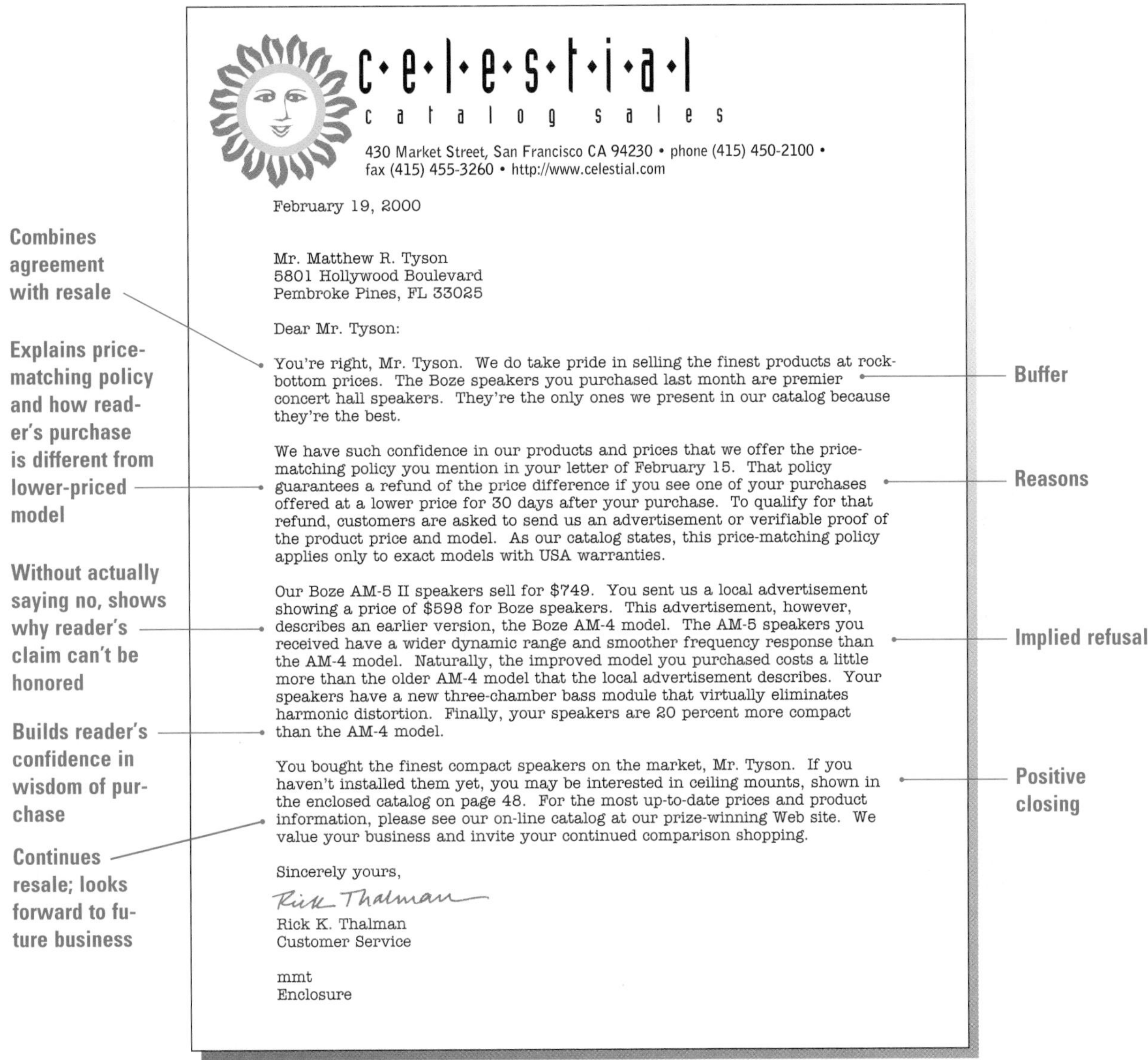

c•e•l•e•s•t•i•a•l
catalog sales
430 Market Street, San Francisco CA 94230 • phone (415) 450-2100 • fax (415) 455-3260 • http://www.celestial.com

February 19, 2000

Mr. Matthew R. Tyson
5801 Hollywood Boulevard
Pembroke Pines, FL 33025

Dear Mr. Tyson:

You're right, Mr. Tyson. We do take pride in selling the finest products at rock-bottom prices. The Boze speakers you purchased last month are premier concert hall speakers. They're the only ones we present in our catalog because they're the best.

We have such confidence in our products and prices that we offer the price-matching policy you mention in your letter of February 15. That policy guarantees a refund of the price difference if you see one of your purchases offered at a lower price for 30 days after your purchase. To qualify for that refund, customers are asked to send us an advertisement or verifiable proof of the product price and model. As our catalog states, this price-matching policy applies only to exact models with USA warranties.

Our Boze AM-5 II speakers sell for $749. You sent us a local advertisement showing a price of $598 for Boze speakers. This advertisement, however, describes an earlier version, the Boze AM-4 model. The AM-5 speakers you received have a wider dynamic range and smoother frequency response than the AM-4 model. Naturally, the improved model you purchased costs a little more than the older AM-4 model that the local advertisement describes. Your speakers have a new three-chamber bass module that virtually eliminates harmonic distortion. Finally, your speakers are 20 percent more compact than the AM-4 model.

You bought the finest compact speakers on the market, Mr. Tyson. If you haven't installed them yet, you may be interested in ceiling mounts, shown in the enclosed catalog on page 48. For the most up-to-date prices and product information, please see our on-line catalog at our prize-winning Web site. We value your business and invite your continued comparison shopping.

Sincerely yours,

Rick Thalman

Rick K. Thalman
Customer Service

mmt
Enclosure

but does not explain the reasons for the denial. Notice how the warm tone reassures the reader that she is respected and that her patronage is valued. The letter implies that her current credit condition is temporary, but it does not raise false hopes by promising future credit.

Effective Letter

Dear Ms. Margolis:

We genuinely appreciate your application of January 12 for a Fashion Express credit account.

Buffer identifies application and shows appreciation for it.

After receiving a report of your current credit record from Experian, we find that credit cannot be extended at this time. To learn more about your record, you may call an Experian credit counselor at (212) 356-0922. We've arranged

Long sentence and passive voice deemphasize bad news. To prevent possible litigation, offers no reason for denial.

for you to take advantage of this service for 60 days from the date of this letter at no charge to you.

Closes cordially and looks forward to continued patronage.

Thanks, Ms. Margolis, for the confidence you've shown in Fashion Express. We invite you to continue shopping at our stores, and we look forward to your reapplication in the future.

Some businesses do provide reasons explaining credit denials (*Credit cannot be granted because your firm's current and long-term credit obligations are nearly twice as great as your firm's total assets*). They may also provide alternatives, such as deferred billing or cash discounts. When the letter denies a credit application that accompanies an order, the message may contain resale information. The writer tries to convert the order from credit to cash.

Whatever form the bad-news letter takes, it's a good idea to have the message reviewed by legal counsel because of the litigation landmines awaiting unwary communicators in this area. The following checklist provides tips on how to craft effective bad-news letters.

Checklist for Delivering Bad News to Customers

Begin indirectly. Express appreciation (but don't thank the reader for requesting something you're about to refuse), show agreement on some point, review facts, or show understanding.

Provide reasons. Except in credit denials, justify the bad news with objective reasons. Use resale, if appropriate, to restore the customer's confidence. Avoid blaming the customer or hiding behind company policy. Look for reader benefits.

Present the bad news. State the bad news objectively or imply it. Although resale or sales promotion is appropriate in order letters, it may offend in claim or credit refusals.

Close pleasantly. Suggest action on an alternative, look forward to future business, offer best wishes, refer to gifts, or use resale sensitively. Don't mention the bad news.

Managing Negative Organization News

7

A tactful tone and a reasons-first approach help preserve friendly relations with customers. These same techniques are useful when delivering bad news to employees and when rejecting job applicants.

Announcing Bad News to Employees

Bad news within organizations might involve declining profits, lost contracts, harmful lawsuits, public relations controversies, and changes in policy. Whether you use a direct or an indirect pattern in delivering that news depends primarily on the anticipated reaction of the receiver. When bad news affects employees personally—such as cutbacks in pay, reduction of benefits, or relocation plans—you can gener-

PROCESS IN PROGRESS

CASE STUDY

Pepsi-Cola Revisited

Cathy Dial, manager of Consumer Relations at Pepsi-Cola, knows that delivering disappointing news while retaining goodwill requires tact, empathy, and good communications skills. When things go wrong or requests must be refused, customers are often upset.

When Dial must deliver disappointing news to consumers or to the public, she generally begins by expressing appreciation. "Any consumer who took the time to call or write us represents many more who did not bother to let us know that something is wrong. And people who take the time to call or write us are usually our most loyal customers. We appreciate their information, and we channel it to our internal partners within the company, such as our buyers, public relations people, marketing managers, quality control experts, and senior management." In her responses Dial usually explains what went wrong or offers reasons to justify a refusal. In some cases, she is able to offer alternatives to soften the bad news. In one promotion, Dial confesses that they underestimated customer response and ran out of gift merchandise. For these unhappy customers, she offered alternative merchandise.

She closes negative-news letters by expressing appreciation again. If the inquiry is about a product, Dial encourages customers to give Pepsi-Cola another try and encloses coupons for free products.

Critical Thinking

- How closely does Cathy Dial's pattern for delivering bad news follow the four-part plan suggested in this chapter?
- Why is consumer feedback, even when it is negative, important to an organization?
- When would form letters make sense for a company such as Pepsi-Cola?

ally lessen its impact and promote better relations by explaining reasons before revealing the bad news.

Internal bad-news memos should use the indirect pattern to convey news that adversely affects employees.

The first version of the following memo, which announces a substantial increase in the cost of employee health care benefits, suffers from many problems.

Ineffective Memo

MEMO TO: Staff

Beginning January 1 your monthly payment for health care benefits will be increased to $109 (up from $42 last year).

Hits readers with bad news without any preparation.

Every year health care costs go up. Although we considered dropping other benefits, Midland decided that the best plan was to keep the present comprehensive package. Unfortunately, we can't do that unless we pass along some of the extra cost to you. Last year the company was forced to absorb the total increase in health care premiums. However, such a plan this year is inadvisable.

Offers no explanation of why health care costs are rising. Action sounds arbitrary. Fails to take credit for absorbing previous increases.

We did everything possible to avoid the sharp increase in costs to you this year. A rate schedule describing the increases in payments for your family and dependents is enclosed.

Sounds defensive; fails to provide reasons.

The improved version of this bad-news memo, shown in Figure 10.6, uses the indirect pattern. Notice that it opens with a relevant, upbeat buffer regarding health

FIGURE 10.6 Announcing Bad News to Employees

The Three Phases of the Writing Process

1 PREWRITING

Analyze: The purpose of this memo is to tell employees that they must share with the company the increasing costs of health care.

Anticipate: The audience will be employees who are unaware of health care costs and, most likely, reluctant to pay more.

Adapt: Because the readers will probably be unhappy and resentful, use the indirect pattern.

2 WRITING

Research: Collect facts and statistics that document health care costs.

Organize: Begin with a buffer describing the company's commitment to health benefits. Provide explanation of health care costs. Announce the bad news. In the closing, focus on the company's major share of the cost.

Compose: Draft the first version on a computer.

3 REVISING

Revise: Remove negativity (*unfortunately, we can't, we were forced, inadvisable, we don't think*). Explain the increase with specifics.

Proofread: Use semicolon before *however.* Use quotes around *defensive* to show its special sense. Spell out *percent* after 300.

Evaluate: Is there any other way to help readers accept this bad news?

DATE: November 6, 2000

TO: Fellow Employees

FROM: David P. Martinez, President DPM

SUBJECT: MAINTAINING QUALITY HEALTH CARE

Health care programs have always been an important part of our commitment to employees at Midland, Inc. We're proud that our total benefits package continues to rank among the best in the country. — **Begins with positive buffer**

Offers reasons explaining why costs are rising — Such a comprehensive package does not come cheaply. In the last decade health care costs alone have risen over 300 percent. We're told that several factors fuel the cost spiral: inflation, technology improvements, increased cost of outpatient services, and "defensive" medicine practiced by doctors to prevent lawsuits.

Reveals bad news clearly but embeds it in paragraph — Just two years ago our monthly health care cost for each employee was $415. It rose to $469 last year. We were able to absorb that jump without increasing your contribution. But this year's hike to $539 forces us to ask you to share the increase. To maintain your current health care benefits, you will be paying $109 a month. The enclosed rate schedule describes the costs for families and dependents.

Ends positively by stressing the company's major share of the costs — Midland continues to pay the major portion of your health care program ($430 each month). We think it's a wise investment.

Enclosure

care—but says nothing about increasing costs. For a smooth transition, the second paragraph begins with a key idea from the opening (*comprehensive package*). The reasons section discusses rising costs with explanations and figures. The bad news (*you will be paying $109 a month*) is clearly presented but embedded within the paragraph. Throughout, the writer strives to show the fairness of the company's position. The ending, which does not refer to the bad news, emphasizes how much the company is paying and what a wise investment it is. Notice that the entire memo demonstrates a kinder, gentler approach than that shown in the first draft. Of prime importance in breaking bad news to employees is providing clear, convincing reasons that explain the decision.

Organizations can sustain employee morale by communicating bad news openly and honestly.

Most organizations involved in a crisis (serious performance problems, major relocation, massive layoffs, management shakeup, or public controversy) prefer to communicate the news openly to employees, customers, and stockholders. Instead of letting rumors distort the truth, they explain the organization's side of the story honestly and early. Morale can be destroyed when employees learn of major events affecting their jobs through the grapevine or from news accounts—rather than from management. For example, Exxon's poor handling of the *Valdez* oil spill—including delaying release of information and downplaying the environmental damage—harmed employee morale, angered stockholders, and lost the company thousands of customers.

Saying *No* to Job Applicants

Being refused a job is one of life's major rejections. The blow is intensified by tactless letters (*Unfortunately, you were not among the candidates selected for . . .*).

Letters that deny applications for employment should be courteous and tactful but free of specifics that could trigger lawsuits.

You can reduce the receiver's disappointment somewhat by using the indirect pattern—with one important variation. In the reasons section it's wise to be vague in explaining why the candidate was not selected. First, giving concrete reasons may be painful to the receiver (*Your grade point average of 2.7 was low compared with GPAs of other candidates*). Second, and more important, providing extra information may prove fatal in a lawsuit. Hiring and firing decisions generate considerable litigation today. To avoid charges of discrimination or wrongful actions, legal advisors warn organizations to keep employment rejection letters general, simple, and short.

The following job refusal letter is tactful but intentionally vague. It implies that the applicant's qualifications don't match those needed for the position, but the letter doesn't reveal anything specific.

Dear Mr. Danson:

Thanks for letting us review your résumé submitted for our advertised management trainee opening.

Shows appreciation. Doesn't indicate good or bad news.

We received a number of impressive résumés for this opening. Although another candidate was selected, your interest in our organization is appreciated. So that you may continue your search for a position at another organization, we are writing to you immediately.

To prevent possible lawsuits, gives no explanation. Places bad news in a dependent clause.

We wish you every success in finding a position that exactly fits your qualifications.

Ends with best wishes.

The following checklist gives tips on how to communicate bad news within an organization.

Checklist for Managing Negative Organization News

 **Start with a relevant, upbeat buffer.** Open with a small bit of good news, praise, appreciation, agreement, understanding, or a discussion of facts leading to the reasons section.

 **Discuss reasons.** Except in job refusal letters, explain what caused the decision necessitating the bad news. Use objective, nonjudgmental, and nondiscriminatory language. Show empathy and fairness.

 **Reveal the bad news.** Make the bad news clear but don't accentuate it. Avoid negative language.

 **Close harmoniously.** End on a positive, friendly note. For job refusals, extend good wishes.

Presenting Bad News in Other Cultures

Communicating bad news in other cultures may require different strategies.

To minimize disappointment, Americans generally prefer to present negative messages indirectly. Other cultures may treat bad news differently.

In Germany, for example, business communicators occasionally use buffers but tend to present bad news directly. British writers also tend to be straightforward with bad news, seeing no reason to soften its announcement. In Latin countries the question is not how to organize negative messages but whether to present them at all. It's considered disrespectful and impolite to report bad news to superiors. Thus, reluctant employees may fail to report accurately any negative messages to their bosses.

In Asian cultures, harmony and peace are sought in all relationships. Disrupting the harmony with bad news is avoided. To prevent discord, Japanese communicators use a number of techniques to indicate *no*—without being forced to say it. In conversation they may respond with silence or with a counter question, such as "Why do you ask?" They may change the subject or tell a white lie to save face for themselves and for the questioner. Sometimes the answer sounds like a qualified *yes*: "I will do my best, but if I cannot, I hope you will understand," "Yes, but . . . ," or "yes" followed by an apology. All of these responses should be recognized as *no*.

In China, Westerners often have difficulty understanding the "hints" given by communicators.

"I agree" might mean "I agree with 15 percent of what you say."

"We might be able to" could mean "Not a chance."

"We will consider" could mean "WE will, but the real decision maker will not."

"That is a little too much" might equate to "That is outrageous."[11]

In Thailand the negativism represented by a refusal is completely alien; the word *no* does not exist. In many cultures negative news is offered with such subtleness or in such a positive light that it may be overlooked or misunderstood by literal-minded Americans. To understand the meaning of what's really being communicated, we must look beyond an individual's actual words, considering the communication style, the culture, and especially the context.

You've now studied the indirect method for revealing bad news and analyzed many examples of messages applying this method. As you observed, business writers generally try to soften the blow; however, they do eventually reveal the bad news. No effort is made to sweep it under the carpet or ignore it totally.

PROCESS TO PRODUCT

CASE STUDY

Applying Your Skills at Pepsi-Cola

Large organizations such as Pepsi-Cola receive many inquiries requesting donations to charities, sponsorship of charitable projects, and contribution of free products. Parent company PepsiCo believes that as a corporate citizen, it has a responsibility to contribute to the quality of life in its community. It sponsors local programs and supports employee volunteer activities including contributions of time, talent, and funds. Each division is responsible for its own giving program, but generally corporate giving is focused on activities in which PepsiCo employees can participate. Its corporate policy is spelled out at its Web site: **www.pepsico.com/corp.overview.html.**

Assume that a recent request came from Direct Relief, one of the largest nonsectarian health assistance agencies in the world. Specifically, Direct Relief asks Pepsi-Cola to make a major contribution toward purchasing a Mobile Surgical Clinic to aid poor people in remote areas of China. Direct Relief sends volunteer physicians and dentists, medical supplies, and food to aid underserved communities and victims of natural and civil disasters in the U.S. and abroad. Although she was impressed by Direct Relief's videotape, literature, and letter appealing for help, Dial must refuse the request because of Pepsi-Cola's corporate giving policy.

Your Job

As an assistant to Cathy Dial, draft a refusal letter to Dr. Melville Haskins, Direct Relief, 27 La Patera Lane, Santa Barbara, CA 93117. Dial is touched by Dr. Haskin's appeal on behalf of Direct Relief, and she tries to think of some way to help. She asks you to check with Pepsi-Cola's newsletter editor to see if she would like to run an article about Direct Relief and perhaps motivate some employees to volunteer to help in its local health assistance programs. (The newsletter editor agrees and asks you to send her any Direct Relief literature you have.) Decide how to handle the refusal based on what you learned in this chapter.

Summary of Learning Objectives

1 **Describe the goals of business communicators in delivering bad news.** Good communicators strive to (a) make the reader understand and accept the bad news, (b) promote and maintain a good image of themselves and their organizations, (c) make the message so clear that additional correspondence is unnecessary, and (d) avoid creating legal liability or responsibility.

2 **Identify the causes of legal problems in business writing.** Abusive language is libelous and actionable when it is false, damages a person's reputation, and is "published"—spoken within the presence of others or written. Even careless language (saying, for instance, that a manufacturing plant is "dangerous") can result in litigation. Moreover, any messages written on company stationery represent that company and can be legally binding.

3 **Explain the components of a bad-news message.** Begin with a buffer, such as a compliment, appreciation, a point of agreement, objective information, understanding, or some part of the message that represents good news. Then

explain the reasons that necessitate the bad news, trying to cite benefits to the reader or others. Choose positive words, and clarify company policy if necessary. Announce the bad news strategically, mentioning a compromise or alternative if possible. Close pleasantly with a forward-looking goodwill statement.

4 **Compare the direct and indirect patterns for breaking bad news.** List situations in which the direct pattern is better. Direct messages begin by announcing the bad news immediately. Indirect messages, on the other hand, begin with a buffer, offer explanation, and then disclose the bad news. The direct pattern is most effective when (a) the receiver may overlook the bad news, (b) organization policy suggests directness, (c) the receiver prefers directness, (d) firmness is necessary, or (e) the bad news is not damaging.

5 **Identify routine requests and describe a strategy for refusing such requests.** Routine requests ask for favors, money, information, action, and other items. When the answer will be disappointing, use the reasons-before-refusal pattern. Open with a buffer; provide reasons; announce the refusal sensitively; suggest possible alternatives; and end with a positive, forward-looking comment.

6 **Describe a strategy for sending bad news to customers while retaining their goodwill.** In addition to using the indirect pattern, consider including resale information (reassuring the customer of a wise choice) or sales promotion (pushing a new product). Be especially careful of the tone of words used. Strive for a warm tone using neutral, objective language. Avoid blaming customers.

7 **Explain the best strategy for managing negative organization news.** When breaking bad news to employees, use the indirect pattern but be sure to provide clear, convincing reasons that explain the decision. In refusing job applicants, however, keep letters short, general, and tactful.

8 **Compare strategies for revealing bad news in different cultures.** American communicators often prefer to break bad news slowly and indirectly. In other low-context cultures, such as Germany and Britain, however, bad news is revealed directly. In high-context cultures, straightforwardness is avoided. In Latin cultures bad news may be totally suppressed. In Asian cultures negativism is avoided and hints may suggest bad news. Subtle meanings must be interpreted carefully.

CHAPTER REVIEW

1. Discuss four goals of a business communicator who must deliver bad news. (Obj. 1)
2. How can business documents in an organization's files become part of a lawsuit? (Obj. 2)
3. Describe the four parts of the indirect message pattern. (Obj. 3)
4. Why should a writer give reasons before revealing bad news? (Obj. 3)
5. Name four or more ways to deemphasize bad news when it is presented. (Obj. 3)

6. What is the most important difference between direct and indirect letters? (Obj. 4)
7. Name five situations in which the direct pattern should be used for bad news. (Obj. 4)
8. Name four kinds of routine requests that businesses must frequently refuse. (Obj. 5)
9. Why should you be especially careful in cushioning the refusal to an invitation? (Obj. 5)
10. What is the major difference between bad-news messages for customers and those for other people? (Obj. 6)
11. List four goals a writer seeks to achieve in writing messages that deny credit to prospective customers. (Obj. 6)
12. Why should a writer be somewhat vague in the reasons section of a letter rejecting a job applicant? (Obj. 7)
13. When organizations must reveal a crisis (such as the Exxon *Valdez* disaster), how should they communicate the news to employees, customers, stockholders, and the public? (Obj. 7)
14. Why is the reasons-before-refusal strategy appropriate for customers who are unhappy with a product or service? (Obj. 6)
15. In Latin countries why may employees sometimes fail to accurately report any negative message to management? (Obj. 8)

CRITICAL THINKING

1. Does bad news travel faster and farther than good news? Why? What implications would this have for companies responding to unhappy customers? (Objs. 1–7)
2. Some people feel that all employee news, good or bad, should be announced directly. Do you agree or disagree? Why? (Objs. 1, 3, and 4)
3. Consider times when you have been aware that others have used the indirect pattern in writing or speaking to you. How did you react? (Objs. 1 and 3)
4. What are the legal and ethical ramifications of using company stationery to write personal letters? (Obj. 2)
5. **Ethical Issue:** In considering negative organization news, should companies immediately reveal grave illnesses of key executives? Or should executives be entitled to keep their health a private matter? Does it matter if the company is public or private? (Objs. 3 and 7)

ACTIVITIES

10.1 Organizational Patterns (Objs. 3–7)

Identify which organizational pattern you would use for the following messages: direct or indirect.

a. A letter refusing a request by a charitable organization asking your restaurant chain to provide refreshments for a large reception.

b. A memo from the manager denying an employee's request for computer access to the Web. Although the employee works closely with the manager on many projects, the employee's work does not require Internet access.

c. An announcement to employees that a fitness specialist has canceled a scheduled lunchtime talk and cannot reschedule.

d. A letter from a bank refusing to fund a company's overseas expansion plan.

e. A form letter from an insurance company announcing new policy requirements that many policyholders may resent. If policyholders do not indicate the plan they prefer, they may lose their insurance coverage.

f. A letter from an amusement park refusing the request of a customer who was unhappy with a substitute concert performer.

g. The last in a series of letters from a collection agency demanding payment of a long-overdue account. The next step will be hiring an attorney.

h. A letter from a computer company refusing to authorize repair of a customer's computer on which the warranty expired six months ago.

i. A memo from an executive refusing a manager's plan to economize by purchasing reconditioned computers. The executive and the manager both appreciate efficient, straightforward messages.

j. A letter informing a customer that the majority of the customer's recent order will not be available for six weeks.

10.2 Passive-Voice Verbs (Obj. 3)

Revise the following sentences to present the bad news with passive-voice verbs.

a. We do not serve meals on any flights other than those during meal times.

b. No one is allowed to park in the yellow zone.

c. Because of our Web site, we are no longer offering a printed catalog.

d. We are unable to grant your request for a loan.

10.3 Subordinating Bad News (Obj. 3)

Revise the following sentences to position the bad news in a subordinate clause. (Hint: Consider beginning the clause with *Although.*) Use passive-voice verbs for the bad news.

a. We cannot refund your purchase price, but we are sending you two coupons toward your next purchase.

b. We appreciate your interest in our organization. Unfortunately, we are unable to extend an employment offer to you at this time.

c. It is impossible for us to ship your complete order at this time. However, we are able to send the four oak desks now; you should receive them within five days.

d. You are able to increase the number of physician visits you make, but we find it necessary to increase the cost of your monthly health benefit contribution.

10.4 Implying Bad News (Obj. 3)

Revise the following statements to *imply* the bad news. Use passive-voice verbs and subordinate clauses to further deemphasize the bad news.

a. I already have an engagement in my appointment calendar for the date you mention. Therefore, I am unable to speak to your group. However, I would like to recommend another speaker who might be able to address your organization.

b. Because of the holiday period, all our billboard space was used this month. Therefore, we are sorry to say that we could not give your charitable group free display space. However, next month, after the holidays, we hope to display your message as we promised.

c. We cannot send you a price list nor can we sell our equipment directly to customers. Our policy is to sell only through dealers, and your dealer is Stereo City, located on Grove Street in Oklahoma City.

10.5 Evaluating Bad-News Statements (Obj. 3)

Discuss the strengths or weaknesses of the following bad-news statements.

a. It's impossible for us to ship your order before May 1.

b. Frankly, we like your résumé, but we were hoping to hire someone a little younger who might be able to stay with us longer.

c. I'm thoroughly disgusted with this entire case, and I will never do business with shyster lawyers like you again.

d. We can assure you that on any return visit to our hotels, you will not be treated so poorly.

e. We must deny your credit application because your record shows a history of late payments, nonpayment, and irregular employment.

f. (*In a confidential company memo:*) I cannot recommend that we promote this young lady into any position where she will meet the public. Her colorful facial decoration, as part of her religion, may offend our customers.

10.6 Negative News in Other Cultures (Obj. 8)

Interview fellow students or work colleagues who are from other cultures. How is negative news handled in their cultures? How would typical individuals refuse a request for a favor, for example? How would a business refuse credit to customers? How would an individual be turned down for a job? Is directness practiced? Report your findings to the class.

10.7 Document for Analysis: Refusal of a Favor Request (Objs. 1, 3, 4, and 6)

Analyze the following letter. List its weaknesses. If your instructor directs, revise it.

Ineffective Letter

Dear Mr. Waters:

Unfortunately, we cannot permit you to apply the lease payments you've been making for the past ten months toward the purchase of your Sako 600 copier.

Company policy does not allow such conversion. Have you ever wondered why we can offer such low leasing and purchase prices? Obviously, we couldn't stay in business long if we agreed to proposals such as yours.

You've had the Sako 600 copier for ten months now, Mr. Waters, and you say you like its versatility and reliability. Perhaps we could interest you in another Sako model—one that's more within your price range. Do give us a call.

10.8 Document for Analysis: Negative News for Customers (Objs. 1, 3, 4, and 6)

Analyze the following letter. List its weaknesses. If your instructor directs, revise it.

Ineffective Letter

Dear Charge Customers:

This letter is being sent to you to announce the termination of in-house charge accounts at Golden West Print and Frame Shop. We are truly sorry that we can no longer offer this service.

Because some customers abused the privilege, we must eliminate local charge accounts. We regret that we must take this action, but we found that carrying our own credit had become quite costly. To continue the service would have meant raising our prices. As a small but growing business, we decided it was more logical to drop the in-house charges. As a result, we are forced to begin accepting bank credit cards, including VISA and MasterCard.

Please accept our apologies in trimming our services somewhat. We hope to see you soon when we can show you our new collection of museum-quality gilded wood frames.

10.9 Document for Analysis: Saying No to a Job Applicant (Objs. 1, 2, 3, and 7)

Analyze the following letter. List its weaknesses. If your instructor directs, revise it.

Ineffective Letter

Dear Mr. Franklin:

Ms. Sievers and I wish to thank you for the pleasure of allowing us to interview you last Thursday. We were delighted to learn about your superb academic record, and we also appreciated your attentiveness in listening to our description of the operations of the Maxwell Corporation.

However, we had many well-qualified applicants who were interested in the advertised position of human resources assistant. As you may have guessed, we were particularly eager to find a minority individual who could help us fill out our Affirmative Action goals. Although you did not fit one of our goal areas, we enjoyed talking with you. We hired a female graduate of Texas Technical University who had most of the qualities we sought.

Although we realize that the job market is difficult at this time, you have our heartfelt wishes for good luck in finding precisely what you are looking for.

10.10 Request Refusal: The End of Free Credit Reports (Obj. 5)

Critical Thinking **Web**

You are part of the customer service team at Experian, the largest supplier of consumer and business credit information in the world. Experian took over TRW Information Systems & Services back in 1996. Experian currently employs over 11,000 people in the United States, United Kingdom, Continental Europe, Africa, and Asia Pacific. As a service to consumers, Experian at one time provided complimentary credit reports. However, it now offers them only in certain states and to certain groups of people.

Experian's Web site explains its new policy in its FAQs (Frequently Asked Questions). Your boss says to you, "I guess not everyone is able to learn about our new policy by going to our Web site because we still receive bundles of requests for free reports. I'm unhappy with the letter we've been using to respond to these requests. I want you to compose a draft of a new form letter that we can send to people who inquire. You should look at our Web site to see who gets free reports and in what states."

Because you are fairly new to Experian, you ask your boss what prompted the change in policy. She sighs and says, "It was a good idea, but it got out of hand. So-called 'credit repair' companies would refer their clients to us for free credit reports, and then they advised their clients to dispute every item on the report. The Federal Trade Commission actually called these companies *fraudulent.* We had to change our policy. But you can read more about it at our Web site." You resolve to study the Experian Web site (**www.experian.com**) closely. Your task is to write a letter refusing the requests of people who want free credit reports. But you must also explain the reasons for the change in policy, as well as its exceptions. Decide whether you should tell consumers how to order a copy and how to pay for it. Although your letter will be used repeatedly for such requests, address your draft to Mrs. Sherry Bennett, 250 Bruce Street, Morrilton, AR 72110. Sign it with your boss's name, Elizabeth Buerkle.

10.11 Request Refusal: Adieu to Cadillacs in Paris (Objs. 5 and 6)

"As I'm sure you've noticed, Cadillac has been on a bit of a roll lately with the world-wide launch of the all-new Seville and the much-awaited launch of the Escalade," began the GM invitation letter. This letter was sent to many of the top automotive journalists in the country inviting them to join GM's executives on a five-day all-expenses paid press trip to Paris. Such junkets were not unusual. Big Three automakers routinely sponsored the trips of reporters to ensure favorable local coverage from the big auto shows in Paris, Frankfurt, Geneva, and Tokyo. GM particularly wanted reporters at the Paris show. This is the show where it hoped to position Cadillac as a global luxury car manufacturer. The invitation letter, mailed in July, promised a "sneak peak at Cadillac's first major concept vehicle in nearly 10 years." But GM had only 20 spots available for the trip, and journalists had to request one of the spots. Suddenly, in late July, GM found itself in the midst of an expensive strike. "All at once, what had seemed like a good idea started to look fiscally irresponsible," said J. Christopher Preuss, Cadillac spokesman. Although exact figures were not available, some estimates held that the Paris trip could easily cost $12,000 per reporter. That's a large bill for a company facing a prolonged, damaging strike.

As an assistant to Mr. Preuss, you are to write to the journalists who signed up for the trip. Announce that GM must back out. About the best thing they can expect now is an invitation to the gala unveiling and champagne reception GM will sponsor in January at the Detroit auto show. At that time GM will brief reporters about Cadillac's "new vision" and unveil the eye-popping Escalade. Mr. Preuss is embarrassed about canceling the Paris trip, but he feels GM must do what is financially prudent. Address the first letter to Rodney M. Puckett, 18543 Haggerty Road, Livonia, MI 48152.[12]

10.12 Request Refusal: Ascending Sales Stars (Obj. 5)

Dustin O'Hair, a magazine editor, asks your organization, Panatronics International, for confidential information regarding the salaries and commissions of your top sales representatives. The magazine, *Marketing Monthly,* plans to spotlight young sales professionals "whose stars are ascending." You've got some great young superstars, as well as many excellent mature sales representatives. Frankly, the publicity would be excellent.

You would agree in a minute except that (1) you don't want to be forced to pick favorites among your sales reps and (2) you can't reveal private salary data. Every sales rep operates under an individual salary contract. During salary negotiations several years ago, an agreement was reached in which both sales staff members and management agreed to keep the terms of these individual contracts confidential. Perhaps the editor would be satisfied with a list that ranks your top sales reps for the past five years. You could also send a fact sheet describing your top reps. You notice that three of the current top sales reps are under the age of thirty-five. Write a refusal that retains the goodwill of *Marketing Monthly,* 145 Fifth Avenue, New York, NY 10011.

10.13 Request Refusal: Saying *No* to Under-21 Crowd on Carnival Cruises (Obj. 5)

Web

The world's largest cruise line finds itself in a difficult position. Carnival climbed to the number one spot by promoting fun at sea and pitching its appeal to younger customers who were drawn to on-board discos, swim-up bars, and hassle-free partying. But apparently the partying of high school and college students went too far. Roving bands of teens had virtually taken over some cruises in recent years. Travel agents complained of "drunken, loud behavior," as reported by Mike Driscall, editor of *Cruise Week.*

To crack down, Carnival raised the drinking age from 18 to 21 and required more chaperoning of school groups. But young individual travelers were still unruly and disruptive. Thus, Carnival instituted a new policy, effective immediately. No one under 21 may travel unless accompanied by an adult over 25. Says Vicki Freed, Carnival's vice president for marketing, "We will turn them back at the docks, and they will not get refunds." As Eric Rivera, a Carnival marketing manager, you must respond to the inquiry of April Corcoran of Counselor Travel, a New York travel agency that features special spring- and summer-break packages for college and high school students.

Counselor Travel has been one of Carnival's best customers. However, Carnival no longer wants to encourage unaccompanied young people. You must refuse the request of Ms. Corcoran to help set up student tour packages. Carnival discourages even chaperoned tours. Its real market is now family packages. You must write to Counselor and break the bad news. Try to promote fun-filled, carefree cruises destined for sunny, exotic ports of call that remove guests from the stresses of everyday life. By the way, Carnival attracts more passengers than any other cruise line—over a million people a year from all over the world. And over 98 percent of Carnival's guests say that they were well satisfied. For more information about Carnival, you might visit its Web site: **www.carnival.com**.

Write your letter to April Corcoran, Counselor Travel Agency, 520 West Third Street, New York, NY 10013. Send her a schedule for spring and summer Caribbean cruises. Tell her you will call during the week of January 5 to help her plan special family tour packages.[13]

10.14 Request Refusal: Turning Down Software Training (Objs. 5 and 6)

As Gail Jones, director of marketing, Trinity Software Systems, 111 Peach Road, Atlanta, GA 30367, you are confronted with the task of denying a favor to a potential customer. Ava Brown, principal, Heritage School, 9201 Magnolia Way, Atlanta, GA 30367, is interested in purchasing your educational software system, but she wants training from Trinity for 65 Heritage teachers and staff. The training costs would be extensive, but the real problem is that Trinity doesn't have the personnel for this huge task. Instead, Trinity would like to train one or two Heritage teachers as on-site trainers. These teacher-trainers then would instruct other Heritage teachers and staff. Trinity also would provide training videotapes and a training program guide.

Using teacher-trainers at other schools has kept Trinity's staff expenses low. Thus far, schools have been satisfied with the result. In fact, schools that use Trinity software enjoy having their own "experts" on hand. Because Trinity maintains an ongoing relationship with them, teacher-trainers are informed of software updates and can get help if they need it. The software is user friendly, and many local schools use it. Other software companies often provide such "hit and run" training that schools have difficulty using their software, even though all teachers supposedly have been trained. These companies offer little to the many teachers who have questions long after most training is over. Write a letter to Mrs. Brown denying her request but keeping her as a potential customer. Send her a training program guide and a training video. Offer to put her in touch with a teacher-trainer from a nearby school. She can reach you at (404) 921-1489.

10.15 Request Refusal: Mountain Bike Race Regrets (Objs. 5 and 6)

As president of CycleWorld you must refuse a request from the North American Biking Association. This group wants your company to become a major sponsor of the first annual Durango World Mountain Bike Championship—to the tune of $30,000! This is one tune you can't dance to. The stakes are just too high. You applaud NABA for its proactive stance in encouraging families to participate in the sport of mountain biking. NABA was also instrumental in opening up ski resorts to mountain bikers during the summer months. Actually, you'd like to support the Durango World Mountain Bike Championship. There's no doubt that such races increase interest in mountain biking and ridership. You have sponsored some bike races in the past, but for small amounts—usually under $500—which paid for trophies. But the NABA wants to offer large cash prizes and pay the expenses of big-name champions to enter.

You are a small Eugene, Oregon, company, and all your current profits are being ploughed into research to compete with the Japanese imports. You're very proud of your newly introduced brake pads and trigger-action shift levers. But these kinds of engineering breakthroughs are costly. You don't have the big bucks NABA wants. You wouldn't mind taking an ad in their program or contributing $500 toward trophies. But that's the limit. Write a refusal to Christopher Van Wijk, North American Biking Association, 8310 Montague Expressway, San Jose, CA 95131.

10.16 Request Refusal: Rock Band Banned for Violating Sound Limits (Obj. 6)

Residents living near the Peachtree Bowl, an outdoor amphitheater, were more than relieved when the rock band Tool was banned from future concerts. At the recent Tool concert, the head-banging band exceeded Bowl sound limits for its entire show. Despite persistent warnings from Bowl personnel, Tool played at levels of over 110 decibels. The Bowl limit is 102. After the performance, Tool was fined $3,000 and banned from future appearances.

Ian Martin, a teenager who had attended the Tool concert, thinks the ban is excessive punishment. In a letter to the general manager of the Peachtree Bowl, Martin implores the bowl to invite Tool back for its summer tour. He argues that a previous INXS concert surpassed decibel limits, but that the band was fined only a few hundred dollars. He also points to a statement from a Bowl spokesman that nearly every performer breaks decibel limits at the Bowl, though admittedly not as badly as Tool did. Moreover, sound limits were established in the 1970s, Martin argues, before bands like Tool learned to rely on volume to deliver their unique sound. "Sound limits just aren't valid anymore," writes Martin, "and they interfere with the artists' creative freedom."

Although Martin's arguments may have some validity, it is Sam Scranton's job to enforce current sound limits, not change them. As general manager of the Peachtree Bowl, he's responsible for informing visiting bands of the sound limits. His crew monitors sound levels and warns bands when they play too loudly. Those that don't comply are fined, says Scranton, but most bands do stay within the limits or exceed them only once or twice during a show. Tool seemed to ignore them completely, although the band was aware of the limits and before the show agreed to comply. The noise was so loud that police reported nearly twice the average number of noise complaints from area residents during the concert.

As Scranton's assistant, it is now your job to reply to Ian Martin. You need to tell Martin about Bowl sound limits and explain that Tool will not be invited back for its summer tour. You think that concert sites away from residential areas would be more inviting for a band like Tool. Incidently, the bowl does have a great summer line-up, including INXS, Matchbox 20, and the Red Hot Chili

Peppers. For Sam Scranton's signature, write a convincing letter to Ian Martin, 1428 Hatton Ford Road, Hartwell, GA 30643.

10.17 Customer Bad News: The StairClimber or the LifeStep? (Obj. 6)

Critical Thinking

You are delighted to receive a large order from Kendra Coleman, Gold's Gym, 2439 Green Street, Champaign, IL 61821. This order includes two Lifecycle Trainers (at $1,295 each), four Pro Abdominal Boards (at $295 each), three Tunturi Muscle Trainers (at $749 each), and three Dual-Action StairClimbers (at $1,545 each)

You could ship immediately except for one problem. The Dual-Action StairClimber is intended for home use, not for gym or club use. Customers like it because they say it's more like scaling a mountain than climbing a flight of stairs. With each step, users exercise their arms to pull or push themselves up. And its special cylinders absorb shock so that no harmful running impact results. However, this model is not what you would recommend for gym use. You feel Ms. Coleman should order your premier stairclimber, the LifeStep (at $2,395 each) This unit has sturdier construction and is meant for heavy use. Its sophisticated electronics provide a selection of customer-pleasing programs that challenge muscles progressively with a choice of workouts. It also quickly multiplies workout gains with computer-controlled interval training. Electronic monitors inform users of step height, calories burned, elapsed time, upcoming levels, and adherence to fitness goals. For gym use the LifeStep is clearly better than the StairClimber. The bad news is that the LifeStep is considerably more expensive.

You get no response when you try to telephone Ms. Coleman to discuss the problem. Should you ship what you can, or hold the entire order until you learn whether she wants the StairClimber or the LifeStep? Or perhaps you should substitute the LifeStep and send only two of them. Decide what to do and write a letter to Ms. Coleman.

10.18 Customer Bad News: Depressed Mattress (Obj. 6)

Team

The following letter was sent in response to a customer's complaint about depressions in your company's BeautyTest mattress. Your company receives enough of these kinds of letters to warrant preparation of a standard response. As an evaluation of your writing skills, your boss asks you and some other interns to come up with a better response. If your letter is better, he may begin using it to pattern similar responses. The problem seems to be that customers don't understand how the unique coil system works. And they have not read the mattress warranty. Get together with your intern team and discuss the faults in this letter before generating a new, more effective letter. Write to Mrs. Shannon Kearney, 1176 53rd Court, West Palm Beach, FL 34624.

Ineffective Letter

Dear Mrs. Kearney:

We have received your letter of May 23 demanding repair or replacement for your newly purchased BeautyTest mattress. You say that you enjoy sleeping on it; but in the morning when you and your husband get up, you claim that the mattress has body impressions that remain all day.

Unfortunately, Mrs. Kearney, we can neither repair nor replace your mattress because those impressions are perfectly normal. If you will read your warranty carefully, you will find this statement: "Slight body impressions will appear with use and are not indicative of structural failure. The body-conforming coils and comfort cushioning materials are beginning to work for you and impressions are caused by the natural settling of these materials."

When you purchased your mattress, I'm sure your salesperson told you that the BeautyTest mattress has a unique, scientifically designed system of individually pocketed coils that provide separate support for each person occupying the bed. This unusual construction, with those hundreds of independently operating coils, reacts to every body contour, providing luxurious comfort. At the same time, this system provides firm support. It is this unique design that's causing the body impressions that you see when you get up in the morning.

Although we never repair or replace a mattress when it merely shows slight impressions, we will send our representative out to inspect your mattress, if it would make you feel better. Please call for an appointment at (800) 322-9800. Remember, on a BeautyTest mattress you get the best night's rest possible.

Cordially,

10.19 Customer Bad News: Wilted Landscaping (Obj. 6)

As Kissandra Powell, owner of Town & Country Landscaping, you must refuse the following request. Mr. and Mrs. Paul Alexander have asked that you replace the landscaping in the home they recently purchased in Kettering. You had landscaped that home nearly a year ago for the former owner, Mrs. Hunter, installing a sod lawn and many shrubs, trees, and flowers. It looked beautiful when you finished, but six months later, Mrs. Hunter sold the property and moved to Dayton. Four months elapsed before the new owners moved in. After four months of neglect and a hot, dry summer, the newly installed landscaping suffered.

You guarantee all your work and normally would replace any plants that do not survive. Under these circumstances, however, you do not feel justified in making any refund because your guarantee necessarily presumes proper maintenance on the part of the property owner. Moreover, your guarantee is made only to the individual who contracted with you—not to subsequent owners. You would like to retain the goodwill of the new owners, since this is an affluent neighborhood and you hope to attract additional work here. On the other hand, you can't afford to replace the materials invested in this job. You believe that the lawn could probably be rejuvenated with deep watering and fertilizer.

You would be happy to inspect the property and offer suggestions to the Alexanders. In reality, you wonder if the Alexanders might not have a claim against the former owner or the escrow agency for failing to maintain the property. Clearly, however, the claim is not against you. Write to Mr. and Mrs. Paul Alexander, 3318 Clearview Drive, Kettering, OH 45429.

10.20 Customer Bad News: Refusing Claim to Evict Noisy Neighbor (Obj. 6)

As Arman Aryai, you must deny the request of Robert Brockway, one of the tenants in your three-story office building. Mr. Brockway, a CPA, demands that you immediately evict a neighboring tenant who plays loud music throughout the day, interfering with Mr. Brockway's conversations with clients and with his concentration. The noisy tenant, Ryan McInnis, seems to operate an entertainment booking agency and spends long hours in his office. You know you can't evict Mr. McInnis immediately because of his lease. Moreover, you hesitate to do anything drastic because paying tenants are hard to find.

After talking with your attorney, you decide that you will call the noisy tenant and ask him to tone in down. If after 30 days the noise persists, you will consider starting eviction proceedings. In the meantime, you must write a response to Mr. Brockway. Deny his request but tell him how you plan to resolve the problem. Write to Robert Brockway, CPA, Suite 203, Pico Building, 1405 Wilshire Boulevard, Santa Monica, CA 90405.

10.21 Customer Bad News: The Sports Connection (Obj. 6)

As manager of the Sports Connection, you must refuse the application of Wendy Takahashi for an extended membership in your athletic club. This is strictly a business decision. You liked Wendy very much when she applied, and she seems genuinely interested in fitness and a healthful lifestyle. However, your "extended membership" plan qualifies the member for all your testing, exercise, aerobics, and recreation programs. This multiservice program is necessarily expensive and requires a solid credit rating. To your disappointment, however, you learned that Wendy's credit rating is decidedly negative. Her credit report indicates that she is delinquent in payments to four businesses, including Holiday Health Spa, your principal competitor.

You do have other programs, including your "Drop In and Work Out" plan that offers use of available facilities on a cash basis. This plan enables a member to reserve space on the racquetball and handball courts; the member can also sign up for exercise and aerobics classes, space permitting. Since Wendy is far in debt, you would feel guilty allowing her to plunge in any more deeply. Refuse her credit application, but encourage her cash business. Suggest that she make an inquiry to the credit reporting company Experian to learn about her credit report. She is eligible to receive a free credit report if she mentions this application. Write to Wendy Takahashi, Mountain View Apartments, Apartment 16E, 1406 North Verdugo Road, Glendale, CA 91401.

10.22 Customer Bad News: Godmother Wants to Cater (Obj. 6)

Revise the following ineffective letter that refuses credit to Mrs. Andria Moreno, GodMother Enterprises, 905 North Gulf Drive, Fort Lauderdale, FL 33334.

Ineffective Letter

Dear Ms. Moreno:

This is to inform you that we have received your recent order. However, we are unable to fill this order because of the bad credit record you have on file at Experian (formerly TRW Information and Reporting Services).

We understand that at this point in time you are opening a new gourmet catering business called "The God-Mother." Our sales rep left us one of your sample menus, and I must say that we were all impressed with your imaginative international selections, including duck lasagna and chicken fettuccine verde. Although we are sure your catering business will be a success, we cannot extend credit because of your poor credit rating.

Did you know that you can find out what's in your credit file? The Fair Credit Reporting Act guarantees you the right to see the information contained in your file. If you would like to see what prevented you from obtaining credit from us, you should call 1-888-EXPERIAN.

We are truly sorry that we cannot fill your initial order totaling $1,430. We pride ourselves on serving most of Fort Lauderdale's finest restaurants and catering services. We would be proud to add the GodMother to our list of discerning customers. Perhaps the best way for you to join that select list is with a smaller order to begin with. We would be happy to serve you on a cash basis. If this plan meets with your approval, do let me know.

Sincerely,

10.23 Customer Bad News: Virus Infects Rocket Launcher (Obj. 6)

Team | **Critical Thinking**

"How could you sell me a program with a virus! I hold your company personally responsible for contaminating my hard drive," wrote Jennifer M. Sage in a letter to software game manufacturer Quixell. Ms. Sage has ample reason to be angry with Quixell. Its Rocket Launcher program carried a computer virus, unknown to Quixell at the time of distribution.

Computer viruses are programs written to perform malicious tasks. They attach themselves secretly to data files and are then copied either by disk or by a computer network. Some viruses are carried on attachments to e-mail. The particular virus contaminating Quixell's program is called "Stoned IV." First reported in Europe, it represents a class of "stealth" viruses. They mask their location and are extremely difficult to detect. Both manufacturers and consumers get stung by viruses. Quixell already had an extensive virus-detection program, but this new virus slipped by. Actually, Quixell has just licensed special digital-signature software that will make it difficult for future viruses to spread undetected. But this new technology won't do much for current angry customers like Ms. Sage.

In the past, courts have generally found that if a company has been reasonably prudent in its production process, that company is not liable for damage caused by a third person (the individual who planted the virus). Nevertheless, Quixell feels an obligation to do whatever is possible—within reason—to rectify the situation. Some customers would like to have software companies like Quixell give them new computers, or at the very least, install new hard drives. Ms. Sage is making what she thinks is a reasonable request. Since she is no computer techie, she wants Quixell to pay for a computer specialist to clean up her hard drive and restore it to its previous uncontaminated state. Such a solution, say most of the Quixell managers, is out of the question. It's much too expensive. Moreover, Quixell can't be sure that her computer doesn't have problems that have nothing to do with the Rocket Launcher virus. When faced with viruses, other software manufacturers have simply offered a clean disk and advice.

Because of its vigilance and concern for product quality, Quixell has never had a virus contaminate any of its 350 products—until Stoned IV. When the virus was discovered, Quixell immediately stopped production and recalled all unsold disks. Like other companies facing virus attacks, Quixell has assigned a specialist to answer specific questions from affected customers. He is Jason John at (415) 344-9901. Quixell has also located an antivirus program, AntiVirus Max by Integrity Software. This program has special routines that detect, remove, and prevent more than 400 viruses, including Stoned IV. AntiVirus Max costs $59.95 and can be purchased by calling Integrity's toll-free number (1-800-690-3220). This program removes the virus and restores the hard drive. Quixell fears that as many as 300 of its customers were affected by the virus. As a small company with a very slim profit margin, Quixell cannot afford to provide the antivirus program to that many customers.

You are part of the customer service team at Quixell that must decide how to handle this request and others. Remember that Quixell cannot afford to have technicians make personal visits. Discuss possible options, make a group decision, and then individually or as a group write a letter to Ms. Jennifer Sage, 2360 Red Rock Road, Hope, AZ 72801.[14]

10.24 Customer Bad News: A Mess With King Fisher and Pick Pocket (Obj. 6)

Assume you are Deborah Pool Dixon, manager, Promotions and Advertising, Seven Flags Lake Point Park. You are upset by the letter you received from Melissa Sledgeman, who complained that she was "taken" by Seven Flags when the park had to substitute performers for King Fisher and the Pick Pocket band concert. Explain to her that the concert was planned by an independent promoter. Your only obligation was to provide the theater facility and advertising. Three days before the event, the promoter left town, taking with him all advance payments from financial backers. As it turned out, many of the artists he had promised to deliver were not even planning to attend.

Left with a pretty messy situation, you decided on Thursday to go ahead with a modified version of the event since you had been advertising it and many would come expecting some kind of talent. At that time you changed your radio advertising to say that for reasons beyond your control, King Fisher and the Pick Pocket band would not be appearing. You described the new talent and posted signs at the entrance and in the parking lot announcing the change. Contrary to Ms. Sledgeman's claim, no newspaper advertising featuring Fisher and Pick Pocket appeared on the day of the concert (at least you did not pay for any to appear that day). Somehow she must have missed your corrective radio advertising and signs at the entrance. You feel you made a genuine effort to communicate the changed program. In your opinion most people who attended the concert thought that Seven Flags had done everything possible to salvage a rather unfortunate situation.

Ms. Sledgeman wants a cash refund of $70 (two tickets at $35 each). Seven Flags has a no-money-back policy on concerts after the event takes place. If Ms. Sledgeman had come to the box office before the event started, you could have returned her money. But she stayed to see the concert. She claims that she didn't know anything about the talent change until after the event was well underway. This sounds unlikely, but you don't quarrel with customers. Nevertheless, you can't give her cash back. You already took a loss on this event. But you can give two complimentary passes to Seven Flags Lake Point Park. Write a refusal letter to Ms. Melissa Sledgeman, 9001 W. Farmington Road, Sandusky, OH 45320. Invite her and a friend to return as guests under happier circumstances.

10.25 Customer Bad News: Refusing Returned Books (Obj. 6)

As the customer service manager of Kent Publishers, you must refuse most of a shipment of books returned from the North West University Bookstore. Your policy is to provide a 100 percent return on books if the books are returned prepaid in *new, unmarked,* and *salable* condition.

The return must be within twelve months of the original invoice date. Old editions of books must be returned within 90 days of your announcement that you will no longer be printing that edition. These conditions are published and sent with every order of books shipped. The return shipment from North West looks as if someone was housecleaning and decided to return all unsold books to you. Fourteen books are not your titles; return them. You could have accepted the 22 copies of Donner's *Introduction to Marketing*—if they were not imprinted with "North West University," the price, and return instructions on the inside cover. The 31 copies of Heigel's *College Writing Handbook* are second editions. Since you've been selling the third edition for 14 months, you can't accept them. Five copies of Quigley's *Business Law* appear to be water damaged; they're unsalable. From the whole mess it looks as if you'll be able to give them credit for 25 copies of Miller's *The Promotable Woman* (wholesale price $31). However, since North West sent no invoice information, you'll have to tack on a 15 percent service charge to cover the effort involved in locating the order in your records.

Write a letter to Christopher Lorenze, manager, North West University Bookstore, 6002 16th Avenue SW, Seattle, WA 98105, that retains his goodwill. North West has been a valued customer in the past. This bookstore placed orders on time and paid on time. Tell Mr. Lorenze what is being returned and how much credit you are allowing. From the credit total, deduct $32.50 for return shipping costs.

10.26 Customer Bad News: No Credit for Cordless Phones (Obj. 6)

As Julie Abrams, sales manager, CyberSound, you are delighted to land a sizeable order for your new 25-channel cordless telephone. This great phone has speed dialing, auto scan to ensure clear conversations, caller ID, and call waiting.

The purchase order comes from High Point Electronics, a retail distributor in High Point, North Carolina. You send the order on to Shane Simmons, your credit manager, for approval of the credit application attached. To your disappointment, Shane tells you that High Point doesn't qualify for credit. Experian, the credit reporting agency that replaced TRW, reports that credit would be risky for High Point.

You decide to write to High Point with the bad news and an alternative. Suggest that High Point order a smaller number of the cordless phones. If it pays cash, it can receive a 2 percent discount. After High Point has sold these fast-moving units, it can place another cash order through your toll-free order number. With your fast delivery system, its inventory will never be depleted. High Point can get the phones it wants now and can replace its inventory almost overnight. Credit Manager Simmons tells you that your company generally reveals to credit applicants the name of the credit reporting service and encourages them to investigate their credit record. Write a credit refusal to Ryan Bardens, High Point Electronics, 3590 Thomasville Road, High Point, NC 28001.

10.27 Customer Bad News: Kodak Refuses Customer's Request to Repeat World Trip (Obj. 6)

Kodak Customer Service manager Charlie Smith can't believe what he reads in a letter from Brian P. Coyle (see Activity 9.17 in Chapter 9). This 27-year-old Orlando resident actually wants Kodak to foot the bill for a repeat round-the-world trip because his Advantix camera malfunctioned and he lost 12 rolls of film! As soon as Smith saw the letter and the returned camera, he knew what was wrong. Of the 2 million Advantix cameras made last year, 20,000 malfunctioned. A supplier squirted too much oil in the shutter mechanism, and the whole lot was recalled. In fact, Kodak spent almost $1 million to remove these cameras from store shelves. Kodak also contacted all customers who could be reached. In addition to the giant recall, the company quickly redesigned the cameras so that they would work even if they had excess oil. But somehow Coyle was not notified of the recall. When Smith checked the warranty files, he learned that this customer had not returned his warranty. Had the customer done so, he would have been notified in August, well before his trip.

Although Customer Service Manager Smith is sorry for the mishap, he thinks that a request for $20,000 to replace "lost memories" is preposterous. Kodak has never assumed any responsibility beyond replacing a camera or film. This customer, however, seems to have suffered more than a routine loss of snapshots. Therefore, Smith decides to sweeten the deal by offering to throw in a digital camera valued at $225, more than double the cost of the Advantix. One of the advantages of a digital camera is that it contains an LCD panel that enables the photographer to view stored images immediately. No chance of losing memories with this digital camera!

As the assistant to Customer Service Manager Smith, you must write a letter that refuses the demand for $20,000 but retains the customer's goodwill. Tell this customer what you will do, and be sure to explain how Kodak reacted immediately when it discovered the Advantix defect. Write a sensitive refusal to Brian P. Coyle, 5942 Bear Crossing Drive, Orlando, FL 32746.[15]

10.28 Employee Bad News: Strikeout for Expanded Office Teams (Obj. 7)

Team **Critical Thinking**

Assume you are Hank James, vice president of Human Resources at Tissue Mills Paper Co., 508 W. Inverary Road, Kingston, Ontario K2G 1V8. Recently several of your employees requested that their spouses or friends be allowed to participate in Tissue Mills' intramural sports teams. Although the teams play only once a week during the season, these employees claim that they can't afford more time away from friends and family. Over 100 employees currently participate in the eight coed volleyball, softball, and tennis teams, which are open to company employees only. The teams were designed to improve employee friendships and to give employees a regular occasion to have fun together.

If nonemployees were to participate, you're afraid that employee interaction would be limited. And while some team members might have fun if spouses or friends were included, you're not so sure all employees would enjoy it. You're not interested in turning intramural sports into "date night." Furthermore, the company would have to create additional teams if many nonemployees joined, and you don't want the administrative or equipment costs of more teams. Adding teams also would require changes to team rosters and game schedules, which could be a problem for some employees. You do understand the need for social time with friends and families, but guests are welcome as spectators at all intramural games. Besides, the company already sponsors a family holiday party and an annual company picnic. Write an e-mail or hard-copy memo to the staff denying the request of several employees to include nonemployees on Tissue Mills' intramural sports teams.

10.29 Employee Bad News: Refusing Christmas (Obj. 7)

In the past your office has always sponsored a Christmas party at a nice restaurant. As your company has undergone considerable downsizing and budget cuts during the past year, you know that no money is available for holiday entertaining. Moreover, as the staff becomes more diverse, you decide that it might be better to celebrate a "holiday" party instead of a Christmas event. As executive vice president, respond to the e-mail request of Dina Gillian, office manager. Dina asks permission to make restaurant reservations for this year's Christmas party. Refuse Dina, but offer some alternatives. How about a potluck dinner?

C.L.U.E. REVIEW 10

Edit the following sentences to correct all language faults, including grammar, punctuation, spelling, and word confusions.

1. Your advertisement in the June second edition of the Boston Globe, caught my attention; because my training and experience matches your requirements.
2. Undoubtlessly the bank is closed at this hour but it's ATM will enable you to recieve the cash you need.
3. A flow chart detailing all sales' procedures in 4 divisions were prepared by our Vice President.
4. The computer and printer was working good yesterday, and appeared to be alright this morning; when I used it for my report.
5. If I was you I would be more concerned with long term not short term returns on the invested capitol.
6. We make a conscience effort by the way to find highly-qualified individuals with up to date computer skills.
7. If your résumé had came earlier I could have showed it to Mr. Sutton and she before your interview.
8. Deborahs report summary is more easier to read then David because she used consistant headings and efficient writing techniques.
9. At McDonald's we ordered 4 big macs 3 orders of french fries, and 5 coca-colas for lunch.
10. Because the budget cuts will severely effect all programs the faculty have unanimously opposed it.

UNIT • 4 •

Reports and Proposals

C H A P T E R • 1 1 •

Report Planning and Research

LEARNING OBJECTIVES

1 Describe nine typical business reports.

2 Distinguish between informational and analytical reports.

3 Identify four report formats.

4 Apply the writing process to reports.

5 Conduct research by locating secondary data.

6 Generate primary data for research projects.

7 Describe three formats for documenting data sources.

COMMUNICATION IN PROCESS

CASE STUDY

Specialized Bicycles Wonders Whether Cycling Is a Men-Only Sport

"Cycling attracts women like ballet attracts men. What cycling lacks in grace, expression, and beauty, it makes up for in blood, guts, and finicky hardware." That's how one biking industry expert explained the lack of participation of women in biking.[1] In other words, cycling may just be a man's sport. But Ariadne Scott, an ardent cyclist, couldn't accept that rationale. Scott is also sales support manager for Specialized Bicycle Components, a northern California company that produces a wide range of high-end bicyles, components, and accessories. She knew that women account for almost half of all cycling participants in the United States. They also control nearly 60 percent of the wealth in this country, and they influence about 80 percent of all purchases.

Armed with these facts, Scott considered female cyclists a market with tremendous growth potential. A survey by *Bicycling Magazine* revealed that millions of female cyclists are not cycling enthusiasts but want to be. The report also showed that those women who did cycle tended to shy away from purchasing their bicycles at specialty shops, where their male counterparts made their purchases.[2]

Scott and a group of other female employees at Specialized, all happy cyclists, set out to learn more about why women ride or don't ride. They hoped to increase female participation in cycling and, of course, to increase awareness of the Specialized brand. Ultimately, they wanted to influence designers to become more responsive to the needs of female cyclists. What started out as a casual lunchtime group of enthusiastic cyclists grew into a team with a mission. To continue its efforts, the team needed company support. Many of the team goals were consistent with company and industry goals. But convincing management to fund a project focused on female cyclists would require considerable persuasion backed up by facts and figures.[3]

www.specialized.com

Clarifying and Classifying Reports

1

Reports are a fact of life in American business. In a high-context culture like that of North America, our values and attitudes seem to prompt us to write reports. We analyze the pros and cons of problems, studying alternatives and assessing facts, figures, and details. We pride ourselves on being practical and logical. We solve problems by applying scientific procedures. When we must persuade management to support a project, as Ariadne Scott at Specialized Bicycle Components wishes to do, we generally write a report laying out the case.

Management decisions in many organizations are based on information submitted in the form of reports. This chapter examines categories, functions, organizational patterns, formats, and writing styles of reports. It also introduces the report-writing process and discusses methods of collecting and documenting data.

Effective business reports solve problems and answer questions systematically.

Because of their abundance and diversity, business reports are difficult to define. They may range from informal half-page trip reports to formal 200-page financial forecasts. Reports may be presented orally in front of a group or electronically on a computer screen. Some reports appear as words on paper in the form of memos and letters. Others are primarily numerical data, such as tax reports or profit-and-loss statements. Some seek to provide information only; others aim to analyze and make recommendations. Although reports vary greatly in length, content, form, and formality level, they all have one common purpose: *Business reports are systematic attempts to answer questions and solve problems.*

Typical Business Reports

In searching for answers and solving problems, organizations prepare thousands of different kinds of reports for managers, employees, customers, and the government. Many of these reports can be grouped into nine categories, briefly described below. Chapters 13 and 14 present "how-to" information and models for writing these reports.

Periodic, situational, investigative, and compliance reports often present data without interpretation.

Periodic Operating Reports. The most common reports in many organizations are written at regular intervals to monitor operations. These operating reports—such as weekly activity reports from sales reps—answer questions about what employees are doing and how effectively the organization is achieving its mission. They monitor and control operations including production, sales, shipping, and customer service.

Situational Reports. Unlike periodic reports, situational reports describe nonrecurring activities. This broad category includes trip, conference, and seminar reports, as well as progress reports for unusual activities, such as sponsoring a mountain bike-riding competition. Since situational reports describe one-time events, writers generally have no ready models to follow. Thus, these reports are usually more challenging, but also more creative, than periodic reports.

Investigative/Informational Reports. Reports that examine situations or problems and supply facts—with little in the way of interpretation or recommendations—are investigative. Assume, for example, that your boss asked you to research the Internal Revenue Service's position on the hiring of independent contractors. You would collect and organize facts into a logical, informational report. Now assume that your boss also wanted you to analyze the status of the independent contractors working for your organization and make recommendations about retaining them. Your report would become more analytical and would be classified differently.

Compliance Reports. Prompted by the government, compliance reports answer such questions as "How much profit did your organization earn and what taxes do you owe?" These reports comply with laws and regulations that protect employees, investors, and customers. Such reports respond to government agencies such as the Internal Revenue Service, the Securities and Exchange Commission, and the Equal Employment Opportunities Commission. A securities prospectus is a compliance report that answers questions from potential stockholders regarding company performance and finances.

Justification/recommendation, yardstick, and feasibility reports analyze alternatives, interpret findings, and often make recommendations.

Justification/Recommendation Reports. When managers and employees must justify or recommend something (such as purchases, changes in operations, new programs, or personnel), they write justification or recommendation reports. These analytical reports usually travel upward to management, where the recommendations are approved or refused. Because these reports analyze alternatives, interpret findings, and make recommendations, they become important tools for managers in solving problems and making decisions.

Yardstick Reports. When a problem has two or more solutions, a helpful way to evaluate the alternatives is to establish consistent criteria—a "yardstick"—by which to measure the alternatives. For example, let's say that a company must decide whether to (1) continue using its outdated mainframe computers, (2) purchase networked personal computers, or (3) hire an outside agency to handle some of its computing needs. A yardstick report assesses the alternatives by applying the same criteria to each, such as cost, service, security, and reliability. Each alternative is measured against the criteria to find the best option.

Feasibility Reports. Feasibility reports use analysis to predict whether projects or alternatives are practical or advisable. They answer questions such as "Should we open a branch office in Panama City?" Feasibility reports examine the benefits and problems connected with the project, as well as its costs and schedule for implementation. The emphasis is on whether to proceed with the venture.

Research Studies. Business organizations sometimes commission research studies that examine problems thoroughly and scientifically. Researchers analyze a problem, suggest ways to solve it (called *hypotheses*), collect data about each possible solution, analyze that data, draw conclusions, and, if requested, make recommendations. The emphasis in these studies is on conducting objective research and interpreting the findings. For example, researchers at the Insurance Institute for Highway Safety studied all police-reported fatal motor vehicle crashes in the United States. It found that 2.5 percent of all fatal crashes are caused by motorists running red lights. It also discovered that red-light violations at intersections with cameras installed to catch offenders had dropped 42 percent.[4] The researchers could then recommend installation of cameras.

Proposals. As attempts to secure new business, proposals offer to solve problems, investigate ideas, or sell products and services. They are organized to answer the receiver's questions regarding the offer and its budget, schedule, and staffing. Another form of proposal is the business plan, a persuasive report that seeks to convince investors to fund a new company. One of the most famous business plans was written in a college class many years ago by Fred Smith, founder of FedEx. It laid the foundation for his hugely successful overnight cargo-delivery business.

Spotlight on **Communicators**

Specialized Bicycle sales support manager Ariadne Scott, standing in the middle, sometimes develops primary data by working directly with the subjects of her reports, as shown here. In writing reports for managers, she says, "I always keep in mind how limited their time is. I start out directly by asking for what I need. Then I follow up with an overview of the entire proposal written in press-release style emphasizing who, what, when, where, and why. If facts or data support my proposal, I always list complete sources."

Functions of Reports

In terms of what they do, most of the reports just described can be placed in two broad categories: informational reports and analytical reports.

2

Informational reports simply present data without analysis or recommendations. Analytical reports provide data, analyses, conclusions, and, if requested, recommendations.

Informational Reports. Reports that present data without analysis or recommendations are primarily informational. Although writers collect and organize facts, they are not expected to analyze the facts for readers. A trip report describing an employee's visit to a trade show, for example, simply presents information. Other reports that present information without analysis involve routine operations, compliance with regulations, and company policies and procedures.

Analytical Reports. Reports that provide data, analyses, and conclusions are analytical. If requested, writers also supply recommendations. Analytical reports may intend to persuade readers to act or to change their beliefs. Assume you're writing a feasibility report that compares several potential locations for a workout/fitness club. After analyzing and discussing alternatives, you might recommend one site, thus attempting to persuade readers to accept this choice.

Direct and Indirect Patterns

Like letters and memos, reports may be organized directly or indirectly. The reader's expectations and the content of a report determine its pattern of development, as il-

FIGURE 11.1 Audience Analysis and Report Organization

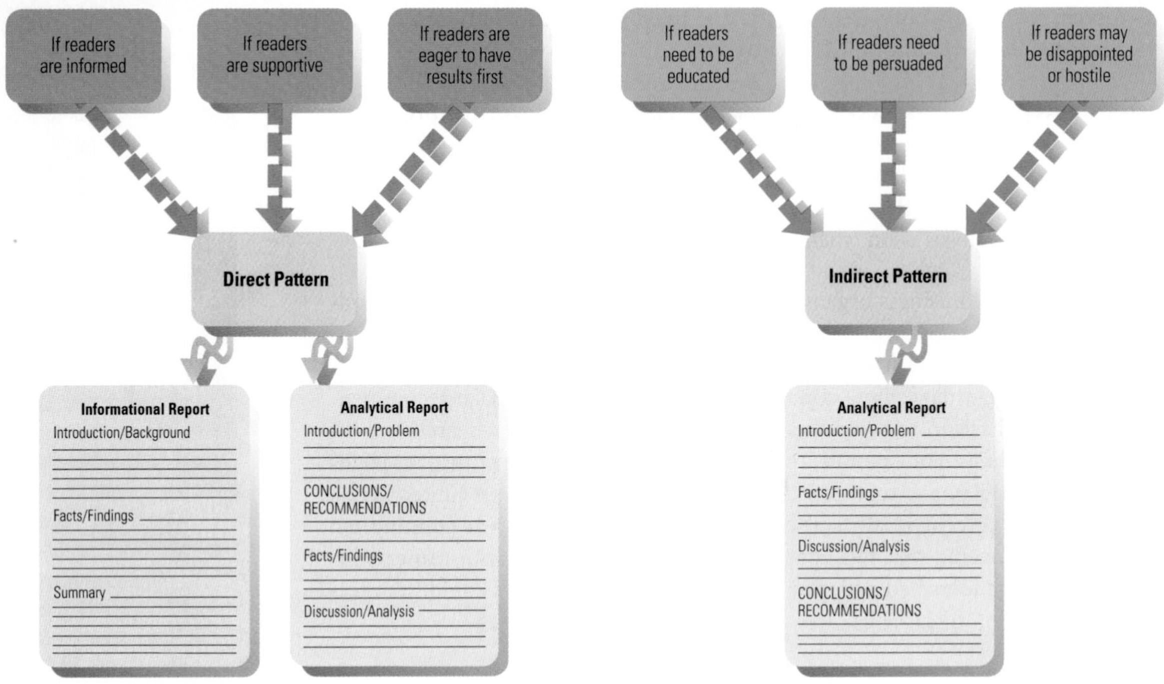

lustrated in Figure 11.1. In long reports, such as corporate annual reports, some parts may be developed directly while other parts are arranged indirectly.

The direct pattern places conclusions and recommendations near the beginning of a report.

Direct Pattern. When the purpose for writing is presented close to the beginning, the organizational pattern is direct. Informational reports, such as the letter report shown in Figure 11.2, are usually arranged directly. They open with an introduction, followed by the facts and a summary. In Figure 11.2 the writer explains a legal services plan. The letter report begins with an introduction. Then it presents the facts, which are divided into three subtopics identified by descriptive headings. The letter ends with a summary and a complimentary close.

Analytical reports may also be organized directly, especially when readers are supportive or are familiar with the topic. Many busy executives prefer this pattern because it gives them the results of the report immediately. They don't have to spend time wading through the facts, findings, discussion, and analyses to get to the two items they are most interested in—conclusions and recommendations. Figure 11.3 illustrates such an arrangement. This analytical memo report describes environmental hazards of a property that a realtor has just listed. The realtor is familiar with the investigation and eager to find out the recommendations. Therefore, the memo is organized directly.

The indirect pattern is appropriate for analytical reports that seek to persuade or that convey bad news.

You should be aware, though, that unless readers are familiar with the topic, they may find the direct pattern confusing. Many readers prefer the indirect pattern because it seems logical and mirrors the way we solve problems.

Indirect Pattern. When the conclusions and recommendations, if requested, appear at the end of the report, the organizational pattern is indirect. Such reports usually begin with an introduction or description of the problem, followed by facts and interpretation from the writer. They end with conclusions and recommendations.

FIGURE 11.2 Informational Report—Letter Format

Tips for Letter Reports

- Use letter format for short informal reports sent to outsiders.
- Organize the facts section into logical divisions identified by consistent headings.
- Single-space the body.
- Double-space between paragraphs.
- Leave two blank lines above each side heading.
- Create side margins of 1 to $1\frac{1}{4}$ inches.
- Add a second-page heading, if necessary, consisting of the addressee's name, the date, and the page number.

Center for Consumers of Legal Services
P.O. Box 260
Richmond, VA 23219

Uses letterhead stationery for an informal report addressed to an outsider

September 7, 2000

Ms. Lisa Burgess, Secretary
Lake Austin Homeowners
3902 Oak Hill Drive
Austin, TX 78134

Dear Ms. Burgess:

As executive director of the Center for Consumers of Legal Services, I'm pleased to send you this information describing how your homeowners' association can sponsor a legal services plan for its members. After an introduction with background data, this report will discuss three steps necessary for your group to start its plan.

Introduction

Presents introduction and facts without analysis or recommendations

A legal services plan promotes preventive law by letting members talk to attorneys whenever problems arise. Prompt legal advice often avoids or prevents expensive litigation. Because groups can supply a flow of business to the plan's attorneys, groups can negotiate free consultation, follow-up, and discounts.

Two kinds of plans are commonly available. The first, a free plan, offers free legal consultation along with discounts for services when the participating groups are sufficiently large to generate business for the plan's attorneys. These plans actually act as a substitute for advertising for the attorneys. The second common type is the prepaid plan. Prepaid plans provide more benefits, but members must pay annual fees, usually of $200 or more a year. Over 30 million people are covered by legal services plans today, and a majority belong to free plans.

Since you inquired about a free plan for your homeowners' association, the following information describes how to set up such a program.

Determine the Benefits Your Group Needs

Arranges facts of report into sections with descriptive headings

The first step in establishing a free legal services plan is to meet with the members of your group to decide what benefits they want. Typical benefits include the following:

Free consultation. Members may consult a participating attorney—by phone or in the attorney's office—to discuss any matter. The number of consultations is unlimited, provided each is about a separate matter. Consultations are generally limited to 30 minutes, but they include substantive analysis and advice.

Emphasizes benefits in paragraph headings with boldface type

Free document review. Important papers—such as leases, insurance policies, and installment sales contracts—may be reviewed with legal counsel. Members may ask questions and receive an explanation of terms.

FIGURE 11.2 Continued

Ms. Lisa Burgess | Page 2 | September 7, 2000

Discount on additional services. For more complex matters, participating attorneys will charge members 75 percent of the attorney's normal fee. However, some organizations choose to charge a flat fee for commonly needed services.

Select the Attorneys for Your Plan

Groups with geographically concentrated memberships have an advantage in forming legal plans. These groups can limit the number of participating attorneys and yet provide adequate service. Generally, smaller panels of attorneys are advantageous.

Assemble a list of candidates, inviting them to apply. The best way to compare prices is to have candidates submit their fees. Your group can then compare fee schedules and select the lowest bidder, if price is important. Arrange to interview attorneys in their offices.

After selecting an attorney or a panel, sign a contract. The contract should include the reason for the plan, what the attorney agrees to do, what the group agrees to do, how each side can end the contract, and the signatures of both parties. You may also wish to include references to malpractice insurance, assurance that the group will not interfere with the attorney-client relationship, an evaluation form, a grievance procedure, and responsibility for government filings.

Publicize the Plan to Your Members

Members won't use a plan if they don't know about it, and a plan will not be successful if it is unused. Publicity must be vocal and ongoing. Announce it in newsletters, meetings, bulletin boards, and flyers.

Persistence is the key. All too frequently, leaders of an organization assume that a single announcement is all that's needed. They expect members to see the value of the plan and remember that it's available. Most organization members, though, are not as involved as the leadership. Therefore, it takes more publicity than the leadership usually expects in order to reach and maintain the desired level of awareness.

Summary

A successful free legal services plan involves designing a program, choosing the attorneys, and publicizing the plan. To learn more about these steps or to order a $25 how-to manual, call me at (804) 355-9901.

Sincerely,

Richard M. Ramos

Richard M. Ramos, Esq.
Executive Director

pas

Identifies second and succeeding pages with headings

Uses parallel side headings for consistency and readability

Includes complimentary close and signature

This pattern is helpful when readers are unfamiliar with the problem. It's also useful when readers must be persuaded or when they may be disappointed with or hostile toward the report's findings. The writer is more likely to retain the reader's interest by first explaining, justifying, and analyzing the facts and then making recommendations. This pattern also seems most rational to readers because it follows the normal thought process: problem, alternatives (facts), solution.

Figure 11.4 shows a portion of an analytical report organized indirectly. Note how readers are introduced, in a background discussion, to the problem of vehicle emissions and smog. Then facts (research findings and proposed solutions to the problem) are presented and analyzed. Finally, the report concludes with recommendations suggesting solutions to the problem.

FIGURE 11.3 Analytical Report—Memo Format

Tips for Memo Reports

- Use memo format for most short (ten or fewer pages) informal reports within an organization.
- Leave side margins of 1 to $1\frac{1}{4}$ inches.
- Sign your initials on the FROM line.
- Use an informal, conversational style.
- For direct analytical reports, put recommendations first.
- For indirect analytical reports, put recommendations last.

Applies memo format for short, informal internal report

Presents recommendations first (direct pattern) because reader is supportive and familiar with topic

Combines findings and analyses in short report

Uses first paragraph as introduction

Atlantic Environmental, Inc.

Interoffice Memo

DATE: March 7, 2000

TO: Kermit Fox, President

FROM: Cynthia M. Rashid, Environmental Engineer CMR

SUBJECT: INVESTIGATION OF MOUNTAIN PARK COMMERCIAL SITE

For Allegheny Realty, Inc., I've completed a preliminary investigation of its Mountain Park property listing. The following recommendations are based on my physical inspection of the site, official records, and interviews with officials and persons knowledgeable about the site.

Recommendations

To reduce its potential environmental liability, Allegheny Realty should take the following steps in regard to its Mountain Park listing:

- Conduct an immediate asbestos survey at the site, including inspection of ceiling insulation material, floor tiles, and insulation around a gas-fired heater vent pipe at 2539 Mountain View Drive.
- Prepare an environmental audit of the generators of hazardous waste currently operating at the site, including Mountain Technology.
- Obtain lids for the dumpsters situated in the parking areas and ensure that the lids are kept closed.

Findings and Analyses

My preliminary assessment of the site and its immediate vicinity revealed rooms with damaged floor tiles on the first and second floors of 2539 Mountain View Drive. Apparently, in recent remodeling efforts, these tiles had been cracked and broken. Examination of the ceiling and attic revealed further possible contamination from asbestos. The insulation for the hot-water tank was in poor condition.

Located on the property is Mountain Technology, a possible hazardous waste generator. Although I could not examine its interior, this company has the potential for producing hazardous material contamination.

In the parking area large dumpsters collect trash and debris from several businesses. These dumpsters were uncovered, thus posing a risk to the general public.

In view of the construction date of the structures on this property, asbestos-containing building materials might be present. Moreover, this property is located in an industrial part of the city, further prompting my recommendation for a thorough investigation. Allegheny Realty can act immediately to eliminate one environmental concern: covering the dumpsters in the parking area.

FIGURE 11.4 Portion of Analytical Report—Manuscript Format

Tips for Manuscript Reports

- Use manuscript format for long, complex, or formal reports and proposals.
- Print the report on plain paper.
- Allow side and bottom margins of 1 to 1¼ inches.
- Display primary and secondary headings appropriately (see Chapter 12).
- Use single or double spacing depending on your organization's preferences.
- Document sources with appropriate citations.

REDUCING VEHICLE EMISSIONS
AND SMOG IN THE LOS ANGELES BASIN

Uses plain paper, title, and manuscript format for long, complex report

INTRODUCTION

Pacific Enterprises, Inc., is pleased to submit this report to the Air Resources Board of Los Angeles County in response to its request of April 18. This report examines the problem of vehicle emissions in the Los Angeles Basin. Moreover, it reviews proposed solutions and recommends a course of action that will lead to a significant reduction in the hydrocarbon and nitrogen oxide emissions of older vehicles.

Background and Discussion of Problem

The County of Los Angeles has battled dirty air for five decades. The largest stationary polluters (manufacturers, petroleum refineries, and electric power plants, for example) are no longer considered a major source of pollution. Today, the biggest smog producers are older automobiles, trucks, and buses. Newer vehicles, as a result of improved technology and government regulation, have sharply reduced their emissions. However, nearly 400,000 pre-1980 vehicles continue to operate on Southern California's streets and freeways. A recent state-funded study (Rutman 37) estimated that 50 percent of the smog generated in Southern California comes from these older vehicles.

Cites author and page number

Yet, many of these vehicles are either undetected or exempted from meeting the clean-air standards. Little has been done to solve this problem because retrofitting these old cars with modern pollution control systems would cost more than many of them are worth. Two innovative solutions were recently proposed.

Uses single spacing to save paper and filing space

Reducing Smog by Eliminating Older Cars

Two large organizations, Unocal and Ford Motor Company, suggested a buy-out program to eliminate older cars. To demonstrate its effectiveness, the two firms bought more than

RECOMMENDATIONS

Organizes data indirectly, with recommendations last, to inform and persuade readers

Based on our findings and the conclusions discussed earlier, we submit the following recommendations to you:

1. Study the progress of Germany's attempt to reduce smog by retrofitting older vehicles with computer-controlled fuel management systems.
2. Encourage Ford Motor Company and Unocal to continue their buy-out programs in exchange for temporary smog credits.
3. Invite Neutronics Enterprises in Carlsbad, California, to test its Lamba emission-control system at your El Monte test center.

Arranges recommendations from least important to most important

Formats of Reports

3

The format of a report is governed by its length, topic, audience, and purpose. After considering these elements, you'll probably choose from among the following four formats:

A report's format depends on its length, audience, topic, and purpose.

- **Letter format.** Use letter format for short (say, ten or fewer pages) informal reports addressed outside an organization. Prepared on office stationery, a letter report contains a date, inside address, salutation, and complimentary close, as shown in Figure 11.2. Although they may carry information similar to that found in correspondence, letter reports usually are longer and show more careful organization than most letters. They also include headings.
- **Memo format.** For short informal reports that stay within organizations, memo format is appropriate. Memo reports begin with DATE, TO, FROM, and SUBJECT, as shown in Figure 11.3. Like letter reports, memo reports differ from regular memos in length, use of headings, and deliberate organization.
- **Manuscript format.** For longer, more formal reports, use manuscript format. These reports are usually printed on plain paper instead of letterhead stationery or memo forms. They begin with a title followed by systematically displayed headings and subheadings, as illustrated in Figure 11.4.
- **Printed forms.** Prepared forms are often used for repetitive data, such as monthly sales reports, performance appraisals, merchandise inventories, and personnel and financial reports. Standardized headings on these forms save time for the writer. Preprinted forms also make similar information easy to locate and ensure that all necessary information is provided.

Writing Style

Reports can be formal or informal depending on the purpose, audience, and setting.

Like other business messages, reports can range from informal to formal, depending on their purpose, audience, and setting. Research reports from consultants to their clients tend to be rather formal. Such reports must project an impression of objectivity, authority, and impartiality. But a report to your boss describing a trip to a conference would probably be informal.

An office worker once called a grammar hot-line service with this problem: "We've just sent a report to our headquarters, and it was returned with this comment, 'Put it in the third person.' What do they mean?" The hot-line experts explained that management apparently wanted a more formal writing style, using third-person constructions (*the company* or *the researcher* instead of *we* and *I*). Figure 11.5, which compares characteristics of formal and informal report-writing styles, can help you decide the writing style that's appropriate for your reports.

4

Applying the 3-×-3 Writing Process to Reports

The best reports grow out of a seven-step process beginning with analysis and ending with proofreading and evaluation.

Because business reports are systematic attempts to answer questions and solve problems, the best reports are developed methodically. The same 3-×-3 writing process that guided memo and letter writing can be applied to reports. Let's channel the process into seven specific steps:

- **Step 1:** Analyze the problem and purpose.
- **Step 2:** Anticipate the audience and issues.
- **Step 3:** Prepare a work plan.

FIGURE 11.5 Report-Writing Styles

	Formal Writing Style	Informal Writing Style
Use	Theses Research studies Controversial or complex reports (especially to outsiders)	Short, routine reports Reports for familiar audiences Noncontroversial reports Most reports for company insiders
Effect	Impression of objectivity, accuracy, professionalism, fairness Distance created between writer and reader	Feeling of warmth, personal involvement, closeness
Characteristics	Absence of first-person pronouns; use of third-person (*the researcher, the writer*) Absence of contractions (*can't, don't*) Use of passive-voice verbs (*the study was conducted*) Complex sentences; long words Absence of humor and figures of speech Reduced use of colorful adjectives and adverbs Elimination of "editorializing" (author's opinions, perceptions)	Use of first-person pronouns (*I, we, me, my, us, our*) Use of contractions Emphasis on active-voice verbs (*I conducted the study*) Shorter sentences; familiar words Occasional use of humor, metaphors Occasional use of colorful speech Acceptance of author's opinions and ideas

- **Step 4:** Research the data.
- **Step 5:** Organize, analyze, interpret, and illustrate the data.
- **Step 6:** Compose the first draft.
- **Step 7:** Revise, proofread, and evaluate.

How much time you spend on each step depends on your report task. A short informational report on a familiar topic might require a brief work plan, little research, and no analysis of the data. A complex analytical report, on the other hand, might demand a comprehensive work plan, extensive research, and careful analysis of the data.

To illustrate the planning stages of a report, we'll watch Diane Camas develop a report she's preparing for her boss, Mike Rivers, at Mycon Pharmaceutical Laboratories. Mike asked Diane to investigate the problem of transportation for sales representatives. Currently, some Mycon reps visit customers (mostly doctors and hospitals) using company-leased cars. A few reps drive their own cars, receiving reimbursements for use. In three months Mycon's leasing agreement for 14 cars expires, and Mike is considering a major change. Diane's task is investigating the choices and reporting her findings to Mike.

Analyzing the Problem and Purpose

The first step in writing a report is understanding the problem or assignment clearly. For complex reports it's wise to prepare a written problem statement. In analyzing her report task, Diane had many questions. Is the problem that Mycon is spending too much money on leased cars? Does Mycon wish to invest in owning a fleet of cars? Is Mike unhappy with the paperwork involved in reimbursing sales reps when they use their own cars? Does he suspect that reps are submitting inflated mileage figures? Before starting research for the report, Diane talked with Mike to define the problem. She learned several dimensions of the situation and wrote the following statement to clarify the problem—both for herself and for Mike.

Before beginning a report, identify in a clear statement the problem to be solved.

Problem Statement: The leases on all company cars will be expiring in three months. Mycon must decide whether to renew them or develop a new policy regarding transportation for sales reps. Expenses and paperwork for employee-owned cars seem excessive.

Diane further defined the problem by writing a specific question that she would try to answer in her report:

Problem Question: What plan should Mycon follow in providing transportation for its sales reps?

Now Diane was ready to concentrate on the purpose of the report. Again, she had questions. Exactly what did Mike expect? Did he want a comparison of costs for buying cars and leasing cars? Should she conduct research to pinpoint exact reimbursement costs when employees drive their own cars? Did he want her to do all the legwork, present her findings in a report, and let him make a decision? Or did he want her to evaluate the choices and recommend a course of action? After talking with Mike, Diane was ready to write a simple purpose statement for this assignment.

A simple purpose statement defines the focus of a report.

Simple Statement of Purpose: To recommend a plan that provides sales reps with cars to be used in their calls.

Preparing a written purpose statement is a good idea because it defines the focus of a report and provides a standard that keeps the project on target. In writing useful purpose statements, choose active verbs telling what you intend to do: *analyze, choose, investigate, compare, justify, evaluate, explain, establish, determine,* and so on. Notice that Diane's statement begins with the active verb *recommend.*

Some reports require only a simple statement of purpose: *to investigate expanded teller hours, to select a manager from among four candidates, to describe the position of accounts supervisor.* Many assignments, though, demand additional focus to guide the project. An expanded statement of purpose considers three additional factors:

- **Scope.** What issues or elements will be investigated? To determine the scope, Diane brainstormed with Mike and others to pin down her task. She learned that Mycon currently had enough capital to consider purchasing a fleet of cars outright. Mike also told her that employee satisfaction was almost as important as cost effectiveness. Moreover, he disclosed his suspicion that employee-owned cars were costing Mycon more than leased cars. Diane had many issues to sort out in setting the boundaries of her report.
- **Significance.** Why is the topic worth investigating at this time? Some topics, after initial examination, turn out to be less important than originally thought. Others involve problems that cannot be solved, making a study useless. For Diane and Mike the problem had significance because Mycon's leasing agreement would expire shortly and decisions had to be made about a new policy for transportation of sales reps.
- **Limitations.** What conditions affect the generalizability and utility of a report's findings? In Diane's case her conclusions and recommendations might apply only to reps in her Kansas City sales district. Her findings would probably not be reliable for reps in Seattle, Phoenix, or Atlanta. Another limitation for Diane is time. She must complete the report in four weeks, thus restricting the thoroughness of her research.

An expanded purpose statement considers scope, significance, and limitations.

Diane decided to expand her statement of purpose to define the scope, significance, and limitations of the report.

Expanded Statement of Purpose: The purpose of this report is to recommend a plan that provides sales reps with cars to be used in their calls. The report will compare costs for three plans: outright ownership, leasing, and compensation for employee-owned cars. It will also measure employee reaction to each plan. The report is significant because Mycon's current leasing agreement expires April 1 and an improved plan could reduce costs and paperwork. The study is limited to costs for sales reps in the Kansas City district.

A. J. Jamal, who hosted the Comedy Channel TV show *Comic Justice,* attributes his successful career to basic problem-solving skills he learned while working for IBM. "Everybody wonders why I am so businesslike with comedy, and it dawned on me that doing comedy is like troubleshooting a technical problem." Jamal explains that IBM taught its employees to break down a big problem into smaller components and look for solutions to each one. This process, called factoring, is also an important first step in outlining the major issues in any report.

After preparing a statement of purpose, Diane checked it with Mike Rivers to be sure she was on target.

Anticipating the Audience and Issues

Once the purpose of a report is defined, a writer must think carefully about who will read the report. A major mistake is concentrating solely on a primary reader. Although one individual may have solicited the report, others within the organization may eventually read it, including upper management and people in other departments. A report to an outside client may first be read by someone who is familiar with the problem and then be distributed to others less familiar with the topic. Moreover, candid statements to one audience may be offensive to another audience. Diane could make a major blunder, for instance, if she mentioned Mike's suspicion that sales reps were padding their mileage statements. If the report were made public—as it probably would be to explain a new policy—the sales reps could feel insulted that their integrity was questioned.

As Diane considered her primary and secondary readers, she asked herself these questions:

- *What do my readers need to know about this topic?*
- *What do they already know?*
- *How will they react to this information?*
- *How can I make this information understandable and readable?*

Answers to these questions help writers determine how much background material to include, how much detail to add, whether to include jargon, what method of organization and presentation to follow, and what tone to use.

Major report problems should be broken into subproblems—or factored—to highlight possible solutions.

In the planning stages a report writer must also break the major investigative problem into subproblems. This process, sometimes called factoring, identifies issues to be investigated or possible solutions to the main problem. In this case Mycon must figure out the best way to transport sales reps. Each possible "solution" or issue that Diane considers becomes a factor or subproblem to be investigated. Diane came up with three tentative solutions to provide transportation to sales reps: (1) purchase cars outright, (2) lease cars, or (3) compensate employees for using their own cars. These three factors form the outline of Diane's study.

Diane continued to factor these main points into the following subproblems for investigation:

What plan should Mycon use to transport its sales reps?

I. Should Mycon purchase cars outright?
   A. How much capital would be required?
   B. How much would it cost to insure, operate, and maintain company-owned cars?
   C. Do employees prefer using company-owned cars?
II. Should Mycon lease cars?
   A. What is the best lease price available?
   B. How much would it cost to insure, operate, and maintain leased cars?
   C. Do employees prefer using leased cars?
III. Should Mycon compensate employees for using their own cars?
   A. How much has it cost in the past to operate employee-owned cars?
   B. How much paperwork is involved in reporting expenses?
   C. Do employees prefer being compensated for using their own cars?

Each subproblem would probably be further factored into additional subproblems. These issues may be phrased as questions, as Diane did, or as statements. In factoring a complex problem, prepare an outline showing the initial problem and its breakdown into subproblems. Make sure your divisions are consistent (don't mix issues), exclusive (don't overlap categories), and complete (don't skip significant issues).

Spotlight on **Communicators**

At Phelps County Bank in Rolla, Missouri, loan processor Peggy Laun helped implement a system of "upward evaluation." She saw a problem, conducted research, collected data, evaluated the results, and then proposed a system that enables employees to review their supervisors. Good research usually begins with a work plan designed to solve a specific problem.

Preparing a Work Plan

After analyzing the problem, anticipating the audience, and factoring the problem, you're ready to prepare a work plan. Preparing a plan forces you to evaluate your resources, set priorities, outline a course of action, and establish a time schedule. Such a plan keeps you on schedule and also gives management a means of measuring your progress. A good work plan includes the following:

- Statement of the problem
- Statement of the purpose including scope, significance, and limitations
- Description of the sources and methods of collecting data
- Tentative outline
- Work schedule

A good work plan provides an overview of a project: resources, priorities, course of action, and schedule.

A work plan gives a complete picture of a project. Because the usefulness and quality of any report rest primarily on its data, you'll want to allocate plenty of time to locate sources of information. For firsthand information you might interview people, prepare a survey, or even conduct a scientific experiment. For secondary information you'll probably search printed materials such as books and magazines as well as electronic materials on the Internet and Web. Your work plan describes how you expect to generate or collect data. Since data collection is a major part of report writing, the next section of this chapter treats the topic more fully.

Figure 11.6 shows a complete work plan for a report that studies safety seals for a food company's products. This work plan is particularly useful because it outlines the issues to be investigated. Notice that considerable thought and discussion and even some preliminary research are necessary to be able to develop a useful work plan.

Although this tentative outline guides investigation, it does not determine the content or order of the final report. You may, for example, study five possible solutions to a problem. If two prove to be useless, your report may discuss only the

FIGURE 11.6 Work Plan for a Formal Report

Tips for Preparing a Work Plan

- Start early; allow plenty of time for brainstorming and preliminary research.
- Describe the problem motivating the report.
- Write a purpose statement that includes its scope, significance, and limitations.
- Describe data collection sources and methods.
- Divide the major problem into subproblems stated as questions to be answered.
- Develop a realistic work schedule citing dates for completion of major tasks.
- Review the work plan with whoever authorized the report.

Statement of Problem

Consumers worry that food and drug products are dangerous as a result of tampering. Our company may face loss of market share and potential liability if we don't protect our products. Many food and drug companies now offer tamper-resistant packaging, but such packaging is costly.

Statement of Purpose

Defines purpose, scope, limits, and significance of report

The purpose of this study is to determine whether tamper-resistant packaging is necessary and/or feasible for our jams, jellies, and preserves. The study will examine published accounts of package tampering and evaluate how other companies have solved the problem. It will also measure consumers' interest in safety-seal packaging, as well as consumers' willingness to pay a slightly higher price for safety lids. We will conduct a market survey limited to a sample of 400 local consumers. Finally, the study will investigate a method for sealing our products and determine the cost for each unit we produce. This study is significant because safety seals could enhance the sales of our products and protect us from possible liability.

Sources and Methods of Data Collection

Describes primary and secondary data sources

Magazine and newspaper accounts of product tampering will be examined for the past 15 years. Articles describing tamper-resistant lids and other safe packaging devices for food and drug manufacturers will be studied. Moreover, our marketing staff will conduct a random telephone survey of local consumers, measuring their interest in safety seals. Finally, our production department will test various devices and determine the most cost-effective method to seal our product safely.

Tentative Outline

Factors problem into manageable chunks

I. Are consumers and producers concerned about product tampering?
   A. What incidents of tampering have been reported in the past 15 years?
   B. How did consumers react to tampered products causing harm?
   C. How did food and drug producers protect their products?
II. How do consumers react to safety seals on products today?
   A. Do consumers prefer food and drug products with safety seals?
   B. Would consumers be more likely to purchase our products if safety-sealed?
   C. Would consumers be willing to pay a few cents extra for safety seals?
III. What kind of safety seal is best for our products?
   A. What devices are other producers using—plastic "blister" packs, foil seals over bottle openings, or bands around lids?
   B. What device would work for our products?

Work Schedule

Estimates time needed to complete report tasks

Task	Dates
Investigate newspaper and magazine articles	Oct. 1-10
Examine safety-seal devices on the market	Oct. 8-18
Interview 400 local consumers	Oct. 8-24
Develop and test devices for our products	Oct. 15-Nov.14
Interpret and evaluate findings	Nov. 15-17
Compose first draft of report	Nov. 18-20
Revise draft	Nov. 21-23
Submit final report	Nov. 24

CASE STUDY

PROCESS IN PROGRESS

Specialized Bicycles Revisited

Why are women less ardent cyclists than men? At Specialized Bicycles Ariadne Scott puzzled over this question, as had much of the cycling industry intermittently for the past 15 years. Scott and other female employees from Specialized decided that they wanted to increase women's awareness of and participation in the sport of cycling. After much discussion and many lunchtime and extracurricular sessions, Scott's team hit on an idea that could achieve their goals—a two-day event targeting women and cycling. This event, called the "Women's Cycling Summit," would combine group rides with workshops, a conference, and riding clinics.

The goals of the Summit were to increase the visibility of women in cycling and to encourage women to view cycling as recreation, sport, fitness, and transportation. Planners also hoped to educate women on various aspects of cycling including fitness and training, life enhancement, products, clubs, safety, repair and maintenance, skills and knowledge, and improving cycling conditions. As part of the conference, Scott's team would distribute a survey that gathered information about such things as why women ride or don't ride, their riding habits, how they select a bike, what they want in cycling products, and what cycling issues are important to them.

Scott's team had big ideas, but they faced many obstacles. Because their small volunteer team was not officially recognized by Specialized, they had no funding. And if they wished to schedule a cycling conference, it had to be staged by the end of August, leaving a scant six months for preparations. Although they knew the event would attract only local participants, they saw the potential for national exposure in the future. As the team's plans crystallized, Scott realized that it was time to report to management and ask for support.

Critical Thinking

- What kind of report would Ariadne Scott and her team write to secure funding and support from management?
- Should Scott's report be developed directly or indirectly? Why? Should it be written formally or informally?
- Describe the major components of a logical work plan for Scott's team to follow in preparing to write a report requesting support.

three winners. Moreover, you will organize the report to accomplish your goal and satisfy the audience. Remember that a busy executive who is familiar with a topic may prefer to read the conclusions and recommendations before a discussion of the findings.

If the report is authorized by someone, be sure to review the work plan with that individual (your manager, client, or professor, for example) before proceeding with the project.

Researching Secondary Data

5

One of the most important steps in the process of writing a report is that of research. Because a report is only as good as its data, the remainder of this chapter describes how to find data and document it. As you analyze a report's purpose and audience, you'll assess the kinds of data needed to support your argument or explain your topic. Do you need statistics, background data, expert opinions, group opinions, or organizational data? Figure 11.7 lists five forms of data and provides questions to guide you in making your research accurate and productive.

FIGURE 11.7 Selecting Report Data

Form of Data	Questions to Ask
Statistical	What is the source? How were these figures derived? In what form do I need the statistics? Must they be converted? How recent are they?
Background or historical	Has this topic been explored before? What have others said about it? What sources did they use?
Expert opinion	Who are the experts? Are their opinions in print? Can they be interviewed? Do we have in-house experts?
Individual or group opinion	Do I need to interview or survey people (such as consumers, employees, or managers)? Do good questionnaires already exist? Can parts of existing test instruments be used or combined?
Organizational	What are the proper channels for obtaining in-house data? Are permissions required? How can I find data about public and private companies?

Primary data come from firsthand experience and observation; secondary data, from reading.

Data fall into two broad categories, primary and secondary. Primary data result from firsthand experience and observation. Secondary data come from reading what others have experienced and observed. Coca-Cola and Pepsi-Cola, for example, produce primary data when they stage taste tests and record the reactions of consumers. These same sets of data become secondary after they have been published and, let's say, a newspaper reporter uses them in an article about soft drinks. Secondary data are easier and cheaper to develop than primary data, which might involve interviewing large groups or sending out questionnaires.

We're going to discuss secondary data first because that's where nearly every research project should begin. Often, something has already been written about your topic. Reviewing secondary sources can save time and effort and prevent you from "reinventing the wheel." Most secondary material is available either in print or electronically.

Print Resources

Print sources are still the most visible part of libraries.

Although we're seeing a steady movement away from print to electronic data, print sources are still the most visible part of nearly all libraries. Much information is available only in print, and you may want to use some of the following print resources.

By the way, if you are an infrequent library user, begin your research by talking with a reference librarian about your project. These librarians won't do your research for you, but they will steer you in the right direction. And they are very accommodating. Several years ago a *Wall Street Journal* poll revealed that librarians are among the friendliest, most approachable people in the working world. Many libraries help you understand their computer, cataloging, and retrieval systems by providing brochures, handouts, and workshops.

Books. Although quickly outdated, books provide excellent historical, in-depth data on subjects. Books can be located through print or computer listings.

- **Card catalog.** Some libraries still maintain card catalogs with all books indexed on 3-by-5 cards alphabetized by author, title, or subject.
- **On-line catalog.** Most libraries today have computerized their card catalogs. Some systems are fully automated, thus allowing users to learn not only whether a book is located in the library but also whether it is currently available.

Periodicals. Magazines, pamphlets, and journals are called *periodicals* because of their recurrent or periodic publication. Journals, by the way, are compilations of scholarly articles. Articles in journals and other periodicals will be extremely useful to you because they are concise, limited in scope, current, and can supplement information in books.

- **Print indexes.** *The Readers' Guide to Periodical Literature* is a valuable index of general-interest magazine article titles. It includes such magazines as *Time, Newsweek, The New Yorker,* and *U.S. News & World Report.* More useful to business writers, though, will be the titles of articles appearing in business and industrial magazines (such as *Forbes, Fortune,* and *Business Week*). For an index of these publications, consult the *Business Periodicals Index.*
- **CD-ROM and Web-based bibliographic indexes.** Automated indexes similar to the print indexes just described are stored in CD-ROM and on-line databases. Many libraries now provide such bibliographic databases for computer-aided location of references and abstracts from magazines, journals, and newspapers, such as *The New York Times.* When using CD-ROM and Web-based on-line indexes, follow the on-screen instructions or ask for assistance from a librarian. It's a good idea to begin with a subject search because it generally turns up more relevant citations than keyword searches (especially when searching for names of people or companies). Once you locate usable references, print a copy of your findings and then check the shelf listings to see if the publications are available.

Spotlight on **Communicators**

Premier management consultant and best-selling author Tom Peters recognizes the value of ongoing research and reporting. He recommends collecting data not only about the performance of your own company but also about that of the competition. To stay abreast of rivals and their techniques, businesses must (1) collect data, (2) update them regularly, and (3) share them widely within the firm.

Electronic Databases

Many researchers today begin by looking in electronic databases.

As a writer of business reports today, you will probably begin your secondary research with electronic resources. Most writers turn to them first because they are fast, cheap, and easy to use. Some are even accessible from remote locations. This means that you can conduct detailed searches without ever leaving your office, home, or dorm room. Although some databases are still offered on CD-ROM, information is increasingly available in on-line databases. They have become the staple of secondary research.

What Is a Database? A database is a collection of information stored electronically so that it is accessible by computer and is digitally searchable. Databases provide both bibliographic (titles of documents and brief abstracts) and full-text documents. Most researchers today, however, prefer full-text documents. Various databases contain a rich array of magazine, newspaper, and journal articles, as well as newsletters, business reports, company profiles, government data, reviews, and directories.

Commercial databases offer articles, reports, and other information on-line.

Who Provides Commercial Databases? Electronic information distributed through commercial databases has been around for over two decades. Throughout the history of on-line information, the product (articles, reports, etc.) has been delivered by an uneasy partnership between the database producers, who create the content, and the on-line services, who distribute the content to the customers. Some of the best-known information producers are Information Access Company (IAC) and UMI (a Bell & Howell Company).[5] See Figure 11.8 for more information about UMI. These companies acquire the rights to the information, develop a variety of databases, and then distribute this information through professional services such as DIALOG and LEXIS-NEXIS and consumer services such as CompuServe, America Online (AOL), and Micosoft Network (MSN). The information producers are like manufacturers who wholesale their product to retailers (DIALOG, LEXIS-NEXIS, and AOL), who then present it in convenient packages at convenient locations for sale to consumers.

With the advent of the Internet, however, many of the information producers are discovering that they don't need the middlemen anymore. They can deliver their product straight to consumers through the Web. Moreover, Web-based information is not restricted to ASCII files. Documents are enriched with charts, graphs, bold and italic fonts, color, and pictures. In the future we can expect to see many more information producers offering their products directly to consumers through their own Web sites.

InfoTrac, ABI/INFORM, and ProQuest are popular on-line databases.

What Kinds of Databases Are Available? You can find an amazing number of databases offered through a variety of interfaces. One of the most popular collections of databases is offered through InfoTrac SearchBank, which serves nearly two thirds of the nation's public and academic libraries.[6] It offers general reference, business, academic, legal, and health-reference products in a variety of formats. Other popular collections of databases are offered by ProQuest Direct, ProQuest European Business, and ProQuest Asian Business. ABI/INFORM is a venerable database that has been providing coverage of business conditions, trends, corporate strategies and tactics, management techniques, competitive and product information, and other topics for more than twenty years.[7] Electric Library offers a collection of journal and newspaper articles, TV and radio transcripts, reference books, maps, and photographs.

LEXIS-NEXIS claims to offer over a billion documents for customers to search. These documents come from news sources and public records. The Lexis service focuses on legal information, while the Nexis service concentrates on business information resources. These include regional, national, and international newspapers; news wires; magazines; trade journals; business publications; and public records.

Libraries pay for on-line services available to walk-in or remote patrons.

Who Pays for the Information? All database information produced by companies such as IAC, ABI, and UMI has a price. As a student or library user, you may not be aware of the cost because your library is footing the bill. Libraries are charged for every commercial database they offer. Many libraries now allow users to connect to their networks to conduct on-line searches from remote locations. Why make a trip to the library when you can do your research from your personal computer? If you wish to have direct access to a consumer database, such as Electric Library or Northern Light, you can arrange for monthly service or per-item downloading. Northern Light, for example, charges $1 to $4 per article.[8]

Many business firms subscribe to specialized, comprehensive databases such as LEXIS-NEXIS, ABI/INFORM, and DIALOG. Firms are generally charged for the length of time required for each search. At this writing DIALOG charges $60 per hour to search the American and Canadian Business Directory files, plus $2 for each

FIGURE 11.8 UMI, Electronic Databases Compiler

UMI, one of the world's largest information archivers and distributors, offers information from more than 20,000 periodicals and 7,000 newspapers worldwide. Its popular ProQuest Direct is a family of electronic databases available at libraries or directly (for a fee) on the Web.

full-text document displayed.[9] Although well stocked and well organized, specialized commercial databases are indeed expensive to use. Many also involve steep learning curves. While learning how to select *keywords* (or *descriptors*) and how to explore the database, you can run up quite a bill.

The Internet

The World Wide Web is a collection of hypertext pages that offer information and links.

The best-known area of the Internet is the World Wide Web. Growing at a dizzying pace, the Web includes an enormous collection of specially formatted documents called Web *pages* located at Web sites around the world. Web offerings include online databases, magazines, newspapers, library resources, job and résumé banks, sound and video files, and many other information resources. Creators of Web pages use a special system of codes (*HTML*, i.e., Hypertext Markup Language) to format their offerings. The crucial feature of these hypertext pages is their use of links to other Web pages. Links are identified by underlined words and phrases or, occasionally, images. When clicked, links connect you to related Web pages. These pages immediately download to your computer screen, thus creating a vast web of resources at your fingertips.

Web Opportunities and Challenges. To a business researcher, the Web offers a wide range of organizational information. You can expect to find such items as product facts, public relations material, mission statements, staff directories, press releases, current company news, government information, selected article reprints, collaborative scientific project reports, and employment information. The Web is unquestionably one of the greatest sources of information now available to anyone needing facts quickly and inexpensively. But finding that information can be frustrating and time-consuming. The constantly changing contents of the Web and its lack of organization make it more problematic for research than searching com-

FIGURE 11.9 Hoover's Online for Company Information

An invaluable resource for business researchers, Hoover's provides free thumbnail sketches of 13,500 U.S. and foreign companies. The capsules, such as this one for PepsiCo, include location, contact information, key officers, sales, industry, and other current information. More comprehensive data is available to subscribers.

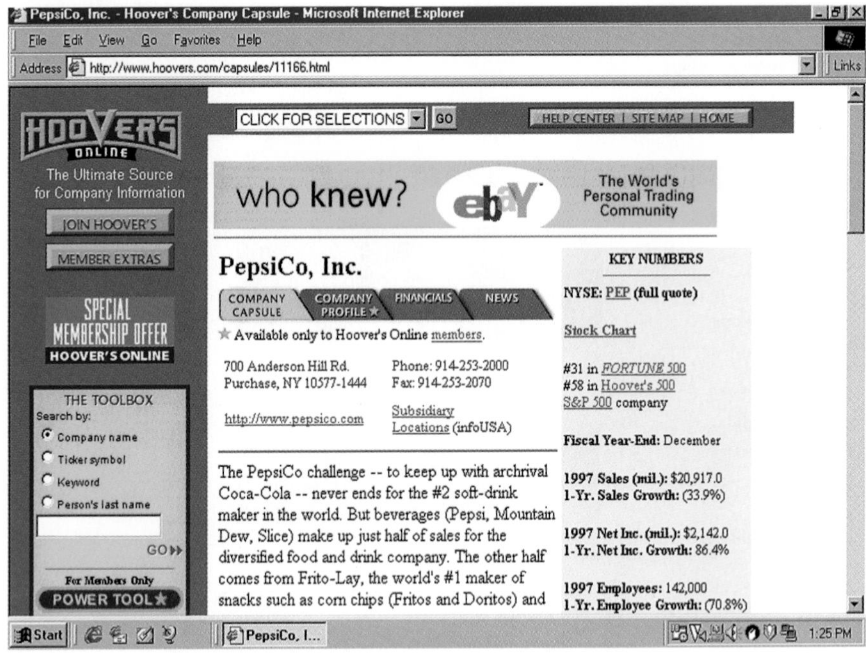

mercial databases. Moreover, Web content is uneven and often the quality is questionable. You'll learn more about evaluating Web sources shortly.

Web browsers are software programs that access Web pages and their links.

Web Browsers and URLs. Searching the Web requires a Web *browser,* such as Netscape Navigator or Microsoft Internet Explorer. Browsers are software programs that enable you to view the graphics and text, as well as access links of Web pages. To locate the Web page of a specific organization, you need its *URL* (*Uniform Resource Locator*). URLs are case and space sensitive, so be sure to type the address exactly as it is printed. For most companies, the URL is *http://www.xyzcompany.com.* (Tip: You can save some keystrokes by omitting "http://"; this portion of the URL is usually unnecessary.) Your goal is to locate the top-level Web page of an organization's site. On this page you'll generally find an overview of the site contents or a link to a site map. If you can't guess a company's URL, you can usually find it quickly at Hoover's **<www.hoovers.com>**. This site, shown in Figure 11.9, indexes and profiles thousands of U.S. and foreign companies.

Search tools such as Yahoo!, AltaVista, and HotBot help you locate specific Web sites and information.

Search Tools. Finding what you are looking for on the Web is like searching for a library book without using the card catalog. Fortunately, a number of search tools—such as Yahoo!, AltaVista, and HotBot—are available at specialized Web sites. These search tools look up words in their indexes. But because of the vastness of the Web, many Web pages are not indexed. One study revealed that the top search engine, HotBot, covered only 34 percent of the estimated pages available on the Web.[10] Even though search tools don't survey everything that's out there on the Web, they usually turn up more information than you want.

Like everything else about the Web, search tools are constantly evolving as developers change their features to attract more users. The following discussion highlights three of the most popular search tools. Please note, however, that keeping current with search engines is like trying to bottle fog. Check the Guffey Web site

FIGURE 11.10 Yahoo! Search Engine

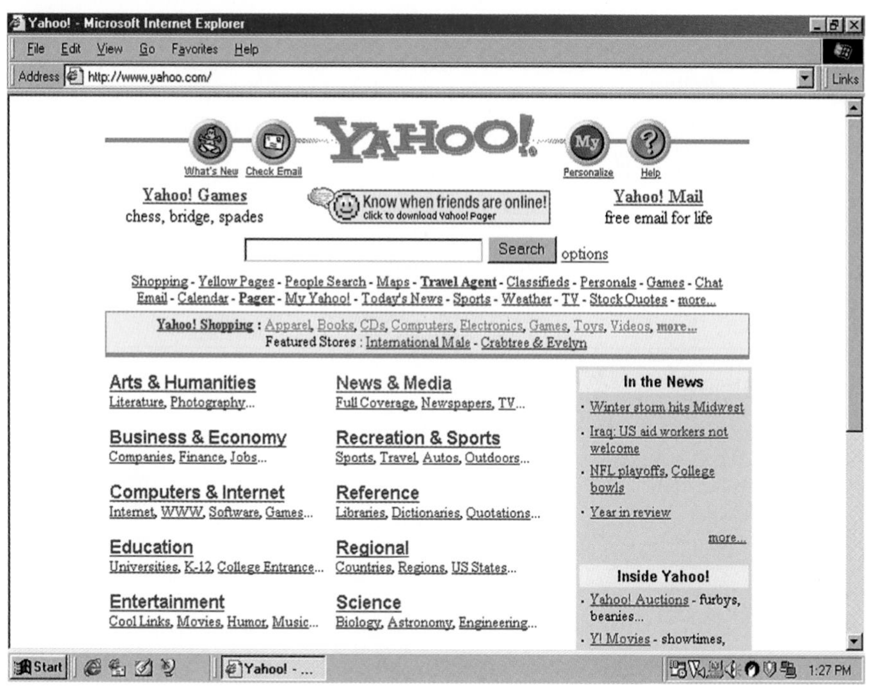

This popular Web tool first searches for matches in its own category indexes and Web sites selected by Yahoo's specialists. If no matches are found, it then automatically performs a Web-wide, full-text document search using the Inktomi search engine. You can customize your search by clicking on bars at the top and bottom of the page.

<www.meguffey.com> to find links to up-to-date reviews of search engines. And always read the help sections of any search engine when you first use it.

Yahoo! sorts Web sites into categories to assist researchers.

Yahoo! **<www.yahoo.com>**, shown in Figure 11.10, is one of the most widely used Web directories. Technically, it's not a "search engine." It uses human researchers to sift through sites and put them into categories, such as *business, sports,* or *computers.* If you have a general idea of what you're looking for and you wish to browse by category, Yahoo! is a good place to begin. It locates "starter" sites, from which you can branch out to more specialized ones. For example, if you are interested in fitness programs, you can start with the "Recreation and Sports" category and drill down to a site describing aerobics. In addition to its indexes, Yahoo! provides keyword searching and now ranks the results of searches in order of the most relevant to the least relevant results. *PC Magazine* rated Yahoo! highly, "With a first-class Web directory, top-notch newsfeeds, and plenty of extras, Yahoo! is a great place to start looking for just about anything."[11]

AltaVista gives the best results for specific searches.

AltaVista **<www.altavista.digital.com>**, shown in Figure 11.11, is considered by many to be the premier Web search engine. It looks for keywords. That's why, if you know what you are seeking, AltaVista consistently delivers better results than category-centered tools such as Yahoo!. AltaVista offers a large index of Web keywords. AltaVista also offers relevancy ranking; that is, the most relevant hits are shown first. Knowing how to phrase your search request precisely can improve results remarkably. In "simple" search mode, you can require or exclude keywords and you can search for precise phrases. See the accompanying Tech Talk box for more advice on structuring search terms. To take full advantage of AltaVista's power and flexibility, you'll want to spend some time learning advanced search syntax in its help pages.

HotBot **<www.hotbot.com>** boasts that it offers the most indexed Web pages of any search engine (54 million URLs at this writing).[12] It's considered a valuable tool for both novice and experienced searchers. Novice searchers will enjoy its helpful graphical query-building aids. Underneath its "Search" box, you'll find easy-to-use

FIGURE 11.11 AltaVista Search Engine

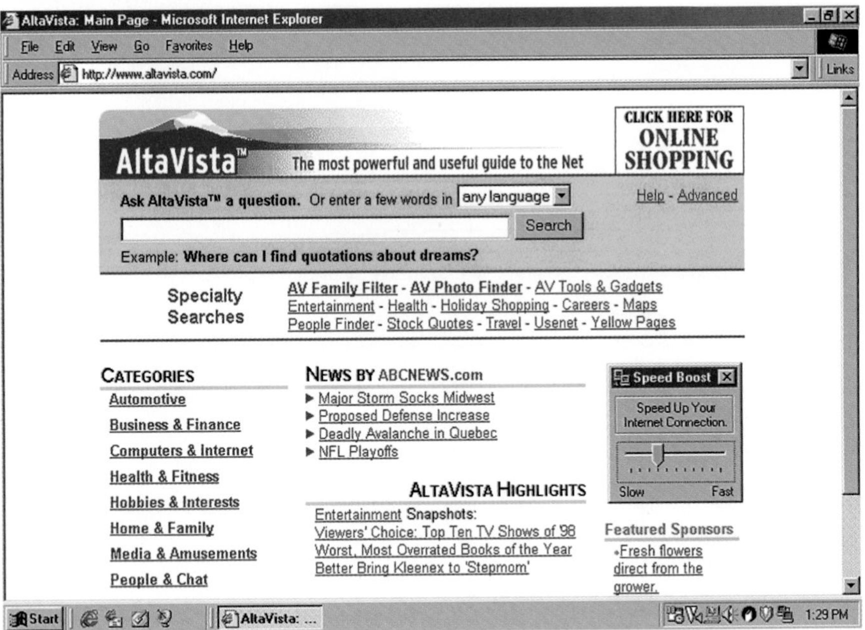

The favorite of many Internet researchers, AltaVista offers both keyword and natural language queries. However, knowledgeable researchers generally prefer keyword searching for more precise responses. Although its main page is somewhat cluttered, the "Help" and "Advanced" icons are useful for tips on pinpointing your search.

natural-language boxes (*all the words, anytime,* and *any language*) that allow you to narrow your search term and thus make it more precise. More experienced searchers can use its advanced searching capabilities, such as Boolean operators, which are described in the accompanying Tech Talk box. HotBot also offers filtering options so that you can, for instance, limit searches by date, geographical area, and media type. You can also filter out pornography sites. A recent addition includes the "Direct Hit Popularity Engine," which supplements your results with a list of the ten most-visited sites for your query.[13]

Excite offers "More like this" feature.

Excite **<www.excite.com>**, a favorite search engine of many specialists, locates items both by keyword and by concept. Concept searches identify documents relevant to the idea you are investigating and not just documents containing the term you enter. Excite searches more than 50 million Web sites. The best part of an Excite search is its "More like this" feature. Once you have made a promising "hit," you can click to see similar listings. Like many other search engines, Excite includes a relevance rating. The closer the rating is to 100 percent, the more confident Excite is that the document will fit your needs.

Other good search engines are *Lycos* **<www.lycos.com>**, *WebCrawler* **<www.crawler.com>**, *Dogpile* **<www.dogpile.com>** (which uses many search engines simultaneously), *Northern Light* **<www.northernlight.com>** (although it charges for its best documents), and Encyclopedia Britannica's *eBlast* **<www.ebig.com>** (which filters out questionable sites).

You must know how to use search engines to make them most effective.

Dumb as Rocks? Internet Search Tips and Techniques. "Search engines are dumber than a box of rocks," claims one Web veteran. For example, he says, "If you ask one to look up *bathing suits,* it will find sites on *bathing* and on *suits.*"[14] But enclosing the phrase in quotation marks tells most search engines to look for the words together. Knowing how to use search engines can transform that dumb box of rocks into a jewel case bulging with gems of useful information. Here's a summary of tips for savvy Internet researchers.[15]

TECH TALK

UNDERSTANDING NATURAL LANGUAGE, KEYWORD, AND BOOLEAN SEARCHING

Natural language searches involve posing a search question as you would normally state it. For example, "Is there a correlation between employee morale and productivity?" Using AltaVista for this search question produced nearly 5 million documents. Although the total is overwhelming, the most relevant "hits" were listed first. And the first ten items were all relevant. An increasing number of Web search engines and databases support natural language searching. It's particularly handy for vague or broad questions.

Keyword searches involve using the principal words in which you are interested. From the above question, you might choose to search on the phrase "employee morale" or "employee productivity." Omit useless words such as articles, conjunctions, and prepositions. Some search tools allow you to enclose keyword sequences (such as *employee morale*) in quotation marks to ensure that the specified words appear together and not separately.

Boolean searches involve joining keywords with "operators" (connectors) that include or exclude specific topics. For example, "employee AND morale." Using Boolean operators enables you to narrow your search and thus improve its precision. The following Boolean operators are most common:

AND Identifies only documents containing all of the specified words. **employee AND productivity AND morale**

OR Identifies documents containing at least one of the specified words: **employee OR productivity OR morale**

NOT Excludes documents containing the specified word: **employee productivity NOT morale**

NEAR Finds documents containing target words or phrases within a specified distance, for instance, within 10 words: **employee NEAR productivity**

Career Application

Using a search engine that supports natural language, keyword, and Boolean searching (such as AltaVista), try an experiment. Explore the same topic using (1) a natural language question, (2) key words, and (3) Boolean operators. Which method produced the most relevant hits?

- **Use two or three search tools.** Different Internet search engines turn up different results. One expert wisely remarked: "Every search engine will give you good results some of the time. Every search engine will give you surprisingly bad results some of the time. No search engine will give you good results all of the time."[16]

Web searches are more productive if you know the tricks.

- **Understand case sensitivity.** Generally use lowercase for your searches, unless you are searching for a term that is generally written in upper- and lowercase, such as a person's name.
- **Understand the AND/OR default and quotation marks.** When searching for a phrase, such as *cost benefit analysis,* most search tools will retrieve documents having all or some of the terms. This AND/OR strategy is the default of most search tools. To locate occurrences of the complete phrase, enclose it in quotation marks.
- **Prefer uncommon words.** Commonly used words make poor search keywords. For example, instead of *keeping employees,* use *employee retention.*
- **Omit articles and prepositions.** These are known as "stop words," and they do not add value to a search. Instead of *request for proposal,* use *proposal request.*
- **Use wild cards.** Most search engines support wildcards, such as asterisks. For example, the search term *cent** will retrieve *cents,* while *cent*** will retrieve both *center* and *centre.*

FIGURE 11.12 HotBot Help Screen

Most search engines offer help/hints screens. You'll find answers to commonly asked questions, tips for using the search engine, and techniques for basic and advanced searches.

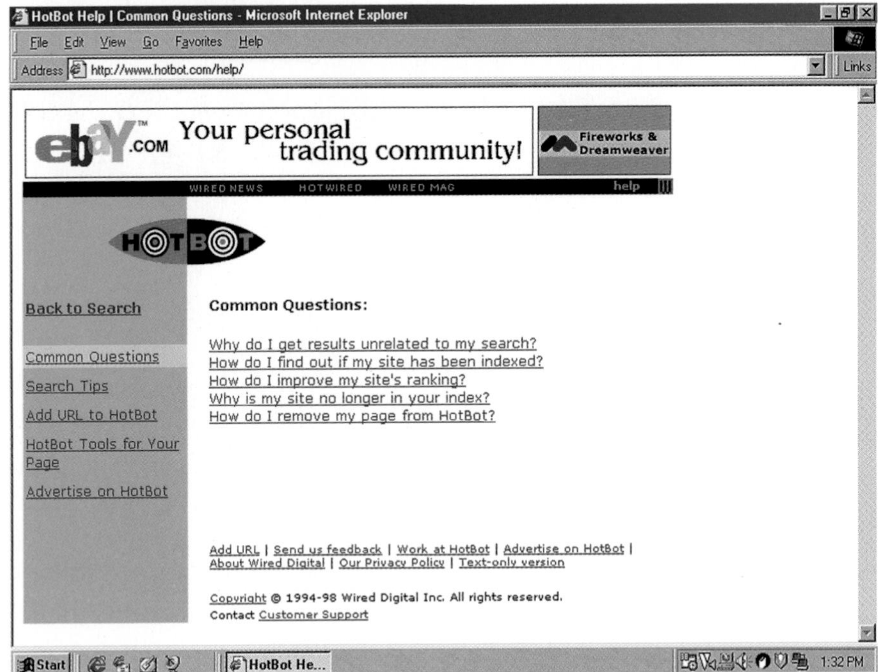

- **Know your search tool.** When connecting to a search service for the first time, always read the description of its service, including its FAQs (Frequently Asked Questions), Help, and How to Search sections, as illustrated in Figure 11.12.
- **Learn basic Boolean search strategies.** You can save yourself a lot of time and frustration by narrowing your search with Boolean operators, as described in the preceding Tech Talk box.
- **Bookmark the best.** To keep better track of your favorite Internet sites, save them on your browser as bookmarks.
- **Keep trying.** If a search produces no results, check your spelling. If you are using Boolean operators, check the syntax of your queries. Try synonyms and variations on words. Try to be less specific in your search term. If your search produces too many hits, try to be more specific. Think of words that uniquely identify what you're looking for. And use as many relevant keywords as possible.
- **Repeat your search a week later.** For the best results, return to your search a couple of days or a week later. The same keywords will probably produce additional results. That's because hundreds of thousands of new pages are being added to the Web every day.

Remember, search tools are "dumb as rocks." Only through clever cybersearching can you uncover the jewels hidden on the Internet.

Evaluating Web Sources. We have a tendency to assume that any information turned up via a search engine has somehow been evaluated as part of a valid selection process.[17] Wrong! The truth is that the Internet is rampant with unreliable sites that reside side by side with reputable sites. Anyone with a computer and an Internet

At Highsmith, Inc., the country's leading mail-order school supply, corporate librarians use the latest cypersearch techniques to track down data. Although head librarian Lisa Guedea Carreno, center, admits that she couldn't do her job without the Internet, she says that "it's a pretty unpredictable, unsophisticated tool." Her list of rules for evaluating Web sites includes asking questions about currency, authority, content, and accuracy.

connection can publish anything on the Web. Unlike library-based research, information at many sites has not undergone the editing or scrutiny of scholarly publication procedures. The information we read in journals and most reputable magazines is reviewed, authenticated, and evaluated. That's why we have learned to trust these sources as valid and authoritative. But information on the Web is much less reliable. Some sites exist to distribute propaganda; others want to sell you something. To use the Web meaningfully, you must scrutinize what you find. For comprehensive, updated information and links to guide you in evaluating Web sources, check the Guffey Web site **<www.meguffey.com>**. Here are specific questions to ask as you examine a site.

Evaluate the currency, authority, content, and accuracy of Web sites carefully.

- **Currency.** What is the date of the Web page? When was it last updated? Is some of the information obviously out of date? If the information is time sensitive and the site has not been updated recently, the site is probably not reliable.
- **Authority.** Who publishes or sponsors this Web page? What makes the presenter an authority? Is a contact address available for the presenter? Learn to be skeptical about data and assertions from individuals whose credentials are not verifiable.
- **Content.** Is the purpose of the page to entertain, inform, convince, or sell? Who is the intended audience, based on content, tone, and style? Can you judge the overall value of the content compared with the other resources on this topic? Web presenters with a slanted point of view cannot be counted on for objective data.
- **Accuracy.** Do the facts that are presented seem reliable to you? Do you find errors in spelling, grammar, or usage? Do you see any evidence of bias? Are footnotes provided? If you find numerous errors and if facts are not referenced, you should be alert that the data may be questionable.

Generating Primary Data

6

Primary data comes from firsthand experience.

Although you'll begin a business report by probing for secondary data, you'll probably need primary data to give a complete picture. Business reports that solve specific current problems typically rely on primary, firsthand data. If, for example, management wants to discover the cause of increased employee turnover in its Seattle office, it must investigate conditions in Seattle by collecting recent information. Providing answers to business problems often means generating primary data through surveys, interviews, observation, or experimentation.

Surveys yield efficient and economical primary data for reports.

Surveys. Surveys collect data from groups of people. When companies develop new products, for example, they often survey consumers to learn their needs. The advantages of surveys are that they gather data economically and efficiently. Mailed surveys reach big groups nearby or at great distances. Moreover, people responding to mailed surveys have time to consider their answers, thus improving the accuracy of the data.

Although mailed surveys may suffer low response rates, they are still useful in generating primary data.

Mailed questionnaires, of course, have disadvantages. Most of us rank them with junk mail, so response rates may be no higher than 10 percent. Furthermore, those who do respond may not represent an accurate sample of the overall population, thus invalidating generalizations from the group. Let's say, for example, that an insurance company sends out a questionnaire asking about provisions in a new policy. If only older people respond, the questionnaire data cannot be used to generalize what people in other age groups might think. A final problem with surveys has to do with truthfulness. Some respondents exaggerate their incomes or distort other facts, thus causing the results to be unreliable. Nevertheless, surveys may be the best way to generate data for business and student reports. Some companies are even using the Internet for gathering survey data, as discussed in the accompanying Tech Talk box. In preparing print or electronic surveys, consider these pointers:

- **Explain why the survey is necessary.** In a cover letter or an opening paragraph, describe the need for the survey. Suggest how someone or something other than you will benefit. If appropriate, offer to send recipients a copy of the findings.
- **Consider incentives.** If the survey is long, persuasive techniques may be necessary. Response rates can be increased by offering money (such as a $1 bill), coupons, gift certificates, free books, or other gifts.
- **Limit the number of questions.** Resist the temptation to ask for too much. Request only information you will use. Don't, for example, include demographic questions (income, gender, age, and so forth) unless the information is necessary to evaluate responses.

Effective surveys target appropriate samples and ask a limited number of specific questions with quantifiable answers.

- **Use questions that produce quantifiable answers.** Check-off, multiple-choice, yes-no, and scale (or rank-order) questions (illustrated in Figure 11.13) provide quantifiable data that are easily tabulated. Responses to open-ended questions (*What should the bookstore do about plastic bags?*) reveal interesting, but difficult-to-quantify, perceptions.[18] To obtain workable data, give interviewees a list of possible responses (as shown in items 5–8 of Figure 11.13). For scale and multiple-choice questions, try to present all the possible answer choices. To be safe, add an "Other" or "Don't know" category in case the choices seem insufficient to the respondent. Many surveys use scale questions because they capture degrees of feelings. Typical scale headings are "agree strongly," "agree somewhat," "neutral," "disagree somewhat," and "disagree strongly."
- **Avoid leading or ambiguous questions.** The wording of a question can dramatically affect responses to it, as shown in a *New York Times*/CBS national poll.[19]

TECH TALK

INTERNET ON-LINE SURVEYS PAY OFF

Gathering customer data by traditional methods usually involves expensive interviews or mailed paper surveys. Advanced Micro Devices (AMD) in Sunnyvale, California, switched to the Internet to quiz customers about satisfaction and found four distinct advantages:

- **Cost.** Because it costs about the same to survey 100 or 1,000 customers, the firm was able to sample a large number for a small cost. The on-line survey replaced costly face-to-face interviews with customers.
- **Speed.** Earlier surveys took at least eight weeks to complete, while the on-line version took just 30 days. In fact, AMD received the expected number of responses (200) in less than 30 days. And the first survey came back in just seven minutes.
- **Convenience.** Responding on-line is easier for customers than having to write answers. The survey took 12 to 15 minutes versus the 45 or 55 minutes needed for phone or in-person interviews. Eliminating manual data entry also made analysis faster and cheaper.
- **Candor.** Customers have more time to think about answers than they would in a face-to-face interview. And anonymity can make them more candid.

Career Application

What are disadvantages of on-line surveys? Examine the suggestions made in this chapter for preparing surveys. Would they be equally applicable for on-line surveys?

When respondents were asked "Are we spending too much, too little, or about the right amount on *assistance to the poor* [emphasis added]?" 13 percent responded "too much." When the same respondents were asked "Are we spending too much, too little, or about the right amount on *welfare* [emphasis added]?" 44 percent responded "too much." Because words have different meanings for different people, you must strive to use objective language and pilot test your questions with typical respondents. Stay away from questions that suggest an answer (*Don't you agree that the salaries of CEOs are obscenely high?*). Instead, ask neutral questions (*Do CEOs earn too much, too little, or about the right amount?*). Also avoid queries that really ask two or more things (*Should the salaries of CEOs be reduced or regulated by government legislation?*). Instead, break them into separate questions (*Should the salaries of CEOs be regulated by government legislation? Should the salaries of CEOs be reduced by government legislation?*).

The way a question is stated influences its response.

- **Select the survey population carefully.** Many surveys question a small group of people (a sample) and project the findings to a larger population. Let's say that a survey of your class reveals that the majority prefer Chicago-style pizza. Can you then say with confidence that all students on your campus (or in the nation) prefer Chicago-style pizza? To be able to generalize from a survey, you need to make the sample as large as possible. In addition, you need to determine whether the sample is like the larger population. For important surveys you will want to consult books on or experts in sampling techniques.

The larger the sample, the more accurate the resulting data is likely to be.

- **Conduct a pilot study.** Try the questionnaire with a small group so that you can remedy any problems. For example, in the survey shown in Figure 11.13, a pilot study revealed that female students generally favored cloth book bags and were willing to pay for them. Male students opposed purchasing cloth bags. By adding a gender category, researchers could verify this finding. The pilot study also

FIGURE 11.13 Preparing a Survey

1 PREWRITING

Analyze: The purpose is to help the bookstore decide if it should replace plastic bags with cloth bags for customer purchases.

Anticipate: The audience will be busy students who will be initially uninterested.

Adapt: Because students will be unwilling to participate, the survey must be simple and clear.

2 WRITING

Research: Ask students how they would react to cloth bags. Use their answers to form question response choices.

Organize: Open by explaining the survey's purpose and importance. Ask clear questions that produce quantifiable answers. Conclude with appreciation and instructions.

Compose: Write the first draft of the questionnaire.

3 REVISING

Revise: Try out the questionnaire with small, representative group. Revise unclear questions.

Proofread: Read for correctness. Be sure that answer choices do not overlap and that they are complete. Provide "other" category if appropriate (as in No. 9).

Evaluate: Is the survey clear, attractive, and easy to complete?

North Shore College Bookstore
STUDENT SURVEY

The North Shore College Bookstore wants to do its part in protecting the environment. Each year we give away 45,000 plastic bags for students to carry off their purchases. We are considering changing from plastic to cloth bags or some other alternative, but we need your views.

Explains need for survey (use cover letter for longer surveys)

Please place checks below to indicate your responses.

Uses groupings that do not overlap (not 9 to 15 and 15 or more)

1. How many units are you presently carrying?
   ___ 15 or more units
   ___ 9 to 14 units
   ___ 8 or fewer units

   ___ Male
   ___ Female

2. How many times have you visited the bookstore this semester?
   ___ 0 times ___ 1 time ___ 2 times ___ 3 times ___ 4 or more times

3. Indicate your concern for the environment.
   ___ Very concerned ___ Concerned ___ Unconcerned

4. To protect the environment, would you be willing to change to another type of bag when buying books?
   ___ Yes
   ___ No

Indicate your feeling about the following alternatives.

Uses scale questions to channel responses into quantifiable alternatives, as opposed to open-ended questions

For major purchases the bookstore should	Agree	Undecided	Disagree
5. Continue to provide plastic bags.	___	___	___
6. Provide no bags; encourage students to bring their own bags.	___	___	___
7. Provide no bags; offer cloth bags at reduced price (about $3).	___	___	___
8. Give a cloth bag with each major purchase, the cost to be included in registration fees.	___	___	___

Allows respondent to add an answer in case choices provided seem insufficient

9. Consider another alternative, such as
   ____

Please return the completed survey form to your instructor or to the survey box at the North Shore College Bookstore exit. Your opinion counts.

Tells how to return survey form

Thanks for your help!

revealed the need to ensure an appropriate representation of male and female students in the survey.

Interviews. Some of the best report information, particularly on topics about which little has been written, comes from individuals. These individuals are usually experts or veterans in their fields. Consider both in-house and outside experts for business reports. Tapping these sources will call for in-person or telephone interviews. To elicit the most useful data, try these techniques:

Interviews with experts yield useful report data, especially when little has been written about a topic.

- **Locate an expert.** Ask managers and individuals working in an area whom they consider to be most knowledgeable. Check membership lists of professional organizations, and consult articles about the topic or related topics. Most people enjoy being experts or at least recommending them. You could also post an inquiry to an Internet *newsgroup.* An easy way to search newsgroups in a topic area is through *Deja News* **<www.dejanews.com>**.
- **Prepare for the interview.** Learn about the individual you're interviewing as well as the background and terminology of the topic. Let's say you're interviewing a corporate communication expert about producing an in-house newsletter. You ought to be familiar with terms such as *font* and software such as QuarkXpress, Adobe Pagemaker, and Ventura Publisher. In addition, be prepared by making a list of questions that pinpoint your focus on the topic. Ask the interviewee if you may record the talk.
- **Make your questions objective and friendly.** Don't get into a debating match with the interviewee. And remember that you're there to listen, not to talk! Use open-ended, rather than yes-or-no, questions to draw experts out.
- **Watch the time.** Tell interviewees in advance how much time you expect to need for the interview. Don't overstay your appointment.
- **End graciously.** Conclude the interview with a general question, such as "Is there anything you'd like to add?" Express your appreciation, and ask permission to telephone later if you need to verify points.

Observation and Experimentation. Some kinds of primary data can be obtained only through firsthand observation and investigation. How long does a typical caller wait before a customer service rep answers the call? How is a new piece of equipment operated? Are complaints of sexual harassment being taken seriously? Observation produces rich data, but that information is especially prone to charges of subjectivity. One can interpret an observation in many ways. Thus, to make observations more objective, try to quantify them. For example, record customer telephone wait-time for 60-minute periods at different times throughout a week. Or compare the number of sexual harassment complaints made with the number of investigations undertaken and the resulting action.

Some of the best report data come from firsthand observation and investigation.

Experimentation produces data suggesting causes and effects. Informal experimentation might be as simple as a pretest and posttest in a college course. Did students expand their knowledge as a result of the course? More formal experimentation is undertaken by scientists and professional researchers who control variables to test their effects. Assume, for example, that the Hershey Company wants to test the hypothesis (which is a tentative assumption) that chocolate lifts people out of the doldrums. An experiment testing the hypothesis would separate depressed individuals into two groups: those who ate chocolate (the experimental group) and those who did not (the control group). What effect did chocolate have? Such experiments are not done haphazardly, however. Valid experiments require sophisticated research designs and careful attention to matching the experimental and control groups.

Documenting Data

7

Documenting data lends credibility, aids the reader, and protects the writer from plagiarism.

Documenting data means revealing and crediting your information sources. Careful documentation in a report serves three purposes:

- **Strengthens your argument.** Including good data from reputable sources will convince readers of your credibility and the logic of your reasoning.
- **Protects you.** Acknowledging your sources keeps you honest. It's unethical and illegal to use others' ideas without proper documentation. The accompanying Ethical Insights box lists specific ways to avoid plagiarism.
- **Instructs the reader.** Citing references enables readers to pursue a topic further and make use of the information themselves.

Three Documentation Formats

Select a suitable format to show textual and bibliographic references for your report sources.

You may choose from three formats to document your data. Select a format that suits your needs and those of your instructor or organization. Many organizations have developed their own in-house documentation styles, which are often a variation of those shown here. Regardless of the format selected, stay with that style throughout your report.

References are usually cited in two places: (1) a brief citation appears in the text and (2) a complete citation appears in a bibliography at the end of the report. The three most common formats for citations and bibliographies are the following: (1) *The Chicago Manual of Style* format, (2) the Modern Language Association (MLA) format, and (3) the American Psychological Association (APA) format. Each has its own style for textual references and bibliography lists, as summarized in Figure 11.14.

The Chicago Manual of Style Format. Report writers who prefer to cite references with a small superscript (raised) number in the text generally follow the format prescribed in *The Chicago Manual of Style,* now in its 14th edition. The superscript refers the reader to the foot of the page, where the complete source appears, as shown in Format 1 of Figure 11.14. At the end of the report, a bibliography lists all the references cited in the report (and perhaps all the references consulted).

An alternative to footnotes is a list of endnotes. Instead of citing references at the bottom of each page, the writer lists them in "Notes" at the end of the report. This method is certainly easier to prepare than footnotes, and pages are less cluttered. References, however, are less convenient for readers. Most high-end word processing programs make both footnotes and endnotes easy to use.

Modern Language Association Format. Writers in the humanities frequently use the MLA format, illustrated in Format 2, Figure 11.14. In parentheses close to the textual reference appears the author's name and page cited. If no author is known, a shortened version of the source title is used. At the end of the report, the writer lists alphabetically all references in a bibliography called "Works Cited." This format is somewhat more efficient than the Chicago style because references appear only once—in "Works Cited." Appendix C contains additional information about the MLA format. To see a long report illustrating MLA documentation, turn to Figure 14.4 in Chapter 14.

American Psychological Association Format. Like the MLA style, the APA style, illustrated in Format 3, Figure 11.14, includes the author's name in the text where the reference appears. The APA format, however, includes the publication date and "p." before the page number of the cited reference. Other variations occur

ETHICAL INSIGHTS

HOW TO AVOID PLAGIARISM

Whether you quote directly or paraphrase (put someone else's ideas into your own words), you must acknowledge the source. Using another person's words or ideas without citing the source is plagiarism, a serious offense in the academic world and elsewhere. Students who plagiarize risk a failing grade in a class and even expulsion from school. Businesspeople, professionals, and politicians caught plagiarizing lose not only their credibility but often their jobs. For example, Boston University Dean H. Joachim Maitre lost his job after it was learned that he plagiarized most of a commencement address. Laura Parker, a newspaper editor in Miami, was fired for copying one of her stories from a news service. And a drama critic in Vancouver, Washington, was fired for pilfering a film review from Roger Ebert. Unskilled researchers can unintentionally plagiarize if they're not careful. Here are some suggestions for collecting data that might prevent an embarrassing moment for you.

- **Take excellent notes.** When you find a good data source, write complete notes on cards or separate sheets of paper. Mark the author's ideas and words carefully. Put your own remarks in parentheses or use a different color. Be sure you distinguish your notes and ideas from the author's.
- **Know what should be documented.** Information that is common knowledge requires no documentation. For example, the statement *The Wall Street Journal is a popular business newspaper* would require no citation. Statements that are not common knowledge, however, must be documented. For example, *The Wall Street Journal is the largest daily newspaper in the United States* would require a citation because most people do not know this fact. Also use citations to document direct quotations and ideas that you summarize or paraphrase in your own words. Moreover, cite sources for proprietary information such as statistics organized and reported by a newspaper or magazine.
- **Use quotations sparingly.** Wise writers and speakers use direct quotations to (1) provide objective background data and establish the severity of a problem as seen by experts; (2) repeat identical phrasing because of its precision, clarity, or aptness; or (3) duplicate exact wording before criticizing. Avoid the tendency of untrained report writers to overuse quotations. Documents that contain pages of spliced-together quotations carry a hidden message: these writers have few ideas of their own.
- **Introduce quotations.** When you must use a long quotation, try to summarize and introduce it in your own words. Readers want to know the gist of a quotation before they tackle it. For example, to introduce a quotation discussing the shrinking staffs of large companies, you could precede it with your words: *In predicting employment trends, Charles Waller believes the corporation of the future will depend on a small core of full-time employees.*
- **Cite quotations and sources properly.** Use quotation marks to enclose exact quotations, such as this: *"The current image,"* says Charles Waller, *"of a big glass-and-steel corporate headquarters on landscaped grounds directing a worldwide army of tens of thousands of employees may soon be a thing of the past."* Select a documentation format, such as superscripts or parenthetical notes, and use it consistently.

Career Track Application

Examine two or more research articles from a professional journal in your career field. How do the writers cite references? Are many quotations used? How are they introduced?

in bibliography formats, the most notable being the emphasis on publication dates in the APA style. For more details about the APA style, see Appendix C. You may see a business report illustrating the APA reference style by turning to Figure 13.6 in Chapter 13.

Model the format for electronic sources on those of print sources.

Citing Electronic Sources. Standards for researchers using electronic sources are still emerging. When citing electronic media, you should hold the same goals as for print sources. That is, you wish to give credit to the authors and to allow others to easily locate the same or updated information. However, traditional formats for identifying authors, publication dates, and page numbers become confusing when

FIGURE 11.14 Three Documentation Formats

Tips for Documentation—Chicago Style

- Use footnotes to place complete references at the bottom of each report page, or use endnotes to place references in a list at the end of the report.
- Place a superscript (raised) number at the end of a sentence citing a reference.
- Include in the reference the author's name, title of publication, date, and page cited.
- Number citations consecutively throughout.
- For footnotes, separate them from the text with a $1\frac{1}{2}$-inch line. Leave one blank line above and below the separating line.
- Supply a list of references (a "Bibliography") at the end of the report.

1.

***Chicago Manual of Style* Documentation Style, Footnotes or Endnotes, Bibliography**

Text Page

Peanut butter was first delivered to the world by a St. Louis physician in 1890, possibly as a protein substitute for elderly patients.[1] However, it was the 1905 Universal Exposition in St. Louis that truly launched peanut butter. Since then, annual peanut butter consumption has zoomed to 3.3 pounds a person in the U.S.[2] America's farmers produce 1.6 million tons of peanuts annually, about half of which is used for oil, nuts, and candy. Lisa Gibbons, executive secretary of the Peanut Advisory Board, says that "peanuts in some form are in four of the top ten candies: Snickers, Reese's Peanut Butter Cups, Peanut M & Ms, and Butterfingers."[3]

---

[1]"History of Peanut Butter," Peanut Advisory Board <http://www.peanutbutterlovers.com/History/index.html> (Retrieved 17 January1999).

[2]Elizabeth Ruth Barrons, "A Comparison of Domestic and International Consumption of Legumes," Journal of Economic Agriculture 23, no. 3 (November 1998): 45.

[3]Mark Allen Meadows, "Peanut Crop Is Anything but Peanuts at Home and Overseas," Business Monthly, 30 September 1997, 32.

Tips for a Bibliography—Chicago Style

- Make the bibliography the last page of a report.
- Center the heading in all capitals 2 inches from the top of the page.
- Include all the references cited in the report and, optionally, all references consulted in your research.
- Arrange items alphabetically by authors' last names or by the first entry of the reference.
- Single-space within and double-space between references.
- Indent the second and succeeding lines of references.

Bibliography

BIBLIOGRAPHY

Barrons, Elizabeth Ruth. "A Comparison of Domestic and International Consumption of Legumes." Journal of Economic Agriculture 23, no 3 (November 1998): 45–49.

"History of Peanut Butter." Peanut Advisory Board. <http://www.peanutbutterlovers.com/History/index.html> (Retrieved 17 January 1999).

Meadows, Mark Allen. "Peanut Crop Is Anything but Peanuts at Home and Overseas." Business Monthly, 30 September 1997, 31–34.

Tips for Documentation—MLA Style

- Document each textual reference with a short source description in parentheses.
- Include the last name of the author(s) and the page number cited. Omit a comma, as (Jones 44).
- If no author is known, refer to the title or a shortened version of it, as (Facts at Fingertips 104).
- At the end of the report, present the complete bibliography ("Works Cited") with entries arranged alphabetically. For more information about MLA reference style, see Appendix C.

2.

Modern Language Association Documentation Style, Parenthetic Notes, Works Cited

Text Page

Peanut butter was first delivered to the world by a St. Louis physician in 1890, possibly as a protein substitute for elderly patients ("History of Peanut Butter"). However, it was the 1905 Universal Exposition in St. Louis that truly launched peanut butter. Since then, annual peanut butter consumption has zoomed to 3.3 pounds a person in the U.S. (Barrons 46). America's farmers produce 1.6 million tons of peanuts annually, about half of which is used for oil, nuts, and candy. Lisa Gibbons, executive secretary of the Peanut Advisory Board, says that "peanuts in some form are in four of the top ten candies: Snickers, Reese's Peanut Butter Cups, Peanut M & Ms, and Butterfingers" (Meadows 32).

Bibliography

Works Cited

Barrons, Elizabeth Ruth. "A Comparison of Domestic and International Consumption of Legumes." Journal of Economic Agriculture 23 (1998): 45–49.

"History of Peanut Butter." Peanut Advisory Board. Retrieved 19 Jan. 1999 <http://www.peanutbutterlovers.com/History/index.html>.

Meadows, Mark Allen. "Peanut Crop Is Anything but Peanuts at Home and Overseas." Business Monthly, 30 September 1997: 31–34.

Tips for Documentation—APA Style

- Document each specific textual source with a short description in parentheses.
- Include the last name of the author(s), date of publication, and page number at an appropriate point in the text, as (Jones, 1998, p. 36).
- If no author is known, refer to the first few words of the reference list entry and the year, as (*Computer Privacy*, 1998, p. 59).
- Omit page numbers for general references, but always include page numbers for direct quotations.
- At the end of the report, present the complete bibliography ("References") with entries arranged alphabetically. For more information about APA reference style, see Appendix C.

3.

American Psychological Association Documentation Style, Parenthetic Notes, References

Text Page

Peanut butter was first delivered to the world by a St. Louis physician in 1890, possibly as a protein substitute for elderly patients (Peanut Advisory Board Web site, no date). However, it was the 1905 Universal Exposition in St. Louis that truly launched peanut butter. Since then, annual peanut butter consumption has zoomed to 3.3 pounds a person in the U.S. (Barrons, 1998, p. 46). America's farmers produce 1.6 million tons of peanuts annually, about half of which is used for oil, nuts, and candy. Lisa Gibbons, executive secretary of the Peanut Advisory Board, says that "peanuts in some form are in four of the top ten candies: Snickers, Reese's Peanut Butter Cups, Peanut M & Ms, and Butterfingers" (Meadows, 1997, p. 32).

Bibliography

References

Barrons, E. (1998). A comparison of domestic and international consumption of legumes. Journal of Economic Agriculture 23, (3), 45–49.

Meadows, M. (1997 September 30). Peanut crop is anything but peanuts at home and overseas. Business Monthly, 14, 31–34.

Peanut Advisory Board (No date). History of peanut butter. Retrieved January 17, 1999 from <http://www.peanutbutterlovers.com/History/index.html>.

CASE STUDY

PROCESS TO PRODUCT

Applying Your Skills at Specialized

Ariadne Scott's team of volunteers at Specialized is convinced that women are underrepresented in cycling and that they hold vast market potential. Her team seeks funding and support for a Women's Cycling Summit, consisting of workshops and seminars on cycling-related issues. As Scott looks ahead, she realizes how big the task is—finding a conference site, publicizing the event, securing top speakers, arranging workshop sessions, recruiting volunteers, coordinating group rides, and locating sponsors. Her team also has to create a survey, tabulate the results, and circulate its findings. Finally, she must follow through on the recommendations made by conference participants.

But her first priority is writing a report that persuades Specialized management to support her team's conference project. To write the report, Scott's team plans to gather information from studies on women and sports, *Bicycling Magazine,* cycling trade journals, business journals, bicycle stores, and interviews with female cyclists.

Your Job

As writing consultants, you and several of your colleagues have been asked by Scott's team to help plan a persuasive report that wins management support. Prepare a work plan that includes a statement of problem, statement of purpose, sources and methods of data collection, tentative outline, and work schedule. The work schedule covers April 1 through April 21. The owner of your consultancy (your instructor) may have suggestions for you in completing this project. Submit your recommendations in a memo or e-mail message to your instructor.

applied to sources on the Internet. Strive to give correct credit for electronic sources by including the author's name (when available), document title, Web page title, Web address, and access date. Formats for some electronic sources are shown in Appendix C. For more comprehensive electronic citation formats, visit the Guffey Web site.

Summary of Learning Objectives

1 **Describe nine typical business reports.** (1) Periodic reports monitor and control business operations, (2) situational reports describe one-time activities, (3) investigative reports examine problems and supply facts without making recommendations, (4) compliance reports satisfy laws and regulations, (5) justification reports analyze problems and make recommendations, (6) yardstick reports evaluate alternatives using consistent criteria, (7) feasibility reports analyze the practicality of alternatives, (8) research studies examine problems scientifically, and (9) proposals offer to solve problems.

2 **Distinguish between informational and analytical reports.** Informational reports collect and organize facts but offer little analysis and no recommendations. Analytical reports provide data, analyses, conclusions, and, if requested, recommendations.

3 **Identify four report formats.** Reports may be written like letters (using company stationery and letter formatting), like memos (opening with TO, FROM, DATE, and SUBJECT), like manuscripts (on plain paper beginning with a title), and on printed forms (with data inserted in appropriate spots).

4 **Apply the writing process to reports.** Report writers begin by analyzing a problem and writing a problem statement, which may include the scope, significance, and limitations of the project. Writers then analyze the audience and define major issues. They prepare a work plan, including a tentative outline and work schedule. They collect, organize, interpret, and illustrate their data. Then they compose the first draft. Finally, they revise (perhaps many times), proofread, and evaluate.

5 **Conduct research by locating secondary data.** Secondary data may be located by searching for books, periodicals, and newspapers through print or electronic indexes. Much report information today is located in electronic databases that are generally offered through professional information services such as DIALOG and LEXIS-NEXIS or through consumer services such as AOL. Much information is also available on the Internet, but searching for it requires knowledge of search tools and techniques. Three popular search tools are Yahoo!, AltaVista, and HotBot. Information obtained on the Internet should be scrutinized for currency, authority, content, and accuracy.

6 **Generate primary data for research projects.** Researchers generate first-hand, primary data through surveys (in-person, print, and on-line), interviews, observation, and experimentation. Surveys are most economical and efficient for gathering information from large groups of people. Interviews are useful when working with experts in a field.

7 **Describe three formats for documenting data sources.** All data sources must be documented. *The Chicago Manual of Style* format prescribes the use of superscript numbers within the text and footnotes or endnotes to record the complete reference. A bibliography at the end of the report lists all references alphabetically. The Modern Language Association format includes the author's name and page reference in parentheses following the citation. A complete list of references, "Works Cited," appears at the end of the report. The American Psychological Association format shows the author, date, and page number in parentheses near the reference. A bibliography at the end of the report is called "References." All three formats have specific sequence and capitalization styles, which must be used consistently. Electronic sources must also be documented, although formats are still evolving.

CHAPTER REVIEW

1. What purpose do most reports serve? (Obj. 1)
2. List nine kinds of typical business reports. (Obj. 1)
3. How do informational and analytical reports differ? (Obj. 2)
4. How do the direct and indirect patterns of development differ? (Obj. 2)
5. Under what circumstances would an analytical report be organized directly? Indirectly? (Obj. 2)
6. Identify four common report formats. (Obj. 3)
7. List the seven steps in the report-writing process. (Obj. 4)
8. What is factoring? (Obj. 4)
9. How do primary data differ from secondary data? Give an original example of each. (Objs. 5 and 6)
10. Should data collection for most business reports begin with primary or secondary research? Why? (Obj. 5)
11. Compare three search tools for the Web. (Obj. 5)
12. Discuss five techniques that you think are most useful in enhancing a Web search. (Obj. 5)
13. In questionnaires what kind of questions produce quantifiable answers? (Obj. 6)
14. What is documentation, and why is it necessary in reports? (Obj. 7)
15. What kind of data require no documentation? (Obj. 7)

CRITICAL THINKING

1. What kinds of reports typically flow upward in an organization? What kinds flow downward? Why? (Obj. 1)
2. Discuss this statement, made by three well-known professional business writers: "Nothing you write will be completely new."[20] (Objs. 5 and 6)
3. For long reports, why is a written work plan a wise idea? (Obj. 4)
4. Is information obtained on the Web as reliable as information obtained from journals, newspapers, and magazines? (Obj. 5)
5. **Ethical Issue:** Discuss this statement: "Let the facts speak for themselves." Are facts always truthful?

ACTIVITIES

11.1 Report Types, Functions, Writing Styles, and Formats (Objs. 1, 2, and 3)

For the following reports, (1) name the report's primary function (informational or analytical), (2) recommend a direct or indirect pattern of development, and (3) select a report format (memo, letter, or manuscript).

a. A persuasive proposal from a construction firm to the Art Institute of Philadelphia describing the contractor's bid to renovate and convert the school's newly purchased 1930s art deco office building into offices, studios, and classrooms.
b. A situational report submitted by a sales rep to her manager describing her attendance at a sports products trade show, including the reactions of visitors to a new noncarbonated sports drink.
c. A recommendation report from a technical specialist to the vice president, Product Development, analyzing ways to prevent piracy of the software company's latest game program. The vice president values straight talk and is familiar with the project.
d. A progress report from a location manager to a Hollywood production company describing safety, fire, and environmental precautions taken for the shooting of a stunt involving blowing up a boat off Marina del Rey.
e. A feasibility report prepared by an outside consultant examining whether a company should invest in a health and fitness center for its employees.
f. A compliance report from a national moving company telling state authorities how it has improved its safety program so that its trucks now comply with state regulations. The report describes but doesn't interpret the program.

11.2 Collaborative Project: Report Portfolio (Objs. 1, 2, and 3)

Team

In teams of four or five, collect four or more sample business reports illustrating at least three report types described in this chapter. (Don't forget corporate annual reports.) For each report identify and discuss the following characteristics:

a. Type
b. Function (informational or analytical)
c. Pattern (primarily direct or indirect)
d. Writing style (formal or informal)
e. Format (memo, letter, manuscript, preprinted form)
f. Effectiveness (clarity, accuracy, expression)

In an informational memo report to your instructor, describe your findings.

11.3 Data Forms and Questions (Objs. 5 and 6)

In conducting research for the following reports, name at least one form of data you will need and the questions you should ask to determine if that set of data is appropriate (see Figure 11.7).

a. A report evaluating the relocation of an Irvine, California, company to Houston, Texas. You find figures in a *USA Today* article showing the average cost of housing for 60 cities, including Irvine and Houston.

b. A market research report to assess fan support for a name ("Sharks") and logo (a shark biting through a hockey stick) selected for a professional hockey team in San Jose.

c. A report examining the effectiveness of ethics codes in American businesses.

11.4 Problem and Purpose Statements (Obj. 4)

The following situations require reports. For each situation write (a) a concise problem question and (b) a simple statement of purpose.

a. The Bank of New Salem is losing money on its Webster branch. A number of branches are being targeted for closure. Management authorizes a report that must recommend a course of action for the Webster branch.

b. New Food and Drug Administration regulations have changed the definitions of common terms such as *fresh, fat free, low in cholesterol,* and *light.* The Big Deal Bakery worries that it must rewrite all its package labels. Big Deal doesn't know whether to hire a laboratory or a consultant for this project.

c. Customers placing telephone orders for clothing with James River Enterprises typically order only one or two items. JRE wonders if it can train telephone service reps to motivate customers to increase the number of items ordered per call.

11.5 Problem and Purpose Statements (Obj. 4)

Identify a problem in your current job or a previous job (such as inadequate equipment, inefficient procedures, poor customer service, poor product quality, or personnel problems). Assume your boss agrees with your criticism and asks you to prepare a report. Write (a) a two- or three-sentence statement describing the problem, (b) a problem question, and (c) a simple statement of purpose for your report.

11.6 Factoring and Outlining a Problem (Obj. 4)

Critical Thinking

Japan Airlines has asked your company, Connections International, to prepare a proposal for a training school for tour operators. JAL wants to know if Burbank would be a good spot for its school. Burbank interests JAL but only if nearby entertainment facilities can be used for tour training. JAL also needs an advisory committee consisting, if possible, of representatives of the travel community and perhaps executives of other major airlines. The real problem is how to motivate these people to cooperate with JAL.

You've heard that NBC Studios in Burbank offers training seminars, guest speakers, and other resources for tour operators. You wonder if Magic Mountain in Valencia would also be willing to cooperate with the proposed school. And you remember that Griffith Park is nearby and might make a good tour training spot. Before JAL will settle on Burbank as its choice, it wants to know if access to air travel is adequate. It's also concerned about available school building space. Moreover, JAL wants to know whether city officials in Burbank would be receptive to this tour training school proposal.

To guide your thinking and research, factor this problem into an outline with several areas to investigate. Further divide the problem into subproblems, phrasing each entry as a question. (See the tentative outline in Figure 11.6.)

11.7 Developing a Work Plan (Obj. 4)

Select a report topic from Activities 13.5–13.19, or 14.1–14.18. For that report prepare a work plan that includes the following:

a. A statement of the problem

b. An expanded statement of purpose (including scope, limitations, and significance)

c. Sources and methods

d. A tentative outline

e. A work schedule (with projected completion dates)

11.8 Using Secondary Sources (Obj. 5)

Conduct research in a library. Prepare a bibliography of the most important magazines and professional journals in your major field of study. Your instructor may ask you to list the periodicals and briefly describe their content, purpose, and audience. In a cover memo to your instructor, describe your bibliography and your research sources (manual or computerized indexes, databases, CD-ROM, and so on).

11.9 Developing Primary Data: Collaborative Survey (Obj. 6)

Team

In teams of three to five, design a survey for your associated student body council. The survey seeks student feedback in addressing the parking problem on campus. Students complain bitterly about lack of parking spaces for them, distance of parking lots from classrooms, and poor condition of the lots. Some solutions have been proposed: limiting parking to full-time students, using auxiliary parking lots farther away with a shuttle bus to campus, encouraging bicycle and moped use, and reducing the number of spaces for visitors. Discuss these solutions and add at least three other possibilities. Then prepare a questionnaire to be distributed on campus. If possible, pilot test the questionnaire before submitting it to your instructor. Be sure to consider how the results will be tabulated and interpreted.

11.10 Surfing the Web for Payroll Data for Tuscaloosa Firm (Obj. 5)

Web

Alisa Robertson, compensation and payroll manager for Gulf States Paper Corporation in Tuscaloosa, Alabama, has been complaining for some time about its complex and outdated payroll processes. "We have over 2,000 employees in nine different locations, and no set deadline for payroll submissions," she says. As a result of her urging, she has been named project manager for the company's "Human Resources/Payroll Business Information Systems Project." Her task is to learn more about payroll software programs that centralize processes, improve security, and reduce human error. As her assistant, you are to begin the research process by using the Web to see what you can turn up. Employ two or more search engines, choose keywords, and search for appropriate sites. Be sure to evaluate each site for currency, authority, content, and accuracy. Select five relevant sites and print a couple of pages of information from each site. Prepare a short memo report to Robertson naming the sites and giving her a brief summary of each.[21]

11.11 Surfing the Web for the Hard Rock Café (Obj. 5)

Web

Just ten years ago, Orlando-based Hard Rock Café International had only five restaurants. Managers considered it a cozy "mom and pop" operation, where everyone knew each other, and information about company goals and initiatives was spread casually through the grapevine. Today, the company has 98 restaurants in 34 countries and more than 14,000 employees. What's more, it plans to add 22 new restaurants this year. With growth, however, came growing pains. "We couldn't be a family-type organization because we were too big. Everybody couldn't know each other," said Mike Shipley, senior director of training at Hard Rock. Along with the CEO, Shipley realized that improving communication and leadership among employees would be critical during this period of rapid growth. Shipley asks you, his assistant, to search the Web for workshops or training programs that might be suitable for improving communication—and producing lasting results. Employ two or more search engines, choose keywords, and search for appropriate sites. Be sure to evaluate each site for currency, authority, content, and accuracy. Select five relevant sites and print a couple of pages of information from each site. Prepare a short memo report to Shipley naming the sites and giving him a brief summary of each.[22]

CHAPTER • 12 •

Report Organization and Presentation

LEARNING OBJECTIVES

1. Use tabulating and statistical techniques to sort and interpret report data.
2. Draw meaningful conclusions from report data.
3. Prepare practical report recommendations.
4. Organize report data logically.
5. Provide cues to aid report comprehension.
6. Develop graphics that create meaning and interest.
7. Incorporate graphics into reports effectively.

CASE STUDY

COMMUNICATION IN PROCESS

J. D. Power and Associates Promises Facts and Analysis

"When it comes to grading quality, J. D. Power and Associates is to cars and trucks what government inspection is to meat," says *Fortune* magazine.[1] As the auto industry's most influential marketing information organization, J. D. Power and Associates regularly surveys car owners to learn what they like and dislike about car models and dealers. Domestic and import carmakers, dealers, and suppliers all rely on its independent studies to compare product quality, monitor retailer service, and discover consumer trends.

As director of Customer Satisfaction and Quality Consulting Services at J. D. Power and Associates, John Humphrey collects, analyzes, and reports data. One study on which he works is the massive Customer Satisfaction Index. In explaining this study, Humphrey says, "Typically, our six-page questionnaire goes to about 72,000 car owners and 30,000 truck owners. We usually get a response rate of 35 percent or better, which is remarkably high for this kind of survey. To 'incentivize,' we sometimes enclose a dollar with each survey. For higher-end models like Porches and some BMW models, we'll include a $5 bill to motivate owners."

When the survey forms come back, they are studied for anything that looks illogical. "While I'm checking the tabulation," says Humphrey, "I'm also warming up to the data, probing for trends or other 'stories' the data might reveal." Although he avoids approaching any study with a rigid set of expectations, he does generally start with a hypothesis or a hunch about what the data might hold. "I avoid strong expectations; it's too easy to get comfortable and try to find things that aren't there. While I do have a preconception of what I will find, I don't let it overwhelm me. It's extremely important to let the data tell the story."

Collecting accurate data that represent a true picture is one very important part of research. But equally important is interpreting that data. What does it mean? What conclusions can be drawn? What recommendations can be made as a result of the findings? John Humphrey and other researchers at J. D. Power and Associates not only study the figures but also must interpret that data and communicate their findings to clients who pay handsomely for authoritative, accurate, and insightful analysis.[2]

www.jdpower.com

Interpreting Data

Interpreting data means sorting, analyzing, combining, and recombining to yield meaningful information.

After collecting data for a report, you, like John Humphrey at J. D. Power and Associates, must sort it and make sense out of it. For informational reports you may organize the facts into a logical sequence, illustrate them, and present a final report. For analytical reports, though, the process is more complex. You'll also interpret the data, draw conclusions, and, if asked, make recommendations.

The data you've collected probably face you in a jumble of printouts, note cards, copies of articles, interview notes, questionnaire results, and statistics. You might feel like a contractor who allowed suppliers to dump all the building materials for a new house in a monstrous pile.[3] Like the contractor you must sort the jumble of raw material into meaningful, usable groups. Unprocessed data become meaningful information through sorting, analysis, combination, and recombination. You'll be examining each item to see what it means by itself and what it means when connected with other data. You're looking for meanings, relationships, and answers to the research questions posed in your work plan.

Tabulating and Analyzing Responses

If you've collected considerable numerical and other information, you must tabulate and analyze it. Fortunately, several tabulating and statistical techniques can help you create order from the chaos. These techniques simplify, summarize, and classify large amounts of data into meaningful terms. From the condensed data you're more likely to be able to draw valid conclusions and make reasoned recommendations.

1

Numerical data must be tabulated and analyzed statistically to bring order out of chaos.

Tables. Numerical data from questionnaires or interviews are usually summarized and simplified in tables. Using systematic columns and rows, tables make quantitative information easier to comprehend. After assembling your data, you'll want to prepare preliminary tables to enable you to see what the information means. Here is a table summarizing the response to one question from a campus survey about student parking:

Question: Should student fees be increased to build parking lots?

	Number	Percent	
Strongly agree	76	11.5	*To simplify the table, combine these items.*
Agree	255	38.5	
No opinion	22	3.3	
Disagree	107	16.1	*To simplify the table, combine these items.*
Strongly disagree	203	30.6	
Total	**663**	**100.0**	

Notice that this preliminary table includes both a total number of responses and a percentage for each response. (To calculate a percentage, divide the figure for each response by the total number of responses.) To simplify the data and provide a broad overview, you can join categories. For example, combining "strongly agree" (11.5 percent) and "agree" (38.5 percent) reveals that 50 percent of the respondents supported the proposal to finance new parking lots with increased student fees.

Sometimes data become more meaningful when *cross-tabulated.* This process allows analysis of two or more variables together. By breaking down our student survey data into male/female responses, shown in the following table, we make an interesting discovery.

Question: Should student fees be increased to build parking lots?

	Total		Male		Female	
	Number	Percent	Number	Percent	Number	Percent
Strongly agree	76	11.5	8	2.2	68	22.0
Agree	255	38.5	54	15.3	201	65.0
No opinion	22	3.3	12	3.4	10	3.2
Disagree	107	16.1	89	25.1	18	5.8
Strongly disagree	203	30.6	191	54.0	12	4.0
Total	**663**	**100.0**	**354**	**100.0**	**309**	**100.0**

Although 50 percent of all student respondents supported the proposal, among females the approval rating was much stronger. Notice that 87 percent of female respondents (combining 22 percent "strongly agree" and 65 percent "agree") endorsed the proposal to increase fees for new parking lots. But among male students, *only 17 percent agreed with the proposal.* You naturally wonder why such a disparity exists. Are female students more unhappy than males with the current parking situa-

Spotlight on **Communicators**

"Because people have limited time, I have to convey considerable information quickly. Instead of a two-page summary, I might draw a simple graph where readers see the results in five seconds." In delivering reports to his clients at J. D. Power and Associates, John Humphrey is careful not to overwhelm them with too much data. Humphrey confesses that he would love to use his computer to put together "complex, multilevel graphs with a thousand spider charts and lines going everywhere." But he reigns in those instincts.

Elliot Goodwin, president of Larry's Shoes, America's largest men's shoe store, displays Ringo Starr's psychedelic sneaker, part of his shoe museum. The museum and other attractions (such as a cappuccino bar, a foot masseuse, and redesigned interiors) resulted from recommendations based on research data collected from shoe shoppers. To find ways to stimulate sales, Goodwin hired a team of market researchers. After tabulating and analyzing surveys and focus group responses, these researchers pinpointed key consumer desires. Potential shoe shoppers said that they wanted a wide variety of shoes, brand names, speedy checkout, easy return policy, and quality shoes at low prices. Interpretation of the data resulted in changes that boosted sales.

tion? If so, why? Is safety a reason? Are male students more concerned with increased fees than females? By cross-tabulating the findings, you sometimes uncover data that may help answer your problem question or that may prompt you to explore other possibilities. Don't, however, undertake cross-tabulation unless it serves more than mere curiosity.

Tables also help you compare multiple data collected from questionnaires and surveys. Figure 12.1 shows, in raw form, responses to several survey items. To convert these data into a more usable form, you need to calculate percentages for each item. Then you can arrange the responses in some rational sequence, such as largest percentage to smallest.

Once the data are displayed in a table, you can more easily draw conclusions. As Figure 12.1 shows, Midland College students apparently are not interested in public transportation or shuttle buses from satellite lots. They want to park on campus, with restricted visitor parking; and only half are willing to pay for new parking lots.

Three statistical concepts—mean, median, and mode—help you describe data.

The Three Ms: Mean, Median, Mode. Tables help you organize data, and the three Ms help you describe it. These statistical terms—mean, median, and mode—are all occasionally used loosely to mean "average." To be safe, though, you should learn to apply these statistical terms precisely.

When people say *average,* they usually intend to indicate the *mean,* or arithmetic average. Let's say that you're studying the estimated starting salaries of graduates from different disciplines, ranging from education to medicine:

Education	$24,000
Sociology	25,000
Humanities	27,000
Biology	30,000

FIGURE 12.1 Converting Survey Data Into Finished Tables

Tips for Converting Raw Data

- Tabulate the responses on a copy of the survey form.
- Calculate percentages (divide the score for an item by the total for all responses to that item; for example, for item 1, divide 331 by 663).
- Round off figures to one decimal point or to whole numbers.
- Arrange items in a logical order, such as largest to smallest percentage.
- Prepare a table with a title that tells such things as who, what, when, where, and why.
- Include the total number of respondents.

Raw Data from Survey Item

INDICATE YOUR FEELINGS TOWARD THE FOLLOWING PROPOSED SOLUTIONS TO THE STUDENT PARKING PROBLEM ON CAMPUS.

	Agree	No opinion	Disagree
1. Increase student fees to build parking lots	331	22	310
2. Limit student parking to satellite lots, providing shuttle buses to campus	52	31	580
3. Offer incentives to use public transportation	111	29	523
4. Restrict visitor parking	612	15	36

Shows raw figures from which percentages are calculated

Finished Table

REACTIONS OF MIDLAND COLLEGE STUDENTS TO FOUR PROPOSED SOLUTIONS TO CAMPUS PARKING PROBLEM*
Spring, 2000
N = 663 students

	Agree	No opinion	Disagree
Restrict visitor parking	92.3%	2.3%	5.4%
Increase student fees to build parking lots	49.9	3.3	46.8
Offer incentives to use public transportation	16.7	4.4	78.9
Limit student parking to satellite lots, providing shuttle buses to campus	7.8	4.7	87.5

*Figures may not equal 100 percent because of rounding.

Orders items from highest to lowest "Agree" percentages

Uses percent sign only at beginning of column

Avoids cluttering the table with total figures

Health sciences	31,000	*Median (middle point in continuum)*
Engineering	33,000	*Mode (figure occurring most frequently)*
Business	33,000	
Law	35,000	*Mean (arithmetic average)*
Medicine	77,000	

To find the mean, you simply add up all the salaries and divide by the total number of items ($315,000 ÷ 9 = $35,000). Thus, the mean salary is $35,000. Means are very useful to indicate central tendencies of figures, but they have one major flaw: extremes at either end cause distortion. Notice that the $77,000 figure makes the mean salary of $35,000 deceptively high. It does not represent a valid average for the group. Because means can be misleading, you should use them only when extreme figures do not distort the result.

The mean is the arithmetic average; the median is the midpoint in a group of figures; the mode is the most frequently occurring figure.

The *median* represents the midpoint in a group of figures arranged from lowest to highest (or vice versa). In our list of salaries, the median is $31,000 (health sciences). In other words, half the salaries are above this point and half are below it. The median is useful when extreme figures may warp the mean. Whereas salaries for medicine distort the mean, the median, at $31,000, is still a representative figure.

The *mode* is simply the value that occurs most frequently. In our list $33,000 (for engineering and business) represents the mode since it occurs twice. The mode has the advantage of being easily determined—just a quick glance at a list of arranged values reveals it. Although mode is infrequently used by researchers, knowing the mode is useful in some situations. Let's say 7-Eleven sampled its customers to determine what drink size they preferred: 12-ounce, 16-ounce, or Big-Gulp 24-ounce. Finding the mode—the most frequently named figure—makes more sense than calculating the median, which might yield a size that 7-Eleven doesn't even offer. (To remember the meaning of *mode,* think about fashion; the most frequent response, the mode, is the most fashionable.)

Mean, median, and mode figures are especially helpful when the range of values is also known. *Range* represents the span between the highest and lowest values. To calculate the range, you simply subtract the lowest figure from the highest. In starting salaries for graduates, the range is $53,000 (77,000 − 24,000). Knowing the range enables readers to put mean and median figures into perspective. This knowledge also prompts researchers to wonder why such a range exists, thus stimulating hunches and further investigation to solve problems.

Correlations between variables suggest possible relationships that will explain research findings.

Correlations. In tabulating and analyzing data, you may see relationships among two or more variables that help explain the findings. If your data for graduates' starting salaries also included years of schooling, you would doubtless notice that graduates with more years of education received higher salaries. For example, beginning teachers, with four years of schooling, earn less than beginning physicians, who have completed nine or more years of education. Thus, a correlation may exist between years of education and starting salary.

Intuition suggests correlations that may or may not prove to be accurate. Is there a relationship between studying and good grades? Between new office computers and increased productivity? Between the rise and fall of hemlines and the rise and fall of the stock market (as some newspaper writers have suggested)? If a correlation seems to exist, can we say that one event caused the other? Does studying cause good grades? Does more schooling guarantee increased salary? Although one event may not be said to *cause* another, the business researcher who sees a correlation begins to ask why and how the two variables are related. In this way, apparent correlations stimulate investigation and present possible problem solutions to be explored.

In reporting correlations, you should avoid suggesting that a cause-and-effect relationship exists when none can be proved. Only sophisticated research methods can statistically prove correlations. Instead, present a correlation as a possible relationship (*The data suggest that beginning salaries are related to years of education*). Cautious statements followed by explanations gain you credibility and allow readers to make their own decisions.

Grids. Another technique for analyzing raw data—especially verbal data—is the grid. Let's say you've been asked by the CEO to collect opinions from all vice presidents about the CEO's four-point plan to build cash reserves. The grid shown in Figure 12.2 enables you to summarize the vice presidents' reactions to each point.

FIGURE 12.2 **Grid to Analyze Complex Verbal Data About Building Cash Reserves**

	Point 1	Point 2	Point 3	Point 4	Overall Reaction
Vice President 1	Disapproves. "Too little, too late."	Strong support. "Best of all points."	Mixed opinion. "Must wait and see market."	Indifferent.	Optimistic, but "hates to delay expansion for 6 months"
Vice President 2	Disapproves. "Creates credit trap."	Approves.	Strong disapproval.	Approves. "Must improve receivable collections."	Mixed support. "Good self-defense plan."
Vice President 3	Strong disapproval.	Approves. "Key to entire plan."	Indifferent.	Approves, but with "caveats."	"Will work only with sale of unproductive fixed assets."
Vice President 4	Disapproves. "Too risky now."	Strong support. "Start immediately."	Approves, "but may damage image."	Approves. "Benefits far outweigh costs."	Supports plan. Suggests focus on Pacific Rim markets.

Grids permit analysis of raw verbal data by grouping and classifying.

Notice how this complex verbal information is transformed into concise, manageable data; readers can see immediately which points are supported and opposed. Imagine how long you could have struggled to comprehend the meaning of this verbal information before plotting it on a grid.

Arranging data in a grid also works for projects such as feasibility studies that compare many variables. Assume you must recommend a new printer to your manager. To see how four models compare, you could lay out a grid with the names of printer models across the top. Down the left side, you would list such significant variables as price, warranty, service, capacity, compatibility, and specifications. As you fill in the variables for each model, you can see quickly which model has the lowest price, longest warranty, and so forth. *Consumer Reports* often uses grids to show information.

In addition, grids help classify employment data. For example, suppose your boss asked you to recommend one individual from among many job candidates. You could arrange a grid with names across the top and distinguishing characteristics—experience, skills, education, and other employment interests—down the left side. When you summarized each candidate's points, you'd have a helpful tool for drawing conclusions and writing a report.

Drawing Conclusions in Reports

2

Conclusions summarize and explain the findings in a report.

The most widely read portions of a report are the sections devoted to conclusions and recommendations. Knowledgeable readers go straight to the conclusions to see what the report writer thinks the data mean. Because conclusions summarize and explain the findings, they represent the heart of a report. Your value in an organization rises considerably if you can draw conclusions that analyze information logically and show how the data answer questions and solve problems.

Any set of data can produce a variety of conclusions. Always bear in mind, though, that the audience for a report wants to know how these data relate to the problem being studied. What do the findings mean in terms of solving the original report problem?

FIGURE 12.3 Report Conclusions and Recommendations

Tips for Writing Conclusions

- Interpret and summarize the findings; tell what they mean.
- Relate the conclusions to the report problem.
- Limit the conclusions to the data presented; do not introduce new material.
- Number the conclusions and present them in parallel form.
- Be objective; avoid exaggerating or manipulating the data.
- Use consistent criteria in evaluating options.

REPORT PROBLEM

Marriott Corporation experienced employee turnover and lowered productivity resulting from conflicting home and work requirements. The hotel conducted a massive survey resulting in some of the following findings.

PARTIAL FINDINGS

1. Nearly 35 percent of employees surveyed have children under age twelve.
2. Nearly 15 percent of employees have children under age five.
3. The average employee with children younger than twelve is absent four days a year and tardy five days because of child-related issues.
4. Within a one-year period, nearly 33 percent of employees who have young children take at least two days off because they can't find a replacement when their child-care plans break down.
5. Nearly 20 percent of employees left a previous employer because of work and family concerns.
6. At least 80 percent of female employees and 78 percent of male employees with young children reported job stress as a result of conflicting work and family roles.
7. Managers perceive family matters to be inappropriate issues for them to discuss at work.

Condenses significant findings in numbered statements

From these and other findings, the following conclusions were drawn.

CONCLUSIONS

1. Home and family responsibilities directly affect job attendance and performance.
2. Time is the crucial issue to balancing work and family issues.
3. Male and female employees reported in nearly equal numbers the difficulties of managing work and family roles.
4. Problems with child-care arrangements increase the employees' level of stress and limit ability to work certain schedules or overtime.
5. A manager supportive of family and personal concerns is central to a good work environment.

Uses conclusion to present sensible analysis without exaggerating or manipulating data

Explains what findings mean in terms of report problem

For example, the Marriott Corporation recognized a serious problem among its employees. Conflicting home and work requirements seemed to be causing excessive employee turnover and decreased productivity. To learn the extent of the problem and to consider solutions, Marriott surveyed its staff.[4] It learned, among other things, that nearly 35 percent of its employees had children under age twelve, and 15 percent had children under age five. Other findings, shown in Figure 12.3, indicated that one third of its staff with young children took time off because of child-care difficulties. Moreover, many current employees left previous jobs because of

FIGURE 12.3 Continued

Tips for Writing Recommendations

- Make specific suggestions for actions to solve the report problem.
- Prepare practical recommendations that will be agreeable to the audience.
- Avoid conditional words such as *maybe* and *perhaps.*
- Present each suggestion separately as a command beginning with a verb.
- Number the recommendations for improved readability.
- If requested, describe how the recommendations may be implemented.
- When possible, arrange the recommendations in an announced order, such as most important to least important.

RECOMMENDATIONS

1. Provide managers with training in working with personal and family matters.
2. Institute a flextime policy that allows employees to adapt their work schedules to home responsibilities.
3. Investigate opening a pilot child development center for preschool children of employees at company headquarters.
4. Develop a child-care resource program to provide parents with professional help in locating affordable child care.
5. Offer a child-care discount program to help parents pay for services.
6. Authorize weekly payroll deductions, using tax-free dollars, to pay for child care.
7. Publish a quarterly employee newsletter devoted to family and child-care issues.

Arranges actions to solve problems from most important to least important

work and family conflicts. The survey also showed that managers did not consider child-care or family problems to be appropriate topics for discussion at work.

A sample of possible conclusions that could be drawn from these findings is shown in Figure 12.3. Notice that each conclusion relates to the initial report problem. Although only a few possible findings and conclusions are shown here, you can see that the conclusions try to explain the causes for the home/work conflict among employees. Many report writers would expand the conclusion section by explaining each item and citing supporting evidence. Even for simplified conclusions, such as those shown in Figure 12.3, you will want to number each item separately and use parallel construction (balanced sentence structure).

Effective report conclusions are objective and bias-free.

Although your goal is to remain objective, drawing conclusions naturally involves a degree of subjectivity. Your goals, background, and frame of reference all color the inferences you make. When Federal Express, for example, tried to expand its next-day delivery service to Europe, it racked up a staggering loss of $1.2 billion in four years of operation.[5] The facts could not be disputed. But what conclusions could be drawn? The CEO might conclude that the competition is greater than anticipated but that FedEx is making inroads; patience is all that is needed. The board of directors and stockholders, however, might conclude that the competition is too well entrenched and that it's time to pull the plug on an ill-fated operation. Findings will be interpreted from the writer's perspective, but they should not be manipulated to achieve a preconceived purpose.

You can make your report conclusions more objective if you use consistent evaluation criteria. Let's say you are comparing computers for an office equipment purchase. If you evaluate each by the same criteria (such as price, specifications, service, and warranty), your conclusions are more likely to be bias-free.

You also need to avoid the temptation to sensationalize or exaggerate your findings or conclusions. Be careful of words like *many, most,* and *all.* Instead of *many of the respondents felt . . . ,* you might more accurately write *some of the respondents. . . .* Examine your motives before drawing conclusions. Don't let preconceptions or wishful thinking color your reasoning.

Writing Report Recommendations

3

Effective report conclusions are objective and bias-free. Effective recommendations offer specific suggestions on how to solve a problem.

Recommendations, unlike conclusions, make specific suggestions for actions that can solve the report problem. Consider the following examples:

Conclusion
Our investments are losing value because the stock market has declined. The bond market shows strength.

Recommendation
Withdraw at least half of our investment in stocks, and invest it in bonds.

Conclusion
The cost of constructing multilevel parking structures for student on-campus parking is prohibitive.

Recommendation
Explore the possibility of satellite parking lots with frequent shuttle buses to campus.

Notice that the conclusions explain what the problem is, while the recommendations tell how to solve it. Typically, readers prefer specific recommendations. They want to know exactly how to implement the suggestions. In addition to recommending satellite parking lots for campus parking, for example, the writer could have discussed sites for possible satellite lots and the cost of running shuttle buses.

Detailed recommendations are written only when the report writer is authorized to do so.

The specificity of your recommendations depends on your authorization. What are you commissioned to do, and what does the reader expect? In the planning stages of your report project, you anticipate what the reader wants in the report. Your intuition and your knowledge of the audience indicate how far your recommendations should be developed.

In the recommendations section of the Marriott employee survey, shown in Figure 12.3, many of the suggestions are summarized. In the actual report each recommendation could have been backed up with specifics and ideas for implementing them. For example, the child-care resource recommendation would be explained: it provides parents with names of agencies and professionals who specialize in locating child care across the country.

A good report provides practical recommendations that are agreeable to the audience. In the Marriott survey, for example, report researchers knew that the company wanted to help employees cope with conflicts between family and work obligations. Thus, the report's conclusions and recommendations focused on ways to resolve the conflict. If Marriott's goal had been merely to reduce employee absenteeism and save money, the recommendations would have been quite different.

If possible, make each recommendation a command. Note in Figure 12.3 that each recommendation begins with a verb. This structure sounds forceful and confident and helps the reader comprehend the information quickly. Avoid words such

PROCESS IN PROGRESS

CASE STUDY

J. D. Power and Associates Revisited

At J. D. Power and Associates, researcher John Humphrey is called on to analyze data collected from surveys and summarize that data in report form. "We describe what we think is happening and discuss any trends. We draw conclusions based on our knowledge of the industry in relation to the current data. In years when customer satisfaction didn't increase much but sales rose dramatically, we might conclude that car dealers lost interest in efforts to satisfy customers. Instead of maintaining customer satisfaction programs, they were more interested in just moving iron," says Humphrey. If asked to make recommendations, he might suggest that dealers think twice before scrapping their customer satisfaction programs.

In studies in which Humphrey acts as both researcher and consultant, he considers it a responsibility to prescribe as well as describe. "Of course, you need to be objective in describing the data. But you also should try to explain any underlying themes, the 'why' of what happened. To make information more valuable, I try to use my expertise in giving an educated guess. For example, in studying a decline in dealership service profits, I might report data showing the decline, explain what I think caused the decline, and suggest specific ways to rectify the problem. Too many researchers get into a groove and report only raw data."

Critical Thinking

- When J. D. Power and Associates conducts massive surveys asking new car and truck owners how they like their new vehicles, why should it do any more than merely report the results (the "raw data")? When would conclusions and recommendations be appropriate?
- What is a hypothesis? Should researchers like those at J. D. Power start with one? Give an example of a hypothesis that a researcher at J. D. Power might have.
- Although J. D. Power and Associates might study customer satisfaction for 40 makes of new cars, it would rank by name only those that are above the mean. All others are listed alphabetically. What is the *mean,* and why do you think this procedure is used?

as *maybe* and *perhaps;* they suggest conditional statements that reduce the strength of recommendations.

Experienced writers may combine recommendations and conclusions. And in short reports, writers may omit conclusions and move straight to recommendations. The important thing about recommendations, though, is that they include practical suggestions for solving the report problem.

Organizing Data

4

After collecting sets of data, interpreting them, and drawing conclusions, you're ready to organize the parts of the report into a logical framework. Poorly organized reports lead to frustration. Readers will not understand, remember, or be persuaded. Wise writers know that reports rarely "just organize themselves." Instead, organization must be imposed on the data.

Informational reports typically are organized in three parts, as shown in Figure 12.4. Analytical reports typically contain four parts and may be organized directly or indirectly. For readers who know about the project, are supportive, or are eager

FIGURE 12.4 Organizing Informational and Analytical Reports

Informational Reports	Analytical Reports: Direct Pattern	Analytical Reports: Indirect Pattern
I. Introduction/background II. Facts/findings III. Summary/conclusion	I. Introduction/problem II. Conclusions/recommendations III. Facts/findings IV. Discussion/analysis	I. Introduction/problem II. Facts/findings III. Discussion/analysis IV. Conclusions/recommendations

The direct pattern is appropriate for informed or receptive readers; the indirect pattern is appropriate when educating or persuading.

to learn the results quickly, the direct method is appropriate. Conclusions—and recommendations, if requested—appear up front. For readers who must be educated or persuaded, the indirect method works better. Conclusions/recommendations appear last, after the findings have been presented and analyzed.

Although every report is different (you'll learn specifics for organizing informal and formal reports in Chapters 13 and 14), the overall organizational patterns described here typically hold true. The real challenge, though, lies in (1) organizing the facts/findings and discussion/analysis sections and (2) providing reader cues.

Ordering Information Logically

Organization by time, component, importance, criteria, or convention helps readers comprehend data.

Whether you're writing informational or analytical reports, the data you've collected must be structured coherently. Five common organizational methods are by time, component, importance, criteria, or convention. Regardless of the method you choose, be sure that it helps the reader understand the data. Reader comprehension, not writer convenience, should govern organization.

Time. Ordering data by time means establishing a chronology of events. Agendas, minutes of meetings, progress reports, and procedures are usually organized by time. For example, a report describing an eight-week training program would most likely be organized by weeks. A plan for step-by-step improvement of customer service would be organized by each step. A monthly trip report submitted by a sales rep might describe customers visited Week 1, Week 2, and so on. Beware of overusing time chronologies, however. Although this method is easy and often mirrors the way data are collected, chronologies—like the sales rep's trip report—tend to be boring, repetitious, and lacking in emphasis. Readers can't always pick out what's important.

Component. Especially for informational reports, data may be organized by components such as location, geography, division, product, or part. For instance, a report detailing company expansion might divide the plan into West Coast, East Coast, and Midwest expansion. The report could also be organized by divisions: personal products, consumer electronics, and household goods. A report comparing profits among makers of athletic shoes might group the data by company: Reebok, Nike, L.A. Gear, and so forth. Organization by components works best when the classifications already exist.

Importance. Organization by importance involves beginning with the most important item and proceeding to the least important—or vice versa. For example, a report discussing the reasons for declining product sales would present the most im-

To reduce alcohol-related accidents, the Federal Highway Administration now requires trucking companies to submit compliance reports. The data in these reports are organized into specific categories such as testing, education, and rehabilitation programs.

portant reason first followed by less important ones. The Marriott report describing work/family conflicts might begin by discussing child care, if the writer considered it the most important issue. Using importance to structure findings involves a value judgment. The writer must decide what is most important, always keeping in mind the readers' priorities and expectations. Busy readers appreciate seeing important points first; they may skim or skip other points. On the other hand, building to a climax by moving from least important to most important enables the writer to focus attention at the end. Thus, the reader is more likely to remember the most important item. Of course, the writer also risks losing the attention of the reader along the way.

Organizing by level of importance saves the time of busy readers and increases the odds that key information will be retained.

Criteria. Establishing criteria by which to judge helps writers to treat topics consistently. Let's say your report compares health plans A, B, and C. For each plan you examine the same standards: Criterion 1, cost per employee; Criterion 2, amount of deductible; and Criterion 3, patient benefits. The resulting data could then be organized either by plans or by criteria:

To evaluate choices or plans fairly, apply the same criteria to each.

By Plan	**By Criteria**
Plan A	Criterion 1
Criterion 1	Plan A
Criterion 2	Plan B
Criterion 3	Plan C
Plan B	Criterion 2
Criterion 1	Plan A
Criterion 2	Plan B
Criterion 3	Plan C
Plan C	Criterion 3
Criterion 1	Plan A
Criterion 2	Plan B
Criterion 3	Plan C

Although you might favor organizing the data by plans (because that's the way you collected the data), the better way is by criteria. When you discuss patient benefits, for example, you would examine all three plans' benefits together. Organizing a report around criteria helps readers make comparisons, instead of forcing them to search through the report for similar data.

Organizing by convention simplifies the organizational task and yields easy-to-follow information.

Convention. Many operational and recurring reports are structured according to convention. That is, they follow a prescribed plan that everyone understands. For example, an automotive parts manufacturer might ask all sales reps to prepare a weekly report with these headings: *Competitive observations* (competitors' price changes, discounts, new products, product problems, distributor changes, product promotions), *Product problems* (quality, performance, needs), and *Customer service problems* (delivery, mailings, correspondence). Management gets exactly the information it needs in easy-to-read form.

Like operating reports, proposals are often organized conventionally. They might use such groupings as background, problem, proposed solution, staffing, schedule, costs, and authorization. As you might expect, reports following these conventional, prescribed structures greatly simplify the task of organization.

Providing Reader Cues

5

When you finish organizing a report, you probably see a neat outline in your mind: major points, supported by subpoints and details. However, readers don't know the material as well as you; they cannot see your outline. To guide them through the data, you need to provide the equivalent of a map and road signs. For both formal and informal reports, devices such as introductions, transitions, and headings prevent readers from getting lost.

Good openers tell readers what topics will be covered in what order and why.

Introductions. The best way to point a reader in the right direction is to provide an introduction that does three things:

- Tells the purpose of the report
- Describes the significance of the topic
- Previews the main points and the order in which they will be developed

The following paragraph includes all three elements in introducing a report on computer security:

> The purpose of this report is to examine the security of our current computer operations and present suggestions for improving security. Lax computer security could mean loss of information, loss of business, and damage to our equipment and systems. Because many former employees, released during recent downsizing efforts, know our systems, major changes must be made. To improve security, I will present three recommendations: (1) begin using *smart cards* that limit access to our computer system, (2) alter sign-on and log-off procedures, (3) move central computer operations to a more secure area.

This opener tells the purpose (examining computer security), describes its significance (loss of information and business, damage to equipment and systems), and outlines how the report is organized (three recommendations). Good openers in effect set up a contract with the reader. The writer promises to cover certain topics in a specified order. Readers expect the writer to fulfill the contract. They want the topics to be developed as promised—using the same wording and presented in the order mentioned. For example, if in your introduction you state that you will discuss the use of *smart cards,* don't change the heading for that section to *access cards.* Remember that the introduction provides a map to a report; switching the names on the map will ensure that readers get lost. To maintain consistency, delay writing the introduction until after you have completed the report. Long, complex reports may require introductions for each section.

Transitions. Expressions like *on the contrary, at the same time,* and *however* show relationships and help reveal the logical flow of ideas in a report. These *transitional expressions* enable writers to tell readers where ideas are headed and how they relate. Notice how abrupt the following two sentences sound without a transition: *American car manufacturers admired Toyota's just-in-time inventory practices. Adopting a JIT system [however] means total restructuring of assembly plants.*

Transitional expressions inform readers where ideas are headed and how they relate.

The following expressions (see Figure 5.7 for a complete list) enable you to show readers how you are developing your ideas.

To Present Additional Thoughts: additionally, again, also, moreover, furthermore

To Suggest Cause and Effect: accordingly, as a result, consequently, therefore

To Contrast Ideas: at the same time, but, however, on the contrary, though, yet

To Show Time and Order: after, before, first, finally, now, previously, then, to conclude

To Clarify Points: for example, for instance, in other words, that is, thus

In using these expressions, recognize that they don't have to sit at the head of a sentence. Listen to the rhythm of the sentence, and place the expression where a natural pause occurs. Used appropriately, transitional expressions serve readers as guides; misused or overused, they can be as distracting and frustrating as too many road signs on a highway.

Headings. Good headings are another structural cue that assist readers in comprehending the organization of a report. They highlight major ideas, allowing busy readers to see the big picture in a glance. Moreover, headings provide resting points for the mind and for the eye, breaking up large chunks of text into manageable and inviting segments.

Good headings provide organizational cues and spotlight key ideas.

Report writers may use functional or talking heads. *Functional heads* (for example, *Background, Findings, Personnel,* and *Production Costs*) describe functions or general topics. They show the outline of a report but provide little insight for readers. Functional headings are useful for routine reports. They're also appropriate for sensitive topics that might provoke emotional reactions. By keeping the headings general, experienced writers hope to minimize reader opposition or response to controversial subjects. *Talking heads* (for example, *Two Sides to Campus Parking Problem* or *Survey Shows Support for Parking Fees*) provide more information and interest. Unless carefully written, however, talking heads can fail to reveal the organization of a report. With some planning, though, headings can be both functional and talking, such as *Parking Recommendations: Shuttle and New Structures.*

To create the most effective headings, follow a few basic guidelines:

Headings should be brief, parallel, and ordered in a logical hierarchy.

- **Use appropriate heading levels.** The position and format of a heading indicate its level of importance and relationship to other points. Figure 12.5 both illustrates and discusses a commonly used heading format for business reports.
- **Capitalize and underline carefully.** Most writers use all capital letters (without underlines) for main titles, such as the report, chapter, and unit titles. For first- and second-level headings, they capitalize only the first letter of main words. For additional emphasis, they use a bold font, as shown in Figure 12.5.

FIGURE 12.5 **Levels of Headings in Reports**

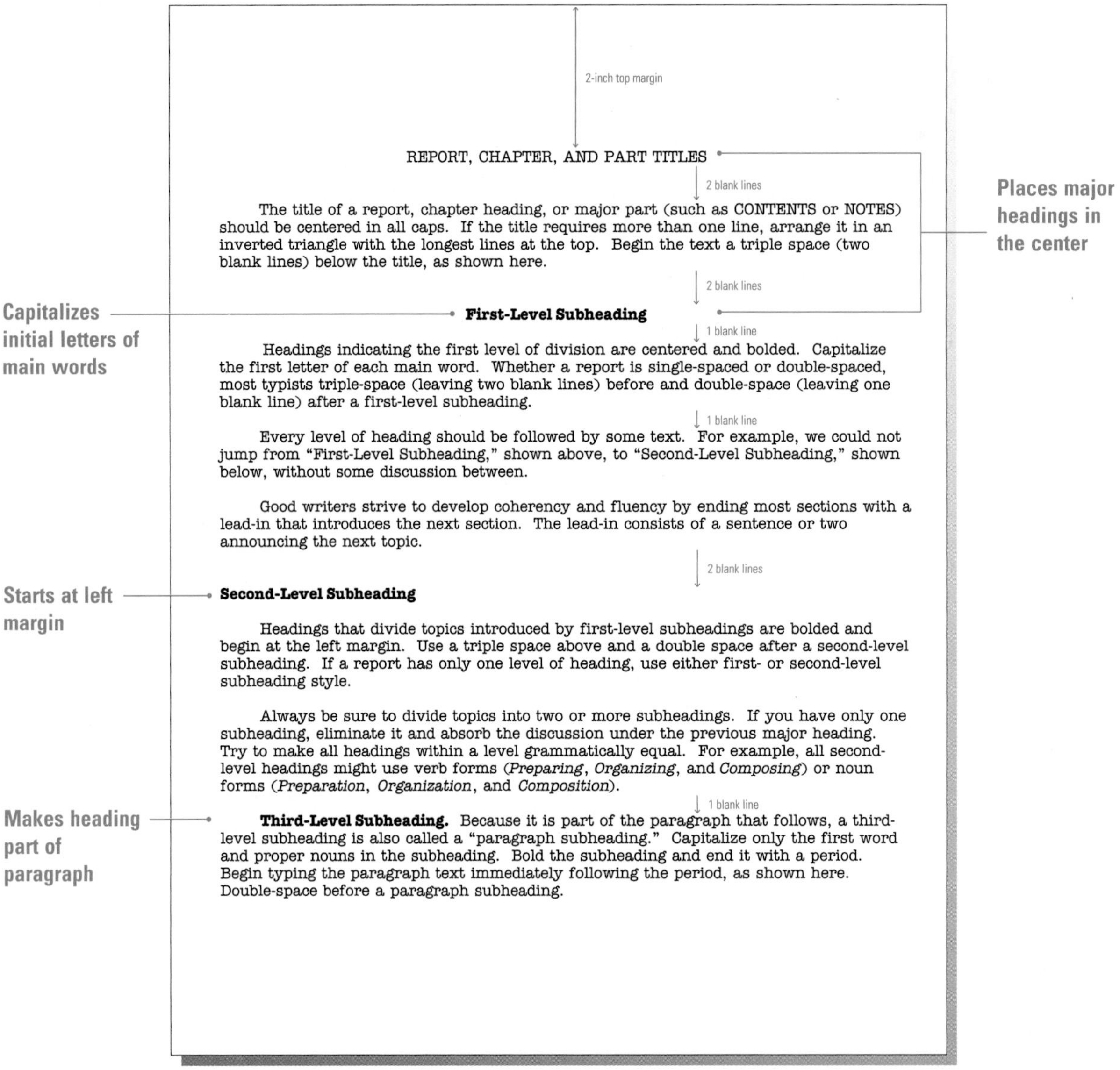

2-inch top margin

REPORT, CHAPTER, AND PART TITLES

2 blank lines

The title of a report, chapter heading, or major part (such as CONTENTS or NOTES) should be centered in all caps. If the title requires more than one line, arrange it in an inverted triangle with the longest lines at the top. Begin the text a triple space (two blank lines) below the title, as shown here.

2 blank lines

First-Level Subheading

1 blank line

Headings indicating the first level of division are centered and bolded. Capitalize the first letter of each main word. Whether a report is single-spaced or double-spaced, most typists triple-space (leaving two blank lines) before and double-space (leaving one blank line) after a first-level subheading.

1 blank line

Every level of heading should be followed by some text. For example, we could not jump from "First-Level Subheading," shown above, to "Second-Level Subheading," shown below, without some discussion between.

Good writers strive to develop coherency and fluency by ending most sections with a lead-in that introduces the next section. The lead-in consists of a sentence or two announcing the next topic.

2 blank lines

Second-Level Subheading

Headings that divide topics introduced by first-level subheadings are bolded and begin at the left margin. Use a triple space above and a double space after a second-level subheading. If a report has only one level of heading, use either first- or second-level subheading style.

Always be sure to divide topics into two or more subheadings. If you have only one subheading, eliminate it and absorb the discussion under the previous major heading. Try to make all headings within a level grammatically equal. For example, all second-level headings might use verb forms (*Preparing*, *Organizing*, and *Composing*) or noun forms (*Preparation*, *Organization*, and *Composition*).

1 blank line

Third-Level Subheading. Because it is part of the paragraph that follows, a third-level subheading is also called a "paragraph subheading." Capitalize only the first word and proper nouns in the subheading. Bold the subheading and end it with a period. Begin typing the paragraph text immediately following the period, as shown here. Double-space before a paragraph subheading.

Places major headings in the center

Capitalizes initial letters of main words

Starts at left margin

Makes heading part of paragraph

- **Balance headings within levels.** All headings at a given level should be grammatically similar. For example, *Developing Quality Circles* and *Presenting Plan to Management* are balanced, but *Development of Quality Circles* is not parallel with *Presenting Plan to Management.*
- **For short reports use first- or second-level headings.** Many business reports contain only one or two levels of headings. For such reports use first-level headings (centered, bolded) and/or second-level headings (flush left, bolded). See Figure 12.5.
- **Include at least one heading per report page.** Headings increase the readability and attractiveness of report pages. Use at least one per page to break up blocks of text.

- **Keep headings short but clear.** One-word headings are emphatic but not always clear. For example, the heading *Budget* does not adequately describe figures for a summer project involving student interns for an oil company in Texas. Try to keep your headings brief (no more than eight words), but make sure they are understandable. Experiment with headings that concisely tell who, what, when, where, and why.
- **Integrate headings gracefully.** Try not to repeat the exact wording from the heading in the sentence immediately following. Also avoid using the heading as an antecedent to a pronoun. For example, don't follow the heading *New Office Systems* with *These will be installed. . . .*

Illustrating Data with Graphics

6

After collecting information and interpreting it, you need to consider how best to present it to your audience. Whether you are delivering your report orally or in writing to company insiders or to outsiders, it will be easier to understand and remember if you include suitable graphics. Appropriate graphics make numerical data meaningful, simplify complex ideas, and provide visual interest. In contrast, readers tend to be bored and confused by text paragraphs packed with complex data and numbers. The same information summarized in a table or chart becomes clear. Tables, charts, graphs, pictures, and other graphics perform three important functions:

Effective graphics clarify numerical data and simplify complex ideas.

- They clarify data.
- They condense and simplify data.
- They emphasize data.

Because the same data can be shown in many different forms (for example, in a chart, table, or graph), you need to recognize how to match the appropriate graphic with your objective. In addition, you need to know how to incorporate graphics into your reports.

Matching Graphics and Objectives

In developing the best graphics, you must first decide what data you want to highlight. Chances are you will have many points you would like to show in a table or chart. But which graphics are most appropriate to your objectives? Tables? Bar charts? Pie charts? Line charts? Surface charts? Flow charts? Organization charts? Pictures? Figure 12.6 summarizes appropriate uses for each type of graphic, the following text discusses each visual in more detail.

Tables. Probably the most frequently used graphic in reports is the table. Because a table presents quantitative or verbal information in systematic columns and rows, it can clarify large quantities of data in small spaces. You may have made rough tables to help you organize the raw data collected from literature, questionnaires, or interviews. In preparing tables for your readers or listeners, though, you'll need to pay more attention to clarity and emphasis. Here are tips for making good tables, one of which is illustrated in Figure 12.7:

Tables permit systematic presentation of large amounts of data, while charts enhance visual comparisons.

- Provide clear heads for the rows and columns.
- Identify the units in which figures are given (percentages, dollars, units per worker hour, and so forth) in the table title, in the column or row head, with the first item in a column, or in a note at the bottom.

FIGURE 12.6 Matching Graphics to Objectives

Graphics		Objective
Table	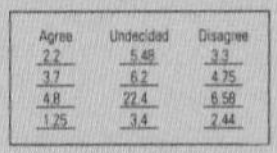	To show exact figures and values
Bar Chart		To compare one item with others
Line Chart		To demonstrate changes in quantitative data over time
Pie Chart		To visualize a whole unit and the proportions of its components
Flow Chart	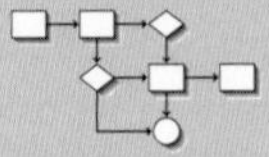	To display a process or procedure
Organization Chart	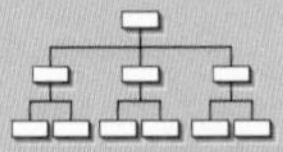	To define a hierarchy of elements
Photograph, Map, Illustration		To create authenticity, to spotlight a location, and to show an item in use

- Arrange items in a logical order (alphabetical, chronological, geographical, highest to lowest) depending on what you need to emphasize.
- Use *N/A* (not available) for missing data.
- Make long tables easier to read by shading alternate lines or by leaving a blank line after groups of five.

FIGURE 12.7 Table Summarizing Precise Data

Figure 1
MPM ENTERTAINMENT COMPANY
Income by Division (in millions of dollars)

	Theme Parks	Motion Pictures	Video	Total
1996	$15.8	$39.3	$11.2	$66.3
1997	18.1	17.5	15.3	50.9
1998	23.8	21.1	22.7	67.6
1999	32.2	22.0	24.3	78.5
2000 (projected)	35.1	21.0	26.1	82.2

Source: *Industry Profiles* (New York: DataPro, 1999), 225.

FIGURE 12.8 Vertical Bar Chart

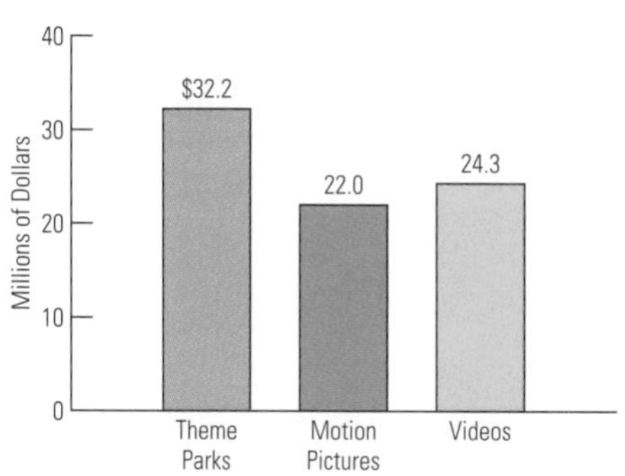

FIGURE 12.9 Horizontal Bar Chart

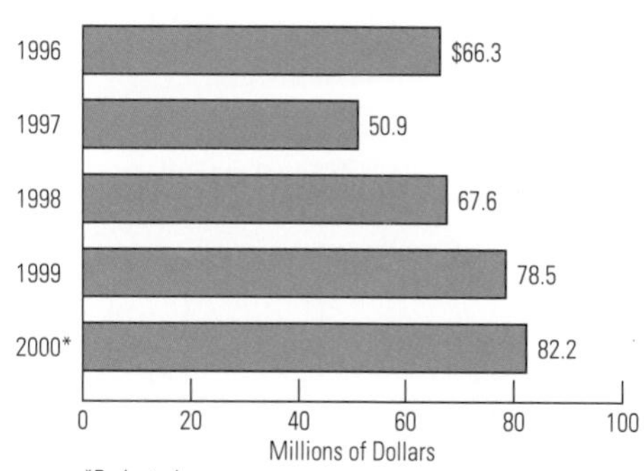

FIGURE 12.10 Grouped Bar Chart

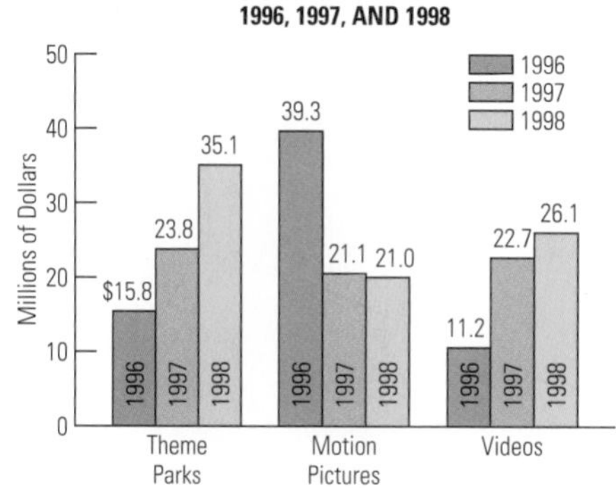

FIGURE 12.11 Segmented 100% Bar Chart

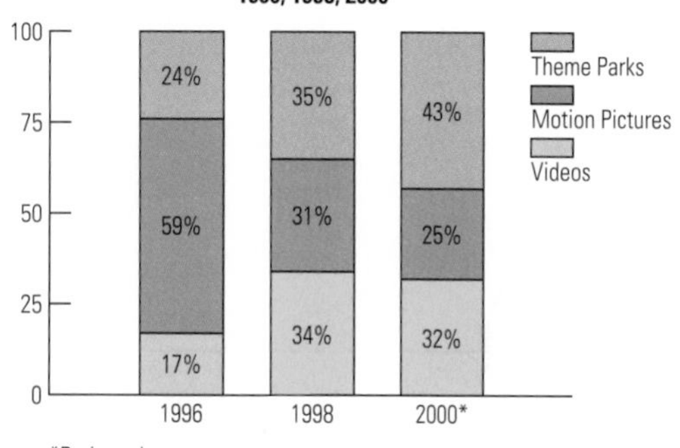

Bar Charts. Although they lack the precision of tables, bar charts enable you to make emphatic visual comparisons. Bar charts can be used to compare related items, illustrate changes in data over time, and show segments as part of a whole. Figures 12.8 through 12.11 show vertical, horizontal, grouped, and segmented bar charts that highlight some of the data shown in the MPM Entertainment Company table (Figure 12.7). Note how the varied bar charts present information in differing ways.

Bar charts enable readers to compare related items, see changes over time, and understand how parts relate to a whole.

Many suggestions for tables also hold true for bar charts. Here are a few additional tips:

- Keep the length of each bar and segment proportional.
- Include a total figure in the middle of a bar or at its end if the figure helps the reader and does not clutter the chart.
- Start dollar or percentage amounts at zero.
- Avoid showing too much information, thus producing clutter and confusion.

FIGURE 12.12 Simple Line Chart

Figure 5

MOTION PICTURE REVENUES
1995 TO 2000

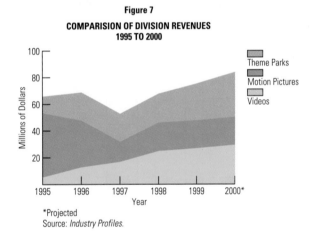

Millions of Dollars

50
40
30
20
10

1995 1996 1997 1998 1999 2000*

*Projected
Source: *Industry Profiles.*

FIGURE 12.13 Multiple Line Chart

Figure 6

COMPARISON OF DIVISION REVENUES
1995 TO 2000

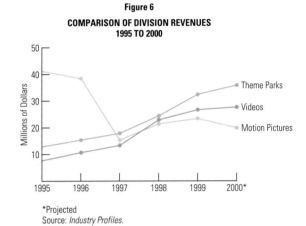

Millions of Dollars

50
40
30
20
10

Theme Parks
Videos
Motion Pictures

1995 1996 1997 1998 1999 2000*

*Projected
Source: *Industry Profiles.*

FIGURE 12.14 Segmented Line (Surface) Chart

Figure 7

COMPARISION OF DIVISION REVENUES
1995 TO 2000

Millions of Dollars

100
80
60
40
20

Theme Parks
Motion Pictures
Videos

1995 1996 1997 1998 1999 2000*
Year

*Projected
Source: *Industry Profiles.*

FIGURE 12.15 Pie Chart

Figure 8

1999 MPM INCOME BY DIVISION

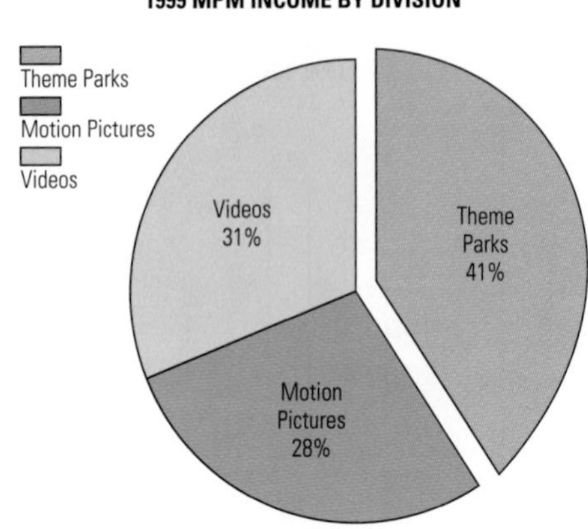

Source: *Industry Profiles.*

Line charts illustrate trends and changes in data over time.

Line Charts. The major advantage of line charts is that they show changes over time, thus indicating trends. Figures 12.12 through 12.14 show line charts that reflect income trends for the three divisions of MPM. Notice that line charts do not provide precise data, such as the 1999 MPM Videos income. Instead, they give an overview or impression of the data. Experienced report writers use tables to list exact data; they use line charts or bar charts to spotlight important points or trends.

Simple line charts (Figure 12.12) show just one variable. Multiple line charts combine several variables (Figure 12.13). Segmented line charts (Figure 12.14), also called *surface* charts, illustrate how the components of a whole change over time. Notice how Figure 12.14 helps you visualize the shift in total MPM income from motion pictures to videos and theme parks. By contrast, tables don't permit such visualization.

Here are tips for preparing a line chart:

- Begin with a grid divided into squares.
- Arrange the time component (usually years) horizontally across the bottom; arrange values for the other variable vertically.

FIGURE 12.16 Flow Chart

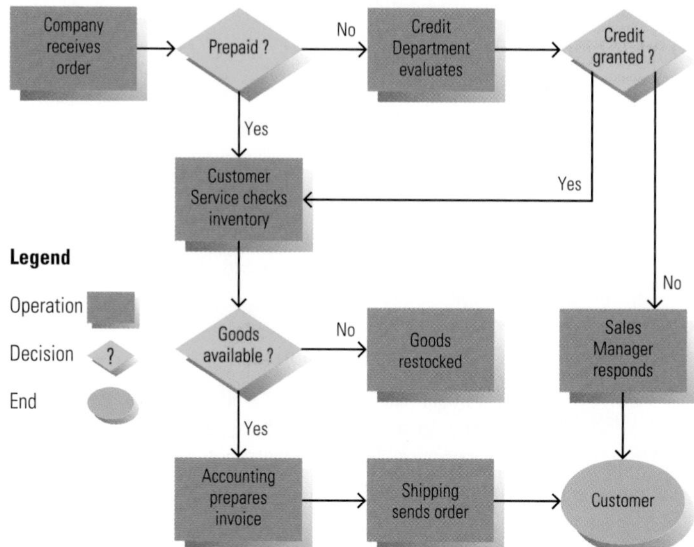

Flow charts are useful to clarify procedures.

- Draw small dots at the intersections to indicate each value at a given year.
- Connect the dots and add color if desired.
- To prepare a segmented (surface) chart, plot the first value (say, video income) across the bottom; add the next item (say, motion picture income) to the first figures for every increment; for the third item (say, theme park income) add its value to the total of the first two items. The top line indicates the total of the three values.

Pie Charts. Pie, or circle, charts enable readers to see a whole and the proportion of its components, or wedges. Although less flexible than bar or line charts, pie charts are useful in showing percentages, as Figure 12.15 illustrates. Notice that a wedge can be "exploded" or popped out for special emphasis, as seen in Figure 12.15.

Pie charts are most useful in showing the proportion of parts to a whole.

For the most effective pie charts, follow these suggestions:

- Begin at the 12 o'clock position, drawing the largest wedge first. (Computer software programs don't always observe this advice, but if you're drawing your own charts, you can.)
- Include, if possible, the actual percentage or absolute value for each wedge.
- Use four to eight segments for best results; if necessary, group small portions into one wedge called "Other."
- Distinguish wedges with color, shading, or cross-hatching.
- Keep all the labels horizontal.

Many software programs help you prepare professional-looking charts with a minimum of effort. See the accompanying Tech Talk box for more information.

Flow Charts. Procedures are simplified and clarified by diagramming them in a flow chart, as shown in Figure 12.16. Whether you need to describe the procedure for handling a customer's purchase order or outline steps in solving a problem, flow

TECH TALK

USING YOUR COMPUTER TO PRODUCE CHARTS

Designing effective bar charts, pie charts, figures, and other images has never been easier than it is now with the use of computer graphics programs.

Spreadsheet programs—such as Excel, Lotus 1-2-3, and Corel QuattroPro—and presentations graphics programs—such as Microsoft PowerPoint and Lotus Freelance Graphics—allow even nontechnical people to design quality graphics. These graphics can be printed directly on paper for written reports or used for transparency masters and slides for oral presentations. The benefits of preparing graphics on a computer are near-professional quality, shorter preparation time, and substantial savings in preparation costs.

To prepare a computer graphic, begin by assembling your data, usually in table form. Let's say you work for Dynamo Products, and you prepared Table 1 below showing the number of Dynamo computers sold in each region for each quarter of the fiscal year.

Next, you must decide what type of chart you want: pie chart, grouped bar chart, vertical bar chart, horizontal bar chart, organization chart, or some other graphic. To make a pie chart showing total computers sold by division for the year, key in the data or select the data from an existing file. Add a title for the chart, as well as any necessary labels. For a bar or line chart, indicate the horizontal and vertical axes (reference lines or beginning points). Most programs will automatically generate legends for figures. If you wish, however, you can easily customize titles and legends.

The finished chart can be printed on paper or inserted into your word processing document to be printed with your finished report. The pie chart and bar chart shown here were created in a spreadsheet program and inserted into a word processing program.

Another useful feature of most word processing programs involves inserting and linking worksheets. Our table showing the total number of computers sold could be created by inserting an Excel worksheet into a Word document. The result is a nicely arranged, easy-to-read table. The table can also be "linked" to the spreadsheet program so that the latest changes made in the worksheet will be automatically reflected in the table as it appears in the word processing document.

Career Track Application

Visit your local software dealer and ask for a demonstration of how to create a pie or bar chart using a computer graphics program. Ask the salesperson to print out a copy of the visual (on a color printer, if available) for you to bring to class for discussion.

DYNAMO PRODUCTS
NUMBER OF COMPUTERS SOLD

Region	1st Qtr.	2nd Qtr.	3rd Qtr.	4th Qtr.	Yearly Totals
Eastern	13,302	15,003	15,550	16,210	60,065
Northern	12,678	11,836	10,689	14,136	49,339
Western	10,345	11,934	10,899	12,763	45,941
Southern	9,345	8,921	9,565	10,256	38,087
Total	45,670	47,694	46,703	53,365	193,432

Figure 1
DYNAMO PRODUCTS
YEARLY SALES

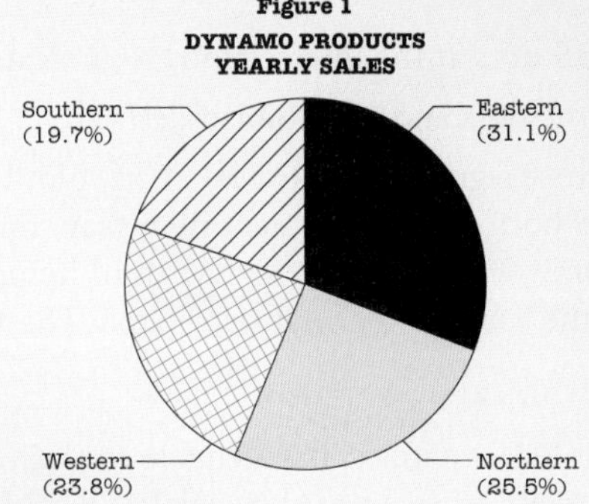

Figure 2
DYNAMO PRODUCTS
1999 QUARTERLY SALES

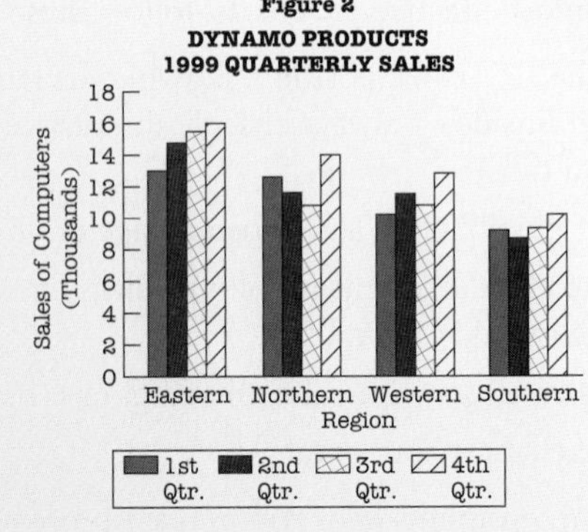

FIGURE 12.17 **Memo With Organization Chart**

Quattro-ATI International
Memorandum

Date: August 12, 1999

To: Deborah Natkin, Facilities Manager

From: David Williams, Post-Acquisition Team Leader

cc: Allison Headrich, Larry Honl, Debra Bohlman, Lin Behmer

The following organizational chart shows how my new Post-Acquisition Team is structured. The acquired employees will be working closely with Allison's group. Please make sure that we have space to keep the eight of them together on the same floor.

I appreciate your help, Deborah, in this challenging post-acquisition period.

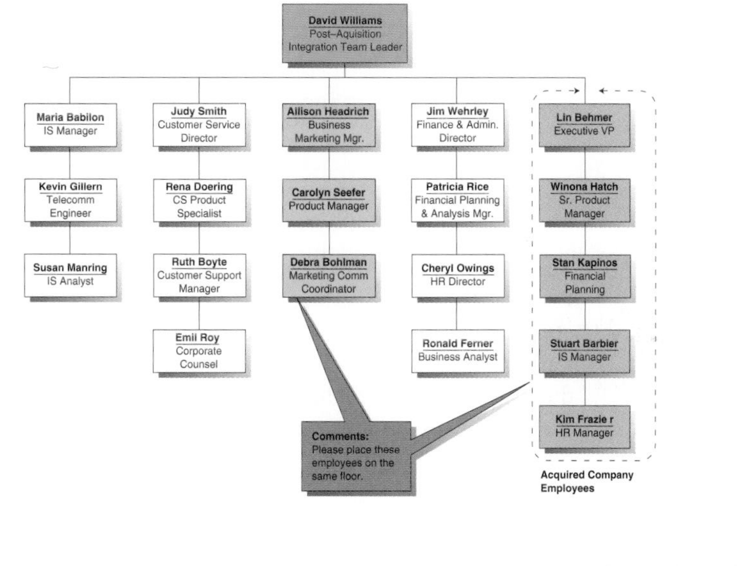

charts help the reader visualize the process. Traditional flow charts use the following symbols:

- Ovals to designate the beginning and end of a process
- Diamonds to denote decision points
- Rectangles to represent major activities or steps

Organization Charts. Many large organizations are so complex that they need charts to show the chain of command, from the boss down to line managers and employees. Organization charts like the one in Figure 1.9 in Chapter 1 provide such information as who reports to whom, how many subordinates work for each manager (the span of control), and what channels of official communication exist. They may also illustrate a company's structure (by function, customer, or product, for example), the work being performed in each job, and the hierarchy of decision making.

Organization charts show the line of command and thus the flow of official communication from management to employees.

Organization charts can also be used in memorandums, such as that shown in Figure 12.17. One company acquired another, and two sets of employees had to be integrated into one organization. The chart in this memo quickly illustrates to readers what employees are to be grouped together. And with today's color printers, the visual grouping becomes even more obvious because of color coding.

Computer technology permits photographs, maps, and illustrations to be scanned directly into a report.

Photographs, Maps, and Illustrations. Some business reports include photographs, maps, and illustrations to serve specific purposes. Pictures, for example, add authenticity and provide a visual record. Dusty Richter, a location manager for a motion picture company, includes pictures in all his scouting reports; and Eliza Cohn, an environmental engineer, documents hazardous sites with her own photographs. With today's computer technology, photographs and images can be scanned directly into business reports.

Maps enable report writers to depict activities or concentrations geographically, such as dots indicating sales reps in states across the country. Your reports might show where an organization's new products will be introduced or what states in the country have income taxes. Office supply stores sometimes carry blank state, national, and global maps; and many computer programs provide maps that you can fill in to highlight locations discussed in your reports.

Illustrations and diagrams are useful in indicating how an object looks or operates. A drawing showing the parts of a VCR with labels describing their functions, for example, is more instructive than a photograph or verbal description. Artists can emphasize critical points and delete distracting details.

Incorporating Graphics in Reports

7

Used appropriately, graphics make reports more interesting and easier to understand. In putting graphics into your reports, follow these suggestions for best effects.

Effective graphics are accurate and ethical, avoid overuse of color or decorations, and include titles.

- **Evaluate the audience.** Size up your readers to determine how many graphics are appropriate. Six charts in an internal report to an executive may seem like overkill; but in a long technical report to outsiders, six may be too few. Evaluate the reader, the content, your schedule, and your budget (graphics take time and money to prepare) in deciding how many graphics to use.
- **Use restraint.** Don't overuse color or decorations. Although color can effectively distinguish bars or segments in charts, too much color can be distracting and confusing. Remember, too, that colors themselves sometimes convey meaning: reds suggest deficits or negative values, blues suggest coolness, and oranges may mean warmth. Also, use decorations (sometimes called "dingbats" or "chartjunk") sparingly, if at all.
- **Be accurate and ethical.** Double-check all graphics for accuracy of figures and calculations. Be certain that your visuals aren't misleading—either accidentally or intentionally. Manipulation of a chart scale can make trends look steeper and more dramatic than they really are. To avoid giving a false picture, experiment with different scales. Then judge whether the resulting trend looks accurate and honest. Also, be sure to cite sources when you use someone else's facts. The accompanying Ethical Insights box discusses in more detail how to make ethical charts and graphics.

Textual graphics should be introduced by statements that help readers interpret them.

- **Introduce a graphic meaningfully.** Refer to every graphic in the text, and place the graphic close to the point where it is mentioned. Most important, though, help the reader understand the significance of a graphic. You can do this by telling the reader what to look for or by summarizing the main point of a graphic. Don't assume the reader will automatically draw the same conclusions you reached from a set of data. Instead of *The findings are shown in Figure 3,* tell the reader what to

ETHICAL INSIGHTS

MAKING ETHICAL CHARTS AND GRAPHICS

Business communicators must present graphical data in the same ethical, honest manner required for all other messages. Remember that the information shown in your charts and graphics will be used to inform others or help them make decisions. If this information is not represented accurately, the reader will be incorrectly informed; any decisions based on the data are likely to be faulty. And mistakes in interpreting such information may have serious and long-lasting consequences.

Chart data can be distorted in many ways. Figure 1 shows advertising expenses displayed on an appropriate scale. Figure 2 shows the same information, but the horizontal scale, from 1992 to 1997, has been lengthened. Notice that the data have not changed, but the increases and decreases are smoothed out, so changes in expenses appear to be slight. In Figure 3 the vertical scale is taller and the horizontal scale is shortened, resulting in what appear to be sharp increases and decreases in expenses.

To avoid misrepresenting data, keep the following pointers in mind when designing your graphics:

- Use an appropriate type of chart or graphic for the message you wish to convey.
- Design the chart so that it focuses on the appropriate information.
- Include all relevant or important data; don't arbitrarily leave out necessary information.
- Don't hide critical information by including too much data in one graphic.
- Use appropriate scales with equal intervals for the data you present.

Career Track Application

Locate one or two graphics in a newspaper, magazine article, or annual report. Analyze the strengths and weaknesses of each graphic. Is the information presented accurately? Select a bar or line chart. Sketch the same chart but change the vertical or horizontal scales on the graphic. How does the message of the chart change?

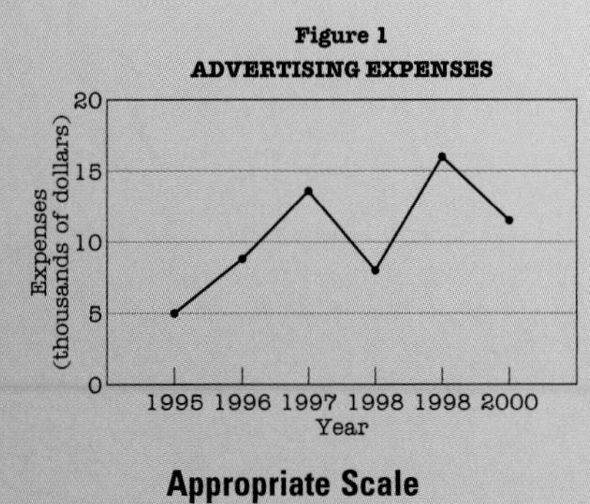

Appropriate Scale

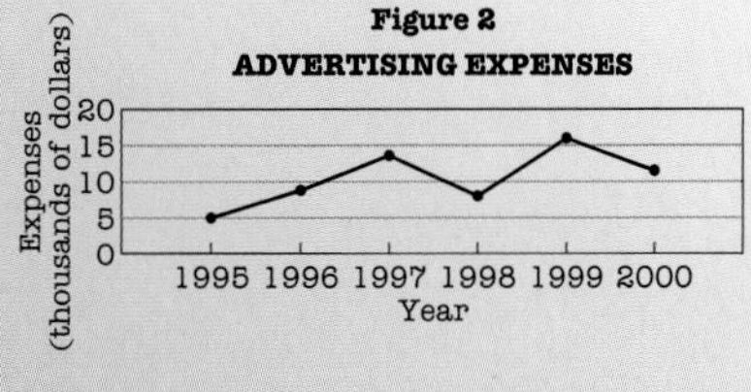

Distorted Scale

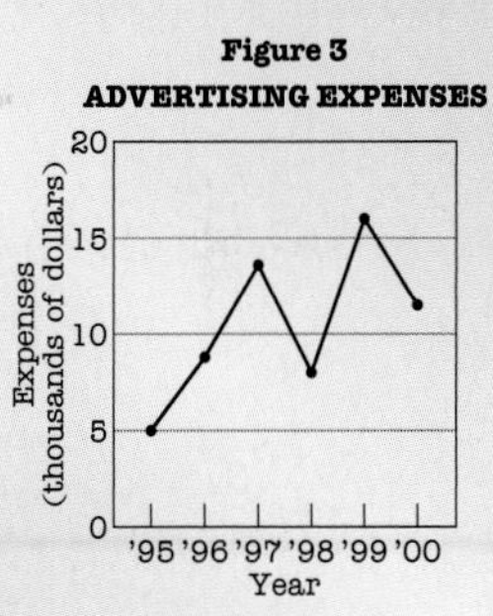

Distorted Scale

look for: *Two thirds of the responding employees, as shown in Figure 3, favor a flextime schedule.* The best introductions for graphics interpret them for readers.

- **Choose an appropriate caption or title style.** Like reports, graphics may use "talking" titles or generic, descriptive titles. "Talking" titles are more persuasive; they tell the reader what to think. Descriptive titles describe the facts more objectively.

Talking Title	**Descriptive Title**
Average Annual Health Care Costs per Worker Rise Steeply As Workers Grow Older	Average Annual Health Care Costs per Worker As Shown by Age Groups

Judge the style you should use by your audience and your company's preferences. Regardless of the style, make the titles consistent and specific.

CASE STUDY

PROCESS TO PRODUCT

Applying Your Skills at J. D. Power and Associates

Most carmakers and franchised dealerships are eager to retain the business of new car buyers. Parts and service can be a big part of the profit picture for most dealers. But many new car owners do not continue to take their cars to a dealership for servicing after their warranties expire. As part of its Vehicle Dependability Study, let's assume that J. D. Power and Associates gathered the following data. In canvassing owners of five-year-old cars, it uncovered many reasons explaining why these owners did not use a franchised dealership for service. Eleven percent said that they had to wait too long for an appointment. Fourteen percent said they had to wait too long while having servicing; 18 percent said they didn't use a franchised dealership because their warranty or service contract had expired. Forty-eight percent said that labor costs were too high at the dealership. Another 31 percent said that parts costs were too high, and 24 percent reported that the location of the dealership was inconvenient. The total does not equal 100 because participants could give more than one reason.

Your Job

As an assistant to researcher and consultant John Humphrey, prepare a table and a bar graph for the data provided. Give the table and graph an appropriate name. What conclusions could you draw from this data? If asked, what recommendations might you make to dealers in regard to retaining the service business of owners of older cars?

Summary of Learning Objectives

1 **Use tabulating and statistical techniques to sort and interpret report data.** Report data become more meaningful when sorted into tables or when analyzed by mean (the arithmetic average), median (the midpoint in a group of figures), and mode (the most frequent response). Range represents a span between the highest and lowest figures. Grids help organize complex data into rows and columns.

2 **Draw meaningful conclusions from report data.** Conclusions tell what the survey data mean—especially in relation to the original report problem. They summarize key findings and may attempt to explain what caused the report problem. They are usually enumerated.

3 **Prepare practical report recommendations.** In reports that call for recommendations, writers make specific suggestions for actions that can solve the report problem. Recommendations should be feasible and potentially agreeable to the audience. They should all relate to the initial problem. Recommendations may be combined with conclusions.

4 **Organize report data logically.** Reports may be organized in many ways, including (1) by time (establishing a chronology or history of events), (2) by component (discussing a problem by geography, division, or product),

(3) by importance (arranging data from most important to least important, or vice versa), (4) by criteria (comparing items by standards), or (5) by convention (using an already established grouping).

5 **Provide cues to aid report comprehension.** Good communicators help receivers understand a topic's organization by using introductions (to spell out topics), transitional expressions (to indicate where a topic is headed), and headings (to highlight major ideas).

6 **Develop graphics that create meaning and interest.** Good graphics improve reports by clarifying, simplifying, and emphasizing data. Tables organize precise data into rows and columns. Bar and line charts enable data to be compared visually. Line charts are especially helpful in showing changes over time. Pie charts show a whole and the proportion of its components. Organization charts, pictures, maps, and illustrations serve specific purposes.

7 **Incorporate graphic aids into reports effectively.** In choosing or crafting graphics, smart communicators evaluate their audience, purpose, topic, and budget to determine the number and kind of graphics. These communicators are accurate, ethical, and restrained in developing graphics. And they are consistent in writing "talking" titles (telling readers what to think about the graphic) or "descriptive" titles (summarizing the topic objectively).

CHAPTER REVIEW

1. Forms that use systematic columns and rows to enable you to summarize and simplify numerical data from questionnaires and interviews are called what? (Obj. 1)
2. What is cross-tabulation? Give an example. (Obj. 1)
3. Calculate the mean, median, and mode for these figures: 3, 4, 4, 4, 10. (Obj. 1)
4. How can a grid help classify material? (Obj. 1)
5. What are the two most widely read sections of a report? (Obj. 2)
6. How do conclusions differ from recommendations? (Objs. 2 and 3)
7. When reports have multiple recommendations, how should they be presented? (Obj. 3)
8. Informational reports typically are organized into what three parts? (Obj. 4)
9. Analytical reports may be organized directly or indirectly. How do the organizational patterns differ? (Obj. 4)
10. Name five methods for organizing report data. Be prepared to discuss each. (Obj. 4)
11. What three devices can report writers use to prevent readers from getting lost in the text? (Obj. 5)
12. Briefly compare the advantages and disadvantages of illustrating data with charts (bar and line) versus tables. (Obj. 6)
13. What is the major advantage of using pie charts to illustrate data? (Obj. 6)
14. What graphic is best for illustrating a process or procedure? (Obj. 6)
15. Describe two kinds of captions or titles for graphics. (Obj. 7)

CRITICAL THINKING

1. Why is audience analysis particularly important in making report recommendations? (Obj. 3)
2. Why is anticipation of the audience's response less important in an informational report than in an analytical report? (Objs. 2 and 3)

3. Should all reports be organized so that they follow the sequence of investigation—that is, describing for the reader the initial problem, analysis of issues, data collection, data analysis, and conclusions? Why or why not? (Obj. 4)

4. Why is it important for reports to contain structural cues clarifying their organization? (Obj. 5)

5. **Ethical Issue:** Discuss the ethics of an annual report that disguises a company's net operating loss by using deceptive graphs. The actual figures, as audited by a CPA, show the loss; but they are buried in long tables within the report. By starting with a base figure below 0, the graphics suggested a profit instead of a loss. Graphics are not audited.

ACTIVITIES

12.1 Tabulation and Interpretation of Survey Results (Obj. 1)

Team | **Critical Thinking**

a. Assume your business communication class at North Shore College was asked by the college bookstore manager, Larry Krause, to conduct a survey (see Figure 11.13). Concerned about the environment, Krause wants to learn students' reactions to eliminating plastic bags, of which 45,000 are given away annually by the bookstore. Students were questioned about a number of proposals, resulting in the following raw data. In groups of four or five, convert the data into a table (see Figure 12.1) with a descriptive title. Arrange the items in a logical sequence.

For major purchases the bookstore should	Agree	Undecided	Disagree
5. Continue to provide plastic bags	132	17	411
6. Provide no bags; encourage students to bring their own bags	414	25	121
7. Provide no bags; offer cloth bags at a reduced price (about $3)	357	19	184
8. Give a cloth bag with each major purchase, the cost to be included in registration fees	63	15	482

b. How could these survey data be cross-tabulated? Would cross-tabulation serve any purpose?

c. Given the conditions of this survey, name at least three conclusions that could be drawn from the data.

d. Prepare three to five recommendations to be submitted to Mr. Krause. How could they be implemented?

12.2 Evaluating Conclusions (Obj. 2)

E-Mail

Read an in-depth article (800 or more words) in *Business Week, Fortune, Forbes,* or *The Wall Street Journal.* What conclusions does the author draw? Are the conclusions valid, based on the evidence presented? In an e-mail message to your instructor, summarize the main points in the article and analyze the conclusions. What conclusions would you have drawn from the data?

12.3 Distinguishing Between Conclusions and Recommendations (Objs. 2 and 3)

For each of the following statements, indicate whether it could be classified as a conclusion or recommendation.

a. In times of recession, individuals spend less money on meals away from home.

b. Our restaurant should offer a menu featuring a variety of low-priced items in addition to the regular menu.

c. Absenteeism among employees with families decreases when they have adequate child care.

d. Nearly 80 percent of our business comes from only 20 percent of our customers.

e. Datatech Company should concentrate its major sales effort on its largest accounts.

f. The length of vacations for employees across the country is directly correlated with their length of employment.

g. The employee vacation schedule of Datatech Company compares favorably with the averages of other similar U.S. companies.

h. Offering outplacement service (assistance in finding jobs) tends to diffuse the anger that goes with involuntary separation (being released from a job).

12.4 Data Organization (Obj. 4)

How could the findings in the following reports be best organized? Consider these methods: time, component, importance, criteria, and convention.

a. A report comparing three sites for a company's new production plant. The report presents figures on property costs, construction costs, proximity to raw materials, state taxes, labor availability, and shipping distances.

b. A report describing the history of the development of dwarf and spur apple trees, starting with the first genetic dwarfs discovered about 100 years ago and progressing to today's grafted varieties on dwarfing rootstocks.

c. An informational brochure for job candidates that describes your company's areas of employment: accounting, finance, information systems, operations management, marketing, production, and computer-aided design.

d. A monthly sales report submitted to the sales manager.

e. A recommendation report, to be submitted to management, presenting four building plans to improve access to your building, in compliance with federal regulations. The plans range considerably in feasibility and cost.

f. A progress report submitted six months into the process of planning the program for your organization's convention.

g. An informational report describing a company's expansion plans in South America, Europe, Australia, and Southeast Asia.

h. An employee performance appraisal submitted annually.

12.5 Evaluating Headings and Titles (Objs. 5 and 7)

Identify the following report headings and titles as "talking" or "functional/descriptive." Discuss the usefulness and effectiveness of each.

a. Problem

b. Need for Tightening Computer ID System

c. Annual Budget

d. How to Implement Quality Circles That Work

e. Case History: Buena Vista Palace Hotel Focuses on Improving Service to Customers

f. Solving Our Records Management Problems

g. Comparing Copier Volume, Ease of Use, and Speed

h. Alternatives

12.6 Selecting Graphics (Obj. 6)

Identify the best kind of graphic to illustrate the following data.

a. Instructions for workers telling them how to distinguish between worker accidents that must be reported to state and federal agencies and those that need not be reported.

b. Figures showing what proportion of every state tax dollar is spent on education, social services, transportation, debt, and other expenses.

c. Data showing the academic, administrative, and operation divisions of a college, from the president to department chairs and division managers.

d. Figures comparing the sales of VCRs, color TVs, and personal computers over the past ten years.

e. Figures showing the operating profit of a company for the past five years.

f. Data showing areas in the United States most likely to have earthquakes.

g. Percentages showing the causes of forest fires (lightning, 73 percent; arson, 5 percent; campfires, 9 percent; and so on) in the Rocky Mountains.

h. Figures comparing the cost of basic TV cable service in ten areas of the United States for the past ten years (the boss wants to see exact figures).

12.7 Evaluating Graphics (Objs. 6 and 7)

Select five graphics from newspapers or magazines. Look in *The Wall Street Journal, USA Today, Business Week, U.S. News & World Report, Fortune,* or other business news publications. In a memo to your instructor, critique each graphic based on what you have learned in this chapter.

12.8 Drawing a Bar Chart (Obj. 6)

Prepare a bar chart comparing the tax rates of eight industrial countries in the world: Canada, 34 percent; France, 42 percent; Germany, 39 percent; Japan, 26 percent; Netherlands, 48 percent; Sweden, 49 percent; United Kingdom, 37 percent; United States, 28 percent. These figures represent a percentage of the gross domestic product for each country. The sources of the figures are the International Monetary Fund and the Japanese Ministry of Finance. Arrange the entries logically. Write two titles: a talking title and a descriptive title. What conclusion might you draw from these figures? What should be emphasized in the graph and title?

12.9 Drawing a Line Chart (Obj. 6)

Prepare a line chart showing the sales of Sidekick Athletic Shoes, Inc., for these years: 1999, $6.7 million; 1998, $5.4 million; 1997, $3.2 million; 1996, $2.1 million; 1995, $2.6 million; 1994, $3.6 million. In the chart title highlight the trend you see in the data.

12.10 Studying Graphics in Annual Reports (Objs. 6 and 7)

In a memo to your instructor, evaluate the effectiveness of graphics in three to five corporation annual reports. Critique their readability, clarity, and success in visualizing data. How were they introduced in the text? What suggestions would you make to improve them?

CHAPTER • 13 •

Typical Business Reports

LEARNING OBJECTIVES

1. Distinguish between informational and analytical reports.
2. Identify periodic reports and describe their major components.
3. Discuss the forms and content of situational reports.
4. Distinguish between investigative and compliance reports.
5. Compare direct and indirect justification/recommendation reports.
6. Describe the purpose and content of feasibility reports.
7. Identify yardstick reports and describe their major components.
8. Discuss the content of research reports.

Nike Scrambles to Restore Image and Profits

After years of unchallenged supremacy in athletic footwear, high-flying Nike Inc. has tumbled a little. No one would question that Nike led the way in making footwear in every sport more fashionable and better engineered than ever before. Beyond revolutionizing footwear, Nike has also changed the entire approach to the athletics market.[1] Instead of focusing totally on developing great footwear, it has branched out into apparel, sports management, sports promotion, sports equipment, and even recycling old sports shoes into sports playing surfaces. For years the Nike name conjured up images of sports heroes like Michael Jordan, Andre Agassi, and Tiger Woods. To many of us, the "swoosh" logo symbolized champions, winning, and doing it our way.

More recently, though, the Nike image has been clouded by allegations of unfair labor practices overseas. To its credit, the company took fast action in responding to and correcting conditions in its factories. Yet, it suffers from lingering ill will and other problems. The Asian economic slump, a glut of expensive merchandise, increased competition from fashion designers, changing footwear fashions, and the continual need for innovative products—all these factors take a toll. What's worse, many young people find it difficult to admire a corporate giant that controls nearly half of the U.S. athletic shoe market and that plasters its logo on everything from ball caps to soccer balls. Suddenly, Nike doesn't seem so cool anymore. One observer says that the "biggest swoosh now is the sound of falling profits."[2]

But successful companies don't sit back and let adversity swallow them up. Nike Chairman Phil Knight, who admits that he has been described as "the perfect corporate villain for these times," has begun to speak out again criticism. He's announced reforms. Moreover, the company continues to expand its range of innovative products and procedures. At every step of the way, Nike relies on information and feedback from researchers, consultants, managers, line employees, suppliers, consumers, and many others. Much of this data and feedback will be in the form of reports.

www.nikebiz.com

Informational Reports

1

Informational reports provide data on periodic and situational activities for readers who do not need to be persuaded.

Nike and all other organizations need information to stay abreast of what's happening inside and outside of their firms. Much of this information will be submitted in the form of reports. This chapter examines both informational and analytical reports.

Informational reports generally deliver data and answer questions without offering recommendations or much analysis. In these reports the emphasis is on facts. Informational reports describe periodic, recurring activities (like monthly sales or weekly customer calls) as well as situational, nonrecurring events (such as trips, conferences, and progress on special projects). They also include routine operating, compliance, and investigative reports. What they have in common is delivering information to readers who do not have to be persuaded. Informational report readers usually are neutral or receptive.

You can expect to write many informational reports as an entry-level or middle-management employee. Because these reports generally deliver nonsensitive data and thus will not upset the reader, they are organized directly. Often they need little background material or introductory comments since readers are familiar with the topics. Although they're generally conversational and informal, informational reports should not be so casual that the reader struggles to find the important points. Main points must be immediately visible. Headings, lists, bulleted items, and other graphic highlighting, as well as clear organization, enable readers to grasp major ideas immediately. The Career Coach box on page 398 provides additional pointers on design features and techniques that can improve your reports.

Periodic Reports

2

Periodic reports keep management informed of operations and activities.

Most businesses—especially larger ones—require periodic reports to keep management informed of operations. These recurring reports are written at regular intervals—weekly, monthly, yearly—so that management can monitor and, if necessary, remedy business strategies. Some periodic reports simply contain figures, such as sales volume, number and kind of customer service calls, shipments delivered, accounts payable, and personnel data. More challenging periodic reports require description and discussion of activities. In preparing a narrative description of their activities, employees writing periodic reports usually do the following:

- Summarize regular activities and events performed during the reporting period.
- Describe irregular events deserving the attention of management.
- Highlight special needs and problems.

Managers naturally want to know that routine activities are progressing normally. They're often more interested, though, in what the competition is doing and in how operations may be affected by unusual events or problems. In companies with open lines of communication, managers expect to be informed of the bad news along with the good news.

Jim Chrisman, sales rep for a West Coast sprinkler manufacturer, worked with a group of fellow sales reps and managers to produce the format for the periodic report shown in Figure 13.1. In Jim's words, "We used to write three- and four-page weekly activity reports that, I hate to admit, rambled all over the place. When our managers complained that they weren't getting the information they wanted, we sat down together and developed a report form with four categories: (1) activity summary, (2) competition update, (3) product problems and comments, and (4) needs. Then one manager wrote several sample reports that we studied. Now, my reports are shorter and more focused. I try to hit the highlights in covering my daily activities, but I really concentrate on product problems and items that I must have to do a better job. Managers tell us that they need this kind of detailed feedback so that they can respond to the competition and also develop new products that our customers want."

Situational Reports

3

Situational reports cover nonrecurring events.

Reports covering nonrecurring situations—trips, conventions, conferences, event planning, and progress—are a little more difficult to write than periodic reports. Because samples are generally unavailable to serve as models, you'll probably devote more attention to organizing your material. Like other informational reports, situational reports are generally prepared as memos. The tone of these reports is informal. The length depends on reader expectations and on the actual situation, but shorter is usually better. Before writing, if possible, ask the person who authorized the report how much detail should be included and how long the report should be. You have nothing to lose by clarifying the assignment. Situational reports usually need introductions (to familiarize the reader with the topic) and closings (to give a sense of ending).

FIGURE 13.1 Periodic Report

1 PREWRITING

Analyze: The purpose of this report is to inform management of the week's activities, customer reactions, and the rep's needs.

Anticipate: The audience is a manager who wants to be able to pick out the report highlights quickly. His reaction will probably be neutral or positive.

Adapt: Introduce the report data in a direct, straightforward manner.

2 WRITING

Research: Verify data for the landscape judging test. Collect facts about competitors. Double-check problems and needs.

Organize: Make lists of items for each of the four report categories. Be sure to distinguish between problems and needs. Emphasize needs.

Compose: Write and print first draft on a computer.

3 REVISING

Revise: Look for ways to eliminate wordiness. For greater emphasis use a bulleted list for *Competition Update* and for *Needs*. Make all items parallel.

Proofread: Run spell checker. Adjust white space around headings.

Evaluate: Does this report provide significant data in an easy-to-read format?

DATE: March 15, 2000

TO: Steve Schumacher

FROM: Jim Chrisman JC

SUBJECT: Weekly Activity Report

Presents internal informational report in memo format

Activity Summary

Condenses weekly activity report into topics requested by management

Highlights of my activities for the week ending March 14 follow:

Fort Worth. On Thursday and Friday I demonstrated our new Rain Stream drip systems at a vendor fair at Benbrook Farm Supply, where over 500 people walked through.

Arlington State College. Over the weekend I was a judge for the Texas Landscape Technician test given on the ASC campus. This certification program ensures potential employers that a landscaper is properly trained. Applicants are tested in such areas as irrigation theory, repair, trouble-shooting, installation, and controller programming. The event proved to be very productive. I was able to talk to my distributors and to several important contractors whose crews were taking the tests.

Competition Update

- Toronado can't seem to fill its open sales position in the west Texas territory.
- RainCo tried to steal the Trinity Country Club golf course contract from us by waiting until the job was spec'd our way and then submitting a lower bid. Fortunately, the Trinity people saw through this ploy and awarded us the contract nevertheless.
- Atlas has a real warranty problem with its 500 series in this area. One distributor had over 200 controllers returned in a seven-week period.

Product Problems, Comments

A contractor in Wichita Falls told me that our Rain Stream No. 250 valves do not hold the adjustment screw in the throttled-down position. Are they designed to do so?

Our Remote Streamer S-100 is generating considerable excitement. Every time I mention it, people come out of the woodwork to request demos. I gave four demos last week and have three more scheduled this week. I'm not sure, though, how quickly these demos will translate into sales because contractors are waiting for our six-month special prices.

Needs

Summarizes needs in abbreviated, easy-to-read form

- More information on xerigation training.
- Spanish training videos showing our products.
- Spray nozzle to service small planter areas, say 6 to 8 feet.

Spotlight on **Communicators**

Reports became an integral part of her existence when Janet Marie Smith helped develop Oriole Park at Camden Yards, the home of the Baltimore Orioles. As vice president of stadium planning and development, she wrote endless situational and investigative reports to keep everyone informed about the construction. "I rely heavily on written communication," she notes, "because it provides records and allows me to send the same information to many different people."

Trip, Convention, and Conference Reports. Employees sent on business trips or to conventions and conferences typically must submit reports when they return. Organizations want to know that their money was well spent in funding the travel. These reports inform management about new procedures, equipment, and laws and supply information affecting products, operations, and service.

The hardest parts of writing these reports are selecting the most relevant material and organizing it coherently. Generally, it's best not to use chronological sequencing (*in the morning we did X, at lunch we heard Y, and in the afternoon we did Z*). Instead, you should focus on three to five topics in which your reader will be interested. These items become the body of the report. Then simply add an introduction and closing, and your report is organized. Here is a general outline for trip, conference, and convention reports:

- Begin by identifying the event (exact date, name, and location) and previewing the topics to be discussed.
- Summarize in the body three to five main points that might benefit the reader.
- Itemize your expenses, if requested, on a separate sheet.
- Close by expressing appreciation, suggesting action to be taken, or synthesizing the value of the trip or event.

Jeff Marchant was recently named employment coordinator in the Human Resources Department of an electronics appliance manufacturer headquartered in central Ohio. Recognizing his lack of experience in interviewing job applicants, he asked permission to attend a one-day conference on the topic. His boss, Angela Taylor, encouraged Jeff to attend, saying, "We all need to brush up on our interviewing techniques. Come back and tell us what you learned." When he returned, Jeff wrote the conference report shown in Figure 13.2. Here's how he describes its preparation: "I know my boss values brevity, so I worked hard to make my report no more than a page and a quarter. The conference saturated me with great ideas, far too many to cover in one brief report. So, I decided to discuss three topics that would be most useful to our staff. Although I had to be brief, I nonetheless wanted to provide as many details—especially about common interviewing mistakes—as possible. By the third draft, I had compressed my ideas into a manageable size without sacrificing any of the meaning."

Progress and interim reports describe ongoing projects to both internal and external readers.

Progress and Interim Reports. Continuing projects often require progress or interim reports to describe their status. These reports may be external (advising customers regarding the headway of their projects) or internal (informing management of the status of activities). Progress reports typically follow this pattern of development:

- Specify in the opening the purpose and nature of the project.
- Provide background information if the audience requires filling in.
- Describe the work completed.
- Explain the work currently in progress, including personnel, activities, methods, and locations.
- Anticipate problems and possible remedies.
- Discuss future activities and provide the expected completion date.

As a location manager in the film industry, Sheila Ryan frequently writes progress reports, such as the one shown in Figure 13.3. Producers want to be informed of what she's doing, and a phone call doesn't provide a permanent record.

FIGURE 13.2 Conference Report

DATE: April 22, 2000
TO: Angela Taylor
FROM: Jeff Marchant JM
SUBJECT: TRAINING CONFERENCE ON EMPLOYMENT INTERVIEWING

I enjoyed attending the "Interviewing People" training conference sponsored by the National Business Foundation. This one-day meeting, held in Columbus on April 19, provided excellent advice that will help us strengthen our interviewing techniques. Although the conference covered many topics, this report concentrates on three areas: structuring the interview, avoiding common mistakes, and responding to new legislation.

Identifies topic and previews how the report is organized

Structuring the Interview

Job interviews usually have three parts. The opening establishes a friendly rapport with introductions, a few polite questions, and an explanation of the purpose for the interview. The body of the interview consists of questions controlled by the interviewer. The interviewer has three goals: (a) educating the applicant about the job, (b) eliciting information about the applicant's suitability for the job, and (c) promoting goodwill about the organization. In closing, the interviewer should encourage the applicant to ask questions, summarize main points, and indicate what actions will follow.

Sets off major topics with centered headings

Avoiding Common Mistakes

Probably the most interesting and practical part of the conference centered on common mistakes made by interviewers, some of which I summarize here:

1. Not taking notes at each interview. Recording important facts enables you to remember the first candidate as easily as you remember the last—and all those in between.

2. Losing control of the interview. Keep control of the interview by digging into the candidate's answers to questions. Probe for responses of greater depth. Don't move on until a question has been satisfactorily answered.

Covers facts that will most interest and help reader

3. Not testing the candidate's communication skills. To be able to evaluate a candidate's ability to express ideas, ask the individual to explain some technical jargon from his or her current position—preferably, something mentioned during the interview.

4. Having departing employees conduct the interviews for their replacements. Departing employees may be unreliable as interviewers because they tend to hire candidates not quite as strong as they are.

5. Failing to check references. As many as 15 percent of all résumés may contain falsified data. The best way to check references is to network: ask the person whose name has been given to suggest the name of another person.

Angela Taylor Page 2 April 22, 2000

Responding to New Legislation

Recently enacted provisions of the Americans With Disabilities Act prohibit interviewers from asking candidates—or even their references—about candidates' disabilities. A question we frequently asked ("Do you have any physical limitations which would prevent you from performing the job for which you are applying?") would now break the law. Interviewers must also avoid asking about medical history; prescription-drug use; prior workers' compensation claims; work absenteeism due to illness; and past treatment for alcoholism, drug use, or mental illness.

Conclusion

This conference provided me with valuable training that I would like to share with other department members at a future staff meeting. Let me know when it can be scheduled.

Here's how she describes her reasoning behind the progress report in Figure 13.3: "I usually include background information in my reports because a director doesn't always know or remember exactly what specifications I was given for a location search. Then I try to hit the high points of what I've completed and what I plan to do next, without getting bogged down in minute details. Although it would be easier to skip them, I've learned to be up front with any problems that I anticipate. I don't tell how to solve the problems, but I feel duty-bound to at least mention them."

Investigative Reports

4

Spotlight on **Communicators**

Regular financial reports keep Protocol Telecommunications squeaky clean. Anthony Miranda, president of Protocol, doesn't wait for his bankers or investors to demand his financials. "I want there to be no question at any time that our financial information was misstated or less than fully disclosed." In addition to systematic financial reports, Protocol employees may submit situational reports describing attendance at trade shows or conferences. Such reports identify the event, summarize relevant information acquired, itemize expenses, and suggest how the information may be applied.

Investigative or informational reports deliver data for a specific situation—without offering interpretation or recommendations. These nonrecurring reports are generally arranged in a direct pattern with three segments: introduction, body, and summary. The body—which includes the facts, findings, or discussion—may be organized by time, component, importance, criteria, or convention. What's important is dividing the topic into logical segments, say, three to five areas that are roughly equal and don't overlap.

The subject matter of the report usually suggests the best way to divide and organize it. Beth Givens, an information specialist for a Minneapolis health care consulting firm, was given the task of researching and writing an investigative report for St. John's Hospital. Her assignment: study the award-winning patient-service program at Good Samaritan Hospital, and report how it improved its patient satisfaction rating from 6.2 to 7.8 in just one year. Beth collected data and then organized her findings into four parts: management training, employee training, patient services, and follow-up program. Although we don't show Beth's complete report here, you can see a similar one in Figure 11.2.

Compliance Reports

Government agencies at local, state, and national levels increasingly require organizations to submit reports verifying compliance with laws. Some of these reports—such as those covering affirmative action, profit and loss, taxation, and occupational safety—consist primarily of data and figures entered on prepared forms. When you must explain actions and operations without the convenience of printed forms, follow these suggestions:

- Collect and report the specific information requested.
- Ensure the accuracy of the data.
- Provide the desired data in an appropriate format and on time.

Mark Thomas, vice president of Allied Trucking in San Jose, found his company in the unhappy position of responding to an unsatisfactory safety rating from the California Highway Patrol. In preparation for a hearing, Mark wrote a letter report, shown in Figure 13.4, to the city attorney explaining the steps his company was taking to achieve and maintain compliance with the law. In explaining his report, Mark said: "An 'unsatisfactory' safety rating from the state highway patrol is a very serious matter for any trucking company. We immediately shifted into high gear and completely revamped our driver and equipment safety programs. My goal in the report was to show the swift and extensive changes we had made. But I couldn't just talk about the changes. I also had to demonstrate them, so I sent examples of all our new inspection routines, equipment checks, and driver reports. I organized the report around the three main areas of change: education, preventive maintenance, and record keeping."

FIGURE 13.3 Progress Report

Tips for Writing Progress Reports

- Identify the purpose and the nature of the project immediately.
- Supply background information only if the reader must be educated.
- Describe the work completed.
- Discuss the work in progress, including personnel, activities, methods, and locations.
- Identify problems and possible remedies.
- Consider future activities.
- Close by telling the expected date of completion.

QuaStar Productions

Interoffice Memo

DATE: January 7, 2000

TO: Rick Willens, Executive Producer

FROM: Sheila Ryan, Location Manager *SR*

SUBJECT: Sites for "Bodega Bay" Telefilm

Identifies project and previews report

This memo describes the progress of my search for an appropriate rustic home, villa, or ranch to be used for the wine country sequences in the telefilm "Bodega Bay." Three sites will be available for you to inspect on January 21, as you requested.

Background: In preparation for this assignment, I consulted Director Dave Durslag, who gave me his preferences for the site. He suggested a picturesque ranch home situated near vineyards, preferably with redwoods in the background. I also consulted Producer Teresa Silva, who told me that the site must accommodate 55 to 70 production crew members for approximately three weeks of filming. Ben Waters, telefilm accountant, requested that the cost of the site not exceed $24,000 for a three-week lease.

Saves space by integrating headings into paragraphs

Work Completed: For the past eight days I have searched the Russian River area in the Northern California wine country. Possible sites include turn-of-the-century estates, Victorian mansions, and rustic farmhouses in the towns of Duncans Mills, Monte Rio, and Guerneville. One exceptional site is the Country Meadow Inn, a 97-year-old farmhouse nestled among vineyards with a breathtaking view of valleys, redwoods, and distant mountains.

Work to Be Completed: In the next five days, I'll search the Sonoma County countryside, including wineries at Korbel, Field Stone, and Napa. Many old wineries contain charming structures that may present exactly the degree of atmosphere and mystery we need. These wineries have the added advantage of easy access. I will also inspect possible structures at the Armstrong Redwoods State Reserve and the Kruse Rhododendron Reserve, both within 100 miles of Guerneville. I've made an appointment with the director of state parks to discuss our project, use of state lands, restrictions, and costs.

Tells the bad news as well as the good

Anticipated Problems: You should be aware of two complications for filming in this area.

1. Property owners seem unfamiliar with the making of films and are suspicious of short-term leases.
2. Many trees won't have leaves again until May. You may wish to change the filming schedule somewhat.

Concludes by giving completion date and describing what follows

By January 14 you'll have my final report describing the three most promising locations. Arrangements will be made for you to visit these sites January 21.

FIGURE 13.4 Compliance Report

ALLIED TRUCKING, INC.
4920 Mountain View Drive
San Jose, California 94320

October 17, 2000

Mr. John R. Arthur
City Attorney
1330 Courthouse Square
San Jose, CA 94350

Dear Mr. Arthur:

SUBJECT: IMPROVED SAFETY COMPLIANCE PROGRAM

After Allied Trucking received an "unsatisfactory" rating on the California Highway Patrol Safety Compliance Report dated June 15, senior management took immediate action. We initiated systematic procedures to achieve and maintain compliance with state safety regulations. This report describes our three-stage program including (1) education, (2) preventive maintenance, and (3) accurate record keeping. The report is accompanied by numerous examples of records that illustrate our compliance with state and federal safety laws.

Provides brief background data because reader is unfamiliar with topic

Previews three major sections of report

Stage 1: Education

Our first step in developing an improved safety program was education. We reviewed publications from (1) the California Highway Patrol, (2) the Department of Motor Vehicles, and (3) the California Trucking Association. Several meetings included not only truck drivers and senior management but also middle management, vehicle dispatchers, and mechanics. Then we developed and implemented a safety program with two important components: preventive maintenance and improved record keeping.

Supplies headings that clearly show outline of ideas

Stage 2: Preventive Maintenance

Transportation safety depends in large part on precautions taken before vehicles are driven. We have developed a rigorous three-part preventive maintenance program that requires drivers' and mechanics' inspections, as well as careful inspection documentation.

Improves readability with ample white space

Drivers' Inspections

As required by law, all drivers will submit a documented daily vehicle inspection report before the vehicle is driven on the highway. All reports will be carefully examined, with all defects corrected before the driver leaves for daily deliveries. An example of one of last month's reports is enclosed.

Mechanics' Inspections

In order to ensure the safe operation of our vehicles, Allied mechanics will inspect our trucks and trailers every 30 days (see enclosed schedule). We are aware that the law allows a maximum inspection interval of 90 days; however, we feel that a 30-day interval best suits our current needs.

Mark's compliance report and other informational reports apply most of the suggestions found in the following checklist.

Checklist for Writing Informational Reports

Introduction

- **Begin directly.** Identify the report and its purpose.
- **Provide a preview.** If the report is over a page long, give the reader a brief overview of its organization.
-  **Supply background data selectively.** When readers are unfamiliar with the topic, briefly fill in the necessary details.

FIGURE 13.4 Continued

Mr. John R. Arthur Page 2 October 17, 2000

Copies of recent mechanics' inspections are enclosed. Please note that all three required systems are being inspected:

a. Brake adjustment
b. Brake system components and leaks
c. Steering and suspension systems

Stage 3: Record Keeping and Compliance Systems

To enable Allied Trucking to be certain that it is complying with all local, state, and federal regulations, we have improved our record keeping in three specific areas.

DMV Pull Notices

All Allied drivers are entered and participate in the Department of Motor Vehicles Pull Notice Program. All pull notice reports are now reviewed, signed, and dated before they are filed. In addition, a new computerized monthly review of current drivers allows us to double-check for the enrollment of new or current drivers and/or the deletion of drivers no longer employed. Current pull notice reports are enclosed for review.

Driver Hours of Service

All driver logs and/or time cards are now continually reviewed in an attempt to adhere to federal and state regulations regarding duty time and rest periods. Moreover, all driver logs and time cards are cross-referenced to ensure accurate recording of driving and duty times. Driver and dispatcher education have been very helpful in achieving and maintaining these objectives. A sample of recent logs and time cards is enclosed.

Driving Proficiency Records

We now keep on file all records of the different types and combinations of vehicles each employee is certified to drive. Samples are enclosed.

Conclusion

We at Allied Trucking believe that the implementation of this three-stage program has helped us attain our twin goals of driver safety and equipment reliability. Should you have questions about this report, please call me at 383-2290.

Sincerely,

Mark W. Thomas

Mark W. Thomas
Vice President

MWT:eeg
Enclosures

Increases credibility by sending copies of relevant documents

Summarizes report objective and adds concluding thought

Body

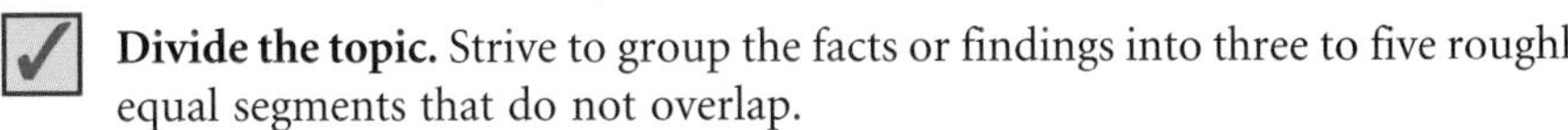
Divide the topic. Strive to group the facts or findings into three to five roughly equal segments that do not overlap.

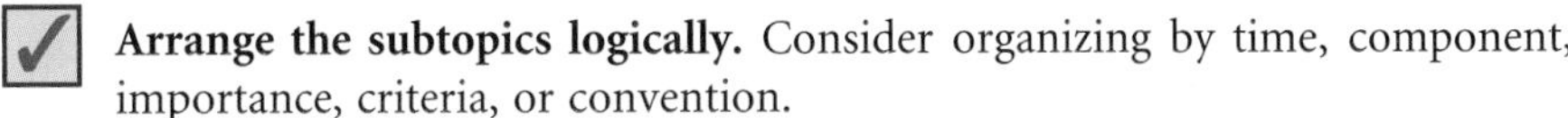
Arrange the subtopics logically. Consider organizing by time, component, importance, criteria, or convention.

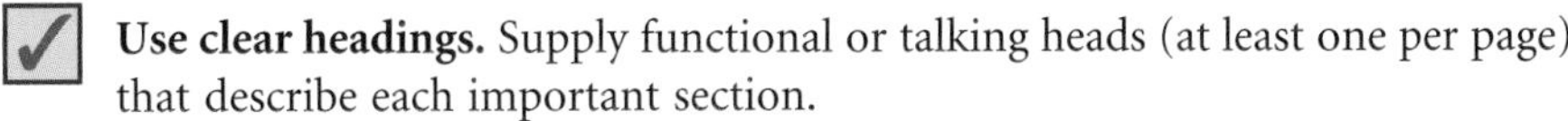
Use clear headings. Supply functional or talking heads (at least one per page) that describe each important section.

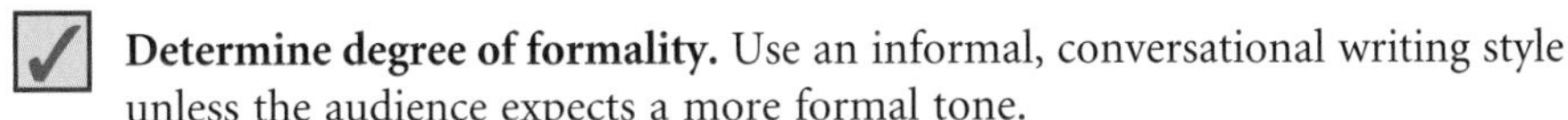
Determine degree of formality. Use an informal, conversational writing style unless the audience expects a more formal tone.

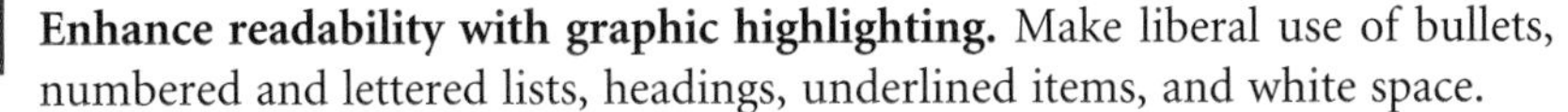
Enhance readability with graphic highlighting. Make liberal use of bullets, numbered and lettered lists, headings, underlined items, and white space.

CAREER COACH

TEN TIPS FOR DESIGNING BETTER DOCUMENTS

Desktop publishing packages, high-level word processing programs, and laser printers now make it possible for you to turn out professional-looking documents. The temptation, though, is to overdo it by incorporating too many features in one document. Here are ten tips for applying good sense and good design principles in "publishing" your documents.

- **Analyze your audience.** Sales brochures and promotional letters can be flashy—with color print, oversized type, and fancy borders—to attract attention. But such effects are out of place for most conservative business documents. Also consider whether your readers will be reading painstakingly or merely browsing. Lists and headings help those readers who are in a hurry.

- **Choose an appropriate type size.** For most business memos, letters, and reports, the body text should be 10 or 11 points tall (a point is 1/72 of an inch). Larger type looks amateurish, and smaller type is hard to read.

- **Use a consistent type font.** Although your software may provide a variety of fonts, stay with a single family of type within one document—at least until you become more expert. The most popular fonts are Times Roman and Helvetica. For emphasis and contrast, you can vary the font size and weight with **bold,** *italic,* ***bold italic,*** and other selections.

- **Generally, don't justify right margins.** Textbooks, novels, newspapers, magazines, and other long works are usually set with justified (even) right margins. However, for shorter works ragged-right margins are recommended because such margins add white space and help readers locate the beginnings of new lines. Slower readers find ragged-right copy more legible.

- **Separate paragraphs and sentences appropriately.** The first line of a paragraph should be indented or preceded by a blank line. To separate sentences, typists have traditionally left two spaces. This spacing is still acceptable for most business documents. If you are preparing a newsletter or brochure, however, you may wish to adopt printer's standards, leaving one space after end punctuation.

- **Design readable headlines.** Presenting headlines and headings in all caps is generally discouraged because solid blocks of capital letters interfere with recognition of word patterns. To further improve readability, select a sans serif typeface (one without cross strokes or embellishment), such as Helvetica.

- **Strive for an attractive page layout.** In designing title pages or graphics, provide for a balance between print and white space. Also consider placing the focal point (something that draws the reader's eye) at the optical center of a page—about three lines above the actual center. Moreover, remember that the average reader scans a page from left to right and top to bottom in a Z pattern. Plan your graphics accordingly.

- **Use graphics and clip art with restraint.** Images created with spreadsheet or graphics programs can be inserted into documents. Original drawings, photographs, and clip art can also be scanned into documents. Use such images, however, only when they are well drawn, relevant, purposeful, and appropriately sized.

- **Avoid amateurish results.** Many beginning writers, eager to display every graphic device a program offers, produce busy, cluttered documents. Too many typefaces, ruled lines, oversized headlines, and images will overwhelm readers. Strive for simple, clean, and forceful effects.

- **Develop expertise.** Learn to use the desktop publishing features of your current word processing software, or investigate one of the special programs, such as Ventura, PageMaker, PowerPoint, or CorelDraw. Although the learning curve for many of these programs is steep, such effort is well spent if you will be producing newsletters, brochures, announcements, visual aids, and promotional literature.

Career Track Application

Buy a book or two on designing documents, and select ten tips that you could share with the class. In teams of three or four, analyze the design and layout of three or four annual reports. Evaluate the appropriateness of typeface and type size, white space, headings, and graphics.

PROCESS IN PROGRESS

CASE STUDY

Nike Inc. Revisited

When allegations of unfair labor practices overseas first surfaced, Nike began immediately to protect its image. It commissioned GoodWorks International to investigate its factories and issue an objective report. The report stated that Nike, while doing a good job, could improve. Nike then set about improving working conditions in factories and publicizing its efforts. Despite taking pains to improve its image, however, Nike still suffers from backlash. Some activists have even posted "rogue" Web sites such as The Official Internet AntiNike Site.[3]

Beyond polishing its image, Nike has other pressing concerns. It is aggressively moving into sports equipment and sports entertainment. It aims to become a full-service sporting goods company, as well as an innovator of new products such as sport-specific watches and sunglasses. "Five years from now," says a Nike official, "You'll see glasses for batting, fielding, volleyball, and running." In the area of services, it is expanding into sports academies and summer camps. Overseas, Nike has seen exciting growth in its European markets. To regain touch with the youth market, Nike is designing a spring collection with plenty of bright colors and modern designs. And while Nike is constantly looking ahead to catch emerging fashion trends, it's also looking over its shoulder at what the competition is doing.

Critical Thinking

- How important to Nike are the collection, organization, and distribution of up-to-date information regarding fashion trends, competition, and product development?
- Should Nike monitor the rogue Web sites that are critical of the company? If so, what kind of reports might be made to management by individuals assigned to the task?
- What kinds of reports would be required from Michael York, a Nike employee assigned to establish a golf camp for parents and children at Pebble Beach, California? What organizational plan would the reports follow?

Summary/Conclusion

When necessary, summarize the report. Briefly review the main points and discuss what action will follow.

Offer a concluding thought. If relevant, express appreciation or describe your willingness to provide further information.

Analytical Reports

5

Analytical reports differ significantly from informational reports. Although both seek to collect and present data clearly, analytical reports also analyze the data and typically try to persuade the reader to accept the conclusions and act on the recommendations. Informational reports emphasize facts; analytical reports emphasize reasoning and conclusions.

For some readers analytical reports may be organized directly with the conclusions and recommendations near the beginning. Directness is appropriate when the reader has confidence in the writer, based on either experience or credentials. Front loading the recommendations also works when the topic is routine or familiar and the reader is supportive.

Spotlight on Communicators

Start at the library, advises Ruth Owades, who has founded two successful companies, Gardener's Eden and Calyx and Corolla. Whether you're considering the feasibility of an action or an entirely new business, you need facts. Extensive research in the card catalog helped her learn about flowers, florists, marketing, and advertising. She also used books to learn how to write a concise business plan that helped finance her $10 million mail-order flower business with headquarters in San Francisco.

Directness can backfire, though. If you announce the recommendations too quickly, the reader may immediately object to a single idea, one that you had no suspicion would trigger a negative reaction. Once the reader is opposed, changing an unfavorable mind-set may be difficult or impossible. A reader may also think you have oversimplified or overlooked something significant if you lay out all the recommendations before explaining how you arrived at them. When the reader must be led through the process of discovering the solution or recommendation, use the indirect method: present conclusions and recommendations last.

Most analytical reports answer questions about specific problems. How can we use a Web site most effectively? Should we close the El Paso plant? Should we buy or lease company cars? How can we improve customer service? Four typical analytical reports answer business questions: justification/recommendation reports, feasibility reports, yardstick reports, and research studies. Because these reports all solve problems, the categories are not mutually exclusive. What distinguishes them is their goals and organization.

Justification/Recommendation Reports

Justification/recommendation reports follow the direct or the indirect pattern depending on the audience and the topic.

Both managers and employees must occasionally write reports that justify or recommend something, such as buying equipment, changing a procedure, hiring an employee, consolidating departments, or investing funds. Large organizations sometimes prescribe how these reports should be organized; they use forms with conventional headings. When you are free to select an organizational plan yourself, however, let your audience and topic determine your choice of direct or indirect structure.

The direct pattern is appropriate for justification/recommendation reports on nonsensitive topics and for receptive audiences.

Direct Pattern. For nonsensitive topics and recommendations that will be agreeable to readers, you can organize directly according to the following sequence:

- Identify the problem or need briefly.
- Announce the recommendation, solution, or action concisely and with action verbs.
- Explain more fully the benefits of the recommendation or steps to be taken to solve the problem.
- Include a discussion of pros, cons, and costs.
- Conclude with a summary specifying the recommendation and action to be taken.

Here's how Justin Brown applied the process in justifying a purchase. Justin is operations manager in charge of a fleet of trucks for a large parcel delivery company in Atlanta. When he heard about a new Goodyear smart tire with an electronic chip, Justin thought his company should give the new tire a try. Because new tires would represent an irregular purchase and because they would require a pilot test, he wrote the justification/recommendation report, shown in Figure 13.5, to his boss. Justin describes his report in this way: "As more and more parcel delivery systems crop up, we have to find ways to cut costs so that we can remain competitive. Although more expensive initially, smart tires may solve a lot of our problems and save us money in the long haul. I knew Bill Montgomery, operations vice president, would be interested in them, particularly if we went slowly and purchased only 24 for a pilot test. Because Bill would be most interested in what they could do for us, I concentrated on benefits. In my first draft the benefits were lost in a couple of long paragraphs. Only after I read what I had written did I see that I was really talking about four separate benefits. Then I looked for words to summarize each one as a heading. So that Bill would know exactly what he should do, I concluded with specifics. All he had to do was say 'Go.'"

FIGURE 13.5 Justification/Recommendation Report: Direct Pattern

The Three Phases of the Writing Process

1 PREWRITING

Analyze: The purpose of this report is to persuade the manager to authorize the purchase and pilot testing of smart tires.

Anticipate: The audience is a manager who is familiar with operations but not with this product. He will probably be receptive to the recommendation.

Adapt: Present the report data in a direct, straightforward manner.

2 WRITING

Research: Collect data on how smart tires could benefit operations.

Organize: Discuss the problem briefly. Introduce and justify the recommendation by noting its cost-effectiveness and paperwork benefits. Explain the benefits of smart tires. Describe the action to be taken.

Compose: Write and print first draft.

3 REVISING

Revise: Revise to break up long paragraphs about benefits. Isolate each benefit in an enumerated list with headings.

Proofread: Double-check all figures. Be sure all headings are parallel.

Evaluate: Does this report make its request concisely but emphatically? Will the reader see immediately what action is required?

DATE: July 19, 2000
TO: Bill Montgomery, Vice President
FROM: Justin Brown, Operations Manager *JB*
SUBJECT: Pilot Testing Smart Tires

Introduces problem briefly

Next to fuel, truck tires are our biggest operating cost. Last year we spent $211,000 replacing and retreading tires for 495 trucks. This year the costs will be greater because prices have jumped at least 12 percent and because we've increased our fleet to 550 trucks. Truck tires are an additional burden since they require labor-intensive paperwork to track their warranties, wear, and retread histories. To reduce our long-term costs and to improve our tire tracking system, I recommend that we do the following:

Presents recommendations immediately

- Purchase 24 Goodyear smart tires.
- Begin a one-year pilot test on six trucks.

How Smart Tires Work

Justifies recommendation by explaining product and benefits

Smart tires have an embedded computer chip that monitors wear, performance, and durability. The chip also creates an electronic fingerprint for positive identification of a tire. By passing a hand-held sensor next to the tire, we can learn where and when a tire was made (for warranty and other identification), how much tread it had originally, and its serial number.

How Smart Tires Could Benefit Us

Although smart tires are initially more expensive than other tires, they could help us improve our operations and save us money in four ways:

1. **Retreads.** Goodyear believes that the wear data is so accurate that we should be able to retread every tire three times, instead of our current two times. If that's true, in one year we could save at least $27,000 in new tire costs.
2. **Safety.** Accurate and accessible wear data should reduce the danger of blowouts and flat tires. Last year, despite our rigorous maintenance program, drivers reported six blowouts.
3. **Record keeping and maintenance.** Smart tires could reduce our maintenance costs considerably. Currently, we use an electric branding iron to mark serial numbers on new tires. Our biggest headache is manually reading those serial numbers, decoding them, and maintaining records to meet safety regulations. Reading such data electronically could save us thousands of dollars in labor.
4. **Theft protection.** The chip can be used to monitor each tire as it leaves or enters the warehouse or yard, thus discouraging theft.

Summary and Action

Explains recommendation in more detail

Specifically, I recommend that you do the following:

- Authorize the special purchase of 24 Goodyear smart tires at $450 each, plus one electronic sensor at $1,200.
- Approve a one-year pilot test in our Atlanta territory that equips six trucks with smart tires and tracks their performance.

Specifies action to be taken

This greenhouse at the famous Keukenhof Gardens in Holland became a key point in the justification report of a tour organizer. In supporting his inclusion of the Keukenhof in a proposed itinerary for an American travel company, the writer argued that tourists can never be rained out. In addition to the 70 acres of outdoor gardens, thousands of flowers bloom under glass. Persuasive justification reports explain fully all the benefits of a recommendation and also anticipate possible reader objections.

The indirect pattern is appropriate for justification/recommendation reports on sensitive topics and for potentially unreceptive audiences.

Indirect Pattern. When a reader may oppose a recommendation or when circumstances suggest caution, don't be in a hurry to reveal your recommendation. Consider using the following sequence for an indirect approach to your recommendations:

- Make a general reference to the problem, not to your recommendation, in the subject line.
- Describe the problem or need your recommendation addresses. Use specific examples, supporting statistics, and authoritative quotes to lend credibility to the seriousness of the problem.
- Discuss alternative solutions, beginning with the least likely to succeed.
- Present the most promising alternative (your recommendation) last.
- Show how the advantages of your recommendation outweigh its disadvantages.
- Summarize your recommendation. If appropriate, specify the action it requires.
- Ask for authorization to proceed, if necessary.

Footnoting sources lends added credibility to justification/recommendation reports.

Diane Adams, an executive assistant at a large petroleum and mining company in Grand Prairie, Texas, received a challenging research assignment. Her boss, the director of Human Resources, asked her to investigate ways to persuade employees to quit smoking. Here's how she describes her task: "We banned smoking many years ago inside our buildings, but we never tried very hard to get smokers to actually kick their habits. My job was to gather information about the problem and how other companies have helped workers stop smoking. The report would go to my boss, but I knew he would pass it along to the management council for approval. If the report were just for my boss, I would put my recommendation right up front, because I'm sure he would support it. But the management council is another story. They need persuasion because of the costs involved—and because some of them are smokers. Therefore, I put the alternative I favored last. To gain credibility, I footnoted my sources. I had enough material for a ten-page report, but I kept it to two pages in keeping with our company report policy."

FIGURE 13.6 Justification/Recommendation Report: Indirect Pattern

1

DATE: October 11, 2000

TO: Damon Moore, Director, Human Resources

FROM: Diane Adams, Executive Assistant *DA*

SUBJECT: MEASURES TO HELP EMPLOYEES STOP SMOKING

At your request, I have examined measures that encourage employees to quit smoking. As company records show, approximately 23 percent of our employees still smoke, despite the antismoking and clean-air policies we adopted in 1991. To collect data for this report, I studied professional and government publications; I also inquired at companies and clinics about stop-smoking programs.

This report presents data describing the significance of the problem, three alternative solutions, and a recommendation based on my investigation.

Significance of Problem: Health Care and Productivity Losses

Employees who smoke are costly to any organization. The following statistics show the effects of smoking for workers and for organizations:

- Absenteeism is 40 to 50 percent greater among smoking employees.
- Accidents are two to three times greater among smokers.
- Bronchitis, lung and heart disease, cancer, and early death are more frequent among smokers (Johns, 1999, p.14).

Although our clean-air policy prohibits smoking in the building, shop, and office, we have done little to encourage employees to stop smoking. Many workers still go outside to smoke at lunch and breaks. Other companies have been far more proactive in their attempts to stop employee smoking. Many companies have found that persuading employees to stop smoking was a decisive factor in reducing their health insurance premiums. Below is a discussion of three common stop-smoking measures tried by other companies, along with a projected cost factor for each.

Alternative 1: Literature and Events

The least expensive and easiest stop-smoking measure involves the distribution of literature, such as "The Ten-Step Plan" from Smokefree Enterprises and government pamphlets citing smoking dangers. Some companies have also sponsored events such as the Great American Smoke-Out, a one-day occasion intended to develop group spirit in spurring smokers to quit. "Studies show, however," says one expert, "that literature

Avoids revealing recommendation immediately

Uses headings that combine function and description

Discusses least effective alternative first

Introduces purpose of report, tells method of data collection, and previews organization

Documents data sources for credibility; uses APA style citing author, date, and page number in the text

Diane single-spaced her report, shown in Figure 13.6, because that's her company's preference. Some companies prefer the readability of double spacing. Be sure to check with your organization for its preference before printing out your reports.

Feasibility Reports

6

Feasibility reports examine the practicality and advisability of following a course of action. They answer this question: Will this plan or proposal work? Feasibility reports typically are internal reports written to advise on matters such as consolidating departments, offering a wellness program to employees, or hiring an outside firm to handle a company's accounting or computing operations. These reports may also be written by consultants called in to investigate a problem. The focus in these reports is on the decision: stopping or proceeding with the proposal. Since your role

FIGURE 13.6 Continued

2

and company-sponsored events have little permanent effect in helping smokers quit" (Woo, 1997, p. 107)

Cost: Negligible

Alternative 2: Stop-Smoking Programs Outside the Workplace

Local clinics provide treatment programs in classes at their centers. Here in Houston we have Smokers' Treatment Center, ACC Motivation Center, and the New-Choice Program for Stopping Smoking. These behavior-modification stop-smoking programs are acknowledged to be more effective than literature distribution or incentive programs. However, studies of companies using off-workplace programs show that many employees fail to attend regularly and do not complete the programs.

Cost: $750 per employee, 3-month individual program (New-Choice Program)
$500 per employee, 3-month group sessions

Highlights costs for easy comparison

Alternative 3: Stop-Smoking Programs at the Workplace

Many clinics offer workplace programs with counselors meeting employees in company conference rooms. These programs have the advantage of keeping a firm's employees together so that they develop a group spirit and exert pressure on each other to succeed. The most successful programs are on company premises and also on company time. Employees participating in such programs had a 72 percent greater success record than employees attending the same stop-smoking program at an outside clinic (Manley, 1998, p. 35). A disadvantage of this arrangement, of course, is lost work time —amounting to about two hours a week for three months.

Arranges alternatives so that most effective is last

Cost: $500 per employee, 3-month program
2 hours per week release time for 3 months

Conclusions and Recommendation

Summarizes findings and ends with specific recommendation

Smokers seem to require discipline, counseling, and professional assistance in kicking the nicotine habit. Workplace stop-smoking programs, on company time, are more effective than literature, incentives, and off-workplace programs. If our goal is to reduce health care costs and lead our employees to healthful lives, we should invest in a workplace stop-smoking program with release time for smokers. Although the program temporarily reduces productivity, we can expect to recapture that loss in lower health care premiums and healthier employees.

Therefore, I recommend that we begin a stop-smoking treatment program on company premises with two hours per week of release time for participants for three months.

Reveals recommendation only after discussing all alternatives

3

Lists all references in APA style

References

Johns, K. (1999, May). No smoking in your workplace. *Business Times*, 14-16.

Manley, D. (1998). Up in smoke: A case study of one company's proactive stance against smoking. *Management Review, 14*, 33-37.

Woo, N. A. (1997). *The last gasp*. New York, NY: Field Publishers.

Magazine

Journal

Book

Making music more accessible to the blind, William McCann uses his music and computer science training. Blind since he was 6, McCann receives support from federal programs, which require well-written proposals for funding. One of his projects involves software that converts a printed musical score to Braille. Before receiving additional funds, however, an applicant like McCann must conduct a feasibility study to determine whether his proposal makes sense and might work.

is not to persuade the reader to accept the decision, you'll want to present the decision immediately. In writing feasibility reports, consider these suggestions:

Feasibility reports analyze whether a proposal or plan will work.

- Announce your decision immediately.
- Provide a description of the background and problem necessitating the proposal.
- Discuss the benefits of the proposal.
- Describe the problems that may result.
- Calculate the costs associated with the proposal, if appropriate.
- Show the time frame necessary for implementation of the proposal.

Elizabeth Webb, customer service manager for a large insurance company in Omaha, Nebraska, wrote the feasibility report shown in Figure 13.7. She describes the report thus: "We had been losing customer service reps (CSRs) after they were trained and were most valuable to us. When I talked with our vice president about the problem, she didn't want me to take time away from my job to investigate what other companies were doing to retain their CSRs. Instead, we hired a consultant who suggested that we use a CSR career progression schedule. The vice president then wanted to know if the consultant's plan was feasible. Although my report is only one page long, it provides all necessary information: approval, background, benefits, problems, costs, and schedule."

A typical feasibility report presents the decision, background information, benefits, problems, costs, and a schedule.

Yardstick Reports

"Yardstick" reports examine problems with two or more solutions. To evaluate the best solution, the writer establishes criteria by which to compare the alternatives. 7
The criteria then act as a yardstick against which all the alternatives are measured. This yardstick approach is effective when companies establish specifications for equipment purchases, and then compare each manufacturer's product with the established specs. The yardstick approach is also effective when exact specifications cannot be established. For example, when the giant aircraft firm McDonnell Douglas considered relocating, it evaluated cities such as Mobile, Fort Worth, Houston, Kansas City, Tulsa, Salt Lake City, and Mesa. For each of these sites, McDonnell

FIGURE 13.7 **Feasibility Report**

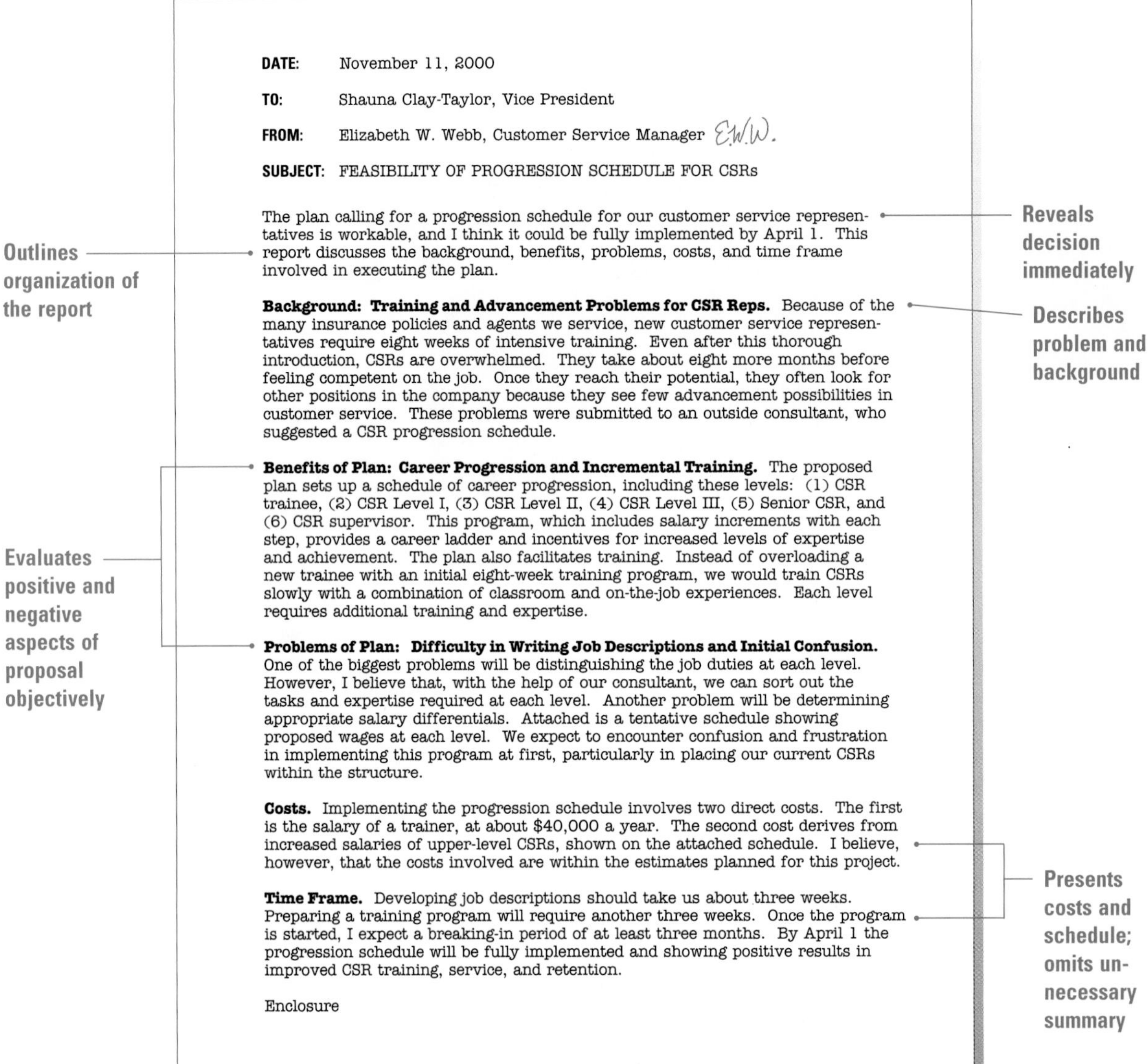

Reveals decision immediately
Outlines organization of the report
Describes problem and background
Evaluates positive and negative aspects of proposal objectively
Presents costs and schedule; omits unnecessary summary

DATE: November 11, 2000

TO: Shauna Clay-Taylor, Vice President

FROM: Elizabeth W. Webb, Customer Service Manager E.W.W.

SUBJECT: FEASIBILITY OF PROGRESSION SCHEDULE FOR CSRs

The plan calling for a progression schedule for our customer service representatives is workable, and I think it could be fully implemented by April 1. This report discusses the background, benefits, problems, costs, and time frame involved in executing the plan.

Background: Training and Advancement Problems for CSR Reps. Because of the many insurance policies and agents we service, new customer service representatives require eight weeks of intensive training. Even after this thorough introduction, CSRs are overwhelmed. They take about eight more months before feeling competent on the job. Once they reach their potential, they often look for other positions in the company because they see few advancement possibilities in customer service. These problems were submitted to an outside consultant, who suggested a CSR progression schedule.

Benefits of Plan: Career Progression and Incremental Training. The proposed plan sets up a schedule of career progression, including these levels: (1) CSR trainee, (2) CSR Level I, (3) CSR Level II, (4) CSR Level III, (5) Senior CSR, and (6) CSR supervisor. This program, which includes salary increments with each step, provides a career ladder and incentives for increased levels of expertise and achievement. The plan also facilitates training. Instead of overloading a new trainee with an initial eight-week training program, we would train CSRs slowly with a combination of classroom and on-the-job experiences. Each level requires additional training and expertise.

Problems of Plan: Difficulty in Writing Job Descriptions and Initial Confusion. One of the biggest problems will be distinguishing the job duties at each level. However, I believe that, with the help of our consultant, we can sort out the tasks and expertise required at each level. Another problem will be determining appropriate salary differentials. Attached is a tentative schedule showing proposed wages at each level. We expect to encounter confusion and frustration in implementing this program at first, particularly in placing our current CSRs within the structure.

Costs. Implementing the progression schedule involves two direct costs. The first is the salary of a trainer, at about $40,000 a year. The second cost derives from increased salaries of upper-level CSRs, shown on the attached schedule. I believe, however, that the costs involved are within the estimates planned for this project.

Time Frame. Developing job descriptions should take us about three weeks. Preparing a training program will require another three weeks. Once the program is started, I expect a breaking-in period of at least three months. By April 1 the progression schedule will be fully implemented and showing positive results in improved CSR training, service, and retention.

Enclosure

Yardstick reports consider alternative solutions to a problem by establishing criteria against which to weigh options.

Douglas compared labor costs, land availability and costs, tax breaks, and housing costs. It also weighed other criteria such as access to markets and transportation costs for raw materials. It did not set up exact specifications for each category; it merely compared each city in these various categories. The real advantage to yardstick reports is that alternatives can be measured consistently using the same criteria.

Reports using a yardstick approach typically are organized this way:

- Begin by describing the problem or need.
- Explain possible solutions and alternatives.
- Establish criteria for comparing the alternatives; tell how they were selected or developed.
- Discuss and evaluate each alternative in terms of the criteria.
- Draw conclusions and make recommendations.

FIGURE 13.8 Yardstick Report

DATE: April 28, 2000

TO: George O. Dawes, Vice President

FROM: Kelly Lopez, Benefits Administrator *KL*

SUBJECT: CHOICE OF OUTPLACEMENT SERVICES

Here is the report you requested April 1 investigating the possibility of CompuTech's use of outplacement services. It discusses the problem of counseling services for discharged staff and establishes criteria for selecting an outplacement agency. It then evaluates three prospective agencies and presents a recommendation based on that evaluation.

Introduces purpose and gives overview of report organization

Problem: Counseling Discharged Staff

Discusses background briefly because readers already know the problem

In an effort to reduce costs and increase competitiveness, CompuTech will begin a program of staff reduction that will involve releasing up to 20 percent of our workforce over the next 12 to 24 months. Many of these employees have been with us for ten or more years, and they are not being released for performance faults. These employees deserve a severance package that includes counseling and assistance in finding new careers.

Uses dual headings, giving function and description

Solution And Alternatives: Outplacement Agencies

Numerous outplacement agencies offer discharged employees counseling and assistance in locating new careers. This assistance minimizes not only the negative feelings related to job loss but also the very real possibility of litigation. Potentially expensive lawsuits have been lodged against some companies by unhappy employees who felt they were unfairly released.

In seeking an outplacement agency, we should find one that offers advice to the sponsoring company as well as to dischargees. Frankly, many of our managers need help in conducting termination sessions. The law now requires certain procedures, especially in releasing employees over 40. CompuTech could unwittingly become liable to lawsuits because our managers are uninformed of these procedures. Here in the metropolitan area, I have located three potential outplacement agencies appropriate to serve our needs: Gray & Associates, Right Access, and Careers Plus.

Announces solution and the alternatives it presents

Establishing Criteria for Selecting Agency

Tells how criteria were selected

In order to choose among the three agencies, I established criteria based on professional articles, discussions with officials at other companies using outplacement agencies, and interviews with agencies. Here are the four groups of criteria I used in evaluating the three agencies:

1. Counseling services—including job search advice, résumé help, crisis management, corporate counseling, and availability of full-time counselors
2. Secretarial and research assistance—including availability of secretarial staff, librarian, and personal computers
3. Reputation—based on a telephone survey of former clients and listing with a professional association
4. Costs—for both group programs and executive services

Creates four criteria to use as yardstick in evaluating alternatives

Kelly Lopez, benefits administrator for computer manufacturer CompuTech, was called on to write a report comparing outplacement agencies. These agencies counsel discharged employees and help find new positions; fees are paid by the former employer. Kelly knew that times were bad for CompuTech and that extensive downsizing would take place in the next two years. Her task was to compare outplacement agencies and recommend one to CompuTech.

After collecting information, Kelly found that her biggest problem was organizing the data and developing a system for making comparisons. All the outplacement agencies she investigated seemed to offer the same basic package of services. Here's how she described her report, shown in Figure 13.8.

Vice President Dawes | Page 2 | April 28, 2000

Discussion: Evaluating Agencies by Criteria

Each agency was evaluated using the four criteria just described. Data comparing the first three criteria are summarized in Table 1.

Table 1

A COMPARISON OF SERVICES AND REPUTATIONS FOR THREE LOCAL OUTPLACEMENT AGENCIES

	Gray & Associates	Right Access	Careers Plus
Counseling services			
Résumé advice	Yes	Yes	Yes
Crisis management	Yes	No	Yes
Corporate counseling	Yes	No	No
Full-time counselors	Yes	No	Yes
Secretarial, research assistance			
Secretarial staff	Yes	Yes	Yes
Librarian, research library	Yes	No	Yes
Personal computers	Yes	No	Yes
Listed by National Association of Career Consultants	Yes	No	Yes
Reputation (telephone survey of former clients)	Excellent	Good	Excellent

Counseling Services

All three agencies offered similar basic counseling services with job-search and résumé advice. They differed, however, in three significant areas.

Right Access does not offer crisis management, a service that puts the discharged employee in contact with a counselor the same day the employee is released. Experts in the field consider this service especially important to help the dischargee begin "bonding" with the counselor immediately. Immediate counseling also helps the dischargee through the most traumatic moments of one of life's great disappointments and helps him or her learn how to break the news to family members. Crisis management can be instrumental in reducing lawsuits because dischargees immediately begin to focus on career planning instead of concentrating on their pain and need for revenge. Moreover, Right Access does not employ full-time counselors; it hires part-timers according to demand. Industry authorities advise against using agencies whose staff members are inexperienced and employed on an "as-needed" basis.

In addition, neither Right Access nor Careers Plus offer regular corporate counseling, which I feel is critical in training our managers to conduct terminal interviews. Careers Plus, however, suggested that it could schedule special workshops if desired.

Secretarial and Research Assistance

Both Gray & Associates and Careers Plus offer complete secretarial services and personal computers. Dischargees have access to staff and equipment to assist them in their job searches. These agencies also provide research libraries, librarians, and databases of company information to help in securing interviews.

Places table close to spot where it is first mentioned

Summarizes complex data in table for easy reading and reference

Highlights the similarities and differences among the alternatives

Does not repeat obvious data from table

Grids are a useful way to organize and compare data for a yardstick report.

"With the information I gathered about three outplacement agencies, I made a big grid listing the names of the agencies across the top. Down the side I listed general categories—such as services, costs, and reputation. Then I filled in the information for each agency. This grid, which began to look like a table, helped me organize all the bits and pieces of information. After studying the grid, I saw that all the information could be grouped into four categories: counseling services, secretarial/research services, reputation, and costs. I made these the criteria I would use to compare agencies. Next, I divided my grid into two parts, which became Table 1 and Table 2. In writing the report, I could have made each agency a separate heading, followed by a discussion of how it measured up to the criteria. Immediately, though, I saw how repetitious that would become. So I used the criteria as headings and discussed

FIGURE 13.8 **Continued**

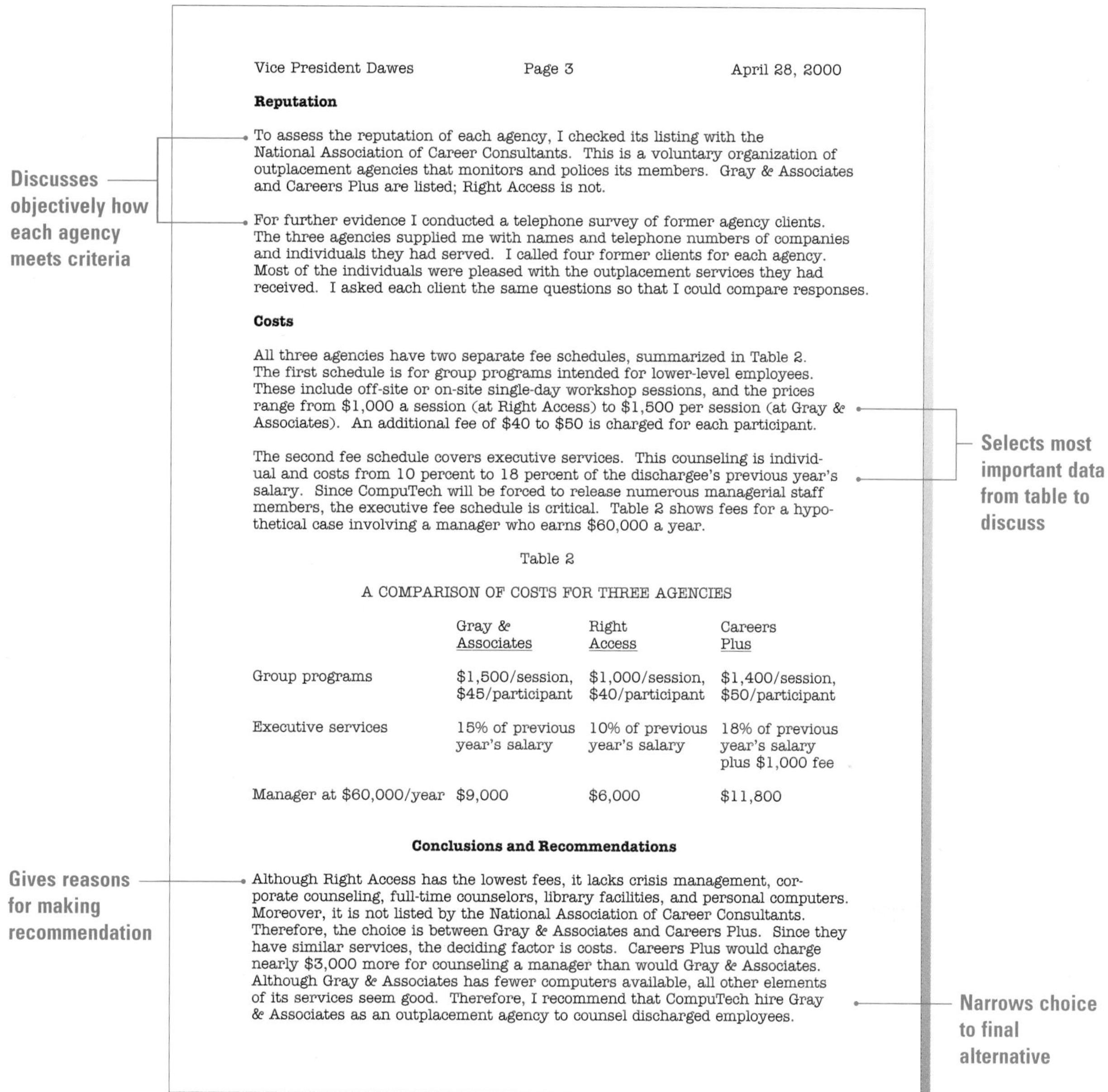

how each agency met that criteria—or failed to meet it. Making a recommendation was easy once I had the tables made and could see how the agencies compared."

Vice President Dawes Page 3 April 28, 2000

Reputation

To assess the reputation of each agency, I checked its listing with the National Association of Career Consultants. This is a voluntary organization of outplacement agencies that monitors and polices its members. Gray & Associates and Careers Plus are listed; Right Access is not.

For further evidence I conducted a telephone survey of former agency clients. The three agencies supplied me with names and telephone numbers of companies and individuals they had served. I called four former clients for each agency. Most of the individuals were pleased with the outplacement services they had received. I asked each client the same questions so that I could compare responses.

Costs

All three agencies have two separate fee schedules, summarized in Table 2. The first schedule is for group programs intended for lower-level employees. These include off-site or on-site single-day workshop sessions, and the prices range from $1,000 a session (at Right Access) to $1,500 per session (at Gray & Associates). An additional fee of $40 to $50 is charged for each participant.

The second fee schedule covers executive services. This counseling is individual and costs from 10 percent to 18 percent of the dischargee's previous year's salary. Since CompuTech will be forced to release numerous managerial staff members, the executive fee schedule is critical. Table 2 shows fees for a hypothetical case involving a manager who earns $60,000 a year.

Table 2

A COMPARISON OF COSTS FOR THREE AGENCIES

	Gray & Associates	Right Access	Careers Plus
Group programs	$1,500/session, $45/participant	$1,000/session, $40/participant	$1,400/session, $50/participant
Executive services	15% of previous year's salary	10% of previous year's salary	18% of previous year's salary plus $1,000 fee
Manager at $60,000/year	$9,000	$6,000	$11,800

Conclusions and Recommendations

Although Right Access has the lowest fees, it lacks crisis management, corporate counseling, full-time counselors, library facilities, and personal computers. Moreover, it is not listed by the National Association of Career Consultants. Therefore, the choice is between Gray & Associates and Careers Plus. Since they have similar services, the deciding factor is costs. Careers Plus would charge nearly $3,000 more for counseling a manager than would Gray & Associates. Although Gray & Associates has fewer computers available, all other elements of its services seem good. Therefore, I recommend that CompuTech hire Gray & Associates as an outplacement agency to counsel discharged employees.

Discusses objectively how each agency meets criteria
Selects most important data from table to discuss
Gives reasons for making recommendation
Narrows choice to final alternative

Research Studies

8

In some business reports the emphasis is on the research. These studies examine a problem, collect data to solve the problem, and reach conclusions growing out of the findings. This scientific approach leads the reader through all the steps to discovering the answer, positive or negative, to a problem. The answer comes as a result of assembling facts and evidence. Throughout the report the emphasis is on educating the reader with objective facts and reasoning.

Research studies educate readers through scientific data collection and analysis.

For example, the cable TV industry hired a research firm to investigate this question: What effect will direct broadcast satellites have on cable TV? Direct broadcast satellite (DBS) systems employ high-power satellites to permit reception by small home-receiving terminals (dishes). Researchers developed three hypotheses. Cable operators would face severe competition if (1) DBS became the first national distributor of high-definition television programs, (2) DBS succeeded in providing low-cost small-antenna home receivers, and (3) DBS was able to offer major network programming. Each of these hypotheses was studied, and data were collected. Researchers described their findings and drew conclusions. One conclusion stated that DBS did, indeed, represent a considerable threat to the cable industry. That cable owners should consider buying into DBS was a natural recommendation following from this conclusion.

Research studies follow the indirect pattern to guide the reader through the research process to the conclusions.

In this kind of research study, the reader must be informed and guided through the research so that the conclusions seem rational. Although an executive summary may reveal the conclusions and recommendations first, the report itself follows an indirect development pattern so that readers can follow the discovery of the answer. This means that the report begins with discussion of the problem and is followed by exploration of possible solutions. It ends with reasons explaining the selection of one course of action.

In writing the results of a research study, follow this organizational plan:

- Discuss the purpose, problem, or need objectively.
- Define the significance, scope, research methodology, and limitations of the project.
- Present the information collected, organizing it around reasons leading to the conclusions.
- Draw conclusions that result naturally from the findings.
- Make recommendations if requested.

An example of a long research study is shown in Chapter 14.

Checklist for Writing Analytical Reports

Introduction

Identify the purpose of the report. Explain why the report is being written. For research studies also include the significance, scope, limitations, and methodology of the investigation.

Preview the organization of the report. Especially for long reports, explain to the reader how the report will be organized.

Summarize the conclusions and recommendations for receptive audiences. Use the direct pattern only if you have the confidence of the reader.

Findings

Discuss pros and cons. In recommendation/justification reports evaluate the advantages and disadvantages of each alternative. For unreceptive audiences consider placing the recommended alternative last.

Establish criteria to evaluate alternatives. In "yardstick" studies create criteria to use in measuring each alternative consistently.

PROCESS TO PRODUCT

Applying Your Skills at Nike Inc.

CASE STUDY

Sales of Nike footwear and apparel have been strong in Europe, but distribution of those items was a big problem. Company executives decided that one or more new distribution centers were needed. A site search team, led by Roger Tragesser, director of European operations, began collecting data and studying possibilities. "We were looking for a site where we could do the most distribution with the least amount of travel time. We knew we didn't want to spend five or six years getting permits . . . and we wanted to be close to good ports, good railroads, and major highways." Other considerations were taxes and labor restrictions. Belgium, for instance, limits the number of staff hours to an average working week of 55 hours.[4] As in the United States, local communities and governments are eager to attract new businesses that bring jobs. Many are willing to offer incentives, such as low-cost land and free training for prospective employees.

Your Job

As assistant to Roger Tragesser, make a list of at least six criteria to use in evaluating sites for the new Nike distribution center. What sources of primary and secondary information would be useful in making a site choice? What kind of report would be best for arriving at a decision and reporting the search team's choice? How should that report be organized?

Support the findings with evidence. Supply facts, statistics, expert opinion, survey data, and other proof from which you can draw logical conclusions.

Organize the findings for logic and readability. Arrange the findings around the alternatives or the reasons leading to the conclusion. Use headings, enumerations, lists, tables, and graphics to focus emphasis.

Conclusions/Recommendations

Draw reasonable conclusions from the findings. Develop conclusions that answer the research question. Justify the conclusions with highlights from the findings.

Make recommendations, if asked. For multiple recommendations prepare a list. Use action verbs. Explain needed action.

Summary of Learning Objectives

1 **Distinguish between informational and analytical reports.** Informational reports provide data and answer questions without offering recommendations or analysis. They may report sales, routine operations, trips, conferences, or compliance. Analytical reports organize data, draw conclusions, and often make recommendations. They may include justification/recommendation, feasibility, yardstick, and research reports.

2 **Identify periodic reports and describe their major components.** Periodic reports—such as sales, accounts payable, and personnel reports—generally summarize regular activities occurring during the reporting period. They also describe irregular events demanding attention and highlight special needs and problems.

3 **Discuss the forms and content of situational reports.** Trip, convention, and conference reports often specify the event, summarize three to five main points of interest to the reader, itemize expenses, and close with appreciation or a suggestion for action. Progress and interim reports identify a project, provide background data, explain the work currently in progress, anticipate problems and remedies, and discuss future activities. Progress reports should always include an expected completion date.

4 **Distinguish between investigative and compliance reports.** Investigative reports examine a topic (such as a production problem) but do not draw conclusions or make recommendations. Compliance reports present data in compliance with local, state, and federal laws. These reports should be honest, accurate, and prompt.

5 **Compare direct and indirect justification/recommendation reports.** Justification/recommendation reports organized directly identify a problem, immediately announce a recommendation or solution, explain and discuss its merits, and summarize the action to be taken. Justification/recommendation reports organized indirectly describe a problem, discuss alternative solutions, prove the superiority of one solution, and ask for authorization to proceed with that solution.

6 **Describe the purpose and content of feasibility reports.** Feasibility reports study the advisability of following a course of action. They generally announce the author's proposal immediately. Then they describe the background, advantages and disadvantages, costs, and schedule for implementing the proposal.

7 **Identify yardstick reports and describe their major components.** "Yardstick" reports compare two or more solutions to a problem by measuring each against a set of established criteria. They usually describe a problem, explain possible solutions, establish criteria for comparing alternatives, evaluate each alternative in terms of the criteria, draw conclusions, and make recommendations. The advantage to yardstick reports is consistency in comparing various alternatives.

8 **Discuss the content of research reports.** Research reports identify a problem, collect data to solve the problem, and reach conclusions drawn from the findings. These scientific reports generally discuss a problem or need objectively; define the significance, scope, methodology, and limitations of the study; gather information; present the data; draw conclusions; and make recommendations, if requested.

CHAPTER REVIEW

1. Name four categories of informational reports. (Obj. 1)
2. Describe periodic reports and what they generally contain. (Obj. 2)
3. Describe situational reports and give two examples. (Obj. 3)
4. What should a progress report include? (Obj. 3)
5. How can the body of an investigative or other informational report be organized? (Obj. 4)
6. What are compliance reports? (Obj. 4)
7. Informational reports emphasize facts. What do analytical reports emphasize? (Objs. 1 and 5)
8. When should an analytical report be organized directly? (Obj. 5)
9. How can directness backfire? (Obj. 5)
10. What sequence should a direct recommendation/justification report follow? (Obj. 5)
11. What sequence should an indirect recommendation/justification report follow? (Obj. 5)
12. What is a feasibility report? (Obj. 6)
13. Are feasibility reports usually intended for internal or external audiences? (Obj. 6)
14. What is a yardstick report? (Obj. 7)
15. How do research studies differ from other problem-solving reports? (Obj. 8)

CRITICAL THINKING

1. Do most reports flow upward or downward? Why? (Objs. 1–7)
2. Why are large companies more likely to require reports than smaller ones? (Objs. 1–7)
3. If you were doubtful about writing a report directly or indirectly, which pattern would be safer? Why? (Obj. 5)
4. What are the major differences between informational and analytical reports? (Objs. 1 and 5)
5. **Ethical Issue:** Discuss the ethics of using persuasive tactics to convince a report's readers to accept its conclusions. Is it ethical to be persuasive only when you believe in the soundness and truth of your conclusions?

ACTIVITIES

13.1 Periodic Reports (Obj. 2)

In a business you know, name five situations that would require periodic reports. If you've had little business experience, imagine a large department store. What kinds of periodic reports would management require of department managers, buyers, and operations staff? Describe how one report might be organized.

13.2 Convention, Conference, and Seminar Reports (Obj. 3)

Select an article from a business publication (such as *The Wall Street Journal, Business Week, Forbes, Fortune,* or *Working Woman*) describing a convention, conference, or seminar. Imagine that you attended that meeting for your company. Outline a report to your boss describing the meeting.

13.3 Situational and Investigative Reports (Objs. 3 and 4)

For each of the following situations, suggest a report type and briefly discuss how the report would be organized.

a. The mail center could save over $10,000 a year if the company would allow it to invest in reusable nylon mail pouches to deliver customer insurance policies to branch offices.

b. Your manager wants a quickie overview of *extranets* (restricted networks that use the Internet to link a company with its customers, suppliers, and other business partners). She knows that other companies are setting up extranets, but she has little knowledge of what they are or how they work. She sees no direct need for the data immediately.

c. Home Depot is considering using shrink wrapping to secure merchandise stored on racks that range from 8 to 16 feet high. Management is concerned about the safety of employees and customers during earthquakes.

d. King Grocery must implement a worker-incentive wage program. This plan would establish standards for warehouse workers and generously reward those who exceed the standard with extra pay and time off. The current wage program pays everyone the same, causing dissension and underachievement. Other wage plans, including a union three-tier system, have drawbacks. Expect management to oppose the worker-incentive plan.

e. Your convention committee has selected a site, set up a tentative program, and is now working on keynote speakers and exhibitors. Report your progress to the organization president.

f. The New Carlisle assembly plant is plagued by high absenteeism and worker turnover. What can be done about eliminating these problems?

13.4 Yardstick Report Criteria (Obj. 7)

Assume you are a benefits analyst who has been assigned the task of investigating three health care plans for your company. You must recommend a plan that the company can afford and that will satisfy employees. Your company is facing a 45 percent cost increase in its basic major medical plan. After doing some research, you find two other options: a health maintenance organization and MedicPlus, a plan that offers choice and is somewhat cheaper than your present carrier. You decide to compare the three plans using the "yardstick" approach. What criteria could you use to compare plans? How would you organize the final report?

13.5 Periodic Report: Filling in the Boss (Obj. 2)

E-Mail

Write a report of your month's accomplishments addressed to your boss. For a job that you currently hold or a previous one, describe your regular activities, discuss irregular events that management should be aware of, and highlight any special needs or problems. Use memo format.

13.6 Trip Report: In Your Dreams (Obj. 3)

From a business periodical select an article describing a conference, seminar, or trip (preferably to an exotic spot) connected with your major area of study. The article must be at least 500 words long. Assume that you attended the meeting or took the trip at the expense of your company. Prepare a memo report to your supervisor.

13.7 Progress Report: Heading Toward That Degree (Obj. 3)

Assume you have made an agreement with your parents (or spouse, relative, or significant friend) that you would submit a progress report at this time describing headway toward your educational goal (such as employment, degree, or certificate). List your specific achievements, and outline what you have left to complete. Prepare a report in letter format.

13.8 Progress Report: Checking In (Obj. 3)

E-Mail

If you are preparing a long report (see Chapter 14), write a progress report informing your instructor of your work. Briefly describe the project (its purpose, scope, limitations, and methodology), work you have completed, work yet to be completed, problems encountered, future activities, and expected completion date. Address the e-mail memo report to your instructor.

13.9 Investigative Report: All You Ever Wanted to Know (Obj. 4)

Web

Investigate a Fortune 500 company for whom you might want to work or one in which you are interested. Start by visiting ⟨www.Hoovers.com⟩ for a thumbnail sketch of the company. Then visit the company's Web site, look at news releases, and review its annual report. Describe its major product, service, or emphasis. Find its Fortune 500 ranking, its current stock price (if listed), and its high and low range for the year. Include its profit-to-earnings ratio. Describe its latest marketing plan, promotion, or product. Identify its home office, major officers, and number of employees. Provide a short history of the company. Address a memo report to your professor.

13.10 Investigative Report: Marketing Abroad (Obj. 4)

You have been asked to help prepare a training program for American companies doing business with (select a country, preferably one for which your library has *Culturgram* materials). Collect data from the Culturgram and from the country's embassy in Washington. Interview on-campus international students. Collect information about formats for written communication, observance of holidays, customary greetings, business ethics, and other topics of interest to businesspeople. For more information about this assignment, see Activity 3.7 in Chapter 3. Remember that your report should promote business, not tourism. Prepare a memo report addressed to Kelly Johnson, editor for the training program materials.

13.11 Investigative Report: Between the Covers (Obj. 4)

As a research assistant in an advertising agency, you must maintain data files about various magazines in which your clients may place ads. Select a business-oriented magazine and examine four to six issues. Collect information about articles (length, seriousness of topics, humor), readability (word, sentence, and paragraph length; formal or informal

tone), format and design (color, white space, glamor), and pictures and graphics. Examine the ads (advertisers, products and services, appeals). Does the magazine accept tobacco and liquor ads? At what audience is the magazine aimed (sex, education, age, income, interests)? Consider other characteristics in which your clients may be interested. Address a memo report to Judy Gold, print media coordinator.

13.12 Justification/Recommendation Report: We Need It (Obj. 5)

Identify a piece of equipment that should be purchased or replaced (photocopier, fax, VCR, computer, printer, digital camera, or the like). Write a memo report addressed to your boss. Assume that you can be direct and straightforward about this request.

13.13 Justification/Recommendation Report: Time for a Change (Obj. 5)

Critical Thinking

Identify a problem or a procedure that must be changed at your job (such as poor scheduling of employees, outdated equipment, slow order processing, failure to encourage employees to participate fully, restrictive rules, inadequate training, or disappointed customers). Using an indirect pattern, write a recommendation report suggesting one or more ways to solve the problem. Address the memo report to your boss.

13.14 Justification/Recommendation Report: Solving a Campus Problem (Obj. 5)

Team

In groups of three to five, investigate a problem on your campus, such as inadequate parking, slow registration, poor class schedules, inefficient bookstore, weak job-placement program, unrealistic degree requirements, or lack of internship programs. Within your group develop a solution to the problem. After reviewing persuasive techniques discussed in Chapter 9, write a group or individual justification/recommendation report(s) addressed to the proper campus official. Decide whether to use direct or indirect patterning based on how you expect the reader to react to your recommendation. With your instructor's approval, send the report.

13.15 Feasibility Report: International Organization (Obj. 6)

Critical Thinking

To fulfill a senior project in your department, you have been asked to submit a letter report to the dean evaluating the feasibility of starting an organization of international students on campus. Find out how many international students there are, what nations they represent, how one goes about starting an organization, and whether a faculty sponsor is needed. Assume that you conducted an informal survey of international students. Of the 39 who filled out the survey, 31 said they would be interested in joining.

13.16 Feasibility Report: Improving Employee Fitness (Obj. 6)

Critical Thinking

Your company is considering ways to promote employee fitness and morale. Select a possibility that seems reasonable for your company (softball league, bowling teams, basketball league, lunchtime walks, lunchtime fitness speakers and demos, company-sponsored health club memberships, workout room, fitness center, fitness director, and so on). Assume that your boss has tentatively agreed to one of the programs and has asked you to write a memo report investigating its feasibility.

13.17 Feasibility Report: Reducing, Reusing, and Recycling (Obj. 6)

Critical Thinking

As a management trainee for a large hotel chain, you have been asked to investigate the feasibility of saving energy and reducing waste within the hotel chain. Your task is to learn how other hotels are improving their environmental record. For example, the Boston Park Plaza eliminated complimentary plastic shower caps and installed thermal windows; the Grand Traverse Resort in Michigan uses a wide array of recycled products and energy-saving utilities; and Days Inn in Fort Myers, Florida, shreds wastepaper for compost mulch. Hotel Inter-Continental, with 100 hotels in 47 countries, has prepared a checklist of 134 actions to help employees "reduce, reuse, and recycle." Your task is not to present specifics on implementing a hotel environmental program, but rather to decide if such a program is feasible. What are the benefits of environmental programs for hotels? Address your memo to Leland Jeffrey, Operations.

13.18 Yardstick Report: Evaluating Equipment (Obj. 7)

Critical Thinking

You recently complained to your boss that you were unhappy with a piece of equipment that you use (printer, computer, copier, fax, or the like). After some thought, the boss decided you were right and told you to go shopping. Compare at least three different manufacturers' models and recommend one. Since the company will be purchasing ten or more units and since several managers must approve the purchase, write a careful report documenting your findings. Establish at least five criteria for comparing the models. Submit a memo report to your boss.

13.19 Yardstick Report: Measuring the Alternatives (Obj. 7)

Critical Thinking

Consider a problem where you work or in an organization you know. Select a problem with several alternative solutions or courses of action (retaining the present status could be one alternative). Develop criteria that could be used to evaluate each alternative. Write a report measuring each alternative by the yardstick you have created. Recommend a course of action to your boss or to the organization head.

CHAPTER • 14 •

Proposals and Formal Reports

LEARNING OBJECTIVES

1. Discuss the components of informal proposals.
2. Discuss the special components in formal proposals.
3. Distinguish between proposals and formal reports.
4. Identify formal report components that precede its introduction.
5. Outline topics that might be covered in the introduction of a formal report.
6. Describe the components of a formal report that follow the introduction.
7. Specify tips that aid writers of formal reports.

CASE STUDY

COMMUNICATION IN PROCESS

Proposals at Hewlett-Packard May Lead to Marriage

Like many multinational companies, Hewlett-Packard faces monumental changes in the way it markets its products. Instead of merely selling computers or measurement equipment, it now must focus on developing a relationship with a customer. This is particularly true of Fortune 500 customers such as Bell Atlantic, Lucent, or Xerox. They want more than a product; they now want a partnership that's almost like a marriage.

This partnership begins with a proposal, which is a written offer to sell services and equipment. Proposals are so important that Hewlett-Packard has a special in-house department devoted wholly to developing them. Mary Piecewicz, Hewlett-Packard proposal manager for Tests and Measurement Proposals in Latin America and the United States, says, "Competition today is tough. Customers are shopping around—especially for big purchases. They want to compare apples to apples, and proposals allow them to do that. Big corporations are now going the proposal route simply because money is tight, and they want to get the most for their dollar. Companies are also trying to protect themselves. Since a proposal is a legally binding document, whatever you put down on paper you have to be able to supply. Proposals allow companies to find the best deal while at the same time giving them protection."[1]

Writing a Hewlett-Packard proposal demands considerable "detective" work. Because customers want to develop a relationship, the HP proposal team must learn all it can about the customer. This means researching such areas as a customer's corporate culture, degree of environmental consciousness, current business strategies, and how it serves its customers. Once the HP proposal team has gathered background information, it is better able to identify the customer's "hot buttons." These are issues that are most important to the customer. Although some customers are interested primarily in low price and high performance, many global customers today are looking for evidence that the two companies are compatible and that a long-lasting partnership will result from the purchase.

www.hp.com

Preparing Formal and Informal Proposals

Proposals are persuasive offers to solve problems, provide services, or sell equipment.

Proposals are written offers to solve problems, provide services, or sell equipment. Although some proposals are internal, often taking the form of justification and recommendation reports, most proposals are external. The external proposals that Mary Piecewicz helps write at Hewlett-Packard are an important means of generating income for the giant computer company.

Because proposals are vital to their success, some businesses hire consultants or maintain specialists, like Piecewicz, who do nothing but write proposals. Such proposals typically tell how a problem can be solved, what procedure will be followed, who will do it, how long it will take, and how much it will cost.

Government agencies and large companies use requests for proposals (RFPs) to solicit competitive bids on projects.

Proposals may be divided into two categories: solicited or unsolicited. When firms know exactly what they want, they prepare a request for proposal (RFP) specifying their requirements. Government agencies and large companies are likely to use RFPs to solicit competitive bids on their projects. As Mary Piecewicz noted, companies today want to be able to compare "apples with apples," and they also want the protection offered by proposals, which are legal contracts. Unsolicited proposals are written when an individual or firm sees a problem to be solved and offers a proposal to do so. Clean-Up Technology, an American waste disposal firm, will be submitting several proposals, for example, to government agencies and firms in

FIGURE 14.1 **Components in Formal and Informal Proposals**

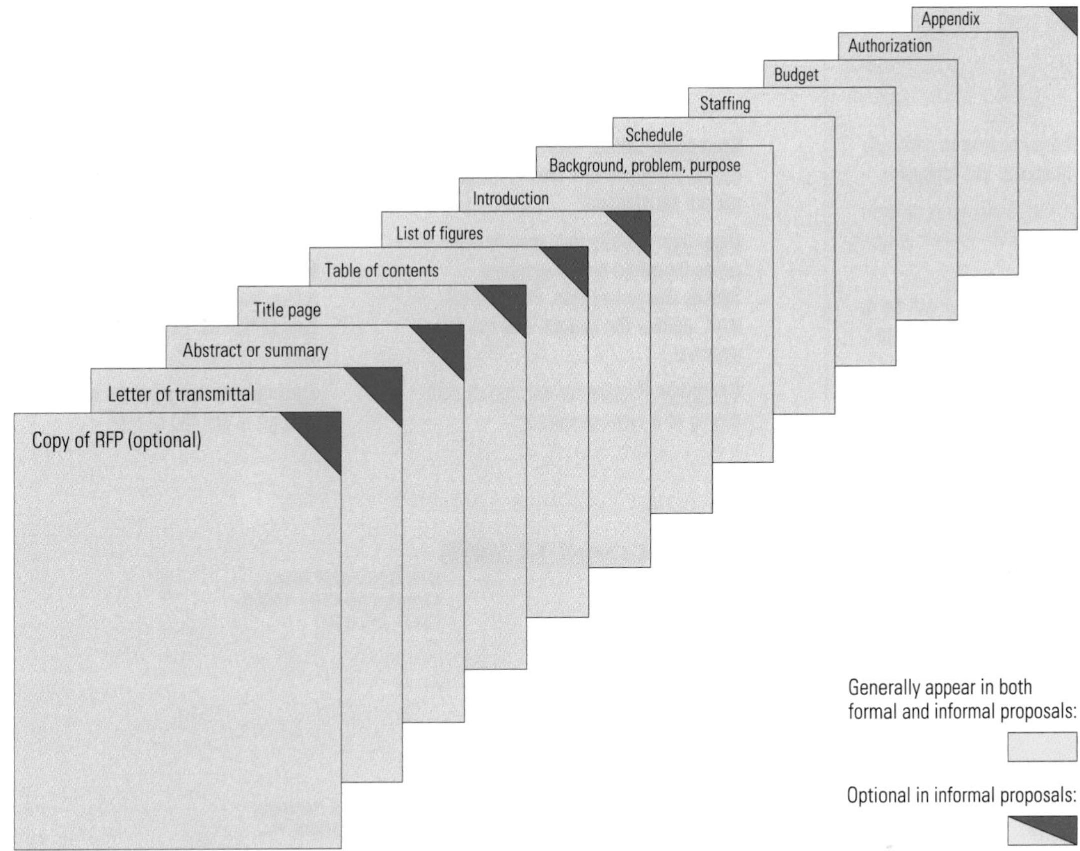

Mexico. Explaining his bid for Mexican business, the waste disposal company president said, "There's obviously a lot of clean-up work to be done in Mexico, and there's not a lot of expertise in our business."[2] Unsolicited proposals, like those of Clean-Up Technology, seize opportunities and capitalize on potential.

The most important point to remember about proposals—whether solicited or unsolicited—is that they are sales presentations. They must be persuasive, not merely mechanical descriptions of what you can do. Among other things, you may recall, effective persuasive sales messages (1) emphasize benefits for the reader, (2) "toot your horn" by detailing your expertise and accomplishments, and (3) make it easy for the reader to understand and respond.

Proposals may be informal or formal; they differ primarily in length and format. Notice in Figure 14.1 that formal proposals, described shortly, have many more components than informal proposals.

Components of Informal Proposals

Informal proposals may be presented in short (two- to four-page) letters. Sometimes called *letter proposals,* they may contain six principal components: introduction, background, proposal, staffing, budget, and authorization request. As you can see in Figure 14.1, both informal and formal proposals contain these six basic parts. Figure 14.2, an informal letter proposal to a Cincinnati dentist to improve patient satisfaction, illustrates the six parts of letter proposals. **1**

FIGURE 14.2 **Informal Proposal**

1 PREWRITING

Analyze: The purpose is to persuade the reader to accept this proposal.

Anticipate: The reader must be convinced that this survey project is worth its hefty price.

Adapt: Because the reader will be resistant at first, use a persuasive approach that emphasizes benefits.

2 WRITING

Research: Collect data about the reader's practice and other surveys of patient satisfaction.

Organize: Identify four specific purposes (benefits) of this proposal. Specify the survey plan. Promote the staff, itemize the budget, and ask for approval.

Compose: Prepare for revision by composing at a word processor.

3 REVISING

Revise: Revise to emphasize benefits. Improve readability with functional headings and lists. Remove jargon and wordiness.

Proofread: Check spelling of client's name. Verify dates and calculation of budget figures. Recheck all punctuation.

Evaluate: Is this proposal convincing enough to sell the client?

MYERS RESEARCH CONSULTANTS

One Riverview Plaza
Cincinnati, Ohio 45268
(513) 356-4300

May 16, 2000

Dr. Matthew M. Calloway
8356 Plainfield Road
Cincinnati, OH 45236

Dear Dr. Calloway:

Myers Research Consultants is pleased to submit the following proposal outlining our plan to analyze your patients and suggest ways to improve your service to them.

[Grabs attention with "hook" that focuses on key benefit] *[Uses opening paragraph in place of introduction]*

Background and Purposes

We understand that you have been incorporating a total quality management system in your practice. Although you have every reason to believe your patients are pleased with the service you provide, you would like to give them an opportunity to discuss what they like and possibly don't like about your service. Specifically, your purposes are to survey your patients to (1) determine the level of their satisfaction with you and your staff, (2) elicit their suggestions for improvement, (3) learn more about how they discovered you, and (4) compare your "preferred" and "standard" patients.

[Identifies four purposes of survey]

Proposed Plan

[Announces heart of proposal]

On the basis of our experience in conducting many local and national customer satisfaction surveys, Myers Research proposes the following plan to you.

[Describes procedure for solving problem or achieving goals]

Survey. We will develop a short but thorough questionnaire probing the data you desire. Although the survey instrument will include both open-ended and closed questions, it will concentrate on the latter. Closed questions enable respondents to answer easily; they also facilitate systematic data analysis. The questionnaire will measure patient reactions to such elements as courtesy, professionalism, accuracy of billing, friendliness, and waiting time. After you approve it, the questionnaire will be sent to a carefully selected sample of 300 patients whom you have separated into groupings of "preferred" and "standard."

[Divides total plan into logical segments for easy reading]

Analysis. Data from the survey will be analyzed by demographic segments, such as patient type, age, and gender. Our experienced team of experts, using state-of-the-art computer systems and advanced statistical measures, will study the (a) degree of patient satisfaction, (b) reasons for satisfaction or dissatisfaction, and (c) relationship between responses of your "preferred" and "standard" patients. Moreover, our team will report to you specific suggestions for making patient visits more pleasant.

Report. You will receive a final report with the key findings clearly spelled out, Dr. Calloway. Our expert staff will also draw conclusions based on these findings. The report will include tables summarizing all responses, broken down into groups of preferred and standard clients.

FIGURE 14.2 Continued

Dr. Matthew Calloway Page 2 May 16, 2000

Schedule. With your approval, the following schedule has been arranged for your patient satisfaction survey:

Questionnaire development and mailing	June 1-6
Deadline for returning questionnaire	June 24
Data tabulation and processing	June 24-26
Completion of final report	July 1

Staffing

Myers Research Consultants is a nationally recognized, experienced research consulting firm specializing in survey investigation. I have assigned your customer satisfaction survey to Dr. Kelly Miller, our director of research. Dr. Miller was trained at Ohio State University and has successfully supervised our research program for the past nine years. Before joining MRC, she was a marketing analyst with Procter & Gamble Company. Assisting Dr. Miller will be a team headed by James Wilson, our vice president for operations. Mr. Wilson earned a bachelor's degree in computer science and a master's degree in marketing from the University of Cincinnati, where he was elected to Phi Delta Mu honor society. Within our organization he supervises our computer-aided telephone interviewing (CATI) system and manages our 30-person professional interviewing staff.

Budget

	Estimated Hours	Rate	Total
Professional and administrative time			
Questionnaire development	3	$150/hr.	$ 450
Questionnaire mailing	4	40/hr.	160
Data processing and tabulation	12	40/hr.	480
Analysis of findings	15	150/hr.	2,250
Preparation of final report	5	150/hr.	750
Mailing costs			
300 copies of questionnaire			120
Postage and envelopes			270
Total costs			$4,480

Authorization

We are convinced, Dr. Calloway, that our professionally designed and administered client satisfaction survey will enhance your practice. Myers Research Consultants can have specific results for you by July 1 if you sign the enclosed duplicate copy of this letter and return it to us with a retainer of $2,300. The prices in this offer are in effect only until September 1.

Sincerely,

Jeffrey W. Myers

Jeffrey W. Myers
President

JWM:pem
Enclosure

Uses past-tense verbs to show that work has already started on the project

This section may be short if only one person is involved

Builds credibility by describing outstanding staff and facilities

Itemizes costs carefully because a proposal is a contract offer

Closes by repeating key qualifications and main benefits

Makes response easy

Provides deadline

Introduction. Most proposals begin by briefly explaining the reasons for the proposal and by highlighting the writer's qualifications. To make your introduction more persuasive, you need to provide a "hook" to capture the reader's interest. One proposal expert suggests these possibilities:[3]

Informal proposals may contain an introduction, background information, the proposal, staffing requirements, a budget, and an authorization request.

- Hint at extraordinary results with details to be revealed shortly.
- Promise low costs or speedy results.
- Mention a remarkable resource (well-known authority, new computer program, well-trained staff) available exclusively to you.
- Identify a serious problem (worry item) and promise a solution, to be explained later.
- Specify a key issue or benefit that you feel is the heart of the proposal.

Spotlight on **Communicators**

"Writer's block is a big problem for sales representatives on a proposal team," says Mary Piecewicz, Hewlett-Packard proposals manager. Since they must prepare the executive summary (the most important part of an HP proposal), Piecewicz offers some coaching. "To conquer writer's block, begin with a bulleted list of what the customer is looking for. This list is like a road map; it gets you started and keeps you headed in the right direction."

For example, Jeffrey Myers, in the introduction for his proposal shown in Figure 14.2, focused on a key benefit. In his proposal to conduct a patient satisfaction survey, Jeffrey thought that Dr. Calloway would be most interested in specific recommendations for improving service to his patients. But Jeffrey didn't hit on this hook until he had written a first draft and had come back to it later. Indeed, it's often a good idea to put off writing the proposal introduction until after you have completed other parts. For longer proposals the introduction also describes the scope and limitations of the project, as well as outlining the organization of the material to come.

Background, Problem, Purpose. The background section identifies the problem and discusses the goals or purposes of the project. In an unsolicited proposal your goal is to convince the reader that a problem exists. Thus, you must present the problem in detail, discussing such factors as monetary losses, failure to comply with government regulations, or loss of customers. In a solicited proposal your aim is to persuade the reader that you understand the problem completely. Thus, if you are responding to an RFP, this means repeating its language. For example, if the RFP asks for the *design of a maintenance program for high-speed mail-sorting equipment,* you would use the same language in explaining the purpose of your proposal. This section might include segments entitled *Basic Requirements, Most Critical Tasks,* and *Most Important Secondary Problems.*

The actual proposal section must give enough information to secure the contract but not so much detail that the services are no longer needed.

Proposal, Plan, Schedule. In the proposal section itself, you should discuss your plan for solving the problem. In some proposals this is tricky because you want to disclose enough of your plan to secure the contract without giving away so much information that your services aren't needed. Without specifics, though, your proposal has little chance, so you must decide how much to reveal. Tell what you propose to do and how it will benefit the reader. Remember, too, that a proposal is a sales presentation. Sell your methods, product, and "deliverables"—items that will be left with the client. In this section some writers specify how the project will be managed and how its progress will be audited. Most writers also include a schedule of activities or timetable showing when events take place.

Staffing. The staffing section of a proposal describes the credentials and expertise of the project leaders. It may also identify the size and qualifications of the support staff, along with other resources such as computer facilities and special programs for analyzing statistics. The staffing section is a good place to endorse and promote your staff. Some firms, like Hewlett-Packard, follow industry standards and include staff qualifications in an appendix. HP also uses generic résumés rather than the actual résumés of key people. This ensures privacy for individuals and also protects the company in case the staff changes after a proposal has been submitted to a customer.

Because a proposal is a legal contract, the budget must be carefully researched.

Budget. A central item in most proposals is the budget, a list of proposed project costs. You need to prepare this section carefully because it represents a contract; you can't raise the price later—even if your costs increase. You can—and should—protect yourself with a deadline for acceptance. In the budget section some writers itemize hours and costs; others present a total sum only. A proposal to install a complex computer system might, for example, contain a detailed line-by-line budget. Similarly, Jeffrey Myers felt that he needed to justify the budget for his firm's patient satisfaction survey, so he itemized the costs, as shown in Figure 14.2. But the budget included for a proposal to conduct a one-day seminar to improve employee communication skills might be a lump sum only. Your analysis of the project will help you decide what kind of budget to prepare.

Authorization Request. Informal proposals often close with a request for approval or authorization. In addition, the closing should remind the reader of key benefits and motivate action. It might also include a deadline date beyond which the offer is invalid. At Hewlett-Packard authorization to proceed is not part of the proposal. Instead, it is usually discussed after the customer has received the proposal. In this way the customer and the sales account manager are able to negotiate terms before a formal agreement is drawn.

Special Components of Formal Proposals

2

Formal proposals might also contain a copy of the RFP, a letter of transmittal, an abstract, a title page, a table of contents, a list of figures, and an appendix.

Formal proposals differ from informal proposals not in style but in size and format. Formal proposals respond to big projects and may range from 5 to 200 or more pages. To facilitate comprehension and reference, they are organized into many parts, as shown in Figure 14.1. In addition to the six basic components just described, formal proposals may contain some or all of the following front and end parts.

Copy of RFP. A copy of the RFP may be included in the opening parts of a formal proposal. Large organizations may have more than one RFP circulating, and identification is necessary.

Letter of Transmittal. A letter of transmittal, usually bound inside formal proposals, addresses the person who is designated to receive the proposal or who will make the final decision. The letter describes how you learned about the problem or confirms that the proposal responds to the enclosed RFP. This persuasive letter briefly presents the major features and benefits of your proposal. Here, you should assure the reader that you are authorized to make the bid and mention the time limit for which the bid stands. You may also offer to provide additional information and ask for action, if appropriate.

An abstract summarizes a proposal's highlights for specialists; an executive summary does so for managers.

Abstract or Executive Summary. An abstract is a brief summary (typically one page) of a proposal's highlights intended for specialists or for technical readers. An executive summary also reviews the proposal's highlights, but it is written for managers and so should be less technically oriented. Formal proposals may contain one or both summaries.

Title Page. The title page includes the following items, generally in this order: title of proposal, name of client organization, RFP number or other announcement, date of submission, author's name, and/or his or her organization.

Table of Contents. Because most proposals don't contain an index, the table of contents becomes quite important. Tables of contents should include all headings and their beginning page numbers. Items that appear before the contents (copy of RFP, letter of transmittal, abstract, and title page) typically are not listed in the contents. However, any appendixes should be listed.

List of Figures. Proposals with many tables and figures often contain a list of figures. This list includes each figure or table title and its page number. If you have just a few figures or tables, however, you may omit this list.

Appendix. Ancillary material of interest to some readers goes in appendixes. Appendix A might include résumés of the principal investigators or testimonial letters. Appendix B might include examples or a listing of previous projects. Other appendixes could include audit procedures, technical graphics, or professional papers cited in the body of the proposal.

Spotlight on **Communicators**

Consultant Thomas Sant advises proposal writers to (1) state the client's key need or problem, (2) spell out why the need must be addressed, (3) present a solution in concrete terms, and (4) fill in the details. Above all, he says, be sure a proposal is client-focused rather than product-focused. If the price tag is hefty, he suggests highlighting long-term savings and cost effectiveness.

Proposals in the past were always paper-based and delivered by mail or special messenger. Today, however, companies increasingly prefer *on-line proposals.* Receiving companies may transmit the electronic proposal to all levels of management without ever printing a page, thus appealing to many environmentally conscious organizations.

Well-written proposals win contracts and business for companies and individuals. Many companies depend entirely on proposals to generate their income, so proposal writing becomes critical. For more information about industry standards and resources, visit the Web site of the Association of Proposal Management Professionals **<www.apmp.org>**.

Checklist for Writing Proposals

Introduction

 **Indicate the purpose.** Specify why the proposal is being made.

 **Develop a persuasive "hook."** Suggest excellent results, low costs, or exclusive resources. Identify a serious problem or name a key issue or benefit.

Background, Problem

 **Provide necessary background.** Discuss the significance of the proposal and its goals or purposes.

 **Introduce the problem.** For unsolicited proposals convince the reader that a problem exists. For solicited proposals show that you fully understand the problem and its ramifications.

Proposal, Plan

 **Explain the proposal.** Present your plan for solving the problem or meeting the need.

 **Discuss plan management and evaluation.** If appropriate, tell how the plan will be implemented and evaluated.

 **Outline a timetable.** Furnish a schedule showing what will be done and when.

Staffing

 **Promote the qualifications of your staff.** Explain the specific credentials and expertise of the key personnel for the project.

 **Mention special resources or equipment.** Show how your support staff and resources are superior to those of the competition.

Budget

 **Show project costs.** For most projects itemize costs. Remember, however, that proposals are contracts.

Include a deadline. Here or in the conclusion present a date beyond which the bid figures are no longer valid.

PROCESS IN PROGRESS

CASE STUDY

Hewlett-Packard Revisited

Staying tuned in to a customer's concerns is the number one focus of proposal writers at Hewlett-Packard. A proposal today, especially in a global environment, involves more than merely supplying a product. Mary Piecewicz, at Hewlett-Packard, says, "It's more like a marriage between two companies. Before we can write a proposal, we need to be detectives and learn as much as possible about the potential partner." HP begins searching for information. From the customer's annual report, news releases, industry reports, and other sources, HP detectives search for specifics about its products, strategies, and company culture. What hot buttons is the company likely to respond to?

In organizing proposals, HP always responds to the customer's outline. If the customer doesn't specify a plan, proposals are arranged as follows: Section 1 includes the executive summary, which is the most important part of the proposal. It spotlights the hot buttons and the proposal criteria set forth in the request for proposal (RFP). Section 2 covers specifications and technical descriptions. Section 3 lists costs, terms, and conditions. Section 4 presents supplemental literature, including generic résumés and staff qualifications. Authorization to proceed is usually discussed after receipt of the proposal. In this way customers are able to negotiate the formal agreement with the sales account manager.

Because of its importance, the executive summary gets special attention. It may open with a brief history of HP, but its primary focus is on the customer's needs. "We address every customer issue and specify our 'differentiators,'" explains Piecewicz. "What makes HP stand out from our competitors? The executive summary is really the selling tool in our proposals, and we spend the most time on it."[4]

Critical Thinking

- Why is it important to become a "detective" before beginning to write a proposal?
- If Hewlett-Packard were preparing a proposal for a Fortune 500 company, what kinds of information should the proposal team investigate and where could it find such information?
- What is the most important part of an HP proposal, and what should it include?

Authorization

 **Ask for approval.** Make it easy for the reader to authorize the project (for example, *Sign and return the duplicate copy*).

Writing Formal Reports

Formal reports are similar to formal proposals in length, organization, and serious tone. Instead of making an offer, however, formal reports represent the end product of thorough investigation and analysis. They present ordered information to decision makers in business, industry, government, and education. In many ways formal reports are extended versions of the analytical business reports presented in Chapter 13. Figure 14.3 shows the components of typical formal reports, their normal sequence, and parts that might be omitted in informal reports.

3

Formal reports discuss the results of a process of thorough investigation and analysis.

Components of Formal Reports

A number of front and end items lengthen formal reports but enhance their professional tone and serve their multiple audiences. Formal reports may be read by

FIGURE 14.3 Components in Formal and Informal Reports

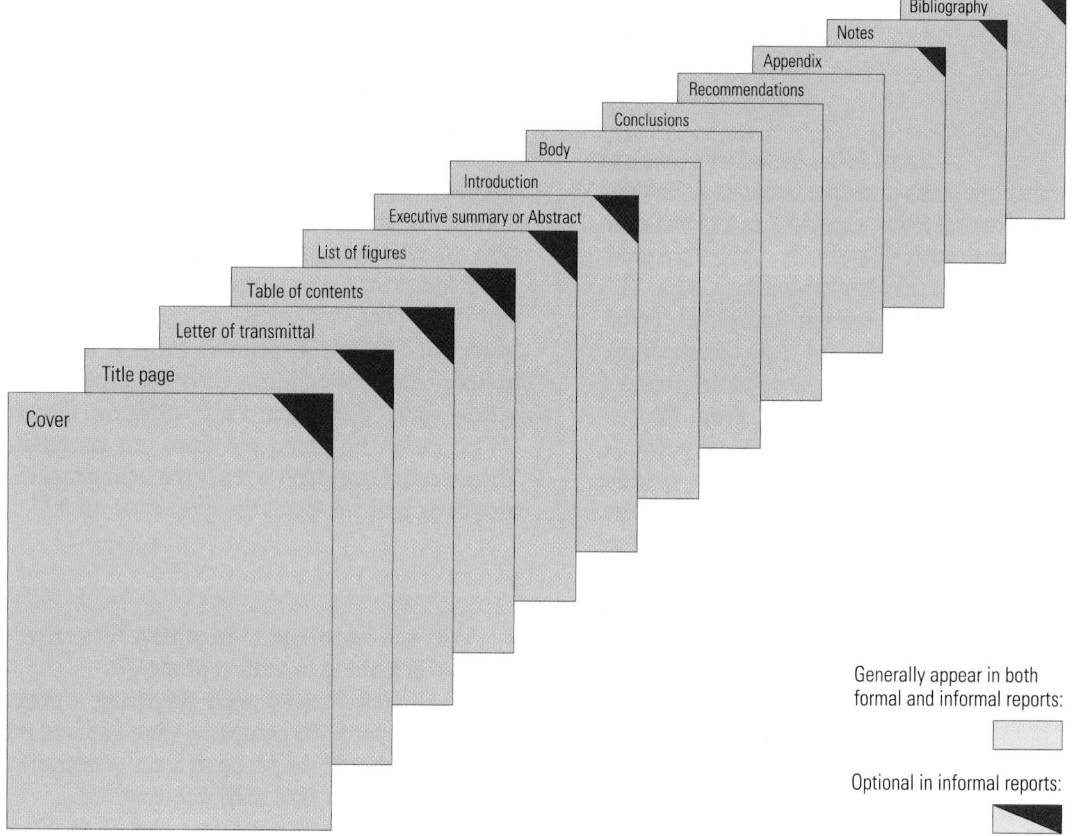

4

Like proposals, formal reports are divided into many segments to make information comprehensible and accessible.

many levels of managers, along with technical specialists and financial consultants. Therefore, breaking a long, formal report into small segments makes its information more accessible and easier to understand for all readers. These segments are discussed here and also illustrated in the model report shown later in the chapter (Figure 14.4). This analytical report studies the recycling program at Sun Coast University and makes recommendations for improving its operation.

Cover. Formal reports are usually enclosed in vinyl or heavy paper binders to protect the pages and to give a professional, finished appearance. Some companies have binders imprinted with their name and logo. The title of the report may appear through a cut-out window or may be applied with an adhesive label. Good stationery and office supply stores usually stock an assortment of report binders and labels.

Title Page. A report title page, as illustrated in the Figure 14.4 model report, begins with the name of the report typed in uppercase letters (no underscore and no quotation marks). Next comes *Presented to* (or *Submitted to*) and the name, title, and organization of the individual receiving the report. Lower on the page is *Prepared by* (or *Submitted by*) and the author's name plus any necessary identification. The last item on the title page is the date of submission. All items after the title are typed in a combination of upper- and lowercase letters.

Photographer David Cupp needed start-up funding for his new online photo business. After taking a course teaching him how to write a business plan, Cupp eventually qualified for a loan from banker James R. Grant. Cupp's advice for business plan writers is simple. Start with a statement of purpose. If you can't explain your venture in 25 words or less, it's probably not a good idea.

Letter or Memo of Transmittal. Generally written on organization stationery, a letter or memorandum of transmittal introduces a formal report. You will recall that letters are sent to outsiders and memos to insiders. A transmittal letter or memo follows the direct pattern and is usually less formal than the report itself (for example, the letter or memo may use contractions and the first-person pronouns *I* and *we*). The transmittal letter or memo typically (1) announces the topic of the report and tells how it was authorized; (2) briefly describes the project; (3) highlights the report's findings, conclusions, and recommendations, if the reader is expected to be supportive; and (4) closes with appreciation for the assignment, instruction for the reader's follow-up actions, acknowledgment of help from others, or offers of assistance in answering questions. If a report is going to different readers, a special transmittal letter or memo should be prepared for each, anticipating what each reader needs to know in using the report.

A letter or memo of transmittal gives a personalized overview of a formal report.

Table of Contents. The table of contents shows the headings in a report and their page numbers. It gives an overview of the report topics and helps readers locate them. You should wait to prepare the table of contents until after you've completed the report. For short reports you should include all headings. For longer reports you might want to list only first- and second-level headings. Leaders (spaced or unspaced dots) help guide the eye from the heading to the page number. Items may be indented in outline form or typed flush with the left margin.

List of Figures. For reports with several figures or illustrations, you may wish to include a list of figures to help readers locate them. This list may appear on the same page as the table of contents, space permitting. For each figure or illustration, include a title and page number. Some writers distinguish between tables and all other illustrations, which are called figures. If you make this distinction, you should also prepare separate lists of tables and figures. Because the model report in Figure 14.4 has few illustrations, the writer labeled them all "figures," a method that simplifies numbering.

The length and complexity of the abstract or executive summary depend on the length of and audience for the report.

Executive Summary or Abstract. Executives and other readers appreciate a summary or abstract highlighting report findings, conclusions, and recommendations. As with proposals, report abstracts are aimed at technical experts and may contain specialized language; executive summaries concentrate on what management needs to know, omitting technical jargon. Whether you are writing an abstract or an executive summary, its length and complexity will be determined by the report. For example, a 100-page report might require a 10-page summary. A 10-page report might need only a 1-page summary—or no summary at all. Longer abstracts may include headings and graphics to adequately highlight main points. Although the executive summary in Figure 14.4 is only one page long, it includes headings to help the reader see the main divisions immediately. Let your organization's practices guide you in determining the length and form of a summary or abstract.

5

Introduction. Formal reports begin with an introduction that sets the scene and announces the subject. Because they contain many parts serving different purposes, formal reports have a degree of redundancy. The same information may be included in the letter of transmittal, summary, and introduction. To avoid sounding repetitious, try to present the data slightly differently. But don't skip the introduction because you've included some of its information elsewhere. You can't be sure that your reader saw the information earlier. A good report introduction typically covers the following elements, although not necessarily in this order:

- **Background.** Describe events leading up to the problem or need.
- **Problem or purpose.** Explain the report topic and specify the problem or need that motivated the report.
- **Significance.** Tell why the topic is important. You may wish to quote experts or cite newspapers, journals, books, and other secondary sources to establish the importance of the topic.
- **Scope.** Clarify the boundaries of the report, defining what will be included or excluded.
- **Organization.** Launch readers by giving them a road map that previews the structure of the report.

Beyond these minimal introductory elements, consider adding any of the following information that is relevant for your readers:

- **Authorization.** Identify who commissioned the report. If no letter of transmittal is included, also tell why, when, by whom, and to whom the report was written.
- **Literature review.** Summarize what other authors and researchers have published on this topic, especially for academic and scientific reports.
- **Sources and methods.** Describe your secondary sources (periodicals, books, databases). Also explain how you collected primary data, including survey size, sample design, and statistical programs used.
- **Definitions of key terms.** Define words that may be unfamiliar to the audience. Also define terms with special meanings, such as *small business* when it specifically means businesses with fewer than 30 employees.

Body. The principal section in a formal report is the body. It discusses, analyzes, interprets, and evaluates the research findings or solution to the initial problem. This is where you show the evidence that justifies your conclusions. Organize the body into main categories following your original outline or using one of the patterns described earlier (such as time, component, importance, criteria, or convention).

Although we refer to this section as the *body,* it doesn't carry that heading. Instead, it contains clear headings that explain each major section. Headings may be functional or talking. Functional heads (such as *Results of the Survey, Analysis of Findings,* or *Discussion*) help readers identify the purpose of the section but don't reveal what's in it. Such headings are useful for routine reports or for sensitive topics that may upset readers. Talking heads (for example, *Recycling Habits of Campus Community*) are more informative and interesting, but they don't help readers see the organization of the report. The model report in Figure 14.4 uses functional heads for organizational sections requiring identification (*Introduction, Conclusions,* and *Recommendations*) and talking heads to divide the body.

Conclusions. This important section tells what the findings mean, particularly in terms of solving the original problem. Some writers prefer to intermix their conclusions with the analysis of the findings—instead of presenting the conclusions separately. Other writers place the conclusions before the body so that busy readers can examine the significant information immediately. Still others combine the conclusions and recommendations. Most writers, though, present the conclusions after the body because readers expect this structure. In long reports this section may include a summary of the findings. To improve comprehension, you may present the conclusions in a numbered or bulleted list.

Recommendations. When requested, you should submit recommendations that make precise suggestions for actions to solve the report problem. Recommendations are most helpful when they are practical and reasonable. Naturally, they should evolve from the findings and conclusions. Don't introduce new information in the conclusions or recommendations. As with conclusions, the position of recommendations is somewhat flexible. They may be combined with conclusions, or they may be presented before the body, especially when the audience is eager and supportive. Generally, though, in formal reports they come last.

Recommendations require an appropriate introductory sentence, such as *The findings and conclusions in this study support the following recommendations.* When making many recommendations, number them and phrase each as a command, such as *Begin an employee fitness program with a workout room available five days a week.* If appropriate, add information describing how to implement each recommendation. Some reports include a timetable describing the who, what, when, where, and how for putting each recommendation into operation.

Appendix. Incidental or supporting materials belong in appendixes at the end of a formal report. These materials are relevant to some readers but not to all. Appendixes may include survey forms, copies of other reports, tables of data, computer printouts, and related correspondence. If additional appendixes are necessary, they would be named *Appendix A, Appendix B,* and so forth.

Works Cited, References, or Bibliography. Readers look in the bibliography section to locate the sources of ideas mentioned in a report. Your method of report documentation determines how this section is developed. If you use the MLA referencing format, all citations would be listed alphabetically in the "Works Cited." If you use the APA format, your list would be called "References." With the *Chicago Manual of Style* format, you would list your references in the "Bibliography." Regardless of the format, you must include the author, title, publication, date of publication, page number, and other significant data for all ideas or quotations used in your report. For electronic references include the preceding information plus a description of the electronic address or path leading to the citation. Also include the

Spotlight on **Communicators**

When former Dallas Cowboys quarterback Roger Staubach launched a commercial real estate business, he started with a business plan, which is a long, formal report necessary to attract investors. He then commissioned another long report, a needs survey of more than 200 customers, architects, developers, and others. Listening to customers, as part of his total quality management program, enables him to analyze data, draw conclusions, and then develop his "Double EE" program centered on ethics and excellence.

The recommendations section of a formal report offers specific suggestions for solving a problem.

The bibliography section of a formal report identifies sources of ideas mentioned in the report.

date on which you located the electronic reference. To see electronic and other citations, examine the list of references at the end of Figure 14.4. Appendix C contains additional documentation information.

Final Writing Tips

7

Formal reports require careful attention to all phases of the 3-×-3 writing process.

Formal reports are not undertaken lightly. They involve considerable effort in all three phases of writing, beginning with analysis of the problem and anticipation of the audience (as discussed in Chapter 4). Researching the data, organizing it into a logical presentation, and composing the first draft (Chapter 5) make up the second phase of writing. Revising, proofreading, and evaluating (Chapter 6) are the third phase. Although everyone approaches the writing process somewhat differently, the following tips offer advice in problem areas faced by most formal report writers.

Smart report writers allow themselves plenty of time, research thoroughly, draw up a useful outline, and work on a computer.

- **Allow sufficient time.** The main reason given by writers who are disappointed with their reports is "I just ran out of time." Develop a realistic timetable and stick to it.
- **Finish data collection.** Don't begin writing until you've collected all the data and drawn the primary conclusions. Starting too early often means backtracking. For reports based on survey data, compile the tables and figures first.
- **Work from a good outline.** A big project such as a formal report needs the order and direction provided by a clear outline, even if the outline has to be revised as the project unfolds.
- **Provide a proper writing environment.** You'll need a quiet spot where you can spread out your materials and work without interruption. Formal reports demand blocks of concentration time.
- **Use a computer.** Preparing a report on a word processor enables you to keyboard quickly, revise easily, and, with most programs, check spelling, grammar, and synonyms readily. A word of warning, though: save your document often and print occasionally so that you have a hard copy. Take these precautions to guard against the grief caused by lost files, power outages, and computer malfunctions.
- **Write rapidly; revise later.** Experts advise writers to record their ideas quickly and save revision until after the first draft is completed. They say that quick writing avoids wasted effort spent in polishing sentences or even sections that may be cut later. Moreover, rapid writing encourages fluency and creativity. However, a quick-and-dirty first draft doesn't work for everyone. Some business writers prefer a more deliberate writing style, so consider this advice selectively.
- **Save difficult sections.** If some sections are harder to write than others, save them until you've developed confidence and rhythm working on easier topics.

Effective formal reports maintain parallelism in verb tenses, avoid first-person pronouns, and use the active voice.

- **Be consistent in verb tense.** Use past-tense verbs to describe completed actions (for example, *the respondents said* or *the survey showed*). Use present-tense verbs, however, to explain current actions (*the purpose of the report is, this report examines, the table shows,* and so forth). When citing references, use past-tense verbs (*Jones reported that*). Don't switch back and forth between present- and past-tense verbs in describing related data.
- **Generally avoid *I* and *we*.** To make formal reports seem as objective and credible as possible, most writers omit first-person pronouns. This formal style sometimes results in the overuse of passive-voice verbs (for example, *periodicals were consulted* and *the study was conducted*). Look for alternative constructions (*periodicals indicated* and *the study revealed*). It's also possible that your organization may allow first-person pronouns, so check before starting your report.

- **Let the first draft sit.** After completing the first version, put it aside for a day or two. Return to it with the expectation of revising and improving it. Don't be afraid to make major changes.
- **Revise for clarity, coherence, and conciseness.** Read a printed copy out loud. Do the sentences make sense? Do the ideas flow together naturally? Can wordiness and flabbiness be cut out? Make sure that your writing is so clear that a busy manager does not have to reread any part. See Chapter 6 for specific revision suggestions.
- **Proofread the final copy three times.** First, read a printed copy slowly for word meanings and content. Then read the copy again for spelling, punctuation, grammar, and other mechanical errors. Finally, scan the entire report to check its formatting and consistency (page numbering, indenting, spacing, headings, and so forth).

Putting It All Together

Formal reports in business generally aim to study problems and recommend solutions. Alan Christopher, business senator to the Office of Associated Students (OAS) at Sun Coast University, was given a campus problem to study, resulting in the formal report shown in Figure 14.4.

The campus recycling program, under the direction of Cheryl Bryant and supported by the OAS, was not attracting the anticipated level of participation. As the campus recycling program began its second year of operation, Cheryl and the OAS wondered if campus community members were sufficiently aware of the program. They also wondered how participation could be increased. Alan volunteered to investigate the problem because of his strong support for environmental causes. He also needed to conduct a research project for one of his business courses, and he had definite ideas for improving the campus OAS recycling program.

Alan's report illustrates many of the points discussed in this chapter. Although it's a good example of typical report format and style, it should not be viewed as the only way to present a report. Wide variation exists in reports.

The following checklist summarizes the report process and report components in one handy list.

Checklist for Preparing Formal Reports

Report Process

Analyze the report problem and purpose. Develop a problem question (*Is sexual harassment affecting employees at DataTech?*) and a purpose statement (*The purpose of this report is to investigate sexual harassment at DataTech and recommend remedies*).

Anticipate the audience and issues. Consider primary and secondary audiences. What do they already know? What do they need to know? Divide the major problem into subproblems for investigation.

Prepare a work plan. Include problem and purpose statements, as well as a description of the sources and methods of collecting data. Prepare a tentative project outline and a work schedule with anticipated dates of completion for all segments of the project.

Text continues on page 444

FIGURE 14.4 **Model Formal Report with MLA Citation Style**

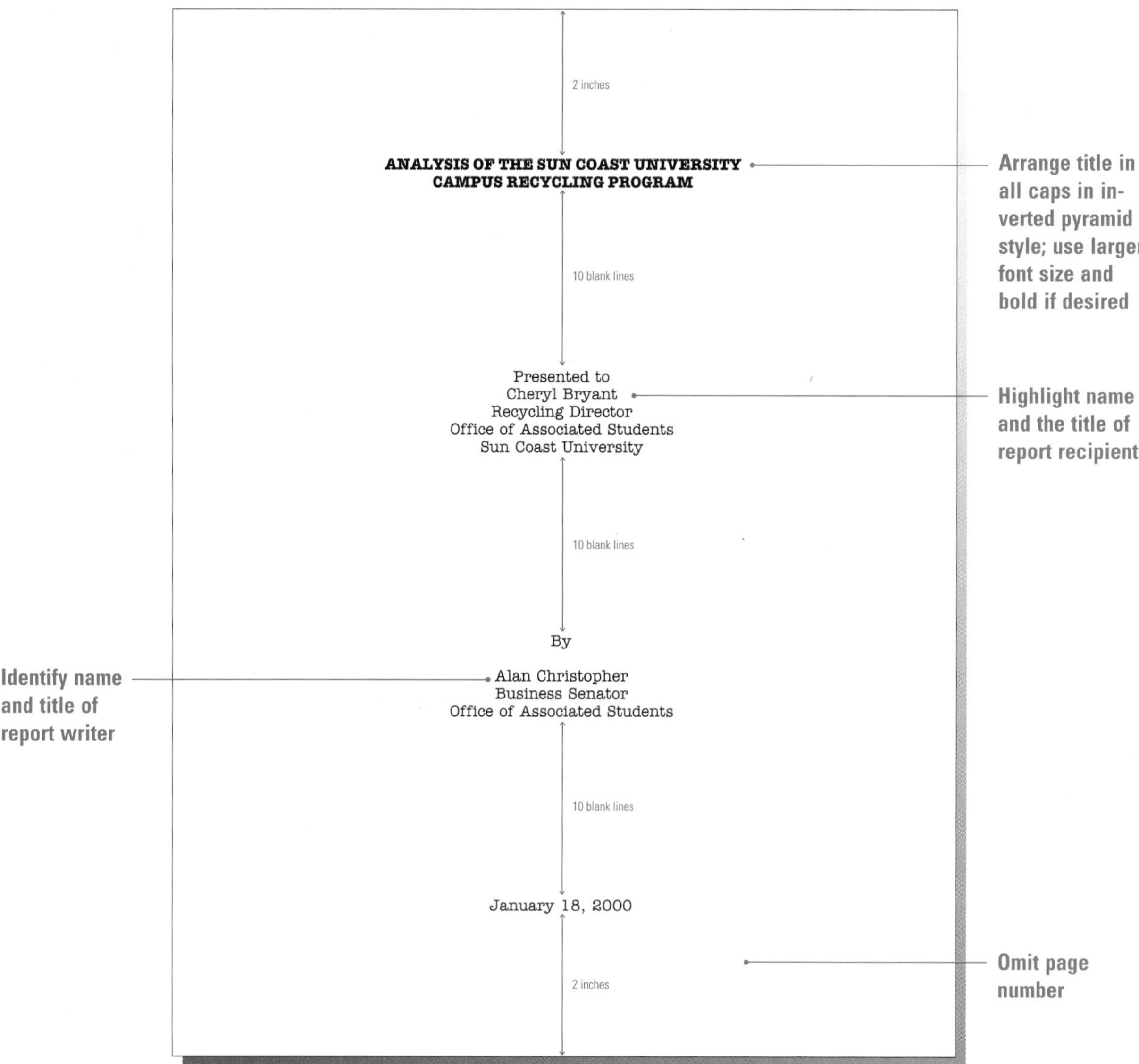

2 inches
ANALYSIS OF THE SUN COAST UNIVERSITY
CAMPUS RECYCLING PROGRAM
Arrange title in all caps in inverted pyramid style; use larger font size and bold if desired
10 blank lines
Presented to
Cheryl Bryant
Recycling Director
Office of Associated Students
Sun Coast University
Highlight name and the title of report recipient
10 blank lines
By
Identify name and title of report writer
Alan Christopher
Business Senator
Office of Associated Students
10 blank lines
January 18, 2000
Omit page number
2 inches

Alan arranges the title page so that the amount of space above the title is equal to the space below the date. If a report is to be bound on the left, move the left margin and center point 1/4 inch to the right. Notice that no page number appears on the title page, although it is counted as page i.

If you use scalable fonts, word processing capabilities, or a laser printer to enhance your report and title page, be careful to avoid anything unprofessional (such as too many type fonts, oversized print, and inappropriate graphics).

FIGURE 14.4 Continued

Includes $1\frac{1}{4}$- to $1\frac{1}{2}$-inch top margin

MEMORANDUM

DATE: January 18, 2000

TO: Cheryl Bryant, Director, Recycling Program
Office of Associated Students

FROM: Alan Christopher, OAS Business Senator

SUBJECT: INCREASING PARTICIPATION IN SUN COAST UNIVERSITY'S RECYCLING PROGRAM

Uses memo format for internal report

Here is the report you requested December 10 about the status of Sun Coast University's recycling program, along with recommendations for increasing its use. The study included both primary and secondary research. The primary study focused on a survey of members of the Sun Coast University campus community.

Announces report and gives broad overview of research conducted

Although the campus recycling program is progressing well, the information gathered shows that with some effort we should be able to increase participation and achieve our goal of setting an excellent example for both campus residents and the local community. Recommendations for increasing campus participation in the program include educating potential users about the program and making recycling on campus easy.

Highlights report findings and recommendations

I am grateful to my business communication class for helping me develop a questionnaire, for pilot testing it, and for distributing it to the campus community. Their enthusiasm and support contributed greatly to the success of this OAS research project.

Acknowledges help of others

Please call, Ms. Bryant, if I may provide additional information or answer questions. I would be happy, at your request, to implement some of the recommendations in this report by developing promotional materials for our recycling campaign.

Establishes warm tone by using the name of the receiver, including first-person pronouns, and volunteering to help

Offers to answer questions and looks forward to follow-up actions.

ii

Uses lowercase roman numeral to indicate second page

Because this report is being submitted within his own organization, Alan uses a memorandum of transmittal. Formal organization reports submitted to outsiders would carry a letter of transmittal printed on company stationery.

The margins for the transmittal should be the same as for the report, about 1¹/₄ inches on all sides. If a report is to be bound, add an extra ¹/₄ inch to the left margin.

FIGURE 14.4 Continued

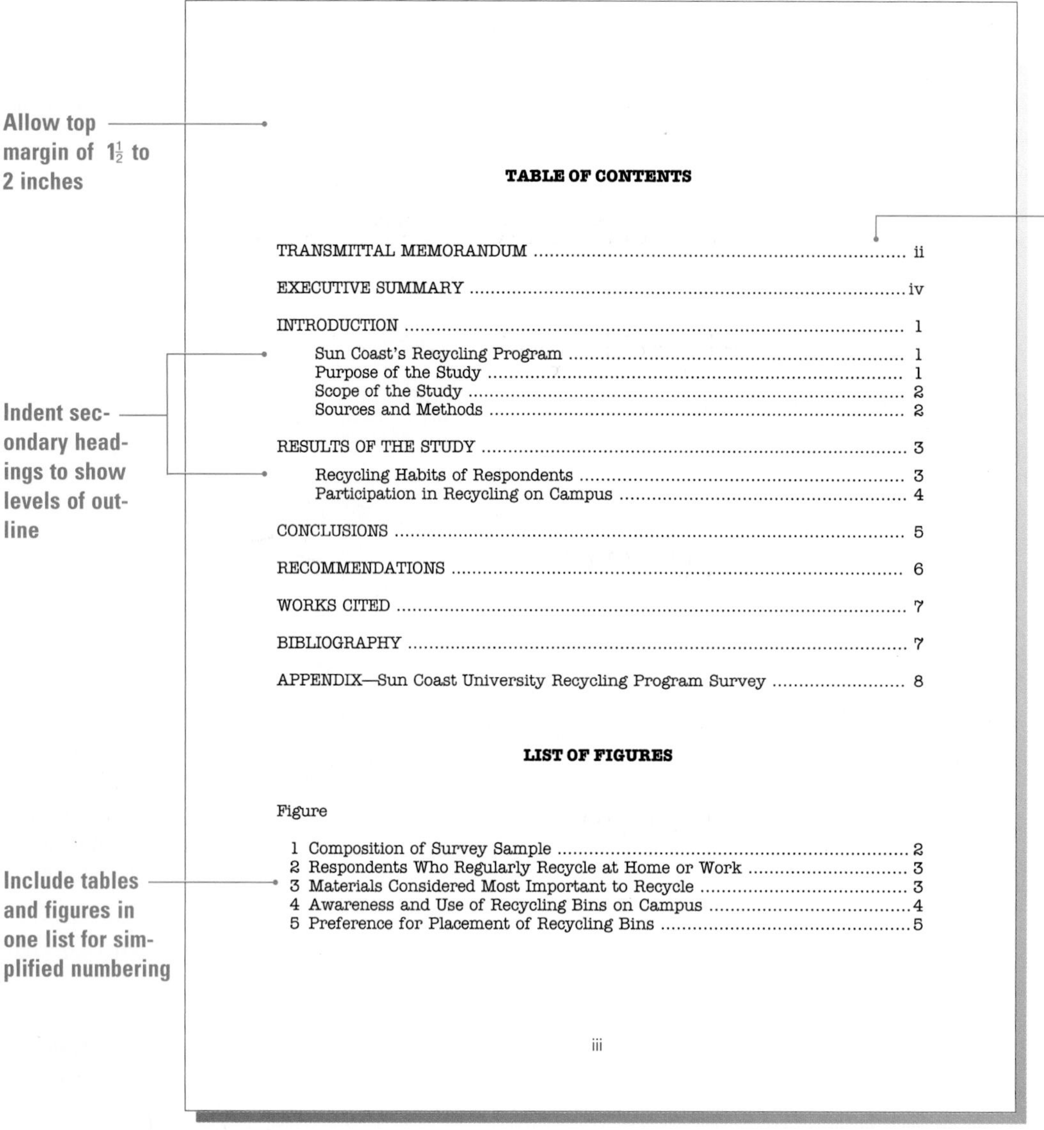

Allow top margin of $1\frac{1}{2}$ to 2 inches

Use leaders to guide eye from heading to page number

Indent secondary headings to show levels of outline

Include tables and figures in one list for simplified numbering

TABLE OF CONTENTS

LIST OF FIGURES

iii

Because Alan's table of contents and list of figures are small, he combines them on one page. Notice that he uses all caps for the titles of major report parts and a combination of upper- and lowercase letters for first-level headings. This duplicates the style within the report.

Advanced word processing capabilities enable you to generate a contents page automatically, including leaders and accurate page numbering—no matter how many times you revise!

FIGURE 14.4 Continued

EXECUTIVE SUMMARY

Purposes of the Report

The purposes of this report are to (1) determine the Sun Coast University campus community's awareness of the campus recycling program and (2) recommend ways to increase participation. Sun Coast's recycling program was intended to respond to the increasing problem of waste disposal, to fulfill its social responsibility as an educational institution, and to meet the demands of legislation requiring individuals and organizations to recycle.

A questionnaire survey was conducted to learn about the campus community's recycling habits and to assess participation in the current recycling program. A total of 220 individuals responded to the survey. Since Sun Coast University's recycling program includes only aluminum, glass, paper, and plastic at this time, these were the only materials considered in this study.

Tells purpose of report and briefly describes survey

Recycling at Sun Coast

Most survey respondents recognized the importance of recycling and stated that they do recycle aluminum, glass, paper, and plastic on a regular basis either at home or at work. However, most respondents displayed a low level of awareness and use of the on-campus program. Many of the respondents were unfamiliar with the location of the bins around campus and, therefore, had not participated in the recycling program. Other responses indicated that the bins were not conveniently located.

Summarizes findings of survey

The results of this study show that more effort is needed to increase participation in the campus recycling program.

Draws primary conclusion

Recommendations for Increasing Recycling Participation

Recommendations for increasing participation in the program include (1) relocating the recycling bins for greater visibility, (2) developing incentive programs to gain the participation of individuals and on-campus student groups, (3) training student volunteers to give on-campus presentations explaining the need for recycling and the benefits of using the recycling program, and (4) increasing advertising about the program.

Concisely enumerates four recommendations using parallel (balanced) phrasing

iv

Numbers pages that precede the body with lowercase roman numerals

For readers who want a quick picture of the report, the executive summary presents its most important elements. Alan has divided the summary into three sections for increased readability.

Executive summaries generally contain little jargon or complex statistics; they condense what management needs to know about a problem and its study. Report abstracts, sometimes written in place of summaries, tend to be more technical and are aimed at specialists rather than management.

FIGURE 14.4 Continued

Leaves 2-inch top margin on first page

ANALYSIS OF THE SUN COAST UNIVERSITY
CAMPUS RECYCLING PROGRAM

INTRODUCTION

Observers criticize America as a "throw-away" society (Cahan 116), and perhaps the criticism is accurate. We discard 11 to 14 billion tons of waste each year, according to the Environmental Protection Agency. Of this sum, 180 million tons comes from households and businesses, areas where recycling efforts could make a difference (Schneider 6). Government specialists Weddle and Klein state that in 1998 "the United States produced enough waste to fill a convoy of garbage trucks reaching halfway to the moon, and the convoy is getting longer every year" (Weddle and Klein 30). Although many individuals would like to send our trash to the moon, unfortunately, most of it finds its way to earthly landfills. With an ever-increasing volume of waste, estimates show that 80 percent of America's landfills will be full by the year 2010 (de Blanc 32).

Begins by establishing the significance of the problem

Builds credibility by documenting statistics with footnote references

To combat the growing waste disposal problem, 32 states have passed legislation aimed at increasing recycling. In addition to legislation at the state level, more than 1,500 communities have enacted regulations requiring residents to separate bottles, cans, and newspapers so that they may be recycled (Schneider 6). Moreover, 35 states are trying other means to reduce waste, including taxes, tax incentives, packaging mandates, and outright product bans (Holusha D2). All levels of government are trying both voluntary and mandatory means of reducing trash sent to landfills.

Uses MLA referencing style

Sun Coast's Recycling Program

Describes background of problem

In order to do its part in reducing trash and to meet the requirements of legislation, Sun Coast University began operating a recycling program one year ago. The program maintains recycling bins to collect aluminum cans, glass, office and computer paper, and plastic containers. The Office of Associated Students oversees the operation of the program, and it relies on promotions, advertisements, and word of mouth to encourage its use by the campus community.

Purposes of the Study

The purposes of this study are to (1) determine the Sun Coast University campus community's awareness of the campus recycling program and (2) recommend ways to increase participation. OAS originally projected that participation in the program would increase to greater levels than it has achieved thus far. Experts say that recycling programs generally must

Includes centered page number on first and succeeding pages

1

The first page of a report generally contains the title printed 2 inches from the top edge. Titles for major parts of a report (such as *Introduction, Results, Conclusion,* and so forth) are centered in all caps. First-level headings are bold and printed with upper- and lowercase letters. Second-level headings begin at the side. For illustration of heading formats, see Figure 12.5.

Notice that Alan's report is single-spaced. Many businesses prefer this space-saving format. However, some organizations prefer double-spacing, especially for preliminary drafts. Page numbers may be centered 1 inch from the bottom of the page or placed 1 inch from the upper right corner at the margin.

FIGURE 14.4 Continued

operate at least a year before results become apparent (de Blanc 33). The OAS program has been in operation one year, yet gains are disappointing. Therefore, OAS authorized this study to determine the campus community's awareness and use of the program. Recommendations for increasing participation in the campus recycling program will be made to the OAS based on the results of this study.

Scope of the Study

Describes what the study includes and excludes

This study investigates potential participants' attitudes toward recycling in general, their awareness of the campus recycling program, their willingness to recycle on campus, and the perceived convenience of the recycling bins. Only aluminum, glass, paper, and plastic are considered in this study, as they are the only materials being recycled on campus at this time. The costs involved in the program were not considered in this study, since a recycling program generally does not begin to pay for itself during the first year. After the first year, the financial benefit is usually realized in reduced disposal costs (Steelman, Desmond, and Johnson 145).

Sources and Methods

Current business periodicals and newspapers were consulted for background information and to learn how other organizations are encouraging use of in-house recycling programs. In addition, a questionnaire survey (shown in the appendix) of administrators, faculty, staff, and students at Sun Coast University campus was conducted to learn about this group's recycling habits. In all, a convenience sample of 220 individuals responded to the self-administered survey. The composition of the sample closely resembles the makeup of the campus population. Figure 1 shows the percentage of students, faculty, staff, and administrators who participated in the survey.

Discusses how the study was conducted

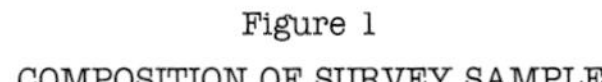

Figure 1

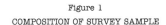

COMPOSITION OF SURVEY SAMPLE

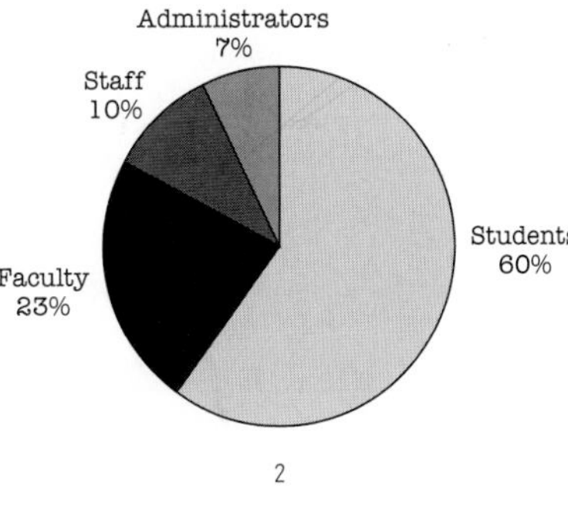

Uses computer-generated pie chart to illustrate makeup of survey

2

Because Alan wants this report to be formal in tone, he avoids *I* and *we*. Notice, too, that he uses present-tense verbs to describe his current writing *(this study investigates)*, but past-tense verbs to indicate research completed in the past *(newspapers were consulted)*.

If you use figures or tables, be sure to introduce them in the text. Although it's not always possible, try to place them close to the spot where they are first mentioned. If necessary to save space, you can print the title of a figure at its side.

FIGURE 14.4 **Continued**

RESULTS OF THE STUDY

Introduces body of report with functional head

The findings of the study will be presented in two categories: recycling habits of the respondents and participation in the Sun Coast University recycling program.

Recycling Habits of Respondents

A major finding of the survey reveals that most respondents are willing to recycle even when not required to do so. Data tabulation shows that 72 percent of the respondents live in an area where neither the city nor the county requires separation of trash. Yet 80 percent of these individuals indicated that they recycle aluminum on a regular basis at home or at work, while another 55 percent said that they recycle paper on a regular basis. Although the percentages are somewhat smaller, many of the respondents also regularly recycle glass (46 percent) and plastic (45 percent). These results, summarized in Figure 2, clearly show that campus respondents are accustomed to recycling the four major materials targeted for the Sun Coast University recycling program.

Interprets and discusses results of survey

Introduces figure as part of another statement

Figure 2

RESPONDENTS WHO REGULARLY RECYCLE AT HOME OR WORK

Summarizes findings of survey question in table

Material	Percentage
Aluminum	80%
Paper	55
Glass	46
Plastic	45

Respondents were asked to rank the importance of recycling the materials collected in the Sun Coast program. Figure 3 shows that they felt aluminum was most important, although most respondents also ranked the other materials (glass, paper, and plastic) either "extremely important" or "somewhat important" to recycle. Respondents were also asked what materials they actually recycled most frequently, and aluminum again ranked first.

Figure 3

MATERIALS CONSIDERED MOST IMPORTANT TO RECYCLE

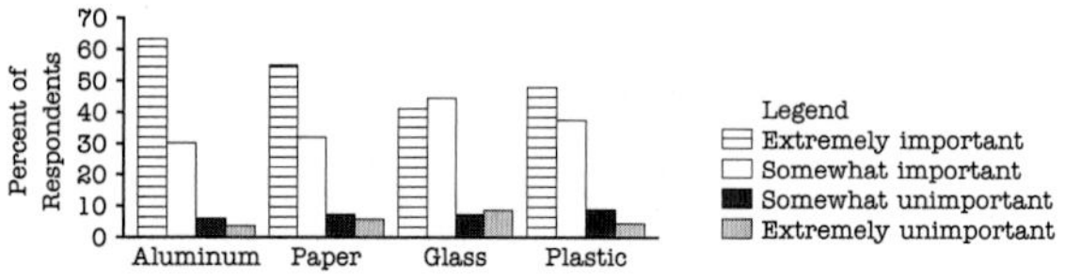

Presents bar chart for visual comparison of responses to survey question

3

Alan selects the most important survey findings to interpret and discuss for readers. Notice that he continues to use present-tense verbs *(the survey reveals* and *these results clearly show)* to discuss the current report.

Because he has few tables and charts, he labels them all as "Figures." Notice that he numbers them consecutively and places the label above each figure. Report writers with a great many tables, charts, and illustrations may prefer to label and number them separately. Tables are labeled as such; everything else is generally called a figure. When tables and figures are labeled separately, tables may be labeled above the table and figures below the figure.

FIGURE 14.4 Continued

Adds personal interpretation

When asked how likely they would be to go out of their way to deposit an item in a recycling bin, 29 percent of the respondents said "very likely," and 55 percent said "somewhat likely." Thus, respondents showed a willingness—at least on paper—to recycle even if it means making a special effort to locate a recycling bin.

Participation in Recycling on Campus

For any recycling program to be successful, participants must be aware of the location of recycling centers and must be trained to use them (de Blanc 33). Another important ingredient in thriving programs is convenience to users. If recycling centers are difficult for users to reach, these centers will be unsuccess-ful. To collect data on these topics, the survey included questions assessing awareness and use of the current bins. The survey also investigated reasons for not participating and the perceived convenience of current bin locations.

Introduces more findings and relates them to the report's purpose

Student Awareness and Use of Bins

Two of the most significant questions in the survey asked whether respondents were aware of the OAS recycling bins on campus and whether they had used the bins. Responses to both questions were disappointing, as Figure 4 illustrates.

Figure 4

AWARENESS AND USE OF RECYCLING BINS ON CAMPUS

Location	Awareness of bins at this location	Use of bins at this location
Social sciences building	38%	21%
Bookstore	29	12
Administration building	28	12
Computer labs	16	11
Library	15	7
Student union	9	5
Department offices	6	3
Campus dormitories	5	3
Unaware of any bins; have not used any bins	20	7

Arranges responses from highest to lowest with "unaware" category placed last

Only 38 percent of the respondents, as shown in Figure 4, were aware of the bins located outside the social sciences building. Even fewer were aware of the bins outside the bookstore (29 percent) and outside the administration building (28 percent). Equally dissatisfying, only 21 percent of the respond-ents had used the most visible recycling bins outside the social sciences

Clarifies and emphasizes meaning of findings

4

In discussing the results of the survey, Alan highlights those that have significance for the purpose of the report.

As you type a report, avoid widows and orphans (ending a page with the first line of a paragraph or carrying a single line of a paragraph to a new page). Strive to start and end pages with at least two lines of a paragraph, even if a slightly larger bottom margin results.

FIGURE 14.4 Continued

building. Other recycling bin locations were even less familiar to the survey respondents and, of course, were little used. These responses plainly show that the majority of the respondents in the Sun Coast campus community have a low awareness of the recycling program and an even lower record of participation.

Reasons for Not Participating

Respondents offered several reasons for not participating in the campus recycling program. Forty-five percent said that the bins are not convenient to use. Thirty percent said that they did not know where the bins were located. Another 25 percent said that they are not in the habit of recycling. Although many reasons for not participating were listed, the primary one appears to center on convenience of bin locations.

Location of Recycling Bins

When asked specifically how they would rate the location of the bins currently in use, only 13 percent of the respondents felt that the bins were extremely convenient. Another 35 percent rated the locations as somewhat convenient. Over half the respondents felt that the locations of the bins were either somewhat inconvenient or extremely inconvenient. Recycling bins are currently located outside nearly all the major campus buildings, but respondents clearly considered these locations inconvenient or inadequate.

Discusses results of other survey questions not represented in tables or charts

In indicating where they would like recycling bins placed (see Figure 5), 42 percent of the respondents felt that the most convenient locations would be outside each building on campus. Placing recycling bins near the food service facilities on campus seemed most convenient to another 33 percent of those questioned, while 15 percent stated that they would like to see the bins placed near the vending machines. Ten percent of the individuals responding to the survey did not seem to think that the locations of the bins would matter to them.

Clarifies results of another survey question with textual discussion accompanied by table

Figure 5

PREFERENCE FOR PLACEMENT OF RECYCLING BINS

Outside each building on campus	42%
Near food service facilities	33
Near vending machines	15
Does not matter	10

CONCLUSIONS

Based on the findings of the recycling survey of members of the Sun Coast University campus community, the following conclusions are drawn:

1. Most members of the campus community are already recycling at home or at work without being required to do so.

5

After completing a discussion of the survey results, Alan articulates what he considers the five most important conclusions to be drawn from this survey. Some writers combine the conclusions and recommendations, particularly when they are interrelated. Alan separated them in his study because the survey findings were quite distinct from the recommendations he would make based on them.

Notice that it is unnecessary to start a new page for the conclusions.

FIGURE 14.4 Continued

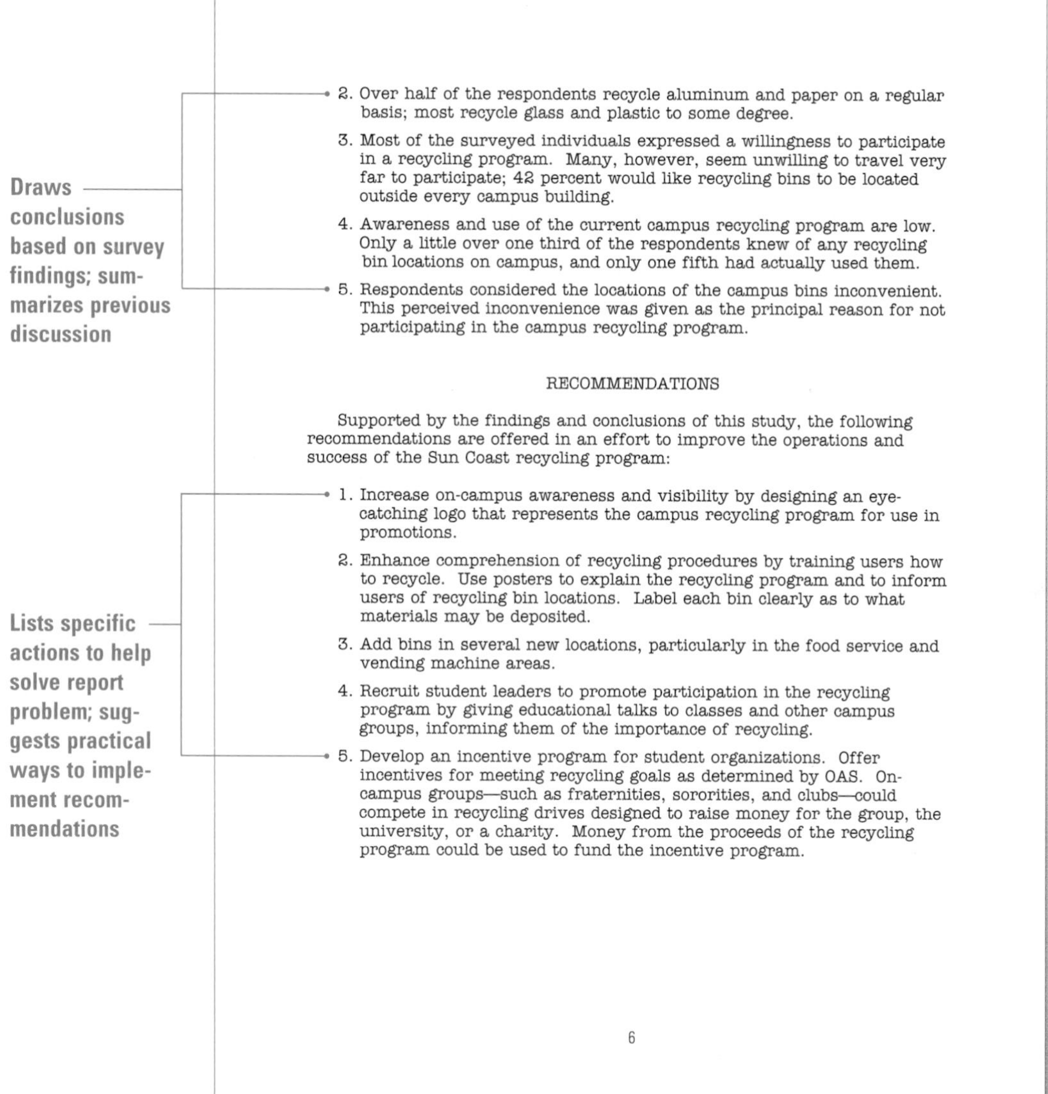

Draws conclusions based on survey findings; summarizes previous discussion
2. Over half of the respondents recycle aluminum and paper on a regular basis; most recycle glass and plastic to some degree.
3. Most of the surveyed individuals expressed a willingness to participate in a recycling program. Many, however, seem unwilling to travel very far to participate; 42 percent would like recycling bins to be located outside every campus building.
4. Awareness and use of the current campus recycling program are low. Only a little over one third of the respondents knew of any recycling bin locations on campus, and only one fifth had actually used them.
5. Respondents considered the locations of the campus bins inconvenient. This perceived inconvenience was given as the principal reason for not participating in the campus recycling program.
RECOMMENDATIONS
Supported by the findings and conclusions of this study, the following recommendations are offered in an effort to improve the operations and success of the Sun Coast recycling program:
Lists specific actions to help solve report problem; suggests practical ways to implement recommendations
1. Increase on-campus awareness and visibility by designing an eye-catching logo that represents the campus recycling program for use in promotions.
2. Enhance comprehension of recycling procedures by training users how to recycle. Use posters to explain the recycling program and to inform users of recycling bin locations. Label each bin clearly as to what materials may be deposited.
3. Add bins in several new locations, particularly in the food service and vending machine areas.
4. Recruit student leaders to promote participation in the recycling program by giving educational talks to classes and other campus groups, informing them of the importance of recycling.
5. Develop an incentive program for student organizations. Offer incentives for meeting recycling goals as determined by OAS. On-campus groups—such as fraternities, sororities, and clubs—could compete in recycling drives designed to raise money for the group, the university, or a charity. Money from the proceeds of the recycling program could be used to fund the incentive program.
6

The most important parts of a report are its conclusions and recommendations. To make them especially clear, Alan enumerated each conclusion and recommendation. Notice that each recommendation starts with a verb and is stated in command language for emphasis and readability.

Report recommendations are most helpful to readers when they not only make suggestions to solve the original research problem but also describe specific actions to be taken. Notice that Alan goes beyond merely listing ideas; instead, he provides practical suggestions for ways to implement the recommendations.

FIGURE 14.4 Continued

Works Cited

Cahan, Vicky. "Waste Not, Want Not? Not Necessarily." Business Week 17 July 1998: 116.

Magazine

de Blanc, Susan. "Paper Recycling: How to Make It Effective." The Office Dec. 1997: 32.

Foster, David. "Recycling: A Green Idea Turns to Gold." The Los Angeles Times. 5 Mar. 1999, Bulldog ed. Metro, CyberTimes. Retrieved 7 Mar. 1999 <http://www.times.com/library/cyber/week/y05dat.html>.

On-line Newspaper

Freeman, Monique M. Personal interview. 2 Nov. 1999.

Interview

Landsburg, Steven E. "Who Shall Inherit the Earth?" Slate 1 May 1997. Retrieved 2 May 1997 <http://www.slate.com/Economics/97-05-01/ Economics.asp>

On-line Magazine

Schneider, Keith. "As Recycling Becomes a Growth Industry, Its Paradoxes Also Multiply." The New York Times, 20 Jan. 1998, sec. 4: 6.

Steelman, James W., Shirley Desmond, and LeGrand Johnson. Facing Global Limitations. New York: Rockford Press, 1998.

Book

Steuteville, Robert. "The State of Garbage in America." Part 1. BioCycle. Apr. 1998. Retrieved 30 Nov. 1999 <http://www.biocycle/recycle/guid.html>.

On-line Magazine

"Tips to Reduce, Reuse, and Recycle." Environmental Recycling Hotline. Retrieved 8 July 1999 <http://www.primenet.com/cgi-bin/erh.pl>.

World Wide Web

Weddle, Bruce, and Edward Klein. "A Strategy to Control the Garbage Glut." EPA Journal 12.2 (1999): 28–34.

Journal

7

On this page Alan lists all the references cited in the text as well as others that he examined during his research. (Some authors list only those works cited in the report.) Alan formats his citations following the MLA referencing style. Notice that all entries are arranged alphabetically. He underlines book and periodical titles, but italics could be used. When referring to on-line items, he shows the full name of the citation and then identifies the path leading to that reference as well as the date on which he accessed the electronic reference.

Most word processing software today automatically updates citation references within the text and prints a complete list for you. For more information about documentation styles, see Chapter 12 and Appendix C.

FIGURE 14.4 Continued

Includes copy of survey questionnaire so that report readers can see actual questions

APPENDIX

SUN COAST UNIVERSITY RECYCLING PROGRAM SURVEY

Sun Coast University recently implemented a recycling program on campus. Please take a few minutes to answer the following questions so that we can make this program as convenient and helpful as possible for you to use.

Explains why survey is necessary, emphasizing "you" view

1. Please indicate which items you recycle on a regular basis at home or at work. (Check *all* that apply.)
   - ☐ Aluminum
   - ☐ Glass
   - ☐ Paper
   - ☐ Plastic
2. Do you live in an area where the city/county requires separation of trash?
   ☐ Yes ☐ No
3. How important is it to you to recycle each of the following:

	Extremely Important	Somewhat Important	Somewhat Unimportant	Extremely Unimportant
Aluminum				
Glass				
Paper				
Plastic				

Provides range of answers that will be easy to tabulate

4. How likely would it be for you to go out of your way to put something in a recycling bin?

Very Likely	Somewhat Likely	Somewhat Unlikely	Very Unlikely

5. Which of the following items do you recycle *most* often? (Choose *one* item only.)
   - ☐ Aluminum
   - ☐ Glass
   - ☐ Paper
   - ☐ Plastic
   - ☐ Other
6. The following are locations of the recycling bins on campus. (Check *all* those of which you are aware.)
   - ☐ Administration building
   - ☐ Bookstore
   - ☐ Campus dorms
   - ☐ Computer labs
   - ☐ Engineering building
   - ☐ Library
   - ☐ Social sciences building
   - ☐ Student union
   - ☐ I'm unaware of any of these recycling bins.

8

Alan had space to add the word "Appendix" to the top of the survey questionnaire. If space were not available, he could have typed a separate page with that title on it. If more than one item were included, he would have named them Appendix A, Appendix B, and so on.

Notice that the appendix continues the report pagination.

FIGURE 14.4 **Continued**

7. Which of the following recycling bins have you actually used? (Check *all* that you have used.)

☐ Administration building ☐ Library
☐ Bookstore ☐ Social sciences building
☐ Campus dorms ☐ Student union
☐ Computer labs ☐ I've not used any of these recycling bins.
☐ Engineering building

8. If you don't recycle on campus, why don't you participate?

☐ I'm not in the habit of recycling.
☐ I don't know where the bins are.
☐ The bins aren't convenient to me.
☐ Other ______________________

9. How do you rate the convenience of the bins' locations?

☐ Extremely convenient
☐ Somewhat convenient
☐ Somewhat inconvenient
☐ Extremely inconvenient

10. Which of the following possible recycling bin locations would be most convenient for you to use? (Check *one* only.)

☐ Outside each building
☐ Near the food service facilities
☐ Near the vending machines
☐ Does not matter
☐ Other ______________________

11. Please indicate:

☐ Student
☐ Faculty
☐ Administrator
☐ Staff

COMMENTS:

Thank you for your responses! Please return the questionnaire in the enclosed, stamped envelope to Sun Coast University, School of Business, Rm. 321. If you have any questions, please call (555) 450-2391.

9

Anticipates responses but also supplies "Other" category

Uses scale questions to capture degrees of feeling

Requests little demographic data to keep survey short

Offers comment section for explanations and remarks

Concludes with appreciation and instructions

 **Collect data.** Begin by searching secondary sources (electronic databases, books, magazines, journals, newspapers) for information on your topic. Then, if necessary, gather primary data by surveying, interviewing, observing, and experimenting.

 **Document data sources.** Prepare note cards or separate sheets of paper citing all references (author, date, source, page, and quotation). Select a documentation format (Chapter 11) and use it consistently.

 **Interpret and organize the data.** Arrange the collected information in tables, grids, or outlines to help you visualize relationships and interpret meanings. Organize the data into an outline (Chapter 5).

Prepare graphics. Make tables, charts, graphs, and illustrations—but *only* if they serve a function. Use graphics to help clarify, condense, simplify, or emphasize your data.

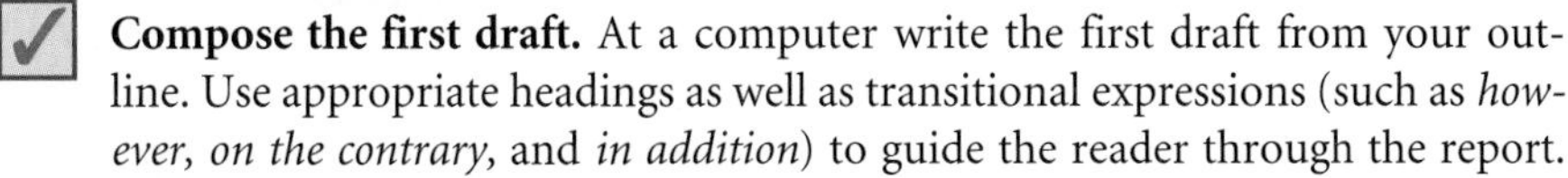

Compose the first draft. At a computer write the first draft from your outline. Use appropriate headings as well as transitional expressions (such as *however, on the contrary,* and *in addition*) to guide the reader through the report.

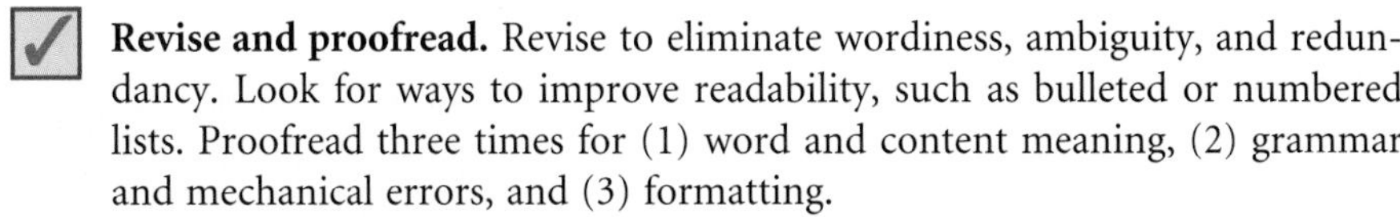

Revise and proofread. Revise to eliminate wordiness, ambiguity, and redundancy. Look for ways to improve readability, such as bulleted or numbered lists. Proofread three times for (1) word and content meaning, (2) grammar and mechanical errors, and (3) formatting.

Evaluate the product. Examine the final report. Will it achieve its purpose? Encourage feedback so that you can learn how to improve future reports.

Report Components

Title page. Balance the following lines on the title page: (1) name of the report (in all caps); (2) name, title, and organization of the individual receiving the report; (3) author's name, title, and organization; and (4) date submitted.

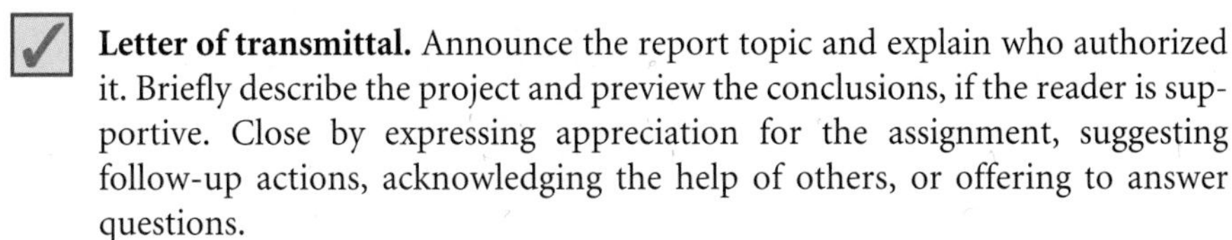

Letter of transmittal. Announce the report topic and explain who authorized it. Briefly describe the project and preview the conclusions, if the reader is supportive. Close by expressing appreciation for the assignment, suggesting follow-up actions, acknowledging the help of others, or offering to answer questions.

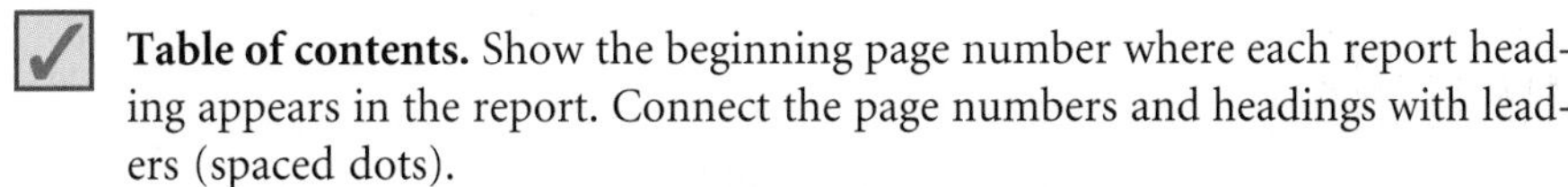

Table of contents. Show the beginning page number where each report heading appears in the report. Connect the page numbers and headings with leaders (spaced dots).

List of illustrations. Include a list of tables, illustrations, or figures showing the title of the item and its page number. If space permits, put these lists on the same page with the table of contents.

Executive summary or abstract. Summarize the report purpose, findings, conclusions, and recommendations. Gauge the length of the summary by the length of the report and by your organization's practices.

Introduction. Explain the problem motivating the report; describe its background and significance. Clarify the scope and limitations of the report. Optional items include a review of relevant literature and a description of data sources, methods, and key terms. Close by previewing the report's organization.

Body. Discuss, analyze, and interpret the research findings or the proposed solution to the problem. Arrange the findings in logical segments following your outline. Use clear, descriptive headings.

Conclusions and recommendations. Explain what the findings mean in relation to the original problem. If requested, make enumerated recommendations that suggest actions for solving the problem.

CASE STUDY

PROCESS TO PRODUCT

Applying Your Skills at Hewlett-Packard

In many ways proposals are similar to long reports. Both are written to solve a problem, and both require research. Assume that you are part of a group of interns being trained by Mary Piecewicz, proposal manager at Hewlett-Packard. She has developed two problems as part of your program. (1) In the first problem, Piecewicz asks your team to compare and contrast proposal components at HP with what you learned in your business communication class in college. (2) As a second problem, she asks you individually to profile a Fortune 500 company in preparation for an HP proposal to that company. Learn about its sales, major products, competitors, history, corporate strategies, corporate culture, and financial picture. Study recent news releases, relevant newspaper articles, and its annual report.

Your Job

Select one of the two problems previously described. (1) As a team, discuss similarities and differences in proposal components at Hewlett-Packard and component suggestions for letter proposals described in your textbook. Submit an individual or group memo to Mary Piecewicz summarizing your comparison. (2) To profile a Fortune 500 company of your choice, conduct research on the Web and in the library. What information would be necessary to enable Hewlett-Packard to develop a relationship with the targeted company? Submit an individual memo report.

 **Appendix.** Include items of interest to some, but not all, readers, such as a data questionnaire or computer printouts.

 **References and bibliography.** If footnotes are not provided in the text, list all references in a section called "Endnotes," "Works Cited," or "References." As an option, include a bibliography showing all the works cited (and perhaps all those consulted) arranged alphabetically.

Summary of Learning Objectives

1 **Discuss the components of informal proposals.** Most informal proposals contain (1) a persuasive introduction that explains the purpose of the proposal and qualifies the writer; (2) background material identifying the problem and project goals; (3) a proposal, plan, or schedule outlining the project; (4) a section describing staff qualifications; (5) a budget showing expected costs; and (6) a request for approval or authorization.

2 **Discuss the special components in formal proposals.** Beyond the six components generally contained in informal proposals, formal proposals may include these additional parts: (1) copy of the RFP (request for proposal), (2) letter of transmittal, (3) abstract or executive summary, (4) title page, (5) table of contents, (6) list of illustrations, and (7) appendix.

3 **Distinguish between proposals and formal reports.** Proposals offer to solve problems, provide services, or sell equipment. Formal reports present ordered information to decision makers in business, industry, government, and education.

4 **Identify formal report components that precede its introduction.** Formal reports may include these beginning components: (1) vinyl or heavy paper cover, (2) title page, (3) letter of transmittal, (4) table of contents, (5) list of illustrations, and (6) executive summary or abstract.

5 **Outline topics that might be covered in the introduction of a formal report.** The introduction to a formal report sets the scene by discussing some or all of the following topics: background material, problem or purpose, significance of the topic, scope and organization of the report, authorization, review of relevant literature, sources and methods, and definitions of key terms.

6 **Describe the components of a formal report that follow the introduction.** The body of a report discusses, analyzes, interprets, and evaluates the research findings or solution to a problem. The conclusion tells what the findings mean and how they relate to the report's purpose. The recommendations tell how to solve the report problem. The last portions of a formal report are the appendix, references, and bibliography.

7 **Specify tips that aid writers of formal reports.** Before writing, develop a realistic timetable and collect all necessary data. During the writing process, work from a good outline, work in a quiet place, and use a computer. Also, try to write rapidly, revising later. While writing, use verb tenses consistently, and avoid *I* and *we.* A few days after completing the first draft, revise to improve clarity, coherence, and conciseness. Proofread the final copy three times.

CHAPTER REVIEW

1. Proposals are written offers to do what? (Obj. 1)
2. What is an RFP? (Objs. 1 and 2)
3. What are the six principal parts of a letter proposal? (Obj. 1)
4. What is a "worry item" in a proposal? (Obj. 1)
5. Why should a proposal budget be prepared very carefully? (Obj. 1)
6. What is generally contained in a letter of transmittal accompanying a formal report? (Obj. 3)
7. What label can a report writer use to describe all illustrations and tables? (Obj. 4)
8. How is an abstract different from an executive summary? (Objs. 2 and 4)
9. What does *scope* mean in relation to a formal report? (Obj. 5)
10. Should the body of a report include the heading *Body*? (Obj. 6)
11. What are the advantages of functional headings? Of talking headings? (Obj. 6)
12. In a formal report where do most writers place the conclusions? (Obj. 6)
13. What materials go in an appendix? (Obj. 6)
14. What environment enhances writing? (Obj. 7)
15. How should a formal report be proofread? (Obj. 7)

CRITICAL THINKING

1. Why are proposals important to many businesses? (Obj. 1)
2. How do formal reports differ from informal reports? (Objs. 4–6)
3. Why do some parts of formal reports tend to be redundant? (Objs. 3 and 5)
4. Discuss the three phases of the writing process in relation to formal reports. What activities take place in each phase? (Objs. 3–7)
5. **Ethical Issue:** Is it ethical to have someone else proofread a report that you will be turning in for a grade?

ACTIVITIES

Consult your instructor to determine the length, format, and emphasis for the following report projects. Some require additional research; others do not.

14.1 Proposal: Outsourcing (Objs. 1–3)

Critical Thinking

Businesses today are doing more "outsourcing" than ever before. This means that they are going outside to find specialists to handle some aspect of their business, such as billing, shipping, or advertising. They're also hiring experts with special training and equipment to solve problems for which they lack the necessary talent and staff. For a business where you have worked or an organization you know, select a problem. Here are some possibilities: poor handling of customer orders, inefficient payroll practices, inadequate computer equipment or software, unsatisfactory inventory control, poor use of sales staff, bad scheduling of employees, poorly trained employees, sexual harassment on the job, Internet misuse, and poor telephone techniques. Assume the boss has asked you as a consultant to either solve the problem or study it and tell the organization what to do. Prepare an informal proposal describing your plan to solve the problem or perform a service. Decide how much you will charge and what staff you will need. Send your letter proposal to your boss.

14.2 Proposal: Profiting From Someone Else's Mistakes (Objs. 1–3)

"It's amazing," says the owner of one of the country's largest trucking companies. "Companies will require a vice president to sign a check for over $50, but the guy or girl in the back can sign for a half million dollars worth of raw material." Freight transportation experts claim that business owners may be losing millions of dollars a year in their shipping and receiving departments. Poorly trained and paid workers make costly blunders that anger customers and eat away at profits.

Your company, United Traffic Services (UTS), offers solutions, especially for businesses without a transportation specialist on the payroll. UTS audits freight bills and provides consulting services. Specifically, you and your staff of nine check all shipping charges (monthly or quarterly) to ensure that trucking companies are charging the correct rates. You also give advice on how to get the lowest shipping rates. You know that, because of competitiveness in the trucking industry, any company that is not getting at least a 50 percent discount is paying too much. You work with both outbound and inbound shipments. One of your services involves selecting a good carrier. Because of your expertise and research capabilities, you can advise any company about the most financially stable and reliable truckers. You also advise businesses about packing and labeling to avoid problems. You know that 98 percent of actual freight claims start at the point of origin because cartons are marked incorrectly.

In addition to auditing shipments, you file freight claims for your clients as well as fight wrongful claims against them. You have saved companies thousands of dollars. Two years ago, a Rancho Dominguez auto products manufacturer was hit by a claim from a trucking company. "In one fell swoop," said the director of operations, "UTS saved us $29,000. We would have owed twice that amount if we didn't have UTS on our side."

Your fee is one half of whatever you save clients on their shipping transactions. They pay nothing if you don't save them money. Write a letter proposal to Steve Hernandez, President, Club Enterprises, 468 Industry Avenue, Covina, CA 91764, proposing your services. Club Enterprises makes a security device for locking the steering column of a car. Club ships out 2 million pounds of products annually, and it receives 1.5 million pounds of raw materials—most of it by truck. President Hernandez has heard of your service and wants to learn more.[5]

14.3 Proposal: Strangers in a Strange Land (Objs. 1–3)

"Probably between $2 billion and $2.5 billion a year is lost from expatriate burnout and failed assignments," said an international personnel expert. Businesses suffer this loss when expatriate employees sent on foreign assignments fail to adjust and pack their bags to come home prematurely. As a result, many cross-cultural training programs are being offered by enterprising consultants. American businesses "are dumb if they don't use cross-cultural training," observed the personnel vice president for overseas branches of Reynolds Metals Company. The expatriate burnout rate for his company dropped to almost zero after it began using cross-cultural training programs.

Global Visions, a consulting firm in Boulder, Colorado, offers a number of training programs for employees being sent to other countries. Global provides previsit orientations, career path counseling, foreign language training, and family cultural immersion programs. Mimi Sams, senior partner in Global Visions, has recently learned that General Motors plans to open a vehicle assembly plant in Kenya. Although the Kenyan government will own 51 percent of the plant and will supply most of the labor force, the plant will be run by GM managers and engineers. Anticipating the need for training the transported staff, Mimi talks to the director of international personnel at GM. He recognizes the benefits of training and would like to consider Global Visions, but he wants a brief written proposal describing the program.

As assistant to Mimi Sams, you have been asked to compose a two-page letter proposal to GM for her approval. Describe your African Total Immersion cross-cultural program. This crash course, conducted at your headquarters in Boulder, includes three full days of intensive training for the employee's entire family. It totally immerses the family, with both group and individual sessions, in African political history, business practices, social customs, and nonverbal communication. The training helps the entire family grasp cultural differences and anticipate culture-shock symptoms such as depression and self-pity.

Because the family's reaction causes more foreign-transfer failure than a manager's work performance, Global Visions focuses on family adjustment. Children and teenagers receive separate training from that of their parents. They sample Indian food, popular in Kenya, and learn how to ride Nairobi public buses and how to speak a little Swahili.

The staff for your African Total Immersion program includes senior trainer Jackson Fox, who was a Peace Corps official in Nigeria for twelve years, responsible for training thousands of new recruits. In addition, you have Idi Midamba, adjunct professor of international relations at Kent State University and son of a Kenyan political leader. Rounding out the staff of African specialists is Innawati Witowalidi, a Kenyan who received an M.S. degree in psychology from the University of Illinois. She specializes in the psychological phases of the process of adjustment. This staff has conducted many successful training sessions for U.S. managers and their families heading for Africa. As part of the program, a former expatriate to Kenya shares his experiences with participants.

Global Visions will tailor a three-day program expressly for the GM managers being sent to Kenya. The sum of $8,000 covers training for four individuals, with $500 for each additional person. The maximum number of trainees for any program is ten. This price includes meals for three days and two nights of lodging at the Grand Peaks Hilton. It also includes a guide book to African social and business customs, along with a Swahili primer. For Mimi Sams's signature write a proposal to Jim Rymers, Director, International Programs, General Motors, Inc., 311 Livonia Place, Bloomfield Hills, MI 48224.[6]

14.4 Proposal: Don't Give Up Your Day Job (Objs. 1–3)

Critical Thinking

As a struggling student, single parent, or budding entrepreneur, you decide to start your own part-time word processing business in your home. Select a company or professional in your city that might need your services. Often, businesses, medical centers, attorneys, and other professionals have overload transcribing or word processing to farm out to a service. Assess your expertise and equipment. Check out the competition. What do other word processing services offer, and what do they charge? Although many apply a flat hourly rate, you may decide to charge more for items that require heavy editing. Find out what a particular company needs. Prepare a letter proposal addressed to a specific individual outlining your plan to offer your services.

14.5 Proposal: Surf's Up in Kansas! (Objs. 1–3)

Amusement parks around the country are constantly searching for sensational new rides to draw crowds. Theme park giants like the Walt Disney Company employ their own staffs to develop hot new rides, but smaller parks can't afford such research. Yet, they need fresh entertainment to attract new thrill-seekers and keep old customers coming back. "The general theory is that you must add a major new ride every two years and a minor one in between," claims one amusement park expert.

Wave Madness, a one-man San Diego company, designs and installs water-related amusement rides. An enormous success for the young company has been Flow Rider, a surfing machine that shoots water against a curved wall creating a wave effect for riders to "surf" down on their stomachs or on boards. At the Schlitterbahn Family Water Park in New Braunsfels, Texas, attendance rose 24 percent, to about 650,000 people, after Flow Rider was installed.

Wave Madness has been approached by the owners of Wichita Fun Park. For next year's summer season, they want a new water ride, similar to the Flow Rider or Waimea Wave, which is popular at the Raging Waters park in Salt Lake City. But they have a limited budget as well as space and energy restrictions. Although water is scarce, they feel that a scaled-down version of Flow Rider or Waimea Wave might be possible. Michael Larson, owner and sole proprietor of Wave Madness, is definitely interested in working with the Wichita people, but he's afraid that he would scare them off if he quoted a price for one of his rides outright. Therefore, he decides to submit a proposal outlining his services as a consultant. At $200 an hour he would be able to talk with them about what they need and how best it can be achieved. If they decide to install one of his rides, his consultation fees would be waived.

In his proposal Larson wants to describe one of his new rides: Master Blaster, a roller coaster using a high-powered stream of water to carry people along. The feeling of being pushed uphill is eerie and exciting, according to users at another park. This new ride is less expensive to install and operate than Flow Rider. On the other hand, he could possibly scale down Flow Rider, which is very popular because of its speed. The surfer moves at only two or three miles an hour down the face of the wall. But the water races past at 20 miles an hour, twice as fast as an ocean wave.

Because the Wichita Fun Park owners want action quickly, Larson develops a tentative schedule. Conferring with the owners would probably take about two days; examining the site and working out the placement of a ride would take about one week; installation of a new ride usually requires thirty working days, weather permitting; testing and adjusting the ride requires two weeks.

Michael Larson comes to you, a writing specialist, to help him with his proposal. His background includes a degree as an attorney and experience as a surfer and real estate developer. When he focused his attention on developing water rides, he obtained technical help at Scripps Institution of Oceanography, a research facility in La Jolla, California. His greatest success thus far has been Flow Rider. He designs and tests every ride himself, never leaving a project until it is installed and working successfully.

Work out a schedule that ensures the ride would be ready for the park's opening May 1. For Michael Larson's signature prepare a proposal addressed to Mr. William Langford, Wichita Entertainment, Inc., 3440 Goddard Avenue, Wichita, KS 67532.[7]

14.6 Research Report: Comparing Car Insurance Carriers (Objs. 4–7)

Web

Costs for car insurance and levels of customer satisfaction vary greatly from one company to another. One of your tasks as a research analyst for Consumers Union is tracking insurance data for state automobile associations. From the most current *Consumer Reports* magazine article on auto insurance, select five representative or well-known insurance carriers that operate within your state. Assume that James Michelin, director of your state automobile association, has asked you to report on these five companies. He's interested in the degree of customer satisfaction, claims problems, nonclaims problems, delayed payments, drop rates, and annual premiums.

To investigate and compare premiums, use the figures provided by *Consumer Reports* at its Web site **<http://www.consumerreports.org/Functions/More/Prodserv/autoins.html>**. If the site has changed addresses go to the *Consumer Reports* home page **<www.consumerreports.org>** and follow the prompts to auto insurance. Compare rates for five carriers and draw conclusions. Make recommendations to Mr. Michelin, who will be distributing your information to members of the automobile association. Address your report to James Michelin, Director, State Automobile Association in the capital of your state.

14.7 Research Report: Work Teams (Objs. 4–7)

Web

Research shows that 60 percent of Fortune 500 firms either have implemented or are experimenting with different types of employee involvement programs, such as work teams, quality circles, and workplace democracy councils. In large and small firms these programs are thought to reap many benefits—from increasing production to boosting morale. Mike Rivera, vice president of operations at DataTech, which employs about 80 electronics assemblers and 30 supporting employees, wants to learn more about these programs. He asks you, his executive assistant, to prepare a report that investigates how other companies have used them. He's particularly interested in safety applications. Could quality circles or work teams improve DataTech's safety record? How are such programs operated at other companies? Collect secondary data including research on the Web. Start by using the search terms "work teams" and "quality circles." Analyze your findings, draw conclusions, and make recommendations in a letter report to Mike Rivera.

14.8 Formal Report: Breaking Through the Glass Ceiling (Objs. 4–7)

Only 3 to 5 percent of all senior executives in corporate America are women. Some observers suggest that a glass ceiling prevents women from breaking through into upper management. You have been asked by the American Management Association to investigate the success of efforts made in the past decade to train and promote female executives. Does a glass ceiling exist? Discuss some of the programs involving mentoring, coaching, women's councils, and management incentives. Develop recommendations directed toward female college students majoring in business or management. Suggest how they can improve their chances for moving up the career ladder when they enter the work world. Address your report to Barbara M. Loring, Chair, Women's Advisory Council, AMA.[8]

14.9 Formal Report: Entrepreneurial Women (Objs. 4–7)

By the year 2005, 40 to 50 percent of all businesses will be owned by women. As an intern at the American

Association of Women in Business, you have been asked to collect information for a booklet to be distributed to women who inquire about starting businesses. Specifically, you have been asked to find articles describing three or four women who have started their own businesses. Examine why they started their businesses, how they did it, and how successful they were. In your report draw conclusions about what kinds of women start businesses, why they do it, what kinds of businesses they are likely to start, and what difficulties they face. Speculate on the dramatic increase in the number of female business owners. Make recommendations to women about starting businesses. You may wish to consult the Small Business Administration's Office of Women's Business Ownership, the National Association of Women Business Owners, and the American Women's Economic Development Corporation. Address your report to Rochelle Robinson, Director, American Association of Women in Business.

14.10 Formal Report: Lending a Helping Hand to the ASO (Objs. 4–7)

Team

Volunteer your class to conduct research aimed at a specific problem facing your campus associated students organization. Ask the president of your campus ASO to visit your class to discuss a problem that requires research. Most ASOs want to learn what students think about their activities, projects, and use of resources. However, ASOs generally lack the expertise and staff needed to gather reliable data. Question the ASO president to isolate the issues to be investigated. For example, the ASO may want students to prioritize activities deserving support. With a limited budget, what activities should the ASO fund: concerts, lectures, intramural sports, movies, a country store, or something else? Other questions may face the leadership: Should the ASO undertake a recycling center? Should it sponsor an adult literacy volunteer program? How should these programs be implemented?

Once a problem for investigation has been selected, divide into groups of three to five to develop a survey questionnaire. Evaluate each group's questionnaire in class, and select the best one. Pilot test the questionnaire. Administer the revised questionnaire to a targeted student group. Tabulate the findings. In teams of three to five or individually, write a report to the ASO president discussing your findings, conclusions, and recommendations.

14.11 Formal Report: Fast-Food Checkup (Objs. 4–7)

Select a fast-food franchise in your area. Assume that the national franchising headquarters has received complaints about the service, quality, and cleanliness of the unit. You have been sent to inspect and to report on what you see. Visit on two or more occasions. Make notes on how many customers were served, how quickly they received their food, and how courteously they were treated. Observe the number of employees and supervisors working. Note the cleanliness of observable parts of the restaurant. Inspect the restroom as well as the exterior and surrounding grounds. Sample the food. Your boss is a stickler for details; he has no use for general statements like *The restroom was not clean.* Be specific. Draw conclusions. Are the complaints justified? If improvements are necessary, make recommendations. Address your report to Lawrence C. Kelsey, President.

14.12 Formal Report: Readability of Insurance Policies (Objs. 4–7)

The 21st Century Insurance Company is concerned about the readability of its policies. State legislators are beginning to investigate complaints of policyholders who say they can't understand their insurance policies. One judge lambasted insurers saying, "The language in these policies is bureaucratic gobbledegook, jargon, double-talk, a form of officialese, federalese, and insurancese that does not qualify as English. The burden upon organizations is to write policies in a manner designed to communicate rather than to obfuscate." Taking the initiative in improving its policies, 21st Century hires you as a consultant to study its standard policy and make recommendations.

Examine a life, fire, or health insurance policy that you own or one from a friend or relative. Select one that is fairly complex. Determine its readability level by calculating its Fog Index (Chapter 6) for several selections. Study the policy for jargon, confusing language, long sentences, and unclear antecedents. Evaluate its format, print size, paper and print quality, amount of white space, and use of headings. Does it have an index or glossary? Are difficult terms defined? How easy is it to find specifics, should a policyholder want to check something?

In addition to the data you collect from your own examination of the policy, 21st Century gives you the data shown in Figure 14.5 from a recent policyholder survey. Prepare a report for Heather Garcia, Vice President, 21st Century Insurance Company, discussing your analysis, conclusions, and recommendations for improving its basic policy.

14.13 Formal Report: Doing Your Own Thing (Objs. 4–7)

In a business, organization, or field you know, think about a problem or issue that needs to be investigated. Assume that a president, owner, supervisor, or executive asks you to examine the problem or issue and analyze its causes and ramifications. Consider ways to solve the problem or define the issue. Draw conclusions based on your analysis. Make

FIGURE 14.5 21st Century Insurance Company Policyholder Survey

RESPONSE TO STATEMENT "I AM ABLE TO READ AND UNDERSTAND THE LANGUAGE AND PROVISIONS OF MY POLICY."

Age Group	Strongly Agree	Agree	Undecided	Disagree	Strongly Disagree
18–34	2%	9%	34%	41%	14%
35–49	2	17	38	33	10
50–64	1	11	22	35	31
65+	1	2	17	47	33

specific recommendations for implementing changes necessary to achieve the solution. You may need to design a questionnaire and circulate it. Be sure to narrow the problem sufficiently so that it can be broken into three to five segments or factors.

14.14 Formal Report: Intercultural Communication (Objs. 4–7)

Team

American businesses are expanding into foreign markets with manufacturing plants, sales offices, and branch offices abroad. Unfortunately, most Americans have little knowledge of or experience with people from other cultures. To prepare for participation in the global marketplace, collect information for a report focused on a Pacific Rim, Latin American, or European country where English is not regularly spoken. Before selecting the country, though, consult your campus international student program for volunteers who are willing to be interviewed. Your instructor may make advance arrangements seeking international student volunteers.

In teams of three to five, collect information about your target country from the library and other sources. Then invite an international student representing your target country to be interviewed by your group. In your primary and secondary research, investigate the topics listed in Figure 14.6. Confirm what you learn in your secondary research by talking with your interviewee. When you complete your research, write a report for the CEO of your company (make up a name and company). Assume that your company plans to expand its operations abroad. Your report should advise the company's executives of social customs, family life, attitudes, religions, education, and values in the target country. Remember that your company's interests are business-oriented; don't dwell on tourist information. Write your report individually or in teams.[9]

14.15 Formal Reports Requiring Secondary Research (Objs. 4–7)

Select one of the following topics for a report. Discuss with your instructor its purpose, scope, length, format, audience, and data sources. For each topic analyze your findings, draw conclusions, and make logical recommendations. Your instructor may ask teams to complete the secondary research.

a. How does the compensation of American executives compare with that of Japanese executives?

b. How are corporations managing employee drug and alcohol abuse?

c. Are corporate fitness programs worth their costs?

d. Has the image of women in advertisements today changed from that shown fifteen years ago?

e. How are businesses dealing with computer fraud and malice?

f. Should McDonald's expand its company-owned and franchise restaurants in Latin America and Asia?

g. Should you invest in an event-planning franchise that specializes in children's parties?

h. What is the best way for you to invest $100,000?

FIGURE 14.6 Intercultural Interview Topics and Questions

Social Customs

1. How do people react to strangers? Friendly? Hostile? Reserved?
2. How do people greet each other?
3. What are the appropriate manners when you enter a room? Bow? Nod? Shake hands with everyone?
4. How are names used for introductions? Is it appropriate to inquire about one's occupation or family?
5. What are the attitudes toward touching?
6. How does one express appreciation for an invitation to another's home? Bring a gift? Send flowers? Write a thank-you note? Are any gifts taboo?
7. Are there any customs related to how or when one sits?
8. Are any facial expressions or gestures considered rude?
9. How close do people stand when talking?
10. What is the attitude toward punctuality in social situations? In business situations?
11. What are acceptable eye contact patterns?
12. What gestures indicate agreement? Disagreement?

Family Life

1. What is the basic unit of social organization? Basic family? Extended family?
2. Do women work outside of the home? In what occupations?

Housing, Clothing, and Food

1. Are there differences in the kind of housing used by different social groups? Differences in location? Differences in furnishings?
2. What occasions require special clothing?
3. Are some types of clothing considered taboo?
4. What is appropriate business attire for men? For women?
5. How many times a day do people eat?
6. What types of places, food, and drink are appropriate for business entertainment? Where is the seat of honor at a table?

Class Structure

1. Into what classes is society organized?
2. Do racial, religious, or economic factors determine social status?
3. Are there any minority groups? What is their social standing?

Political Patterns

1. Are there any immediate threats to the political survival of the country?
2. How is political power manifested?
3. What channels are used for expression of popular opinion?
4. What information media are important?
5. Is it appropriate to talk politics in social situations?

Religion and Folk Beliefs

1. To which religious groups do people belong? Is one predominant?
2. Do religious beliefs influence daily activities?
3. Which places have sacred value? Which opjects? Which events?
4. How do religious holidays affect business activities?

Economic Institutions

1. What are the country's principal products?
2. Are workers organized in unions?
3. How are businesses owned? By family units? By large public corporations? By the government?
4. What is the standard work schedule?
5. Is it appropriate to do business by telephone?
6. Is participatory management used?
7. Are there any customs related to exchanging business cards?
8. How is status shown in an organization? Private office? Secretary? Furniture?
9. Are businesspersons expected to socialize before conducting business?

Value Systems

1. Is competitiveness or cooperation more prized?
2. Is thrift or enjoyment of the moment more valued?
3. Is politeness more important than factual honesty?
4. What are the attitudes toward education?
5. Do women own or manage businesses? If so, how are they treated?
6. What are your people's preceptions of Americans? Do Americans offend you? What has been hardest for you to adjust to in America? How could Americans make this adjustment easier for you?

i. Should environmentalists engage in junk-mail promotions to advertise their causes?

j. Of three locations, which is the best for a new McDonald's (or Dairy Queen, Subway, or franchise of your choice)?

k. What magazines represent the best advertising choice for Reebok (or a product with which you are familiar)?

l. What effects do aromas have on the senses, and how can aromas be used to advantage in the workplace?

14.16 Formal Reports Requiring Primary Research (Objs. 4–7)

Select one of the following topics for a report. Discuss with your instructor its purpose, scope, length, format, audience, and data sources. For each topic analyze your findings, draw conclusions, and make logical recommendations. Your instructor may ask teams to complete the primary research.

a. How can your community improve its image and attract new businesses?

b. How can your community improve its recycling efforts?

c. Does your campus need to add or improve a student computer lab?

d. How can the associated student organization (or a club of your choice) increase its membership and support on this campus?

e. Can the registration process at your college or university be improved?

f. Are the requirements for a degree in your major realistic and relevant?

g. How can drug and alcohol abuse be reduced in your community?

h. What is a significant student problem on your campus, and how can it be solved?

i. What does an analysis of local and national newspapers reveal about employment possibilities for college graduates?

j. What demographic characteristics (age, sex, income, major, socioeconomic status, family, employment, interests, and so forth) does the typical student have on your campus?

14.17 Formal Report: The Perfect Résumé (Objs. 4–7)

What do personnel administrators and recruiters really want to see in the résumés of job applicants? Assume that the American Association of Personnel Administrators conducts continuing research to answer that very question. Each year this organization samples its members regarding résumé preferences. Some of the data collected for 1989, 1994, and 1998 are shown in Figure 14.7. The AAPA uses a stratified random sample ensuring that an appropriate number of personnel administrators from small, medium, and large businesses are included (small businesses employ fewer than 100 people; medium, 100–999; and large, 1,000 plus). Each year 500 questionnaires are sent; this year 378 usable questionnaires were returned, and this figure is similar to that received in previous surveys.

As a research assistant for the AAPA, analyze the data and prepare a report to be submitted to your boss, Dr. Nancy M. Taylor. Eventually, the report will be distributed to AAPA members, college placement offices, and the news media. The AAPA résumé report has become a popular tool among colleges, who use it to keep their students informed of current résumé practices. Your boss expects you to interpret the findings and speculate about why personnel administrators have responded as they have. Dr. Taylor may add her ideas to the report later, but she wants your analysis first. In addition to the data for 1989, 1994, and 1998, the most recent survey (1998) posed two new questions, shown in Figures 14.8 and 14.9 on page 456. These questions dealt with correctness and length of résumés as well as the average time each personnel administrator spends reading a résumé.

Draw conclusions and make recommendations for job applicants. Define any terms that college students, a primary audience for the report, may not understand. Write a memo report to Dr. Nancy M. Taylor, director of research.

FIGURE 14.7 AAPA Survey on the Importance of Résumé Items and Formats

	Percentage of respondents who considered résumé items important		
Résumé Item	**1989**	**1994**	**1998**
Name, address, telephone number	100%	100%	100%
Degree	100	100	100
Name of college	100	100	100
Titles of jobs held	99	99	100
Names of previous employers	98	97	100
Special aptitudes, skills	90	91	95
Job, career objective	73	84	92
Awards, scholarships, honors, achievements	88	89	91
Grade point average	85	89	91
Willingness to relocate	74	82	90
Work experience achievements (learning, contributions, accomplishments)	72	81	89
Professional organizations	67	74	84
College activities	85	83	84
References shown on résumé	79	51	32
Note saying that references would be supplied on request	35	21	20
Summary of qualifications	25	42	72
Reasons for leaving jobs	54	37	29
Name of high school	20	14	4
High school grades	18	15	5
High school activities, awards	19	14	5
List of college courses completed	42	34	21
Social security number	32	35	18
Religion, race	10	5	1
Photograph	16	11	2
Marital status	30	19	2
Height/weight	25	11	1
Church involvement	13	8	0
Birthdate	21	17	3
Health	34	19	6
Résumé Format			
Preference for traditional, chronological format	78	81	88
Preference for functional, skills-oriented format	22	19	12

FIGURE 14.8 AAPA Survey on Résumé Correctness and Length

RESPONSE TO STATEMENT "THE FOLLOWING FACTOR WOULD CAUSE ME TO LOSE INTEREST IN A CANDIDATE."

Factor	Strongly Agree	Agree	Neutral	Disagree	Strongly Disagree	Not sure
Poor grammar	63%	34%	1%	1%	0%	1%
More than one spelling error	51	42	4	2	0	1
Incorrect word choice	15	51	26	6	0	2
One spelling error	13	37	31	18	1	0
Use of abbreviations	4	18	49	22	4	3
More than one typing error	39	44	10	6	0	1
Poorly reproduced	21	44	25	7	1	2
Poor margins	7	30	42	13	4	4
One typing error	11	27	41	18	2	1
Poor organization	26	52	18	2	1	1
Too long	23	33	30	11	1	2
Too condensed	11	35	35	13	1	5

FIGURE 14.9 AAPA Survey on Average Reading Time Per Résumé

Time in Seconds	Percentage of Recruiters
1–29	1%
30–60	26
61–90	15
91–120	16
121–180	28
181+	11
No response	3

14.18 Formal Report: Writing Skills for CPAs (Objs. 4–7)

For years practitioners from all types and sizes of accounting firms have complained about the weak communication skills of those entering the profession. Assume that the American Association of Certified Public Accountants conducted a study investigating the communication skills of new accountants. In a survey questionnaire distributed to managing partners of 150 of the largest accounting firms in the United States, 97 partners responded. Some of the results from the study are shown in Figure 14.10.

As a research analyst for the AACPA, interpret the findings and make recommendations to the association. Two issues are particularly important to the AACPA, although these issues were not addressed directly in the survey. The first issue concerns the essay portion of the CPA examination. The exam currently contains essay questions covering auditing theory and business laws, as well as accounting problems for which narrative solutions must be written. Critics want to eliminate all essay questions, contending that the exam is too long, too expensive to administer, and too subjective. A second issue concerns recommendations for colleges offering accounting education. Should the AACPA recommend accounting curricula to colleges and universities that include more or fewer communication courses? In your analysis consider the profession as a whole in addition to the two issues presented here. Address your report to Richard M. Tarsky, Executive Director, American Association of Certified Public Accountants.

FIGURE 14.10 Survey Results of American Association of CPAs

1. How important are the following communication tasks and skills for "new" accountants?

	Very Important	Somewhat Important	Somewhat Unimportant	Totally Unimportant	Don't Know; No Response
Written Communication					
Audit reports	11%	18%	34%	12%	25%
Articles for publication	9	10	43	21	17
Memos, e-mail	31	48	11	4	6
Reports	42	38	10	3	7
Letters	28	31	25	6	10
Proposals	16	23	42	13	6
Oral Communication					
Meeting, conference skills	45	33	13	4	5
Interviewing	38	35	16	7	4
Presentations	24	38	21	11	6
Formal speechmaking	7	14	49	23	7

2. Evaluate the level of communication ability of the "new" accountants who have joined your firm.

	Inadequate	Satisfactory	Very Satisfactory	Excellent	Don't Know; No Response
Written Communication					
Reports	79%	10%			11%
Memos, e-mail	55	31	5%		9
Letters	53	39			8
Proposals	81	7			12
Audit reports	71	18			11
Articles for publication	86	2	2		10
Oral Communication					
Speeches	52	31	5		12
Presentations	39	45	7		9
Meetings/conferences	47	39	5		9
Client interviews	58	34			8

3. Indicate your agreement with the following statement:

	Agree	Disagree	No Opinion
The primary mission of accounting education should be			
a. preparation for the CPA examination	14%	80%	6%
b. development of well-rounded individuals	91	4	5

4. If you could design a college course or program to develop communication skills, what would it contain?

Representative answers: "More emphasis on writing skills," "extensive case studies requiring brief, concise explanations," "require considerably more nontechnical classes to prepare the accountant for his environment as part of the graduation requirement for a 5-year curriculum," "courses to develop written and oral communication skills in college and continued in training sessions by employers in workshop fashion," "more required written reports in schools to be graded skillfully and critically by competent teachers." The overall emphasis was on "more communication course work."

UNIT •5•

Presentations

CHAPTER • 15 •

Speaking Skills

LEARNING OBJECTIVES

1 Discuss two important first steps in preparing an effective oral presentation.

2 Explain the major elements in the introduction, body, and conclusion of an oral presentation and discuss the importance of verbal signposts.

3 Identify appropriate visual aids and handouts for a presentation.

4 Review techniques for designing an electronic presentation.

5 Specify delivery techniques for use before, during, and after a presentation.

6 Discuss effective techniques for adapting oral presentations to cross-cultural audiences.

7 List techniques for improving telephone and voice-mail effectiveness.

CASE STUDY

COMMUNICATION IN PROCESS

Walt Disney Imagineering Sells Tokyo Disneyland on Winnie the Pooh

Tokyo Disneyland, the largest amusement park in Japan, draws nearly as many visitors each year as the Magic Kingdom here in the United States.[1] But like all theme parks, the Tokyo park understood the need to offer fresh attractions and exciting new rides to keep the crowds coming back year after year. In its search for dynamic new ideas to expand its already popular park, Tokyo Disneyland turned to Walt Disney Imagineering.

Generating and implementing new ideas for the Disney theme parks are tasks of Walt Disney Imagineering, the research, design, and engineering subsidiary of Walt Disney Attractions. Although Tokyo Disneyland is a Disney theme park and Disney retains creative control of the park, the park is actually owned and operated by the Oriental Land Company. This company makes all financial and investment decisions. While creative concepts come from Disney Imagineering teams, those ideas are not automatically accepted by theme park owners. Imagineering teams not only had to dream up exciting new concepts for the Tokyo park, but they also had to *sell* the ideas and win the approval of Japanese owners. Millions of dollars in contracts and hundreds of jobs in the United States and in Japan rested on successful presentations to the owners of Tokyo Disneyland.

Jon Georges, lead show producer for the Tokyo Disneyland Project, was part of a talented Imagineering team that came up with a totally new attraction and restaurant concept for the Disney theme park. Based on Winnie the Pooh and Alice in Wonderland characters, the creative project involved two phases. The first was a theme restaurant called the "Queen of Hearts Banquet Hall." The second was a major ride attraction based on Winnie the Pooh characters. Both concepts required considerable persuasion to win approval.

Traditionally, the Japanese park owners had accepted only attractions that had proved technically successful in other theme parks. Naturally, they were reluctant to try a restaurant concept and a ride technology that were both brand new. Selling the Japanese on the new concepts required exceptional oral presentations from Jon Georges and the Imagineering team.[2]

Preparing an Effective Oral Presentation

At some point everyone in business has to sell an idea, and such persuasion is often done in person. Like most of us, Jon Georges at Walt Disney Imagineering does not consider himself a professional speaker. He admits that he once was so afraid of public speaking that he started a couple of speech courses as part of his degree program at UCLA but always dropped out. Finally, he took a night class in speaking and began to get over his fears.

1

Many businesspeople must make presentations as part of their careers.

Many future businesspeople fail to take advantage of opportunities in college to develop speaking skills. Yet, such skills often play an important role in a successful career. You might, for example, need to describe your company's expansion plans to your banker, or you might need to persuade management to support your proposed marketing strategy. You might have to make a sales pitch before customers or speak to a professional gathering. This chapter develops speaking skills in making oral presentations and in using the telephone and voice mail to advantage.

Spotlight on **Communicators**

"Before every formal presentation, I suffer butterflies," confesses Jon Georges, lead show producer, Walt Disney Imagineering. But after taking courses and getting some experience, he reports that he is able to channel his surging adrenalin into an increased level of excitement. "It's no longer fear. I look on it as enthusiasm, and it actually helps me perform better."

For any presentation, you can reduce your fears and lay the foundation for a professional performance by focusing on four areas: preparation, organization, visual aids, and delivery.

Knowing Your Purpose

The most important part of your preparation is deciding what you want to accomplish. Do you want to sell a health care program to a prospective client? Do you want to persuade management to increase the marketing budget? Do you want to inform customer service reps of three important ways to prevent miscommunication? Whether your goal is to persuade or to inform, you must have a clear idea of where you are going. At the end of your presentation, what do you want your listeners to remember or do?

Eric Evans, a loan officer at First Fidelity Trust, faced such questions as he planned a talk for a class in small business management. Eric's former business professor had asked him to return to campus and give the class advice about borrowing money from banks in order to start new businesses. Because Eric knew so much about this topic, he found it difficult to extract a specific purpose statement for his presentation. After much thought he narrowed his purpose to this: *To inform potential entrepreneurs about three important factors that loan officers consider before granting start-up loans to launch small businesses.* His entire presentation focused on ensuring that the class members understood and remembered three principal ideas.

Knowing Your Audience

A second key element in preparation is analyzing your audience, anticipating its reactions, and making appropriate adaptations. Many factors influence a presentation. A large audience, for example, usually requires a more formal and less personalized approach. Other elements, such as age, gender, education, experience, and attitude toward the subject, will also affect your style and message content. Analyze these factors to determine your strategy, vocabulary, illustrations, and level of detail. Here are specific questions to consider:

Audience analysis issues include number of people, age, gender, experience, attitude, and expectations.

- *How will this topic appeal to this audience?*
- *How can I relate this information to their needs?*
- *How can I earn respect so that they accept my message?*
- *Which of the following would be most effective in making my point? Statistics? Graphic illustrations? Demonstrations? Case histories? Analogies? Cost figures?*
- *What measures must I take to ensure that this audience remembers my main points?*

Organizing the Content

2

Once you have determined your purpose and analyzed the audience, you're ready to collect information and organize it logically. Good organization and conscious repetition are the two most powerful keys to audience comprehension and retention. In fact, many speech experts recommend the following admittedly repetitious, but effective, plan:

- **Step 1:** Tell them what you're going to say.
- **Step 2:** Say it.
- **Step 3:** Tell them what you've just said.

In other words, repeat your main points in the introduction, body, and conclusion of your presentation. Although it sounds deadly, this strategy works surprisingly well. Let's examine how to construct the three parts of a presentation and add appropriate verbal signposts to ensure that listeners understand and remember.

Introduction

The opening of your presentation should strive to accomplish three specific goals:

- Capture listeners' attention and get them involved.
- Identify yourself and establish your credibility.
- Preview your main points.

If you're able to appeal to listeners and involve them in your presentation right from the start, you're more likely to hold their attention until the finish. Consider some of the same techniques that you used to open sales letters: a question, a startling fact, a joke, a story, or a quotation. Some speakers achieve involvement by opening with a question or command that requires audience members to raise their hands or stand up. Additional techniques to gain and keep audience attention are presented in the accompanying Career Coach box.

To establish your credibility, you need to describe your position, knowledge, or experience—whatever qualifies you to speak. Try also to connect with your audience. Listeners are particularly drawn to speakers who reveal something of themselves and identify with them. A consultant addressing office workers might reminisce about how she started as a clerk-typist; a CEO might tell a funny story in which the joke is on himself.

After capturing attention and establishing yourself, you'll want to preview the main points of your topic, perhaps with a visual aid. You may wish to put off actually writing your introduction, however, until after you have organized the rest of the presentation and crystallized your principal ideas.

Take a look at Eric Evans' introduction, shown in Figure 15.1, to see how he integrated all the elements necessary for a good opening.

Spotlight on **Communicators**

"Know your audience" is advice frequently given by Les Brown, former Ohio legislator and now a motivational speaker for Fortune 500 companies. Before he addresses a company he reads trade magazines and questions owners and employees to learn what they expect from each other. This "holistic" approach to addressing a group of people enables him to speak their language and relate to their issues.

The best oral presentations focus on a few key ideas.

Body

The biggest problem with most oral presentations is a failure to focus on a few principal ideas. Thus, the body of your short presentation (20 or fewer minutes) should include a limited number of main points, say, two to four. Develop each main point with adequate, but not excessive, explanation and details. Too many details can obscure the main message, so keep your presentation simple and logical. Remember, listeners have no pages to leaf back through should they become confused.

When Eric Evans began planning his presentation, he realized immediately that he could talk for hours on his topic. He also knew that listeners are not good at separating major and minor points. Thus, instead of submerging his listeners in a sea of information, he sorted out a few principal ideas. In the mortgage business, loan officers generally ask the following three questions of each applicant for a small business loan: (1) Are you ready to "hit the ground running" in starting your business? (2) Have you done your homework? and (3) Have you made realistic projections of potential sales, cash flow, and equity investment? These questions would become his main points, but Eric wanted to streamline them further so that his audience would be sure to remember them. He capsulized the questions in three words: *experience, preparation,* and *projection.* As you can see in Figure 15.1, Eric prepared a sentence outline showing these three main ideas. Each is supported by examples and explanations.

CAREER COACH

NINE TECHNIQUES FOR GAINING AND KEEPING AUDIENCE ATTENTION

Experienced speakers know how to capture the attention of an audience and how to maintain that attention during a presentation. Here are eight proven techniques.

- **A promise.** Begin with a promise that keeps the audience expectant (for example, "By the end of this presentation I will show you how you can increase your sales by 50 percent").
- **Drama.** Open by telling an emotionally moving story or by describing a serious problem that involves the audience. Throughout your talk include other dramatic elements, such as a long pause after a key statement. Change your vocal tone or pitch. Professionals use high-intensity emotions such as anger, joy, sadness, and excitement.
- **Eye contact.** As you begin, command attention by surveying the entire audience to take in all listeners. Take two to five seconds to make eye contact with as many people as possible.
- **Movement.** Leave the lectern area whenever possible. Walk around the conference table or between the aisles of your audience. Try to move toward your audience, especially at the beginning and end of your talk.
- **Questions.** Keep listeners active and involved with rhetorical questions. Ask for a show of hands to get each listener thinking. The response will also give you a quick gauge of audience attention.
- **Demonstrations.** Include a member of the audience in a demonstration (for example, "I'm going to show you exactly how to implement our four-step customer courtesy process, but I need a volunteer from the audience to help me").
- **Samples/gimmicks.** If you're promoting a product, consider using items to toss out to the audience or to award as prizes to volunteer participants. You can also pass around product samples or promotional literature. Be careful, though, to maintain control.
- **Visuals.** Give your audience something to look at besides yourself. Use a variety of visual aids in a single session. Also consider writing the concerns expressed by your listeners on a flipchart or on the board as you go along.
- **Self-interest.** Review your entire presentation to ensure that it meets the critical "What's-in-it-for-me?" audience test. Remember that people are most interested in things that benefit them.

Career Track Application

Watch a lecture series speaker on campus, a department store sales presentation, a TV "infomercial," or some other speaker. Note and analyze specific techniques used to engage and maintain the listener's attention. Which techniques would be most effective in a classroom presentation? Before your boss or work group?

Main ideas can be organized according to time, component, importance, criteria, or conventional groupings.

How to organize and sequence main ideas may not be immediately obvious when you begin working on a presentation. Let's review the five organizational methods employed for written reports in Chapter 12, because those methods are equally appropriate for oral presentations. You could structure your ideas by the following elements:

- **Time.** Example: A presentation describing the history of a problem, organized from the first sign of trouble to the present.
- **Component.** Example: A sales report organized by divisions or products.
- **Importance.** Example: A report describing operating problems arranged from the most important to the least.
- **Criteria.** Example: A presentation evaluating equipment by comparing each model against a set of specifications.
- **Conventional groupings.** Example: A report comparing asset size, fees charged, and yields of mutual funds arranged by these existing categories.

FIGURE 15.1 Oral Presentation Outline

Analyze: The purpose of this report is to inform listeners of three critical elements in securing business loans.

Anticipate: The audience members are aspiring businesspeople who are probably unfamiliar with loan operations.

Adapt: Because the audience will be receptive but uninformed, explain terms and provide examples. Repeat the main ideas to ensure comprehension.

Research: Analyze previous loan applications; interview other loan officers. Gather critical data.

Organize: Group the data into three major categories. Support with statistics, details, and examples. Plan visual aids.

Compose: Prepare a sentence outline. Consider using presentation software to outline your talk.

Revise: Develop transitions between topics. Prepare note cards or speaker's notes.

Practice: Rehearse the entire talk and time it. Practice enunciating words and projecting your voice. Practice using your visual aids. Develop natural hand motions.

Evaluate: Tape record or videotape a practice session to evaluate your movements, voice tone, enunciation, and timing.

What Makes a Loan Officer Say "Yes"?

I. INTRODUCTION

A. How many of you expect one day to start your own businesses? How many of you have all the cash available to capitalize that business when you start? — **Captures attention**

B. Like you, nearly every entrepreneur needs cash to open a business, and I promise you that by the end of this talk you will have inside information on how to make a loan application that will be successful. — **Involves audience**

C. As a loan officer at First Fidelity Trust, which specializes in small-business loans, I make decisions on requests from entrepreneurs like you applying for start-up money. — **Identifies speaker**

<u>Transition</u>: Your professor invited me here today to tell you how you can improve your chances of getting a loan from us or from any other lender. I have suggestions in three areas: experience, preparation, and projection. — **Previews three main points**

II. BODY

Establishes main points (A, B, C)

A. First, let's consider experience. You must show that you can hit the ground running.

1. Demonstrate what experience you have in your proposed business.
2. Include your résumé when you submit your business plan.
3. If you have little experience, tell us whom you would hire to supply the skills that you lack.

<u>Transition</u>: In addition to experience, loan officers will want to see that you have researched your venture thoroughly.

B. My second suggestion, then, involves preparation. Have you done your homework?

1. Talk to local businesspeople, especially those in related fields.
2. Conduct traffic counts or other studies to estimate potential sales.
3. Analyze the strengths and weaknesses of the competition.

<u>Transition</u>: Now that we've discussed preparation, we're ready for my final suggestion.

C. My last tip is the most important one. It involves making a realistic projection of your potential sales, cash flow, and equity.

1. Present detailed monthly cash-flow projections for the first year.
2. Describe "what-if" scenarios indicating both good and bad possibilities.
3. Indicate that you intend to supply at least 25 percent of the initial capital yourself.

<u>Transition</u>: The three major points I've just outlined cover critical points in obtaining start-up loans. Let me review them for you.

Develops coherence with planned transitions (transitions)

III. CONCLUSION

A. Loan officers are most likely to say "Yes" to your loan application if you do three things: (1) prove that you can hit the ground running when your business opens, (2) demonstrate that you've researched your proposed business seriously, and (3) project a realistic picture of your sales, cash flow, and equity. — **Summarizes main points**

B. Experience, preparation, and projection, then, are the three keys to launching your business with the necessary start-up capital so that you can concentrate on where your customers, not your funds, are coming from. — **Provides final focus**

FIGURE 15.2 **Using an Outline Feature in Presentation Software**

Prepared in PowerPoint™, this outline shows some of the major ideas of a presentation on the topic of recycling shown in Figure 15.6.

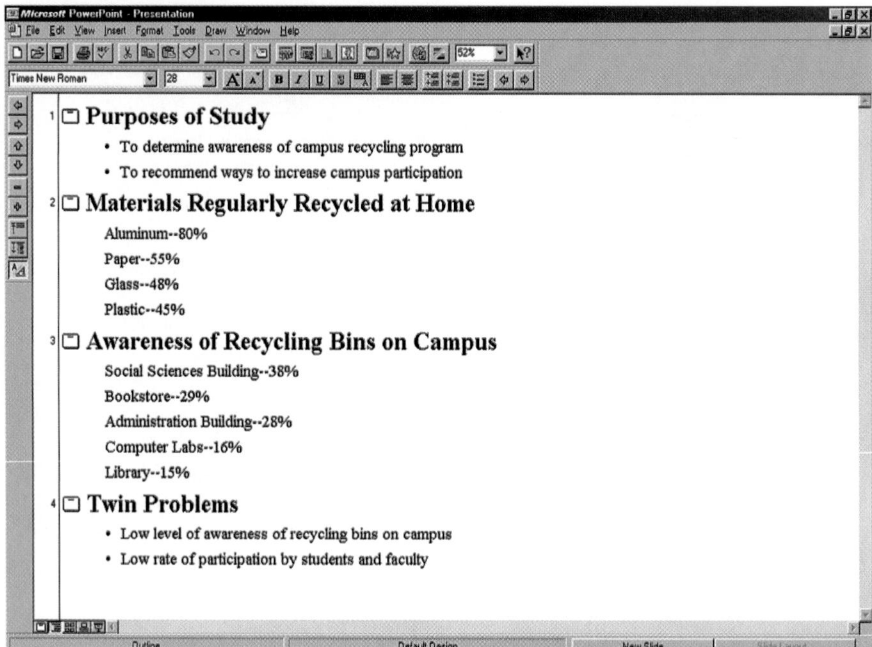

In his presentation Eric arranged the main points by importance, placing the most important point last where it had maximum effect.

In organizing any presentation, prepare a little more material than you think you will actually need. Savvy speakers always have something useful in reserve (such as an extra handout, transparency, or idea)—just in case they finish early. To help you visualize the organization of your presentation, consider using the outline feature of a software presentation program, as shown in Figure 15.2. You'll learn more about preparing electronic presentations shortly.

Conclusion

Effective conclusions summarize main points and focus on a goal.

You should prepare the conclusion carefully because this is your last chance to drive home your main points. Don't end limply with comments like "I guess that's about all I have to say." Skilled speakers use the conclusion to review the main themes of the presentation and focus on a goal. They concentrate on what they want the audience to do, think, or remember. Even though they were mentioned earlier, important ideas must be repeated. Notice how Eric Evans, in the conclusion shown in Figure 15.1, summarized his three main points and provided a final focus to listeners.

When they finish, most speakers encourage questions. If silence ensues, you can prime the pump with "One question that I'm frequently asked is . . .". You can also remark that you will be happy to answer questions individually after the presentation is completed.

Verbal Signposts

Speakers must remember that listeners, unlike readers of a report, cannot control the rate of presentation or flip back through pages to review main points. As a result, listeners get lost easily. Knowledgeable speakers help the audience recognize the organization and main points in an oral message with verbal signposts. They keep listeners on track by including helpful previews, summaries, and transitions, such as these:

To Preview
The next segment of my talk presents three reasons for . . .

Let's now consider the causes of . . .

To Summarize
Let me review with you the major problems I've just discussed . . .

You see, then, that the most significant factors are . . .

To Switch Directions
Thus far we've talked solely about . . . ; now let's move to . . .

I've argued that . . . and . . ., but an alternate view holds that . . .

Knowledgeable speakers provide verbal signposts to spotlight organization and key ideas.

You can further improve any oral presentation by including appropriate transitional expressions such as *first, second, next, then, therefore, moreover, on the other hand, on the contrary,* and *in conclusion.* These expressions lend emphasis and tell listeners where you are headed. Notice in Eric Evans' outline, in Figure 15.1, the specific transitional elements designed to help listeners recognize each new principal point.

Planning Visual Aids and Handouts

3

Before you make a business presentation, consider this wise Chinese proverb: "Tell me, I forget. Show me, I remember. Involve me, I understand." Because your goals as a speaker are to make listeners understand, remember, and act on your ideas, include visual aids to get them interested and involved. Some authorities suggest that we acquire 85 percent of all our knowledge visually. Therefore, an oral presentation that incorporates visual aids is far more likely to be understood and retained than one lacking visual enhancement.

Visual aids clarify points, improve comprehension, and aid retention.

Good visual aids have many purposes. They emphasize and clarify main points, thus improving comprehension and retention. They increase audience interest, and they make the presenter appear more professional, better prepared, and more persuasive. Furthermore, research shows that the use of visual aids actually shortens meetings.[3] Visual aids are particularly helpful for inexperienced speakers because the audience concentrates on the aid rather than on the speaker. Good visuals also serve to jog the memory of a speaker, thus improving self-confidence, poise, and delivery.

Fortunately for today's speakers, many forms of visual media are available to enhance a presentation. Figure 15.3 describes a number of visual aids and compares their cost, degree of formality, and other considerations. Three of the most popular visuals are overhead transparencies, computer visuals, and handouts.

Overhead Transparencies

Student and professional speakers alike rely on the overhead projector for many reasons. Most meeting areas are equipped with projectors and screens. Moreover, acetate transparencies for the overhead are cheap, easily prepared on a computer or copier, and simple to use. And, because rooms need not be darkened, a speaker using transparencies can maintain eye contact with the audience. A word of caution,

FIGURE 15.3 Presentation Enhancers

Medium	Cost	Audience Size	Formality Level	Advantages and Disadvantages
Overhead projector	Low	2–200	Formal or informal	Transparencies are easy and inexpensive to produce. Speaker keeps contact with audience.
Flipchart	Low	2–200	Informal	Easels and charts are readily available and portable. Speaker can prepare the display in advance or on the spot.
Write-and-wipe board	Medium	2–200	Informal	Procelain-on-steel surface replaces messy chalkboard. Speaker can wipe clean with cloth.
Slide projector	Medium	2–500	Formal	Slides provide excellent graphic images. Darkened room may put audience to sleep. Slides demand expertise, time, and equipment to produce.
Video monitor	Medium	2–100	Formal or informal	A VCR display features motion and sound. Videos require skill, time, and equipment to prepare.
Computer slides	Low	2–200	Formal or informal	Computers generate slides, transparencies, or multimedia visuals. Presentation software programs are easy to use, and they create dazzling results.
Handouts	Varies	Unlimited	Formal or informal	Audience appreciates take-home items such as outlines, tables, charts, reports, brochures, or summaries. However, handouts can divert attention from speaker.

though: stand to the side of the projector so that you don't obstruct the audience's view.

Handouts

You can enhance and complement your presentations by distributing pictures, outlines, brochures, articles, charts, summaries, or other supplements. Speakers who use computer presentation programs often prepare a set of their slides along with notes to hand out to viewers. Timing the distribution of any handout, though, is tricky. If given out during a presentation, your handouts tend to distract the audience, causing you to lose control. Thus, it's probably best to discuss most handouts during the presentation but delay distributing them until after you finish.

Computer Visuals

With today's excellent software programs—such as PowerPoint, Freelance Graphics, and Corel Presentations—you can create dynamic, colorful presentations with your PC. The output from these programs is generally shown on a PC monitor, a TV monitor, an LCD (liquid crystal display) panel, or a screen. With a little expertise and advanced equipment, you can create a multimedia presentation that includes stereo sound, videos, and hyperlinks, as described in the following discussion of electronic presentations.

Designing an Electronic Presentation

The content of most presentations today hasn't changed, but the medium certainly has. At meetings and conferences smart speakers now use computer programs, such as PowerPoint, to present, defend, and sell their ideas most effectively. Business speakers have switched to computer presentations because they are economical, flexible, and easy to prepare. Changes can be made right up to the last minute. Most important, though, such presentations make even amateurs look like real pros.

4

Computer-aided presentations are economical, flexible, professional, and easy to prepare.

Using Templates

Many novice presenters begin by using one of the professionally designed templates that come with a software program such as PowerPoint. These templates combine harmonious colors, borders, and fonts for pleasing visual effects. Templates also provide guidance in laying out each slide, as shown in Figure 15.4. You can select a layout for a title page, a bulleted list, a bar chart, a double-column list, an organization chart, and so on.

Working With Color

Background and text colors depend on lightness of room.

You don't need training in color theory to create presentation images that impress your audience rather than confuse them. You can use the color schemes from the design templates that come with your presentation program, as shown in Figure 15.5, or you can alter them. Generally, you're smart to use a color palette of five or fewer colors for an entire presentation. Use warm colors—reds, oranges, and yellows—to highlight important elements. Use the same color for like elements. For example, all slide titles should be the same color. The color for backgrounds and text depends on where the presentation will be given. Use light text on a dark back-

FIGURE 15.4 Selecting a Slide Layout

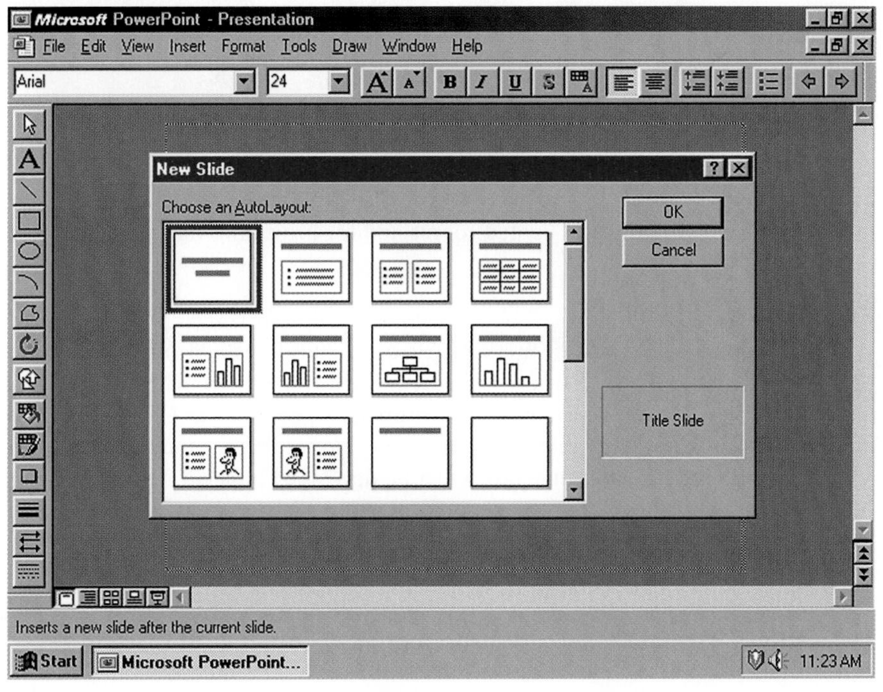

You may choose from a variety of slide layout plans, or you may design your own slide to fit your material.

FIGURE 15.5 **Choosing a Color Scheme**

Tips for Choosing the Best Colors in Visuals

- Develop a color palette of five or fewer colors.
- Use warm colors to highlight important elements.
- Use the same color for similar elements.
- Use dark text on a light background for presentations in bright rooms.
- Use light text on a dark background for presentations in darkened rooms.
- Use dark text on a light background for transparencies.
- Beware of light text on light backgrounds and dark text on dark backgrounds.

ground for presentations in darkened rooms. Use dark text on a light background for computer presentations in lighted rooms and for projecting transparencies.

Building Bullet Points

When you prepare your slides, translate the major headings in your presentation outline into titles for slides. For example, Alan Christopher prepared a PowerPoint presentation based on his research report featured in Figure 14.4 in Chapter 14. Part of his presentation slides are shown in Figure 15.6. Notice that the major topics from his outline became the titles of slides. Then he developed bulleted items for major subpoints. As you learned earlier, bulleted items must be constructed in parallel form. They should be phrases or key words, not complete sentences.

One of the best features about electronic presentation programs is the "build" capability. You can focus the viewer's attention on each specific item as you add bullet points line by line. The bulleted items may "fly" in from the left, right, top, or bottom. They can also build or dissolve from the center. As each new bullet point

FIGURE 15.6 **Making a PowerPoint™ Presentation**

Tips for Preparing and Using Slides

- Keep all visuals simple; spotlight major points only.
- Use the same font size and style for similar headings.
- Apply the Rule of Seven: No more than seven words on a line, seven total lines, and 7 × 7 or 49 total words.
- Be sure that everyone in the audience can see the slides.
- Show a slide, allow audience to read it, then paraphrase it. Do NOT read from a slide.
- Rehearse by practicing talking to the audience, not to the slides.
- Bring back-up transparencies in case of equipment failure.

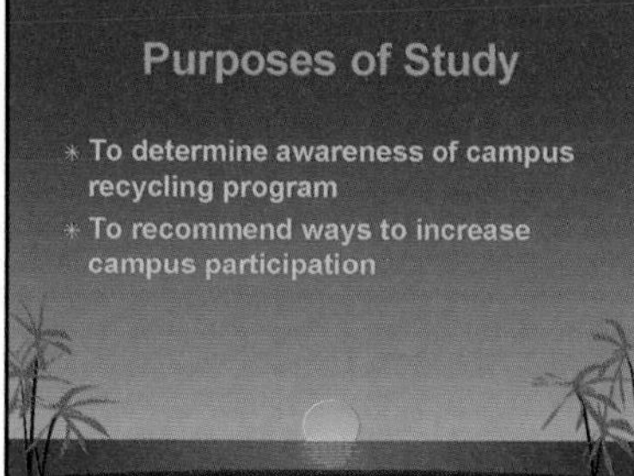

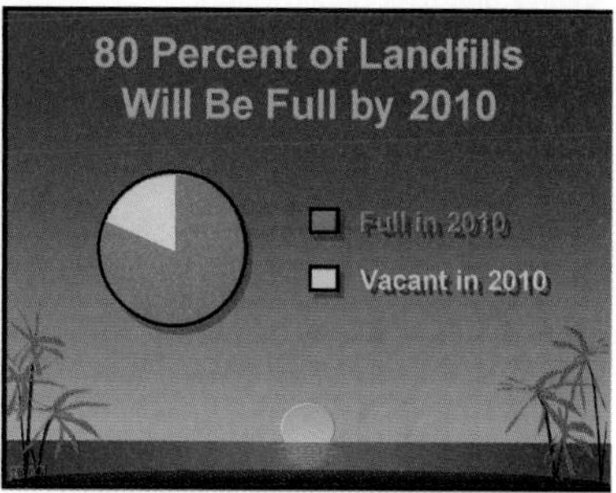

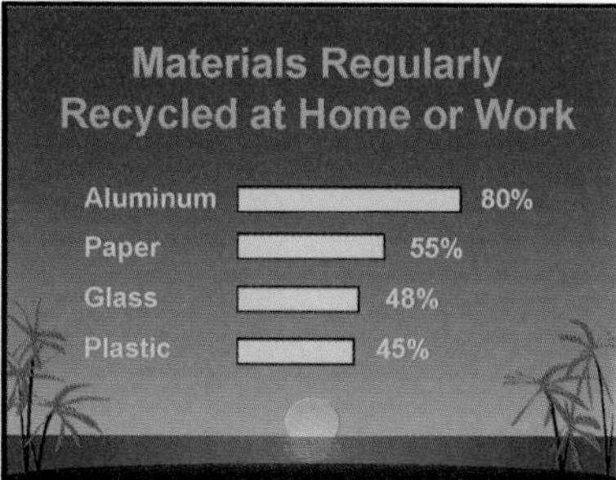

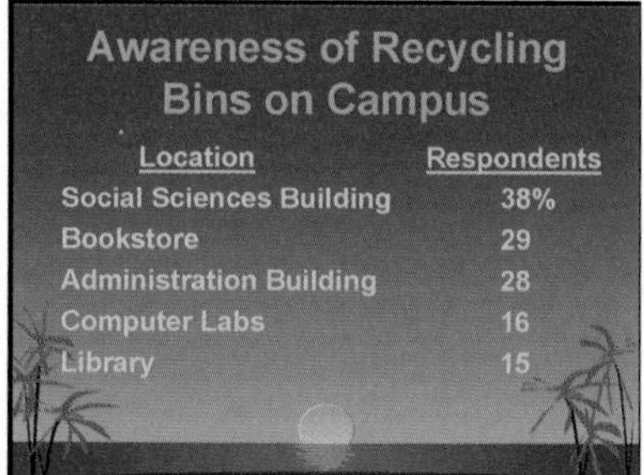

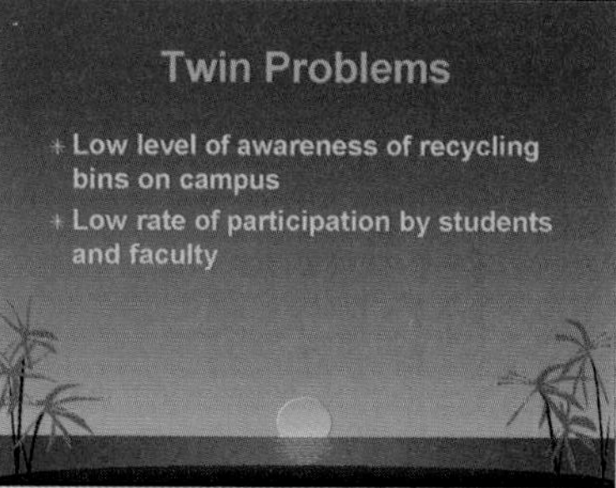

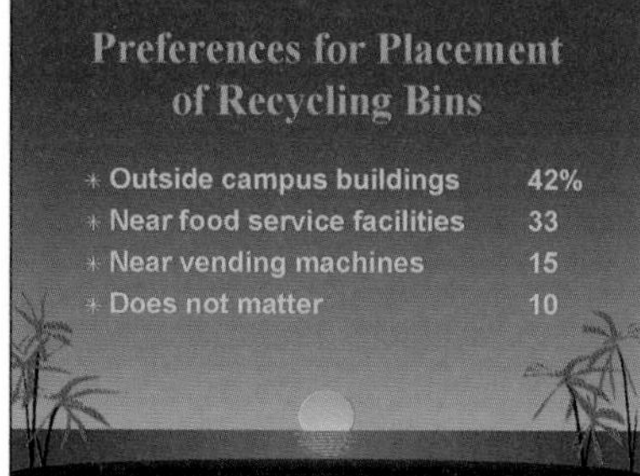

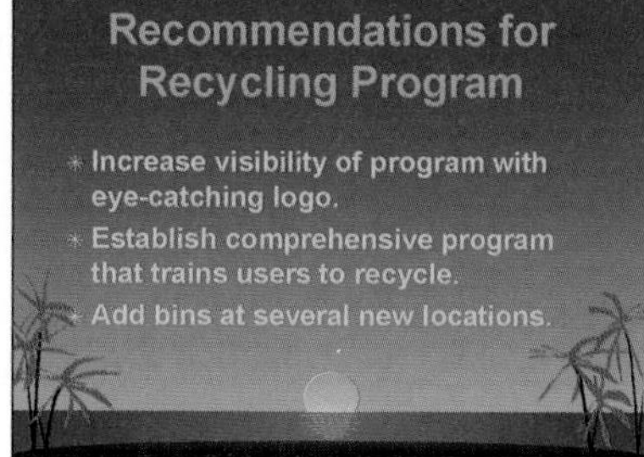

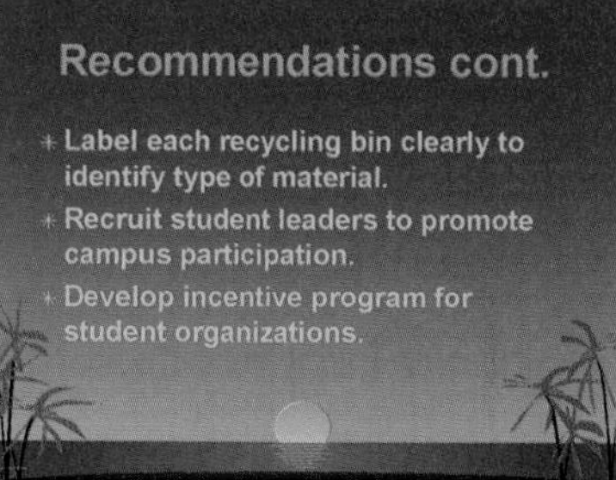

is added, leave the previous ones on the slide but show them in lightened text. In building bulleted points or in moving from one slide to the next, you can use *slide transition* elements, such as "wipe outs," glitter, ripple, liquid, and vortex effects. But don't overdo it. Experts suggest choosing one transition effect and applying it consistently.[4]

For the most readable slides, apply the *Rule of Seven.* Each slide should include no more than seven words in a line, no more than seven total lines, and no more

FIGURE 15.7 Making Speaker's Notes for an Electronic Presentation

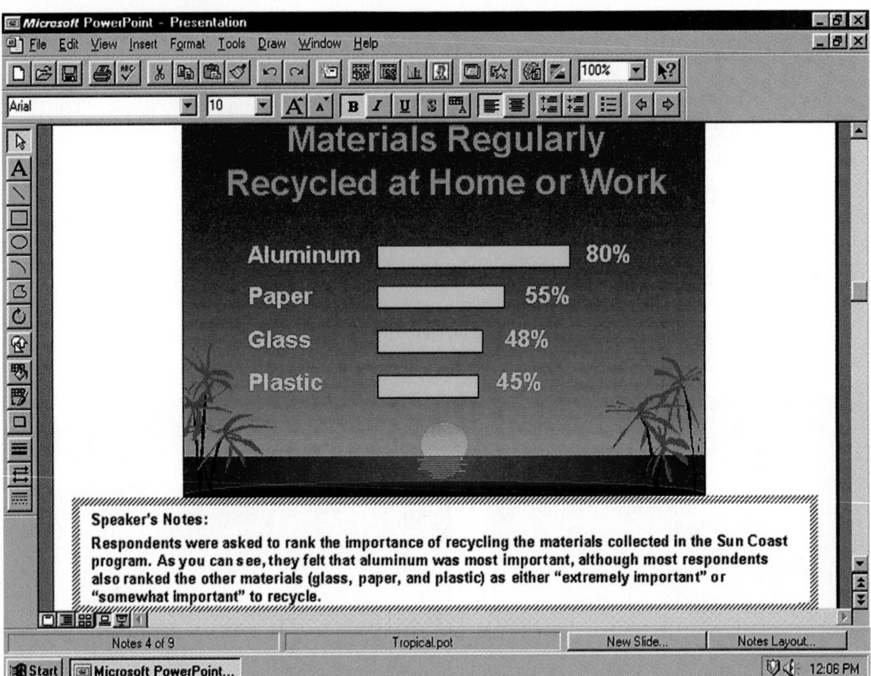

Speaker's notes enable you to print discussion items beneath each slide, thus providing handy review material for practice.

than 7 × 7 or 49 total words. And remember that presentation slides summarize; they don't tell the whole story. That's the job of the presenter.

Adding Multimedia and Other Effects

Multimedia elements include sound, animation, and video features.

Many presentation programs also provide libraries of *multimedia* features to enhance your content. These include sound, animation, and video elements. For example, you could use sound effects to "reward" correct answers from your audience. But using the sound of screeching tires in a Department of Motor Vehicles presentation is probably unwise. Similarly, video clips—when used judiciously—can add excitement and depth to a presentation. You might use video to capture attention in a stimulating introduction, to show the benefits of a product in use, or to bring the personality of a distant expert or satisfied customer right into the meeting room.

Another way to enliven a presentation is with real-life photographic images, which are now easy to obtain thanks to the prevalence of new low-cost scanners and digital cameras. Some programs are also capable of generating hyperlinks ("hot" spots on the screen) that allow you to instantly jump to relevant data or multimedia content.

Producing Speaker's Notes and Handouts

Most electronic presentation programs offer a variety of presentation options. In addition to printouts of your slides, you can make speaker's notes, as shown in Figure 15.7. These are wonderful aids for practicing your talk; they remind you of the supporting comments for the abbreviated material in your slides. Many programs allow you to print miniature versions of your slides with numerous slides to a page, if you wish. These miniatures are handy if you want to preview your talk to a sponsoring organization or if you wish to supply the audience with a summary of your presentation.

Developing Web-Based Presentations and Electronic Handouts

Because of recent technological improvements, you can now give a talk without even traveling off-site. In other words, you can put your slides "on the road." Web presentations with slides, narration, and speaker control are emerging as a less expensive alternative to *videoconferencing,* which was discussed in Chapter 2. For example, you could initiate a meeting via a conference call, narrate using a telephone, and have participants see your slides from the browsers on their computers. If you prefer, you could skip the narration and provide a prerecorded presentation. Web-based presentations have many applications, including providing access to updated training or sales data whenever needed.[5] Larry Magid, computer expert and noted speaker, suggests still another way that speakers can use the Web. He recommends posting your slides on the Web even if you are giving a face-to-face presentation. Attendees appreciate these *electronic handouts* because they don't have to lug them home.[6]

Avoiding Being Upstaged by Your Slides

Although electronic presentations supply terrific sizzle, they cannot replace the steak. In developing a presentation, don't expect your slides to carry the show. They merely summarize important points. As the speaker, you must explain the analyses leading up to the major points. You must explain what the major points mean. Slides provide you with talking points. For each slide you should have one or more paragraphs of narration to present to your audience. Make use of the speaker's notes feature to capture your supporting ideas while you make the slides. And don't let a PowerPoint presentation "steal your thunder." You must maintain control of the presentation rather than allowing the electronics to take over. In addition to your narration, you can maintain control by using a laser pen or pointer to connect you with the screen. Keep in mind that your slides and transparencies merely supply a framework for your presentation. Your audience came to see and hear you.

Spotlight on Communicators

Novice speakers often speed up their delivery, perhaps out of nervousness or eagerness to sit down. Justice Sandra Day O'Connor, shortly after becoming the first woman on the Supreme Court, revealed a trick she uses when she has important words to speak: "I taught myself early on to speak very slowly—enunciating every word—when I wanted someone's undivided attention."

Polishing Your Delivery

5

Once you've organized your presentation and prepared visuals, you're ready to practice delivering it. Here are suggestions for selecting a delivery method, along with specific techniques to use before, during, and after your presentation.

Delivery Method

Inexperienced speakers often feel that they must memorize an entire presentation to be effective. Unless you're an experienced performer, however, you will sound wooden and unnatural. Moreover, forgetting your place can be disastrous! Therefore, memorizing an entire oral presentation is not recommended. However, memorizing significant parts—the introduction, the conclusion, and perhaps a meaningful quotation—can be dramatic and impressive.

If memorizing won't work, is reading your presentation the best plan? Definitely not! Reading to an audience is boring and ineffective. Because reading suggests that you don't know your topic very well, the audience loses confidence in your exper-

CAREER COACH

HOW TO AVOID STAGE FRIGHT

Ever get nervous before giving a speech? Everyone does! And it's not all in your head, either. When you face something threatening or challenging, your body reacts in what psychologists call the *fight-or-flight response.* This response provides your body with increased energy to deal with threatening situations. It also creates those sensations—dry mouth, sweaty hands, increased heartbeat, and stomach butterflies—that we associate with stage fright. The fight-or-flight response arouses your body for action—in this case, giving a speech.

Since everyone feels some form of apprehension before speaking, it's impossible to eliminate the physiological symptoms altogether. But you can help reduce their effects with the following techniques:

- Use deep breathing to ease your fight-or-flight symptoms. Inhale to a count of ten, hold this breath to a count of ten, and exhale to a count of ten. Concentrate on your counting and your breathing; both activities reduce your stress.
- Don't view your sweaty palms and dry mouth as evidence of fear. Interpret them as symptoms of exuberance, excitement, and enthusiasm to share your ideas.
- Feel confident about your topic. Select a topic that you know well and that is relevant to your audience.
- Use positive self-talk. Remind yourself that you know your topic and are prepared. Tell yourself that the audience is on your side—because it is!
- Shift the spotlight to your visuals. At least some of the time the audience will be focusing on your slides, transparencies, handouts, or whatever you have prepared—and not on you.
- Ignore any stumbles. Don't apologize or confess your nervousness. If you keep going, the audience will forget any mistakes quickly.

When you're finished, you'll be surprised at how good you feel. You can take pride in what you've accomplished, and your audience will reward you with applause and congratulations. And, of course, your body will call off the fight-or-flight response and return to normal!

Career Track Application

Interview someone in your field or in another business setting who must make oral presentations. How did he or she develop speaking skills? What advice can this person suggest to reduce stage fright? When you next make a class presentation, try some or all of the techniques described above and note which are most effective for you

tise. Reading also prevents you from maintaining eye contact. You can't see audience reactions; consequently, you can't benefit from feedback.

Neither the memorizing nor the reading method creates very convincing presentations. The best plan, by far, is a "notes" method. Plan your presentation carefully and talk from note cards or an outline containing key sentences and major ideas. By preparing and then practicing with your notes, you can talk to your audience in a conversational manner. Your notes should be neither entire paragraphs nor single words. Instead, they should contain a complete sentence or two to introduce each major idea. Below the topic sentence(s), outline subpoints and illustrations. Note cards will keep you on track and prompt your memory, but only if you have rehearsed the presentation thoroughly.

Delivery Techniques

Nearly everyone experiences some degree of stage fright when speaking before a group. "If you hear someone say he or she isn't nervous before a speech, you're talking either to a liar or a very boring speaker," says corporate speech consultant Dianna Booher.[7] Being afraid is quite natural and results from actual physiological changes occurring in your body. Faced with a frightening situation, your body responds with the fight-or-flight response, discussed more fully in the accompanying Career Coach box. You can learn to control and reduce stage fright, as well as to incorporate techniques for effective speaking, by using the following strategies and techniques before, during, and after your presentation.

Before Your Presentation

- **Prepare thoroughly.** One of the most effective strategies for reducing stage fright is knowing your subject thoroughly. Research your topic diligently and prepare a careful sentence outline. Those who try to "wing it" usually suffer the worst butterflies—and make the worst presentations.
- **Rehearse repeatedly.** When you rehearse, practice your entire presentation, not just the first half. Place your outline sentences on separate cards. You may also wish to include transitional sentences to help you move to the next topic. Use these cards as you practice, and include your visual aids in your rehearsal. Record your rehearsal on audio- or videotape so that you can evaluate your effectiveness.
- **Time yourself.** Most audiences tend to get restless during longer talks. Thus, try to complete your presentation in no more than 20 minutes. Set a timer during your rehearsal to measure your speaking time.
- **Request a lectern.** Every beginning speaker needs the security of a high desk or lectern from which to deliver a presentation. It serves as a note holder and a convenient place to rest wandering hands and arms.
- **Check the room.** Before you talk, make sure that a lectern has been provided. If you are using sound equipment or a projector, be certain they are operational. Check electrical outlets and the position of the viewing screen. Ensure that the seating arrangement is appropriate to your needs.
- **Practice stress reduction.** If you feel tension and fear while you are waiting your turn to speak, use stress reduction techniques, such as deep breathing. Additional techniques to help you conquer stage fright are presented in the accompanying Career Coach box.

During Your Presentation

- **Begin with a pause.** When you first approach the audience, take a moment to adjust your notes and make yourself comfortable. Establish your control of the situation.
- **Present your first sentence from memory.** By memorizing your opening, you can immediately establish rapport with the audience through eye contact. You'll also sound confident and knowledgeable.
- **Maintain eye contact.** If the size of the audience overwhelms you, pick out two individuals on the right and two on the left. Talk directly to these people.
- **Control your voice and vocabulary.** This means speaking in moderated tones but loudly enough to be heard. Eliminate verbal static, such as *ah, er, you know,* and *um.* Silence is preferable to meaningless fillers when you are thinking of your next idea.
- **Put the brakes on.** Many novice speakers talk too rapidly, displaying their nervousness and making it very difficult for audience members to understand their ideas. Slow down and listen to what you are saying.

Spotlight on Communicators

To give rhythm and punch to your presentations, says corporate speech consultant Dianna Booher, make ample use of these three techniques: *triads* ("we are one nation—black, white, brown; we are Protestants, Jews, and Catholics"; *alliteration* ("we wish you health, happiness, and hope"); and *rhyme* ("American business must automate, emigrate, or evaporate").

Stage fright is both natural and controllable.

Thorough preparation, extensive rehearsal, and stress-reduction techniques can lessen stage fright.

Eye contact, a moderate tone of voice, and natural movements enhance a presentation.

ETHICAL INSIGHTS

THE "WORST DEADLY SIN" IN A PRESENTATION

Audiences appreciate speakers with polished delivery techniques, but they are usually relatively forgiving when mistakes occur. One thing they don't suffer gladly, though, is unethical behavior. Executives in a comprehensive research survey agreed that the "worst deadly sin" a speaker can commit in a presentation is demonstrating a lack of integrity.[8]

What kinds of unethical behavior do audiences reject? They distrust speakers who misrepresent, exaggerate, and lie. They also dislike cover-ups and evasiveness. Everyone expects a speaker who is trying to "sell" a product or idea to emphasize its strong points. Promotion, however, becomes unethical when the speaker intentionally seeks to obscure facts or slant issues to deceive the audience. The following situations clearly signal trouble for speakers because of the unethical actions involved:

- A sales rep, instead of promoting his company's products, suggests that his competitor's business is mismanaged, is losing customers, or offers seriously flawed products.
- A manager distorts a new employee insurance plan, underemphasizing its deficiencies and overemphasizing its strengths.
- An accountant for a charity suggests that management should authorize loose bookkeeping practices in order to mislead the public regarding the use of donors' money.
- A sales rep fabricates an answer to a tough question instead of admitting ignorance.
- A financial planner tries to prove her point by highlighting an irrelevant statistic.
- A real estate broker compares dissimilar properties and locations to inflate the value of some property.
- A speaker deliberately uses excessively technical language to make an idea or proposal seem more important and complex than it is.
- A project manager claims personal credit for a proposal developed largely by consultants.

How can you make certain that your own presentations are ethical? The best strategy, of course, is to present your information honestly, fairly, and without deception. Be aware of your own biases and prejudices so that you don't unconsciously distort data. Remember that the goals of an ethical communicator, discussed in Chapter 1, include telling the truth, labeling opinions so that they can be distinguished from facts, being objective, writing clearly, and giving credit when you use others' ideas or words.

Career Track Application

Watch TV or read news stories about congressional debates. Note how proponents on each side of an issue (usually Democrats and Republicans) present their views in a positive light and cast their opponents' views in a negative light. Make notes of any unethical presentation techniques.

The time to answer questions, distribute handouts, and reiterate main points is after a presentation.

- **Move naturally.** You can use the lectern to hold your notes so that you are free to move about casually and naturally. Avoid fidgeting with your notes, your clothing, or items in your pockets. Learn to use your body to express a point.
- **Use visual aids effectively.** You should discuss and interpret each visual aid for the audience. Move aside as you describe it so that it can be seen fully. Use a pointer if necessary.
- **Avoid digressions.** Stick to your outline and notes. Don't suddenly include clever little anecdotes or digressions that occur to you on the spot. If it's not part of your rehearsed material, leave it out so that you can finish on time. Remember, too, that your audience may not be as enthralled with your topic as you are.
- **Summarize your main points.** Conclude your presentation by reiterating your main points or by emphasizing what you want the audience to think or do. Once

you have announced your conclusion, proceed to it directly. Don't irritate the audience by talking for five or ten more minutes.

After Your Presentation

- **Distribute handouts.** If you prepared handouts with data the audience will need, pass them out when you finish.
- **Encourage questions.** If the situation permits a question-and-answer period, announce it at the beginning of your presentation. Then, when you finish, ask for questions. Set a time limit for questions and answers.
- **Repeat questions.** Although the speaker may hear the question, audience members often do not. Begin each answer with a repetition of the question. This also gives you thinking time. Then, direct your answer to the entire audience.
- **Reinforce your main points.** You can use your answers to restate your primary ideas ("I'm glad you brought that up because it gives me a chance to elaborate on . . ."). In answering questions, avoid becoming defensive or debating the questioner.
- **Keep control.** Don't allow one individual to take over. Keep the entire audience involved.
- **End with a summary and appreciation.** To signal the end of the session before you take the last question, say something like "We have time for just one more question." As you answer the last question, try to work it into a summary of your main points. Then, express appreciation to the audience for the opportunity to talk with them.

Preparing and organizing an oral presentation, as summarized in the concluding checklist, requires attention to content and strategy. Along with the care you devote to developing your talk, consider also its ethics, so that you won't be guilty of committing the "worst deadly sin" spotlighted in the accompanying Ethical Insights box.

PROCESS IN PROGRESS

CASE STUDY

Walt Disney Imagineering Revisited

Jon Georges and a Walt Disney Imagineering design team worked intensively on a new creative concept for one of the world's most-visited theme parks, Tokyo Disneyland. But the entire project would come to a screeching halt without a successful presentation before the owners of Tokyo Disneyland. The Imagineering team had to convince the assembled Japanese that new Winnie the Pooh feature attractions, as well as associated merchandise shops and a major restaurant, would be exciting and profitable additions to the existing theme park.

Understanding the audience and anticipating its reaction were integral parts of Jon's preparation for a presentation. For the Tokyo Disneyland project, Jon and the Imagineering team wanted to present their concepts in broad terms to see if the financiers liked the total idea. But Jon also knew that this audience would be detail oriented. "Japanese businessmen tend to want particulars—like the color of the concrete, the number of restrooms, and the exact location where visitors would exit an attraction."

Other adaptations Jon made for the Tokyo presentation involved choice of language and presentation style. Carefully avoiding Disney and design jargon, he consciously used common words and simple sentences, which the translator had little trouble converting to Japanese. In making his presentation, Jon kept in mind three important elements: organization, visuals, and focus. Although he had thousands of details in mind, he forced himself to keep his presentation logical and simple. He concentrated on one powerful point: convincing his Japanese listeners that the new attractions would enhance the value of Tokyo Disneyland and would draw more visitors through the turnstiles.

Critical Thinking

- What questions should Jon Georges ask himself in anticipating the audience for the Tokyo Disneyland presentation?
- Why is simplicity important in an oral presentation and why was it particularly important for the Tokyo Disneyland presentation?
- Why are visual aids critical for both local and international audiences?

Adapting to International and Cross-Cultural Audiences

Addressing cross-cultural audiences requires a speaker to consider audience expectations and cultural conventions.

Every good speaker adapts to the audience, and cross-cultural presentations call for special adjustments and sensitivity. When working with an interpreter or speaking before individuals whose English is limited, you'll need to be very careful about your language. For his presentation in Tokyo, Jon Georges spoke slowly, used simple English, avoided jargon and clichés, and used short sentences.

Beyond these basic language adaptations, however, more fundamental sensitivity is often necessary. In organizing a presentation for a cross-cultural audience, think twice about delivering your main idea up front. Many people (notably those in Japanese, Latin American, and Arabic cultures) consider such directness to be brash and inappropriate. Remember that others may not share our cultural emphasis on straightforwardness.

Also consider breaking your presentation into short, discrete segments. In Japan, Jon Georges divided his talk into three distinct topics: theme park attractions, merchandise shops, and food services. He developed each topic separately, encouraging discussion periods after each. Such organization enables participants to ask questions and digest what has been presented. This technique is especially effective in cultures where people communicate in "loops." In the Middle East, for example, Arab speakers "mix circuitous, irrelevant (by American standards) conversations with short dashes of information that go directly to the point." Presenters who are patient, tolerant, and "mature" (in the eyes of the audience) will make the sale or win the contract.[9]

Remember, too, that some cultures prefer greater formality than Americans exercise. Writing on a flipchart or transparency seems natural and spontaneous in this country. Abroad, though, such informal techniques may suggest that the speaker does not value the audience enough to prepare proper visual aids in advance.[10]

This caution aside, you'll still want to use visual aids to communicate your message. These visuals should be written in both languages, so that you and your audience understand them. Never use numbers without writing them out for all to see. If possible, say numbers in both languages. Distribute translated handouts, summarizing your important information, when you finish. Finally, be careful of your body language. Looking people in the eye suggests intimacy and self-confidence in this country, but in other cultures such eye contact may be considered disrespectful.

Checklist for Preparing and Organizing Oral Presentations

Getting Ready to Speak

Identify your purpose. Decide what you want your audience to believe, remember, or do when you finish. Aim all parts of your talk toward this purpose.

Analyze the audience. Consider how to adapt your message (its organization, appeals, and examples) to your audience's knowledge and needs.

Organizing the Introduction

- ☑ **Get the audience involved.** Capture the audience's attention by opening with a promise, story, startling fact, question, quote, relevant problem, or self-effacing joke.

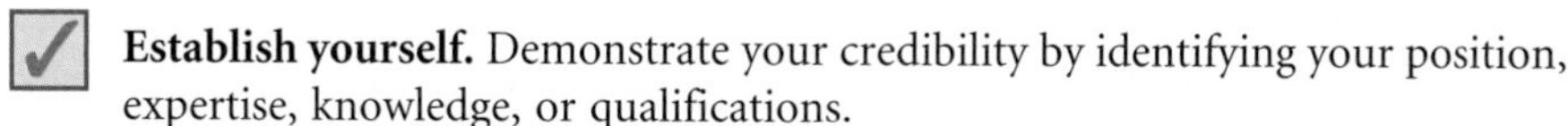

- ☑ **Establish yourself.** Demonstrate your credibility by identifying your position, expertise, knowledge, or qualifications.

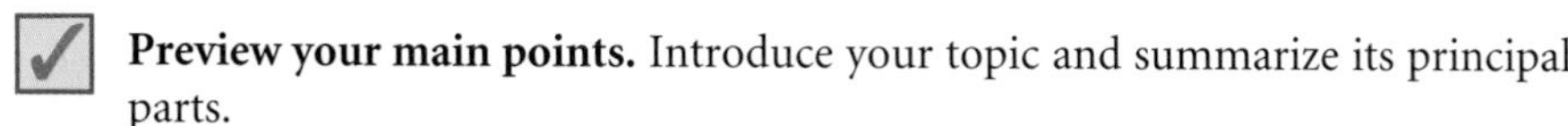

- ☑ **Preview your main points.** Introduce your topic and summarize its principal parts.

Organizing the Body

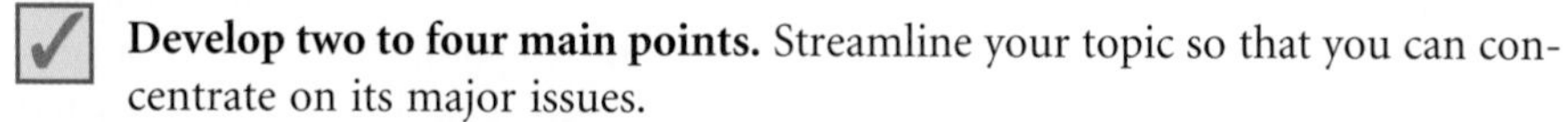

- ☑ **Develop two to four main points.** Streamline your topic so that you can concentrate on its major issues.

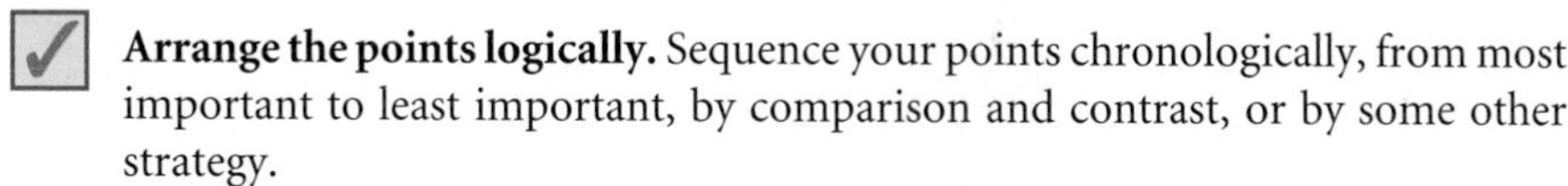

- ☑ **Arrange the points logically.** Sequence your points chronologically, from most important to least important, by comparison and contrast, or by some other strategy.

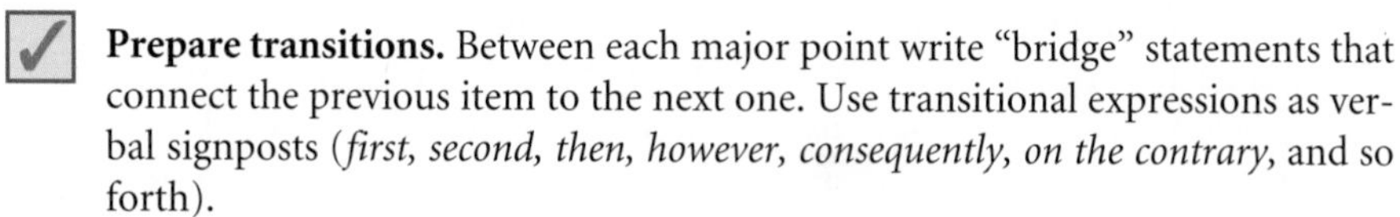

- ☑ **Prepare transitions.** Between each major point write "bridge" statements that connect the previous item to the next one. Use transitional expressions as verbal signposts (*first, second, then, however, consequently, on the contrary,* and so forth).

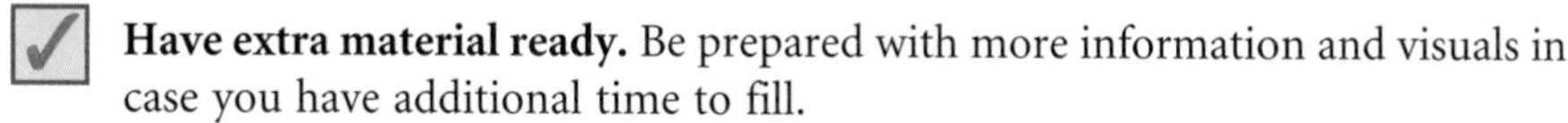

- ☑ **Have extra material ready.** Be prepared with more information and visuals in case you have additional time to fill.

Organizing the Conclusion

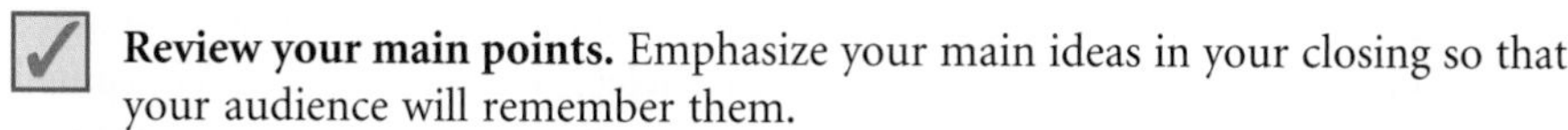

- ☑ **Review your main points.** Emphasize your main ideas in your closing so that your audience will remember them.
- ☑ **Provide a final focus.** Tell how your listeners can use this information, why you have spoken, or what you want them to do.

Designing Visual Aids

- ☑ **Select your medium carefully.** Consider the size of your audience, degree of formality desired, cost and ease of preparation, and potential effectiveness.
- ☑ **Highlight main ideas.** Use visual aids to illustrate major concepts only. Keep them brief and simple.
- ☑ **Use aids skillfully.** Talk to the audience, not to the visuals. Paraphrase their contents.

Developing Electronic Presentations

- ☑ **Learn to use your software program.** Study template and slide layout designs to see how you can adapt them to your purposes.
- ☑ **Select a pleasing color palette.** Work with five or fewer colors for your entire presentation.

 **Use bulleted points for major headings.** Make sure your points are all parallel and observe the Rule of Seven.

 **Make speaker's notes.** Jot down the narrative supporting each slide and use these notes to practice your presentation.

 **Maintain control.** Don't let your slides upstage you. Use a laser pointer to connect you to the slides and your audience.

Telephones and Voice Mail

The telephone is the most universal—and, some would say, one of the most important—pieces of equipment in offices today.[11] The telephone has spawned an entire new industry—voice-mail systems, which are rapidly replacing switchboards and receptionists. These computerized message systems save labor costs and provide sophisticated capabilities and flexibility unavailable in the past. Regardless of their advanced technology, though, telephones and voice mail are valuable business tools only when they generate goodwill and increase productivity. Poor communication techniques can easily offset any benefits arising from improved equipment. What good is an extensive voice-mail system if callers hang up in frustration after waiting through a long list of menu options without learning what they need? Here are suggestions aimed at helping business communicators make the best use of telephone and voice-mail equipment.

Telephones and voice mail should promote goodwill and increase productivity.

Making Productive Telephone Calls

Before making a telephone call, decide whether the intended call is really necessary. Could you find the information yourself? If you wait a while, would the problem resolve itself? Perhaps your message could be delivered more efficiently by some other means. One West Coast company found that telephone interruptions consumed about 18 percent of staff members' workdays. Another study found that two thirds of all calls were less important than the work they interrupted.[12] Alternatives to telephone calls include e-mail, memos, or calls to voice-mail systems. If a telephone call must be made, consider using the following suggestions to make it fully productive.

Making productive telephone calls means planning an agenda, identifying the purpose, being courteous and cheerful, and avoiding rambling.

- **Plan a mini-agenda.** Have you ever been embarrassed when you had to make a second telephone call because you forgot an important item the first time? Before placing a call, jot down notes regarding all the topics you need to discuss. Following an agenda guarantees not only a complete call but also a quick one. You'll be less likely to wander from the business at hand while rummaging through your mind trying to remember everything.
- **Use a three-point introduction.** When placing a call, immediately (1) name the person you are calling, (2) identify yourself and your affiliation, and (3) give a brief explanation of your reason for calling. For example: "May I speak to Larry Lopez? This is Hillary Dahl of Sebastian Enterprises, and I'm seeking information about a software program called Power Presentations." This kind of introduction enables the receiving individual to respond immediately without asking further questions.
- **Be cheerful and accurate.** Let your voice show the same kind of animation that you radiate when you greet people in person. In your mind try to envision the individual answering the telephone. A smile can certainly affect the tone of your voice, so smile at that person. Moreover, be accurate about what you say. "Hang

on a second; I'll be right back" rarely is true. Better to say, "It may take me two or three minutes to get that information. Would you prefer to hold or have me call you back?"

- **Bring it to a close.** The responsibility for ending a call lies with the caller. This is sometimes difficult to do if the other person rambles on. You may need to use suggestive closing language, such as "I've certainly enjoyed talking with you," "I've learned what I needed to know, and now I can proceed with my work," "Thanks for your help," or "I must go now, but may I call you again in the future if I need. . . ?"
- **Avoid telephone tag.** If you call someone who's not in, ask when it would be best for you to call again. State that you will call at a specific time—and do it. If you ask a person to call you, give a time when you can be reached—and then be sure you are in at that time.
- **Leave complete voice-mail messages.** Remember that there's no rush when you leave a voice-mail message. Always enunciate clearly. And be sure to provide a complete message, including your name, telephone number, and the time and date of your call. Explain your purpose so that the receiver can be ready with the required information when returning your call.

Spotlight on **Communicators**

Instead of commanding telephone callers to "Hold, please," ask politely if the caller is *able* to hold, advises Telephone Doctor Nancy Friedman. She helps companies improve their employees' telephone skills. One phrase she prohibits is "I don't know." It's better to say, "I'll find out." She also recommends that people smile *before* they answer the phone. That prevents "emotional leakage," taking personal frustration out on a caller.

Receiving Productive Telephone Calls

Receiving productive telephone calls means identifying oneself, acting responsive, being helpful, and taking accurate messages.

With a little forethought you can make your telephone a productive, efficient work tool. Developing good telephone manners also reflects well on you and on your organization.

- **Identify yourself immediately.** In answering your telephone or someone else's, provide your name, title or affiliation, and, possibly, a greeting. For example, "Larry Lopez, Proteus Software. How may I help you?" Force yourself to speak clearly and slowly. Remember that the caller may be unfamiliar with what you are saying and fail to recognize slurred syllables.
- **Be responsive and helpful.** If you are in a support role, be sympathetic to callers' needs. Instead of "I don't know," try "That's a good question; let me investigate." Instead of "We can't do that," try "That's a tough one; let's see what we can do." Avoid "No" at the beginning of a sentence. It sounds especially abrasive and displeasing because it suggests total rejection.
- **Be cautious when answering calls for others.** Be courteous and helpful, but don't give out confidential information. Better to say, "She's away from her desk" or "He's out of the office" than to report a colleague's exact whereabouts.
- **Take messages carefully.** Few things are as frustrating as receiving a potentially important phone message that is illegible. Repeat the spelling of names and verify telephone numbers. Write messages legibly and record their time and date. Promise to give the messages to intended recipients, but don't guarantee return calls.
- **Explain what you're doing when transferring calls.** Give a reason for transferring, and identify the extension to which you are directing the call in case the caller is disconnected.

Making the Best Use of Voice Mail

Voice mail eliminates telephone tag, inaccurate message-taking, and time-zone barriers; it also allows communicators to focus on essentials.

Voice mail links a telephone system to a computer that digitizes and stores incoming messages. Some systems also provide functions such as automated attendant menus, allowing callers to reach any associated extension by pushing specific buttons on a touch-tone telephone. Interactive systems allow callers to receive verbal

CASE STUDY

PROCESS TO PRODUCT

Applying Your Skills at Walt Disney Imagineering

As a lead show producer at Walt Disney Imagineering, Jon Georges develops new ideas for theme park attractions. He and other members of Imagineering teams are constantly doing research to gather ideas for new projects or for fleshing out current ideas. Staff members are also keeping track of what others are doing in the area of themed environments. How are other parks attracting big crowds? What's happening in Las Vegas? What kind of new theme restaurants are opening—and closing? Imagineering teams "benchmark" (compare) their efforts against those of similar developers of entertainment concepts. In presenting new ideas and in reporting on the competition, team members occasionally must make informal or formal presentations to their teams or to management. Although presenters sometimes use film clips, they have not made extensive use of electronic presentation software. Jon wonders whether Imagineering presentations might be more effective if speakers used a program such as PowerPoint.

Your Job

Jon Georges knows that you and other Imagineering interns have been learning about PowerPoint in your college classes. He asks your group to collaborate in preparing a presentation that demonstrates how PowerPoint works. Before your group makes the full presentation to selected Imagineering teams, Jon wants to see an outline. If it looks good, you'll make the complete demonstration. Prepare an outline based on what you learned about PowerPoint in this chapter. Apply the suggestions for making presentations.

information from a computer database. For example, a ski resort in Colorado uses voice mail to answer routine questions that once were routed through an operator: "Welcome to Snow Paradise. For information on accommodations, touch 1; for snow conditions, touch 2; for ski equipment rental, touch 3," and so forth.

Voice mail serves many functions, but the most important is message storage. Because half of all business calls require no discussion or feedback, the messaging capabilities of voice mail can mean huge savings for businesses. Incoming information is delivered without interrupting potential receivers and without all the niceties that most two-way conversations require. Stripped of superfluous chit-chat, voice-mail messages allow communicators to focus on essentials. Voice mail also eliminates telephone tag, inaccurate message-taking, and time-zone barriers. Critics complain, nevertheless, that automated systems seem cold and impersonal and are sometimes confusing and irritating.

In any event, here are some ways that you can make voice mail work more effectively for you.

- **Announce your voice mail.** If you rely principally on a voice-mail message system, identify it on your business stationery and cards. Then, when people call, they will be ready to leave a message.
- **Prepare a warm and informative greeting.** Make your mechanical greeting sound warm and inviting, both in tone and content. Identify yourself and your organization so that callers know they have reached the right number. Thank the caller and briefly explain that you are unavailable. Invite the caller to leave a message or, if appropriate, call back. Here's a typical voice-mail greeting: "Hi! This is Larry

Lopez of Proteus Software, and I appreciate your call. You've reached my voice mailbox because I'm either working with customers or talking on another line at the moment. Please leave your name, number, and reason for calling so that I can be prepared when I return your call." Give callers an idea of when you will be available, such as "I'll be back at 2:30" or "I'll be out of my office until Wednesday, May 20." If you screen your calls as a time-management technique, try this message: "I'm not near my phone right now, but I should be able to return calls after 3:30."

- **Test your message.** Call your number and assess your message. Does it sound inviting? Sincere? Understandable? Are you pleased with your tone? If not, says one consultant, have someone else, perhaps a professional, record a message for you.

Summary of Learning Objectives

1 **Discuss two important first steps in preparing an effective oral presentation.** First, identify what your purpose is and what you want the audience to believe or do so that you can aim the entire presentation toward your goal. Second, know your audience so that you can adjust your message and style to its knowledge and needs.

2 **Explain the major elements in the introduction, body, and conclusion of an oral presentation and discuss the importance of verbal signposts.** The introduction of a good presentation should capture the listener's attention, identify the speaker, establish credibility, and preview the main points. The body should discuss two to four main points, with appropriate explanations, details, and verbal signposts to guide listeners. The conclusion should review the main points and provide a final focus. Good speakers provide verbal signposts to preview, summarize, and switch directions.

3 **Identify appropriate visual aids and handouts for a presentation.** Use simple, easily understood visual aids to emphasize and clarify main points. Choose transparencies, flipcharts, slides, or other visuals depending on audience size, degree of formality desired, and budget. Generally, it's best to distribute handouts after a presentation.

4 **Review techniques for designing an electronic presentation.** Speakers employing a program such as PowerPoint use templates, layout designs, and bullet points to produce effective slides. A presentation may be enhanced with slide transitions, sound, animation, and video elements. Speaker's notes and handouts may be generated from slides. Web-based presentations allow speakers to narrate and show slides without leaving their home bases. Increasing numbers of speakers are using the Web to provide copies of their slides as electronic handouts.

5 **Specify delivery techniques for use before, during, and after a presentation.** Before your talk prepare a sentence outline on note cards or speaker's notes and rehearse repeatedly. Check the room, lectern, and equipment. During the presentation consider beginning with a pause and presenting your first sentence from memory. Make eye contact, control your voice, speak and move naturally, and avoid digressions. After your talk distribute handouts and answer questions. End gracefully and express appreciation.

6 **Discuss effective techniques for adapting oral presentations to cross-cultural audiences.** In presentations before groups whose English is limited, speak slowly, use simple English, avoid jargon and clichés, and use short sentences. Consider building up to your main idea rather than announcing it immediately. Also consider breaking the presentation into short segments to allow participants to ask questions and digest small parts separately. Beware of appearing too spontaneous and informal. Use visual aids to help communicate your message, but also distribute translated handouts summarizing the most important information.

7 **List techniques for improving telephone and voice-mail effectiveness.** You can improve your telephone calls by planning a mini-agenda and using a three-point introduction (name, affiliation, and purpose). Be cheerful and responsive, and use closing language to end a conversation. Avoid telephone tag by leaving complete messages. In answering calls, identify yourself immediately, avoid giving out confidential information when answering for others, and take careful messages. In setting up an automated-attendance voice-mail menu, limit the number of choices. For your own message prepare a warm and informative greeting. Tell when you will be available. Evaluate your message by calling it yourself.

CHAPTER REVIEW

1. The planning of an oral presentation should begin with serious thinking about what two factors? (Obj. 1)
2. Name three goals to be achieved in the introduction of an oral presentation. (Obj. 2)
3. For a 20-minute presentation, how many main points should be developed? (Obj. 2)
4. What should the conclusion to an oral presentation include? (Obj. 2)
5. Name three ways for a speaker to use verbal signposts in a presentation. Illustrate each. (Obj. 2)
6. Why are visual aids particularly useful to inexperienced speakers? (Obj. 3)
7. Why are transparencies a favorite visual aid? (Obj. 3)
8. Name three specific advantages of electronic presentation software. (Obj. 4)
9. What is a *template* and how is it useful? (Obj. 4)
10. How is the Rule of Seven applied in preparing bulleted points? (Obj. 4)
11. What delivery method is most effective for speakers? (Obj. 5)
12. Why should speakers deliver the first sentence from memory? (Obj. 5)
13. How might presentations before international or cross-cultural audiences be altered to be most effective? (Obj. 6)
14. What is a three-point introduction for a telephone call? (Obj. 7)
15. What is voice mail? (Obj. 7)

CRITICAL THINKING

1. Why is it necessary to repeat key points in an oral presentation? (Objs. 2 and 5)
2. How can a speaker make the most effective use of visual aids? (Obj. 3)
3. How can speakers prevent electronic presentation software from stealing their thunder? (Obj. 4)
4. Discuss effective techniques for reducing stage fright. (Obj. 5)
5. **Ethical Issue:** How can business communicators ensure that their oral presentations are ethical?

ACTIVITIES

15.1 Critiquing a Speech (Objs. 1–4)

Visit your library and select a speech from Vital Speeches of Our Day. Write a memo report to your instructor critiquing the speech in terms of the following:

- **a.** Effectiveness of the introduction, body, and conclusion
- **b.** Evidence of effective overall organization
- **c.** Use of verbal signposts to create coherence
- **d.** Emphasis of two to four main points
- **e.** Effectiveness of supporting facts (use of examples, statistics, quotations, and so forth)

15.2 Preparing an Oral Presentation From an Article (Objs. 1, 2, 3 and 5)

Select a newspaper or magazine article and prepare an oral report based on it. Submit your outline, introduction, and conclusion to your instructor, or present the report to your class.

15.3 Overcoming Stage Fright (Obj. 5)

In a class discussion develop a list of reasons for being fearful when making a presentation before class. What makes you nervous? Being tongue-tied? Fearing all eyes on you? Messing up? Forgetting your ideas and looking silly? Then, in groups of three or four discuss ways to overcome these fears. Your instructor may ask you to write a memo (individual or collective) summarizing your suggestions, or you may break out of your small groups and report your best ideas to the entire class.

15.4 Investigating Oral Communication in Your Field (Objs. 1 and 5)

Interview one or two individuals in your professional field. How is oral communication important in this profession? Does the need for oral skills change as one advances? What suggestions can these people make to newcomers to the field for developing proficient oral communication skills? Discuss your findings with your class.

15.5 Outlining an Oral Presentation (Objs. 1 and 2)

One of the hardest parts of preparing an oral presentation is developing the outline. Select an oral presentation topic from the list in Activity 15.7 or suggest an original topic. Prepare an outline for your presentation using the following format.

Title	
Purpose	
	I. INTRODUCTION
Gain attention of audience	A.
Involve audience	B.
Establish credibility	C.
Preview main points	D.
Transition	
	II. BODY
Main point	A.
Illustrate, clarify, contrast	1.
	2.
	3.
Transition	
Main point	B.
Illustrate, clarify, contrast	1.
	2.
	3.
Transition	
Main point	C.
Illustrate, clarify, contrast	1.
	2.
	3.
Transition	
	III. CONCLUSION
Summarize main points	A.
Provide final focus	B.
Encourage questions	C.

15.6. Discovering Presentation Tips on the Internet (Objs. 2–5)

Web

Using your favorite search engine and the search term "presentation tips," visit at least three Web sites that provide suggestions for giving presentations. If possible, print the most relevant findings. Select at least eight good tips or techniques that you did not learn from this chapter. Your instructor may ask you to bring them to class for discussion or submit a short memo report outlining your tips.

15.7 Choosing a Topic for an Oral Presentation (Objs. 1–6)

Select a topic from the list below or from the report topics in Activities 14.15 and 14.16 for a five- to ten-minute oral presentation. Consider yourself an expert who has been called in to explain some aspect of the topic before a group of interested people. Since your time is limited, prepare a concise yet forceful presentation with effective visual aids.

- **a.** What kinds of employment advertisements are legal, and what kinds are potentially illegal?
- **b.** How can the Internet be used to find a job?
- **c.** What graphics package should your fellow students use to prepare visual aids for reports?

d. What is the employment outlook in three career areas of interest to you?

e. What is telecommuting, and for what kind of workers is it an appropriate work alternative?

f. How much choice should parents have in selecting schools for their young children (parochial, private, and public)?

g. What travel location would you recommend for college students at Christmas (or another holiday or in summer)?

h. What is the economic outlook for a given product (such as domestic cars, laptop computers, economy cameras, fitness equipment, or a product of your choice)?

i. How can your organization or institution improve its image?

j. Why should people invest in a company or scheme of your choice?

k. What brand and model of computer and printer represent the best buy for college students today?

l. What franchise would offer the best investment opportunity for an entrepreneur in your area?

m. How should a job candidate dress for an interview?

n. Why should you be hired for a position for which you have applied?

o. How do the accounting cycles in manual and computerized systems compare?

p. How is an administrative assistant different from a secretary?

q. Where should your organization hold its next convention?

r. What is your opinion of the statement "Advertising steals our time, defaces the landscape, and degrades the dignity of public institutions"?[13]

s. How can individuals reduce their income tax responsibilities?

t. What is the outlook for real estate (commercial or residential) investment in your area?

u. What are the pros and cons of videoconferencing for [name an organization]?

v. What do the personal assistants for celebrities do, and how does one become a personal assistant? (Investigate the Association of Celebrity Personal Assistants.)

w. What kinds of gifts are appropriate for businesses to give clients and customers during the holiday season?

x. What scams are on the Federal Trade Commission's List of Top 10 Consumer Scams and how can consumers avoid falling for them?

y. How are businesses and conservationists working to protect the world's dwindling tropical forests?

z. Should employees be able to use computers in a work environment for anything other than work-related business?

15.8 Improving Telephone Skills by Role Playing (Obj. 7)

Your instructor will divide the class into pairs. For each scenario take a moment to read and rehearse your role silently. Then play the role with your partner. If time permits, repeat the scenarios, changing roles.

	Partner 1	Partner 2
A.	You are the personnel manager of Datatronics, Inc. Call Elizabeth Franklin, office manager at Computers Plus. Inquire about a job applicant, Chelsea Chavez, who listed Ms. Franklin as a reference.	You are the receptionist for Computers Plus. The caller asks for Elizabeth Franklin, who is home sick today. You don't know when she will be able to return. Answer the call appropriately.
B.	Call Ms. Franklin again the following day to inquire about the same job applicant, Chelsea Chavez. Ms. Franklin answers today, but she talks on and on, describing the applicant in great detail. Tactfully close the conversation.	You are now Ms. Franklin, office manager. Describe Chelsea Chavez, an imaginary employee. Think of someone with whom you've worked. Include many details, such as her ability to work with others, her appearance, her skills at computing, her schooling, her ambition, and so forth.
C.	You are now the receptionist for Tom Wing, of Wing Imports. Answer a call for Mr. Wing, who is working in another office, at ext. 134, where he will accept calls.	You are now an administrative assistant for attorney Michael Murphy. Call Tom Wing to verify a meeting date Mr. Murphy has with Mr. Wing. Use your own name in identifying yourself.
D.	You are now Tom Wing, owner of Wing Imports. Call your attorney, Michael Murphy, about a legal problem. Leave a brief, incomplete message.	You are now the receptionist for attorney Michael Murphy. Mr. Murphy is skiing in Aspen and will return in two days, but he doesn't want his clients to know where he is. Take a message.
E.	Call Mr. Murphy again. Leave a message that will prevent telephone tag.	Take a message again.

CHAPTER • 16 •

Employment Communication

LEARNING OBJECTIVES

1. Prepare for employment by identifying your interests, evaluating your assets, recognizing the changing nature of jobs, choosing a career path, and studying traditional and electronic job search techniques.

2. Compare and contrast chronological, functional, and combination résumés.

3. Organize, format, and produce a persuasive résumé.

4. Identify techniques that prepare a résumé for computer scanning, posting at a Web site, faxing, and e-mailing.

5. Write a persuasive letter of application to accompany your résumé.

6. Write effective employment follow-up letters and other messages.

7. Evaluate successful job interview strategies.

CASE STUDY

COMMUNICATION IN PROCESS

Carnival Captures Cruise Market and Shoreside Job Applicants

Carnival Cruise Lines, "The Most Popular Cruise Line in the World," just keeps growing and growing. After its debut in 1972 with one ship, Carnival launched increasingly larger and more luxurious ships. It expects to introduce five new ships over the next four years, bringing its total fleet to 18. These new "mega-liners" are floating palaces where guests enjoy multidecked glass atriums, marble-topped bars, Venetian-glass sculptures, a variety of dining options, spas, casinos, discos, jazz clubs, Las Vegas style entertainment, video arcades, bountiful buffets, and even swimming pools such as that shown on the Lido Deck of Carnival's Paradise.

In recent years Carnival has essentially reinvented all aspects of its "Fun Ship"™ cruise experience while continually striving to deliver the best "bang for the buck" in the industry. Firmly rooted in Miami, Carnival is one of the area's largest employers. Just as guests eagerly sign up for "Fun Ship"™ vacations, job applicants flock to fill its shoreside staff openings.

Carnival recruiting specialist Bonnie Gesualdi-Chao and her department examine between 12,000 and 13,000 résumés annually. Most of these résumés are generated by newspaper advertisements or by referrals made by employees, travel and tourism schools, colleges, and universities. Bonnie Gesualdi-Chao's primary task is recruiting employees for positions in the call center, which receives thousands of daily telephone inquiries regarding cruise options. Many Carnival managers start in call center positions because they are a good way to get to know the company.

Looking over thousands of résumés has taught Bonnie some quick scanning techniques. She reads each one-page résumé rapidly looking for education, skills, and experience. She's not interested in job descriptions. She wants to see results. What did the applicant accomplish in a previous job, internship, or coursework? How do those accomplishments equip the candidate for a Carnival job? A well-written résumé tailored to a specific opening immediately grabs Bonnie's attention. She's also impressed by applicants who have done their homework and show that they know something about Carnival.[1]

www.carnival.com

Preparing for Employment

1

Finding a satisfying career means learning about oneself, the job market, and the employment process.

One day you may be sending your résumé to a recruiting specialist like Bonnie Chao, who reads thousands of such résumés annually. What can you do to make your résumé and cover letter stand out? This chapter provides many tips for writing dynamite résumés and cover letters, as well as suggestions for successful interviewing. But the job search process actually begins long before you are ready to write a résumé. Whether you are looking for an internship, applying for a full-time position, searching for a part-time job, competing for a promotion, or changing careers, you must invest time and effort preparing yourself. You can't hope to find the position of your dreams without first (1) knowing yourself, (2) knowing the job market, and (3) knowing the employment process.

One of the first things you should do is obtain career information and choose a specific job objective. At the same time, you should be studying the job market and becoming aware of substantial changes in the nature of work. You'll want to understand how to use the latest Internet resources in your job search. Finally, you'll need to design a persuasive résumé and letter of application appropriate for small

FIGURE 16.1 The Employment Search

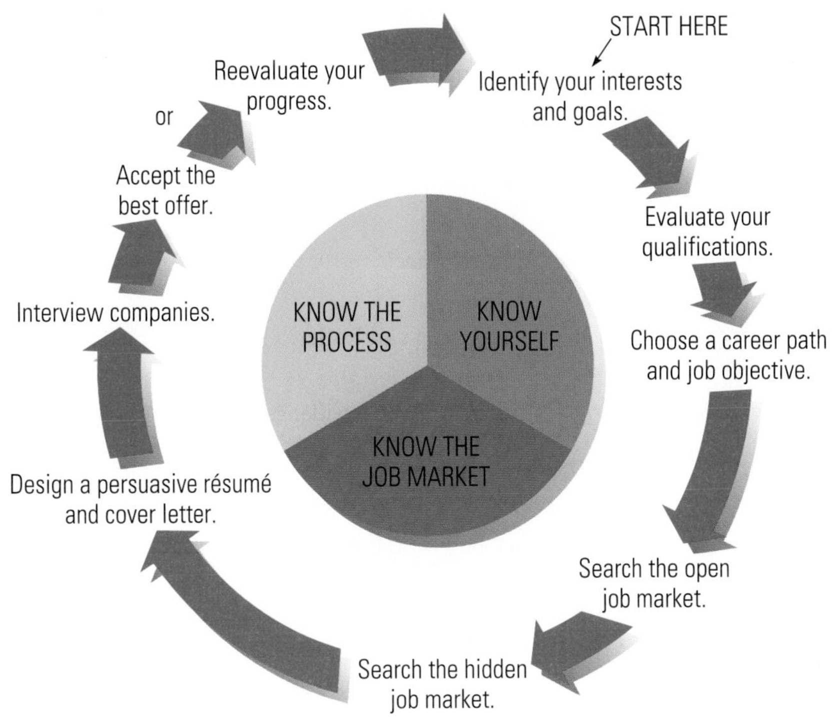
START HERE
Identify your interests and goals.
Evaluate your qualifications.
Choose a career path and job objective.
Search the open job market.
Search the hidden job market.
Design a persuasive résumé and cover letter.
Interview companies.
Accept the best offer.
or
Reevaluate your progress.
KNOW THE PROCESS
KNOW YOURSELF
KNOW THE JOB MARKET

businesses as well as for larger organizations that may be using résumé-scanning programs. Following these steps, summarized in Figure 16.1 and described in this chapter, gives you a master plan for landing a job you really want.

Identifying Your Interests

The employment process begins with introspection. This means looking inside yourself to analyze what you like and dislike so that you can make good employment choices. Career counselors charge large sums for helping individuals learn about themselves. You can do the same kind of self-examination—without spending a dime. For guidance in choosing a field that eventually proves to be satisfying, answer the following questions. If you have already chosen a field, think carefully about how your answers relate to that choice.

- *Do I enjoy working with people, data, or things?*
- *How important is it to be my own boss?*
- *How important are salary, benefits, and job stability?*
- *How important are working environment, colleagues, and job stimulation?*
- *Would I rather work for a large or small company?*
- *Must I work in a specific city, geographical area, or climate?*
- *Am I looking for security, travel opportunities, money, power, or prestige?*
- *How would I describe the perfect job, boss, and coworkers?*

Spotlight on **Communicators**

Bonnie Gesualdi-Chao, recruiting specialist for Carnival Cruise Lines, suggests that applicants "dress their résumés for the job they want—not for the job they already have." In other words, instead of merely listing current job duties, tailor your statements to relate to the targeted position. Before you can target a position, however, you must identify your interests and evaluate your qualifications.

Spotlight on **Communicators**

Computer mogul Michael Dell says that he learned one lesson early. Don't hire someone based on the company's immediate job needs. Because the nature of jobs is changing constantly, Dell prefers to hire a candidate based on that person's potential to grow and develop. Dell started his computer company in his University of Texas dorm room with $1,000 in capital in 1983. He now oversees a thriving company with more than 24,000 employees.

Evaluating Your Qualifications

In addition to your interests, assess your qualifications. Employers today want to know what assets you have to offer them. Your responses to the following questions will target your thinking as well as prepare a foundation for your résumé. Remember, though, that employers seek more than empty assurances; they will want proof of your qualifications.

- *What computer skills can I offer?* Employers are often interested in specific software programs.
- *What other skills have I acquired in school, on the job, or through activities?* How can I demonstrate these skills?
- *Do I work well with people?* What proof can I offer? Consider extracurricular activities, clubs, and jobs.
- *Am I a leader, self-starter, or manager?* What evidence can I offer?
- *Do I speak, write, or understand another language?*
- *Do I learn quickly? Am I creative?* How can I demonstrate these characteristics?
- *Do I communicate well in speech and in writing?* How can I verify these talents?

Recognizing the Changing Nature of Jobs

As you learned in Chapter 1, the nature of the workplace is changing. One of the most significant changes involves the concept of the "job." Following the downsizing in the early years of the 1990s and the movement toward flattened organizations, fewer people are employed in permanent positions. Many employees are feeling less job security although they are doing more work.

People feel less job security after downsizing and movement to flatter organizations.

In his best-selling book *JobShift,* William Bridges describes the disappearance of the traditional job. The notion of a full-time permanent job with a specific job description, he claims, is giving way to more flexible work arrangements. Work is completed by teams assigned to projects, or work is outsourced to a group that's not even part of an organization.[2] He sees the migration of work away from fixed "boxes" that we've always called jobs.

At the same time that work is becoming more flexible, big companies are no longer the main employers. Only 20 percent of new jobs are created by big companies.[3] And only one third of people currently employed work for companies with 500 or more employees.[4] People seem to be working for smaller companies, or they are becoming consultants or specialists who work on tasks or projects under arrangements too fluid to be called "jobs." And because new technologies can spring up overnight making today's skills obsolete, employers are less willing to hire people into jobs with narrow descriptions.

"Jobs" are becoming more flexible and less permanent.

What do these changes mean for you? For one thing, you should probably no longer think in terms of a lifelong career with a single company. In fact, you can't even expect reasonably permanent employment for work well done. This social contract between employer and employee is no longer a given. And predictable career paths within companies have largely disappeared. Career advancement is in your own hands.[5] In the new workplace you can expect to work for multiple employers on flexible job assignments associated with teams and projects. Finally, never become complacent about your position or job skills. Be prepared for constant retraining and updating of your skills. People who learn quickly and adapt to change are "high-value-added" individuals who will always be in demand even in a climate of surging change.

Choosing a Career Path

There's no escaping the fact that the employment picture today is much different from that of a decade or two ago. As a new college graduate, you can expect to have eight to ten jobs in as many as three different careers during your lifetime.[6] Some of you probably have not yet settled on your first career choice; others are returning to college to retrain for a new career. Although you may be changing jobs in the future, you still need to train for a specific career area now. In choosing an area, you'll make the best decisions when you can match your interests and qualifications with the requirements and rewards in specific careers. But where can you find career data? Here are some suggestions:

- **Visit your campus career center.** Most have literature, inventories, software programs, and Internet connections that allow you to investigate such fields as accounting, finance, office technology, information systems, hotel management, and so forth.
- **Search the Web.** Many job search sites on the Web offer career-planning information and resources. For example, at JobWeb you can link to Career/Life Planning sites for college students. Updated descriptions of and links to the best career counseling and job search Web sites may be found at the Guffey Student Web site **<meguffey.com>**. Click on "Jobs."
- **Use your library.** Many print and on-line resources are especially helpful. Consult the latest edition of the *Dictionary of Occupational Titles, Occupational Outlook Handbook,* and *The Jobs Rated Almanac* for information about career duties, qualifications, salaries, and employment trends.
- **Take a summer job, internship, or part-time position in your field.** Nothing is better than trying out a career by actually working in it or an allied area. Many companies offer internships and temporary jobs to begin training college students and to develop relationships with them. These relationships sometimes blossom into permanent positions. Jon Georges, spotlighted in Chapter 15, commuted 90 minutes each way to work at Disneyland while in high school and college. That tenacity undoubtedly helped his résumé stand out from the hundreds that Disney Imagineering received.
- **Interview someone in your chosen field.** People are usually flattered when asked to describe their careers. Inquire about needed skills, required courses, financial and other rewards, benefits, working conditions, future trends, and entry requirements.
- **Monitor the classified ads.** Early in your college career, begin monitoring want ads and Web sites of companies in your career area. Check job availability, qualifications sought, duties, and salary range. Don't wait until you're about to graduate to see how the job market looks.
- **Join professional organizations in your field.** Frequently, professional organizations offer student membership status and reduced rates. You'll get an inside track on issues, career news, and possibly jobs.

Spotlight on Communicators

"Know then thyself; presume not the Web to scan, until you know what you love to do, and have evolved a plan." Those wise words (with apologies to the poet Alexander Pope) came from Richard Nelson Bolles, author of *What Color Is Your Parachute?* This is the best-selling job hunting book in the world. One way to learn what you love, he suggests, is through informational interviewing. This involves talking with someone who has the kind of job you want—but not necessarily the person who does the hiring.

Summer and part-time jobs and internships are good opportunities to learn about different careers.

Using Traditional Job Search Techniques

Finding the perfect job requires an early start and a determined effort. Whether you use traditional or on-line job search techniques, you should be prepared to launch an aggressive campaign. And you can't start too early. Some universities now require first- and second-year students to take an employment seminar called "Reality 101." Students are told early on that a college degree alone doesn't guarantee a job. They

CAREER COACH

HOW TO USE TRADITIONAL AND ON-LINE NETWORKING TO EXPLORE THE HIDDEN JOB MARKET

Not all jobs are advertised in classified ads or listed in job databases. The "hidden" job market, according to some estimates, accounts for as much as two thirds of all positions available. Companies don't always announce openings publicly because it's time-consuming to interview all the applicants, many of whom are not qualified. But the real reason that companies resist announcing a job is that they dislike hiring "strangers." One recruiter explains, "If I'm in a hiring position, I'm first going to look around among my friends and acquaintances. If I can't find anybody, I'll look around for their friends and acquaintances. Only if I can't find anybody will I advertise."[7] Employers are much more comfortable hiring a person they know.

The key to finding a good job, then, is converting yourself from a "stranger" into a known quantity. One way to become a known quantity is by networking. You can use either traditional methods or on-line resources.

Traditional Networking

Step 1: Develop a List. Make a list of anyone who would be willing to talk with you about finding a job. List your friends, relatives, former employers, former coworkers, classmates from grade school and high school, college friends, members of your church, people in social and athletic clubs, present and former teachers, neighbors, and friends of your parents.

Step 2: Make Contacts. Call the people on your list or, even better, try to meet with them in person. To set up a meeting, say "Hi, Aunt Martha! I'm looking for a job and I wonder if you could help me out. When could I come over to talk about it?" During your visit be friendly, well organized, polite, and interested in what your contact has to say. Provide a copy of your résumé, and try to keep the conversation centered on your job search area. Your goal is to get two or more referrals. In pinpointing your request, ask two questions. "Do you know of anyone who might have an opening for a person with my skills?" If not, "Do you know of anyone else who might know of someone who would?"

Step 3: Follow Up on Your Referrals. Call the people whose names are on your referral list. You might say something like, "Hello. I'm Carlos Ramos, a friend of Connie Cole. She suggested that I call and ask you for help. I'm looking for a position as a marketing trainee, and she thought you might be willing to see me and give me a few ideas." Don't ask for a job. During your referral interview ask how the individual got started in this line of work, what he or she likes best (or least) about the work, what career paths exist in the field, and what problems must be overcome by a newcomer. Most important, ask how a person with your background and skills might get started in the field. Send an informal thank-you note to anyone who helps you in your job search, and stay in touch with the most promising contacts. Ask if you may call every three weeks or so during your job search.

On-Line Networking

Like traditional networking, the goal is to make connections with people who are advanced in their field. Ask for their advice about finding a job. Most people like talking about themselves, and asking them about their experiences is an excellent way to begin an on-line correspondence. "Hanging out" at an on-line forum or newsgroup where industry professionals can be found is also a great way to keep tabs on the latest business trends and potential job leads.

- **Web-Based Forums.** Forum One **<www.forumone.com>** is a Web site that allows you to search over 260,000 Web forum discussion groups. For example, the search term "business" brings up hundreds of groups where professionals are discussing their fields.
- **Mailing Lists and Newsgroups.** LISZT **<www.liszt.com>** is the premier directory of publicly accessible mailing lists, with over 90,000 listings, 178 of which are devoted to business topics. For information and postings of Usenet newsgroups, try Deja News **<www.dejanews.com>**.

Career Coach Application

Begin developing your network. Conduct at least one referral interview or join one professional mailing list or newsgroup. Ask your instructor to recommend an appropriate mailing list or newsgroup for your field. Take notes, and report your reactions and findings to your class.

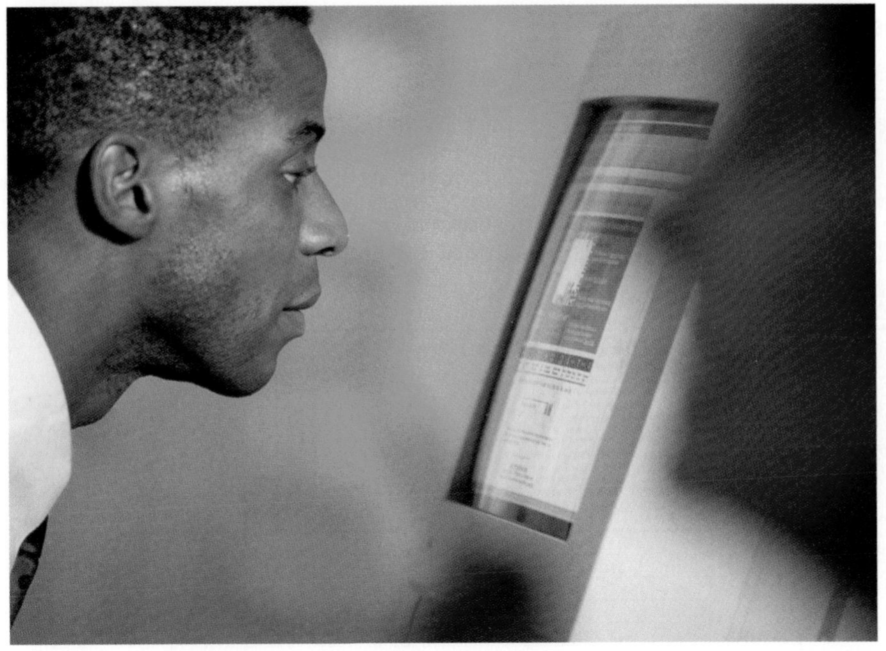

Preparing for a career begins long before you search the Web or want ads and write your résumé. Some of the best ways to learn about career paths involve talking with a campus counselor, taking a summer or part-time job, or signing up for an internship. Most often internships and part-time jobs in your field don't just fall in your lap. They require determination and effort.

are cautioned that grade-point averages make a difference to employers. And they are advised of the importance of experience. Here are some traditional steps that job candidates take:

- **Check classified ads in local and national newspapers.** Be aware, though, that classified ads are only one small source of jobs, as discussed in the accompanying Career Coach box.
- **Check announcements in publications of professional organizations.** If you do not have a student membership, ask your professors to share current copies of professional journals, newsletters, and so on. Your college library is another good source.
- **Contact companies in which you're interested, even if you know of no current opening.** Write an unsolicited letter and include your résumé. Follow up with a telephone call. Check the company's Web site for employment possibilities and procedures.
- **Sign up for campus interviews with visiting company representatives.** Campus recruiters may open your eyes to exciting jobs and locations.
- **Ask for advice from your professors.** They often have contacts and ideas for expanding your job search.
- **Develop your own network of contacts.** Networking still accounts for most of the jobs found by candidates. Therefore, plan to spend a considerable portion of your job search time developing a personal network. The Career Coach box gives you step-by-step instructions for traditional networking as well as some ideas for on-line networking.

Spotlight on **Communicators**

Michael Saafir tried everything to land a job, including wearing a sandwich board and passing out résumés to passing motorists. What eventually worked for him, though, was networking. A cousin had heard of job openings at a bank and suggested that Michael apply. He got the job. Developing an extensive personal network is one of the most effective job search tactics for any candidate.

Using Electronic Job Search Techniques

Just as the Internet has changed the way the world works, it's also changing the nature of the job search. One software maker observed, "Employers are more proactive now, and there's less 'pounding the pavement' for job seekers."[8] Increasing num-

FIGURE 16.2 **Using the Web to Search for a Job**

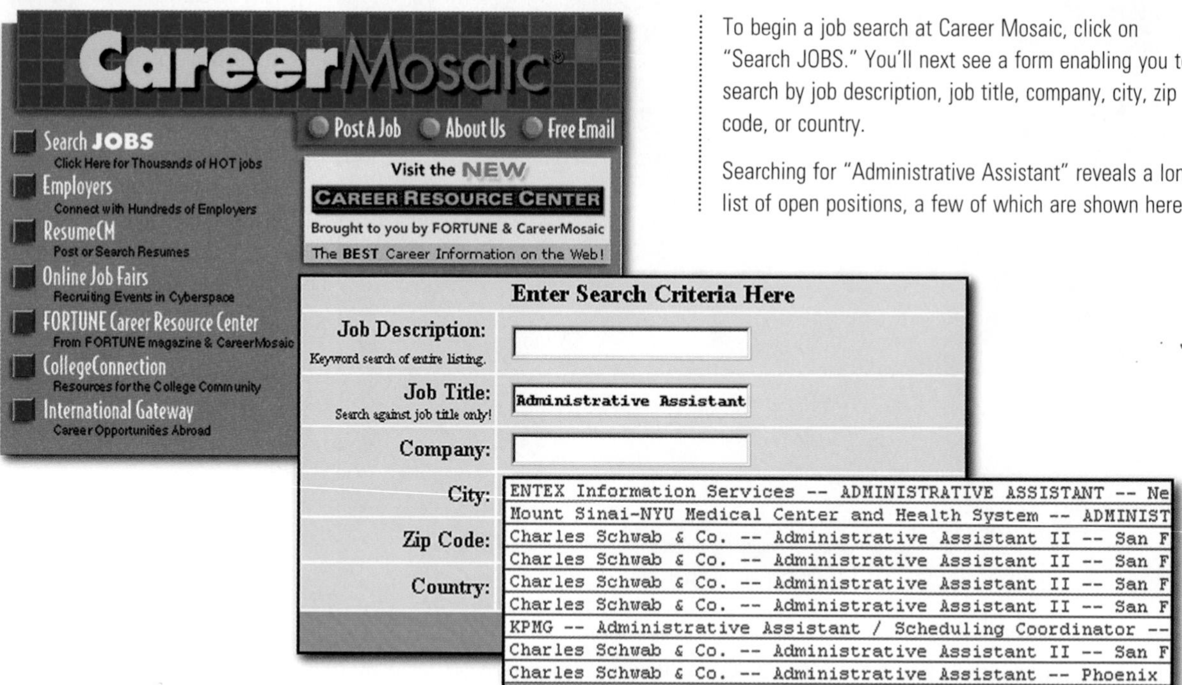

To begin a job search at Career Mosaic, click on "Search JOBS." You'll next see a form enabling you to search by job description, job title, company, city, zip code, or country.

Searching for "Administrative Assistant" reveals a long list of open positions, a few of which are shown here.

An electronic job-search campaign includes searching career and company Web sites for job listings.

bers of employers are listing their job openings at special Web sites that are similar to newspaper classified ads. Companies are also listing job openings at their own Web sites providing a more direct connection to employment opportunities. Although we will describe six of the best Internet job sites here, you can find a more extensive and continuously updated list with clickable hot links at the Guffey Student Web site **<meguffey.com>**. Our site includes many job lists for recent college graduates and entry-level positions.

- **America's Job Bank** is a partnership between the U.S. Department of Labor and the state-operated Public Employment Service. It lists more than 850,000 opportunities across the country, and its service is free.
- **Career Mosaic** offers a job database and employer profiles. It also breaks down listings by city and even by ZIP codes so that you can find a job in a particular part of town, as shown in Figure 16.2.
- **CareerPath** allows you to search help-wanted ads from 20 major newspapers. You can search by newspaper, job category, or by keywords.
- **College Grad Job Hunter** offers job postings and helpful hints for novices to the job market, such as how to write a résumé, interview, and negotiate.
- **E-Span's JobOptions** offers a searchable jobs database, links to homepages of potential employers, and an opportunity to post a résumé. After you submit a profile, E-span will keep you posted on new jobs that match your profile.
- **Monster Board** offers access to information on more than 50,000 jobs worldwide. It will find job listings that match your profile and e-mail them to you once a week. Although most of its jobs are aimed at experienced candidates, it also has plenty of entry-level positions.

Perhaps even better are the job openings listed at company Web sites. Check out your favorite companies to see what positions are open. What's the fastest way to find a company's Web address? We recommend Hoover's **<www.hoovers.com>** for quick company information and Web site links. If that fails, use your favorite search engine to see if a company has its own Web site. Some companies even have on-line résumé forms that encourage job candidates to submit their qualifications immediately. For example, Texas Instruments provides a convenient form at **<http://www.ti.com/recruit/docs/resume-form.html>**.

Hundreds of job sites now flood the Internet, and increasing numbers of companies offer on-line recruiting. However, the harsh reality is that landing a job still depends largely on personal contacts. One employment expert said, "On-line recruiting is a little like computer dating. People may find dates that way, but they don't get married that way."[9] Another professional placement expert said, "If you think just [posting] your résumé will get you a job, you're crazy. [Electronic services are] just a supplement to a core strategy of networking your buns off."[10]

Many jobs are posted on the Internet, but most jobs are still found through networking.

The Persuasive Résumé

2

After using both traditional and on-line resources to learn about the employment market and to develop job leads, you'll focus on writing a persuasive résumé. Such a résumé does more than merely list your qualifications. It packages your assets into a convincing advertisement that sells you for a specific job. The goal of a persuasive résumé is winning an interview. Even if you are not in the job market at this moment, preparing a résumé now has advantages. Having a current résumé makes you look well organized and professional should an unexpected employment opportunity arise. Moreover, preparing a résumé early helps you recognize weak qualifications and gives you two or three years in which to bolster them.

Choosing a Résumé Style

Your qualifications and career goal will help you choose from among three résumé styles: chronological, functional, and combination.

Chronological. Most popular with recruiters is the chronological résumé, shown in Figure 16.3. It lists work history job by job, starting with the most recent position. As Bonnie Chao at Carnival Cruise Lines pointed out, recruiters favor the chronological style because such résumés quickly reveal a candidate's education and experience record. Another corporate recruiter said, "I'm looking for applicable experience; chronological résumés are the easiest to assess."[11] The chronological style works well for candidates who have experience in their field of employment and for those who show steady career growth. But for many college students and others who lack extensive experience, the functional résumé format may be preferable.

Chronological résumés focus on past employment; functional résumés focus on skills.

Functional. The functional résumé, shown in Figure 16.4, focuses attention on a candidate's skills rather than on past employment. Like a chronological résumé, the functional résumé begins with the candidate's name, address, telephone number, job objective, and education. Instead of listing jobs, though, the functional résumé groups skills and accomplishments in special categories, such as *Supervisory and Management Skills* or *Retailing and Marketing Experience.* This résumé style highlights accomplishments and can de-emphasize a negative employment history. People who have changed jobs frequently or who have gaps in their employment records may prefer the functional résumé. Recent graduates with little employment experience often find the functional résumé useful.

FIGURE 16.3 Chronological Résumé

Analyze: The purpose is to respond to a job advertisement and win an interview.

Anticipate: The reader probably sees many résumés and will skim this one quickly. He or she will be indifferent and must be persuaded to read on.

Adapt: Emphasize the specific skills that the targeted advertisement mentions.

Research: Investigate the targeted company and its needs. Find the name of the person who will be receiving this résumé.

Organize: Make lists of all accomplishments and skills. Select those items most appropriate for the targeted job.

Compose: Experiment with formats to achieve readability, emphasis, and attractiveness.

Revise: Use present-tense verbs to describe current experience. Bullet experience items. Check for parallel phrasing. Adjust spacing for best effect.

Proofread: Run spell checker. Read for meaning. Have a friend proofread and critique.

Evaluate: Will this résumé impress a recruiter in 30 seconds?

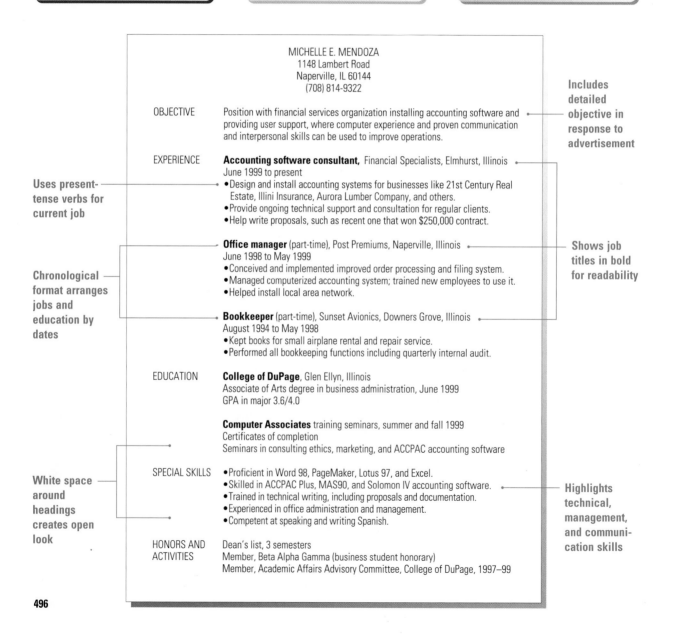

MICHELLE E. MENDOZA
1148 Lambert Road
Naperville, IL 60144
(708) 814-9322

OBJECTIVE
Position with financial services organization installing accounting software and providing user support, where computer experience and proven communication and interpersonal skills can be used to improve operations.

Includes detailed objective in response to advertisement

EXPERIENCE
Accounting software consultant, Financial Specialists, Elmhurst, Illinois
June 1999 to present
- Design and install accounting systems for businesses like 21st Century Real Estate, Illini Insurance, Aurora Lumber Company, and others.
- Provide ongoing technical support and consultation for regular clients.
- Help write proposals, such as recent one that won $250,000 contract.

Uses present-tense verbs for current job

Office manager (part-time), Post Premiums, Naperville, Illinois
June 1998 to May 1999
- Conceived and implemented improved order processing and filing system.
- Managed computerized accounting system; trained new employees to use it.
- Helped install local area network.

Shows job titles in bold for readability

Chronological format arranges jobs and education by dates

Bookkeeper (part-time), Sunset Avionics, Downers Grove, Illinois
August 1994 to May 1998
- Kept books for small airplane rental and repair service.
- Performed all bookkeeping functions including quarterly internal audit.

EDUCATION
College of DuPage, Glen Ellyn, Illinois
Associate of Arts degree in business administration, June 1999
GPA in major 3.6/4.0

Computer Associates training seminars, summer and fall 1999
Certificates of completion
Seminars in consulting ethics, marketing, and ACCPAC accounting software

SPECIAL SKILLS
- Proficient in Word 98, PageMaker, Lotus 97, and Excel.
- Skilled in ACCPAC Plus, MAS90, and Solomon IV accounting software.
- Trained in technical writing, including proposals and documentation.
- Experienced in office administration and management.
- Competent at speaking and writing Spanish.

White space around headings creates open look

Highlights technical, management, and communication skills

HONORS AND ACTIVITIES
Dean's list, 3 semesters
Member, Beta Alpha Gamma (business student honorary)
Member, Academic Affairs Advisory Committee, College of DuPage, 1997–99

FIGURE 16.4 Functional Résumé

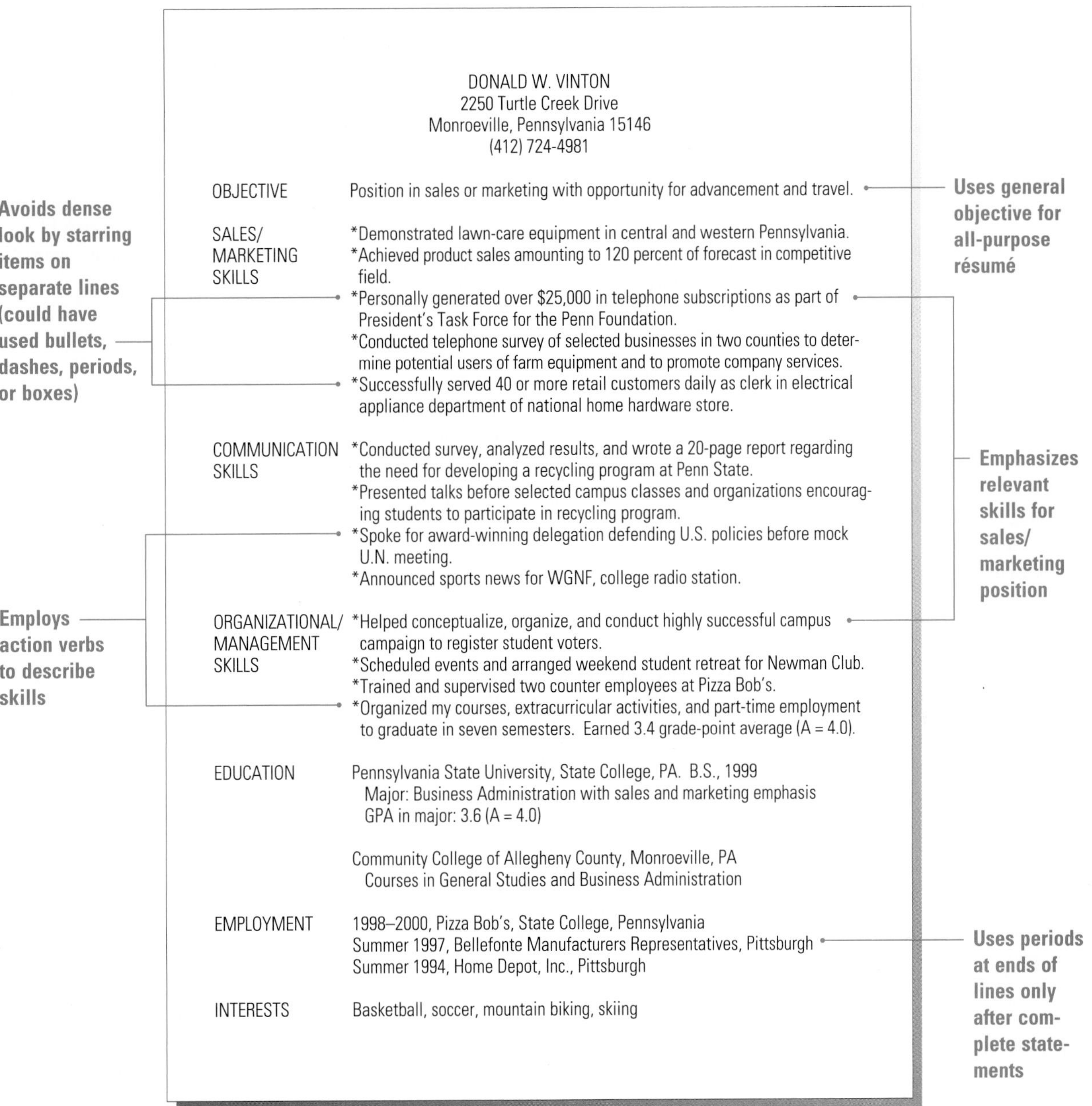
Donald, a recent graduate, chose this functional format to de-emphasize his meager work experience and emphasize his potential in sales and marketing. He included an employment section to satisfy recruiters.

DONALD W. VINTON
2250 Turtle Creek Drive
Monroeville, Pennsylvania 15146
(412) 724-4981

OBJECTIVE
Position in sales or marketing with opportunity for advancement and travel.

SALES/ MARKETING SKILLS
*Demonstrated lawn-care equipment in central and western Pennsylvania.
*Achieved product sales amounting to 120 percent of forecast in competitive field.
*Personally generated over $25,000 in telephone subscriptions as part of President's Task Force for the Penn Foundation.
*Conducted telephone survey of selected businesses in two counties to determine potential users of farm equipment and to promote company services.
*Successfully served 40 or more retail customers daily as clerk in electrical appliance department of national home hardware store.

COMMUNICATION SKILLS
*Conducted survey, analyzed results, and wrote a 20-page report regarding the need for developing a recycling program at Penn State.
*Presented talks before selected campus classes and organizations encouraging students to participate in recycling program.
*Spoke for award-winning delegation defending U.S. policies before mock U.N. meeting.
*Announced sports news for WGNF, college radio station.

ORGANIZATIONAL/ MANAGEMENT SKILLS
*Helped conceptualize, organize, and conduct highly successful campus campaign to register student voters.
*Scheduled events and arranged weekend student retreat for Newman Club.
*Trained and supervised two counter employees at Pizza Bob's.
*Organized my courses, extracurricular activities, and part-time employment to graduate in seven semesters. Earned 3.4 grade-point average (A = 4.0).

EDUCATION
Pennsylvania State University, State College, PA. B.S., 1999
Major: Business Administration with sales and marketing emphasis
GPA in major: 3.6 (A = 4.0)

Community College of Allegheny County, Monroeville, PA
Courses in General Studies and Business Administration

EMPLOYMENT
1998–2000, Pizza Bob's, State College, Pennsylvania
Summer 1997, Bellefonte Manufacturers Representatives, Pittsburgh
Summer 1994, Home Depot, Inc., Pittsburgh

INTERESTS
Basketball, soccer, mountain biking, skiing

Avoids dense look by starring items on separate lines (could have used bullets, dashes, periods, or boxes)
Employs action verbs to describe skills
Uses general objective for all-purpose résumé
Emphasizes relevant skills for sales/ marketing position
Uses periods at ends of lines only after complete statements

Functional résumés are also called *skill* résumés. Although the functional résumé of Donald Vinton shown in Figure 16.4 concentrates on skills, it does include a short employment section because recruiters expect it. Notice that Donald breaks his skills into three categories. An alternative—and easier—method is to make one large list, perhaps with a title such as *Areas of Accomplishment, Summary of Qualifications,* or *Areas of Expertise and Ability.*

FIGURE 16.5 Combination Résumé

Because Susan wanted to highlight her skills and capabilities along with her experience, she combined the best features of functional and traditional résumés. This résumé style is becoming increasingly popular. Although it's not standard practice, Susan included references because employers in her area expected them.

Note: For more résumé models, see Figures 16.10–16.13.

SUSAN R. SNOW
Route 2, Box 180
Dodgeville, Wisconsin 53533

Residence: (608) 935-3196 | Messages: (608) 935-4399

SKILLS AND CAPABILITIES

- Key board 70 wpm with accuracy.
- Take symbol shorthand at 90 wpm with accurate transcription.
- Skilled in the production of legal documents and correspondence.
- Competent in producing mailable copy from machine transcription.
- Experienced in personal computer use, including the following software: Word 98, Lotus 97, and Excel.
- Ability to perform office tasks and interact effectively using excellent written and oral communication skills.

EXPERIENCE

Word Processing Operator 1, Limited-term employee
University of Wisconsin—Madison, May 1999 to August 1999
- Transcribed confidential letters, memos, reports, and other documents from machine dictation using Word98.
- Proofread documents for other operators, marking grammar and content errors.

Student assistant
Southwest Wisconsin Technical College, Fennimore, WI 53809, June 1998 to August 1998
- Typed memos and input financial aid data on terminal to mainframe; printed and verified monthly report totals for $70,000 budget.
- Helped financial aid applicants understand and complete five-page form.
- Screened incoming telephone calls for supervisor and three counselors.

Part-time cook and cashier
Souprrr Subs, Fennimore, WI 53809, May 1997 to May 1998
- Prepared menu items, accepted customer payments, and balanced cash drawer.

EDUCATION

Southwest Wisconsin Technical College, Fennimore, WI 53809
Major: Office assistant and word processing specialist programs
AA degree expected May 2000. GPA in major: 3.6 (4.0 = A)

ACTIVITIES AND AWARDS

- Received the Fennimore Times award from Southwest Wisconsin Technical College Foundation for academic excellence and contribution to campus life.
- Elected secretary of Business Professionals of America Club. Represented SWTC chapter at state and national competitions.

REFERENCES

Ms. Shirley A. Yost	Professor Lois Wagner	Mr. James W. Loy
College of Letters & Science	SW Wisconsin Technical College	SW Wisconsin Technical College
University of Wisconsin	Highway 18 East	Highway 18 East
Madison, WI 53489	Fennimore, WI 53809	Fennimore, WI 53809
(413) 390-4491	(608) 822-8931	(608) 822-8749

Omits objective to keep all options open

Focuses on skills and aptitudes that employers seek

Arranges employment by job title for easy reading

Combines activities and awards to fill out section

Includes references because local employers expect them (most résumés today omit references)

Combination. The combination résumé style, shown in Figure 16.5, draws on the best features of the chronological and functional résumés. It emphasizes a candidate's capabilities while also including a complete job history. For recent graduates the combination résumé is a good choice because it enables them to profile what they can do for a prospective employer. If the writer has a specific job in mind, the items should be targeted to that job description.

Arranging the Parts

Although résumés have standard parts, their arrangement and content should be strategically planned. The most persuasive résumés emphasize skills and achievements aimed at a particular job or company. They show a candidate's most important qualifications first, and they de-emphasize any weaknesses. In arranging the parts, try to create as few headings as possible; more than six generally looks cluttered. No two résumés are ever exactly alike, but most writers consider the following parts.

3

The parts of résumés must be arranged with the most important qualifications first.

Main Heading. Your résumé should always begin with your name, address, and telephone number. If possible, include a number where messages may be left for you. Prospective employers tend to call the next applicant when no one answers. Avoid showing both permanent and temporary addresses; some specialists say that dual addresses immediately identify about-to-graduate college students. Keep the main heading as uncluttered and simple as possible. And don't include the word *résumé*; it's like putting the word *letter* above correspondence.

Résumés targeted to specific positions have the best chance of being read.

Career Objective. Opinion is divided on the effect of including a career objective on a résumé. Recruiters think such statements indicate that a candidate has made a commitment to a career. Moreover, career objectives make the recruiter's life easier by quickly classifying the résumé. But such declarations can also disqualify a candidate if the stated objective doesn't match a company's job description.[12] One expert warned that putting a job objective on a résumé has "killed more opportunities for candidates . . . than typos."[13]

You have four choices regarding career objectives. One option is to include a career objective when applying for a specific, targeted position. For example, the following responds to an advertised position: *Objective: To work in the health care industry as a human resources trainee with exposure to recruiting, training, and benefit administration.* A second choice—one that makes sense if you are preparing an all-purpose résumé—is to omit the career objective. A third possibility involves using a general statement, such as *Objective: Challenging position in urban planning* or *Job Goal: Position in sales/marketing.* A fourth possibility is omitting an objective on the résumé but including it in the cover letter, where it can be tailored to a specific position.[14]

Some consultants warn against using the words *entry-level* in your objective, as these words emphasize lack of experience. Many aggressive job applicants today prepare individual résumés that are targeted for each company or position sought. Thanks to word processing, the task is easy.

Spotlight on **Communicators**

Résumé consultant and author Yana Parker recommends a "lean and focused" résumé. Skip the clutter of overly precise dates by listing only years. Short periods of unemployment need not be explained, but longer periods should be accounted for in a positive statement telling what you were doing. "Remember," she says, "that a résumé is a marketing piece, not an historical document or a confessional." She advises including a specific job objective, perhaps even a job title. Then, recruiters don't have to guess what you're looking for.

Education. The next component is your education—if it is more noteworthy than your work experience. In this section you should include the name and location of schools, dates of attendance, major fields of study, and degrees received. Your grade-point average and/or class ranking are important to prospective employers. One way to enhance your GPA is to calculate it in your major courses only (for example, *3.6/4.0 in major*). By the way, it is not unethical to showcase your GPA in your major—so long as you clearly indicate what you are doing. Some applicants want to list all their courses, but such a list makes for very dull reading. Refer to courses only if you can relate them to the position sought. When relevant, include certificates earned, seminars attended, and workshops completed. Because employers are interested in your degree of self-sufficiency, you might wish to indicate the percentage of your education for which you paid. If your education is incomplete, include such statements as *B.S. degree expected 6/01* or *80 units completed in 120-unit program.* Entitle this section *Education, Academic Preparation,* or *Professional Training.*

FIGURE 16.6 Action Verbs for Persuasive Résumés*

Management Skills	Communication Skills	Research Skills	Technical Skills	Teaching Skills
administered	addressed	clarified	assembled	adapted
analyzed	arbitrated	collected	built	advised
consolidated	arranged	critiqued	calculated	clarified
coordinated	collaborated	diagnosed	computed	coached
delegated	<u>convinced</u>	evaluated	designed	communicated
developed	developed	examined	devised	coordinated
directed	drafted	extracted	engineered	developed
evaluated	edited	identified	executed	enabled
<u>improved</u>	explained	inspected	fabricated	encouraged
<u>increased</u>	formulated	interpreted	maintained	evaluated
organized	interpreted	interviewed	operated	explained
oversaw	negotiated	investigated	<u>overhauled</u>	facilitated
planned	persuaded	organized	programmed	guided
prioritized	promoted	summarized	remodeled	informed
recommended	publicized	surveyed	repaired	instructed
scheduled	recruited	systematized	solved	persuaded
<u>strengthened</u>	translated		<u>upgraded</u>	set goals
supervised	wrote			trained

*The <u>underlined</u> words are especially good for pointing out **accomplishments.**

The work experience section of a résumé should list specifics and quantify achievements.

Work Experience or Employment History. If your work experience is significant and relevant to the position sought, this information should appear before education. List your most recent employment first and work backwards, including only those jobs that you think will help you win the targeted position. A job application form may demand a full employment history, but your résumé may be selective. (Be aware, though, that time gaps in your employment history will probably be questioned in the interview.) For each position show the following:

- Employer's name, city, and state
- Dates of employment
- Most important job title
- Significant duties, activities, accomplishments, and promotions

Describe your employment achievements concisely but concretely. Avoid generalities like *Worked with customers.* Be more specific, with statements such as *Served 40 or more retail customers a day, Successfully resolved problems about custom stationery orders,* or *Acted as intermediary among customers, printers, and suppliers.* If possible, quantify your accomplishments, such as *Conducted study of equipment needs of 100 small businesses in Phoenix; Personally generated orders for sales of $90,000 annually; Keyboarded all the production models for a 250-page employee procedures manual;* or *Assisted editor in layout, design, and news writing for 12 issues of division newsletter.* One professional recruiter said, "I spend a half hour every day screening 50

FIGURE 16.6 Continued

Financial Skills	Creative Skills	Helping Skills	Clerical or Detail Skills	More Verbs for Accomplishments
administered	acted	assessed	approved	achieved
allocated	conceptualized	assisted	catalogued	expanded
analyzed	created	clarified	classified	improved
appraised	customized	coached	collected	pioneered
audited	designed	counseled	compiled	reduced (losses)
balanced	developed	demonstrated	generated	resolved (problems)
budgeted	directed	diagnosed	inspected	restored
calculated	established	educated	monitored	spearheaded
computed	founded	expedited	operated	transformed
developed	illustrated	facilitated	organized	
forecasted	initiated	familiarized	prepared	
managed	instituted	guided	processed	
marketed	introduced	motivated	purchased	
planned	invented	referred	recorded	
projected	originated	represented	screened	
researched	performed		specified	
	planned		systematized	
	revitalized		tabulated	

Source: Adapted from Yana Parker, *The Damn Good Résumé Guide* (Berkeley, CA:Ten Speed Press, 1996). Reprinted with permission.

résumés or more, and if I don't spot some [quantifiable] results in the first 10 seconds, the résumé is history."[15]

In addition to technical skills, employers seek individuals with communication, management, and interpersonal capabilities. This means you'll want to select work experiences and achievements that illustrate your initiative, dependability, responsibility, resourcefulness, and leadership. Employers also want people who can work together in teams. Thus, include statements like *Collaborated with interdepartmental task force in developing 10-page handbook for temporary workers* and *Headed student government team that conducted most successful voter registration in campus history.*

Statements describing your work experience can be made forceful and persuasive by using action verbs, such as those listed in Figure 16.6 and demonstrated in Figure 16.7.

Capabilities and Skills. Recruiters want to know specifically what you can do for their companies. Therefore, list your special skills, such as *Proficient in preparing correspondence and reports using Word 98.* Include your ability to use computer programs, office equipment, foreign languages, or sign language. Describe proficiencies you have acquired through training and experience, such as *Trained in computer accounting, including general ledger, accounts receivable, accounts payable, and payroll.* Use expressions like *competent in, skilled in, proficient with, experienced in,* and *ability to*; for example, *Competent in typing, editing, and/or proofreading reports, tables, letters, memos, manuscripts, and business forms.*

Emphasize the skills and aptitudes that recommend you for a specific position.

FIGURE 16.7 Using Action Verbs to Strengthen Your Résumé

Identified weaknesses in internship program and **researched** five alternate programs.

Reduced delivery delays by an average of three days per order.

Streamlined filing system, thus reducing 400-item backlog to 0.

Organized holiday awards program for 1200 attendees and 140 awardees.

Created a 12-point checklist for managers to use when requesting temporary workers.

Designed five posters announcing new employee suggestion program.

Calculated shipping charges for overseas deliveries and **recommended** most economical rates.

Managed 24-station computer network linking data and employees in three departments.

Distributed and **explained** voter registration forms to over 500 prospective student voters.

Praised by top management for enthusiastic teamwork and achievement.

Secured national recognition from National Arbor Foundation for tree project.

You'll also want to highlight exceptional aptitudes, such as working well under stress and learning computer programs quickly. If possible, provide details and evidence that back up your assertions; for example, *Mastered PhotoShop in 25 hours with little instruction.* Search for examples of your writing, speaking, management, organizational, and interpersonal skills—particularly those talents that are relevant to your targeted job.

For recent graduates, this section can be used to give recruiters evidence of your potential. Instead of *Capabilities,* the section might be called *Skills and Abilities.*

Awards, honors, and activities are appropriate for résumés; most personal data are not.

Awards, Honors, and Activities. If you have three or more awards or honors, highlight them by listing them under a separate heading. If not, put them with activities. Include awards, scholarships (financial and other), fellowships, honors, recognition, commendations, and certificates. Be sure to identify items clearly. Your reader may be unfamiliar, for example, with Greek organizations, honoraries, and awards; tell what they mean. Instead of saying *Recipient of Star award,* give more details: *Recipient of Star award given by Pepperdine University to outstanding graduates who combine academic excellence and extracurricular activities.*

It's also appropriate to include school, community, and professional activities. Employers are interested in evidence that you are a well-rounded person. This section provides an opportunity to demonstrate leadership and interpersonal skills. Strive to use action statements. For example, instead of saying *Treasurer of business club,* explain more fully: *Collected dues, kept financial records, and paid bills while serving as treasurer of 35-member business management club.*

Omit personal data not related to job qualifications.

Personal Data. Today's résumés omit personal data, such as birth date, marital status, height, weight, and religious affiliation. Such information doesn't relate to genuine occupational qualifications, and recruiters are legally barred from asking for such information. Some job seekers do, however, include hobbies or interests (such as skiing or photography) that might grab the recruiter's attention or serve as conversation starters. Naturally, you wouldn't mention dangerous pastimes (such as bungee jumping or sports car racing) or time-consuming interests. But you should indicate your willingness to travel or to relocate, since many companies will be interested.

References. Listing references on a résumé is favored by some recruiters and opposed by others.[16] Such a list takes up valuable space. Moreover, it is not normally instrumental in securing an interview—few companies check references before the interview. Instead, they prefer that a candidate bring to the interview a list of individuals willing to discuss her or his qualifications. If you do list them, use parallel form. For example, if you show a title for one person (*Professor, Dr., Mrs.*), show titles for all. Include addresses and telephone numbers.

Whether or not you include references on your résumé, you should have their names available when you begin your job search. Ask three to five instructors or previous employers whether they will be willing to answer inquiries regarding your qualifications for employment. Be sure, however, to provide them with an opportunity to refuse. No reference is better than a negative one. Do not include personal or character references, such as friends or neighbors, because recruiters rarely consult them. Companies are more interested in the opinions of objective individuals.

References are unnecessary for the résumé, but they should be available for the interview.

One final note: personnel officers see little reason for including the statement *References furnished upon request.* "It's like saying the sun comes up every morning," remarked one human resources professional.[17]

Preparing for Computer Scanning

4

Thus far we've aimed our résumé advice at human readers. However, the first reader of your résumé may well be a computer. Hiring companies now use computer programs in two ways to reduce costs of hiring and to make résumé information more accessible.

Applicant-Tracking Programs

Applicant-tracking programs scan incoming résumés and store the information for future hiring.

The first method involves software that helps large companies track incoming résumés. Sport shoe manufacturer Nike, for example, was deluged with thousands of unsolicited résumés. As a result, confessed Karen Cross, Nike employment specialist, "nobody ever looked at the résumé files because they were just too huge."[18] Then Nike installed a computer-based *applicant-tracking program.* This program uses optical-character recognition to scan incoming résumés. Such programs scan résumés, identify job categories, and even rank applicants. Most programs then generate letters of rejection or prepare interview offers for the lucky applicants whose résumés match job openings. Finally, these applicant-tracking programs store résumé information for future hiring. When a job opens up, a hiring manager tells the system what the position requires. The computer then searches to find résumés with words that match the request. Electronic searches offer ease and precision, unlike the hopelessness of searching manually through thousands of résumés in file cabinets. The process of a résumé-scanning program is shown in Figure 16.8.

Résumé Databanks

A second way hiring companies use computers is through *résumé databanks.* Smaller companies can't afford the big bucks required for applicant-tracking software. They are therefore turning to résumé databanks. These databanks store thousands of electronic résumés submitted by eager job candidates. Hiring companies no longer must recruit, advertise, and interview extensively. Experts estimate that it costs an employer $35,300 to hire a professional or managerial person if a private recruiting firm is used. But an electronic search costs only a fraction of that sum. Small wonder that employers are increasingly using résumé banks to find new employees.[19]

Spotlight on **Communicators**

Lee Morrison of Oklahoma City; Kathleen Korzan of North Haven, Connecticut; and Gary Hernandez of Bloomfield, New Jersey, all found jobs in Las Vegas through a computer database. For a $99 fee SkillSearch of Nashville <www.skillsearch.com> maintains career profiles of job applicants and matches them with employment requests from companies. SkillSearch differs from other electronic job services in that it preserves the confidentiality and security of both applicants and employers while serving as a matchmaker in the employment process.

FIGURE 16.8 What A Résumé-Scanning Program Does

Reads résumé with scanner

Identifies job categories and ranks applicants

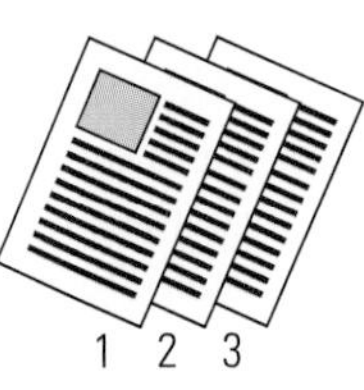

Generates letters of rejection or interview offers

Stores information or actual résumé image for future searches

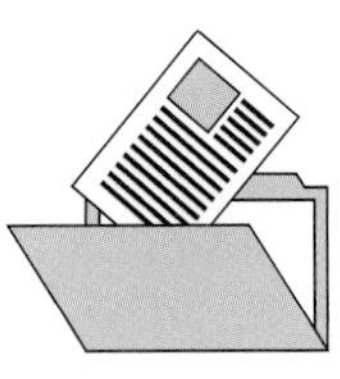

Making Your Résumé Computer Friendly

What does this all mean for you and your résumé? First, don't panic. It doesn't mean that you will have to hire a résumé specialist to write an entirely new résumé. It does mean, though, that you should consider the possibility that your résumé might be scanned. How can you know? One simple solution is to call any company where you plan to apply. Ask if it scans résumés electronically. What if you can't get a clear answer? If you have even the slightest suspicion that your résumé might be read electronically, you'll be smart to prepare a plain, scannable version. A scannable résumé must sacrifice many of the graphics possibilities that savvy writers employ. Computers aren't impressed by graphics. Computers prefer "vanilla" résumés—free of graphics and fancy fonts. To make a computer-friendly "vanilla" résumé, you'll want to apply the following suggestions about its physical appearance.

Computer-friendly résumés are free of graphics and fancy fonts.

- **Avoid unusual typefaces, underlining, and italics.** Moreover, don't use boxing, shading, or other graphics to highlight text. These features don't scan well. Most applicant-tracking programs, however, can accurately read bold print, solid bullets, and asterisks.
- **Use 10- to 14-point type.** Because touching letters or unusual fonts are likely to be misread, it's safest to use a large, well-known font, such as 12-point Times Roman or Helvetica. This may mean that your résumé will require two pages. After printing, inspect your résumé to see if any letters touch—especially in your name.
- **Use smooth white paper, black ink, and quality printing.** Avoid colored and textured papers as well as dot-matrix printing.
- **Be sure that your name is the first line on the page.** Don't use fancy layouts that may confuse a scanner.
- **Provide white space.** To ensure separation of words and categories, leave plenty of white space. For example, instead of using parentheses to enclose a telephone area code, insert blank spaces, such as 212 799-2415. Leave blank lines around headings.
- **Avoid double columns.** When listing job duties, skills, computer programs, and so forth, don't tabulate items into two- or three-column lists. Scanners read across and may convert tables into gobbledygook.
- **Don't fold or staple your résumé.** Send it in a large envelope so that you can avoid folds. Words that appear on folds may not be scanned correctly. Avoid staples because the indentions left after they are removed may cause pages to stick.

FIGURE 16.9 **Interpersonal Keywords Most Requested by Employers Using Résumé-Scanning Software***

Ability to delegate	Creative	Leadership	Self-accountable
Ability to implement	Customer oriented	Multitasking	Self-managing
Ability to plan	Detail minded	Open communication	Setting priorities
Ability to train	Ethical	Open minded	Supportive
Accurate	Flexible	Oral communication	Takes initiative
Adaptable	Follow instructions	Organizational skills	Team building
Aggressive worker	Follow through	Persuasive	Team player
Analytical ability	Follow up	Problem solving	Tenacious
Assertive	High energy	Public speaking	Willing to travel
Communication skills	Industrious	Results oriented	
Competitive	Innovative	Safety conscious	

*Reported by Resumix, a leading producer of résumé-scanning software.

Source: Joyce Lain Kennedy and Thomas J. Morrow, *Electronic Résumé Revolution* (New York: John Wiley & Sons, 1994), 70. Reprinted by permission of John Wiley & Sons, Inc.

- **Use abbreviations carefully.** Minimize unfamiliar abbreviations, but maximize easily recognized abbreviations—especially those within your field, such as CAD, COBRA, or JIT. When in doubt, though, spell out! Computers are less addled by whole words.
- **Include all your addresses and telephone numbers.** Be sure your résumé contains your electronic mail address, as well as your land address, telephone numbers, and fax number, if available.
- **Be prepared to send your résumé in ASCII.** Pronounced "AS-kee," this format offers text only and is immediately readable by all computer programs. It eliminates italics, bold, underlining, and unusual keyboard characters.

Emphasizing Keywords

Keywords are usually nouns that describe specific candidate traits or job requirements.

In addition to paying attention to the physical appearance of your résumé, you must also be concerned with keywords. These are usually nouns that describe what an employer wants. Suppose a supervisor at Nike wants to hire an administrative assistant with special proficiencies. That supervisor might submit the following keywords to the Nike applicant-tracking system: *Administrative Assistant, Computer Skills, Word 98, Self-Starter, Report Writing, Proofreading, Communication Skills.* The system would then search through all the résumés on file to see which ones best match the requirements.

Joyce Lain Kennedy, nationally syndicated career columnist and author of *Electronic Résumé Revolution,*[20] suggests using a *keyword* summary. On your résumé this list of keyword descriptors immediately follows your name and address.

A keyword summary should contain your targeted job title and alternative labels, as well as previous job titles, skills, software programs, and selected jargon known in your field. It concentrates on nouns rather than on verbs or adjectives.

To construct your summary, go through your core résumé and mark all relevant nouns. Also try to imagine what eight to ten words an employer might use to describe the job you want. Then select the 25 best words for your summary. Because interpersonal traits are often requested by employers, consult Figure 16.9. It shows the most frequently requested interpersonal traits, as reported by Resumix, one of the leaders in résumé-scanning software.

You may entitle your list "Keyword Summary," "Keyword Profile," or "Keyword Index." Here's an example of a possible keyword summary for a junior accountant:

A computer-friendly résumé may contain a keyword summary filled with words (usually nouns) that describe the job or candidate.

Keyword Summary
Accountant: Public. Junior. Staff. AA, Delgado Community College—Business Administration. BA, Nicholls State University—Accounting. Payables. Receivables. Payroll Experience. Quarterly Reports. Unemployment Reports. Communication Skills. Computer Skills. Excel. Word 98. PCs. Mainframes. Internet. Web. Networks. J. D. Edwards Software. Ability to learn software. Accurate. Dean's List. Award of Merit. Team player. Willing to travel. Relocate.

After an introductory keyword summary, your résumé should contain the standard parts discussed in this chapter. Remember that the keyword section merely helps ensure that your résumé will be selected for inspection. Then human eyes take over. Therefore, you'll want to observe the other writing tips you've learned to make your résumé attractive and forceful. Figures 16.10 through 16.12 show additional examples of chronological and combination résumés. Notice that the scannable résumé in Figure 16.13 is not drastically different from the others. It does, however, include a keyword summary.

Preparing an On-Line, Hypertext Résumé

To give your résumé life and make it stand out from others, you might wish to prepare an on-line résumé. This is actually an HTML (Hypertext Markup Language) document located at a Web site. Posting an on-line résumé has some distinct advantages—and a few disadvantages.

An on-line résumé contains hypertext links to work samples or a portfolio of additional information.

On the plus side, merely preparing an on-line résumé suggests that you have exceptional technical savvy. (You would, of course, give credit for any borrowed graphics or code.) An on-line résumé can be viewed whenever it is convenient for an employer, and it can be seen by many individuals in an organization without circulating a paper copy. But the real reason for preparing an on-line résumé is that it can become an electronic portfolio with links to examples of your work.

You could include clickable links to reports you have written, summaries of projects completed, a complete list of your coursework, letters of recommendation (with permissions from your recommenders), and extra information about your work experience. An advanced portfolio might include links to electronic copies of your artwork, film projects, blueprints, and photographs of classwork that might otherwise be difficult to share with potential employers. Moreover, you can include razzle-dazzle effects such as color, animation, sound, and graphics. An on-line résumé provides ample opportunity to show off your creative talents, but only if the position calls for creativity.

On the minus side, on-line résumés must be more generic than print résumés. They cannot be easily altered if you apply for different positions. Moreover, they present a security problem unless password protected. You may wish to include only an e-mail address instead of offering your address and telephone number.

Perhaps the best approach is to submit a traditional résumé and letter of application and treat your on-line résumé only as a portfolio of your work. For assistance in preparing an on-line or hypertext résumé, go to Wired Resumes **<www.wired-resume.com>**. This Web site, sponsored by the publisher of this textbook, helps subscribers design and develop an on-line résumé even if they have no knowledge of HTML.

FIGURE 16.10 Enhanced Résumé

Although Jeffrey had little paid work experience off campus, his résumé looks impressive because of his relevant summer, campus, and extern experiences. He describes specific achievements related to finance, his career goal. This version of his résumé is enhanced with desktop publishing features because he knows it will not be scanned.

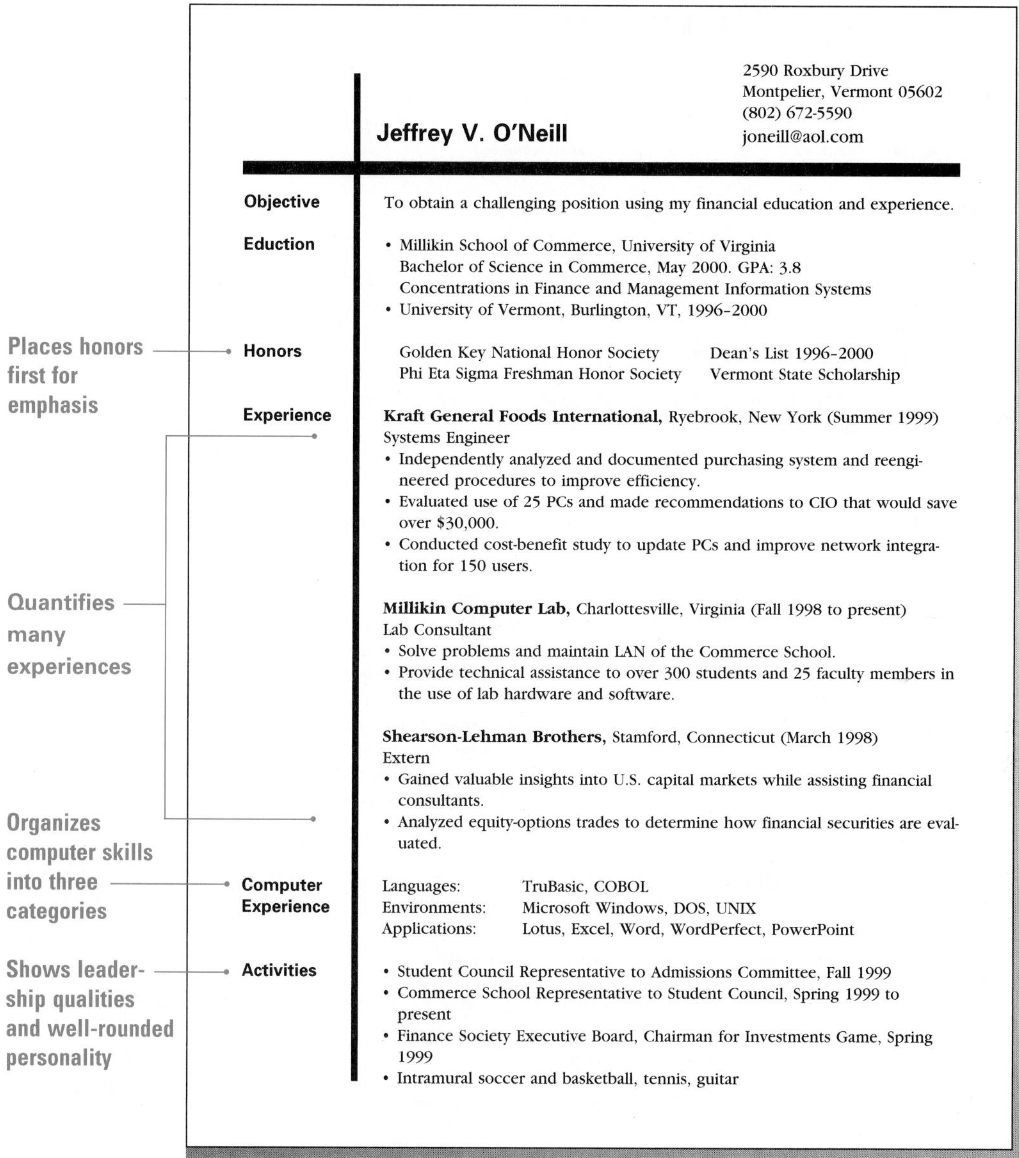

Jeffrey V. O'Neill

2590 Roxbury Drive
Montpelier, Vermont 05602
(802) 672-5590
joneill@aol.com

Objective

To obtain a challenging position using my financial education and experience.

Eduction

- Millikin School of Commerce, University of Virginia
  Bachelor of Science in Commerce, May 2000. GPA: 3.8
  Concentrations in Finance and Management Information Systems
- University of Vermont, Burlington, VT, 1996–2000

Places honors first for emphasis → **Honors**

Golden Key National Honor Society — Dean's List 1996–2000
Phi Eta Sigma Freshman Honor Society — Vermont State Scholarship

Experience

Kraft General Foods International, Ryebrook, New York (Summer 1999)
Systems Engineer
- Independently analyzed and documented purchasing system and reengineered procedures to improve efficiency.
- Evaluated use of 25 PCs and made recommendations to CIO that would save over $30,000.
- Conducted cost-benefit study to update PCs and improve network integration for 150 users.

Quantifies many experiences

Millikin Computer Lab, Charlottesville, Virginia (Fall 1998 to present)
Lab Consultant
- Solve problems and maintain LAN of the Commerce School.
- Provide technical assistance to over 300 students and 25 faculty members in the use of lab hardware and software.

Shearson-Lehman Brothers, Stamford, Connecticut (March 1998)
Extern
- Gained valuable insights into U.S. capital markets while assisting financial consultants.
- Analyzed equity-options trades to determine how financial securities are evaluated.

Organizes computer skills into three categories → **Computer Experience**

Languages: TruBasic, COBOL
Environments: Microsoft Windows, DOS, UNIX
Applications: Lotus, Excel, Word, WordPerfect, PowerPoint

Shows leadership qualities and well-rounded personality → **Activities**

- Student Council Representative to Admissions Committee, Fall 1999
- Commerce School Representative to Student Council, Spring 1999 to present
- Finance Society Executive Board, Chairman for Investments Game, Spring 1999
- Intramural soccer and basketball, tennis, guitar

Applying the Final Touches

Because your résumé is probably the most important message you will ever write, you'll revise it many times. With so much information in concentrated form and with so much riding on its outcome, your résumé demands careful polishing, proofreading, and critiquing.

As you revise, be certain to verify all the facts, particularly those involving your previous employment and education. Don't be caught in a mistake, or worse, dis-

FIGURE 16.11 **Combination Résumé**

Rick's résumé responds to an advertisement specifying skills for a staff accountant. He uses the combination format to allow him to highlight the skills his education and limited experience have provided. To make the résumé look professional, he uses the italics, bold, and scalable font features of his word processing program.

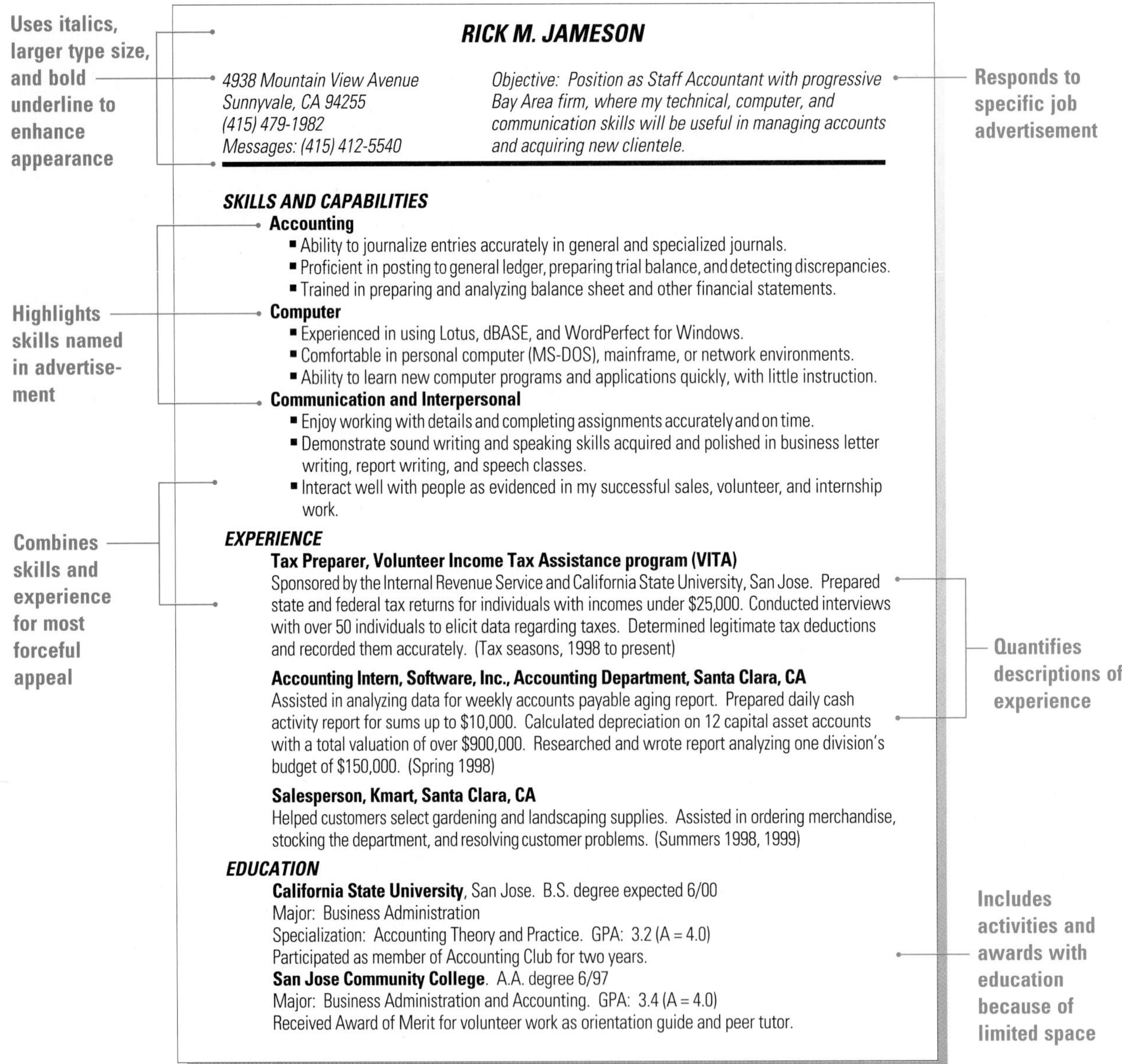

Uses italics, larger type size, and bold underline to enhance appearance

Responds to specific job advertisement

Highlights skills named in advertisement

Combines skills and experience for most forceful appeal

Quantifies descriptions of experience

Includes activities and awards with education because of limited space

RICK M. JAMESON

4938 Mountain View Avenue
Sunnyvale, CA 94255
(415) 479-1982
Messages: (415) 412-5540

Objective: Position as Staff Accountant with progressive Bay Area firm, where my technical, computer, and communication skills will be useful in managing accounts and acquiring new clientele.

SKILLS AND CAPABILITIES

Accounting

- Ability to journalize entries accurately in general and specialized journals.
- Proficient in posting to general ledger, preparing trial balance, and detecting discrepancies.
- Trained in preparing and analyzing balance sheet and other financial statements.

Computer

- Experienced in using Lotus, dBASE, and WordPerfect for Windows.
- Comfortable in personal computer (MS-DOS), mainframe, or network environments.
- Ability to learn new computer programs and applications quickly, with little instruction.

Communication and Interpersonal

- Enjoy working with details and completing assignments accurately and on time.
- Demonstrate sound writing and speaking skills acquired and polished in business letter writing, report writing, and speech classes.
- Interact well with people as evidenced in my successful sales, volunteer, and internship work.

EXPERIENCE

Tax Preparer, Volunteer Income Tax Assistance program (VITA)
Sponsored by the Internal Revenue Service and California State University, San Jose. Prepared state and federal tax returns for individuals with incomes under $25,000. Conducted interviews with over 50 individuals to elicit data regarding taxes. Determined legitimate tax deductions and recorded them accurately. (Tax seasons, 1998 to present)

Accounting Intern, Software, Inc., Accounting Department, Santa Clara, CA
Assisted in analyzing data for weekly accounts payable aging report. Prepared daily cash activity report for sums up to $10,000. Calculated depreciation on 12 capital asset accounts with a total valuation of over $900,000. Researched and wrote report analyzing one division's budget of $150,000. (Spring 1998)

Salesperson, Kmart, Santa Clara, CA
Helped customers select gardening and landscaping supplies. Assisted in ordering merchandise, stocking the department, and resolving customer problems. (Summers 1998, 1999)

EDUCATION

California State University, San Jose. B.S. degree expected 6/00
Major: Business Administration
Specialization: Accounting Theory and Practice. GPA: 3.2 (A = 4.0)
Participated as member of Accounting Club for two years.
San Jose Community College. A.A. degree 6/97
Major: Business Administration and Accounting. GPA: 3.4 (A = 4.0)
Received Award of Merit for volunteer work as orientation guide and peer tutor.

tortion of previous jobs and dates of employment. These items likely will be checked. And the consequences of puffing up a résumé with deception or flat-out lies are simply not worth the risk. Other ethical traps you'll want to avoid are described in the accompanying Ethical Insights box.

As you continue revising, look for other ways to improve your résumé. For example, consider consolidating headings. By condensing your information into as few

FIGURE 16.12 Chronological Résumé

Because Rachel has many years of experience and seeks high-level employment, she focuses on her experience. Notice how she includes specific achievements and quantifies them whenever possible.

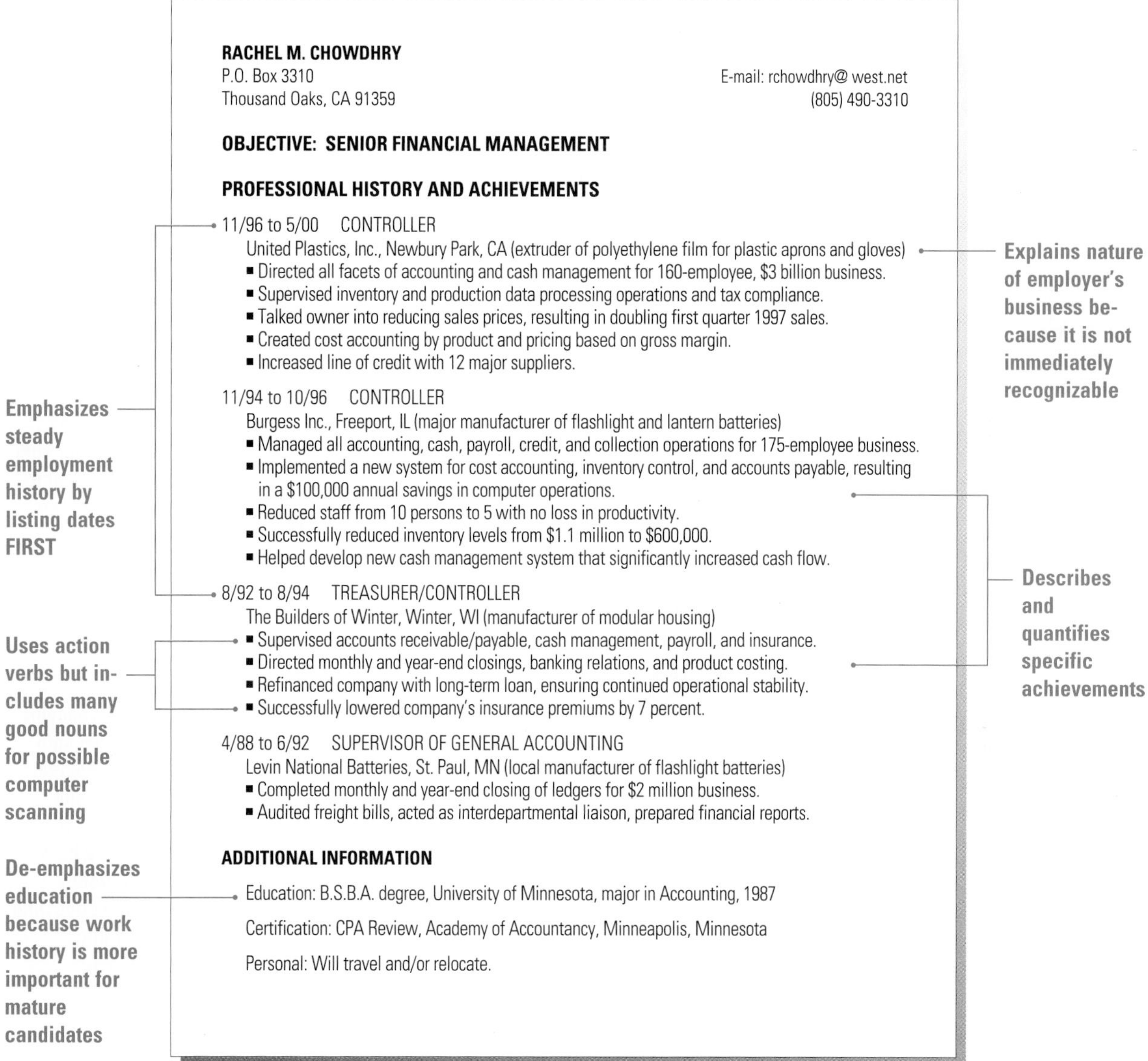

RACHEL M. CHOWDHRY
P.O. Box 3310 — E-mail: rchowdhry@ west.net
Thousand Oaks, CA 91359 — (805) 490-3310

OBJECTIVE: SENIOR FINANCIAL MANAGEMENT

PROFESSIONAL HISTORY AND ACHIEVEMENTS

11/96 to 5/00 CONTROLLER
United Plastics, Inc., Newbury Park, CA (extruder of polyethylene film for plastic aprons and gloves)
- Directed all facets of accounting and cash management for 160-employee, $3 billion business.
- Supervised inventory and production data processing operations and tax compliance.
- Talked owner into reducing sales prices, resulting in doubling first quarter 1997 sales.
- Created cost accounting by product and pricing based on gross margin.
- Increased line of credit with 12 major suppliers.

11/94 to 10/96 CONTROLLER
Burgess Inc., Freeport, IL (major manufacturer of flashlight and lantern batteries)
- Managed all accounting, cash, payroll, credit, and collection operations for 175-employee business.
- Implemented a new system for cost accounting, inventory control, and accounts payable, resulting in a $100,000 annual savings in computer operations.
- Reduced staff from 10 persons to 5 with no loss in productivity.
- Successfully reduced inventory levels from $1.1 million to $600,000.
- Helped develop new cash management system that significantly increased cash flow.

8/92 to 8/94 TREASURER/CONTROLLER
The Builders of Winter, Winter, WI (manufacturer of modular housing)
- Supervised accounts receivable/payable, cash management, payroll, and insurance.
- Directed monthly and year-end closings, banking relations, and product costing.
- Refinanced company with long-term loan, ensuring continued operational stability.
- Successfully lowered company's insurance premiums by 7 percent.

4/88 to 6/92 SUPERVISOR OF GENERAL ACCOUNTING
Levin National Batteries, St. Paul, MN (local manufacturer of flashlight batteries)
- Completed monthly and year-end closing of ledgers for $2 million business.
- Audited freight bills, acted as interdepartmental liaison, prepared financial reports.

ADDITIONAL INFORMATION

Education: B.S.B.A. degree, University of Minnesota, major in Accounting, 1987

Certification: CPA Review, Academy of Accountancy, Minneapolis, Minnesota

Personal: Will travel and/or relocate.

Emphasizes steady employment history by listing dates FIRST
Uses action verbs but includes many good nouns for possible computer scanning
De-emphasizes education because work history is more important for mature candidates
Explains nature of employer's business because it is not immediately recognizable
Describes and quantifies specific achievements

headings as possible, you'll produce a clean, professional-looking document. Study other résumés for valuable formatting ideas. Ask yourself what graphics highlighting techniques you can use to improve readability: capitalization, underlining, indenting, and bulleting. Experiment with headings and styles to achieve a pleasing, easy-to-read message. Moreover, look for ways to eliminate wordiness. For example, instead of *Supervised two employees who worked at the counter,* try *Supervised two counter employees.* Review Chapter 6 for more tips.

FIGURE 16.13 Computer-Friendly Résumé

Casandra prepared this "vanilla" resume (free of graphics and fancy formatting) so that it would scan well if read by a computer. Notice that she begins with a keyword summary that contains job titles, skills, traits, and other descriptive words. She hopes that some of these keywords will match those submitted by an employer. To improve accurate scanning, she avoids italics, vertical and horizontal lines, and double columns.

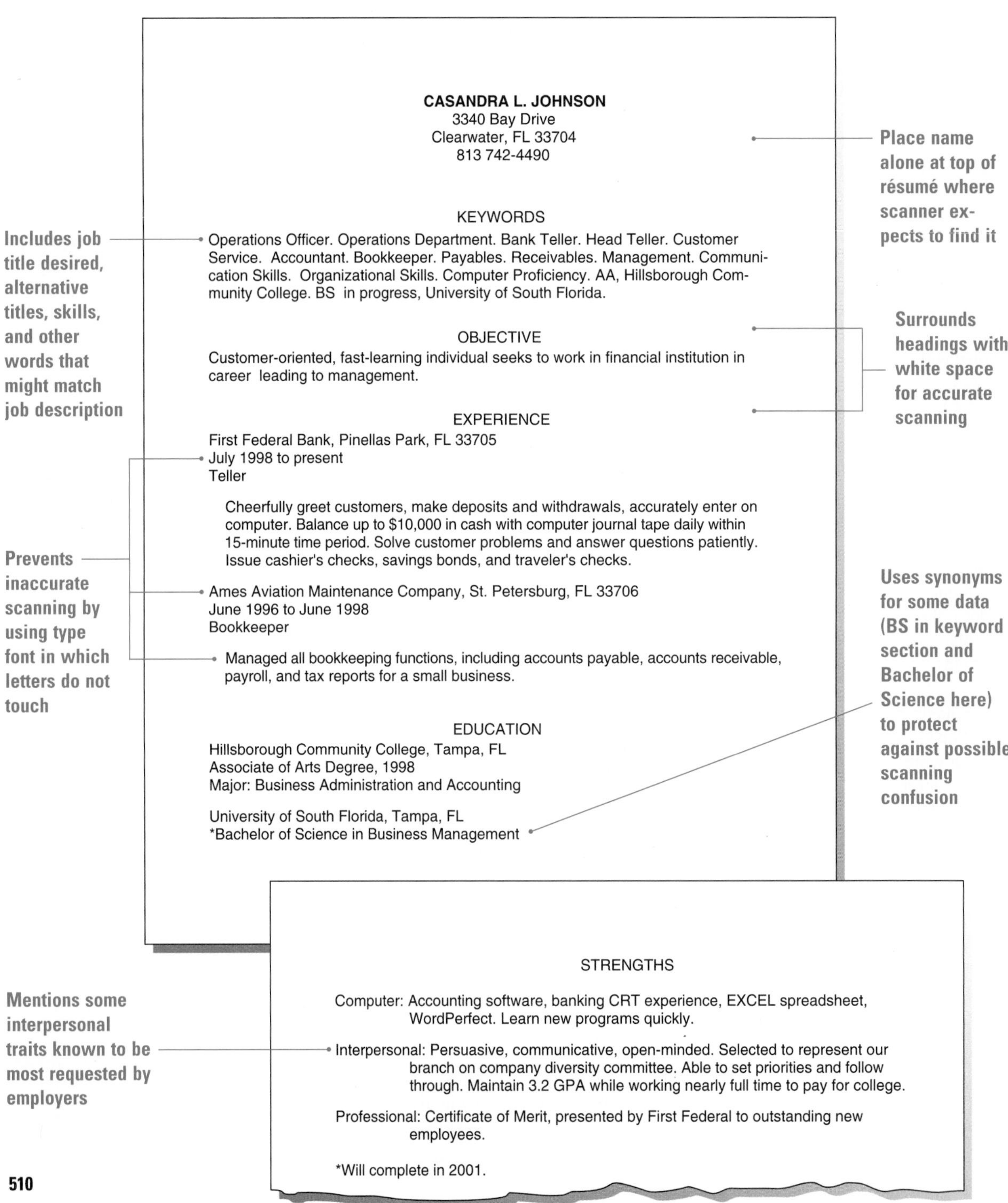
CASANDRA L. JOHNSON
3340 Bay Drive
Clearwater, FL 33704
813 742-4490

KEYWORDS
Operations Officer. Operations Department. Bank Teller. Head Teller. Customer Service. Accountant. Bookkeeper. Payables. Receivables. Management. Communication Skills. Organizational Skills. Computer Proficiency. AA, Hillsborough Community College. BS in progress, University of South Florida.

OBJECTIVE
Customer-oriented, fast-learning individual seeks to work in financial institution in career leading to management.

EXPERIENCE
First Federal Bank, Pinellas Park, FL 33705
July 1998 to present
Teller

Cheerfully greet customers, make deposits and withdrawals, accurately enter on computer. Balance up to $10,000 in cash with computer journal tape daily within 15-minute time period. Solve customer problems and answer questions patiently. Issue cashier's checks, savings bonds, and traveler's checks.

Ames Aviation Maintenance Company, St. Petersburg, FL 33706
June 1996 to June 1998
Bookkeeper

Managed all bookkeeping functions, including accounts payable, accounts receivable, payroll, and tax reports for a small business.

EDUCATION
Hillsborough Community College, Tampa, FL
Associate of Arts Degree, 1998
Major: Business Administration and Accounting

University of South Florida, Tampa, FL
*Bachelor of Science in Business Management

STRENGTHS

Computer: Accounting software, banking CRT experience, EXCEL spreadsheet, WordPerfect. Learn new programs quickly.

Interpersonal: Persuasive, communicative, open-minded. Selected to represent our branch on company diversity committee. Able to set priorities and follow through. Maintain 3.2 GPA while working nearly full time to pay for college.

Professional: Certificate of Merit, presented by First Federal to outstanding new employees.

*Will complete in 2001.

Place name alone at top of résumé where scanner expects to find it
Includes job title desired, alternative titles, skills, and other words that might match job description
Surrounds headings with white space for accurate scanning
Prevents inaccurate scanning by using type font in which letters do not touch
Uses synonyms for some data (BS in keyword section and Bachelor of Science here) to protect against possible scanning confusion
Mentions some interpersonal traits known to be most requested by employers

Above all, make your résumé look professional. Avoid anything humorous or "cute," such as a help-wanted poster with your name or picture inside. Eliminate the personal pronoun *I*. The abbreviated, objective style of a résumé precludes the use of personal pronouns. Use white, off-white, or buff-colored heavy bond paper (24-pound) and a first-rate printer.

After revising, proofread, proofread, and proofread again: for spelling and mechanics, for content, and for format. Then, have a knowledgeable friend or relative proofread it again. This is one document that must be perfect.

Because résumés must be perfect, they should be proofread many times.

By now you may be thinking that you'd like to hire someone to write your résumé. Don't. First, you know yourself better than anyone else could know you. Second, you'll end up with either a generic or a one-time résumé. A generic résumé in today's highly competitive job market will lose out to a targeted résumé nine times out of ten. Equally useless is a one-time résumé aimed at a single job. What if you don't get that job? Because you will need to revise your résumé many times as you seek a variety of jobs, be prepared to write (and rewrite) it yourself.

A final word about résumé-writing services. Some tend to produce eye-catching, elaborate documents with lofty language, fancy borders, and fuzzy thinking. Here's an example of empty writing: "Seeking a position which will utilize academic achievements and hands-on experience while providing for career-development opportunities."[21] Save your money and buy a good interview suit instead.

Faxing or E-Mailing Your Résumé

In this hurry-up world, employers increasingly want information immediately. If you must fax or e-mail your résumé, take a second look at it. The key to success is SPACE. Without it, letters and character blur. Underlines blend with the words above, and bold print may look like an ink blot.[25] How can you improve your chances of making a good impression when you must fax or e-mail your résumé?

Résumés to be faxed should have ample space between letters, be printed in 12-point or larger font, and avoid underlines.

If you are faxing your printed résumé, select a font with adequate space between each character. Thinner fonts—such as Times, Palatino, New Century Schoolbook, Courier, and Bookman—are clearer than thicker ones. Use a 12-point or larger font, and avoid underlines, which may look broken or choppy when faxed. To be safe, get a transmission report to ensure that all pages were transmitted satisfactorily. Finally, follow up with your polished, printed résumé.

If you are e-mailing your résumé, you may wish to prepare an ASCII version (text only). It will eliminate bold, italics, underlining, tabulated indentions, and unusual characters. To prevent lines from wrapping at awkward spots, keep your line length to 65 characters or less. You can, of course, transmit a fully formatted, attractive résumé if you send it as an attachment and your receiver is using a compatible e-mail program.

Résumés that are sent by e-mail transmit best as ASCII (text-only) files without tabs, underlines, italics, bold, or unusual characters.

Nearly everyone writes a résumé by adapting a model, such as those in Figures 16.3 through 16.5 and 16.10 through 16.13. The chronological résumé for Rachel shown in Figure 16.12 is typical of candidates with considerable working experience. Although she describes four positions that span a 14-year period, she manages to fit her résumé on one page. However, two-page résumés are justified for people with long work histories.

As you prepare to write your current résumé, consult the following checklist to review the job search process and important résumé-writing techniques.

ETHICAL INSIGHTS

ARE INFLATED RÉSUMÉS WORTH THE RISK?

A résumé is expected to showcase a candidate's strengths and minimize weaknesses. For this reason, recruiters expect a certain degree of self-promotion. But some résumé writers step over the line that separates honest self-marketing from deceptive half-truths and flat-out lies. Distorting facts on a résumé is unethical; lying is illegal. And either practice can destroy a career.

Although recruiters can't check everything, most will verify previous employment and education before hiring candidates. Over half will require official transcripts. And after hiring, the checking process may continue. At one of the nation's top accounting firms, the human resources director described the posthiring routine: "If we find a discrepancy in GPA or prior experience due to an honest mistake, we meet with the new hire to hear an explanation. But if it wasn't a mistake, we terminate the person immediately. Unfortunately, we've had to do that too often."[22]

No job seeker wants to be in the unhappy position of explaining résumé errors or defending misrepresentation. Avoiding the following common problems can keep you off the hot seat:

- **Inflated education, grades, or honors.** Some job candidates claim degrees from colleges or universities when in fact they merely attended classes. Others increase their grade-point averages or claim fictitious honors. Any such dishonest reporting is grounds for dismissal when discovered.

- **Enhanced job titles.** Wishing to elevate their status, some applicants misrepresent their titles. For example, one technician called himself a "programmer" when he had actually programmed only one project for his boss. A mail clerk who assumed added responsibilities conferred upon herself the title of "supervisor." Even when the description seems accurate, it's unethical to list any title not officially granted.

- **Puffed-up accomplishments.** Some job seekers inflate their employment experience or achievements. One clerk, eager to make her photocopying duties sound more important, said that she assisted the *vice president in communicating and distributing employee directives.* An Ivy

Checklist for Writing a Persuasive Résumé

Preparation

Research the job market. Learn about available jobs, common qualifications, and potential employers. The best résumés are targeted for specific jobs with specific companies.

Analyze your strengths. Determine what aspects of your education, experience, and personal characteristics will be assets to prospective employers.

Study models. Look at other résumés for formatting and element placement ideas. Experiment with headings and styles to achieve an artistic, readable product.

Heading and Objective

Identify yourself. List your name, address, and telephone number. Skip the word *résumé.*

Include a career objective for a targeted job. If this résumé is intended for a specific job, include a statement tailored to it (*Objective: Cost accounting position in the petroleum industry*).

League graduate who spent the better part of six months watching rented videos on his VCR described the activity as *Independent Film Study.* The latter statement may have helped win an interview, but it lost him the job.[23] In addition to avoiding puffery, guard against taking sole credit for achievements that required many people. When recruiters suspect dubious claims on résumés, they nail applicants with specific—and often embarrassing—questions during their interviews.[24]

- **Altered employment dates.** Some candidates extend the dates of employment to hide unimpressive jobs or to cover up periods of unemployment and illness. Let's say that several years ago Cindy was unemployed for fourteen months between working for Company A and being hired by Company B. To make her employment history look better, she adds seven months to her tenure with Company A and seven months to Company B. Now her employment history has no gaps, but her résumé is dishonest and represents a potential booby trap for her.

The employment process can easily lure you into ethical traps, such as those described in Chapter 1. Beware of these specific temptations:

- **The relative-filth trap:** "A little fudging on my GPA is nothing compared with the degrees that some people buy in degree mills."
- **The rationalization trap:** "I deserve to call myself 'manager' because that's what I really did."
- **The self-deception trap:** "Giving myself a certificate from the institute is OK because I really intended to finish the program, but I got sick."

Falling into these ethical traps risks your entire employment future. If your honest qualifications aren't good enough to get you the job you want, start working now to improve them.

Career Track Application

As a class, discuss the ethics of writing résumés. What's the difference between honest self-marketing and deception? What are some examples from your experience? Where could college students go wrong in preparing their résumés? Is a new employee "home free" if an inflated résumé is not detected in the hiring process? Are job candidates obligated to describe every previous job on a résumé? How can candidates improve an unimpressive résumé without resorting to "puffing it up"?

Education

 **Name your degree, date of graduation, and institution.** Emphasize your education if your experience is limited.

 **List your major and GPA.** Give information about your studies, but don't inventory all your courses.

Work Experience

 **Itemize your jobs.** Start with your most recent job. Give the employer's name and city, dates of employment (month, year), and most significant job title.

 **Describe your experience.** Use action verbs to summarize achievements and skills relevant to your targeted job.

 **Present nontechnical skills.** Give evidence of communication, management, and interpersonal talents. Employers want more than empty assurances; try to quantify your skills and accomplishments (*Collaborated with six-member task force in producing 20-page mission statement*).

Special Skills, Achievements, and Awards

 **Highlight computer skills.** Remember that nearly all employers seek employees who are proficient in using the Internet, e-mail, word processing, databases, and spreadsheets.

CASE STUDY

PROCESS IN PROGRESS

Carnival Cruise Lines Revisited

Bonnie Gesualdi-Chao, recruiting specialist at Carnival Cruise Lines, prefers one-page chronological résumés because they're easy to read and provide a quick history of a candidate. "I'm generally recruiting for entry-level positions; and I want to see their education, internships, summer jobs, and experience lined up in chronological order," says Bonnie. "I'm also very interested in skills and training—such as computer knowledge, a second language, travel and tourism courses, seminars, and symposiums. Because I'm scanning many résumés quickly, the chronological format is best for me."

In regard to experience and training, Bonnie is most interested in achievements that relate to Carnival and its job requirements. For example, if a position were open in group sales reservations, she would look for someone who had worked in a travel agency or who had attended travel and tourism school or who had coordinated special events for large groups. For entry-level positions, Bonnie says, "I'm not expecting a whole lot of experience, but I do look to see whether an applicant's college classes relate to the job and whether the person was interested enough in the field to complete an internship. Since we are the 'Fun Ships' and we're in the vacation industry, we're also looking for people who are enthusiastic, eager, and ready to have fun. But we'd also like them to be hardworking and dedicated."

Critical Thinking

- If job recruiters seem to prefer one-page, chronological résumés, why should candidates use any other format?
- Why not prepare one excellent résumé, and use the same one for all applications?
- How can a candidate with little actual work experience prepare a chronological résumé that doesn't look skimpy?

 **Show that you are a well-rounded individual.** List awards, experiences, and extracurricular activities—particularly if they demonstrate leadership, teamwork, reliability, loyalty, industry, initiative, efficiency, and self-sufficiency.

Final Tips

 **Consider omitting references.** Have a list of references available for the interview, but don't include them or refer to them unless you have a specific reason to do so.

 **Look for ways to condense your data.** Omit all street addresses except your own. Consolidate your headings. Study models and experiment with formats to find the most readable and efficient groupings.

 **Double-check for parallel phrasing.** Be sure that all entries have balanced construction, such as similar verb forms (*Organized files, trained assistants, scheduled events*).

 **Make your résumé scannable.** If there's a chance it will be read by a computer, add a keyword summary, use a common font, and remove graphics.

 **Project professionalism and quality.** Avoid personal pronouns and humor. Use 24-pound bond paper and a high-quality printer.

 **Proofread, proofread, proofread.** Make this document perfect by proofreading at least three times.

The Persuasive Letter of Application

5

Letters of application introduce résumés, relate writer strengths to reader benefits, and seek an interview.

To accompany your résumé, you'll need a persuasive letter of application (also called a *cover letter*). The letter of application has three purposes: (1) introducing the résumé, (2) highlighting your strengths in terms of benefits to the reader, and (3) gaining an interview. In many ways your letter of application is a sales letter; it sells your talents and tries to beat the competition. It will, accordingly, include many of the techniques you learned for sales presentations (Chapter 9).

Personnel professionals disagree on how long to make the letter of application. Many prefer short letters with no more than four paragraphs; instead of concentrating on the letter, these readers focus on the résumé. Others desire longer letters that supply more information, thus giving them a better opportunity to evaluate a candidate's qualifications. The latter personnel professionals argue that hiring and training new employees is expensive and time-consuming; therefore, they welcome extra data to guide them in making the best choice the first time. Follow your judgment in writing a brief or a lengthier letter of application. If you feel, for example, that you need space to explain in more detail what you can do for a prospective employer, do so.

Regardless of its length, a letter of application should have three primary parts: (1) an opening that gains attention, (2) a body that builds interest and reduces resistance, and (3) a closing that motivates action.

Gaining Attention in the Opening

The opener in a letter of application gains attention by addressing the receiver by name.

The first step in gaining the interest of your reader is addressing that individual by name. Rather than sending your letter to the "Personnel Manager" or "Human Resources Department," try to identify the name of the appropriate individual. Make it a rule to call the organization for the correct spelling and the complete address. This personal touch distinguishes your letter and demonstrates your serious interest.

How you open your letter of application depends largely on whether the application is solicited or unsolicited. If an employment position has been announced and applicants are being solicited, you can use a direct approach. If you do not know whether a position is open and you are prospecting for a job, use an indirect approach. Whether direct or indirect, the opening should attract the attention of the reader. Strive for openings that are more imaginative than *Please consider this letter an application for the position of . . .* or *I would like to apply for. . . .*

Openers for solicited jobs refer to the source of the information, the job title, and qualifications for the position.

Openings for Solicited Jobs. Here are some of the best techniques to open a letter of application for a job that has been announced:

- **Refer to the name of an employee in the company.** Remember that employers always hope to hire known quantities rather than complete strangers:

  Mitchell Sims, a member of your Customer Service Department, told me that IntriPlex is seeking an experienced customer service representative. The attached summary of my qualifications demonstrates my preparation for this position.

  At the suggestion of Ms. Jennifer Larson of your Human Resources Department, I submit my qualifications for the position of staffing coordinator.

- **Refer to the source of your information precisely.** If you are answering an advertisement, include the exact position advertised and the name and date of the publication. For large organizations it's also wise to mention the section of the newspaper where the ad appeared:

Your advertisement in Section C-3 of the June 1 *Daily News* for an accounting administrator greatly appeals to me. With my accounting training and computer experience, I believe I could serve Quad Graphics well.

The September 10 issue of *The Washington Post* reports that you are seeking a mature, organized, and reliable administrative assistant with excellent communication skills.

Susan Butler, placement director at Sierra University, told me that DataTech has an opening for a technical writer with knowledge of Web design and graphics.

- **Refer to the job title and describe how your qualifications fit the requirements.** Personnel directors are looking for a match between an applicant's credentials and the job needs:

Will an honors graduate with a degree in recreation and two years of part-time experience organizing social activities for a convalescent hospital qualify for your position of activity director?

Because of my specialized training in computerized accounting at Boise State University, I feel confident that I have the qualifications you described in your advertisement for a cost accountant trainee.

Openers for unsolicited jobs show interest in and knowledge of the company, as well as spotlighting reader benefits.

Openings for Unsolicited Jobs. If you are unsure whether a position actually exists, you may wish to use a more persuasive opening. Since your goal is to convince this person to read on, try one of the following techniques:

- **Demonstrate interest in and knowledge of the reader's business.** Show the personnel director that you have done your research and that this organization is more than a mere name to you:

Since Signa HealthNet, Inc., is organizing a new information management team for its recently established group insurance division, could you use the services of a well-trained information systems graduate who seeks to become a professional systems analyst?

- **Show how your special talents and background will benefit the company.** Personnel directors need to be convinced that you can do something for them:

Could your rapidly expanding publications division use the services of an editorial assistant who offers exceptional language skills, an honors degree from the University of Maine, and two years' experience in producing a campus literary publication?

In applying for an advertised job, Nancy Gutierrez James wrote the solicited letter of application shown in Figure 16.14. Notice that her opening identifies the position and the newspaper completely so that the reader knows exactly what advertisement Nancy means. More challenging are unsolicited letters of application, such as Donald Vinton's shown in Figure 16.15. Because he hopes to discover or create a job, his opening must grab the reader's attention immediately. To do that, he capitalizes on company information appearing in the newspaper. Notice, too, that Donald purposely kept his cover letter short and to the point because he anticipated that a busy executive would be unwilling to read a long, detailed letter.

Donald's unsolicited letter "prospects" for a job. Some job candidates feel that such letters may be even more productive than efforts to secure advertised jobs, since "prospecting" candidates face less competition.

FIGURE 16.14 **Solicited Letter of Application**

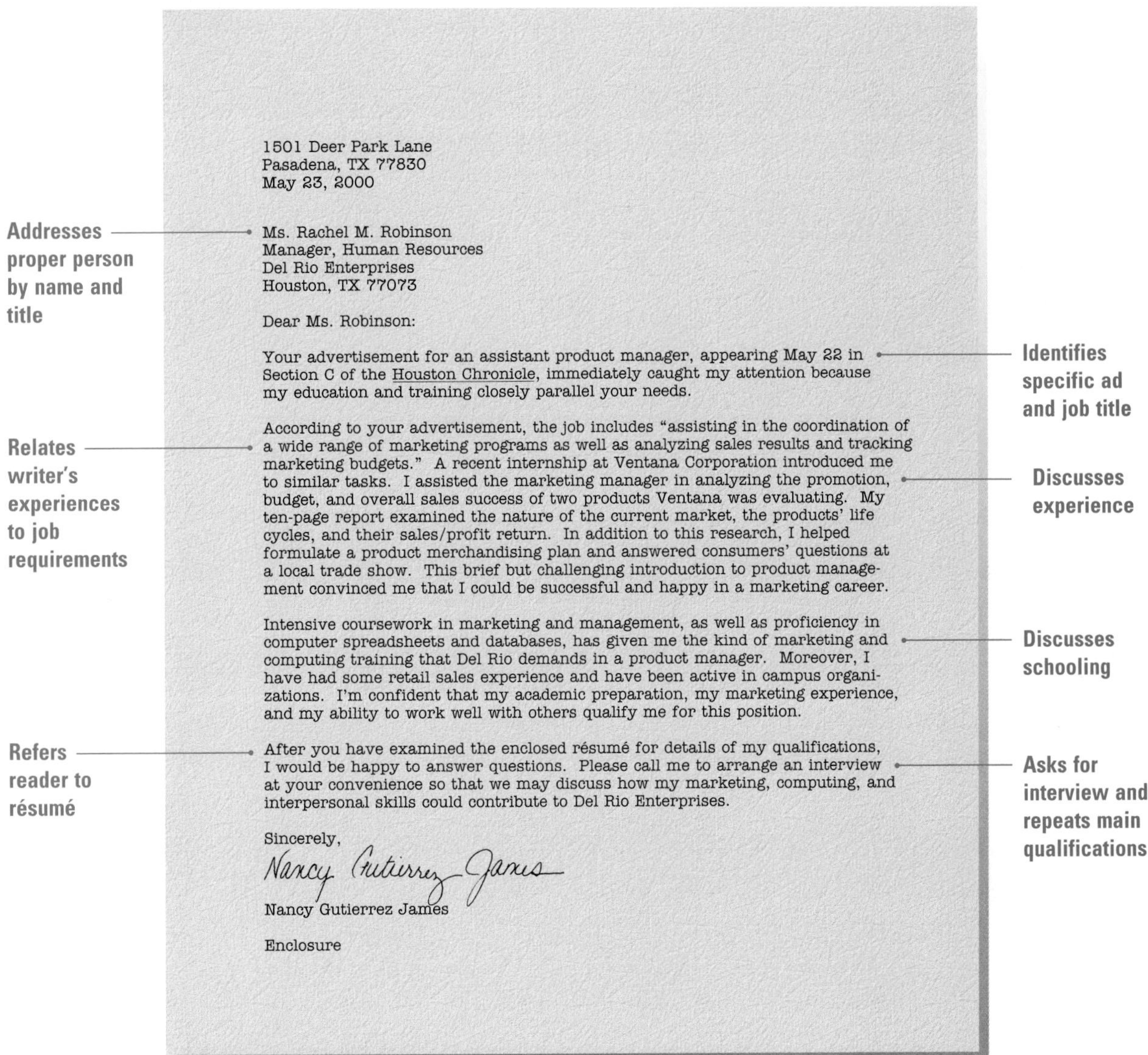

Addresses proper person by name and title
Relates writer's experiences to job requirements
Refers reader to résumé
Identifies specific ad and job title
Discusses experience
Discusses schooling
Asks for interview and repeats main qualifications

1501 Deer Park Lane
Pasadena, TX 77830
May 23, 2000

Ms. Rachel M. Robinson
Manager, Human Resources
Del Rio Enterprises
Houston, TX 77073

Dear Ms. Robinson:

Your advertisement for an assistant product manager, appearing May 22 in Section C of the Houston Chronicle, immediately caught my attention because my education and training closely parallel your needs.

According to your advertisement, the job includes "assisting in the coordination of a wide range of marketing programs as well as analyzing sales results and tracking marketing budgets." A recent internship at Ventana Corporation introduced me to similar tasks. I assisted the marketing manager in analyzing the promotion, budget, and overall sales success of two products Ventana was evaluating. My ten-page report examined the nature of the current market, the products' life cycles, and their sales/profit return. In addition to this research, I helped formulate a product merchandising plan and answered consumers' questions at a local trade show. This brief but challenging introduction to product management convinced me that I could be successful and happy in a marketing career.

Intensive coursework in marketing and management, as well as proficiency in computer spreadsheets and databases, has given me the kind of marketing and computing training that Del Rio demands in a product manager. Moreover, I have had some retail sales experience and have been active in campus organizations. I'm confident that my academic preparation, my marketing experience, and my ability to work well with others qualify me for this position.

After you have examined the enclosed résumé for details of my qualifications, I would be happy to answer questions. Please call me to arrange an interview at your convenience so that we may discuss how my marketing, computing, and interpersonal skills could contribute to Del Rio Enterprises.

Sincerely,

Nancy Gutierrez James

Nancy Gutierrez James

Enclosure

Building Interest in the Body

The body of a letter of application should build interest, reduce resistance, and discuss relevant personal traits.

Once you have captured the attention of the reader, you can use the body of the letter to build interest and reduce resistance. Keep in mind that your résumé emphasizes what you have *done*; your application letter stresses what you *can do* for the employer.

Your first goal is to relate your remarks to a specific position. If you are responding to an advertisement, you'll want to explain how your preparation and experience fill the stated requirements. If you are prospecting for a job, you may not know the exact requirements. Your employment research and knowledge of your field, however, should give you a reasonably good idea of what is expected for this position.

FIGURE 16.15 Unsolicited Letter of Application

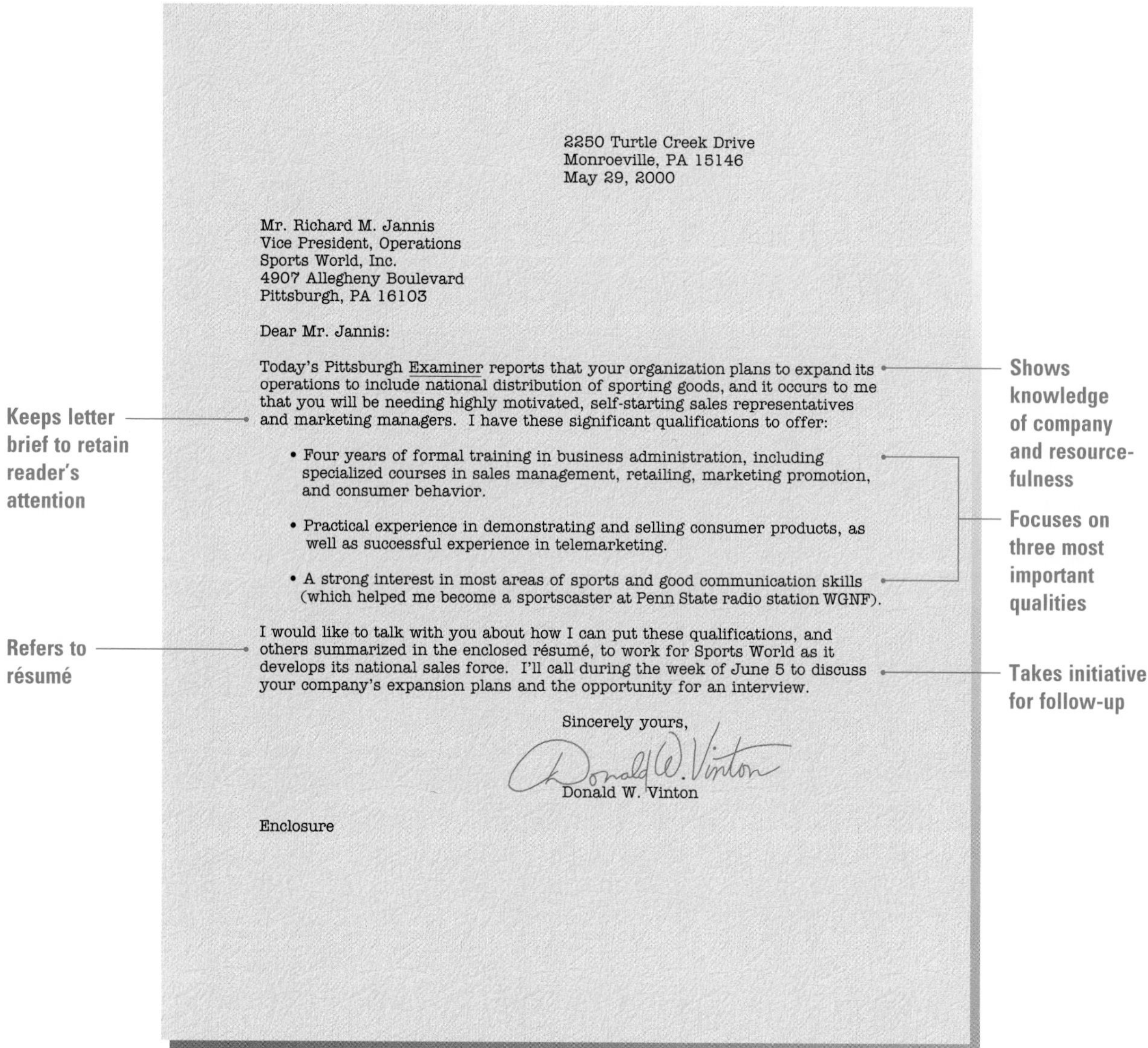

2250 Turtle Creek Drive
Monroeville, PA 15146
May 29, 2000

Mr. Richard M. Jannis
Vice President, Operations
Sports World, Inc.
4907 Allegheny Boulevard
Pittsburgh, PA 16103

Dear Mr. Jannis:

Today's Pittsburgh Examiner reports that your organization plans to expand its operations to include national distribution of sporting goods, and it occurs to me that you will be needing highly motivated, self-starting sales representatives and marketing managers. I have these significant qualifications to offer:

- Four years of formal training in business administration, including specialized courses in sales management, retailing, marketing promotion, and consumer behavior.
- Practical experience in demonstrating and selling consumer products, as well as successful experience in telemarketing.
- A strong interest in most areas of sports and good communication skills (which helped me become a sportscaster at Penn State radio station WGNF).

I would like to talk with you about how I can put these qualifications, and others summarized in the enclosed résumé, to work for Sports World as it develops its national sales force. I'll call during the week of June 5 to discuss your company's expansion plans and the opportunity for an interview.

Sincerely yours,

Donald W. Vinton

Enclosure

Keeps letter brief to retain reader's attention
Refers to résumé
Shows knowledge of company and resourcefulness
Focuses on three most important qualities
Takes initiative for follow-up

It's also important to emphasize reader benefits. In other words, you should describe your strong points in relation to the needs of the employer. In one employment survey many personnel professionals expressed the same view: "I want you to tell me what you can do for my organization. This is much more important to me than telling me what courses you took in college or what 'duties' you performed on your previous jobs."[26] Instead of *I have completed courses in business communication, report writing, and technical writing,* try this:

Spotlighting reader benefits means matching personal strengths to employer needs.

> Courses in business communication, report writing, and technical writing have helped me develop the research and writing skills required of your technical writers.

Choose your strongest qualifications and show how they fit the targeted job. And remember, students with little experience are better off spotlighting their education and its practical applications, as these candidates did:

Because you seek an architect's apprentice with proven ability, I submit a drawing of mine that won second place in the Sinclair College drafting contest last year.

Successfully transcribing over 100 letters and memos in my college transcription class gave me experience in converting the spoken word into the written word, an exacting communication skill demanded of your administrative assistants.

In the body of your letter, you'll also want to discuss relevant personal traits. Employers are looking for candidates who, among other things, are team players, take responsibility, show initiative, and learn easily. Notice how the following paragraph uses action verbs to paint a picture of a promising candidate:

The body of a letter of application may describe such traits as taking responsibility, showing initiative, and learning easily.

In addition to developing technical and academic skills at Mid-State University, I have gained interpersonal, leadership, and organizational skills. As vice president of the business students' organization, Gamma Alpha, I helped organize and supervise two successful fund-raising events. These activities involved conceptualizing the tasks, motivating others to help, scheduling work sessions, and coordinating the efforts of 35 diverse students in reaching our goal. I enjoyed my success with these activities and look forward to applying such experience in your management trainee program.

Finally, in this section or the next, you should refer the reader to your résumé. Do so directly or as part of another statement, as shown here:

Please refer to the attached résumé for additional information regarding my education, experience, and references.

As you will notice from my résumé, I will graduate in June with a bachelor's degree in business administration.

Motivating Action in the Closing

After presenting your case, you should conclude with a spur to action. This is where you ask for an interview. If you live in a distant city, you may request an employment application or an opportunity to be interviewed by the organization's nearest representative. However, never ask for the job. To do so would be presumptuous and naive. In requesting an interview, suggest reader benefits or review your strongest points. Sound sincere and appreciative. Remember to make it easy for the reader to agree by supplying your telephone number and best times to call you. And keep in mind that some personnel directors prefer that you take the initiative to call them. Here are possible endings:

The closing of a letter of application should include a request for an interview.

I hope this brief description of my qualifications and the additional information on my résumé indicate to you my genuine desire to put my skills in accounting to work for you. Please call me at (405) 488-2291 before 10 a.m. or after 3 p.m. to arrange an interview.

To add to your staff an industrious, well-trained administrative assistant with proven word processing and communication skills, call me at (350) 492-1433 to arrange an interview. I can meet with you at any time convenient to your schedule.

Next week, after you have examined the attached résumé, I will call you to discuss the possibility of arranging an interview.

Final Tips

A letter of application should look professional and suggest quality.

As you revise your letter of application, notice how many sentences begin with *I*. Although it's impossible to talk about yourself without using *I*, you can reduce "I" domination with this writing technique. Make activities and outcomes, and not yourself, the subjects of sentences. For example, rather than *I took classes in business communication and computer applications,* say *Classes in business communication and computer applications prepared me to . . .* Instead of *I enjoyed helping customers,* say *Helping customers was a real pleasure.*

Like the résumé, your letter of application must look professional and suggest quality. This means using a traditional letter style, such as block or modified block. Also, be sure to print it on the same bond paper as your résumé. And, as with your résumé, proofread it several times yourself; then, have a friend read it for content and mechanics. The following checklist provides a quick summary of suggestions to review when you compose and proofread your cover letter.

Checklist for Writing a Persuasive Letter of Application

Opening

 **Use the receiver's name.** Whenever possible, address the proper individual by name.

 **Identify your information source, if appropriate.** In responding to an advertisement, specify the position advertised as well as the date and publication name. If someone referred you, name that person.

 **Gain the reader's attention.** Use one of these techniques: (1) tell how your qualifications fit the job specifications, (2) show knowledge of the reader's business, (3) describe how your special talents will be assets to the company, or (4) use an original and relevant expression.

Body

 **Describe what you can do for the reader.** Demonstrate how your background and training fill the job requirements.

 **Highlight your strengths.** Summarize your principal assets from education, experience, and special skills. Avoid repeating specific data from your résumé.

 **Refer to your résumé.** In this section or the closing, direct the reader to the attached résumé. Do so directly or incidentally as part of another statement.

Closing

 **Ask for an interview.** Also consider reviewing your strongest points or suggesting how your assets will benefit the company.

 **Make it easy to respond.** Tell when you can be reached during office hours or announce when you will call the reader. Note that some recruiters prefer that you call them.

Follow-Up Letters and Other Employment Documents

Although the résumé and letter of application are your major tasks, other important letters and documents are often required during the employment process. You may need to make requests, write follow-up letters, or fill out employment applications. Because each of these tasks reveals something about you and your communication skills, you'll want to put your best foot forward. These documents often subtly influence company officials to extend an interview or offer a job.

Reference Request

Most employers expect job candidates at some point to submit names of individuals who are willing to discuss the candidates' qualifications. Before you list anyone as a reference, however, be sure to ask permission. Try to do this in person. Ask an instructor, for example, if he or she would be willing and has the time to act as your recommender. If you detect any sign of reluctance, don't force the issue. Your goal is to find willing individuals who think well of you.

To get good letters of recommendation, find willing people and provide ample data about yourself.

What your recommenders need most is information about you. What should they stress to prospective employers? Let's say you're applying for a specific job that requires a letter of recommendation. Professor Smith has already agreed to be a reference for you. To get the best letter of recommendation from Professor Smith, help her out. Write a letter telling her about the position, its requirements, and the recommendation deadline. Include a copy of your résumé. You might remind her of a positive experience with you (*You said my report was well organized*) that she could use in the recommendation. Remember that recommenders need evidence to support generalizations. Give them appropriate ammunition, as the student has done in the following request:

Dear Professor Smith:

Recently I applied for the position of administrative assistant in the Human Resources Department of Host International. Because you kindly agreed to help me, I am now asking you to write a letter of recommendation to Host.

Identify the target position and company. Tell immediately why you are writing.

The position calls for good organizational, interpersonal, and writing skills, as well as computer experience. To help you review my skills and training, I enclose my résumé. As you may recall, I earned an A in your business communication class; and you commended my long report for its clarity and organization.

Specify the job requirements so that the recommender knows what to stress in the letter. Also, supply data to jog the memory of the writer.

Please send your letter before July 1 in the enclosed stamped, addressed envelope. I'm grateful for your support, and I promise to let you know the results of my job search.

Provide a stamped, addressed envelope.

Application Request Letter

Some organizations consider candidates only when they submit a completed application form. To secure a form, write a routine letter of request. But provide enough information about yourself, as shown in the following example, to assure the reader that you are a serious applicant:

Dear Mr. Adams:

Please send me an application form for work in your Human Resources Department. In June I will be completing my studies in psychology and communications at Northwestern University in Evanston, Illinois. My program included courses in public relations, psychology, and communications.

Because you expect a positive response, announce your request immediately.

Supply an end date, if it seems appropriate. End on a forward-looking note.

I would appreciate receiving this application by May 15 so that I may complete it before making a visit to your city in June. I'm looking forward to beginning a career in personnel management.

Application or Résumé Follow-Up Letter

If your letter or application generates no response within a reasonable time, you may decide to send a short follow-up letter like the one below. Doing so (1) jogs the memory of the personnel officer, (2) demonstrates your serious interest, and (3) allows you to emphasize your qualifications or to add new information.

Dear Ms. Lopez:

Open by reminding the reader of your interest.

Please know I am still interested in becoming an administrative support specialist with Quad, Inc.

Substitute *letter* or *résumé* if appropriate. Use this opportunity to review your strengths or to add new qualifications.

Since I submitted an application in May, I have completed my schooling and have been employed as a summer replacement for office workers in several downtown offices. This experience has honed my word processing and communication skills. It has also introduced me to a wide range of office procedures.

Close by looking forward positively; avoid accusations that make the reader defensive.

Please keep my application in your active file and let me know when I may put my formal training, technical skills, and practical experience to work for you.

Interview Follow-Up Letter

After a job interview you should always send a brief letter of thanks. This courtesy sets you apart from other applicants (most of whom will not bother). Your letter also reminds the interviewer of your visit as well as suggesting your good manners and genuine enthusiasm for the job.

Follow-up letters are most effective if sent immediately after the interview. In your letter refer to the date of the interview, the exact job title for which you were interviewed, and specific topics discussed. Avoid worn-out phrases, such as *Thank you for taking the time to interview me.* Be careful, too, about overusing *I*, especially to begin sentences. Most important, show that you really want the job and that you are qualified for it. Notice how the following letter conveys enthusiasm and confidence:

Dear Ms. Cogan:

Mention the interview date and specific position.

Talking with you Thursday, May 23, about the graphic designer position was both informative and interesting.

Show appreciation, good manners, and perseverance —traits that recruiters value.

Thanks for describing the position in such detail and for introducing me to Ms. Thomas, the senior designer. Her current project designing the annual report in four colors on a Macintosh sounds fascinating as well as quite challenging.

Personalize your letter by mentioning topics discussed in the interview. Highlight a specific skill you have for the job.

Now that I've learned in greater detail the specific tasks of your graphic designers, I'm more than ever convinced that my computer and creative skills can make a genuine contribution to your graphic productions. My training in Macintosh design and layout ensures that I could be immediately productive on your staff.

You will find me an enthusiastic and hard-working member of any team effort. I'm eager to join the graphics staff at your Santa Barbara headquarters, and I look forward to hearing from you soon.

Remind the reader of your interpersonal skills as well as your enthusiasm and eagerness for this job.

Rejection Follow-Up Letter

If you didn't get the job and you think it was perfect for you, don't give up. Employment consultant Patricia Windelspecht advises, "You should always respond to a rejection letter . . . I've had four clients get jobs that way." In a rejection follow-up letter, it's okay to admit you're disappointed. Be sure to add, however, that you're still interested and will contact them again in a month in case a job opens up. Then follow through for a couple of months—but don't overdo it. "There's a fine line between being professional and persistent and being a pest," adds consultant Windelspecht.[27] Here's an example of an effective rejection follow-up letter:

Dear Mr. Crenshaw:

Although I'm disappointed that someone else was selected for your accounting position, I appreciate your promptness and courtesy in notifying me.

Subordinate your disappointment to your appreciation at being notified promptly and courteously.

Because I firmly believe that I have the technical and interpersonal skills needed to work in your fast-paced environment, I hope you will keep my résumé in your active file. My desire to become a productive member of your Transamerica staff remains strong.

Emphasize your continuing interest. Express confidence in meeting the job requirements.

I enjoyed our interview, and I especially appreciate the time you and Mr. Samson spent describing your company's expansion into international markets. To enhance my qualifications, I've enrolled in a course in International Accounting at CSU.

Refer to specifics of your interview. If possible, tell how you are improving your skills.

Should you have an opening for which I am qualified, you may reach me at (818) 719-3901. In the meantime, I will call you in a month to discuss employment possibilities.

Take the initiative; tell when you will call for an update.

Application Form

Some organizations require job candidates to fill out job application forms instead of submitting résumés. This practice permits them to gather and store standardized data about each applicant. Here are some tips for filling out such forms:

- Carry a card summarizing those vital statistics not included on your résumé. If you are asked to fill out an application form in an employer's office, you will need a handy reference to the following data: social security number, graduation dates, beginning and ending dates of all employment; salary history; full names, titles, and present work addresses of former supervisors; and full names, occupational titles, occupational addresses, and telephone numbers of persons who have agreed to serve as references.
- Look over all the questions before starting. Fill out the form neatly, printing if your handwriting is poor.
- Answer all questions. Write *Not applicable* if appropriate.
- Be prepared for a salary question. Unless you know what comparable employees are earning in the company, the best strategy is to suggest a salary range or to write in *Negotiable* or *Open.*
- Ask if you may submit your résumé in addition to the application form.

A job interview gives you a chance to explain your résumé and sell your technical expertise as well as your communication and interpersonal skills. But the interview also allows the recruiter to promote his company and explain the duties of the position. Be prepared to ask meaningful questions.

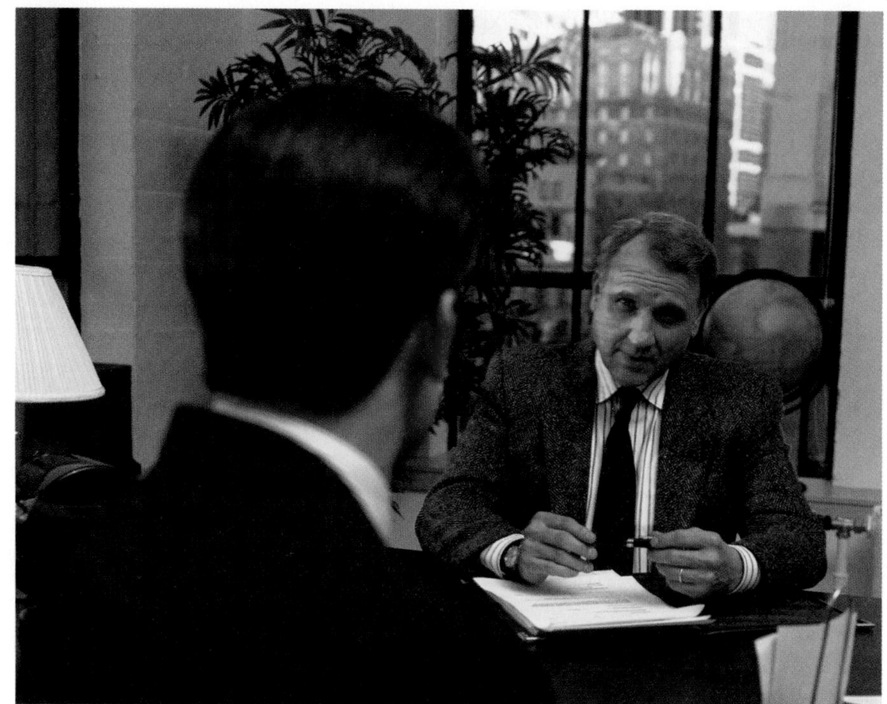

Interviewing for Employment

7

Job interviews, for most of us, are intimidating; no one enjoys being judged and, possibly, rejected. You can overcome your fear of the interview process by knowing how it works and how to prepare for it.

Trained recruiters generally structure the interview in three separate activities: (1) establishing a cordial relationship, (2) eliciting information about the candidate, and (3) giving information about the job and company. During the interview its participants have opposing goals. The interviewer tries to uncover any negative information that would eliminate a candidate. The candidate, of course, tries to minimize faults and emphasize strengths to avoid being eliminated.

You can become a more skillful player in the interview game if you know what to do before, during, and after the interview.

Before the Interview

Prior to an interview, applicants should research the organization and plan answers to potential questions.

- **Research the organization.** Never enter an interview cold. Visit the library or use your computer to search for information about the target company or its field, service, or product. Visit the company's Web site and read everything. Call the company to request annual reports, catalogs, or brochures. Ask about the organization and possibly the interviewer. Learn something about the company's size, number of employees, competitors, reputation, and strengths and weaknesses.
- **Learn about the position.** Obtain as much specific information as possible. What are the functions of an individual in this position? What is the typical salary range? What career paths are generally open to this individual? What did the last person in this position do right or wrong?

- **Plan to sell yourself.** Identify three to five of your major selling points regarding skills, training, personal characteristics, and specialized experience. Memorize them; then in the interview be certain to find a place to insert them.
- **Prepare answers to possible questions.** Imagine the kinds of questions you may be asked and work out sample answers. Although you can't anticipate precise questions, you can expect to be asked about your education, skills, experience, and availability. The accompanying Career Coach box shows ten of the most common questions and suggests responses.
- **Prepare success stories.** Rehearse two or three incidents that you can relate about your accomplishments. These may focus on problems you have solved, promotions you have earned, or recognition or praise you have received.
- **Arrive early.** Get to the interview five or ten minutes early. If you are unfamiliar with the area where the interview is to be held, you might visit it before the scheduled day. Locate the building, parking facilities, and office. Time yourself.
- **Dress appropriately.** Heed the advice of one expert: "Dress and groom like the interviewer is likely to dress—but cleaner."[28] Don't overdo perfume, jewelry, or after-shave lotion. Avoid loud colors; strive for a coordinated, natural appearance. Favorite "power" colors for interviews are gray and dark blue. It's not a bad idea to check your appearance in a restroom before entering the office.

During the Interview

During an interview, applicants should act confident, focus on their strengths, and sell themselves.

- **Establish the relationship.** Shake hands firmly. Don't be afraid to offer your hand first. Address the interviewer formally ("Hello, Mrs. Jones"). Allow the interviewer to put you at ease with small talk.
- **Act confident but natural.** Establish and maintain eye contact, but don't get into a staring contest. Sit up straight, facing the interviewer. Don't cross your arms and legs at the same time (review body language cues in Chapter 2). Don't manipulate objects, like a pencil or keys, during the interview. Try to remain natural and at ease.
- **Don't criticize.** Avoid making negative comments about previous employers, instructors, or others. Such criticism may be taken to indicate a negative personality. Employers are not eager to hire complainers. Moreover, such criticism may suggest that you would do the same to this organization.
- **Stay focused on your strengths.** If the interviewer asks a question that does not help you promote your strongest qualifications, answer briefly. Alternatively, try to turn your response into a positive selling point, such as this: "I have not had extensive paid training in that area, but I have completed a 50-hour training program that provided hands-on experience using the latest technology and methods. My recent training taught me to be open to new ideas and showed me how I can continue learning on my own. I was commended for being a quick learner."

Asking questions about the job helps applicants learn whether this position is right for them.

- **Find out about the job early.** Because your time will be short, try to learn all you can about the target job early in the interview. Ask about its responsibilities and the kinds of people who have done well in the position before. Inquiring about the company's culture will help you decide if your personality fits with this organization.
- **Prepare for salary questions.** Remember that nearly all salaries are negotiable, depending on your qualifications. Knowing the typical salary range for the target position helps. The recruiter can tell you the salary ranges—but you will have to ask. If you've had little experience, you will probably be offered a salary some-

CAREER COACH

ANSWERING TEN FREQUENTLY ASKED INTERVIEW QUESTIONS

Interviewers want to learn about your job experiences and education so that they can evaluate who you are and predict how you might perform on the job. Study each of the following frequently asked interview questions and the strategies for answering them successfully.

- **Why do you want to work for us?** Questions like this illustrate the need for you to research an organization thoroughly before the interview. Go to the company's Web site, read its annual report, conduct library research, ask friends, and read the company's advertisements and other printed materials to gather data. Describe your desire to work for them not only from your perspective but also from their point of view. What have you to offer them?
- **Why should we hire you?** Here is an opportunity for you to sell your strong points in relation to this specific position. Describe your skills, academic preparation, and relevant experience. If you have little experience, don't apologize—the interviewer has read your résumé. Emphasize strengths as demonstrated in your education, such as initiative and persistence in completing assignments, ability to learn quickly, self-sufficiency, and excellent attendance.
- **What can you tell me about yourself?** Use this chance to promote yourself. Stick to professional or business-related strengths; avoid personal or humorous references. Be ready with at least three success stories illustrating characteristics important to this job. Demonstrate responsibility you have been given; describe how you contributed as a team player.
- **What are your strongest (or weakest) personal qualities?** Stress your strengths, such as "I believe I am conscientious, reliable, tolerant, patient, and thorough." Add examples that illustrate these qualities: "My supervisor said that my research was exceptionally thorough." If pressed for a weakness, give a strength disguised as a weakness: "Perhaps my greatest fault is being too painstaking with details." Or, "I am impatient when tasks are not completed on time." Don't admit weaknesses, not even to sound human. You'll be hired for your strengths, not your weaknesses.
- **What do you expect to be doing ten years from now?** Formulate a realistic plan with respect to your present age and situation. The important thing is to be prepared for this question.
- **Do you prefer working with others or by yourself?** This question can be tricky. Provide a middle-of-the-road answer that not only suggests your interpersonal qualities but also reflects an ability to make independent decisions and work without supervision.
- **Have you ever changed your major during your education? Why?** Another tricky question. Don't admit weaknesses or failures. In explaining changes, suggest career potential and new aspirations awakened by your expanding education, experience, or maturity.
- **What have been your most rewarding or disappointing work (or school) experiences?** If possible, concentrate on positive experiences such as technical and interpersonal skills you acquired. Avoid dwelling on negative or unhappy topics. Never criticize former employers. If you worked for an ungrateful, penny-pinching slave driver in a dead-end position, say that you learned all you could from that job. Move the conversation to the prospective position and what attracts you to it.
- **Have you established any new goals lately?** Watch out here. If you reveal new goals, you may inadvertently admit deficiencies. Instead of "I've resolved to finally learn something about graphics design," try "Although I'm familiar with simple graphics programs, I decided to get serious about graphics design by mastering the tools of Adobe PhotoShop and Illustrator."
- **What are your long- and short-term goals?** Suggest realistic goals that you have consciously worked out before the interview. Know what you want to do with your future. To admit to an interviewer that you're not sure what you want to do is a sign of immaturity, weakness, and indecision.

Career Track Application

In teams of two to four, role-play an employment interview. Take turns playing interviewer and interviewee. Each student should answer four to five questions. Imagine a company where you'd like to work and answer accordingly. For more interviewing tips and questions, see the Employment Interviewing Kit in the Study Guide for this textbook or go to the Guffey Student Web site and click on the bonus chapter "Interviewing."

where between the low point and the midpoint in the range. With more experience you can negotiate for a higher figure. A word of caution, though. One personnel manager warns that candidates who emphasize money are suspect because they may leave if offered a few thousand dollars more elsewhere.

- **Be ready for inappropriate questions.** If you are asked a question that you think is illegal, politely ask the interviewer how that question is related to this job. Ask the purpose of the question. Perhaps valid reasons exist that are not obvious.
- **Ask your own questions.** Often, the interviewer concludes an interview with "Do you have any questions about the position?" Inquire about career paths, orientation or training for new employees, or the company's promotion policies. Have a list of relevant questions prepared. If the interview has gone well, ask the recruiter about his or her career in the company.
- **Conclude positively.** Summarize your strongest qualifications, show your enthusiasm for obtaining this position, and thank the interviewer for a constructive interview. Be sure you understand the next step in the employment process.

CASE STUDY

PROCESS TO PRODUCT

Applying Your Skills at Carnival Cruise Lines

As an assistant to Bonnie Gesualdi-Chao at Carnival Cruise Lines, you have been asked to help her prepare "before" and "revised" résumé examples. Bonnie is making a presentation at a nearby college regarding good résumé practices. Her goal is to show students how to improve their résumés so that they are more likely to get them the jobs they want. You know that in the experience section of a résumé, Bonnie wants to see specific results and achievements rather than a job title or a list of duties. She shows you one example:

Résumé statement from applicant for a customer service representative opening:

BEFORE
Front Desk Clerk
Responsible for telephones and assisting counselors.

REVISED

- Cheerfully answered telephone and in-person questions from parents and students.
- Scheduled appointments, greeted visitors, and maintained student files for 12 counselors.

Your Job

Based on what you learned in this chapter, use your own experience or your imagination to prepare at least four additional examples of "before" and "revised" examples for Bonnie to use in her presentation. You may use examples from any career area but try to quantify the examples and strive to relate the statements to a targeted career area or actual position, such as accountant, sales representative, product manager, management trainee, or administrative assistant.

After the Interview

Keeping notes of the meeting helps candidates remember what happened.

- **Make notes on the interview.** While the events are fresh in your mind, jot down the key points—good and bad.
- **Write a thank-you letter.** Immediately write a letter thanking the interviewer for a pleasant and enlightening discussion. Be sure to spell his or her name correctly.

For more information about employment interviewing, visit the Guffey Student Web site **<meguffey.com>** and click on the bonus chapter "Interviewing." You'll find 50 all-time favorite interview questions along with strategic answers for some of them.

Summary of Learning Objectives

1 Prepare for employment by identifying your interests, evaluating your assets, recognizing the changing nature of jobs, choosing a career path, and studying traditional and electronic job search techniques. The employment process begins with an analysis of your likes and your qualifications. Because the nature of jobs is changing, your future work may include flexible work assignments, multiple employers, and constant retraining. You can learn more about career opportunities through your campus career center, the Web, your library, internships, part-time jobs, interviews, classified ads, and professional organizations. Traditional job search techniques range from newspaper ads to developing your own network of friends and relatives. Electronic job search techniques include visiting Internet job sites and company Web sites.

2 Compare and contrast chronological, functional, and combination résumés. Chronological résumés, listing work and education by dates, rank highest with recruiters. Functional résumés, highlighting skills instead of jobs, appeal to people changing careers or those having negative employment histories. Combination résumés, including a complete job history along with skill areas, are increasingly popular.

3 Organize, format, and produce a persuasive résumé. Target your résumé for a specific job. Study models to arrange most effectively your main heading, career objective (optional), education, work experience, capabilities, awards and activities, personal data, and references (optional). Use action verbs to show how your assets will help the target organization.

4 Identify techniques that prepare a résumé for computer scanning, posting at a Web site, faxing, and e-mailing. Computer-friendly résumés avoid unusual typefaces, underlining, and italics. They use 10- to 14-point type, smooth white paper, and quality printing. The applicant's name appears on the first line. The résumé includes ample white space, avoids double columns, and is not folded or stapled. It emphasizes keywords, which are nouns that an employer might use to describe the position and skills desired. Résumés posted at Web sites must be prepared in HTML (Hypertext Markup Language). They may include links to résumé extras such as work samples and letters of recommendation. Faxed résumés must avoid small fonts and underlining. E-mailed résumés should probably be sent in ASCII (text-only format). Follow up faxed and e-mail résumés with polished copies.

5 **Write a persuasive letter of application to accompany your résumé.** Gain attention in the opening by mentioning the job or a person who referred you. Build interest in the body by stressing what you can do for the targeted company. Refer to your résumé, request an interview, and motivate action in the closing.

6 **Write effective employment follow-up letters and other messages.** Follow up all your employment activities with appropriate messages. After submitting your résumé or after an interview, even after being rejected, follow up with letters that express your appreciation and continuing interest.

7 **Evaluate successful job interview strategies.** Learn about the job and the organization. Prepare answers to possible questions and be ready with success stories. Act confident and natural. Be prepared to ask or answer salary questions. Have a list of your own questions, summarize your key strengths, and stay focused on your strong points. Afterwards, send a thank-you letter.

CHAPTER REVIEW

1. Name at least five questions that you should ask yourself to identify your employment interests. (Obj. 1)
2. List five sources of career information. (Obj. 1)
3. How are most jobs likely to be found? Through classified ads? The Internet? Employment agencies? Networking? (Obj. 1)
4. What is the goal of your résumé? (Obj. 2)
5. Describe a chronological résumé and discuss its advantages. (Obj. 2)
6. Describe a functional résumé and discuss its advantages. (Obj. 2)
7. What are the disadvantages of a functional résumé? (Obj. 2)
8. When does it make sense to include a career objective on your résumé? (Obj. 3)
9. On a chronological résumé what information should you include for the jobs you list? (Objs. 2 and 3)
10. In addition to technical skills, what traits and characteristics do employers seek? (Objs. 2 and 3)
11. What changes must be made in a typical résumé to make it effective for computer scanning? (Obj. 4)
12. What are the three purposes of a letter of application? (Obj. 5)
13. How can you make it easy for a recruiter to reach you? (Obj. 5)
14. Other than a letter of application, name five kinds of letters you might need to write in the employment process. (Obj. 6)
15. What information should a candidate gather in preparing for a job interview? (Obj. 7)

CRITICAL THINKING

1. How has the concept of the "job" changed, and how will it affect your employment search? (Obj. 1)
2. How is a résumé different from a company employment application? (Objs. 1 and 2)
3. Some job candidates think that applying for unsolicited jobs can be more fruitful than applying for advertised openings. Discuss the advantages and disadvantages of letters that "prospect" for jobs. (Obj. 5)
4. How do the interviewer and interviewee play opposing roles during job interviews? What strategies should the interviewee prepare in advance? (Obj. 7)

5. **Ethical Issue:** Job candidate Karen accepts a position with Company A. One week later she receives a better offer from Company B. She wants very much to accept it. What should she do?

ACTIVITIES

16.1 Identifying Your Employment Interests (Obj. 1)

In a memo addressed to your instructor, answer the questions in the section "Identifying Your Interests" at the beginning of the chapter. Draw a conclusion from your answers. What kind of career, company, position, and location seem to fit your self-analysis?

16.2 Evaluating Your Qualifications (Objs. 1, 2, and 3)

Prepare four worksheets that inventory your qualifications in these areas: employment, education, capabilities and skills, and honors and activities. Use active verbs when appropriate.

a. *Employment.* Begin with your most recent job or internship. For each position list the following information: employer, job title, dates of employment, and three to five duties, activities, or accomplishments. Emphasize activities related to your job goal. Strive to quantify your achievements.

b. *Education.* List degrees, certificates, and training accomplishments. Include courses, seminars, or skills that are relevant to your job goal. Calculate your grade-point average in your major.

c. *Capabilities and skills.* List all capabilities and skills that recommend you for the job you seek. Use words like *skilled, competent, trained, experienced,* and *ability to.* Also list five or more qualities or interpersonal skills necessary for a successful individual in your chosen field. Write action statements demonstrating that you possess some of these qualities. Empty assurances aren't good enough; try to show evidence (*Developed teamwork skills by working with a committee of eight to produce a . . .*).

d. *Awards, honors, and activities.* Explain any awards so that the reader will understand them. List campus, community, and professional activities that suggest you are a well-rounded individual or possess traits relevant to your target job.

16.3 Choosing a Career Path (Obj. 1)

Visit your college library, local library, or campus career center. In bound form or on CD-ROM, consult the *Dictionary of Occupational Titles.* Find the description for a position for which you could apply in two to five years. Photocopy or print the pages from the *Occupational Outlook Handbook* that describe employment in the area in which you are interested. If your instructor directs, attach these copies to the letter of application you will write in Activity 16.8.

16.4 Searching the Job Market (Obj. 1)

Clip a job advertisement from the classified section of a newspaper or print one from a career site on the Web. Select an ad describing the kind of employment you are seeking now or plan to seek when you graduate. Save this advertisement to attach to the résumé you will write in Activity 16.8.

16.5 Posting a Résumé on the Web (Obj. 4)

Web

Prepare a list of at least three Web sites where you could post your résumé. Describe the procedure involved and the advantages for each site.

16.6 Draft Document: Résumé (Objs. 2 and 3)

Analyze the following résumé. Discuss its strengths and weaknesses. Your instructor may ask you to revise sections of this résumé before showing you an improved version.

Wendy Lee Cox
5349 East Zion Place
Tulsa, OK 74115-3394
Phone: (d) (918) 834-4583 (n) (918) 594-2985

Seeking to be hired at Mead Products as an intern in Accounting

SKILLS: Accounting, Internet, Windows 98, Excel, PowerPoint, Freelance Graphics

EDUCATION
Now working on B.S. in Business Administration. Major, Management and Accounting; GPA is 3.5. Expect to graduate in June, 2001.

EXPERIENCE:
Assistant Accountant, 1996 to present. March and McLennan, Inc., Bookkeeping/Tax Service, Tulsa. I keep accounting records for several small businesses accurately. I prepare 150 to 200 individual income tax returns each year. For Hill and Hill Truck Line I maintain accurate and up-to-date A/R records. And I prepare payroll records for 16 employees at three firms.

Peterson Controls Inc., Tulsa. Data Processing Internship, 2000 to present. I design and maintain spreadsheets and also process weekly and monthly information for production uptime and downtime. I prepare graphs to illustrate uptime and downtime data.

Tulsa Country Club. Accounts Payable Internship, 1999 to 2000. Took care of accounts payable including filing system for the club. Responsible for processing monthly adjusting entries for general ledger. Worked closely with treasurer to give the Board budget/disbursement figures regularly.

Langston University, Tulsa. I marketed the VITA program to Langston students and organized volunteers and supplies. Official title: Coordinator of Volunteer Income Tax Assistance Project.

COMMUNITY SERVICE: March of Dimes Drive, Central Park High School; All Souls Unitarian Church, coordinator for Children's Choir

16.7 Draft Document: Letter of Application (Obj. 5)

Analyze each section of the following letter of application written by an accounting major about to graduate.

Dear Human Resources Director:

Please consider this letter as an application for the position of staff accountant that I saw advertised in the *Houston Post.* Although I have had no paid work experience in this field, accounting has been my major in college and I'm sure I could be an asset to your company.

For four years I have studied accounting, and I am fully trained for full-charge bookkeeping as well as electronic accounting. I have taken 36 units of college accounting and courses in business law, economics, statistics, finance, management, and marketing.

In addition to my course work, during the tax season I have been a student volunteer for VITA. This is a project to help individuals in the community prepare their income tax returns, and I learned a lot from this experience. I have also received some experience in office work and working with figures when I was employed as an office assistant for Copy Quick, Inc.

I am a competent and responsible person who gets along pretty well with others. I have been a member of some college and social organizations and have even held elective office.

I feel that I have a strong foundation in accounting as a result of my course work and my experience. Along with my personal qualities and my desire to succeed, I hope that you will agree that I qualify for the position of staff accountant with your company.

Sincerely,

16.8 Résumé (Objs. 2 and 3)

Using the data you developed in Activity 16.2, write your résumé. Aim it at a full-time job, part-time position, or internship. Attach a job listing for a specific position (from Activity 16.4). Use a computer. Revise your résumé until it is perfect.

16.9 Letter of Application (Obj. 5)

Write a cover letter introducing your résumé. Again, use a computer. Revise your cover letter until it is perfect.

16.10 Interview Follow-Up Letter (Obj. 6)

Assume you were interviewed for the position you seek. Write a follow-up thank-you letter.

16.11 Reference Request (Obj. 6)

Your favorite professor has agreed to recommend you. Write to the professor and request that he or she send a letter of recommendation to a company where you are applying for a job. Provide data about the job description and about yourself so that the professor can target its content.

16.12 Résumé Follow-Up Letter (Obj. 6)

A month has passed since you sent your résumé and letter of application in response to a job advertisement. Write a follow-up letter that doesn't offend the reader or damage your chances of employment.

16.13 Application Request (Obj. 6)

Select a company for which you'd like to work. Write a letter requesting an employment application, which the company requires for all job seekers.

16.14 Rejection Follow-Up Letter (Obj. 6)

Assume you didn't get the job. Although someone else was selected, you hope that other jobs may become available. Write a follow-up letter that keeps the door open.

APPENDIX A

C.L.U.E. Competent Language Usage Essentials

A Business Communicator's Guide

In the business world, people are often judged by the way they speak and write. Using the language competently can mean the difference between individual success and failure. Often a speaker sounds accomplished; but when that same individual puts ideas in print, errors in language usage destroy his or her credibility. One student observed, "When I talk, I get by on my personality; but when I write, the flaws in my communication show through. That's why I'm in this class."

What C.L.U.E. Is

This appendix provides a condensed guide to competency in language usage essentials (C.L.U.E.). Fifty guidelines review sentence structure, grammar, usage, punctuation, capitalization, and number style. These guidelines focus on the most frequently used—and abused—language elements. Presented from a business communicator's perspective, the guidelines also include realistic tips for application. And frequent checkpoint exercises enable you to try out your skills immediately. In addition to the 50 language guides in this appendix, you'll find a list of 160 frequently misspelled words plus a quick review of selected confusing words.

The concentrated materials in this guide will help novice business communicators focus on the major areas of language use. The guide is not meant to teach or review *all* the principles of English grammar and punctuation. It focuses on a limited number of language guidelines and troublesome words. Your objective should be mastery of these language principles and words, which represent a majority of the problems typically encountered by business writers.

How to Use C.L.U.E.

Your instructor may give you a language diagnostic test to help you assess your competency. After taking this test, read and work your way through the 50 guidelines. Concentrate on areas where you are weak. Memorize the spelling list and definitions for the confusing words located at the end of this appendix.

Two kinds of exercises are available for your practice. (1) *Checkpoints,* located in this appendix, focus on a small group of language guidelines. Use them to test your comprehension as you complete each section. (2) *Review exercises,* located in

Chapters 1 through 10, cover all guidelines, spelling words, and confusing words. Use the review exercises to reinforce your language skills at the same time you are learning about the processes and products of business communication. As you complete the following review exercises, you may wish to use the standard proofreading marks shown in Appendix D (p. A-50).

Many students want all the help they can get in improving their language skills. For additional assistance with grammar and language fundamentals, try these resources:

- **On-Line Interactive Skill Builders.** At the Guffey Web site **<meguffey.com>**, you will find sentence competency drills that are similar to the following C.L.U.E. exercises. Click on Book Support, *Business English,* and Skill Builders. You can also work on your spelling and vocabulary skills at this Web site.
- **Reference Books.** More comprehensive treatment of grammar and punctuation guidelines can be found in Clark and Clark's *A Handbook for Office Workers* and Guffey's *Business English.*
- **Study Guide C.L.U.E. Exercises.** The Student Study Guide accompanying this textbook provides many additional C.L.U.E. review exercises, and the answers are available for immediate checking.

Guidelines: Competent Language Usage Essentials

Sentence Structure

GUIDE 1: Express ideas in complete sentences. You can recognize a complete sentence because it (a) includes a subject (a noun or pronoun that interacts with a verb), (b) includes a verb (a word expressing action or describing a condition), and (c) makes sense (comes to a closure). A complete sentence is an independent clause. One of the most serious errors a writer can make is punctuating a fragment as if it were a complete sentence. A fragment is a broken-off part of a sentence.

Fragment	**Improved**
Because 90 percent of all business transactions involve written messages. Good writing skills are critical.	Because 90 percent of all business transactions involve written messages, good writing skills are critical.
The recruiter requested a writing sample. Even though the candidate seemed to communicate well.	The recruiter requested a writing sample, even though the candidate seemed to communicate well.

Tip. Fragments often can be identified by the words that introduce them—words like *although, as, because, even, except, for example, if, instead of, since, so, such as, that, which,* and *when.* These words introduce dependent clauses. Make sure such clauses are always connected to independent clauses.

DEPENDENT CLAUSE — INDEPENDENT CLAUSE

Since she became supervisor, she had to write more memos and reports.

GUIDE 2: Avoid run-on (fused) sentences. A sentence with two independent clauses must be joined by a coordinating conjunction (*and, or, nor, but*) or by a semicolon (;). Without a conjunction or a semicolon, a run-on sentence results.

Run-on	Improved
Robin visited resorts of the rich and the famous he also dropped in on luxury spas.	Robin visited resorts of the rich and famous, and he also dropped in on luxury spas.
	Robin visited resorts of the rich and famous; he also dropped in on luxury spas.

GUIDE 3: Avoid comma-splice sentences. A comma splice results when a writer joins (splices together) two independent clauses—without using a coordinating conjunction (*and, or, nor, but*).

Comma Splice	Improved
Disney World operates in Orlando, EuroDisney serves Paris.	Disney World operates in Orlando; EuroDisney serves Paris.
	Disney World operates in Orlando, and EuroDisney serves Paris.
Visitors wanted a resort vacation, however they were disappointed.	Visitors wanted a resort vacation; however, they were disappointed.

Tip. In joining independent clauses, beware of using a comma and words like *consequently, furthermore, however, therefore, then, thus,* and so on. These conjunctive adverbs require semicolons.

✓ Checkpoint

Revise the following to rectify sentence fragments, comma splices, and run-ons.

1. When McDonald's tested pizza, Pizza Hut fought back. With aggressive ads ridiculing McPizza.
2. Aggressive ads can backfire, consequently, marketing directors consider them carefully.
3. Corporations study the legality of attack advertisements they also retaliate with counterattacks.
4. Although Pizza Hut is the country's number one pizza chain. Domino's Pizza leads in deliveries.
5. About half of the 6,600 outlets make deliveries, the others concentrate on walk-in customers.

For all the Checkpoint sentences, compare your responses with the answers at the end of Appendix A (page A-22).

Grammar

Verb Tense

GUIDE 4: Use present tense, past tense, and past participle verb forms correctly.

Present Tense	**Past Tense**	**Past Participle**
(Today I ______)	(Yesterday I ______)	(I have ______)
am	was	been
begin	began	begun
break	broke	broken
bring	brought	brought
choose	chose	chosen
come	came	come
do	did	done
give	gave	given
go	went	gone
know	knew	known
pay	paid	paid
see	saw	seen
steal	stole	stolen
take	took	taken
write	wrote	written

The package *came* yesterday, and Kevin *knew* what it contained.

If I *had seen* the shipper's bill, I *would have paid* it immediately.

I *know* the answer now; I wish I *had known* it yesterday.

Tip. Probably the most frequent mistake in tenses results from substituting the past participle form for the past tense. Notice that the past participle tense requires auxiliary verbs such as *has, had, have, would have,* and *could have.*

Faulty	**Correct**
When he *come* over last night, he *brung* pizza.	When he *came* over last night, he *brought* pizza.
If he *had came* earlier, we *could have saw* the video.	If he *had come* earlier, we *could have seen* the video.

Verb Mood

GUIDE 5: Use the subjunctive mood to express hypothetical (untrue) ideas. The most frequent misuse of the subjunctive mood involves using *was* instead of *were* in clauses introduced by *if* and *as though* or containing *wish.*

If I *were* (not *was*) you, I would take a business writing course.

Sometimes I wish I *were* (not *was*) the manager of this department.

He acts as though he *were* (not *was*) in charge of this department.

Tip. If the statement could possibly be true, use *was.*

If I *was* to blame, I accept the consequences.

 **Checkpoint**

Correct faults in verb tenses and mood.

6. If I was in your position, I would have wrote the manager a letter.
7. You could have wrote a better résumé if you have read the chapter first.
8. When Trevor seen the want ad, he immediately contacted the company.
9. I wish I was able to operate a computer so that I could have went to work there.
10. Because she had took many computer courses, Maria was able to chose a good job.

Verb Voice

For a discussion of active- and passive-voice verbs, see page 139 in Chapter 5.

Verb Agreement

GUIDE 6: Make subjects agree with verbs despite intervening phrases and clauses. Become a detective in locating *true* subjects. Don't be deceived by prepositional phrases and parenthetic words that often disguise the true subject.

Our study of annual budgets, five-year plans, and sales proposals *is* (not *are*) progressing on schedule. (The true subject is *study.*)

The budgeted item, despite additions proposed yesterday, *remains* (not *remain*) as submitted. (The true subject is *item.*)

A salesperson's evaluation of the prospects for a sale, together with plans for follow-up action, *is* (not *are*) what we need. (The true subject is *evaluation.*)

Tip. Subjects are nouns or pronouns that control verbs. To find subjects, cross out prepositional phrases beginning with words like *about, at, by, for, from, of,* and *to.* Subjects of verbs are not found in prepositional phrases. Also, don't be tricked by expressions introduced by *together with, in addition to,* and *along with.*

GUIDE 7: Subjects joined by *and* require plural verbs. Watch for true subjects joined by the conjunction *and.* They require plural verbs.

The CEO and one of his assistants *have* (not *has*) ordered a limo.

Considerable time and money *were* (not *was*) spent on remodeling.

Exercising in the gym and jogging every day *are* (not *is*) how he keeps fit.

GUIDE 8: Subjects joined by *or* or *nor* may require singular or plural verbs. The verb should agree with the closest subject.

Either the software or the printer *is* (not *are*) causing the glitch. (The verb is controlled by closer subject, *printer.*)

Neither St. Louis nor Chicago *has* (not *have*) a chance of winning. (The verb is controlled by *Chicago.*)

Tip. In joining singular and plural subjects with *or* or *nor,* place the plural subject closer to the verb. Then, the plural verb sounds natural. For example, *Either the manufacturer or the distributors are responsible.*

GUIDE 9: Use singular verbs for most indefinite pronouns. For example: *anyone, anybody, anything, each, either, every, everyone, everybody, everything, neither, nobody, nothing, someone, somebody,* and *something* all take singular verbs.

Everyone in both offices *was* (not *were*) given a bonus.

Each of the employees *is* (not *are*) being interviewed.

GUIDE 10: Use singular or plural verbs for collective nouns, depending on whether the members of the group are operating as a unit or individually. Words like *faculty, administration, class, crowd,* and *committee* are considered *collective* nouns. If the members of the collective are acting as a unit, treat them as singular subjects. If they are acting individually, it's usually better to add the word *members* and use a plural verb.

Correct
The Finance Committee *is* working harmoniously. (*Committee* is singular because its action is unified.)

The Planning Committee *are* having difficulty agreeing. (*Committee* is plural because its members are acting individually.)

Improved
The Planning Committee members *are* having difficulty agreeing. (Add the word *members* if a plural meaning is intended.)

Tip. In America collective nouns are generally considered singular. In Britain these collective nouns are generally considered plural.

 **Checkpoint**

Correct the errors in subject-verb agreement.

11. A manager's time and energy has to be focused on important issues.
12. Promotion of women, despite managerial training programs and networking efforts, are disappointingly small.
13. We're not sure whether Mr. Murphy or Ms. Wagner are in charge of the program.
14. Each of the Fortune 500 companies are being sent a survey regarding women in management.
15. Our CEO, like other good executives, know how to be totally informed without being totally involved.

Pronoun Case

GUIDE 11: Learn the three cases of pronouns and how each is used. Pronouns are substitutes for nouns. Every business writer must know the following pronoun cases.

Nominative or Subjective Case	Objective Case	Possessive Case
Used for subjects of verbs and subject complements	Used for objects of prepositions and objects of verbs	Used to show possession
I	me	my, mine
we	us	our, ours

Nominative or Subjective Case	Objective Case	Possessive Case
you	you	you, yours
he	him	his
she	her	her, hers
it	it	its
they	them	their, theirs
who, whoever	whom, whomever	whose

GUIDE 12: Use nominative case pronouns as subjects of verbs and as complements. Complements are words that follow linking verbs (such as *am, is, are, was, were, be, being,* and *been*) and rename the words to which they refer.

She and *I* (not *her* and *me*) prefer easy-riding mountain bikes. (Use nominative case pronouns as the subjects of the verb *prefer.*)

We think that *she* and *he* (not *her* and *him*) will win the race. (Use nominative case pronouns as the subjects of the verb *will win.*)

It must have been *she* (not *her*) who called last night. (Use a nominative case pronoun as a subject complement.)

Tip. If you feel awkward using nominative pronouns after linking verbs, rephrase the sentence to avoid the dilemma. Instead of *It is she who is the boss,* say *She is the boss.*

GUIDE 13: Use objective case pronouns as objects of prepositions and verbs.

Please order stationery for *her* and *me* (not *she* and *I*). (The pronouns *her* and *me* are objects of the preposition *for.*)

The CEO appointed *him* (not *he*) to the position. (The pronoun *him* is the object of the verb *appointed.*)

Tip. When a pronoun appears in combination with a noun or another pronoun, ignore the extra noun or pronoun and its conjunction. Then, the case of the pronoun becomes more obvious.

Jason asked Jennifer and *me* (not *I*) to lunch. (Ignore *Jennifer and.*)

The waiter didn't know whether to give the bill to Jason or *her* (not *she*). (Ignore *Jason or.*)

Tip. Be especially alert to the following prepositions: *except, between, but,* and *like.* Be sure to use objective pronouns as their objects.

Just between you and *me* (not *I*), that mineral water comes from the tap.

Computer grammar checkers work well for writers like Lee and *him* (not *he*).

GUIDE 14: Use possessive case pronouns to show ownership. Possessive pronouns (such as *hers, yours, whose, ours, theirs,* and *its*) require no apostrophes.

All reports except *yours* (not *your's*) have to be rewritten.

The printer and *its* (not *it's*) fonts produce exceptional copy.

Tip. Don't confuse possessive pronouns and contractions. Contractions are shortened forms of subject-verb phrases (such as *it's* for *it is, there's* for *there is, who's* for *who is,* and *they're* for *they are*).

Checkpoint

Correct errors in pronoun case.

16. Although my friend and myself are interested in this computer, it's price seems high.

17. Letters addressed to he and I were delivered to you and Ann in error.

18. Just between you and I, the mail room and its procedures need improvement.

19. Several applications were lost; your's and her's were the only ones delivered.

20. It could have been her who sent the program update to you and I.

GUIDE 15: Use *self*-ending pronouns only when they refer to previously mentioned nouns or pronouns.

> The president *himself* ate all the M & Ms.
>
> Send the package to Marcus or *me* (not *myself*).

Tip. Trying to sound less egocentric, some radio and TV announcers incorrectly substitute *myself* when they should use *I.* For example, "Jerry and *myself* (should be *I*) are cohosting the telethon."

GUIDE 16: Use *who* or *whoever* for nominative case constructions and *whom* or *whomever* for objective case constructions. In determining the correct choice, it's helpful to substitute *he* for *who* or *whoever* and *him* for *whom* or *whomever.*

> For *whom* was this software ordered? (The software was ordered for *him.*)
>
> *Who* did you say called? (You did say *he* called?)
>
> Give the supplies to *whoever* asked for them. (In this sentence the clause *whoever asked for them* functions as the object of the preposition *to.* Within the clause *whoever* is the subject of the verb *asked.* Again, try substituting *he: he asked for them.*)

Checkpoint

Correct any errors in the use of *self*-ending pronouns and *who/whom.*

21. The boss herself is willing to call whoever we nominate for the position.

22. Who would you like to see nominated?

23. These supplies are for whomever ordered them.

24. The meeting is set for Tuesday; however, Jeff and myself cannot attend.

25. Incident reports are to be written by whomever experiences a sales problem.

Pronoun Reference

GUIDE 17: Make pronouns agree in number and gender with the words to which they refer (their antecedents). When the gender of the antecedent is obvious, pronoun references are simple.

One of the boys lost *his* (not *their*) new tennis shoes. (The singular pronoun *his* refers to the singular *One.*)

Each of the female nurses was escorted to *her car* (not *their cars*). (The singular pronoun *her* and singular noun *car* are necessary because they refer to the singular subject *Each.*)

Somebody on the girls' team left *her* (not *their*) headlights on.

When the gender of the antecedent could be male or female, sensitive writers today have a number of options.

Faulty

Every employee should receive *their* check Friday. (The plural pronoun *their* does not agree with its singular antecedent *employee.*)

Improved

All employees should receive *their* checks Friday. (Make the subject plural so that the plural pronoun *their* is acceptable. This option is preferred by many writers today.)

All employees should receive checks Friday. (Omit the possessive pronoun entirely.)

Every employee should receive *a* check Friday. (Substitute *a* for a pronoun.)

Every employee should receive *his* or *her* check Friday. (Use the combination *his* or *her.* However, this option is wordy and should be avoided.)

GUIDE 18: Be sure that pronouns such as *it, which, this,* and *that* refer to clear antecedents. Vague pronouns confuse the reader because they have no clear single antecedent. The most troublesome are *it, which, this,* and *that.* Replace vague pronouns with concrete nouns, or provide these pronouns with clear antecedents.

Faulty

Our office recycles as much paper as possible because *it* helps the environment. (Does *it* refer to *paper, recycling,* or *office*?)

The disadvantages of local area networks can offset their advantages, *which* merits further evaluation. (What merits evaluation: advantages, disadvantages, or offsetting of one by the other?)

Improved

Our office recycles as much paper as possible because *such efforts* help the environment. (Replace *it* with *such efforts.*)

The disadvantages of local area networks can offset their advantages, a *fact* which merits further evaluation. (*Fact* supplies a clear antecedent for *which.*)

Faulty	**Improved**
Negotiators announced an expanded health care plan, reductions in dental coverage, and a proposal of on-site child care facilities. *This* caused employee protests. (What exactly caused employee protests?)	Negotiators announced an expanded health care plan, reductions in dental coverage, and a proposal of on-site child care facilities. *This* reduction in dental coverage caused employee protests. (The pronoun *This* now has a clear reference.)

Tip. Whenever you use the words *this, that, these,* and *those* by themselves, a red flag should pop up. These words are dangerous when they stand alone. Inexperienced writers often use them to refer to an entire previous idea, rather than to a specific antecedent, as shown in the preceding example. You can often solve the problem by adding another idea to the pronoun (such as *this announcement*).

Checkpoint

Correct the faulty and vague pronoun references in the following sentences. Numerous remedies exist.

26. Every employee is entitled to have their tuition reimbursed.

27. Flexible working hours may mean slower career advancement, but it appeals to me anyway.

28. Any subscriber may cancel their subscription at any time.

29. Every voter must have their name and address verified at the polling place.

30. Obtaining agreement on job standards, listening to coworkers, and encouraging employee suggestions all helped to open lines of communication. This is particularly important in team projects.

Adjectives and Adverbs

GUIDE 19: Use adverbs, not adjectives, to describe or limit the action of verbs.

Andrew said he did *well* (not *good*) on the exam.

After its tune-up, the engine is running *smoothly* (not *smooth*).

Don't take the manager's criticism *personally* (not *personal*).

GUIDE 20: Hyphenate two or more adjectives that are joined to create a compound modifier before a noun.

Follow the *step-by-step* instructions to construct the *low-cost* bookshelves.

A *well-designed* keyboard is part of their *state-of-the-art* equipment.

Tip. Don't confuse adverbs ending in *-ly* with compound adjectives: *newly enacted* law and *highly regarded* CEO would not be hyphenated.

Checkpoint

Correct any problems in the use of pronouns, adjectives, and adverbs.

31. My manager and myself prepared a point by point analysis of the proposal.

32. Because we completed the work so quick, we were able to visit the recently-opened snack bar.

33. If I do good on the placement exam, I qualify for many part time jobs and a few full time positions.

34. The vice president told him and I not to take the announcement personal.

35. In the not too distant future, we may enjoy interactive television.

Punctuation

GUIDE 21: Use commas to separate three or more items (words, phrases, or short clauses) in a series.

> Downward communication delivers job instructions, procedures, and appraisals.
>
> In preparing your résumé, try to keep it brief, make it easy to read, and include only job-related information.
>
> The new ice cream flavors include cookie dough, chocolate raspberry truffle, cappuccino, and almond amaretto.

Tip. Some professional writers omit the comma before *and.* However, most business writers prefer to retain that comma because it prevents misreading the last two items as one item. Notice in the previous example how the final two ice cream flavors could have been misread if the comma had been omitted.

GUIDE 22: Use commas to separate introductory clauses and certain phrases from independent clauses. This guideline describes the comma most often omitted by business writers. Sentences that open with dependent clauses (often introduced by words such as *since, when, if, as, although,* and *because*) require commas to separate them from the main idea. The comma helps readers recognize where the introduction ends and the big idea begins. Introductory phrases of more than five words or phrases containing verbal elements also require commas.

> If you recognize introductory clauses, you will have no trouble placing the comma. (Comma separates introductory dependent clause from main clause.)
>
> When you have mastered this rule, half the battle with commas will be won.
>
> As expected, additional explanations are necessary. (Use a comma even if the introductory clause omits the understood subject: *As we expected.*)
>
> In the spring of last year, we opened our franchise. (Use a comma after a phrase containing five or more words.)
>
> Having considered several alternatives, we decided to invest. (Use a comma after an introductory verbal phrase.)
>
> To invest, we needed $100,000. (Use a comma after an introductory verbal phrase, regardless of its length.)

Tip. Short introductory prepositional phrases (four or fewer words) require no commas. Don't clutter your writing with unnecessary commas after introductory phrases such as *by 2000, in the fall,* or *at this time.*

GUIDE 23: Use a comma before the coordinating conjunction in a compound sentence. The most common coordinating conjunctions are *and, or, nor,* and *but.* Occasionally, *for* and *so* may also function as coordinating conjunctions. When coordinating conjunctions join two independent clauses, commas are needed.

> The investment sounded too good to be true, *and* many investors were dubious. (Use a comma before the coordinating conjunction *and* in a compound sentence.)

> Southern California is the financial fraud capital of the world, *but* some investors refuse to heed warning signs.

Tip. Before inserting a comma, test the two clauses. Can each of them stand alone as a complete sentence? If either is incomplete, skip the comma.

> Promoters said the investment offer was for a limited time and couldn't be extended even one day. (Omit a comma before *and* because the second part of the sentence is not a complete independent clause.)

> Home is a place you grow up wanting to leave but grow old wanting to return to. (Omit a comma before *but* because the second half of the sentence is not a complete clause.)

 **Checkpoint**

Add appropriate commas.

36. Before he entered this class Jeff used to sprinkle his writing with commas semicolons and dashes.
37. After studying punctuation he learned to use commas more carefully and to reduce his reliance on dashes.
38. At this time Jeff is engaged in a strenuous body-building program but he also finds time to enlighten his mind.
39. Next spring Jeff may enroll in accounting and business law or he may work for a semester to earn money.
40. When he completes his degree he plans to apply for employment in San Diego Orlando or Seattle.

GUIDE 24: Use commas appropriately in dates, addresses, geographical names, degrees, and long numbers.

> September 30, 1963, is her birthday. (For dates use commas before and after the year.)

> Send the application to James Kirby, 20045 45th Avenue, Lynnwood, WA 98036, as soon as possible. (For addresses use commas to separate all units except the two-letter state abbreviation and the zip code.)

> She expects to move from Cupertino, California, to Sonoma, Arizona, next fall. (For geographical areas use commas to enclose the second element.)

> Karen Munson, CPA, and Richard B. Larsen, Ph.D., were the speakers. (For professional designations and academic degrees following names, use commas to enclose each item.)

> The latest census figures show the city's population to be 342,000. (In figures use commas to separate every three digits, counting from the right.)

GUIDE 25: Use commas to set off internal sentence interrupters. Sentence interrupters may be verbal phrases, dependent clauses, contrasting elements, or parenthetical expressions (also called transitional phrases). These interrupters often provide information that is not grammatically essential.

> Harvard researchers, working steadily for 18 months, developed a new cancer therapy. (Use commas to set off an interrupting verbal phrase.)
>
> The new therapy, which applies a genetically engineered virus, raises hopes among cancer specialists. (Use commas to set off nonessential dependent *clauses.*)
>
> Dr. James C. Morrison, who is one of the researchers, made the announcement. (Use commas to set off nonessential dependent clauses.)
>
> It was Dr. Morrison, not Dr. Arturo, who led the team effort. (Use commas to set off a contrasting element.)
>
> This new therapy, by the way, was developed from a herpes virus. (Use commas to set off a parenthetical expression.)

Tip. Parenthetical (transitional) expressions are helpful words that guide the reader from one thought to the next. Here are representative parenthetical expressions that require commas:

as a matter of fact	in addition	of course
as a result	in the meantime	on the other hand
consequently	nevertheless	therefore
for example		

Tip. Always use *two* commas to set off an interrupter, unless it begins or ends a sentence.

Checkpoint

Insert necessary commas.

41. Sue listed 222 Georgetown Road Jacksonville NC 28540 as her forwarding address.
42. The personnel director felt nevertheless that the applicant should be given an interview.
43. Employment of paralegals which is expected to increase 32 percent next year is growing rapidly because of the expanding legal services industry.
44. The contract was signed April 1 1996 and remained in effect until January 1 1999.
45. As a matter of fact the average American drinks enough coffee to require 12 pounds of coffee beans annually.

GUIDE 26: Avoid unnecessary commas. Do not use commas between sentence elements that belong together. Don't automatically insert commas before every *and* or at points where your voice might drop if you were saying the sentence out loud.

> **Faulty**
> Growth will be spurred by the increasing complexity of business operations, and by large employment gains in trade and services. (A comma unnecessarily precedes *and.*)

All students with high grades, are eligible for the honor society. (A comma unnecessarily separates the subject and verb.)

One of the reasons for the success of the business honor society is, that it is very active. (A comma unnecessarily separates the verb and its complement.)

Our honor society has, at this time, over 50 members. (Commas unnecessarily separate a prepositional phrase from the sentence.)

✓ Checkpoint

Remove unnecessary commas. Add necessary ones.

46. Businesspeople from all over the world, gathered in Las Vegas for the meeting.

47. When shopping for computer equipment consider buying products that have been on the market for at least a year.

48. The trouble with talking fast is, that you sometimes say something before you've thought of it.

49. We think on the other hand, that we must develop management talent pools with the aim of promoting women minorities and people with disabilities.

50. A powerful reason for mail-order purchasing is, that customers make big savings.

Semicolons, Colons

GUIDE 27: Use a semicolon to join closely related independent clauses. Mature writers use semicolons to show readers that two thoughts are closely associated. If the ideas are not related, they should be expressed as separate sentences. Often, but not always, the second independent clause contains a conjunctive adverb (such as *however, consequently, therefore,* or *furthermore*) to show the relation between the two clauses.

Learning history is easy; learning its lessons is almost impossible.

He was determined to complete his degree; consequently, he studied diligently.

Most people want to be delivered from temptation; they would like, however, to keep in touch.

Tip. Don't use a semicolon unless each clause is truly independent. Try the sentence test. Omit the semicolon if each clause could not stand alone as a complete sentence.

Faulty	**Improved**
There's no point in speaking; unless you can improve on silence. (The second half of the sentence is a dependent clause. It could not stand alone as a sentence.)	There's no point in speaking unless you can improve on silence.
Although I cannot change the direction of the wind; I can adjust my sails to reach my destination. (The first clause could not stand alone.)	Although I cannot change the direction of the wind, I can adjust my sails to reach my destination.

GUIDE 28: Use a semicolon to separate items in a series when one or more of the items contains internal commas.

Representatives from as far away as Blue Bell, Pennsylvania; Bowling Green, Ohio; and Phoenix, Arizona, attended the conference.

Stories circulated about Henry Ford, founder, Ford Motor Company; Lee Iacocca, CEO, Chrysler Motor Company; and Shoichiro Toyoda, chief, Toyota Motor Company.

GUIDE 29: Use a colon after a complete thought that introduces a list of items. Words such as *these, the following,* and *as follows* may introduce the list or they may be implied.

The following cities are on the tour: Louisville, Memphis, and New Orleans.

An alternate tour includes several western cities: Seattle, San Francisco, and San Diego.

Tip. Be sure that the statement before a colon is grammatically complete. An introductory statement that ends with a preposition (such as *by, for, at,* and *to*) or a verb (such as *is, are,* or *were*) is incomplete. The list following a preposition or a verb actually functions as an object or as a complement to finish the sentence.

Faulty	**Improved**
Three Big Macs were ordered by: Pam, Jim, and Lee. (Do not use a colon after an incomplete statement.)	Three Big Macs were ordered by Pam, Jim, and Lee.
Other items that they ordered were: fries, Cokes, and salads. (Do not use a colon after an incomplete statement.)	Other items that they ordered were fries, Cokes, and salads.

GUIDE 30: Use a colon after business letter salutations and to introduce long quotations.

Dear Mr. Duran: Dear Lisa:

The Asian consultant bluntly said: "Americans tend to be too blabby, too impatient, and too informal for Asian tastes. To succeed in trade with Pacific Rim countries, Americans must become more willing to adapt to native cultures."

Tip. Use a comma to introduce short quotations. Use a colon to introduce long one-sentence quotations and quotations of two or more sentences.

✓ Checkpoint

Add appropriate semicolons and colons.

51. My short-term goal is an entry-level job my long-term goal however is a management position.
52. Reebok interviewed the following candidates Joni Sims Auburn University James Jones University of Georgia and Madonna Farr Louisiana Tech.
53. The recruiter was looking for three qualities initiative versatility and enthusiasm.

54. Reebok seeks experienced individuals however it will hire recent graduates who have excellent records.
55. Portland is an expanding area therefore many business opportunities are available.

Apostrophe

GUIDE 31: **Add an apostrophe plus *s* to an ownership word that does not end in an *s* sound.**

We hope to show a profit in one year's time. (Add *'s* because the ownership word *year* does not end in an *s*.)

The company's assets rose in value. (Add *'s* because the ownership word *company* does not end in *s*.)

All the women's votes were counted. (Add *'s* because the ownership word *women* does not end in *s*.)

GUIDE 32: **Add only an apostrophe to an ownership word that ends in an *s* sound—unless an extra syllable can be pronounced easily.**

Some workers' benefits will cost more. (Add only an apostrophe because the ownership word *workers* ends in an *s*.)

Several months' rent are now due. (Add only an apostrophe because the ownership word *months* ends in an *s*.)

The boss's son got the job. (Add *'s* because an extra syllable can be pronounced easily.)

Tip. To determine whether an ownership word ends in an *s*, use it in an *of* phrase. For example, *one month's salary* becomes *the salary of one month.* By isolating the ownership word without its apostrophe, you can decide if it ends in an *s*.

GUIDE 33: **Use *'s* to make a noun possessive when it precedes a gerund, a verb form used as a noun.**

We all protested *Laura's* (not *Laura*) smoking.

His (not *Him*) talking interfered with the movie.

I appreciate *your* (not *you*) answering the telephone while I was gone.

✓ Checkpoint

Correct erroneous possessives.

56. Both companies presidents received huge salaries, even when profits were falling.
57. Within one months time we were able to verify all members names and addresses.
58. Bryans supporters worry that there's little chance of him being elected.
59. The position requires five years experience in waste management.
60. Ms. Jackson car is serviced every six months.

GUIDE 34: Use a period to end a statement, command, indirect question, or polite request.

Everyone must row with the oars that he or she has. (Statement)

Send the completed report to me by June 1. (Command)

Stacy asked whether she could use the car next weekend. (Indirect question)

Will you please send me an employment application. (Polite request)

Tip. Polite requests often sound like questions. To determine the punctuation, apply the action test. If the request prompts an action, use a period. If it prompts a verbal response, use a question mark.

Faulty	**Improved**
Could you please correct the balance on my next statement? (This polite request prompts an action rather than a verbal response.)	Could you please correct the balance on my next statement.

GUIDE 35: Use a question mark after a direct question and after statements with questions appended.

Is it illegal to duplicate training videotapes?

Most of their training is in-house, isn't it?

GUIDE 36: Use a dash to (a) set off parenthetical elements containing internal commas, (b) emphasize a sentence interruption, or (c) separate an introductory list from a summarizing statement. The dash has legitimate uses. However, some writers use it whenever they know that punctuation is necessary, but they're not sure exactly what. The dash can be very effective, if not misused.

Three top students—Gene Engle, Donna Hersh, and Mika Sato—won awards. (Use dashes to set off elements with internal commas.)

Executives at IBM—despite rampant rumors in the stock market—remained quiet regarding dividend earnings. (Use dashes to emphasize a sentence interruption.)

Dell, Compaq, and Apple—these were the three leading computer manufacturers. (Use a dash to separate an introductory list from a summarizing statement.)

GUIDE 37: Use parentheses to set off nonessential sentence elements, such as explanations, directions, questions, or references.

Researchers find that the office grapevine (see Chapter 1 for more discussion) carries surprisingly accurate information.

Only two dates (February 15 and March 1) are suitable for the meeting.

Tip. Careful writers use parentheses to de-emphasize and the dash to emphasize parenthetical information. One expert said, "Dashes shout the news; parentheses whisper it."

GUIDE 38: Use quotation marks to (a) enclose the exact words of a speaker or writer; (b) distinguish words used in a special sense, such as slang; or (c) enclose titles of articles, chapters, or other short works.

"If you make your job important," said the consultant, "it's quite likely to return the favor."

The recruiter said that she was looking for candidates with good communication skills. (Omit quotation marks because the exact words of the speaker are not quoted.)

This office discourages "rad" hair styles and clothing. (Use quotes for slang.)

In *Business Week* I saw an article entitled "Communication for Global Markets." (Use quotation marks around the title of an article; use all caps, underlines, or italics for the name of the publication.)

Tip. Never use quotation marks arbitrarily, as in *Our "spring" sale starts April 1.*

 **Checkpoint**

Add appropriate punctuation.

61. Will you please send me your latest catalog as soon as possible

62. (Direct quote) The only thing you get in a hurry said the professor is trouble

63. (De-emphasize) Two kinds of batteries see page 16 of the instruction booklet may be used in this camera.

64. (Emphasize) The first three colors that we tested red, yellow, and orange were selected.

65. All letters with erroneous addresses were reprinted weren't they

Capitalization

GUIDE 39: Capitalize proper nouns and proper adjectives. Capitalize the *specific* names of persons, places, institutions, buildings, religions, holidays, months, organizations, laws, races, languages, and so forth. Don't capitalize common nouns that make *general* references.

Proper Nouns	**Common Nouns**
Michelle DeLuca	the manufacturer's rep
Everglades National Park	the wilderness park
College of the Redwoods	the community college
Empire State Building	the downtown building
Environmental Protection Agency	the federal agency
Persian, Armenian, Hindi	modern foreign languages
Proper Adjectives	
Hispanic markets	Italian dressing
Xerox copy	Japanese executives
Swiss chocolates	Reagan economics

GUIDE 40: Capitalize only specific academic courses and degrees.

Professor Jane Mangrum, Ph.D., will teach Accounting 121 next spring.

James Barker, who holds bachelor's and master's degrees, teaches marketing.

Jessica enrolled in classes in management, English, and business law.

GUIDE 41: Capitalize courtesy, professional, religious, government, family, and business titles when they precede names.

Mr. Jameson, Mrs. Alvarez, and Ms. Robinson (Courtesy titles)
Professor Andrews, Dr. Lee (Professional titles)
Rabbi Cohen, Pastor Williams, Pope John (Religious titles)
Senator Tom Harrison, Major Jackson (Government titles)
Uncle Edward, Mother Teresa, Cousin Vinney (Family titles)
Vice President Morris, Budget Director Lopez (Business titles)

Do not capitalize a title when it is followed by an appositive (that is, when the title is followed by a noun that renames or explains it).

Only one professor, Jonathan Marcus, favored a tuition hike.

Local candidates counted on their president, Bill Clinton, to raise funds.

Do not capitalize titles following names unless they are part of an address:

Mark Yoder, president of Yoder Enterprises, hired all employees.

Paula Beech, director of Human Resources, interviewed all candidates.

Send the package to Amanda Harr, Advertising Manager, Cambridge Publishers, 20 Park Plaza, Boston, MA 02116.

Generally, do not capitalize a title that replaces a person's name.

Only the president, his chief of staff, and one senator made the trip.

The director of marketing and the sales manager will meet at 1 p.m.

Do not capitalize family titles used with possessive pronouns.

my mother, his father, your cousin

GUIDE 42: Capitalize the principal words in the titles of books, magazines, newspapers, articles, movies, plays, songs, poems, and reports. Do *not* capitalize articles (*a, an, the*) and prepositions of fewer than four letters (*in, to, by, for*) unless they begin or end the title.

I enjoyed the book *A Customer Is More Than a Name.*

Did you read the article entitled "Companies in Europe Seeking Executives With Multinational Skills"?

We liked the article entitled "Advice From a Pro: How to Say It With Pictures."

(Note that the titles of books are underlined or italicized while the titles of articles are enclosed in quotation marks.)

GUIDE 43: Capitalize *north, south, east, west,* and their derivatives only when they represent specific geographical regions.

from the Pacific Northwest	heading northwest on the highway
living in the East	east of the city
Midwesterners, Southerners	western Oregon, southern Ohio

GUIDE 44: Capitalize the names of departments, divisions, or committees within your own organization. Outside your organization capitalize only *specific* department, division, or committee names.

Attorneys in our Legal Assistance Department handle numerous cases.

Samsung offers TVs in its Consumer Electronics Division.

We volunteered for the Employee Social Responsibility Committee.

You might send an application to their personnel department.

GUIDE 45: Capitalize product names only when they refer to trademarked items. Don't capitalize the common names following manufacturers' names.

Sony portable television	Skippy peanut butter	NordicTrack treadmill
Eveready Energizer	Norelco razor	Kodak color copier
Coca-Cola	Apple computer	Big Mac sandwich

GUIDE 46: Capitalize most nouns followed by numbers or letters (except in page, paragraph, line, and verse references).

Room 14	Exhibit A	Flight 12, Gate 43
Figure 2.1	Plan No. 1	Model Z2010

 **Checkpoint**

Capitalize all appropriate words.

66. vice president ellis bought a toshiba computer for use on her trips to europe.

67. our director of research brought plan no. 1 with him to the meeting in our engineering research department.

68. proceed west on highway 10 until you reach the mt. vernon exit.

69. you are booked on american airlines flight 164 leaving from gate 5 at newark international airport.

70. to improve their english, many hispanics purchased the book entitled *the power of language is yours.*

Number Usage

GUIDE 47: Use word form to express (a) numbers *ten* and under and (b) numbers beginning sentences. General references to numbers *ten* and under should be expressed in word form. Also use word form for numbers that begin sentences. If the resulting number involves more than two words, however, the sentence should be recast so that the number does not fall at the beginning.

We answered *six* telephone calls for the *four* sales reps.

Fifteen customers responded to the *three* advertisements today.

A total of 155 cameras were awarded as prizes. (Avoid beginning the sentence with a long number such as *one hundred fifty-five.*)

GUIDE 48: Use words to express general references to ages, small fractions, and periods of time.

When she reached *twenty-one,* she received *one half* of the estate.

James owns a *one-third* interest in the electronics business. (Note that fractions are hyphenated only when they function as adjectives.)

That business was founded *thirty-five* years ago.

Tip. Exact ages and specific business terms may be expressed in figures.

Both Meredith Jones, 55, and Jack Jones, 57, appeared in the article.

The note is payable in 60 days.

GUIDE 49: Use figures to express most references to numbers *11* and over.

Over *150* people from *53* companies attended the two-day workshop.

A four-ounce serving of Haagen-Dazs toffee crunch ice cream contains *300* calories and *19* grams of fat.

GUIDE 50: Use figures to express money, dates, clock time, decimals, and percents. Use a combination of words and figures to express sums of 1 million and over.

One item cost only *$1.95*; most, however, were priced between *$10* and *$35.* (Omit the decimals and zeros in even sums of money.)

A total of *3,700* employees approved the contract *May 12* at *3 p.m.*

When U.S. sales dropped *4.7* percent, net income fell *9.8* percent. (Use the word *percent* instead of the % symbol.)

Orion lost *$62.9 million* in the latest fiscal year on revenues of *$584 million.* (Use a combination of words and figures for sums 1 million and over.)

Tip. To ease your memory load, concentrate on the numbers normally expressed in words: numbers *ten* and under, numbers at the beginning of a sentence, and small fractions. Nearly everything else in business is generally written with figures.

 **Checkpoint**

Correct any inappropriate expression of numbers.

71. McDonald's former McLean Deluxe, priced at one dollar and fifty-nine cents, had only three hundred ten calories and nine percent fat.

72. 175 employees will attend the meeting January tenth at one p.m.

73. The Nordstrom family, which owns forty percent of the company's stock, recently added four co-presidents.

74. Our three branch offices, with a total of ninety-six workers, needs to add six computers and nine printers.

75. On March eighth we paid thirty-two dollars a share to acquire one third of the stocks.

Key to C.L.U.E. Checkpoint Exercises in Appendix A

This key shows all corrections. If you marked anything else, double-check the appropriate guideline.

1. Pizza Hut fought back with
2. backfire; consequently,
3. advertisements; they
4. chain, Domino's
5. deliveries; the
6. If I *were* . . . I would have *written*
7. could have *written* . . . if you *had* read
8. When Trevor *saw*
9. I wish I *were* . . . could have *gone*
10. she had *taken* . . . able to *choose*
11. energy *have*
12. efforts, *is* disappointingly
13. Ms. Wagner *is* in charge
14. companies *is* being
15. *knows* how
16. my friend and *I* . . . *its* price
17. to *him* and *me*
18. between you and *me*
19. *yours* and *hers*
20. could have been *she* . . . to you and *me*
21. *whomever* we nominate
22. *Whom* would you
23. *whoever* ordered
24. Jeff and *I*
25. by *whoever* experiences
26. to have *his or her* tuition; to have *the* tuition; *all employees are entitled to have their tuition reimbursed*
27. but *this advancement plan* appeals (*Revise to avoid vague pronoun* it.)
28. may cancel *his or her* subscription; may cancel *the* subscription; *subscribers* may cancel *their* subscriptions
29. *his or her* name and address; *all voters must have their names and addresses*
30. *These activities are* particularly important (*Revise to avoid the vague pronoun* this.)

31. my manager and *I* . . . point-by-point

32. completed the work so *quickly* . . . recently opened (*Omit hyphen.*)

33. If I do *well* . . . part-time . . . full-time

34. told him and *me* . . . *personally*

35. *not-too-distant* future

36. class, Jeff . . . commas, semicolons, and

37. punctuation, (*No comma before* and!)

38. program, but

39. business law, or

40. degree, he . . . San Diego, Orlando, or

41. 222 Georgetown Road, Jacksonville, NC 28540, as her

42. felt, nevertheless,

43. paralegals, which . . . year,

44. April 1, 1996, . . . January 1, 1999.

45. As a matter of fact,

46. (*Remove comma.*)

47. equipment,

48. (*Remove comma.*)

49. think, on the other hand, . . . women, minorities, and

50. (*Remove comma.*)

51. entry-level job; my . . . goal, however,

52. candidates: Joni Sims, Auburn University; James Jones, University of Georgia; and Madonna Farr, Louisiana Tech.

53. qualities: initiative, versatility, and

54. individuals; however,

55. area; therefore,

56. companies'

57. one month's time . . . members'

58. Bryan's . . . *his* being elected

59. years' experience

60. Jackson's car

61. possible.

62. "The only thing you get in a hurry," said the professor, "is trouble."

63. batteries (see page 16 of the instruction booklet) may be

64. tested—red, yellow, and orange—were selected.

65. reprinted, weren't they?

66. Vice President Ellis . . . Toshiba computer . . . Europe

67. Our . . . Plan No. 1 . . . Engineering Research Department

68. Proceed . . . Highway 10 . . . Mt. Vernon exit.

69. You . . . American Airlines Flight 164 . . . Gate 5 at Newark International Airport.

70. To improve their English, many Hispanics . . . *The Power of Language Is Yours.*

71. priced at $1.59, had only 310 calories and 9 percent fat.

72. A total of 175 employees . . . January 10 at 1 p.m.

73. 40 percent

74. 96 workers

75. March 8 . . . $32

Confusing Words

accede:	to agree or consent
exceed:	over a limit
accept	to receive
except	to exclude; (prep) but
advice:	suggestion, opinion
advise:	to counsel or recommend
affect:	to influence
effect:	(n) outcome, result; (v) to bring about, to create
all ready:	prepared
already:	by this time
all right:	satisfactory
alright:	unacceptable variant spelling
altar:	structure for worship
alter:	to change
appraise:	to estimate
apprise:	to inform
assure:	to promise
ensure:	to make certain
insure:	to protect from loss
capital:	(n) city that is seat of government; wealth of an individual; (adj) chief
capitol:	building that houses state or national lawmakers
cereal:	breakfast food
serial:	arranged in sequence
cite:	to quote; to summon
site:	location
sight:	a view; to see
complement:	that which completes
compliment:	to praise or flatter
conscience:	regard for fairness
conscious:	aware
council:	governing body
counsel:	to give advice; advice
desert:	arid land; to abandon
dessert:	sweet food
device:	invention or mechanism
devise:	to design or arrange
disburse:	to pay out
disperse:	to scatter widely
elicit:	to draw out
illicit:	unlawful
every day:	each single day
everyday:	ordinary
farther:	a greater distance
further:	additional
formally:	in a formal manner
formerly:	in the past
hole:	an opening
whole:	complete
imply:	to suggest indirectly
infer:	to reach a conclusion
liable:	legally responsible
libel:	damaging written statement
loose:	not fastened
lose:	to misplace
miner:	person working in a mine
minor:	a lesser item; person under age
patience:	calm perseverance
patients:	people receiving medical treatment
personal:	private, individual
personnel:	employees
precede:	to go before
proceed:	to continue
precedence:	priority
precedents:	events used as an example
principal:	(n) capital sum; school official; (adj) chief
principle:	rule of action
stationary:	immovable
stationery:	writing material
than:	conjunction showing comparison
then:	adverb meaning "at that time"
their:	possessive form of *they*
there:	at that place or point

they're:	contraction of *they are*	*two:*	a number
to:	a preposition; the sign of the infinitive	*waiver:*	abandonment of a claim
too:	an adverb meaning "also" or "to an excessive extent"	*waver:*	to shake or fluctuate

160 Frequently Misspelled Words

absence
accommodate
achieve
acknowledgment
across
adequate
advisable
analyze
annually
appointment
argument
automatically
bankruptcy
becoming
beneficial
budget
business
calendar
canceled
catalog
changeable
column
committee
congratulate
conscience
conscious
consecutive
consensus
consistent
control
convenient
correspondence
courteous
criticize
decision
deductible
defendant
definitely
dependent
describe
desirable
destroy
development
disappoint
dissatisfied
division
efficient
embarrass
emphasis
emphasize
employee
envelope
equipped
especially
evidently
exaggerate
excellent
exempt
existence
extraordinary
familiar
fascinate
feasible
February
fiscal
foreign
forty
fourth
friend
genuine
government
grammar
grateful
guarantee
harass
height
hoping
immediate
incidentally
incredible
independent
indispensable
interrupt
irrelevant
itinerary
judgment
knowledge
legitimate
library
license
maintenance
manageable
manufacturer
mileage
miscellaneous
mortgage
necessary
nevertheless
ninety
ninth
noticeable
occasionally
occurred
offered
omission
omitted
opportunity
opposite
ordinarily
paid
pamphlet
permanent
permitted
pleasant
practical
prevalent
privilege
probably
procedure
profited
prominent
qualify
quantity
questionnaire
receipt
receive
recognize
recommendation
referred
regarding
remittance
representative
restaurant
schedule
secretary
separate
similar
sincerely
software
succeed
sufficient
supervisor
surprise
tenant
therefore
thorough
though
through
truly
undoubtedly
unnecessarily
usable
usage
using
usually
valuable
volume
weekday
writing
yield

APPENDIX B

Guide to Document Formats

Business documents carry two kinds of messages. Verbal messages are conveyed by the words chosen to express the writer's ideas. Nonverbal messages are conveyed largely by the appearance of a document. If you compare an assortment of letters and memos from various organizations, you will notice immediately that some look more attractive and more professional than others. The nonverbal message of the professional-looking documents suggests that they were sent by people who are careful, informed, intelligent, and successful. Understandably, you're more likely to take seriously documents that use attractive stationery and professional formatting techniques.

Over the years certain practices and conventions have arisen regarding the appearance and formatting of business documents. Although these conventions offer some choices (such as letter and punctuation styles), most business letters follow standardized formats. To ensure that your documents carry favorable nonverbal messages about you and your organization, you'll want to give special attention to the stationery and formatting of your letters, envelopes, memos, e-mail messages, and fax cover sheets.

Stationery

Most organizations use high-quality stationery for business documents. This stationery is printed on select paper that meets two qualifications: weight and cotton-fiber content.

Paper is measured by weight and may range from 9 pounds (thin onionskin paper) to 32 pounds (thick card and cover stock). Most office stationery is in the 16- to 24-pound range. Lighter 16-pound paper is generally sufficient for internal documents including memos. Heavier 20- to 24-pound paper is used for printed letterhead stationery.

Paper is also judged by its cotton-fiber content. Cotton fiber makes paper stronger, softer in texture, and less likely to yellow. Good-quality stationery contains 25 percent or more cotton fiber.

Letter Placement

The easiest way to place letters on the page is to use the defaults of your word processing program. These are usually set for side margins of 1 inch. Many companies today find these margins quite acceptable.

If you wish to adjust your margins to better balance shorter letters, use the following chart.

Words in Body of Letter	**Side Margins**	**Blank Lines After Date**
Under 200	1½ inches	4 to 10
Over 200	1 inch	2 to 3

By the way, experts say that a "ragged" right margin is easier to read than a justified (even) margin. Consider turning off the justification feature of your word processing program if it automatically justifies the right margin.

Letter Parts

Professional-looking business letters are arranged in a conventional sequence with standard parts. Following is a discussion of how to use these letter parts properly. Figure B.1 illustrates the parts in a block-style letter. (See Chapter 7 for additional discussion of letters and their parts.)

Letterhead. Most business organizations use 8½- by 11-inch paper printed with a letterhead displaying their official name, address, and telephone and fax numbers. The letterhead may also include a logo and an advertising message.

Dateline. On letterhead paper you should place the date one blank line below the last line of the letterhead or 2 inches from the top edge of the paper (line 13). On plain paper place the date immediately below your return address. Since the date goes on line 13, start the return address an appropriate number of lines above it. The most common dateline format is as follows: *June 9, 2000.* Don't use *th* (or *rd*) when the date is written this way. For European or military correspondence, use the following dateline format: *9 June 2000.* Notice that no commas are used.

Addressee and Delivery Notations. Delivery notations such as *FAX TRANSMITTAL, FEDERAL EXPRESS, MESSENGER DELIVERY, CONFIDENTIAL,* or *CERTIFIED MAIL* are typed in all capital letters one blank line above the inside address.

Inside Address. Type the inside address—that is, the address of the organization or person receiving the letter—single-spaced, starting at the left margin. The number of lines between the dateline and the inside address depends on the size of the letter body, the type size (point or pitch size), and the length of the typing lines. Generally, one to nine blank lines are appropriate.

Be careful to duplicate the exact wording and spelling of the recipient's name and address on your documents. Usually, you can copy this information from the letterhead of the correspondence you are answering. If, for example, you are responding to *Jackson & Perkins Company,* don't address your letter to *Jackson and Perkins Corp.*

Always be sure to include a courtesy title such as *Mr., Ms., Mrs., Dr.,* or *Professor* before a person's name in the inside address—for both the letter and the envelope.

FIGURE B.1 Block and Modified Block Letter Styles

Block style
Open punctuation

Letterhead — *islandgraphics*
893 Dillingham Boulevard Honolulu, HI 96817-8817

Dateline — September 13, 1997 ↓ line 13 or 1 blank line below letterhead

↓ 1 to 9 blank lines

Inside address — Mr. T. M. Wilson, President
Visual Concept Enterprises
1901 Kaumualii Highway
Lihue, HI 96766

↓ 1 blank line

Salutation — Dear Mr. Wilson

↓ 1 blank line

Subject line — SUBJECT: BLOCK LETTER STYLE

↓ 1 blank line

This letter illustrates block letter style, about which you asked. All typed lines begin at the left margin. The date is usually placed two inches from the top edge of the paper or two lines below the last line of the letterhead, whichever position is lower.

Body — This letter also shows open punctuation. No colon follows the salutation, and no comma follows the complimentary close. Although this punctuation style is efficient, we find that most of our customers prefer to include punctuation after the salutation and the complimentary close.

If a subject line is included, it appears two lines below the salutation. The word *SUBJECT* is optional. Most readers will recognize a statement in this position as the subject without an identifying label. The complimentary close appears two lines below the end of the last paragraph.

↓ 1 blank line

Complimentary close — Sincerely

↓ 3 blank lines

Signature block — Mark H. Wong
Graphics Designer

↓ 1 blank line

MHW:pil

Modified block style
Mixed punctuation

In the modified block-style letter shown at the left, the date is centered or aligned with the complimentary close and signature block, which start at the center. Mixed punctuation includes a colon after the salutation and a comma after the complimentary close, as shown at the left.

Although many women in business today favor *Ms.*, you'll want to use whatever title the addressee prefers.

Remember that the inside address is not included for readers who already know who and where they are. It's there to help writers accurately file a copy of the message.

In general, avoid abbreviations (such as *Ave.* or *Co.*) unless they appear in the printed letterhead of the document being answered.

Attention Line. An attention line allows you to send your message officially to an organization but to direct it to a specific individual, officer, or department. However, if you know an individual's complete name, it's always better to use it as the first line of the inside address and avoid an attention line. Here are two common formats for attention lines:

MultiMedia Enterprises
931 Calkins Road
Rochester, NY 14301

ATTENTION MARKETING DIRECTOR

MultiMedia Enterprises
Attention: Marketing Director
931 Calkins Road
Rochester, NY 14301

Attention lines may be typed in all caps or with upper- and lowercase letters. The colon following *Attention* is optional. Notice that an attention line may be placed one blank line below the address block or printed as the second line of the inside address. You'll want to use the latter format if you're composing on a word processor because the address block may be copied to the envelope and the attention line will not interfere with the last-line placement of the zip code. (Mail can be sorted more easily if the zip code appears in the last line of a typed address.)

Whenever possible, use a person's name as the first line of an address instead of putting that name in an attention line. Some writers use an attention line because they fear that letters addressed to individuals at companies may be considered private. They worry that if the addressee is no longer with the company, the letter may be forwarded or not opened. Actually, unless a letter is marked "Personal" or "Confidential," it will very likely be opened as business mail.

Salutation. For most letter styles place the letter greeting, or salutation, one blank line below the last line of the inside address or the attention line (if used). If the letter is addressed to an individual, use that person's courtesy title and last name (Dear Mr. Lanham). Even if you are on a first-name basis (Dear Leslie), be sure to add a colon (not a comma or a semicolon) after the salutation. Do not use an individual's full name in the salutation (not Dear Mr. Leslie Lanham) unless you are unsure of gender (Dear Leslie Lanham).

For letters with attention lines or those addressed to organizations, the selection of an appropriate salutation has become more difficult. Formerly, *Gentlemen* was used generically for all organizations. With increasing numbers of women in business management today, however, *Gentlemen* is problematic. Because no universally acceptable salutation has emerged as yet, you'll probably be safest with *Ladies and Gentlemen* or *Gentlemen and Ladies.*

One way to avoid the salutation dilemma is to address a document to a specific person. Another alternative is to use the simplified letter style, which conveniently omits the salutation (and the complimentary close).

Subject and Reference Lines. Although experts suggest placing the subject line one blank line below the salutation, many businesses actually place it above the salutation. Use whatever style your organization prefers. Reference lines often show policy or file numbers; they generally appear one blank line above the salutation.

Body. Most business letters and memorandums are single-spaced, with double line spacing between paragraphs. Very short messages may be double-spaced with indented paragraphs.

Complimentary Close. Typed one blank line below the last line of the letter, the complimentary close may be formal (Very truly yours) or informal (Sincerely yours or Cordially). The simplified letter style omits a complimentary close.

Signature Block. In most letter styles the writer's typed name and optional identification appear three to four blank lines below the complimentary close. The combination of name, title, and organization information should be arranged to achieve a balanced look. The name and title may appear on the same line or on separate lines, depending on the length of each. Use commas to separate categories within the same line, but not to conclude a line.

Sincerely yours,

Jeremy M. Wood

Jeremy M. Wood, Manager
Technical Sales and Services

Cordially yours,

Casandra Baker-Murillo

Casandra Baker-Murillo
Executive Vice President

Courtesy titles (*Ms., Mrs., or Miss*) should be used before female names that are not readily dinstinguishable as male or female. They should also be used before names containing only initials and international names. The title is usually placed in parentheses, but it may appear without them.

Yours truly,

K. C. Tripton

(Ms.) K. C. Tripton
Project Manager

Sincerely,

Leslie Hill

(Mr.) Leslie Hill
Public Policy Department

Some organizations include their names in the signature block. In such cases the organization name appears in all caps two lines below the complimentary close, as shown here.

Cordially,

LITTON COMPUTER SERVICES

Shelina A. Simpson

Shelina A. Simpson
Executive Assistant

Reference Initials. If used, the initials of the typist and writer are typed one blank line below the writer's name and title. Generally, the writer's initials are capitalized and the typist's are lowercased, but this format varies.

Enclosure Notation. When an enclosure or attachment accompanies a document, a notation to that effect appears one blank line below the reference initials. This notation reminds the typist to insert the enclosure in the envelope, and it reminds the recipient to look for the enclosure or attachment. The notation may be spelled out (*Enclosure, Attachment*), or it may be abbreviated (*Enc., Att.*). It may indicate the number of enclosures or attachments, and it may also identify a specific enclosure (*Enclosure: Form 1099*).

Copy Notation. If you make copies of correspondence for other individuals, you may use *cc* to indicate carbon copy, *pc* to indicate photocopy, or merely *c* for any kind of copy. A colon following the initial(s) is optional.

Second-Page Heading. When a letter extends beyond one page, use plain paper of the same quality and color as the first page. Identify the second and succeeding pages with a heading consisting of the name of the addressee, the page number, and the date. Use either of the following two formats:

Ms. Rachel Ruiz 2 May 3, 2000

Ms. Rachel Ruiz
Page 2
May 3, 2000

Both headings appear on line 7 followed by two blank lines to separate them from the continuing text. Avoid using a second page if you have only one line or the complimentary close and signature block to fill that page.

Plain-Paper Return Address. If you prepare a personal or business letter on plain paper, place your address immediately above the date. Do not include your name; you will type (and sign) your name at the end of your letter. If your return address contains two lines, begin typing it on line 11 so that the date appears on line 13. Avoid abbreviations except for a two-letter state abbreviation.

580 East Leffels Street
Springfield, OH 45501
December 14, 2000

Ms. Ellen Siemens
Escrow Department
TransOhio First Federal
1220 Wooster Boulevard
Columbus, OH 43218-2900

Dear Ms. Siemens:

For letters prepared in the block style, type the return address at the left margin. For modified block-style letters, start the return address at the center to align with the complimentary close.

Letter Styles

Business letters are generally prepared in one of three formats. The most popular is the block style, but the simplified style has much to recommend it.

Block Style. In the block style, shown earlier in Figure B.1, all lines begin at the left margin. This style is a favorite because it is easy to format.

Modified Block Style. The modified block style differs from block style in that the date and closing lines appear in the center, as shown at the bottom of Figure B.1. The date may be (1) centered, (2) begun at the center of the page (to align with the closing lines), or (3) backspaced from the right margin. The signature block—including the complimentary close, writer's name and title, or organization identification—begins at the center. The first line of each paragraph may begin at the left margin or may be indented five or ten spaces. All other lines begin at the left margin.

Simplified Style. Introduced by the Administrative Management Society a number of years ago, the simplified letter style, shown in Figure B.2, requires little formatting. Like the block style, all lines begin at the left margin. A subject line appears in all caps two blank lines below the inside address and two blank lines above the first paragraph. The salutation and complimentary close are omitted. The signer's name and identification appear in all caps four blank lines below the last paragraph. This letter style is efficient and avoids the problem of appropriate salutations and courtesy titles.

Punctuation Styles

Two punctuation styles are commonly used for letters. *Open* punctuation, shown with the block-style letter in Figure B.1, contains no punctuation after the salutation or complimentary close. *Mixed* punctuation, shown with the modified block-style letter in Figure B.1, requires a colon after the salutation and a comma after the complimentary close. Many business organizations prefer mixed punctuation, even in a block-style letter.

If you choose mixed punctuation, be sure to use a colon—not a comma or semicolon—after the salutation. Even when the salutation is a first name, the colon is appropriate.

Envelopes

An envelope should be printed on the same quality and color of stationery as the letter it carries. Because the envelope introduces your message and makes the first impression, you need to be especially careful in addressing it. Moreover, how you fold the letter is important.

Return Address. The return address is usually printed in the upper left corner of an envelope, as shown in Figure B.3. In large companies some form of identification (the writer's initials, name, or location) may be typed above the company name and return address. This identification helps return the letter to the sender in case of nondelivery.

On an envelope without a printed return address, single-space the return address in the upper-left corner. Beginning on line 3 on the fourth space (½ inch) from the left edge, type the writer's name, title, company, and mailing address.

Mailing Address. On legal-sized No. 10 envelopes (4⅛ by 9½ inches), begin the address on line 13 about 4¼ inches from the left edge, as shown in Figure B.3. For small envelopes (3⅝ by 6½ inches), begin typing on line 12 about 2½ inches from the left edge.

The U.S. Postal Service recommends that addresses be typed in all caps without any punctuation. This Postal Service style, shown in the small envelope in Figure

FIGURE B.2 Simplified Letter Style

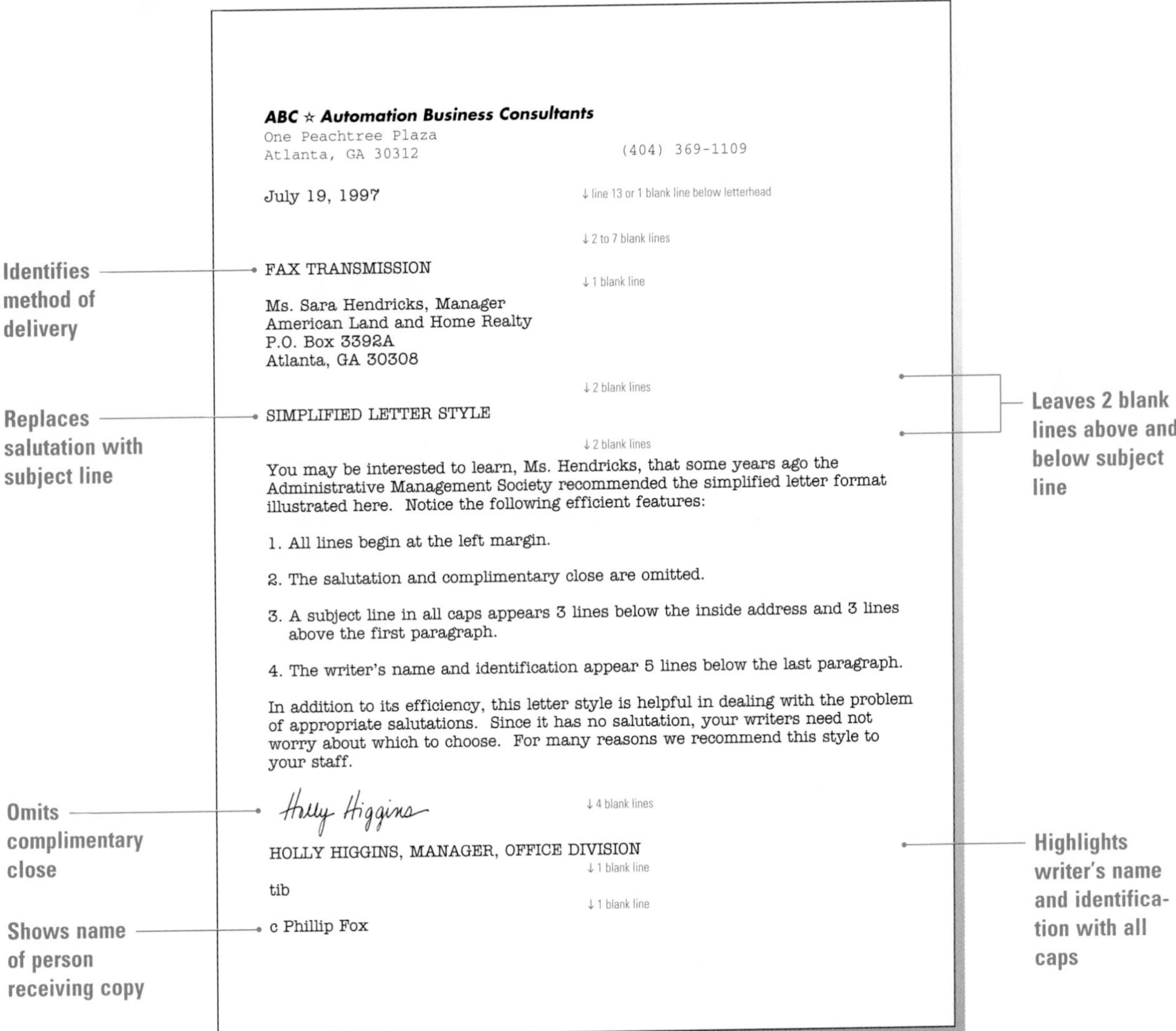

ABC ☆ Automation Business Consultants
One Peachtree Plaza
Atlanta, GA 30312 (404) 369-1109

July 19, 1997 ↓ line 13 or 1 blank line below letterhead

↓ 2 to 7 blank lines

FAX TRANSMISSION

↓ 1 blank line

Ms. Sara Hendricks, Manager
American Land and Home Realty
P.O. Box 3392A
Atlanta, GA 30308

↓ 2 blank lines

SIMPLIFIED LETTER STYLE

↓ 2 blank lines

You may be interested to learn, Ms. Hendricks, that some years ago the Administrative Management Society recommended the simplified letter format illustrated here. Notice the following efficient features:

1. All lines begin at the left margin.
2. The salutation and complimentary close are omitted.
3. A subject line in all caps appears 3 lines below the inside address and 3 lines above the first paragraph.
4. The writer's name and identification appear 5 lines below the last paragraph.

In addition to its efficiency, this letter style is helpful in dealing with the problem of appropriate salutations. Since it has no salutation, your writers need not worry about which to choose. For many reasons we recommend this style to your staff.

Holly Higgins ↓ 4 blank lines

HOLLY HIGGINS, MANAGER, OFFICE DIVISION
↓ 1 blank line

tib

↓ 1 blank line

c Phillip Fox

Identifies method of delivery
Replaces salutation with subject line
Omits complimentary close
Shows name of person receiving copy
Leaves 2 blank lines above and below subject line
Highlights writer's name and identification with all caps

B.3, was originally developed to facilitate scanning by optical character readers. Today's OCRs, however, are so sophisticated that they scan upper- and lowercase letters easily. Many companies today do not follow the Postal Service format because they prefer to use the same format on the envelope as for the inside address. If the same format is used, writers can take advantage of word processing programs to "copy" the inside address to the envelope, thus saving keystrokes and reducing errors. Having the same format on both the inside address and the envelope also looks more professional and consistent. For these reasons you may choose to use the familiar upper- and lowercase combination format. But you will want to check with your organization to learn its preference.

In addressing your envelopes for delivery in this country or in Canada, use the two-letter state and province abbreviations shown in Figure B.4. Notice that these abbreviations are in capital letters without periods.

FIGURE B.3 Envelope Formats

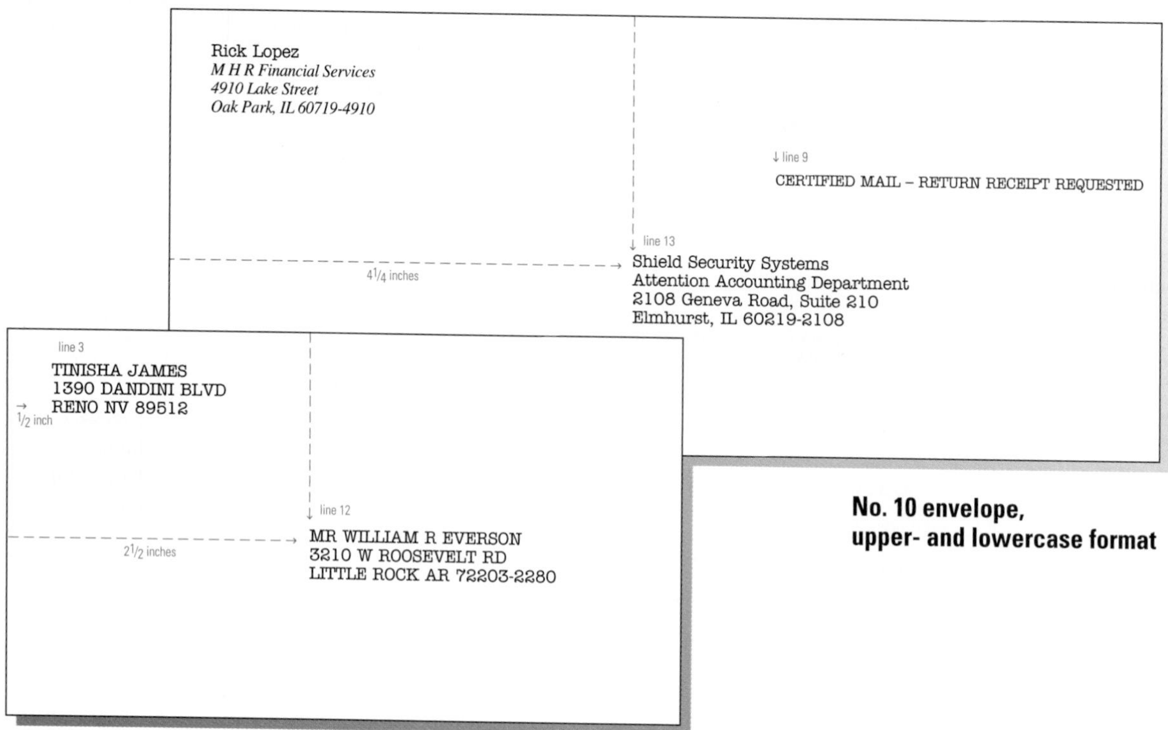

Rick Lopez
M H R Financial Services
4910 Lake Street
Oak Park, IL 60719-4910
line 9
CERTIFIED MAIL – RETURN RECEIPT REQUESTED
line 13
4¼ inches
Shield Security Systems
Attention Accounting Department
2108 Geneva Road, Suite 210
Elmhurst, IL 60219-2108
line 3
TINISHA JAMES
1390 DANDINI BLVD
RENO NV 89512
½ inch
line 12
2½ inches
MR WILLIAM R EVERSON
3210 W ROOSEVELT RD
LITTLE ROCK AR 72203-2280

No. 10 envelope, upper- and lowercase format

No. 6¾ envelope, Postal Service uppercase format

Folding. The way a letter is folded and inserted into an envelope sends additional nonverbal messages about a writer's professionalism and carefulness. Most businesspeople follow the procedures shown here, which produce the least number of creases to distract readers.

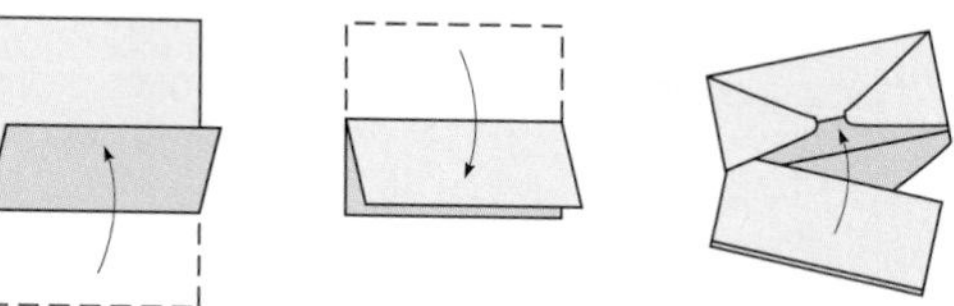

For large No. 10 envelopes, begin with the letter face up. Fold slightly less than one third of the sheet toward the top, as shown above. Then fold down the top third to within ⅓ inch of the bottom fold. Insert the letter into the envelope with the last fold toward the bottom of the envelope.

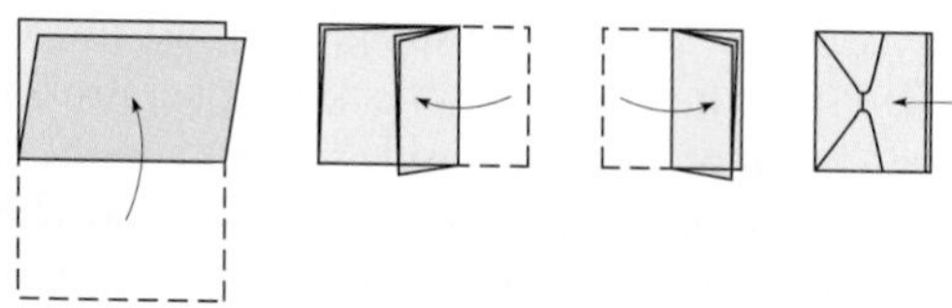

For small No. 6¾ envelopes, begin by folding the bottom up to within ⅓ inch of the top edge. Then fold the right third over to the left. Fold the left third to within ⅓ inch from the last fold. Insert the last fold into the envelope first.

FIGURE B.4 **Abbreviations of States, Territories, and Provinces**

State or Territory	Two-Letter Abbreviation	State or Territory	Two-Letter Abbreviation	State or Territory	Two-Letter Abbreviation
Alabama	AL	Michigan	MI	Vermont	VT
Alaska	AK	Minnesota	MN	Virgin Islands	VI
Arizona	AZ	Mississippi	MS	Virginia	VA
Arkansas	AR	Missouri	MO	Washington	WA
California	CA	Montana	MT	West Virginia	WV
Canal Zone	CZ	Nebraska	NE	Wisconsin	WI
Colorado	CO	Nevada	NV	Wyoming	WY
Connecticut	CT	New Hampshire	NH		
Delaware	DE	New Jersey	NJ		
District of Columbia	DC	New Mexico	NM	**Canadian Province**	**Two-letter Abbreviation**
Florida	FL	New York	NY		
Georgia	GA	North Carolina	NC	Alberta	AB
Guam	GU	North Dakota	ND	British Columbia	BC
Hawaii	HI	Ohio	OH	Labrador	LB
Idaho	ID	Oklahoma	OK	Manitoba	MB
Illinois	IL	Oregon	OR	New Brunswick	NB
Indiana	IN	Pennsylvania	PA	Newfoundland	NF
Iowa	IA	Puerto Rico	PR	Northwest Territories	NT
Kansas	KS	Rhode Island	RI	Nova Scotia	NS
Kentucky	KY	South Carolina	SC	Ontario	ON
Louisiana	LA	South Dakota	SD	Prince Edward Island	PE
Maine	ME	Tennessee	TN	Quebec	PQ
Maryland	MD	Texas	TX	Saskatchewan	SK
Massachusetts	MA	Utah	UT	Yukon Territory	YT

Memorandums

As discussed in Chapter 8, memorandums deliver messages within organizations. Many offices use memo forms imprinted with the organization name and, optionally, the department or division names, as shown in Figure B.5. Although the design and arrangement of memo forms vary, they usually include the basic elements of TO, FROM, DATE, and SUBJECT. Large organizations may include other identifying headings, such as FILE NUMBER, FLOOR, EXTENSION, LOCATION, and DISTRIBUTION.

Because of the difficulty of aligning computer printers with preprinted forms, many business writers store memo formats in their computers and call them up when preparing memos. The guide words are then printed with the message, thus eliminating alignment problems.

If no printed or stored computer forms are available, memos may be typed on company letterhead or on plain paper, as shown in Figure B.6. On a full sheet of paper, start the guide words on line 13; on a half sheet, start on line 7. Double-space and type in all caps the guide words: TO:, FROM:, DATE:, SUBJECT:. Align all the

FIGURE B.5 Printed Memo Forms

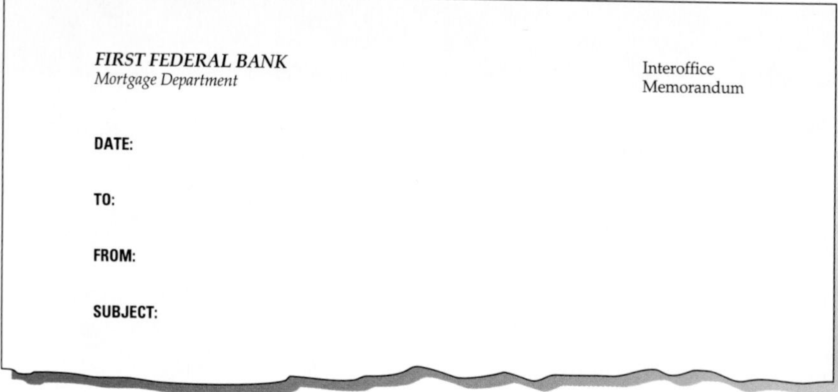
FIRST FEDERAL BANK
Mortgage Department

Interoffice
Memorandum

DATE:

TO:

FROM:

SUBJECT:

TMB
USA Inc.

Internal Memo

TO: DATE:

FROM: FILE:

SUBJECT:

fill-in information two spaces after the longest guide word (SUBJECT:). Leave three lines between the last line of the heading and the first line of the memo. Like business letters, memos are single-spaced.

Memos are generally formatted with side margins of 1¼ inches, or they may conform to the printed memo form. (For more information about memos, see Chapter 8.)

FIGURE B.6 Memo on Plain Paper

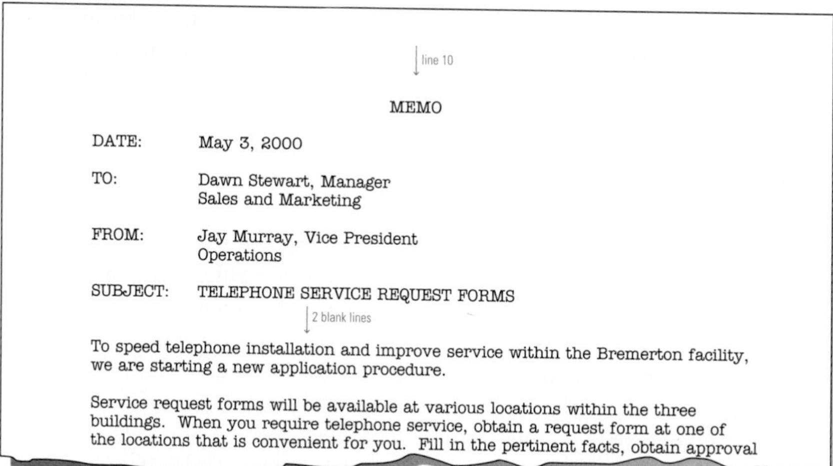

MEMO

DATE: May 3, 2000

TO: Dawn Stewart, Manager
Sales and Marketing

FROM: Jay Murray, Vice President
Operations

SUBJECT: TELEPHONE SERVICE REQUEST FORMS

To speed telephone installation and improve service within the Bremerton facility, we are starting a new application procedure.

Service request forms will be available at various locations within the three buildings. When you require telephone service, obtain a request form at one of the locations that is convenient for you. Fill in the pertinent facts, obtain approval

FIGURE B.7 E-mail Message

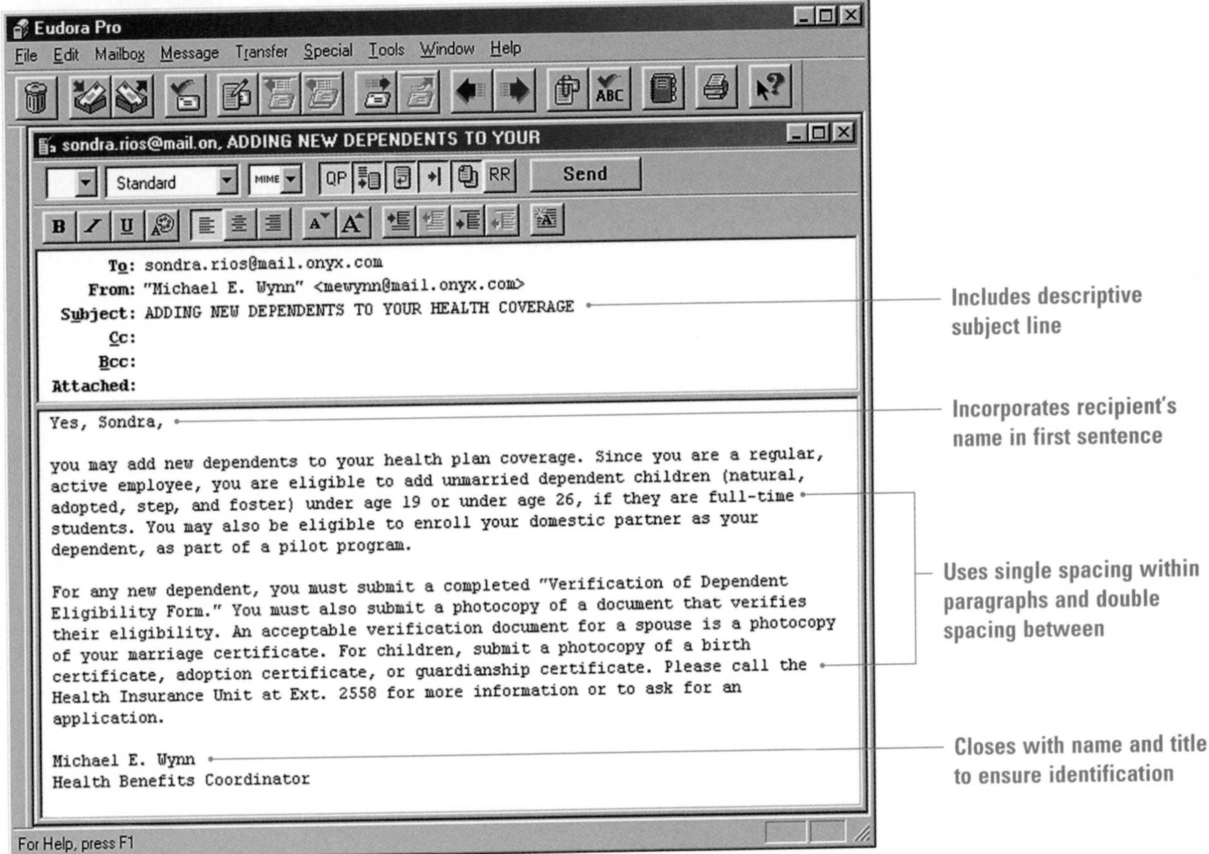

E-Mail Messages

Because e-mail is a developing communication medium, formatting and usage are still fluid. The following suggestsions, illustrated in Figure B.7 and also in Figure 8.3 in Chapter 8, may guide you in setting up the parts of an e-mail message. Always check, however, with your organization so that you can follows its practices.

***To* Line.** Include the receiver's e-mail address after *To.* If the receiver's address is recorded in your address book, you just have to click on it. Be sure to enter all addresses very carefully since one mistyped letter prevents delivery.

***From* Line.** Most mail programs automatically include your name and e-mail address after *From.*

Cc* and *Bcc. Insert the e-mail address of anyone who is to receive a copy of the message. *Cc* stands for carbon copy or courtesy copy. Don't be tempted, though, to send needless copies just because it's so easy. *Bcc* stands for *blind carbon copy.* Some writers use this to send a copy of the message without the addressee's knowledge. Sending blind carbon copies, however, is dangerous because you just might make an address error; and the addressee could learn of the intended *bcc.*

Subject. Identify the subject of the e-mail message with a brief but descriptive summary of the topic. Be sure to include enough information to be clear and compelling. Capitalize the initial letters of principal words, or capitalize the entire line if space permits.

Salutation. Include a brief greeting, if you like. Some writers use a salutation such as *Dear Sondra* followed by a comma or a colon. Others are more informal with *Hi, Sondra!,* or *Good morning* or *Greetings.* Some writers stimulate a saluation by including the name of the receiver in an abbreviated first line, as shown in Figure B.7. Other writers treat an e-mail message like a memo and skip the salutation entirely.

Message. Cover just one topic in your message, and try to keep your total message under two screens in length. Single-space and be sure to use both upper- and lower-case letters. Double-space between paragraphs.

Closing. Conclude an external message, if you like, with *Cheers, Best wishes,* or *Warm regards,* followed by your name and e-mail address (because some programs and routers do not transmit your address automatically). If the recipient is unlikely to know you, it's not a bad idea to include your title and organization. Some veteran e-mail users include a *signature file* with identifying information embellished with keyboard art. Use restraint, however, because signature files take up precious space. Writers of e-mail messages sent within organizations may omit a closing and even skip their names at the ends of messages because receivers recognize them from indentification in the opening lines.

Attachment. Use the attachment window or button to select the path and file name of any file you wish to send with your e-mail message. You can also attach a Web page to your message.

Fax Cover Sheet

Documents transmitted by fax are usually introduced by a cover sheet, such as that shown in Figure B.8. As with memos, the format varies considerably. Important items to include are (1) the name and fax number of the receiver, (2) the name and fax number of the sender, (3) the number of pages being sent, and (4) the name and telephone number of the person to notify in case of unsatisfactory transmission.

When the document being transmitted requires little explanation, you may prefer to attach an adhesive note (such as a Post-It fax transmittal form) instead of a full cover sheet. These notes carry essentially the same information as shown in our printed fax cover sheet. They are perfectly acceptable in most business organizations and can save considerable paper and transmission costs.

FIGURE B.8 Fax Cover Sheet

FAX TRANSMISSION

DATE: ______________________________

TO: ______________________________ FAX NUMBER: ____________________

____

____

FROM: ______________________________ FAX NUMBER: ____________________

____

____

NUMBER OF PAGES TRANSMITTED INCLUDING THIS COVER SHEET: ____________________

MESSAGE:

If any part of this fax transmission is missing or not clearly received, please call:

NAME: ______________________________

PHONE: ______________________________

APPENDIX C

Documentation Formats

For many reasons careful writers take pains to properly document report data. Citing sources strengthens a writer's argument, as you learned in Chapter 11. Acknowledging sources also shields writers from charges of plagiarism. Moreover, good references help readers pursue further research. Fortunately, word processing programs have taken much of the pain out of documenting data, particularly for footnotes and endnotes.

Before we discuss specific documentation formats, you must understand the difference between *source* notes and *content* notes. Source notes identify quotations, paraphrased passages, and author references. They lead readers to the sources of cited information, and they must follow a consistent format. Content notes, on the other hand, enable writers to add comments, explain information not directly related to the text, or refer readers to other sections of a report. Because content notes are generally infrequent, most writers identify them in the text with a raised asterisk (*). At the bottom of the page, the asterisk is repeated with the content note following. If two content notes appear on one page, a double asterisk identifies the second reference.

Your real concern will be with source notes. These identify quotations or paraphrased ideas in the text, and they direct readers to a specific endnote or footnote or to the complete list (bibliography) of references at the end of your report. Researchers have struggled for years to develop the perfect documentation system, one that is efficient for the writer and crystal clear to the reader. As a result, many systems exist, each with its advantages. The important thing for you is to adopt one system and use it consistently.

Students frequently ask, "But what documentation system is most used in business?" Actually, no one method dominates. Many businesses have developed their own hybrid systems. These companies generally supply guidelines illustrating their in-house style to employees. Before starting any research project on the job, you'll want to inquire about your organization's preferred documentation style. You can also look in the files for examples of previous reports.

To give you guidance for your academic papers, we'll concentrate on three common documentation formats: American Psychological Association (APA) style, Modern Language Association (MLA) style, and *The Chicago Manual of Style* (CMS) documentary style. These three systems have two primary goals: to cite sources of data, ideas, and quotations; and to interrupt the text as little as possible. Generally, a short citation is inserted into the text. It may be a superscript number or the author's name and reference page number. This in-text citation guides the reader to a list with complete bibliographical references located at the end of the work. But the reference formats differ in each of the three systems. The following discussion will show sample references illustrating (1) **in-text citations** and (2) **bibliography** references for all three systems.

An important development in documentation is the increasing use of electronic research. We'll show current formats, but remember that these formats may change as technology progresses and standards are introduced.

APA Style—American Psychological Association

Popular in the social and physical sciences, the American Psychological Association (APA) documentation style uses parenthetic citations. That is, each author reference is shown in parentheses when cited in the text. Below are selected distinguishing features of the APA style. For more information see the *Publication Manual of the American Psychological Association,* Fourth Edition (Washington, DC: American Psychological Association, 1994).

In-Text Citation. In-text citations consist of the author's last name, year of publication, and pertinent page number(s). These items appear in parentheses usually at the end of a clause or end of a sentence in which material is cited. This parenthetic citation, as shown in the following illustration, directs readers to a reference list at the end of the report where complete bibliographic information is recorded.

> The strategy of chicken king Don Tyson was to expand aggressively into other "center-of-the-plate" proteins, such as pork, fish, and turkey (Berss, 1998, p. 64).

Bibliography. All reference sources are alphabetized in a bibliography called a "Reference List." Below are selected guidelines summarizing important elements of the APA bibliographic format:

- Include authors' names with the last name first followed by initials, such as **Smith, M. A.** First and middle names are not used.
- Show the date of publication in parentheses such as **Smith, M. A. (1999).**
- Underline the titles of books and use "sentence-style" (sometimes called *down style*) capitalization. This means that only the first word of a title, proper nouns, or the first word after an internal colon is capitalized. Book titles are followed by the place of publication and publisher's name, such as **Smith, M. A. (1999). <u>Communication for managers</u>, Elmsford, NY: Pergamon Press.**
- Type the titles of magazine and journal articles without underlining or quotation marks. Use sentence-style capitalization for article titles. However, underscore the names of magazines and journals and capitalize the initial letters of all important words. Also underscore the volume number, such as **Cheung, H. K. and Burn, J. M. (1997). Distributing global information systems resources in multinational companies—a contingency model. <u>Journal of Global Information Management, 2</u>(3), 14–27.** ["2(3), 14–27" indicates volume 2, issue 3, pages 14–27]
- Space only once following periods and colons.
- Underline appropriate items in manuscripts being submitted for publication. Such underlines, according to APA guidelines, indicate words that will be italicized when printed. For student reports, however, you may wish to use italics instead of underlines.

Electronic References. When print information is available, APA suggests placing it first followed by on-line information. For example, a newspaper article: **Schellhardt, T. D. (1999, March 4). In a factory schedule, where does religion fit in? *The Wall Street Journal,* pp. B1, B12. Retrieved 5 March 1999 from <http://interactive.wsj.com>**. For additional discussion and examples, visit the APA Web site **<http://www.apa.org/journals/webref.html>**. Because formats for electronic references are still evolving, consult the Guffey Web site **<meguffey.com>** for current business-oriented examples.

Figure C.1 shows the format of an APA Reference List. To see a business report prepared using APA documentation, look at Figure 13.6 in Chapter 13.

FIGURE C.1 Model APA Bibliography Sample References

References

American Airlines. (1999). 1999 Annual Report. Fort Worth, TX: AMR Corporation. — **Annual report**

Berss, M. (1998, October 24). Protein man. Forbes, 154, 64-66. — **Magazine article**

Globalization often means that the fast track leads overseas. (1998, June 16). The Washington Post, p. A10. — **Newspaper article, no author**

Huang, J. (1994). Solid waste disposal. Microsoft Encarta'95 [CD-ROM]. Redmon, WA: Microsoft. — **CD-ROM encyclopedia article**

Lancaster, H. (1998, February 7). When taking a tip from a job network, proceed with caution. The Wall Street Journal, p. B1. — **Newspaper article, one author**

Markoff, J. (1999, June 5). Voluntary rules proposed to help insure privacy for Internet users. *The New York Times.* Retrieved 9 June 1999 from <http://www.nytimes.com/library/cyber/week/y05dat.html>. — **On-line newspaper article**

Murphy, H.L. (1997, March 4). Saturn's orbit still high with consumers. *Marketing News Online*. Retrieved 13 May 1998 from <http://www.ama.org/pubs/mn/0818n1.htm>. — **On-line magazine article**

Pinkerton Investigation Services. (1998). The employer's guide to investigation services (3rd ed.) [Brochure]. Atlanta: Pinkerton Information Center. — **Brochure**

Rose, R. C. & Garrett, E. M. (1998). How to make a buck and still be a decent human being. New York, HarperCollins. — **Book, two authors**

Tips to reduce, reuse, and recycle. (1999). Environmental Recycling Hotline. Retrieved 8 July 1999 from <http://www.primenet.com/cgi-bin/erh.pl. — **World Wide Web**

U.S. Department of Labor. (1999). Child care as a workforce issue: An update. Washington, DC: U.S. Government Printing Office. — **Government publication**

Wetherbee, J. C., Vitalari, N. P., & Milner, A. (1998). Key trends in systems development in Europe and North America. Journal of Global Information Management, 3(2), 5-20. ["3(2)" signifies volume 3, series or issue 2] — **Journal article with volume and issue numbers**

MLA Style—Modern Language Association

The MLA style is favored by writers and researchers in the humanities. Like the APA documentation style, the MLA style uses parenthetic author references in the text. These in-text citations guide the reader to a bibliography called "Works Cited." Following are selected distinguishing characteristics of the MLA style. For more information consult Joseph Gibaldi, *MLA Handbook for Writers of Research Papers,* Fourth Edition (New York: The Modern Language Association of America, 1995).

In-Text Citation. The author's last name and relevant page reference appear in parentheses after the information cited, such as **(Smith 310)**. Unlike the APA style, the date and separating comma are omitted. If the author's name is mentioned in the text, cite only the page number in parentheses. Neither the word *page* nor the abbreviations *p.* or *pp.* are used as shown in the following example:

> Although listing your résumé with an electronic job bank is wise, don't stop there. George Crosby of the Human Resources Network says, "If you think just sending out your resume will get you a job, you're crazy. [These services are] just a supplement to a core strategy of networking your buns off" (Lancaster B1).

Bibliograpy. A bibliography called "Works Cited" lists all references cited in a report. Some writers also include all works consulted. Below are selected guidelines summarizing important elements of the MLA bibliographic format:

- Underline the titles of books and use "headline style" (up style) for capitalization. This means that the initial letters of all main words are capitalized, as **Peters, Thomas J., and Robert H. Waterman, Jr. In Search of Excellence. New York: Warner Books, 1983.**
- For the titles of magazine articles include the date of publication but omit volume and issue numbers, such as **Lee, Mary M. "Investing in International Relationships." Business Monthly 18 Feb. 1999: 23–24.**
- For journal articles follow the same format as for magazine articles except include the volume number, issue number (if needed), and the year of publication inside parentheses: **Taylor, Chris L. "Nonverbal Communication," The Journal of Business Ethics 10:2 (1999): 23–29.** ["10:2" indicates volume 10, issue 2]

Electronic References. For MLA references to electronic sources, include print information, if available, along with as much other information as necessary for a reader to locate a source. Underline the title of a database, periodical, or professional or personal Web site. For sites without titles, underline a description such as *Home page.* Although MLA style does not suggest including the word "Retrieved" before the access date, we include it to distinguish the retrieval date from the publication date. The Modern Language Association promises a new editon of its *MLA Handbook* shortly. Thus, check the Guffey Web site for the latest revisions to electronic reference formats **<meguffey.com>**.

Figure C.2 shows the format of a MLA "Works Cited" bibliography and many sample references. To see a complete report using MLA documentation, turn to Figure 14.4 in Chapter 14.

FIGURE C.2 Model MLA Bibliography Sample References

Works Cited

American Airlines. 1999 Annual Report. Fort Worth, TX: AMR Corporation.	Annual report
Berss, Marcia. "Protein Man." Forbes 24 Oct. 1998: 64-66.	Magazine article
"Globalization Often Means That the Fast Track Leads Overseas." The Washington Post 16 June 1999: A10.	Newspaper article, no author
Huang, Jerry Y. C. "Solid Waste Disposal," Microsoft Encarta '95. CD-ROM. Redmond, WA: Microsoft, 1994.	CD-ROM encyclopedia article, one author
Lancaster, Hal. "When Taking a Tip From a Job Network, Proceed With Caution." The Wall Street Journal 7 Feb. 1998: B1.	Newspaper article, one author
Markoff, John. "Voluntary Rules Proposed to Help Insure Privacy for Internet Users." The New York Times. 5 June 1999, business sec., CyberTimes. Retrieved 9 June 1999 <http://www.times.com/library/cyber/week/y05dat.html>.	On-line newspaper article
Murphy, H. Lee. "Saturn's Orbit Still High With Consumers." Marketing News Online. 31 Aug. 1998. Retrieved 1 Sept. 1998 <http://www.ama.org/pubs/mn/0818/n1.htm>.	On-line magazine article
Pinkerton Investigation Services. The Employer's Guide to Investigation Services, 2nd ed. Atlanta: Pinkerton Information Center, 1998.	Brochure
Rivera, Francisco. Personal interview. 16 May 1999.	Interview
Rose, Richard C., and Echo Montgomery Garrett. How to Make a Buck and Still Be a Decent Human Being. New York: HarperCollins, 1998.	Book, two authors
"Tips to Reduce, Reuse, and Recycle." Environmental Recycling Hotline. Retrieved 8 July 1999. <http://www.primenet.com/cgi-bin/erh.pl>.	World Wide Web
U.S. Dept. of Labor. Child Care as a Workforce Issue: An Update. Washington, DC: GPO, 1999.	Government publication
Wetherbee, James C., Nicholas P. Vitalari, and Andrew Milner. "Key Trends in Systems Development in Europe and North America." Journal of Global Information Management 3.2 (1998): 5-20. ["3.2" signifies volume 3, issue 2]	Journal article with volume and issue numbers

CMS Style—The Chicago Manual of Style

The Chicago Manual of Style has guided researchers for many decades. In the 14th edition it now shows two different formats. The first is the traditional documentary-note or humanities style. Favored by many in literature, history, and the arts, this style employs superscript (raised) numbers in the text to mark references. The reader is directed to a complete bibliographic citation appearing either in a footnote or in an endnote. Some readers like footnotes because relevant citations appear at the bottom of each page and are immediately available. Others dislike footnotes because they clutter the page. Instead of footnotes, many writers today use endnotes, which list all citations at the end of the report. Advanced word processing programs contain features that make footnotes or endnotes easy to accomplish. A second format now featured in the *Chicago Manual* is the author-date system, which is said to be gaining favor both in the social sciences and the humanities. For our purposes, however, we will concentrate on the traditional documentary-note style and illustrate its in-text citation and bibliographic form. For more information about CMS formats, see *The Chicago Manual of Style,* 14th edition, John Grossman, ed., pp. 487 to 635.

In-Text Citation. At the end of a quotation or reference, a superscript (raised) number, shown below, marks the reference. It guides the reader to a complete reference at the bottom of the page or to a list at the end of the report.

> Cross-border business alliances are difficult. "Simple things like scheduling meetings," said one manager, "became ballets of clashing customs."[4]

Endnote or Footnote Citation. This note refers the reader to a specific page or electronic screen showing the specific reference. These notes begin with the first name of the author. Incidentally, don't be alarmed if your word processing program numbers the endnotes in large numbers in parentheses instead of small superscript figures. Either form is acceptable.

> [4]Francisco Rivera, production manager, Waste Control Management, Inc. Interview with author, 16 May 1999. White Plains, NY.

Bibliography. In addition to footnotes or endnotes, a "Bibliography" lists all references cited. The bibliography may also contain all references consulted. While endnotes are arranged in order of their appearance in the text, the bibliography is alphabetical. The bibliography does not list references to specific pages cited in notes. Instead, it gives broad publication information. The following guidelines illustrate important elements for preparing a CMS-style bibliography:

- Arrange entries alphabetically by the author's last name. If no author is known, alphabetize by the initial letter of the first important title word.
- Use hanging indented form with the second and succeeding lines indented.
- Enclose titles of magazine, newspaper, and journal articles in quotation marks and capitalize important words.
- Italicize the names of books, newspapers, journals, and other complete publications. Capitalize important words.

Electronic References. The editors of *The Chicago Manual of Style* do not expect to revise the 14th edition until at least 2002, and they provide no guidance for electronic citation formats at their Web site. Thus, the examples you see here are extrapolated from the existing print models and the limited examples of electronic forms in the 14th edition. To cite most electronic references, include as much of the following information as is available: author (or name of Web site), document or page title, date of Internet publication, URL, and date of retrieval.

Figure C.3 shows a set of endnotes formatted by CMS guidelines, and Figure C.4 shows a CMS bibliography.

FIGURE C.3 ***The Chicago Manual of Style*** **Sample Endnotes/Footnotes**

Endnotes

1 American Airlines, *1998 Annual Report* (Fort Worth, TX: AMR Corporation), 7.	Annual report
2 Marcia Berss, "Protein Man," *Forbes,* 24 October 1998, 65.	Magazine article
3 "Globalization Often Means That the Fast Track Leads Overseas," *The Washington Post,* 16 June 1998, A10.	Newspaper article, no author
4 Jerry Y. C. Huang, "Solid Waste Disposal," *Microsoft Encarta '95.* (Redmond, WA: Microsoft, 1994) [CD-ROM].	CD-ROM encyclopedia article
5 Hal Lancaster, "When Taking a Tip From a Job Network, Proceed With Caution," *The Wall Street Journal,* 7 February 1998, B1.	Newspaper article, one author
6 John Markoff, "Voluntary Rules Proposed to Help Insure Privacy for Internet Users," *The New York Times,* business sec., 5 June 1999, Cybertimes, <http:www.times/com/library/cyber/week/y05dat.html> (Retrieved 9 June 1999).	On-line newspaper article
7 H. Lee Murphy, "Saturn's Orbit Still High With Consumers," *Marketing News Online,* 4 March 1997 <http://www.ama.org/pubs/mn/0818/n1.htm> (Retrieved 13 May 1998).	On-line magazine article
8 Francisco Rivera, production manager, Waste Control Management, Inc., 16 May 1999. Interview by author, White Plains, NY.	Interview
9 Richard C. Rose and Echo Montgomery Garrett, *How to Make a Buck and Still Be a Decent Human Being* (New York: HarperCollins, 1998), 192.	Book, two authors
10 "Tips to Reduce, Reuse, and Recycle," *Environmental Recycling Hotline* <http://www.primenet.com/cgi-bin/erh.pl> (Retrieved 8 July 1999).	World Wide Web
11 U.S. Department of Labor. *Child Care as a Workforce Issue: An Update* (Washington, DC: GPO, 1999), 138.	Government publication
12 James C. Wetherbee, Nicholas P. Vitalari, and Andrew Milner, "Key Trends in Systems Development in Europe and North America," *Journal of Global Information Management* 3, no. 2 (Spring 1998): 6.	Journal article with volume and issue numbers

FIGURE C.4 ***The Chicago Manual of Style* Sample Bibliography**

Bibliography

American Airlines. 1999 *Annual Report*. Fort Worth, TX: AMR Corporation, 7. — Annual report

Berss, Marcia. "Protein Man." *Forbes*. (24 October 1998): 64-66. — Magazine article

"Globalization Often Means That the Fast Track Leads Overseas." *The Washington Post,* 16 June 1998, A10. — Newspaper article, no author

Huang, Jerry Y. C. "Solid Waste Disposal." *Microsoft Encarta '95.* Redmond, WA: Microsoft, 1994. [CD-ROM]. — CD-ROM encyclopedia article

Lancaster, Hal. "When Taking a Tip From a Job Network, Proceed With Caution." *The Wall Street Journal,* 7 February 1998, B1. — Newspaper article, one author

Markoff, John. "Voluntary Rules Proposed to Help Insure Privacy for Internet Users." *The New York Times,* business sec., Cybertimes. 5 June 1999 <http://www.times/com/library/cyber/week/y05dat.html> (Retrieved 9 June 1999). — On-line newspaper article

Murphy, H. Lee. "Saturn's Orbit Still High With Consumers." *Marketing News Online,* 4 March 1997 <http://www.ama.org/pubs/mn/0818/n1.htm> (Retrieved 13 May 1998). — On-line magazine article

Rivera, Francisco. Interview by author. White Plains, NY, 16 May 1999. — Interview

Rose, Richard C. and Echo Montgomery Garrett. *How to Make a Buck and Still Be a Decent Human Being.* New York: HarperCollins, 1998. — Book, two authors

"Tips to Reduce, Reuse, and Recycle." *Environmental Recycling Hotline.* <http://www.primenet.com/cgi-bin/erh.pl> (Retrieved 8 July 1999). — World Wide Web

U. S. Department of Labor. *Child Care as a Workforce Issue: An Update.* Washington: GPO, 1999: 38. — Government publication

Wetherbee, James C., Nicholas P. Vitalari, and Andrew Milner. "Key Trends in Systems Development in Europe and North America." *Journal of Global Information Management* 3, no. 2 (Spring 1998): 6. — Journal article with volume and issue numbers

APPENDIX D

Correction Symbols

In marking your papers, your instructor may use the following symbols or abbreviations to indicate writing weaknesses. You'll find that studying these symbols and suggestions will help you understand your instructor's remarks. Knowing this information can also help you evaluate and improve your own letters, memos, reports, and other writing. For specific writing guidelines and self-help exercises, see Appendix A, Competent Language Usage Essentials (C.L.U.E.).

Strategy and Organization

Coh Develop coherence between ideas. Repeat key idea or add transitional expression.
DS Use direct strategy. Start with main idea or good news.
IS Use indirect strategy. Explain before introducing main idea.
Org Improve organization. Keep similar topics together.
Plan Apply appropriate plan for message.
Trans Include transition to join ideas.

Content and Style

Acc Verify accuracy of names, places, amounts, and other data.
ACE Avoid copying examples.
ACP Avoid copying case problems.
Act Use active voice.
AE Use action ending that tells reader what to do.
Awk Rephrase to avoid awkward or unidiomatic expression.
Asn Check assignment for instructions or facts.
Chop Use longer sentences to avoid choppiness. Vary sentence patterns.
Cl Improve clarity of ideas or expression.
Con Condense into shorter form.
Emp Emphasize this idea.
Eth Use language that projects honest, ethical business practices.
Exp Explain more fully or clearly.
Inc Expand an incomplete idea.
Jar Avoid jargon or specialized language that reader may not know.
Log Remedy faulty logic.
Neg Revise negative expression with more positive view.

Obv Avoid saying what is obvious.
Par Use parallel (balanced) expression.
PV Express idea from reader's point of view.
RB Show reader benefits. What's in it for reader?
Rdn Revise to eliminate redundant idea or expression.
Rep Avoid unintentional repetition of word, idea, or sound.
Sin Use language that sounds sincere.
Spec Develop idea with specific details.
Sub Subordinate this point to lessen its impact.
SX Avoid sexist language.
Tone Use more conversational or positive tone.
You Emphasize *you*-view.
Var Vary sentences with different patterns.
Vag Avoid vague pronoun. Don't use *they, that, this, which, it,* or other pronouns unless their references are clear.
Vb Use correct verb tense. Avoid verb shift.
W Condense to avoid wordiness.
WC Improve word choice. Find a more precise word.

Grammar and Mechanics

Abv Avoid most abbreviations in text. Use correct abbreviation if necessary.
Agr Make each subject and verb or pronoun and noun agree.
Apos Use an apostrophe to show possession or contraction.
Art Choose a correct article (*a, an,* or *the*).
Cap Capitalize appropriately.
Cm Use a comma.
CmConj Use a comma preceding coordinating conjunction (*and, or, nor, but*) that joins independent clauses.
CmIntro Use a comma following introductory dependent clause or long phrase.
CmSer Use commas to separate items in a series.
CS Rectify a comma splice by separating independent clauses with a period or a semicolon.
Div Improve word division by hyphenating between syllables.
DM Rectify a dangling modifier by supplying a clear subject for modifying element.
Exp Avoid expletives such as *there is, there are,* and *it is.*
Frag Revise fragment to form complete sentence.
Gram Use correct grammar.
Hyp Hyphenate a compound adjective.
lc Use lower case instead of capital.
MM Correct misplaced modifier by moving modifier closer to word it describes or limits.
Num Express numbers in correct word or figure form.
Pn Use correct punctuation.
Prep Correct use of preposition.
RO Rectify run-on sentence with comma or semicolon to separate independent clauses.
Sem Use semicolon to join related independent clauses.
Sp Check spelling.
SS Shorten sentences.
UnCm Avoid unnecessary comma.

Format

Cen Center a document appropriately on the page.
DSp Insert a double space, or double-space throughout.
F Choose appropriate format for this item or message.
GH Use graphic highlighting (bullets, lists, indentions, and headings) to improve readability.
Mar Improve margins to frame a document on the page.
SSp Insert a single space, or single-space throughout.
TSp Insert a triple space.

PROOFREADING MARKS

Proofreading Mark	Draft Copy	Final Copy
Align horizontally	TO: Rick Munoz	TO: Rick Munoz
Align vertically	166.32 132.45	166.32 132.45
Capitalize	Coca-cola runs on ms-dos	Coca-Cola runs on MS-DOS
Close up space	meeting at 3 p. m.	meeting at 3 p.m.
Center	Recommendations	Recommendations
Delete	in my final judgement	in my judgment
Insert apostrophe	our companys product	our company's product
Insert comma	you will of course	you will, of course,
Insert hyphen	tax free income	tax-free income
Insert period	Ms Holly Hines	Ms. Holly Hines
Insert quotation mark	shareholders receive a bonus.	shareholders receive a "bonus."
Insert space	wordprocessing program	word processing program
Lowercase (remove capitals)	the Vice President HUMAN RESOURCES	the vice president Human Resources
Move to left	I. Labor costs	I. Labor costs
Move to right	A. Findings of study	A. Findings of study
Spell out	aimed at 2 depts	aimed at two departments
Start new paragraph	Keep the screen height of your computer at eye level.	Keep the screen height of your computer at eye level.
Stet (don't delete)	officials talked openly	officials talked openly
Transpose	accounts recievable	accounts receivable
Use boldface	Conclusions bf	**Conclusions**
Use italics	The Perfect Résumé ital	*The Perfect Résumé*

Key to C.L.U.E. Exercises

Chapter 1

1. After he checked many statements our Accountant found the error in ~~colume~~ 2 of the balance sheet.
2. Because Mr. Lockwoods business owned considerable property We were serprised by it's lack of liquid assets.
3. The mortgage company checked all property titles separatly however it found no discrepancies.
4. When Ms. Diaz finished the audit she wrote 3 letters To appraise the owners of her findings.
5. Just between you and I whom do you think could have ordered all this stationary.
6. Assets and liabilities is what the 4 buyers want to see consequently we are preparing this years statements.
7. Next spring my brother and ~~myself~~ plan to enroll in the following courses marketing english and history.
8. Dan felt that he had done ~~good~~ on the exam but he wants to do even better when it's given again next Fall.
9. Our records show that your end of the month balance was ~~ninety-six dollars and 30 cents~~.
10. When the ~~principle~~ in the account grows to large we must make annual withdrawals.

Chapter 2

1. If swimming is especialy good for ~~you're~~ figure how do you explain whales.
2. Although you may be on the right track you can get run over if you just ~~set~~ there.
3. Ellen and ~~myself~~ examined all simlar accounts on a case by case basis.
4. Although both reports ~~was wrote~~ by Jeff and I, they carried the bosses signature.
5. The Vice President said, "Meetings are places where minutes may be kept but hours are lost."
6. At least ~~fourteen~~ patience were admitted after the accident however only ~~four~~ required treatment.
7. If the company is sold about ~~one hundred and fifty~~ employees will be out of work.
8. The meeting is scheduled for 4:00 p.m. consaquently Melissa and ~~myself~~ may be a little late.

9. Did you know that seventy percent of americans have visited disneyland or disney world.

10. I have allready checked the Web but I visited only one Government cite.

Chapter 3

1. To avoid embarassing any employee the personell manager and myself has decided to talk personal to each individual.

2. 3 assistants were sent on a search and destroy mission in a conscience effort to remove at least fifteen thousand old documents from the files.

3. Electronic mail, now used by 3/4 of Americas largest companys transmits messages quick and cheap.

4. An article entitled whats new with managers appeared in reader's digest which is read by 60,000,000 americans.

5. Your account is now sixty days overdue consequently we have only 1 alternative left.

6. The marketing managers itinrary listed the following three destinations seattle portland and eugene.

7. Each of the beautifully printed books available at pickwick book company have been reduced to thirty dollars.

8. We reccommend therefor that a committee study our mail procedures for a 3 week period and submit a report of it's findings.

9. Their going to visit there relatives in columbus ohio over the memorial day holiday.

10. The hotel can acommodate three hundred convention guests but it has parking facilities for only one hundred cars.

Chapter 4

1. If I was you I would schedule the conference for one of these cities Atlanta Memphis or Nashville.

2. The committees next meeting is scheduled for May fifth at three p.m. and should last about two hours.

3. Were not asking you to altar the figures, we are asking you to check there accuracy.

4. Will you please fax me a list of our independant contractors names and addresses.

5. The vacation calender fills up quick for the Summer months, therefore you should make your plans early.

6. After the inspector issues the waver we will be able to procede with the architects plan.

7. If we can't give out neccessary information what is the point in us answering the telephone.

8. Every new employee will receive their orientation packet and be told about their parking priviledges.

9. About eighty-five percent of all new entrants into the workforce in the 2000s is expected to be women, minorities and immigrants.

10. Our Vice President in the Human Resources Development Department asked the Manager and I to come to her office at three-thirty p.m.

Chapter 5

1. Although, we formally used a neighborhood printer for all our print jobs we are now saving almost five hundred dollars a month by using desktop publishing.

2. Powerful softwear however cannot garantee a good final product.

3. To develop a better sense of design we collected desireable samples from: books, magazines, brochures, and newsletters.

4. We noticed that poorly designed projects often was filled with cluttered layouts, incompatible typefaces, and to many typefaces.

5. Our layout design are usually formal but ocasionally we use an informal layout design which is shown in figure six.

6. We usually prefer a black and white design; because color printing is much more costly.

7. Expensive color printing jobs are sent to foreign countries, for example china Italy and Japan.

8. Jeffreys article which he entitled "The Shaping of a corporate image" was excepted for publication in "the journal of communication."

9. Every employee will persanally receive a copy of his Performance Evaluation which the President said will be the principle basis for promotion.

10. We will print three hundred and fifty copies of the newsletter to be sent to whomever is currently listed in our database.

Chapter 6

1. Business documents must be written clear to insure that readers comprehend the message quick.

2. We expect Mayor Wilson to visit the govenor in an attempt to increase the cities share of State funding.

3. The caller could have been him but we don't know for sure, since he didn't leave his name.

4. The survey was sited in an article entitled "Whats new in softwear, however I can't locate it now.

5. All three of our companys auditors—Jim Lucus, Doreen Delgado, and Brad Kirby—critisized there accounting procedures.

6. Anyone of the auditors are authorized to procede with an independant action however only a member of the management counsel can alter policy.

7. Because our printer has been broke everyday this week, were looking at new models.

8. Have you all ready ordered the following: a dictionary a reference manual and a style book.

9. In the morning Mrs. Williams ordinarilly opens the office in the evening Mr. Williams usualy closes it.

10. When you travel in england and ireland I advice you to charge purchases to your visa credit card.

Chapter 7

1. The extrordinary increase in sales is related to us placing the staff on a commission basis and the increase also effected our stock value.

2. She acts as if she was the only person who ever received a complement about their business writting. [OR omit **his or her**.]

3. Karen is interested in working for the U.S. foreign service, since she is hopping to travel.

4. Major Hawkins whom I think will be elected has all ready served three consecative terms as a member of the gulfport city counsel.

5. After Mr. Freeman and him returned from lunch the customer's were handled more quick.

6. Our new employees cafeteria, which opened six months ago has a salad bar that everyone definitly likes.

7. On Tuesday Ms. Adams can see you at two p.m. on Wednesday she has a full skedule.

8. His determination courage and sincerity could not be denied however his methods were often questioned.

9. After you have checked the matter farther report to the CEO and I.

10. Mr. Garcia and her advised me not to dessert my employer at this time. Although they were quite sympathetic to my personel problems.

Chapter 8

1. Mr. Krikorian always tries however to wear a tie and shirt that has complimentary colors.

2. The federal trade commission are holding hearings to illicit information about IBMs request to expand marketing in twenty-one city's.

3. Consumer buying and spending for the past 5 years is being studied by a Federal team of analysts.

4. Because we recommend that students bring there own supplies, the total expense for the trip should be a miner amount.

5. Wasnt it Mr Cohen not Ms Lyons who asked for a tuition waver.

6. As soon as we can verify the figures either my sales manager or myself will call you nevertheless, you must continue to disperse payroll funds.

7. Our human resources department which was formerally in room 35 has moved it's offices to room 5.

8. We have arranged interviews on the following dates, Wednesday at 330 pm Thursday at 1030 am and Friday at 415 pm.

9. The Post Dispatch our local newspaper featured as its principle article a story entitled Smarter E-Mail is here.

10. Every one on the payroll, which includes all dispatchers and supervisers were cautioned to maintain careful records everyday.

Chapter 9

1. 2 loans made to Consumer products corporation must be repaid within 90 days, Or the owners will be in default.

2. One loan was for property apprised at forty thousand dollars, the other was for property estimated to be worth ten thousand dollars.

3. Our Senior Marketing Director and the sales manager are quite knowledgable about communications hardware, therefore they are traveling to the Computer show in northern California.

4. We congradulate you on winning the award and hope that you will continue to experience simular success in the future.

5. Mr. Salazar left three million dollars to be divided among 4 heirs, one of whom is a successful manufacture.

6. If the CEO and him had behaved more professional the chances of a practicle settlement would be considerably greater.

7. Just inside the entrance is the desk of the receptionist and a complete directory of all departments.

8. Every new employee must recieve their permit to park in lot 5-A or there car will be sited. OR Every new employee must submit a permit to park in Lot 5-A, or his or her car will be cited.

9. When we open our office in Montreal we will need at least 3 people whom are fluent in french and english.

10. Most companys can boost profits almost one hundred percent by retaining just 5% more of there permenent customers.

Chapter 10

1. Your advertisement in the June second edition of the Boston Globe caught my attention because my training and experience matches your requirements.

2. Undoubtlessly the bank is closed at this hour but it's ATM will enable you to recieve the cash you need.

3. A flow chart detailing all sales procedures in 4 divisions were prepared by our vice president.

4. The computer and printer was working good yesterday and appeared to be alright this morning when I used it for my report.

5. If I was you I would be more concerned with long term not short term returns on the invested capitol.

6. We make a conscience effort by the way to find highly qualified individuals with up to date computer skills.

7. If your résumé had came earlier I could have showed it to Mr. Sutton and she before your interview.

8. Deborahs report summary is more easier to read then David because she used consistant headings and efficient writing techniques.

9. At McDonald's we ordered 4 big macs 3 orders of french fries, and 5 coca-colas for lunch.

10. Because the budget cuts will severely effect all programs the faculty have unanimously opposed it.

Endnotes

CHAPTER 1

1. Gillian Flynn, "Pillsbury's Recipe Is Candid Talk," *Workforce,* February 1998, 57–58.
2. Suzanne Bidlake, "Burger King's Euro Push," *Marketing,* 20 February 1992, 2.
3. Hal Lancaster, "Learning to Manage in a Global Workplace," *The Wall Street Journal,* 2 June 1998, B1.
4. Barbara Booth, "Beg to Differ," *International Business,* November 1996, 28.
5. Faye Rice, "Champions of Communication," *Fortune,* 3 June 1991, 112.
6. Paula Jacobs, "Strong Writing Skills Essential for Success, Even in IT," *Infoworld,* 6 July 1998, 86.
7. "Team Player: No More 'Same-Ol' Same-Ol,'" *Business Week,* 17 October 1994, 95.
8. Sharon Helldorfer and Michael Daly, "Reengineering Brings Together Units," *Best's Review,* October 1993, 82–85.
9. Barbara DePompa, "Start Your Engines," *Success,* December 1990, 24.
10. Paula Jacobs, "Writing Skills Essential for Success, Even in IT," *InfoWorld,* 6 July 1998, 86.
11. Eric Rolfe Greenberg, "E-mail Usurps the Phone as Communication Tool," *HR Focus,* May 1998, 2.
12. Kirk Johnson, "Limits on the Work-at-Home Life," *The New York Times,* 17 December 1997, A20.
13. Lesley Meall, "Workers With Reservations," *Accountancy,* March 1997, 54–55.
14. Hal Lancaster, "Hiring a Full Staff May Be the Next Fad in Management," *The Wall Street Journal,* 4 April 1998, B1.
15. Andrew Denka, "New Office Etiquette Dilemmas," *CPA Journal,* August 1996, 13.
16. Sharon Nelton, "Nurturing Diversity," *Nation's Business,* June 1995, 25–27.
17. Laurie J. Bassi, George Benson, and Scott Cheney, "The Top Ten Trends," *Training & Development,* November 1996, 28–42.
18. Patrick Carnevale, as quoted by Genevieve Capowski, "Managing Diversity," *Management Review,* June 1996, 6.
19. Alvin Toffler, *PowerShift* (New York: Bantam Books, 1990), 238. See also Oren Harari, "Flood Your Organization With Knowledge," *Management Review,* November 1997, 33–37.
20. Peter Drucker, "New Realities, New Ways of Managing," *Business Month,* May 1989, 50–51.
21. G. A. Marken, "New Approach to Moving up the Corporate Ladder," *Public Relations Quarterly,* Winter 1996, 47.
22. Barrett J. Mandel and Judith Yellen, "Mastering the Memo," *Working Woman,* September 1989, 135.
23. Based on Terry Thompson, "Pillsbury to Recall Cookie Dough With Undeclared Walnuts: Second Alert," Pillsbury PR Newswire, 9 October 1998. <http://pillsbury/story?StoryID=Cn2kqbWbtu5gmde0&FQ=%22The%20Pillsbury%20Company%22&Title=> (Retrieved 26 October 1998).
24. Cheryl Hamilton with Cordell Parker, *Communicating for Results* (Belmont, CA: Wadsworth, 1997), 7.
25. Jerry Sullivan, Naoki Karmeda, and Tatsuo Nobu, "Bypassing in Managerial Communication," *Business Horizons,* January/February 1991, 72.
26. Peter Drucker, *Managing the Non-Profit Organization: Practices and Principles* (New York: Harper-Collins, 1990), 46.
27. Genevieve Wilkinson, "Stop Reading! Check Your Messages," *Investor's Business Daily,* 28 May 1998, A9.
28. Kenneth Hein, "Communication Breakdown," *Incentive,* July 1997, 24–27.
29. Wilkinson, "Stop Reading!"
30. Tom Geddie, "Technology: It's About Time," *Communication World,* Special Issue Supplement, March 1998, 26–28.
31. Leslie Walker, as quoted in "Coping With Communication Overload," *Association Management,* October 1997, 32–33.
32. Mitch Betts and Tim Ouellette, "Taming the E-mail Shrew," *Computerworld,* 6 November 1995, 1, 32.
33. Marken, "New Approach to Moving Up the Corporate Ladder," *Public Relations Quarterly,* Winter 1996, 47.
34. Thomas J. Hackett, "Giving Teams a Tune-Up: Reviving Work Teams," *HR Focus,* November 1997.
35. "Who Told You That?" *The Wall Street Journal,* 23 May 1985, 33.
36. Robert L. Dilenschneider, "Cultivating the Corporation Grapevine," *The New York Times,* 2 July 1995, F14.

37. Marilyn Moats Kennedy, "Who Pruned the Grapevine?" *Across the Board,* March 1997), 55–56.
38. Stephanie Zimmermann, Beverly Davenport, and John W. Haas, "A Communication Metamyth in the Workplace: The Assumption That More Is Better," *Journal of Business Communication,* April 1996, 185–204.
39. Bob Nelson, "How to Energize Everyone in the Company," *Bottom Line/Business,* October 1997, 3.
40. Robert McGarvey, "Do the Right Thing," *Entrepreneur,* October 1992, 140.
41. Max M. Thomas, "Classroom Conundrum: Profits + Ethics = ?" *Business Month,* February 1990, 6.
42. Tina Kelley, "Charting a Course to Ethical Profits," *The New York Times,* 8 February 1998, BU1.
43. Samuel Greengard, "50 Percent of Your Employees Are Lying, Cheating, and Stealing," *Workforce,* October 1997, 46–47.
44. Martha Groves, "Ethics at Work: Honor System," *Los Angeles Times,* 3 November 1997, Careers sec., 3, 15. See also Alison Boyd, "Employee Traps—Corruption in the Workplace," *Management Review,* September 1997, 9.
45. Mary E. Guy, *Ethical Decision Making in Everyday Work Situations* (New York: Quorum Books, 1990), 3.
46. Based on Michael Josephson's remarks reported in Alison Bell, "What Price Ethics?" *Entrepreneurial Woman,* January/February, 1991, 68.
47. Amy Harmon, "On the Office PC, Bosses Opt for All Work, and No Play," *The New York Times,* 22 September 1997, A1, C11.
48. Diane Cole, "Ethics: Companies Crack Down on Dishonesty," *The Wall Street Journal,* Spring 1991, Managing Your Career, sec. 8.
49. David Stewart, "Deception, Materiality, and Survey Research: Some Lessons From Kraft," *Journal of Public Policy & Marketing,* Spring 1995, 15–28.
50. J. Craig Andrews and Thomas J. Maronick, "Advertising Research Issues From FTC Versus Stouffer Foods Corporation," *Journal of Public Policy & Marketing,* Fall 1995, 301–309.
51. Michael Schroeder, "Get Firm 'Abs' in a Few Hours? Don't Believe It," *The Wall Street Journal,* 18 June 1997, B1.
52. Jane Applegate, "Women Starting Small Businesses Twice as Fast as Men," *The Washington Post,* 2 September 1991, W10.
53. "Faxpoll," *Business Month,* December 1989, 7.

CHAPTER 2

1. Patricia Buhler, "Managing in the 90s: Creating Flexibility in Today's Workplace," *Supervision,* January 1996, 24–26.
2. Jon R. Katzenbach and Douglas K. Smith, *The Wisdom of Teams* (New York: HarperBusiness and Harvard Business School Press, 1994), 19.
3. Charles Parnell, "Teamwork: Not a New Idea, But It's Transforming the Workplace," *Executive Speeches,* December 1997/January 1998, 35–40.
4. Harvey Robbins and Michael Finley, *Why Teams Don't Work: What Went Wrong and How to Make It Right* (Princeton, NJ: Peterson's/Pacesetter Books, 1995), 11–12.
5. Katzenbach and Smith, *The Wisdom of Teams,* 14.
6. The discussion of Tuckman's model is adapted from Robbins and Finley, *Why Teams Don't Work,* Chapter 22. See also Jane Henderson-Loney, "Tuckman and Tears: Developing Teams During Profound Organizational Change," *Supervision,* May 1996, 3–5.
7. Allen C. Amason, Wayne A. Hochwarter, Kenneth R. Thompson, and Allison W. Harrison, "Conflict: An Important Dimension in Successful Management Teams," *Organizational Dynamics,* Autumn 1995, 20–35.
8. Kathleen M. Eisenhardt, Jean L. Kahwajy, and L. J. Bourgeois, III, "Conflict and Strategic Choice: How Top Management Teams Disagree," *California Management Review,* Winter, 1997, 42–62.
9. I. L. Janis, *Groupthink: Psychological Studies on Policy Decisions and Fiascoes* (Boston: Houghton Mifflin, 1982). See also Shaila M. Miranda and Carol Saunders, "Group Support Systems: An Organization Development Intervention to Combat Groupthink," *Public Administration Quarterly,* Summer 1995, 193–216.
10. Amason, Hochwater, "Conflict," 1.
11. Parnell, "Teamwork: Not a New Idea," 36–40.
12. Katzennbach and Smith, *Wisdom of Teams,* 45.
13. Joel Makower, "Managing Diversity in the Workplace," *Business and Society Review,* Winter 1995, 48–54.
14. Katzenbach and Smith, *Wisdom of Teams,* 50.
15. Jon Hanke, "Presenting as a Team," *Presentations,* January 1998, 74–82.
16. Clyde Fessler, "Rotating Leadership at Harley-Davidson: From Hierarchy to Interdependence," *Strategy & Leadership,* July/August 1997, 42–43.
17. Robbins and Finley, *Why Teams Don't Work,* 123.
18. Tom W. Harris, "Listen Carefully," *Nation's Business,* June 1989, 78.
19. L. K. Steil, L. I. Barker, and K. W. Watson, *Effective Listening: Key to Your Success* (Reading, MA: Addison-Wesley, 1983).
20. Eric H. Nelson and Jan Gypen, "The Subordinate's Predicament," *Harvard Business Review,* September/October 1979, 133.
21. Stephen Golen, "A Factor Analysis of Barriers to Effective Listening," *The Journal of Business Communication,* Winter 1990, 25–37.
22. "Effective Communication," *Training Tomorrow,* November 1994, 32–33.
23. Albert Mehrabian, *Silent Messages* (Belmont, CA: Wadsworth, 1971), 44.

24. J. Burgoon, D. Coker, and R. Coker, "Communication Explanations," *Human Communication Research,* 12 (1986), 463–494.
25. Michael Tarsala, "Remec's Ronald Ragland: Drawing Rivals to His Team by Making Their Concerns His," *Investor's Business Daily,* 7 November 1997, A1.
26. Ray Birdwhistel, *Kinesics and Context* (Philadelphia: University of Pennsylvlania Press, 1970).
27. "What's A-O.K. in the U.S.A. Is Lewd and Worthless Beyond," *The New York Times,* 18 August 1996, E-7.
28. Dorothy Leeds, "Body Language: Actions Speak Louder Than Words," *National Underwriter,* 1 May 1995, 18–19.
29. Anne Russell, "Fine Tuning Your Corporate Image," *Black Enterprise,* May 1992, 80.
30. Hal Lancaster, "Learning Some Ways to Make Meetings Slightly Less Awful," *The Wall Street Journal,* 26 May 1998, B1.
31. Tom McDonald, "Minimizing Meetings," *Successful Meetings,* June 1996, 24.
32. Lancaster, "Learning Some Ways," B1.
33. John C. Bruening, "There's Good News About Meetings," *Managing Office Technology,* July 1996, 24–25.
34. Kirsten Schabacker, "A Short, Snappy Guide to Meaningful Meetings," *Working Women,* June 1991, 73.
35. J. Keith Cook, "Try These Eight Guidelines for More Effective Meetings," *Communication Briefings Bonus Item,* April 1995, 8a. See also Morey Stettner, "How to Manage a Corporate Motormouth, *Investor's Business Daily,* 8 October 1998, A1.
36. Mary Munter, "Meeting Technology: From Low-Tech to High-Tech," *Business Communication Quarterly,* June 1998, 84–85.
37. Thomas C. Hayes, "Doing Business Screen to Screen," *The New York Times,* 21 February 1991, C1.
38. Bob Filipczak, "The Soul of the Hog," *Training,* February 1996, 38–42.

CHAPTER 3

1. Anthony DePalma, "It Takes More Than a Visa to Do Business in Mexico," *The New York Times,* 26 June 1994, F5.
2. Joseph B. White, "There Are No German or U.S. Companies, Only Successful Ones,'" *The Wall Street Journal,* 17 May 1998, A1.
3. Alecia Swasy, "Don't Sell Thick Diapers in Tokyo," *The New York Times,* 3 October 1993, F9.
4. Raju Narisetti, "Can Rubbermaid Crack Foreign Markets?" *The Wall Street Journal,* 20 June 1996, B1.
5. E. S. Browning, "In Pursuit of the Elusive Euroconsumer," *The Wall Street Journal,* 23 April 1992, B1.
6. Gabriella Stern, "Heinz Aims to Export Taste for Ketchup," *The Wall Street Journal,* 21 November 1992, B1.
7. Mary O'Hara-Devereaux and Robert Johansen, *GlobalWork: Bridging Distance, Culture and Time* (San Francisco: Jossey-Bass Publishers, 1994), 245.
8. Sari Kalin, "Global Net Knits East to West at Liz Claiborne," *Computerworld,* 9 June 1997, G4–G6.
9. Kalin, Sari. "The Importance of Being Multiculturally Correct," *ComputerWorld,* 6 October 1997, G16–G17.
10. Andrea Colburn, "Immigration and Housing," *Housing Economics,* July 1998, 11–14.
11. Howard Gleckman, "A Rich Stew in the Melting Pot," *Business Week,* 31 August 1998, 76.
12. Andrew Pollack, "Barbie's Journey in Japan," *The New York Times,* 22 December 1996, E3.
13. Lennie Copeland and Lewis Griggs, *Going International* (New York: Plume Books, 1985), 14.
14. Edward T. Hall and Mildred Reed Hall, *Understanding Cultural Differences* (Yarmouth, ME: Intercultural Press, 1987), 183–184.
15. Kathleen K. Reardon, *Where Minds Meet* (Belmont, CA: Wadsworth, 1987), 199.
16. Vivienne Luk, Mumtaz Patel, and Kathryn White, "Personal Attributes of American and Chinese Business Associates," *The Bulletin of the Association for Business Communication,* December 1990, 67.
17. Cynthia Gallois and Victor Callan, *Communication and Culture* (New York: John Wiley Sons, 1997), 24.
18. Susan S. Jarvis, "Preparing Employees to Work South of the Border," *Personnel,* June 1990, 763.
19. Gallois and Callan, *Communication and Culture,* 29.
20. Copeland and Griggs, *Going International,* 94.
21. Copeland and Griggs, *Going International,* 108.
22. Copeland and Griggs, *Going International,* 12.
23. Jeff Copeland, "Stare Less, Listen More," *American Way,* American Airlines, 15 December 1990.
24. E. S. Browning, "Computer Chip Project Brings Rivals Together, But the Cultures Clash," *The Wall Street Journal,* 3 May 1994, A1, A11.
25. M. J. Buoyant, "Towards Ethnorelativism: A Developmental Model of Intercultural Sensitivity," in Guo-Ming Chen and William J. Starosta, *Foundations of Intercultural Communication* (Boston: Allyn and Bacon, 1998, 233.
26. M. J. Bennett, in Chen and Starosta, *Foundations of Intercultural Communication,* 231.
27. S. Ishii and T. Bruneau, "Silence and Silences in Cross-cultural Perspective: Japan and the United States." In *Intercultural Communication: A Reader* (Belmont, CA: Wadsworth, 1994), 266.
28. Copeland and Griggs, *Going International,* 111.
29. M. R. Hammer, "Intercultural Communication Competence," in Chen and Starosta, *Foundations of Intercultural Communication,* 247.
30. Lillian H. Chaney and Jeanette S. Martin, *Intercultural Business Communication* (Englewood Cliffs, NJ: Prentice Hall Career and Technology, 1995), 67.
31. *Do's and Taboos Around the World,* 2E (New York: Wiley, 1990), 71.

32. Robert McGarvey, "Foreign Exchange," *USAir Magazine,* June 1992, 64.
33. Andrew W. Singer, "Ethics: Are Standards Lower Overseas?" *Across the Board,* September 1991, 31–34.
34. Singer, "Ethics," 31.
35. Edmund L. Andrews, "29 Nations Agree to Outlaw Bribing Foreign Officials," *The New York Times,* 21 October 1997, C1–C2.
36. Kent Hodgson, "Adapting Ethical Decisions to a Global Marketplace," *Management Review,* May 1992, 56.
37. Charlene Marmer Solomon, "Put Your Ethics to a Global Test," *Personnel Journal,* January 1996, 66–74. See also Larry R. Smeltzer and Marianne M. Jennings, "Why an International Code of Business Ethics Would Be Good for Business," *Journal of Business Ethics,* January 1998, 57–66.
38. Based on Kent Hodgson, "Adapting Ethical Decisions," 54.
39. Anna M. Rappaport and others, "Population Trends and the Labor Force in the Years Ahead," *Benefits Quarterly,* Fourth Quarter, 1998, 8–17.
40. Jack Neff, "Diversity," *Advertising Age,* 16 February 1998, S1.
41. Rae Andre, "Diversity Stress as Morality Stress," *Journal of Business Ethics,* June 1995, 489–496.
42. Genevieve Capowski, "Managing Diversity," *Management Review,* June 1996, 16.
43. Joel Makower, "Managing Diversity in the Workplace," *Business and Society Review,* Winter 1995, 48–54.
44. George Simons and Darlene Dunham, "Making Inclusion Happen," *Managing Diversity,* December 1995. <http://www.jalmc.org/mk-incl.htm> (Retrieved 9 August 1996).
45. Anthony Patrick Carnevale and Susan Carol Stone, *The American Mosaic* (New York: McGraw-Hill, 1995), 60.
46. Michele Wucker, "Keep on Trekking," *Working Woman,* December/January 1998, 32–36.
47. Karl Schoenberger, "Motorola Bets Big on China," *Fortune,* 27 May 1996, 116–124.
48. Rita Thomas Noel, "International Training Manual," *The Bulletin of the Association for Business Communication,* March 1992, 26–28.
49. Based on Rose Knotts and Mary S. Thibodeaux, "Verbal Skills in Cross-Culture Managerial Communication," *European Business Review,* 92, no. 2, 1992, v–vii.
50. Keith Martin and Sheila M. Walsh, "Beware the Foreign Corrupt Practices Act," October 1996, 25–27.
51. Joel Makower, "Managing Diversity."
52. Sari Kalin, "The Importance of Being Multiculturally Correct," *Computerworld,* 6 October 1997, G16–G17.
53. Jayne Tear, "They Just Don't Understand Gender Dynamics," *The Wall Street Journal,* 20 November 1995, A12; Anne Roiphe, "Talking Trouble," *Working Woman,* October 1994, 28–31; Cristina Stuart, "Why Can't a Woman Be More Like a Man?" *Training Tomorrow,* February 1994, 22–24; and Alan Wolfe, "Talking From 9 to 5: How Women's and Men's Conversational Styles Affect Who Gets Heard, Who Gets Credit, and What Gets Done at Work," *New Republic,* 12 December 1994.

CHAPTER 4

1. Michael H. Martin, "Kinko's," *Fortune,* 8 July 1996, 102.
2. Ann Marsh, "Kinko's Grows Up—Almost," *Forbes,* 1 December 1997, 270–272.
3. Marsh, "Kinko's Grows Up," 270–272.
4. Hugh Hay-Roe, "The Secret of Excess," *Executive Excellence,* January 1995, 20.
5. Charles C. Manz, Christopher P. Neek, James Mancuso, and Karen P. Manz, *For Team Members Only* (New York: AMACOM American Management Association, 1997), 3–4. See also Edward M. Marshall, *Transforming the Way We Work* (New York: AMACOM American Management Association, 1995), 5.
6. A. Lunsford and L. Ede, "Audience Addressed/Audience Invoked: The Role of Audience in Composition Theory and Pedagogy," *College Composition and Communication,* May 1984, 2; and A. Lunsford and L. Ede, "Why Write . . . Together: A Research Update," *Rhetoric Review,* Fall 1986, 1.
7. Earl N. Harbert, "Knowing Your Audience," in *The Handbook of Executive Communication,* ed. John L. DiGaetani (Homewood, IL: Dow Jones/Irwin, 1986), 3.
8. Vanessa Dean Arnold, "Benjamin Franklin on Writing Well," *Personnel Journal,* August 1986, 17.
9. Mark Bacon, quoted in "Business Writing: One-on-One Speaks Best to the Masses," *Training,* April 1988, 95. See also Elizabeth Danziger, "Communicate Up," *Journal of Accountancy,* February 1998, 67.
10. For more information see Marilyn Schwartz, *Guidelines for Bias-Free Writing* (Bloomington, Indiana: University Press, 1994).
11. Leslie Matthies, as mentioned in Carl Heyel, "Policy and Procedure Manuals," *The Handbook of Executive Communication,* 212.
12. Parts of this section are based on Kristin R. Woolever's "Corporate Language and the Law: Avoiding Liability in Corporate Communications," *IEE Transactions on Professional Communication,* 2 June 1990, 95–98.
13. Victor E. Schwartz, "Continuing Duty to Warn: An Opportunity for Liability Prevention or Exposure," *Journal of Public Policy & Marketing,* Spring 1998, 124.
14. Lisa Jenner, "Develop Communication and Training With Literacy in Mind," *HR Focus,* March 1994, 14.
15. Woolever, "Corporate Language," 96.
16. Woolever, "Corporate Language," 95.

17. Lisa Jenner, "Employment-at-Will Liability: How Protected Are You?" *HR Focus,* March 1994, 11.
18. Judy E. Pickens, "Communication: Terms of Equality: A Guide to Bias-Free Language," *Personnel Journal,* August 1985, 5.

CHAPTER 5

1. Andree Conrad and Faye Musselman, "The State of the Industry," *Apparel Industry Magazine,* April 1998, 28–32.
2. James A. Morrissey, "Industry Mulls Issue of Apparel Sweatshops," *Textile World,* August 1997, 94.
3. Kimberly Paterson, "The Writing Process," *Rough Notes,* April 1998, 59–60.
4. Andrew Fluegelman and Jeremy Joan Hewes, "The Word Processor and the Writing Process," in *Strategies for Business and Technical Writing,* 4th ed. Kevin J. Harty (San Diego: Harcourt Brace Jovanovich, 1989), 43. See also Lynn Quitman Troyka, *Simon & Schuster Handbook for Writers,* 4th ed. (Upper Saddle River, NJ: Prentice Hall, 1996), 49.
5. Maryann V. Piotrowski, *Effective Business Writing* (New York: HarperPerennial, 1996), 12.
6. Robert W. Goddard, "Communication: Use Language Effectively," *Personnel Journal,* April 1989, 32.
7. Frederick Crews, *The Random House Handbook,* 4th ed. (New York: Random House, 1991), 152.

CHAPTER 6

1. Nancy Brumback, "Yo Quiero Mexican Food," *Restaurant Business,* 1 September 1998, 43–44.
2. Laura Yee, "Border Crossing," *Restaurants and Institutions,* 15 April 1998, 39–61.
3. Peter Elbow, *Writing With Power: Techniques for Mastering the Writing Process* (Oxford: Oxford University Press, 1998), 30.
4. John S. Fielden, "What Do You Mean You Don't Like My Style?" *Harvard Business Review,* May/June 1982, 128.
5. Sonia Von Matt Stoddard, "Proofreading for Perfection," *Legal Assistant Today,* March/April 1997, 84–85.
6. Ralph Brown, "Add Some Informal Polish to Your Writing," *Management,* March 1998, 12.
7. Richard E. Neff, "CEOs Want Information, Not Just Words," *Communication World,* April/May 1997, 22–25.
8. Claire K. Cook, *Line by Line* (Boston: Houghton Mifflin, 1985), 17.
9. William Power and Michael Siconolfi, "Memo to: Mr. Ball, RE: Your Messages, Sir: They're Weird," *The Wall Street Journal,* 30 November 1990, 1; Ralph Brown, "Add Some Informal Polish to Your Writing," *Management,* March 1998, 12.
10. Al Neuharth, "Why Washington Is Lost in the Fog," *USA Today,* 12 October 1990, A13.
11. Louise Lague, *People* Magazine editor, interview with Mary Ellen Guffey, 5 February 1992.
12. Joel Shore, "Suites Still Depend on 'Feature Creep' to Grow," *Computer Reseller News,* 11 November 1996, 202.
13. Spell checker poem has appeared in many publications without attribution.

CHAPTER 7

1. Alice Blachly, interview with Mary Ellen Guffey, 12 January 1993. See also Cheryl Strauss Einhorn, "Commodities Corner: Fat City," *Barron's,* 17 August 1998; Lori Anne Marotta and Paul W. Cockerham, "Ben & Jerry's Dilbert's World," *Frozen Food Age,* August 1998, 22; Craig Smith, "Ben & Jerry's Double-Dip," *Marketing,* 27 August 1998, 25; Molly Farrell, "From Ice Cream to Nuts in Food Residuals Composting," *BioCycle,* October 1998, 43–47.
2. Malcolm Forbes, "How to Write a Business Letter," International Paper Company, reprinted in *Strategies for Business and Technical Writing,* 4th ed., ed. Kevin Harty (Boston: Allyn and Bacon, 1999), 108.
3. Bill Knapp, "Communication Breakdown," *World Wastes,* February 1998, 16.
4. Hugh Hay-Roe, "The Secret of Excess," *Executive Excellence,* January 1995, 20.
5. Dennis Chambers, *Writing to Get Action* (Bristol, VT: Velocity Business Publishing, 1998), 12.
6. *Business Week,* 6 July 1981, 107.
7. Alice Blachly, interview.
8. Geoffrey Brewer, "The Customer Stops Here," *Sales & Marketing Management,* March 1998, 30–36.
9. Amy Saltzman, "Suppose They Sue? Why Companies Shouldn't Fret So Much About Bias Cases," *U.S. News & World Report,* 22 September 1997, 69.
10. "A 'Catch 22' in Honesty," *The Wall Street Journal,* 2 December 1990, F25. See also Brian Gill, "Establishing Job References Policies," *American Printer,* January 1998, 66.
11. Stephen B. Knouse, "Confidentiality and the Letter of Recommendation: A New Approach," *The Bulletin of the Association for Business Communication,* September 1987, 7.
12. Robert J. Aalberts and Lorraine A. Krajewski, "Claim and Adjustment Letters: Theory Versus Practice and Legal Implications," *The Bulletin of the Association for Business Communication,* September 1987, 5.
13. Gary L. Clark, Peter F. Kaminski, and David R. Rink, "Consumer Complaints: Advice on How Companies Should Respond Based on an Empirical Study," *Journal of Services Marketing,* Winter 1992, 41–50.
14. Robert Klara, "Press 1 to Gripe," *Restaurant Business,* 15 May 1998, 96–102.
15. "Foiling the Rogues: 'Anti' Web Sites Are Great for Angry Customers, But Now Companies Are Trying to Fight Back," *Newsweek,* 27 October 1997, 80; Roberta Furger, "Don't Get Mad, Get Online," *PC World,* October 1997, 37.

16. "Grove's Internet Apology," *Computer Reseller News,* 5 December 1994, 313.
17. Marcia Mascolini, "Another Look at Teaching the External Negative Message," *The Bulletin of the Association of Business Communication,* June 1994, 46; Robert J. Aalberts and Lorraine A. Krajewski, "Claim and Adjustment Letters," *The Bulletin of the Association for Business Communication,* September 1987, 2.
18. Elizabeth Blackburn Brockman and Kelly Belanger, "You-Attitude and Positive Emphasis: Testing Received Wisdom in Business Communication," *The Bulletin of the Association for Business Communication,* June 1993, 1–5; C. Goodwin and I. Ross, "Consumer Evaluations of Responses to Complaints: What's Fair and Why," *Journal of Consumer Marketing,* 7, 1990, 39–47; Marcia Mascolini, "Another Look at Teaching the External Negative Message," *The Bulletin of the Association for Business Communication,* June 1994, 46.
19. Pamela Gilbert, "Two Words That Can Help a Business Thrive," *The Wall Street Journal,* 30 December 1996, A12.
20. Saburo Haneda and Hirosuke Shima, "Japanese Communication Behavior as Reflected in Letter Writing," *The Journal of Business Communication,* 1 (1982): 29. See also Iris I. Varner and Linda Beamer, Intercultural Communication (Chicago: Irwin, 1995), 120.
21. Wolfgang Manekeller, as cited in Iris I. Varner, "Internationalizing Business Communication Courses," *The Bulletin of the Association for Business Communication,* December 1987, 10.
22. Dr. Annette Luciani-Samec, French instructor, and Dr. Pierre Samec, French businessman, interviews with the author, Palo Alto, California, May 1995.
23. Retha H. Kilpatrick, "International Business Communication Practices," *The Journal of Business Communication,* Fall 1984, 42–43.
24. Based on articles by Nora Wood, "1998 Motivators of the Year," *Incentive,* April 1998, 27–36; Feliza Mirasol, "Warner-Lambert and Pfizer lead Pharma Earnings," *Chemical Market Reporter,* 3 August 1998, 4, 9; Brian O'Reilly, "The Pills That Saved Warner-Lambert," *Fortune,* 13 October 1997, 94–95; Jennifer J. Laabs, "Warner-Lambert Sends a Global Thank-You to Employees Worldwide," *Workforce,* March 1998, 13–14.
25. Based on articles by Frank Edward Allen, "McDonald's to Reduce Waste in Plan Developed With Environmental Group," *The Wall Street Journal,* 17 April 1991, B1; Martha T. Moore, "McDonald's Trashes Sandwich Boxes," *USA Today,* 2 November 1990, 1; Michael Parrish, "McDonald's to Do Away With Foam Packages," *Los Angeles Times,* 2 November 1990, 1; and Mark Hamstra, "McD Supersizes Efforts to Cut Down on Costs," *Nation's Restaurant News,* 29 June 1998, 1, 60.

CHAPTER 8

1. Cathy Trimble, interview with Mary Ellen Guffey, 8 February 1995. Other information from *Guide to Hospital Services at Shore Memorial Hospital* (Somers Point, NJ: Shore Memorial Hospital, 1994); "1998 Calendar of Events, Wellness and The Center for Women's Health at Shore Memorial Hospital." <http://www.shorememorial.org/welnessf.htm> (Retrieved 1 December 1998).
2. See G. A. Marken, "Think Before You Click," *Office Systems,* March 1998, 44–46; Christopher B. Sullivan, "Preferences for Electronic Mail in Organizational Communication Tasks," *The Journal of Business Communication,* January 1995, 49–65; Mary K. Kirtz and Diana C. Reep, "A Survey of the Frequency, Types, and Importance of Writing Tasks in Four Career Areas," *The Bulletin of the Association for Business Communication,* December 1990, 3.
3. Marken, "Think," 44.
4. Barb Cole-Gomolski, "E-Mail Traffic, Costs Hit High-Speed Lane," *Computerworld,* 14 April 1997.
5. Sana Reynolds, "Composing Effective E-Mail Messages," *Communication World,* July 1997, 8–9.
6. Reynolds, "Composing Effective E-Mail," 8.
7. Paula Jacobs, "Strong Writing Skills Essential for Success, Even in IT," *InfoWorld,* 6 July 1998, 86.
8. Rosalind Gold, "Reader-Friendly Writing," *Supervisory Management,* January 1989, 40.
9. Marken, "Think," 44.
10. Linda Himelstein, "Exhibit A: The Telltale Computer Tape," *Business Week,* 15 August 1994, 8; and Lawrence Dietz, "E-Mail Is Wonderful But It Has Risks," *Bottom Line/Business* (published by Boardroom, Inc.), 15 June 1995, 3–4; Jenny C. McCune, "Get the Message," *Management Review,* January 1997.
11. Peter H. Lewis, "What's on Your Hard Drive?" *The New York Times,* 8 October 1998, G1.
12. Leslie Helm, "The Digital Smoking Gun," *Los Angeles Times,* 16 June 1994, El.
13. John Fielden, "Clear Writing Is Not Enough," *Management Review,* April 1989, 51.
14. Michael Siconolfi and Jonathan Auerbach, "Trading Obscenities: Brokers Are Told to Curb Gutter Talk," *The Wall Street Journal,* 19 September 1996, A1, A6.
15. Roberta Maynard, "The Lighter Side of Promotions," *Nation's Business,* July 1996, 4.
16. Laura Liebeck, "Novelty Hasn't Worn Off for Candy Manufacturers," *Discount Store News,* 13 July 1998, 8, 110.
17. Based on Maggie Jackson, "Casual Day a Bad Fit?" *Los Angeles Times Careers,* 19 January 1998, 27–28.
18. Based on Charles Waltner, "Web Watchers," *Informationweek,* 27 April 1998, 121–126; and Howard

Millman, "Easy EDI for Everyone," *InfoWorld*, 17 August 1998, 38–39.

19. George D. Webster, "Internal Communications Issues," *Association Management*, May 1995, 150–153.

CHAPTER 9

1. Based on Kathleen Doler, "Interview: Jeff Bezos, Founder and CEO of Amazon.com Inc." *Inside*, September 1998, 76–80; Joshua Macht, "Amazon.com; A Moving Target," *Inc.*, October 1998, 18; Dylan Tweney, "No Mere Bookstore, Amazon Wants to be an Online Retail Giant," *InfoWorld*, 10 August 1998, 46; and Jodi Mardesich and Marc Gunther, "Is Competition Closing in on Amazon.com?" *Fortune*, 9 November 1998, 229–234.
2. Raymond A. Dumont and John Lannon, *Business Communications*, 3rd ed. (Glenview, IL: Scott, Foresman, Little, Brown, 1990), 33.
3. Seth Faison, "Trying to Play by the Rules," *The New York Times*, 22 December 1991, sec. 3, 1.
4. "How to Ask For—And Get—What You Want!" *Supervision*, February 1990, 11.
5. Rob Yogel, "Sending Your Message Electronically," *Target Marketing*, June 1998, 77–78.
6. Dean Rieck, "Great Letters and Why They Work," *Direct Marketing*, June 1998, 20–24.
7. Dennis Chambers, *The Agile Manager's Guide to Writing to Get Action* (Bristol, VT: Velocity Press, 1998), 86.
8. Kevin McLaughlin, "Words of Wisdom," *Entrepreneur*, October 1990, 101.
9. Based on Richard Gibson, "Merchants Mull the Long and the Short of Lines," *The Wall Street Journal*, 3 September 1998, B1.
10. Laura Johannes, "Globe-Trotting Shutterbug Slaps Kodak With the Bill for a Reshoot," *The Wall Street Journal*, 24 April 1998, B1.
11. Based on Ashlea Ebeling, "The Three Icons of the Old West," *Forbes*, 17 November 1997, 152–154.
12. Based on "U.S. Company Pays Big Bucks for Used Athletic Footwear," *Sporting Goods Business*, 23 January 1998; "Your Feet Are Paved With Gold," *Canadian Business*, October 1996, 113.

CHAPTER 10

1. Cathy C. Dial, manager, Consumer Relations, Pepsi-Cola Company, interview with Mary Ellen Guffey, 11 November 1994 and 5 January 1995. Other information from Adrienne Mand, "DDB Interactive Creates 'One' World for Pepsi," *Brandweek*, 12 October 1998, 332; PepsiCo Web site <www.pepsico.com> (Retrieved 5 December 1998); *50 Years and Counting: Direct Relief . . . A Half Century of Health & Healing* (Santa Barbara, CA 1998).
2. Mohan R. Limaye, "Further Conceptualization of Explanations in Negative Messages," *Business Communication Quarterly*, June 1997, 46.
3. Robert Mirguet, information security manager, Eastman Kodak Co., Rochester, New York, quoted in *Computerworld*, cited in "Telecommunicating," *Boardroom Reports*, 1 March 1995, 15; Sandy Sampson, "Wild Wild Web: Legal Exposure on the Internet," *Software Magazine*, November 1997, 75–78.
4. Elizabeth A. McCord, "The Business Writer, the Law, and Routine Business Communication: A Legal and Rhetorical Analysis," *Journal of Business and Technical Communication*, April 1991, 183.
5. Phillip M. Perry, "E-Mail Hell: The Dark Side of the Internet Age," *Folio: The Magazine for Magazine Management*, June 1998, 74–75.
6. McCord, "The Business Writer," 183, 193.
7. Marcia Mascolini, "Another Look at Teaching the External Negative Message," *The Bulletin of the Association for Business Communication*, June 1994, 47.
8. "Letters to Lands' End," *February 1991 Catalog* (Dodgeville, WI: Lands' End, 1991), 100.
9. Carol David and Margaret Ann Baker, "Rereading Bad News: Compliance-Gaining Features in Management Memos," *The Journal of Business Communication*, 31, no. 4, 268.
10. Malcolm Forbes, "How to Write a Business Letter," International Paper Company, reprinted in *Strategies for Business and Technical Writing*, 4th ed., ed. Kevin Harty (Boston: Allyn and Bacon, 1999), 108.
11. Jeanette W. Gilsdorf, "Metacommunication Effects on International Business Negotiating in China," *Business Communication Quarterly*, June 1997, 27.
12. Based on Robert L. Simison, "'Forget Paris,' GM Tells Journalists; Instead They Get to Visit Detroit," *The Wall Street Journal*, 12 August 1998, B1.
13. Based on Gene Sloan, "Under 21? Carnival Says Cruise Is Off," *USA Today*, 29 November 1996; Jill Jordan Sieder, "Full Steam Ahead: Carnival Cruise Line Makes Boatloads of Money by Selling Fun," *U.S. News & World Report*, 16 October 1995, 72, on-line [1 December 1996]; "What to Expect on Carnival Cruises," Bon Vivant Travel <http://www.bvt-usa.com/cruises/c-expect.html> (Retrieved 2 December 1996).
14. Based on Julia King, "SunGard Stung by Virus," *Computerworld*, 6 February 1995, 73; Gary H. Anthes, "PowerMac Users Warned: Threat of Viruses Increases If Users Run Both Macintosh and PC Applications," *Computerworld*, 23 January 1995, 41; and Mark Henricks, "Attack of the Killer Virus," *Office Systems*, July 1998, 38–41.
15. Laura Johannes, "Globe-Trotting Shutterbug Slaps Kodak With the Bill for a Reshoot," *The Wall Street Journal*, 24 April 1998, B1.

CHAPTER 11

1. Don Cuerdon, "Girls Don't Rule," *Mountain Bike*, November 1997, 16.

2. "How Women Buy Their Bikes," 1997 report compiled by *Bicycling Magazine,* Rodale Press, Inc.
3. Ariadne Delon Scott, sales support manager, Specialized Bicycle Components, interview with Mary Ellen Guffey, 14 January 1999.
4. Catherine Strong, "Deaths in Red-Light Running Rise 15 Percent, Study Says," *Santa Barbara News-Press,* 21 May 1998, A1.
5. Mick O'Leary, "IAC Offers Double Web Package," *Information Today,* October 1996, 16, 54.
6. "IAC Calls Usage Growth of InfoTrac SearchBank 'Explosive,'" *Information Today,* February 1997, 34.
7. "International Content, Color Enhance UMI's Proquest Direct," *Information Today,* January 1998, 1, 53.
8. "Northern Light Special Collection: Overview." <http://www.northernlight.com/docs.specoll_help_overview.html> (Retrieved 28 December 1998).
9. Mary Ellen Bates, "American Business Information: Here, There, and Everywhere," *Database,* April/May 1997, 45–50.
10. Thomas E. Weber, "Web's Vastness Foils Even Best Search Engines," *The Wall Street Journal,* 3 April 1998, B1.
11. David Lidsky and others, "Searching the Net (36 Internet search sites)," *PC Magazine,* 2 December 1997, 227.
12. Randolph E. Hock, "Sizing Up HotBot," *Online,* November-December, 1997.
13. Nancy Sirapyan, "HotBot," *PC Magazine,* 1 December 1998.
14. H. B. Koplowitz, "The Nature of Search Engines," *Link-Up,* September/October 1998, 28.
15. Based on Konnie G. Kustron, "Searching the World Wide Web," *Records Management Quarterly,* July 1997, 8–12.
16. Susan Feldman quoted in Annette Skov, "Internet Quality," *Database,* August/September 1998.
17. M. Theodore Farries, II, Jeanne D. Maes, and Ulla K. Bunz, "References and Bibliography: Citing the Internet," *Journal of Applied Business Research,* Summer 1998, 33–36.
18. Christopher Velotta, "How to Design and Implement a Questionnaire," *Technical Communication,* Fall 1991.
19. Robin Toner, "Politics of Welfare: Focusing on the Problems," *The New York Times,* 5 July 1991, 1.
20. Gerald J. Alred, Walter E. Oliu, and Charles T. Brusaw, *The Professional Writer* (New York: St. Martin's Press, 1992), 78.
21. "Gulf States Centralizes HR/Payroll Functions," *Workforce,* December 1998, 70.
22. "Hard Rock Café Rocks Even Harder With The 7 Habits," *Workforce,* December 1998, 72.

CHAPTER 12

1. Alex Taylor, III, "And the Best Car Plant in North America Is . . ." *Fortune,* 26 October 1998, 46.
2. John Humphrey, interviews with Mary Ellen Guffey, 1 November 1994 and 12 January 1999. Other information from *The Power Report,* J. D. Power and Associates, July 1994; and Taylor, *Fortune,* 26 October 1998.
3. Walter Wells, *Communications in Business* (Boston: PWS/Kent, 1988), 471.
4. Charlene Marmer Solomon, "Marriott's Family Matters," *Personnel Journal,* October 1991, 40–42; Jennifer Laabs, "They Want More Support—Inside and Outside of Work," *Workforce,* November 1998, 54–56.
5. Chuck Hawkins, "FedEx: Europe Nearly Killed the Messenger," *Business Week,* 25 May 1992, 124–126.

CHAPTER 13

1. Oren Harari, "Lessons From the Swoosh," *Management Review,* July/August 1998, 39.
2. William McCall, "Nike Battles Backlash From Overseas Sweatshops," *Marketing News,* 9 November 1998, 14.
3. Leslie Goff, "<YourCompanyName-Here>sucks.com," *Computerworld,* 20 July 1998, 57–58.
4. "A Swift Decision; Nike Chooses Site of Its New Distribution Centre," *Corporation Location,* November/December 1995, 19.

CHAPTER 14

1. Mary Piecewicz, interview with Mary Ellen Guffey, 12 January 1999. Other information from Hewlett-Packard, *1992 Annual Report* (Palo Alto, CA: Hewlett-Packard, 1992), 1–21.
2. Mary Piecewitz, interview, 12 January 1999.
3. Nancy Rivera Brooks and Jesus Sanchez, "U.S. Firms Map Ways to Profit From the Accord," *Los Angeles Times,* 13 August 1992, D1, D2.
4. Herman Holtz, *The Consultant's Guide to Proposal Writing* (New York: John Wiley, 1990), 188.
5. Based on Jane Applegate, "Weigh Freight Expenses Carefully," *Los Angeles Times,* 14 August 1992, D3.
6. Based on Joann S. Lublin, "Companies Use Cross-Cultural Training to Help Their Employees Adjust Abroad," *The Wall Street Journal,* 4 August 1992, B1.
7. Based on John R. Emshwiller, "Designer of Surfing Ride Catches a Wave of Success," *The Wall Street Journal,* 12 August 1992, B2.
8. Based on Barbara Ettorre, "Breaking the Glass . . . or Just Window Dressing," *Management Review,* March 1992, 16–22; and Janet Guyon, "The Global Glass Ceiling and Ten Women Who Broke Through," *Fortune,* 12 October 1998, 109–103.
9. Based on Karen S. Sterkel, "Integrating Intercultural Communication and Report Writing in the Communication Class," *The Bulletin of the Association for Business Communication,* September 1988, 14–16.

CHAPTER 15

1. Miki Tanikawa, "Fun in the Sun," *Far Eastern Economic Review,* 29 May 1997, 56–57.

2. Jon Georges interview with Mary Ellen Guffey, 3 February 1999. Other information from "Disney's $600 Million Royalties Securitization Dwarfs the Market," *Asset Finance International,* May 1997, 8.
3. Wharton Applied Research Center, "A Study of the Effects of the Use of Overhead Transparencies on Business Meetings, Final Report" cited in "Short, Snappy Guide to Meaningful Presentations," *Working Woman,* June 1991, 73.
4. Jim Endicott, "For Better Presentations, Avoid PowerPoint Pitfalls," *Presentations,* June 1998, 36–37.
5. Victoria Hall Smith, "Gigs by the Gigabyte," *Working Woman,* May 1998, 114.
6. Smith, "Gigs," 115.
7. Dianna Booher, *Executive's Portfolio of Model Speeches for All Occasions* (Englewood Cliffs, NJ: Prentice-Hall, 1991), 259.
8. Raymond Slesinski, "Giving a Topnotch Executive Presentation," *Management,* April 1990, 16.
9. Ronald E. Dulek, John S. Fielden, and John S. Hill, "International Communication: An Executive Primer," *Business Horizons,* January/February 1991, 23.
10. Dulek, Fielden, and Hill, "International Communication," 22.
11. Patricia A. LaRosa, "Voice Messaging Is Quality 'Lip Service,'" *The Office, May 1992, 10.*
12. "Did You know That . . . ," *Boardroom Reports,* 15 August 1992, 15.
13. Michael Jackson, quoted in "Garbage In, Garbage Out," *Consumer Reports,* December 1992, 755.

CHAPTER 16

1. Bonnie Gesualdi-Chao, interview with Mary Ellen Guffey, 22 February 1999. Other information from Vance Gullicksin, Carnival Cruise Lines Public Relations; William G. Flanagan, "Thanks for the Subsidies," *Forbes,* 7 July 1997, 120; and "About Carnival," Carnival Cruise Lines <http://www.carnival.com/aboutccl.aboutccl.asp> (Retrieved 15 February 1999).
2. Caitlin P. Williams, "The End of the Job As We Know It," *Training & Development,* January 1999, 52–54. See also Manuel London, "Redeployment and Continuous Learning in the 21st Century: Hard Lessons and Positive Examples from the Downsizing Era," *Academy of Management Executive,* November 1996, 67–79.
3. Maarten Mittner, "The Brave New World of Work," *Finance Week,* 30 October 1998, 77.
4. Cary L. Cooper, "The 1998 Crystal Lecture: The Future of Work—A Strategy for Managing the Pressures," *Journal of Applied Management Studies,* December 1998, 275–281.
5. George B. Weathersby, "Responding to Change," *Management Review,* October 1998, 5.
6. Sharon Voros, "Managing Your Career: The New Realities," *Communication World,* February 1997, 28–30.
7. Judith Schroer, "Seek a Job With a Little Help From Your Friends," *USA Today,* 19 November 1990, B1.
8. Michele Pepe, "ResumeMaker Turns a Complete Circle," *Computer Reseller News,* 29 September 1997, 173.
9. Professor Mark Granovetter, quoted in Susan J. Wells, "Many Jobs on Web," *The New York Times,* 12 March 1998, A12.
10. George Crosby of the Human Resources Network, as quoted in Hal Lancaster, "When Taking a Tip From a Job Network, Proceed With Caution," *The Wall Street Journal,* 7 February 1995, B1.
11. Dan Moreau, "Write a Résumé That Works," *Changing Times,* June 1990, 91. See also Naralie Bortoli, "Resumes in the Right: New Rules Make Writing a Winner Easy," *Manage,* August 1997, 20–21.
12. Bortoli, "Resumes in the Right," 20.
13. H. B. Crandall, quoted in Jacqueline Trace, "Teaching Résumé Writing the Functional Way," *The Bulletin of the Association for Business Communication,* June 1985, 41.
14. Bortoli, "Resumes in the Right," 20.
15. Tom Washington, "Improve Your Résumé 100 Percent," <http://www.nbew.com/archive/961001–001.html> (Retrieved 27 September 1998).
16. Robert Lorentz, James W. Carland, and Jo Ann Carland, "The Résumé: What Value Is There in References?" *Journal of Technical Writing and Communication,* Fall 1993, 371.
17. "As Graduation Approaches . . . ," *Personnel,* June 1991, 14.
18. Margaret Mannix, "Writing a Computer-Friendly Résumé," *U.S. News & World Report,* 26 October 1992, 90.
19. Tim Ouellette, "Résumé Site Eases Hiring," *ComputerWorld,* 13 April 1998, 47–50.
20. Joyce Lain Kennedy and Thomas J. Morrow, *Electronic Résumé Revolution* (New York: John Wiley & Sons, 1994), Chapter 3.
21. Marc Silver, "Selling the Perfect You," *U.S. News & World Report,* 5 February 1990, 70–72.
22. Diane Cole, "Ethics: Companies Crack Down on Dishonesty," *The Wall Street Journal,* Managing Your Career supplement, Spring 1991, 8.
23. "Managing Your Career," *National Business Employment Weekly,* Fall 1989, 29.
24. Joan E. Rigdon, "Deceptive Resumes Can Be Door-Openers but Can Become an Employee's Undoing," *The Wall Street Journal,* 17 June 1992, B1. See also Barbara Solomon, "Too Good to be True?" *Management Review,* April 1998, 28.
25. Rhonda D. Findling, "The Résumé Fax-periment," *Résumé Pro Newsletter,* Fall 1994, 10.
26. Harriett M. Augustin, "The Written Job Search: A Comparison of the Traditional and a Nontraditional Approach," *The Bulletin of the Association for Business Communication,* September 1991, 13.
27. Julia Lawlor, "Networking Opens More Doors to Jobs," *USA Today,* 19 November 1990, B7.
28. J. Michael Farr, *The Very Quick Job Search* (Indianapolis, IN: JIST Works, 1991), 158.

Acknowledgments

Text, Figures, Captions

p. 3 Case study based on Gillian Flynn, "Pillsbury's Recipe Is Candid Talk," *Workforce,* February 1998, 56-59; "Profile," Pillsbury Web site <http://pillsbury.com/community/community/html>; Paul S. Nadler, "Snapshots of a Downsizing Era," *Secured Lender,* July/August 1998, 16-18; Clare Conley, "UK Pillsbury Boss Moves Abroad," *Marketing Week,* 18 June 1998, 10; Stephanie Thompson, "Pillsbury Sings Freshness Theme With Bread Dough, Coffee Cakes," *Brandweek,* 16 February 1998, 4; Bob Nelson, "The Care of the Un-downsized," *Training and Development,* April 1997, 40-43; John E. Jacobs, "Re-thinking the Basics," *Executive Excellence,* October 1997, 3-4; Ian P. Murphy, " Pillsbury Proves Charity, Marketing Begin at Home," *Marketing News,* 17 February 1997, 16; Bill Trahant and W. Warner Burke, "Traveling Through Transitions," *Training and Development,* February 1996, 37-41; Craig Dreilinger, "Fear and Loathing After Downsizing . . . What Can Managers Do?" *Tapping the Network Journal,* Summer 1994, 8-10; Theresa Howard, "BK Plan Targets Job Cuts, Corporate Restructuring," *Nation's Restaurant News,* 7 March 1994, 1, 4; and Suzanne Bidlake, "Burger King's Euro Push," *Marketing,* 20 February 1992, 2. **p. 9** Spotlight caption based on Oren Harari, "Flood Your Organization With Knowledge," *Management Review,* November 1997, 33. **p. 12** Spotlight caption based on Sandra Kurtzig and Tom Parker, *CEO* (New York: W. W. Norton, 1991). **p. 19** Chart courtesy of Pitney Bowes Inc. **p. 22** Spotlight caption based on Noel M. Tichy and Stratford Sherman, *Control Your Destiny or Someone Else Will* (New York: Bantam Doubleday Dell Publishing, 1993), as reported in "Jack Welch's Lessons for Success," *Fortune,* 25 January 1993, 92; John A. Bryne, "Jack: A Close-up Look at How America's #1 Manager Runs GE," *Business Week,* 8 June 1998, 92-108. **p. 25** Picture caption based on Samuel Greengard, "Lockheed Martin Is Game for Ethics," *Workforce,* October 1997, 51; Martha Groves, "Honor System," *Los Angeles Times,* "Careers," 3 November 1997, 3, 15. **p. 26** Spotlight caption based on Ingrid Abramovitch, "The Trust Factor," *Success* (March 1993), 18. **p. 37** Case study based on Stuart F. Brown, "Gearing Up for the Cruiser Wars," *Fortune,* 3 August 1998, 128B-128D; Barbara M. Schmitz, "Computer Simulation Helps Improve Motorcycle Handling," *Computer-Aided Engineering,* September 1998, 8-10; Peter Bradley, "Harley-Davidson Keeps Its Eyes on the Road," *Logistics Management & Distribution Report,* August 1998, 68-73; Tim Minahan, "Harley-Davidson Revs Up Development Process," *Purchasing,* 7 May 1998, 44S18-44S23; Aaron Baar, "Harley-Davidson Aims Younger," *Adweek,* 10 August 1998, 4; Robert J. Bowman, "All That It's Cracked Up to Be?" *World Trade,* July 1998, 75-76; Paul Nolan, "Prepaid Gas Card Fuels Harley-Davidson Anniversary Promotion," *Potentials in Marketing,* September 1998, 18; Aaron Baar, "Colle & McVoy Helping Revive Norton Cycles," *Adweek,* 13 July 1998, 4; David Kiley, "Harley-Davidson," *Mediaweek,* 14 July 1997, 32-33; Clyde Fessler, "Rotating Leadership at Harley-Davidson: From Hierarchy to Interdependence," *Strategy & Leadership,* July-August, 1997, 42-43; Laura Koss-Feder, "Be Reborn to Be Wild on Today's Powerful Retro Motorcycles," *Money,* April 1997, 174; Richard A. Melcher, "Tune-Up Time for Harley: It Must Soothe Impatient Customers and Fight Imitators," *Business Week,* 8 April 1996, 90-94; and Bob Filipczak, "The Soul of the Hog," *Training,* February 1996, 38-42. **p. 38** Spotlight based on Charles Parnell, "Teamwork: Not a New Idea, But It's Transforming the Workplace," *Executive Speeches,* December 1997/January 1998, 35-40. **pp. 38-41** Discussion of four phases of team development, role of conflict, and characteristics of successful teams based on Jon R. Katzenbach and Douglas K. Smith, *The Wisdom of Teams* (New York: HarperCollins, 1994); Harvey Robbins and Michael Finley, *Why Teams Don't Work* (Peterson's/Pacesetter, 1995); Jon R. Katzenbach, *Teams at the Top* (Boston: Harvard Business School Press, 1997); Laurel Kieffer, "Building a Team," *Nonprofit World,* July/August 1997, 39-41; Stephanie Reynolds, "Managing Conflict Through a Team Intervention and Training Strategy," *Employee Relations Today,* Winter 1998, 57-64; Odette Pollar, "Sticking Together," *Successful Meetings,* January 1997, 87-90; Kathleen M. Eisenhardt, "How Management Teams Can Have a Good Fight," *Harvard Business Review,* July/August 1997, 77-85; Charles Parnell, " Teamwork: Not a New Idea, But It's Transforming the Workplace," *Executive Speeches,* December 1997/January 1998, 38-40; Patricia Buhler, "Managing in the 90s: Creating Flexibility in Today's Workplace," *Supervision,* January 1996, 24-26; Erich Brockmann, "Removing the Paradox of Conflict from Group Decisions," *Academy of Management Executive,* May 1996, 61-62; Peter Jackson, "Getting the Group to Work," *CA Magazine,* January/February 1998, 41-43; Judith Bogert and David Butt, " Opportunities Lost, Challenges Met: Understanding and Applying Group Dynamics in Writing Projects," *The Bulletin,* June 1990, 51-58; Sandra J. Nelson and Douglas C. Smith, "Maximizing Cohesion and Minimizing Conflict in Collaborative Writing Groups," *The Bulletin,* June 1990, 59-62; Allen C. Amason, Wayne A. Hochwarter, Kenneth R. Thompson, and Allison W. Harrison, "Conflict: An Important Dimension in Successful Management Teams," *Organizational Dynamics,* Autumn 1995, 20-35; Allen C. Amason, "Distinguishing the Effects of Functional and Dysfunctional Conflict on Strategic Decision Making: Resolving a Paradox for Top Management Teams," *Academy of Management Journal,* February 1996, 123-148; Kathleen M. Eisenhardt, Jean L. Kahwajy, and L. J. Bourgeois, III,

"Conflict and Strategic Choice: How Top Management Teams Disagree," *California Management Review*, Winter 1997, 42-62; Jane Henderson-Loney, "Tuckman and Tears: Developing Teams During Profound Organizational Change," *Supervision*, May 1996, 3-5; Christopher P. Neck and Charles C. Manz, "From Groupthink to Teamthink: Toward the Creation of Constructive Thought Patterns in Self-Managing Work Teams," *Human Relations*, August 1994, 929-952; Shaila M. Miranda and Carol Saunders, "Group Support Systems: An Organization Development Intervention to Combat Groupthink," *Public Administration Quarterly*, Summer 1995, 193-216; Christopher P. Neck and Gregory Moorhead, "Groupthink Remodeled: The Importance of Leadership, Time Pressure, and Methodical Decision-Making Procedures," *Human Relations*, May 1995, 537-557. **p. 41** Spotlight based on "CEOs Speak Out," *Keying In*, Newsletter of the National Business Education Association, November 1996, 5. **p. 42** Portions of Career Coach box reprinted with permission of Peterson's, a division of International Thomson Publishing, FAX 800-730-2215. Adapted from *Why Teams Don't Work* © 1995 by Harvey A. Robbins and Michael Finley. **p. 43** Portions of discussion for organizing effective written and oral team presentations based on Frank Jossi, "Putting It All Together: Creating Presentations as a Team," *Presentations*, July 1996, 18-26; Jon Rosen, "10 Ways to Make Your Next Team Presentation a Winner," *Presentations*, August 1997, 31; Jon Hanke, "Presenting as a Team," *Presentations*, January 1998, 74-82. **p. 47** Portions of discussion on tips for better team listening based on Hal Lancaster, "It's Time to Stop Promoting Yourself and Start Listening," *The Wall Street Journal*, 10 June 1997, B1; "Good Ideas Go Unheard," *Management Review*, February 1998, 7; Morey Stettner, "Angry? Slow Down and Listen to Others," *Investor's Business Daily*, 19 January 1998, A1; "Effective Communication," *Training Tomorrow*, November 1994, 32-33; John W. Haas and Christa L. Arnold, "An Examination of the Role of Listening in Judgments of Communication," *Journal of Business Communication*, April 1995, 123-139; Richard L. Papiernik, "Diversity Demands New Understanding," *Nation's Restaurant News*, 30 October 1995, 54, 84; and Kenneth Kaye, "The Art of Listening," *HR Focus*, October 1994, 24. **p. 48** Spotlight based on Leslie Marshall, "The Intentional Oprah," *InStyle*, November 1998, 341. **pp. 54-58** Portions of discussion based on Hal Lancaster, "Learning Some Ways to Make Meetings Slightly Less Awful," *The Wall Street Journal*, 26 May 1998, B1; Melinda Ligos, "Why Your Meetings Are a Total Bore," *Sales & Marketing Management*, May 1998, 84; Jana M. Kemp, "The Writing's on the Wall," *Successful Meetings*, August 1996, 74; Charles R. McConnell, "The Chairperson's Guide to Effective Meetings," *Health Care Supervisor*, March 1997, 1-9; John C. Bruening, "There's Good News About Meetings," *Managing Office Technology*, July 1996, 24-25; Tom McDonald, "Minimizing Meetings," *Successful Meetings*, June 1996, 24; Robert E. Levasseur, "Breaking the Silence," *Successful Meetings*, December 1995, 61-63; Sharon M. Lippincott, "Better Meetings," *Bottom Line/Business*, 15 August 1995, 3; Carol M. Barnum, "Here's How to Manage Your Meetings Effectively," *Communication Briefings* Bonus Item, April 1994, 8a-b; J. Keith Cook, "Try These Eight Guidelines for More Effective Meetings," *Communication Briefings* Bonus Item, April 1995, 8a-b; Larry D. Lauer, "A New Way to Look at Meetings," *Nonprofit World*, March/April 1995, 55-58. **pp. 59-61** Portions of discussion based on Mary Munter, "Meeting Technology: From Low-Tech to High-Tech," *Business Communication Quarterly*, June 1998, 80-87; Jon Hanke, "Presenting as a Team," *Presentations*, January 1998, 74-82; Sacha Cohen, "@ Work," *Predictions*, April 1998, 18-19; Michelle Mitterer, "Taming the Waves," *Successful Meetings*, March 1998, 112; Mary E. Thyfault, "Videoconferencing Boost," *Informationweek*, 4 May 1998, 148; Thomas Love, "A High-Tech Way to Save Time and Money," *Nation's Business*, June 1998; Phil Jones, *Official Netscape Communicator 4 Book* (Research Triangle Park, NC: Ventana, 1997), Chapter 11; Bryan Pfaffenberger, *Official Microsoft Internet Explorer 4 Book* (Redmond, WA: Microsoft Press, 1997), Chapter 17; William R. Pape, "A Meeting of Minds," *Inc*, Technology Supplement, 16 September 1997, 29-30; Jon Rosen, "10 Ways to Make Your Next Team Presentation a Winner," *Presentations*, August 1997, 31; Heath Row, "Real-time Collaboration Tools," *CIO*, 1 April 1997, 90-99; Larry Tuck, "Brave New Meetings," *Presentations*, September 1996, 30-36; Michael C. Brandon, "From Need to Know to Need to Know," *Communication World*, October/November, 1996, 18-19; Nancy R. Daly, "Reaching Board Decisions Online," *Association Management*, January 1996, L53-L56+; Leonard M. Jessup and David Van Over, "When a System Must Be All Things to All People: The Functions, Components and Costs of a Multi-purpose Group Support System Facility," *Journal of Systems Management*, July/August 1996, 14-21; Frank Jossi, "Putting It All Together: Creating Presentations as a Team," *Presentations*, July 1996, 18-26; Jim Clark and Richard Koonce, "Meetings Go High-Tech," *Training & Development*, November 1995; 32-38; Paul Dishman and Kregg Aytes, "Exploring Group Support Systems in Sales Management Applications," *Journal of Personal Selling & Sales Management*, Winter 1996, 65-77; Barbara Langham, "Mediated Meetings," *Successful Meetings*, January 1995, 75-76; M. Suzanne C. Berry, "Conducting Conference Calls," *Association Management*, January 1995, L-58 to L-60. **p. 68** Case study based on Anthony DePalma, "It Takes More Than a Visa to Do Business in Mexico," *Los Angeles Times*, 26 June 1996, F5. **p. 70** Figure caption based on Sari Kalin, "The Importance of Being Multiculturally Correct," *Computerworld*, 6 October 1997, G16-G17. **p. 71** Tech Talk box based on Sari Kalin, "The Importance of Being Multiculturally Correct," *Computer world*, 6 October 1997, G16-17; B. G. Yovovich, "Making Sense of all the Web's Numbers," *Editor & Publisher*, Mediainfo.com Supplement, November 1998, 30-31; Laura Morelli, "Writing for a Global Audience on the Web," *Marketing News*, 17 August 1998, 16. **p. 73** Picture caption based on Orlando Ramirez, "Ad Strategists Go After Hispanic Shoppers," *Santa Barbara News Press*, 1 September 1996, F1. **p. 75** Figure 3.2 based on J. Chung's analysis appearing in Guo-Ming Chen and William J. Starosta, *Foundations of Intercultural Communication* (Boston: Allyn and Bacon, 1998), 51; and Mary O'Hara-Devereaux and Robert Johansen, *Globalwork: Bridging Distance, Culture, and Time* (San Francisco: Jossey-Bass, 1994), 55. **p. 77** Spotlight based on Minda Zetlin, "When 99 Percent Isn't Enough," *Management Review*, March 1993, 52. **p. 83** Figure 3.4 based on Sondra Ostheimer, "Internationalize Yourself," *Business Education Forum* (February 1995), 45. Reprinted with permission of Sondra Ostheimer, Southwest Wisconsin Technical College. **p. 85** Figure 3.5 based on William Horton, "The Almost Universal Language: Graphics for International Documents," *Technical Communication*, Fourth Quarter, 1993, 690. **p. 87** Figure 3.6 reprinted with permission of *The New York Times*. **p. 101** Case study on Kinko's based on "Accounts in Review/2," *Adweek*, 15 June 1998, 12; "Kinko's

Strengthens Office Products Assortment," *Discount Store News,* 17 November 1997, 6, 70; Michele Marchetti, "Getting the Kinks Out," *Sales and Marketing Management,* March 1997, 56-64; Ann Marsh, "Kinko's Grows Up—Almost," *Forbes,* 1 December 1997, 270-272; Chad Rubel, "Treating Coworkers Right Is the Key to Kinko's Success," *Marketing News,* 29 January 1996, 2; Laurie Flynn, "Kinko's Adds Internet Services to Its Copying Business," *The New York Times,* 18 March 1996, C5; Michael H. Martin, "Kinko's," *Fortune,* 8 July 1996, 102; Zina Moukheiber, "'I'm Just a Peddler,'" *Forbes,* 17 July 1995, 42-43; "Collegiate Hall of Fame," *Inc.,* August 1996, 34; Edmond M. Rosenthal, "Kinko's Tries to Copy Campus Success With Business Clients," *Advertising Age's Business Marketing,* October 1996, 3, 12; Nanette Byrnest, "Kinko's Goes Corporate," *Business Week,* 19 August 1996, 58-59; Rob Gilhooly, "Kinko's Duplicating Firm's Success in Japan," *Japan Times Weekly International Edition,* 13 November 1995, 13. **p. 104** Spotlight based on Warren Buffet's remarks appearing in the Preface to *A Plain English Handbook* (Washington, DC: Office of Investor Education and Assistance, U.S. Securities and Exchange Commission, 1997), <http://www.sec.gov/consumer/plaine.htm#A9 (Retrieved 4 April 1997). **p. 111** Spotlight based on "Ebony's John H. Johnson: How He Went From a Tin-Roof Shack to the Forbes 400," *Investor's Business Daily,* 26 March 1998, 1. **p. 113** Spotlight caption based on Judy Flander, "Catching Up With Katie Couric," *The Saturday Evening Post,* September/October 1992, 38-42; Peter Kafka, "Anchors Away," *Forbes* (22 March 1998), 248. **116** Spotlight caption based on Tricia Devers, "Her Personal Focus Is Personal Finance," *Editor & Publisher,* 13 May 1989, 46; Jane Bryant Quinn, *Making the Most of Your Money* (New York: Simon & Schuster, 1991). **p. 152** Case study based on Philip Michaels, "Chihuahua, Chicken Sandwiches Recharge Chain," *Investor's Business Daily,* 16 February 1999, A10; Nancy Brumback, "Yo Quiero Mexican Food," *Restaurant Business,* 1 September 1998, 43-44; Mark Hamstra, "Operators See Potential in Tricon's Newest Prototype," *Nation's Restaurant News,* 5 October 1998, 3, 170; Richard Martin, "Anne Albertine: Taco Bell's Top Toque Stirs up Corporate Cuisine," *Nation's Restaurant News,* 14 September 1998, 113; Karen Benezra, "Dog's Day," *Brandweek,* 8 June 1998, 46; Nancy Brumback, "Big Enchilada," *Restaurant Business,* 1 September 1998, 46-48; Theresa Howard, "Taco Bell Aims to Inspire Holiday Feeding Frenzy With Plush Chihuahuas," *Brandweek,* 14 September 1998, 4; Gregg Cebrynski, "Taco Bell Ad: Gordita Whips the Whopper," *Nation's Restaurant News,* 20 July 1998, 3, 185; Mark Hamstra, "Tricon's Triple Play: Link Brands to Chase McD," *Nation's Restaurant News,* 19 October 1998, 3, 125; Gregg Cebrzynski, "El Pollo Loco, Del Taco Take Aim at Taco Bell's Gorditas," *Nation's Restaurant News,* 22 June 1998, 18, 32; Clint Smith, "For Whom the Bell Tolls," *Restaurant Business,* 1 September 1998, 122; Laura Yee, "Border Crossing," *Restaurants & Institutions,* 15 April 1998, 39-61; Jacque Kochak, "A Mexican Standoff," *Restaurant Business,* 15 October 1997, 63-68; Bob Garfield, "Taco Bell Fills the Bill for Teens' Tummies," *Advertising Age,* 4 August 1997, 43; Bill McDowell, "Taco Bell Plans Overhaul to Get Beyond Low Prices," *Advertising Age,* 10 February 1997, 2; Seth Lubove, "Flea Bites Elephant," *Forbes,* 5 May 1997, 72; Brad A. Johnson, "Nuevo Latino," *Restaurants & Institutions,* 15 March 1997, 58-68; Bill McDowell, "Fast-Food Chains Warm Up to New 'Wrap' Sandwiches: Non-Burger Product Lures Major Players Like Taco Bell," *Advertising Age,* 28 October 1996, 55; Brad A. Johnson, "The New Southwest," *Restaurants & Institutions,* 1 October 1996, 32-47; and Ron Ruggless, "Fine Dining Discovers New-World Flavors of 'Nuevo Latino' Cuisine," *Nation's Restaurant News,* 16 December 1996, 36-39. **p. 153** Spotlight caption based on "Quotations from Chairman Powell: A Leadership Primer," *Management Review,* December 1996, 36. **p. 154** Spotlight caption based on Jeff Moad, "Mike Simmons: A CIO With No Apologies," *Datamation,* 1 August 1990, 73-75. **p. 155** Picture caption based on J. Peder Zane, "For Investors, an Initial Public Offering of English," *The New York Times,* 25 August 1996; U. S. Securities and Exchange Commission, *A Plain English Handbook,* Washington, DC, 13 January 1997. **p. 156** Spotlight caption based on "Sam Walton in His Own Words," *Fortune,* 29 June 1992, 98-106. **p. 160** Spotlight caption for William Raspberry based on *Washington Post* column, "Words to the Wise on Students' Speech" as quoted in *Writing Concepts,* April 1998, 3. **p. 163** Tech Talk box based in part on Joel Shore, "Suites Still Depend on 'Feature Creep' to Grow," *Computer Reseller News,* 11 November 1996, 202. **p. 165** Tech Talk box based on Herb Brody, "Managers Turn to Grammar, Style Checkers," *PC World,* August 1990, 72; Rubin Rabinovitz, "New Windows Grammar Checkers Improve Error-Catching Rates," *PC Magazine,* 16 June 1992; Lisa Picarille, "Word 97 Goal: Simplify," *Computerworld,* 7 October 1996, 57; Steven R. Knowlton, "Grammar Aid for Those Who/Whom Need It," *The New York Times,* 23 July 1998. **p. 177** Case study based on interview with Alice Blachley, Ben & Jerry's, used with permission. **p. 192** Ethical Insights box based on Lauren Picker, "Job References: To Give or Not to Give," *Working Woman,* February 1992, 21; Amy Saltzman, "News You Can Use: Suppose They Sue," *U.S. News & World Report,* 22 September 1997, 68-70; and Jeffrey L. Seglin, "Too Much Ado About Giving References," *The New York Times,* 21 February 1999, BU4. **pp. 195-197.** Discussion on claim and adjustment letters based on Jeffry J. Roth, "When the Customer's Got a Beef," *ABA Banking Journal,* July 1998, 24-29; Geoffrey Brewer, "The Customer Stops Here," *Sales & Marketing Management,* March 1998, 30-36; Bill Knapp, "Communication Breakdown," *World Wastes,* February 1998, 16; Stephen S. Tax, Stephen W. Brown, and Murali Chandrashekaran, "Customer Evaluations of Service Complaint Experiences: Implications for Relationship Marketing," *Journal of Marketing,* April 1998, 60-76; Edmund S. Fine, "Are You Listening to Your Customers?" *Quality Progress,* January 1998, 120; Robert Klara, "Press 1 to Gripe," *Restaurant Business,* 15 May 1998, 96-102; "Foiling the Rogues: 'Anti' Web Sites Are Great for Angry Customers, But Now Companies Are Trying to Fight Back," *Newsweek,* 27 October 1997, 80; Roberta Furger, "Don't Get Mad, Get Online," *PC World,* October 1997, 37; Gary Hren, "The Sales Behind the Scowl," *American Demographics, Marketing Tools Supplement,* March/April 1996, 14-17; Gwendolyn N. Smith, Rebecca F. Nolan, and Young Dai, "Job-Refusal Letters: Readers' Affective Responses to Direct and Indirect Organizational Plans," *Business Communication Quarterly,* March 1996, 67-73; Carol David and Margaret Ann Baker, "Rereading Bad News: Compliance-Gaining Features in Management Memos," *The Journal of Business Communications,* October 1994, 267-290; "Grove's Internet Apology," *Computer Reseller News,* 5 December 1994, 313; Denise T. Smart and Charles L. Martin, "Consumers Who Correspond With Business: A Profile and Measure of Satisfaction With Responses," *Journal of Applied Business Research,* Spring 1993, 30-42; Gary L. Clark, Peter F. Kaminski, and David R.

Rink, "Consumer Complaints: Advice on How Companies Should Respond Based on an Empirical Study," *Journal of Services Marketing,* Winter 1992, 41-50; "How to Turn Complaints Into Business," *Agency Sales Magazine,* August 1990, 41-45; and Robert J. Aalberts and Lorraine A. Krajewski, "Claim and Adjustment Letters: Theory Versus Practice and Legal Implications," *The Bulletin of the Association of Business Communication,* September 1987, 1-5. **p. 200** Spotlight caption based on Brent Frei, "Taking the Pain Out of Growing," *Nation's Business,* December 1998, 6. **p. 201** Spotlight caption based on Andrew S. Grove, "The Fine Art of Feedback," *Working Woman,* February 1992, 26. **p. 218** Case study based on interview with Cathy Trimble, Wellness Center coordinator, Shore Memorial Hospital. **p. 220** Figure 8.1 provided by Cathy Trimble, Shore Memorial Hospital. **p. 222** Tech Talk box based on William M. Bulkeley, "Advances in Networking and Software Push Firms Closer to Paperless Office," *The Wall Street Journal,* 5 August 1993, B1; and Ted Needleman, "Not Exactly a Paperless Office, But Close," *Investor's Business Daily,* 4 December 1998, A1. **pp. 224-228** Text discussion and Career Coach box based on "Surviving Information Glut," *Communication Briefings,* September 1998, 2; Margaret Boles and Brenda Paik Sunoo, "Don't Let E-Mail Botch Your Career," *Workforce,* February 1998, 21; Brenda Paik Sunoo, "What if Your E-Mail Ends Up in Court?" *Workforce,* July 1998, 36-41; G. A. Marken, "Think Before You Click," *Office Systems,* March 1998, 44-46; Hubert B. Van Hoof and Marja J. Verbeeten, "E-Mail, Web Site Most Commonly Used Internet Tools," *Hotel & Motel Management,* 15 June 1998, 34; Howard Millman, "Easy EDI for Everyone," *InfoWorld,* 17 August 1998, 38-39; Joe Dysart, "Establishing an Internet Policy," *Credit Union Executive,* May/June 1998, 18-22; "Do's and Don'ts for E-Mail Use," *CA Magazine,* June/July 1998, 40; Sana Reynolds, "Composing Effective E-Mail Messages," *Communication World,* July 1997, 8-9; Laura K. Romei, "ee cummings was a punk!" *Managing Office Technology,* February 1997, 9; Jenny C. McCune, "Get the Message," *Management Review,* January 1997, 10-11; John Edwards, "The Six Most Common Mistakes in Sending E-Mail," *Bottom Line/Business,* October 1997, 8; Mark Gibbs, "Where Do You Want Your E-Mail To Go Today?" *Network World,* 28 April 1997, 74; Barb Cole-Gomolski, "E-Mail Traffic, Costs Hit High-Speed Lane," *Computerworld,* 14 April 1997, 14; Marianne Kolbasuk McGee, "E-Mail Study Shows Few Constraints," *Informationweek,* 9 December 1996, 103-105; Elizabeth J. Hunt, "*A Matter of 'Netiquette,'" Business Quarterly,* Winter 1996, 13-14. **p. 226** Web site caption based on Jenny C. McCune, "Get the Message," *Management Review,* January 1997, 10-11. **p. 227** Spotlight caption based on Ivor Davis, "Patriot Gains," *Working Woman,* October 1998, 58-59. **p. 237** Spotlight caption based on Susan Caminiti, "America's Most Successful Businesswoman," *Fortune,* 15 June 1992, 102-108; J. P. Donlon, "Queen of Cash Flow," *Chief Executive,* January/February 1994, 38-42. **pp. 251-252** Career Coach box based on Michael E. Hattersley and Linda McJannet, *Management Communication* (New York: McGraw-Hill, 1996), 78-84, David W. Ewing, "Strategies of Persuasion," *Writing for Results* (New York: Wiley, 1979); and Joseph Mancuso, *Winning With the Power of Persuasion* (Dearborn, MI: Enterprise, 1993). **p. 253** Picture caption based on Roberta Maynard, "The Heat Is On," *Nation's Business,* October 1997, 12-13. **p. 255** Picture caption based on Dennis Blank, "Riding High on Theme Parks," *Nation's Business,* August 1998, 51. **p. 257** Ethical Insights box based on Lynn Quitman Troyka, *Simon & Schuster Handbook for Writers* (Upper Saddle River, NJ: Prentice Hall, 1996), 144-146; Frederick Crews, *The Random House Handbook* (New York: Random House, 1987), 76-78; and Stephen Downes, "Stephen's Guide to the Logical Fallacies" <www.assiniboinec.mb.ca/user/downes/fallacy/falla.htm> (Retrieved 6 December 1998). **p. 266** Spotlight caption based on Ron Stodghill, "Kathleen Synnott: Shaping the Mailrooms of Tomorrow," *Business Week,* 16 November 1992, 66. **p. 267** Spotlight caption based on, "Beware the Impossible Guarantee," *Inc.,* November 1992, 30. **p. 268** Spotlight caption based on Bob Weinstein, "The Buck Stops Here: Going for Broke, Charles Schwab & Co.," *Entrepreneur,* February 1993, 127-131; Erick Schonfeld, " Schwab Puts It All Online," *Fortune,* 7 December 1998, 94-100. **pp. 271, 273** Picture and news release reprinted with permission of Brad Daniel. **p. 285** Picture caption based on Minda Zetlin, "A Slow Takeoff," *Management Review,* July 1996, 24-26; Shari Caudron, "A Day in the Life of," *Workforce,* June 1998, 82-83. **p. 287** Spotlight caption based on Peter Krass, "Entrepreneur Estee Lauder," *Investor's Business Daily,* 6 April 1998, A3. **p. 289** Spotlight caption based on Malcolm Forbes, "How to Write a Business Letter," *Strategies for Business and Technical Writing,* Kevin J. Harty, ed., 4th edition (Boston: Allyn and Bacon, 1998) 108. **p. 293** Figure 10.3 reprinted with permission of FedEx Corporation, Memphis, Tennessee. **p. 322** Spotlight based on interview with Ariadne Delon Scott. **pp. 325-26** Figure 11.2 based on William A. Bolger, "How to Start a Free Legal Services Plan for Your Group" (Gloucester, VA: National Resource Center for Consumers of Legal Services, 1987). **p. 332** Photo caption based on Tom Ehrenfeld, "Out of the Blue," *Inc.,* July 1995, 70. **p. 333** Spotlight caption based on John Case, "The Best Small Companies to Work for in America," *Inc.,* November 1992, 96. **p. 337** Spotlight captio n based on Tom Peters, *Thriving on Chaos* (New York: Knopf, 1991), 230-231. **p. 345** Picture caption based on Leigh Buchanan, "The Smartest Little Company in America," *Inc.,* January 1999, 43-54. **p. 347** Discussion in Tech Talk box based on "How Internet Surveys Pay Off," *Communication Briefings,* December 1998, 1. **p. 351** Discussion in Ethics Insights box based on data from Gregg Easterbrook, "The Sincerest Flattery," *Newsweek,* 29 July 1991, 45-46; William A. Henry, III, "Recycling in the Newsroom," *Time,* 29 July 1991, 59; and M. L. Stein, "Drama Critic Fired for Copying Review," *Editor & Publisher,* 13 April 1996, 55. **p. 361** Spotlight caption based on interview with John Humphrey, 12 January 1999. **pp. 366-67** Figure 12.3 based on Charlene Marmer Solomon, "Marriott's Family Matters," *Personnel Journal,* October 1991, 40-42; Suzanne Gordon, "Helping Corporations Care," *Working Woman,* January 1993, 30. **p. 371** Picture caption based on Julie Candler, "A Sobering Law for Truckers," *Nation's Business,* January 1996, 26-27. **p. 374** Figure 12.5 based on James Clark and Lyn Clark, *A Handbook for Office Workers,* 8e (Cincinnati: South-Western, 1998), 358-359. **p. 381** Figure 12.17 based on memo shown in advertisement presented by Visio Corporation, 520 Pike Street, Seattle, Washington. **p. 389** Case study based on "Oren Harari, "Lessons From the Swoosh," *Management Review,* July/August 1998, 39; Sharon R. King, "Flying the Swoosh and Stripes," *The New York Times,* 19 March 1998, C1; Mark Tedeschi, "What Crisis? With Footwear Slowing, Nike Turns to Other Markets in Its Stable," *Sporting Goods Business,* 2 June 1997, 22; William McCall, "Nike Battles Backlash From Overseas Sweatshops," *Marketing News,* 9 November 1998, 14; Erika Rasmusson, "Defending a

Brand Name," *Sales & Marketing Management,* September 1997, 22; Philip Knight, "Global Manufacturing: The Nike Story Is Just Good Business," *Vital Speeches of the Day,* 1 August 1998, 637-640; "A Swift Decision: Nike Chooses Site of Its New Distribution Centre," *Corporate Location* November/December 1995, 19; Leslie Goff, "<YourCompanyNameHere> Sucks.Com, *Computerworld,* 20 July 1998, 57-58; Terry Lefton, "Nike Stretches," *Brandweek,* 23 November 1998, 1, 6; Brad Wolverton, "Today's Training Ground for Tomorrow's Jocks," *Business Week,* 12 May 1997, 152; **p. 392** Spotlight caption based on telephone interview with Janet Marie Smith, used with permission; **p. 394** Picture caption based on Jill Andresky Fraser, "He Asks to be Audited—Often," *Inc.,* December 1994, and personal telephone interview 16 August 1995; **p. 398** Career Coach box based on Pat R. Graves and Jack E. Murry, "Enhancing Communication With Effective Page Design and Typography," *Delta Pi Epsilon* Instructional Strategies Series, Summer 1990; **p. 400** Spotlight caption based on Leslie Brokaw, "Twenty-Eight Steps to a Strategic Alliance," *Inc.,* April 1993, 96-104; **p. 405** Picture caption based on Sharon Nelton, "Innovative Spark From Uncle Sam," *Nation's Business,* December 1998, 50; **p. 418** Case study based on interviews with Mary Piecewicz, 16 November 1995 and 14 January 1999; **p. 422** Spotlight caption based on interview with Mary Piecewicz, 14 January 1999; **p. 424** Spotlight caption based on Thomas Sant, "Powerful Proposals," *Entrepreneur,* February 1993, 54-55; **p. 427** Picture caption based on Susan Hodges, "One Giant Step Toward a Loan," *Nation's Business,* August 1997, 34; **p. 429** Spotlight caption based on Albert G. Holzinger, "How to Succeed by Really Trying," *Nation's Business,* August 1992, 50-52; **p. 462** Spotlight caption based on interview with Jon Georges, 3 February 1999; **p. 463** Spotlight caption based on Les Brown, *Live Your Dreams* (New York: Morrow, 1992); **p. 464** Career Coach box based on Bert Decker, "Successful Presentations: Simple and Practical," *HR Focus,* February 1992, 19; Lawrence Stevens, "The Proof Is in the Presentation," *Nation's Business,* July 1991, 33; Hal Lancaster, "Practice and Coaching Can Help You Improve Um, Y'Know, Speeches," *The Wall Street Journal,* 9 January 1996, B1. **pp. 469-473** based on Scott Heimes, "Add Some Visual Thunder to Your Presentations," *Presentations,* March 1998, 11-12; Stuart Kahan, "Capturing Clients Through High-Powered Presentations," *Practical Accountant,* February 1997, 39-42; Nancy Ferris, "Brief the Boss, Dazzle the Audience," *Government Executive,* February 1998, 61-62; David Fine, "Chart a Clear Course for Better Financial Graphics," *Presentations,* June 1998, 40-41; "How to Put Together a Great Presentation," *Supervisory Management,* November 1995, 6; Jim Endicott, "For Better Presentations, Avoid PowerPoint Pitfalls," *Presentations,* June 1998, 36-37; Victoria Hall Smith, "Gigs by the Gigabyte," *Working Woman,* May 1998, 114-115. **p. 475** Spotlight caption based on Dianna Booher, *Executive's Portfolio of Model Speeches for All Occasions* (Englewood Cliffs, NJ: Prentice Hall 1991), 252. **p. 481** Spotlight caption based on Barbara Marsh, "Oh, It's You, We Were Hoping You'd Call, Please Hold," *The Wall Street Journal,* 9 June 1994, and personal interview 2 February 1999. **p. 489** Spotlight caption based on personal interview with Bonnie Gesualdi-Chao, **p. 490** Spotlight caption based on Nick Turner, *Investor's Business Daily,* "Entrepreneur Michael Dell," 1 March 1999, A8. **p. 491** Spotlight caption based on *The 1999 What Color Is Your Parachute?* (Berkeley, CA: Ten Speed Press, 1999); and interview with Richard Nelson Bolles in Bob Rosner, "What Color Is HP's Parachute?" *Workforce,* September 1999, 50-52. **p. 492** Career Coach box based on J. Michael Farr, *The Very Quick Job Search* (Indianapolis: JIST Works, Inc., 1991), Bob Rosner, "What Color Is HR's Parachute?," *Workforce,* September 1998, 50-51; and Rebecca Smith, "NetKnocking," *Computer Bits,* January 1997, <http://www.computerbits.com/archive, 9701/netknock.htm> (Retrieved 14 February 1999). **pp. 493-494** Discussion on electronic job searching based on Rebecca Quick, "Your CyberCareer: Using the Internet to Find a Job," *The Wall Street Journal,* 5 March 1998, B7; Michele Pepe, "Online Job-Search Sites Flourish, Prosper," *Computer Reseller News,* 18 May 1998, 169; "Beyond Company Web Sites," *InfoWorld,* 22 June 1998, 103. **p. 499** Spotlight caption based on personal interview and on Yana Parker, author of *Damn Good Résumé Guide* (Berkeley: Ten Speed Press, 1996). **p. 504** Spotlight caption based on "Give Your Résumé to a Computer," *Fortune,* 15 June 1992, 12.

Photo Credits

p. 1 © SuperStock. **p. 2** © Richard Hamilton Smith/Corbis. **p. 8** Walter Hodges/Tony Stone Images. **p. 9** © Carl Cox 1998. **p. 12** Courtesy of the ASK Companies. **p. 22** Courtesy of the General Electric Company. **p. 25** Los Angeles Times Photo, Spencer Weiner. **p. 26** © Michael Barley. **p. 36:** © Ralf Schultheiss/Tony Stone Images. **p. 38** AP/Wide World Photos. **p. 39** © AP/Wide World Photos. **p. 41** © Southwire Corporation. **p. 48** © Arnaldo Magnani/Gamma Liaison International. **p. 49:** Photo courtesy of Students in Free Enterprise. **p. 60** © Reuters/Archive Photos. **p. 65** © PhotoDisc, Inc. **p. 67** © Grilly Bernard/Tony Stone Images. **p. 73** © Michael Newman/PhotoEdit. **p. 77** © Brian Willar. **p. 89** © Charles Gupton/Tony Stone Images. **p. 96** © PhotoDisc, Inc. **p. 97** Photo Courtesy of William Curry. **p. 99** © SuperStock. **p. 100** Photo Courtesy Dr. Mary Ellen Guffey. **p. 104** © Reuters/Str/Archive Photos. **p. 108** © Peter Cade/Tony Stone Images. **p. 111** © Michael Krasowitz/FPG International. **p. 111** © AP/Wide World Photos. **p. 113** © John Harrington. **p. 116** Courtesy of Jane Bryant Quinn. **p. 125** © Bernard Gotfryd/Archive Photos. **p. 128** Courtesy of MTV Networks. **p. 139** Printed with permission of The Writing Center. **p. 151** © Corbis/Mitch Gerber. **p. 153** © AP/Wide World Photos. **p. 154** Courtesy Mike Simmons. **p. 155** © Doug Armand/Tony Stone Images. **p. 156** © Steven Pumphrey. **p. 160** © AP/Wide World Photos. **p. 162** © Corbis/Tony Arruza. **p. 171** © PhotoDisc, Inc. **p. 175** © SuperStock. **p. 176** © Corbis/Richard T. Nowitz. **p. 200** © Paul Souders. **p. 201** Courtesy of Intel Corp. **p. 210** © PhotoDisc, Inc. **p. 215** © PhotoDisc, Inc. **p. 217** Courtesy of Shore Memorial Hospital. **p. 219** © Dan Bosler/Tony Stone Images. **p. 226** Printed by permission of Hallmark. **p. 227** © American Tours International. **p. 237** © Larry Ford. **p. 243** Photo Disc, Inc. **p. 248** © Souders/Gamma Liaison International. **p. 253** © 1997 Robert Holmgren Photography. **p. 255** © T. Michael Keza. **p. 266** Courtesy of Pitney Bowes. **p. 267** Courtesy of Southwest Airline Company. **p. 268** © Menuez/Reportage. **p. 271** © Ken Touchton. **p. 280** © PhotoDisc, Inc. **p. 283** © Morton Beebe-S.F./Corbis. **p. 285** © Denver International A P Marketing. **p. 287** © William Coupon/Gamma Liaison International. **p. 299** © Bruce Ayers/Tony Stone Images. **p. 300** © E. Adams/Sygma. **p. 313** © Corbis/Alex Fevzer. **p. 319** © SuperStock. **p. 320** Courtesy of Specialized Bicycles. **p. 323** Courtesy of Specialized Bicycles. **p. 332** © Eric Millette. **p. 333** © Mark Katzman. **p. 337** Courtesy of the Tom Peters Group. **p. 345** © Marc Hauser. **p. 359** © AP/Wide World Photos. **p. 361** Courtesy of John Humphrey. **p. 362** © Danny Turner. **p. 371**

© Bob Daemmrich Photo, Inc. **p. 388** © Reuters/Jeff Topping/Archive Photos. **p. 392** © 1992, Janice E. Rettaliata. **p. 392** © 1992 Janice E. Rettaliata. **p. 394** © Amy Etra. **p. 400** © Doug Menez/Reportage. **p. 402** Photo Courtesy Dr. Mary Ellen Guffey. **p. 405** © T. Michael Keza. **p. 415** © PhotoDisc, Inc. **p. 417** © Jim Krantz/Tony Stone Images. **p. 422** Courtesy Mary Piecewicz. **p. 424** Courtesy Thomas Sant. **p. 427** © Larry Hammill. **p. 429** Courtesy of Roger Staubach. **p. 243** © PhotoDisk, Inc. **p. 452** Photo Courtesy Shirley Finkenbiner. **p. 454** © PhotoDisc, Inc. **p. 459** © SuperStock. **p. 460** © 1989 The Walt Disney Company. **p. 462** Courtesy of Walt Disney Imagineering. **p. 463** © 1993 Anthony Loew. **p. 473** © Corbis/Roger Ressmeyer. **p. 475** Courtesy of Booher Consultants, Inc. **p. 481** Courtesy of Nancy Friedman. **p. 487** Courtesy of Carnival. Photo by Andy Newman/CCL. **p. 489** Courtesy Bonnie Chao. **p. 490** © AP/Wide World Photos. **p. 491** Courtesy Richard N. Bolles. **p. 493** © PhotoDisc, Inc. **p. 493** © Linda Sue Scott. **p. 499** © Don Melandry. **p. 504** © Hank Delespinasse. **p. 524** © PhotoDisc, Inc. **p. 530** © PhotoDisc, Inc. **p. 531** © PhotoDisc, Inc.

Index

Page numbers in *italics* refer to figures.

A

B

C

D

E

F

G

H

I

J

K

L

M

N

O

P

Q

R

S

T

U

V

W

Y

Z